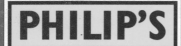

GW00418765

STREET ATLAS
Cambridgeshire
and Peterborough

First published in 2001 by

Philip's, a division of
Octopus Publishing Group Ltd
2-4 Heron Quays, London E14 4JP

Second edition 2005
First impression 2005

ISBN-10   0-540-08735-1 (spiral)
ISBN-13   978-0-540-08735-8 (spiral)

© Philip's 2005

Ordnance Survey®

This product includes mapping data licensed
from Ordnance Survey® with the permission of
the Controller of Her Majesty's Stationery Office.
© Crown copyright 2005. All rights reserved.
Licence number 100011710.

No part of this publication may be reproduced,
stored in a retrieval system or transmitted in any
form or by any means, electronic, mechanical,
photocopying, recording or otherwise, without
the permission of the Publishers and the
copyright owner.

To the best of the Publishers' knowledge, the
information in this atlas was correct at the time
of going to press. No responsibility can be
accepted for any errors or their consequences.

The representation in this atlas of a road, track
or path is no evidence of the existence of a right
of way.

Ordnance Survey and the OS Symbol are
registered trademarks of Ordnance Survey, the
national mapping agency of Great Britain.

Post Office is a trade mark of Post Office Ltd
in the UK and other countries.

Printed and bound in Italy by Rotolito

Contents

III **Key to map symbols**

IV **Key to map pages**

VI **Route planning**

X **Administrative and Postcode boundaries**

1 **Street maps** at 3½ inches to 1 mile

208 **Street maps** at 1¾ inches to 1 mile

239 **Street maps** at 3½ inches to 1 mile

246 **Street map of Cambridge city centre**
at 7 inches to 1 mile

247 **Index** of towns and villages

249 **Index** of streets, hospitals, industrial estates, railway
stations, schools, shopping centres, universities
and places of interest

Digital Data

The exceptionally high-quality mapping found in this atlas is available as digital data in TIFF
format, which is easily convertible to other bitmapped (raster) image formats.

The index is also available in digital form as a standard database table. It contains all the details
found in the printed index together with the National Grid reference for the map square in which
each entry is named.

For further information and to discuss your requirements, please contact Philip's on
020 7644 6932 or james.mann@philips-maps.co.uk

Key to map symbols

III

Motorway with junction number (22a)	**Ambulance station**
Primary route – dual/single carriageway	**Coastguard station**
A road – dual/single carriageway	**Fire station**
B road – dual/single carriageway	**Police station**
Minor road – dual/single carriageway	**Accident and Emergency entrance to hospital**
Other minor road – dual/single carriageway	**Hospital**
Road under construction	**Place of worship**
Tunnel, covered road	**Information Centre** (open all year)
Rural track, private road or narrow road in urban area	**Shopping Centre**
Gate or obstruction to traffic (restrictions may not apply at all times or to all vehicles)	**Parking, Park and Ride**
Path, bridleway, byway open to all traffic, road used as a public path	**Post Office**
Pedestrianised area	**Camping site, caravan site**
Postcode boundaries DY7	**Golf course**
County and unitary authority boundaries	**Picnic site**
Railway, tunnel, railway under construction	**Important buildings, schools, colleges, universities and hospitals** Prim Sch
Tramway, tramway under construction	**Built up area**
Miniature railway	**Woods**
Railway station Walsall	**Tidal water, water name** River Ouse
Private railway station	**Non-tidal water** – lake, river, canal or stream
Metro station South Shields	**Lock, weir, tunnel**
Tram stop, tram stop under construction	**Non-Roman antiquity** Church
Bus, coach station	**Roman antiquity** ROMAN FORT
	Adjoining page indicators and overlap bands 87 246 The colour of the arrow and the band indicates the scale of the adjoining or overlapping page (see scales below)

Acad	**Academy**	Inst	**Institute**	Recn Gd	**Recreation Ground**		
Allot Gdns	**Allotments**	Ct	**Law Court**				
Cemy	**Cemetery**	L Ctr	**Leisure Centre**	Resr	**Reservoir**		
C Ctr	**Civic Centre**	LC	**Level Crossing**	Ret Pk	**Retail Park**		
CH	**Club House**	Liby	**Library**	Sch	**School**		
Coll	**College**	Mkt	**Market**	Sh Ctr	**Shopping Centre**		
Crem	**Crematorium**	Meml	**Memorial**	TH	**Town Hall/House**		
Ent	**Enterprise**	Mon	**Monument**	Trad Est	**Trading Estate**		
Ex H	**Exhibition Hall**	Mus	**Museum**	Univ	**University**		
Ind Est	**Industrial Estate**	Obsy	**Observatory**	W Twr	**Water Tower**		
IRB Sta	**Inshore Rescue Boat Station**	Pal	**Royal Palace**	Wks	**Works**		
		PH	**Public House**	YH	**Youth Hostel**		

Enlarged mapping only

	Railway or bus station building
	Place of interest
	Parkland

■ The small numbers around the edges of the maps identify the 1 kilometre National Grid lines
■ The dark grey border on the inside edge of some pages indicates that the mapping does not continue onto the adjacent page

The scale of the maps on the pages numbered in blue is 5.52 cm to 1 km • 3½ inches to 1 mile • 1: 18103	0 ¼ ½ ¾ 1 mile / 0 250 m 500 m 750 m 1 kilometre
The scale of the maps on pages numbered in green is 2.76 cm to 1 km • 1¾ inches to 1 mile • 1: 36206	0 ¼ ½ ¾ 1 mile / 0 250m 500m 750m 1kilometre
The scale of the maps on pages numbered in red is 11.04 cm to 1 km • 7 inches to 1 mile • 1: 9051	0 220 yards 440 yards 660 yards ½ mile / 0 125m 250m 375m ½ kilometre

Key to map pages

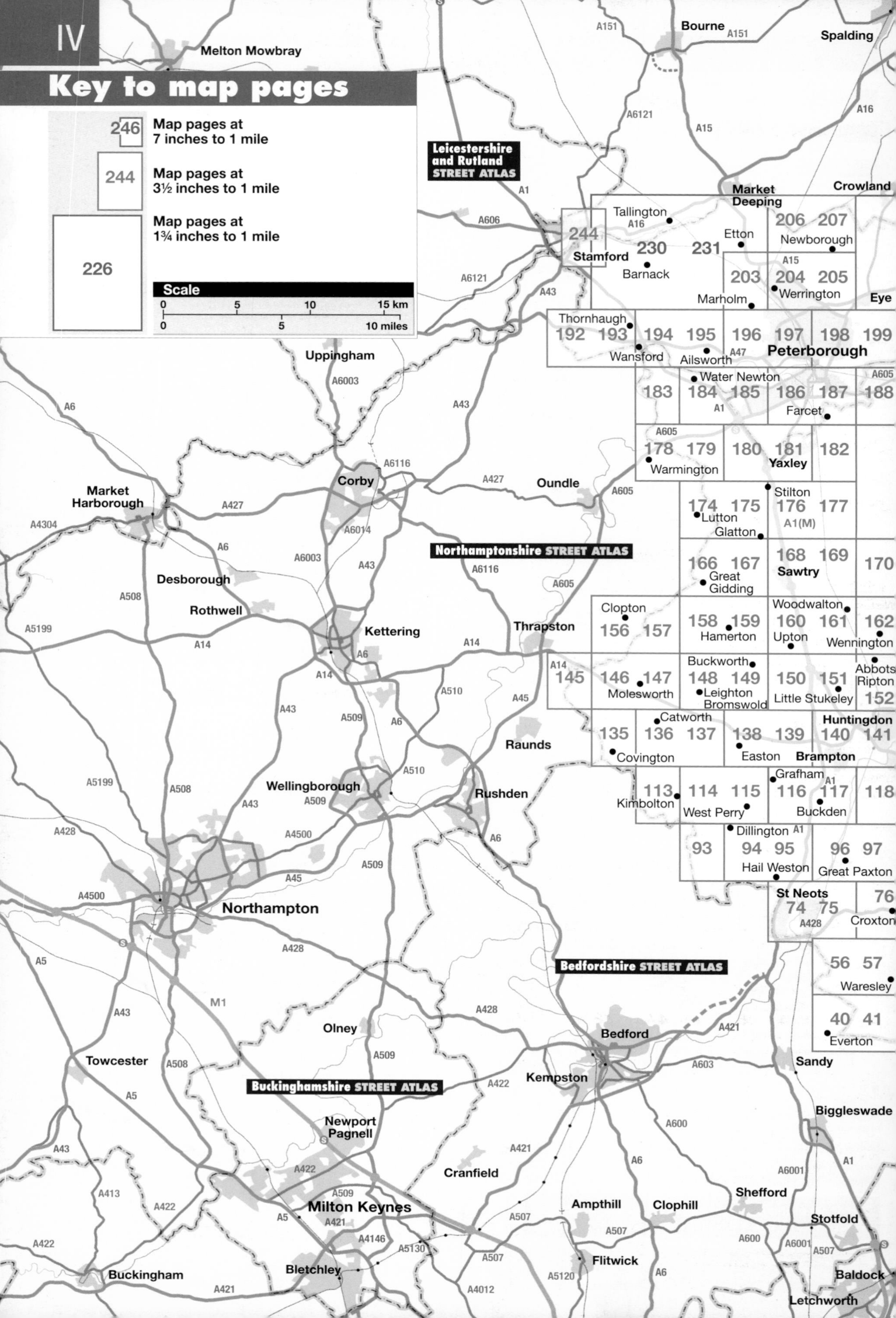
246
Map pages at
7 inches to 1 mile
244
Map pages at
3½ inches to 1 mile
226
Map pages at
1¾ inches to 1 mile
Scale
0
5
10
15 km
0
5
10 miles
Leicestershire and Rutland STREET ATLAS
Northamptonshire STREET ATLAS
Bedfordshire STREET ATLAS
Buckinghamshire STREET ATLAS
Melton Mowbray
Bourne
Spalding
A151
A16
A15
A6121
A1
A606
Crowland
Market Deeping
Tallington
Etton
206
207
Newborough
244
230
231
Stamford
Barnack
203
204
205
Werrington
Marholm
Eye
A6121
A43
Thornhaugh
192
193
194
195
196
197
198
199
Wansford
Ailsworth
A47
Peterborough
Uppingham
A6003
Water Newton
A605
183
184
185
186
187
188
Farcet
A6
A43
178
179
180
181
182
Warmington
Yaxley
Corby
A6116
A427
Oundle
A605
Stilton
174
175
176
177
Lutton
A1(M)
Glatton
Market Harborough
A427
A4304
A6014
A6
A6003
A43
A6116
166
167
168
169
170
Great Gidding
Sawtry
Desborough
A508
Rothwell
A605
Clopton
Woodwalton
156
157
158
159
160
161
162
Hamerton
Upton
Wennington
Thrapston
Kettering
A5199
A14
A6
A14
Abbots Ripton
145
146
147
148
149
150
151
152
Buckworth
Molesworth
Leighton Bromswold
Little Stukeley
A14
A510
A45
A43
A509
A6
Catworth
Huntingdon
135
136
137
138
139
140
141
Covington
Easton
Brampton
Raunds
Grafham
A5199
A508
Wellingborough
A509
A510
Rushden
113
114
115
116
117
118
Kimbolton
West Perry
Buckden
A428
A43
A4500
A6
Dillington
93
94
95
96
97
Hail Weston
Great Paxton
A509
A45
St Neots
74
75
76
A428
Croxton
A4500
Northampton
A428
A5
56
57
Waresley
M1
A428
A43
40
41
Everton
Olney
Bedford
A421
Towcester
A508
A509
A603
Sandy
A5
A422
Kempston
Newport Pagnell
A600
Biggleswade
A43
A422
A421
A6
A6001
A1
Cranfield
A413
A422
A509
Milton Keynes
Ampthill
Clophill
Shefford
A5
A421
A507
A507
Stotfold
A422
A4146
A5130
A600
A6001
A507
A507
Buckingham
Bletchley
Flitwick
A421
A4012
A5120
A6
Baldock
Letchworth

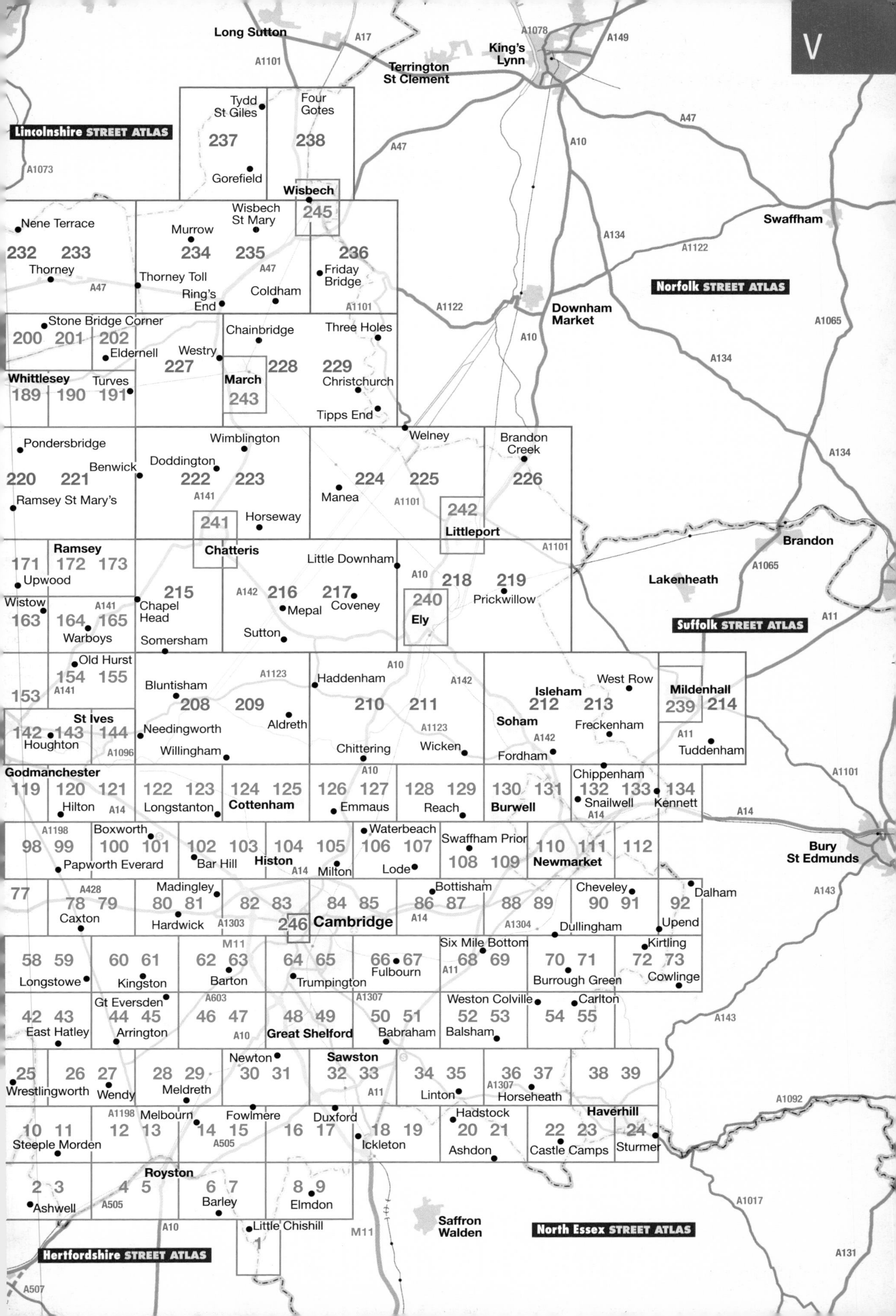

V

Long Sutton

A1078 King's Lynn

A17 Terrington St Clement

A149

A1101

Lincolnshire STREET ATLAS

Tydd St Giles Four Gotes

237 **238**

Gorefield

A1073

A47

A10

Swaffham

A134

A1122

Wisbech

245

Nene Terrace Murrow Wisbech St Mary

232 **233** **234** **235** **236**
Thorney Friday Bridge

Thorney Toll Coldham

Ring's End

A47 A47

A1101 A1122 A1122

Norfolk STREET ATLAS

Downham Market

A10

A1065

Stone Bridge Corner Chainbridge Three Holes

200 **201** **202** **227** **228** **229**
Eldernell Westry

Whittlesey Christchurch

189 **190** **191** March **243** Tipps End

Turves

A134

Pondersbridge Wimblington Welney Brandon Creek

Benwick Doddington

220 **221** **222** **223** **224** **225** **226**
Ramsey St Mary's Manea

A141 Horseway A1101

241 **242**

Chatteris Littleport

Ramsey Little Downham A1101

171 **172** **173** **215** **216** **217** **218** **219**
Upwood Chapel Head Mepal Coveney Prickwillow

Wistow A142 **240**

163 **164** **165** Somersham Sutton Ely
Warboys

Lakenheath Brandon

A1065

A11

Old Hurst Haddenham A10 Isleham West Row **Suffolk STREET ATLAS**

154 **155** **208** **209** **210** **211** **212** **213** **239** **214**
Bluntisham Aldreth Soham Freckenham Mildenhall

153 Needingworth Chittering Wicken Fordham Tuddenham

St Ives Willingham A1123 A142 A11

142 **143** **144**
Houghton A1096

A1101

Godmanchester Chippenham A14

119 **120** **121** **122** **123** **124** **125** **126** **127** **128** **129** **130** **131** **132** **133** **134**
Hilton Longstanton Cottenham Emmaus Reach Burwell Snailwell Kennett

A14 A14

Bury St Edmunds

A1198 Boxworth Waterbeach Swaffham Prior

98 **99** **100** **101** **102** **103** **104** **105** **106** **107** **108** **109** **110** **111** **112**
Papworth Everard Bar Hill Histon Milton Lode Newmarket

A14

A143

A428 Madingley Bottisham Cheveley Dalham

77 **78** **79** **80** **81** **82** **83** **84** **85** **86** **87** **88** **89** **90** **91** **92**
Caxton Hardwick Cambridge Dullingham Upend

A1303 **246** A14 A1304

M11 Six Mile Bottom Kirtling

58 **59** **60** **61** **62** **63** **64** **65** **66** **67** **68** **69** **70** **71** **72** **73**
Longstowe Kingston Barton Trumpington Fulbourn Burrough Green Cowlinge

A11

Gt Eversden A603 A1307 Weston Colville Carlton

42 **43** **44** **45** **46** **47** **48** **49** **50** **51** **52** **53** **54** **55**
East Hatley Arrington Great Shelford Babraham Balsham

A10 A143

Newton Sawston

25 **26** **27** **28** **29** **30** **31** **32** **33** **34** **35** **36** **37** **38** **39**
Wrestlingworth Wendy Meldreth Linton Horseheath Haverhill

A11 A1307

A1092

Melbourn Fowlmere Duxford Hadstock Haverhill

10 **11** **12** **13** **14** **15** **16** **17** **18** **19** **20** **21** **22** **23** **24**
Steeple Morden Ickleton Ashdon Castle Camps Sturmer

A1198 A505 A505

A1017

Royston

2 **3** **4** **5** **6** **7** **8** **9**
Ashwell Barley Elmdon

A505 A10

Little Chishill Saffron Walden

1

M11 **North Essex STREET ATLAS**

Hertfordshire STREET ATLAS

A507 A131

Route Planning

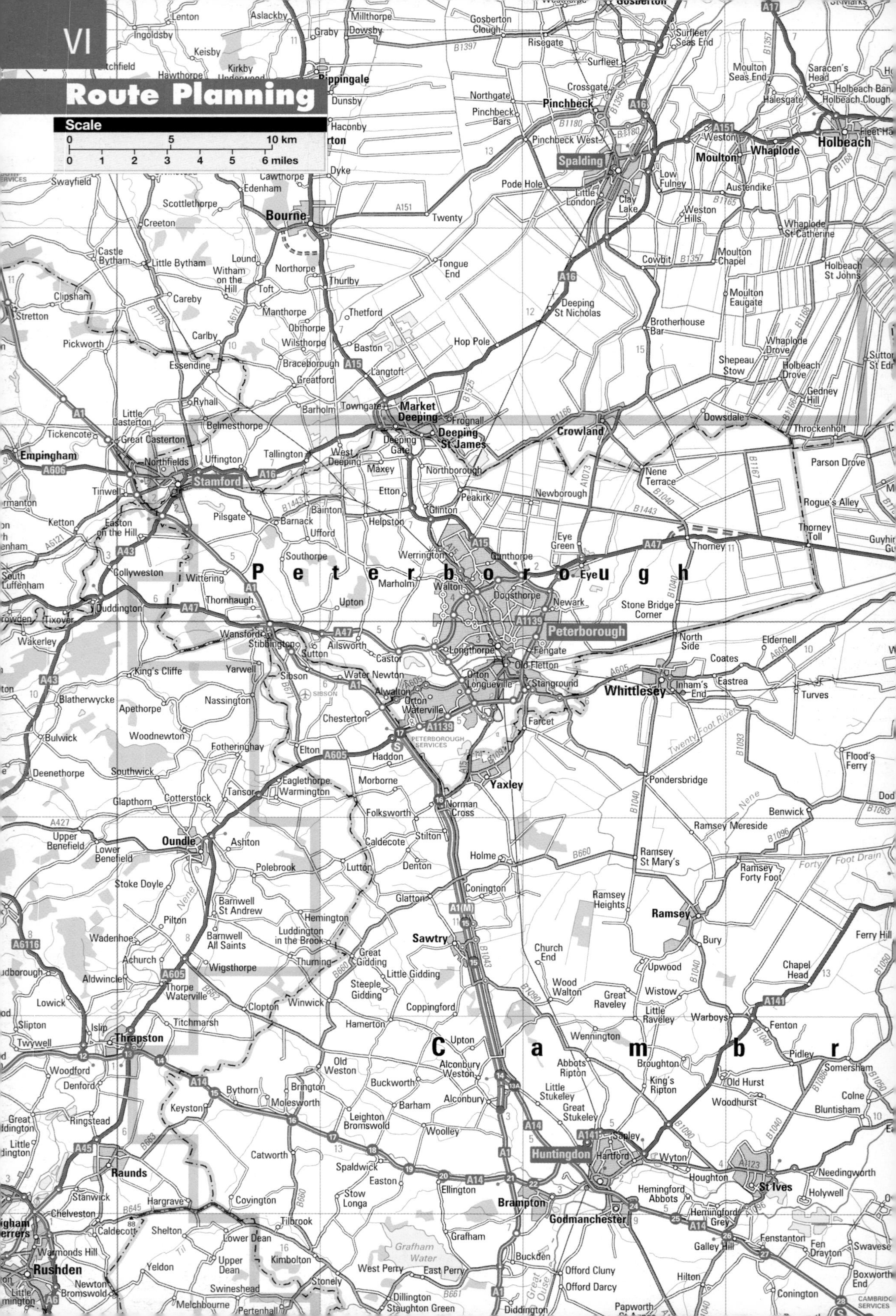
Scale
0 5 10 km
0 1 2 3 4 5 6 miles
Lenton
Aslackby
Millthorpe
Gosberton Clough
Gosberton
Surfleet Seas End
Ingoldsby
Graby
Dowsby
Risegate
Surfleet
Moulton Seas End
Saracen's Head
Keisby
B1397
B1357
A17
Hawthorpe
Kirkby Underwood
Rippingale
Crossgate
Holbeach Bank
Holbeach Clough
Halesgate
Northgate
Pinchbeck
Pinchbeck Bars
B1356
A16
Dunsby
B1180
A151
Fleet Hargate
Weston
Moulton
Whaplode
Holbeach
Haconby
Pinchbeck West
Spalding
Swayfield
Cawthorpe
Dyke
Low Fulney
Edenham
Pode Hole
Little London
Clay Lake
Austendike
Scottlethorpe
Bourne
A151
Twenty
Weston Hills
B1165
Whaplode St Catherine
Creeton
B1168
Castle Bytham
Little Bytham
Lound
Northorpe
Tongue End
Cowbit
B1357
Moulton Chapel
Holbeach St Johns
Witham on the Hill
Thurlby
A16
Clipsham
Toft
Careby
Deeping St Nicholas
Moulton Eaugate
Stretton
B1176
A6121
Manthorpe
Thetford
Brotherhouse Bar
Obthorpe
Carlby
Wilsthorpe
Baston
Hop Pole
Whaplode Drove
Pickworth
Braceborough
Shepeau Stow
Holbeach Drove
Sutton St Edmund
Essendine
A15
Langtoft
Greatford
B1525
Gedney Hill
Ryhall
Barholm
Towngate
Market Deeping
B1166
Little Casterton
Frognall
Crowland
Dowsdale
Throckenholt
Belmesthorpe
Tickencote
Great Casterton
Deeping Gate
Deeping St James
Empingham
Tallington
West Deeping
B1167
Parson Drove
Uffington
Northfields
Maxey
Northborough
Nene Terrace
A606
A16
Stamford
A1073
Tinwell
Etton
Peakirk
Newborough
B1040
Rogue's Alley
Ketton
Pilsgate
Bainton
Glinton
B1443
B1443
Easton on the Hill
Barnack
Helpston
Ufford
Thorney Toll
A6121
A43
Southorpe
Werrington
A15
Gunthorpe
Eye Green
A47
Thorney
Guyhirn
South Luffenham
Collyweston
Wittering
Peterborough
Marholm
Walton
Dogsthorpe
Eye
Newark
Stone Bridge Corner
Thornhaugh
A1
Duddington
Upton
A47
Tixover
Wansford
A47
A1139
Peterborough
Wakerley
Stibbington
Ailsworth
North Side
Eldernell
Sutton
Castor
Longthorpe
Fengate
Coates
King's Cliffe
Yarwell
Old Fletton
A605
Sibson
Water Newton
Orton Longueville
Stanground
Whittlesey
Inham's End
Eastrea
Turves
A43
Blatherwycke
Apethorpe
Nassington
A1
SIBSON
Alwalton
A605
Orton Waterville
Twenty Foot River
Chesterton
A1139
Farcet
Bulwick
Woodnewton
PETERBOROUGH SERVICES
Fotheringhay
Elton
A605
Haddon
B1093
Flood's Ferry
Deenethorpe
Southwick
Yaxley
Pondersbridge
Eaglethorpe
Warmington
Tansor
Morborne
Glapthorn
Cotterstock
Norman Cross
B1040
Nene
Benwick
A427
Folksworth
Ramsey Mereside
B1093
Upper Benefield
Lower Benefield
Oundle
Ashton
Caldecote
Stilton
B1096
Polebrook
Lutton
Denton
Holme
B660
Ramsey St Mary's
Forty Foot Drain
Ramsey Forty Foot
Stoke Doyle
Conington
Ramsey Heights
Barnwell St Andrew
Nene
Glatton
A1(M)
Ramsey
Pilton
Hemington
Wadenhoe
Barnwell All Saints
Luddington in the Brook
Sawtry
B1043
Bury
Ferry Hill
A6116
Great Gidding
Church End
Achurch
Thurning
B660
Upwood
Chapel Head
Aldwincle
Wigsthorpe
Little Gidding
B1040
Steeple Gidding
Wood Walton
Great Raveley
Wistow
B1050
Lowick
A605
Thorpe Waterville
B662
B1090
Clopton
Winwick
Coppingford
Little Raveley
Warboys
A141
Slipton
Islip
Titchmarsh
Hamerton
Fenton
Twywell
Thrapston
Upton
Wennington
Pidley
B1040
Old Weston
Alconbury Weston
Abbots Ripton
Broughton
Somersham
Woodford
A14
Buckworth
King's Ripton
Old Hurst
B1086
Denford
Bythorn
Brington
Little Stukeley
Colne
Keyston
Molesworth
Barham
Alconbury
Woodhurst
Bluntisham
Great Stukeley
Great Addington
Ringstead
Leighton Bromswold
Woolley
A14
B1040
Little Addington
A141
Sapley
B1090
A45
B663
Catworth
Huntingdon
Hartford
Wyton
Raunds
Spaldwick
A1
A1123
Needingworth
Easton
B660
Ellington
A14
Houghton
St Ives
Stanwick
Hargrave
Covington
Stow Longa
Brampton
Hemingford Abbots
Holywell
Chelveston
B645
Tilbrook
Godmanchester
Hemingford Grey
A14
Higham Ferrers
Caldecott
Shelton
Lower Dean
Grafham
Fenstanton
Fen Drayton
Swavesey
Grafham Water
Galley Hill
Warmonds Hill
Upper Dean
Kimbolton
West Perry
East Perry
Buckden
Rushden
Yeldon
Offord Cluny
Boxworth End
Hilton
Newton Bromswold
Swineshead
Stonely
Offord Darcy
Great Ouse
Little Irthlingborough
A6
Melchbourne
Pertenhall
Dillington
Staughton Green
B661
A1
Diddington
Papworth
Conington
CAMBRIDGE SERVICES
Cambr

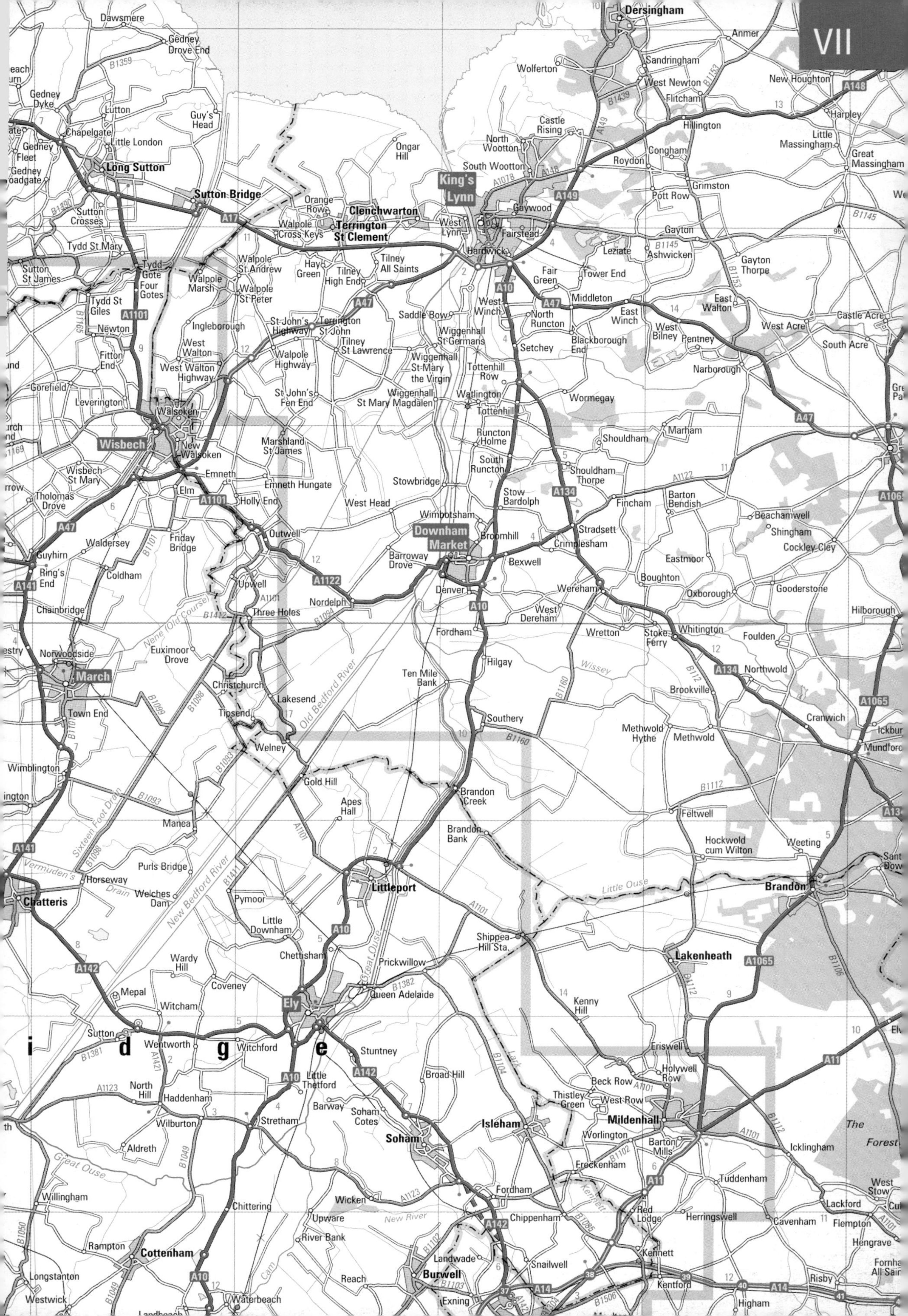
Dawsmere
Gedney Drove End
Dersingham
Anmer
Sandringham
Wolferton
West Newton
Flitcham
New Houghton
Harpley
Gedney Dyke
Lutton
Guy's Head
Chapelgate
Little London
Gedney
Fleet
Long Sutton
Ongar Hill
Castle Rising
North Wootton
Hillington
Little Massingham
Great Massingham
Congham
Roydon
South Wootton
King's Lynn
Grimston
Sutton Bridge
Pott Row
Gaywood
Orange Row
Clenchwarton
Terrington St Clement
Walpole Cross Keys
West Lynn
Fairstead
Gayton
Sutton Crosses
Tydd St Mary
Hardwick
Leziate
Ashwicken
Gayton Thorpe
Sutton St James
Tydd Gote
Four Gotes
Walpole St Andrew
Walpole Marsh
Walpole St Peter
Hay Green
Tilney High End
Tilney All Saints
Fair Green
Tower End
Middleton
East Walton
Tydd St Giles
Newton
Ingleborough
St John's Highway
Terrington St John
Tilney St Lawrence
Saddle Bow
West Winch
North Runcton
East Winch
West Bilney
Pentney
Castle Acre
West Acre
South Acre
Fitton End
West Walton
West Walton Highway
Walpole Highway
Wiggenhall St Germans
Wiggenhall St Mary the Virgin
Setchey
Blackborough End
Narborough
Gorefield
Leverington
St John's Fen End
Wiggenhall St Mary Magdalen
Tottenhill Row
Watlington
Tottenhill
Wormegay
Walsoken
Wisbech
New Walsoken
Marshland St James
Runcton Holme
Shouldham
Marham
Wisbech St Mary
Emneth
Emneth Hungate
South Runcton
Shouldham Thorpe
Stowbridge
Tholomas Drove
Elm
Holly End
West Head
Stow Bardolph
Fincham
Barton Bendish
Beachamwell
Wimbotsham
Shingham
Outwell
Downham Market
Broomhill
Stradsett
Crimplesham
Cockley Cley
Waldersey
Friday Bridge
Guyhirn
Barroway Drove
Bexwell
Eastmoor
Ring's End
Coldham
Upwell
Denver
Boughton
Nordelph
Wereham
Oxborough
Gooderstone
Chainbridge
Three Holes
West Dereham
Hilborough
Fordham
Wretton
Stoke Ferry
Whitington
Foulden
Norwoodside
Euximoor Drove
Hilgay
March
Christchurch
Ten Mile Bank
Northwold
Brookville
Town End
Lakesend
Tipsend
Southery
Methwold Hythe
Methwold
Cranwich
Mundford
Welney
Wimblington
Gold Hill
Brandon Creek
Apes Hall
Feltwell
Manea
Brandon Bank
Hockwold cum Wilton
Weeting
Purls Bridge
Horseway
Welches Dam
Littleport
Brandon
Chatteris
Pymoor
Little Downham
Shippea Hill Sta.
Chettisham
Lakenheath
Prickwillow
Wardy Hill
Coveney
Queen Adelaide
Mepal
Witcham
Kenny Hill
Ely
Sutton
Wentworth
Witchford
Stuntney
Eriswell
Little Thetford
Broad Hill
Holywell Row
North Hill
Haddenham
Beck Row
Thistley Green
West Row
Barway
Soham Cotes
Wilburton
Stretham
Isleham
Mildenhall
Soham
Worlington
Barton Mills
The Forest
Icklingham
Aldreth
Freckenham
Tuddenham
Fordham
Wicken
West Stow
Willingham
Chittering
Lackford
Upware
Chippenham
Red Lodge
Herringswell
Cavenham
Flempton
Rampton
River Bank
Hengrave
Cottenham
Landwade
Kennett
Snailwell
Longstanton
Burwell
Reach
Kentford
Risby
Westwick
Waterbeach
Exning
Higham
Sixteen Foot Drain
Vermuden's Drain
New Bedford River
Old Bedford River
Nene (Old Course)
Great Ouse
Little Ouse
Wissey
Lark
Kennett
Cam
New River
i
d
g
e

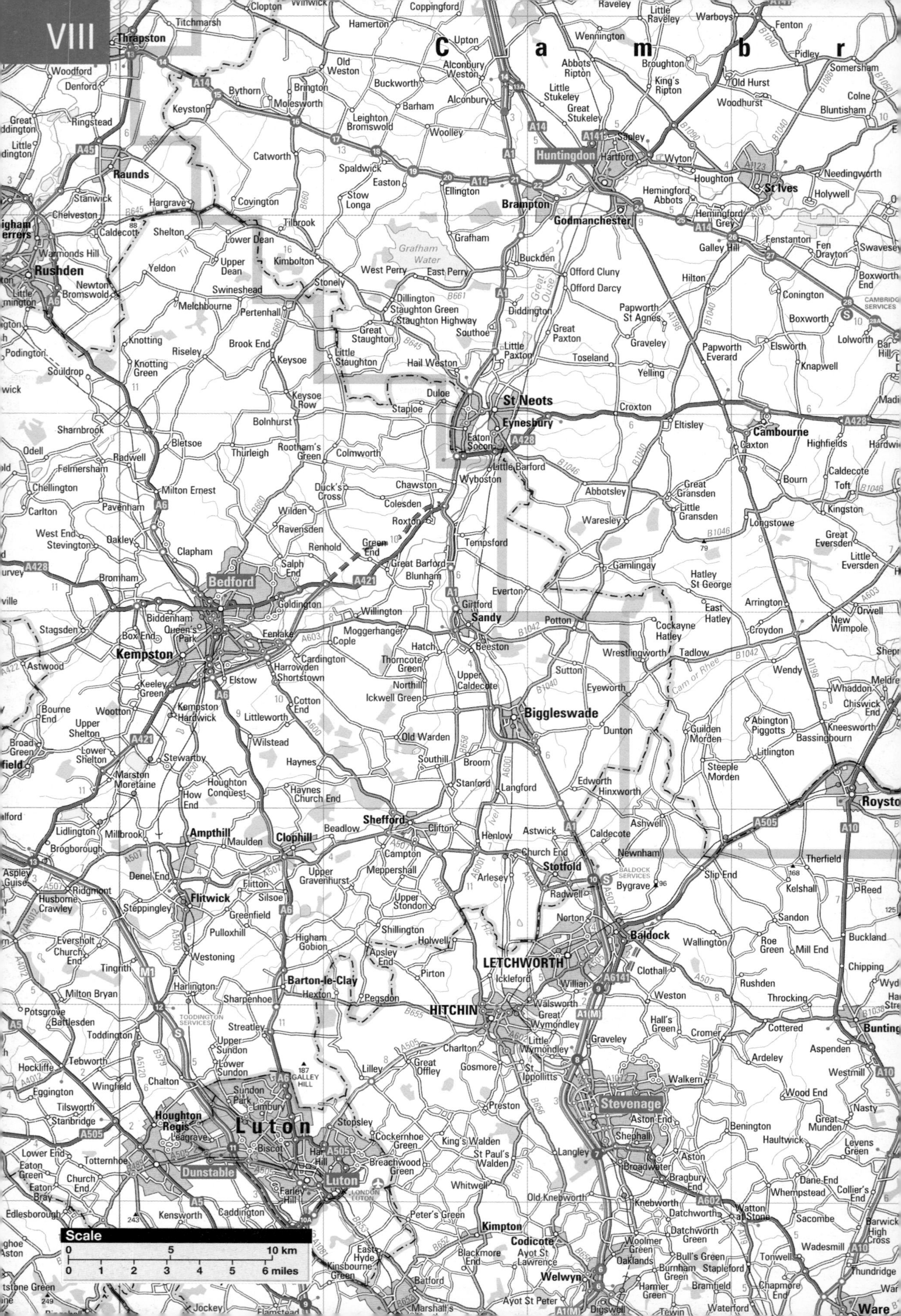
VIII
Cambr
Thrapston
Titchmarsh
Clopton
Winwick
Coppingford
Hamerton
Upton
Raveley
Little Raveley
Warboys
Fenton
Wennington
Woodford
Denford
Old Weston
Alconbury Weston
Abbots Ripton
Broughton
King's Ripton
Pidley
Somersham
Old Hurst
Colne
Bluntisham
Woodhurst
Bythorn
Brington
Buckworth
Alconbury
Little Stukeley
Great Stukeley
Keyston
Molesworth
Barham
Leighton Bromswold
Woolley
Sapley
Hartford
Wyton
Huntingdon
Great Addington
Ringstead
Little Addington
Raunds
Catworth
Spaldwick
Easton
Ellington
Brampton
Godmanchester
Houghton
Hemingford Abbots
Hemingford Grey
St Ives
Needingworth
Holywell
Stanwick
Hargrave
Covington
Stow Longa
Chelveston
Higham Ferrers
Caldecott
Shelton
Tilbrook
Lower Dean
Grafham
Grafham Water
Galley Hill
Fenstanton
Fen Drayton
Swavesey
Warmonds Hill
Rushden
Yeldon
Upper Dean
Kimbolton
West Perry
East Perry
Buckden
Offord Cluny
Offord Darcy
Hilton
Boxworth End
Newton Bromswold
Little Irchester
Swineshead
Stonely
Dillington
Staughton Green
Staughton Highway
Great Ouse
Diddington
Papworth St Agnes
Conington
Cambridge Services
Melchbourne
Pertenhall
Southoe
Great Paxton
Boxworth
Great Staughton
Little Paxton
Graveley
Papworth Everard
Elsworth
Lolworth
Bar Hill
Knotting
Riseley
Brook End
Keysoe
Little Staughton
Hail Weston
Toseland
Yelling
Knapwell
Podington
Souldrop
Knotting Green
Keysoe Row
Duloe
St Neots
Staploe
Eynesbury
Croxton
Eltisley
Cambourne
Bolnhurst
Sharnbrook
Bletsoe
Thurleigh
Rootham's Green
Colmworth
Eaton Socon
Caxton
Highfields
Odell
Radwell
Felmersham
Little Barford
Caldecote
Chellington
Milton Ernest
Duck's Cross
Chawston
Wyboston
Abbotsley
Great Gransden
Little Gransden
Bourn
Toft
Carlton
Pavenham
Wilden
Colesden
Roxton
Waresley
Kingston
Longstowe
West End
Stevington
Oakley
Ravensden
Renhold
Green End
Tempsford
Great Eversden
Little Eversden
Clapham
Bedford
Salph End
Great Barford
Blunham
Gamlingay
Hatley St George
Bromham
Goldington
Everton
Girtford
Sandy
Potton
Arrington
Orwell
Biddenham
Queen's Park
Willington
East Hatley
New Wimpole
Stagsden
Box End
Fenlake
Moggerhanger
Cople
Cockayne Hatley
Croydon
Kempston
Cardington
Hatch
Beeston
Tadlow
Wrestlingworth
Astwood
Harrowden
Shortstown
Thorncote Green
Elstow
Upper Caldecote
Sutton
Wendy
Keeley Green
Northill
Eyeworth
Cam or Rhee
Whaddon
Bourne End
Wootton
Kempston Hardwick
Cotton End
Ickwell Green
Biggleswade
Chiswick End
Meldreth
Upper Shelton
Littleworth
Dunton
Guilden Morden
Abington Piggotts
Kneesworth
Bassingbourn
Wilstead
Old Warden
Broad Green
Lower Shelton
Stewartby
Haynes
Southill
Broom
Litlington
Steeple Morden
Marston Moretaine
Houghton Conquest
How End
Stanford
Langford
Edworth
Hinxworth
Royston
Haynes Church End
Ashwell
Lidlington
Millbrook
Ampthill
Maulden
Clophill
Beadlow
Shefford
Clifton
Henlow
Astwick
Caldecote
Brogborough
Campton
Church End
Stotfold
Newnham
Therfield
Aspley Guise
Ridgmont
Denel End
Flitton
Meppershall
Upper Gravenhurst
Arlesey
Baldock Services
Bygrave
Slip End
Kelshall
Reed
Husborne Crawley
Flitwick
Silsoe
Upper Stondon
Radwell
Steppingley
Greenfield
Norton
Sandon
Eversholt
Pulloxhill
Shillington
Holwell
Baldock
Wallington
Roe Green
Mill End
Buckland
Church End
Higham Gobion
Apsley End
Letchworth
Clothall
Chipping
Tingrith
Westoning
Pirton
Ickleford
William
Milton Bryan
Harlington
Barton-le-Clay
Hexton
Pegsdon
Weston
Rushden
Throckings
Potsgrove
Sharpenhoe
Hitchin
Walsworth
Great Wymondley
Toddington Services
Battlesden
Streatley
Hall's Green
Cromer
Cottered
Buntingford
Toddington
Upper Sundon
Little Wymondley
Graveley
Charlton
Ardeley
Aspenden
Hockliffe
Tebworth
Lower Sundon
187 Galley Hill
Great Offley
Gosmore
St Ippollitts
Walkern
Westmill
Eggington
Wingfield
Chalton
Lilley
Wood End
Tilsworth
Sundon Park
Limbury
Stevenage
Nasty
Stanbridge
Houghton Regis
Luton
Stopsley
Preston
Aston End
Benington
Great Munden
Leagrave
Cockernhoe Green
King's Walden
Shephall
Haultwick
Levens Green
Lower End
Totternhoe
Biscot
Hart Hill
St Paul's Walden
Langley
Aston
Eaton Green
Dunstable
Breachwood Green
Broadwater
Bragbury End
Dane End
Collier's End
Church End
Eaton Bray
Farley Hill
London Luton
Whitwell
Whempstead
Edlesborough
Kensworth
Caddington
Old Knebworth
Knebworth
Datchworth
Watton at Stone
Sacombe
Barwick
High Cross
Peter's Green
Kimpton
Datchworth Green
Codicote
Woolmer Green
Ayot St Lawrence
Wadesmill
East Hyde
Blackmore End
Oakland
Bull's Green
Tonwell
Kinsbourne Green
Burnham Green
Stapleford
Thundridge
Welwyn
Batford
Harmer Green
Bramfield
Chapmore End
Ware
Whipsnade
Jockey End
Flamstead
Marshall's
Ayot St Peter
Digswell
Tewin
Waterford
Scale
0 5 10 km
0 1 2 3 4 5 6 miles

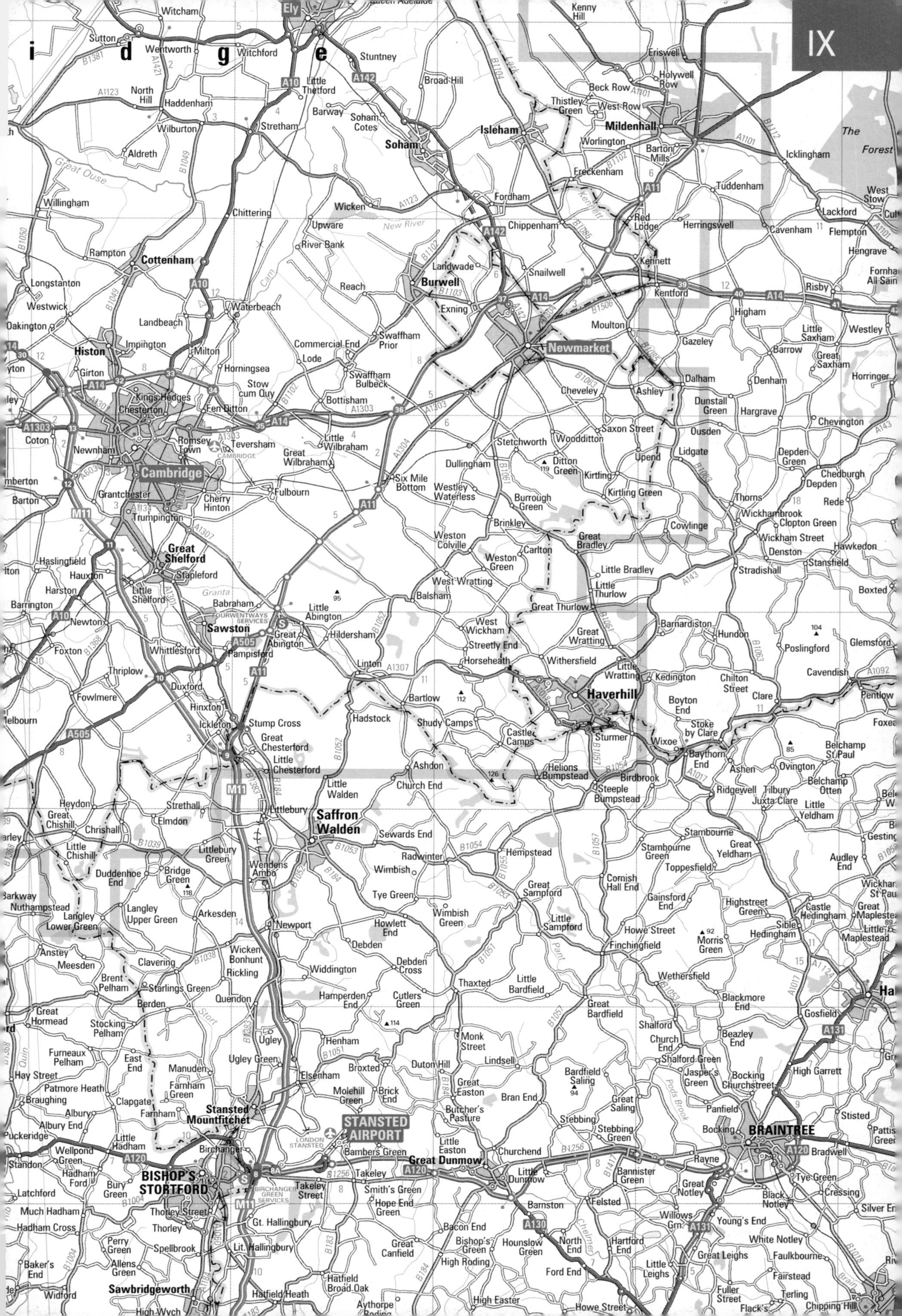

IX
Ely
Witcham
Sutton
Wentworth
Witchford
Stuntney
Little Thetford
Broad Hill
A10
A142
North Hill
Haddenham
Barway
Soham Cotes
Soham
Stretham
Wilburton
Aldreth
Great Ouse
Willingham
Chittering
Wicken
A1123
Upware
New River
River Bank
Rampton
Cottenham
Longstanton
Westwick
Oakington
Landbeach
Waterbeach
Histon
Impington
Milton
Girton
Horningsea
Kings Hedges
Chesterton
Stow cum Quy
Fen Ditton
A14
A1303
Coton
Newnham
Romsey Town
Teversham
Cambridge
Grantchester
Cherry Hinton
Fulbourn
Trumpington
Barton
M11
Great Shelford
Stapleford
Haslingfield
Hauxton
Harston
Little Shelford
Barrington
Newton
Foxton
Whittlesford
Thriplow
Fowlmere
Duxford
Hinxton
Ickleton
Babraham
Sawston
Pampisford
Great Abington
Little Abington
Hildersham
A505
A11
Reach
Burwell
Landwade
Exning
Swaffham Prior
Commercial End
Lode
Swaffham Bulbeck
Bottisham
Little Wilbraham
Great Wilbraham
Six Mile Bottom
Isleham
Fordham
Chippenham
Snailwell
Newmarket
Moulton
Kentford
Kennett
Red Lodge
Freckenham
Worlington
Mildenhall
Barton Mills
Beck Row
Thistley Green
West Row
Holywell Row
Eriswell
Kenny Hill
Icklingham
Tuddenham
Herringswell
Cavenham
Lackford
Flempton
Hengrave
West Stow
Risby
Higham
Gazeley
Little Saxham
Great Saxham
Barrow
Westley
Denham
Dalham
Ashley
Cheveley
Dunstall Green
Hargrave
Chevington
Ousden
Saxon Street
Woodditton
Stetchworth
Dullingham
Ditton Green
Kirtling
Upend
Lidgate
Depden Green
Depden
Chedburgh
Kirtling Green
Burrough Green
Westley Waterless
Brinkley
Thorns
Rede
Wickhambrook
Clopton Green
Cowlinge
Wickham Street
Denston
Hawkedon
Stansfield
Stradishall
Great Bradley
Little Bradley
Little Thurlow
Great Thurlow
Carlton
Weston Colville
Weston Green
West Wratting
Balsham
West Wickham
Streetly End
Horseheath
Great Wratting
Withersfield
Little Wratting
Haverhill
Kedington
Barnardiston
Hundon
Poslingford
Glemsford
Cavendish
Chilton Street
Clare
Boyton End
Stoke by Clare
Wixoe
Sturmer
Linton
Bartlow
Hadstock
Shudy Camps
Castle Camps
Helions Bumpstead
Steeple Bumpstead
Birdbrook
Baythorn End
Ashen
Ovington
Belchamp St Paul
Belchamp Otten
Ridgewell
Tilbury Juxta Clare
Little Yeldham
Pentlow
Stump Cross
Great Chesterford
Little Chesterford
Ashdon
Church End
Little Walden
Saffron Walden
Littlebury
Strethall
Elmdon
Heydon
Great Chishill
Chrishall
Little Chishill
Littlebury Green
Wendens Ambo
Sewards End
Radwinter
Wimbish
Hempstead
Duddenhoe End
Bridge Green
Barkway
Nuthampstead
Langley Lower Green
Langley Upper Green
Arkesden
Newport
Tye Green
Wimbish Green
Howlett End
Debden
Great Sampford
Little Sampford
Stambourne
Stambourne Green
Great Yeldham
Toppesfield
Cornish Hall End
Gainsford End
Highstreet Green
Castle Hedingham
Sible Hedingham
Howe Street
Finchingfield
Morris Green
Anstey
Meesden
Clavering
Wicken Bonhunt
Rickling
Widdington
Debden Cross
Brent Pelham
Starlings Green
Berden
Quendon
Hamperden End
Cutlers Green
Thaxted
Little Bardfield
Great Bardfield
Wethersfield
Blackmore End
Gosfield
Great Hormead
Stocking Pelham
Ugley
Henham
Monk Street
Shalford
Church End
Beazley End
Furneaux Pelham
East End
Manuden
Ugley Green
Elsenham
Duton Hill
Lindsell
Bardfield Saling
Shalford Green
Jasper's Green
Bocking Churchstreet
High Garrett
Hay Street
Patmore Heath
Braughing
Farnham Green
Farnham
Clapgate
Albury
Albury End
Molehill Green
Broxted
Brick End
Great Easton
Bran End
Great Saling
Panfield
Stansted Mountfitchet
STANSTED AIRPORT
Butcher's Pasture
Stebbing
Stebbing Green
Bocking
BRAINTREE
Stisted
Puckeridge
Little Hadham
Wellpond Green
Standon
Hadham Ford
Birchanger
Bambers Green
Little Easton
Churchend
Great Dunmow
Little Dunmow
Bannister Green
Rayne
A120
Bradwell
Tye Green
BISHOP'S STORTFORD
Bury Green
Latchford
Takeley
Takeley Street
Smith's Green
Hope End Green
Barnston
Felsted
Great Notley
Black Notley
Cressing
Much Hadham
Hadham Cross
Thorley Street
Thorley
Gt. Hallingbury
Lit. Hallingbury
Bacon End
Bishop's Green
Hounslow Green
North End
Hartford End
Willows Grn.
Young's End
Silver End
White Notley
Perry Green
Spellbrook
Great Canfield
High Roding
A130
A131
Great Leighs
Faulkbourne
Baker's End
Allens Green
Little Leighs
Fairstead
Sawbridgeworth
Hatfield Broad Oak
Ford End
Widford
Hatfield Heath
High Easter
Fuller Street
Terling
High Wych
Aythorpe Roding
Howe Street
Flack's
Chipping Hill

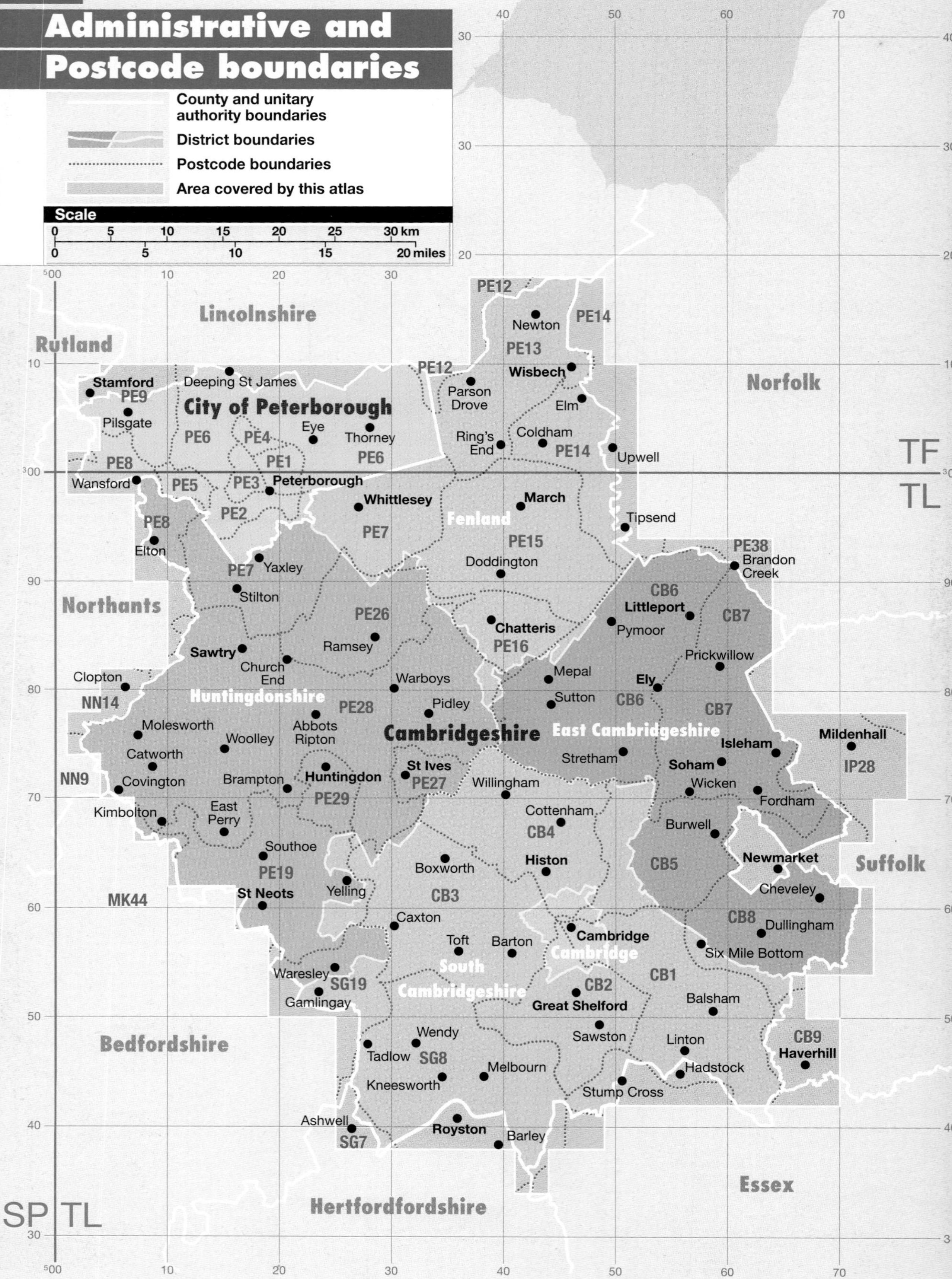

Administrative and Postcode boundaries

County and unitary authority boundaries

District boundaries

Postcode boundaries

Area covered by this atlas

Scale

| 0 | 5 | 10 | 15 | 20 | 25 | 30 km |

| 0 | 5 | 10 | 15 | 20 miles |

Lincolnshire

Rutland

Norfolk

Stamford
PE9
Pilsgate

Deeping St James

PE12

City of Peterborough

PE12
Parson Drove

PE13

Newton

PE14

Wisbech

Elm

PE6

PE4

Eye

Thorney

PE1

PE6

Ring's End

Coldham

PE14

Upwell

TF

TL

Wansford

PE8

PE5

PE3

Peterborough

PE2

Whittlesey

March

PE7

Fenland

Tipsend

PE8
Elton

PE15

PE38
Brandon Creek

PE7

Yaxley

Stilton

Doddington

CB6

Littleport

Pymoor

CB7

Northants

PE26

Ramsey

Chatteris

PE16

Mepal

Prickwillow

Sawtry
Church End

Warboys

Sutton

Ely

CB7

Clopton

NN14

Huntingdonshire

PE28

Pidley

Cambridgeshire

East Cambridgeshire

CB6

Molesworth

Woolley

Abbots Ripton

Stretham

Isleham

Mildenhall

Catworth

Brampton

Huntingdon

St Ives

Willingham

Soham

Wicken

IP28

NN9

Covington

PE29

Fordham

Kimbolton

East Perry

Cottenham

CB4

Burwell

Southoe

Histon

CB5

Newmarket

Suffolk

PE19

Boxworth

Cheveley

MK44

St Neots

Yelling

Caxton

CB3

Six Mile Bottom

CB8

Dullingham

Toft

Barton

Cambridge

CB1

Cambridge

Waresley

SG19

South Cambridgeshire

CB2

Balsham

Gamlingay

Great Shelford

Wendy

Sawston

Linton

CB9

Haverhill

Bedfordshire

Tadlow

SG8

Melbourn

Hadstock

Kneesworth

Stump Cross

Ashwell

Royston

Barley

SG7

Essex

SP TL

Hertfordshire

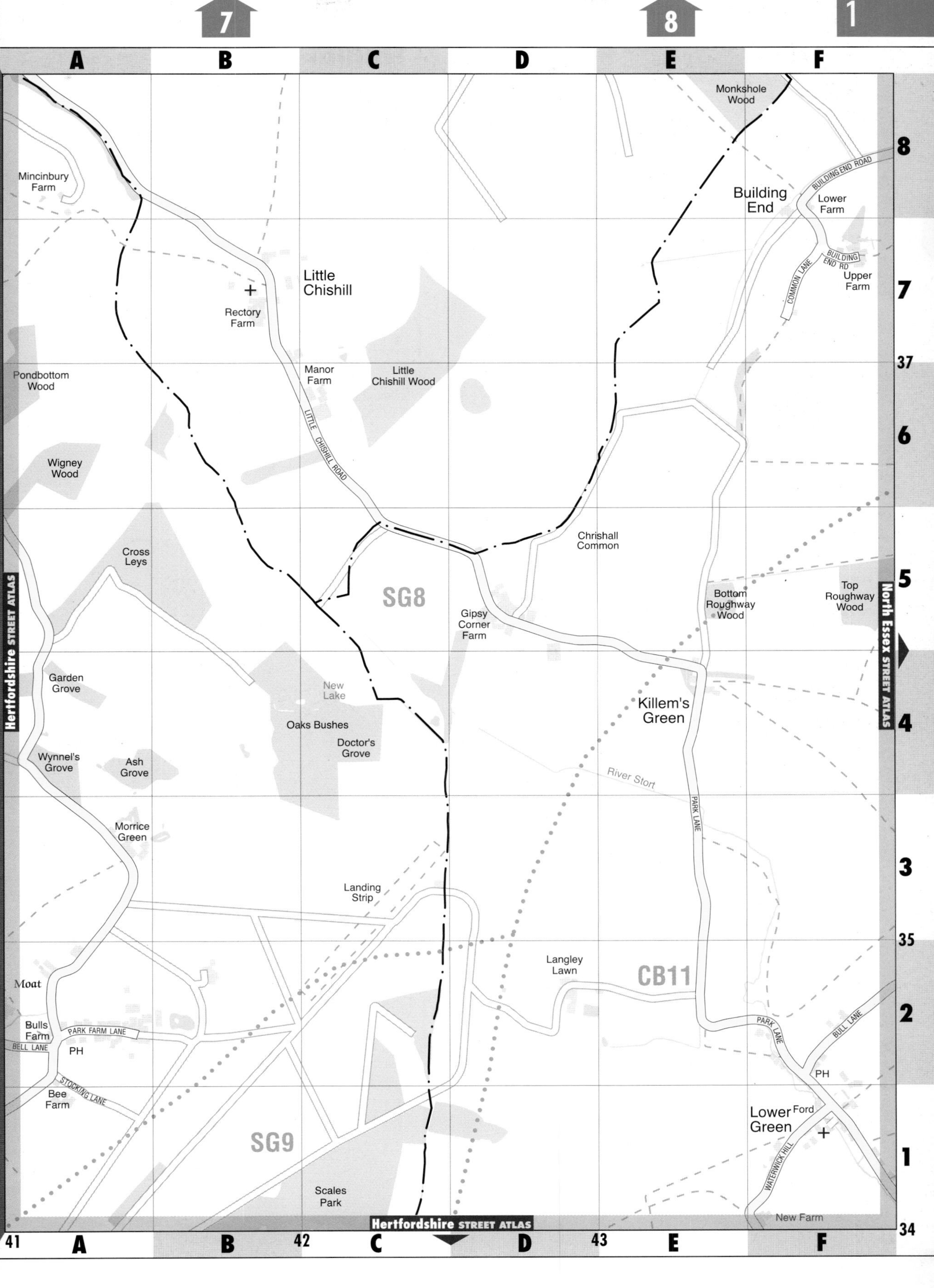

A   B   C   D   E   F

8
7
37
6
5
4
3
35
2
1
34

Mincinbury Farm

Building End

Monkshole Wood

BUILDING END ROAD
Lower Farm
COMMON LANE
BUILDING END RD
Upper Farm

Little Chishill

Rectory Farm

Pondbottom Wood

Manor Farm

Little Chishill Wood

LITTLE CHISHILL ROAD

Wigney Wood

Chrishall Common

Cross Leys

SG8

Gipsy Corner Farm

Bottom Roughway Wood

Top Roughway Wood

Garden Grove

New Lake

Killem's Green

Wynnel's Grove

Ash Grove

Oaks Bushes

Doctor's Grove

River Stort

PARK LANE

Morrice Green

Landing Strip

Moat

Langley Lawn

CB11

Bulls Farm

PARK FARM LANE

PH

BELL LANE

PARK LANE

BULL LANE

PH

Bee Farm

STOCKING LANE

Lower Green

Ford

WATERWICK HILL

SG9

Scales Park

New Farm

A **B** **C** **D** **E** **F**

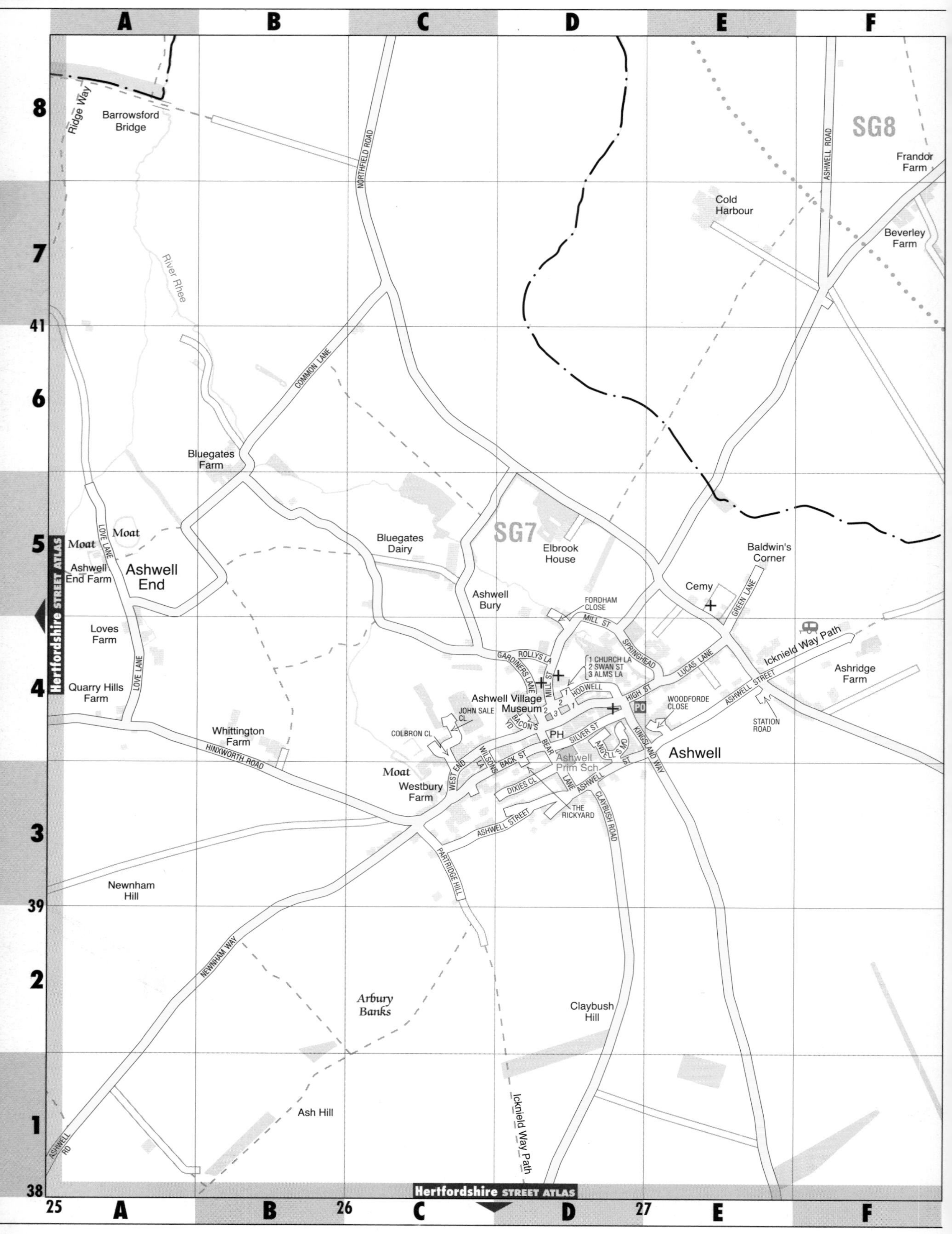

8

7

41

6

5

4

39

3

2

1

38

Ridge Way

Barrowsford Bridge

Northfield Road

River Rhee

Common Lane

SG8

Ashwell Road

Frandor Farm

Beverley Farm

Cold Harbour

Bluegates Farm

Bluegates Dairy

Moat

Moat

Love Lane

Ashwell End Farm

Ashwell End

Loves Farm

Love Lane

Quarry Hills Farm

SG7

Elbrook House

Ashwell Bury

Baldwin's Corner

Green Lane

Cemy

FORDHAM CLOSE

MILL ST

ROLLYS LA

GARDINERS LANE

MILL ST

Ashwell Village Museum

JOHN SALE CL

BACON'S

COLBRON CL

WEST END

WILSONS LA

BACK ST

PH

Moat

Westbury Farm

DIXIES CL

SILVER ST

THE RICKYARD

CLAYBUSH ROAD

ASHWELL LANE

HODWELL

SPRINGHEAD

HIGH ST

LUCAS LANE

1 CHURCH LA
2 SWAN ST
3 ALMS LA

Icknield Way Path

WOODFORDE CLOSE

KINGSLAND WAY

PO

Ashwell Prim Sch

MUSW..

Ashwell

Ashridge Farm

ASHWELL STREET

STATION ROAD

Whittington Farm

HINXWORTH ROAD

ASHWELL STREET

PARTRIDGE HILL

Newnham Hill

NEWNHAM WAY

Arbury Banks

Claybush Hill

ASHWELL RD

Ash Hill

Icknield Way Path

25 **A** **B** 26 **C** **D** 27 **E** **F**

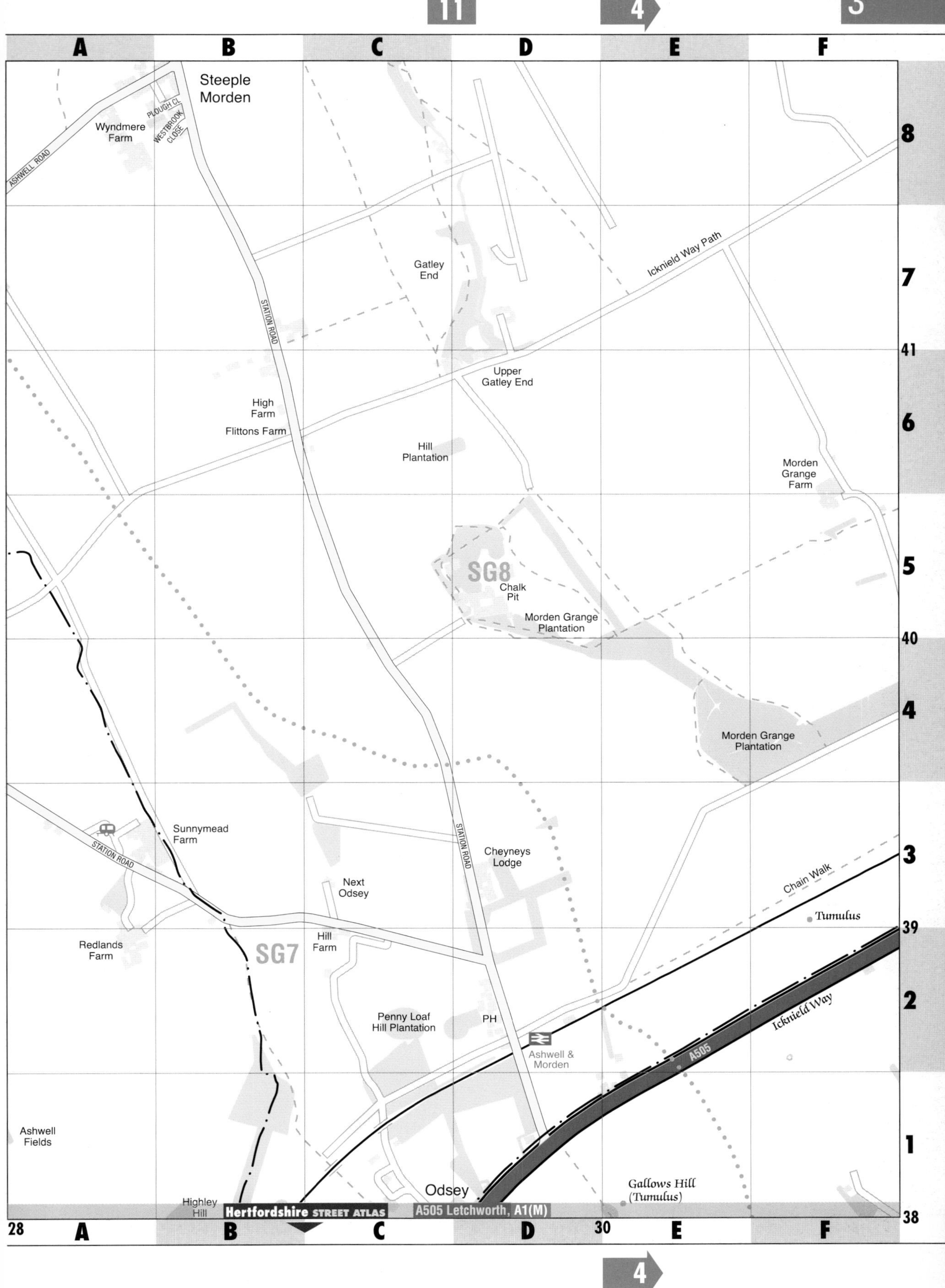
11
4
A
B
C
D
E
F
8
7
41
6
5
40
4
3
39
2
1
38
28
30
Steeple
Morden
Wyndmere
Farm
PLOUGH CL
WESTBROOK
CLOSE
ASHWELL ROAD
STATION ROAD
Gatley
End
Icknield Way Path
Upper
Gatley End
High
Farm
Flittons Farm
Hill
Plantation
Morden
Grange
Farm
SG8
Chalk
Pit
Morden Grange
Plantation
Morden Grange
Plantation
Sunnymead
Farm
STATION ROAD
Cheyneys
Lodge
Next
Odsey
Chain Walk
Tumulus
Redlands
Farm
SG7
Hill
Farm
Penny Loaf
Hill Plantation
PH
Ashwell &
Morden
A505
Icknield Way
Ashwell
Fields
Gallows Hill
(Tumulus)
Odsey
Highley
Hill
Hertfordshire STREET ATLAS
A505 Letchworth, A1(M)
4

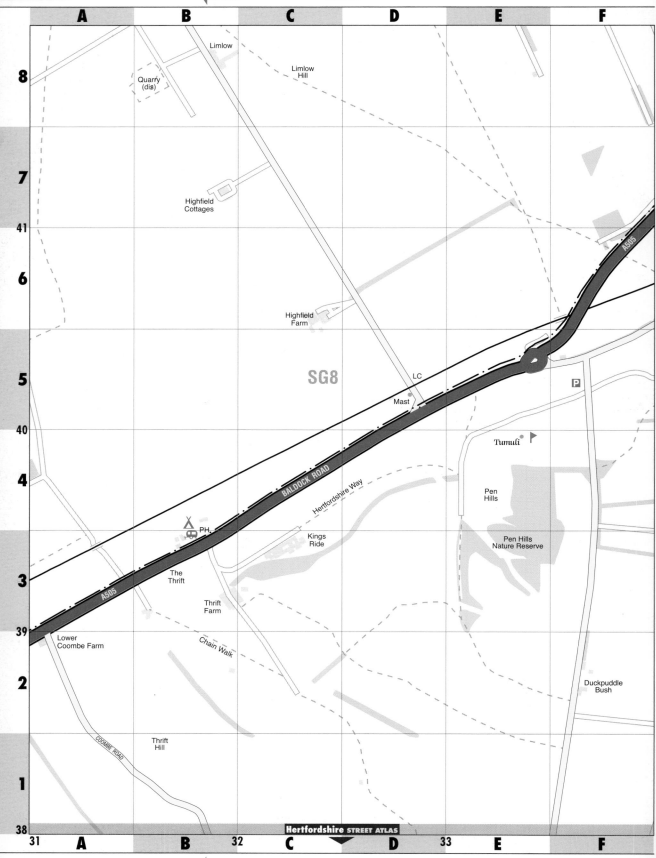

A B C D E F

8

7

41

6

5

40

4

3

39

2

1

38

31 A B 32 C D 33 E F

Limlow

Quarry
(dis)

Limlow
Hill

Highfield
Cottages

Highfield
Farm

SG8

LC

Mast

Tumuli

Pen
Hills

Pen Hills
Nature Reserve

BALDOCK ROAD

Hertfordshire Way

PH

Kings
Ride

The
Thrift

Thrift
Farm

A505

Chain Walk

Lower
Coombe Farm

Duckpuddle
Bush

Thrift
Hill

COOMBE ROAD

A505

Hertfordshire STREET ATLAS

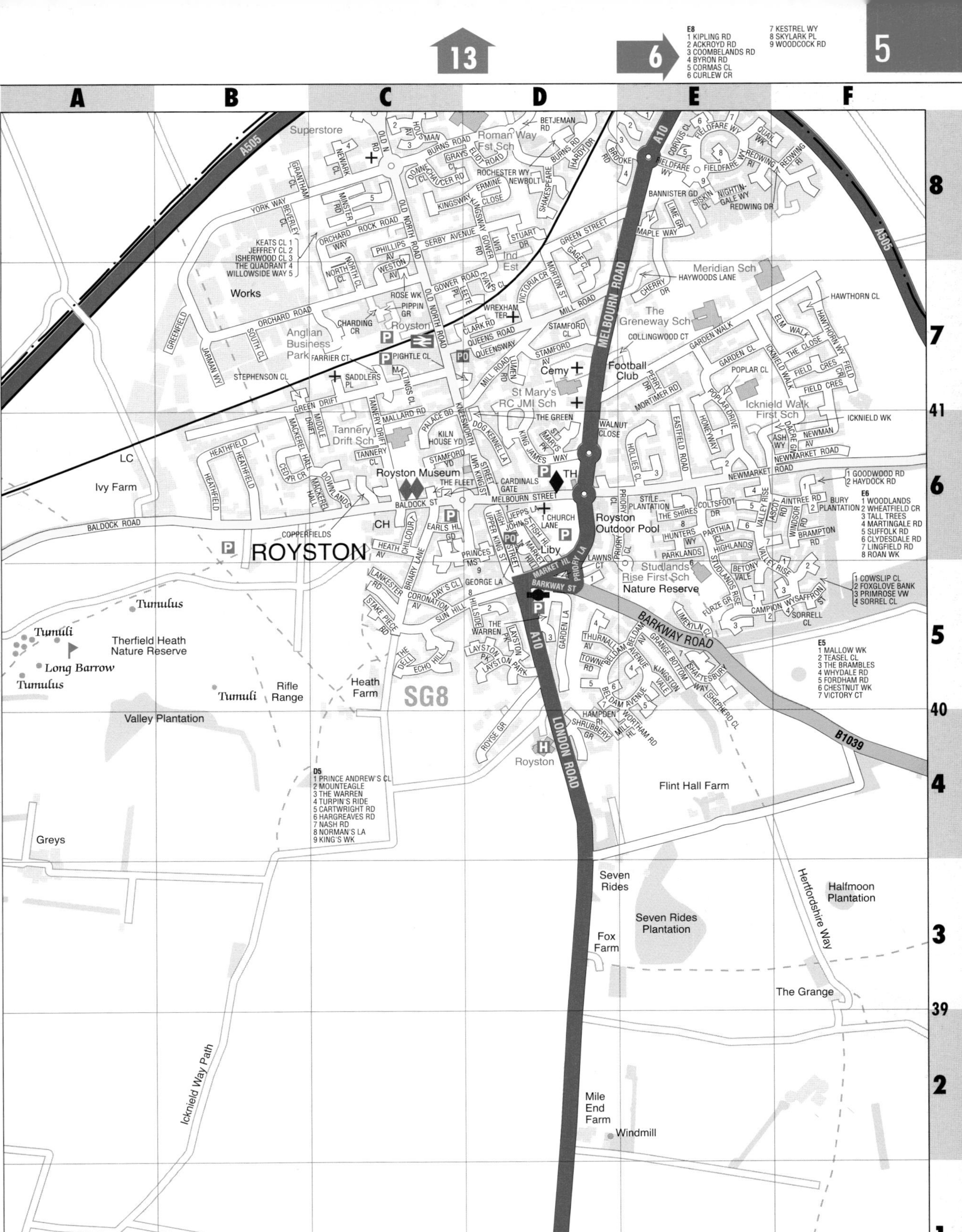

13

6

5

E8
1 KIPLING RD
2 ACKROYD RD
3 COOMBELANDS RD
4 BYRON RD
5 CORMAS CL
6 CURLEW CR

7 KESTREL WY
8 SKYLARK PL
9 WOODCOCK RD

A B C D E F

8

7

41

6

5

40

4

3

39

2

1

38

Superstore

Roman Way
Fst Sch

Meridian Sch

The
Greneway Sch

Football
Club

Icknield Walk
First Sch

ICKNIELD WK

E6
1 GOODWOOD RD
2 HAYDOCK RD

E6
1 WOODLANDS
2 WHEATFIELD CR
3 TALL TREES
4 MARTINGALE RD
5 SUFFOLK RD
6 CLYDESDALE RD
7 LINGFIELD RD
8 ROAN WK

1 COWSLIP CL
2 FOXGLOVE BANK
3 PRIMROSE VW
4 SORREL CL

E5
1 MALLOW WK
2 TEASEL CL
3 THE BRAMBLES
4 WHYDALE RD
5 FORDHAM RD
6 CHESTNUT WK
7 VICTORY CT

B1039

Works

KEATS CL 1
JEFFREY CL 2
ISHERWOOD CL 3
THE QUADRANT 4
WILLOWSIDE WAY 5

Anglian Business
Park

St Mary's
RC JMI Sch

Royston Museum

The Fleet

ROYSTON

Royston
Outdoor Pool

Studlands
Rise First Sch

Nature Reserve

Tannery
Drift Sch

Tannery

COPPERFIELDS

LC

Ivy Farm

BALDOCK ROAD

Tumulus

Tumuli

Long Barrow

Tumuli

Therfield Heath
Nature Reserve

Tumuli

Rifle
Range

Heath
Farm

SG8

Valley Plantation

D5
1 PRINCE ANDREW'S CL
2 MOUNTEAGLE
3 THE WARREN
4 TURPIN'S RIDE
5 CARTWRIGHT RD
6 HARGREAVES RD
7 NASH RD
8 NORMAN'S LA
9 KING'S WK

Greys

Royston

Flint Hall Farm

Seven
Rides

Fox
Farm

Seven Rides
Plantation

Halfmoon
Plantation

Hertfordshire Way

The Grange

Mile
End
Farm

Windmill

Icknield Way Path

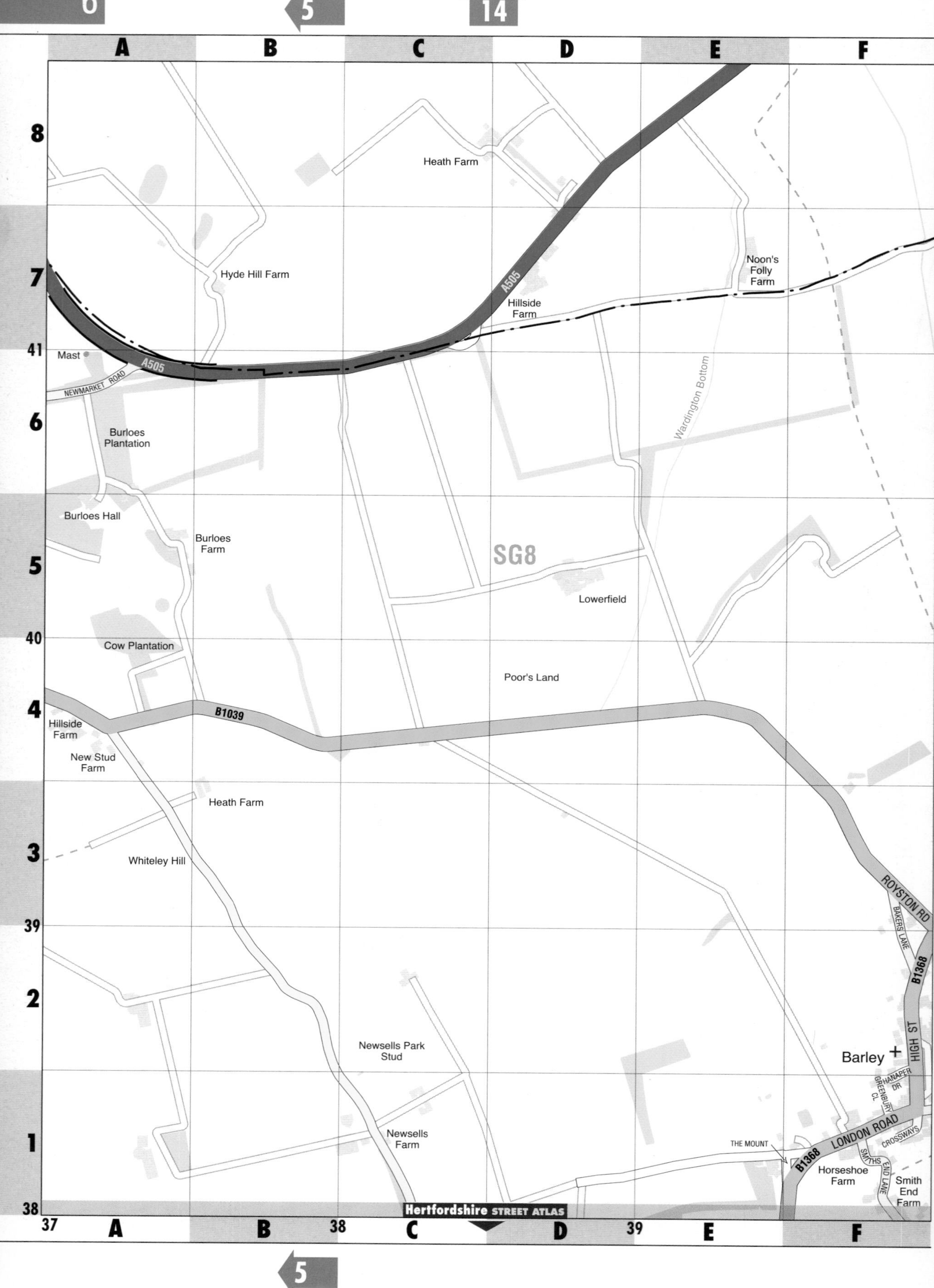

A   B   C   D   E   F

8

Heath Farm

7

Hyde Hill Farm

Noon's
Folly
Farm

A505

Hillside
Farm

41

Mast

A505

NEWMARKET ROAD

Wardington Bottom

6

Burloes
Plantation

Burloes Hall

Burloes
Farm

SG8

5

Lowerfield

40

Cow Plantation

Poor's Land

4

B1039

Hillside
Farm

New Stud
Farm

Heath Farm

3

Whiteley Hill

ROYSTON RD

BAKERS LANE

39

B1368

2

Newsells Park
Stud

Barley

HIGH ST

GREENACRE
DR

GREENBURY
CL

1

Newsells
Farm

THE MOUNT

B1368

LONDON ROAD

SMITHS

END LANE

CROSSWAYS

Horseshoe
Farm

Smith End
Farm

38

37   A   38   B   C   38   D   39   E   F

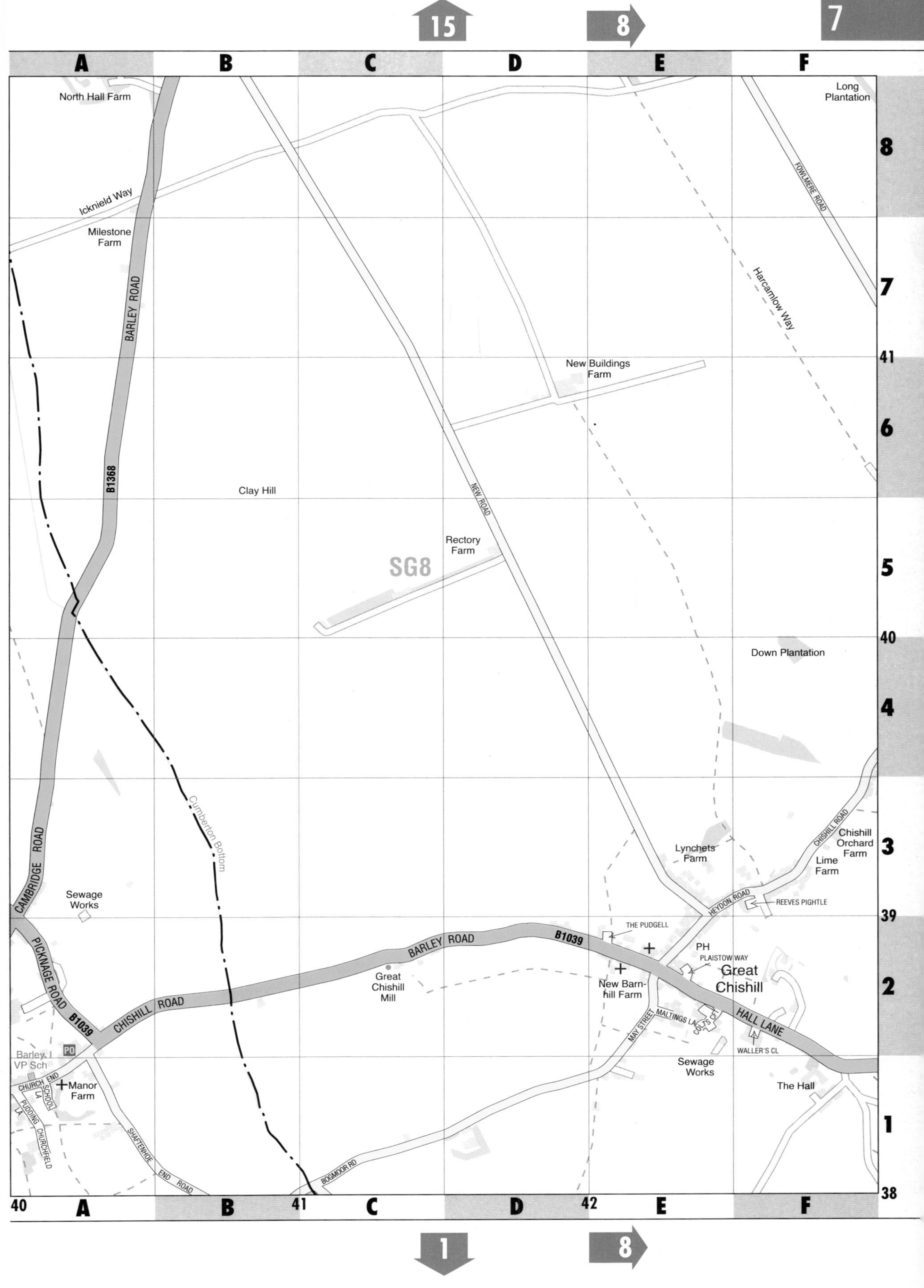
15
8
A
B
C
D
E
F
North Hall Farm
Long Plantation
8
FOWLMERE ROAD
Icknield Way
Milestone Farm
7
Harcamlow Way
BARLEY ROAD
41
New Buildings Farm
6
B1368
Clay Hill
NEW ROAD
Rectory Farm
SG8
5
40
Down Plantation
4
Cumberton Bottom
CAMBRIDGE ROAD
Lynchets Farm
CHISHILL ROAD
Chishill Orchard Farm
3
Lime Farm
Sewage Works
HEYDON ROAD
REEVES PIGHTLE
39
THE PUDGELL
B1039
BARLEY ROAD
PICKNAGE ROAD
PH
PLAISTOW WAY
Great Chishill
2
Great Chishill Mill
New Barnhill Farm
CHISHILL ROAD
B1039
MALTINGS LA
COLTS CFT
HALL LANE
MAY STREET
WALLER'S CL
PO
Barley I VP Sch
Sewage Works
CHURCH END
SCHOOL LA
Manor Farm
The Hall
PUDDING LA
CHURCHFIELD
SHAFTENHOE END ROAD
1
BOGMOOR RD
38
40
41
42
1
8

A B C D E F

8
Long Plantation

Redlands

Anthonyhill Plantation
Anthony Hill

7

41

Strip Lynchets

Reeve Hill

6

Valley Plantation

Heydon Valley Farm

SG8

Pightle Farm

CB11

5
Heydon

MILL CAUSEWAY
Hillside Farm

Crawley End

Lane Farm
HEYDON LANE

PINKENEYS

ENGLERIC

CRAWLEY END

HERTFORD LANE

Earthwork

40

HIGH CL
FOWLMERE RD

Moat

Castle Grove

4

CHISHILL ROAD

ABRAM'S LANE

Arrow Plantation

Wire Farm

Chrishall

HEYDON LA

PH
PO

Martinholme Farm

Woodgreen Animal Shelter

Broad Green Farm

PALMERS LANE

Broad Green

King's Grove

3

Wisdom's Grove

PH
PO

HOG'S LA

Park Farm

CHURCH ROAD

Icknield Way Path

P

HIGH STREET

BRICK ROW

39

Park Wood

2

Barnard's Wood

Parsonage Farm

Moat

CHALKY LANE

HOLLOW ROAD

Glebe Farm

BURY LANE

1

B1039

New Farm

BUILDING END ROAD

38
Monkshole Wood

North Essex STREET ATLAS

43 A B 44 C D 45 E F

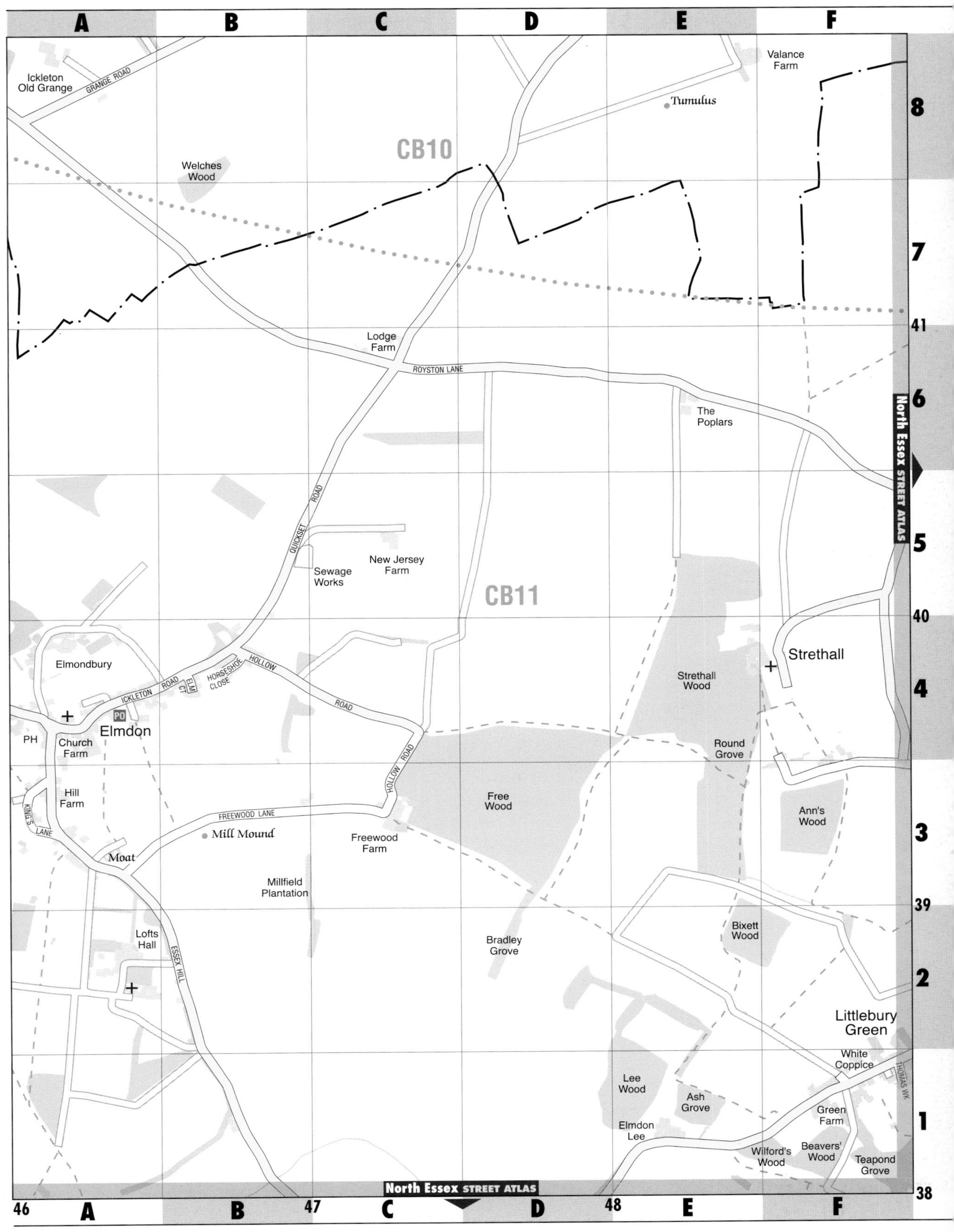

A   B   C   D   E   F

Ickleton
Old Grange
GRANGE ROAD

CB10

Welches
Wood

Valance
Farm

Tumulus

41

7

Lodge
Farm

ROYSTON LANE

6

The
Poplars

QUICKSET ROAD

Sewage
Works

New Jersey
Farm

CB11

5

40

Strethall
Wood

Strethall

Elmondbury

HORSESHOE CLOSE

ICKLETON ROAD

HIGH ST

HOLLOW ROAD

PO

Elmdon

Round
Grove

4

PH

Church
Farm

Ann's
Wood

Hill
Farm

KING'S LANE

FREEWOOD LANE

Mill Mound

HOLLOW ROAD

Free
Wood

3

Moat

Freewood
Farm

Millfield
Plantation

39

Bradley
Grove

Bixett
Wood

Lofts
Hall

ESSEX HILL

2

Littlebury
Green

White
Coppice

THOMAS WLK

Lee
Wood

Ash
Grove

Green
Farm

1

Elmdon
Lee

Beavers'
Wood

Wilford's
Wood

Teapond
Grove

38

46   A   B   47   C   D   48   E   F

North Essex STREET ATLAS

North Essex STREET ATLAS

8

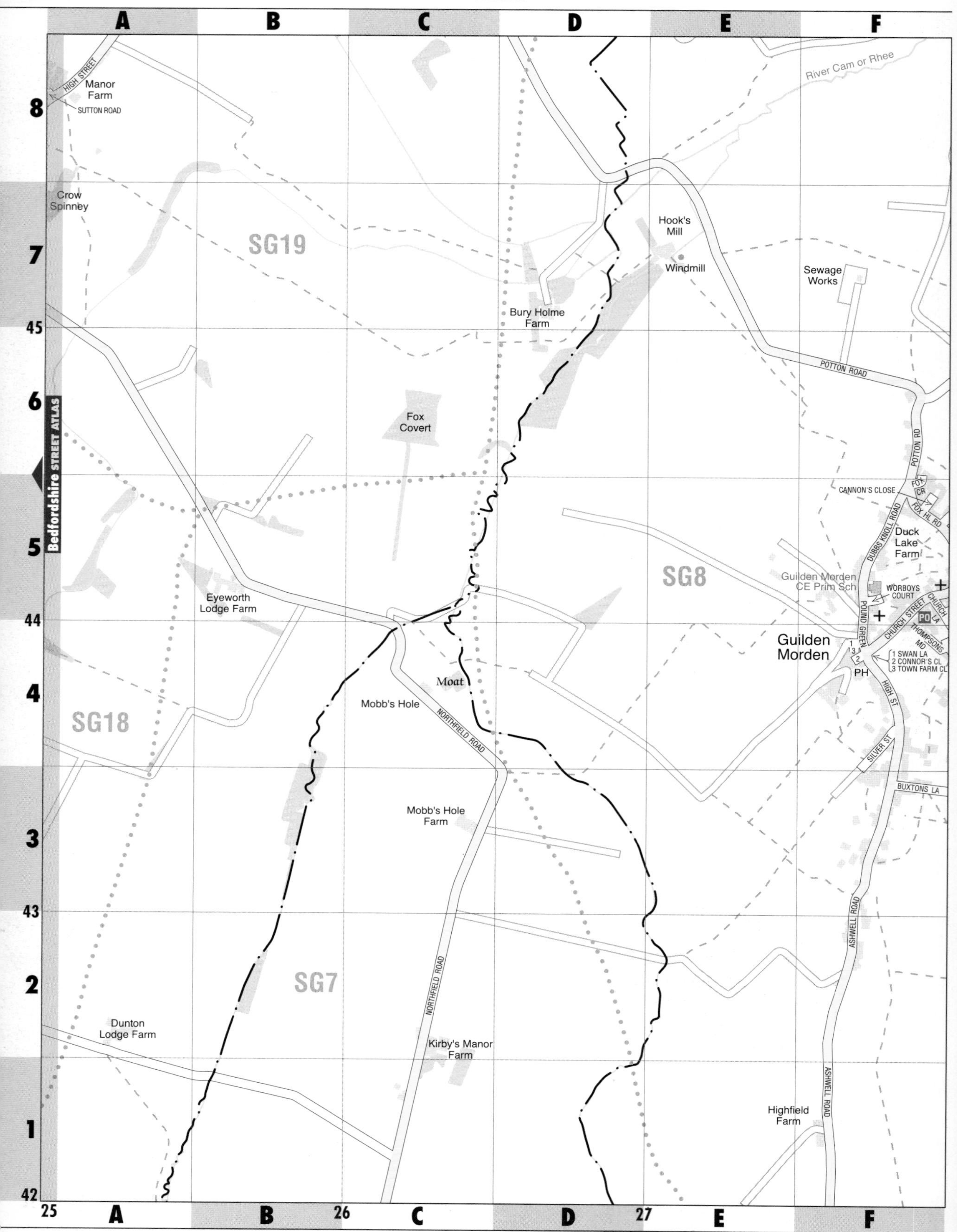

Bedfordshire STREET ATLAS

A B C D E F

8

7

45

6

5

44

4

43

3

2

1

42

25 A B 26 C D 27 E F

High Street
Manor Farm
SUTTON ROAD

Crow Spinney

SG19

Bury Holme Farm

Fox Covert

Eyeworth Lodge Farm

SG18

Moat
Mobb's Hole

NORTHFIELD ROAD

Mobb's Hole Farm

SG7

Dunton Lodge Farm

Kirby's Manor Farm

NORTHFIELD ROAD

River Cam or Rhee

Hook's Mill

Windmill

Sewage Works

POTTON ROAD

POTTON RD
FOX CR
FOX HL RD
CANNON'S CLOSE

DUBBS KNOLL ROAD

Duck Lake Farm

SG8

Guilden Morden CE Prim Sch

WORBOYS COURT

POUND GREEN

Guilden Morden

CHURCH LA
CHURCH ST
PO
MD
THOMPSON'S RD

1 SWAN LA
2 CONNOR'S CL
3 TOWN FARM CL

PH

HIGH ST

SILVER ST

BUXTONS LA

ASHWELL ROAD

Highfield Farm

ASHWELL ROAD

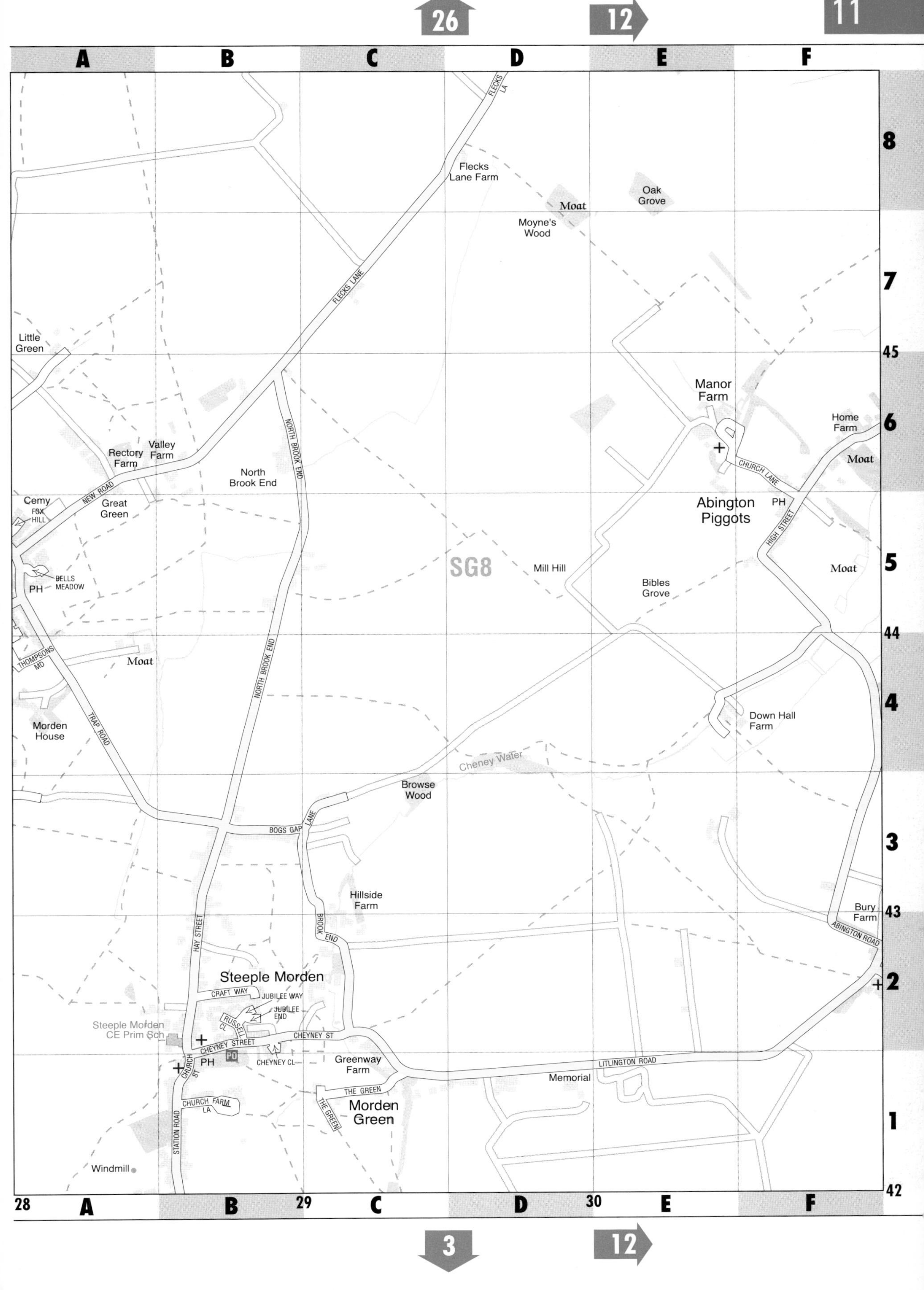

A B C D E F

8

7

45

6

45

44

4

3

43

2

1

42

Flecks Lane Farm

Moat

Oak Grove

Moyne's Wood

FLECKS LA

FLECKS LANE

Little Green

NORTH BROOK END

Manor Farm

Home Farm

Moat

CHURCH LANE

Rectory Farm

Valley Farm

North Brook End

NEW ROAD

Cemy FOX HILL

Great Green

Abington Piggots

HIGH STREET

PH

Moat

PH

BELLS MEADOW

SG8

Mill Hill

Bibles Grove

Moat

THOMPSONS MD

Moat

NORTH BROOK END

Down Hall Farm

TRAP ROAD

Morden House

Cheney Water

Browse Wood

BOGS GAP LANE

Bury Farm

ABINGTON ROAD

Hillside Farm

BROOK END

HAY STREET

Steeple Morden

CRAFT WAY

JUBILEE WAY

JUBILEE END

Steeple Morden CE Prim Sch

RUSSELL CL

CHEYNEY STREET

CHEYNEY ST

Greenway Farm

LITLINGTON ROAD

Memorial

PH

PO

CHEYNEY CL

CHURCH ST

CHURCH FARM LA

THE GREEN

Morden Green

STATION ROAD

THE GREEN

Windmill

11
27

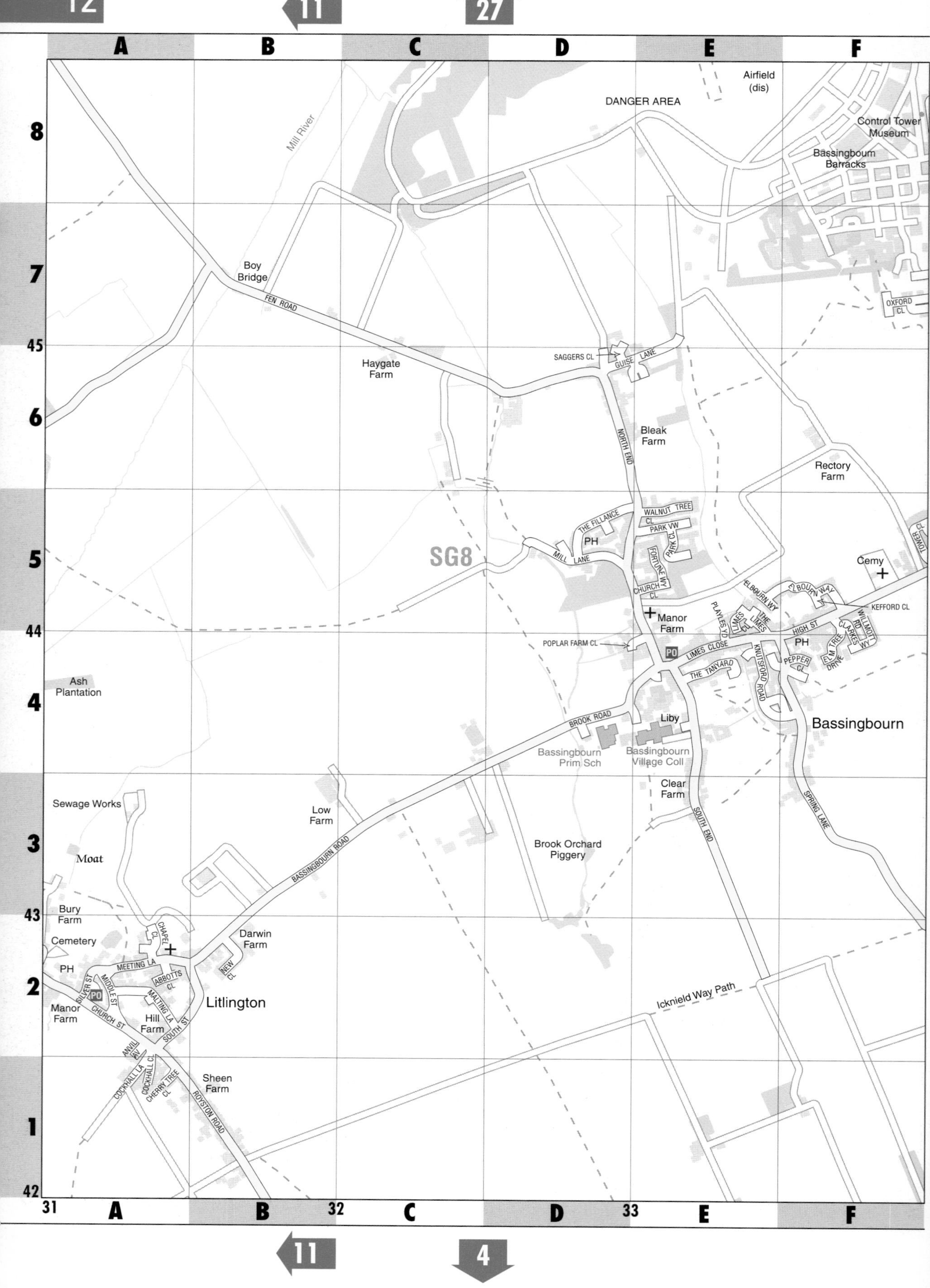
A
B
C
D
E
F
8
7
45
6
5
44
4
3
43
2
1
42
31
32
33
Airfield
(dis)
DANGER AREA
Control Tower
Museum
Bassingbourn
Barracks
Mill River
Boy
Bridge
FEN ROAD
OXFORD
CL
Haygate
Farm
SAGGERS CL
GUISE
LANE
Bleak
Farm
NORTH END
Rectory
Farm
WALNUT TREE
CL
THE FILLANCE
PARK VW
PH
PARK CL
FORTUNE WY
SG8
MILL LANE
CHURCH
CL
Cemy
TOWER CL
ELBOURN WY
ELBOURN WAY
KEFFORD CL
Manor
Farm
PLAYLES YD
LIMES CL
THE LIMES
HIGH ST
WILLMOTT RD
CLARKES WY
PH
ELM TREE
DRIVE
POPLAR FARM CL
PO
LIMES CLOSE
KNUTSFORD ROAD
PEPPER
CL
THE TANYARD
Ash
Plantation
BROOK ROAD
Liby
Bassingbourn
Bassingbourn
Prim Sch
Bassingbourn
Village Coll
Clear
Farm
SPRING LANE
Sewage Works
Low
Farm
SOUTH END
Moat
Brook Orchard
Piggery
BASSINGBOURN ROAD
Bury
Farm
Darwin
Farm
CHAPEL
CL
Cemetery
PH
MEETING LA
ABBOTTS
CL
NEW
CL
PO
SILVER ST
MIDDLE ST
MALTING LA
Litlington
Icknield Way Path
Manor
Farm
CHURCH ST
Hill
Farm
SOUTH ST
ANVIL
AV
Sheen
Farm
COCKHALL LA
COCKHALL CL
CHERRY TREE
CL
ROYSTON ROAD

11
4

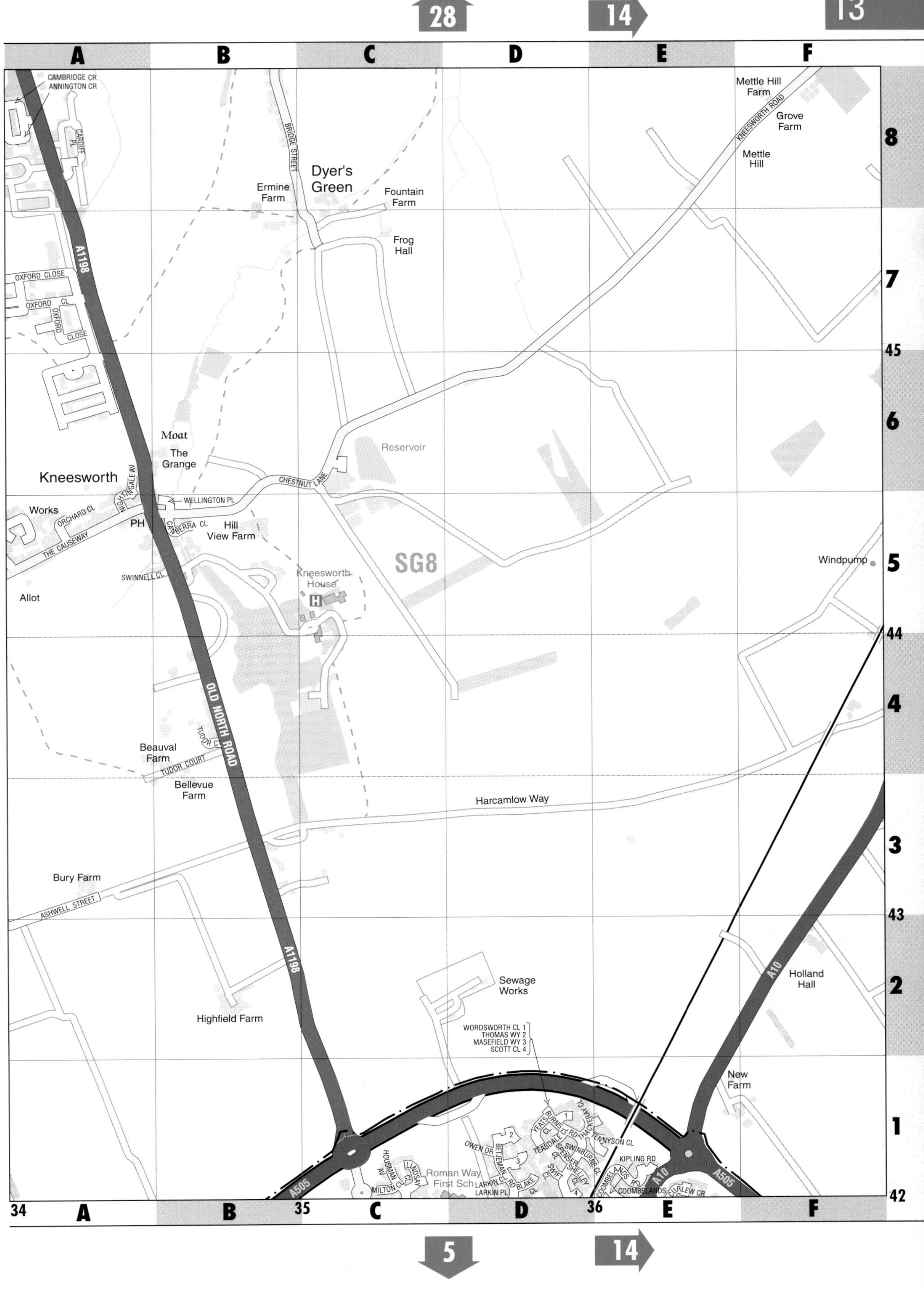
28
14
A
B
C
D
E
F
CAMBRIDGE CR
ANNINGTON CR
CARDIFF PL
BRIDGE STREET
Dyer's Green
Ermine Farm
Fountain Farm
Frog Hall
Mettle Hill Farm
KNEESWORTH ROAD
Grove Farm
Mettle Hill
8
7
45
6
5
44
4
3
43
2
1
42
A1198
OXFORD CLOSE
OXFORD CL
OXFORD CLOSE
Moat
The Grange
Kneesworth
NIGHTINGALE AV
WELLINGTON PL
CHESTNUT LANE
Reservoir
Works
ORCHARD CL
PH
CANBERRA CL
Hill View Farm
THE CAUSEWAY
SG8
Kneesworth House
H
Windpump
SWINNELL CL
Allot
OLD NORTH ROAD
TUDOR CL
Beauval Farm
TUDOR COURT
Bellevue Farm
Harcamlow Way
Bury Farm
ASHWELL STREET
A1198
Sewage Works
Highfield Farm
WORDSWORTH CL 1
THOMAS WY 2
MASEFIELD WY 3
SCOTT CL 4
A10
Holland Hall
New Farm
YEATS CL
BURNS RD
THACKERAY CL
TENNYSON CL
TEASDALE CL
SWINBURNE CL
SPENSER
SHELLEY CL
SWIFT CL
OWEN DR
BETJEMAN RD
HOUSMAN AV
LINDSAY CL
MILTON CL
Roman Way First Sch
LARKIN CL
LARKIN PL
BLAKE CL
KIPLING RD
COOMBELANDS RD
COOMBELANDS
CURLEW CR
A10
A505
A505
34
35
36
5
14

13
29

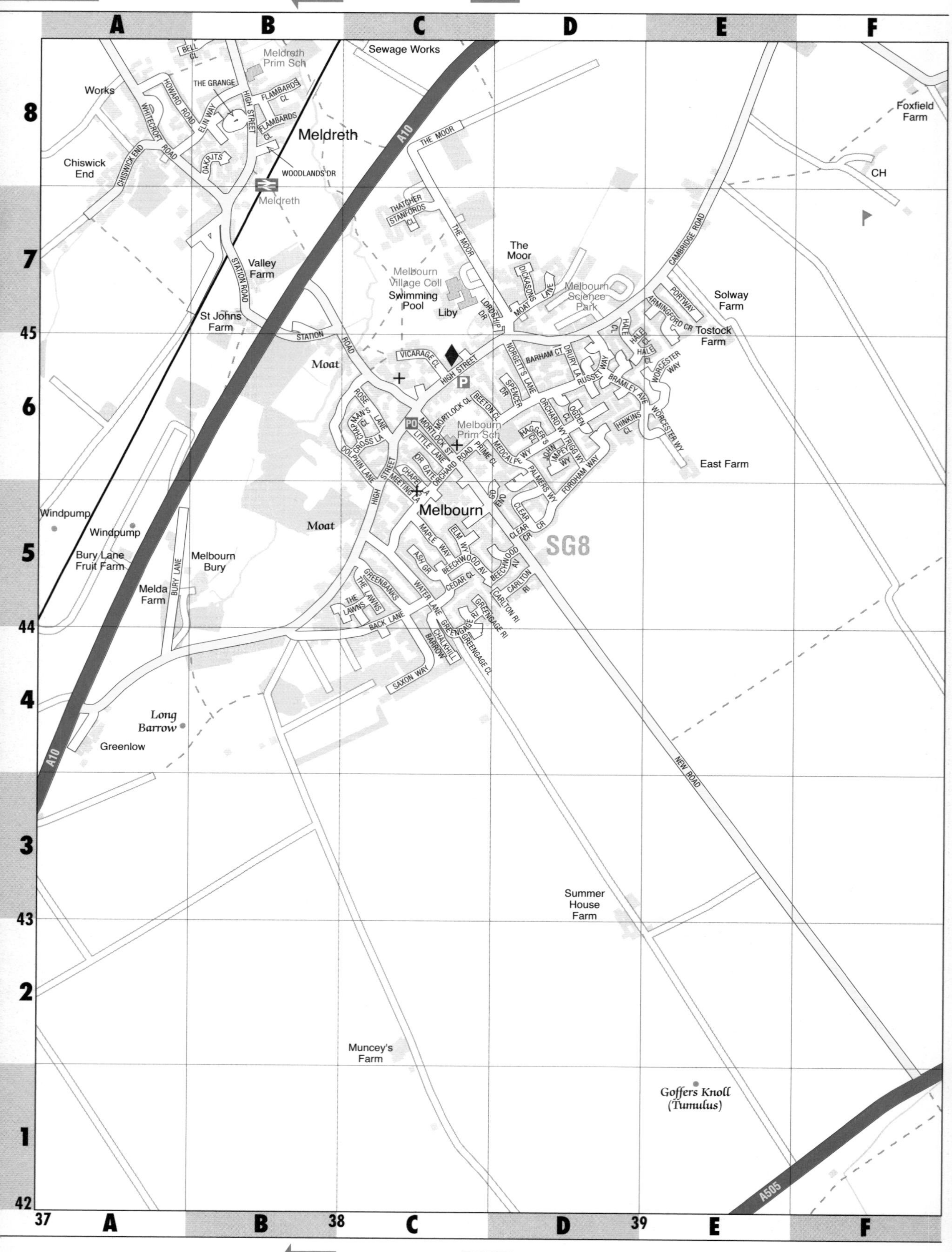
A
B
C
D
E
F
8
7
45
6
5
44
4
3
43
2
1
42
37
38
39
Sewage Works
Meldreth Prim Sch
Works
Meldreth
Chiswick End
Meldreth
Valley Farm
St Johns Farm
The Moor
Melbourn Village Coll
Swimming Pool
Liby
Melbourn Science Park
Solway Farm
Tostock Farm
Foxfield Farm
CH
Moat
Melbourn Prim Sch
Melbourn
East Farm
SG8
Windpump
Windpump
Bury Lane Fruit Farm
Melbourn Bury
Melda Farm
Moat
Long Barrow
Greenlow
A10
NEW ROAD
CAMBRIDGE ROAD
STATION ROAD
HIGH STREET
Summer House Farm
Muncey's Farm
Goffers Knoll (Tumulus)
A505

13
6

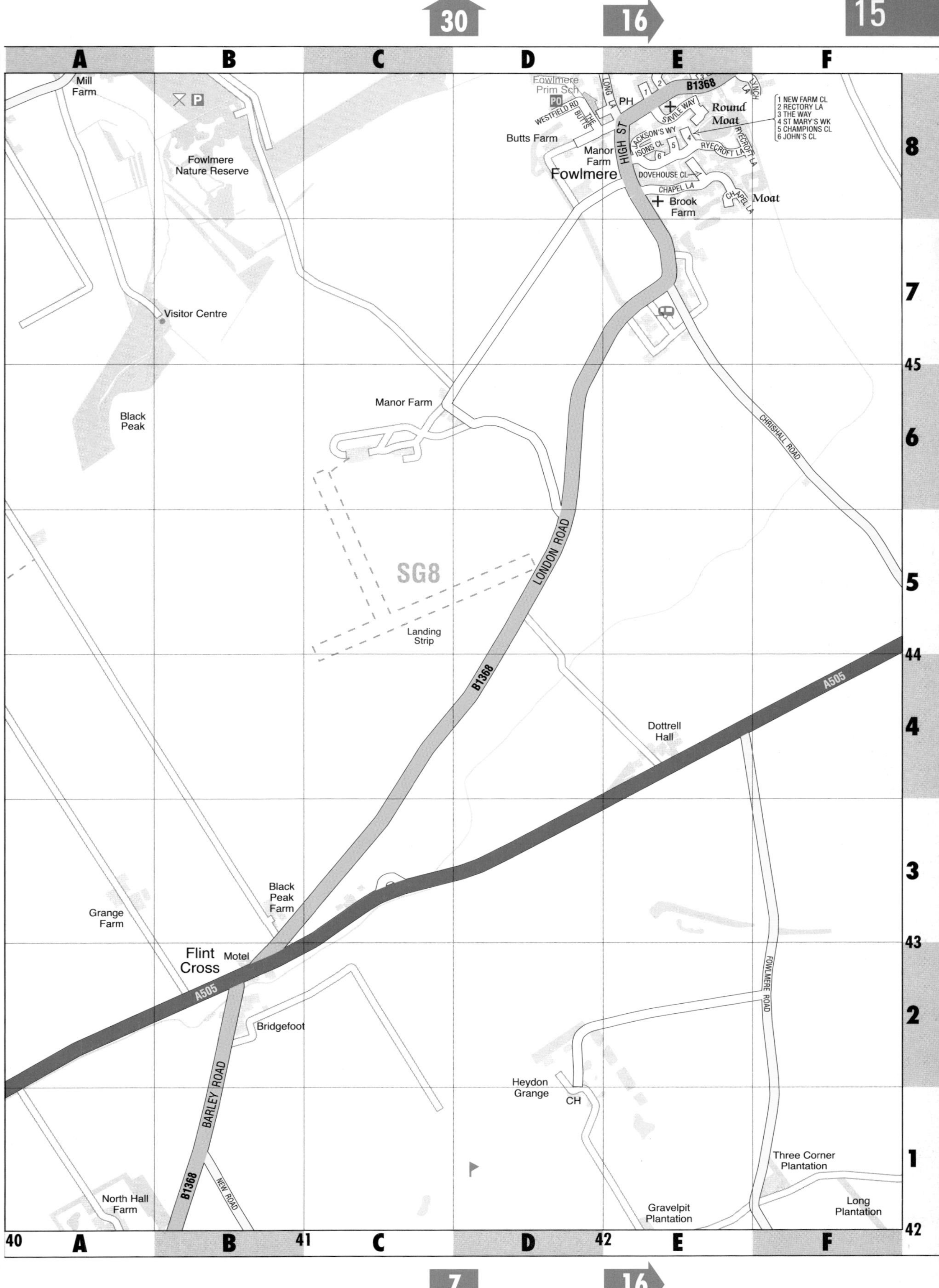

A B C D E F

Mill Farm

P

Fowlmere Nature Reserve

Fowlmere Prim Sch

PO

WESTFIELD RD

BUTTS

LONG LA

HIGH ST

PH

SAVILE WAY

JACKSON'S WY

ISONS CL

B1368

Round Moat

LYNCH

RYECROFT LA

1 NEW FARM CL
2 RECTORY LA
3 THE WAY
4 ST MARY'S WK
5 CHAMPIONS CL
6 JOHN'S CL

8

Butts Farm

Manor Farm

Fowlmere

DOVEHOUSE CL

CHAPEL LA

CHAPEL LA

Moat

Brook Farm

Visitor Centre

7

45

Black Peak

Manor Farm

CHRISHALL ROAD

6

LONDON ROAD

SG8

5

Landing Strip

B1368

A505

44

Dottrell Hall

4

Grange Farm

Black Peak Farm

3

43

Flint Cross

Motel

A505

FOWLMERE ROAD

Bridgefoot

2

Heydon Grange

CH

BARLEY ROAD

North Hall Farm

B1368

NEW ROAD

Three Corner Plantation

1

Gravelpit Plantation

Long Plantation

42

15
31

A B C D E F

8
7
45
6
5
44
4
3
43
2
1
42

Newditch Plantation
American Air Museum
Long Plantation
The Royal Anglian Regiment Museum
A505
GRAVEL PIT HILL
Gravelpit Hill Plantation
Heath Farm
CB2
Home Plantation
Grange Farm
Duxford Grange House
CHRISHALL ROAD
A505
Forty Acre Plantation
Round Plantation
SG8
Chrishall Grange
Chrishall Grange Plantation
Laburnum Plantation
CB10

43 A B 44 C D 45 E F

15
8

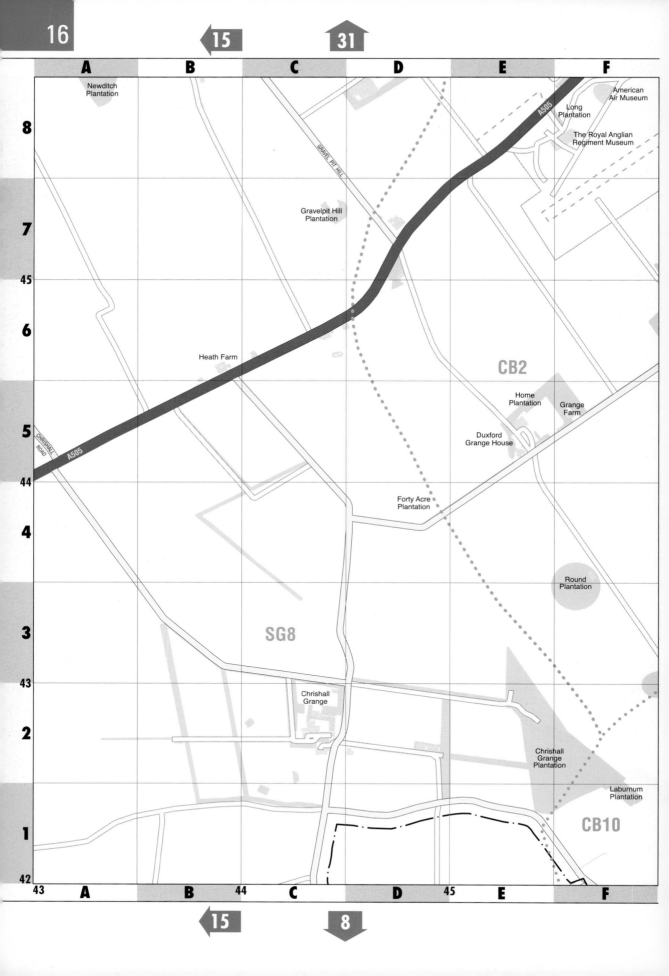

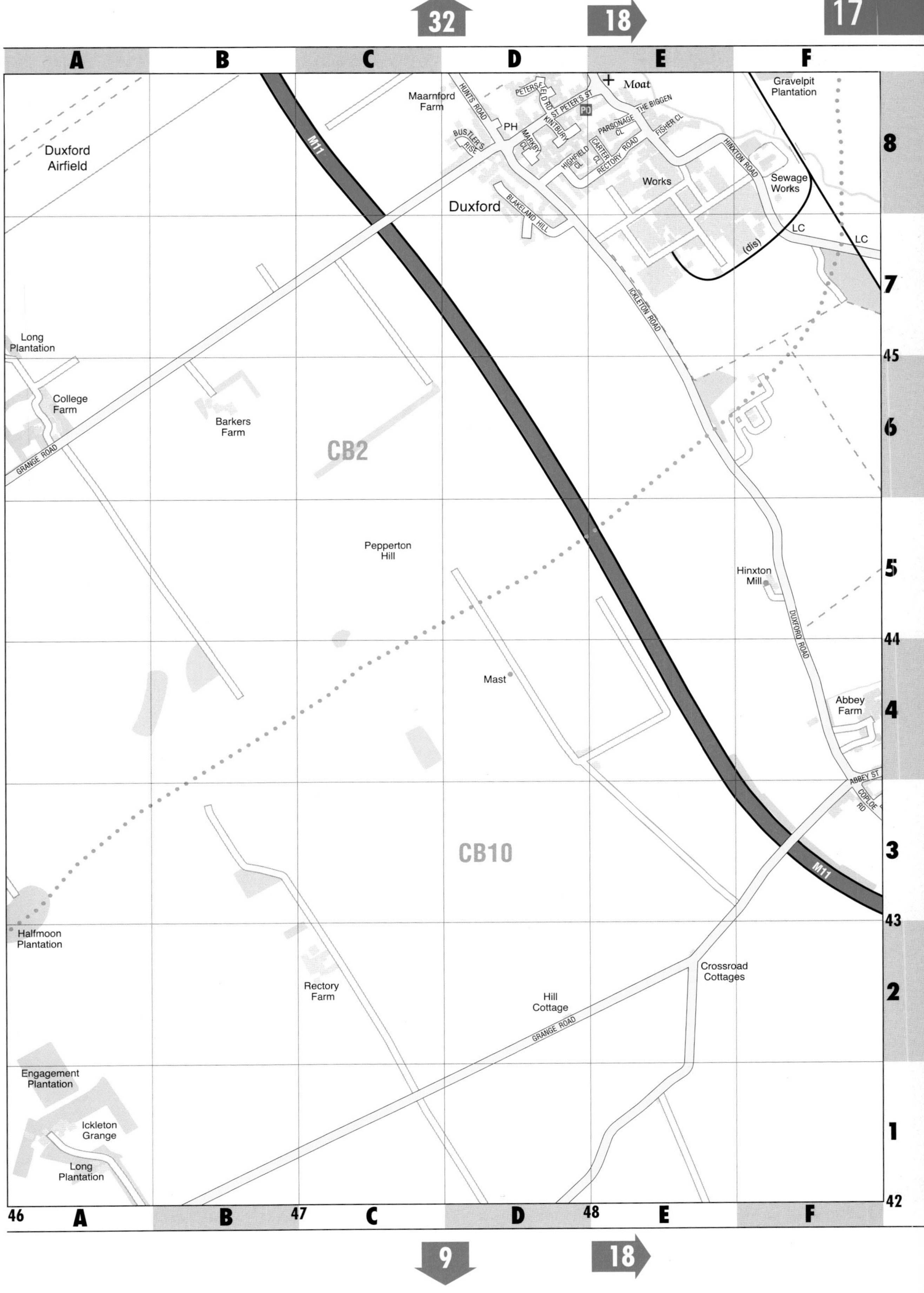
32
18
A
B
C
D
E
F
Maarnford Farm
HUNTS ROAD
PETERSFIELD RD
ST PETER'S ST
Moat
THE BIGGEN
PH
PO
KINTBURY
BUSTLER'S RISE
MARKBY CL
PARSONAGE CL
FISHER CL
HIGHFIELD CL
CARTER CL
RECTORY ROAD
HINXTON ROAD
Gravelpit Plantation
Sewage Works
Works
Duxford Airfield
Duxford
BLAKELAND HILL
M11
LC
(dis)
8
7
45
6
5
44
4
3
43
2
1
42
Long Plantation
College Farm
Barkers Farm
GRANGE ROAD
CB2
ICKLETON ROAD
Pepperton Hill
Hinxton Mill
DUXFORD ROAD
Mast
Abbey Farm
ABBEY ST
COPLOE RD
CB10
Halfmoon Plantation
Crossroad Cottages
Rectory Farm
Hill Cottage
Engagement Plantation
Ickleton Grange
46
47
48
9

17 33

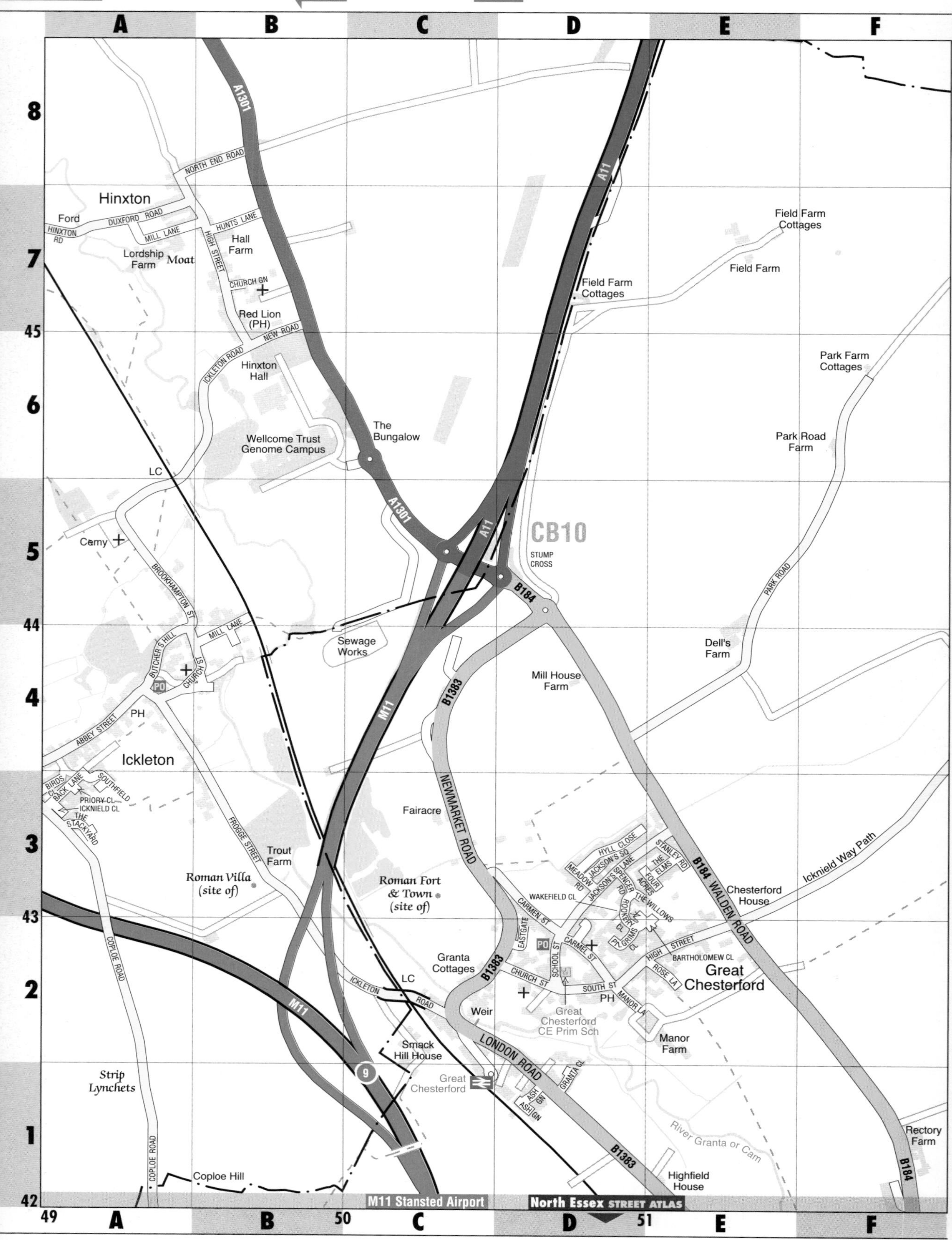
A
B
C
D
E
F
8
7
45
6
5
44
4
3
43
2
1
42
49
50
51
Hinxton
Ford
HINXTON RD
DUXFORD ROAD
MILL LANE
NORTH END ROAD
HUNTS LANE
HIGH STREET
Hall Farm
Lordship Farm
Moat
CHURCH GN
Red Lion (PH)
NEW ROAD
ICKLETON ROAD
Hinxton Hall
A1301
Wellcome Trust Genome Campus
The Bungalow
A11
Field Farm Cottages
Field Farm
Park Farm Cottages
Park Road Farm
CB10
STUMP CROSS
B184
LC
Cemy
BROOKHAMPTON ST
MILL LANE
BUTCHER'S HILL
CHURCH ST
PO
PH
ABBEY STREET
Ickleton
BIRDS CL
BACK LANE
SOUTHFIELD
PRIORY CL
ICKNIELD CL
THE STACKYARD
Sewage Works
M11
B1383
Mill House Farm
Dell's Farm
PARK ROAD
Fairacre
NEWMARKET ROAD
FROGGE STREET
Trout Farm
Roman Villa (site of)
Roman Fort & Town (site of)
HYLL CLOSE
JACKSON'S SQ
MEADOW RD
JACKSON'S LANE
SPENCER RD
STANLEY RD
THE ELMS
FOUR ACRES
THE WILLOWS
ROOKERY CL
GRIMS CL
PL
B184 WALDEN ROAD
Chesterford House
Icknield Way Path
WAKEFIELD CL
CARMEN ST
EASTGATE
SCHOOL ST
CARMEL ST
HIGH STREET
BARTHOLOMEW CL
ROSE LA
Great Chesterford
Granta Cottages
CHURCH ST
SOUTH ST
MANOR LA
ICKLETON ROAD
COPLOE ROAD
Weir
Great Chesterford CE Prim Sch
Manor Farm
Smack Hill House
LONDON ROAD
GRANTA CL
Great Chesterford
ASH GN
9
Strip Lynchets
River Granta or Cam
Rectory Farm
B1383
Highfield House
Coploe Hill
M11 Stansted Airport
North Essex STREET ATLAS

17

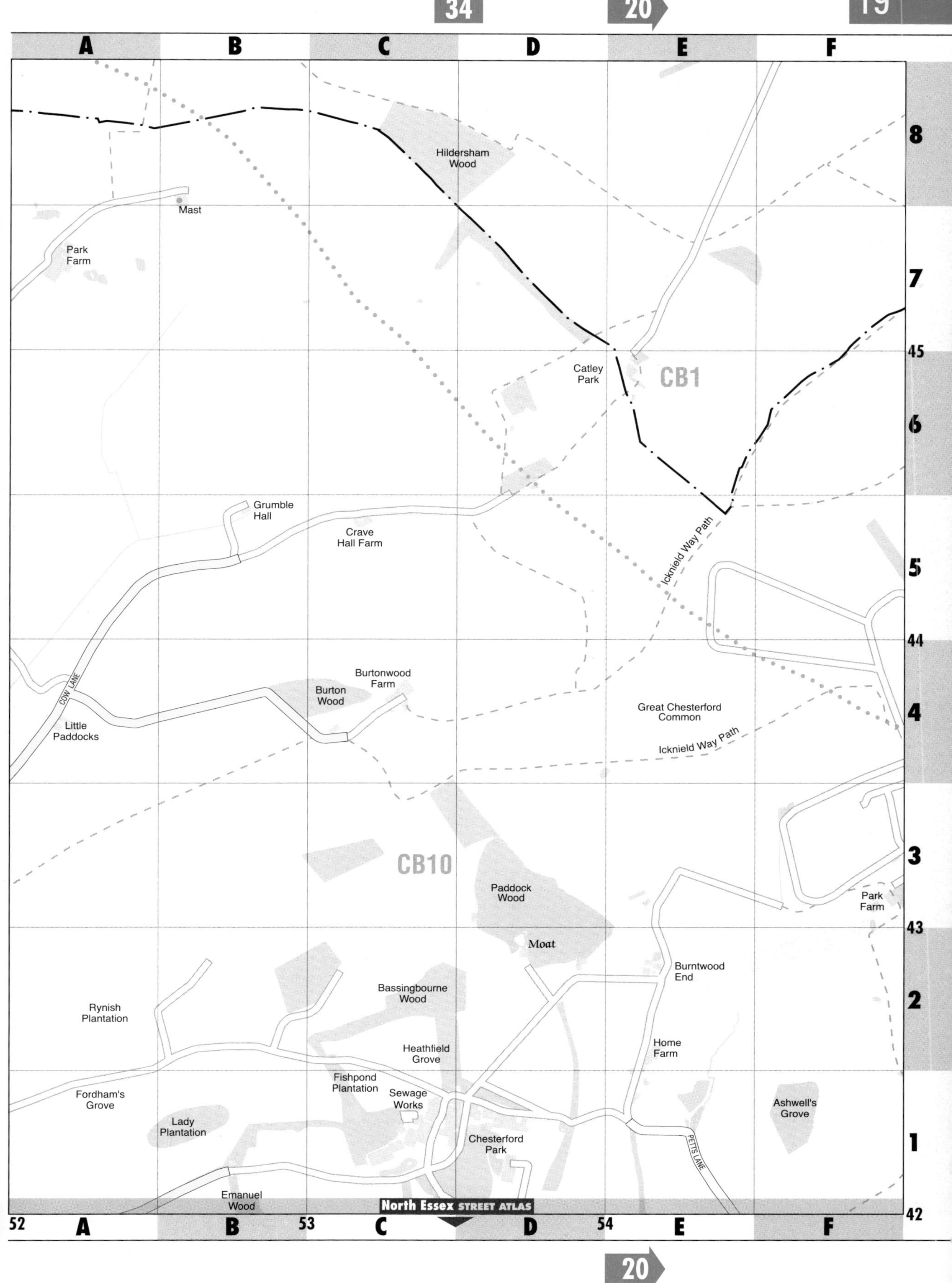

A B C D E F

8

Park Farm

Mast

Hildersham Wood

7

45

Catley Park

CB1

6

Grumble Hall

Crave Hall Farm

Icknield Way Path

5

COW LANE

44

Burtonwood Farm

Burton Wood

Great Chesterford Common

4

Little Paddocks

Icknield Way Path

CB10

3

Paddock Wood

Park Farm

43

Moat

Burntwood End

Rynish Plantation

2

Bassingbourne Wood

Heathfield Grove

Home Farm

Fordham's Grove

Fishpond Plantation

Sewage Works

Ashwell's Grove

1

Lady Plantation

Chesterford Park

PETTS LANE

Emanuel Wood

North Essex STREET ATLAS

42

19
35

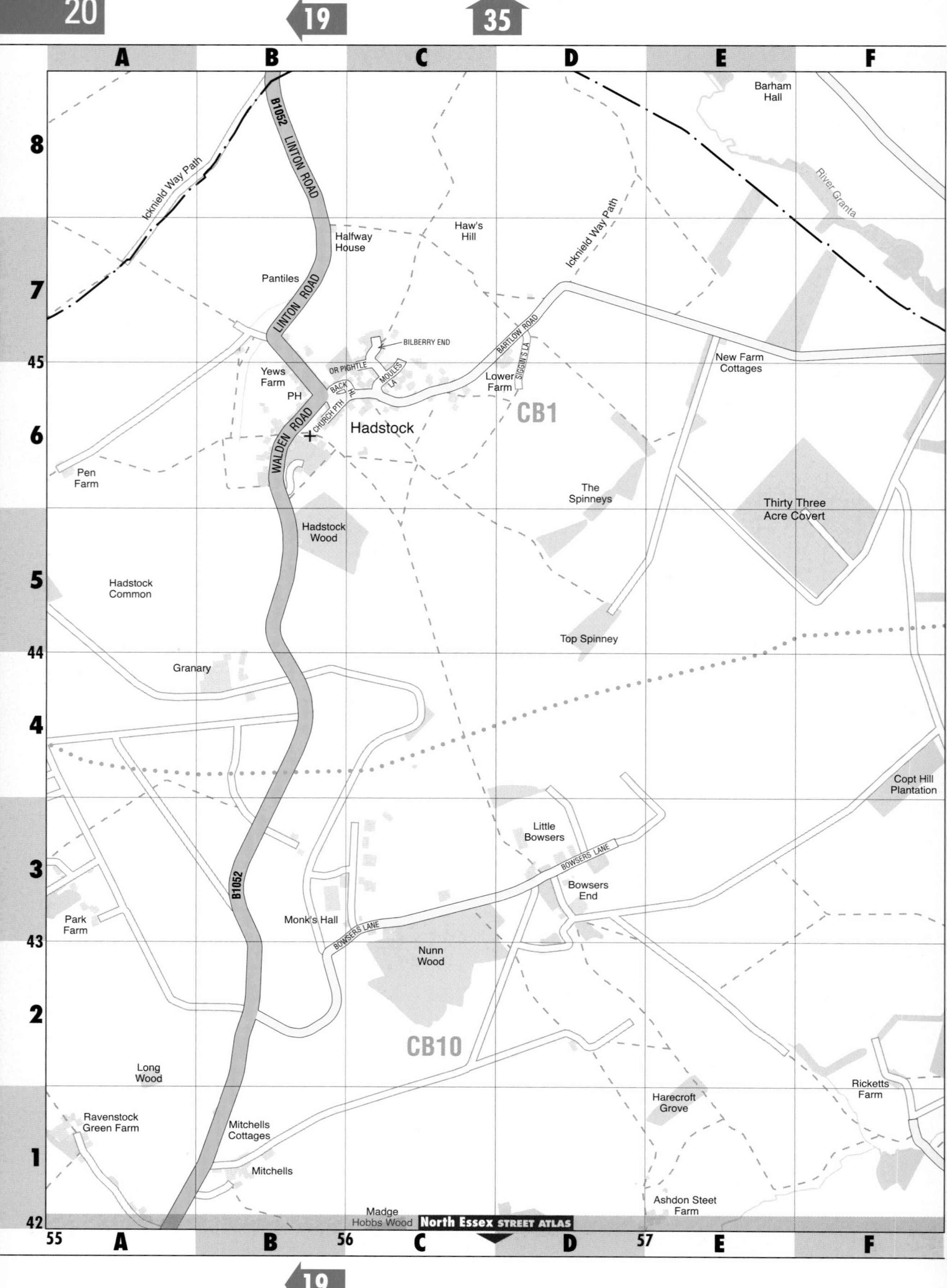
A
B
C
D
E
F
8
7
45
6
5
44
4
3
43
2
1
42
55
56
57
B1052
LINTON ROAD
Icknield Way Path
Barham Hall
River Granta
Halfway House
Haw's Hill
Pantiles
BILBERRY END
BARTLOW ROAD
OR PIGHTLE
MOULES LA
SIGGIN'S LA
BACK LA
New Farm Cottages
Yews Farm
PH
Lower Farm
CB1
WALDEN ROAD
CHURCH PTH
Hadstock
Pen Farm
The Spinneys
Thirty Three Acre Covert
Hadstock Wood
Hadstock Common
Top Spinney
Granary
Copt Hill Plantation
Little Bowsers
BOWSERS LANE
Bowsers End
Park Farm
Monk's Hall
Nunn Wood
CB10
Long Wood
Ricketts Farm
Harecroft Grove
Ravenstock Green Farm
Mitchells Cottages
Mitchells
Ashdon Steet Farm
Madge Hobbs Wood

19

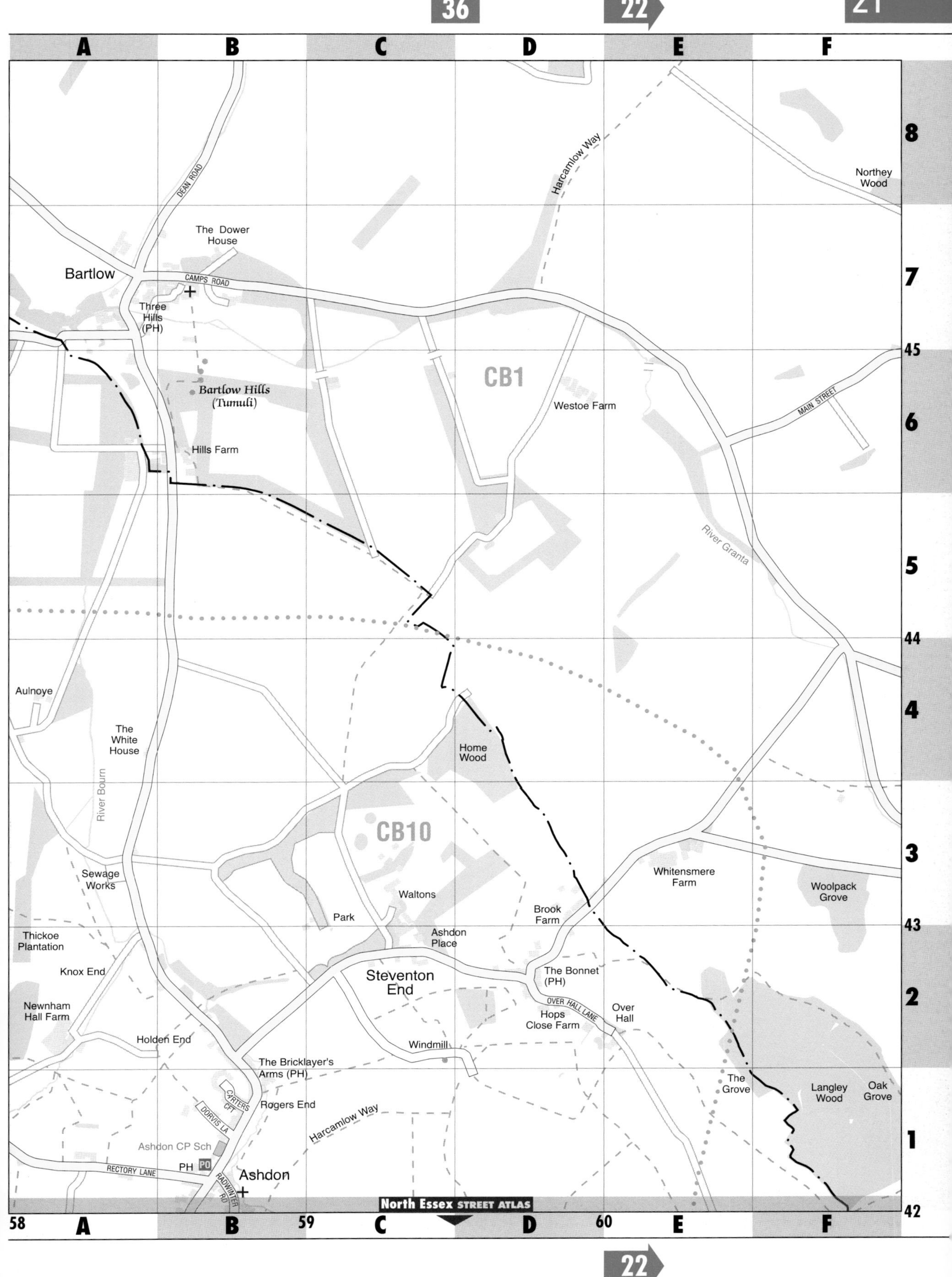

A B C D E F

8

DEAN ROAD

The Dower
House

Bartlow

CAMPS ROAD

7

Three
Hills
(PH)

45

CB1

Bartlow Hills
(Tumuli)

Westoe Farm

MAIN STREET

6

Hills Farm

River Granta

5

44

Aulnoye

4

The
White
House

Home
Wood

River Bourn

CB10

3

Sewage
Works

Waltons

Whitensmere
Farm

Woolpack
Grove

Thickoe
Plantation

Park

Brook
Farm

43

Knox End

Ashdon
Place

The Bonnet
(PH)

Steventon
End

OVER HALL LANE

2

Newnham
Hall Farm

Hops
Close Farm

Over
Hall

Holden End

Windmill

The Bricklayer's
Arms (PH)

The
Grove

Langley
Wood

Oak
Grove

CARTERS
CFT

Rogers End

Harcamlow Way

DORVIS LA

1

Ashdon CP Sch

PH PO

RECTORY LANE

Ashdon

RADWINTER RD

Harcamlow Way

Northey
Wood

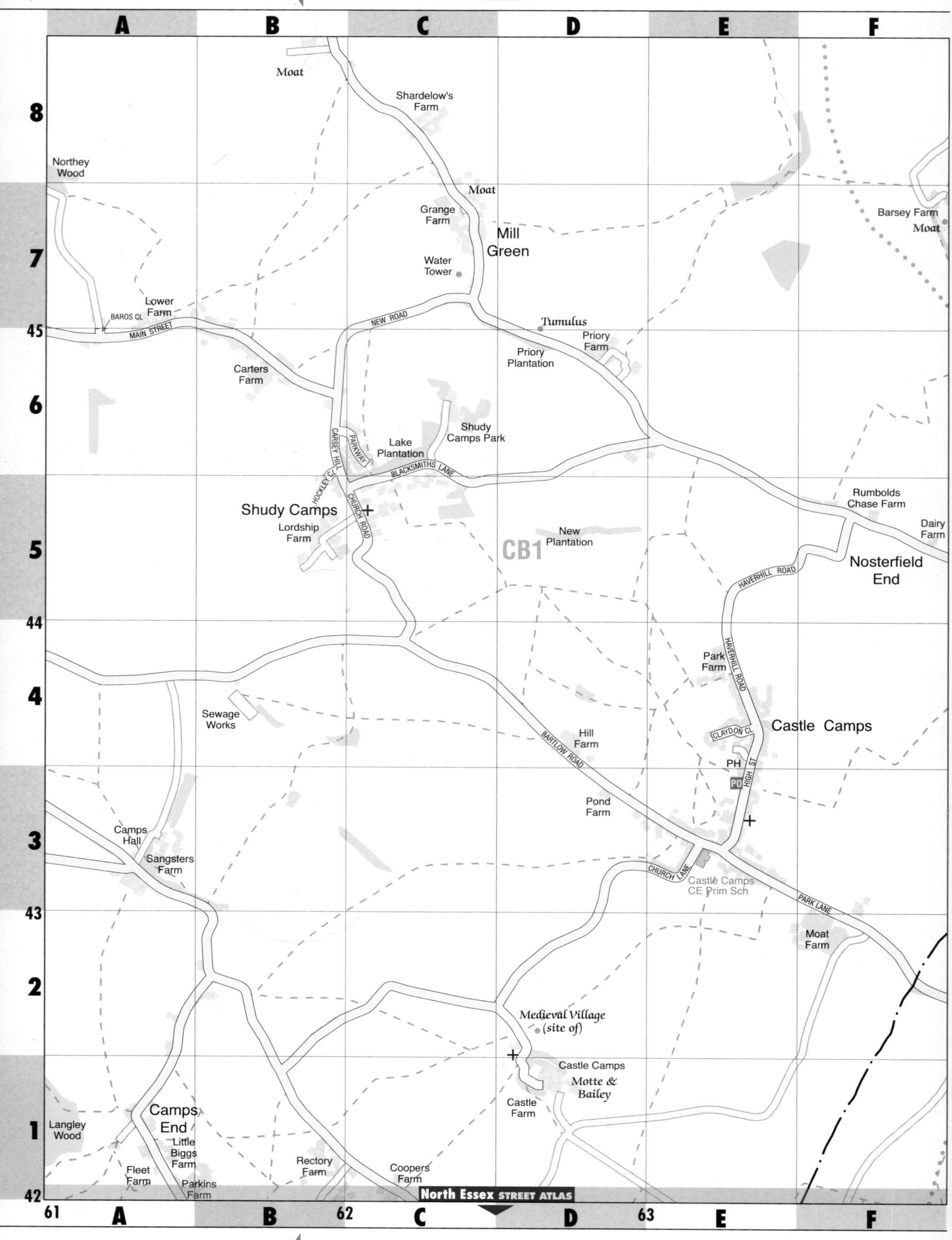

A B C D E F

8

Moat

Shardelow's Farm

Northey Wood

Moat

Grange Farm

Mill Green

Barsey Farm
Moat

7

Water Tower

Lower Farm

BAROS CL

MAIN STREET

NEW ROAD

Tumulus

Priory Farm

45

Carters Farm

Priory Plantation

6

CARSEY HILL

PARKWAY

Lake Plantation

Shudy Camps Park

HOCKLEY CL

CHURCH ROAD

BLACKSMITHS LANE

Rumbolds Chase Farm

Dairy Farm

Shudy Camps

Lordship Farm

CB1

New Plantation

5

HAVERHILL ROAD

Nosterfield End

44

Park Farm

4

Sewage Works

BARTLOW ROAD

Hill Farm

HAVERHILL ROAD

CLAYDON CL

Castle Camps

HIGH ST

PH

PO

Pond Farm

Camps Hall

Sangsters Farm

3

CHURCH LANE

Castle Camps CE Prim Sch

PARK LANE

43

Moat Farm

2

Medieval Village (site of)

Camps End

Castle Camps
Motte & Bailey

Langley Wood

1

Little Biggs Farm

Castle Farm

Fleet Farm

Rectory Farm

Coopers Farm

Parkins Farm

42

E7
1 GREENWOOD CL
2 PARSONAGE GDNS
3 YERRIL GDN
4 HORSESHOE LA
5 RUTLAND CT
6 WARREN CT
7 SHIRE CT
8 FALLOWFIELD CT
9 SHEPHERDS CT
10 RYE CT
11 HAREWOOD TERR
12 ALDHAM CT
13 BLAXHALL CT
14 BURES CT
15 WELLINGTON TERR
16 SOMERSET CT
17 SHAFTESBURY CT
18 WELLUM CL
19 MARLBOROUGH CT
20 BOXFORD CT
21 ALDEBURGH CL

38

E8
1 ARUNDEL WK
2 WARWICK CT
3 BODIAN WK
4 BELVOIR CT
5 BALMORAL DR
6 WENTWORTH TERR
7 QUEENS CT
8 BISHOPS CT
9 ST JAMES CT

24

F7
1 SALISBURY CT
2 TREFOIL CT
3 BEAUFORT CT
4 BEACONSFIELD CT
5 BEDFORD CT
6 CLAYHIVE DR
7 OLD CLEMENTS LA
8 BELMONT CT
9 MONTFORT CT

23

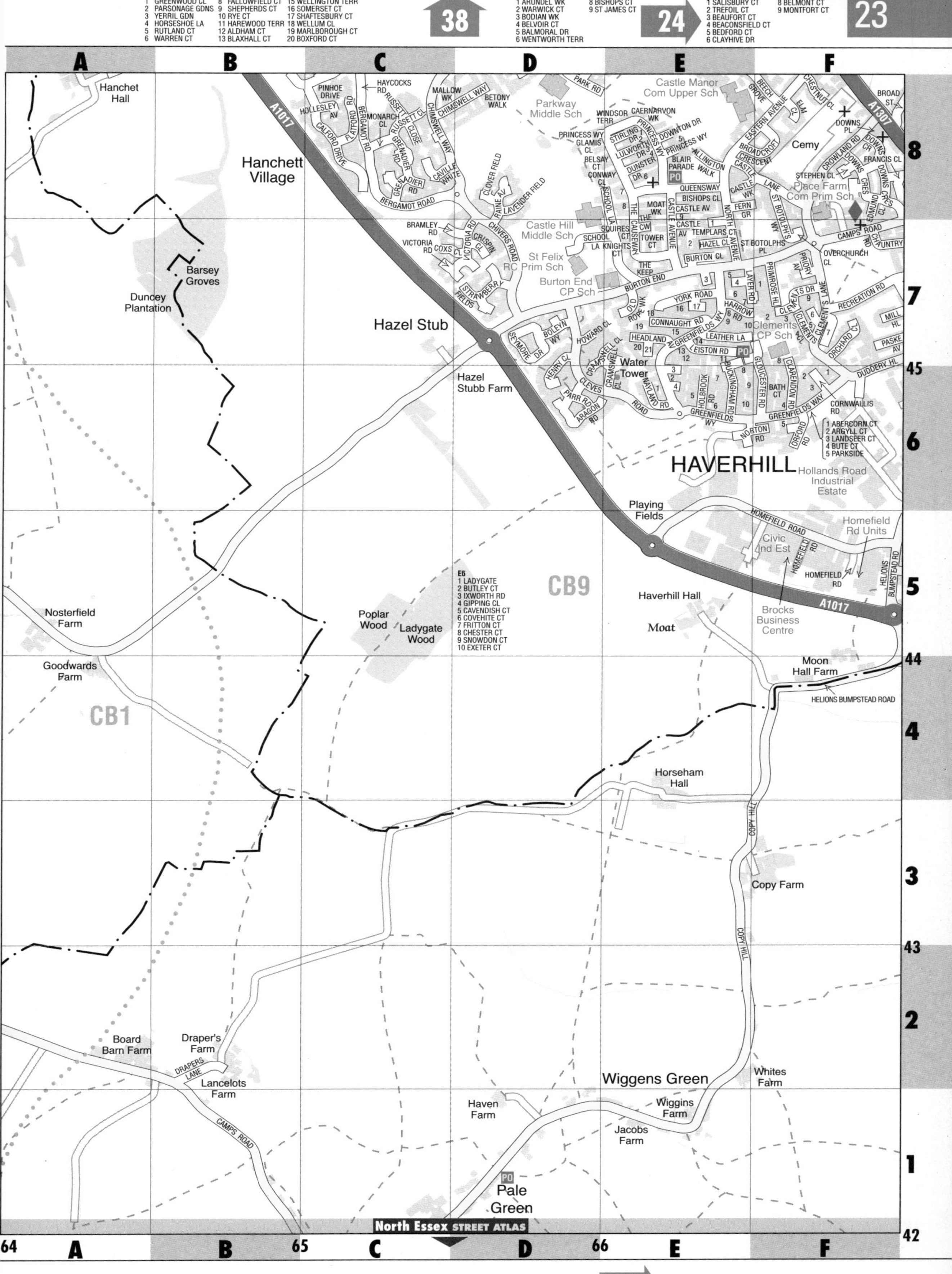

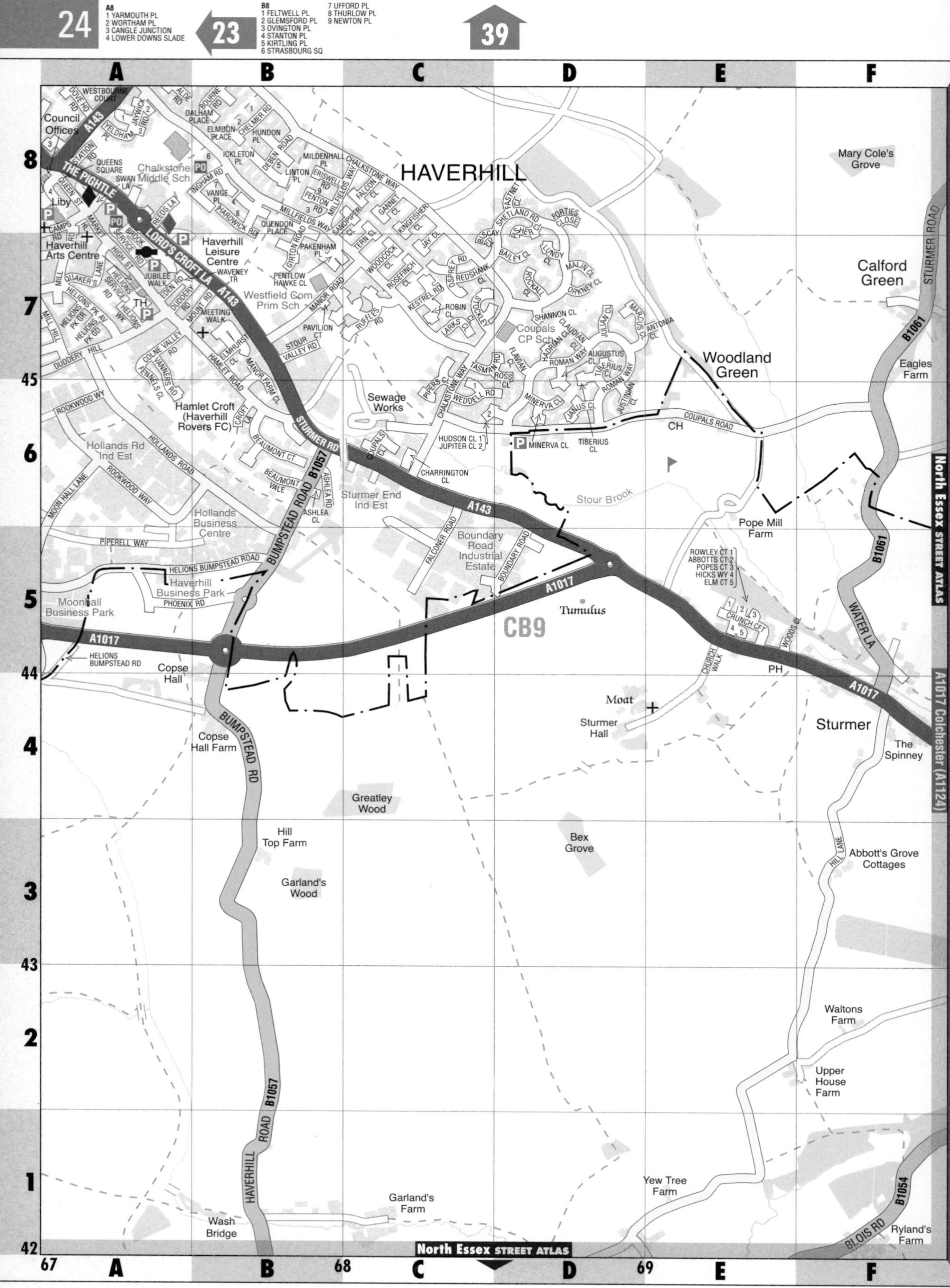
A
B
C
D
E
F
8
7
45
6
5
44
4
3
43
2
1
42
67
68
69
HAVERHILL
Council Offices
Chalkstone Middle Sch
Liby
Haverhill Arts Centre
Haverhill Leisure Centre
Westfield Com Prim Sch
Coupals CP Sch
Woodland Green
Mary Cole's Grove
Calford Green
Eagles Farm
Sewage Works
Hamlet Croft (Haverhill Rovers FC)
Hollands Rd Ind Est
Hollands Business Centre
Sturmer End Ind Est
Boundary Road Industrial Estate
Pope Mill Farm
Haverhill Business Park
Moonhall Business Park
Copse Hall
Copse Hall Farm
Tumulus
CB9
Moat
Sturmer Hall
Sturmer
The Spinney
Greatley Wood
Hill Top Farm
Bex Grove
Garland's Wood
Abbott's Grove Cottages
Waltons Farm
Upper House Farm
Yew Tree Farm
Garland's Farm
Wash Bridge
Ryland's Farm
Stour Brook
A143
A1017
B1057
B1061
B1054
THE PIGHTLE
LORD'S CROFT LA
STURMER RD
BUMPSTEAD ROAD
BUMPSTEAD RD
HAVERHILL ROAD
COUPALS ROAD
WATER LA
HILL LANE
BLOIS RD
STURMER ROAD
CHURCH WALK
HELIONS BUMPSTEAD ROAD
HELIONS BUMPSTEAD RD
PIPERELL WAY
PHOENIX RD
ROOKWOOD WY
ROOKWOOD WAY
HOLLANDS ROAD
MOON HALL LANE
DUDDERY HILL
CHALKSTONE WAY
MILLFIELDS WAY
FALCONER ROAD
BOUNDARY ROAD
ROMAN WAY
HUDSON CL 1
JUPITER CL 2
ROWLEY CT 1
ABBOTTS CT 2
POPES CT 3
HICKS WY 4
ELM CT 5
CRUNCH CFT
WOODS CL
CH
PH
TH
PO
North Essex STREET ATLAS
A1017 Colchester (A1124)

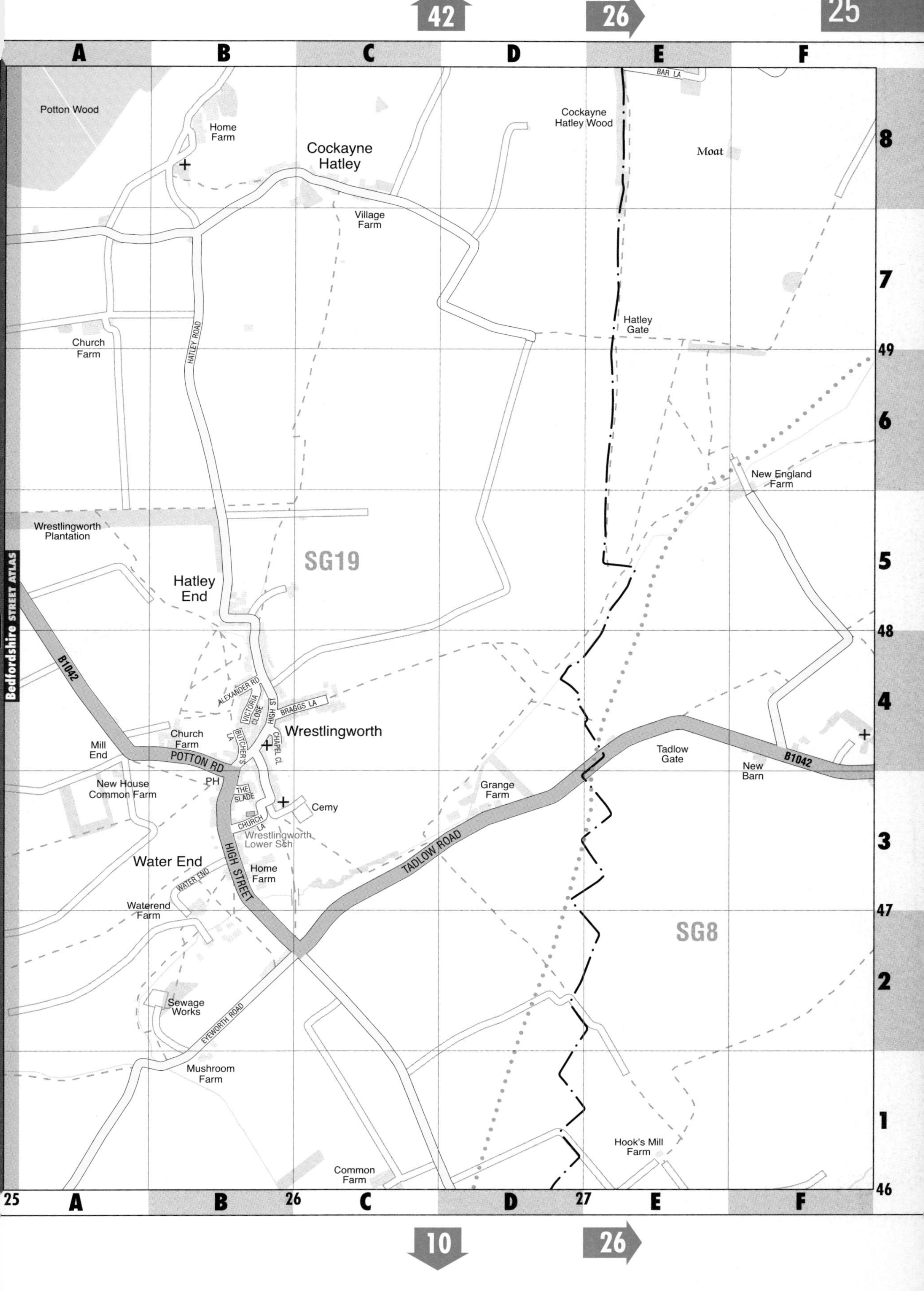

A B C D E F

8

Potton Wood

Home Farm

Cockayne Hatley

Cockayne Hatley Wood

BAR LA

Moat

Village Farm

7

Church Farm

Hatley Gate

49

HATLEY ROAD

6

Wrestlingworth Plantation

New England Farm

SG19

Hatley End

5

48

B1042

ALEXANDER RD
VICTORIA CLOSE
LS HIGH
BRAGGS LA
CHAPEL CL.
BUTCHER'S LA

4

Mill End

Church Farm

Wrestlingworth

Tadlow Gate

New Barn

B1042

POTTON RD

PH

New House Common Farm

THE SLADE

Cemy

CHURCH LA

Grange Farm

Water End

Wrestlingworth Lower Sch

TADLOW ROAD

3

HIGH STREET

WATER END

Home Farm

47

Waterend Farm

SG8

2

Sewage Works

EYEWORTH ROAD

1

Mushroom Farm

Hook's Mill Farm

Common Farm

46

25 A B 26 C D 27 E F

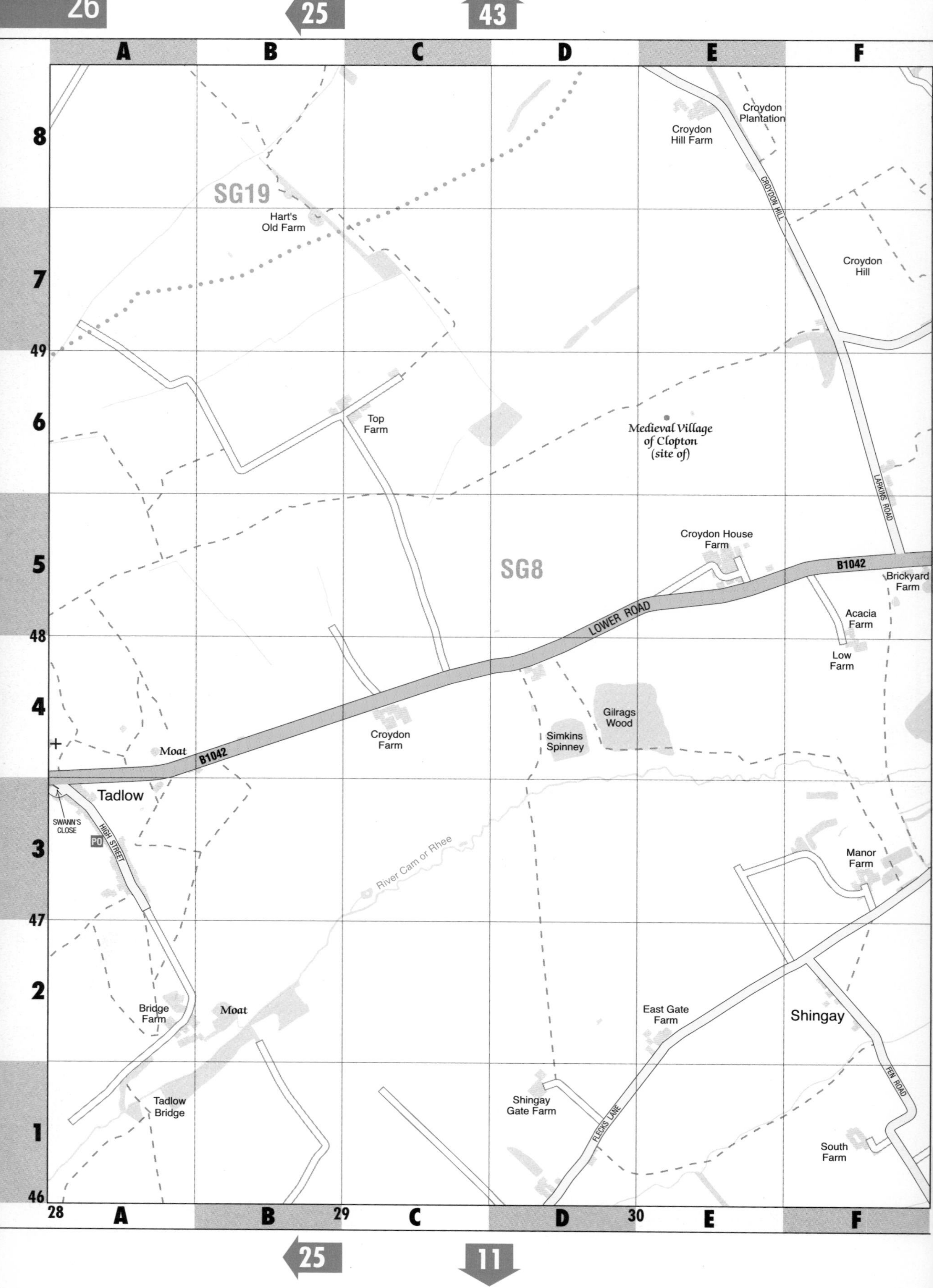

A B C D E F

8

SG19

Hart's
Old Farm

Croydon
Hill Farm

Croydon
Plantation

CROYDON HILL

7

Croydon
Hill

49

Top
Farm

6

Medieval Village
of Clopton
(site of)

LARKINS ROAD

SG8

Croydon House
Farm

B1042

Brickyard
Farm

5

LOWER ROAD

Acacia
Farm

48

Low
Farm

4

Gilrags
Wood

Moat

B1042

Croydon
Farm

Simkins
Spinney

Tadlow

SWANN'S
CLOSE

PO

HIGH STREET

River Cam or Rhee

Manor
Farm

3

47

Shingay

2

Bridge
Farm

Moat

East Gate
Farm

FEN ROAD

Tadlow
Bridge

Shingay
Gate Farm

FLECKS LANE

1

South
Farm

46

28 A B 29 C D 30 E F

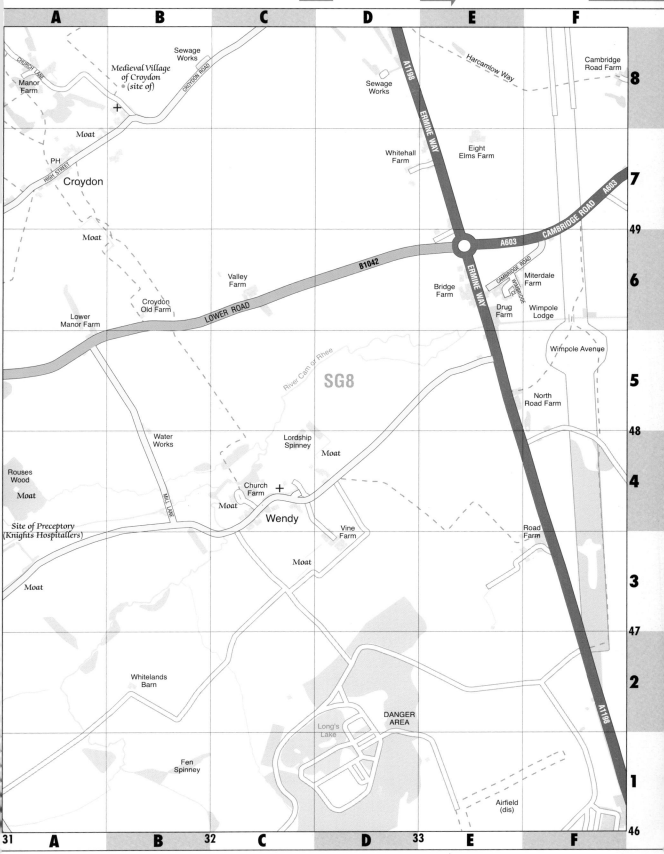

27
45

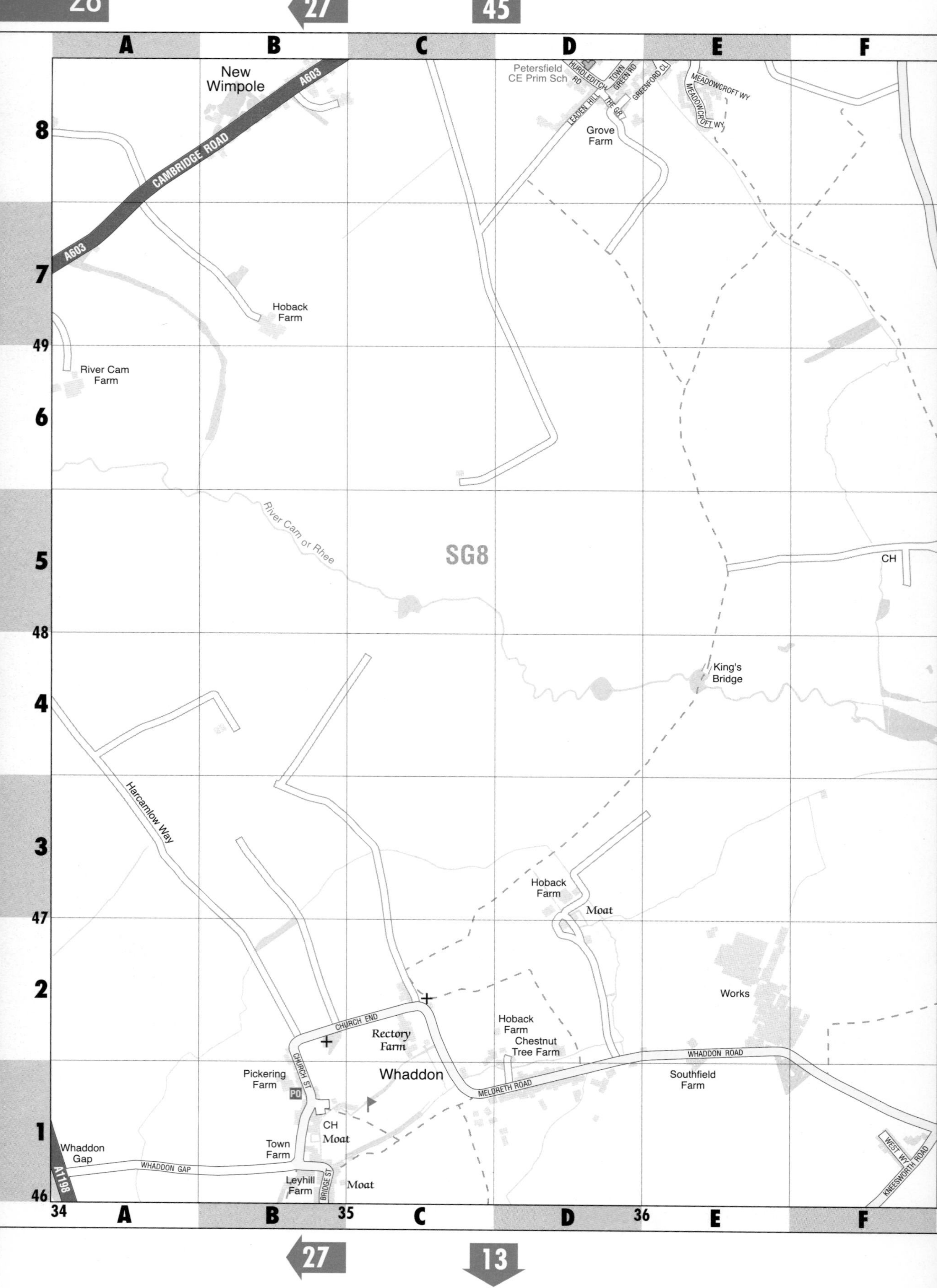
A
B
C
D
E
F
New Wimpole
A603
CAMBRIDGE ROAD
Petersfield CE Prim Sch
HURDLEDITCH RD
TOWN GREEN RD
GREENFORD CL
MEADOWCROFT WY
LEADEN HILL
THE GR
Grove Farm
8
7
49
6
5
48
4
3
47
2
1
46
Hoback Farm
River Cam Farm
River Cam or Rhee
SG8
CH
King's Bridge
Harcamlow Way
Moat
Works
CHURCH END
Rectory Farm
Chestnut Tree Farm
WHADDON ROAD
MELDRETH ROAD
CHURCH ST
Pickering Farm
PO
Whaddon
Southfield Farm
Whaddon Gap
WHADDON GAP
A1198
Town Farm
Leyhill Farm
BRIDGE ST
WEST WY
KNEESWORTH ROAD
34
35
36

27
13

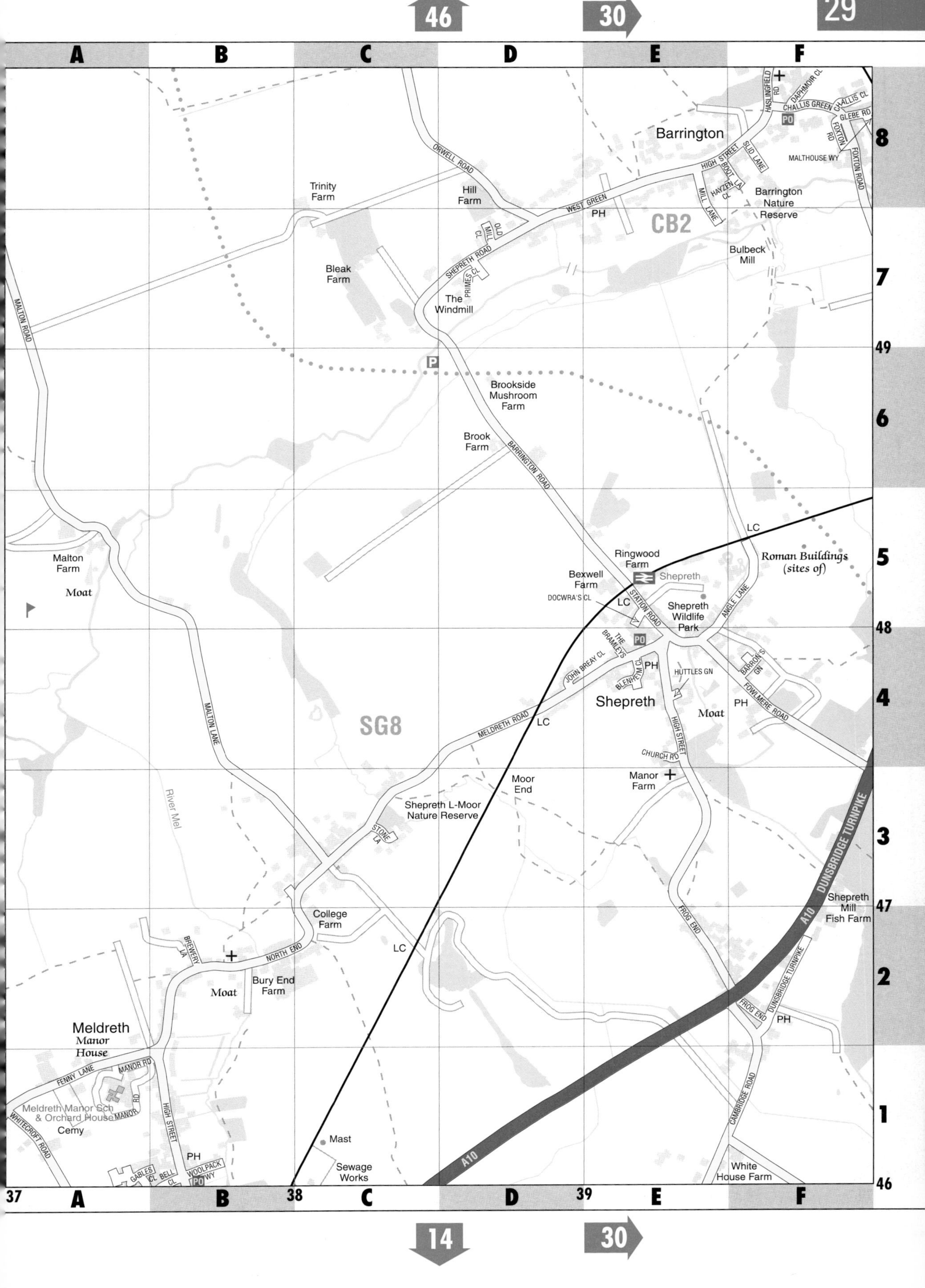
A
B
C
D
E
F
Barrington
HASLINGFIELD RD
DAPHMOIR CL
CHALLIS GREEN
CHALLIS CL
GLEBE RD
FOXTON RD
FOXTON ROAD
MALTHOUSE WY
HIGH STREET
SLID LANE
BOOT LA
HAYZEN CL
MILL LANE
Barrington Nature Reserve
CB2
Bulbeck Mill
ORWELL ROAD
Hill Farm
WEST GREEN
PH
Trinity Farm
OLD MILL CL
SHEPRETH ROAD
PRIMES CL
Bleak Farm
The Windmill
MALTON ROAD
Brookside Mushroom Farm
Brook Farm
BARRINGTON ROAD
LC
Roman Buildings (sites of)
Ringwood Farm
Bexwell Farm
Shepreth
DOCWRA'S CL
STATION ROAD
Shepreth Wildlife Park
ANGLE LANE
Malton Farm
Moat
THE BRAMLEYS
JOHN BREAY CL
BLENHEIM CL
HUTTLES GN
BARRONS GN
FOWLMERE ROAD
Shepreth
Moat
MELDRETH ROAD
SG8
MALTON LANE
HIGH STREET
CHURCH RD
Manor Farm
Moor End
River Mel
Shepreth L-Moor Nature Reserve
STONE LA
DUNSBRIDGE TURNPIKE
Shepreth Mill Fish Farm
College Farm
FROG END
A10
BREWERY LA
NORTH END
Bury End Farm
Moat
Meldreth
Manor House
FENNY LANE
MANOR RD
Meldreth Manor Sch & Orchard House
Cemy
WHITECROFT ROAD
HIGH STREET
GABLES CL
BELL CL
WOOLPACK WY
Mast
Sewage Works
CAMBRIDGE ROAD
White House Farm
8
7
49
6
5
48
4
3
47
2
1
46
37
38
39

A   B   C   D   E   F

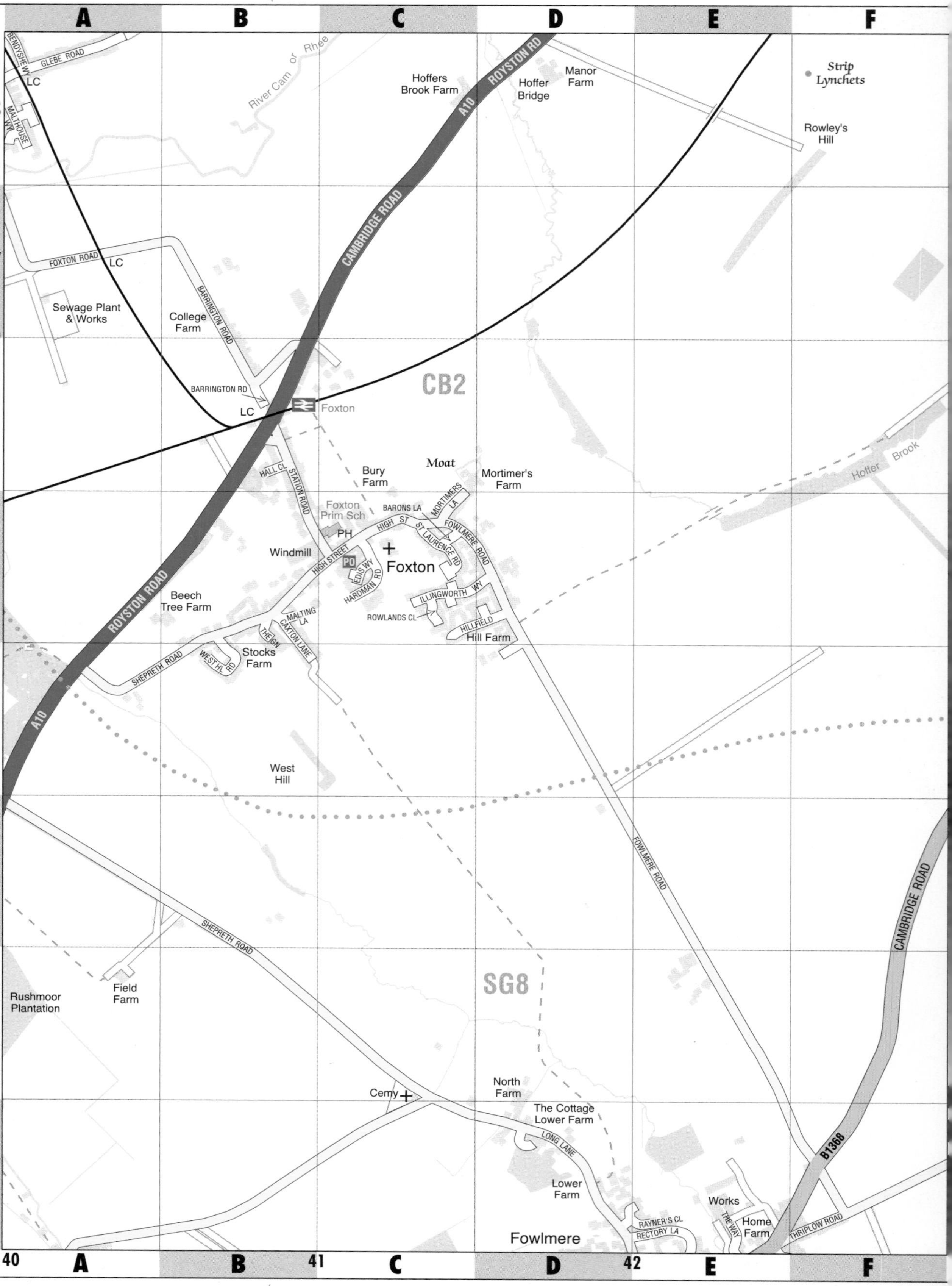

BENDYSHE WY
GLEBE ROAD
LC
MALTHOUSE WY

River Cam of Rhee

Hoffers Brook Farm

ROYSTON RD
A10

Hoffer Bridge

Manor Farm

Strip Lynchets

Rowley's Hill

8

FOXTON ROAD
LC

CAMBRIDGE ROAD

7

Sewage Plant & Works

College Farm

BARRINGTON ROAD

49

CB2

BARRINGTON RD

LC

Foxton

6

Hoffer Brook

HALL CL
STATION ROAD

Bury Farm

Moat

Mortimer's Farm

ROYSTON ROAD

Foxton Prim Sch

BARONS LA
HIGH ST
ST LAURENCE RD
MORTIMERS LA
FOWLMERE ROAD

PH

Windmill

HIGH STREET
LEYS WY
PO
HARDMAN RD

Foxton

5

Beech Tree Farm

ILLINGWORTH WY

ROWLANDS CL

MALTING LA
THE GN
FOXTON LANE

Stocks Farm

HILLFIELD
Hill Farm

A10

SHEPRETH ROAD
WEST PL RD

48

4

West Hill

3

SHEPRETH ROAD

47

Rushmoor Plantation

Field Farm

SG8

FOWLMERE ROAD

CAMBRIDGE ROAD

2

Cemy

North Farm

The Cottage
Lower Farm

LONG LANE

B1368

1

Lower Farm

Works

THE WAY
Home Farm

Fowlmere

RAYNER'S CL
RECTORY LA

THRIPLOW ROAD

46

40   A   B   41   C   D   42   E   F

48
32

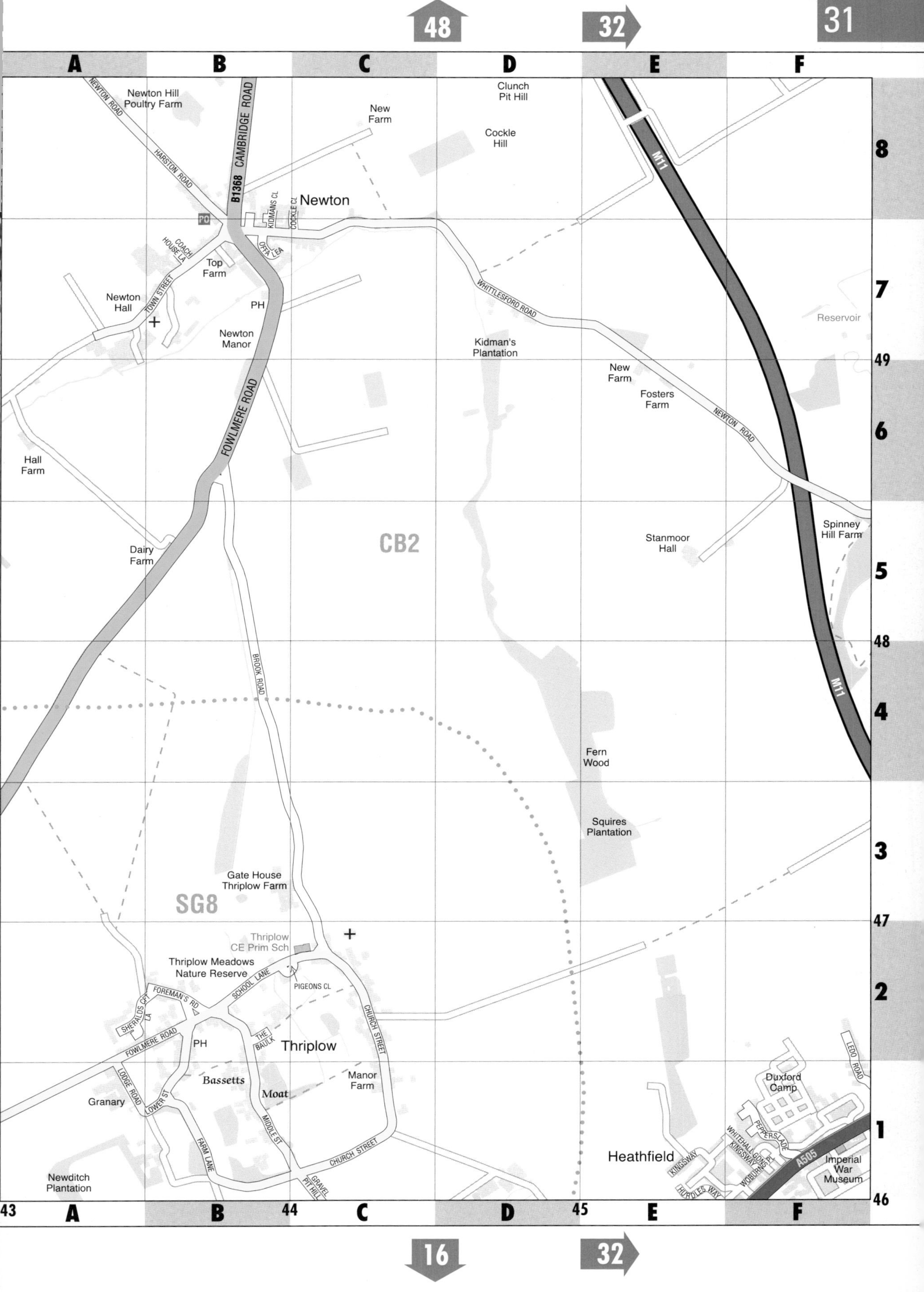
A
B
C
D
E
F
Newton Hill
Poultry Farm
NEWTON ROAD
HARSTON ROAD
CAMBRIDGE ROAD
B1368
Clunch
Pit Hill
New
Farm
Cockle
Hill
M11
Newton
KIDMANS CL
COCKLE CL
PO
COACH HOUSE LA
OFFA LEA
Top
Farm
TOWN STREET
Newton
Hall
PH
Newton
Manor
WHITTLESFORD ROAD
Kidman's
Plantation
Reservoir
FOWLMERE ROAD
New
Farm
Fosters
Farm
NEWTON ROAD
Hall
Farm
CB2
Dairy
Farm
Stanmoor
Hall
Spinney
Hill Farm
BROOK ROAD
M11
Fern
Wood
Squires
Plantation
Gate House
Thriplow Farm
SG8
Thriplow
CE Prim Sch
Thriplow Meadows
Nature Reserve
PIGEONS CL
FOREMAN'S RD
SCHOOL LANE
SHERALDS CFT LA
FOWLMERE ROAD
CHURCH STREET
PH
THE BAULK
Thriplow
LEDO ROAD
Bassetts
Moat
Manor
Farm
Duxford
Camp
LODGE ROAD
LOWER ST
Granary
MIDDLE ST
FARM LANE
CHURCH STREET
PEPPERSLADE
WHITEHALL GDNS
KINGSWAY
WOBURN PL
Heathfield
KINGSWAY
A505
Imperial
War
Museum
Newditch
Plantation
GRAVEL PIT HILL
HURDLES WAY
8
7
49
6
5
48
4
3
47
2
1
46
43
44
45

16
32

31
49

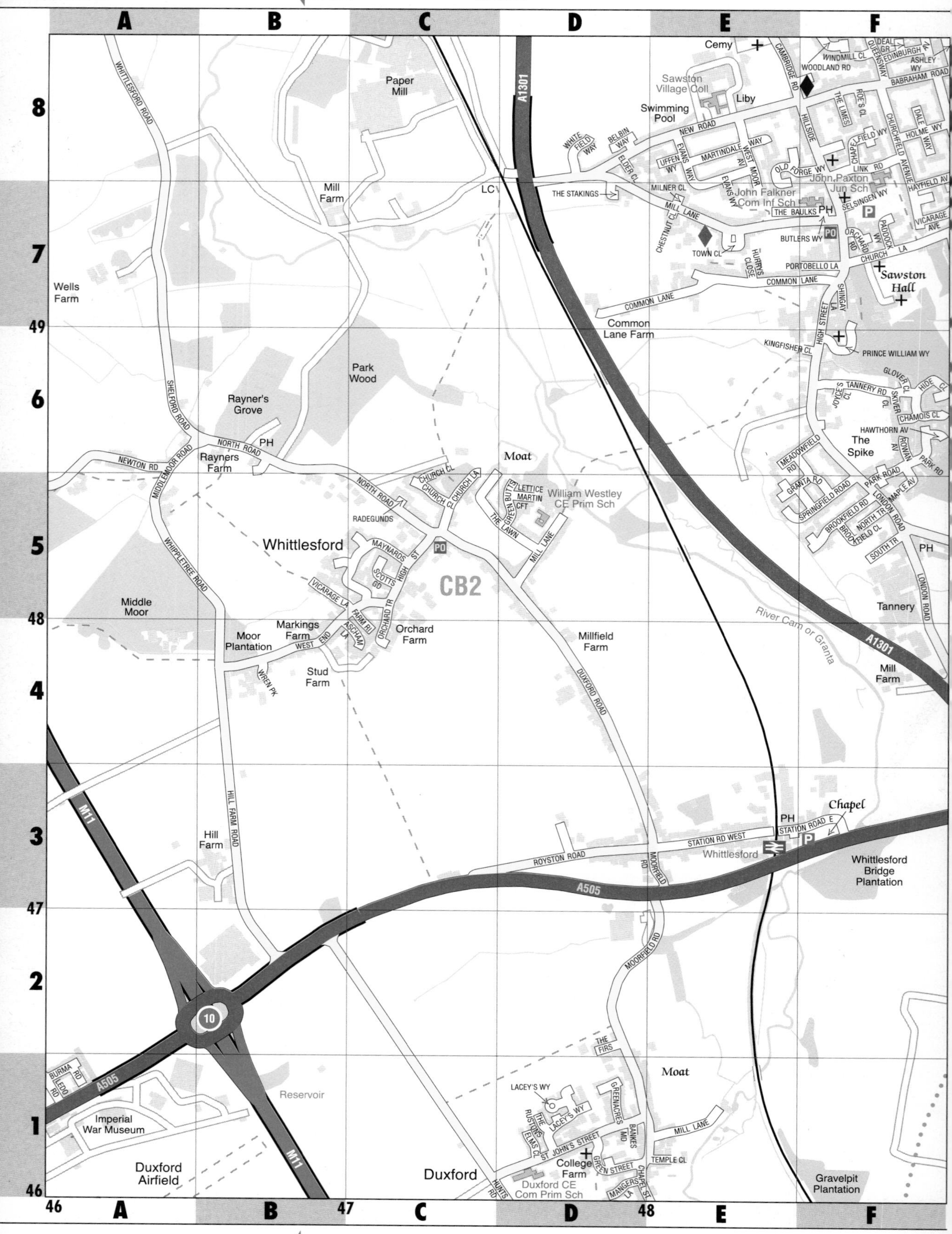
A
B
C
D
E
F
8
7
49
6
5
48
4
3
47
2
1
46
46
47
48
Cemy
Sawston Village Coll
Liby
Swimming Pool
Paper Mill
Mill Farm
LC
A1301
WHITTLESFORD ROAD
CAMBRIDGE RD
WOODLAND RD
WINDMILL CL
QUEENSWAY
DEAL GR
EDINBURGH AV
ASHLEY WY
BABRAHAM ROAD
THE LIMES
ROE'S CL
HILLSIDE
NEW ROAD
WHITE FIELD WAY
BELBIN WAY
EVANS WAY
LUFFEN WY
MARTINDALE WAY
WEST MOOR AV
ELDER CL
CHAPEL FIELD WY
CHURCHFIELD AVENUE
DALE WAY
HOLME WY
OLD FORGE WY
LINK RD
John Paxton Jun Sch
HAYFIELD AV
MILNER CL
THE STAKINGS
John Falkner Com Inf Sch
EVANS WY
MILL LANE
SELSINGEN WY
PH
THE BAULKS
CHESTNUT CL
BUTLERS WY
PO
ORCHARD RD
PADDOCK WY
VICARAGE AVE
TOWN CL
HURRYS CLOSE
CHURCH LA
PORTOBELLO LA
COMMON LANE
Sawston Hall
Wells Farm
SHINGAY LA
HIGH STREET
Common Lane Farm
KINGFISHER CL
PRINCE WILLIAM WY
Park Wood
GLOVER CL
HIDE CL
TANNERY RD
JOYCE'S CL
SKIVER CL
CHAMOIS CL
SHELFORD ROAD
Rayner's Grove
HAWTHORN AV
The Spike
NORTH ROAD
PH
ROWAN AV
PARK RD
MEADOWFIELD RD
NEWTON RD
MIDDLEMOOR ROAD
Rayners Farm
Moat
CHURCH CL
CHURCH LA
LETTICE MARTIN CFT
William Westley CE Prim Sch
GRANTA RD
SPRINGFIELD ROAD
PARK ROAD
MAPLE AV
GREEN BUTTS
THE LAWN
BROOKFIELD RD
NORTH TR
LONDON ROAD
RADEGUNDS
BROOKFIELD CL
Whittlesford
MAYNARDS
MILL LANE
SOUTH TR
PH
WHIPPLETREE ROAD
HIGH ST
PO
SCOTTS GD
CB2
LONDON ROAD
Middle Moor
VICARAGE LA
Tannery
River Cam or Granta
FARM RI
ORCHARD TR
Markings Farm
Orchard Farm
Millfield Farm
Moor Plantation
WEST END
ASCHAM LA
A1301
Mill Farm
Stud Farm
WREN PK
DUXFORD ROAD
M11
Chapel
PH
STATION ROAD E
HILL FARM ROAD
P
Hill Farm
STATION RD WEST
Whittlesford
Whittlesford Bridge Plantation
ROYSTON ROAD
MOORFIELD RD
A505
MOORFIELD RD
10
THE FIRS
BURMA RD
LEDO RD
Moat
A505
Reservoir
LACEY'S WY
GREENACRES
Imperial War Museum
THE RUSTONS
LACEY'S WY
ELMS CL
ST JOHN'S STREET
MILL LANE
BANKES MD
TEMPLE CL
College Farm
GREEN STREET
M11
Duxford Airfield
Duxford
HUNTS RD
Duxford CE Com Prim Sch
MANGERS LA
CHAPEL ST
Gravelpit Plantation

31
17

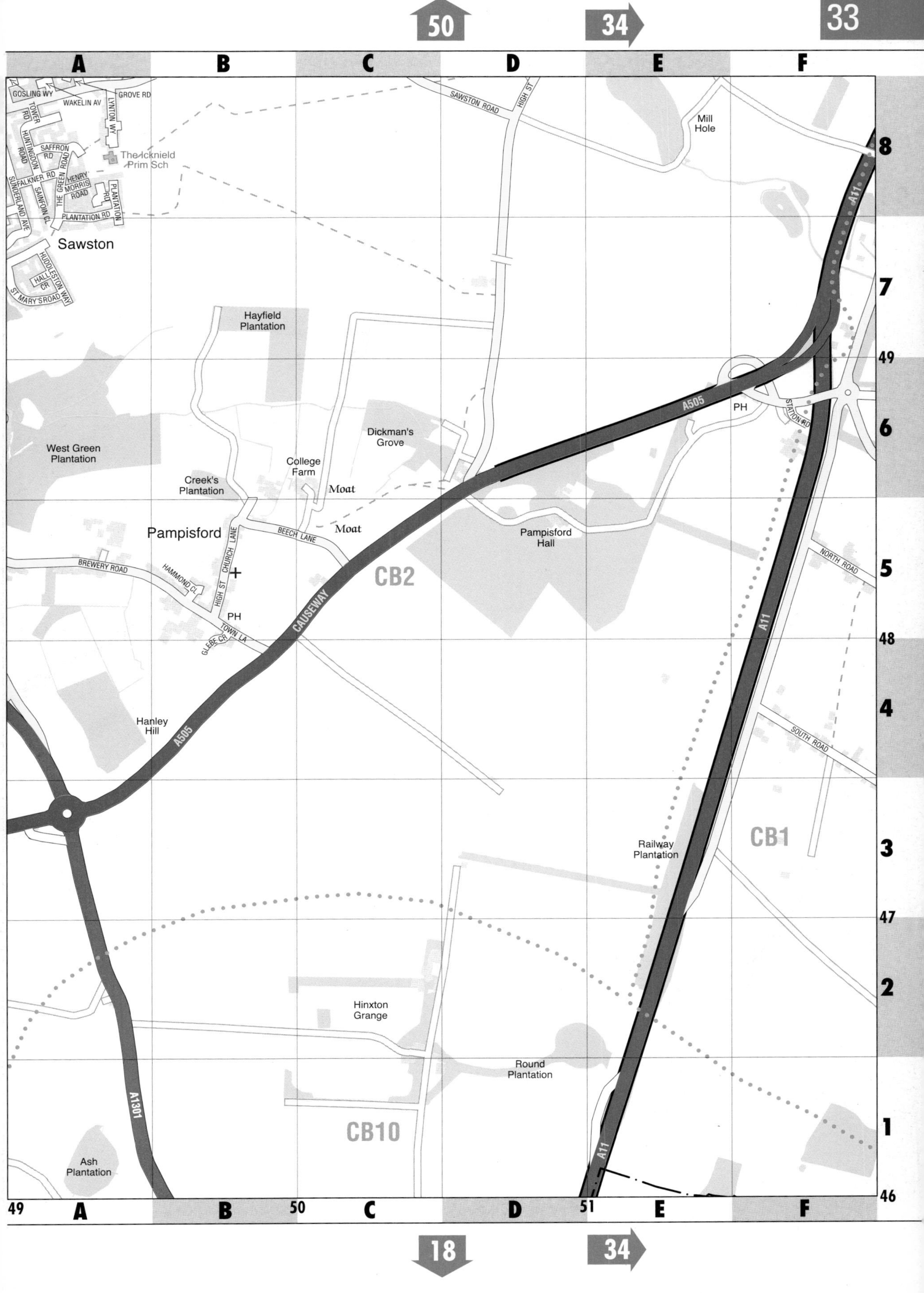
50
34
A
B
C
D
E
F
GOSLING WY
WAKELIN AV
GROVE RD
TOWER RD
HUNTINGDON ROAD
LYNTON WY
SAFFRON RD
THE GREEN ROAD
The Icknield Prim Sch
FALKNER RD
HENRY MORRIS ROAD
SAINFOIN CL
PLANTATION RD
SUNDERLAND AVE
PLANTATION RD
Sawston
HUDDLESTON WAY
HALL CR
ST MARY'S ROAD
SAWSTON ROAD
HIGH ST
Mill Hole
A11
Hayfield Plantation
A505
PH
STATION RD
West Green Plantation
Dickman's Grove
College Farm
Creek's Plantation
Moat
Moat
Pampisford
BEECH LANE
CHURCH LANE
Pampisford Hall
BREWERY ROAD
HAMMOND CL
HIGH ST
CB2
NORTH ROAD
PH
TOWN LA
GLEBE CR
CAUSEWAY
A11
Hanley Hill
A505
SOUTH ROAD
CB1
Railway Plantation
Hinxton Grange
Round Plantation
A1301
CB10
A11
Ash Plantation
8
7
49
6
5
48
4
3
47
2
1
46
49
50
51
18
34

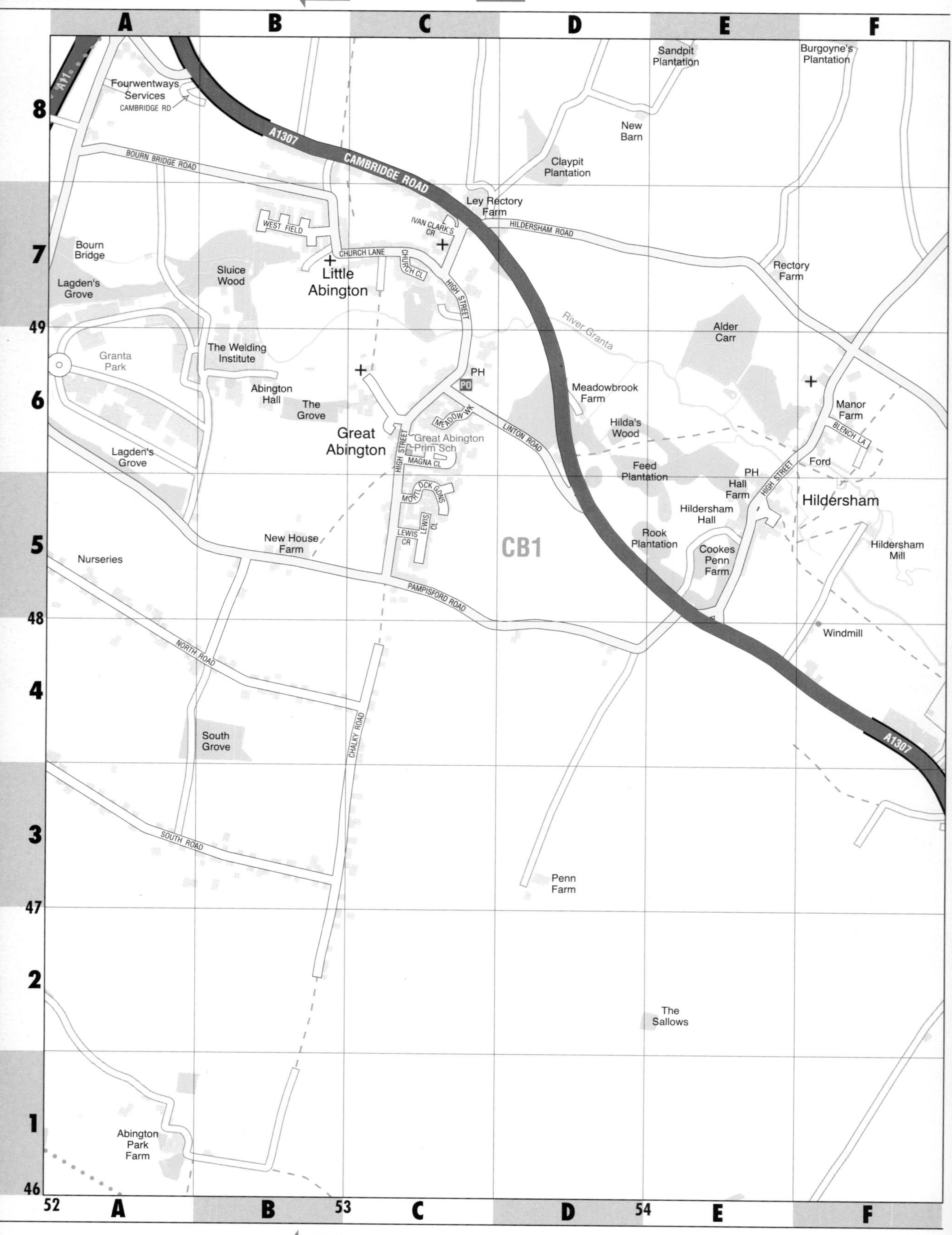

A   B   C   D   E   F

8

Fourwentways
Services
CAMBRIDGE RD

A1307

CAMBRIDGE ROAD

Sandpit
Plantation

Burgoyne's
Plantation

New
Barn

BOURN BRIDGE ROAD

Claypit
Plantation

7

Bourn
Bridge

WEST FIELD

Ley Rectory
Farm

HILDERSHAM ROAD

IVAN CLARK'S
CR

CHURCH LANE

Rectory
Farm

Sluice
Wood

Little
Abington

CHURCH CL

Lagden's
Grove

HIGH STREET

49

River Granta

Alder
Carr

The Welding
Institute

Granta Park

Abington
Hall

The
Grove

PH

PO

Meadowbrook
Farm

Manor
Farm

6

Great
Abington

MEADOW WK

BLENCH LA

Hilda's
Wood

Great Abington
Prim Sch

HIGH STREET

LINTON ROAD

MAGNA CL

Feed
Plantation

PH
Hall
Farm

HIGH STREET

Ford

Lagden's
Grove

Hildersham

MORTLOCK GDNS

Hildersham
Hall

LEWIS
CL

5

New House
Farm

LEWIS
CR

CB1

Rook
Plantation

Cookes
Penn
Farm

Hildersham
Mill

Nurseries

PAMPISFORD ROAD

48

NORTH ROAD

Windmill

4

CHALKY ROAD

South
Grove

A1307

3

SOUTH ROAD

Penn
Farm

47

2

The
Sallows

1

Abington
Park
Farm

46

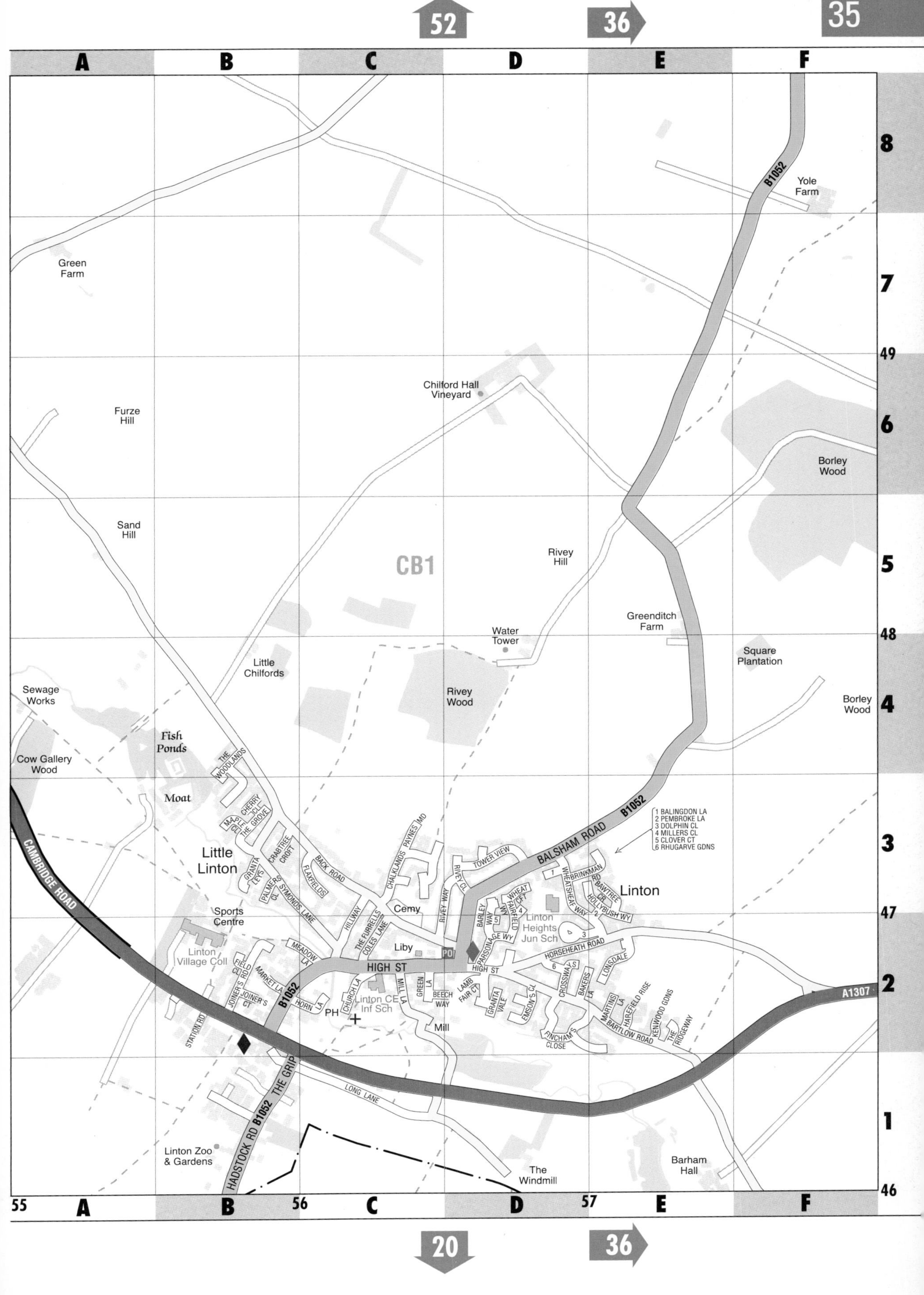

A B C D E F

8

Yole
Farm

B1052

7

49

Green
Farm

Furze
Hill

6

Borley
Wood

Chilford Hall
Vineyard

Sand
Hill

CB1

Rivey
Hill

5

Greenditch
Farm

48

Square
Plantation

Water
Tower

Borley
Wood

4

Little
Chilfords

Rivey
Wood

Sewage
Works

Cow Gallery
Wood

Fish
Ponds

Moat

THE WOODLANDS
CHERRY HOLT
THE GROVE
MAPLE CL

1 BALINGDON LA
2 PEMBROKE LA
3 DOLPHIN CL
4 MILLERS CL
5 CLOVER CT
6 RHUGARVE GDNS

BALSHAM ROAD B1052

Linton

3

Little
Linton

CRABTREE
CROFT

GRANTA LEYS

PALMERS CL
SYMONDS LANE

BACK ROAD

FLAXFIELDS

HILLWAY

CHALKLANDS

PAYNES MD

TOWER VIEW

RIVEY CL

BUSY WAY

BARLEY WAY

WHEAT CFT

PARSONAGE WY

HIGH ST

FAIRFIELD

BRINKMAN RD
BAWTREE CL
HOLLYBUSH WY
WHEATSHEAF WAY

Linton
Heights
Jun Sch

47

Sports
Centre

Linton
Village Coll

THE FURRELLS
COLES LANE

Cemy

Liby

PO

HORSEHEATH ROAD

LONGDALE

MEADOW LA

FIELD CL RD

MARKET LA

HIGH ST

GREEN LA

LAMB LA

Mill

FINCHAM
CLOSE

MARTINS LA

HAREFIELD RISE

KENWOOD GDNS

THE RIDGEWAY

2

JOINERS RD

JOINER'S CT

B1052

HORN LA

PH

CHURCH LA

Linton CE
Inf Sch

BEECH WAY

GRANTA VALE

FAIR CT

CROSSWAY

SAXON'S CL

BAKERS LA

BARTLOW ROAD

A1307

STATION RD

THE GRIP

HADSTOCK RD B1052

LONG LANE

1

Linton Zoo
& Gardens

The
Windmill

Barham
Hall

46

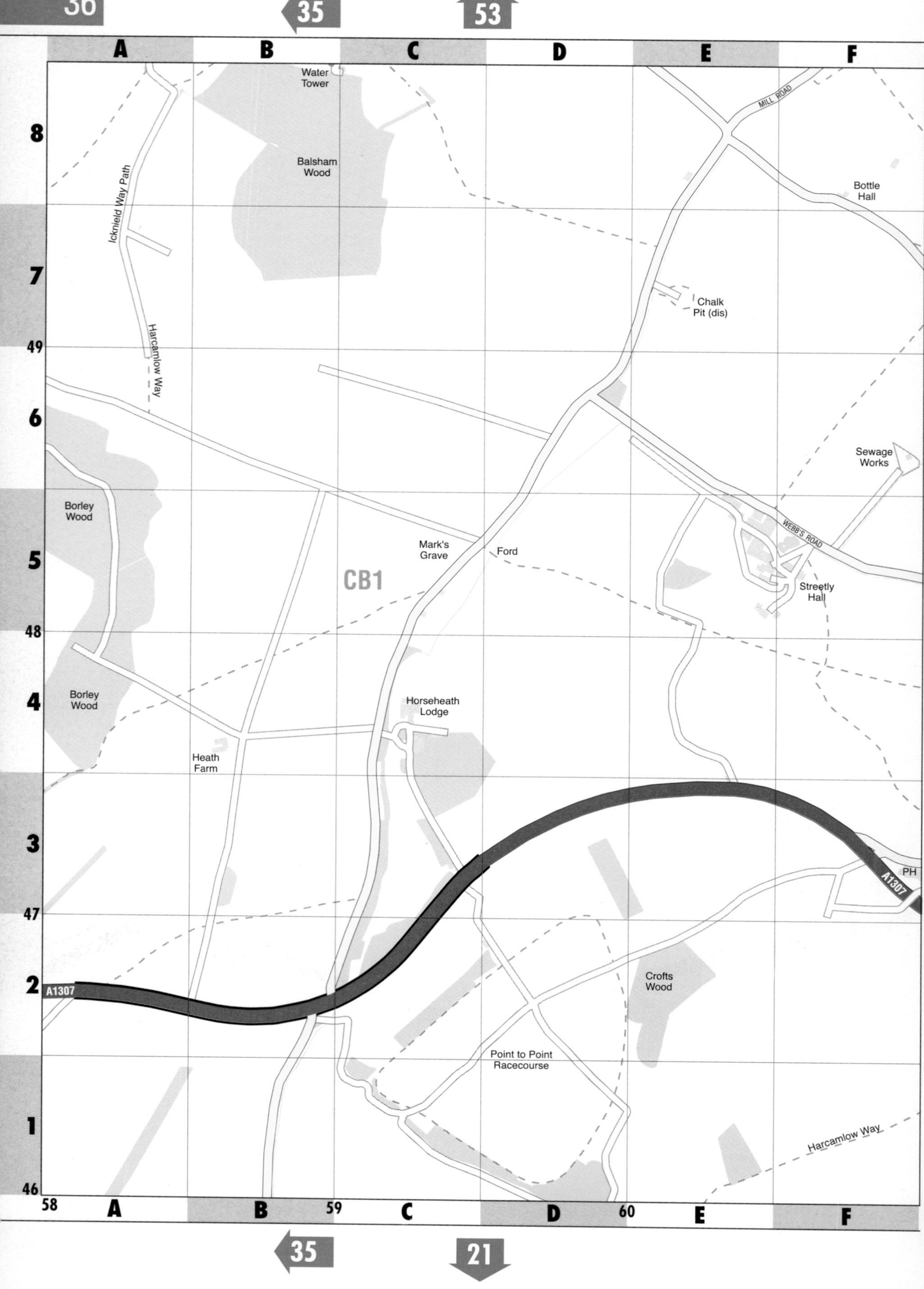

A   B   C   D   E   F

8

Water
Tower

Balsham
Wood

MILL ROAD

Bottle
Hall

7

Chalk
Pit (dis)

49

Harcamlow Way

Icknield Way Path

6

Sewage
Works

Borley
Wood

WEBB'S ROAD

Mark's
Grave

Ford

CB1

Streetly
Hall

5

48

Borley
Wood

4

Horseheath
Lodge

Heath
Farm

A1307

PH

3

47

Crofts
Wood

A1307

2

Point to Point
Racecourse

Harcamlow Way

1

46

58   A   B   59   C   D   60   E   F

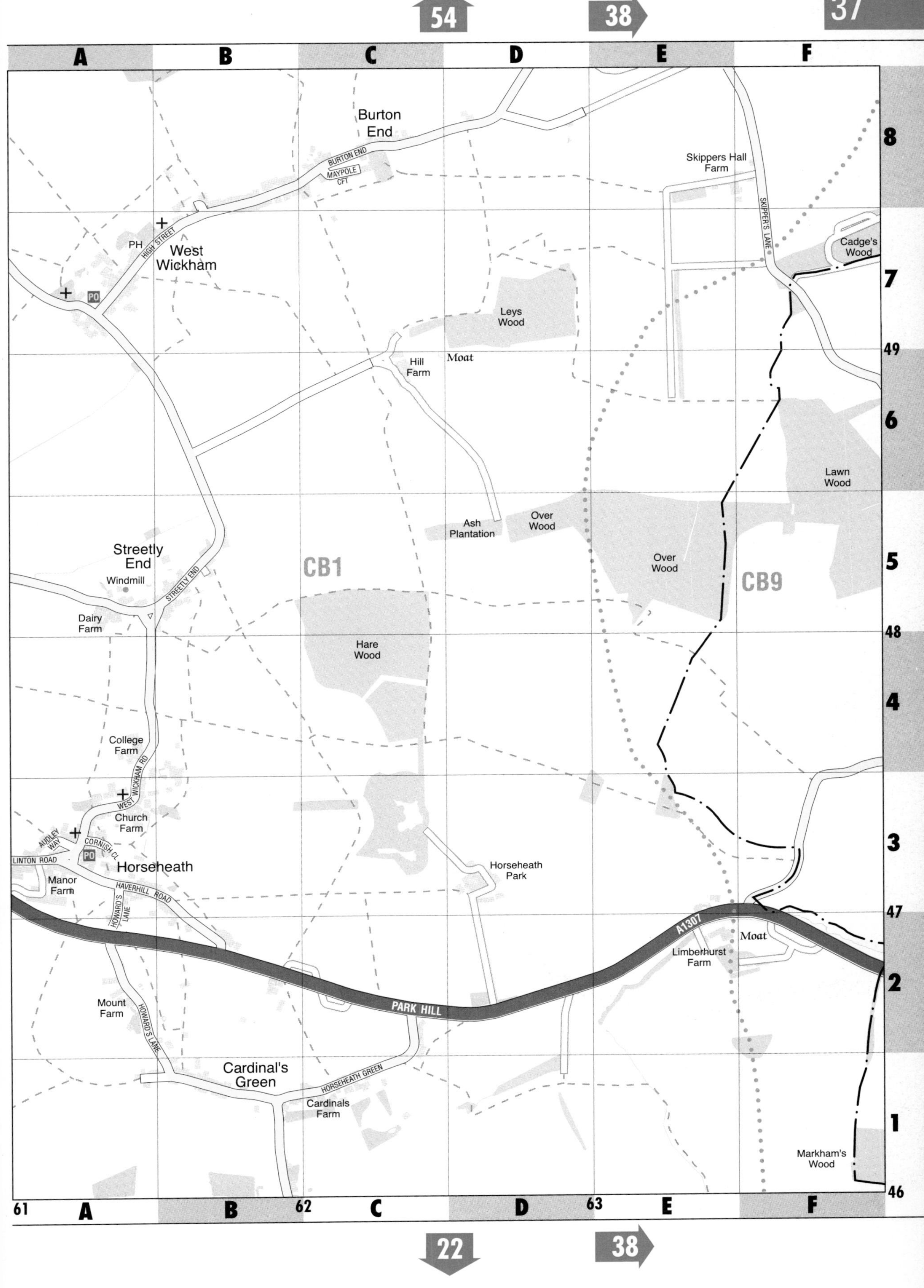

A B C D E F

8

Burton
End

Skippers Hall
Farm

BURTON END
MAYPOLE
CFT

SKIPPER'S LANE

Cadge's
Wood

PH

West
Wickham

HIGH STREET

7

PO

49

Leys
Wood

Hill
Farm

Moat

6

Lawn
Wood

Ash
Plantation

Over
Wood

Over
Wood

5

CB1

CB9

Streetly
End

Windmill

STREETLY END

48

Dairy
Farm

Hare
Wood

4

College
Farm

WEST WICKHAM RD

Church
Farm

AUDLEY
WAY

CORNISH CL

3

Horseheath
Park

Horseheath

PO

47

A1307

Moat

LINTON ROAD

Manor
Farm

HAVERHILL ROAD

HOWARD'S LANE

Limberhurst
Farm

2

Mount
Farm

HOWARD'S LANE

PARK HILL

Cardinal's
Green

HORSEHEATH GREEN

Cardinals
Farm

1

Markham's
Wood

46

61 A B 62 C D 63 E F

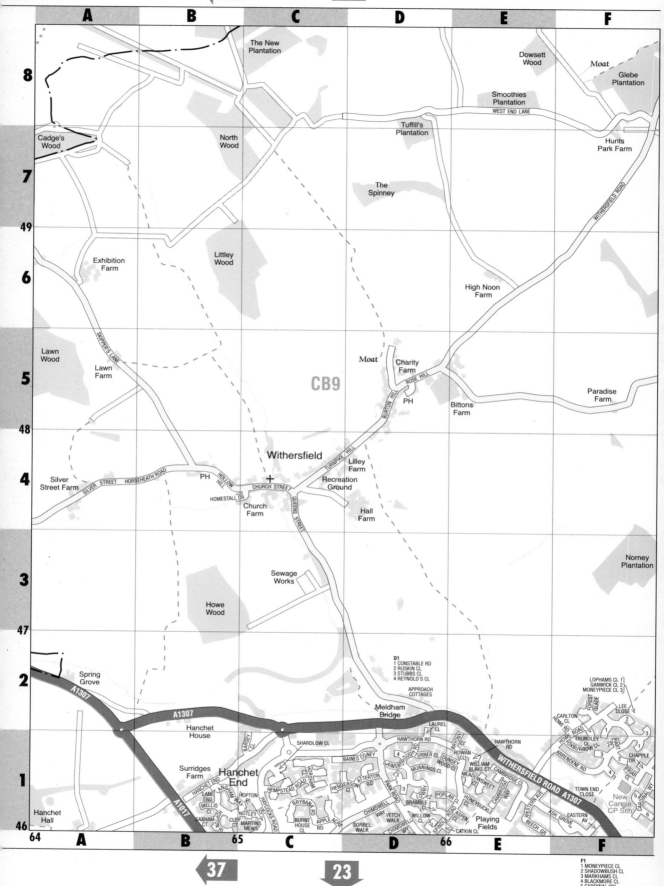

The New Plantation

Dowsett Wood

Moat

Glebe Plantation

Smoothies Plantation

WEST END LANE

Cadge's Wood

North Wood

Tuffill's Plantation

Hunts Park Farm

The Spinney

WITHERSFIELD ROAD

Exhibition Farm

Littley Wood

High Noon Farm

SKIPPER'S LANE

Lawn Wood

Lawn Farm

CB9

Moat

Charity Farm

ROSE HILL

BURTON HILL

PH

Bittons Farm

Paradise Farm

Silver Street Farm

SILVER STREET   HORSEHEATH ROAD

PH

HOLLOW HILL

HOMESTALL DR

Withersfield

CHURCH STREET

Church Farm

TURNPIKE HILL

Lilley Farm

Recreation Ground

QUEENS STREET

Hall Farm

Sewage Works

Howe Wood

Norney Plantation

D1
1 CONSTABLE RD
2 RUSKIN CL
3 STUBBS CL
4 REYNOLD'S CL

APPROACH COTTAGES

Spring Grove

A1307

A1307

Meldham Bridge

LOPHAMS CL 1
GANWICK CL 2
MONEYPIECE CL 3

Hanchet House

LAUREL CL

HAWTHORN RD

HAWTHORN RD

CARLTON CL

FOREST GLADE

LEE CLOSE

A1017

Surridges Farm

Hanchet End

SHARDLOW CL

BAINES CONEY

BRITONY CT

ROWAN CL

DUNSBY WOOD CL

WILLIAM BLAKE CT

MEADOWSWEET

CAMBRIDGE CL

HOWE RD

TRUNDLEY CL

FOXBURROW CL

ARRENDENE RD

CAMBRIDGE WAY

WESTERN AVE

HART CL

CHAPPLE DR

CHAPLE CL

FRIAR CL

HANCHET END

LANE END

BARSBY CL

HORSHAM RD

HEMPSTEAD RD

HENDERSON CT

ATTERTON RD

TURNER CL

GAINSBOROUGH CL

PARK ROAD

MUNNINGS CL

LOWRY CT

BRAMBLE CL

POPLAR CL

ASPEN CL

HONEYSUCKLE CL

TOWN END CLOSE

Hanchet Hall

MELLIS CL

NOTLEY CL

CLEV CT

MARTINS MEWS

HOPTON CL

BRYBANK RD

BURNT HOUSE CL

APPLE ACRE RD

CHIMSWELL WAY

VETCH WALK

SORREL WALK

CHIMSWELL WY

WILLOW CL

SPINDLE

CATKIN CL

Playing Fields

BEECH GR

ASH GROVE

EASTERN AV

CARDINAL WY

New Cangle CP Sch

SAXHAM CT

CAMBRIDGE

WESTERN AVE

WITHERSFIELD ROAD A1307

F1
1 MONEYPIECE CL
2 SHADOWBUSH CL
3 MARKHAMS CL
4 BLACKMORE CL
5 CARDINAL WY
6 CHAPLAINS CL

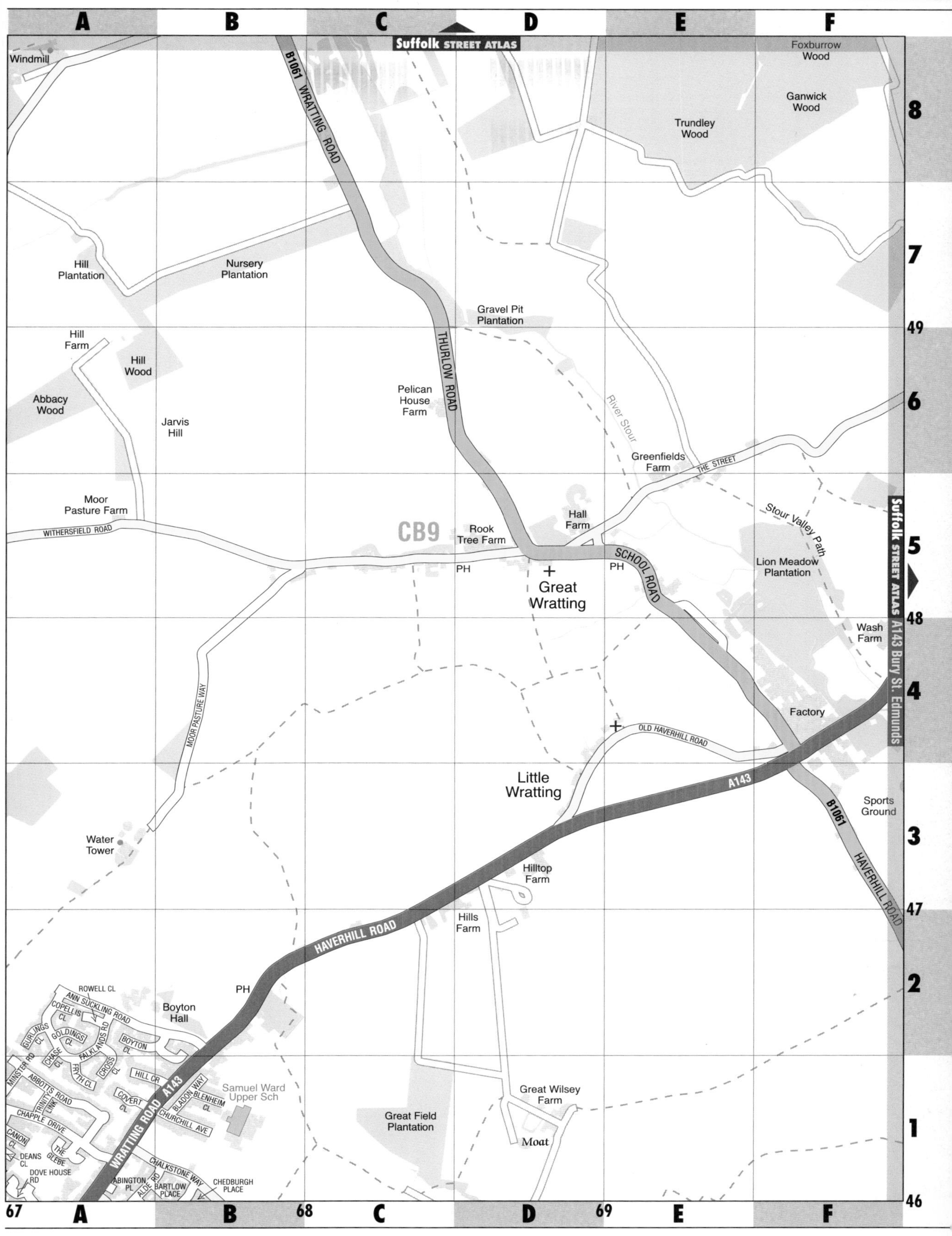

Windmill

B1061 WRATTING ROAD

Foxburrow Wood

Ganwick Wood

Trundley Wood

8

Hill Plantation

Nursery Plantation

7

Gravel Pit Plantation

49

Hill Farm

THURLOW ROAD

Hill Wood

Pelican House Farm

River Stour

6

Abbacy Wood

Jarvis Hill

Greenfields Farm

THE STREET

Stour Valley Path

Moor Pasture Farm

WITHERSFIELD ROAD

CB9

Rook Tree Farm

Hall Farm

Lion Meadow Plantation

5

48

PH

PH

SCHOOL ROAD

+ Great Wratting

Wash Farm

MOOR PASTURE WAY

Factory

4

Little Wratting

+ OLD HAVERHILL ROAD

A143

B1061

Sports Ground

HAVERHILL ROAD

3

Water Tower

Hilltop Farm

47

Hills Farm

HAVERHILL ROAD

ROWELL CL

PH

2

Ann Suckling Road

Boyton Hall

COPELLIS CL

BURLINGS CL

GOLDINGS CL

FALKLANDS RD

BOYTON CL

FRYTH CL

CHASE CL

CROSS

HILL CR

Great Wilsey Farm

MINSTER RD

ABBOTTS ROAD

WRATTING ROAD A143

COVERT CL

BLADON WAY

BLENHEIM CL

CHURCHILL AVE

Samuel Ward Upper Sch

1

TRINITY CL

CHAPPLE DRIVE

CANON CL

DEANS CL

THE GLEBE

DOVE HOUSE RD

ABINGTON PL

CHALKSTONE WAY

CHEDBURGH PLACE

BARTLOW PLACE

Great Field Plantation

Moat

46

67 A   B 68 C   D 69 E   F

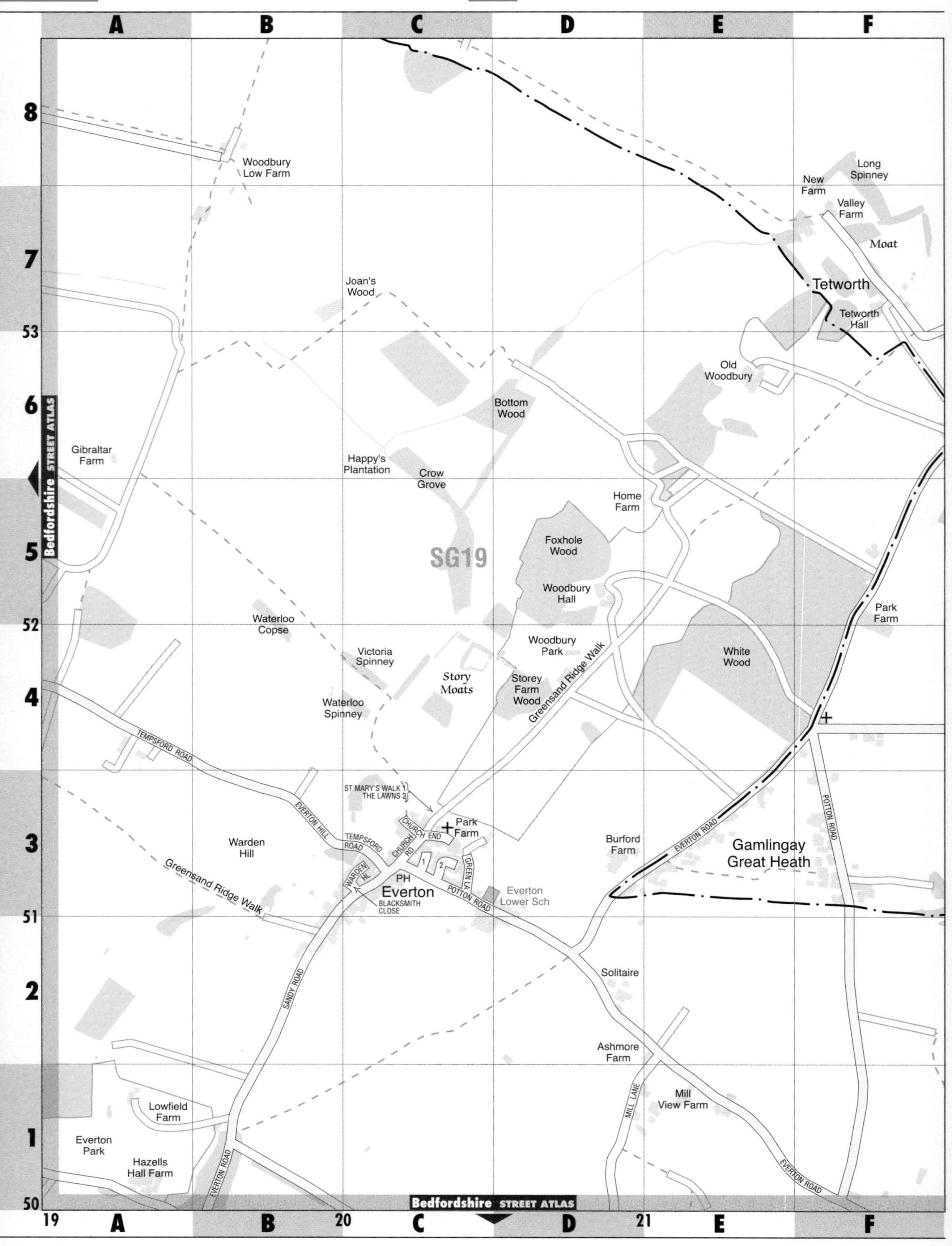

Woodbury Low Farm

Joan's Wood

Tetworth

New Farm

Long Spinney

Valley Farm

Moat

Tetworth Hall

Old Woodbury

Bottom Wood

Gibraltar Farm

Happy's Plantation

Crow Grove

Home Farm

SG19

Foxhole Wood

Woodbury Hall

Park Farm

Waterloo Copse

Victoria Spinney

Woodbury Park

White Wood

Story Moats

Storey Farm Wood

Greensand Ridge Walk

Waterloo Spinney

TEMPSFORD ROAD

EVERTON HILL

ST MARY'S WALK 1
THE LAWNS 2

CHURCH END

Park Farm

Warden Hill

TEMPSFORD ROAD

CHURCH RD

GREEN LA

Burford Farm

EVERTON ROAD

Gamlingay Great Heath

POTTON ROAD

Greensand Ridge Walk

WARDEN LA

PH

Everton

BLACKSMITH CLOSE

POTTON ROAD

Everton Lower Sch

SANDY ROAD

Solitaire

Ashmore Farm

MILL LANE

Mill View Farm

EVERTON ROAD

Lowfield Farm

Everton Park

Hazells Hall Farm

EVERTON ROAD

Bedfordshire STREET ATLAS

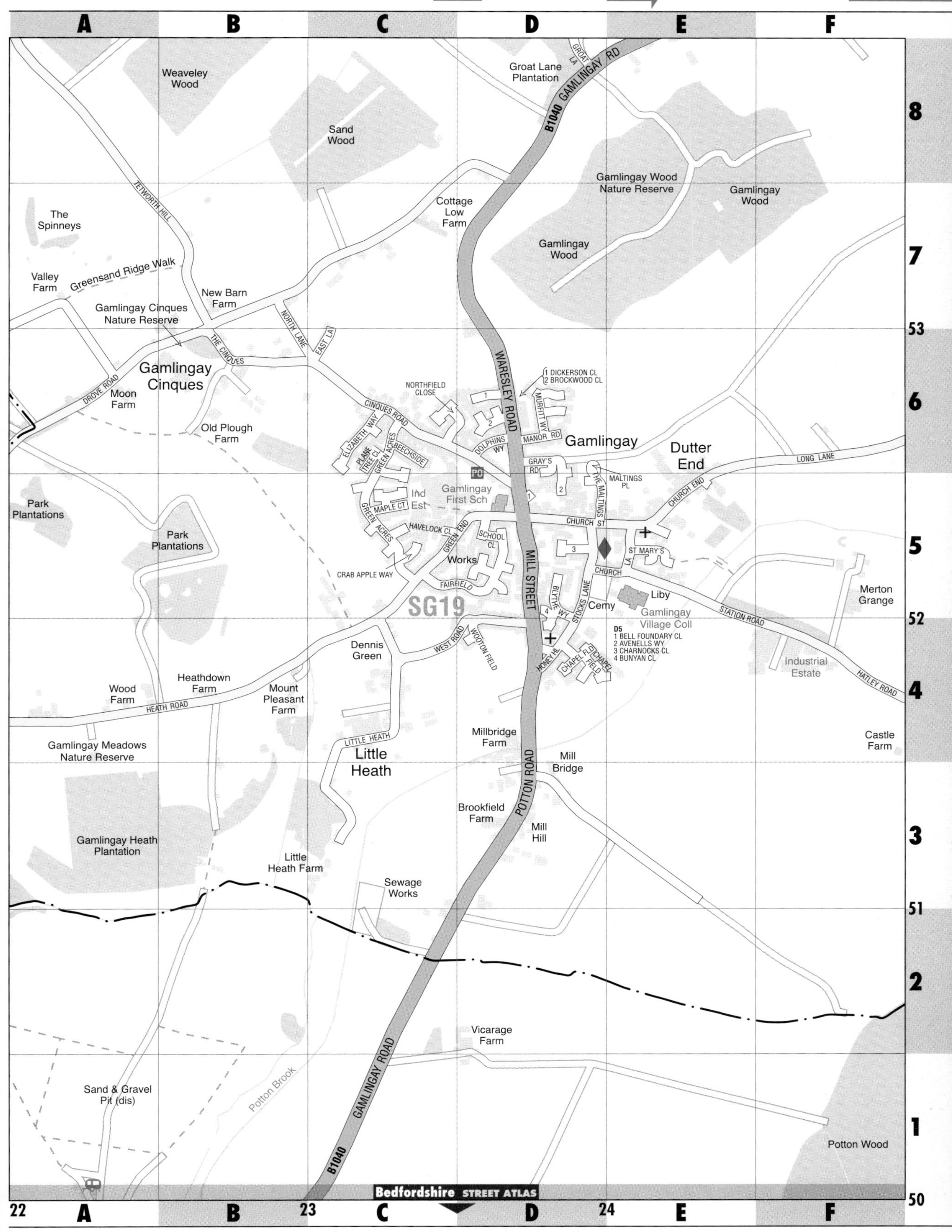

A B C D E F

8

7

53

6

5

52

4

3

51

2

1

50

Weaveley
Wood

Sand
Wood

Groat Lane
Plantation

Gamlingay Wood
Nature Reserve

Gamlingay
Wood

The
Spinneys

Cottage
Low
Farm

Gamlingay
Wood

Valley
Farm

Greensand Ridge Walk

New Barn
Farm

TETWORTH HILL

Gamlingay Cinques
Nature Reserve

NORTH LANE

EAST LA

THE CINQUES

Gamlingay
Cinques

Moon
Farm

DROVE ROAD

Old Plough
Farm

CINQUES ROAD

NORTHFIELD
CLOSE

DOLPHINS WY

WARESLEY ROAD

MURFITT WY

1 DICKERSON CL
2 BROCKWOOD CL

MANOR RD

Gamlingay

Dutter
End

LONG LANE

Park
Plantations

ELIZABETH WAY

PLANE TREE CL

GREEN ACRES

BEECHSIDE

GRAY'S
RD

THE MALTINGS

MALTINGS
PL

CHURCH END

Park
Plantations

MAPLE CT

Ind
Est

Gamlingay First Sch

CHURCH ST

Works

GREEN ACRES

HAVELOCK CL

GREEN END

SCHOOL
CL

CHURCH

St Mary's

Liby

Merton
Grange

CRAB APPLE WAY

FAIRFIELD

MILL STREET

BLYTHE WY

STOCKS LANE

Cemy

Gamlingay
Village Coll

STATION ROAD

SG19

Dennis
Green

WEST ROAD

WOOTTON FIELD

MONEY HL

CHAPEL FIELD

CHAPEL FIELD

D5
1 BELL FOUNDARY CL
2 AVENELLS WY
3 CHARNOCKS CL
4 BUNYAN CL

Industrial
Estate

HATLEY ROAD

Heathdown
Farm

Mount
Pleasant
Farm

Wood
Farm

HEATH ROAD

Gamlingay Meadows
Nature Reserve

LITTLE HEATH

Little
Heath

Millbridge
Farm

Mill
Bridge

POTTON ROAD

Castle
Farm

Little
Heath Farm

Brookfield
Farm

Mill
Hill

Gamlingay Heath
Plantation

Sewage
Works

Vicarage
Farm

Sand & Gravel
Pit (dis)

Potton Brook

GAMLINGAY ROAD

B1040

Potton Wood

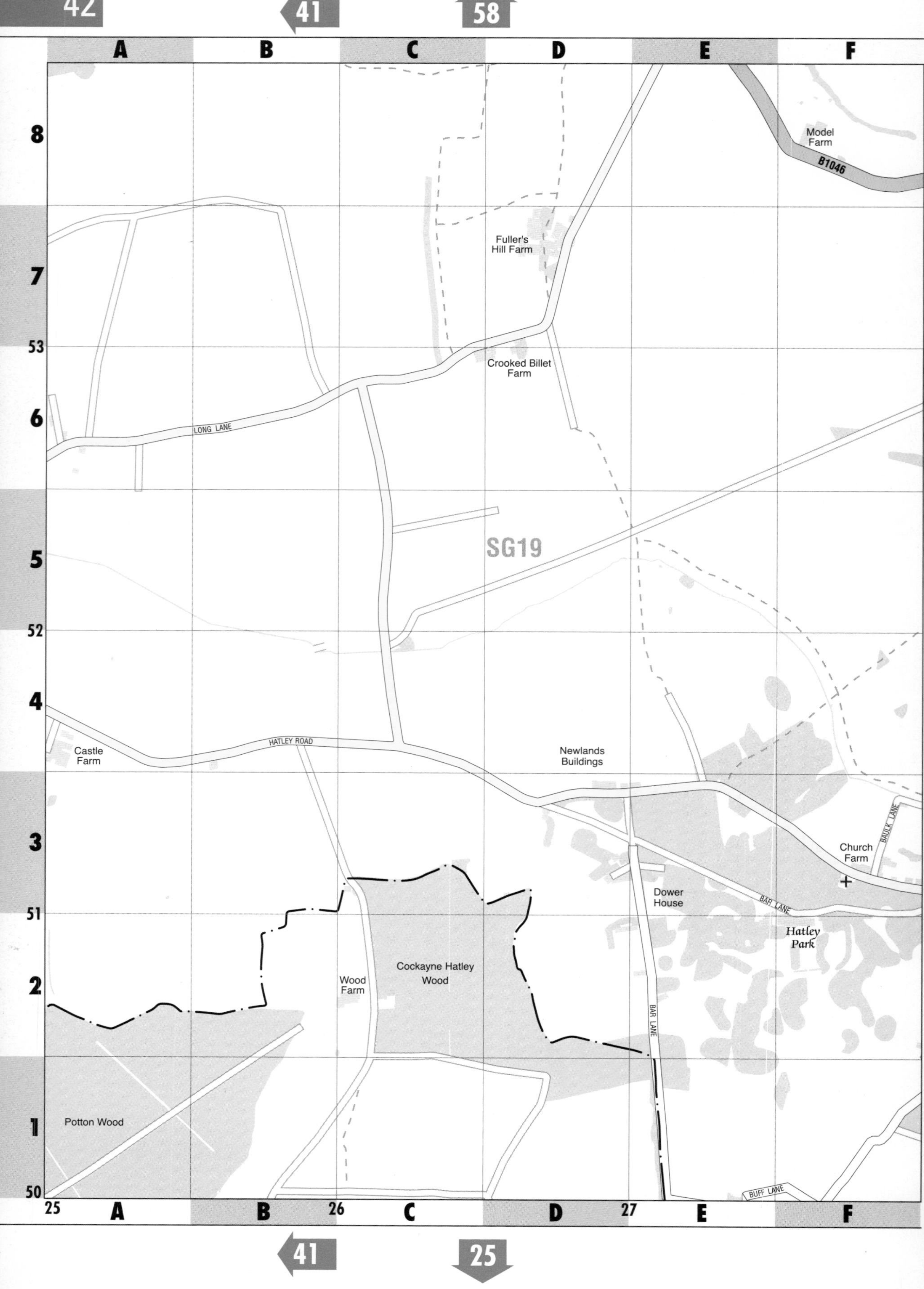

A   B   C   D   E   F

8

7

53

6

5

52

4

3

51

2

1

50

Model Farm

B1046

Fuller's Hill Farm

Crooked Billet Farm

LONG LANE

SG19

Castle Farm

HATLEY ROAD

Newlands Buildings

Church Farm

BRIDLE LANE

Dower House

BAR LANE

Hatley Park

Wood Farm

Cockayne Hatley Wood

BAR LANE

Potton Wood

BUFF LANE

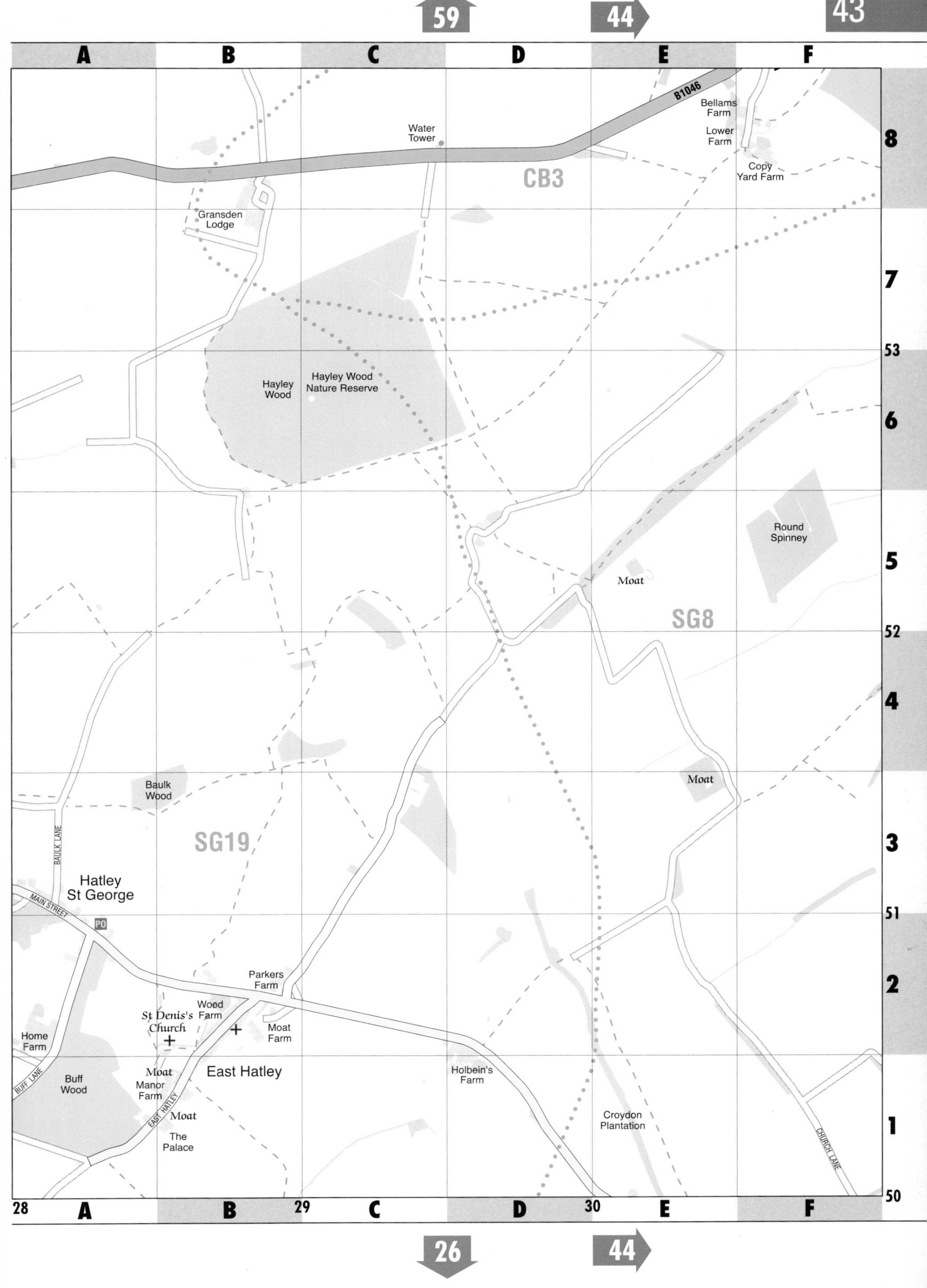
59
44
A
B
C
D
E
F
8
7
53
6
5
52
4
3
51
2
1
50
28
29
30
B1046
Bellams
Farm
Lower
Farm
Copy
Yard Farm
Water
Tower
CB3
Gransden
Lodge
Hayley
Wood
Hayley Wood
Nature Reserve
Round
Spinney
Moat
SG8
Baulk
Wood
Moat
SG19
BAULK LANE
Hatley
St George
MAIN STREET
PO
Parkers
Farm
Wood
Farm
St Denis's
Church
Moat
Farm
Home
Farm
Buff
Wood
BUFF LANE
Moat
Manor
Farm
East Hatley
EAST HATLEY
Moat
The
Palace
Holbein's
Farm
Croydon
Plantation
CHURCH LANE
26
44

43
60

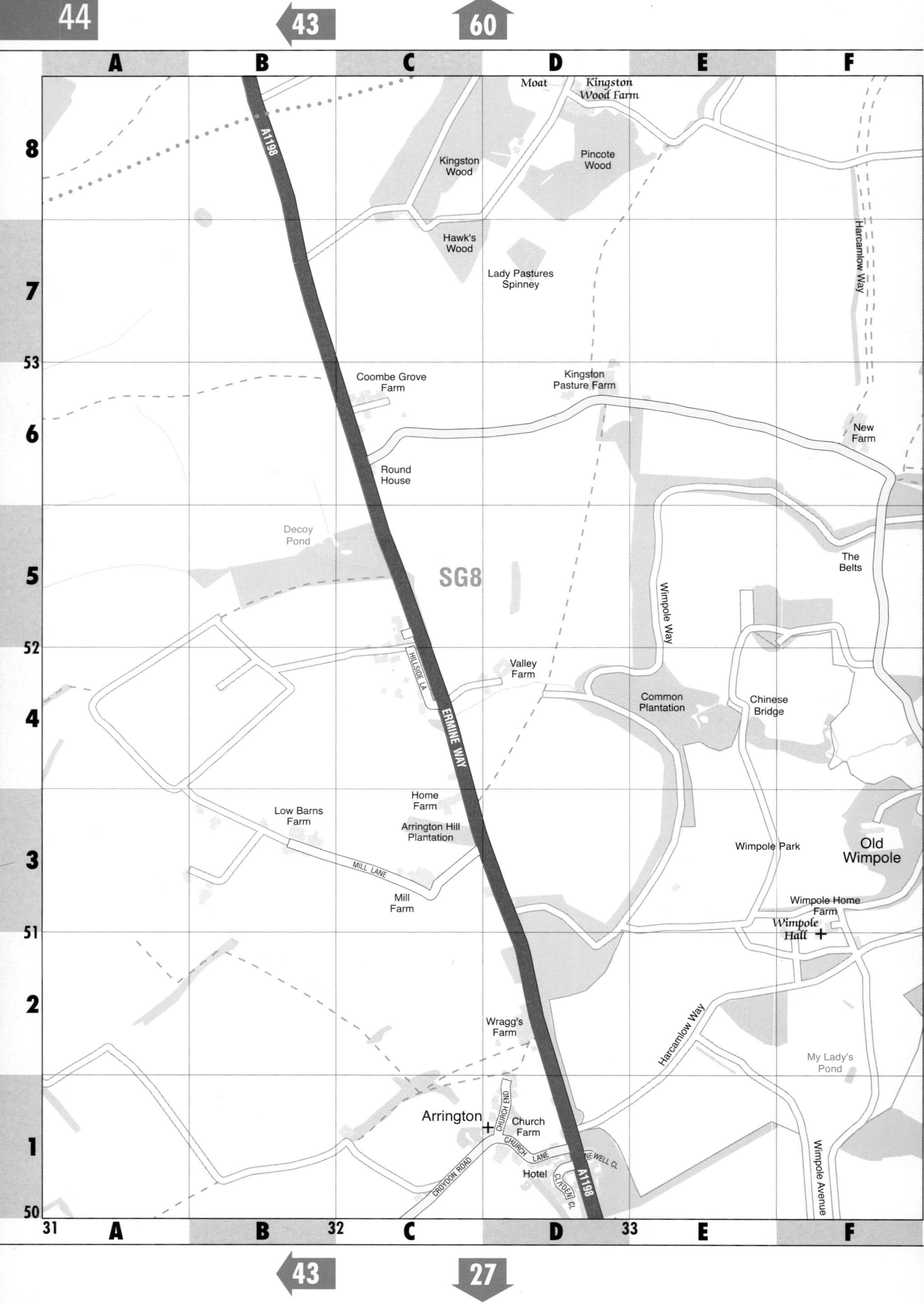
A
B
C
D
E
F
Moat
Kingston Wood Farm
8
A1198
Kingston Wood
Pincote Wood
Hawk's Wood
Harcamlow Way
7
Lady Pastures Spinney
53
Coombe Grove Farm
Kingston Pasture Farm
6
New Farm
Round House
Decoy Pond
The Belts
5
SG8
Wimpole Way
52
Valley Farm
HILLSIDE LA
4
ERMINE WAY
Common Plantation
Chinese Bridge
Home Farm
Low Barns Farm
Arrington Hill Plantation
Old Wimpole
3
Wimpole Park
MILL LANE
Mill Farm
Wimpole Home Farm
51
Wimpole Hall
2
Wragg's Farm
Harcamlow Way
My Lady's Pond
Arrington
CHURCH END
Church Farm
1
CHURCH LANE
NEWELL CL
CROYDON ROAD
Hotel
CLYDEN CL
A1198
Wimpole Avenue
50
31
32
33

43
27

61
46

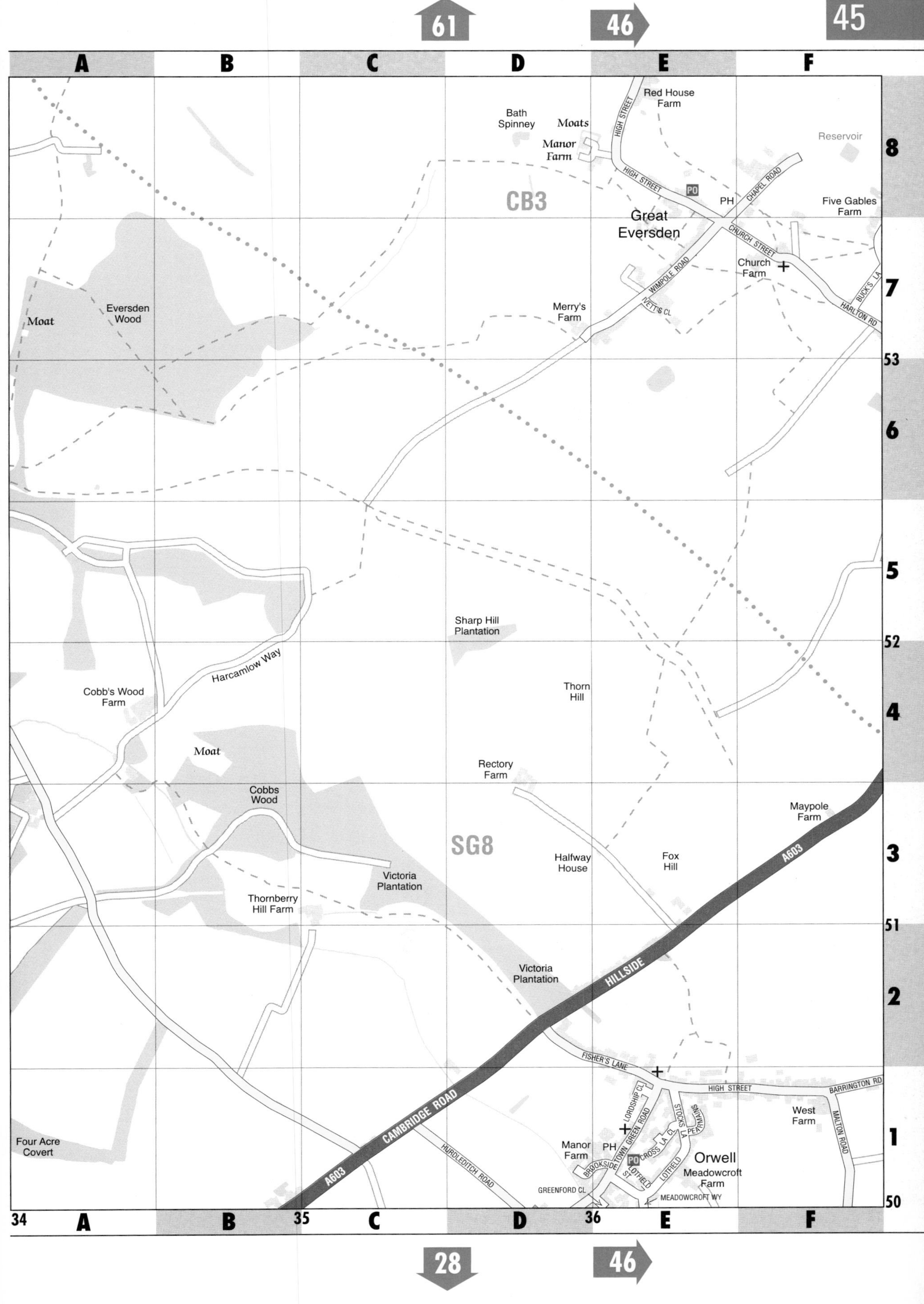
A
B
C
D
E
F
Red House Farm
Bath Spinney
Moats
Manor Farm
HIGH STREET
Reservoir
8
CB3
PO
PH
CHAPEL ROAD
Five Gables Farm
Great Eversden
CHURCH STREET
Church Farm
WIMPOLE ROAD
BUCK'S LA
7
Eversden Wood
Moat
Merry's Farm
IVETT'S CL
HARLTON RD
53
6
5
Sharp Hill Plantation
52
Harcamlow Way
Cobb's Wood Farm
Thorn Hill
4
Moat
Rectory Farm
Cobbs Wood
Maypole Farm
SG8
Halfway House
Fox Hill
3
A603
Victoria Plantation
Thornberry Hill Farm
51
HILLSIDE
Victoria Plantation
2
FISHER'S LANE
HIGH STREET
BARRINGTON RD
LORDSHIP CL
TOWN GREEN ROAD
STOCKS LA
PEARMAINS
West Farm
MALTON ROAD
1
CROSS LA CL
Four Acre Covert
CAMBRIDGE ROAD
Manor Farm
PH
BROOKSIDE
PO
ST LOTFIELD
LOTFIELD
Orwell
Meadowcroft Farm
HURDLEDITCH ROAD
A603
GREENFORD CL
MEADOWCROFT WY
50
34
A
B
35
C
D
36
E
F

28
46

45
62

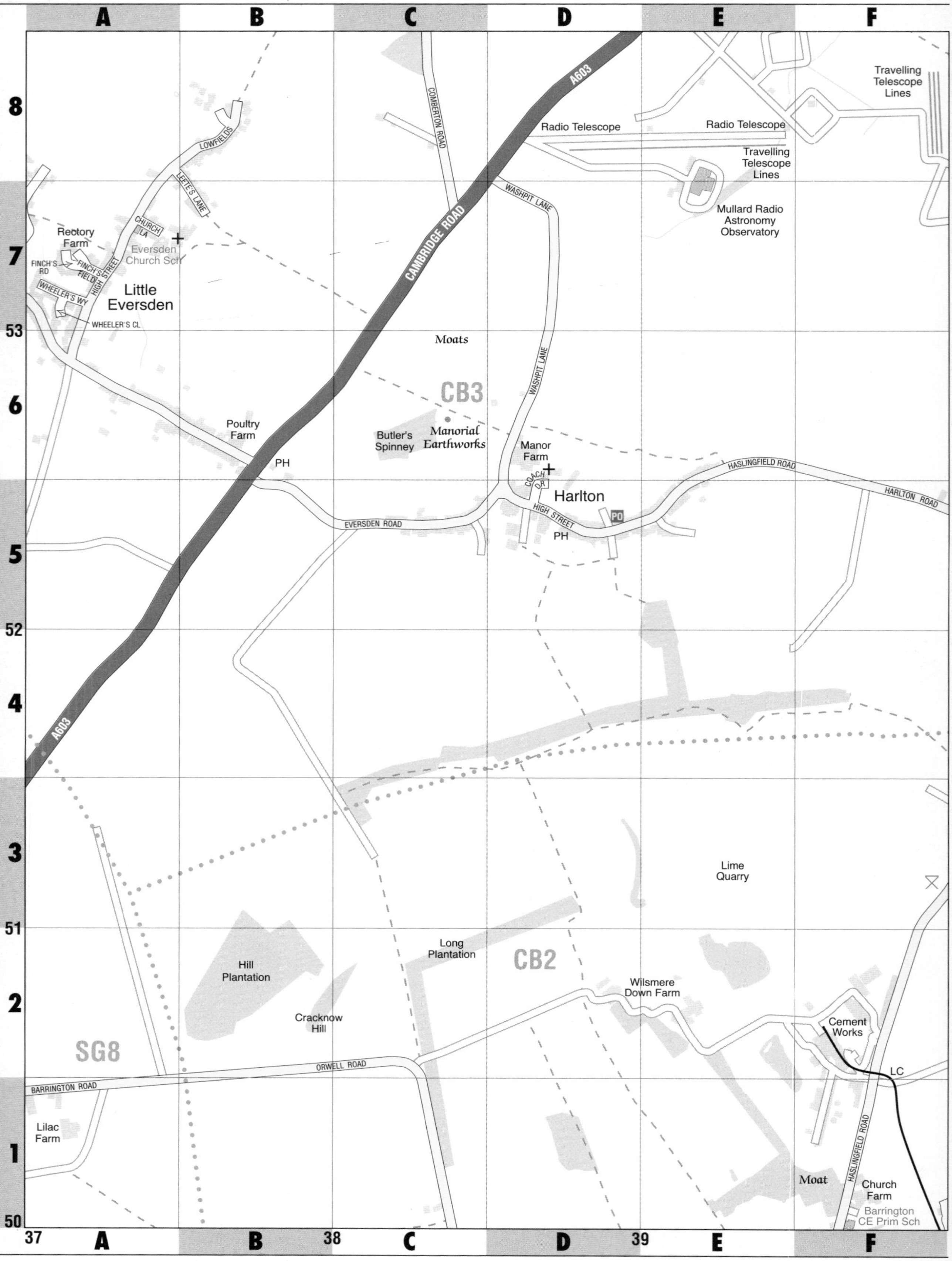

A B C D E F

8

Travelling Telescope Lines

A603

COMBERTON ROAD

Radio Telescope

Radio Telescope

Travelling Telescope Lines

WASHPIT LANE

Mullard Radio Astronomy Observatory

7

Rectory Farm

CHURCH LA

Eversden Church Sch

LOWFIELDS

LEFFE'S LANE

FINCH'S RD

FINCH'S FIELD

HIGH STREET

WHEELER'S WY

Little Eversden

CAMBRIDGE ROAD

WASHPIT LANE

53

WHEELER'S CL

Moats

6

CB3

Poultry Farm

PH

Butler's Spinney

Manorial Earthworks

Manor Farm

HASLINGFIELD ROAD

HARLTON ROAD

COACH DR

Harlton

PO

EVERSDEN ROAD

HIGH STREET

PH

5

52

4

A603

3

Lime Quarry

51

Hill Plantation

Long Plantation

CB2

Wilsmere Down Farm

2

Cracknow Hill

Cement Works

SG8

ORWELL ROAD

LC

BARRINGTON ROAD

HASLINGFIELD ROAD

1

Lilac Farm

Moat

Church Farm

50

Barrington CE Prim Sch

37 A B 38 C D 39 E F

45
29

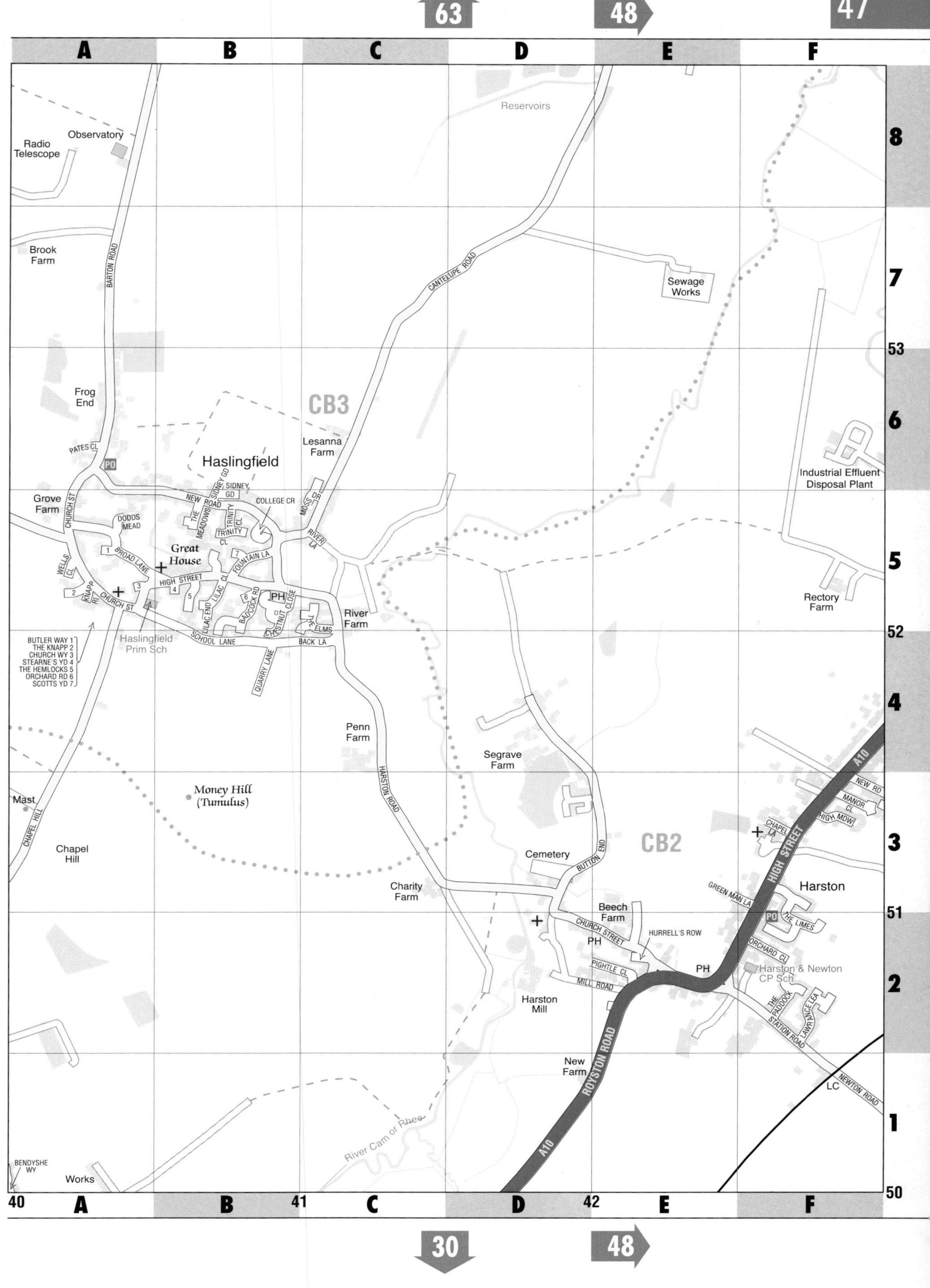

A   B   C   D   E   F

8

7

53

6

5

52

4

3

51

2

1

50

Reservoirs

Radio
Telescope

Observatory

Brook
Farm

BARTON ROAD

CANTELUPE ROAD

Sewage
Works

Frog
End

PATES CL

PO

CB3

Lesanna
Farm

Haslingfield

Grove
Farm

CHURCH ST

NEW ROAD

SIDNEY GD

SIDNEY GD

COLLEGE CR

MOLE ST

RIVER LA

DR

Industrial Effluent
Disposal Plant

DODDS
MEAD

THE MEADOWS

TRINITY CL

TRINITY CL

Great
House

WELLS CL

KNAPP

BROAD LANE

1

HIGH STREET

3

4

5

LILAC END

LILAC CL

FOUNTAIN LA

BADDOCK RD

6

PH

THE ELMS

River
Farm

Rectory
Farm

BUTLER WAY 1
THE KNAPP 2
CHURCH WY 3
STEARNE'S YD 4
THE HEMLOCKS 5
ORCHARD RD 6
SCOTTS YD 7

CHURCH ST

Haslingfield
Prim Sch

SCHOOL LANE

CHESTNUT CLOSE

BACK LA

QUARRY LANE

Penn
Farm

HARSTON ROAD

Segrave
Farm

CB2

Mast

CHAPEL HILL

Chapel
Hill

Money Hill
(Tumulus)

Cemetery

BUTTON END

A10

NEW RD

MANOR CL

HIGH MDW

CHAPEL LA

HIGH STREET

Harston

GREEN MAN LA

PO

THE LIMES

Charity
Farm

Beech
Farm

CHURCH STREET

PH

HURRELL'S ROW

ORCHARD CL

PH

Harston & Newton
CP Sch

PIGHTLE CL

MILL ROAD

Harston
Mill

THE PADDOCK

STATION ROAD

LAWRANCE LA

BENDYSHE
WY

Works

New
Farm

ROYSTON ROAD

A10

River Cam or Rhee

LC

NEWTON ROAD

40   A   B   41   C   D   42   E   F   50

47
64

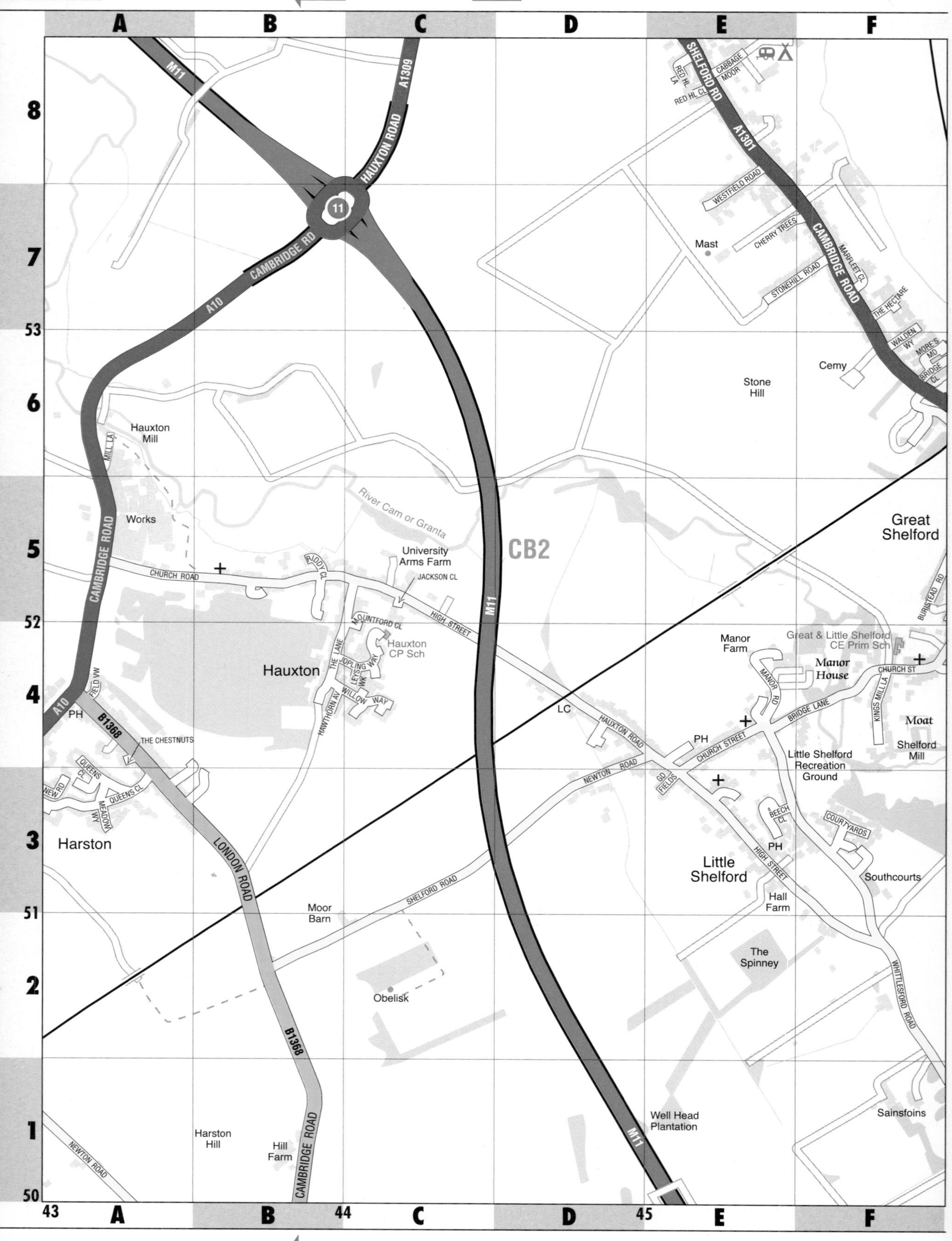
A
B
C
D
E
F
8
7
53
6
5
52
4
3
51
2
1
50
43
44
45
M11
A1309
HAUXTON ROAD
11
CAMBRIDGE RD
A10
SHELFORD RD
RED HL LA
CABBAGE MOOR
RED HL CL
A1301
WESTFIELD ROAD
CHERRY TREES
Mast
CAMBRIDGE ROAD
STONEHILL ROAD
MARFLEET CL
THE HECTARE
WALDEN WY
MORE'S MD
BRIDGE CL
Cemy
Stone Hill
Hauxton Mill
MILL LA
Works
CAMBRIDGE ROAD
River Cam or Granta
CB2
Great Shelford
University Arms Farm
RIDDY CL
JACKSON CL
CHURCH ROAD
HIGH STREET
MOUNTFORD CL
Hauxton CP Sch
THE LANE
OPLING WAY
LEYS WK
WILLOW WAY
HAWTHORN AV
Hauxton
FIELD VW
A10
PH
B1368
THE CHESTNUTS
QUEENS CL
NEW RD
MEADOW WY
Harston
LONDON ROAD
LC
HAUXTON ROAD
NEWTON ROAD
GD FIELDS
CHURCH STREET
PH
BRIDGE LANE
Manor Farm
MANOR RD
Manor House
Great & Little Shelford CE Prim Sch
CHURCH ST
KINGS MILL LA
BURNSTEAD RD
Moat
Shelford Mill
Little Shelford Recreation Ground
BEECH CL
COURTYARDS
PH
HIGH STREET
Little Shelford
Southcourts
Hall Farm
SHELFORD ROAD
Moor Barn
The Spinney
Obelisk
WHITTLESFORD ROAD
B1368
Well Head Plantation
Sainsfoins
M11
Harston Hill
Hill Farm
CAMBRIDGE ROAD
NEWTON ROAD

47
31

65
50

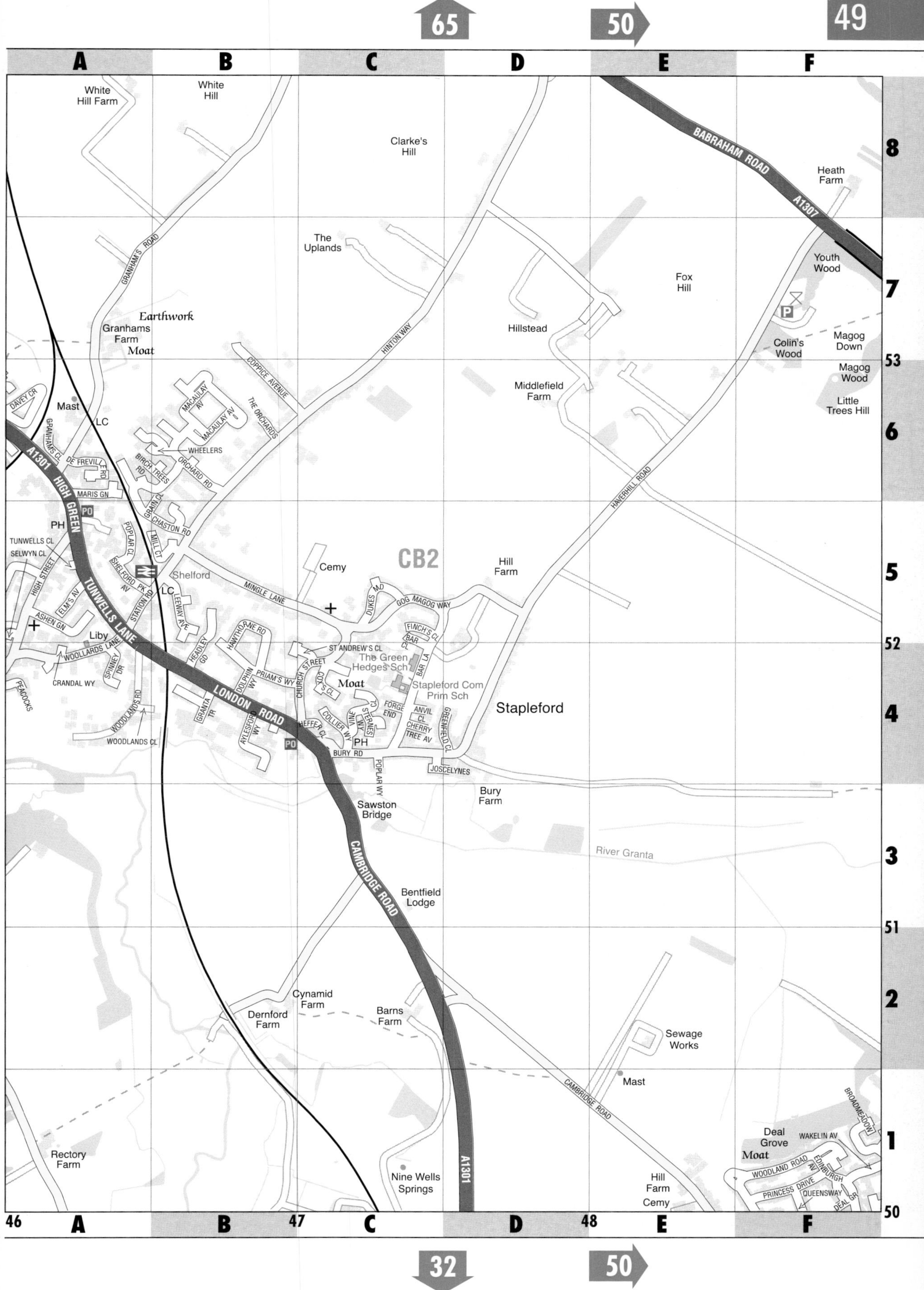
A
B
C
D
E
F
White Hill Farm
White Hill
Clarke's Hill
BABRAHAM ROAD
A1307
Heath Farm
8
The Uplands
GRANHAM'S ROAD
Youth Wood
Fox Hill
7
Earthwork
Granhams Farm
Moat
Hillstead
HINTON WAY
Colin's Wood
Magog Down
53
COPPICE AVENUE
Middlefield Farm
Magog Wood
DAVEY CR
Mast
LC
MACAULAY AV
THE ORCHARDS
Little Trees Hill
6
GRANHAMS CL
A1301
HIGH GREEN
DE FREVILLE RD
BIRCH TREES RD
WHEELERS
ORCHARD RD
MARIS GN
PO
PH
GRAIN CL
CHASTON RD
HAVERHILL ROAD
TUNWELLS CL
SELWYN CL
POPLAR CL
MILL CT
CB2
Cemy
Hill Farm
5
HIGH STREET
SHELFORD AV
PK
Shelford
LC
MINGLE LANE
DUKES MD
GOG MAGOG WAY
ELM'S AV
TUNWELLS LANE
STATION RD
LEEWAY AV
ASHEN GN
FINCH'S CL
Liby
HAWTHORNE RD
BAR CL
52
WOOLLARDS LANE
HEADLEY GD
ST ANDREW'S CL
The Green Hedges Sch
BAR LA
CRANDAL WY
SPINNEY DR
PRIAM'S WY
CHURCH STREET
COX'S CL
Moat
Stapleford Com Prim Sch
PEACOCKS
LONDON ROAD
DOLPHIN WY
Stapleford
4
WOODLANDS RD
GRANTA TR
COLLIER WY
VINE WY
STERNES CL
FORGE END
ANVIL CL
GREENFIELD CL
WOODLANDS CL
AYLESFORD WY
HEFFER CL
CHERRY TREE AV
PO
PH
BURY RD
JOSCELYNES
POPLAR WY
Bury Farm
Sawston Bridge
River Granta
3
CAMBRIDGE ROAD
Bentfield Lodge
51
Cynamid Farm
2
Dernford Farm
Barns Farm
Sewage Works
Mast
CAMBRIDGE ROAD
BROADMEADOW
1
Deal Grove
WAKELIN AV
Moat
Rectory Farm
WOODLAND ROAD
EDINBURGH AV
A1301
Nine Wells Springs
Hill Farm
PRINCESS DRIVE
QUEENSWAY
DEAL GR
Cemy
50
46
A
B
47
C
D
48
E
F

32
50

49
66

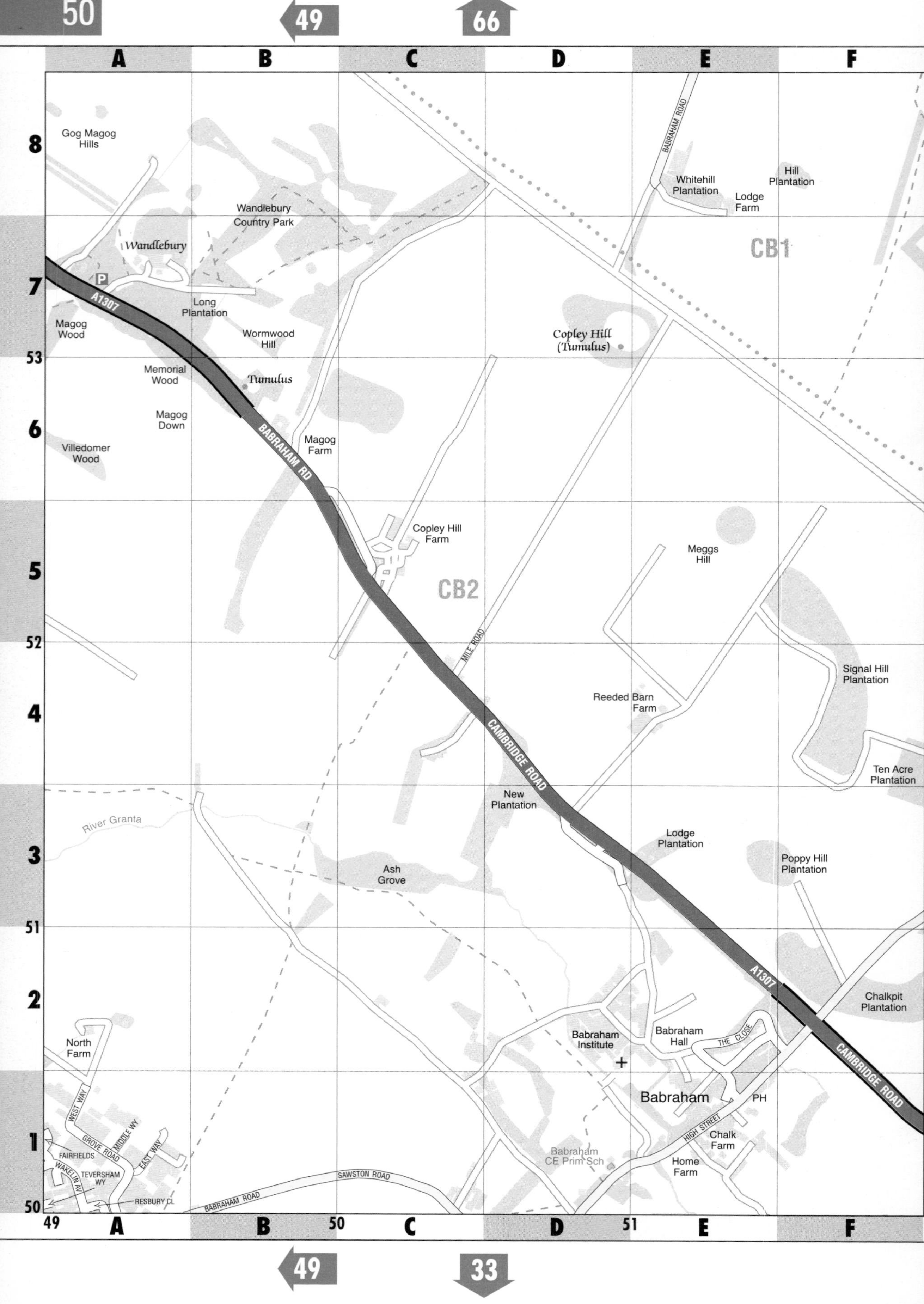
A
B
C
D
E
F
8
7
53
6
5
52
4
3
51
2
1
50
49
50
51
Gog Magog
Hills
Wandlebury
Country Park
Wandlebury
P
A1307
Long
Plantation
Magog
Wood
Wormwood
Hill
Memorial
Wood
Tumulus
Magog
Down
Villedomer
Wood
BABRAHAM RD
Magog
Farm
Copley Hill
Farm
CB2
MILE ROAD
BABRAHAM ROAD
Whitehill
Plantation
Hill
Plantation
Lodge
Farm
CB1
Copley Hill
(Tumulus)
Meggs
Hill
Signal Hill
Plantation
Reeded Barn
Farm
Ten Acre
Plantation
CAMBRIDGE ROAD
New
Plantation
River Granta
Lodge
Plantation
Ash
Grove
Poppy Hill
Plantation
A1307
Chalkpit
Plantation
North
Farm
Babraham
Institute
Babraham
Hall
THE CLOSE
CAMBRIDGE ROAD
Babraham
PH
WEST WAY
GROVE ROAD
MIDDLE WY
EAST WAY
FAIRFIELDS
WAKELIN AV
TEVERSHAM
WY
RESBURY CL
BABRAHAM ROAD
SAWSTON ROAD
Babraham
CE Prim Sch
HIGH STREET
Chalk
Farm
Home
Farm

49
33

A   B   C   D   E   F

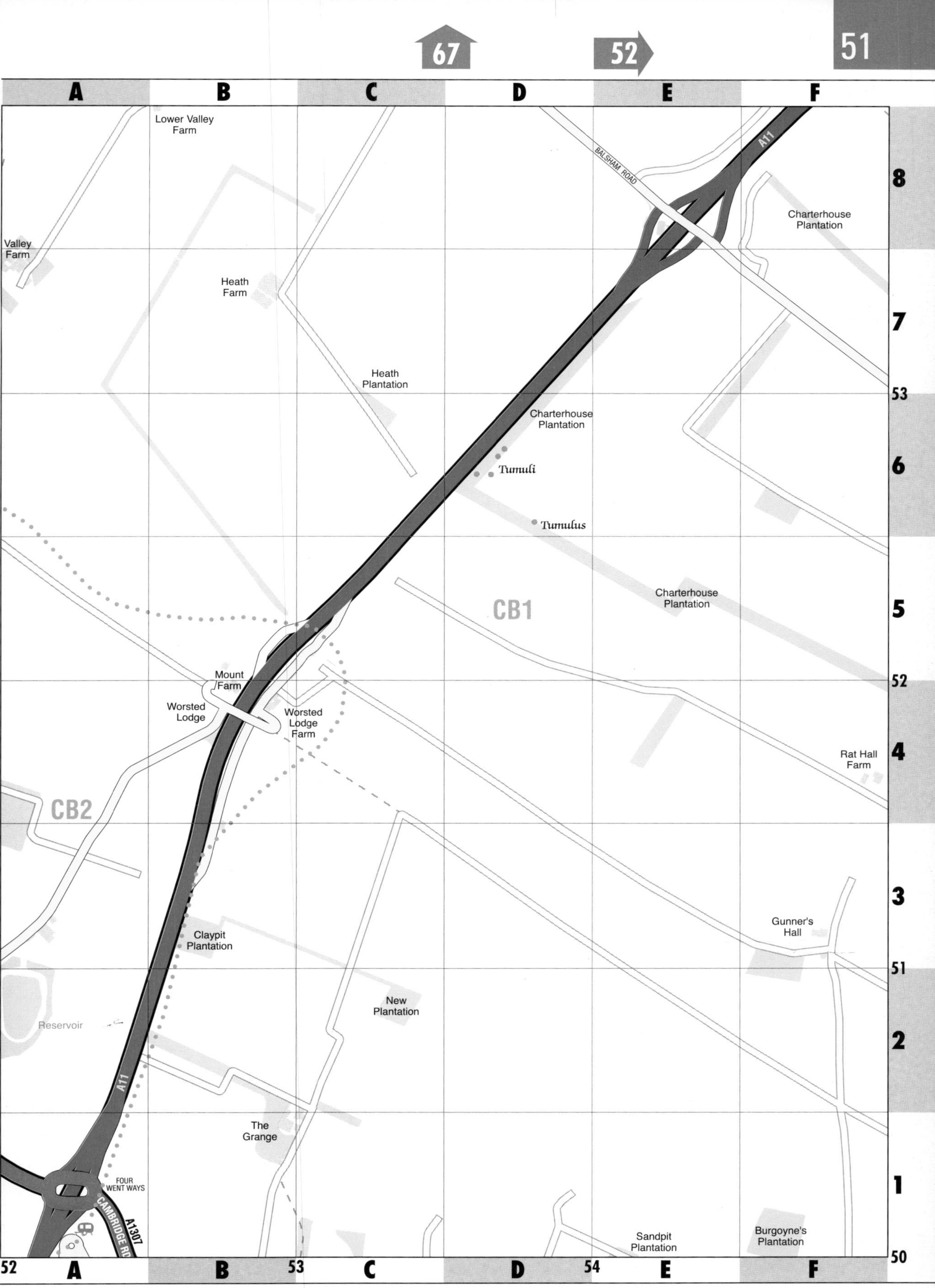

Lower Valley Farm

Valley Farm

Heath Farm

Heath Plantation

Charterhouse Plantation

Charterhouse Plantation

Tumuli

Tumulus

Charterhouse Plantation

CB1

BALSHAM ROAD

A11

CB2

Mount Farm

Worsted Lodge

Worsted Lodge Farm

Rat Hall Farm

Claypit Plantation

Gunner's Hall

Reservoir

New Plantation

A11

The Grange

FOUR WENT WAYS

CAMBRIDGE RD

A1307

Sandpit Plantation

Burgoyne's Plantation

8
7
53
6
5
52
4
3
51
2
1
50

51
68

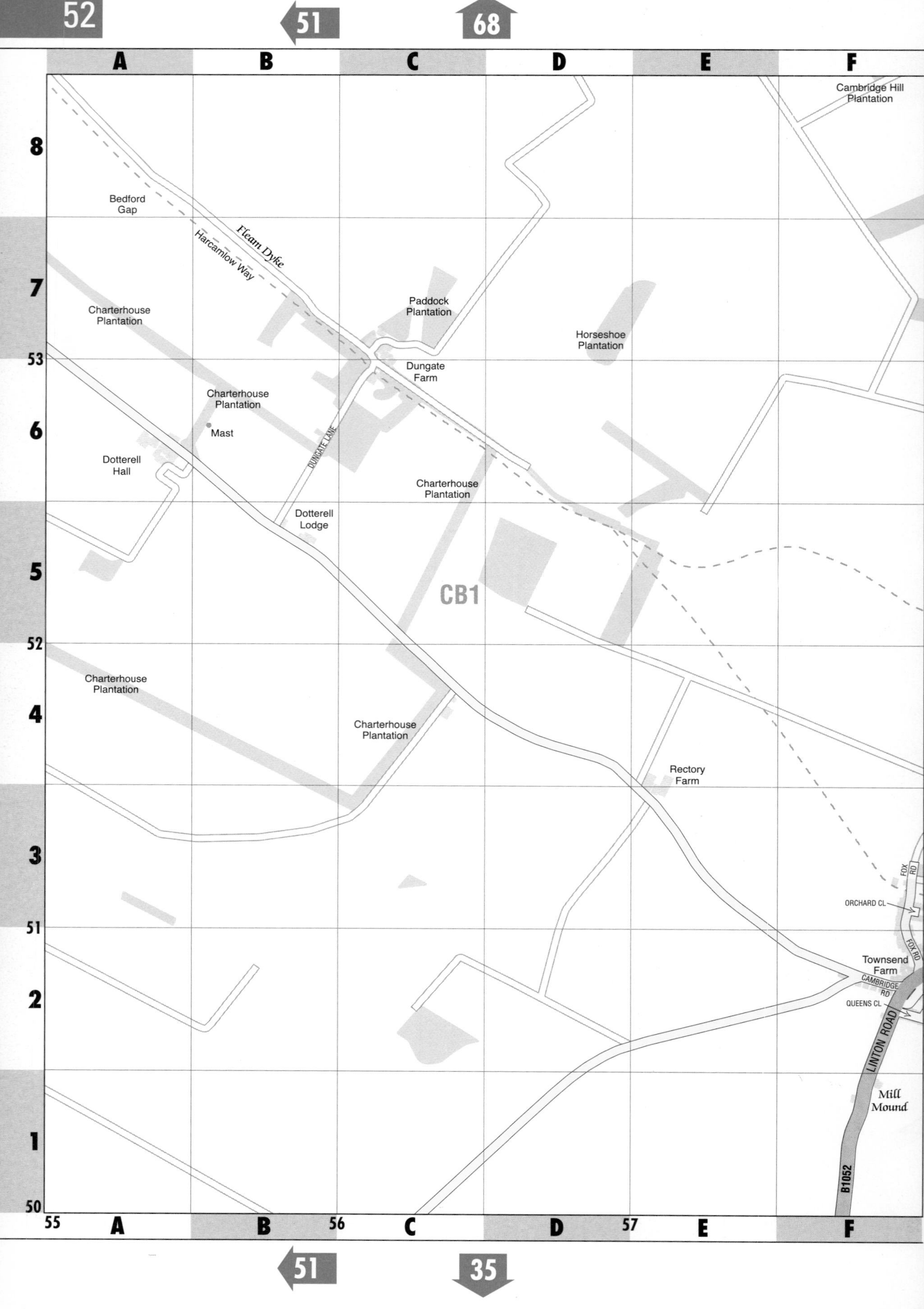
A
B
C
D
E
F
8
7
53
6
5
52
4
3
51
2
1
50
55
56
57
Cambridge Hill Plantation
Bedford Gap
Fleam Dyke
Harcamlow Way
Charterhouse Plantation
Paddock Plantation
Horseshoe Plantation
Dungate Farm
Charterhouse Plantation
Mast
Dotterell Hall
DUNGATE LANE
Charterhouse Plantation
Dotterell Lodge
CB1
Charterhouse Plantation
Charterhouse Plantation
Rectory Farm
FOX RD
ORCHARD CL
FOX RD
Townsend Farm
CAMBRIDGE RD
QUEENS CL
LINTON ROAD
Mill Mound
B1052

51
35

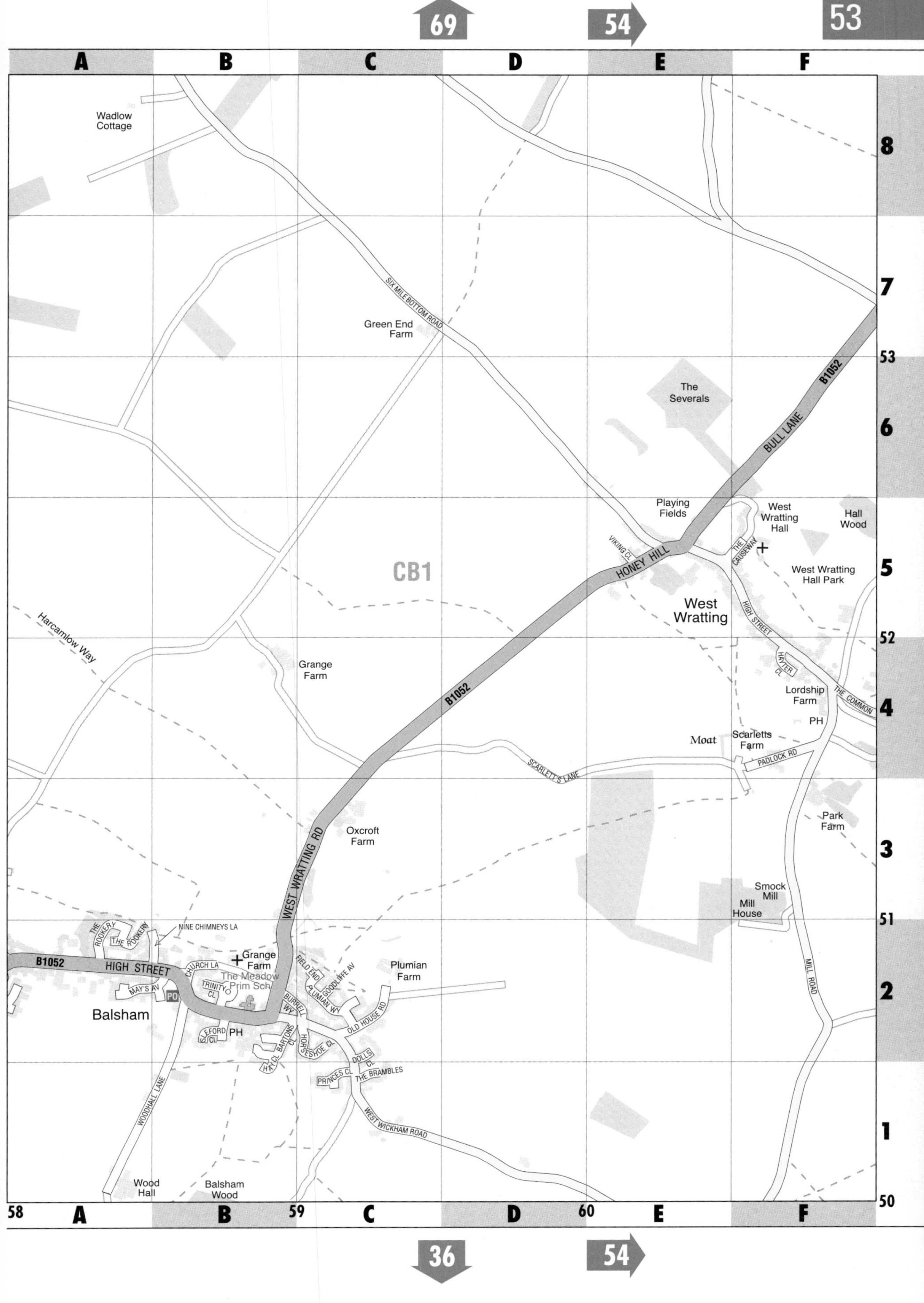

A B C D E F

8
7
53
6
5
52
4
3
51
2
1
50

Wadlow
Cottage

SIX MILE BOTTOM ROAD

Green End
Farm

The
Severals

B1052

BULL LANE

Playing
Fields

West
Wratting
Hall

Hall
Wood

West Wratting
Hall Park

VIKING CL

HONEY HILL

West
Wratting

HIGH STREET

HAYTER CL

THE CAUSEWAY

THE COMMON

CB1

Harcamlow Way

Grange
Farm

B1052

Lordship
Farm

PH

Moat

Scarletts
Farm

SCARLETT'S LANE

PADLOCK RD

Park
Farm

Oxcroft
Farm

WEST WRATTING RD

Smock
Mill

Mill
House

MILL ROAD

THE ROOKERY

THE ROOKERY

NINE CHIMNEYS LA

Grange
Farm

B1052 HIGH STREET

CHURCH LA

The Meadow
Prim Sch

MAY'S AV

PO

TRINITY
CL

Balsham

FIELD END

GOODLIFE AV

ALLMAN WY

Plumian
Farm

BURRELL
WY

S. FORD
CL

PH

HATCL

BARTONS

HORSESHOE CL

OLD HOUSE RD

DOLLS
CL

THE BRAMBLES

PRINCES CL

WEST WICKHAM ROAD

WOODHALL LANE

Wood
Hall

Balsham
Wood

53
70

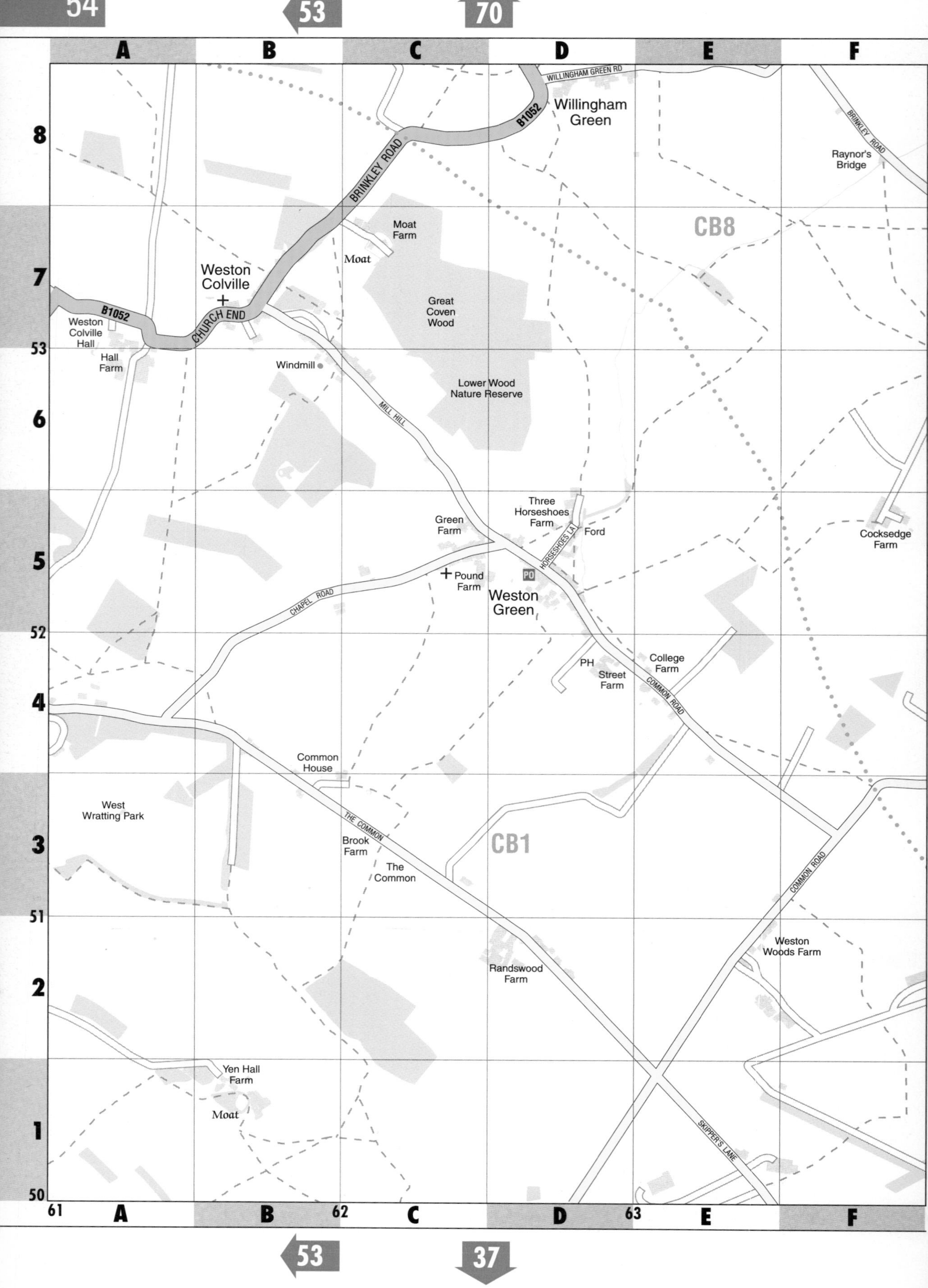
A
B
C
D
E
F
8
7
53
6
5
52
4
3
51
2
1
50
61
62
63
WILLINGHAM GREEN RD
B1052
Willingham Green
BRINKLEY ROAD
Raynor's Bridge
Moat Farm
Moat
CB8
Weston Colville
B1052
CHURCH END
Weston Colville Hall
Hall Farm
Great Coven Wood
Windmill
Lower Wood Nature Reserve
MILL HILL
Three Horseshoes Farm
Green Farm
Ford
HORSESHOES LA
Cocksedge Farm
PO
Pound Farm
CHAPEL ROAD
Weston Green
PH
College Farm
Street Farm
COMMON ROAD
Common House
West Wratting Park
THE COMMON
Brook Farm
The Common
CB1
COMMON ROAD
Weston Woods Farm
Randswood Farm
Yen Hall Farm
Moat
SKIPPER'S LANE

53
37

71

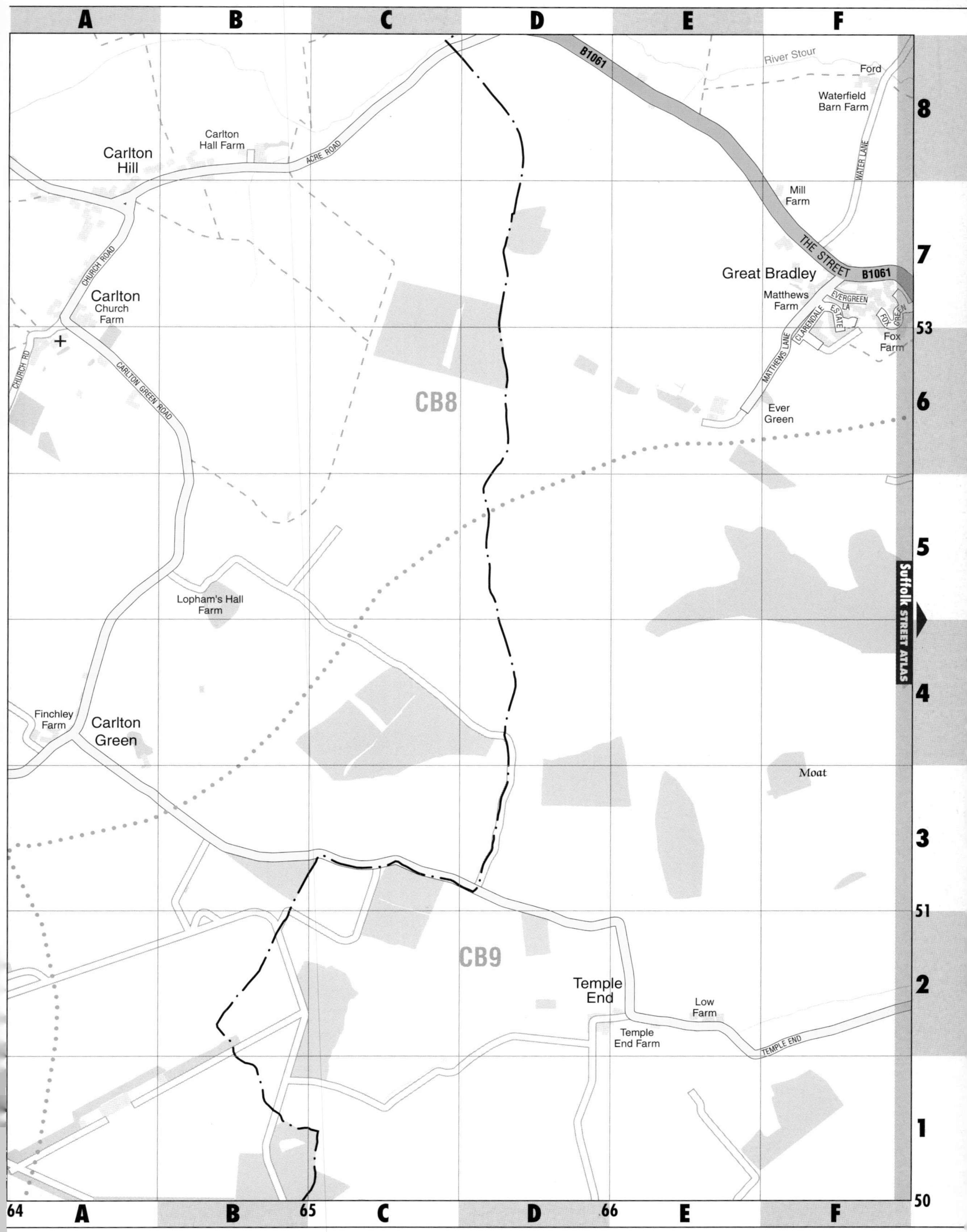

A
B
C
D
E
F
8
7
53
6
5
4
3
51
2
1
50
64
65
66
River Stour
Ford
Waterfield Barn Farm
B1061
Carlton Hill
Carlton Hall Farm
ACRE ROAD
WATER LANE
Mill Farm
THE STREET
CHURCH ROAD
Great Bradley
B1061
Matthews Farm
EVERGREEN LA
ESTATE
CLARENDALE
FOX GREEN
Fox Farm
MATTHEWS LANE
Carlton Church Farm
CHURCH RD
CARLTON GREEN ROAD
CB8
Ever Green
Lopham's Hall Farm
Suffolk STREET ATLAS
Finchley Farm
Carlton Green
Moat
CB9
Temple End
Low Farm
Temple End Farm
TEMPLE END

38

75

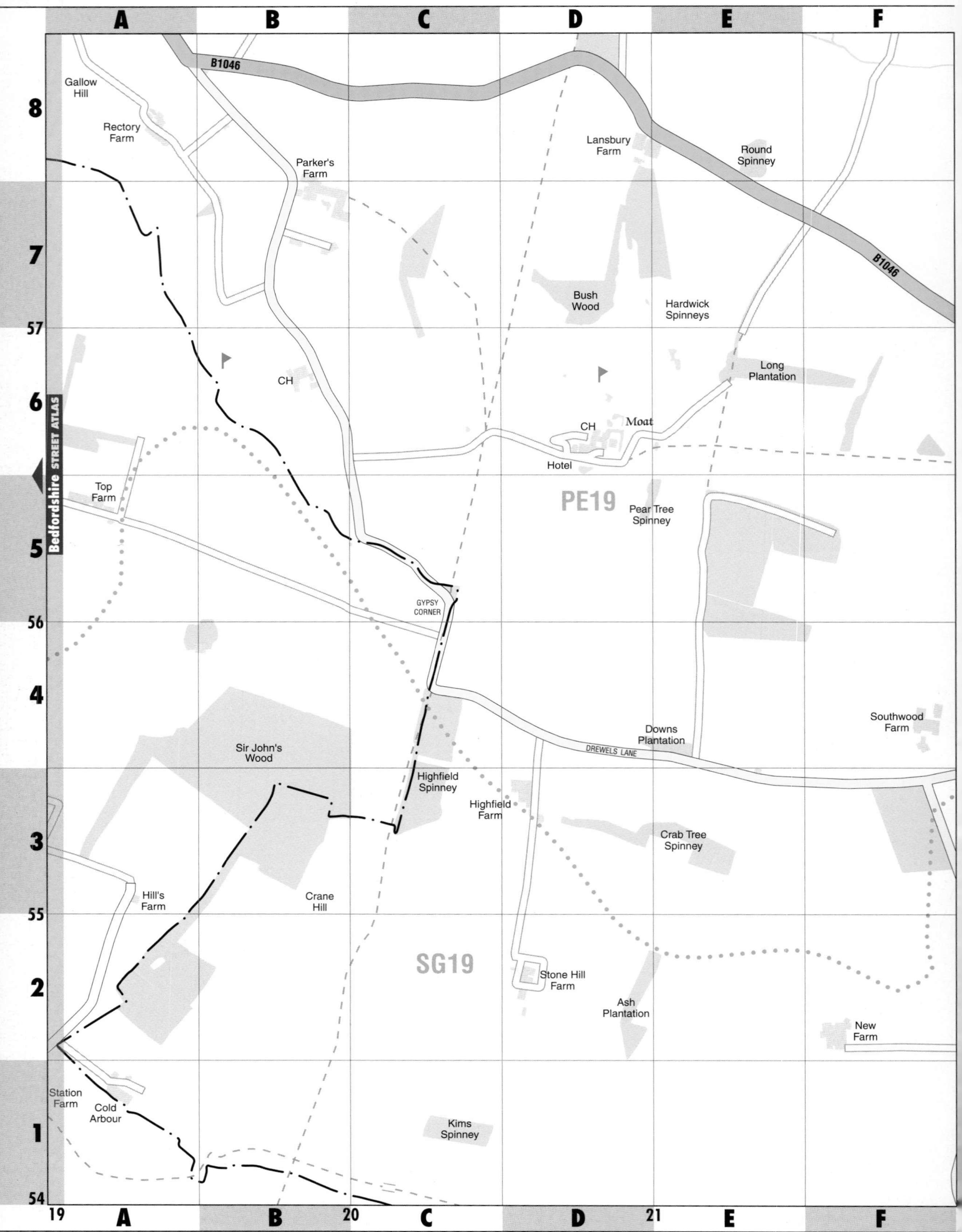

A
B
C
D
E
F
8
7
57
6
5
56
4
3
55
2
1
54
19
20
21
Bedfordshire STREET ATLAS
B1046
Gallow Hill
Rectory Farm
Parker's Farm
Lansbury Farm
Round Spinney
Bush Wood
Hardwick Spinneys
Long Plantation
CH
CH
Moat
Hotel
Top Farm
PE19
Pear Tree Spinney
GYPSY CORNER
Southwood Farm
Downs Plantation
DREWELS LANE
Sir John's Wood
Highfield Spinney
Highfield Farm
Crab Tree Spinney
Hill's Farm
Crane Hill
SG19
Stone Hill Farm
Ash Plantation
New Farm
Station Farm
Cold Arbour
Kims Spinney

40

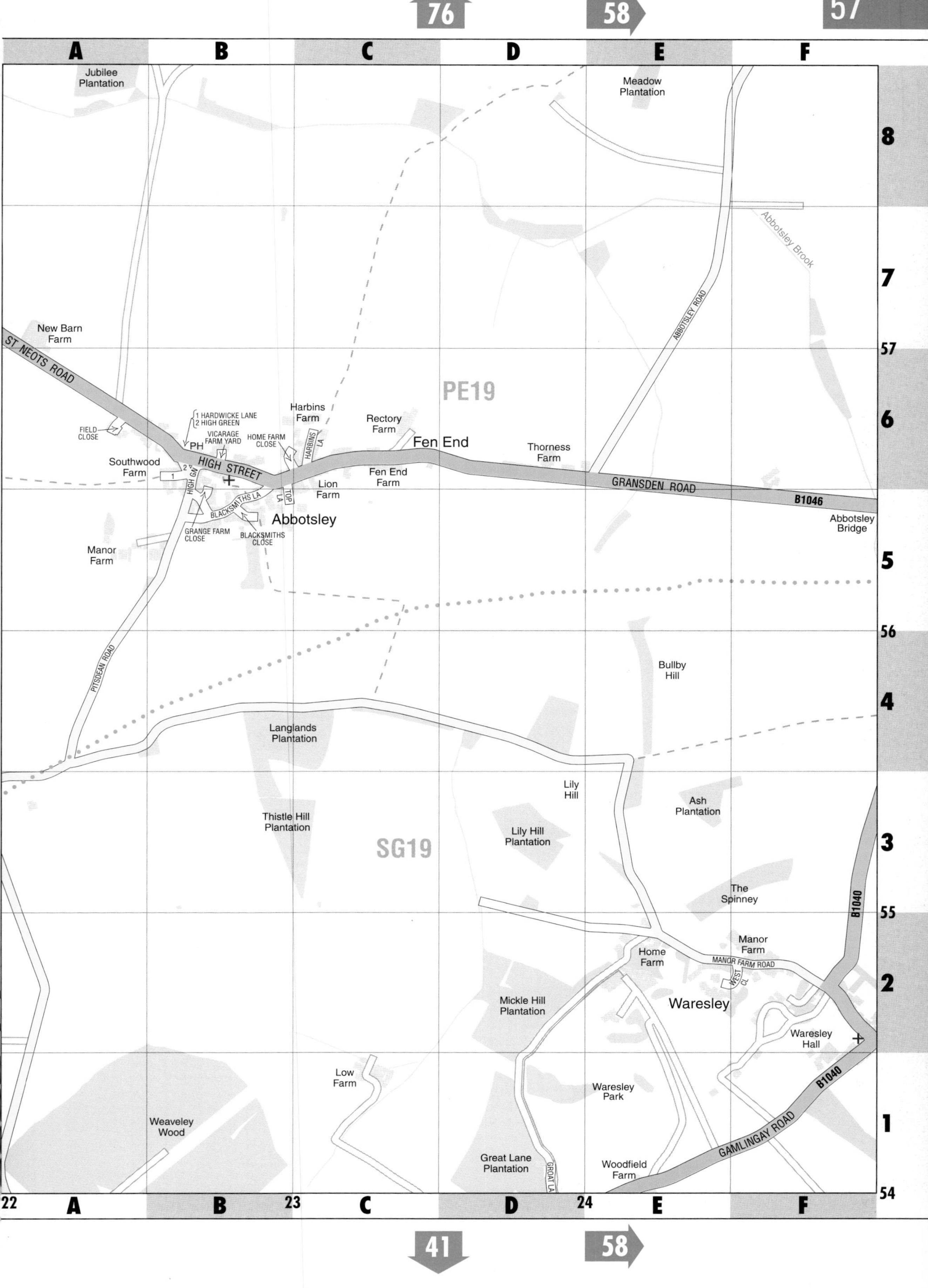

A B C D E F

8

7

57

6

5

56

4

3

55

2

1

54

Jubilee
Plantation

Meadow
Plantation

Abbotsley Brook

New Barn
Farm

ST NEOTS ROAD

PE19

ABBOTSLEY ROAD

FIELD
CLOSE

1 HARDWICKE LANE
2 HIGH GREEN

Harbins
Farm

Rectory
Farm

VICARAGE
FARM YARD

HOME FARM
CLOSE

PH

HARBINS LA

Fen End

Thorness
Farm

Southwood
Farm

HIGH STREET

1

2

HIGH GN

Lion
Farm

Fen End
Farm

GRANSDEN ROAD

B1046

Abbotsley
Bridge

BLACKSMITHS LA

TOP LA

Abbotsley

Manor
Farm

GRANGE FARM
CLOSE

BLACKSMITHS
CLOSE

PITSDEAN ROAD

Bullby
Hill

Langlands
Plantation

Lily
Hill

Ash
Plantation

Thistle Hill
Plantation

SG19

Lily Hill
Plantation

The
Spinney

B1040

Manor
Farm

MANOR FARM ROAD

WEST CL

55

Home
Farm

Mickle Hill
Plantation

Waresley

Waresley
Hall

B1040

Low
Farm

Waresley
Park

GREAT LA

GAMLINGAY ROAD

Weaveley
Wood

Great Lane
Plantation

Woodfield
Farm

A B C D E F

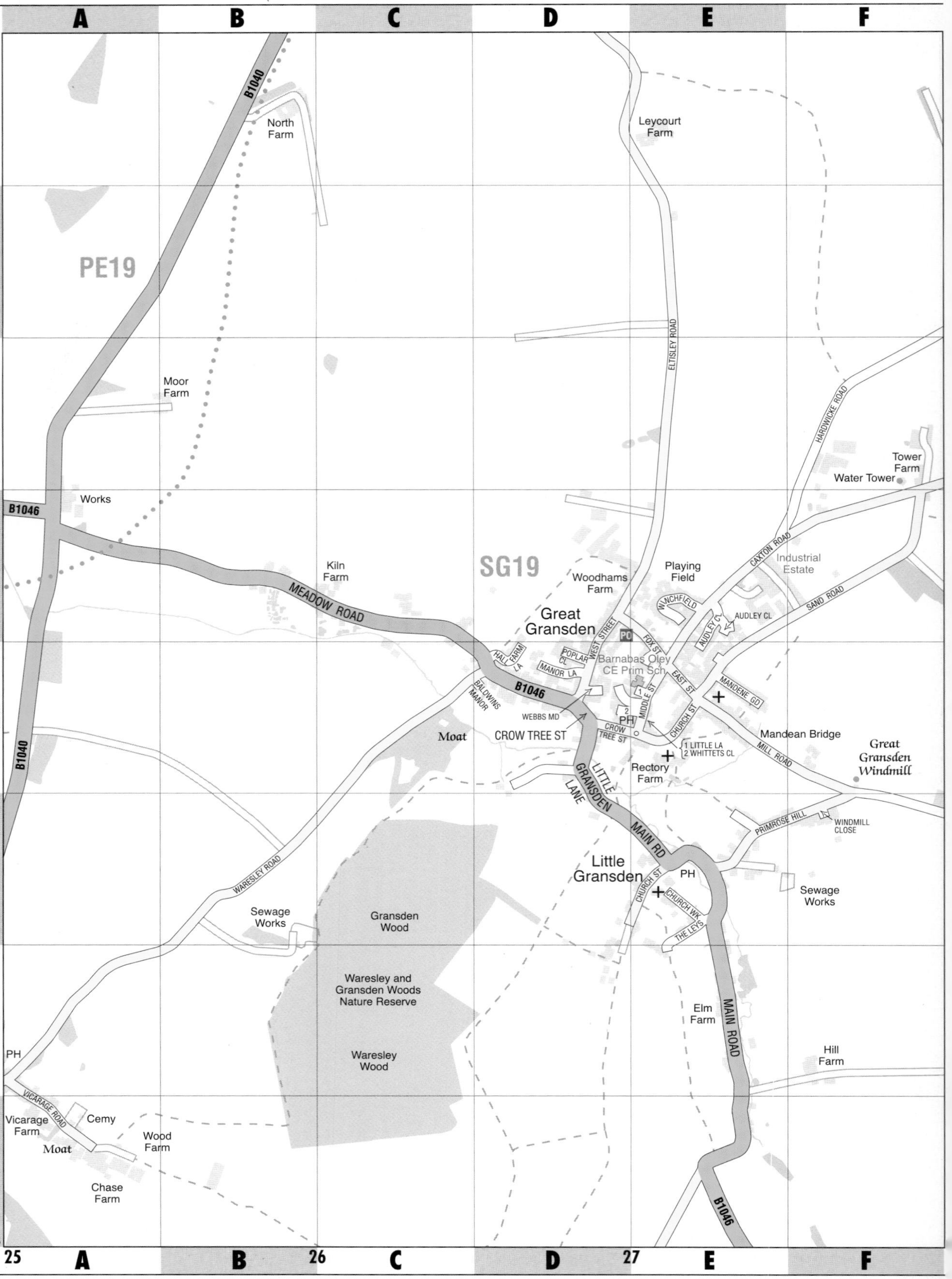

8

7

PE19

57

6

B1046

5

56

4

B1040

3

55

2

1

54

25 A B 26 C D 27 E F

B1040

North Farm

Leycourt Farm

Moor Farm

ELTISLEY ROAD

HARDWICKE ROAD

Tower Farm

Water Tower

Works

Kiln Farm

SG19

MEADOW ROAD

Woodhams Farm

Playing Field

CAXTON ROAD

Industrial Estate

SAND ROAD

Great Gransden

WINCHFIELD

WEST STREET

FOX ST

AUDLEY CL

AUDLEY CL

PO

HALL FARM LA

POPLAR CL

MANOR LA

Barnabas Oley CE Prim Sch

EAST ST

MANDENE GD

BALDWINS MANOR

B1046

WEBBS MD

PH

CROW TREE ST

2

MIDDLE ST

CHURCH ST

CROW TREE ST

Mandean Bridge

Moat

CROW TREE ST

1 LITTLE LA
2 WHITTETS CL

MILL ROAD

Great Gransden Windmill

LITTLE GRANSDEN LANE

Rectory Farm

PRIMROSE HILL

WINDMILL CLOSE

WARESLEY ROAD

MAIN RD

CHURCH ST

PH

Sewage Works

Little Gransden

CHURCH WK

Sewage Works

Gransden Wood

THE LEYS

Waresley and Gransden Woods Nature Reserve

Elm Farm

MAIN ROAD

Hill Farm

Waresley Wood

PH

VICARAGE ROAD

Vicarage Farm

Cemy

Wood Farm

Moat

Chase Farm

B1046

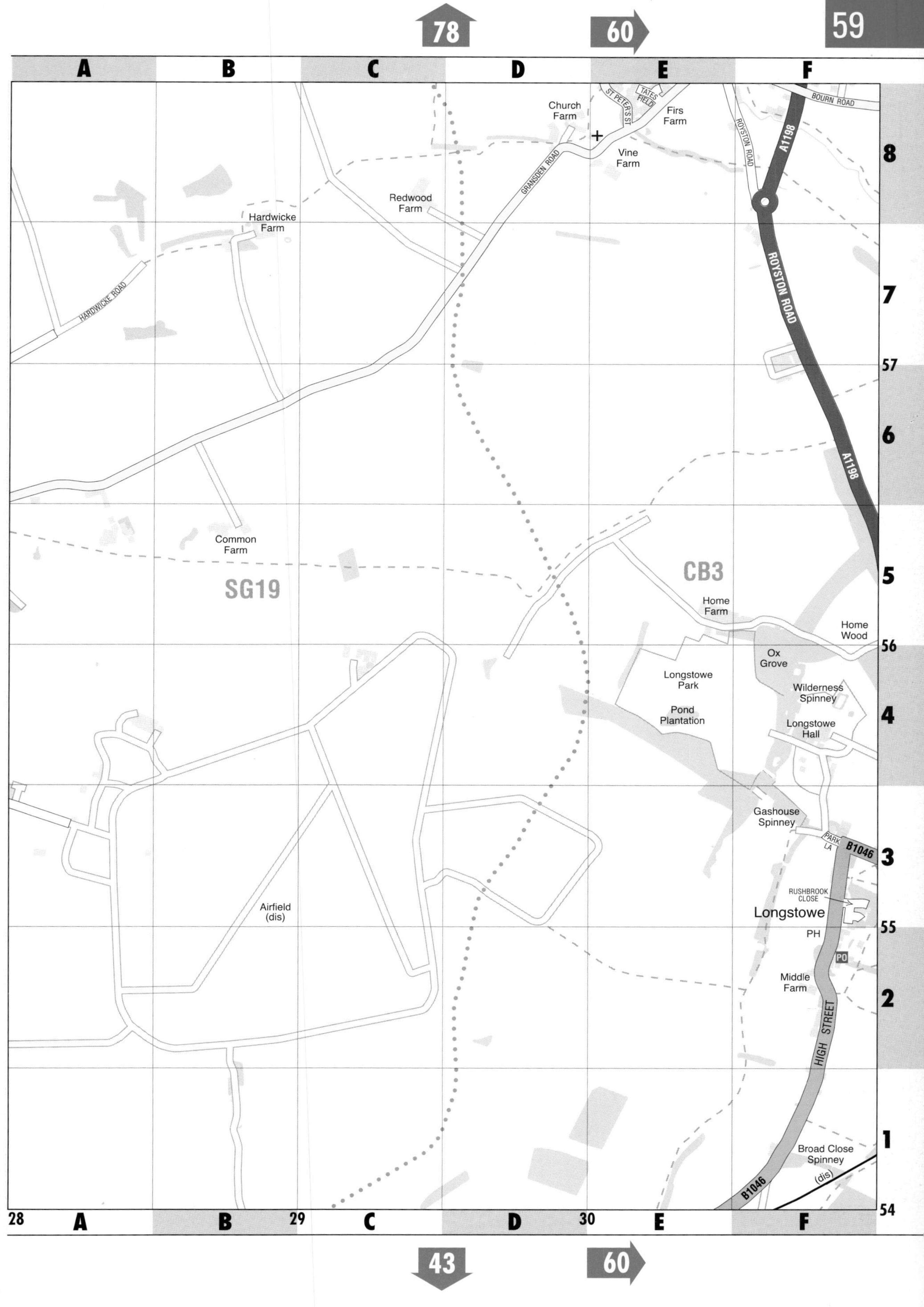
78
60
A
B
C
D
E
F
8
7
57
6
5
56
4
3
55
2
1
54
28
29
30
Church Farm
ST PETER'S ST
TATES FIELD
Firs Farm
Vine Farm
BOURN ROAD
ROYSTON ROAD
A1198
GRANSDEN ROAD
Redwood Farm
Hardwicke Farm
HARDWICKE ROAD
ROYSTON ROAD
A1198
Common Farm
SG19
CB3
Home Farm
Home Wood
Ox Grove
Longstowe Park
Wilderness Spinney
Pond Plantation
Longstowe Hall
Gashouse Spinney
PARK LA
B1046
RUSHBROOK CLOSE
Longstowe
PH
PO
Middle Farm
Airfield (dis)
HIGH STREET
Broad Close Spinney
(dis)
B1046
43
60

59
79

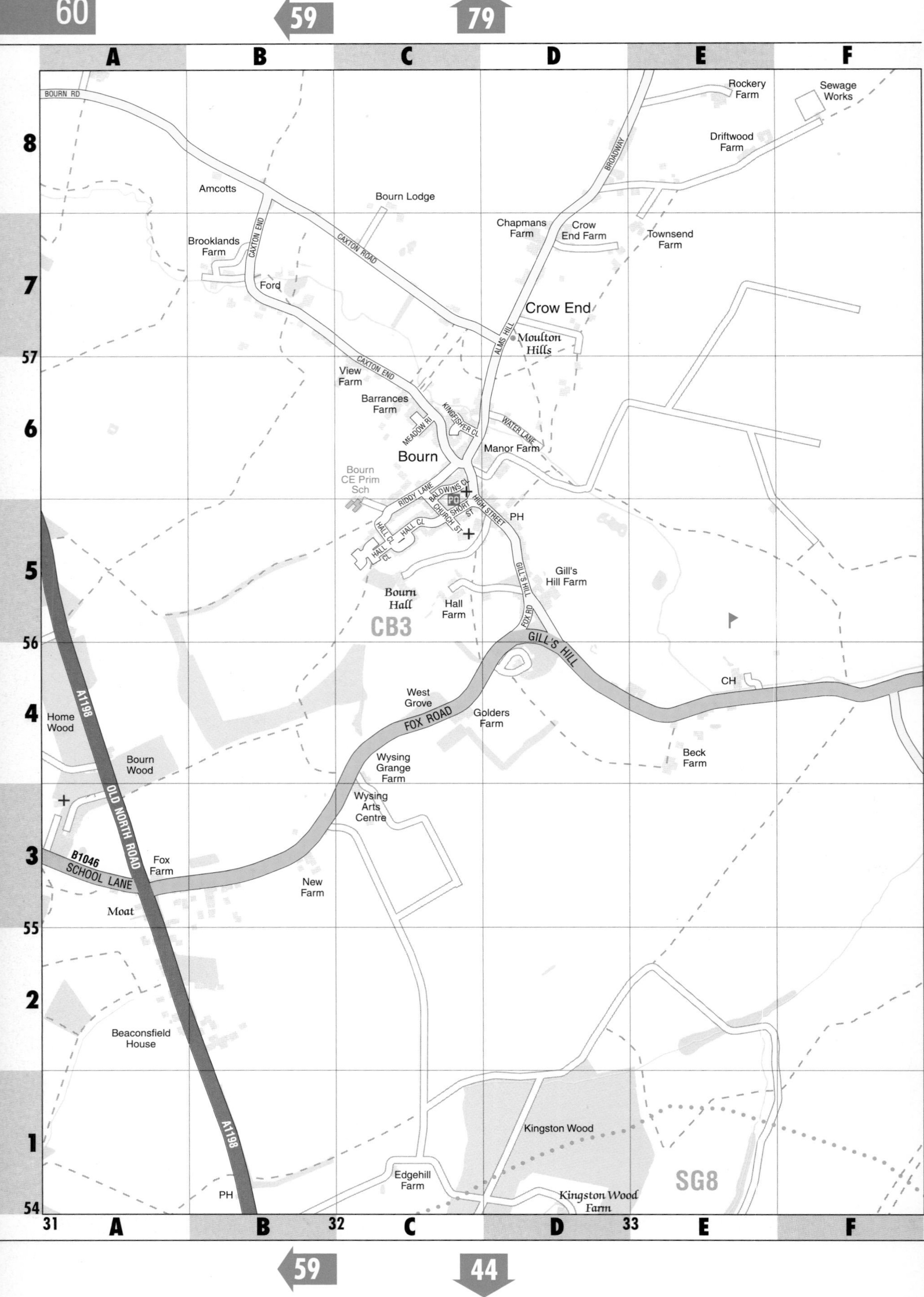
A
B
C
D
E
F
8
7
57
6
5
56
4
3
55
2
1
54
31
32
33
BOURN RD
Rockery Farm
Sewage Works
Driftwood Farm
BROADWAY
Amcotts
Bourn Lodge
Chapmans Farm
Crow End Farm
Townsend Farm
Brooklands Farm
CAXTON END
CAXTON ROAD
Ford
Crow End
ALMS HILL
Moulton Hills
CAXTON END
View Farm
Barrances Farm
KINGFISHER CL
WATER LANE
MEADOW RI
Manor Farm
Bourn
Bourn CE Prim Sch
RIDDY LANE
BALDWINS CL
PO
HIGH STREET
SHORT ST
CHURCH ST
PH
HALL CL
HALL CL
HALL CL
GILL'S HILL
Gill's Hill Farm
Bourn Hall
Hall Farm
CB3
FOX RD
GILL'S HILL
CH
West Grove
A1198
Home Wood
FOX ROAD
Golders Farm
Bourn Wood
Wysing Grange Farm
Beck Farm
OLD NORTH ROAD
Wysing Arts Centre
B1046
SCHOOL LANE
Fox Farm
New Farm
Moat
Beaconsfield House
Kingston Wood
A1198
Edgehill Farm
SG8
PH
Kingston Wood Farm

59
44

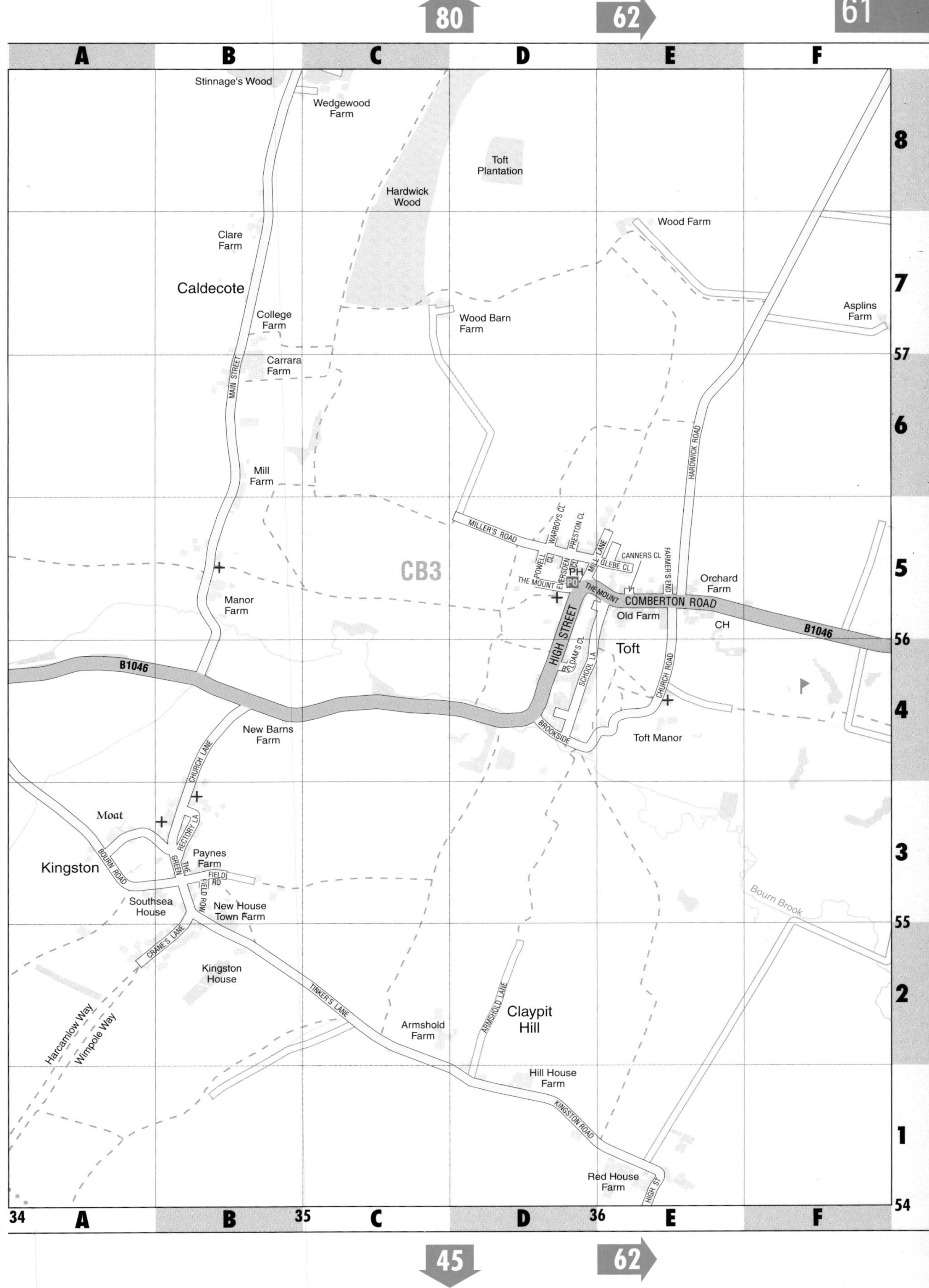
80
62
A
B
C
D
E
F
8
7
57
6
5
56
4
3
55
2
1
54
34
35
36
Stinnage's Wood
Wedgewood Farm
Toft Plantation
Hardwick Wood
Clare Farm
Wood Farm
Caldecote
College Farm
Wood Barn Farm
Asplins Farm
Carrara Farm
MAIN STREET
HARDWICK ROAD
Mill Farm
MILLER'S ROAD
WARBOYS CL
PRESTON CL
MILL LANE
CANNERS CL
GLEBE CL
FARMER'S END
POWELL CL
EVERSDEN CL
PH
PO
THE MOUNT
CB3
Orchard Farm
Manor Farm
COMBERTON ROAD
Old Farm
CH
B1046
HIGH STREET
ADAM'S CL
SCHOOL LA
Toft
CHURCH ROAD
B1046
BROOKSIDE
Toft Manor
New Barns Farm
CHURCH LANE
Moat
RECTORY LA
Kingston
BOURN ROAD
THE GREEN
Paynes Farm
FIELD RD
FIELD ROW
Southsea House
New House Town Farm
Bourn Brook
CRANE'S LANE
Kingston House
TINKER'S LANE
Harcamlow Way
Wimpole Way
Armshold Farm
ARMSHOLD LANE
Claypit Hill
Hill House Farm
KINGSTON ROAD
Red House Farm
HIGH ST
45
62

61
81

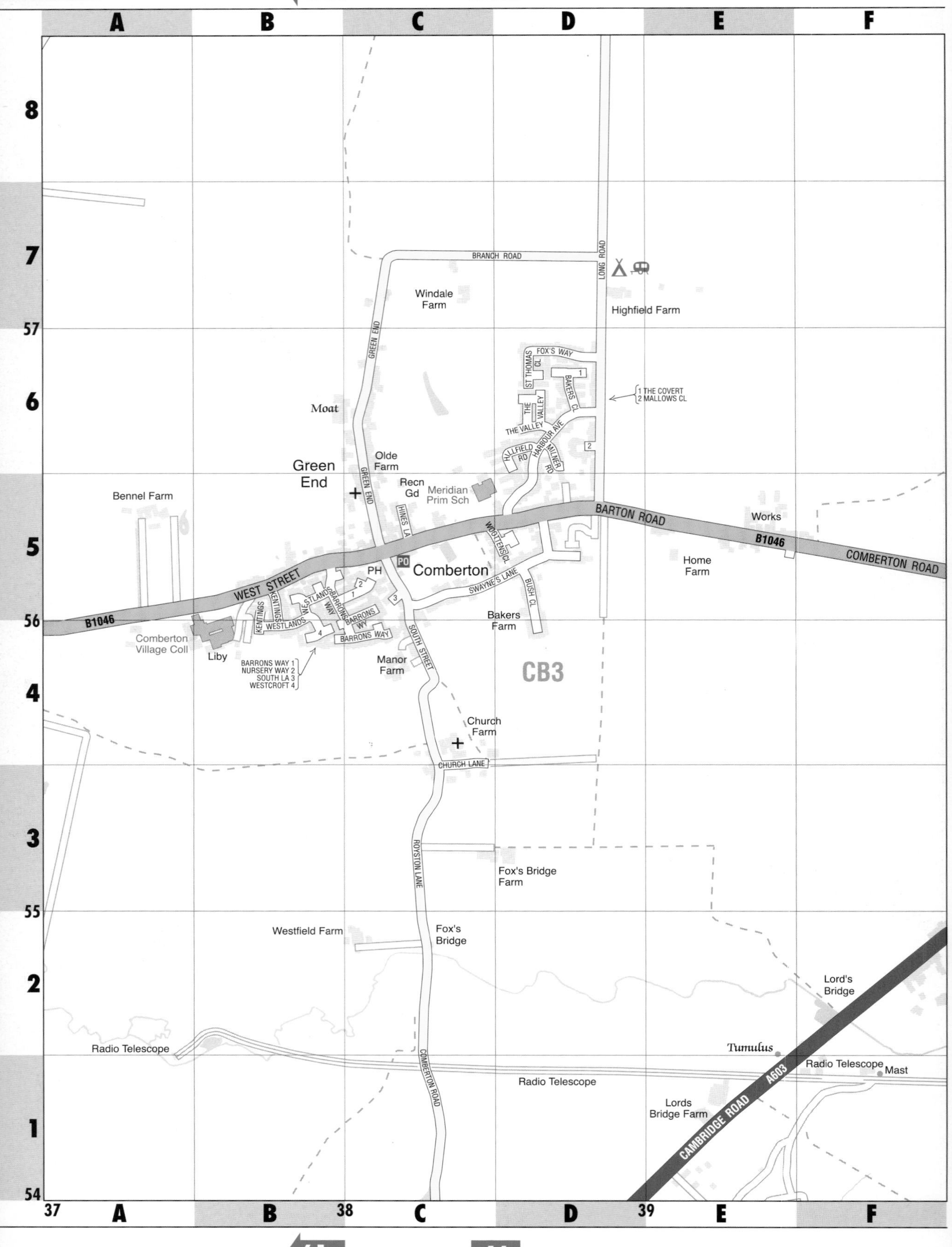
A
B
C
D
E
F
8
7
57
6
5
56
4
3
55
2
1
54
37
38
39
BRANCH ROAD
LONG ROAD
Windale
Farm
Highfield Farm
GREEN END
FOX'S WAY
ST THOMAS CL
BAKERS CL
1 THE COVERT
2 MALLOWS CL
THE VALLEY
HARBOUR AVE
HALLFIELD RD
MILNER RD
Moat
Green
End
Olde
Farm
Recn
Gd
Meridian
Prim Sch
Bennel Farm
HINES LA
WOOTENS CL
BARTON ROAD
B1046
COMBERTON ROAD
Works
Home
Farm
PO
Comberton
PH
WEST STREET
SWAYNE'S LANE
BUSH CL
KENTINGS
WESTLANDS
BARRONS WAY
BARRONS WY
SOUTH STREET
Bakers
Farm
Comberton
Village Coll
Liby
BARRONS WAY 1
NURSERY WAY 2
SOUTH LA 3
WESTCROFT 4
Manor
Farm
CB3
Church
Farm
CHURCH LANE
ROYSTON LANE
Fox's Bridge
Farm
Westfield Farm
Fox's
Bridge
Lord's
Bridge
Radio Telescope
Tumulus
Radio Telescope
Mast
Radio Telescope
COMBERTON ROAD
Lords
Bridge Farm
A603
CAMBRIDGE ROAD

61
46

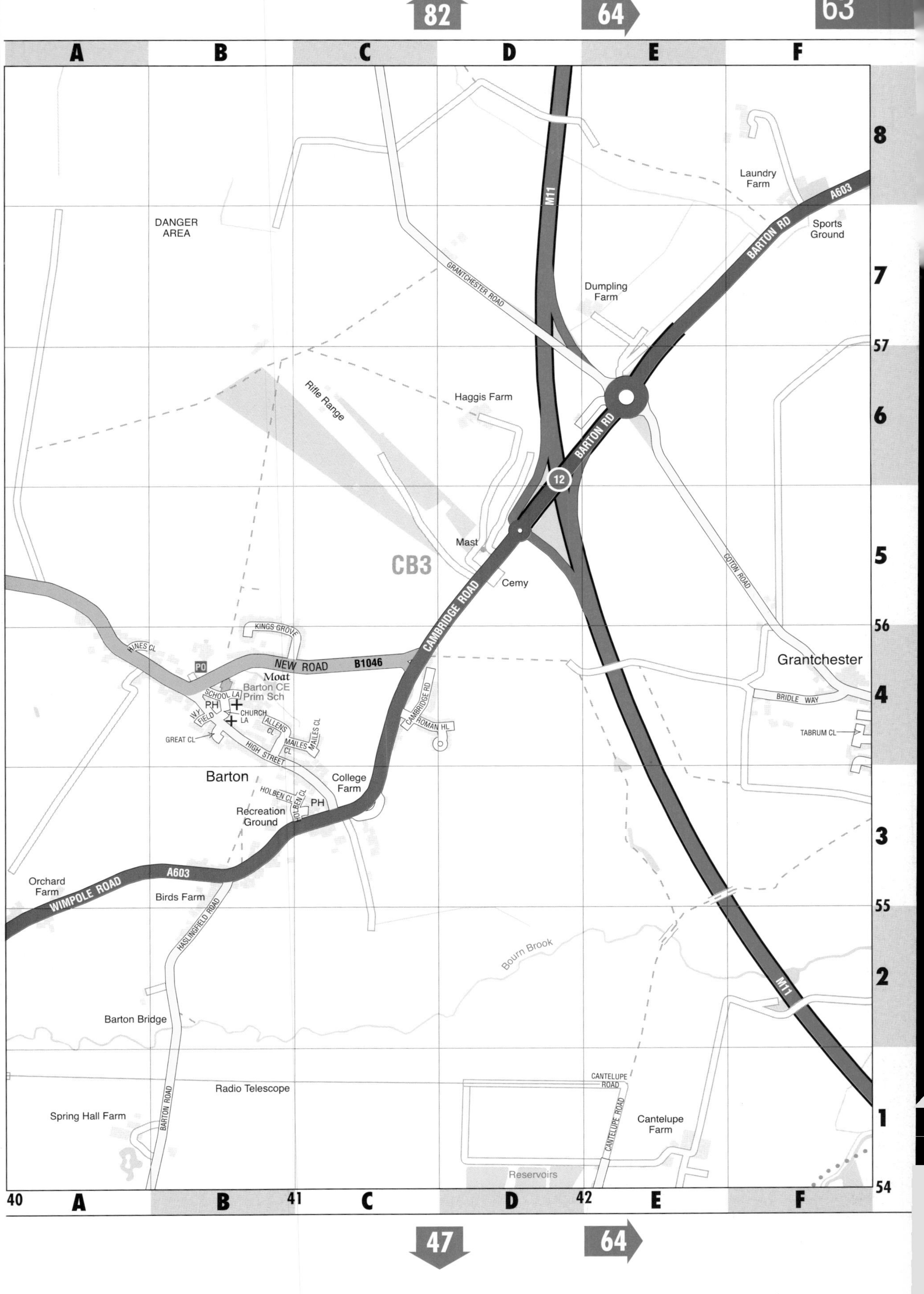

A B C D E F

8
7
57
6
5
56
4
3
55
2
1
54

DANGER AREA

Laundry Farm

Sports Ground

BARTON RD

A603

M11

Dumpling Farm

GRANTCHESTER ROAD

Rifle Range

Haggis Farm

BARTON RD

12

CB3

Mast

Cemy

SOUTH ROAD

CAMBRIDGE ROAD

KINGS GROVE

HINES CL

PO

NEW ROAD

B1046

Moat

Barton CE Prim Sch

SCHOOL LA

PH

CHURCH LA

ALLENS CL

MAILES CL

CAMBRIDGE RD

ROMAN HL

56

Grantchester

BRIDLE WAY

TABRUM CL

W.Y. FIELD

GREAT CL

MAILES CL

HIGH STREET

Barton

HOLBEN CL

HOLBEN CL

PH

College Farm

Recreation Ground

Orchard Farm

WIMPOLE ROAD

A603

Birds Farm

HASLINGFIELD ROAD

Bourn Brook

M11

Barton Bridge

BARTON ROAD

Radio Telescope

CANTELUPE ROAD

CANTELUPE ROAD

Cantelupe Farm

Spring Hall Farm

Reservoirs

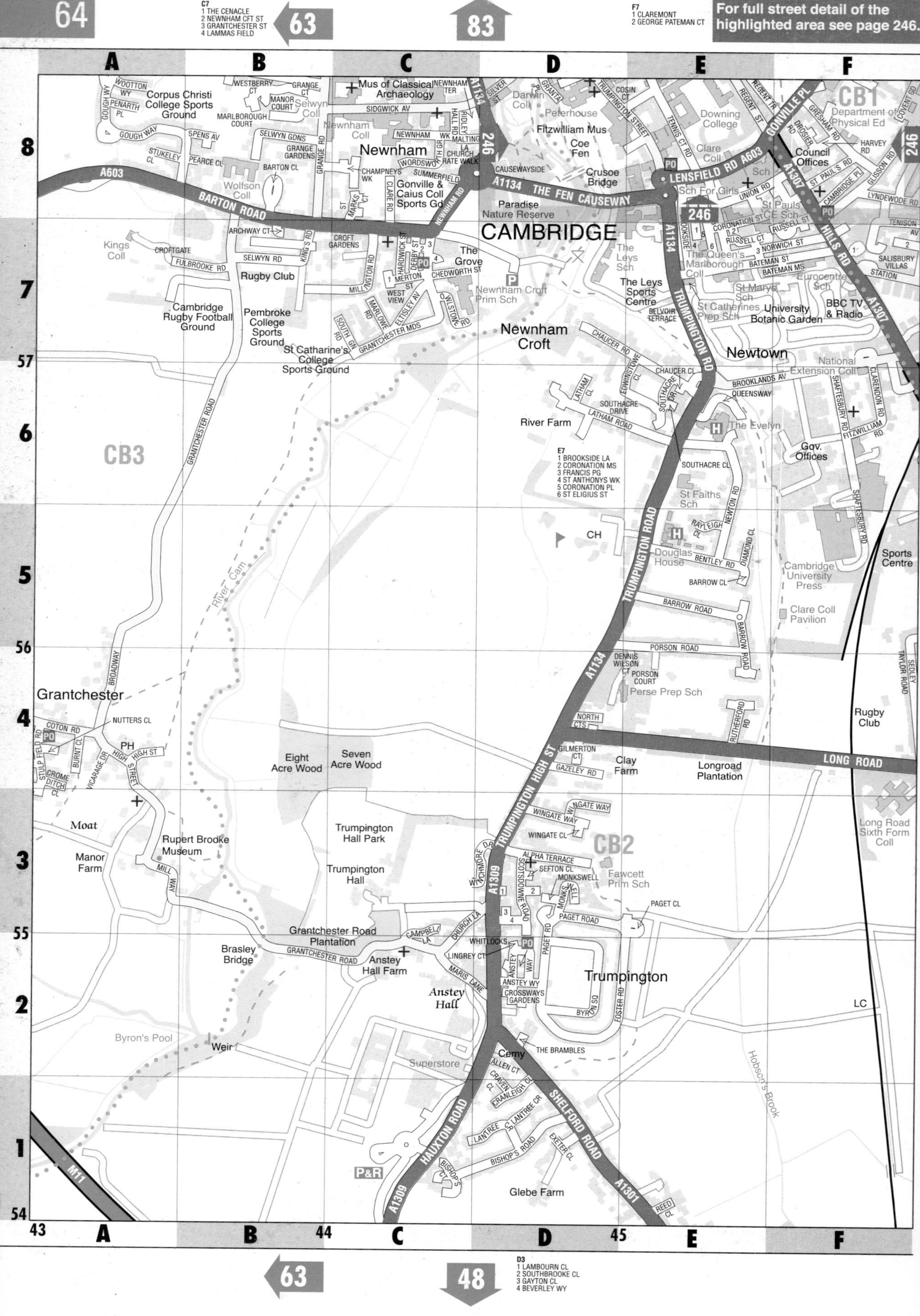

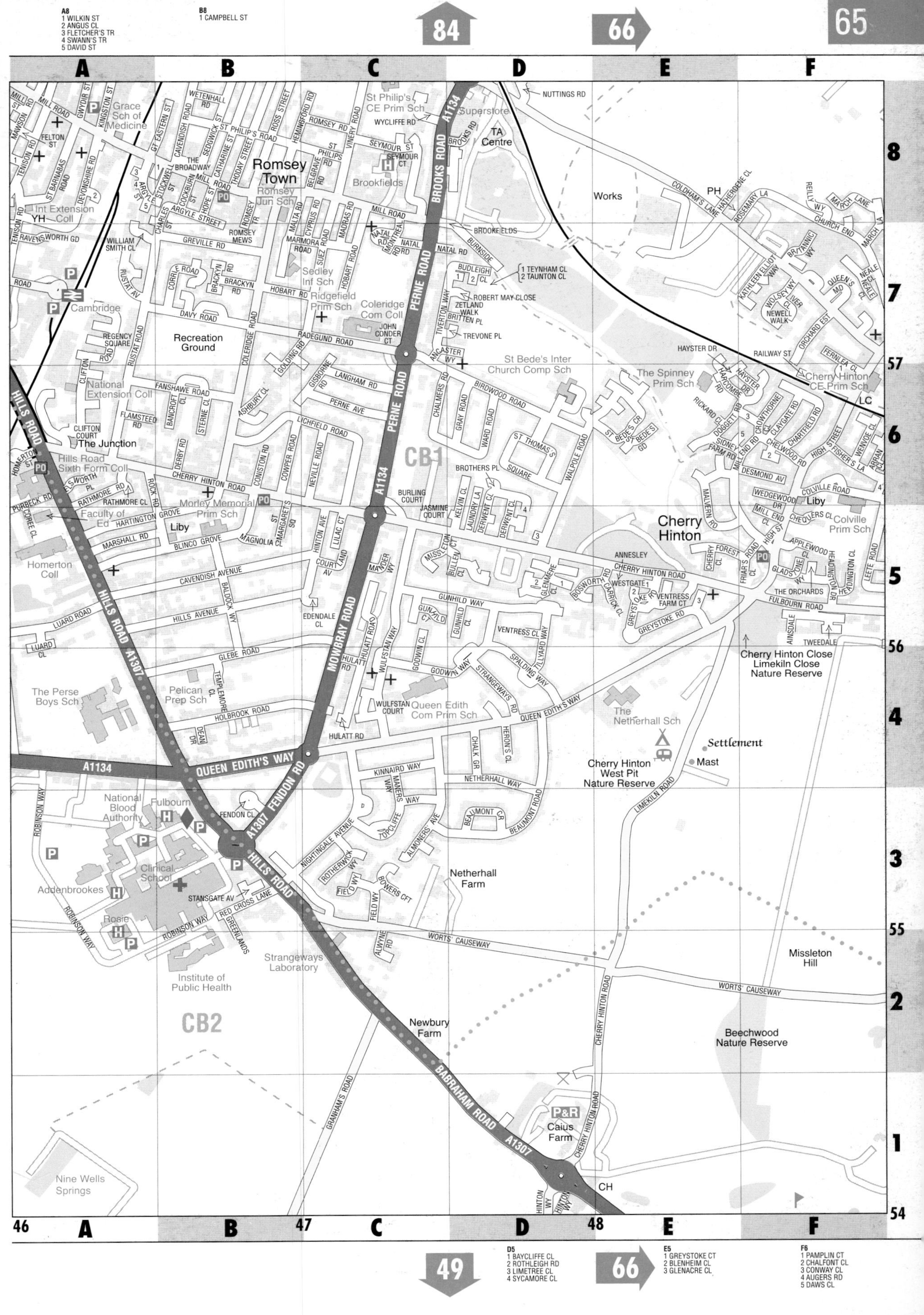

A8
1 WILKIN ST
2 ANGUS CL
3 FLETCHER'S TR
4 SWANN'S TR
5 DAVID ST
B8
1 CAMPBELL ST
84
66
65
A
B
C
D
E
F
8
7
57
6
5
56
4
3
55
2
1
54
46
47
48
Romsey Town
Romsey Jun Sch
Brookfields
St Philip's CE Prim Sch
Superstore
TA Centre
Works
Grace Sch of Medicine
Int Extension Coll
Cambridge
Sedley Inf Sch
Ridgefield Prim Sch
Coleridge Com Coll
Recreation Ground
National Extension Coll
The Junction
Hills Road Sixth Form Coll
Faculty of Ed
Morley Memorial Prim Sch
Homerton Coll
St Bede's Inter Church Comp Sch
The Spinney Prim Sch
Cherry Hinton CE Prim Sch
Cherry Hinton
Colville Prim Sch
CB1
The Perse Boys Sch
Pelican Prep Sch
Queen Edith Com Prim Sch
The Netherhall Sch
Settlement
Mast
Cherry Hinton West Pit Nature Reserve
Cherry Hinton Close Limekiln Close Nature Reserve
National Blood Authority
Fulbourn
Clinical School
Addenbrookes
Rosie
Netherhall Farm
Strangeways Laboratory
Institute of Public Health
Missleton Hill
CB2
Newbury Farm
Beechwood Nature Reserve
Caius Farm
Nine Wells Springs
HILLS ROAD
A1307
A1134
PERNE ROAD
BROOKS ROAD
MOWBRAY ROAD
QUEEN EDITH'S WAY
FENDON RD
BABRAHAM ROAD
CHERRY HINTON ROAD
MILL ROAD
COLDHAM'S LANE
FULBOURN ROAD
LIMEKILN ROAD
WORTS' CAUSEWAY
CHERRY HINTON ROAD
GRANHAM'S ROAD
RADEGUND ROAD
BIRDWOOD ROAD
CAVENDISH AVENUE
HILLS AVENUE
GLEBE ROAD
HOLBROOK ROAD
NIGHTINGALE AVENUE
D5
1 BAYCLIFFE CL
2 ROTHLEIGH RD
3 LIMETREE CL
4 SYCAMORE CL
49
66
E5
1 GREYSTOKE CT
2 BLENHEIM CL
3 GLENACRE CL
F6
1 PAMPLIN CT
2 CHALFONT CL
3 CONWAY CL
4 AUGERS RD
5 DAWS CL

A B C D E F

8

Manor Farm

Moat

Caudle Ditch

1 PANTHER WAY
2 ANTELOPE WAY
3 WINDEREMERE CL
4 BROXBOURNE CI
5 LANGDALE CL

Manor Farm

FERNDALE

TEVERSHAM DRIFT

CHERRY HINTON RD

AIRPORT WY

CARIBOU WY

DOLPHIN CL

BUFFALO

GAZELLE WAY

IMPALA DR

Cherry Hinton

7

FULBOURN ROAD

CAPUCHIN

TEVERSHAM DRIFT

CHERRY END

HIGH ST

KELSEY CR

LEYBURN RD

SABLE CT

ROEBER CL

MANDRILL CL

ELAND WY

LYNX

THE

LEMUR DR

LORIS CL

FENNEC CL

Fernleigh Farm

Colbrook

57

TERBY

BLISS

LILY

HIGHD...

FULBOURN OLD DRIFT

BIRCHAM

TAMARIN GD

TAMARIN GD

Cherry Hinton Com Jun Sch

GAZELLE WAY

WELSTEAD RD

SUNMEAD
WALK

LISLE
WALK

RUSH CL

JAMES NURSE CL

Caudle Corner Farm

LC

Breckenwood Rd

Barnbury Farm

HIGHFIELD GATE

6

LC

SPEEDWELL CL

YARROW RD

Superstore

FULBOURN OLD DRIFT

Ida Darwin

THOMAS

RALPH

TEVERSHAM ROAD

COX'S DRO

COW LANE

STANSFIELD GD

N.THORPE ST

GREATER FOXES

GREATER FOXES

HIGH ST

FISHER'S CL

PEN CL

SHEPHERD

LUCERNE

SPEEDWELL

LUCERNE CL

COLVILLE RD

KEATES RD

PRIMROSE CL

VIOLET CT

TEASEL WY

SWAN CT

CLOVER

BRIDEWELL RD

DRAYTON CL

BRAMBLE CL

YARROW RD

The Windmill Sch

BRUNSWICK CT

PH

CHERRY CR

WESTON GR

CARAWAY RD

Hinton Road

THE MAPLES

BIRD FARM RD

THE CROFT

PIERCE LANE

THE HAVEN

Fulbourn Prim Sch

PO

5

MALLETTS RD

DRAYTON RD

COMFREY CT

COL'SFOOT

Fulbourn

CB1

CHERRY DR

CARAWAY RD

CARAWAY RD

MARCH'S CL

WINDMILL LA

OSCAR'S CL

DUNMOWE WY

CHAPLIN'S CL

FARMER'S ROW

SWIFTS CR

HAGGIS GAP

ALL SAINT'S RD

S.S. RD

VIGOR'S RD

SCHOOL LA

St Liby

56

Peterhouse Technology Park

CAMBRIDGE RD

CAMBRIDGE ROAD

Fulbourn Smock Mill

Mill Hill

GRANDRIDGE CL

HUNT'S HILL

FROMONT CL

WRIGHTS GR

PETTITS CL

HOLLMANS CL

4

Westbourn Farm

Highfield Farm

Fulbourn

DOGGET LA

3

SHELFORD ROAD

Limepit Hill

BABRAHAM ROAD

55

Bishop's Farm

2

WORTS CAUSEWAY

Mast

Hill Farms

Rectory Farm

Grange Farm

1

CB2

Mag's Hill

54

49 A B 50 C D 51 E F

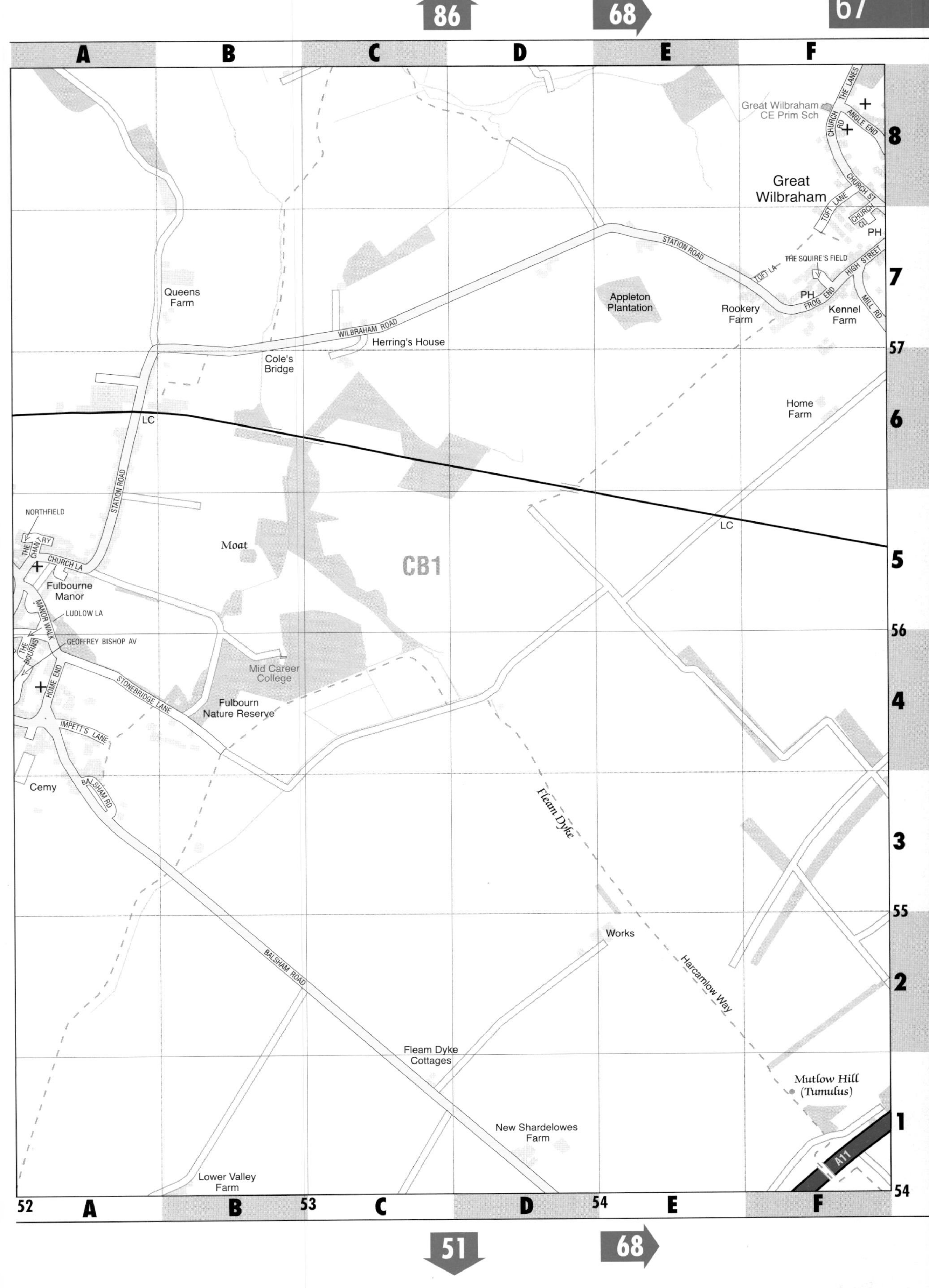
86
68
A
B
C
D
E
F
Great Wilbraham CE Prim Sch
THE LANES
CHURCH RD
ANGLE END
Great Wilbraham
CHURCH ST
TOFT LANE
CHURCH CL
PH
STATION ROAD
THE SQUIRE'S FIELD
TOFT LA
HIGH STREET
Queens Farm
Appleton Plantation
Rookery Farm
PH
FROG END
Kennel Farm
MILL RD
WILBRAHAM ROAD
Herring's House
Cole's Bridge
Home Farm
LC
STATION ROAD
NORTHFIELD
THE CHANTRY
Moat
CB1
LC
CHURCH LA
Fulbourne Manor
MANOR WALK
LUDLOW LA
THE BOURNS
GEOFFREY BISHOP AV
Mid Career College
HOME END
STONEBRIDGE LANE
Fulbourn Nature Reserve
IMPETT'S LANE
Cemy
BALSHAM RD
Fleam Dyke
Works
BALSHAM ROAD
Harcamlow Way
Fleam Dyke Cottages
Mutlow Hill (Tumulus)
A11
New Shardelowes Farm
Lower Valley Farm
8
7
57
6
5
56
4
3
55
2
1
54
52
53
54
51
68

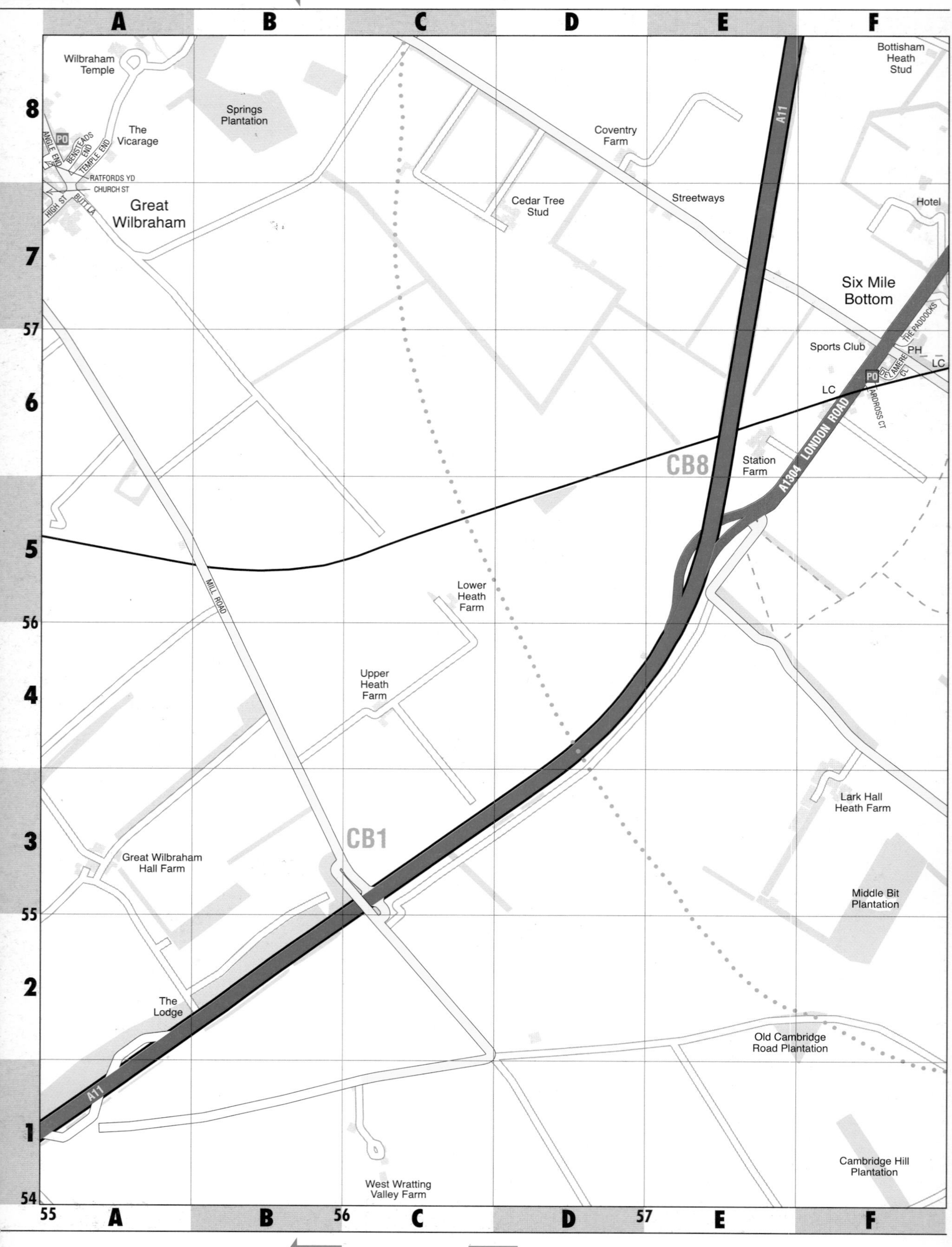

A B C D E F

8

7

57

6

5

56

4

3

55

2

1

54

Wilbraham Temple

Springs Plantation

Coventry Farm

Bottisham Heath Stud

The Vicarage

PO

ANGLE END

BENSTEADS END

TEMPLE END

RATFORDS YD

CHURCH ST

HIGH ST

BUTT LA

Great Wilbraham

Cedar Tree Stud

Streetways

Hotel

Six Mile Bottom

A11

Sports Club

THE PADDOCKS

PH

LC

PO

PELHAMERE

CLOSE

CT

LC

A1304 LONDON ROAD

CARDROSS CT

CB8

Station Farm

MILL ROAD

Lower Heath Farm

Upper Heath Farm

CB1

Great Wilbraham Hall Farm

Lark Hall Heath Farm

Middle Bit Plantation

The Lodge

Old Cambridge Road Plantation

A11

Cambridge Hill Plantation

West Wratting Valley Farm

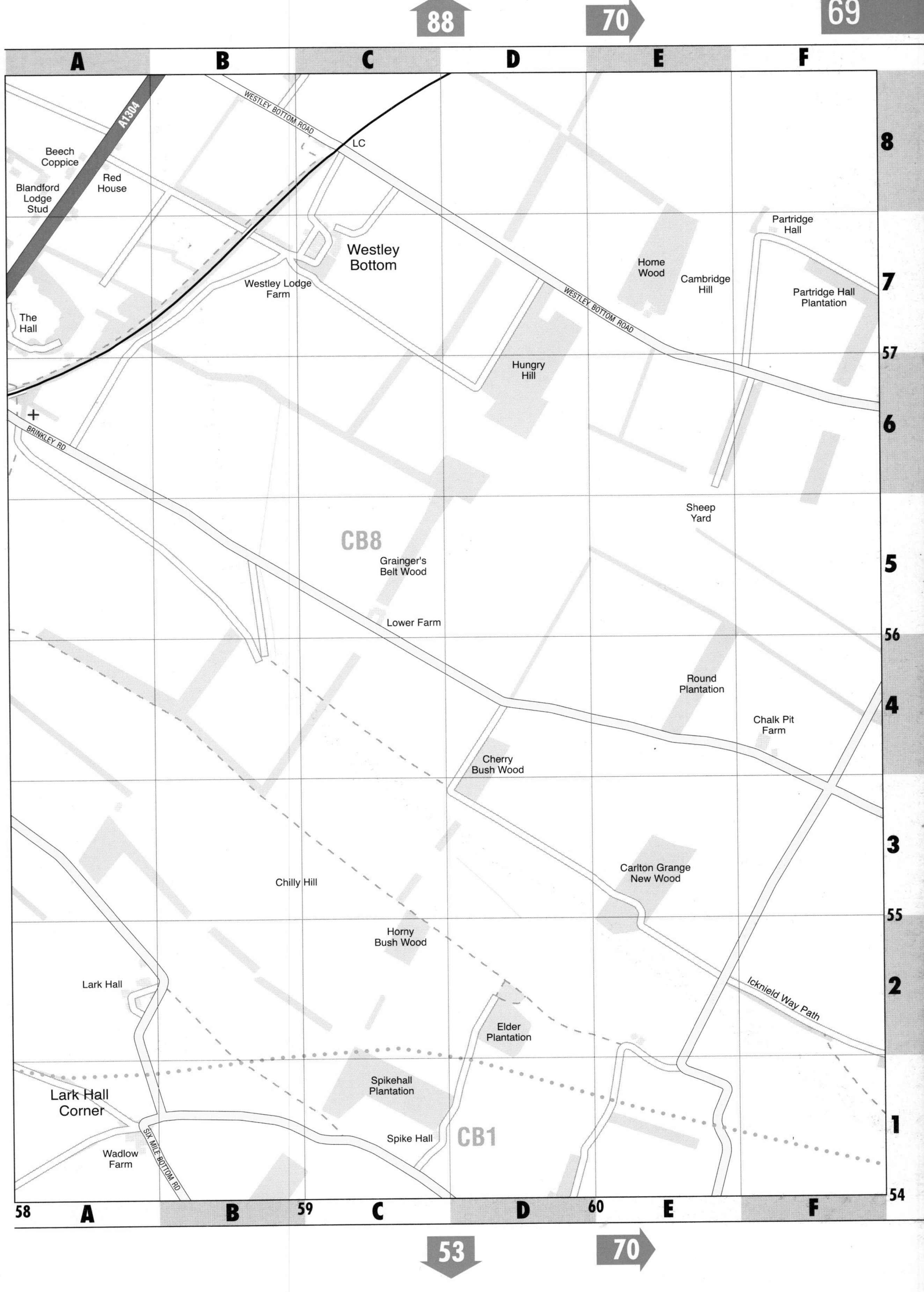

A   B   C   D   E   F

A1304

Beech
Coppice

Blandford
Lodge
Stud

Red
House

WESTLEY BOTTOM ROAD

LC

Westley
Bottom

Westley Lodge
Farm

The
Hall

Home
Wood

Cambridge
Hill

Partridge
Hall

Partridge Hall
Plantation

WESTLEY BOTTOM ROAD

8

7

57

BRINKLEY RD

Hungry
Hill

6

Sheep
Yard

CB8

Grainger's
Belt Wood

Lower Farm

Round
Plantation

Chalk Pit
Farm

5

56

4

Cherry
Bush Wood

Chilly Hill

Carlton Grange
New Wood

3

55

Horny
Bush Wood

Icknield Way Path

2

Lark Hall

Elder
Plantation

Lark Hall
Corner

Spikehall
Plantation

CB1

Wadlow
Farm

SIX MILE BOTTOM RD

Spike Hall

1

54

58   A   B   59   C   D   60   E   F

69
89

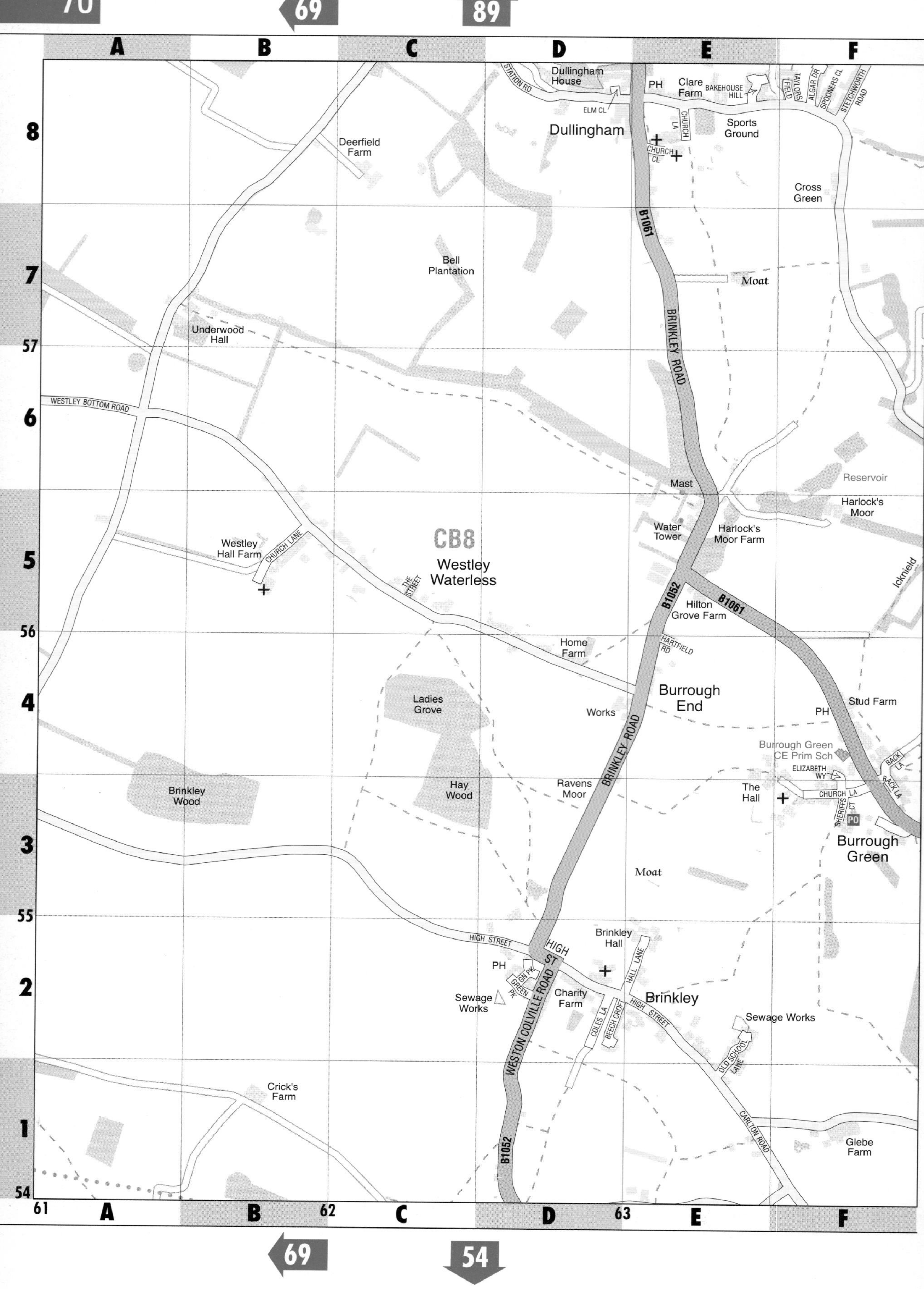
A
B
C
D
E
F
8
7
57
6
5
56
4
3
55
2
1
54
61
62
63
Dullingham House
STATION RD
ELM CL
PH
Clare Farm
BAKEHOUSE HILL
TAYLORS FIELD
ALGAR DR
SPOONERS CL
STETCHWORTH ROAD
CHURCH LA
Sports Ground
Dullingham
CHURCH CL
Deerfield Farm
Cross Green
B1061
Bell Plantation
Moat
BRINKLEY ROAD
Underwood Hall
WESTLEY BOTTOM ROAD
Mast
Reservoir
Harlock's Moor
Water Tower
Harlock's Moor Farm
CB8
Westley Hall Farm
CHURCH LANE
Westley Waterless
THE STREET
Icknield
B1052
Hilton Grove Farm
B1061
HARTFIELD RD
Home Farm
Burrough End
Ladies Grove
Works
PH
Stud Farm
Burrough Green CE Prim Sch
BACK LA
ELIZABETH WY
BACK LA
Brinkley Wood
Hay Wood
Ravens Moor
BRINKLEY ROAD
The Hall
CHURCH LA
SHERIFFS CT
PO
Burrough Green
Moat
HIGH STREET
HIGH ST
Brinkley Hall
PH
GN PK
GREEN PK
HALL LANE
Sewage Works
WESTON COLVILLE ROAD
Charity Farm
Brinkley
COLES LA
BEECH CROFT
HIGH STREET
Sewage Works
OLD SCHOOL LANE
Crick's Farm
CARLTON ROAD
Glebe Farm
B1052

69
54

90
72

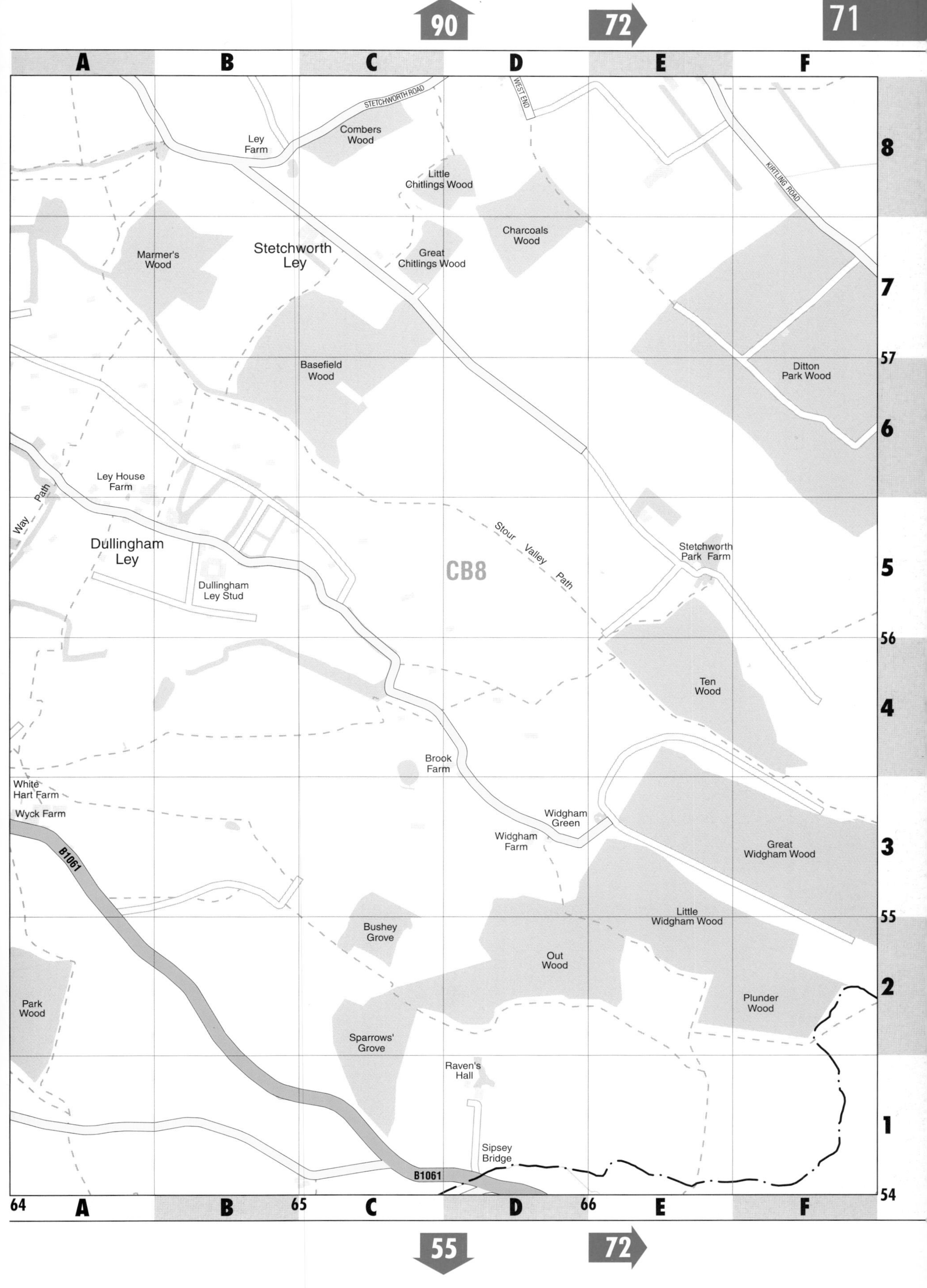
A
B
C
D
E
F
8
7
57
6
5
56
4
3
55
2
1
54
64
65
66
STETCHWORTH ROAD
WEST END
KIRTLING ROAD
Ley
Farm
Combers
Wood
Little
Chitlings Wood
Charcoals
Wood
Marmer's
Wood
Stetchworth
Ley
Great
Chitlings Wood
Basefield
Wood
Ditton
Park Wood
Ley House
Farm
Way
Path
Dullingham
Ley
Dullingham
Ley Stud
Stour
Valley
Path
CB8
Stetchworth
Park Farm
Ten
Wood
Brook
Farm
White
Hart Farm
Wyck Farm
B1061
Widgham
Green
Widgham
Farm
Great
Widgham Wood
Little
Widgham Wood
Bushey
Grove
Out
Wood
Park
Wood
Plunder
Wood
Sparrows'
Grove
Raven's
Hall
Sipsey
Bridge
B1061

55
72

A   B   C   D   E   F

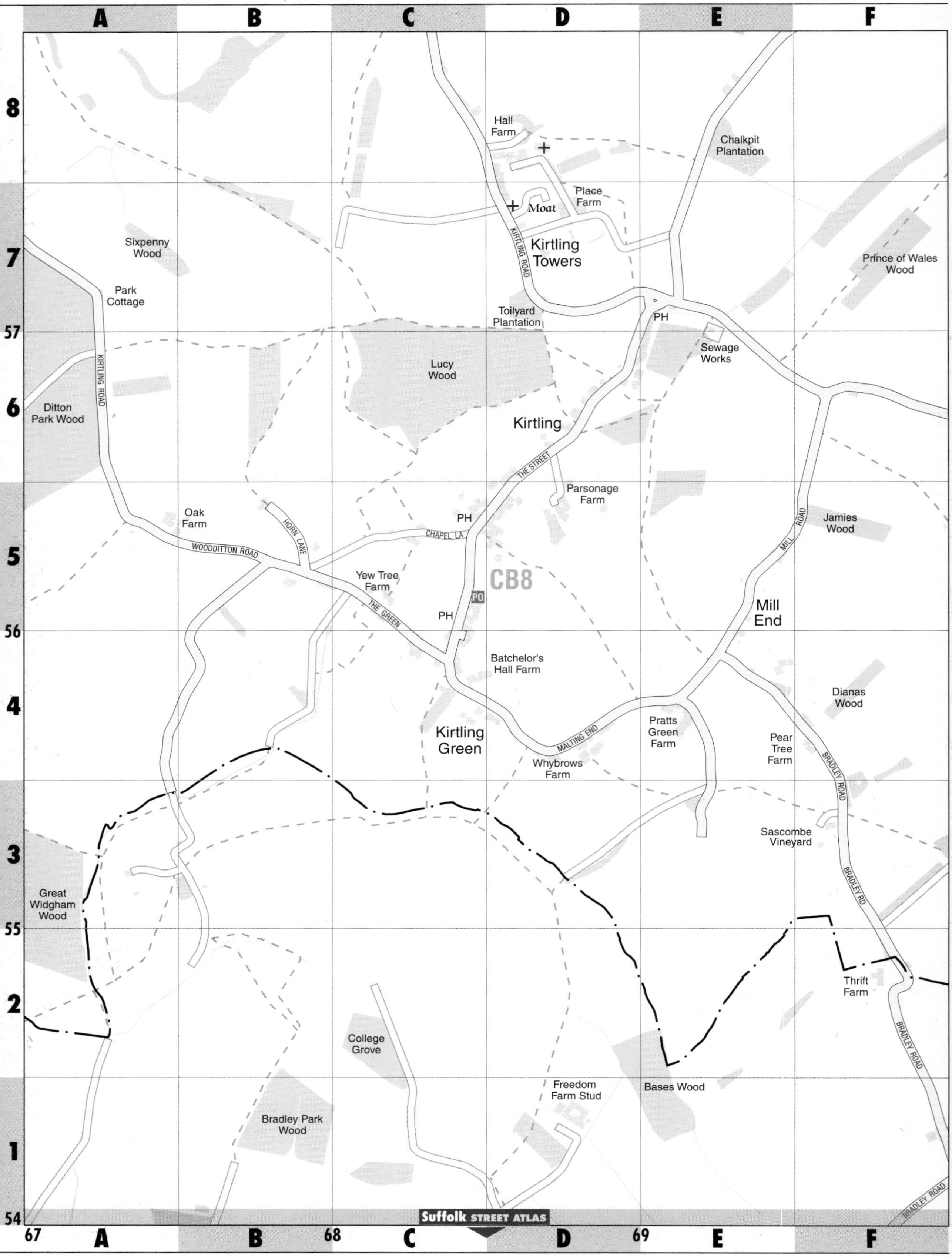

8

Hall Farm

Chalkpit Plantation

Place Farm

Moat

Kirtling Towers

7

Sixpenny Wood

Prince of Wales Wood

Park Cottage

KIRTLING ROAD

Toilyard Plantation

PH

57

Sewage Works

6

Ditton Park Wood

Lucy Wood

Kirtling

THE STREET

Parsonage Farm

MILL ROAD

Jamies Wood

Oak Farm

HORN LANE

WOODDITTON ROAD

CHAPEL LA.

PH

5

Yew Tree Farm

THE GREEN

PH

PO

CB8

Mill End

56

PH

Batchelor's Hall Farm

4

Kirtling Green

MALTING END

Pratts Green Farm

Dianas Wood

Whybrows Farm

Pear Tree Farm

BRADLEY ROAD

Sascombe Vineyard

3

Great Widgham Wood

55

Thrift Farm

2

College Grove

BRADLEY ROAD

Freedom Farm Stud

Bases Wood

Bradley Park Wood

1

54

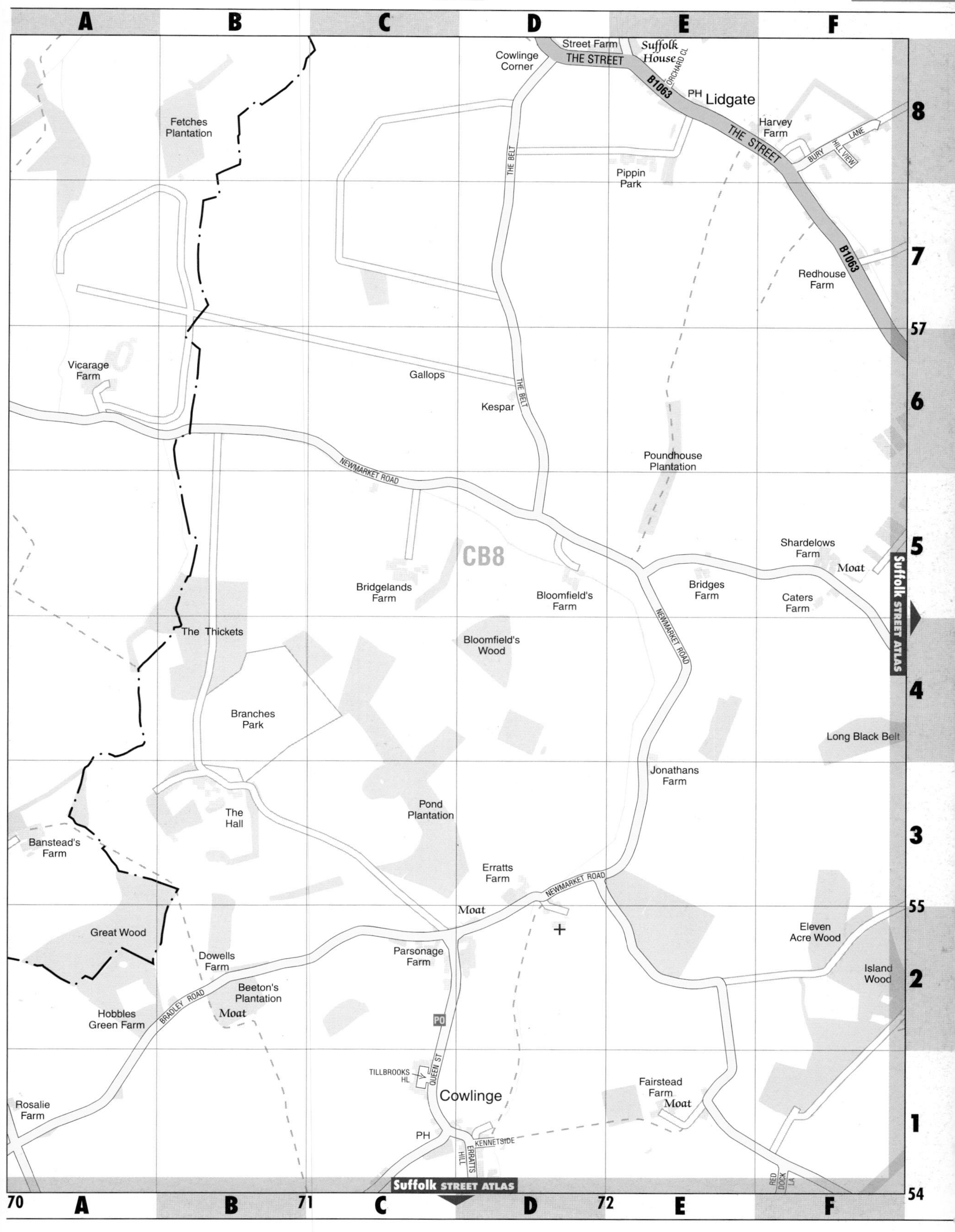

A B C D E F

8

7

57

6

5

4

55

3

2

1

54

70 A B 71 C D 72 E F

Fetches
Plantation

Street Farm
Cowlinge
Corner
THE STREET

Suffolk
House
PH Lidgate
B1063
THE STREET
Harvey
Farm
BURY LANE
HILL VIEW
ORCHARD CL

Pippin
Park

B1063

Redhouse
Farm

THE BELT

Vicarage
Farm

Gallops

Kespar

THE BELT

Poundhouse
Plantation

NEWMARKET ROAD

CB8

Shardelows
Farm
Moat

Bridgelands
Farm

Bloomfield's
Farm

Bridges
Farm

Caters
Farm

The Thickets

Bloomfield's
Wood

NEWMARKET ROAD

Suffolk STREET ATLAS

Long Black Belt

Branches
Park

The
Hall

Pond
Plantation

Jonathans
Farm

Banstead's
Farm

Errats
Farm

NEWMARKET ROAD

Moat

Eleven
Acre Wood

Great Wood

Dowells
Farm

Parsonage
Farm

Island
Wood

BRADLEY ROAD

Beeton's
Plantation
Moat

PO

Hobbles
Green Farm

Fairstead
Farm
Moat

TILLBROOKS
HL
QUEEN ST

Rosalie
Farm

Cowlinge

PH

KENNETSIDE
ERRATTS
HILL

RED
DOCK
LA

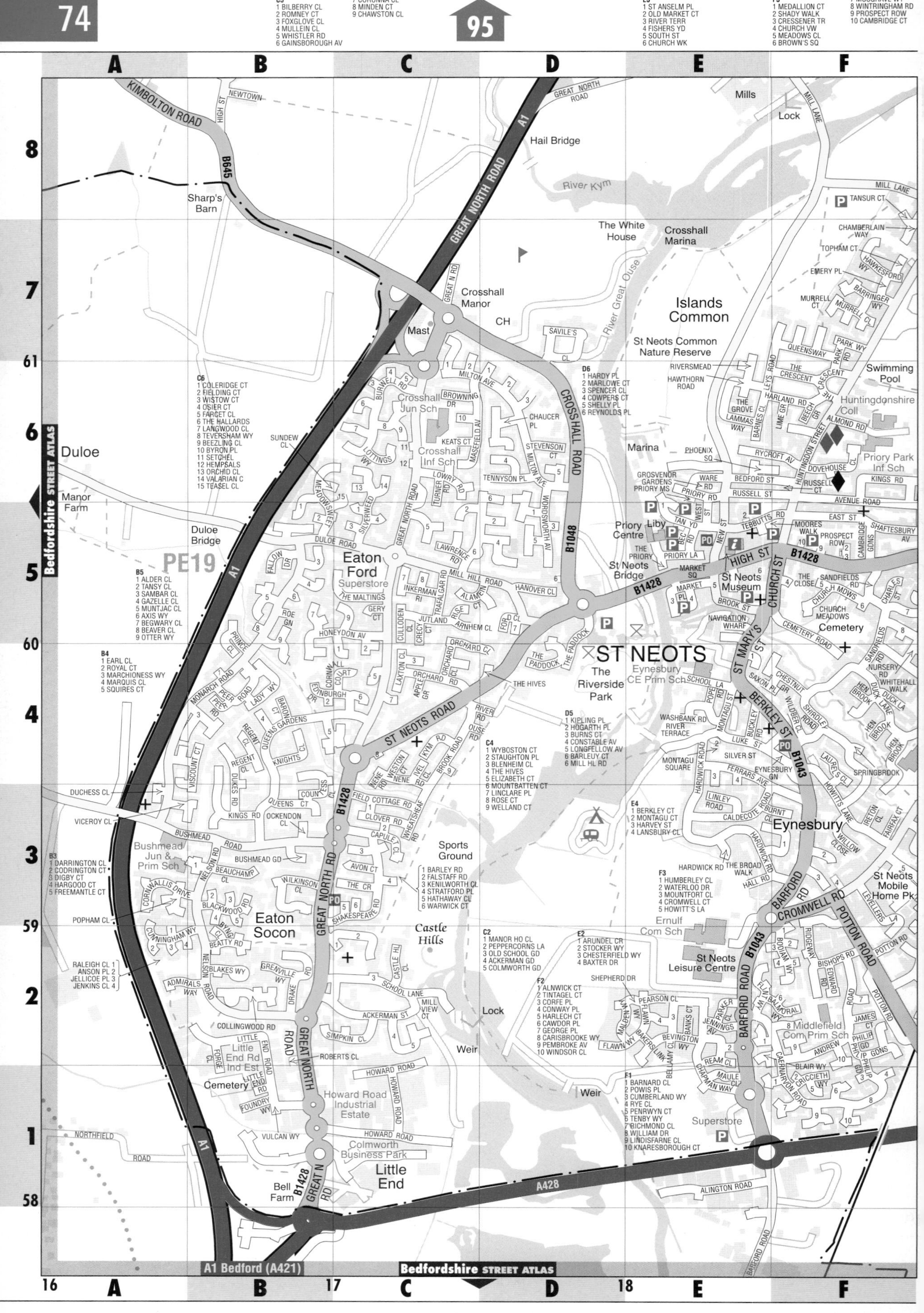

C5
1 BILBERRY CL
2 ROMNEY CT
3 FOXGLOVE CL
4 MULLEIN CL
5 WHISTLER RD
6 GAINSBOROUGH AV

7 CORUNNA CL
8 MINDEN CT
9 CHAWSTON CL

E5
1 ST ANSELM PL
2 OLD MARKET CT
3 RIVER TERR
4 FISHERS YD
5 SOUTH ST
6 CHURCH WK

F5
1 MEDALLION CT
2 SHADY WALK
3 CRESSENER TR
4 CHURCH VW
5 MEADOWS CL
6 BROWN'S SQ

7 MUSGRAVE WY
8 WINTRINGHAM RD
9 PROSPECT ROW
10 CAMBRIDGE CT

C6
1 COLERIDGE CT
2 FIELDING CT
3 WISTOW CT
4 OSIER CT
5 FARGET CL
6 THE HALLARDS
7 LANGWOOD CL
8 TEVERSHAM WY
9 BEEZLING CL
10 BYRON PL
11 SETCHEL
12 HEMPSALS
13 ORCHID CL
14 VALARIAN C
15 TEASEL CL

D6
1 HARDY PL
2 MARLOWE CT
3 SPENCER CL
4 COWPERS CT
5 SHELLY PL
6 REYNOLDS PL

B5
1 ALDER CL
2 TANSY CL
3 SAMBAR CL
4 GAZELLE CL
5 MUNTJAC CL
6 AXIS WY
7 BEGWARY CL
8 BEAVER CL
9 OTTER WY

B4
1 EARL CL
2 ROYAL CT
3 MARCHIONESS WY
4 MARQUIS CL
5 SQUIRES CT

D5
1 KIPLING PL
2 HOGARTH PL
3 BURNS CT
4 CONSTABLE AV
5 LONGFELLOW AV
6 BARLEUY CT
7 MILL HL RD

C4
1 WYBOSTON CT
2 STAUGHTON PL
3 BLENHEIM CL
4 THE HIVES
5 ELIZABETH CT
6 MOUNTBATTEN CT
7 LINCLARE PL
8 ROSE CT
9 WELLAND CT

B3
1 DARRINGTON CL
2 CODRINGTON CT
3 DIGBY CT
4 HARGOOD CT
5 FREEMANTLE CT

C3
1 BARLEY RD
2 FALSTAFF RD
3 KENILWORTH CL
4 STRATFORD PL
5 HATHAWAY CL
6 WARWICK CT

E4
1 BERKLEY CT
2 MONTAGU CT
3 HARVEY ST
4 LANSBURY CT

F3
1 HUMBERLEY CL
2 WATERLOO DR
3 MOUNTFORT CL
4 CROMWELL CT
5 HOWITT'S LA

C2
1 MANOR HO CL
2 PEPPERCORNS LA
3 OLD SCHOOL GD
4 ACKERMAN GD
5 COLMWORTH GD

E2
1 ARUNDEL CR
2 STOCKER WY
3 CHESTERFIELD WY
4 BAXTER DR

D2
1 ALNWICK CT
2 TINTAGEL CT
3 CORFE PL
4 CONWAY WY
5 HARLECH CT
6 CAWDOR PL
7 GEORGE PL
8 CARISBROOKE WY
9 PEMBROKE AV
10 WINDSOR CL

F1
1 BARNARD CL
2 POWIS PL
3 CUMBERLAND WY
4 RYE CL
5 PENRWYN CT
6 TENBY WY
7 RICHMOND CL
8 WILLIAM DR
9 LINDISFARNE CL
10 KNARESBOROUGH CL

A B C D E F

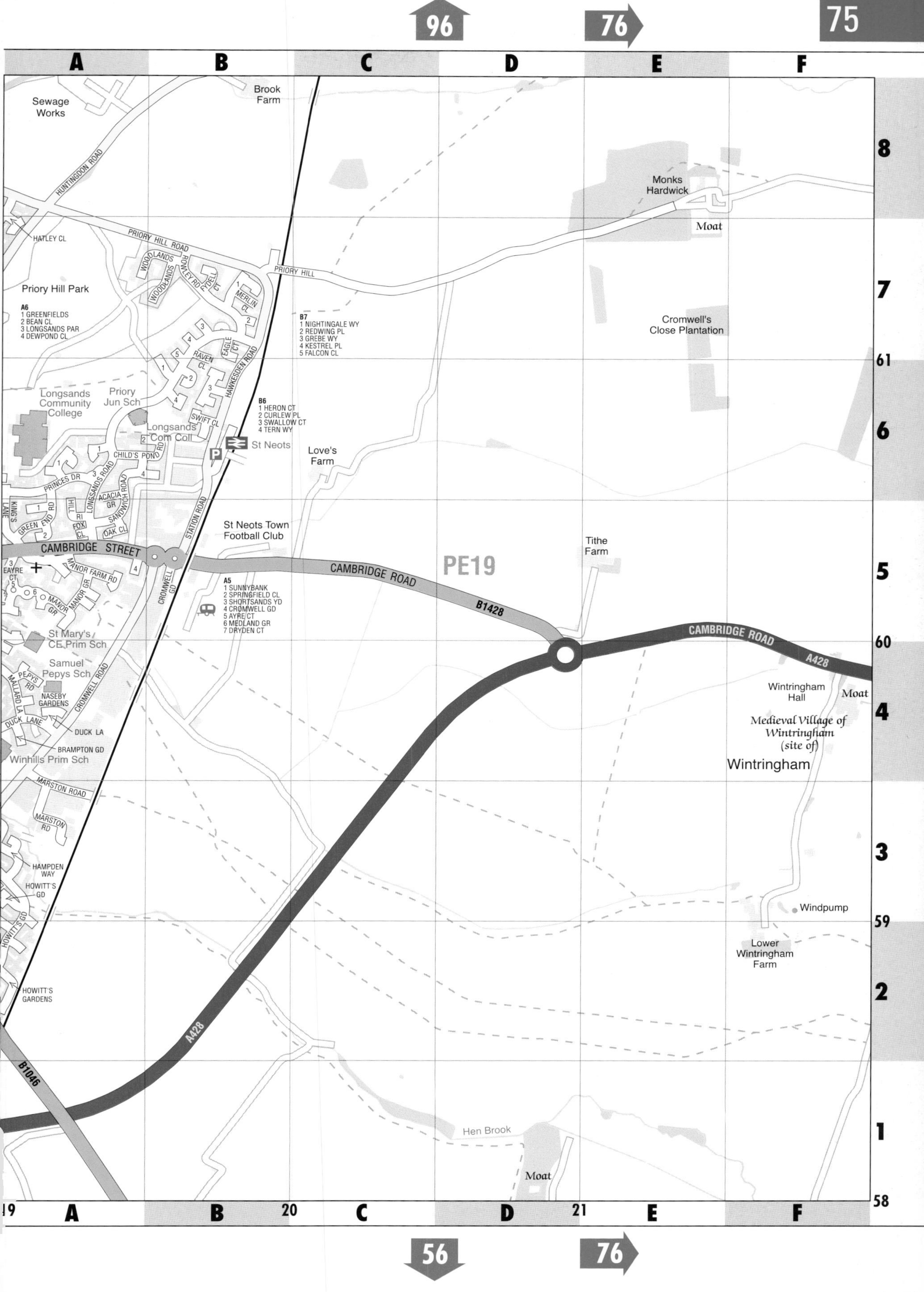

8

Sewage Works

Brook Farm

Monks Hardwick

Moat

HATLEY CL

PRIORY HILL ROAD

PRIORY HILL

7

Priory Hill Park

A6
1 GREENFIELDS
2 BEAN CL
3 LONGSANDS PAR
4 DEWPOND CL

WOODLANDS

WOODLANDS

RINKLEY RD

DELL

MERLIN CL

Cromwell's Close Plantation

B7
1 NIGHTINGALE WY
2 REDWING PL
3 GREBE WY
4 KESTREL PL
5 FALCON CL

61

Longsands Community College

Priory Jun Sch

RAVEN CL

HAWKESDEN ROAD

SWIFT CL

EAGLE CT

B6
1 HERON CT
2 CURLEW PL
3 SWALLOW CT
4 TERN WY

6

Longsands Com Coll

Child's Pond

P

St Neots

Love's Farm

PRINCES DR

LONGSANDS ROAD

ACACIA GR

SANDWICH ROAD

HILL RI

FOX CL

OAK CL

St Neots Town Football Club

CAMBRIDGE ROAD

PE19

Tithe Farm

5

KING'S LANE

GREEN END RD

CAMBRIDGE STREET

STATION ROAD

CROMWELL RD

B1428

A5
1 SUNNYBANK
2 SPRINGFIELD CL
3 SHORTSANDS YD
4 CROMWELL GD
5 AYRE CT
6 MEDLAND GR
7 DRYDEN CT

CAMBRIDGE ROAD

A428

60

EAYRE CT

MANOR FARM RD

MANOR GR

MANOR GR

St Mary's C E Prim Sch

Samuel Pepys Sch

CROMWELL ROAD

NASEBY GARDENS

DUCK LA

Wintringham Hall

Moat

Medieval Village of Wintringham (site of)

Wintringham

4

MALLARD LA

PEPYS RD

DUCK LANE

BRAMPTON GD

Winhills Prim Sch

MARSTON ROAD

MARSTON RD

Windpump

3

HAMPDEN WAY

HOWITT'S GD

59

Lower Wintringham Farm

HOWITT'S GD

A428

HOWITT'S GARDENS

2

B1046

Hen Brook

1

Moat

58

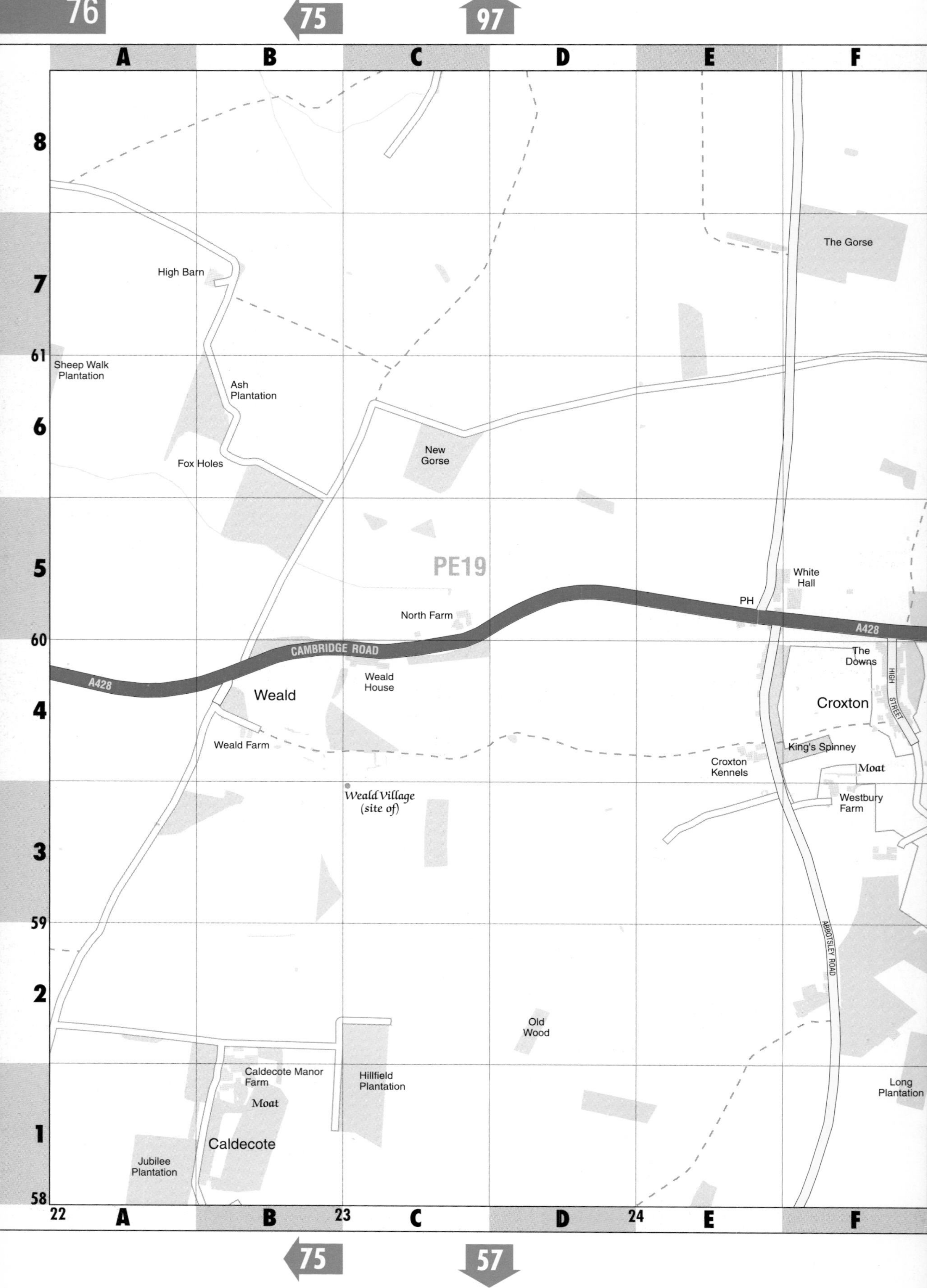

A B C D E F

8
7
61
6
5
60
4
3
59
2
1
58

High Barn

Sheep Walk
Plantation

Ash
Plantation

Fox Holes

New
Gorse

The Gorse

PE19

North Farm

White
Hall

PH

A428

CAMBRIDGE ROAD

A428

Weald

Weald
House

Croxton

The Downs

HIGH STREET

Weald Farm

Weald Village
(site of)

King's Spinney

Croxton
Kennels

Moat

Westbury
Farm

Old
Wood

ABBOTSLEY ROAD

Caldecote Manor
Farm

Hillfield
Plantation

Moat

Long
Plantation

Caldecote

Jubilee
Plantation

98
78

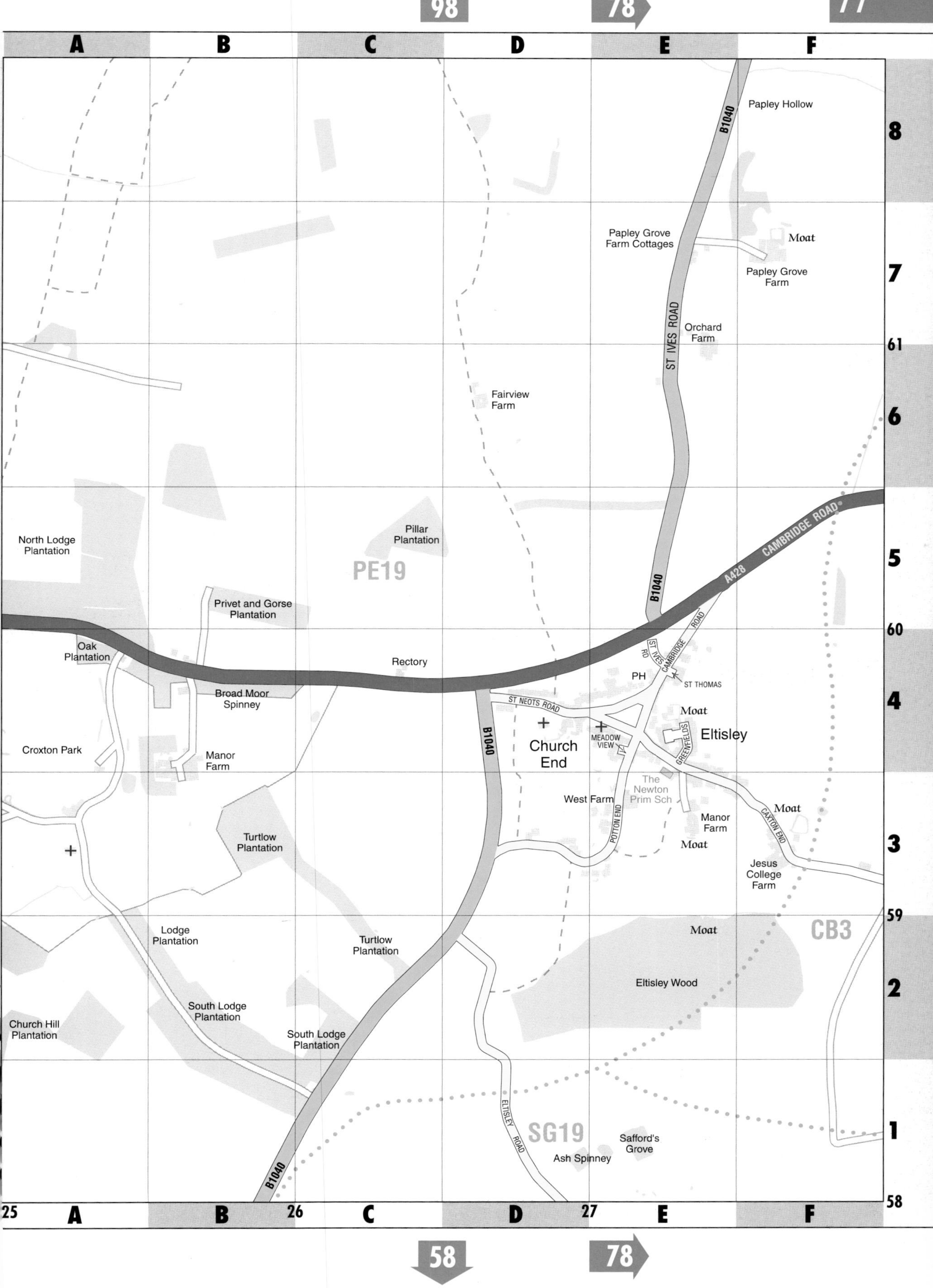
A
B
C
D
E
F
Papley Hollow
B1040
8
Papley Grove
Farm Cottages
Moat
Papley Grove
Farm
7
ST IVES ROAD
Orchard
Farm
61
Fairview
Farm
6
North Lodge
Plantation
Pillar
Plantation
PE19
CAMBRIDGE ROAD
A428
5
B1040
Privet and Gorse
Plantation
60
Oak
Plantation
Rectory
ST IVES RD
CAMBRIDGE ROAD
PH
ST THOMAS
Broad Moor
Spinney
ST NEOTS ROAD
Moat
4
B1040
Church
End
MEADOW
VIEW
GREENFIELDS
Eltisley
Croxton Park
Manor
Farm
The
Newton
Prim Sch
West Farm
Moat
CAXTON END
Manor
Farm
POTTON END
Moat
Turtlow
Plantation
3
Jesus
College
Farm
59
Moat
CB3
Lodge
Plantation
Turtlow
Plantation
Eltisley Wood
2
South Lodge
Plantation
Church Hill
Plantation
South Lodge
Plantation
ELTISLEY ROAD
SG19
Safford's
Grove
Ash Spinney
1
B1040
58
25
A
B
26
C
D
27
E
F

58
78

A B C D E F

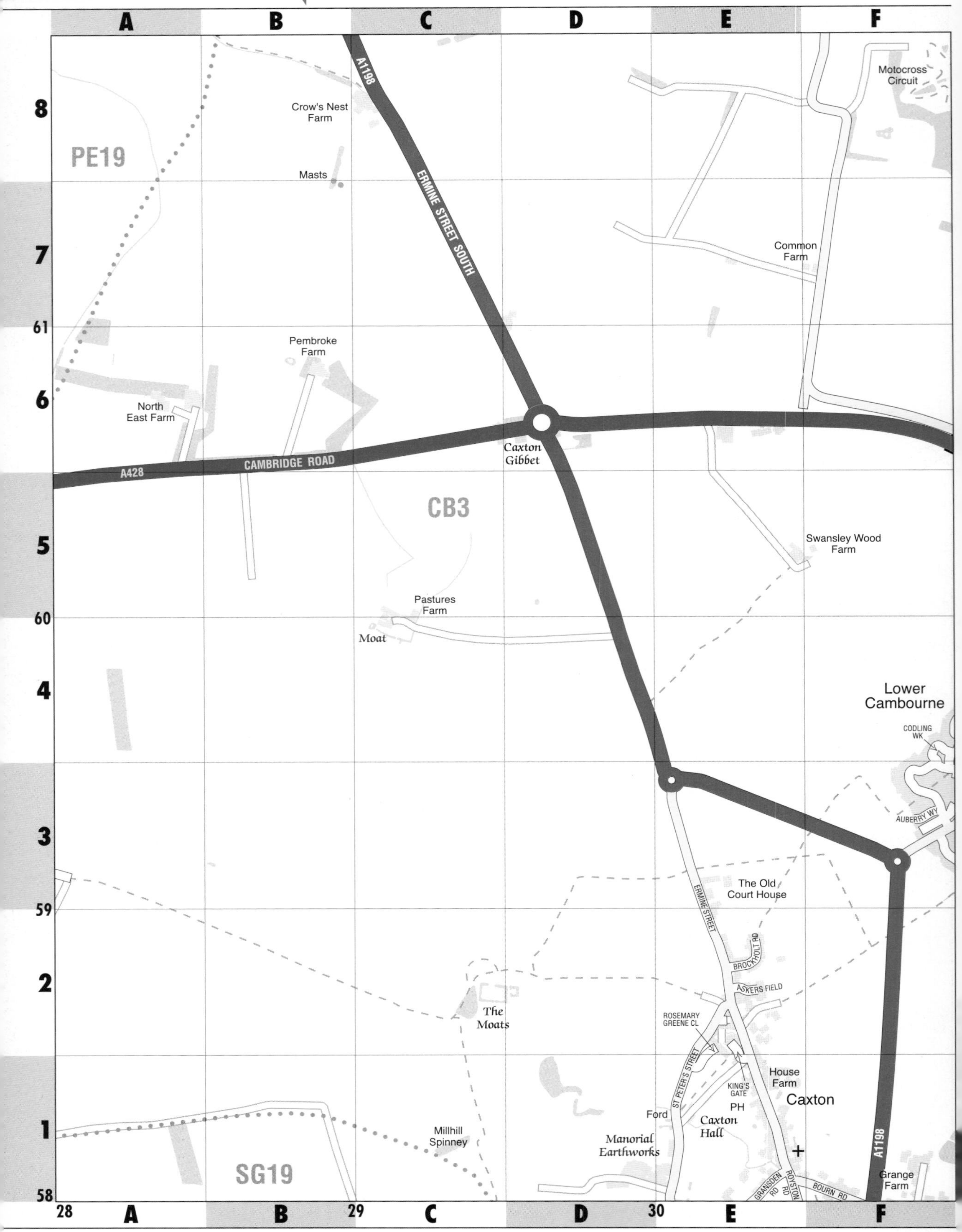

8

PE19

Crow's Nest
Farm

Masts

A1198

ERMINE STREET SOUTH

7

Motocross
Circuit

Common
Farm

61

Pembroke
Farm

6

North
East Farm

Caxton
Gibbet

A428

CAMBRIDGE ROAD

CB3

Swansley Wood
Farm

5

Pastures
Farm

Moat

60

4

Lower
Cambourne

CODLING
WK

AUBERRY WY

3

The Old
Court House

59

ERMINE STREET

BROCKHOLT RD

2

ASKERS FIELD

The
Moats

ROSEMARY
GREENE CL

ST PETER'S STREET

KING'S
GATE

House
Farm

Caxton

1

Millhill
Spinney

Ford

PH

Caxton
Hall

Manorial
Earthworks

A1198

Grange
Farm

SG19

GRANSDEN RD

ROYSTON RD

BOURN RD

58

28   **A**   **B**   29   **C**   **D**   30   **E**   **F**

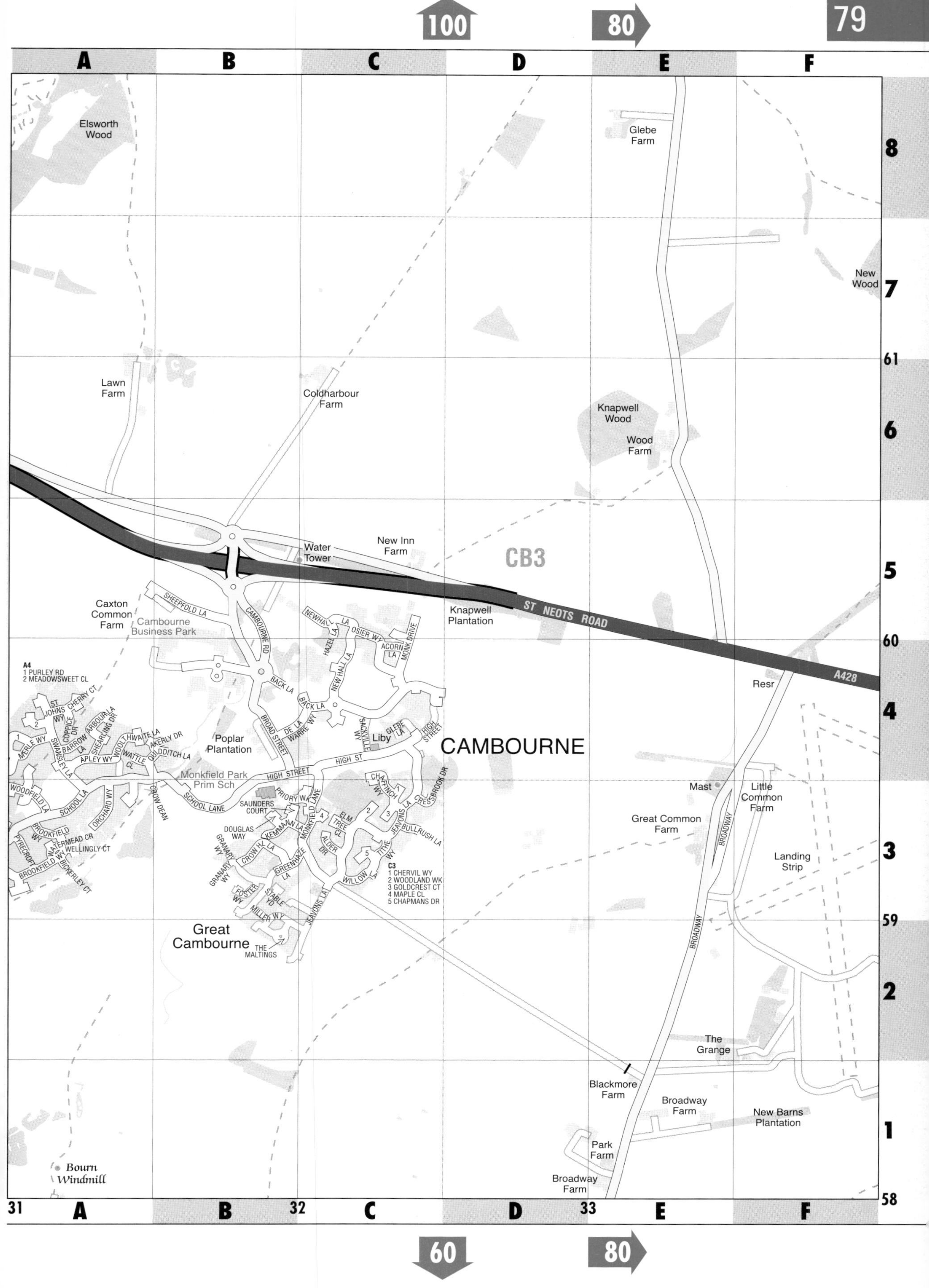
A
B
C
D
E
F
8
7
61
6
5
60
4
3
59
2
1
58
31
32
33
Elsworth Wood
Glebe Farm
New Wood
Lawn Farm
Coldharbour Farm
Knapwell Wood
Wood Farm
Water Tower
New Inn Farm
CB3
Caxton Common Farm
Cambourne Business Park
SHEEPFOLD LA
CAMBOURNE RD
Knapwell Plantation
ST NEOTS ROAD
A428
NEWHALL LA
HAZEL LA
OSIER WY
MONK DRIVE
ACORN LA
NEW HALL LA
BACK LA
DE LA WARRE WY
SACKVILLE WY
GLEBE LA
HIGH STREET
Liby
CAMBOURNE
Resr
A4
1 PURLEY RD
2 MEADOWSWEET CL
ST JOHNS WY
CHERRY CT
COPPICE DR
ARBOURLA
SHEARLING DR
BARROW LA
SWANSLEY LA
MERLE WY
APLEY WY
WOOLTHWAITE LA
AKERLY DR
WATTLE CL
GOLDDITCH LA
Poplar Plantation
BROAD STREET
HIGH ST
Monkfield Park Prim Sch
HIGH STREET
SCHOOL LANE
SCHOOL LA
CROW DEAN
WOODFIELD LA
ORCHARD WY
BROOKFIELD WY
WATERMEAD CR
WELLINGLY CT
PYRECROFT
BROOKFIELD WY
BICKERLEY CT
SAUNDERS COURT
PRIORY WA
DOUGLAS WAY
KEMMANN LA
CROW HL LA
GRANARY WY
GREENHAZE LA
MONKFIELD LANE
ALDER DR
ELM TREE CL
CHAFFINCH WY
CRESSBROOK DR
JEAVONS LA
BULLRUSH LA
TITHE WY
WILLOW LA
C3
1 CHERVIL WY
2 WOODLAND WK
3 GOLDCREST CT
4 MAPLE CL
5 CHAPMANS DR
FOSTER WY
STABLE YD
MILLER WY
JEAVONS LA
Great Cambourne
THE MALTINGS
Mast
Little Common Farm
Great Common Farm
BROADWAY
Landing Strip
BROADWAY
The Grange
Blackmore Farm
Broadway Farm
New Barns Plantation
Park Farm
Broadway Farm
Bourn Windmill

A B C D E F

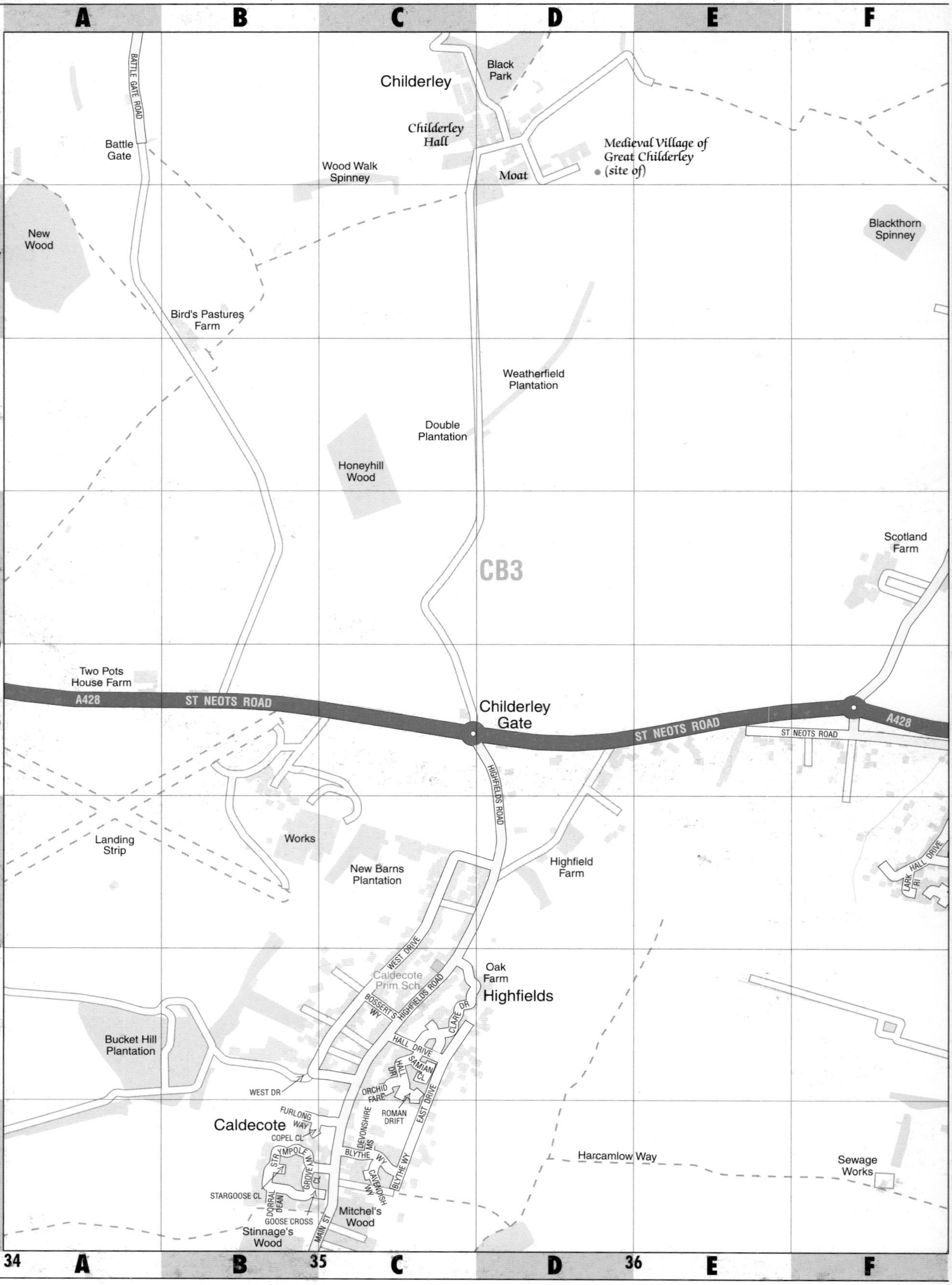

8

Childerley

Black Park

Childerley Hall

Medieval Village of Great Childerley
(site of)

Blackthorn Spinney

7

New Wood

BATTLE GATE ROAD

Battle Gate

Wood Walk Spinney

Moat

Bird's Pastures Farm

61

Weatherfield Plantation

6

Double Plantation

Honeyhill Wood

5

CB3

Scotland Farm

60

Two Pots House Farm

4

A428 ST NEOTS ROAD

Childerley Gate

ST NEOTS ROAD

ST NEOTS ROAD

A428

LARK HALL DRIVE

Landing Strip

Works

New Barns Plantation

HIGHFIELDS ROAD

Highfield Farm

3

59

WEST DRIVE

Caldecote Prim Sch

Oak Farm

Highfields

2

Bucket Hill Plantation

BOSSERT WY

HIGHFIELDS ROAD

CLARE DR

HALL DRIVE

WEST DR

ORCHID FARE

HALL DR

CAXTON CL

EAST DRIVE

Caldecote

FURLONG WAY

DEVONSHIRE MS

ROMAN DRIFT

Harcamlow Way

Sewage Works

COPEL CL

STRYMPOLE WY

BLYTHE WY

CAVENDISH WY

BLYTHE WY

1

STARGOOSE CL

GODFRAY BANK

GROVE WY

Mitchel's Wood

MAIN ST

GOOSE CROSS

Stinnage's Wood

58

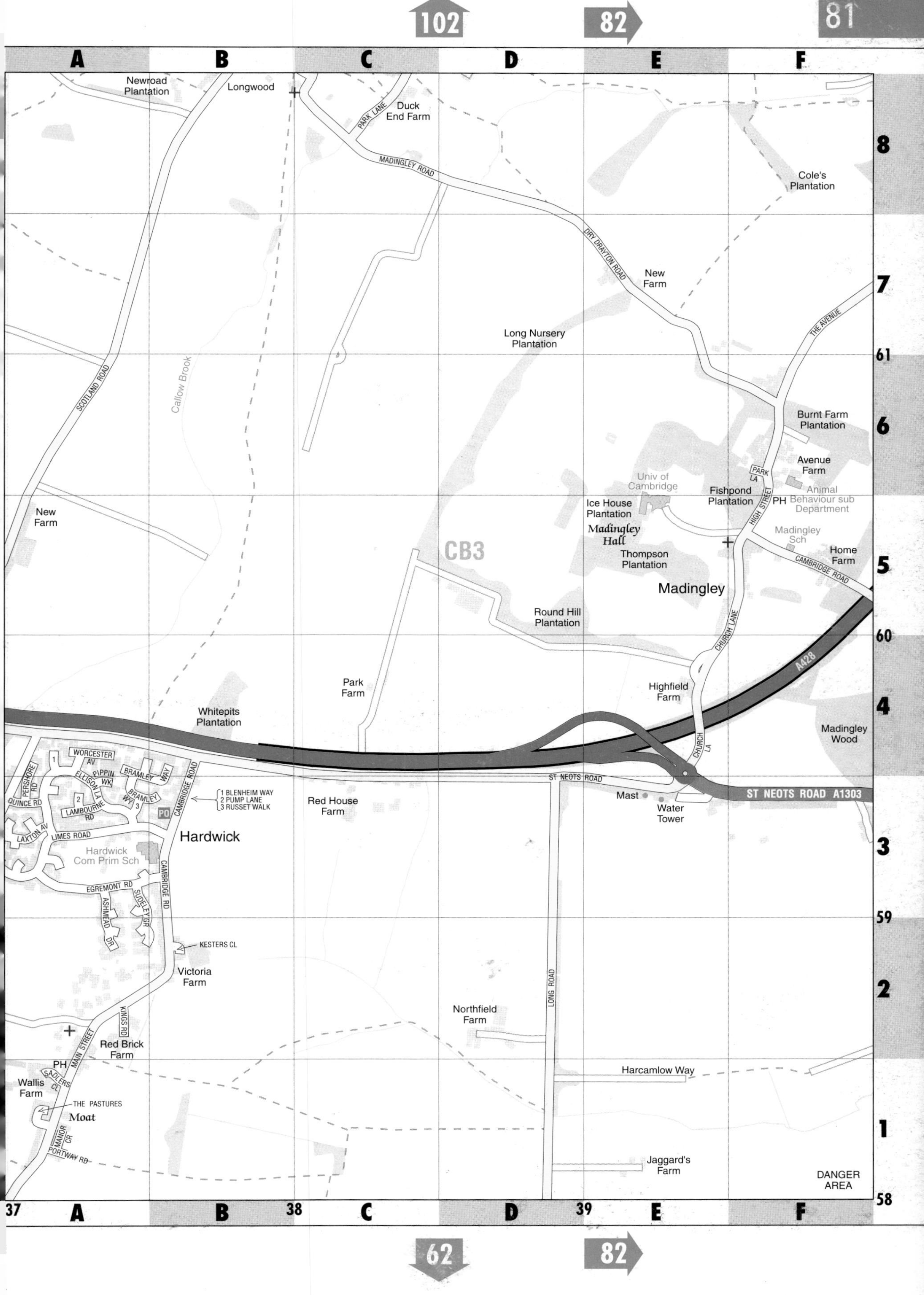

102
82
Newroad Plantation
Longwood
Duck End Farm
PARK LANE
MADINGLEY ROAD
Cole's Plantation
DRY DRAYTON ROAD
New Farm
THE AVENUE
Long Nursery Plantation
SCOTLAND ROAD
Callow Brook
Burnt Farm Plantation
PARK LA
Avenue Farm
Univ of Cambridge
Animal Behaviour sub Department
Fishpond Plantation
HIGH STREET
PH
Ice House Plantation
Madingley Hall
Madingley Sch
New Farm
CB3
Thompson Plantation
Home Farm
CAMBRIDGE ROAD
Madingley
Round Hill Plantation
CHURCH LANE
A428
Park Farm
Highfield Farm
Whitepits Plantation
Madingley Wood
CHURCH LA
WORCESTER AV
PERSHORE RD
PIPPIN WK
BRAMLEY WAY
ELLISON LA
BRAMLEY WY
CAMBRIDGE ROAD
QUINCE RD
LAMBOURNE RD
PO
1 BLENHEIM WAY
2 PUMP LANE
3 RUSSET WALK
Red House Farm
ST NEOTS ROAD
Mast
Water Tower
ST NEOTS ROAD A1303
LAXTON AV
LIMES ROAD
Hardwick
Hardwick Com Prim Sch
EGREMONT RD
ASHMEAD DR
SUDELEY GR
CAMBRIDGE RD
KESTERS CL
Victoria Farm
LONG ROAD
Northfield Farm
KINGS RD
MAIN STREET
Red Brick Farm
PH
SADLERS CL
Harcamlow Way
Wallis Farm
THE PASTURES
Moat
MANOR CR
PORTWAY RD
Jaggard's Farm
DANGER AREA
37
38
39
58
59
60
61
62
82

81
103

A **B** **C** **D** **E** **F**

8

Beck Brook Farm

THE AVENUE

Hanchard Plantation

M11

WASHPIT ROAD

LAWRENCE CL
DUCK END
CHURCH LANE
HICKS LANE
WHITEGATE CL
REDGATE RD
CAMBRIDGE ROAD
MAYFIELD RD

Orchard Farm

CHERRY BOUNDS
ST VINCENT'S CL
GIFFORD'S CL
ST VINCENT'S CLOSE
PEPYS WAY

Girton

WEST FIELD

7

A14

A1307

14

Biotechnology Centre

GRANGE DRIVE
ORCHARD DRIVE
ORCHARD DRIVE
HUNTINGDON ROAD
GIRTON ROAD
WELLBROOK WY.
THORNTON ROAD
WILDERSPIN CL
ST MARGARET'S ROAD
BANDON RD
THORNTON CT
THORNTON ROAD

61

Cambridge University Farm

Girton Coll

A1307

6

A1303

Ladybush Close

5

A428

Wrangling Corner

Trinity Farm

60

CB3

Pheasant Plantation

4

Madingley Wood

Cambridge American Cemetery

CAMBRIDGE ROAD

Moor Barns Farm

Mill Farm Windmill

Trinity
• *Conduit Head*

3

A1303

A1303

ST NEOTS ROAD

MADINGLEY ROAD

13

P&R

BRADRUSHE FIELDS

LANSDOWNE ROAD
CONDUIT HEAD RD

PO

CAMBRIDGE ROAD

Rectory Farm

British Antarctic Survey

Schlumberger Laboratories

Dept of Veterinary Medicine

Merton Hall Farm

THOMPSON AVE

59

Coton CE Prim Sch

HIGH ST
CHURCH END
SADLER'S CL
ST CATHARINES Hall
PH
THE FOOTPATH

High Cross

Coton

2

WHITWELL WAY
BENNY'S WAY
ST PETER'S ROAD
ST JOHN'S ROAD
SILVERDALE CL
SILVERDALE AVE
BROOKFIELD RD

Manor Farm

BROOK LANE

Rec Gnd

Harcamlow Way

1

Whitwell Farm

DANGER AREA

GRANTCHESTER ROAD

Bin Brook

M11

58

40 **A** **B** **41** **C** **D** **42** **E** **F**

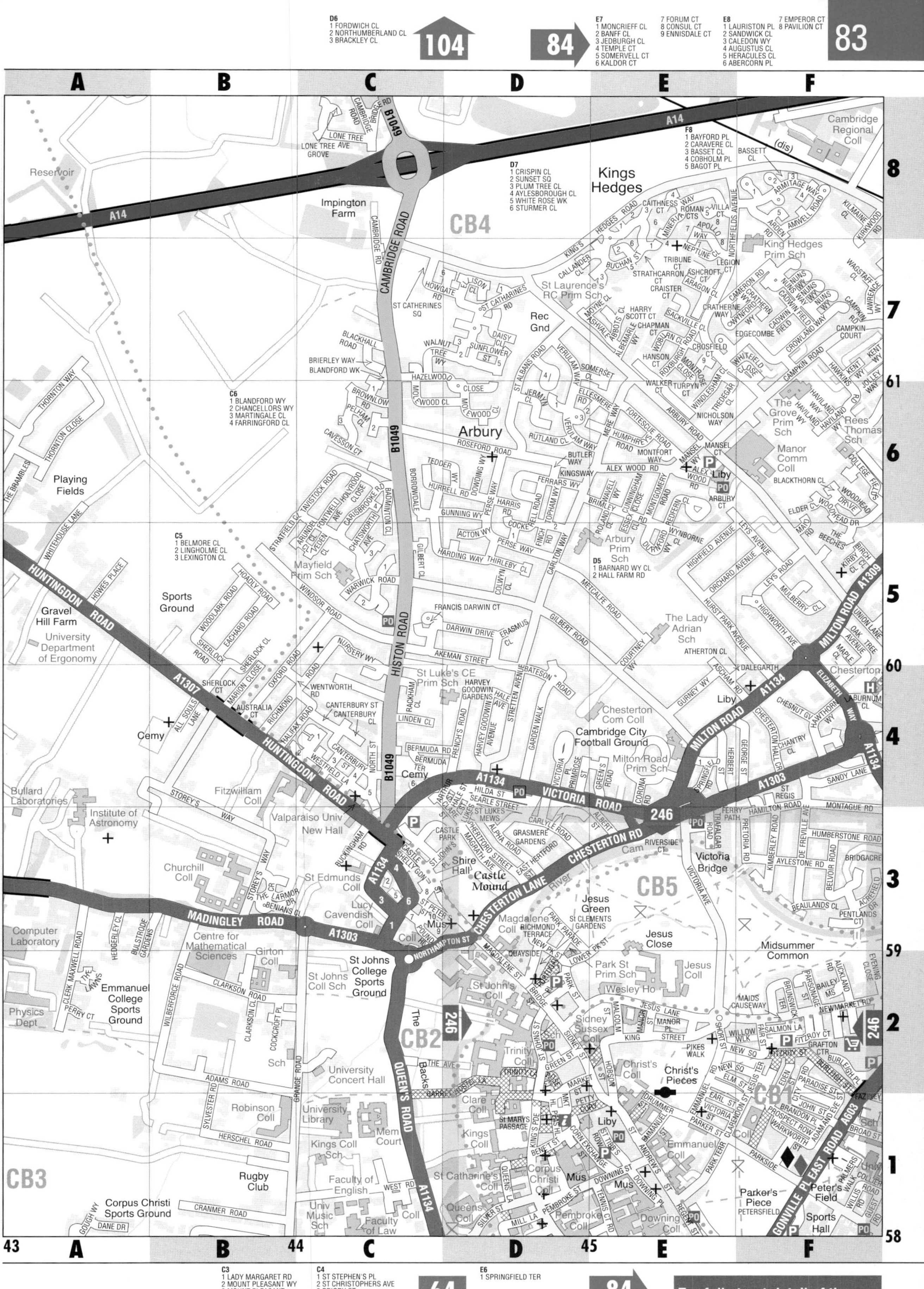

83
105

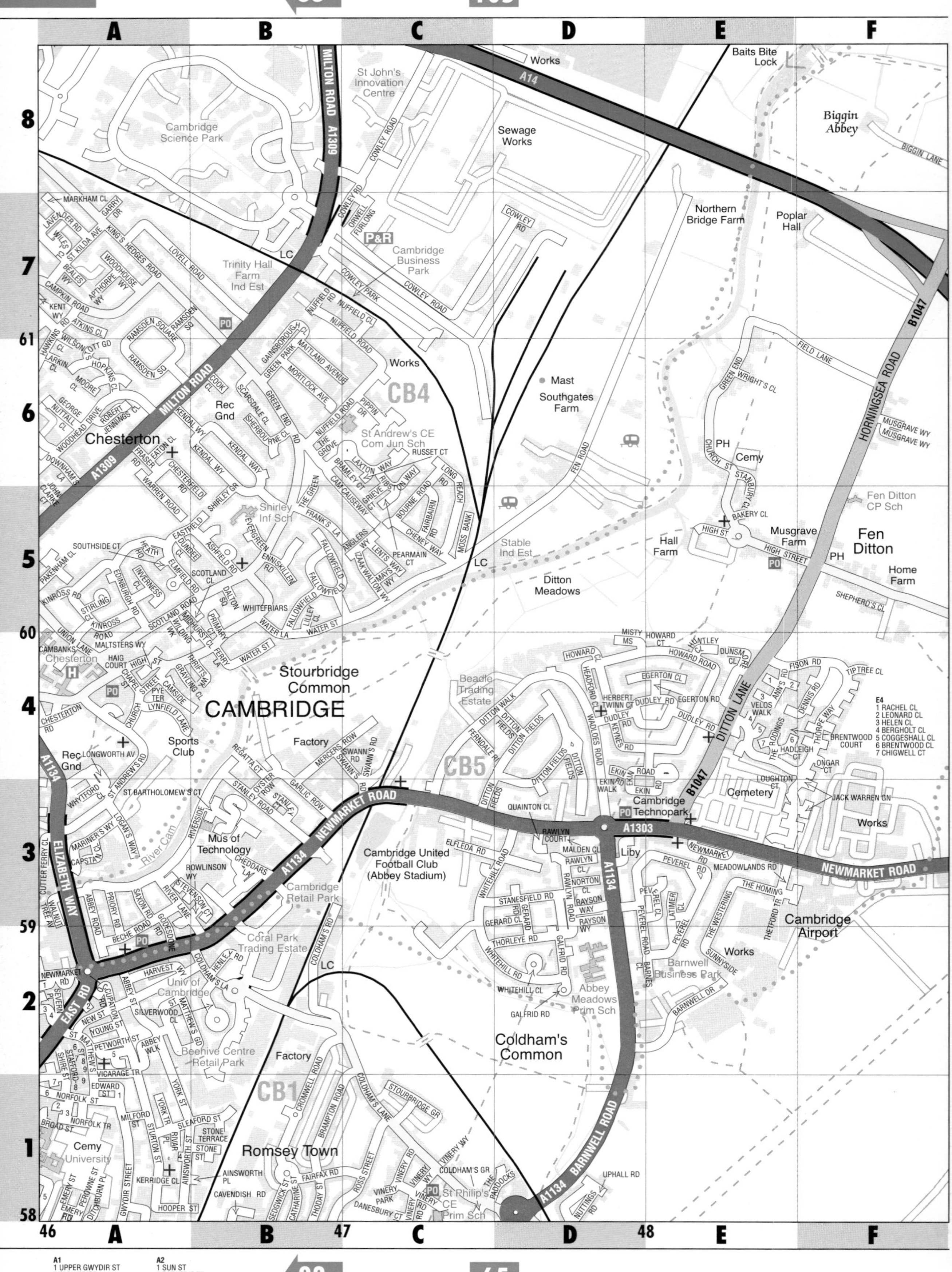

83
65

A1
1 UPPER GWYDIR ST
2 FLOWER ST
3 BLOSSOM ST
4 AINSWORTH CT
5 MACKENZIE RD
6 ASHLEY CT
7 STAFFORDSHIRE GD
8 ATHLONE
9 BRAY

A2
1 SUN ST
2 PARKER'S TR
3 WELLINGTON CT
4 WELLINGTON ST
5 ST MATTHEW'S CT
6 HOLLYMOUNT
7 ENFIELD
8 FARRAN
9 CARLOW

106
86

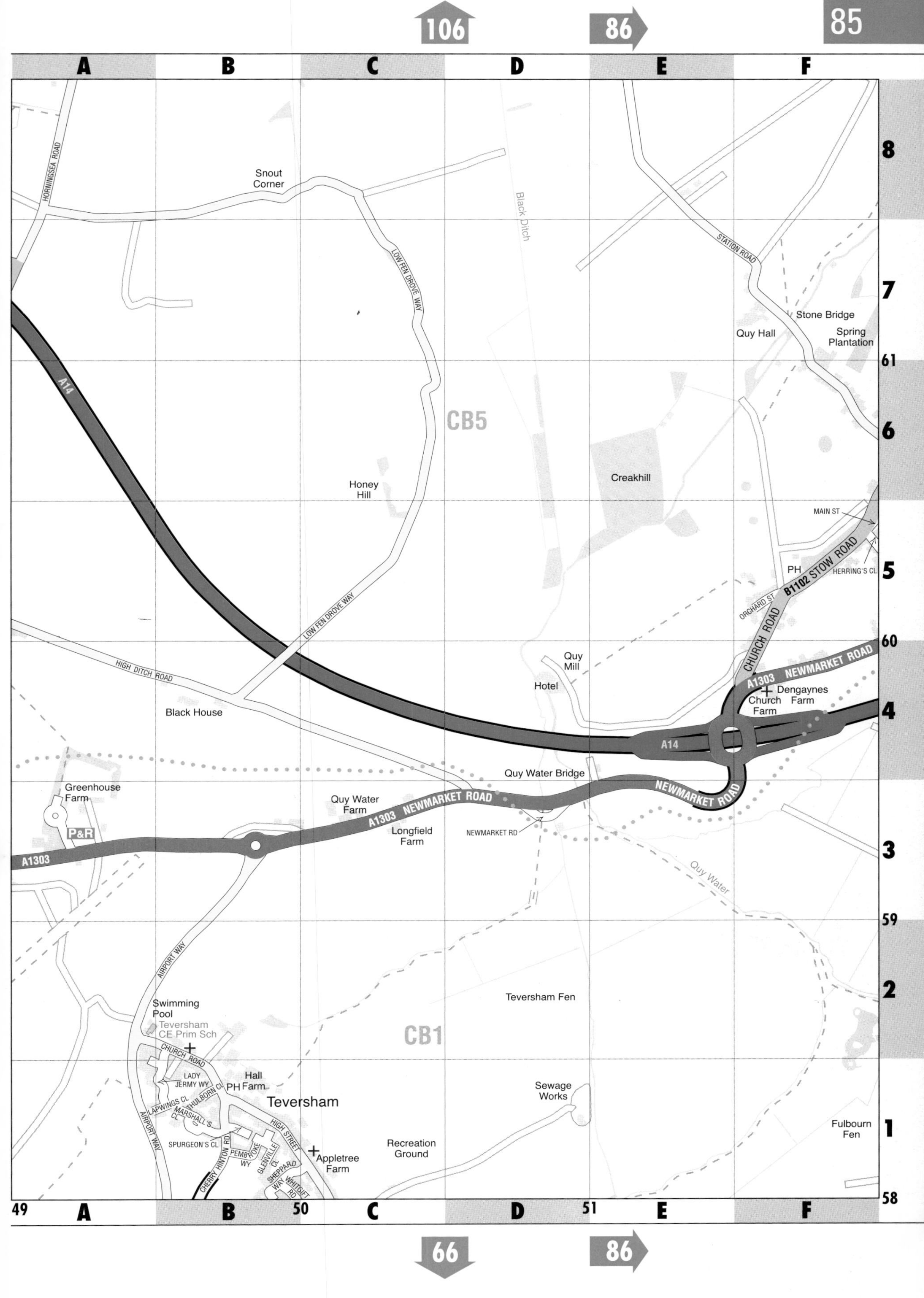
A
B
C
D
E
F
8
7
61
6
5
60
4
3
59
2
1
58
49
50
51
Snout
Corner
HORNINGSEA ROAD
Black Ditch
STATION ROAD
LOW FEN DROVE WAY
Stone Bridge
Quy Hall
Spring
Plantation
A14
CB5
Creakhill
Honey
Hill
MAIN ST
B1102 STOW ROAD
PH
HERRING'S CL
ORCHARD ST
CHURCH ROAD
A1303 NEWMARKET ROAD
Quy
Mill
Hotel
Dengaynes
Farm
Church
Farm
HIGH DITCH ROAD
Black House
Quy Water Bridge
Greenhouse
Farm
P&R
Quy Water
Farm
A1303 NEWMARKET ROAD
NEWMARKET ROAD
Longfield
Farm
NEWMARKET RD
A1303
Quy Water
AIRPORT WAY
Teversham Fen
Swimming
Pool
Teversham
CE Prim Sch
CB1
CHURCH ROAD
LADY
JERMY WY
THULBORN CL
PH
Hall
Farm
LAPWINGS CL
MARSHALL'S CL
Teversham
Sewage
Works
HIGH STREET
SPURGEON'S CL
CHERRY HINTON RD
PEMBROKE WY
GLENVILLE CL
SHEPPARD WAY
WHITGIFT RD
Appletree
Farm
Recreation
Ground
Fulbourn
Fen

66
86

85
107

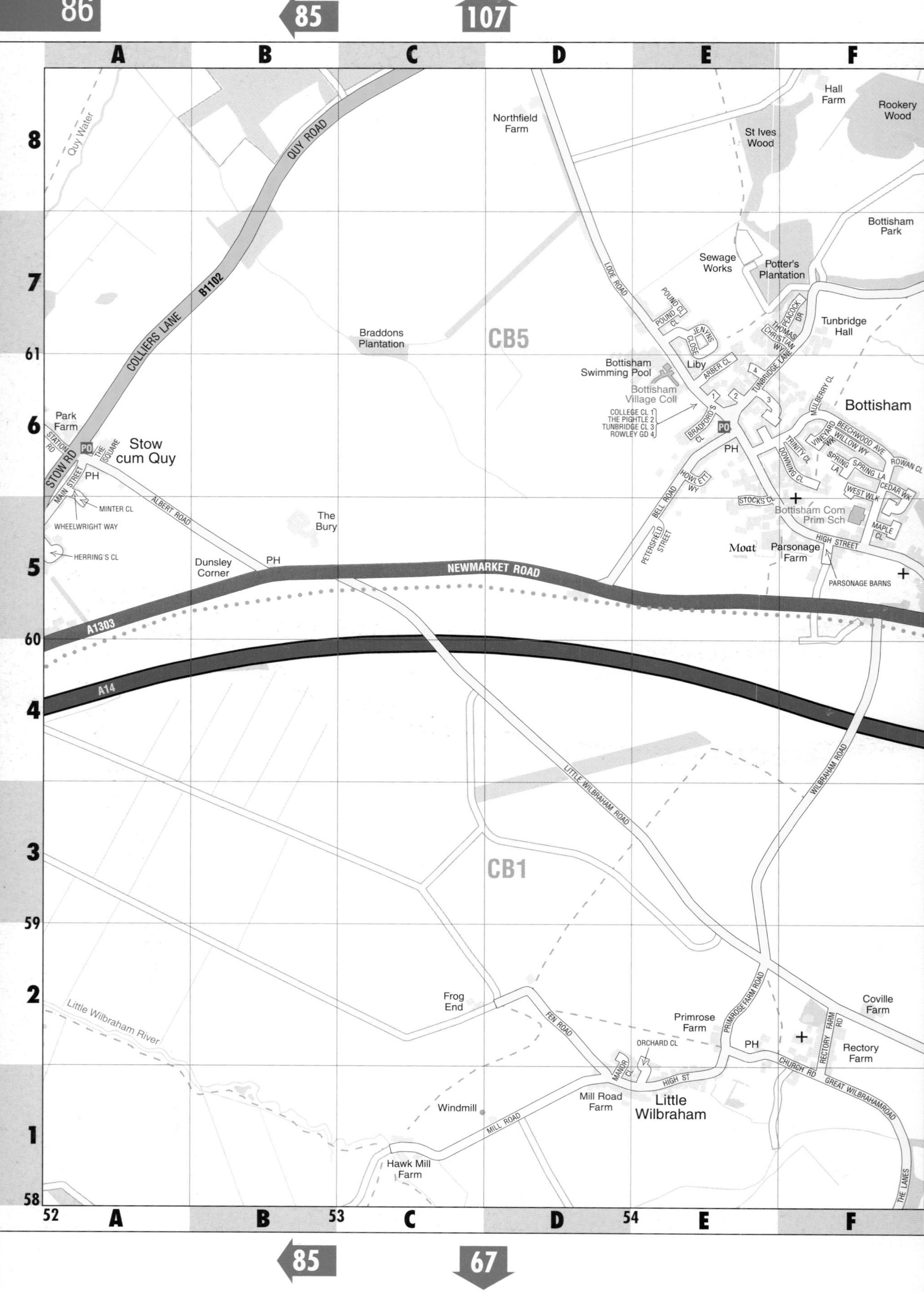
A B C D E F
8 7 61 6 5 60 4 3 59 2 1 58
52 53 54
Quy Water
QUY ROAD
B1102
COLLIERS LANE
Northfield Farm
Hall Farm
Rookery Wood
St Ives Wood
Bottisham Park
Sewage Works
Potter's Plantation
LODE ROAD
POUND CL
JENYNS CLOSE
PEACOCK DR
THOMAS CHRISTIAN WY
Tunbridge Hall
Braddons Plantation
CB5
Bottisham Swimming Pool
Liby
ARBER CL
TUNBRIDGE LANE
MULBERRY CL
Bottisham
Bottisham Village Coll
COLLEGE CL 1
THE PIGHTLE 2
TUNBRIDGE CL 3
ROWLEY GD 4
BRADFORD'S CL
PO
PH
BEECHWOOD AVE
VINEYARD WK
WILLOW WY
TRINITY CL
SPRING LA
ROWAN CL
DOWNING CL
CEDAR WK
WEST WLK
HOWLETT WY
BELL ROAD
STOCKS CL
Bottisham Com Prim Sch
MAPLE CL
PETERSFIELD STREET
HIGH STREET
Moat
Parsonage Farm
PARSONAGE BARNS
Park Farm
STATION RD
STOW RD
THE SQUARE
Stow cum Quy
MAIN STREET
MINTER CL
WHEELWRIGHT WAY
ALBERT ROAD
HERRING'S CL
The Bury
Dunsley Corner
NEWMARKET ROAD
A1303
A14
LITTLE WILBRAHAM ROAD
WILBRAHAM ROAD
CB1
Frog End
FEN ROAD
Primrose Farm
PRIMROSE FARM ROAD
Coville Farm
ORCHARD CL
MANOR CL
HIGH ST
RECTORY FARM RD
Rectory Farm
CHURCH RD
GREAT WILBRAHAM ROAD
Little Wilbraham River
Windmill
MILL ROAD
Mill Road Farm
Little Wilbraham
Hawk Mill Farm
THE LANES

85
67

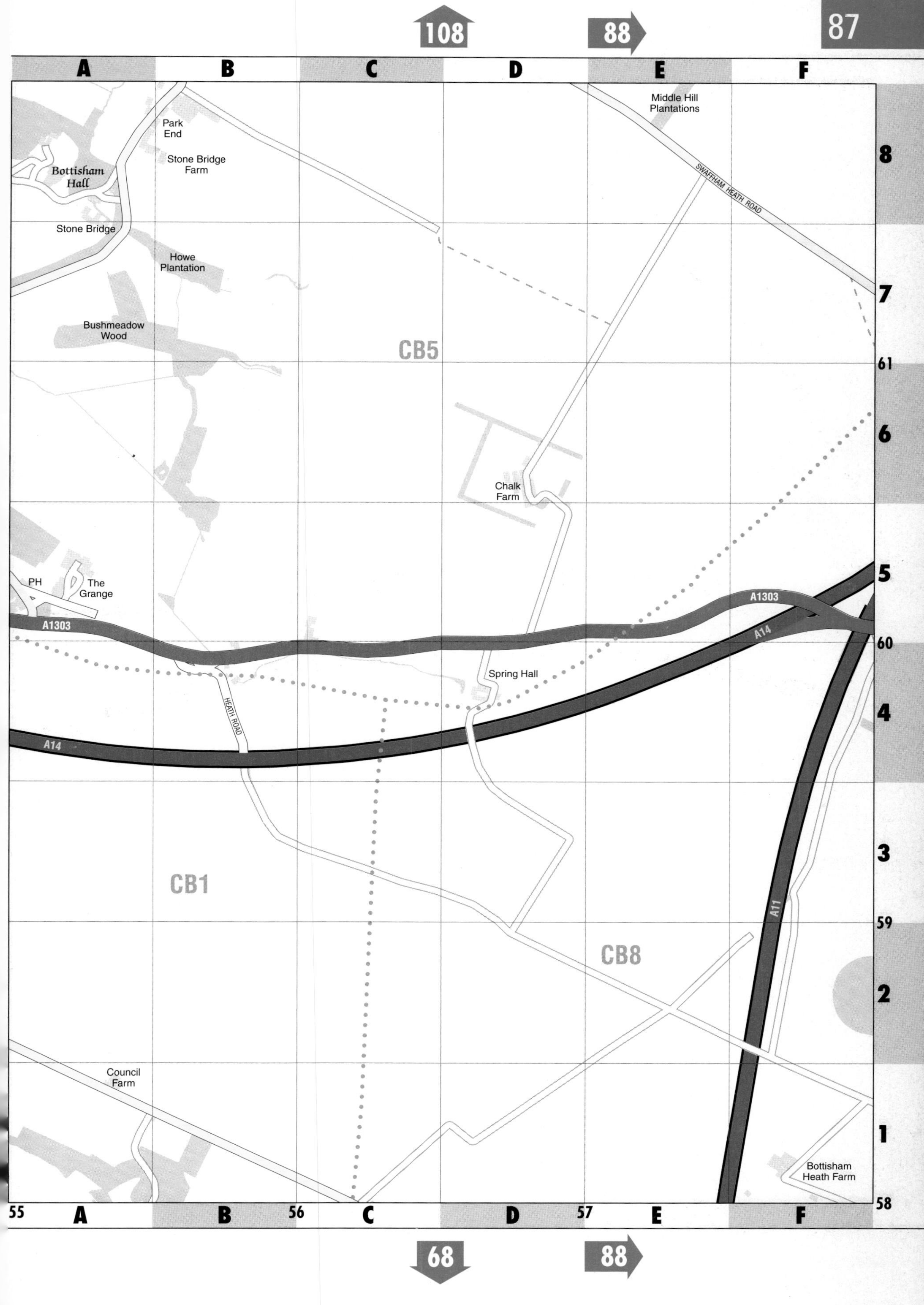

A B C D E F

8

Middle Hill
Plantations

SWAFFHAM HEATH ROAD

Park
End

Stone Bridge
Farm

Bottisham
Hall

Stone Bridge

7

Howe
Plantation

CB5

Bushmeadow
Wood

61

6

Chalk
Farm

5

A1303

PH

The
Grange

A1303

A14

60

HEATH ROAD

Spring Hall

4

A14

3

A11

CB1

59

2

CB8

Council
Farm

1

Bottisham
Heath Farm

58

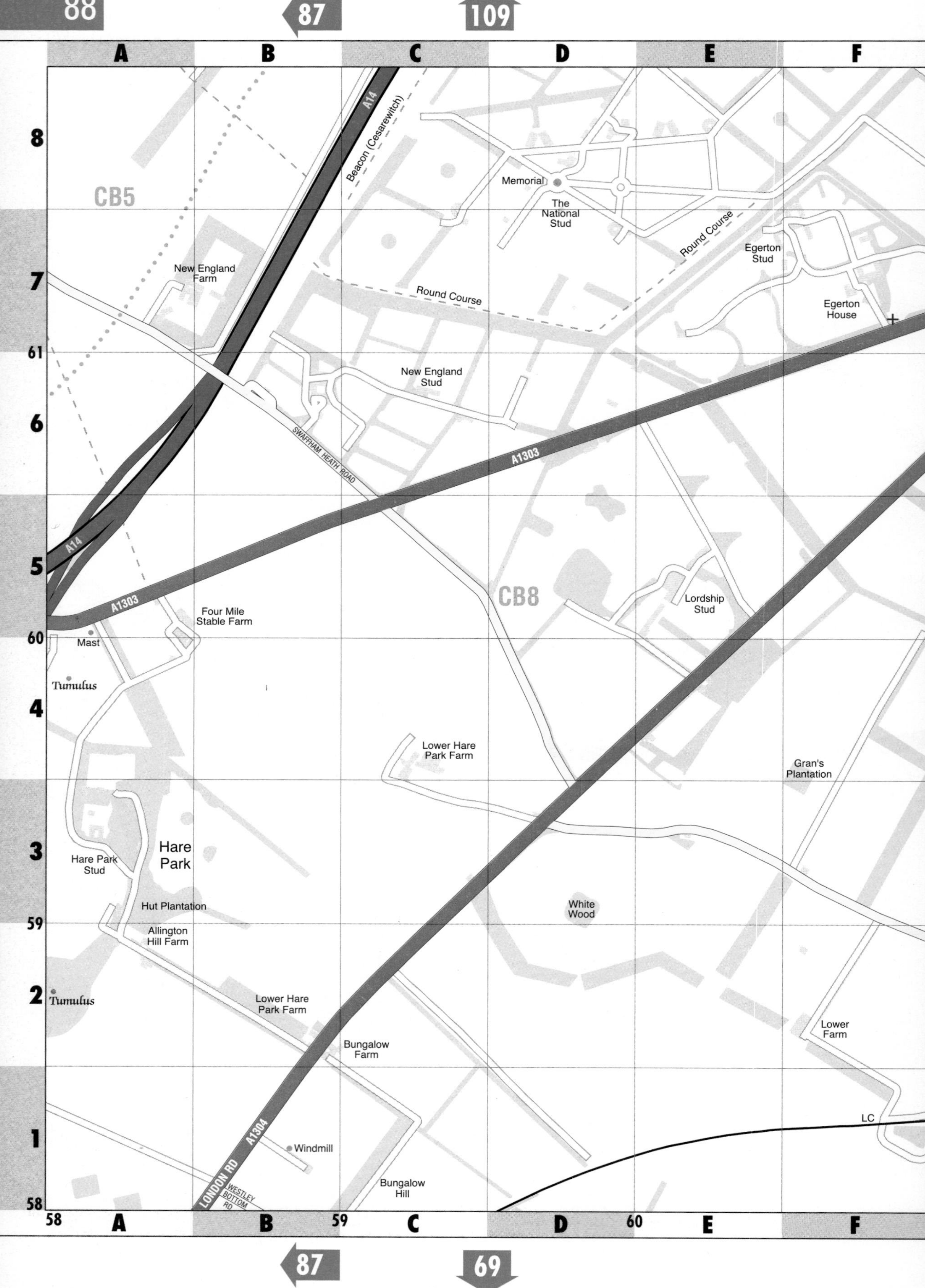

A B C D E F

8

CB5

New England Farm

7

61

Round Course

6

A14

SWAFFHAM HEATH ROAD

A1303

5

A14

A1303

Four Mile Stable Farm

60

Mast

Tumulus

4

Lower Hare Park Farm

3

Hare Park

Hare Park Stud

Hut Plantation

59

Allington Hill Farm

2

Tumulus

Lower Hare Park Farm

Bungalow Farm

1

A1304

LONDON RD

WESTLEY BOTTOM RD

Windmill

Bungalow Hill

58

58 A B 59 C D 60 E F

Beacon (Cesarewitch)

Memorial

The National Stud

Round Course

Egerton Stud

Egerton House

New England Stud

CB8

Lordship Stud

Gran's Plantation

White Wood

Lower Farm

LC

110
90

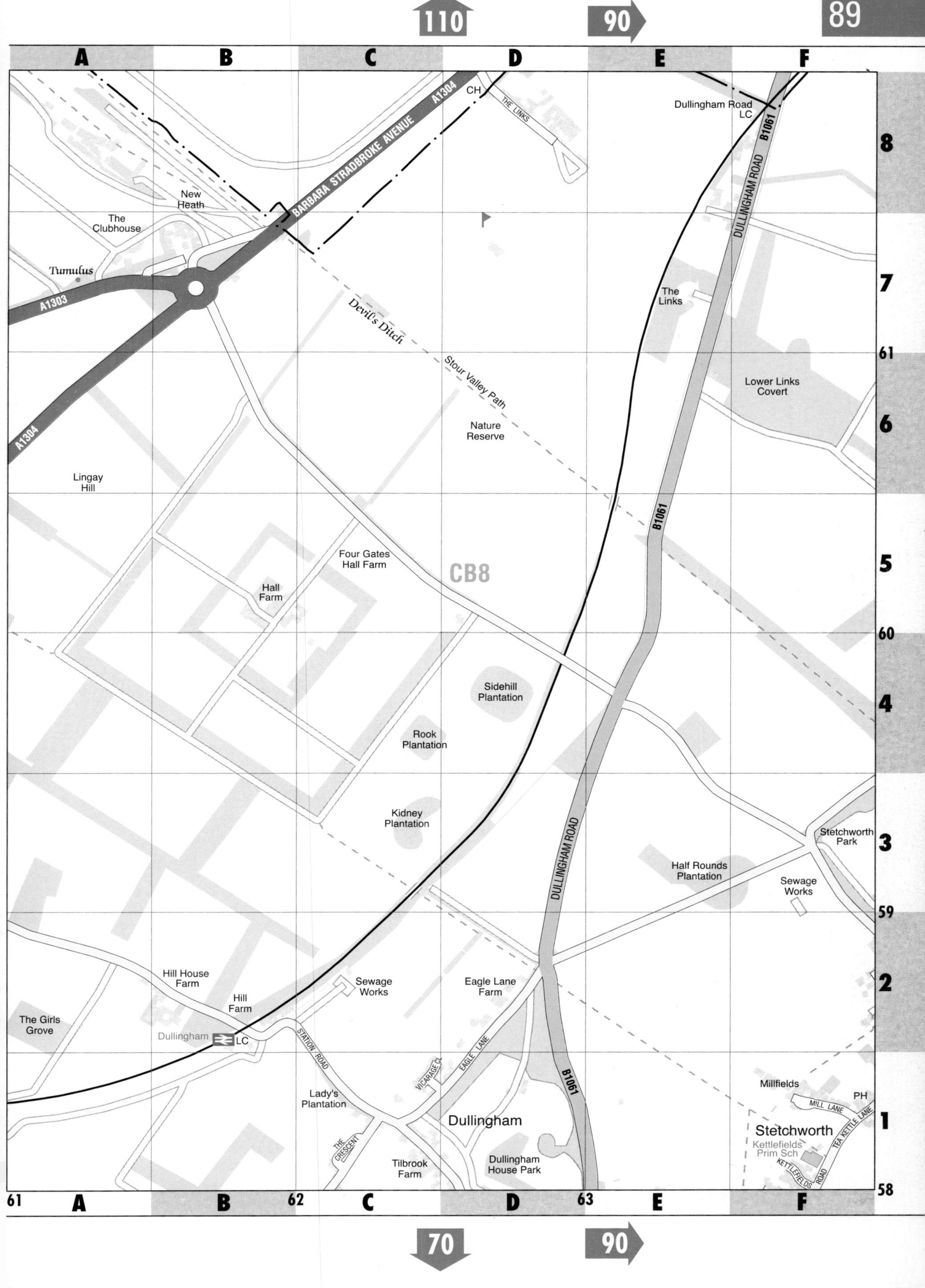
A
B
C
D
E
F
8
7
61
6
5
60
4
3
59
2
1
58
61
62
63
CH
THE LINKS
Dullingham Road
LC
B1061
A1304
BARBARA STRADBROKE AVENUE
DULLINGHAM ROAD
New
Heath
The
Clubhouse
Tumulus
A1303
The
Links
Devil's Ditch
Stour Valley Path
Lower Links
Covert
Nature
Reserve
A1304
Lingay
Hill
B1061
Four Gates
Hall Farm
CB8
Hall
Farm
Sidehill
Plantation
Rook
Plantation
Kidney
Plantation
Stetchworth
Park
DULLINGHAM ROAD
Half Rounds
Plantation
Sewage
Works
Hill House
Farm
Sewage
Works
Eagle Lane
Farm
Hill
Farm
The Girls
Grove
Dullingham
LC
STATION ROAD
EAGLE LANE
VICARAGE CL
B1061
Millfields
PH
MILL LANE
TEA KETTLE LANE
Lady's
Plantation
Dullingham
Stetchworth
Kettlefields
Prim Sch
KETTLEFIELDS
ROAD
THE CRESCENT
Tilbrook
Farm
Dullingham
House Park

70
90

89
111

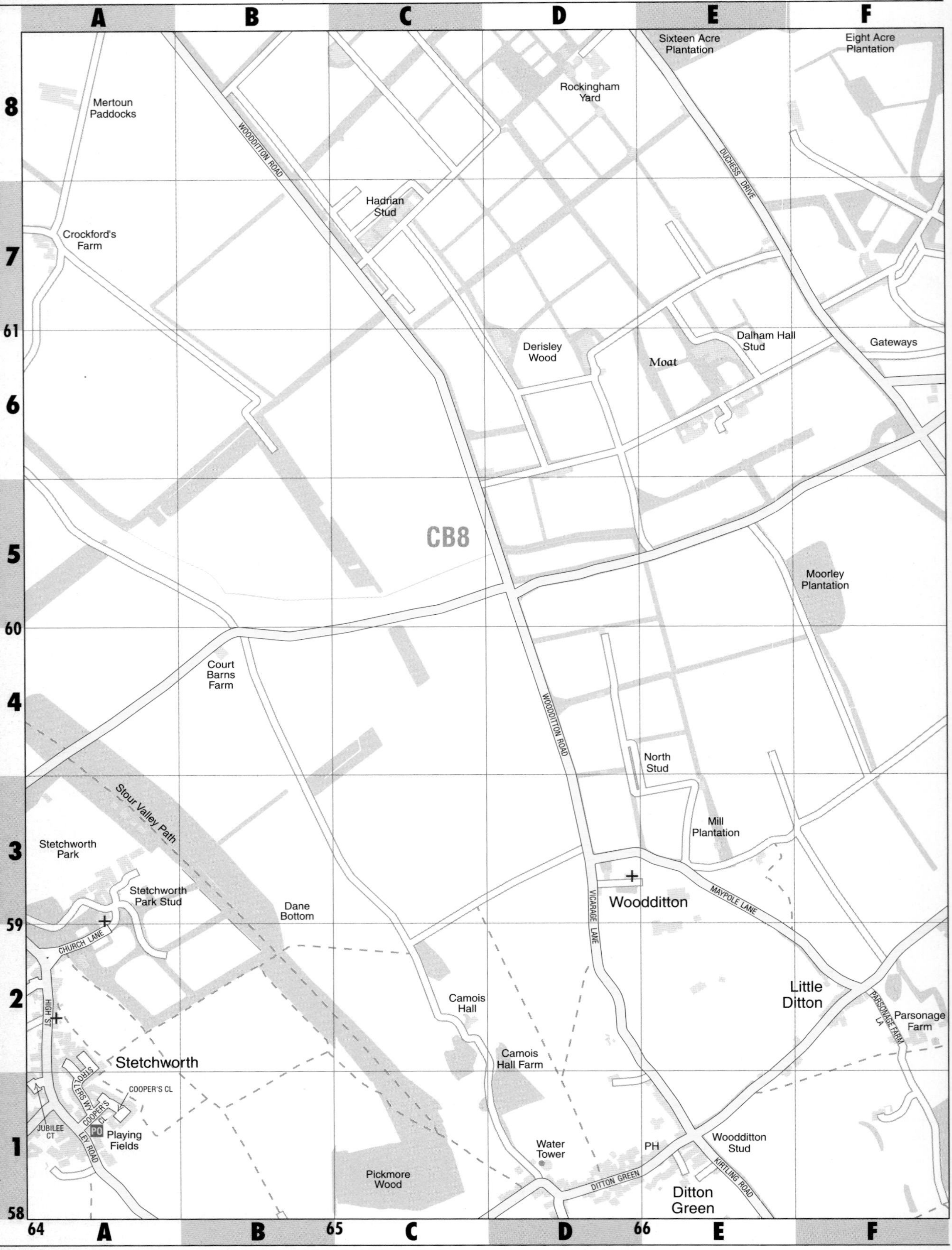

A   B   C   D   E   F

8

Mertoun
Paddocks

WOODDITTON ROAD

Sixteen Acre
Plantation

Eight Acre
Plantation

Rockingham
Yard

Hadrian
Stud

Crockford's
Farm

7

DUCHESS DRIVE

61

Derisley
Wood

Moat

Dalham Hall
Stud

Gateways

6

CB8

Moorley
Plantation

5

60

Court Barns
Farm

4

WOODDITTON ROAD

North
Stud

Mill
Plantation

Stour Valley Path

3

Stetchworth
Park

VICARAGE LANE

Woodditton

MAYPOLE LANE

Stetchworth
Park Stud

Dane
Bottom

59

CHURCH LANE

Little
Ditton

PARSONAGE FARM LA

2

HIGH ST

Camois
Hall

Parsonage
Farm

Stetchworth

COOPER'S CL

Camois
Hall Farm

COOPERS IVY CL

COOPER'S CL

JUBILEE CT

PO

Playing
Fields

Water
Tower

PH

Wood ditton
Stud

KIRTLING ROAD

1

LEY ROAD

Pickmore
Wood

DITTON GREEN

Ditton
Green

58

64   A   B   65   C   D   66   E   F

89
71

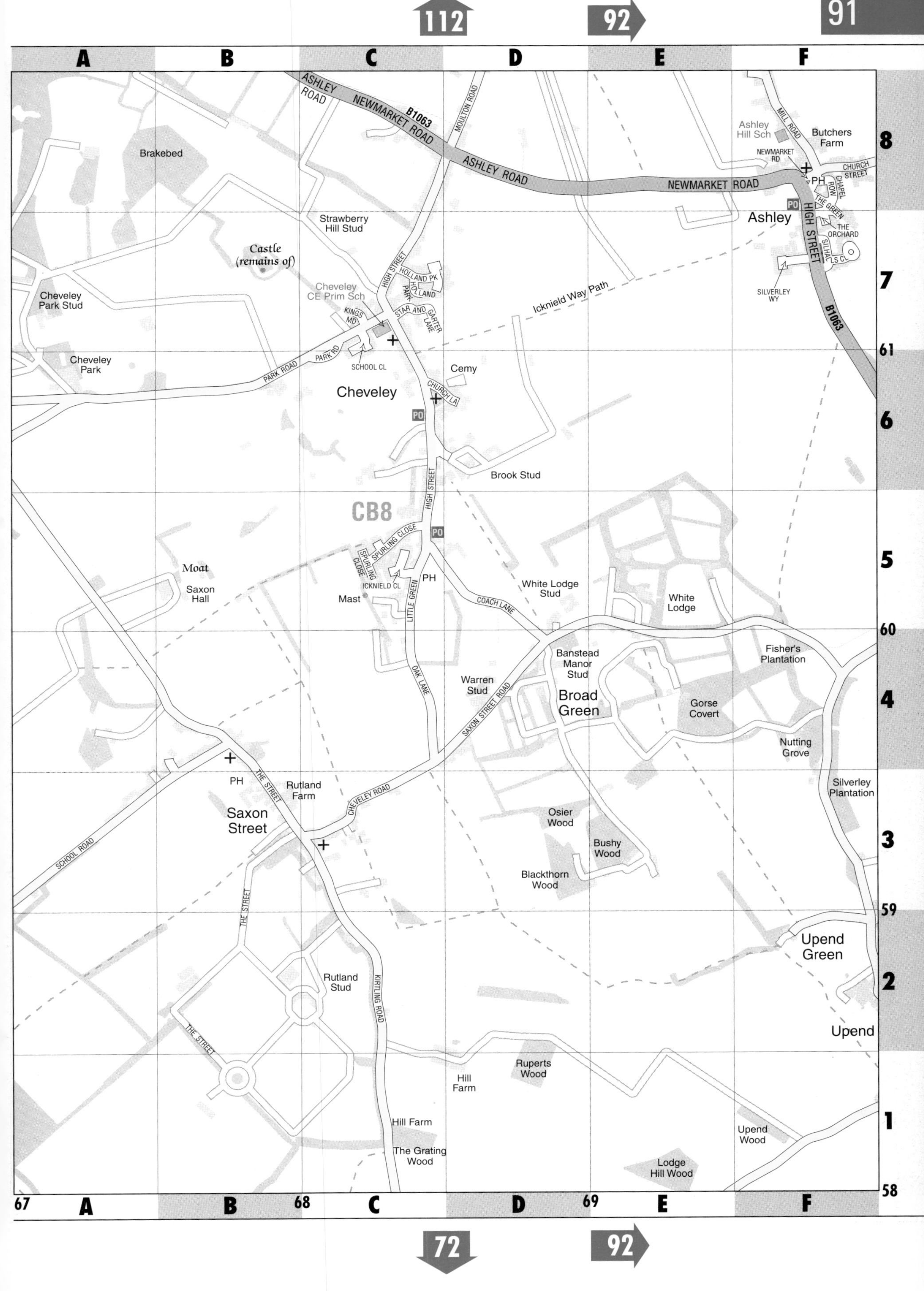
112
92
A
B
C
D
E
F
ASHLEY ROAD
NEWMARKET ROAD
B1063
MOULTON ROAD
ASHLEY ROAD
NEWMARKET ROAD
Brakebed
Strawberry Hill Stud
Castle (remains of)
Cheveley Park Stud
Cheveley CE Prim Sch
HIGH STREET
HOLLAND PK
HOLLAND PARK
STAR AND GARTER LANE
KINGS MD
PARK ROAD
PARK RD
SCHOOL CL
Cheveley Park
Cemy
Cheveley
CHURCH LA
PO
Brook Stud
HIGH STREET
CB8
SPURLING CLOSE
ICKNIELD CL
PH
Mast
Moat
Saxon Hall
LITTLE GREEN
COACH LANE
White Lodge Stud
White Lodge
Icknield Way Path
Ashley Hill Sch
Butchers Farm
MILL ROAD
NEWMARKET RD
CHURCH STREET
CHAPEL ROW
THE GREEN
Ashley
THE ORCHARD
SILHALLS CL
SILVERLEY WY
B1063
Banstead Manor Stud
Broad Green
Warren Stud
OAK LANE
SAXON STREET ROAD
Gorse Covert
Fisher's Plantation
Nutting Grove
Silverley Plantation
Rutland Farm
THE STREET
Saxon Street
CHEVELEY ROAD
SCHOOL ROAD
Osier Wood
Bushy Wood
Blackthorn Wood
Upend Green
Upend
Rutland Stud
KIRTLING ROAD
THE STREET
Ruperts Wood
Hill Farm
Hill Farm
The Grating Wood
Upend Wood
Lodge Hill Wood
8
7
61
6
5
60
4
3
59
2
1
58
67
68
69
72
92

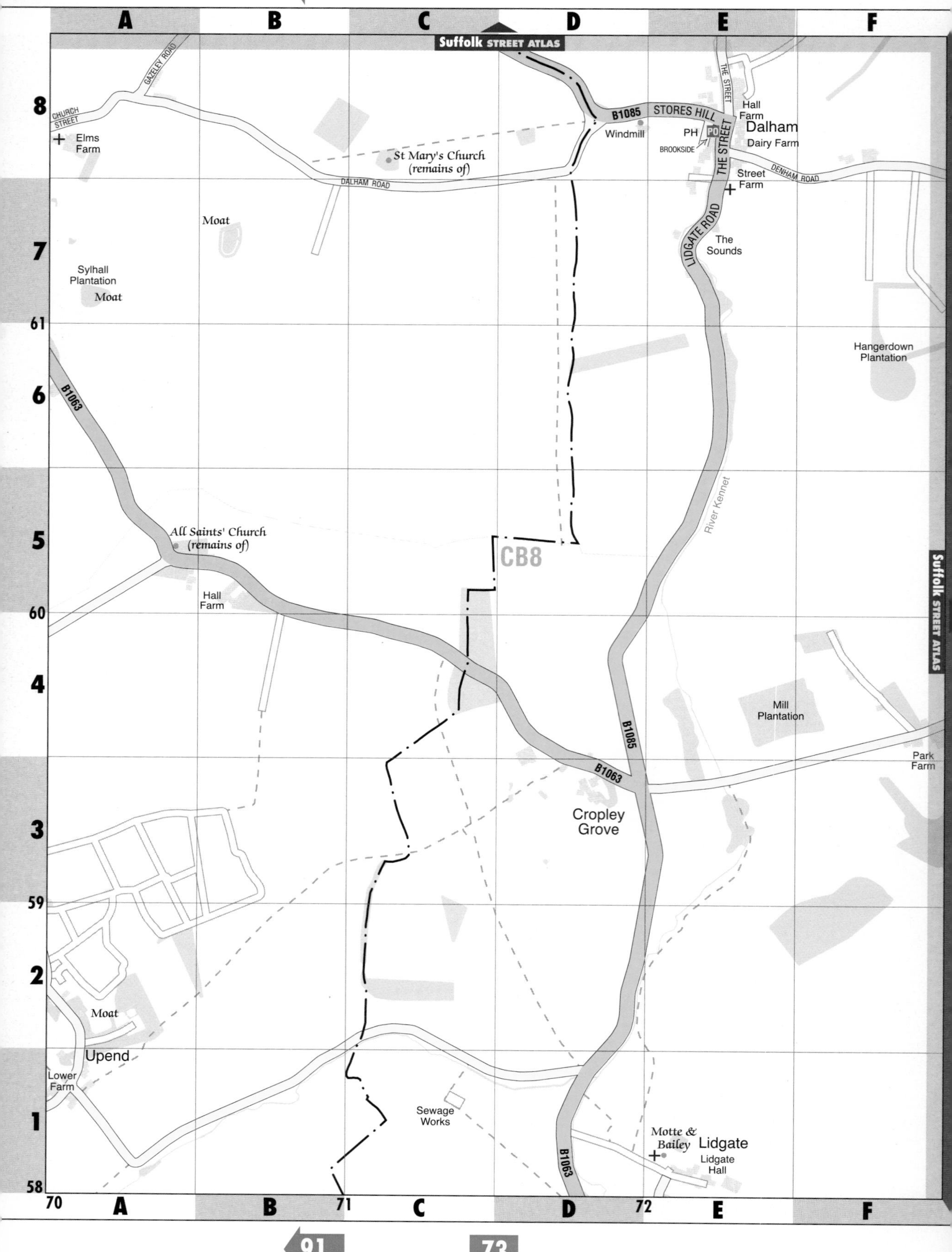

Suffolk STREET ATLAS

A B C D E F

8

CHURCH
STREET
GAZELEY ROAD
Elms
Farm

B1085 STORES HILL
Windmill

Hall
Farm
Dalham
PH
P
Dairy Farm
BROOKSIDE
THE STREET

DALHAM ROAD
St Mary's Church
(remains of)

Street
Farm
DENHAM ROAD

7

Moat

Sylhall
Plantation
Moat

The
Sounds
LIDGATE ROAD

Hangerdown
Plantation

61

6

B1063

River Kennet

5

All Saints' Church
(remains of)
CB8

60

4

Hall
Farm

Mill
Plantation

B1085

Park
Farm

3

Cropley
Grove

59

2

Moat

1

Upend

Lower
Farm

Sewage
Works

B1063
Motte &
Bailey
Lidgate
Lidgate Hall

58

70 A B 71 C D 72 E F

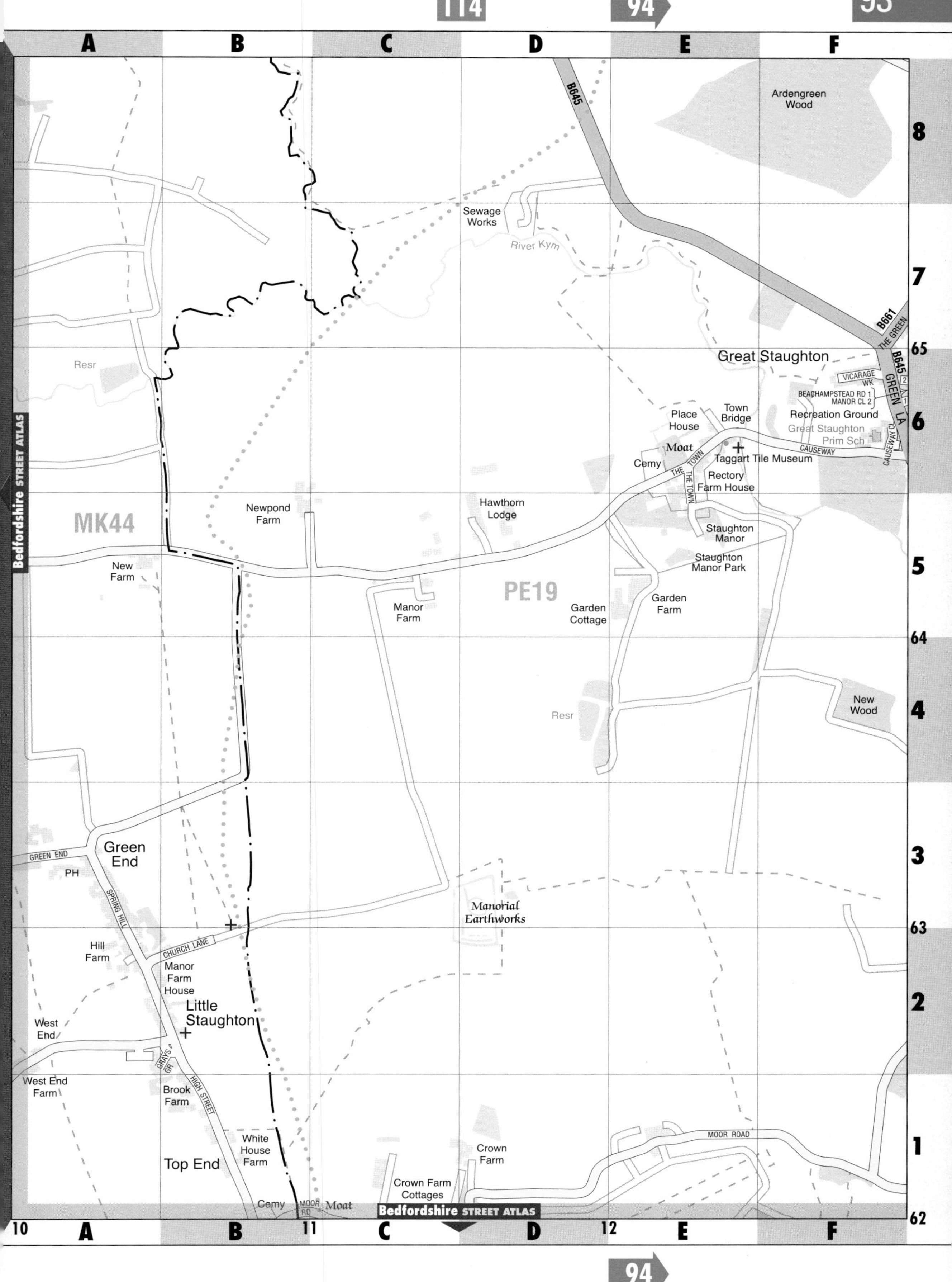

A   B   C   D   E   F

8

Ardengreen
Wood

7

B645

Sewage
Works

River Kym

65

Great Staughton

B661

THE GREEN

GREEN LA

B645

CAUSEWAY

VICARAGE
WK

BEACHAMPSTEAD RD 1
MANOR CL 2

Recreation Ground

Great Staughton
Prim Sch

6

Place
House

Town
Bridge

Moat

Cemy

Taggart Tile Museum

THE TOWN

Rectory
Farm House

Newpond
Farm

Hawthorn
Lodge

Staughton
Manor

MK44

New
Farm

Manor
Farm

PE19

Garden
Cottage

Staughton
Manor Park

Garden
Farm

5

64

Resr

New
Wood

4

Green End

PH

Green
End

SPRING HILL

CHURCH LANE

Manorial
Earthworks

3

63

Hill
Farm

Manor
Farm
House

West
End

Little
Staughton

2

West End
Farm

GRAY'S
DR

Brook
Farm

HIGH STREET

MOOR ROAD

Crown
Farm

Crown Farm
Cottages

Top End

White
House
Farm

MOOR
RD

Moat

Cemy

1

62

Bedfordshire STREET ATLAS

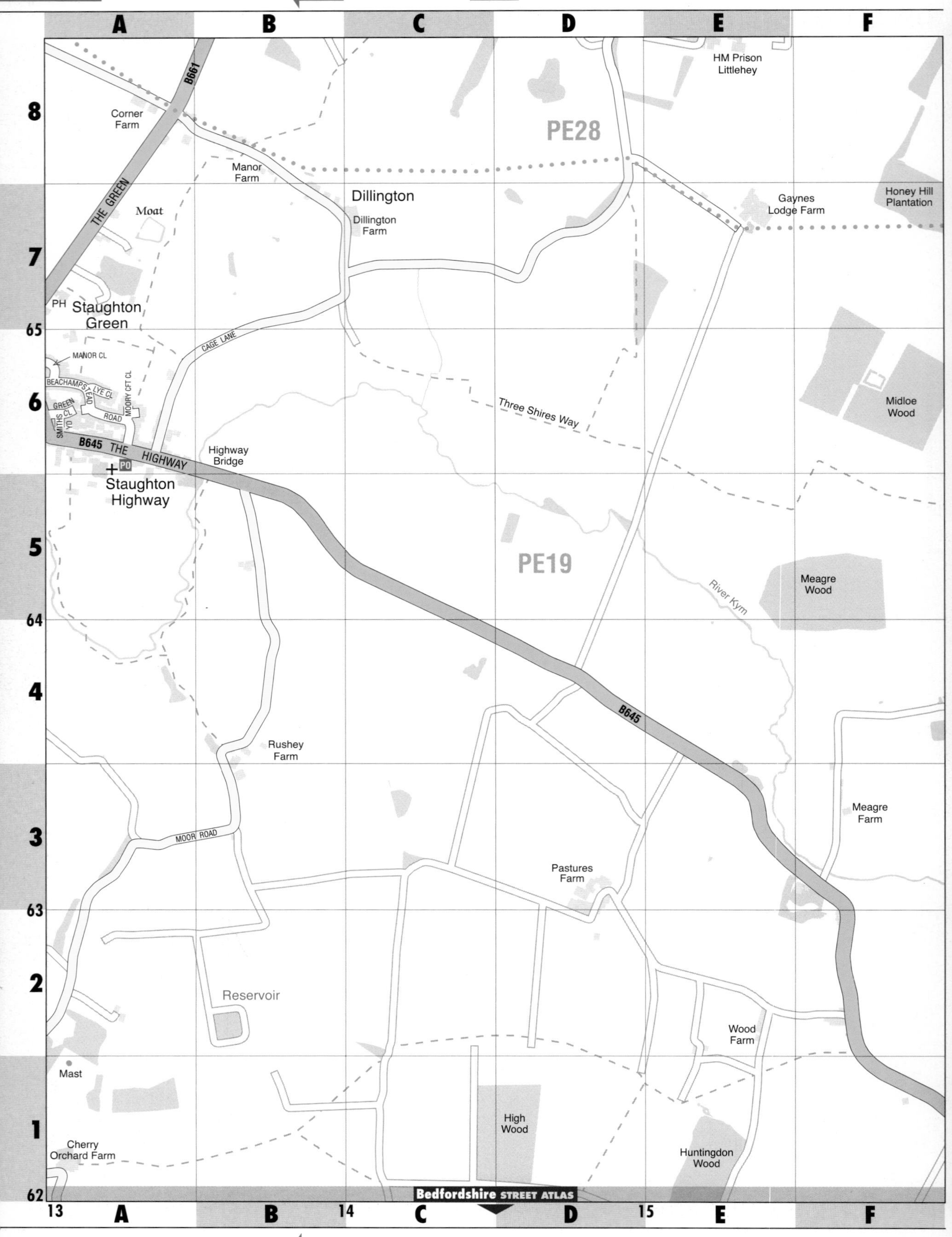

A B C D E F

Corner Farm

PE28

HM Prison Littlehey

Manor Farm

Honey Hill Plantation

Dillington

Gaynes Lodge Farm

Moat

Dillington Farm

PH Staughton Green

CAGE LANE

MANOR CL

Midloe Wood

Three Shires Way

B645 THE HIGHWAY

Highway Bridge

Staughton Highway

PE19

River Kym

Meagre Wood

B645

Rushey Farm

Meagre Farm

MOOR ROAD

Pastures Farm

Reservoir

Wood Farm

Mast

High Wood

Cherry Orchard Farm

Huntingdon Wood

116
96

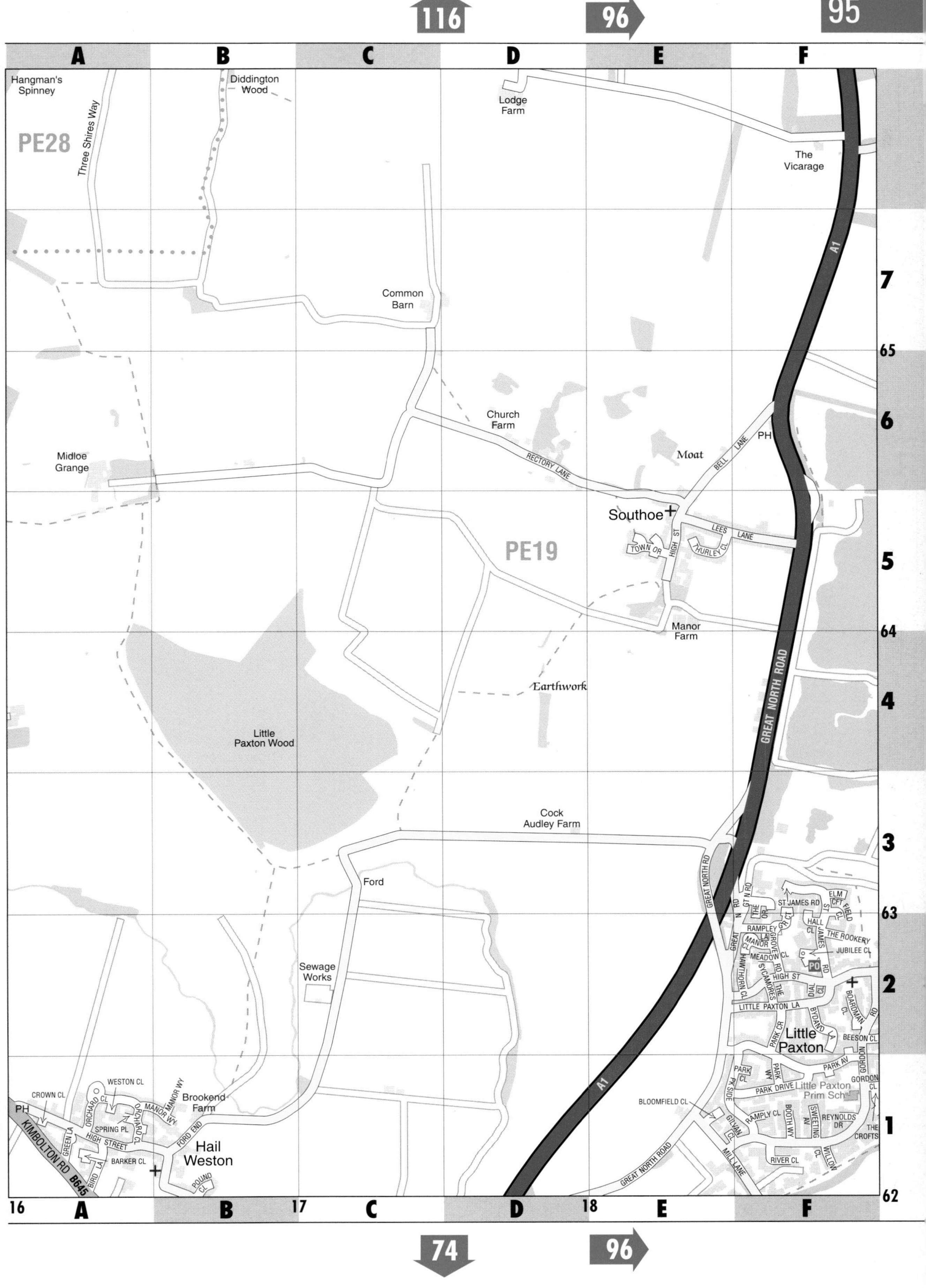
A
B
C
D
E
F
Hangman's Spinney
Diddington Wood
PE28
Three Shires Way
Lodge Farm
The Vicarage
A1
7
Common Barn
65
Church Farm
6
Midloe Grange
Moat
PH
BELL LANE
RECTORY LANE
Southoe
LEES LANE
TOWN OR
HIGH ST
HURLEY CL
PE19
5
Manor Farm
64
GREAT NORTH ROAD
Earthwork
4
Little Paxton Wood
Cock Audley Farm
3
Ford
GREAT NORTH RD
ST JAMES RD
ELM CFT
FIELD
HALL CL
JAMES ST
RAMPLEY LA
GROVE
MANOR CL
THE ROOKERY
JUBILEE CL
MEADOW CL
HAWTHORN CL
SYCAMORES
HIGH ST
DIAL CL
PO
63
Sewage Works
LITTLE PAXTON LA
BOARDMAN CL
BYDAND
PARK CR
Little Paxton
BEESON CL
GORDON RD
2
PARK AV
PARK CL
PARK WY
PARK DRIVE
PK SIDE
Little Paxton Prim Sch
GORDON CL
BLOOMFIELD CL
RAMPLY CL
BOOTH WY
SWEETING AV
REYNOLDS DR
THE CROFTS
GILVAN CL
MILL LANE
RIVER CL
WILLOW CL
GREAT NORTH ROAD
1
WESTON CL
CROWN CL
PH
ORCHARD CL
MANOR WY
Brookend Farm
SPRING PL
HIGH STREET
FORD END
GREEN LA
KIMBOLTON RD
B645
BARKER CL
BIRD LA
Hail Weston
POUND CL
62
16
17
18

74
96

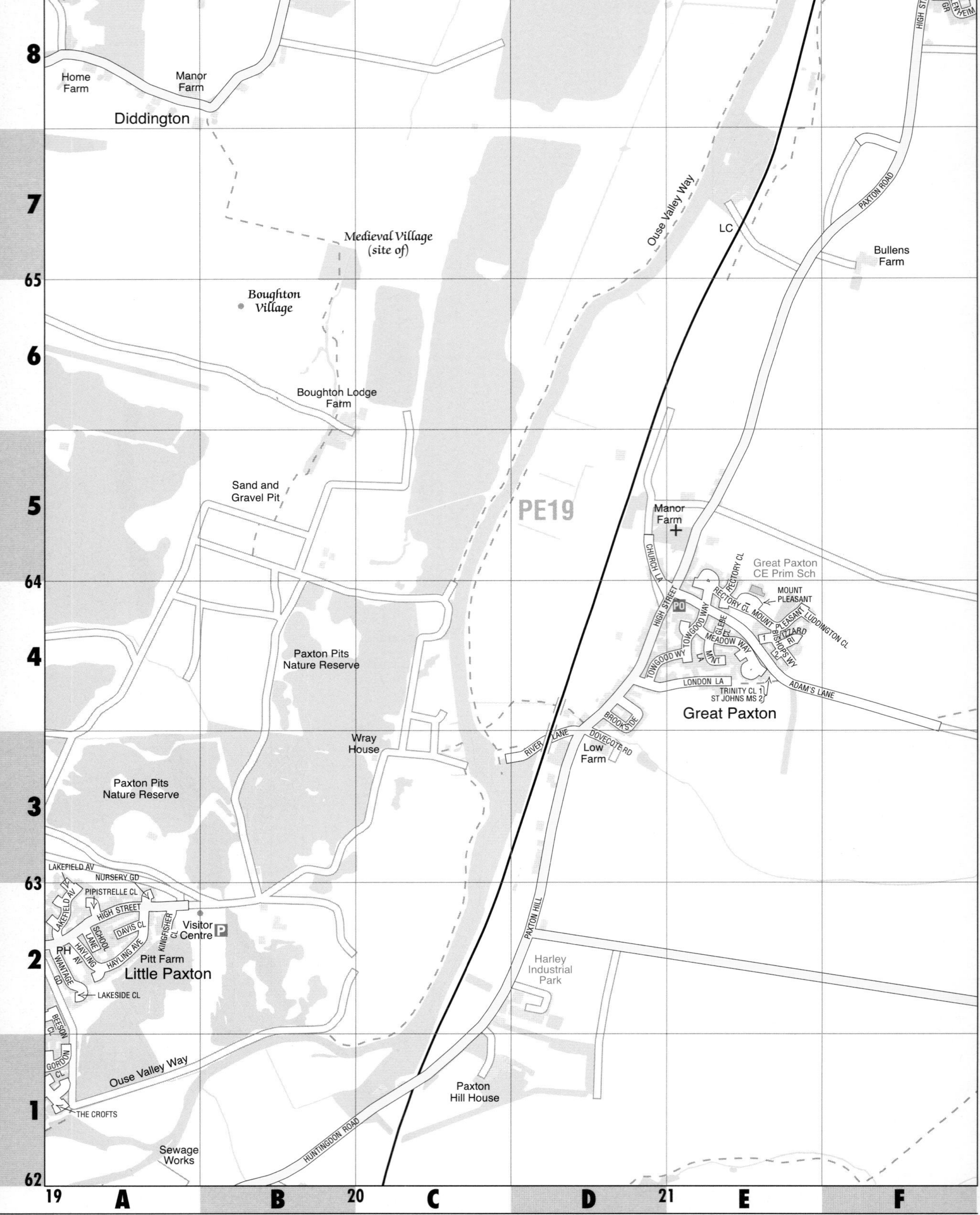

8

Home
Farm

Manor
Farm

Diddington

High Street

APPLE
CL

BLENHEIM
GR

7

Ouse Valley Way

LC

Paxton Road

Bullens
Farm

Medieval Village
(site of)

65

Boughton
Village

6

Boughton Lodge
Farm

Sand and
Gravel Pit

PE19

Manor
Farm

Great Paxton
CE Prim Sch

5

64

RECTORY CL

MOUNT
PLEASANT

LUDDINGTON CL

CHURCH LA

HIGH STREET

PO

TOWGOOD WAY

RECTORY CL

GLEBE
CL

BISHOPS WY

BUZZARD
CL

Paxton Pits
Nature Reserve

4

MEADOW WAY

TOWGOOD WY

LONDON LA

TRINITY CL 1
ST JOHNS MS 2

ADAM'S LANE

Great Paxton

Wray
House

RIVER LANE

BROOK'S
DE

DOVECOTE RD

Low
Farm

3

Paxton Pits
Nature Reserve

63

LAKEFIELD AV

NURSERY GD

PIPISTRELLE CL

LAKEFIELD AV

HIGH STREET

DAVIS CL

KINGFISHER
CL

Visitor
Centre

P

SCHOOL
LANE

2

PH

HAYLING AVE

WANTAGE
GD

Pitt Farm

Little Paxton

Paxton Hill

Harley
Industrial
Park

LAKESIDE CL

BEESON
CL

GORDON
CL

Ouse Valley Way

1

THE CROFTS

Paxton
Hill House

Sewage
Works

HUNTINGDON ROAD

62

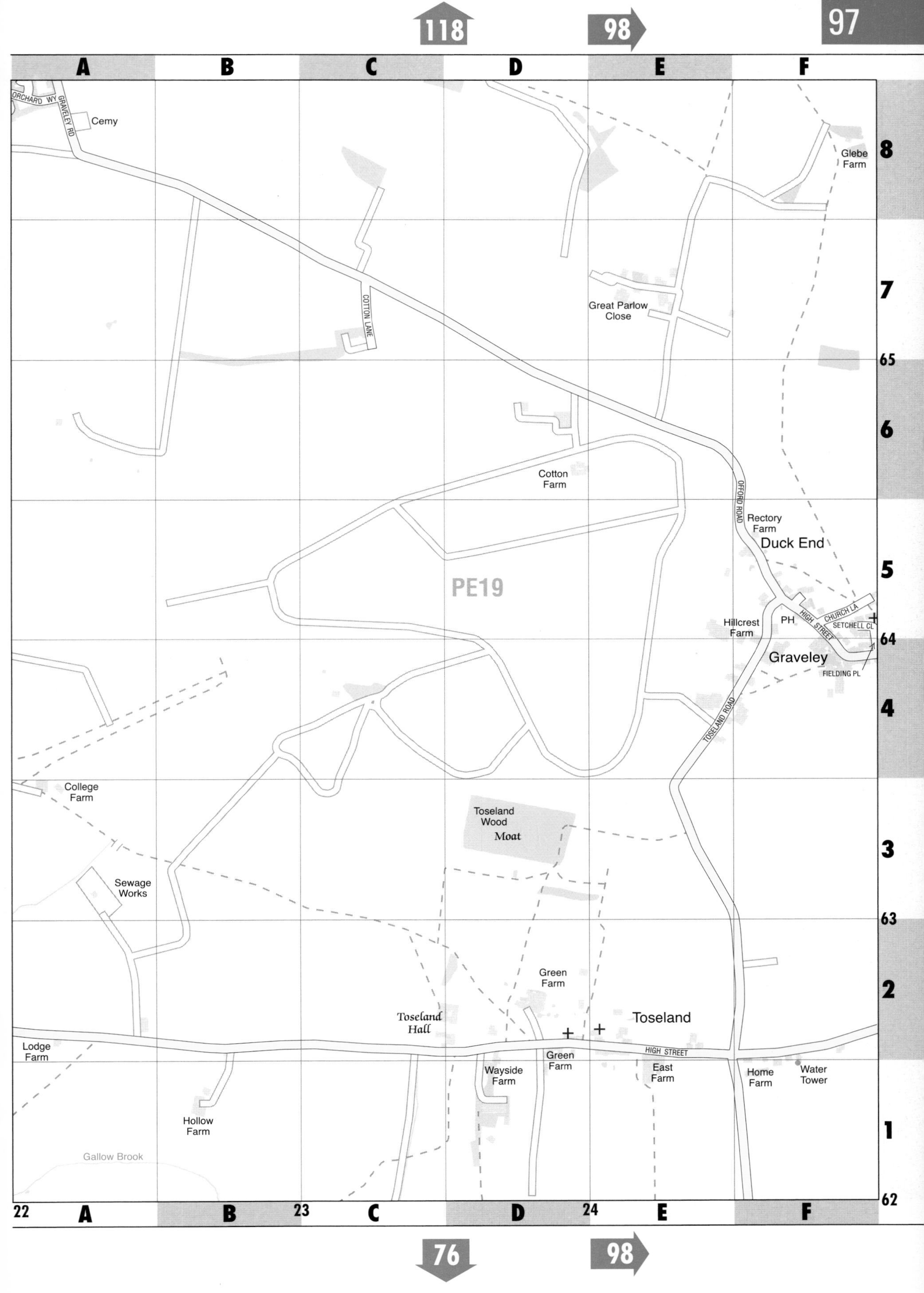

A B C D E F

ORCHARD WY
GRAVELEY RD

Cemy

8

COTTON LANE

7

65

6

Cotton
Farm

OFFORD ROAD

Rectory
Farm

Duck End

5

PE19

Great Parlow
Close

Hillcrest
Farm

PH.

HIGH STREET

CHURCH LA

SETCHELL CL

Graveley

64

FIELDING PL

4

TOSELAND ROAD

College
Farm

Toseland
Wood
Moat

3

Sewage
Works

63

Green
Farm

2

Toseland
Hall

Toseland

Lodge
Farm

Green
Farm

HIGH STREET

East
Farm

Home
Farm

Water
Tower

Wayside
Farm

Hollow
Farm

1

Gallow Brook

62

97
119

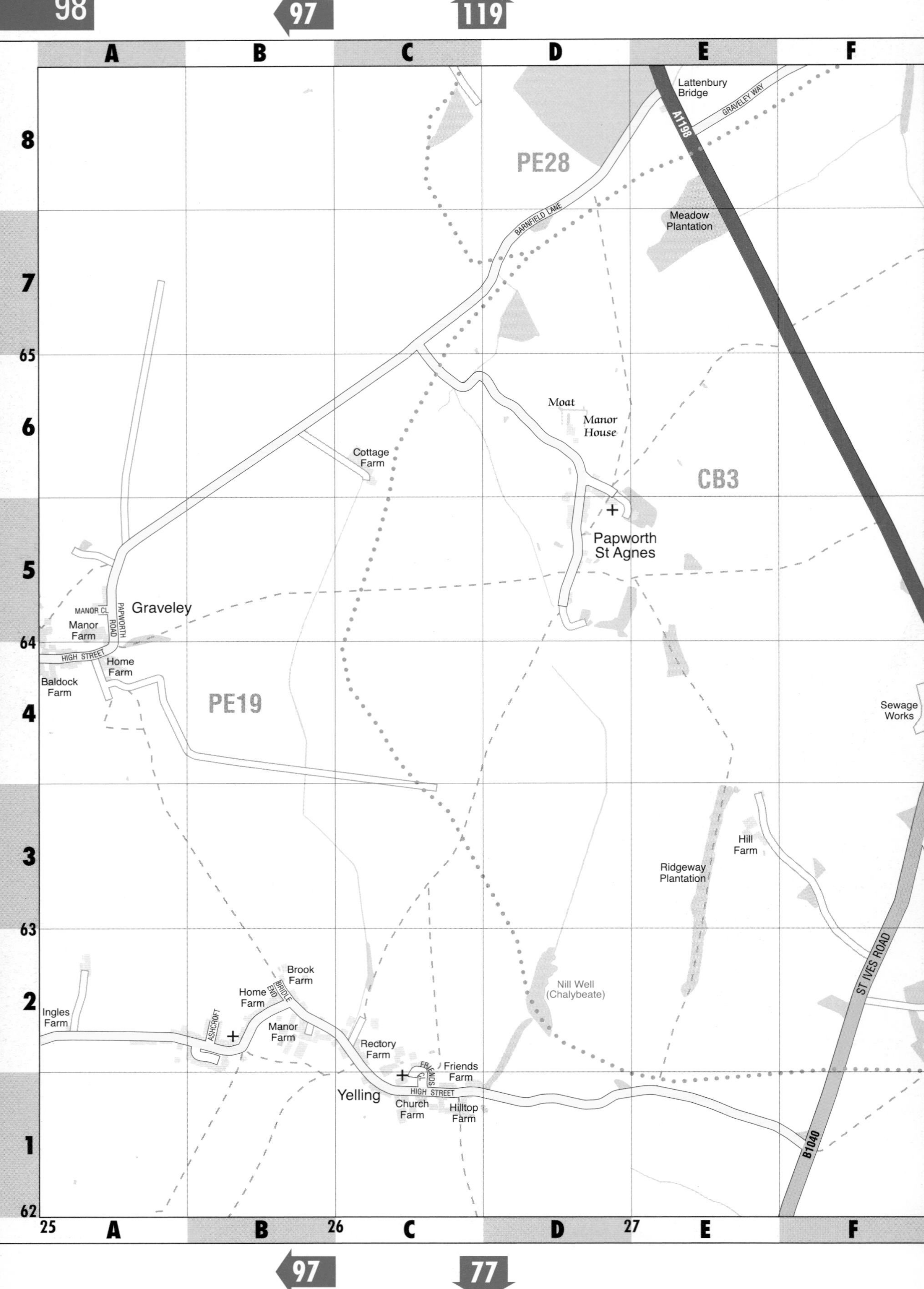
A
B
C
D
E
F
8
7
65
6
5
64
4
3
63
2
1
62
25
26
27
Lattenbury Bridge
GRAVELEY WAY
A1198
PE28
BARNFIELD LANE
Meadow Plantation
Moat
Manor House
Cottage Farm
CB3
Papworth St Agnes
Graveley
MANOR CL
PAPWORTH ROAD
Manor Farm
HIGH STREET
Home Farm
Baldock Farm
PE19
Sewage Works
Hill Farm
Ridgeway Plantation
ST IVES ROAD
Nill Well (Chalybeate)
Brook Farm
Home Farm
END
BRIDLE
Ingles Farm
ASHCROFT
Manor Farm
Rectory Farm
FRIENDS CL
Friends Farm
HIGH STREET
Yelling
Church Farm
Hilltop Farm
B1040

97
77

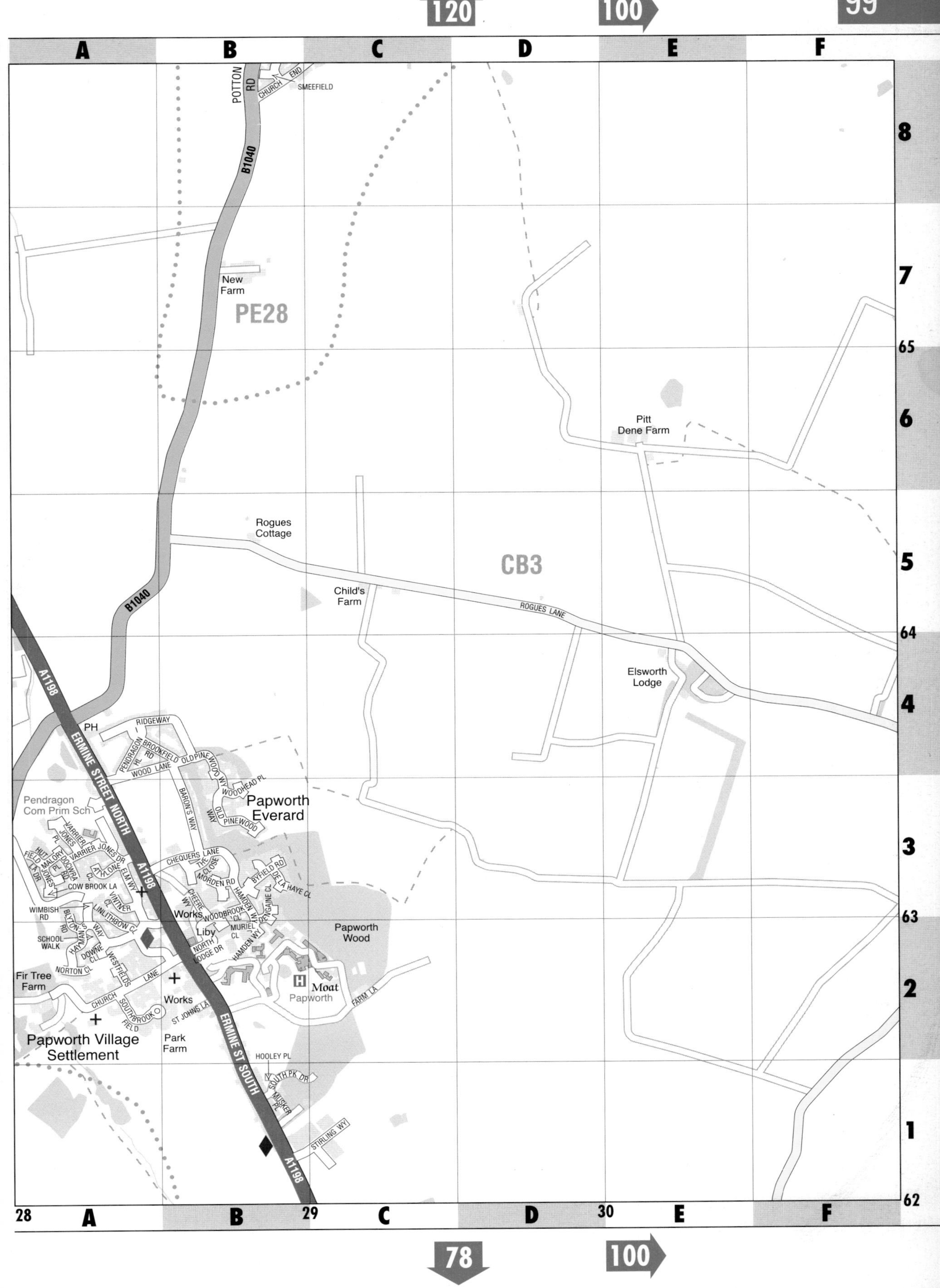

120
100
A
B
C
D
E
F
8
7
65
6
5
64
4
3
63
2
1
62
28
29
30
POTTON RD
CHURCH
END
SMEEFIELD
B1040
New Farm
PE28
Pitt Dene Farm
Rogues Cottage
CB3
Child's Farm
ROGUES LANE
Elsworth Lodge
A1198
PH
RIDGEWAY
ERMINE STREET NORTH
PENDRAGON HL
BROOKFIELD RD
OLD PINE WOOD WY
WOOD LANE
WOODHEAD PL
BARON'S WAY
OLD WAY
PINEWOOD
Papworth Everard
Pendragon Com Prim Sch
VARRIER JONES PL
VARRIER JONES DR
HUTFIELD DR
MALORY PL
DOCWRA RD
ATHLONE CL
ELM WY
CHEQUERS LANE
THE CLOSE
MORDEN RD
BYFIELD RD
DE LA HAYE CL
COW BROOK LA
VINTNER
WIMBISH RD
CHEERE WY
WOODBROOK CL
HAMDEN WY
PENGAINE CL
LINLITHGOW CL
Works
Liby
MURIEL CL
SCHOOL WALK
HAYMANS WAY
DOWNE CL
NORTH LODGE DR
HAMDEN WY
Papworth Wood
NORTON CL
WESTFIELDS
LANE
Fir Tree Farm
CHURCH
SOUTHBROOK FIELD
Works
H
Moat
Papworth
FARM LA
ST JOHNS LA
Papworth Village Settlement
Park Farm
ERMINE ST SOUTH
HOOLEY PL
SOUTH PK DR
MUSKER PL
STIRLING WY
A1198

78
100

99
121

| A | B | C | D | E | F |

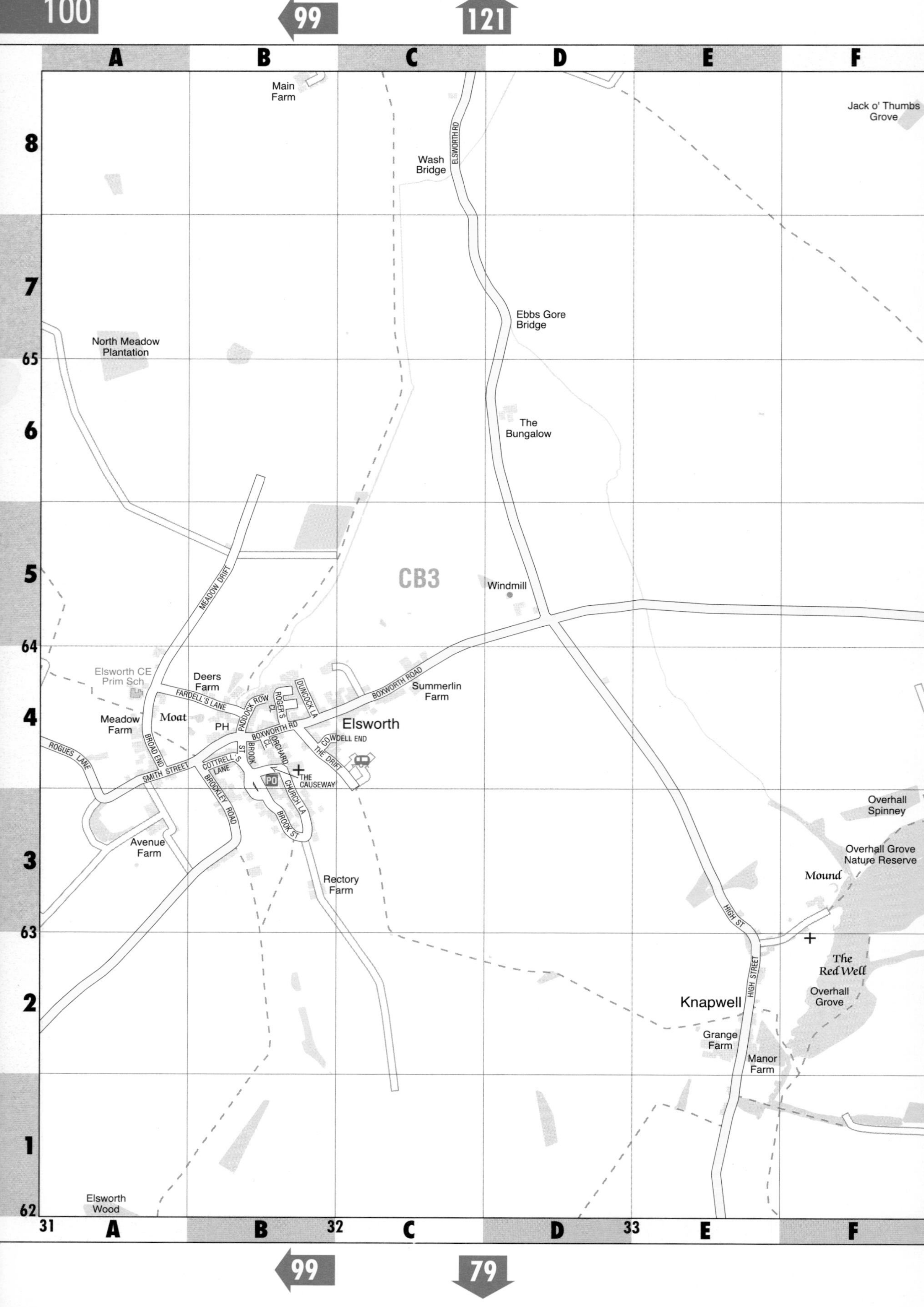

8

Main Farm

Jack o' Thumbs Grove

ELSWORTH RD

Wash Bridge

7

Ebbs Gore Bridge

North Meadow Plantation

65

6

The Bungalow

5

CB3

Windmill

64

Elsworth CE Prim Sch

Deers Farm

Boxworth Road

Summerlin Farm

4

Meadow Farm

FARDELL'S LANE

DUNCOCK LA

ROGER'S CL

Moat

PH

PADDOCK ROW

BOXWORTH RD

Elsworth

ROGUES LANE

BROAD END RD

SMITH STREET

COTTRELL'S LANE

BROOKLEY ROAD

BROOK ST'S

ST'S

ORCHARD

BROOK

THE DRIFT

COWDELL END

PO

THE CAUSEWAY

CHURCH LA

Overhall Spinney

Overhall Grove Nature Reserve

3

Avenue Farm

BROOK ST'S

Rectory Farm

Mound

63

Overhall Grove

The Red Well

2

Knapwell

HIGH ST

HIGH STREET

Grange Farm

Manor Farm

1

Elsworth Wood

62

| 31 | A | B | 32 | C | D | 33 | E | F |

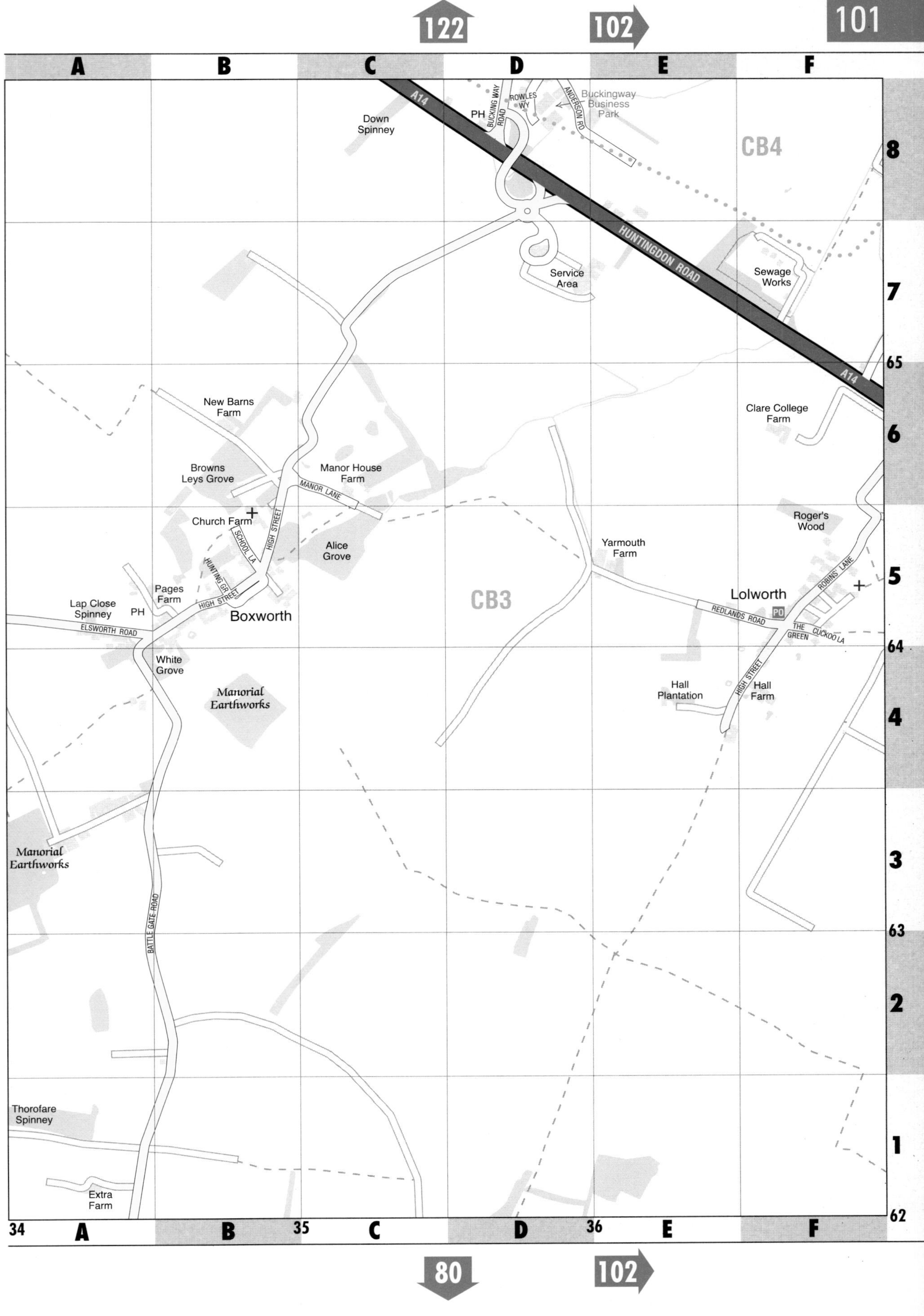
101
122
102
80
102
A
B
C
D
E
F
8
7
65
6
5
64
4
3
63
2
1
62
34
35
36
A14
HUNTINGDON ROAD
PH
BUCKING WAY ROAD
ROWLES WY
ANDERSON RD
Buckingway Business Park
Down Spinney
CB4
Service Area
Sewage Works
New Barns Farm
Clare College Farm
Browns Leys Grove
Manor House Farm
MANOR LANE
Church Farm
HIGH STREET
SCHOOL LA
Alice Grove
Roger's Wood
Yarmouth Farm
HUNTING GR
Pages Farm
Lap Close Spinney
PH
HIGH STREET
Boxworth
ELSWORTH ROAD
CB3
Lolworth
ROBINS' LANE
REDLANDS ROAD
PO
THE GREEN
CUCKOO LA
White Grove
Manorial Earthworks
Hall Plantation
HIGH STREET
Hall Farm
Manorial Earthworks
BATTLE GATE ROAD
Thorofare Spinney
Extra Farm

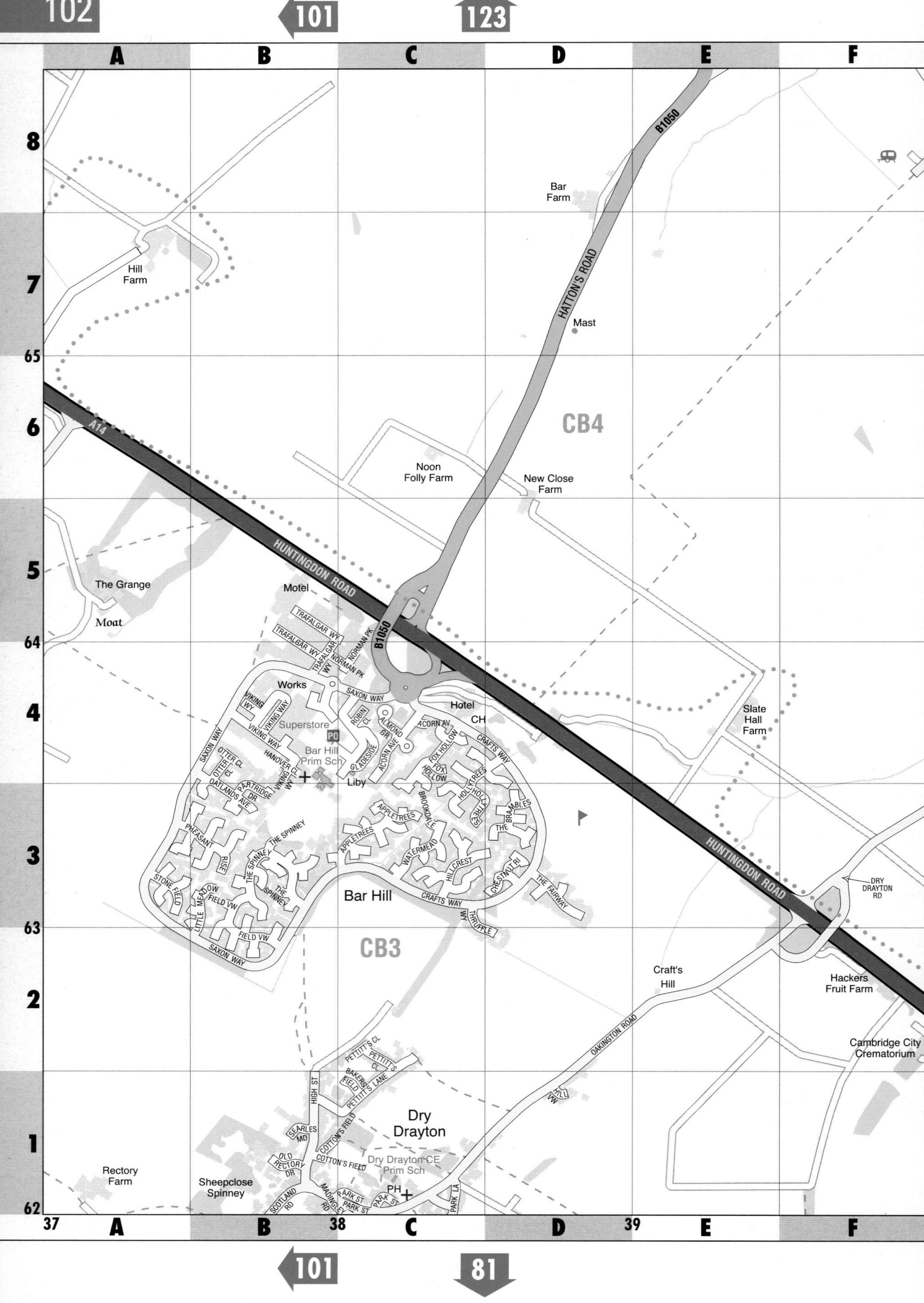

A B C D E F

8

7

65

6

CB4

5

64

4

3

63

2

1

62

37 A B 38 C D 39 E F

B1050

Bar
Farm

HATTON'S ROAD

Mast

A14

Huntingdon Road

Hill
Farm

Noon
Folly Farm

New Close
Farm

The Grange

Moat

Motel

TRAFALGAR WY

TRAFALGAR WY

TRAFALGAR WY

NORMAN PK

B1050

SAXON WAY

VIKING WY

VIKING WAY

VIKING WAY

SAXON WAY

OTTER CL

OTTER CL

HANOVER CL

PARTRIDGE DR

VIKING CT

OATLANDS AVE

PHEASANT

RISE

THE SPINNEY

THE SPINNEY

THE SPINNEY

THE SPINNEY

STONE FIELD

LITTLE MEADOW

FIELD VW

FIELD VW

SAXON WAY

Works

Superstore

PO

Bar Hill
Prim Sch

Liby

ROBIN

ALMOND GR

GLADESIDE

ACORN AV

ACORN AV

FOX HOLLOW

FOX
HOLLOW

Hotel
CH

APPLETREES

APPLETREES

WATERMEAD

BROOKDALE

HOLLYTREES

HOLLYTREES

THE

CRAFTS WAY

THE BRAMBLES

HILLCREST

CHESTNUT CL

CRAFTS WAY

THE FAIRWAY

WY

THROSTLE

Slate
Hall
Farm

Huntingdon Road

DRY
DRAYTON
RD

Bar Hill

CB3

Craft's
Hill

Hackers
Fruit Farm

Cambridge City
Crematorium

OAKINGTON ROAD

FEN

PETTITT'S CL

PETTITT'S
CL

BAKER'S

FIELD

PETTITT'S LANE

HIGH ST

SEARLES
MD

COTTON'S FIELD

COTTON'S FIELD

OLD
RECTORY
DR

SCOTLAND RD

MADINGLEY RD

PARK ST

PARK ST

PARK LA

PARK LA

PH

Dry
Drayton

Dry Drayton CE
Prim Sch

Rectory
Farm

Sheepclose
Spinney

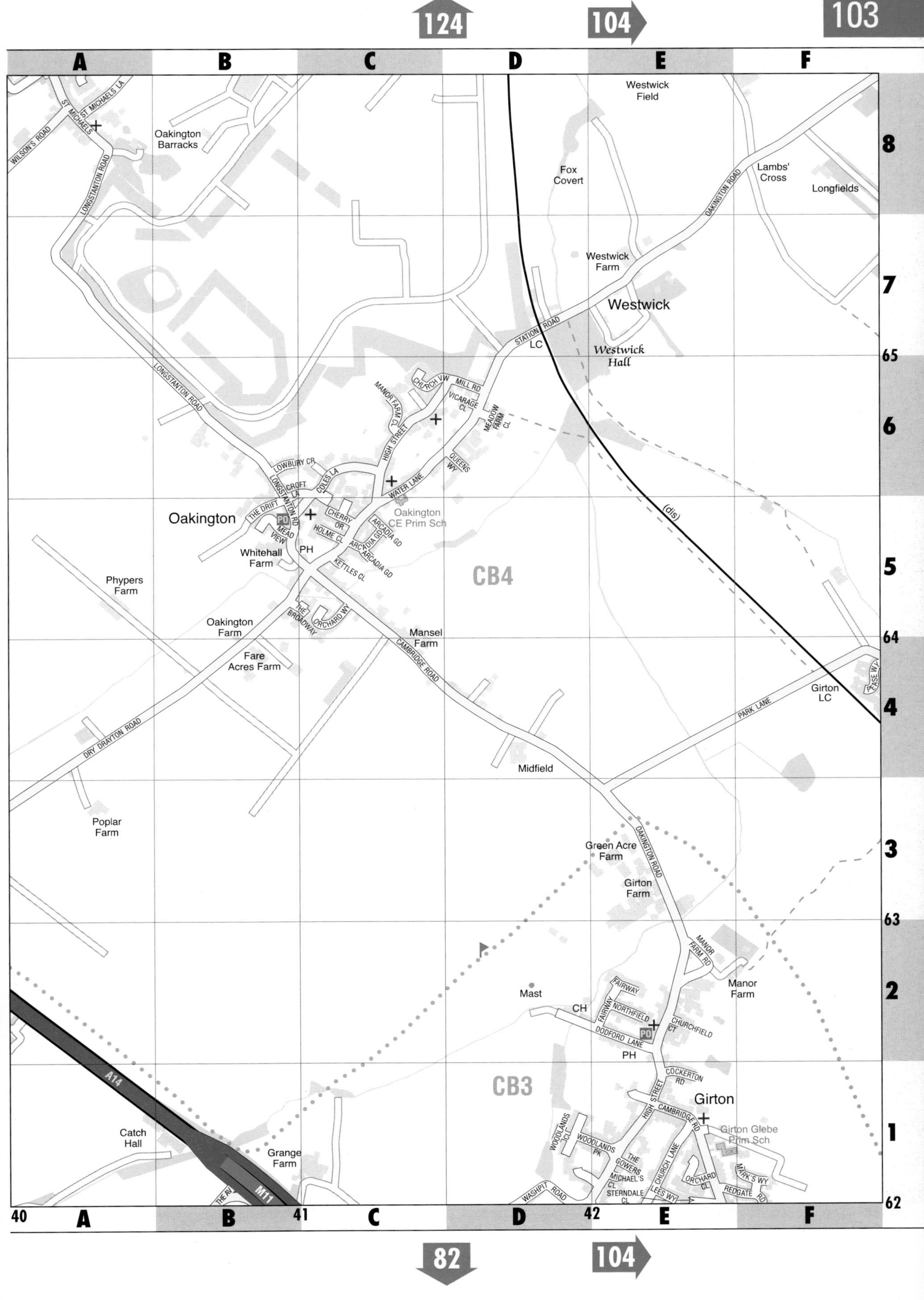
124
104
A
B
C
D
E
F
8
7
65
6
5
64
4
3
63
2
1
62
40
41
42
82
104
Westwick Field
Oakington Barracks
Fox Covert
Lambs' Cross
Longfields
Westwick Farm
Westwick
Westwick Hall
LC
Oakington
Whitehall Farm
Oakington CE Prim Sch
PH
CB4
Phypers Farm
Oakington Farm
Fare Acres Farm
Mansel Farm
Midfield
Girton LC
Poplar Farm
Green Acre Farm
Girton Farm
Manor Farm
Mast
CH
PH
CB3
Girton
Girton Glebe Prim Sch
Catch Hall
Grange Farm
ST MICHAELS LA
ST MICHAELS
WILSON'S ROAD
LONGSTANTON ROAD
STATION ROAD
OAKINGTON ROAD
CHURCH VW
MILL RD
VICARAGE CL
MANOR FARM CL
HIGH STREET
MEADOW FARM CL
QUEENS WY
LOWBURY CR
COLES LA
CROFT LA
WATER LANE
THE DRIFT
MEAD VIEW
CHERRY OR
HOLME CL
ARCADIA GD
KETTLES CL
THE BROADWAY
ORCHARD WY
CAMBRIDGE ROAD
DRY DRAYTON ROAD
PARK LANE
PEASE WY
(dis)
A14
M11
THE AV
MANOR FARM RD
FAIRWAY
NORTHFIELD
CHURCHFIELD CT
DODFORD LANE
COCKERTON RD
HIGH STREET
CAMBRIDGE RD
WOODLANDS CL
WOODLANDS PK
THE GOWERS
MICHAEL'S CL
STERNDALE CL
CHURCH LANE
LEES WY
ORCHARD CL
REDGATE RD
MARK'S WY
WASHPIT ROAD

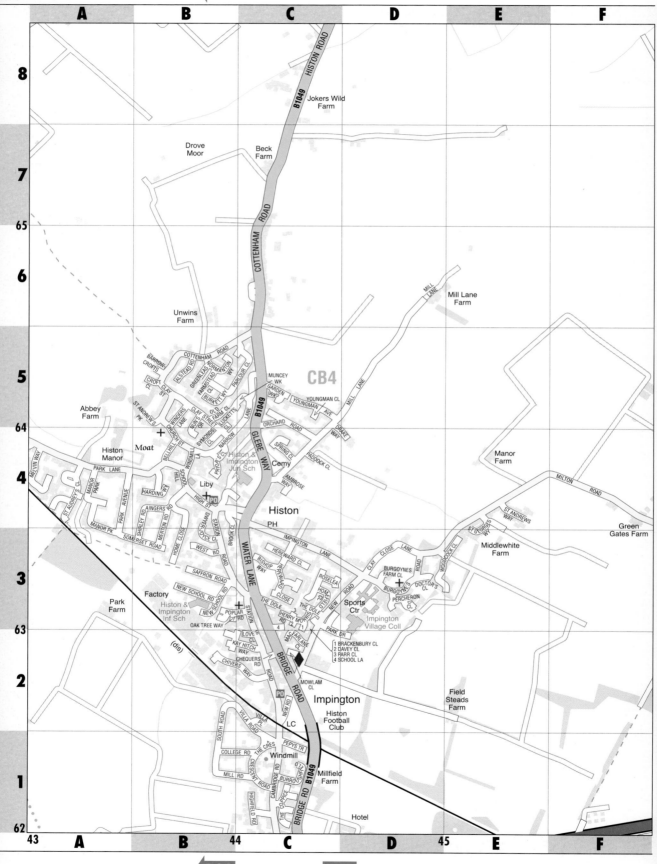

126
106

A B C D E F

8
7
65
6
5
64
4
3
63
2
1
62

Denny End
DENNY END ROAD
CONVENT DR
PEMBROKE AV
A10 ELY ROAD
COTTENHAM ROAD
North Farm
GREEN END
Beach Farm
Manorial Earthworks
BECHE WAY
Manor Farm
REUBENS RD
SPALDINGS LA
CHAPMANS CL
Rectory Farm
Landbeach
Sandal Wood
COCKFEN LANE
Rectory Farm
Site of Medieval Village Moat
MATTHEW PARKER CL
WATERBEACH ROAD
CAMBRIDGE RD
PH
ABRAHAMS CL
BANWORTH LA
CAR DYKE RD
CB5
HIGH STREET
Middle Farm
AKEMAN STREET
Oldfield Farm
Punch Farm
Old Field Farm
Lime Farm
The Hawks
Hall Farm
ELY ROAD
Bedlam Farm
CB4
LANDBEACH ROAD
Hepworth Farm
Stanton Farm
A10
Penfold Farm
Cemy
Rectory Farm
BURLING CL 1
STARLING CL 2
TOWNSEND CL 3
Mereway Farm
Sun Close Farm
New Close Farm
BUTT LANE
BULTEEL CL 1
BUTCHER CL 2
CONDER CL 3
GARNER CL 4
LANDER CL 5
College of West Anglia
ELY ROAD
LANDBEACH RD
FROMENT WAY
BALLARD CL
SUTTON CL
HUMPHRIES WAY
DAVID BULL WAY
CHERRY CL
HIGH ST
KNIGHTS WAY
MANSFIELD CL
LYNDHURST CL
WILLOW CRES
HIGH ST
COULSON CL
BUTT LANE
WOODMANS WAY
GUNNELL CL
Milton CE Prim Sch
FOX'S CL
PO
CHURCH LA
Milton
FAULKNER CL
PETER GOODIN CL
THE ELMS
THE OAKS
EDMUND CL
HIGH STREET
PH
ROAD
HALL END
GODING WY
Fen Farm
THE SYCAMORES
THE ROWANS
WILSON WAY
OLD SCHOOL LANE
THE ROWANS
WALKING WY
COLES
PRYOR CL
SHIRLEY CL
FEN ROAD
THE ROWANS
RECREATION CL
PEARSON CL
A10
Playing Field
BENET CL
ROAD
BARNABAS CT
Works
LC
THE ROWANS
CAMBRIDGE
Superstore
WINSHIP ROAD
Milton Country Park
Crane Industrial Estate
A14
Visitor Centre
P
Baits Bite Lock

46 A B 47 C D 48 E F

84
106

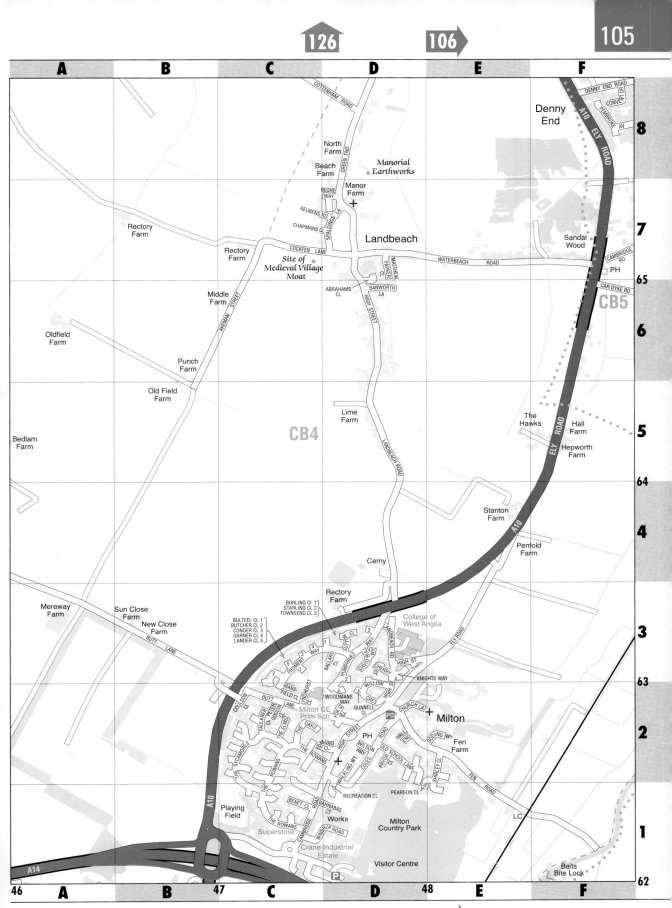

105
127

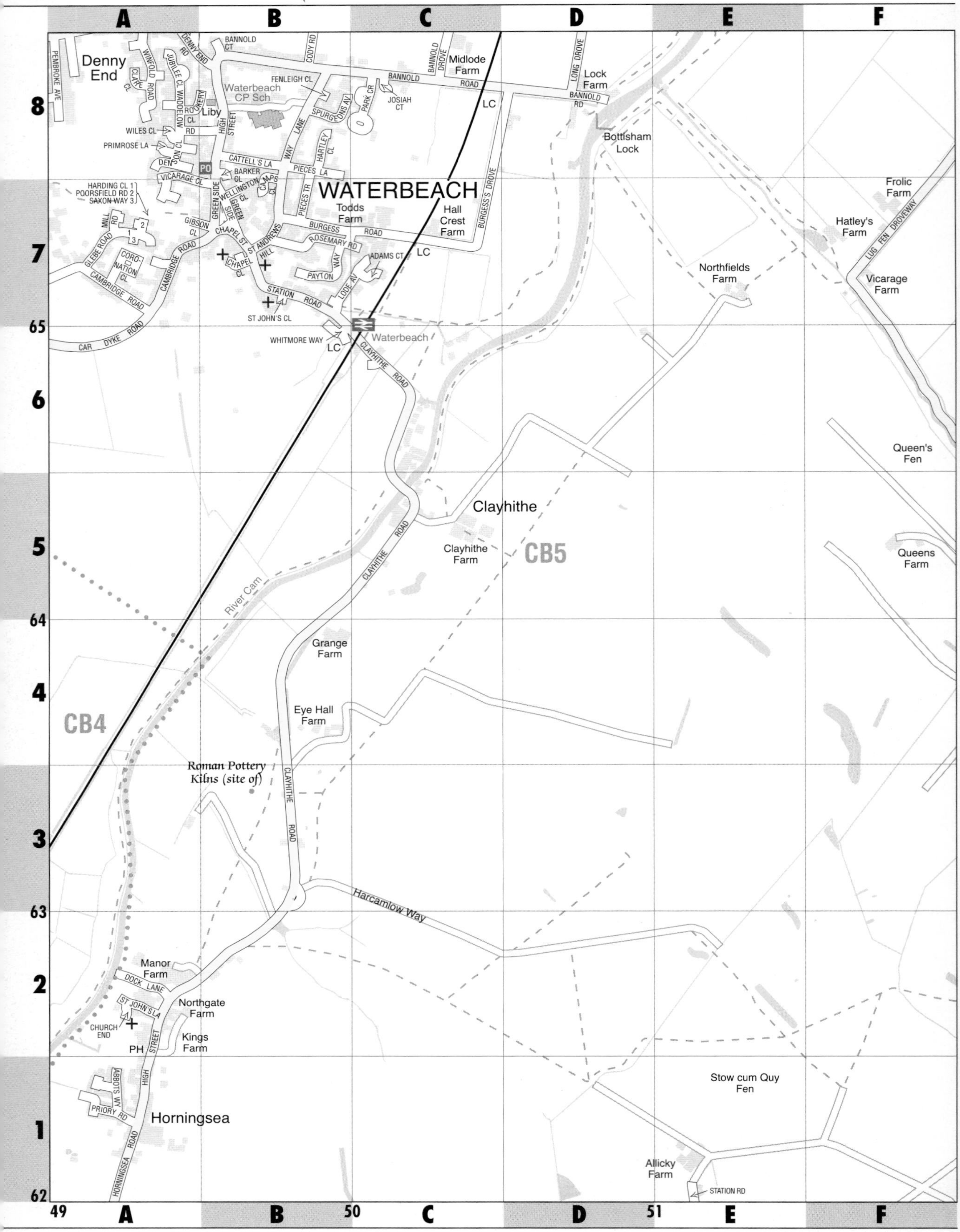

A **B** **C** **D** **E** **F**

Denny
End

BANNOLD
CT

DENNY END

WINFOLD
RD

CLAYS

JUBILEE CL
WADELOW

ROUNES
CL

FENLEIGH CL

CODY RD

Waterbeach
CP Sch

Midlode
Farm

BANNOLD
DROVE

BANNOLD
ROAD

LONG DROVE

Lock
Farm

8

Liby

WILES CL

DENS CL

RD

HIGH STREET

PARK CR

JOSIAH
CT

SPURGEONS AV

LC

BANNOLD
RD

Bottisham
Lock

PRIMROSE LA

PO

VICARAGE CL

CATTELL'S LA

BARKER
CL

CAMPS

PIECES TR

WAY LANE

HARTLEY CL

WATERBEACH

HARDING CL 1
POORSFIELD RD 2
SAXON WAY 3

GIBSON
CL

GREEN SIDE

WELLINGTON
CL

CHAPEL ST

ST ANDREWS

GREEN

Todds
Farm

BURGESS
ROAD

Hall
Crest
Farm

BURGESS'S DROVE

Frolic
Farm

7

MILL ROAD

GLEBE ROAD

CORO-
NATION
CL

1
2
3

CAMBRIDGE ROAD

CHAPEL
HILL

ROSEMARY RD

WAY

PAYTON

ADAMS CT

LC

Northfields
Farm

Hatley's
Farm

LUG FEN DROVEWAY

Vicarage
Farm

CAMBRIDGE ROAD

LODE AV

CAR DYKE ROAD

ST JOHN'S CL

STATION
ROAD

65

WHITMORE WAY

LC

Waterbeach

6

CLAYHITHE ROAD

Queen's
Fen

River Cam

CLAYHITHE ROAD

Clayhithe

CB5

5

Clayhithe
Farm

Queens
Farm

64

Grange
Farm

4

CB4

Eye Hall
Farm

CLAYHITHE ROAD

Roman Pottery
Kilns (site of)

Harcamlow Way

3

63

Manor
Farm

DOCK LANE

2

ST JOHN'S LA

Northgate
Farm

HIGH STREET

CHURCH
END

PH

Kings
Farm

Stow cum Quy
Fen

ABBOTS WM SLOBBY

PRIORY RD

1

HORNINGSEA ROAD

Horningsea

Allicky
Farm

STATION RD

62

49   50   51

A B C D E F

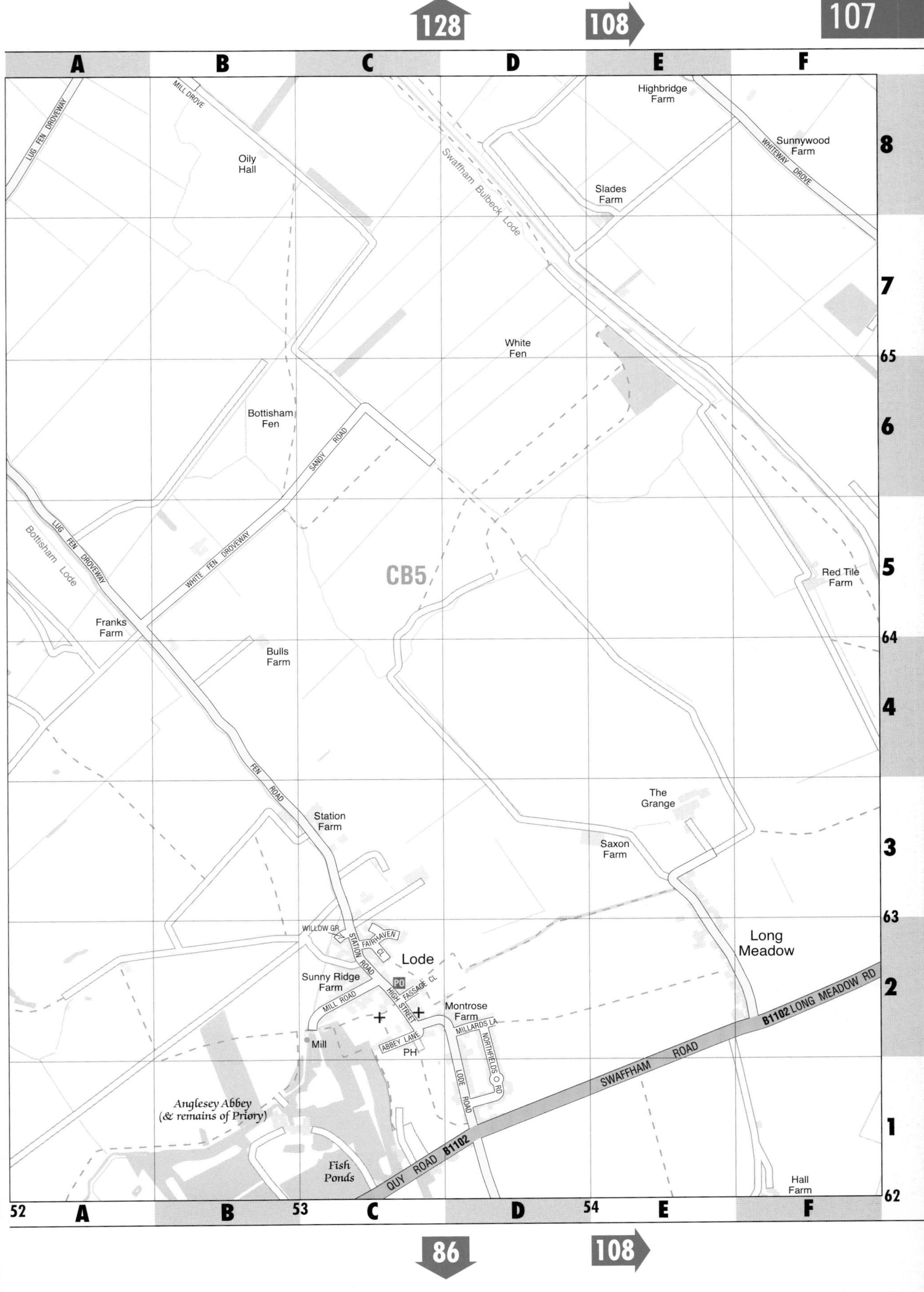

8
7
65
6
5
64
4
3
63
2
1
62

MILL DROVE

Oily Hall

Swaffham Bulbeck Lode

Highbridge Farm

Sunnywood Farm

WHITEWAY DROVE

Slades Farm

LUG FEN DROVEWAY

Bottisham Fen

White Fen

SANDY ROAD

STATION ROAD

WHITE FEN DROVEWAY

CB5

Bottisham Lode

Red Tile Farm

Franks Farm

Bulls Farm

FEN ROAD

Station Farm

The Grange

Saxon Farm

Long Meadow

WILLOW GR

FAIRHAVEN CL

Lode

Sunny Ridge Farm

MILL ROAD

HIGH STREET

PASSAGE CL

PO

Montrose Farm

MILLARDS LA

NORTHFIELDS RD

B1102 LONG MEADOW RD

SWAFFHAM ROAD

Mill

ABBEY LANE

PH

LODE ROAD

Anglesey Abbey
(& remains of Priory)

Fish Ponds

QUY ROAD B1102

Hall Farm

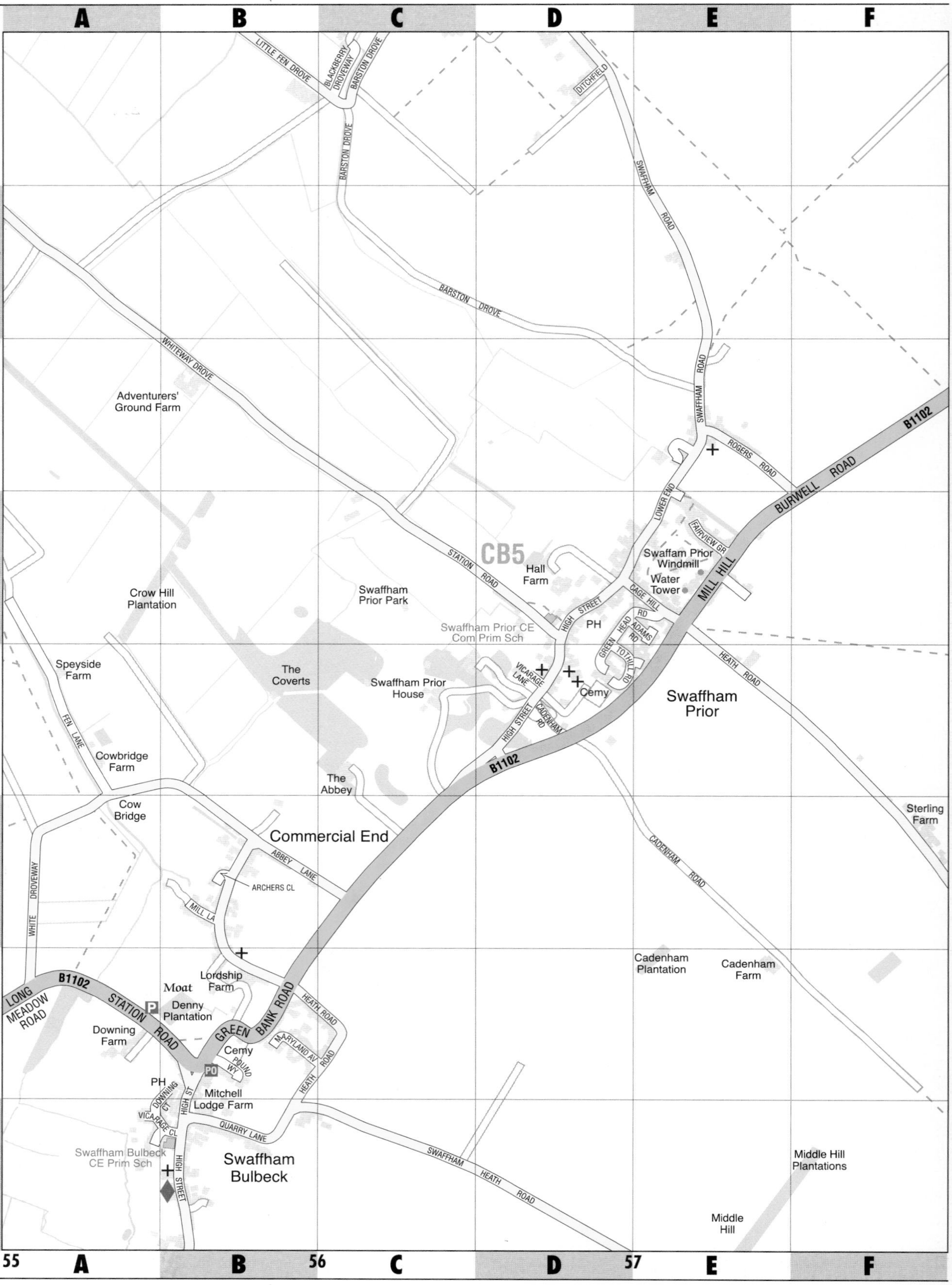

A B C D E F

8

7

65

6

5

64

4

3

63

2

1

62

Little Fen Drove
Blackberry Droveway
Barston Drove
Ditchfield
Swaffham Road
Whiteway Drove
Barston Drove
Adventurers' Ground Farm
B1102
Burwell Road
Rogers Road
Lower End
Fairview Gr
Station Road
CB5
Hall Farm
Swaffham Prior Windmill
Water Tower
Mill Hill
Crow Hill Plantation
Swaffham Prior Park
Swaffham Prior CE Com Prim Sch
High Street
PH
Page Hill
Green Head Rd
Adams Rd
Tothill Rd
Heath Road
Speyside Farm
The Coverts
Swaffham Prior House
Vicarage Lane
High Street
Cadenham Rd
Cemy
Swaffham Prior
Cowbridge Farm
Fen Lane
B1102
The Abbey
Sterling Farm
Cow Bridge
Cadenham Road
Commercial End
White Droveway
Abbey Lane
ARCHERS CL
MILL LA
Cadenham Plantation
Cadenham Farm
Long Meadow Road
B1102
Station Road
Moat
Lordship Farm
Denny Plantation
Green Bank Road
Heath Road
Downing Farm
Cemy
MARYLAND AV
POUND DY
PO
PH
Mitchell Lodge Farm
Heath Road
DOWNING CT
HIGH ST
VICARAGE CL
QUARRY LANE
Swaffham Heath Road
Swaffham Bulbeck CE Prim Sch
Swaffham Bulbeck
HIGH STREET
Middle Hill Plantations
Middle Hill

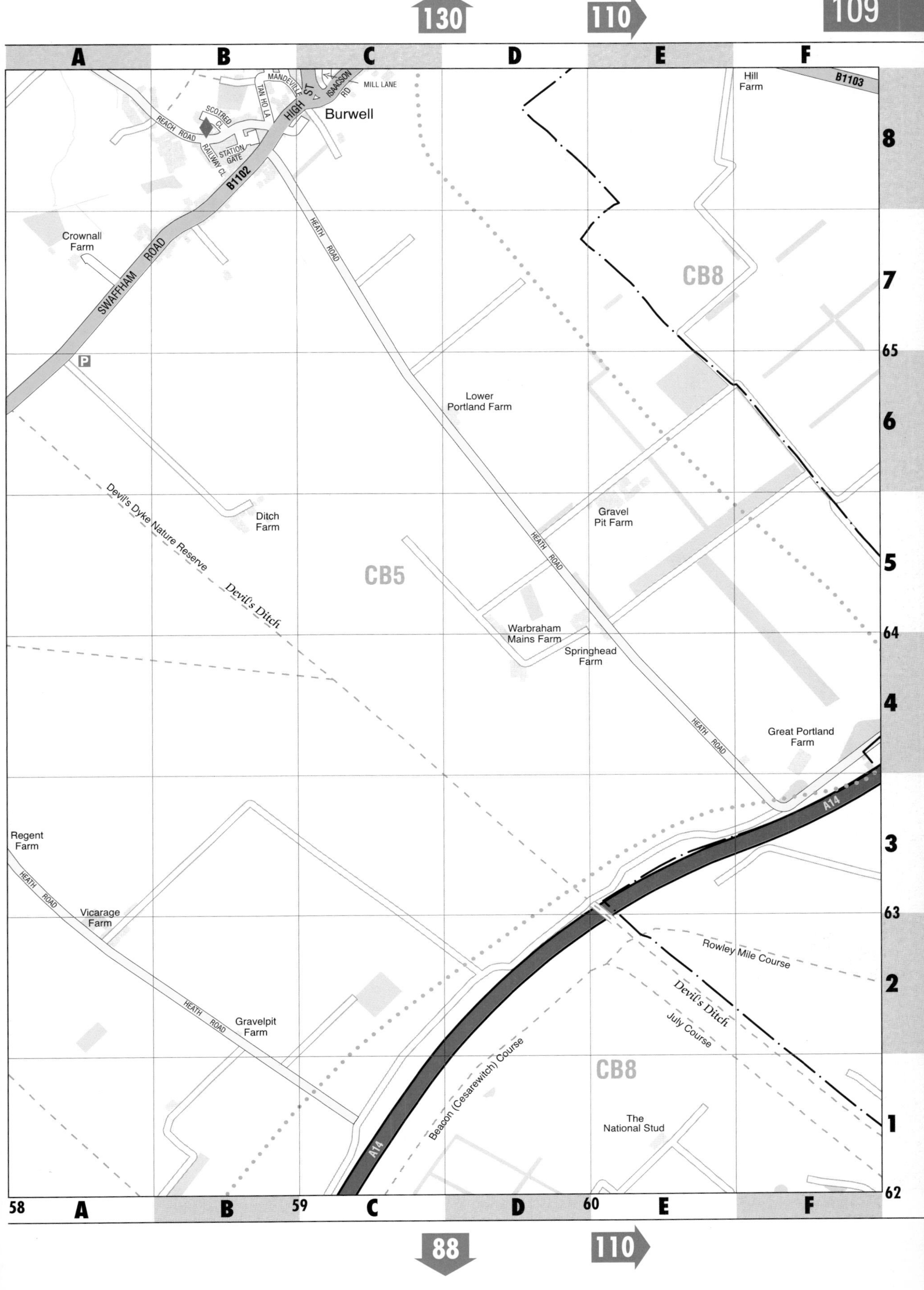
130
110
A
B
C
D
E
F
MANDEVILLE
ISAACSON RD
MILL LANE
TAN HO LA
HIGH ST
Burwell
SCOTRED CL
REACH ROAD
STATION GATE
RAILWAY CL
B1102
B1103
Hill Farm
8
HEATH ROAD
Crownall Farm
SWAFFHAM ROAD
CB8
7
65
P
Lower Portland Farm
6
Devil's Dyke Nature Reserve
Ditch Farm
Gravel Pit Farm
CB5
Devil's Ditch
5
Warbraham Mains Farm
Springhead Farm
64
4
Great Portland Farm
A14
Regent Farm
3
Vicarage Farm
63
Rowley Mile Course
2
Gravelpit Farm
July Course
Beacon (Cesarewitch) Course
CB8
The National Stud
1
62
58
59
60
88
110

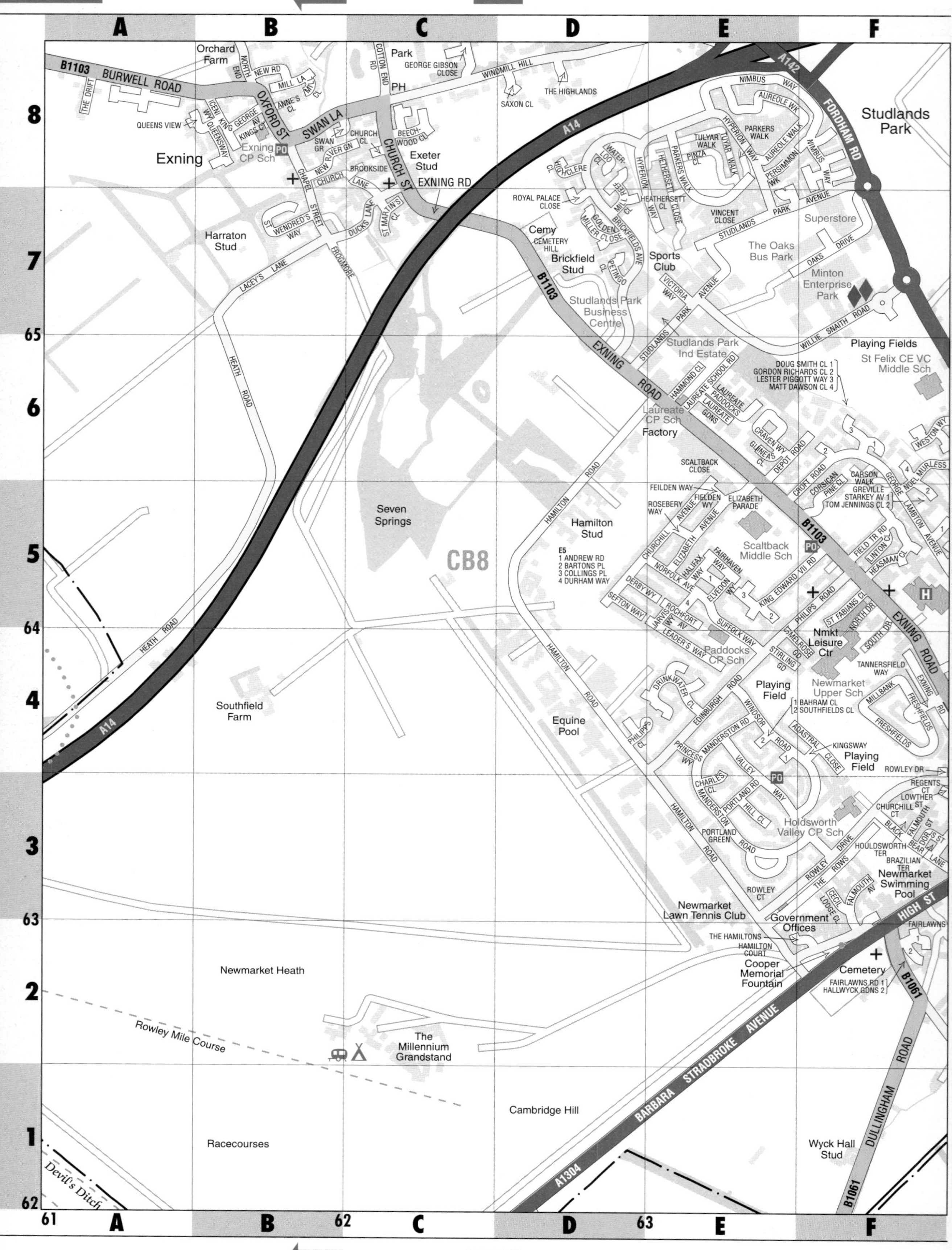

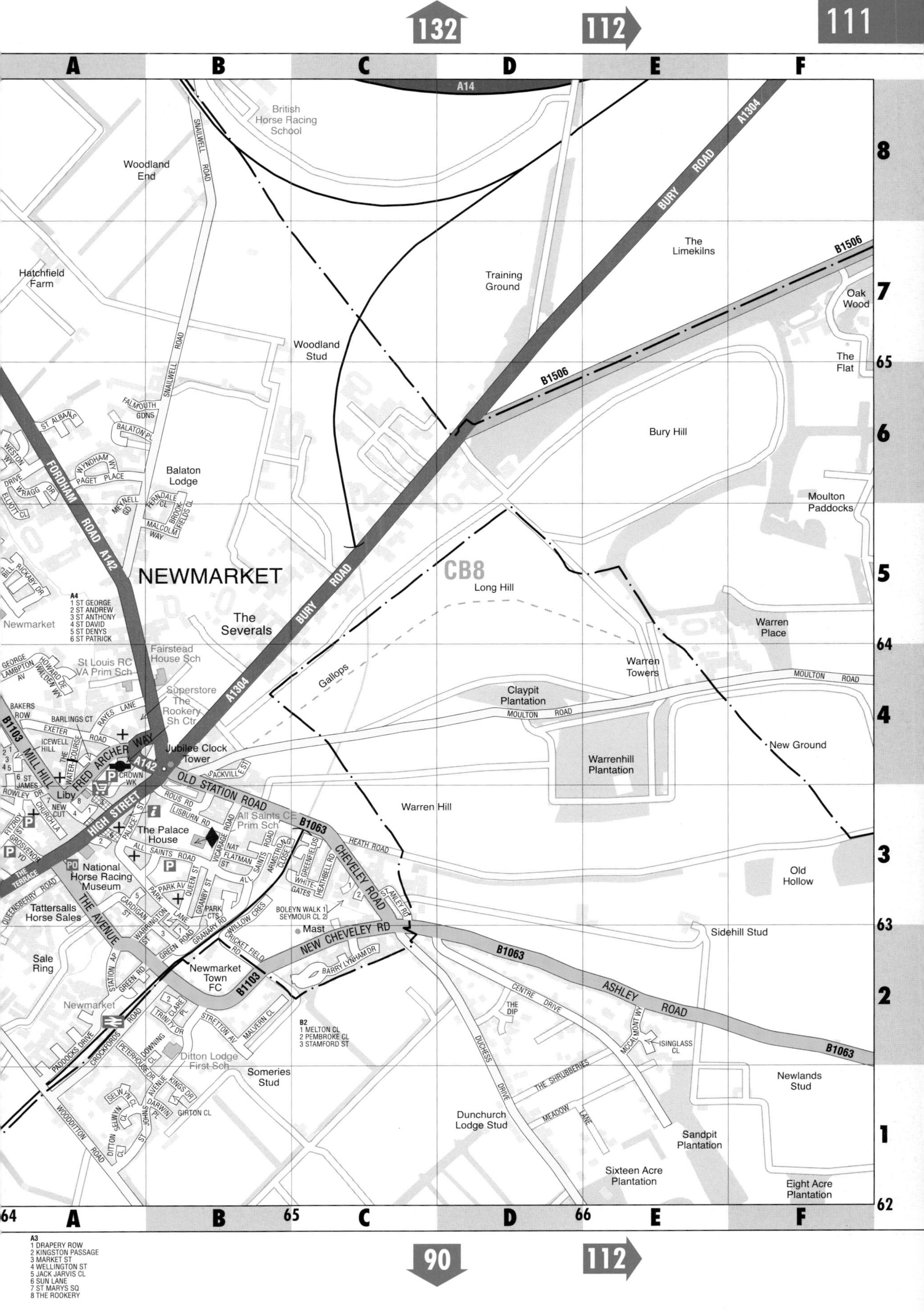

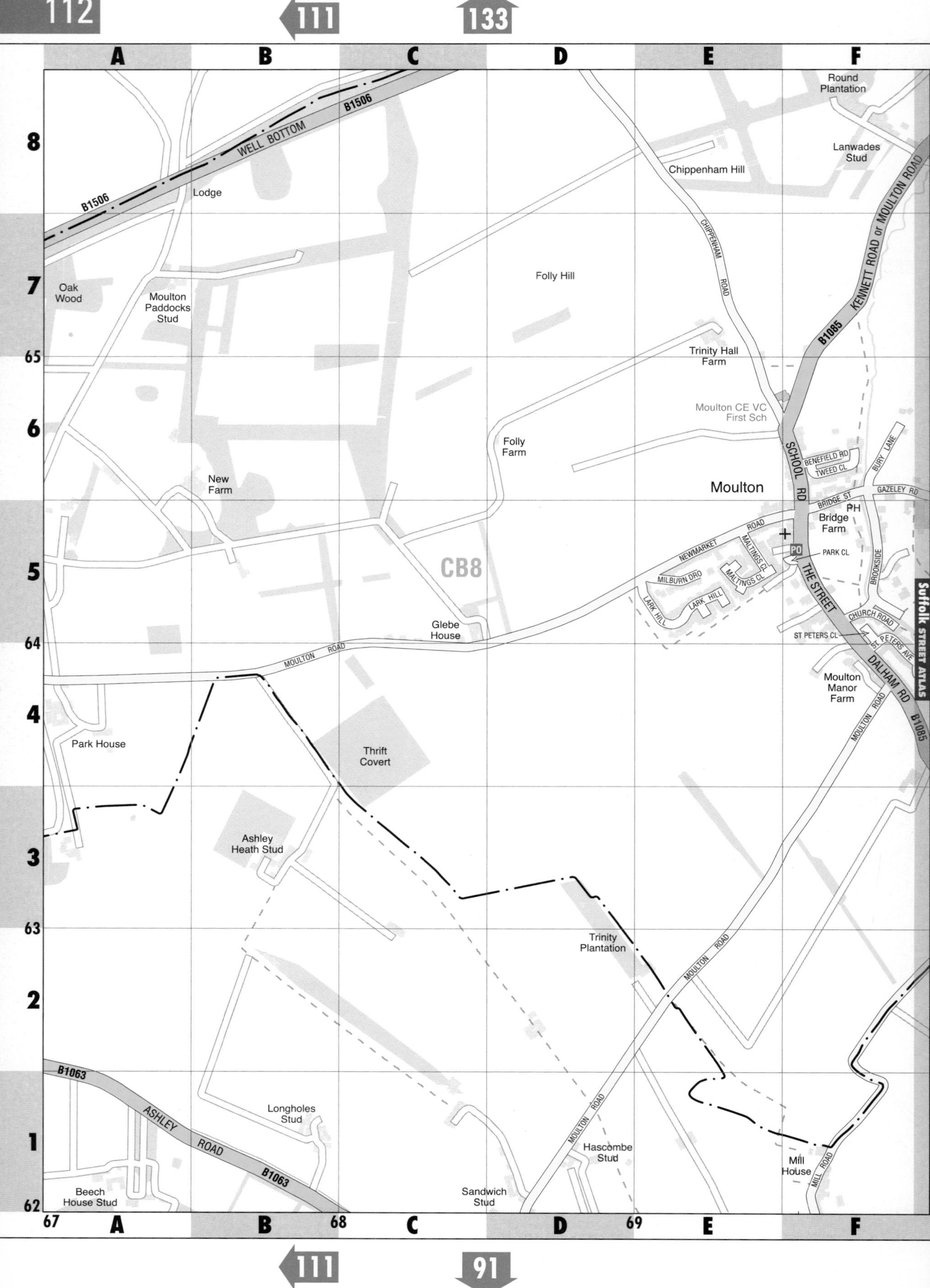

A B C D E F

8

Round Plantation

WELL BOTTOM

B1506

B1506

Lodge

Chippenham Hill

Lanwades Stud

7

Oak Wood

Moulton Paddocks Stud

Folly Hill

CHIPPENHAM ROAD

B1085

65

Trinity Hall Farm

Moulton CE VC First Sch

6

New Farm

Folly Farm

Moulton

SCHOOL RD

Benefield Rd
TWEED CL

BURY LANE

GAZELEY RD

BRIDGE ST
PH
Bridge Farm

NEWMARKET ROAD

MALTINGS CL

5

CB8

MILBURN DRO

MALTINGS CL

LARK HILL

LARK HILL

PO PARK CL

THE STREET

BROOKSIDE

Glebe House

CHURCH ROAD

64

MOULTON ROAD

ST PETERS CL

St PETERS AVE

St Peters Cl

Moulton Manor Farm

DALHAM RD

B1085

4

Park House

Thrift Covert

MOULTON ROAD

3

Ashley Heath Stud

63

Trinity Plantation

MOULTON ROAD

2

B1063

Longholes Stud

ASHLEY ROAD

MOULTON ROAD

MILL ROAD

Mill House

1

B1063

Hascombe Stud

Beech House Stud

Sandwich Stud

62

67 A B 68 C D 69 E F

Suffolk STREET ATLAS

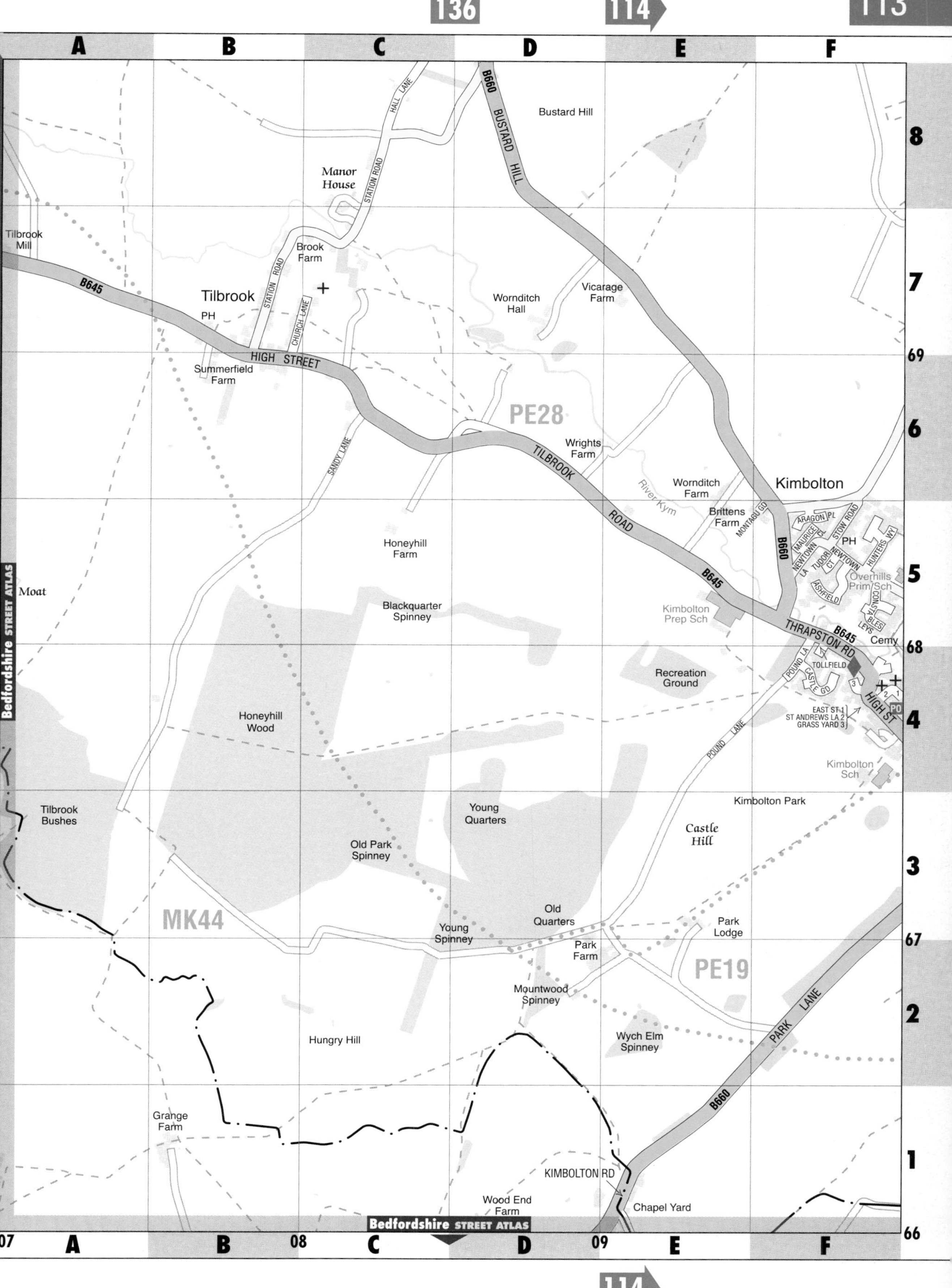

A B C D E F

Bustard Hill

B660 BUSTARD HILL

Manor House

HALL LANE

STATION ROAD

Brook Farm

Tilbrook

Wornditch Hall

Vicarage Farm

PH

CHURCH LANE

HIGH STREET

Summerfield Farm

PE28

Tilbrook Mill

B645

Wrights Farm

TILBROOK ROAD

River Kym

Wornditch Farm

Kimbolton

MONTAGU GD

Brittens Farm

B660

ARAGON PL

MAURICE CT

NEWTOWN LA

TUDOR LA

NEWTOWN CT

PH

STOW ROAD

HUNTERS WY

CONSTABLES

Moat

SANDY LANE

Honeyhill Farm

Blackquarter Spinney

B645

Kimbolton Prep Sch

ASHFIELD

Overhills Prim Sch

THRAPSTON RD

B645

Cemy

Honeyhill Wood

Recreation Ground

POUND LA

CASTLE GD

TOLLFIELD

EAST ST 1
ST ANDREWS LA 2
GRASS YARD 3

HIGH ST

PO

Kimbolton Sch

Tilbrook Bushes

POUND LANE

MK44

Old Park Spinney

Young Quarters

Old Quarters

Kimbolton Park

Castle Hill

Park Lodge

PE19

Young Spinney

Park Farm

Mountwood Spinney

Wych Elm Spinney

PARK LANE

Hungry Hill

Grange Farm

B660

KIMBOLTON RD

Wood End Farm

Chapel Yard

Bedfordshire STREET ATLAS

113
137

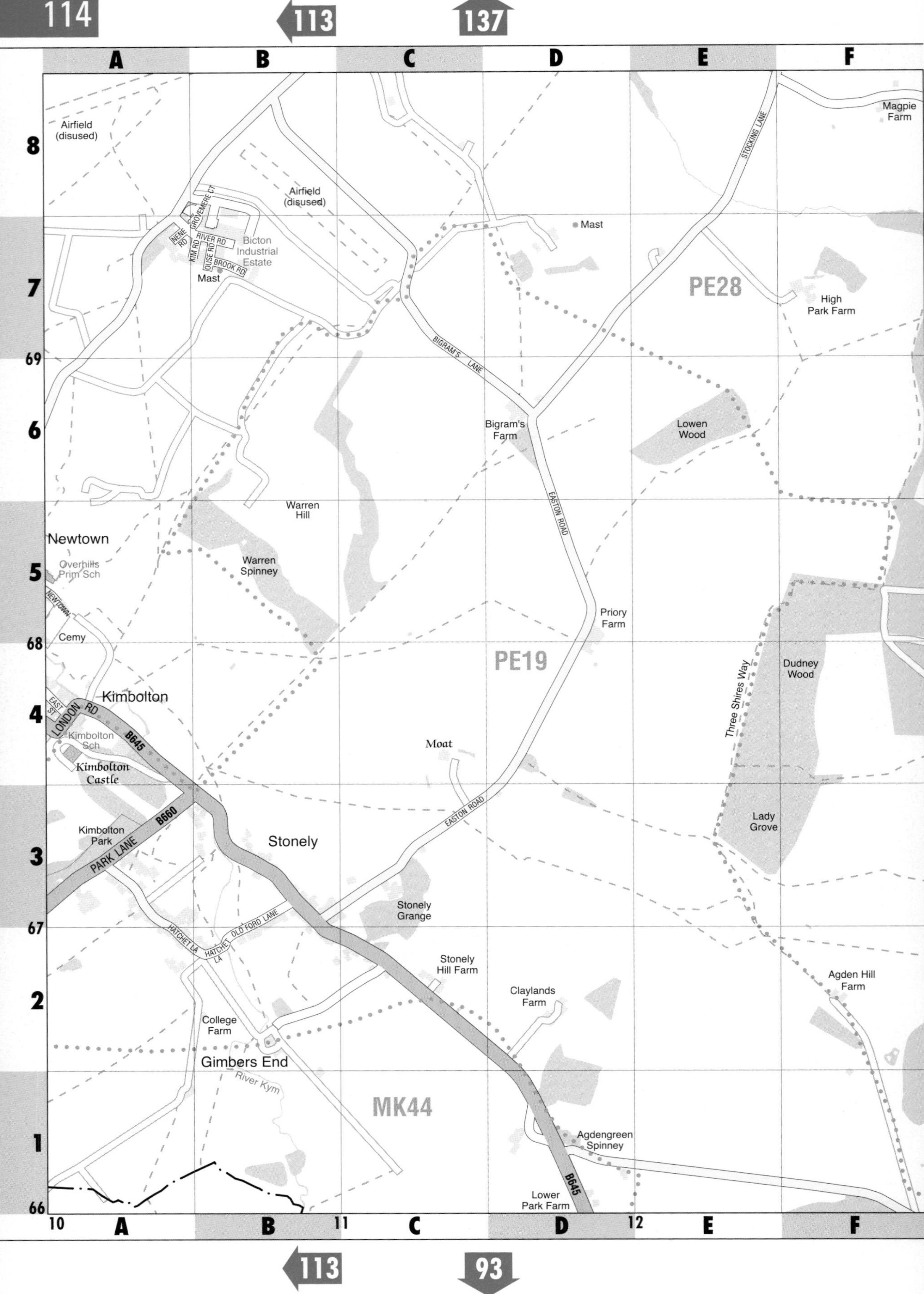
A
B
C
D
E
F
8
7
69
6
5
68
4
3
67
2
1
66
10
11
12
Airfield
(disused)
Airfield
(disused)
GROVEMERE CT
NENE RD
RIVER RD
KIM RD
OUSE RD
BROOK RD
Bicton
Industrial
Estate
Mast
Mast
STOCKING LANE
Magpie
Farm
PE28
High
Park Farm
BIGRAM'S LANE
Bigram's
Farm
Lowen
Wood
Warren
Hill
EASTON ROAD
Newtown
Overhills
Prim Sch
Warren
Spinney
NEWTOWN
Cemy
Priory
Farm
PE19
Dudney
Wood
Three Shires Way
Kimbolton
EAST ST
LONDON RD
B645
Kimbolton
Sch
Kimbolton
Castle
Moat
Lady
Grove
EASTON ROAD
Kimbolton
Park
B660
PARK LANE
Stonely
Stonely
Grange
OLD FORD LANE
HATCHET LA
HATCHET LA
Stonely
Hill Farm
Claylands
Farm
Agden Hill
Farm
College
Farm
Gimbers End
River Kym
MK44
Agdengreen
Spinney
B645
Lower
Park Farm

113
93

138
116

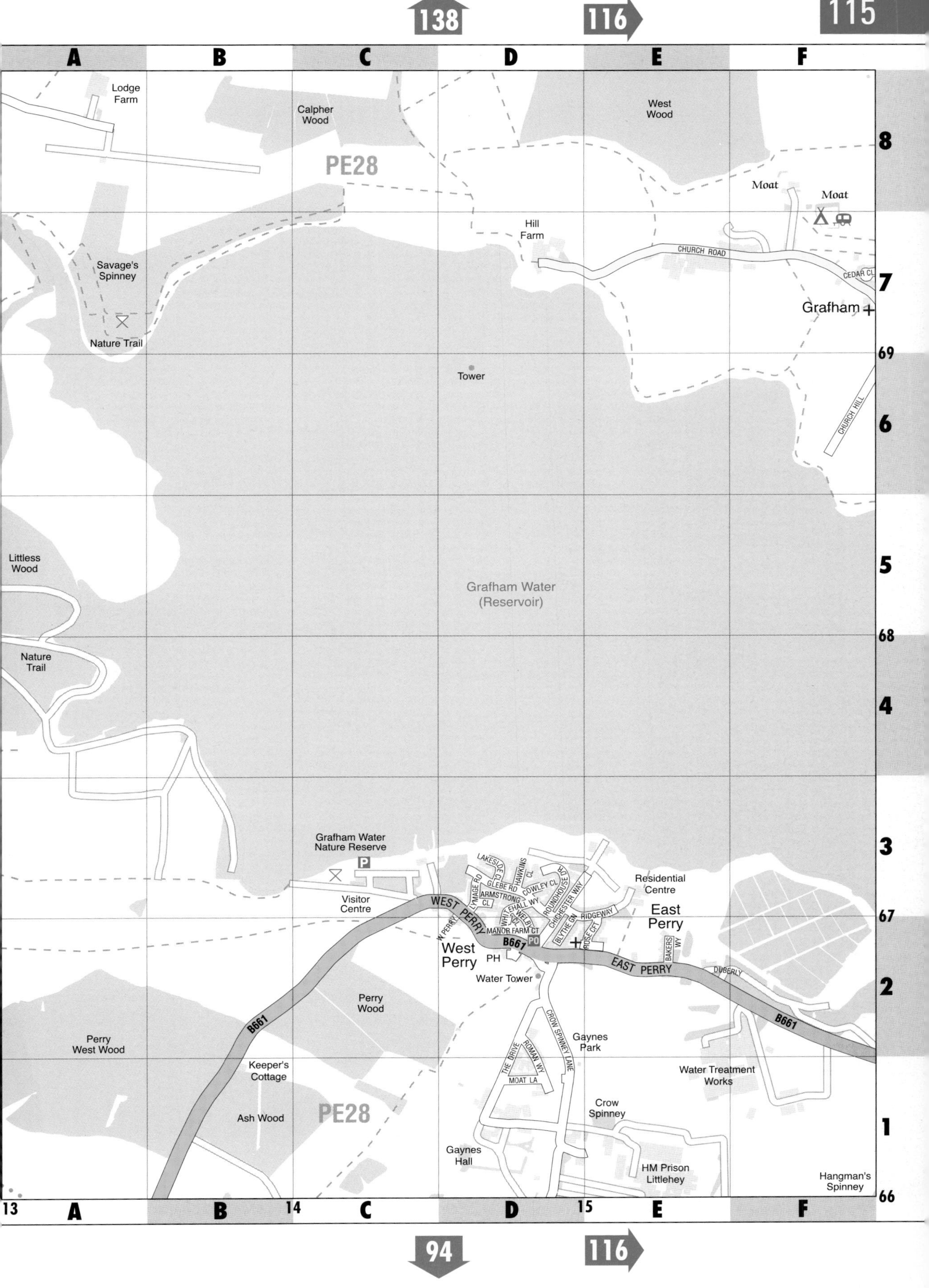
A
B
C
D
E
F
Lodge Farm
Calpher Wood
West Wood
PE28
Moat
Moat
Hill Farm
CHURCH ROAD
CEDAR CL
Savage's Spinney
Grafham
Nature Trail
Tower
CHURCH HILL
Littless Wood
Grafham Water (Reservoir)
Nature Trail
Grafham Water Nature Reserve
P
Visitor Centre
LAKESIDE CL
HAWKINS CL
LYMAGE RD
GLEBE RD
ARMSTRONG CL
COWLEY CL
ROUNDHOUSE DR
CHICHESTER WAY
WHITEHALL WY
RIDGEWAY
Residential Centre
East Perry
WEST PERRY
W PERRY
MANOR FARM CT
BLYTHE GN
ROSE CFT
BAKERS WY
B661
PO
West Perry
PH
EAST PERRY
DUBERLY
Water Tower
Perry Wood
CROW SPINNEY LANE
Gaynes Park
B661
Perry West Wood
B661
THE DRIVE
ROMAN WY
MOAT LA
Keeper's Cottage
Water Treatment Works
Ash Wood
PE28
Crow Spinney
Gaynes Hall
HM Prison Littlehey
Hangman's Spinney
8
7
69
6
5
68
4
3
67
2
1
66
13
14
15

94
116

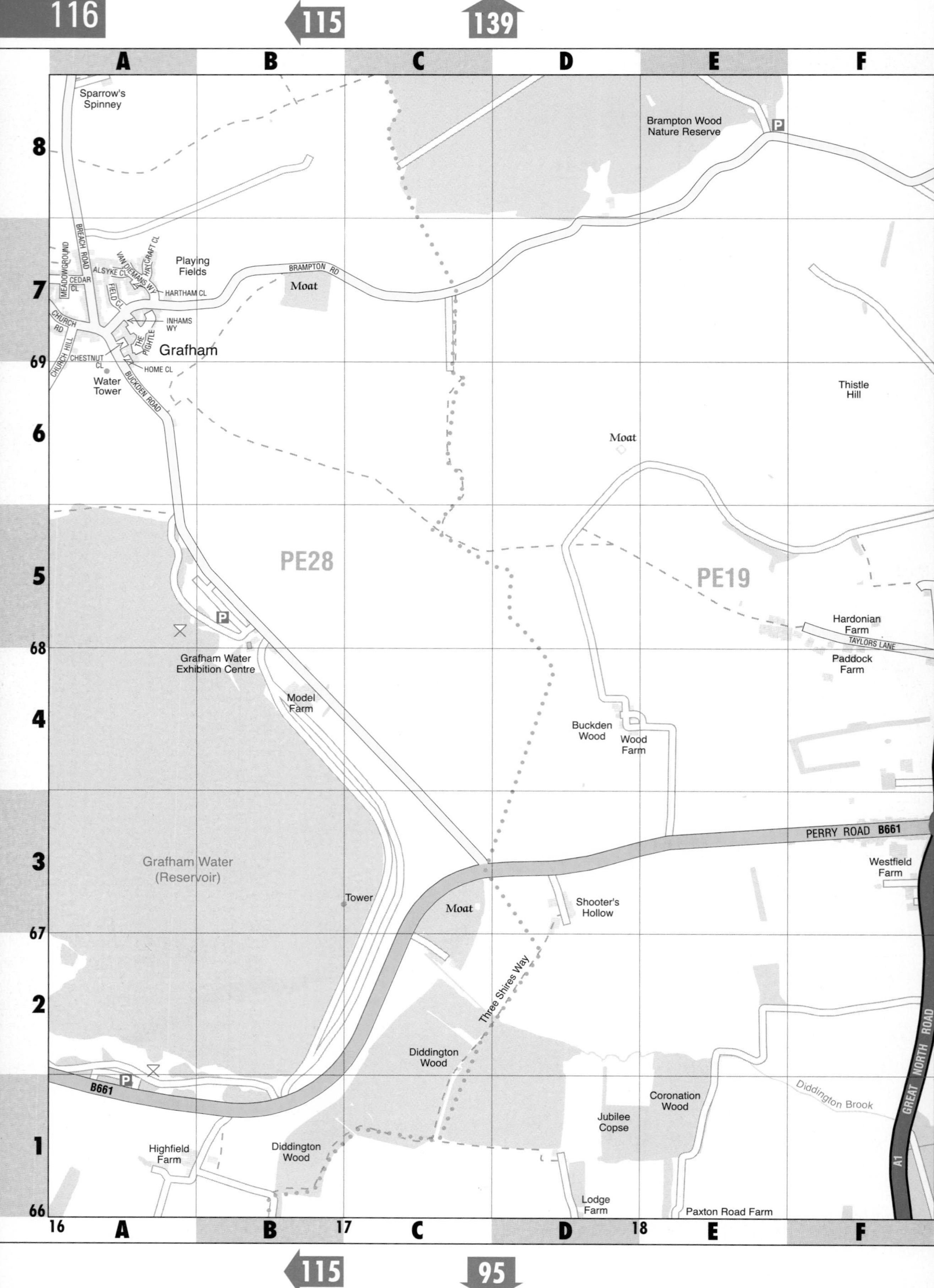

A   **B**   **C**   **D**   **E**   **F**

Sparrow's
Spinney

8

Brampton Wood
Nature Reserve

P

BREACH ROAD

MEADOWGROUND

VAN DIEMANS WY

ALSYKE CL

HAYCRAFT CL

CEDAR
CL

FIELD CL

Playing
Fields

BRAMPTON RD

HARTHAM CL

Moat

7

CHURCH
RD

THE PIGHTLE

INHAMS
WY

Thistle
Hill

69

CHURCH HILL

CHESTNUT
CL

Grafham

HOME CL

Water
Tower

BUCKDEN ROAD

Moat

6

Moat

PE28

PE19

5

Hardonian
Farm

TAYLORS LANE

P

Paddock
Farm

68

Grafham Water
Exhibition Centre

Model
Farm

4

Buckden
Wood

Wood
Farm

PERRY ROAD **B661**

Westfield
Farm

3

Grafham Water
(Reservoir)

Tower

Moat

Shooter's
Hollow

67

Three Shires Way

2

Diddington
Brook

GREAT NORTH ROAD

A1

B661

P

Diddington
Wood

Coronation
Wood

1

Highfield
Farm

Diddington
Wood

Jubilee
Copse

Lodge
Farm

Paxton Road Farm

66

16   **A**   **B**   **17**   **C**   **D**   **18**   **E**   **F**

140
118

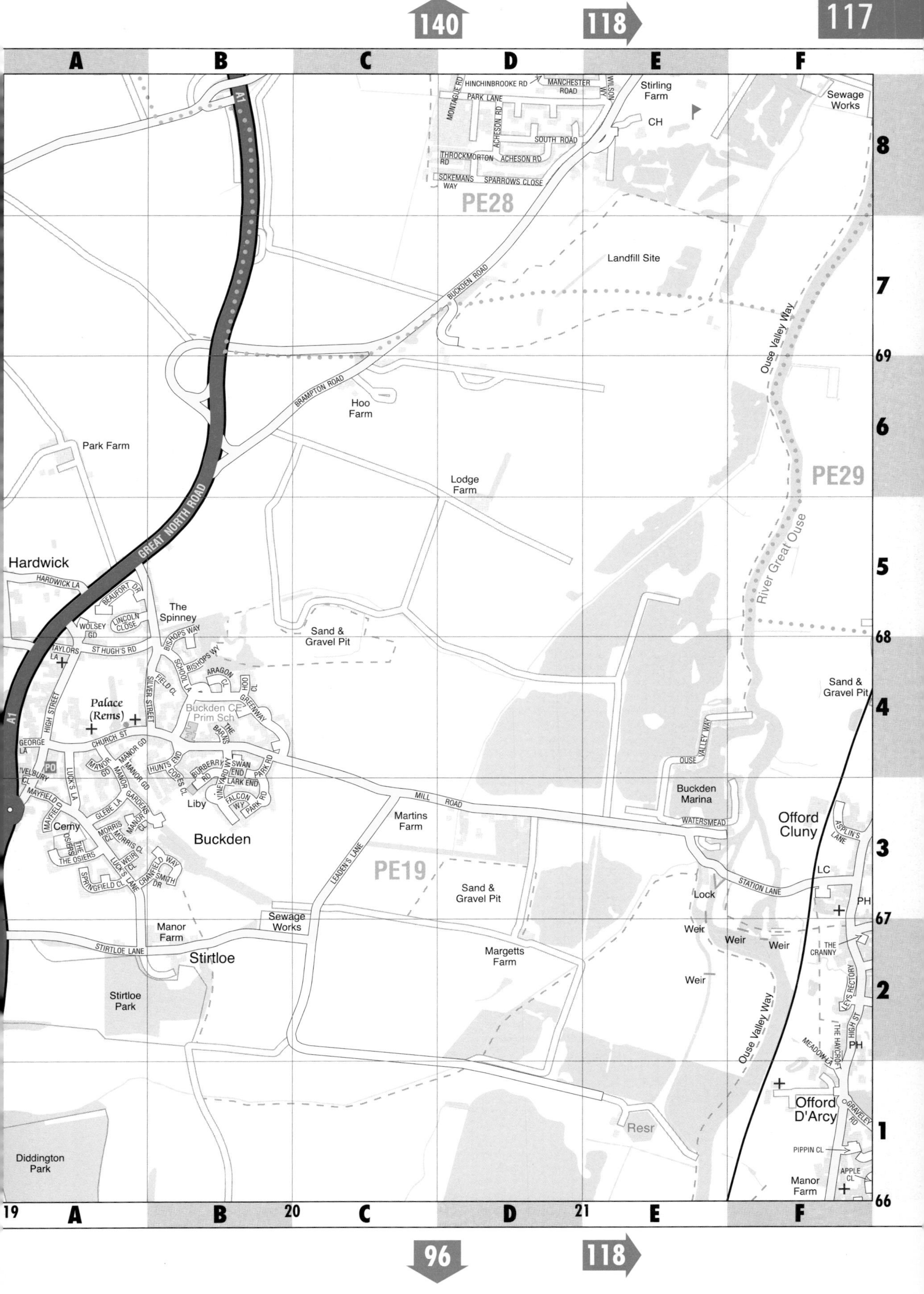
A
B
C
D
E
F
8
7
69
6
5
68
4
3
67
2
1
66
19
20
21
HINCHINBROOKE RD
MANCHESTER ROAD
WILSON WY
MONTAGUE RD
PARK LANE
ACHESON RD
SOUTH ROAD
THROCKMORTON RD
ACHESON RD
SOKEMANS WAY
SPARROWS CLOSE
PE28
Stirling Farm
CH
Sewage Works
A1
Landfill Site
BUCKDEN ROAD
Ouse Valley Way
BRAMPTON ROAD
Hoo Farm
Park Farm
Lodge Farm
PE29
GREAT NORTH ROAD
River Great Ouse
Hardwick
HARDWICK LA
BEAUFORT DR
The Spinney
LINCOLN CLOSE
WOLSEY GD
BISHOPS WAY
Sand & Gravel Pit
TAYLORS LA
ST HUGH'S RD
BISHOPS WY
SCHOOL LA
ARAGON CL
HOO CL
FIELD CL
SILVER STREET
GREENWAY
HIGH STREET
Palace (Rems)
Buckden CE Prim Sch
THE BARNS
Sand & Gravel Pit
GEORGE LA
CHURCH ST
MANOR GD
OUSE VALLEY WAY
PO
MANOR GD
HUNTS END
COPES CL
BURBERRY RD
SWAN END
PARK RD
IVELBURY CL
LUCK'S LA
MANOR GARDENS
LARK END
VINEYARD WY
MAYFIELD
GLEBE LA
FALCON WY
PARK RD
MILL ROAD
Buckden Marina
Liby
Martins Farm
WATERSMEAD
Offord Cluny
MAYFIELD
Cemy
MORRIS CL
MANOR CL
ASPLIN'S LANE
THE OSIERS
MORRIS CL
Buckden
WEIR CL
THE OSIERS
LUCK'S LANE
CRANFIELD WAY
SMITH DR
LEADEN'S LANE
PE19
LC
STATION LANE
SPRINGFIELD CL
Sand & Gravel Pit
Lock
PH
Sewage Works
Manor Farm
Weir
Weir
Weir
THE CRANNY
STIRTLOE LANE
Stirtloe
Margetts Farm
Weir
EYS RECTORY
Stirtloe Park
Ouse Valley Way
THE HAYCROFT
HIGH ST
PH
MEADOW LA
Offord D'Arcy
GRAVELEY RD
Resr
PIPPIN CL
Diddington Park
APPLE CL
Manor Farm
19
A
B
20
C
D
21
E
F

96
118

117
141

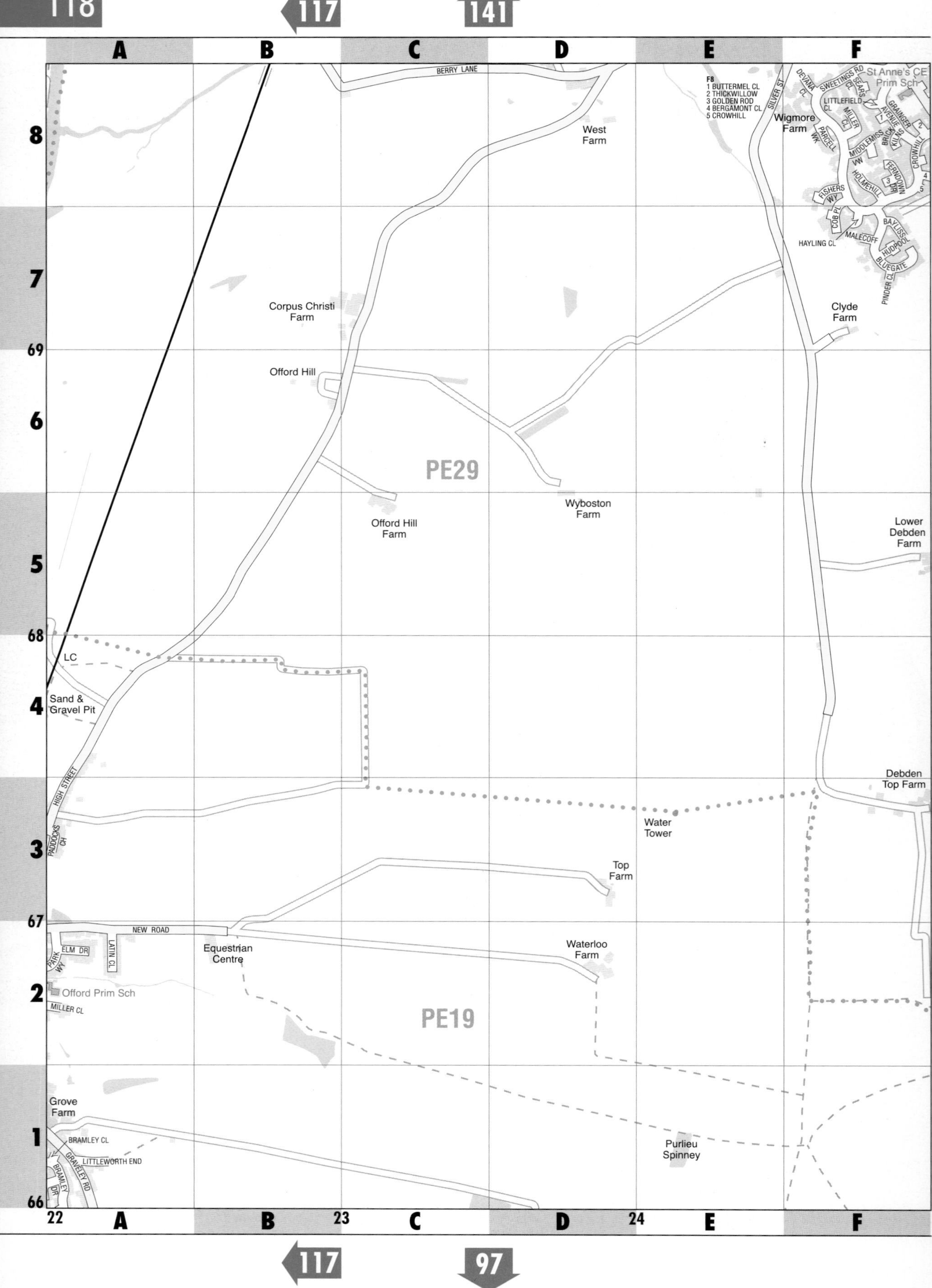

A   B   C   D   E   F

8

7

69

6

PE29

5

68

LC

4   Sand &
Gravel Pit

3

67

2

PE19

1   Grove
Farm

66

BERRY LANE

West
Farm

F8
1 BUTTERMEL CL
2 THICKWILLOW
3 GOLDEN ROD
4 BERGAMONT CL
5 CROWHILL

St Anne's CE
Prim Sch

Wigmore
Farm

Corpus Christi
Farm

HAYLING CL

Clyde
Farm

Offord Hill

Offord Hill
Farm

Wyboston
Farm

Lower
Debden
Farm

Debden
Top Farm

Water
Tower

Top
Farm

HIGH STREET

PADDOCKS CH

NEW ROAD

PARK WY
ELM DR
LATIN CL

Offord Prim Sch

MILLER CL

Equestrian
Centre

Waterloo
Farm

Purlieu
Spinney

BRAMLEY CL

GRAVELEY RD
BRAMLEY DR
LITTLEWORTH END

22   A   B   23   C   D   24   E   F

117   97

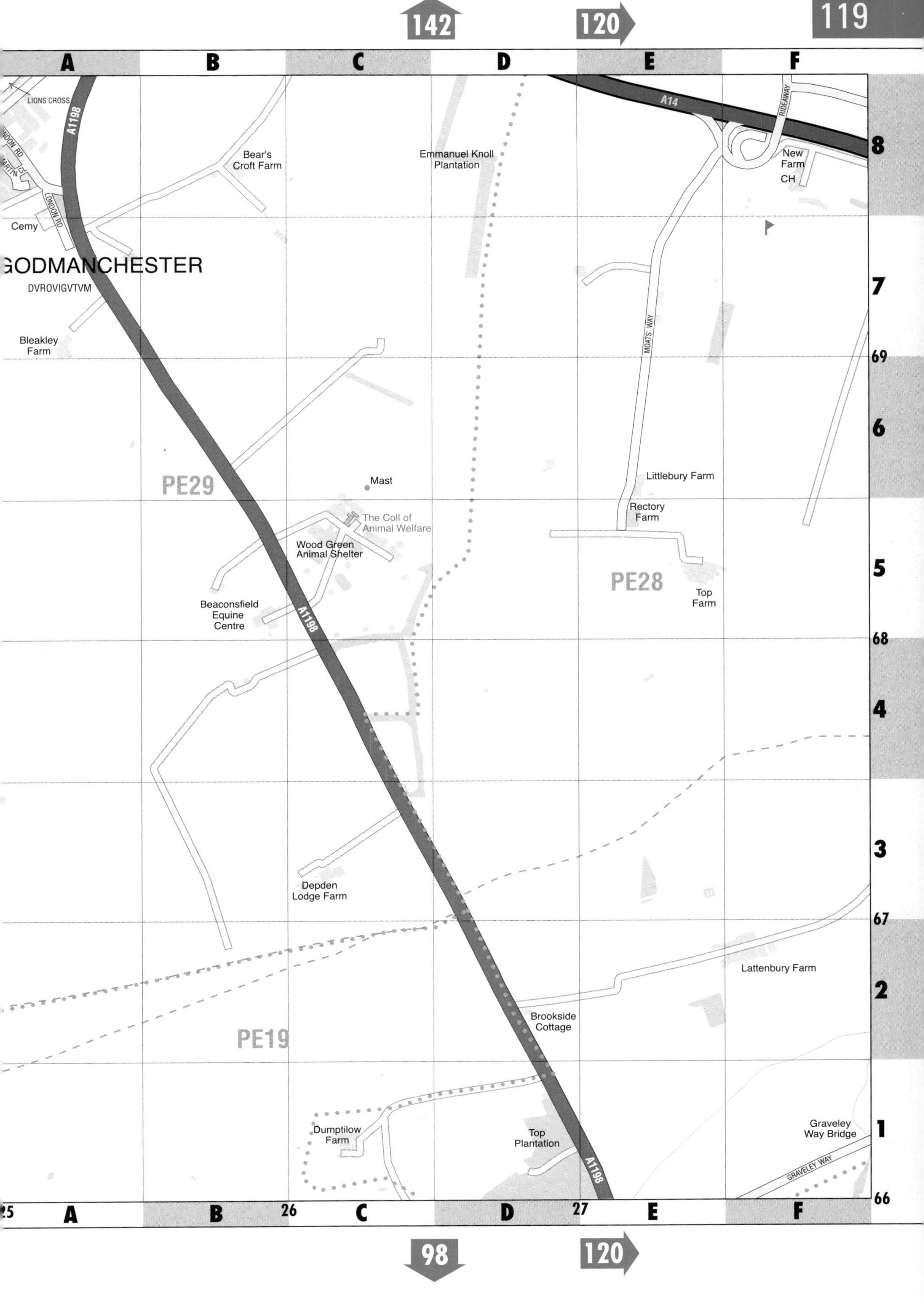

A   B   C   D   E   F

LIONS CROSS

Bear's
Croft Farm

Emmanuel Knoll
Plantation

A14

RIDGEWAY

New
Farm
CH

8

Cemy

GODMANCHESTER

DVROVIGVTVM

7

Bleakley
Farm

69

PE29

6

MOATS WAY

Littlebury Farm

Mast

The Coll of
Animal Welfare

Rectory
Farm

Wood Green
Animal Shelter

PE28

5

Beaconsfield
Equine
Centre

Top
Farm

68

A1198

4

3

Depden
Lodge Farm

67

Lattenbury Farm

2

Brookside
Cottage

PE19

Dumptilow
Farm

Top
Plantation

A1198

Graveley
Way Bridge

1

GRAVELEY WAY

66

25   A   B   26   C   D   27   E   F

119
143

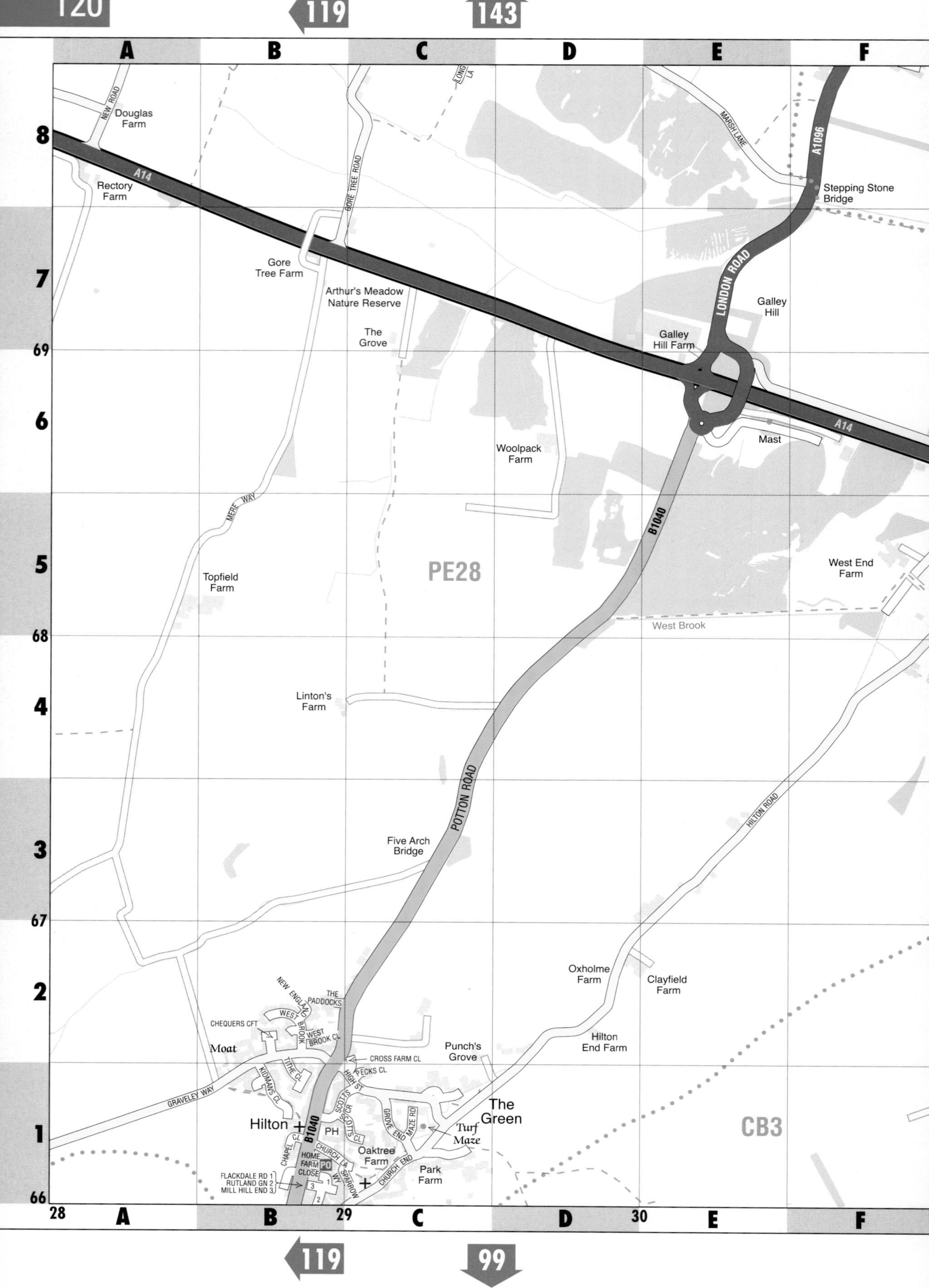
A
B
C
D
E
F
8
7
69
6
5
68
4
3
67
2
1
66
28
29
30
NEW ROAD
Douglas Farm
A14
Rectory Farm
LONG LA
GORE TREE ROAD
Gore Tree Farm
Arthur's Meadow Nature Reserve
The Grove
MARSH LANE
A1096
Stepping Stone Bridge
LONDON ROAD
Galley Hill
Galley Hill Farm
Mast
Woolpack Farm
MERE WAY
B1040
Topfield Farm
PE28
West End Farm
West Brook
Linton's Farm
POTTON ROAD
HILTON ROAD
Five Arch Bridge
Oxholme Farm
Clayfield Farm
NEW ENGLAND
THE PADDOCKS
WEST BROOK
CHEQUERS CFT
WEST BROOK CL
Moat
CROSS FARM CL
Punch's Grove
Hilton End Farm
PECKS CL
TITHE CL
KIDMANS CL
HIGH ST
GRAVELEY WAY
SCOTTS CR
SCOTTS CL
GROVE END
MAZE RD
The Green
Turf Maze
Hilton
PH
CHAPEL CL
CHURCH LA
Oaktree Farm
HOME FARM CLOSE
PO
SPARROW WY
CHURCH END
Park Farm
FLACKDALE RD 1
RUTLAND GN 2
MILL HILL END 3
CB3

119
99

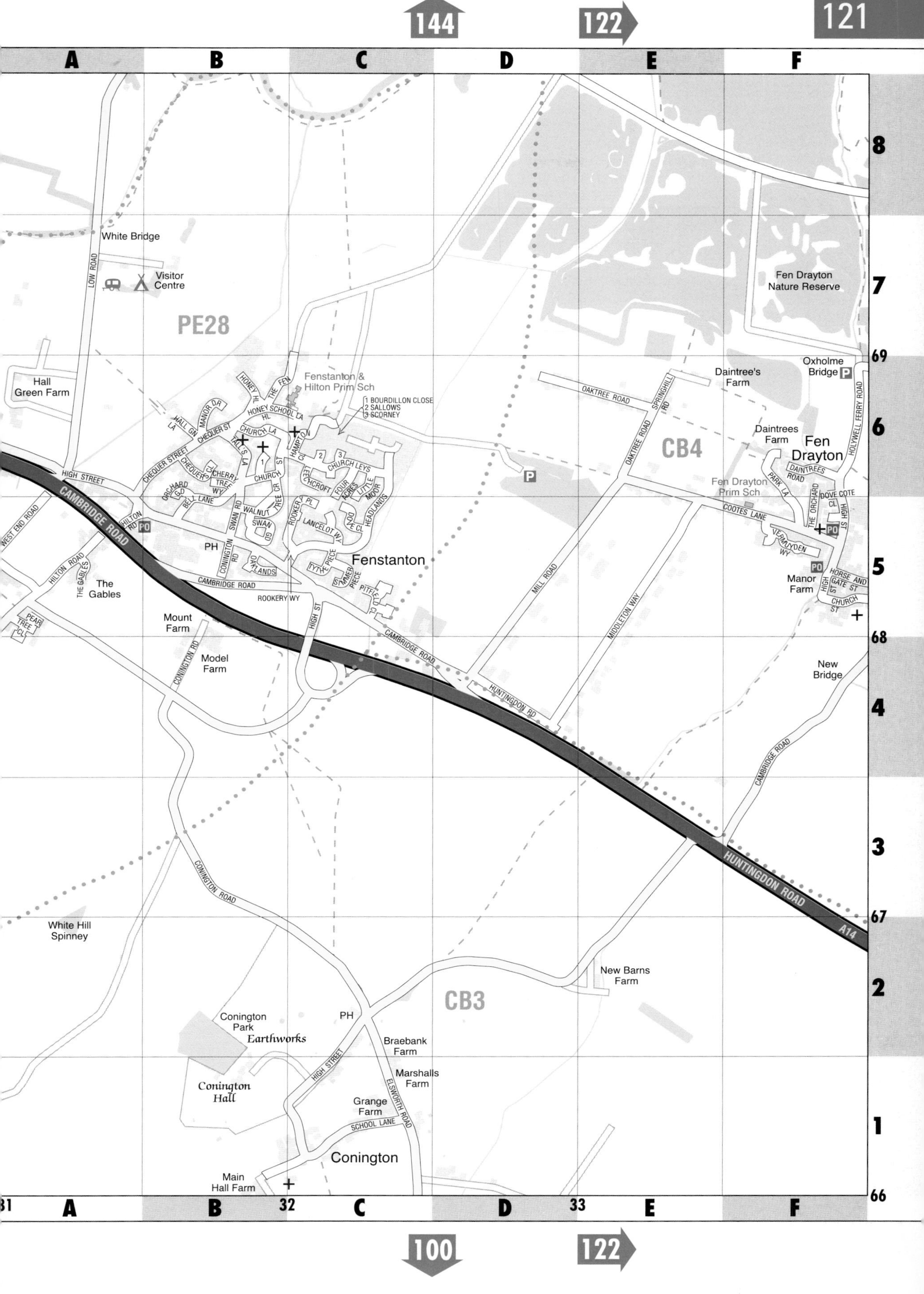
144
122
A
B
C
D
E
F
8
7
6
5
4
3
2
1
69
68
67
66
31
32
33
100
122
White Bridge
LOW ROAD
Visitor Centre
PE28
Hall Green Farm
Fenstanton & Hilton Prim Sch
1 BOURDILLON CLOSE
2 SALLOWS
3 SCORNEY
HIGH STREET
CAMBRIDGE ROAD
WEST END ROAD
HILTON ROAD
THE GABLES
The Gables
PEAR TREE CL
PH
Fenstanton
ROOKERY WY
Mount Farm
Model Farm
CONINGTON RD
HIGH ST
CAMBRIDGE ROAD
HUNTINGDON RD
MILL ROAD
MIDDLETON WAY
OAKTREE ROAD
SPRINGHILL RD
CB4
Daintree's Farm
Oxholme Bridge
HOLYWELL FERRY ROAD
Daintrees Farm
Fen Drayton
DAINTREES ROAD
Fen Drayton Prim Sch
COOTES LANE
PARK LA
THE ORCHARD
DOVE COTE CL
VERMUYDEN WY
Manor Farm
HORSE AND GATE ST
CHURCH ST
Fen Drayton Nature Reserve
New Bridge
CAMBRIDGE ROAD
HUNTINGDON ROAD
A14
CONINGTON ROAD
White Hill Spinney
CB3
New Barns Farm
Conington Park
Earthworks
PH
Braebank Farm
Marshalls Farm
HIGH STREET
ELSWORTH ROAD
Conington Hall
Grange Farm
SCHOOL LANE
Conington
Main Hall Farm

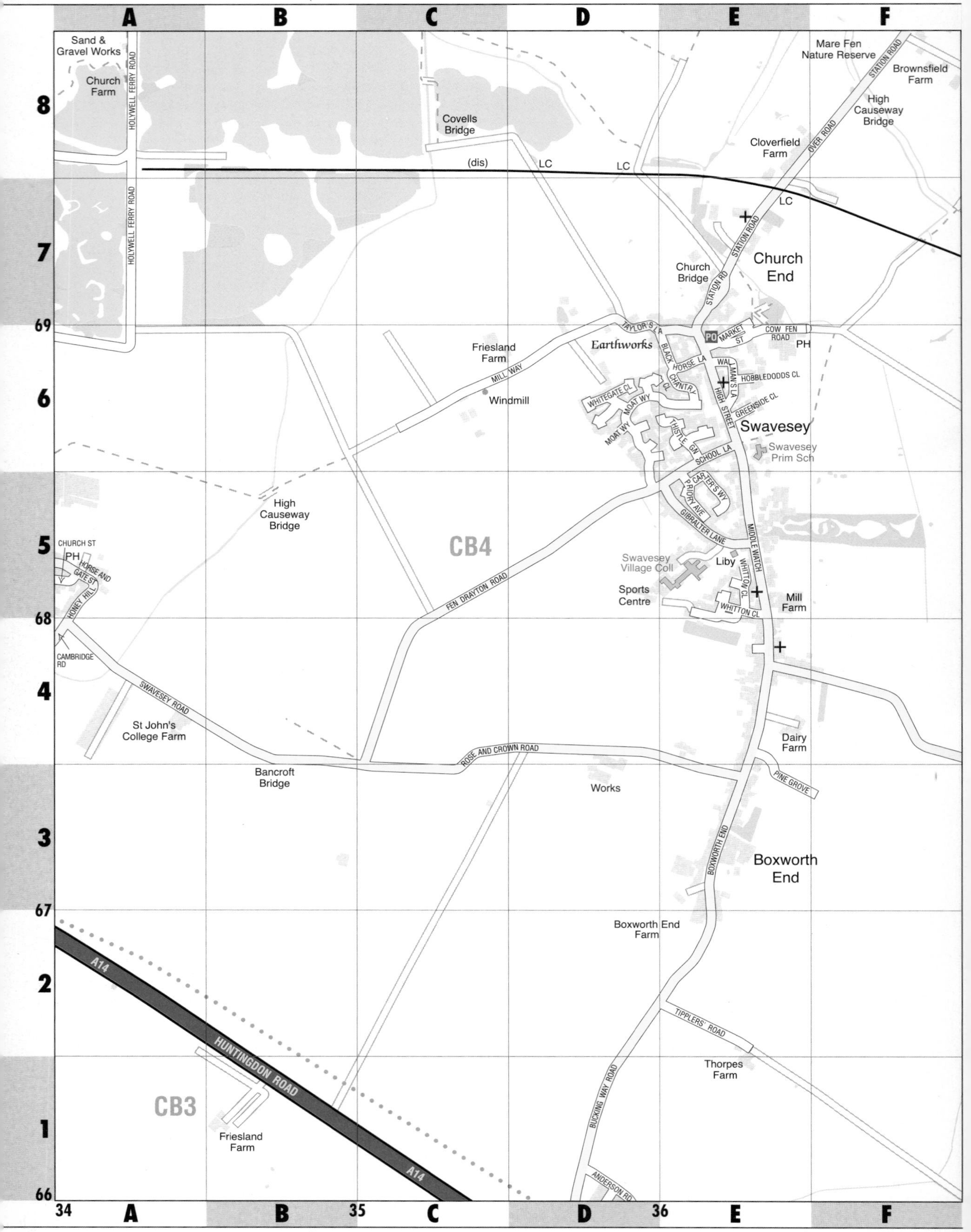

A B C D E F

8

Sand & Gravel Works

Church Farm

HOLYWELL FERRY ROAD

Covells Bridge

Mare Fen Nature Reserve

Brownsfield Farm

High Causeway Bridge

Cloverfield Farm

OVER ROAD

STATION ROAD

(dis)   LC   LC   LC

7

HOLYWELL FERRY ROAD

Church Bridge

STATION RD

Church End

STATION ROAD

Swavesey

69

Friesland Farm

MILL WAY

Earthworks

TAYLOR'S LA

BLACK CHANTRY

HORSE LA

PO

MARKET ST

COW FEN ROAD

PH

6

Windmill

WHITEGATE CL

MOAT WY

MOAT WY

HISTLE GIN

CHANTRY CL

HIGH STREET

WAL

MAIN'S LA

HOBBLEDODDS CL

GREENSIDE CL

SCHOOL LA

Swavesey Prim Sch

CB4

High Causeway Bridge

CARTER'S WY

PRIORY AVE

GIBRALTER LANE

Swavesey

MIDDLE WATCH

Liby

5

CHURCH ST

PH

HORSE AND GATE ST

Swavesey Village Coll

Sports Centre

WHITTON CL

WHITTON CL

Mill Farm

68

HONEY HILL

CAMBRIDGE RD

FEN DRAYTON ROAD

4

SWAVESEY ROAD

St John's College Farm

Dairy Farm

PINE GROVE

Bancroft Bridge

ROSE AND CROWN ROAD

Works

3

BOXWORTH END

Boxworth End

67

A14

Boxworth End Farm

2

A14

HUNTINGDON ROAD

TIPPLERS' ROAD

BUCKING WAY ROAD

Thorpes Farm

1

CB3

Friesland Farm

ANDERSON RD

66

34   A   B   35   C   D   36   E   F

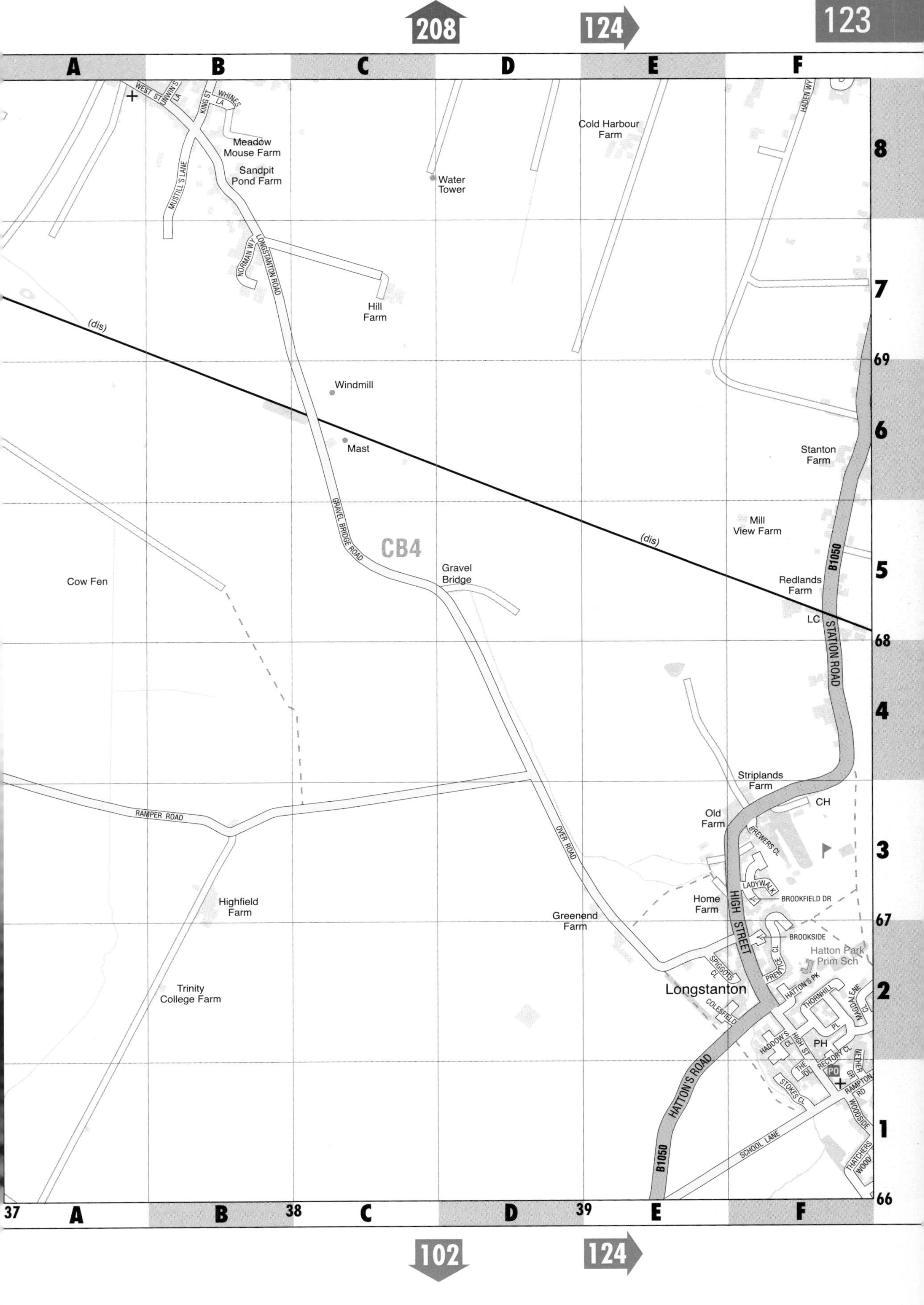

A B C D E F

8
7
69
6
5
68
4
67
3
2
1
66

West St
Mustill's La
King St
Whines La

+

Meadow Mouse Farm

Sandpit Pond Farm

Cold Harbour Farm

Water Tower

Norman Wy

Longstanton Road

Hill Farm

Windmill

Mast

(dis)

Gravel Bridge Road

CB4

Gravel Bridge

Cow Fen

(dis)

Stanton Farm

Mill View Farm

Redlands Farm

B1050

LC

Station Road

Ramper Road

Over Road

Striplands Farm

CH

Old Farm

Brewers Cl

Highfield Farm

Greenend Farm

Home Farm

Ladywalk

Brookfield Dr

High Street

Brookside

Hatton Park Prim Sch

Trinity College Farm

Longstanton

Spinolds Cl

to PH

Hatton's Pk

Thornhill Pl

Maygate La

Colesfield

Haddon's Cl

The Idl

High St

Rectory Cl

PH

Nether Rd

Hatton's Road

PO

+

Stokes Cl

Woodside

Rampton Rd

B1050

School Lane

Thatchers Wood

Haden Wy

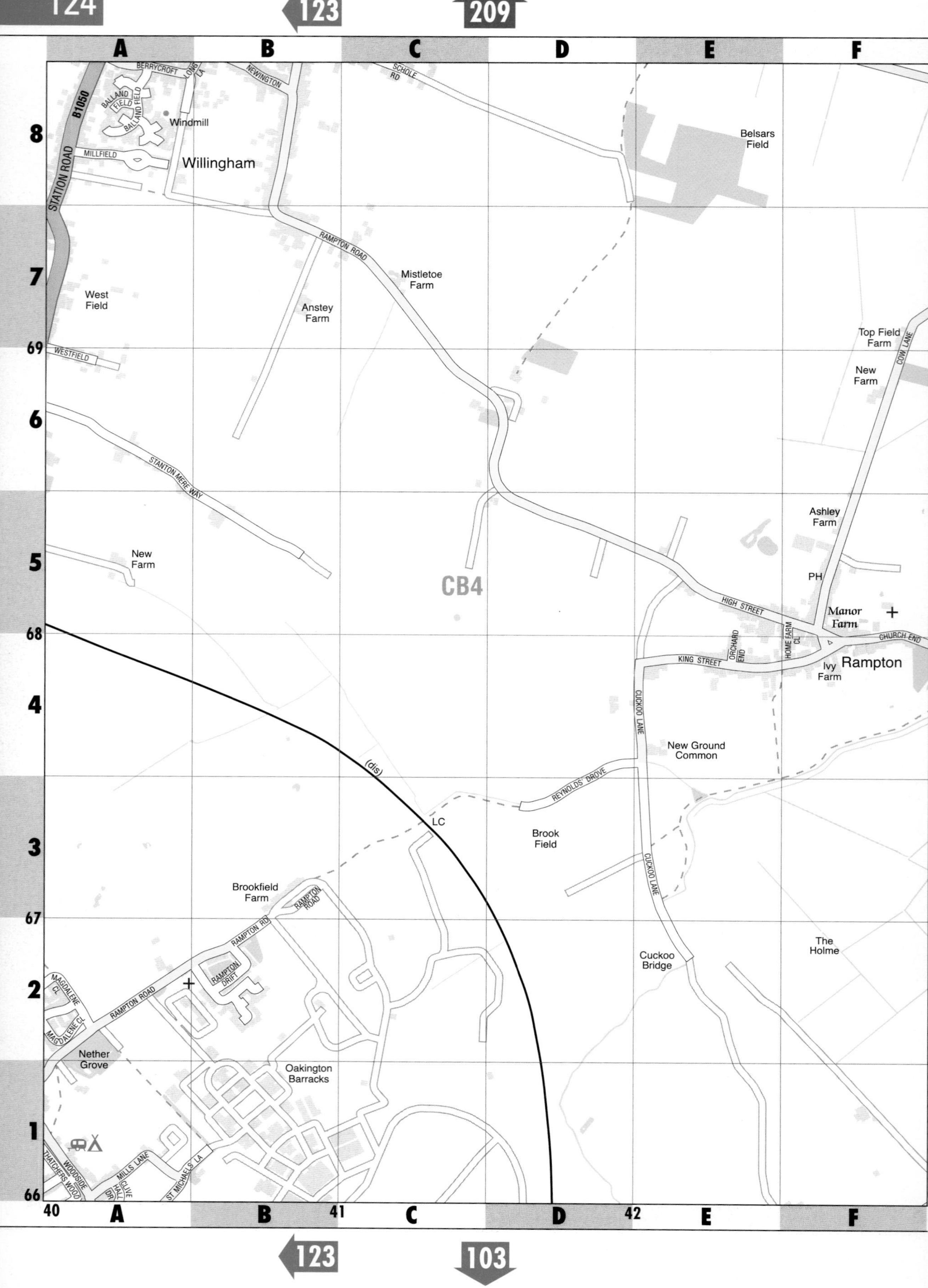

123
209

A **B** **C** **D** **E** **F**

B1050

Berrycroft

Long La

Newington

Schole Rd

Balland Field

Millfield Field

Windmill

8

Willingham

Belsars Field

Rampton Road

West Field

7

Mistletoe Farm

Anstey Farm

Top Field Farm

69

Westfield

New Farm

Cow Lane

6

Stanton Mere Way

Ashley Farm

5

New Farm

CB4

PH

Manor Farm

High Street

Orchard End

Home Farm Dr

Church End

68

Ivy Farm

Rampton

King Street

4

Cuckoo Lane

New Ground Common

(dis)

Reynolds Drove

LC

Brook Field

3

Cuckoo Lane

Brookfield Farm

Rampton Rd

Rampton Road

67

The Holme

Cuckoo Bridge

Magdalene Cl

Rampton Drift

2

Rampton Road

Magdalene Cl

Nether Grove

Oakington Barracks

Woodside

1

Thatchers Wood

Mills Lane

St Michaels La

Clive Hall Dr

66

40 **A** **B** 41 **C** **D** 42 **E** **F**

123
103

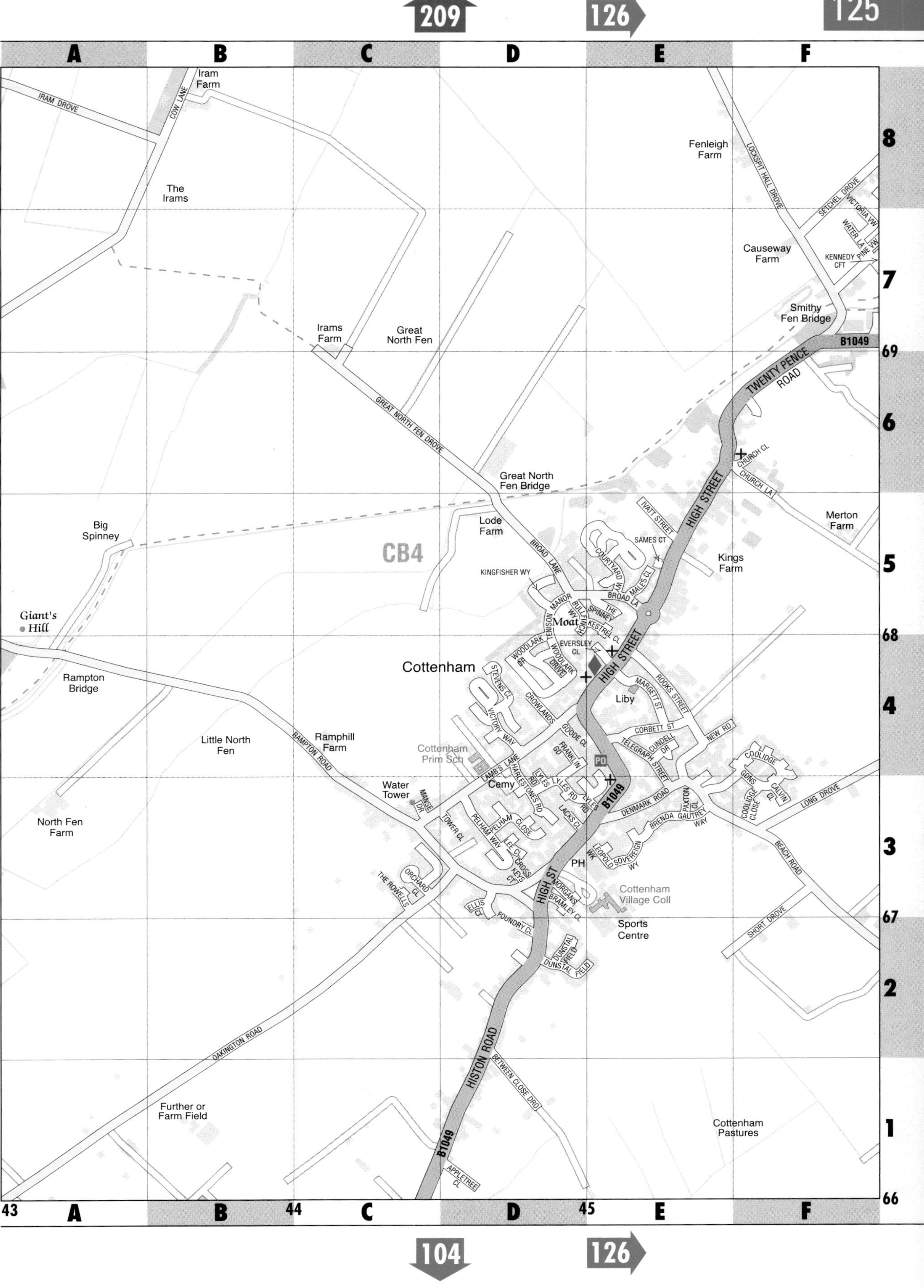

209
126

A B C D E F

8

7

Fenleigh
Farm

IRAM DROVE

Iram
Farm

COW LANE

The
Irams

Causeway
Farm

LOCKSPIT HALL DROVE

SETCHEL DROVE

VICTORIA TW

WATER LA

PINE TW

KENNEDY
CFT

Smithy
Fen Bridge

B1049

69

6

Irams
Farm

Great
North Fen

GREAT NORTH FEN DRIVE

TWENTY PENCE ROAD

CHURCH CL

CHURCH LA

Merton
Farm

5

Big
Spinney

CB4

Great North
Fen Bridge

Lode
Farm

BROAD LANE

KINGFISHER WY

IVATT STREET

SAMES CT

HIGH STREET

BROAD MALES CL

Kings
Farm

Giant's
Hill

MANOR WY

THE SPINNEY

BILLY KESTREL CL

MUSSELL WOOD BR

WOODLARK BR

WOODLARK DRIVE

68

4

Rampton
Bridge

Little North
Fen

RAMPTON ROAD

Ramphill
Farm

STEVENS CT

Moat

Cottenham

EVERSLEY
CL

HIGH STREET

Liby

ROOKS STREET

MARGETT ST

CORBETT ST

CUNDELL DR

TELEGRAPH STREET

NEW RD

COOLIDGE

BONS

CALTON

North Fen
Farm

Cottenham
Prim Sch

VICTORY WAY

CROMWELLS

LAMB'S LANE

PELHAM WAY

HARLESTONES RD

LYLES RD

GOODE CL

FRANKLIN RD

PO

B1049

DENMARK ROAD

BRENDA GAUTREY WY

PAXTON WAY

COOLIDGE CLOSE

LONG DROVE

BEACH ROAD

3

67

Water
Tower

Cemy

MANSE DR

TOWER CL

ORCHARD CL

THE ROWELLS

ELLIS CL

FOUNDRY CL

LEE CL

CROSS KEYS

LACKS CT

HIGH ST

WK

LEOPOLD

SOVEREIGN WY

MORGANS

BRAMLEY CL

PH

Cottenham
Village Coll

Sports
Centre

SHORT DROVE

2

OAKINGTON ROAD

HISTON ROAD

BETWEEN CLOSE DROJ

DUNSTAL FIELD

Cottenham
Pastures

1

Further or
Farm Field

B1049

APPLETREE CL

66

43 A B 44 C D 45 E F

125
210

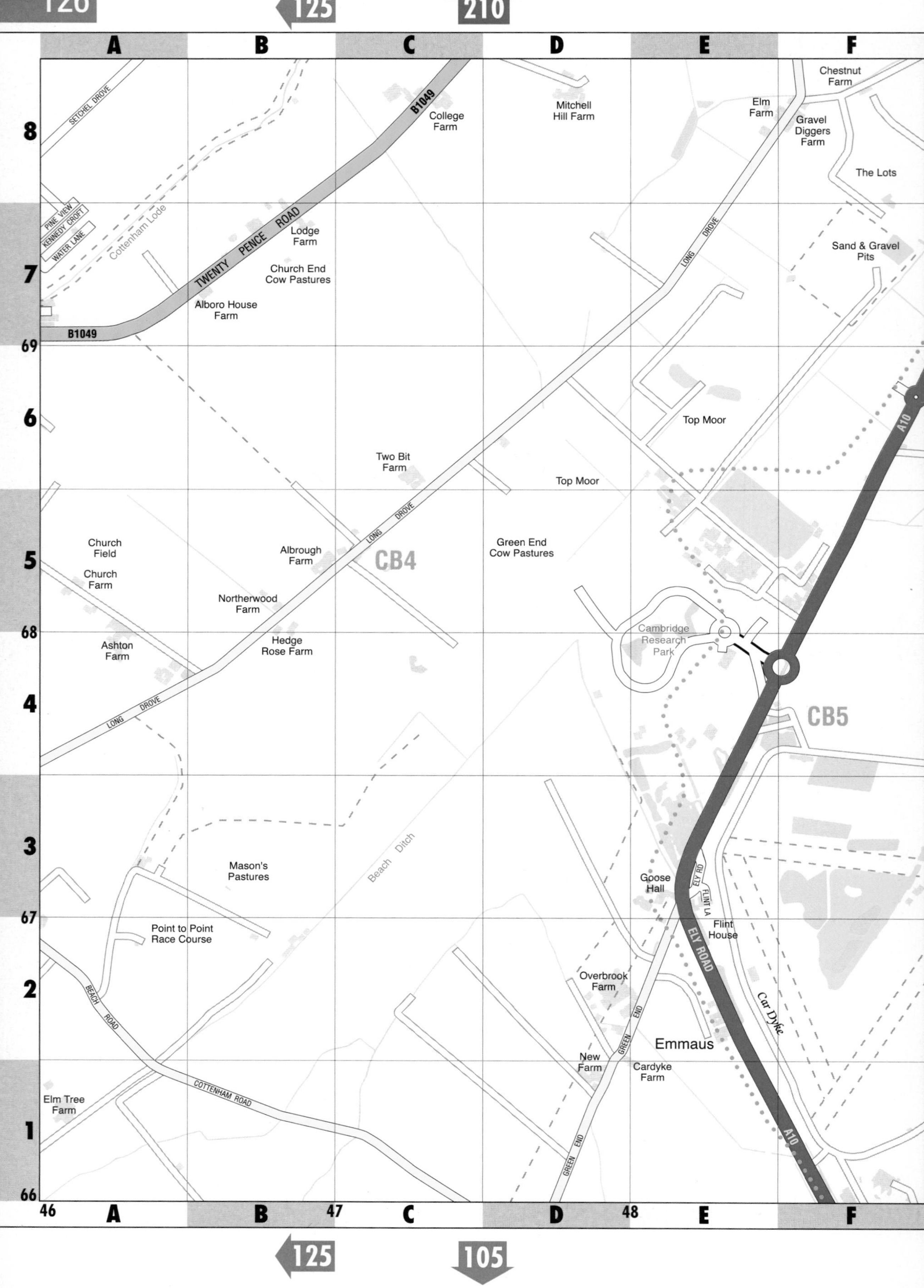
A
B
C
D
E
F
8
7
69
6
5
68
4
3
67
2
1
66
46
47
48
SETCHEL DROVE
B1049
College Farm
Mitchell Hill Farm
Elm Farm
Chestnut Farm
Gravel Diggers Farm
The Lots
PINE VIEW
KENNEDY CROFT
WATER LANE
Cottenham Lode
TWENTY PENCE ROAD
Lodge Farm
Church End Cow Pastures
Alboro House Farm
LONG DROVE
Sand & Gravel Pits
Top Moor
Two Bit Farm
Top Moor
A10
Church Field
Church Farm
Albrough Farm
CB4
Green End Cow Pastures
Northerwood Farm
Hedge Rose Farm
Ashton Farm
Cambridge Research Park
CB5
Beach Ditch
Mason's Pastures
Goose Hall
ELY RD
FLINT LA
Flint House
Point to Point Race Course
ELY ROAD
Car Dyke
Overbrook Farm
BEACH ROAD
GREEN END
Emmaus
New Farm
Cardyke Farm
COTTENHAM ROAD
Elm Tree Farm

125
105

A B C D E F

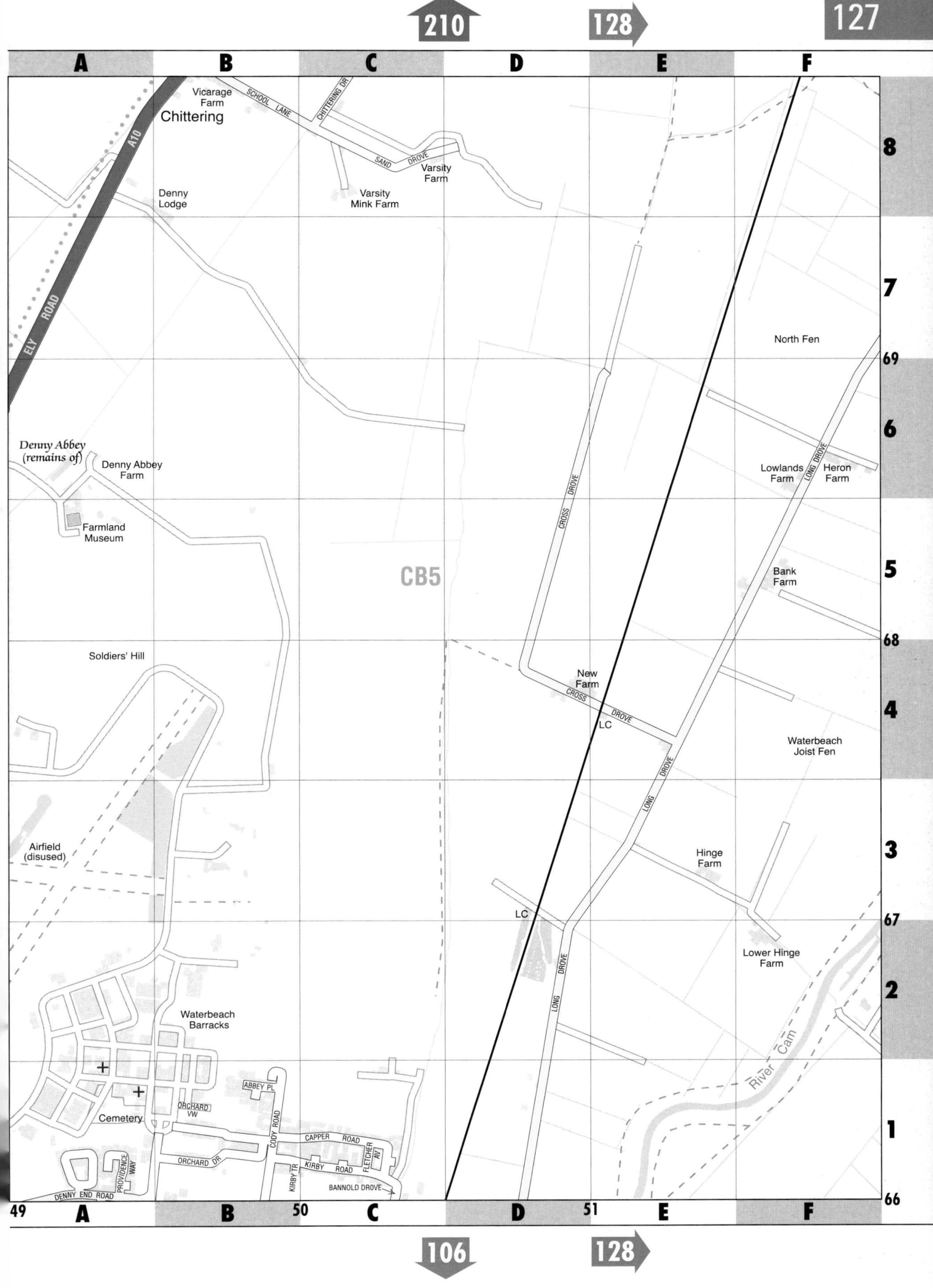

8

7

69

6

5

68

4

3

67

2

1

66

Vicarage Farm
SCHOOL LANE
CHITTERING DR
Chittering
SAND DROVE
Varsity Farm

Denny Lodge

Varsity Mink Farm

North Fen

Denny Abbey (remains of)
Denny Abbey Farm

Lowlands Farm
LONG DROVE
Heron Farm

Farmland Museum

CB5

Bank Farm

Soldiers' Hill

CROSS DROVE

New Farm
CROSS DROVE
LC

Waterbeach Joist Fen

Airfield (disused)

LONG DROVE

Hinge Farm

LC

Lower Hinge Farm

River Cam

Waterbeach Barracks

LONG DROVE

Cemetery
ORCHARD VW
ABBEY PL
CODY ROAD
CAPPER ROAD
KIRBY TR
KIRBY ROAD
FLETCHER AV
ORCHARD DR
PROVIDENCE WAY
DENNY END ROAD
BANNOLD DROVE

ELY ROAD
A10

127
211

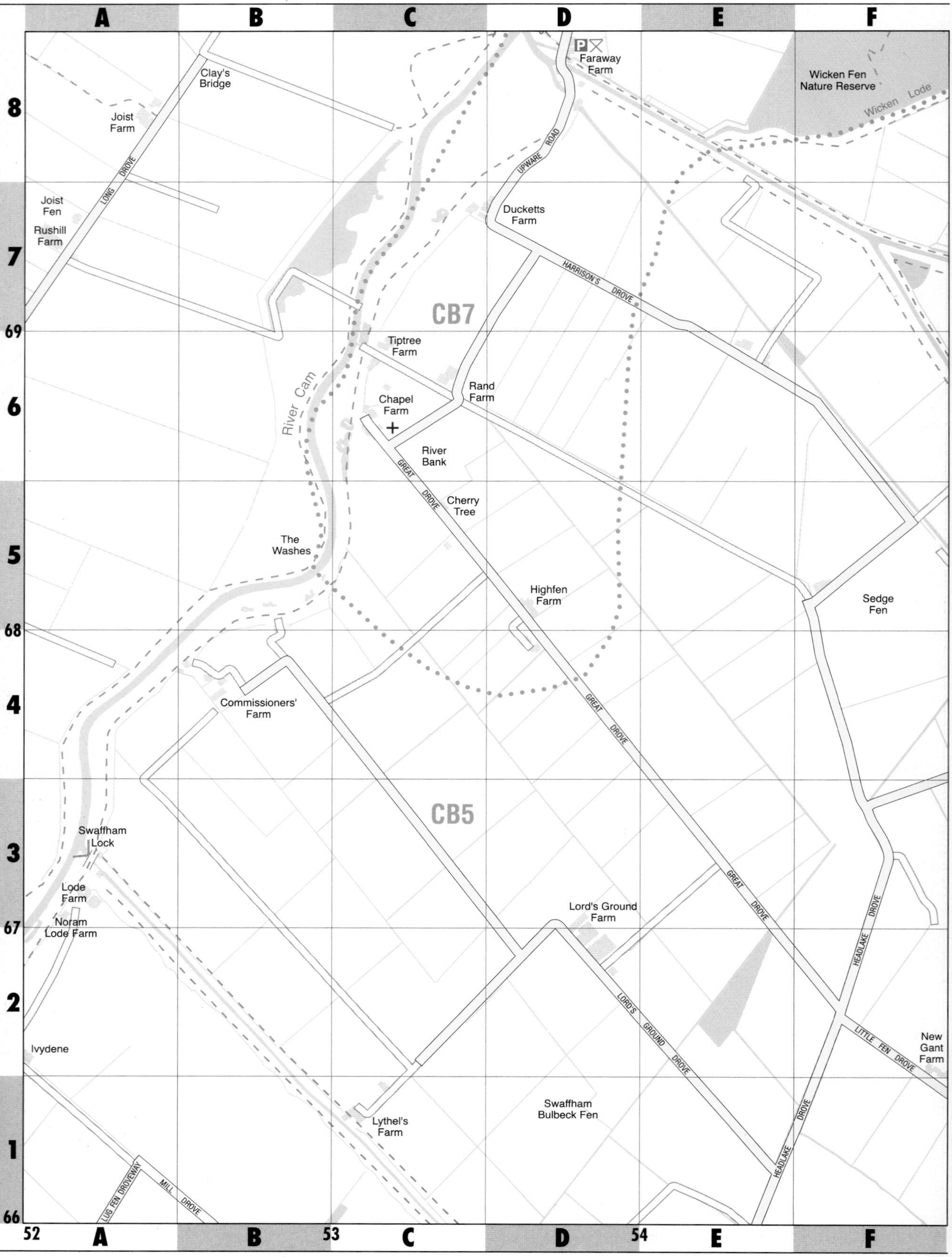

A B C D E F

8

Clay's
Bridge

Joist
Farm

Joist
Fen

Rushill
Farm

7

LONG DROVE

UPWARE ROAD

Faraway
Farm

Wicken Fen
Nature Reserve

Wicken Lode

Ducketts
Farm

HARRISON'S DROVE

CB7

69

Tiptree
Farm

River Cam

Rand
Farm

6

Chapel
Farm

River
Bank

GREAT DROVE

Cherry
Tree

The
Washes

5

Highfen
Farm

Sedge
Fen

68

Commissioners'
Farm

GREAT DROVE

4

CB5

Swaffham
Lock

3

Lode
Farm

Lord's Ground
Farm

GREAT DROVE

HEADLAKE DROVE

Noram
Lode Farm

67

2

Ivydene

LORD'S GROUND DROVE

LITTLE FEN DROVE

New
Gant
Farm

Swaffham
Bulbeck Fen

HEADLAKE DROVE

Lythel's
Farm

1

66

LUS FEN DROVEWAY

MILL DROVE

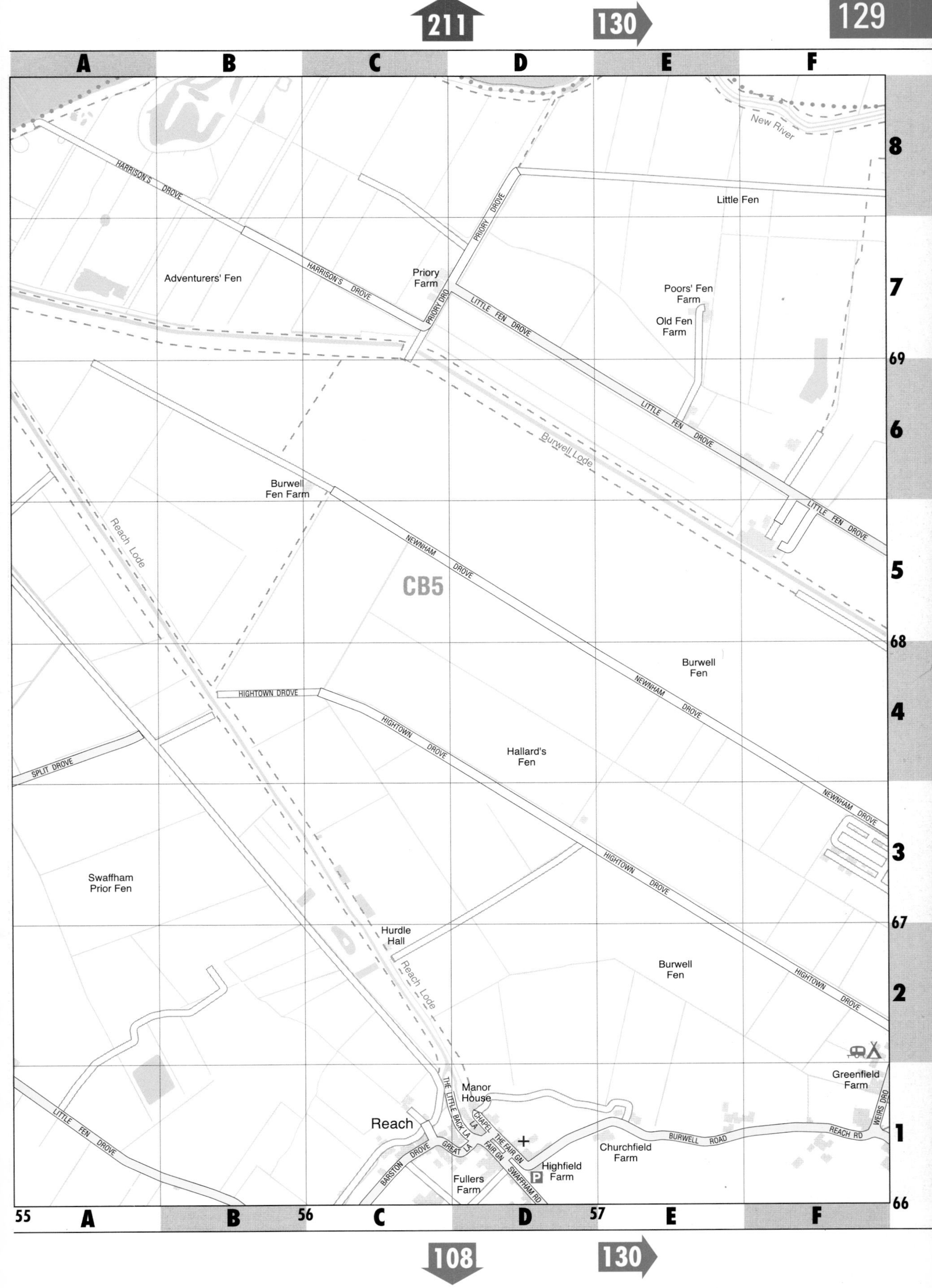

A   B   C   D   E   F

8

New River

Little Fen

HARRISON'S DROVE

7

Adventurers' Fen

HARRISON'S DROVE

Priory
Farm

PRIORY DRO

PRIORY DROVE

LITTLE FEN DROVE

Poors' Fen
Farm

Old Fen
Farm

69

6

Burwell Lode

LITTLE FEN DROVE

Reach Lode

Burwell
Fen Farm

NEWNHAM DROVE

CB5

LITTLE FEN DROVE

5

68

Burwell
Fen

HIGHTOWN DROVE

HIGHTOWN DROVE

Hallard's
Fen

NEWNHAM DROVE

NEWNHAM DROVE

4

SPLIT DROVE

3

Swaffham
Prior Fen

HIGHTOWN DROVE

Burwell
Fen

67

Hurdle
Hall

Reach Lode

HIGHTOWN DROVE

2

Greenfield
Farm

LITTLE FEN DROVE

Manor
House

THE LITTLE BACK LA

Reach

BARSTON DROVE

GREAT

CHAPEL LA

THE FAIR GN

FAIR GN

SWAFFHAM RD

P

Highfield
Farm

Churchfield
Farm

BURWELL ROAD

REACH RD

WEIRS DRO

1

Fullers
Farm

66

55   A   B   56   C   D   57   E   F

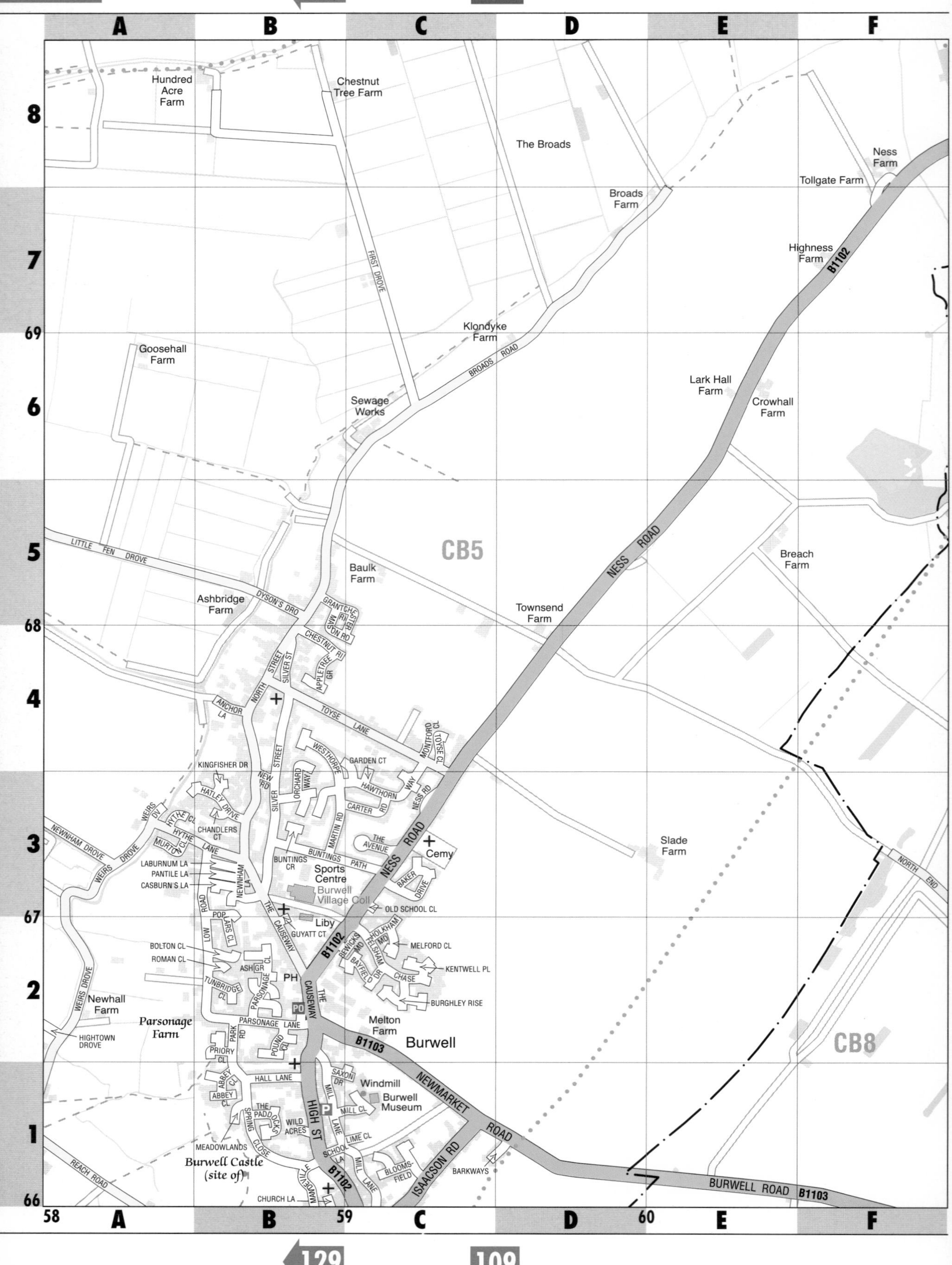

A B C D E F

8
7
69
6
5
68
4
3
67
2
1
66

Hundred Acre Farm
Chestnut Tree Farm
The Broads
Broads Farm
Ness Farm
Tollgate Farm
Highness Farm
B1102
Klondyke Farm
BROADS ROAD
Goosehall Farm
Lark Hall Farm
Crowhall Farm
Sewage Works
FIRST DROVE
CB5
NESS ROAD
Breach Farm
LITTLE FEN DROVE
Baulk Farm
Townsend Farm
Ashbridge Farm
DYSON'S DRO
GRANTCHE
PL
SILVER ST
CHESTNUT RI
APPLETREE GR
NORTH STREET
Slade Farm
NORTH END
ANCHOR LA
TOYSE LANE
MONTFORD CL
TOYSE CL
KINGFISHER DR
WESTHORPE
GARDEN CT
NEW RD
ORCHARD WAY
CARTER RD
HAWTHORN RD
NESS ROAD
HATLEY DRIVE
SILVER STREET
MARTIN RD
THE AVENUE
NEWNHAM DROVE
WEIRS DV
HYTHE CL
CHANDLERS CT
BUNTINGS PATH
Cemy
WEIRS DROVE
MURTON
HYTHE LANE
BUNTINGS CR
Sports Centre
LABURNUM LA
PANTILE LA
CASBURN'S LA
NEWNHAM LA
Burwell Village Coll
BAKER DRIVE
NEWNHAM
OLD SCHOOL CL
POP CL
JAS CL
Liby
THE CAUSEWAY
GUYATT CT
BOLTON CL
ROMAN CL
LOW ROAD
ASH GR
B1102
MELFORD CL
HOLKHAM
FEESHAM
FELDGATE
BENTOCK RD
CHASE
KENTWELL PL
PH
TUNBRIDGE CL
PARSONAGE CL
Newhall Farm
Parsonage Farm
PARSONAGE LANE
THE CAUSEWAY
POUND
BURGHLEY RISE
HIGHTOWN DROVE
PARK RD
PO
Melton Farm
Burwell
PRIORY CL
B1103
ABBEY CL
HALL LANE
SAXON DR
MILL
Windmill
Burwell Museum
NEWMARKET
MEADOWLANDS
THE PADDOCKS
SPRING CLOSE
WILD ACRES
P
HIGH ST
MILL LANE
MILL CL
LIME CL
ROAD
Burwell Castle (site of)
SCHOOL LA
B1102
MILL LANE
BLOOMS FIELD
ISAACSON RD
BARKWAYS
CHURCH LA
REACH ROAD
BURWELL ROAD
B1103
CB8

58 59 60

A B C D E F

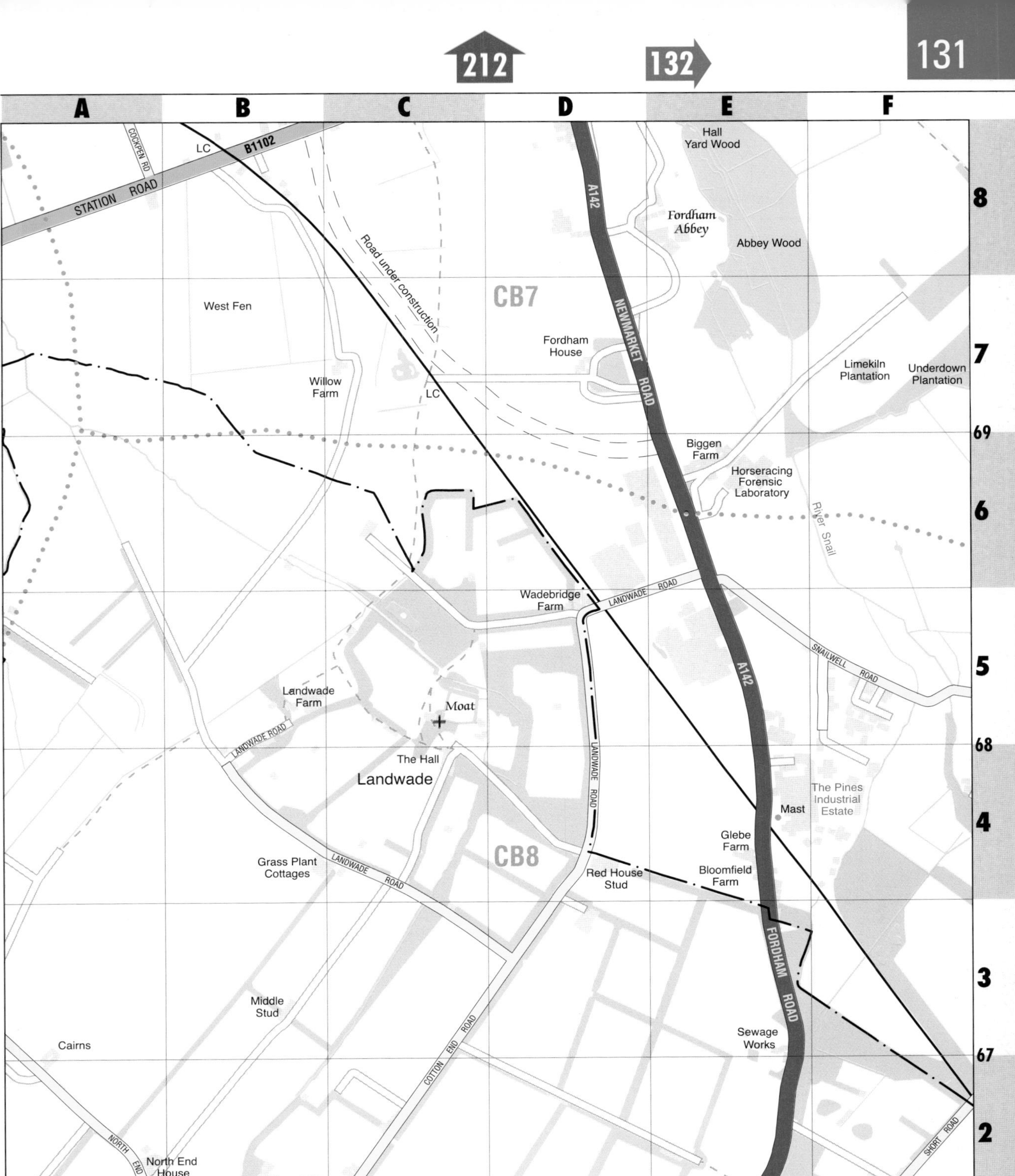

A B C D E F

8
7
69
6
5
68
4
3
67
2
1
66

COCKPEN RD
LC B1102
STATION ROAD

Road under construction

CB7

Hall Yard Wood

Fordham Abbey

Abbey Wood

West Fen

Willow Farm

LC

Fordham House

NEWMARKET ROAD

A142

Limekiln Plantation

Underdown Plantation

Biggen Farm

Horseracing Forensic Laboratory

River Snail

Wadebridge Farm

LANDWADE ROAD

SNAILWELL ROAD

Landwade Farm

LANDWADE ROAD

Moat

The Hall

Landwade

LANDWADE ROAD

Grass Plant Cottages

LANDWADE ROAD

CB8

Red House Stud

Glebe Farm

Bloomfield Farm

A142

Mast

The Pines Industrial Estate

Middle Stud

COTTON END ROAD

Sewage Works

FORDHAM ROAD

Cairns

NORTH END

North End House

Sheepcote Stud

Plantation Stud

SHORT ROAD

COTTON END ROAD

WINDMILL HILL

A142

SNAILWELL SHORT ROAD

Northmore Stud Farm

Rose Hall

MILL LA

GEORGE GIBSON CL

A14

61 A B 62 C D 63 E F

← 131
↑ 213

A	B	C	D	E	F

Chippenham

8

HIGH STREET   PH   NEW STREET

PALACE LANE

B1085

PARKSIDE

Chippenham
Lodge

Underdown
Plantation

Forty
Acre Wood

Gifford
Wood

Chippenham
Hall

7

Chippenham Fen
National
Nature Reserve

The Canal

Jerusalem
Wood

Ash
Wood

69

Chippenham
Park

6

Park
Farm

High Park
Corner

5

CB7

FORDHAM ROAD

68

Foxburrow
Plantation

Coachroad
Plantation

Hundred Acre
Plantation

4

PH

Manor
Farm

Snailwell

CHIPPENHAM   ROAD

Four
Ponds

THE STREET

CHURCH LANE

Church
Farm

THE GREEN

Gravelpit
Plantation

3

SHORT   ROAD

Snailwell
Stud

Sounds
Plantation

67

CB8

2

Lower
Yard

NEWMARKET   ROAD

1

A14

A14

A1304

66

64	A	B	65	C	D	66	E	F

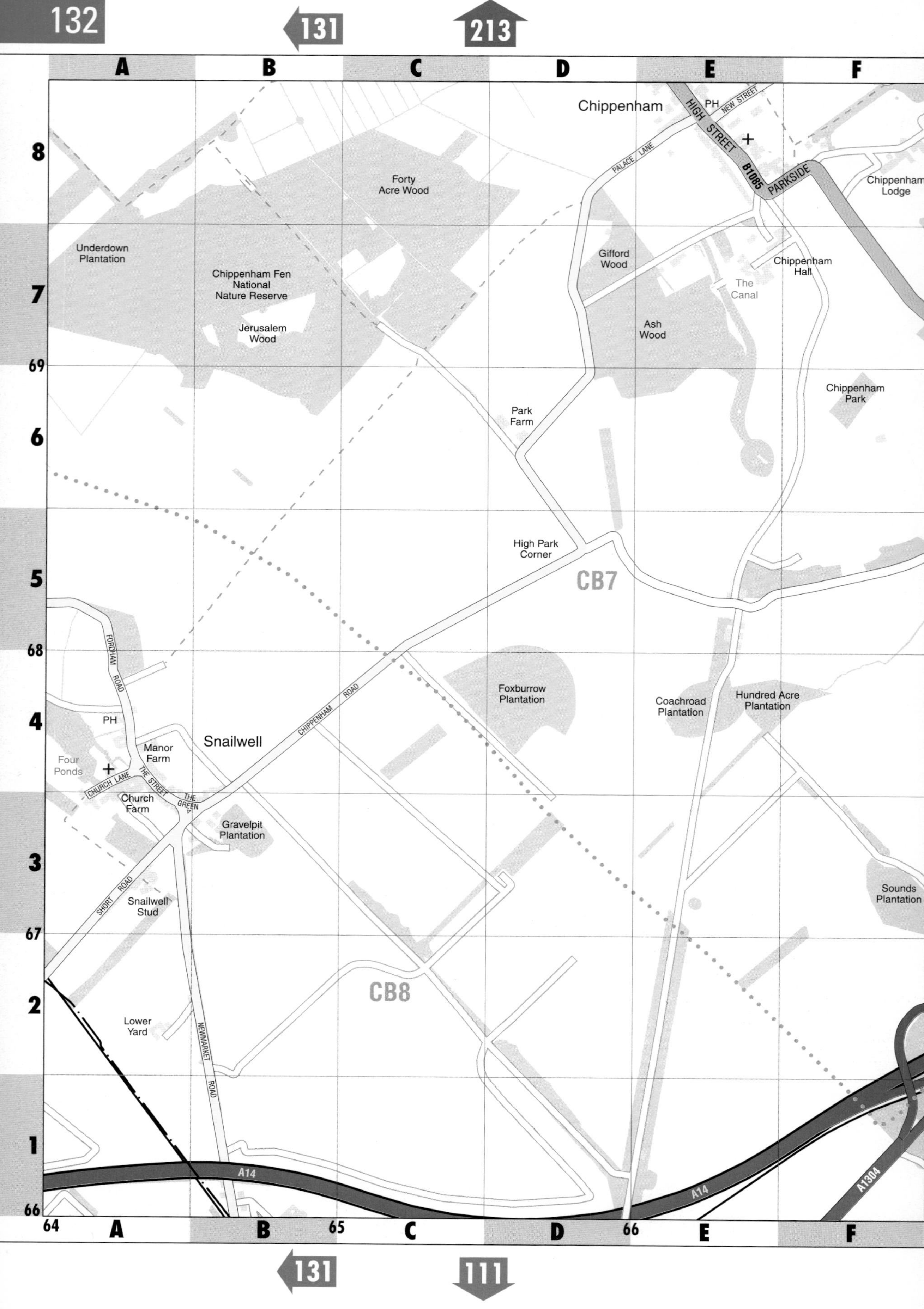

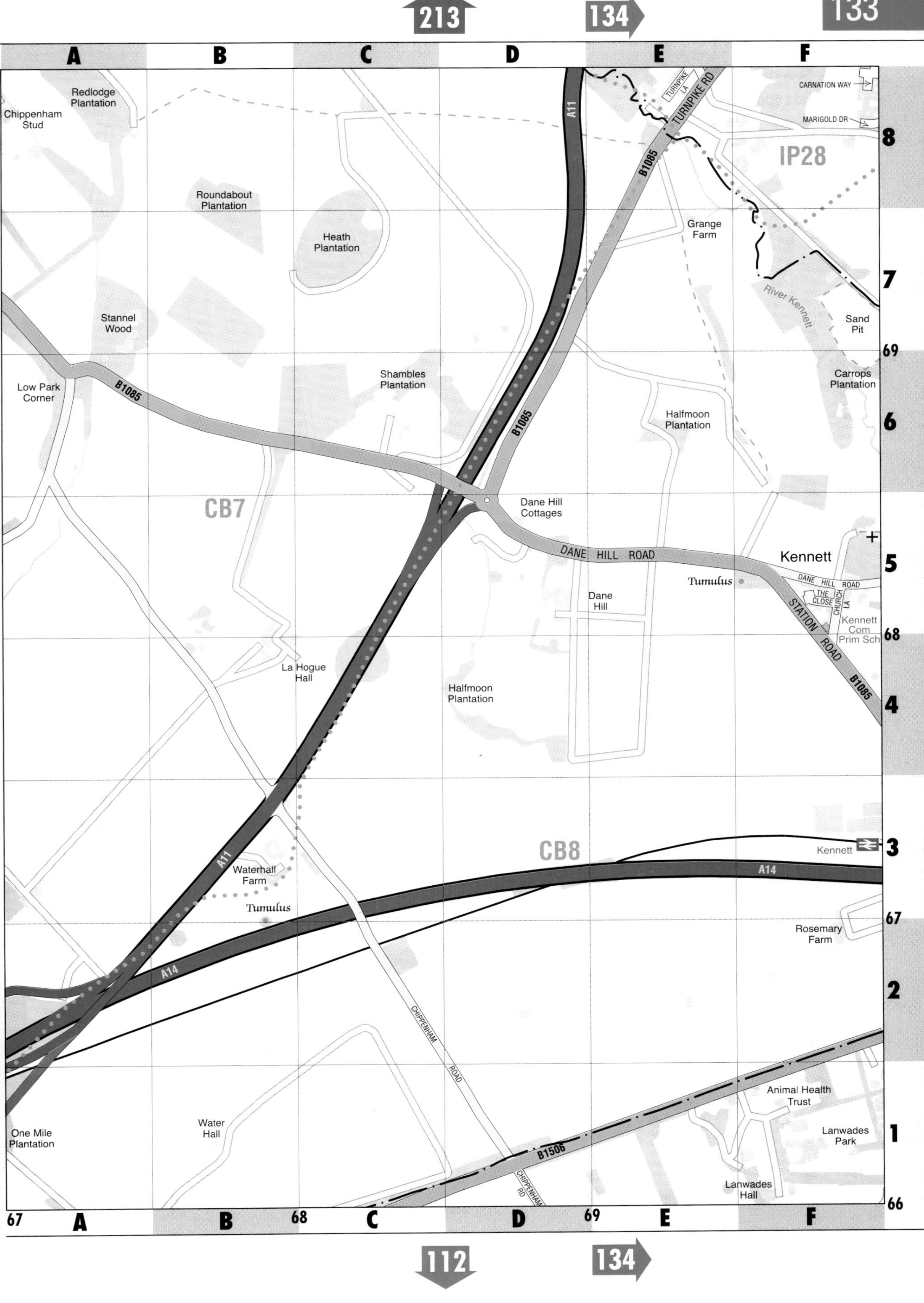

Chippenham Stud

Redlodge Plantation

CARNATION WAY

MARIGOLD DR

IP28

8

Roundabout Plantation

Heath Plantation

Grange Farm

River Kennett

Sand Pit

7

69

Stannel Wood

Shambles Plantation

Halfmoon Plantation

Carrops Plantation

6

Low Park Corner

B1085

B1085

CB7

Dane Hill Cottages

DANE HILL ROAD

Tumulus

Kennett

DANE HILL ROAD

THE CLOSE

Kennett Com Prim Sch

STATION ROAD

B1085

5

68

La Hogue Hall

Dane Hill

Halfmoon Plantation

4

A11

CB8

Kennett

3

Waterhall Farm

Tumulus

A14

Rosemary Farm

67

A14

Water Hall

One Mile Plantation

CHIPPENHAM ROAD

Animal Health Trust

Lanwades Park

2

B1506

CHIPPENHAM RD

Lanwades Hall

1

66

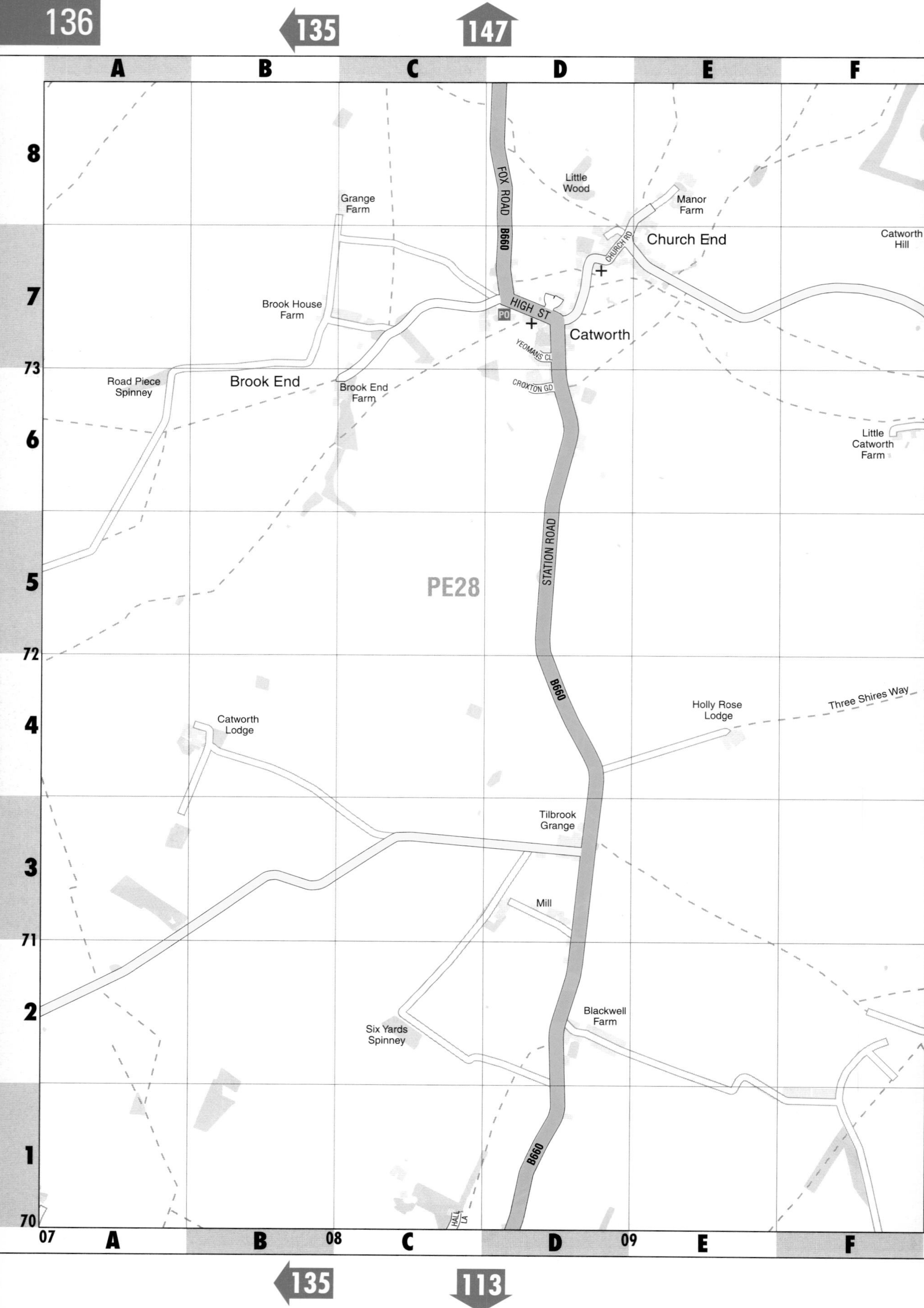

A   B   C   D   E   F

8

7

73

6

5

72

4

3

71

2

1

70

07   A   B   08   C   D   09   E   F

Grange Farm

Little Wood

Manor Farm

Church End

Catworth Hill

FOX ROAD

B660

CHURCH RD

Brook House Farm

HIGH ST

PO

Catworth

Road Piece Spinney

Brook End

Brook End Farm

YEOMANS CL

CROXTON GD

Little Catworth Farm

STATION ROAD

PE28

B660

Holly Rose Lodge

Three Shires Way

Catworth Lodge

Tilbrook Grange

Mill

Six Yards Spinney

Blackwell Farm

B660

HALL LA

148
138

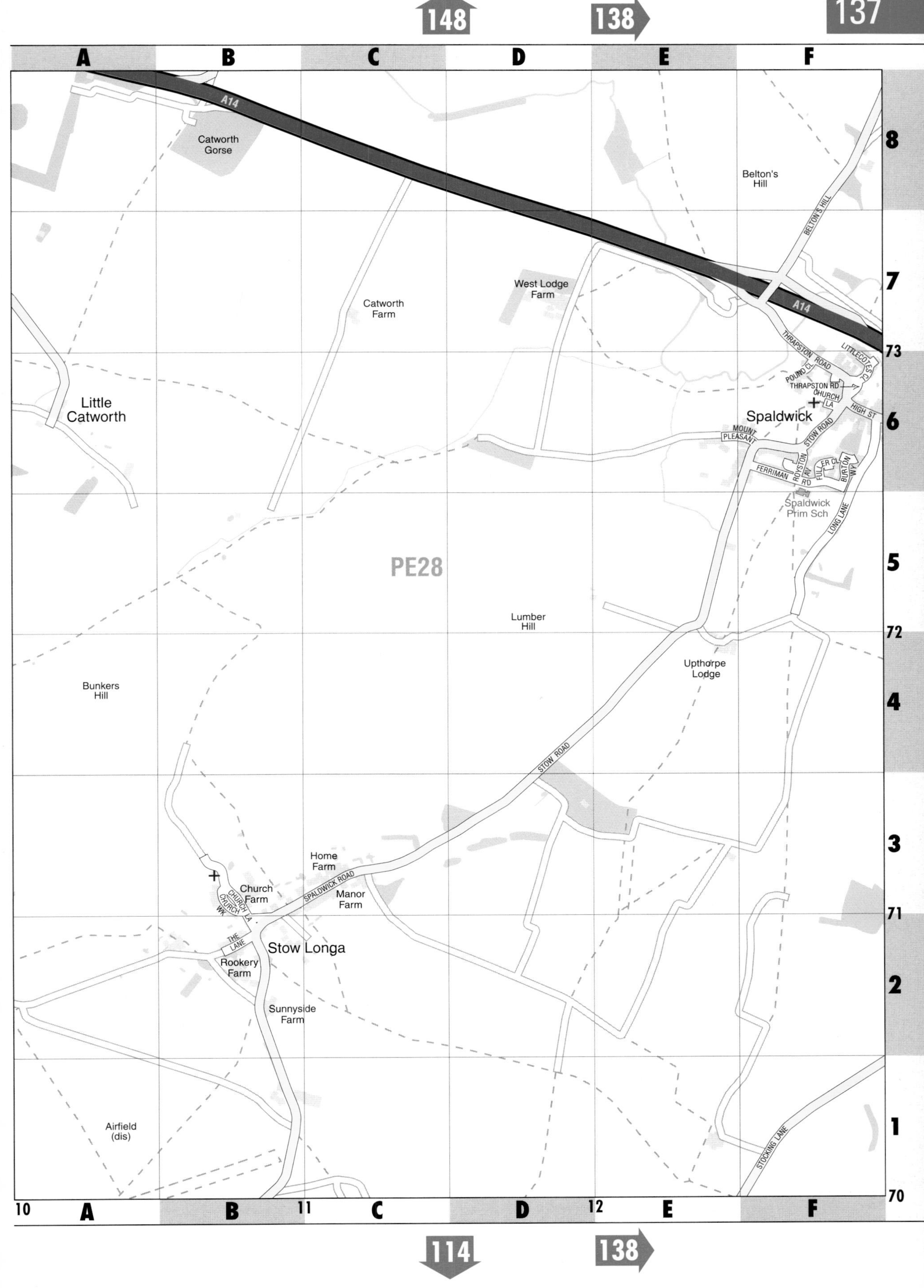
A
B
C
D
E
F
A14
Catworth
Gorse
Belton's
Hill
BELTON'S HILL
West Lodge
Farm
Catworth
Farm
Little
Catworth
THRAPSTON ROAD
LITTLECOTES CL
POUND CL
THRAPSTON RD
CHURCH
LA
HIGH ST
Spaldwick
MOUNT
PLEASANT
STOW ROAD
ROYSTON
AV
FULLER CL
BURTON
WY
FERRIMAN
RD
Spaldwick
Prim Sch
LONG LANE
PE28
Lumber
Hill
Upthorpe
Lodge
Bunkers
Hill
STOW ROAD
Home
Farm
Church
Farm
SPALDWICK ROAD
Manor
Farm
CHURCH LA
CHURCH
WK
THE
LANE
Stow Longa
Rookery
Farm
Sunnyside
Farm
Airfield
(dis)
STOCKING LANE
8
7
73
6
5
72
4
3
71
2
1
70
10
11
12

114
138

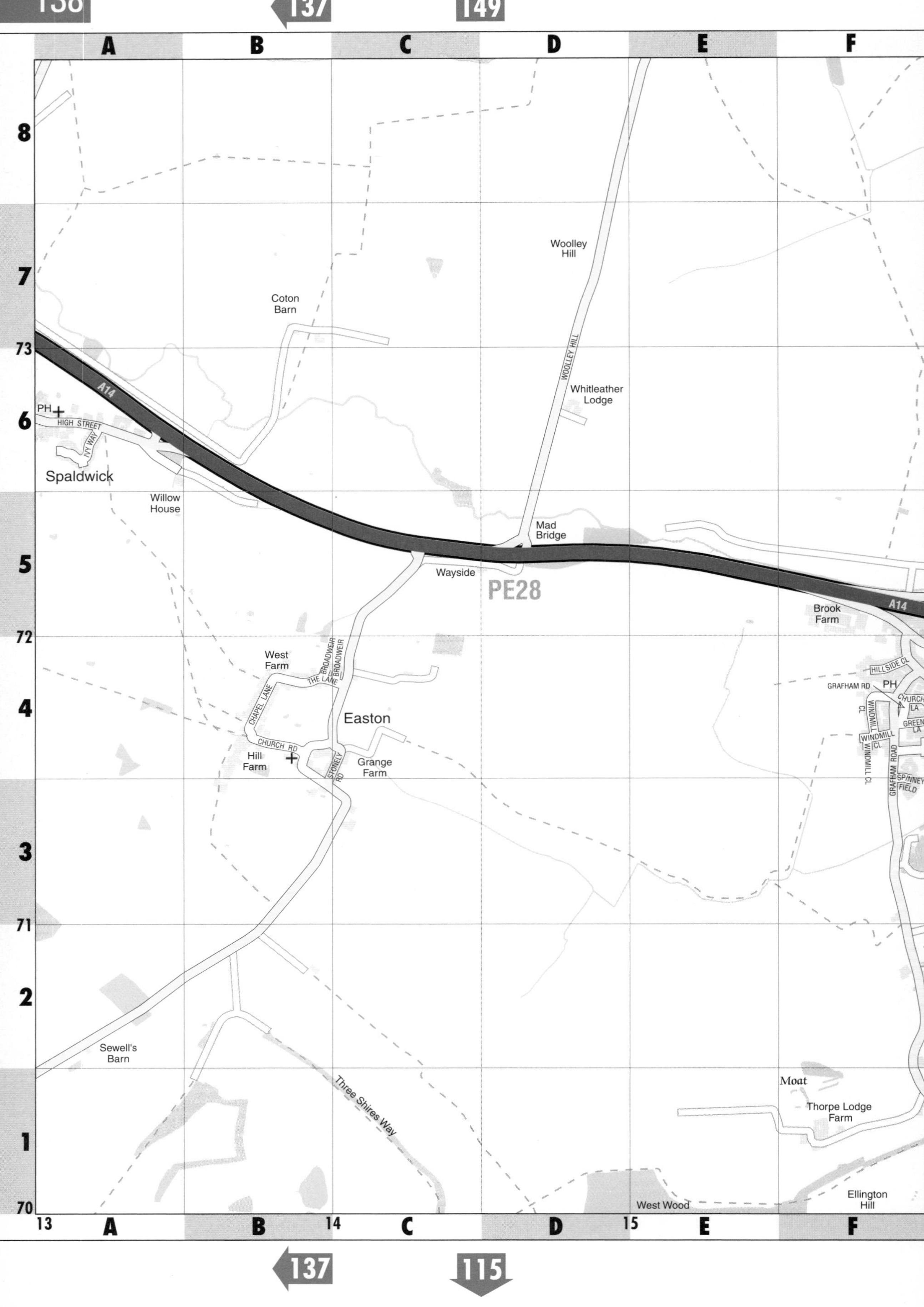

A B C D E F

8

7

73

6

PH ┿
HIGH STREET
IVY WAY

A14

Spaldwick

Willow
House

Coton
Barn

Woolley
Hill

WOOLLEY HILL

Whitleather
Lodge

5

Wayside

Mad
Bridge

PE28

A14

Brook
Farm

72

West
Farm

BROADWAY
BROADWER
THE LANE

HILLSIDE CL

GRAFHAM RD

PH

CHURCH LA

4

CHAPEL LANE

Easton

CHURCH RD

Hill
Farm ┿

STONELY RD

Grange
Farm

WINDMILL CL

WINDMILL CL

GREEN LA

GRAFHAM ROAD

SPINNEY
FIELD

3

71

2

Sewell's
Barn

Three Shires Way

Moat

Thorpe Lodge
Farm

1

70

West Wood

Ellington
Hill

13   A   B   14   C   D   15   E   F

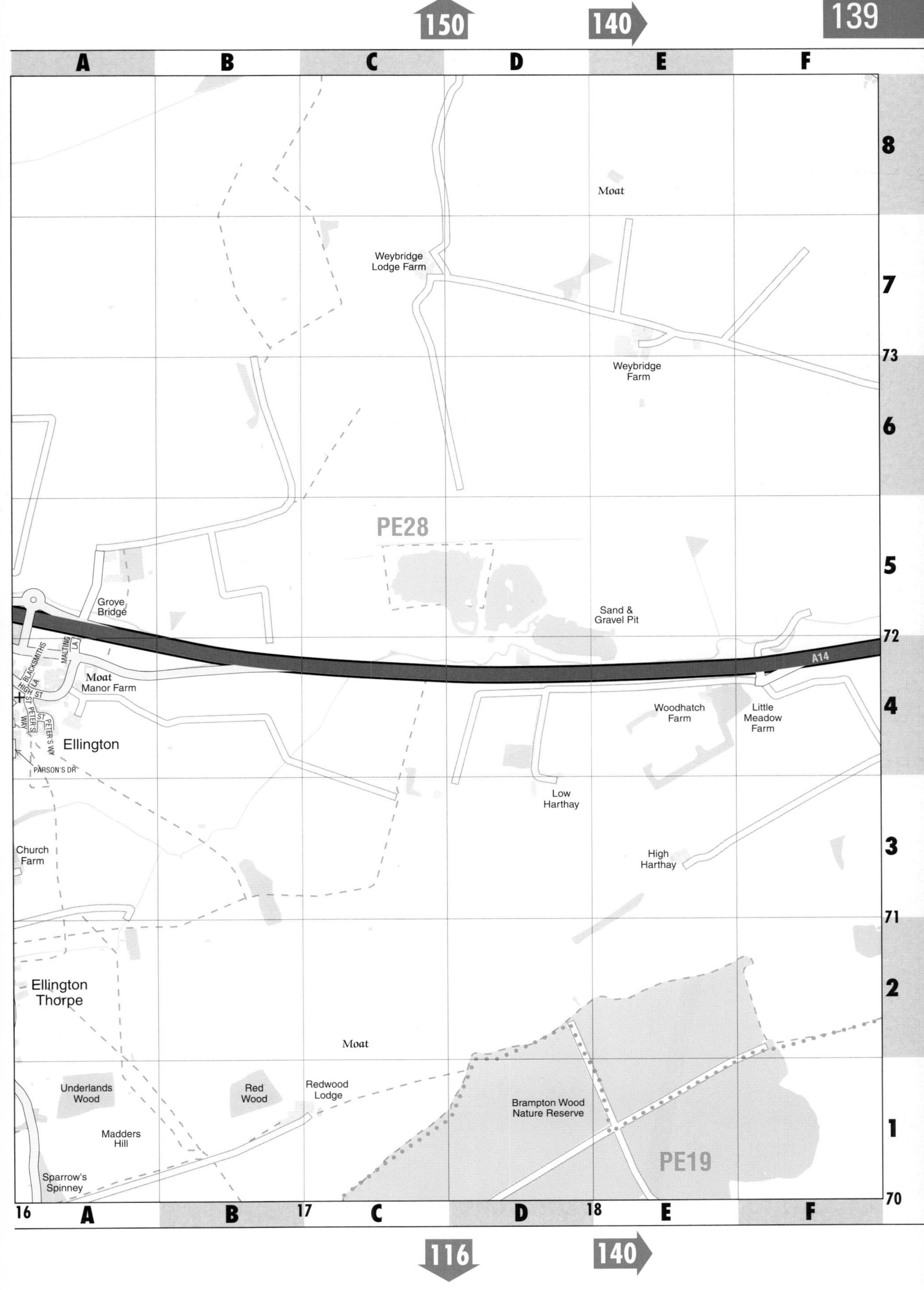
150
140
A
B
C
D
E
F
8
Moat
Weybridge
Lodge Farm
7
73
Weybridge
Farm
6
PE28
5
Grove
Bridge
Sand &
Gravel Pit
72
A14
MALTING LA
BLACKSMITHS LA
HIGH ST
Moat
Manor Farm
ST PETER'S WAY
ST PETER'S WAY
Ellington
PARSON'S DR
Woodhatch
Farm
Little
Meadow
Farm
4
Low
Harthay
Church
Farm
High
Harthay
3
71
Ellington
Thorpe
2
Moat
Underlands
Wood
Red
Wood
Redwood
Lodge
Brampton Wood
Nature Reserve
1
Madders
Hill
PE19
Sparrow's
Spinney
70
16
17
18
116
140

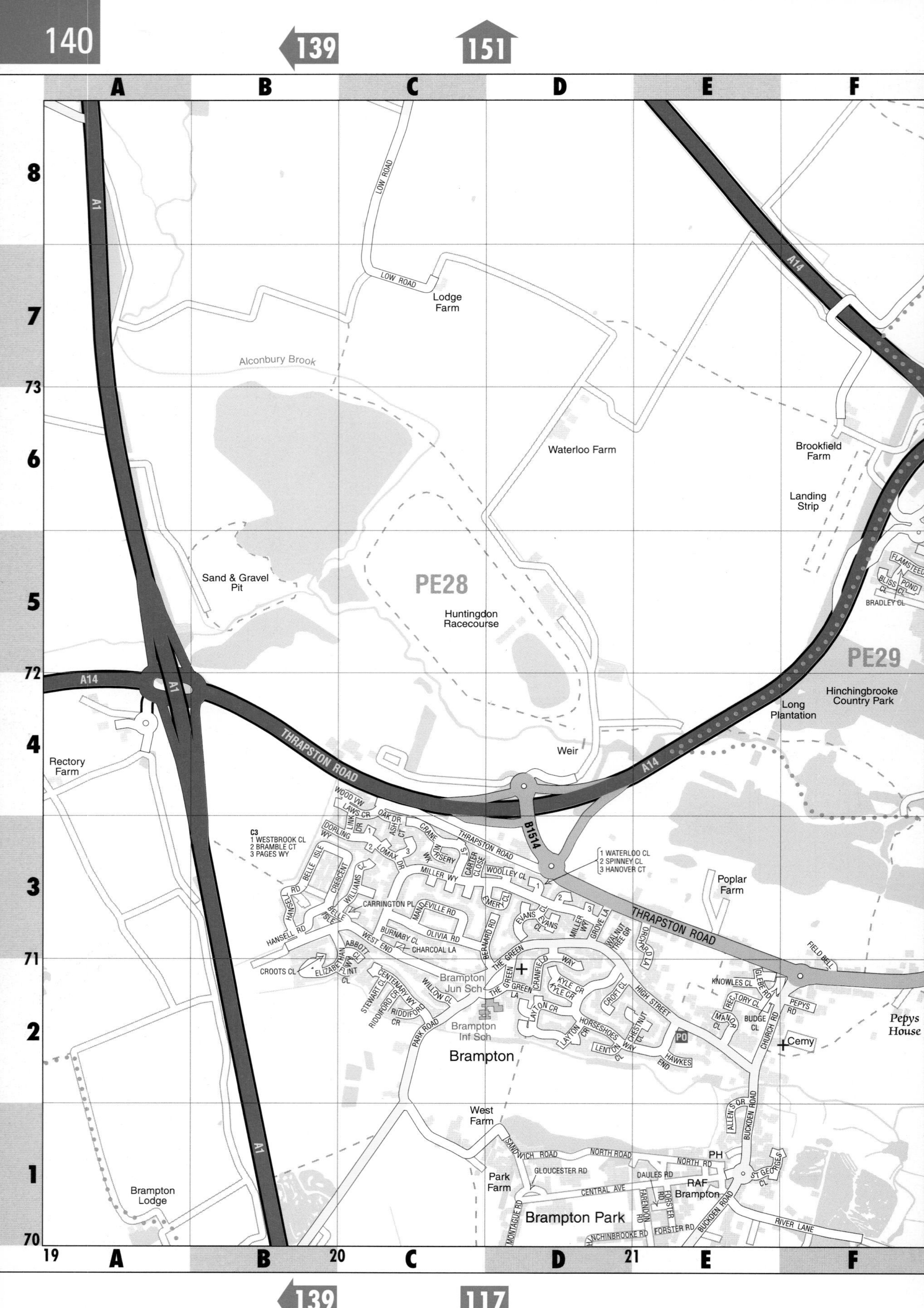

A   B   C   D   E   F

8

7

73

6

5

72

4

3

71

2

1

70

A1

A14

A1

A14

A14

Low Road

Low Road

Lodge Farm

Alconbury Brook

Waterloo Farm

Brookfield Farm

Landing Strip

Sand & Gravel Pit

PE28

Huntingdon Racecourse

PE29

Rectory Farm

Thrapston Road

Weir

A14

Hinchingbrooke Country Park

Long Plantation

FLAMSTEED
BLISS CL
POND
BRADLEY CL

B1514

C3
1 WESTBROOK CL
2 BRAMBLE CT
3 PAGES WY

1 WATERLOO CL
2 SPINNEY CL
3 HANOVER CT

WOOD VW
LAWS CR
LINK DR
OAK DR
ASH CL
CRANE
NURSERY
CARTER CLOSE
WOOLLEY CL
THRAPSTON ROAD

DORLING WY
LOMAX
MILLER WY

Poplar Farm

THRAPSTON ROAD

BELLE ISLE
CRESCENT
WILLIAMS
NURSERY
MAN...
NEVILLE RD
OLIVIA RD
CARRINGTON PL
SOMER CL
BERNARD RD
EVANS CL
EVANS
MILLER WY
GROVE LA
WALNUT
TREE CL
ORCHARD LA

Field Bell

HANSELL RD
HANSELL RD
BELLE ISLE
BURNABY RD
WEST END
CHARCOAL LA
THE GREEN
CRANFIELD
WAY

KNOWLES CL
RECTORY CL
PEPYS RD

CROOTS CL
ELIZABETH WY
ABBOTT CL
FLINT CL
STEWART CL
CENTENARY WY
RIDDIFORD CR
WILLOW CL
Brampton Jun Sch
THE GREEN
THE GREEN
LAYTON CR
KYLE CR
KYLE CR
CROFT CL
HIGH STREET

Pepys House

PARK ROAD
Brampton Inf Sch
LAYTON CR
HORSESHOES WAY
CHESTNUT CL
LENTON CL
PO
HAWKES END

MANOR CL
BUDGE CL
CHURCH RD
Cemy

Brampton

West Farm

ALLEN'S DR
BUCKDEN ROAD

SANDWICH ROAD
NORTH ROAD
NORTH RD
PH
DAULES RD
ST GEORGES CL

Park Farm
GLOUCESTER RD
CENTRAL AVE
RAF Brampton
FORSTER RD

MONTAGUE RD
Brampton Park
HINCHINBROOKE RD
FARNDON
FORSTER RD
BUCKDEN ROAD
RIVER LANE

Brampton Lodge

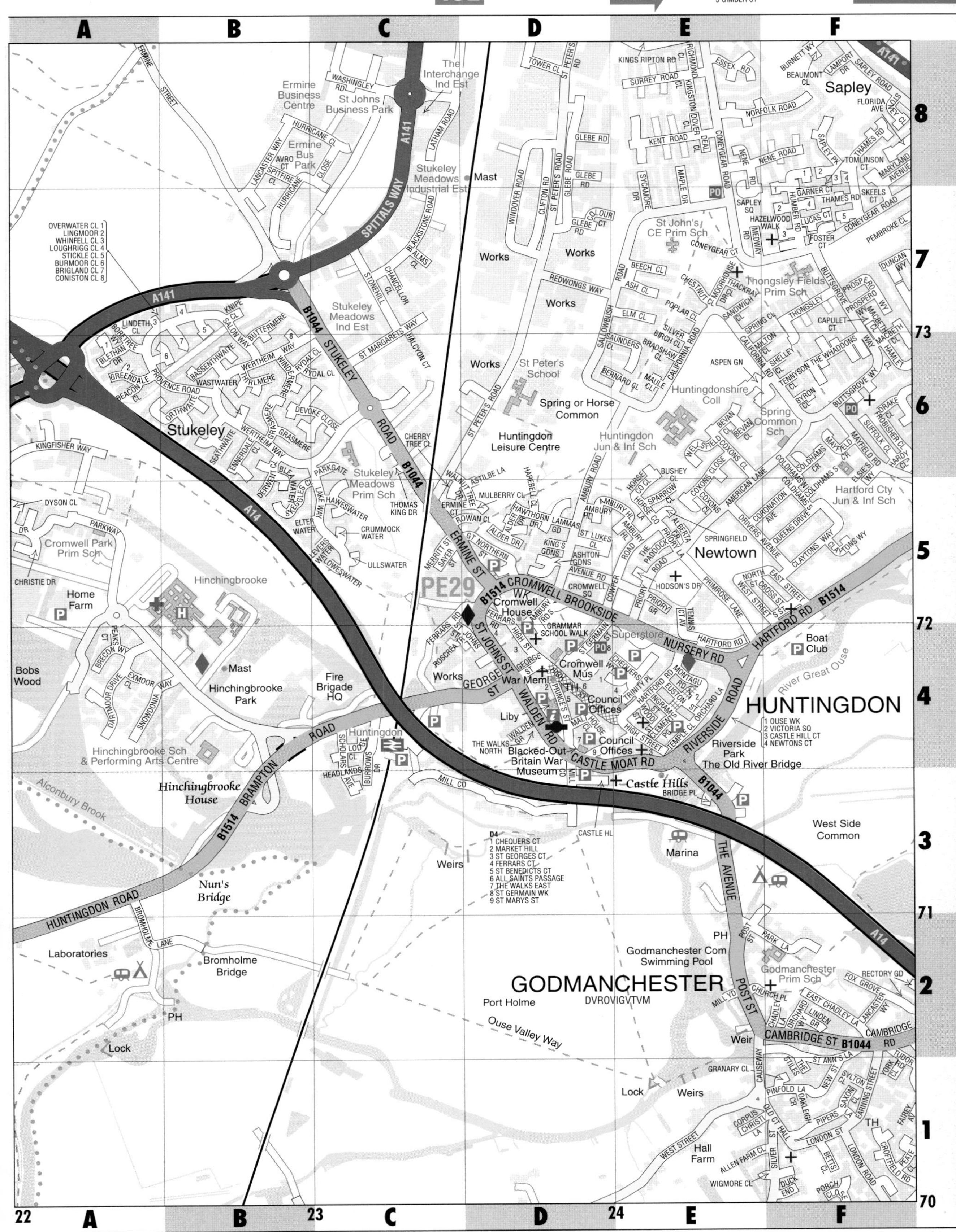

← 152

142 →

141

F7
1 COTTON CT
2 SELBY CT
3 ST BARNABAS CT
4 LAVENDER CT
5 GIMBER CT

F8
1 ARMSTRONG CT
2 BEALE CT
3 JUDSON CT
4 GODEBY CT

A   B   C   D   E   F

8
73
7
6
5
72
4
3
71
2
70
1

22   A   B   23   C   D   24   E   F

OVERWATER CL 1
LINGMOOR 2
WHINFELL CL 3
LOUGHRIGG CL 4
STICKLE CL 5
BURMOOR CL 6
BRIGLAND CL 7
CONISTON CL 8

Ermine
Business
Centre

St Johns
Business Park

The
Interchange
Ind Est

WASHINGLEY
RD

LATHAM ROAD

Stukeley
Meadows
Industrial Est

Mast

KINGS RIPTON RD

TOWER CL

ST PETER'S
RD

ESSEX RD

RICHMOND
RD

BURNETT WY

BEAUMONT CT

Sapley

LAMPORT
DR

SAPLEY ROAD

FLORIDA
AVE

A141

SURREY ROAD

KINGSTON DOVER RD

DEAL

NORFOLK ROAD

CONEYGEAR ROAD

NENE RD

NENE ROAD

TOMLINSON
CT

MAITLAND
AVENUE

THAMES RD

SKEELS
CT

Ermine
Bus
Park

Stukeley
Meadows
Ind Est

WINDOVER ROAD

CLIFTON RD

ST PETER'S ROAD

GLEBE RD

GLEBE
RD

GLEBE
RD

COLOUR
CT

KENT ROAD

MAPLE DR

SYCAMORE

PO

SAPLEY
SQ

HAZELWOOD
WALK

GARNER CT

THAMES RD

LUCAS CT

CONEYGEAR ROAD

FOSTER

PEMBROKE CT

Works

Works

REDWONGS WAY

BEECH CL

ASH CL

CHESTNUT CL

St John's
CE Prim Sch

CONEYGEAR RD

NORTHDENE
THACKRAY

Thongsley Fields
Prim Sch

PROSPER RD

DUNCAN CT

Works

ELM CL

POPLAR CL

SILVER
BIRCH CL

SANDWICH

THONGSLEY

SPRING CL

CAPULET
CT

Works

St Peter's
School

SAUNDERS

BRADSHAW CL

CALIFORNIA

HAMILTON

SHELLEY

TENNYSON

THE WHADDONS

BYRON

BUTTSGROVE WY

Spring or Horse
Common

Huntingdon
Leisure Centre

BERNARD CL

MAULE
CL

ASPEN GN

Huntingdonshire
Coll

BEVAN

BEVAN

Spring
Common
Sch

PO

Stukeley
Meadows
Prim Sch

THOMAS
KING DR

WALNUT TREE

ERMINE
CL

ASTILBE LA

MULBERRY CL

HAWTHORN
CL

ALDER DR

ROWAN DR

KING'S
GDNS

ST LUKES

AMBURY
RD

AMBURY
HLL

HORSE
CL

BUSHEY
CL

WELD
CL

COLMANS
CL

AMERICAN LANE

COLDHAMS CT

COLDHAMS RD

Hartford Cty
Jun & Inf Sch

CROMWELL
PARK PRIM SCH

Stukeley

Huntingdon
Jun & Inf Sch

ASHTON
GDNS

AVENUE RD

SPARROW

COONS
CL

CORONATION
AVE

QUEENS DRIVE

MAYFD CL

SUFFOLK CL

Huntingdon

CHERRY
TREE CL

B1044

STUKELEY ROAD

ST MARGARETS WAY

WALTON CT

DEVOKE CLOSE

MERRITT ST

GT NORTHERN ST

GT GEORGE ST

HARBELL CL

Newtown

THE PADDOCK

PRIORY
RD

HODSON'S DR

SPRINGFIELD

CLAYTONS WY

PAXTONS WY

A141

B1514

HARTFORD RD

B1514

Hinchingbrooke

PE29

CROMWELL
WK

BROOKSIDE

Superstore

NURSERY RD

Boat
Club

River Great Ouse

Home
Farm

H

Hinchingbrooke
Park

Mast

Fire
Brigade
HQ

P

Huntingdon

SCHOLARS WY

P

GEORGE ST

ST JOHN'S ST

WALDEN RD

War Meml

TH

Cromwell
Mus

Council
Offices

MONTAGU

Riverside
Park

The Old River Bridge

HUNTINGDON

1 OUSE WK
2 VICTORIA SQ
3 CASTLE HILL CT
4 NEWTONS CT

Bobs
Wood

BRECON WY

DARTMOOR DR

DARTMOOR CL

EXMOOR WAY

SNOWDONIA WAY

Hinchingbrooke Sch
& Performing Arts Centre

Hinchingbrooke
House

BRAMPTON ROAD

BURROWS
AVE

HEADLANDS

P

THE WALKS
NORTH

Liby

P

Blacked-Out
Britain War
Museum

CASTLE MOAT RD

Council
Offices

RIVERSIDE ROAD

Castle Hills

BRIDGE PL

B1044

P

West Side
Common

Alconbury Brook

B1514

HUNTINGDON ROAD

Nun's
Bridge

BROMHOLME LANE

Laboratories

Bromholme
Bridge

MILL CO

CASTLE HL

CASTLE HILL

D4
1 CHEQUERS CT
2 MARKET HILL
3 ST GEORGES CT
4 FERRARS CT
5 ST BENEDICTS CT
6 ALL SAINTS PASSAGE
7 THE WALKS EAST
8 ST GERMAIN WK
9 ST MARYS ST

Weirs

Marina

THE AVENUE

PH

Godmanchester Com
Swimming Pool

Godmanchester
Prim Sch

RECTORY GD

FOX GROVE

A14

PH

Lock

Port Holme

Ouse Valley Way

GODMANCHESTER

DVROVIGVTVM

POST ST

MILL YD

CHURCH PL

EAST CHADLEY LA

LANCASTER

LINDEN
CL

Weir

CAMBRIDGE ST

B1044

CAMBRIDGE
RD

GRANARY CL

CAUSEWAY

PINFOLD LA

ST ANN'S LA

NEW ST

CORPUS
CHRISTI
LA

MAXIM

PIPERS

TUDOR

FROTFIELD RD

Lock

Weirs

Hall
Farm

WEST STREET

ALLEN FARM LA

WIGMORE CL

DUCK
END

PORCH
CLO

LONDON ST

BETSI

TH

EARNING STREET

LONDON ROAD

FARM
GATE

141
153

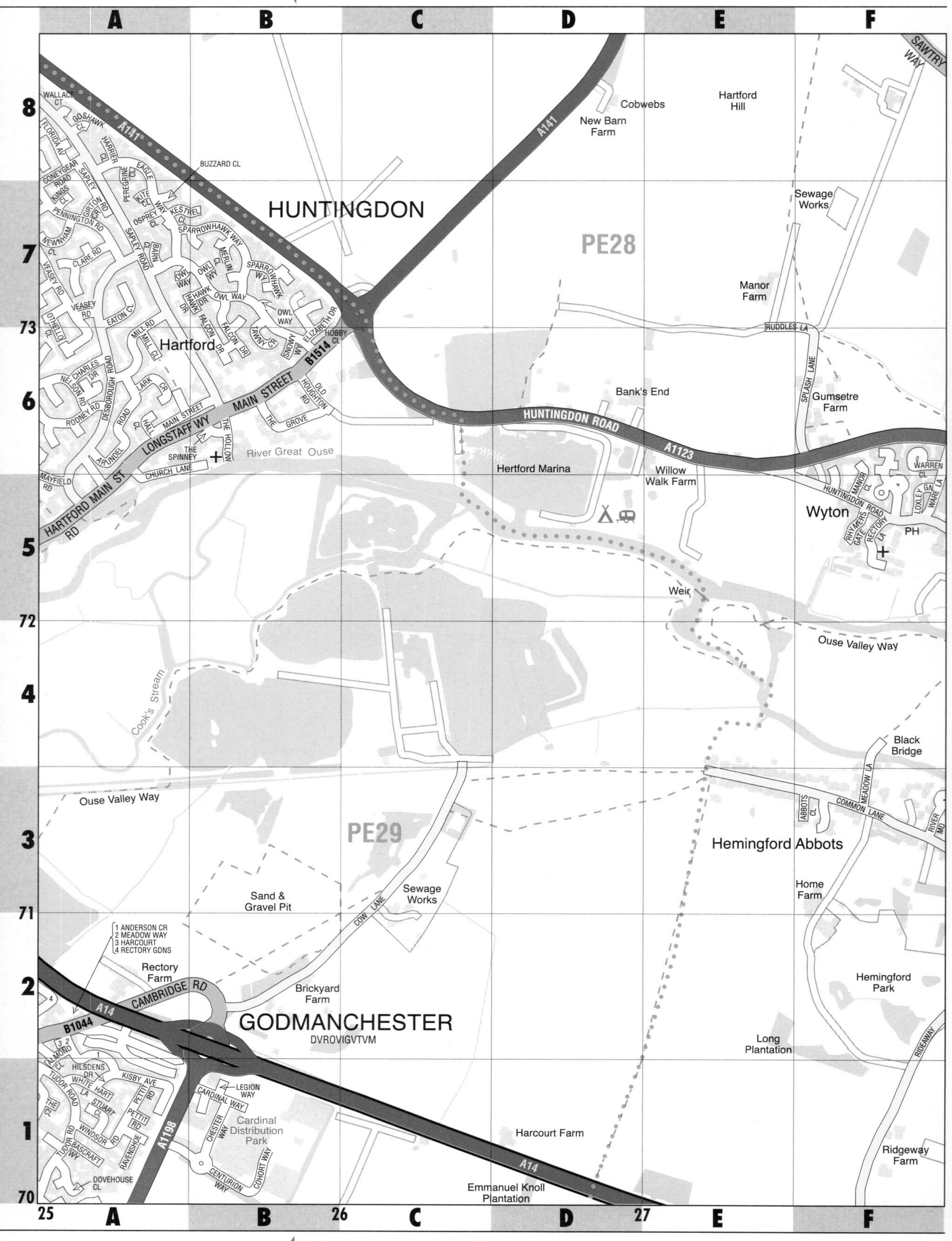
HUNTINGDON
Hartford
PE28
Cobwebs
New Barn Farm
Hartford Hill
Sewage Works
Manor Farm
Bank's End
Gumsetre Farm
HUNTINGDON ROAD
A1123
A141
B1514
MAIN STREET
LONGSTAFF WY
River Great Ouse
Hertford Marina
Willow Walk Farm
Wyton
PH
Weir
Ouse Valley Way
Cook's Stream
Black Bridge
PE29
Hemingford Abbots
COMMON LANE
Home Farm
Sand & Gravel Pit
Sewage Works
COW LANE
1 ANDERSON CR
2 MEADOW WAY
3 HARCOURT
4 RECTORY GDNS
Rectory Farm
CAMBRIDGE RD
A14
B1044
Brickyard Farm
GODMANCHESTER
DVROVIGVTVM
Hemingford Park
Long Plantation
Cardinal Distribution Park
A1198
Harcourt Farm
Emmanuel Knoll Plantation
Ridgeway Farm
HARTFORD MAIN ST
CHURCH LANE
THE SPINNEY
THE HOLLOW
HOUGHTON RD
THE GROVE
BUZZARD CL
SAWTRY WAY
RUDDLES LA
SPLASH LANE
HUNTINGDON ROAD
WARREN CL
ABBOTS CL
MEADOW LA
RIDGEAWAY
CARDINAL WAY
LEGION WAY
CENTURION WAY
COHORT WAY
CHESTER WAY
DOVEHOUSE CL
TUDOR ROAD
KISBY AVE
WINDSOR RD
RAVENSHOE

A B C D E F
8 7 73 6 5 72 4 3 71 2 1 70
25 26 27

141
119

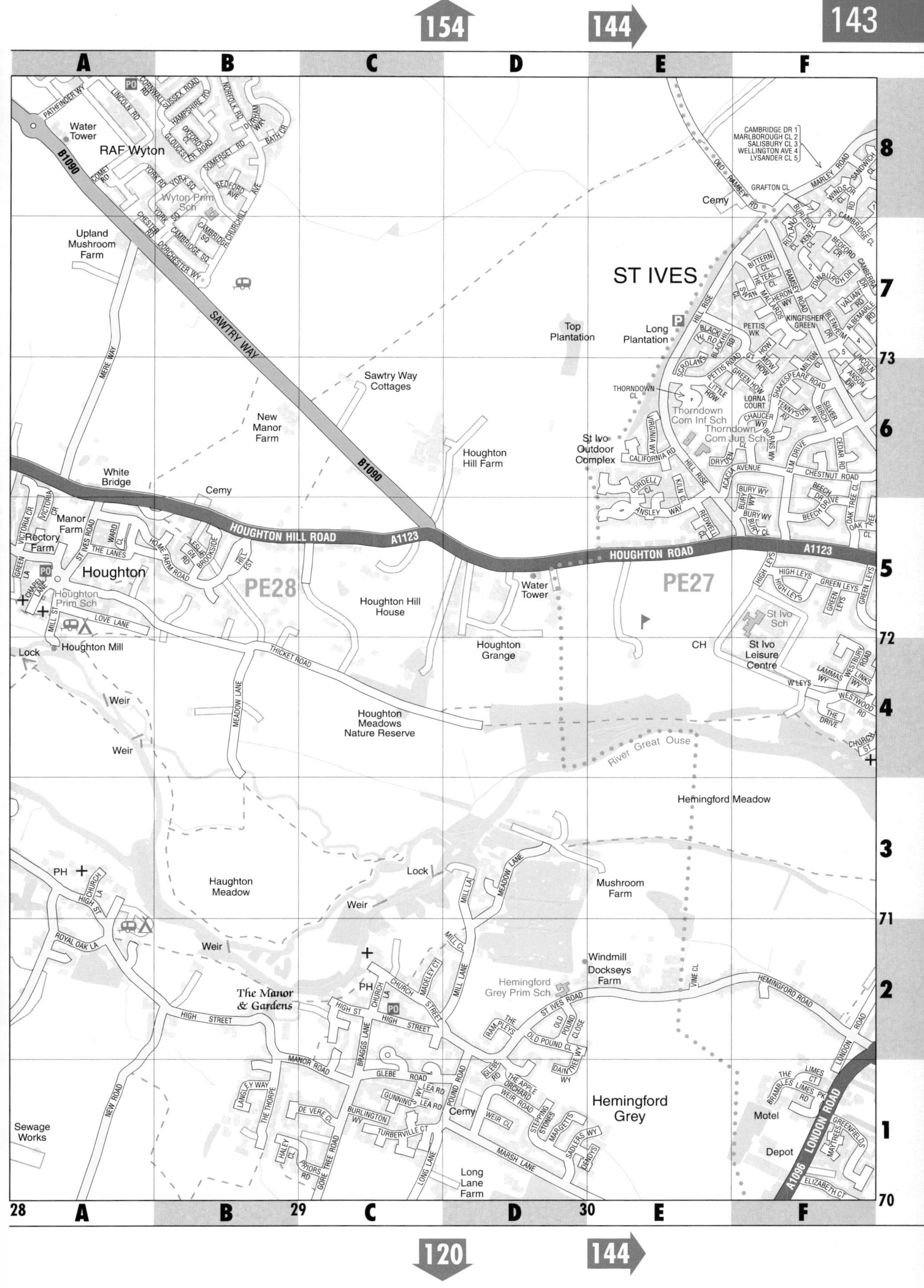

154
144
A
B
C
D
E
F
8
7
73
6
5
72
4
3
71
2
1
70
28
29
30
RAF Wyton
Water Tower
Wyton Prim Sch
Upland Mushroom Farm
SAWTRY WAY
B1090
MERE WAY
ST IVES
Top Plantation
Long Plantation
Cemy
Sawtry Way Cottages
New Manor Farm
Houghton Hill Farm
St Ivo Outdoor Complex
Thorndown Com Inf Sch
Thorndown Com Jun Sch
White Bridge
HOUGHTON HILL ROAD
A1123
HOUGHTON ROAD
Manor Farm
Rectory Farm
Houghton
Houghton Prim Sch
PE28
PE27
Houghton Hill House
Water Tower
Houghton Grange
St Ivo Sch
St Ivo Leisure Centre
CH
Lock
Houghton Mill
THICKET ROAD
Weir
MEADOW LANE
Houghton Meadows Nature Reserve
River Great Ouse
Hemingford Meadow
Haughton Meadow
Lock
Mushroom Farm
PH
Windmill
Dockseys Farm
Hemingford Grey Prim Sch
The Manor & Gardens
HIGH STREET
HEMINGFORD ROAD
Hemingford Grey
Sewage Works
Motel
Depot
LONDON ROAD
A1096
Long Lane Farm
CAMBRIDGE DR 1
MARLBOROUGH CL 2
SALISBURY CL 3
WELLINGTON AVE 4
LYSANDER CL 5

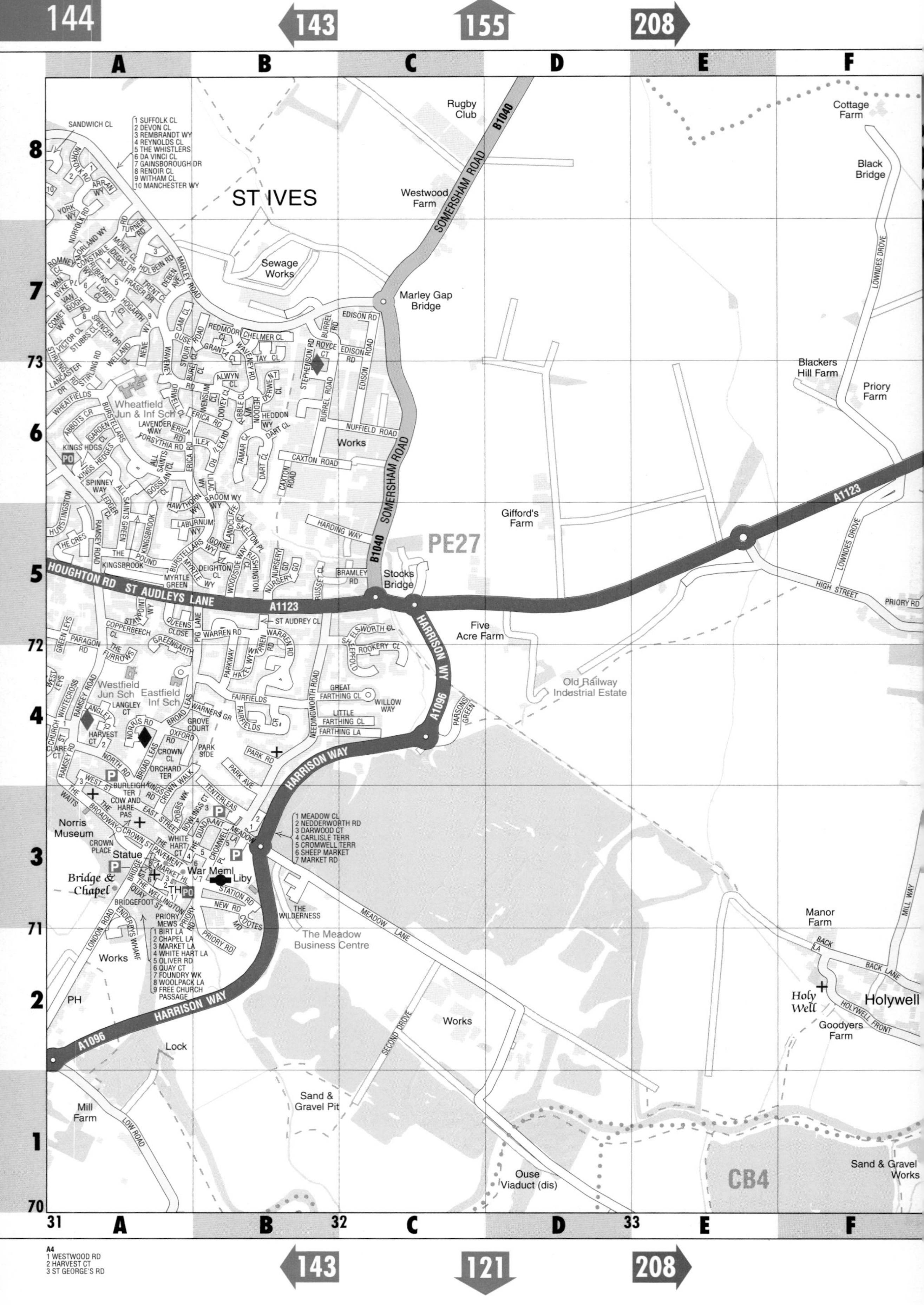
143
155
208
A
B
C
D
E
F
8
7
73
6
5
72
4
3
71
2
1
70
31
32
33
SANDWICH CL
1 SUFFOLK CL
2 DEVON CL
3 REMBRANDT WY
4 REYNOLDS CL
5 THE WHISTLERS
6 DA VINCI CL
7 GAINSBOROUGH DR
8 RENOIR CL
9 WITHAM CL
10 MANCHESTER WY
ST IVES
Rugby Club
B1040
SOMERSHAM ROAD
Westwood Farm
Cottage Farm
Black Bridge
Sewage Works
Marley Gap Bridge
LOWNDES DROVE
MARLEY ROAD
EDISON RD
CHELMER CL
ROYCE CT
EDISON RD
Blackers Hill Farm
Priory Farm
Wheatfield Jun & Inf Sch
NUFFIELD ROAD
Works
CAXTON ROAD
Gifford's Farm
A1123
HARDING WAY
PE27
HOUGHTON RD
ST AUDLEYS LANE
Stocks Bridge
LOWNDES DROVE
HIGH STREET
PRIORY RD
ST AUDREY CL
ELSWORTH CL
HARRISON WAY
Five Acre Farm
ROOKERY CL
Old Railway Industrial Estate
Westfield Jun Sch
Eastfield Inf Sch
GREAT FARTHING CL
WILLOW WAY
LITTLE FARTHING CL
FARTHING LA
A1096
PARSONS GREEN
Norris Museum
1 MEADOW CL
2 NEDDERWORTH RD
3 DARWOOD CT
4 CARLISLE TERR
5 CROMWELL TERR
6 SHEEP MARKET
7 MARKET RD
Statue
War Meml
Liby
Bridge & Chapel
TH
THE WILDERNESS
MEADOW LANE
The Meadow Business Centre
1 BIRT LA
2 CHAPEL LA
3 MARKET LA
4 WHITE HART LA
5 OLIVER RD
6 QUAY CT
7 FOUNDRY WK
8 WOOLPACK LA
9 FREE CHURCH PASSAGE
Works
Manor Farm
BACK LA
BACK LANE
MILL WAY
PH
Holy Well
Holywell
HOLYWELL FRONT
Goodyers Farm
Works
SECOND DROVE
Lock
Mill Farm
LOW ROAD
Sand & Gravel Pit
Ouse Viaduct (dis)
CB4
Sand & Gravel Works
A4
1 WESTWOOD RD
2 HARVEST CT
3 ST GEORGE'S RD
143
121
208

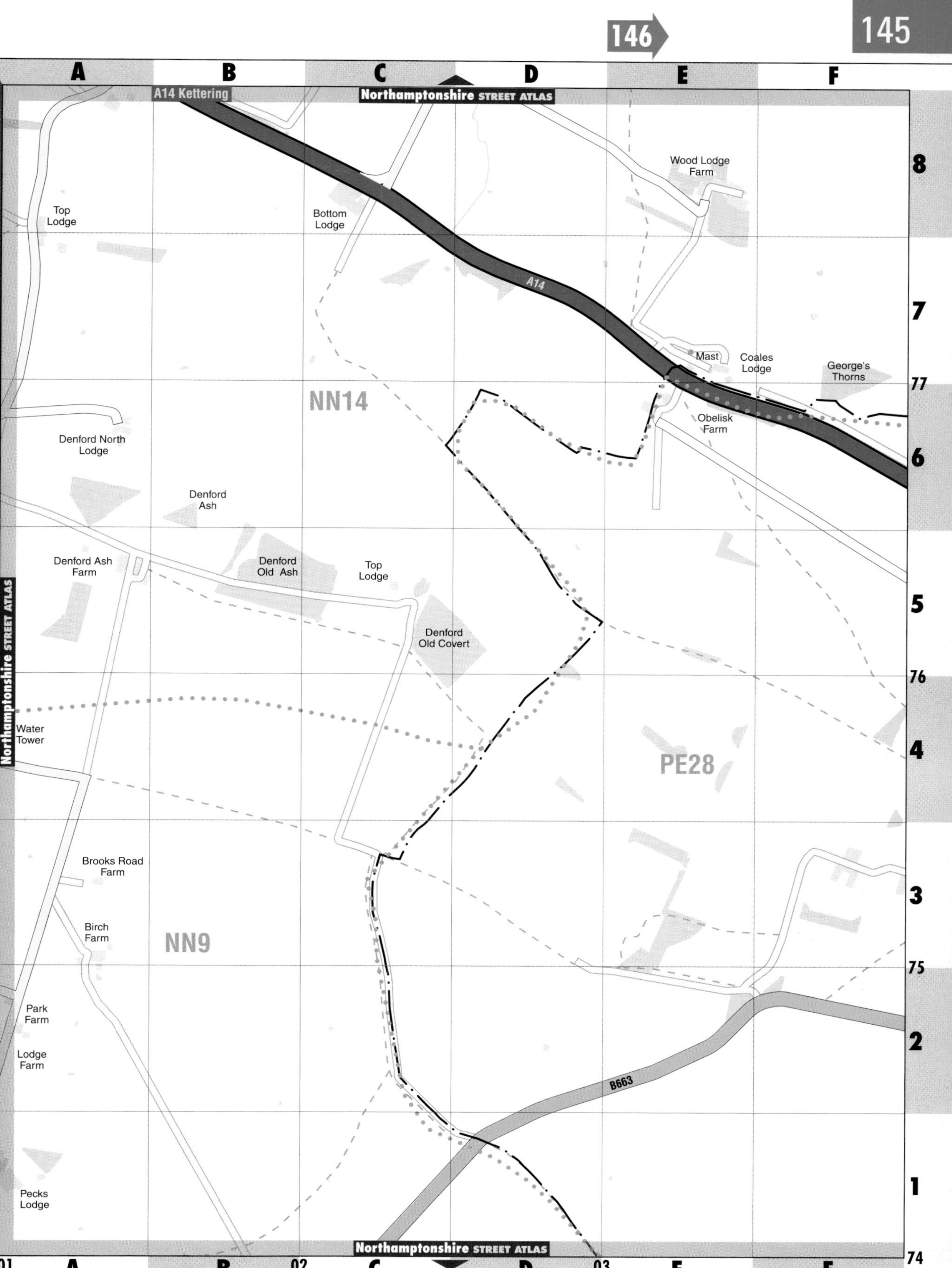

Top
Lodge

Bottom
Lodge

Wood Lodge
Farm

A14

Mast

Coales
Lodge

George's
Thorns

NN14

Denford North
Lodge

Obelisk
Farm

Denford
Ash

Denford Ash
Farm

Denford
Old Ash

Top
Lodge

Denford
Old Covert

PE28

Water
Tower

Brooks Road
Farm

Birch
Farm

NN9

Park
Farm

Lodge
Farm

B663

Pecks
Lodge

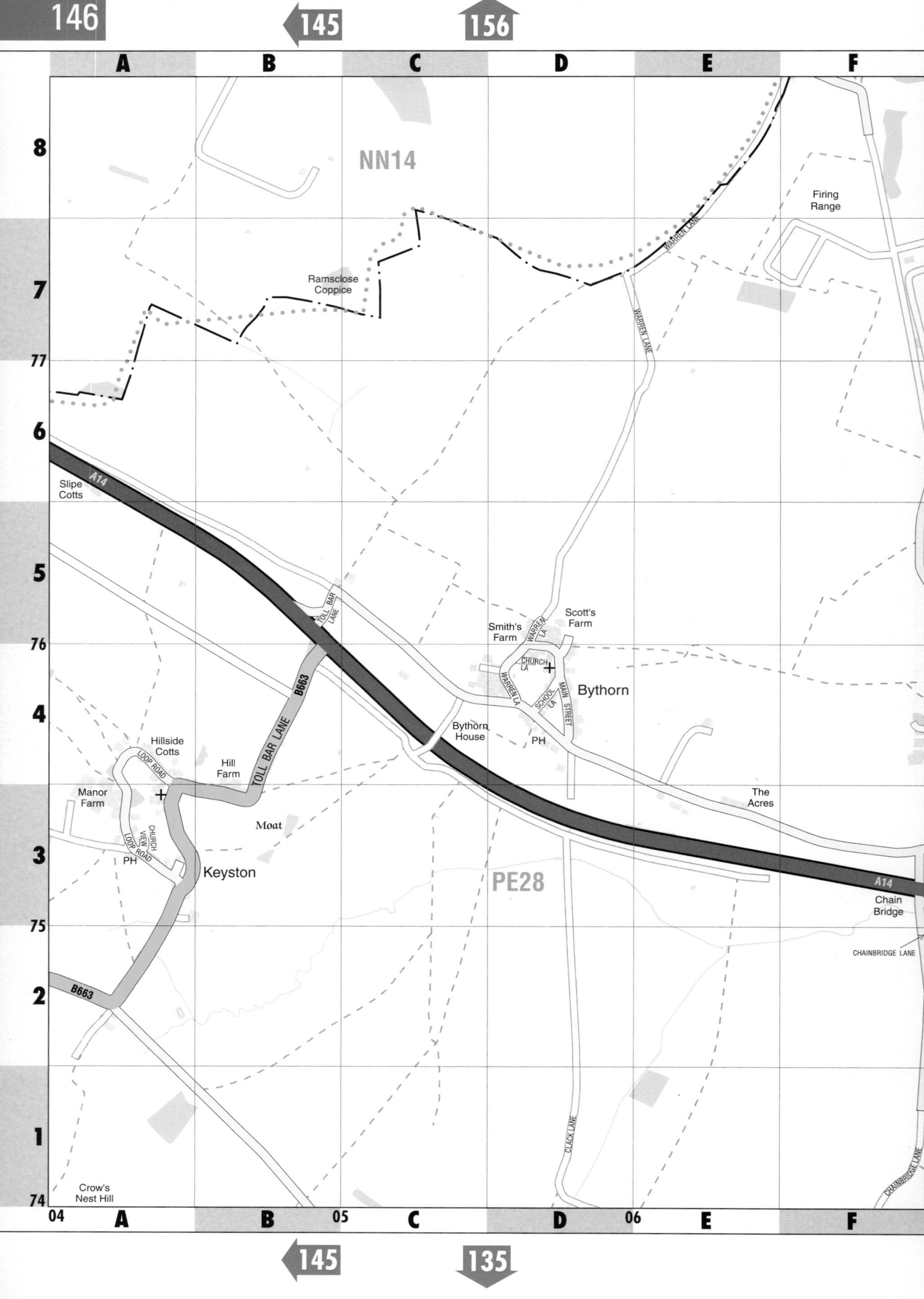

A   B   C   D   E   F

8

NN14

7

77

6

Slipe
Cotts

A14

5

Toll Bar Lane

76

B663

Smith's
Farm

Scott's
Farm

WARREN LA

CHURCH LA

Bythorn

4

Hillside
Cotts

Hill
Farm

LOOP ROAD

TOLL BAR LANE

B663

Bythorn
House

WARREN LA

SCHOOL LA

MAIN STREET

PH

The
Acres

Manor
Farm

Moat

CHURCH
VIEW

LOOP ROAD

PH

Keyston

PE28

3

A14

Chain
Bridge

75

CHAINBRIDGE LANE

2

B663

CLACK LANE

CHAINBRIDGE LANE

1

Crow's
Nest Hill

74

04   A   B   05   C   D   06   E   F

Ramsclose
Coppice

Firing
Range

WARREN LANE

WARREN LANE

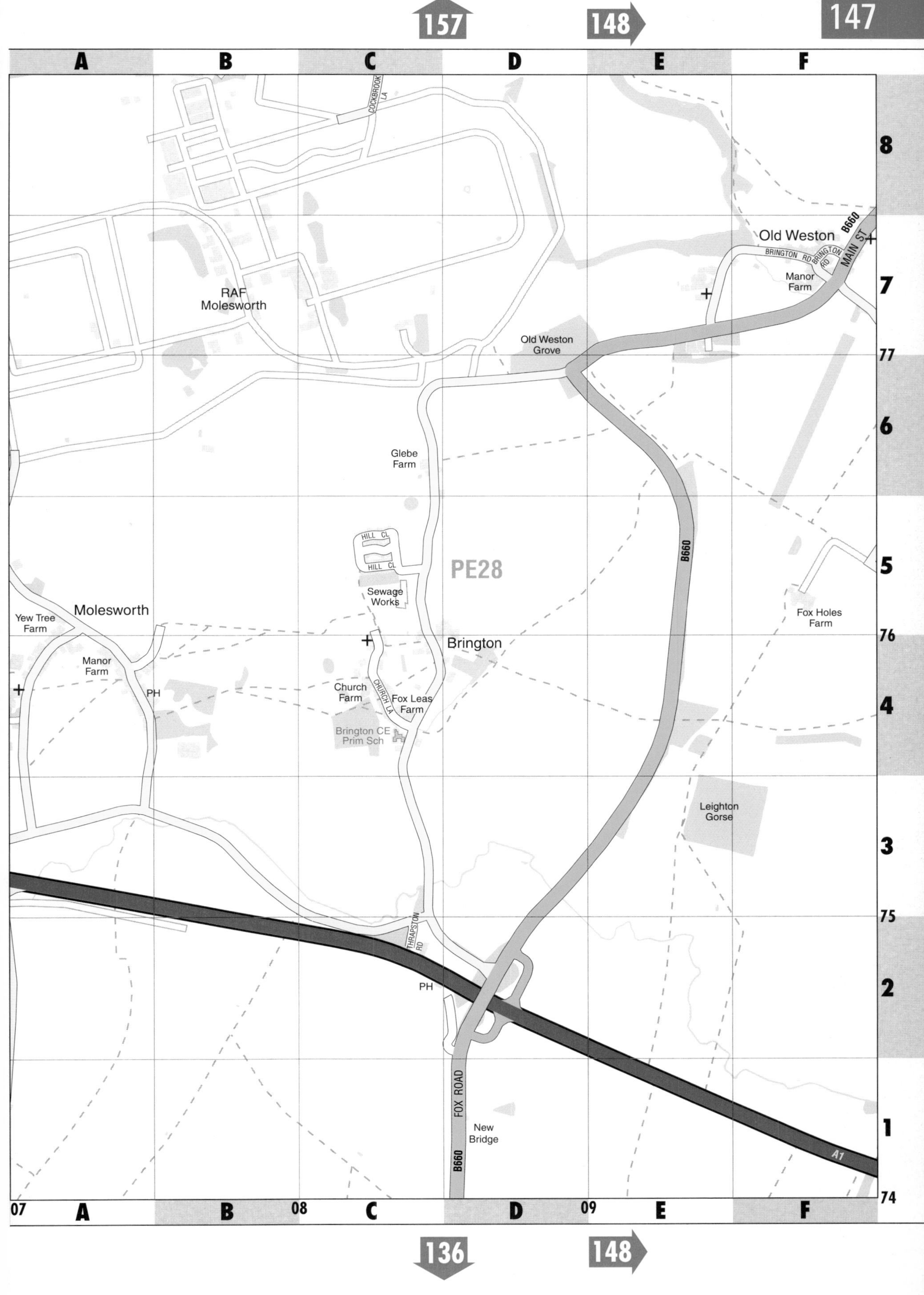

A B C D E F

8 7 77 6 5 76 4 3 75 2 1 74

07 08 09

COCKBROOK LA

RAF
Molesworth

Old Weston

B660

BRINGTON RD
BRINGTON RD
MAIN ST

Manor
Farm

Old Weston
Grove

Glebe
Farm

PE28

HILL CL
HILL CL

Sewage
Works

B660

Fox Holes
Farm

Molesworth

Yew Tree
Farm

Brington

Manor
Farm

PH

Church
Farm

CHURCH LA

Fox Leas
Farm

Brington CE
Prim Sch

Leighton
Gorse

THRAPSTON RD

PH

A1

FOX ROAD

B660

New
Bridge

147
158

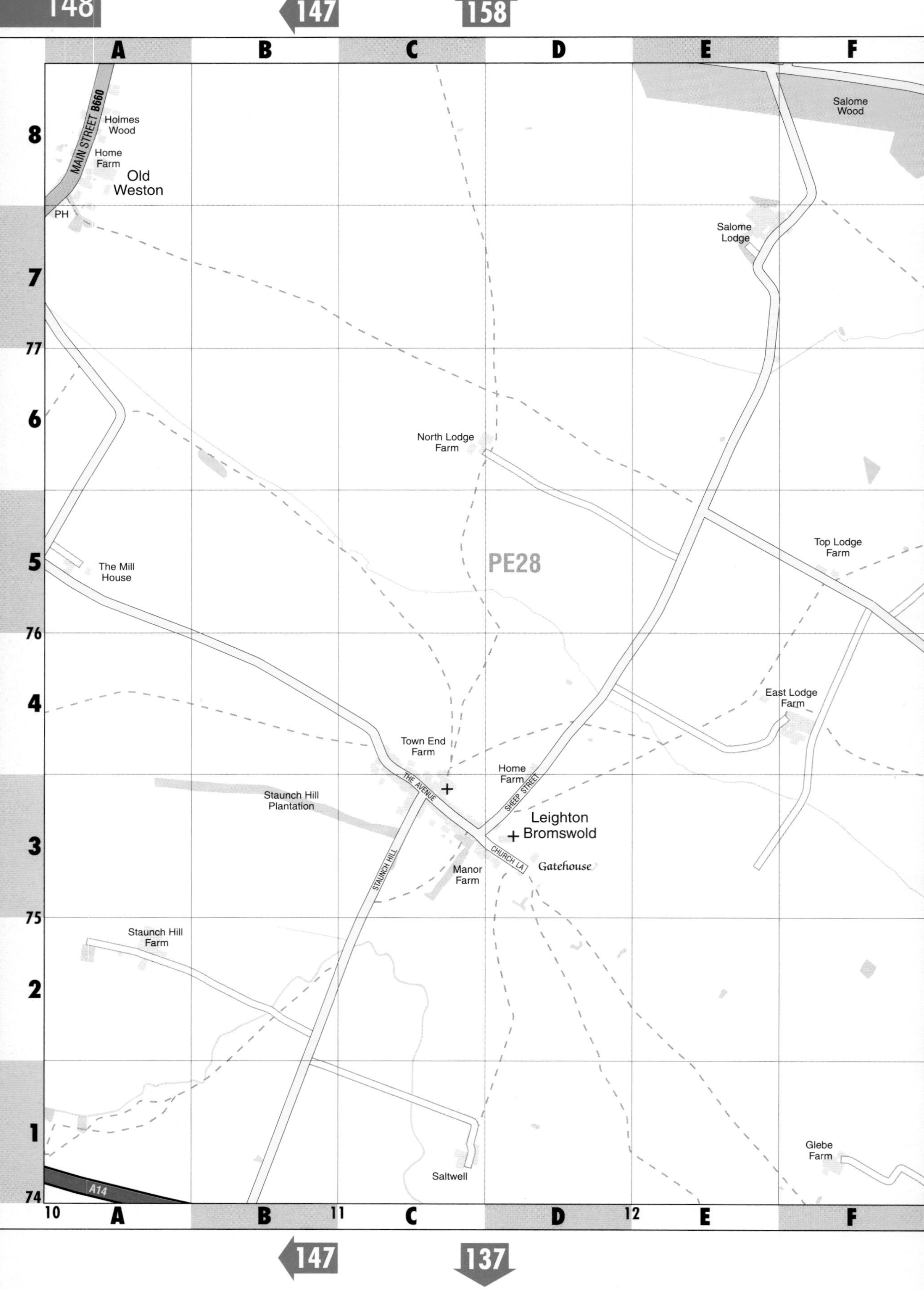
A
B
C
D
E
F
8
7
77
6
5
76
4
3
75
2
1
74
10
11
12
MAIN STREET B660
Holmes Wood
Home Farm
Old Weston
PH
Salome Wood
Salome Lodge
North Lodge Farm
PE28
The Mill House
Top Lodge Farm
East Lodge Farm
Town End Farm
Home Farm
THE AVENUE
SHEEP STREET
Staunch Hill Plantation
Leighton Bromswold
CHURCH LA
Gatehouse
Manor Farm
STAUNCH HILL
Staunch Hill Farm
Glebe Farm
Saltwell
A14

147
137

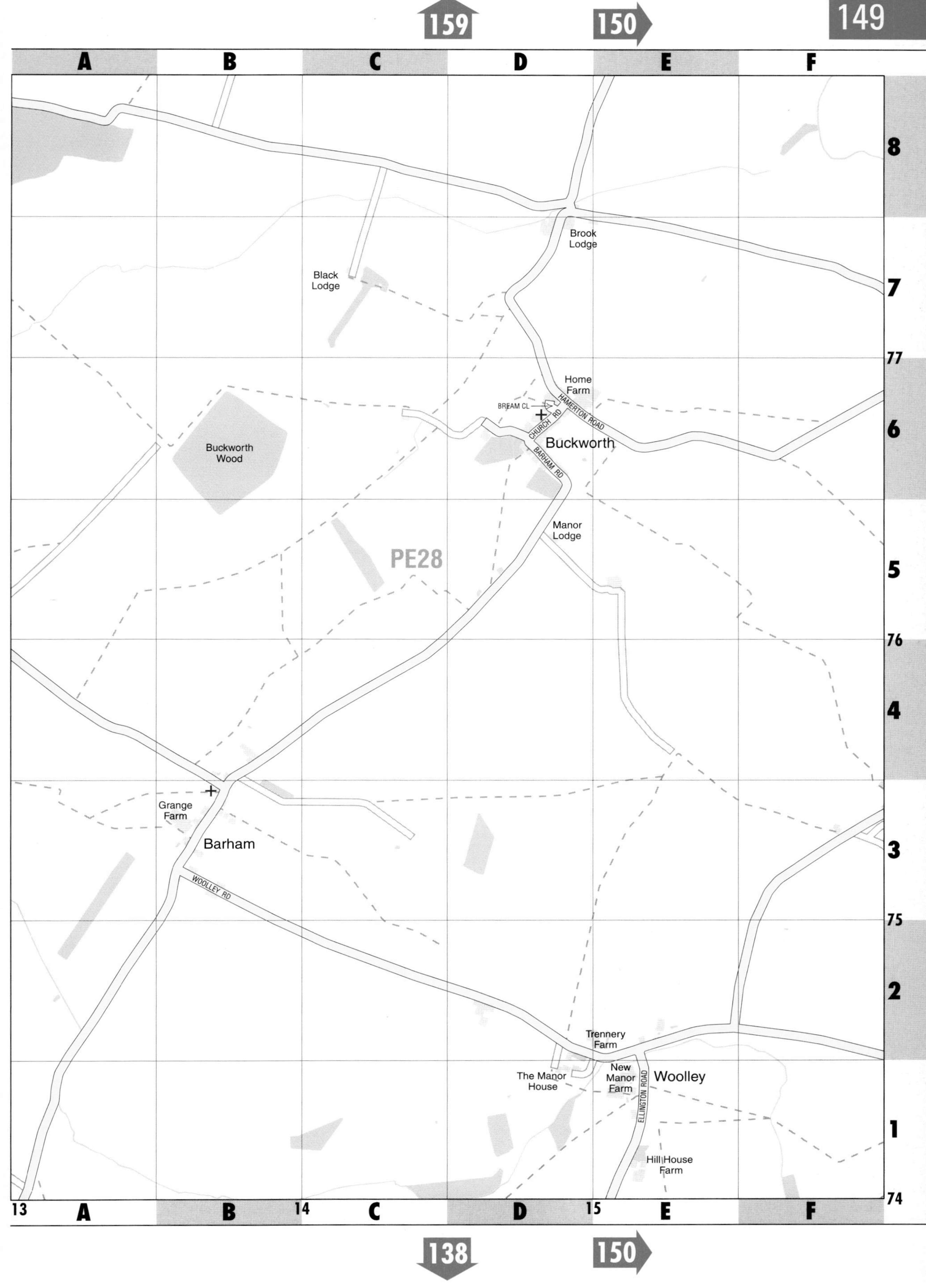

A B C D E F

8

Brook
Lodge

7

Black
Lodge

77

Home
Farm

BREAM CL
HAMERTON ROAD

Buckworth
Wood

CHURCH RD

Buckworth

6

BARHAM RD

Manor
Lodge

PE28

5

76

4

Grange
Farm

Barham

3

WOOLLEY RD

75

2

Trennery
Farm

New
Manor
Farm

Woolley

The Manor
House

ELLINGTON ROAD

1

Hill House
Farm

74

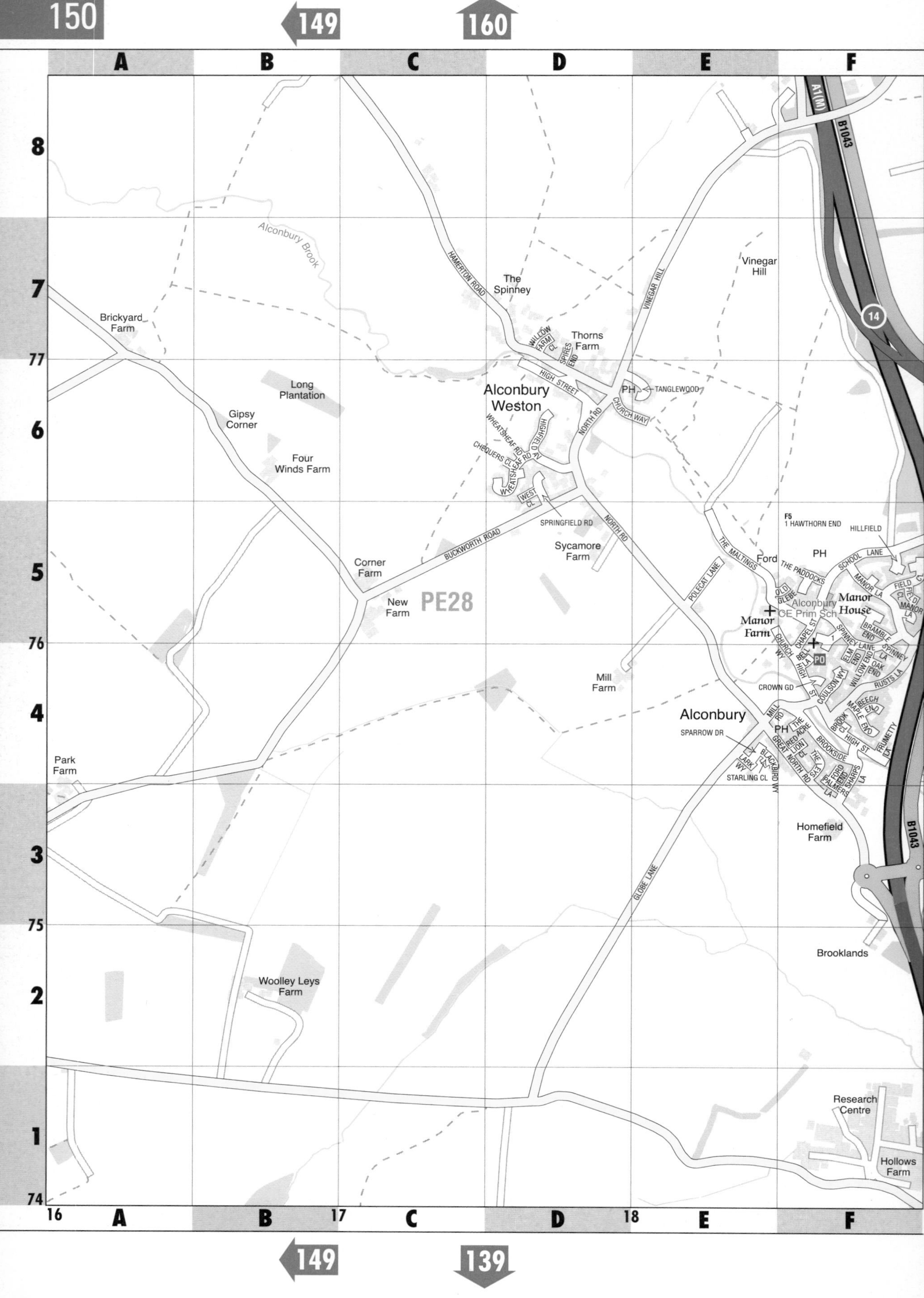

A B C D E F

8

7

77

6

5

76

4

75

2

1

74

Alconbury Brook

Brickyard Farm

Long Plantation

Gipsy Corner

Four Winds Farm

HAMERTON ROAD

The Spinney

WILLOW FARM CL
SPIRES END

Thorns Farm

Alconbury Weston

HIGH STREET

WHEATSHEAF RD
HIGHFIELD RD
CHEQUERS CL
WHEATSHEAF RD
WEST CL

NORTH RD

CHURCH WAY

PH

Tanglewood

Vinegar Hill

VINEGAR HILL

A1(M)

B1043

14

F5
1 HAWTHORN END

HILLFIELD

Corner Farm

New Farm

PE28

BUCKWORTH ROAD

SPRINGFIELD RD

NORTH RD

Sycamore Farm

Ford

POLECAT LANE

THE MALTINGS

THE PADDOCKS

OLD GLEBE

Manor Farm

Alconbury CE Prim Sch

CHAPEL ST
BELL LA
SQUARE
CHURCH LA

PH

SCHOOL LANE
MANOR LA

Manor House

MANOR CL
FIELD CL
THE CL DR
MANOR CL

BRAMBLE
SPINNEY
SPINNEY LANE
ELM END
OAK END
WILLOW END
MAPLE END
BROOK CL

RUSTS LA

CROWN GD

Mill Farm

Alconbury

SPARROW DR

PH

MILL RD
RED ACRE
GREAT NORTH RD
BLACKBIRD WY
LARK WY
STARLING CL

THE LION
THE CL
BROOKSIDE
FORD
PALMERS LA
HIGH ST
SHARPS LA
MAPLE END

BEECH END

TRUMETTY

Park Farm

Woolley Leys Farm

GLOBE LANE

Homefield Farm

B1043

Brooklands

Research Centre

Hollows Farm

16 A B 17 C D 18 E F

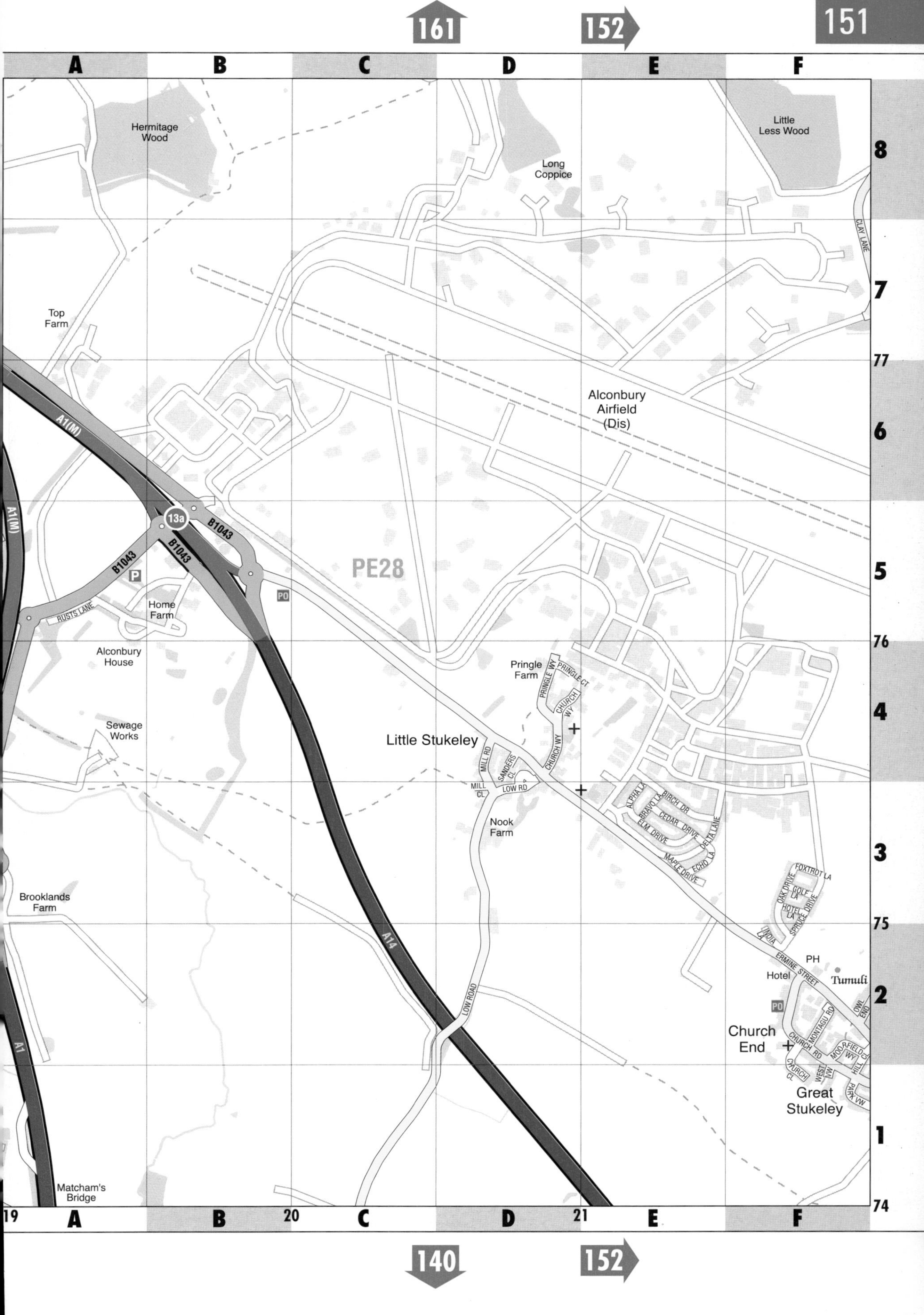
A
B
C
D
E
F
Hermitage Wood
Little Less Wood
Long Coppice
CLAY LANE
Top Farm
Alconbury Airfield (Dis)
A1(M)
13a
B1043
PE28
P
PO
RUSTS LANE
Home Farm
Alconbury House
Pringle Farm
PRINGLE WY
PRINGLE CT
CHURCH WY
Sewage Works
Little Stukeley
MILL RD
SANDERS CL
MILL CL
LOW RD
Nook Farm
ALPHA LA
BRAVO LA
BIRCH DR
CEDAR DRIVE
ELM DRIVE
DELTA LANE
ECHO LA
MAPLE DRIVE
FOXTROT LA
OAK DRIVE
GOLF LA
HOTEL LA
SPRUCE DRIVE
INDIA
Brooklands Farm
A14
ERMINE STREET
PH
Hotel
Tumuli
LOW ROAD
OWL END
MONTAGU RD
Church End
CHURCH RD
MOORFIELD
CHURCH CL
WEST VW
HILL
PARK VW
Great Stukeley
A1
Matcham's Bridge
8
7
77
6
5
76
4
3
75
2
1
74
19
20
21

151
162

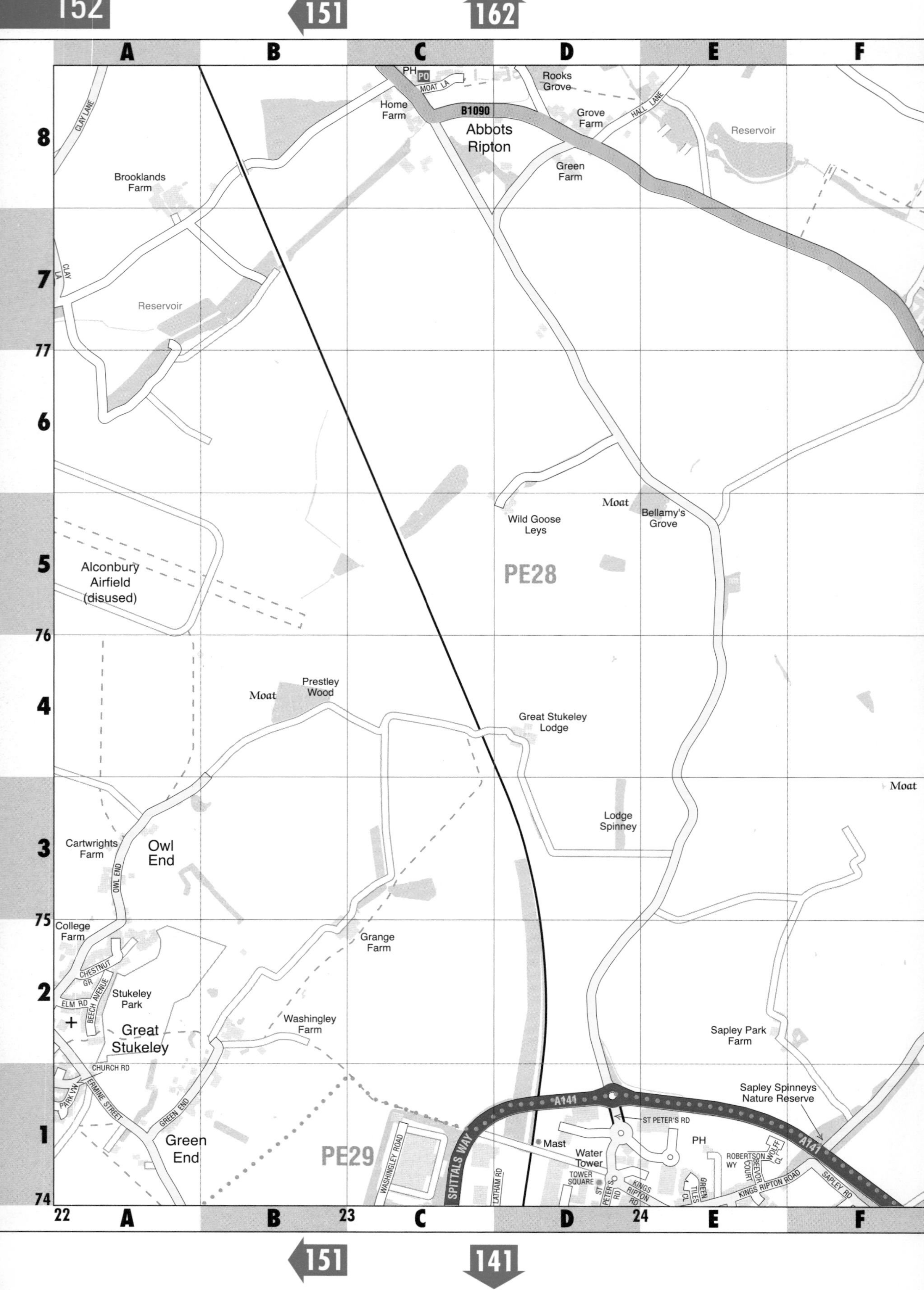
A
B
C
D
E
F
8
7
77
6
5
76
4
3
75
2
1
74
22
23
24
PH
PO
MOAT LA
Rooks Grove
Home Farm
B1090
Abbots Ripton
Grove Farm
HALL LANE
Reservoir
CLAY LANE
Green Farm
Brooklands Farm
CLAY LA
Reservoir
Moat
Bellamy's Grove
Wild Goose Leys
Alconbury Airfield (disused)
PE28
Moat
Prestley Wood
Great Stukeley Lodge
Moat
Lodge Spinney
Cartwrights Farm
Owl End
OWL END
College Farm
Grange Farm
CHESTNUT GR
ELM RD
BEECH AVENUE
Stukeley Park
Great Stukeley
Washingley Farm
Sapley Park Farm
CHURCH RD
PARK VW
ERMINE STREET
GREEN END
Green End
A141
ST PETER'S RD
Sapley Spinneys Nature Reserve
Mast
Water Tower
PH
PE29
WASHINGLEY ROAD
SPITTALS WAY
LATHAM RD
TOWER SQUARE
ST PETERS RD
KINGS RIPTON RD
GREEN TILES
CL
ROBERTSON WY
BEEVOR COURT
WOLFF CL
KINGS RIPTON ROAD
SAPLEY RD

151
141

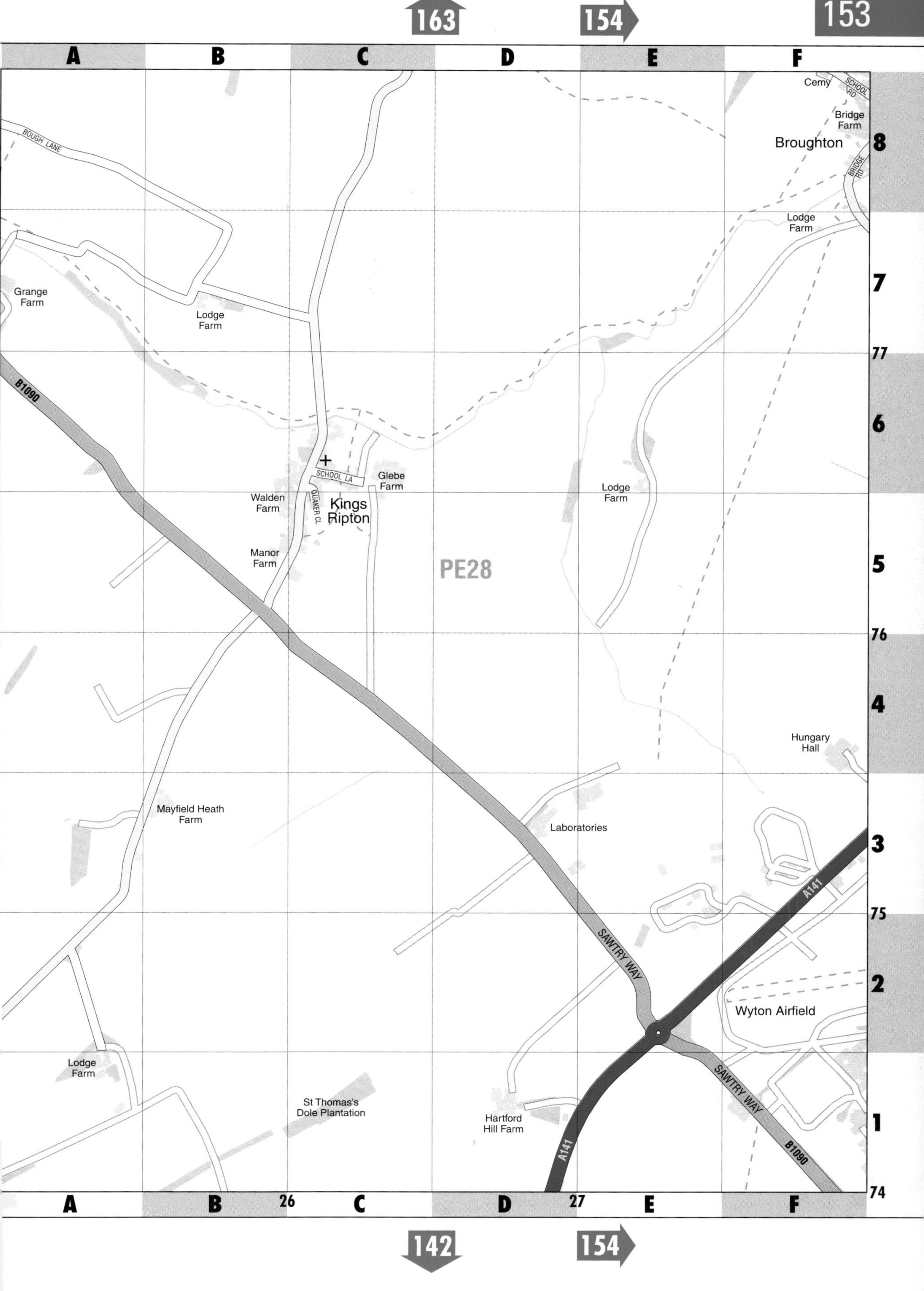
A
B
C
D
E
F
BOUGH LANE
Cemy
SCHOOL RD
Bridge Farm
Broughton
BRIDGE RD
8
Lodge Farm
7
Grange Farm
Lodge Farm
77
B1090
6
SCHOOL LA
Glebe Farm
Walden Farm
QUAKER CL
Kings Ripton
Lodge Farm
Manor Farm
PE28
5
76
4
Hungary Hall
Mayfield Heath Farm
Laboratories
3
A141
75
SAWTRY WAY
2
Wyton Airfield
Lodge Farm
St Thomas's Dole Plantation
Hartford Hill Farm
A141
SAWTRY WAY
B1090
1
74
A
B
26
C
D
27
E
F

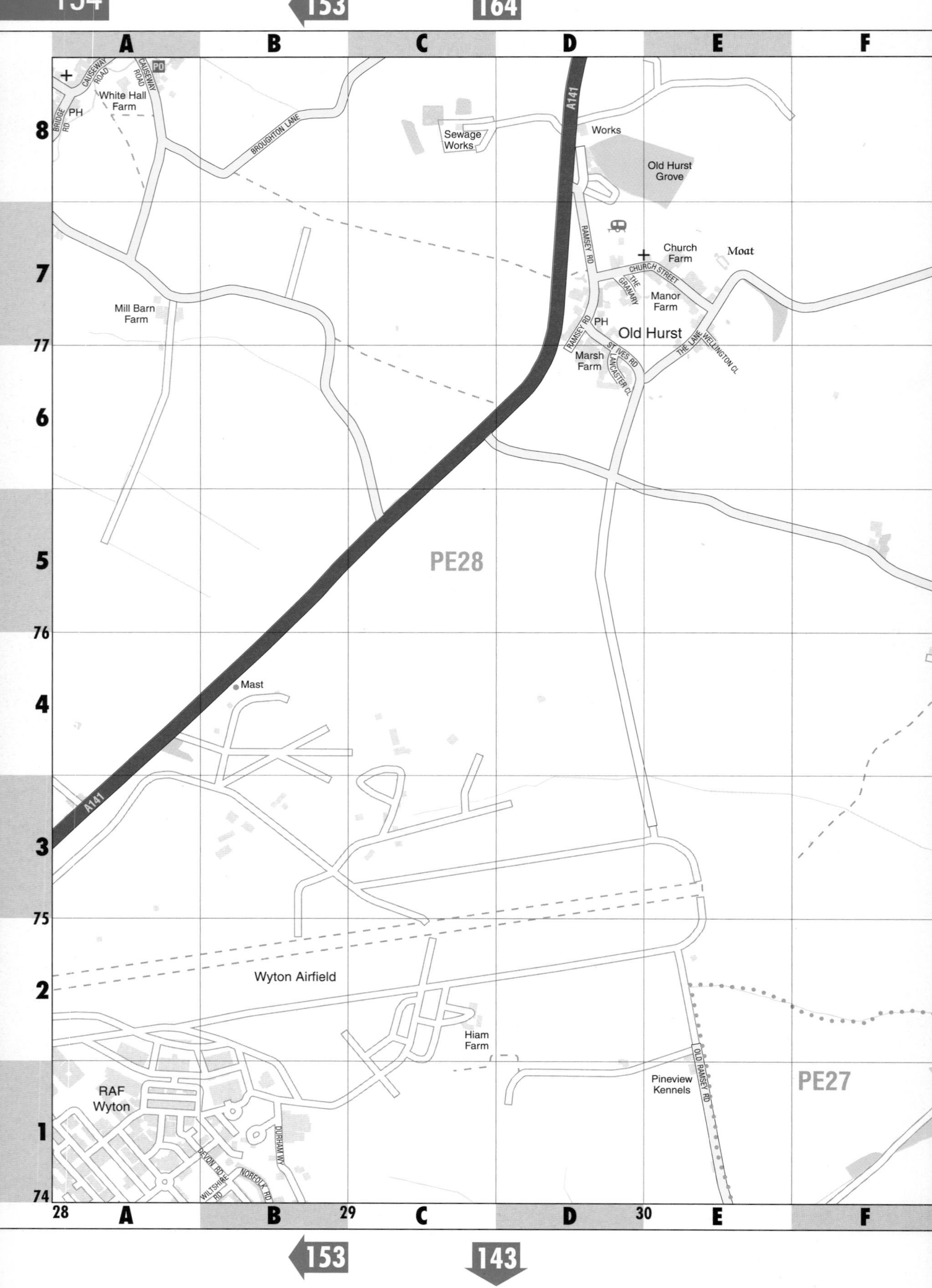
A
B
C
D
E
F
8
7
77
6
5
76
4
3
75
2
1
74
28
29
30
CAUSEWAY ROAD
CAUSEWAY ROAD
PO
White Hall Farm
BRIDGE RD
PH
BROUGHTON LANE
Sewage Works
A141
Works
Old Hurst Grove
RAMSEY RD
Church Farm
Moat
CHURCH STREET
THE GRANARY
Manor Farm
Mill Barn Farm
RAMSEY RD
PH
Old Hurst
Marsh Farm
ST IVES RD
LANCASTER CL
THE LANE
WELLINGTON CL
PE28
Mast
A141
Wyton Airfield
Hiam Farm
OLD RAMSEY RD
Pineview Kennels
PE27
RAF Wyton
DURHAM WY
DEVON RD
WILTSHIRE RD
NORFOLK RD

A B C D E F

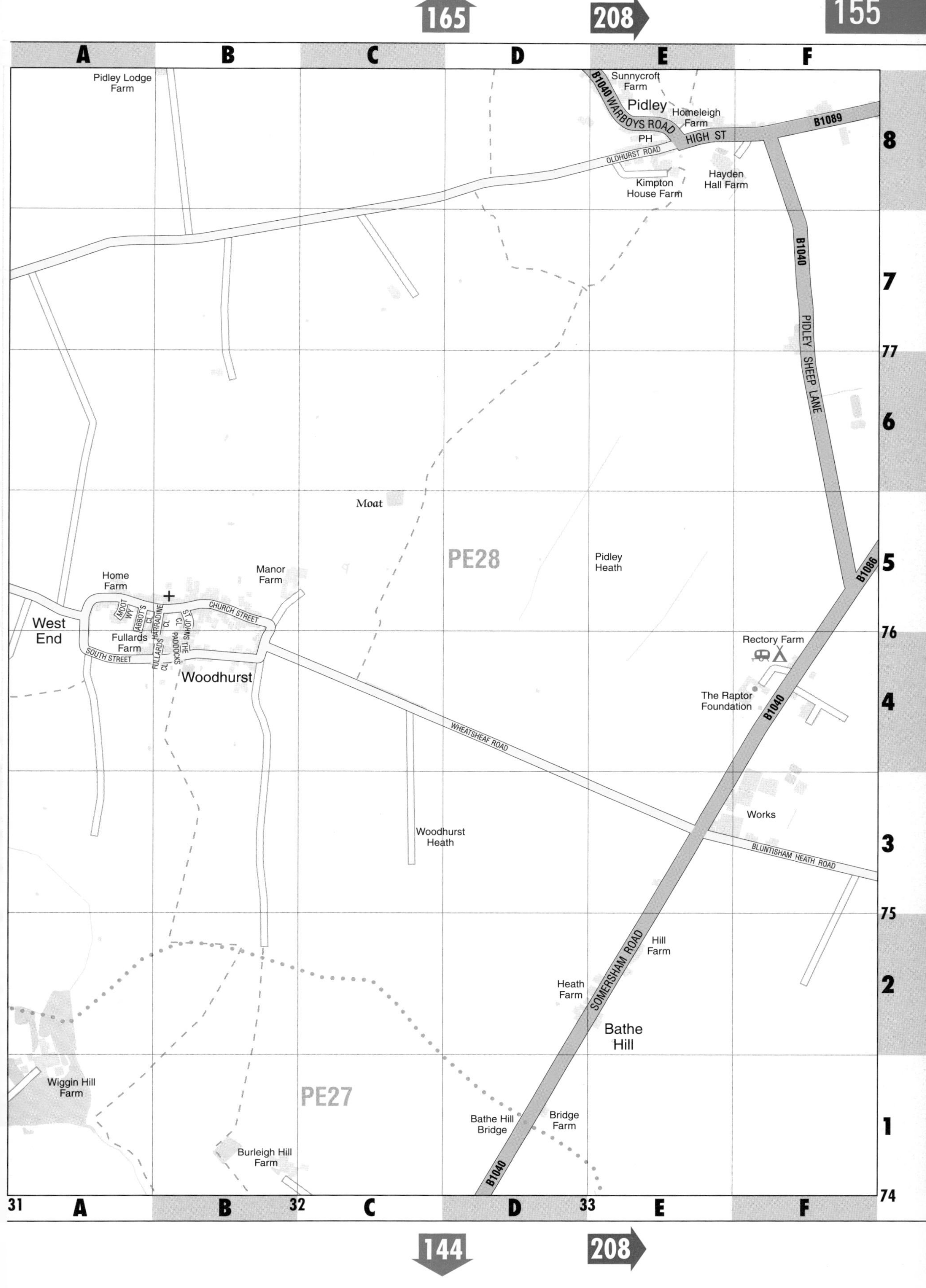

Pidley Lodge Farm

Sunnycroft Farm

Pidley

Homeleigh Farm

B1040 WARBOYS ROAD

PH

HIGH ST

B1089

OLDHURST ROAD

Kimpton House Farm

Hayden Hall Farm

B1040

PIDLEY SHEEP LANE

Moat

PE28

Pidley Heath

B1086

Home Farm

Manor Farm

West End

CHURCH STREET

Rectory Farm

Fullards Farm

ABBOT'S CL

MARRADINE CL

ST JOHN'S CL

PADDOCKS

THE

B1040

The Raptor Foundation

SOUTH STREET

Woodhurst

WHEATSHEAF ROAD

B1040

Works

Woodhurst Heath

BLUNTISHAM HEATH ROAD

SOMERSHAM ROAD

Hill Farm

Heath Farm

Bathe Hill

Wiggin Hill Farm

PE27

Bathe Hill Bridge

Bridge Farm

Burleigh Hill Farm

B1040

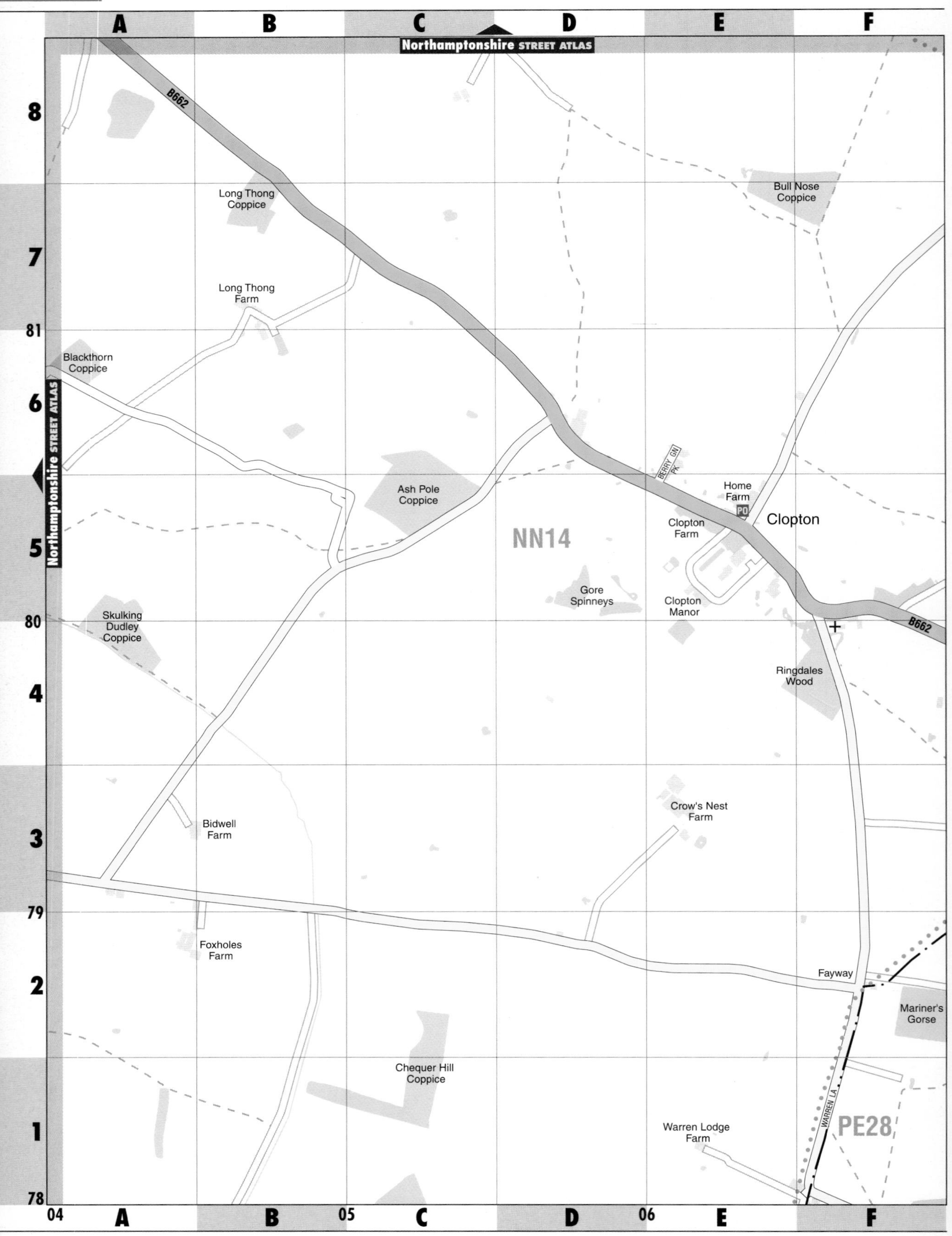

Northamptonshire STREET ATLAS

B662

8

7

81

Long Thong
Coppice

Long Thong
Farm

Blackthorn
Coppice

6

Ash Pole
Coppice

NN14

Home
Farm

Clopton
Farm

Clopton

5

Gore
Spinneys

Clopton
Manor

Skulking
Dudley
Coppice

80

Ringdales
Wood

B662

4

Bidwell
Farm

Crow's Nest
Farm

3

79

Foxholes
Farm

Fayway

2

Mariner's
Gorse

Chequer Hill
Coppice

WARREN LA

Warren Lodge
Farm

PE28

1

78

Bull Nose
Coppice

BERRY DN
PK

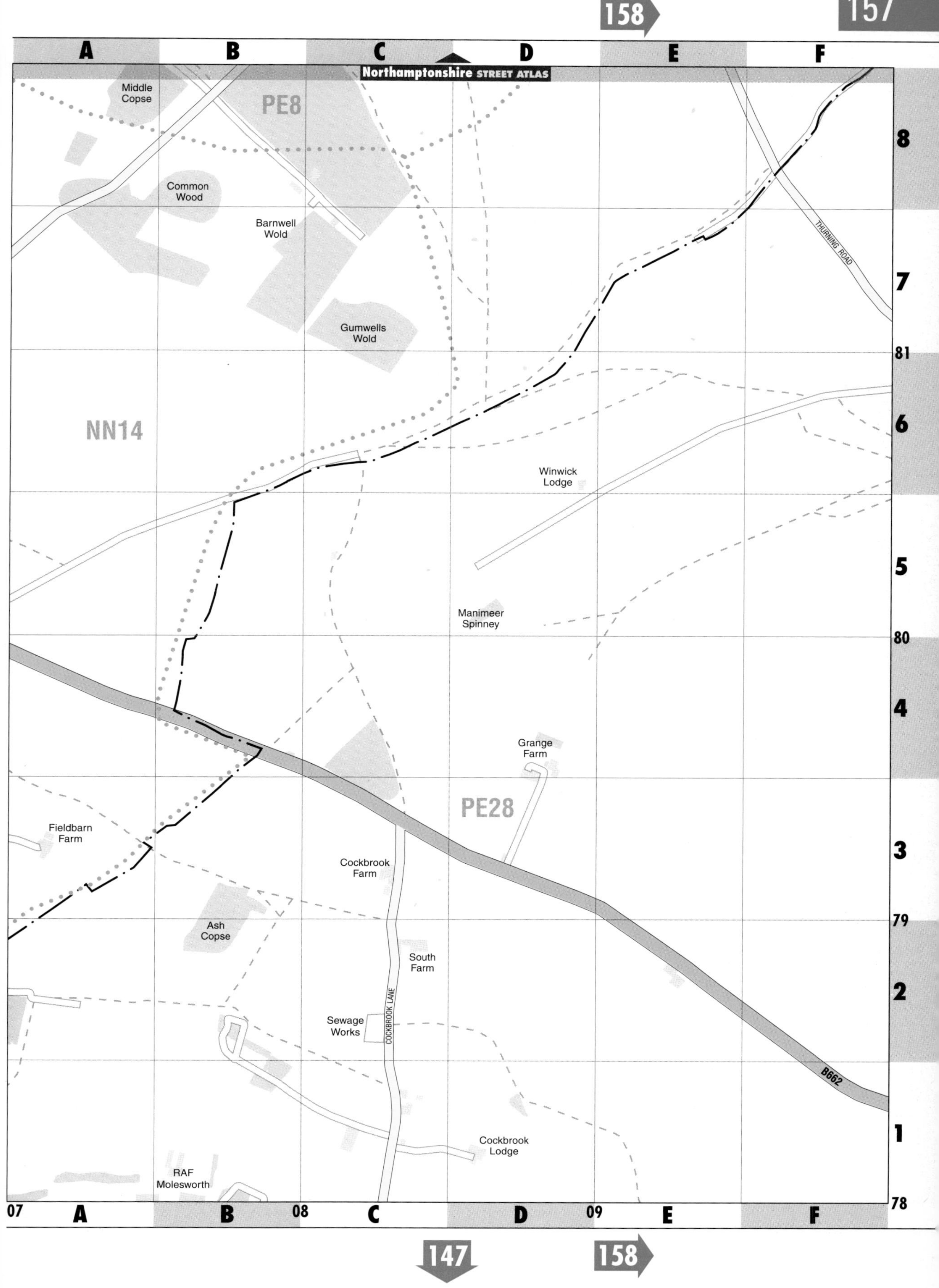

158

Northamptonshire STREET ATLAS

A B C D E F

8

7

81

6

5

80

4

3

79

2

1

78

PE8

Middle Copse

Common Wood

Barnwell Wold

Gumwells Wold

NN14

THURNING ROAD

Winwick Lodge

Manimeer Spinney

Grange Farm

PE28

Fieldbarn Farm

Cockbrook Farm

Ash Copse

South Farm

COCKBROOK LANE

Sewage Works

Cockbrook Lodge

RAF Molesworth

B662

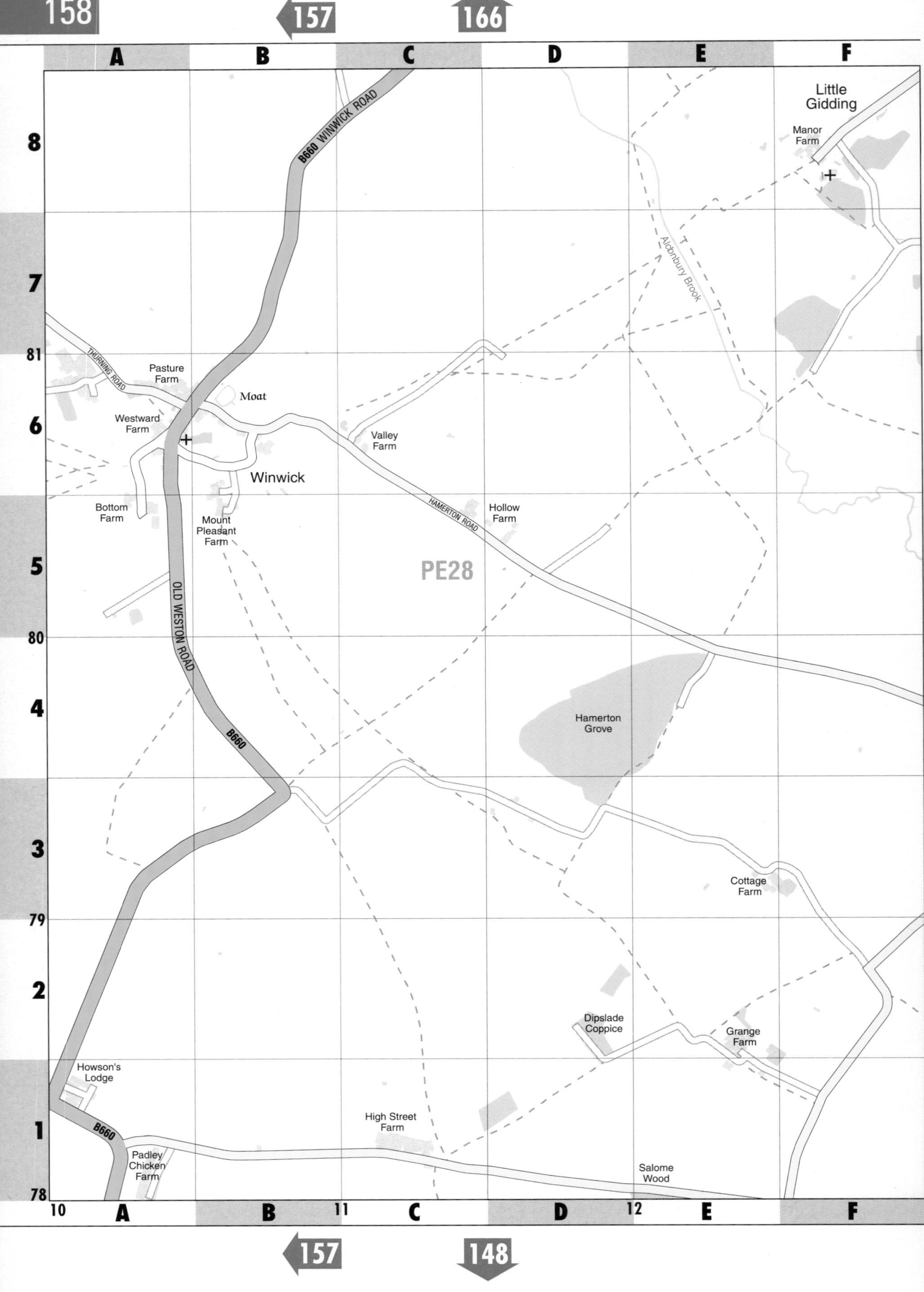

8

7

81

6

5

80

4

3

79

2

1

78

A B C D E F

B660 WINWICK ROAD

Little Gidding

Manor Farm

Aldenbury Brook

THURNING ROAD

Pasture Farm

Moat

Westward Farm

Winwick

Valley Farm

HAMERTON ROAD

Hollow Farm

Bottom Farm

Mount Pleasant Farm

OLD WESTON ROAD

PE28

Hamerton Grove

B660

Cottage Farm

Dipslade Coppice

Grange Farm

Howson's Lodge

B660

High Street Farm

Padley Chicken Farm

Salome Wood

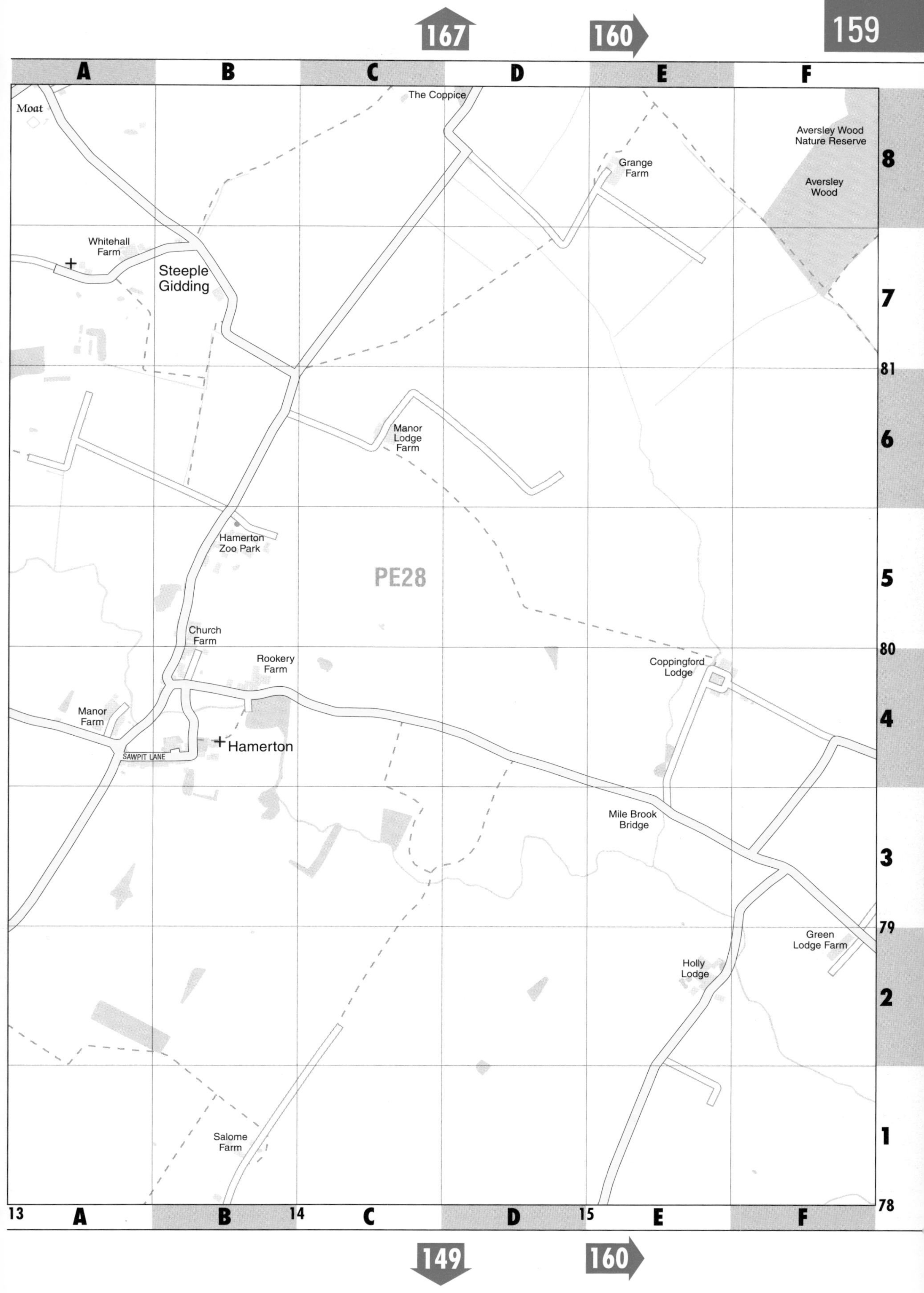

167
160
A
B
C
D
E
F
Moat
The Coppice
Aversley Wood
Nature Reserve
Grange
Farm
Aversley
Wood
8
Whitehall
Farm
Steeple
Gidding
7
81
Manor
Lodge
Farm
6
Hamerton
Zoo Park
PE28
5
Church
Farm
Rookery
Farm
80
Coppingford
Lodge
Manor
Farm
4
SAWPIT LANE
Hamerton
Mile Brook
Bridge
3
79
Green
Lodge Farm
Holly
Lodge
2
Salome
Farm
1
78
13
14
15
149
160

159

A **B** **C** **D** **E** **F**

Aversley Wood

Whitehall

Whitehall Farm

ST JUDITH'S LANE

B1043

A1(M)

B1090

8

Manorial Earthworks

Brickyard Farm

7

Archers Wood Farm

Archers Wood Nature Reserve

81

Archer's Wood

6

ST JUDITH'S LANE

Hill Top Farm

Hermitage Grove

PE28

Motel

5

Mast

Coppingford Wood

Top Farm

Moat

80

Coppingford

Tumulus

4

Stangate Hill

Upton Wood

Upton Lodge Farm

3

Monks' Wood Farm

79

Glebe Farm

2

Top Farm

GREEN LANE

College Farm

Manor Farm

Upton

A1(M)

B1043

UPTON HILL

South Farm

1

78

16 **A** **B** 17 **C** **D** 18 **E** **F**

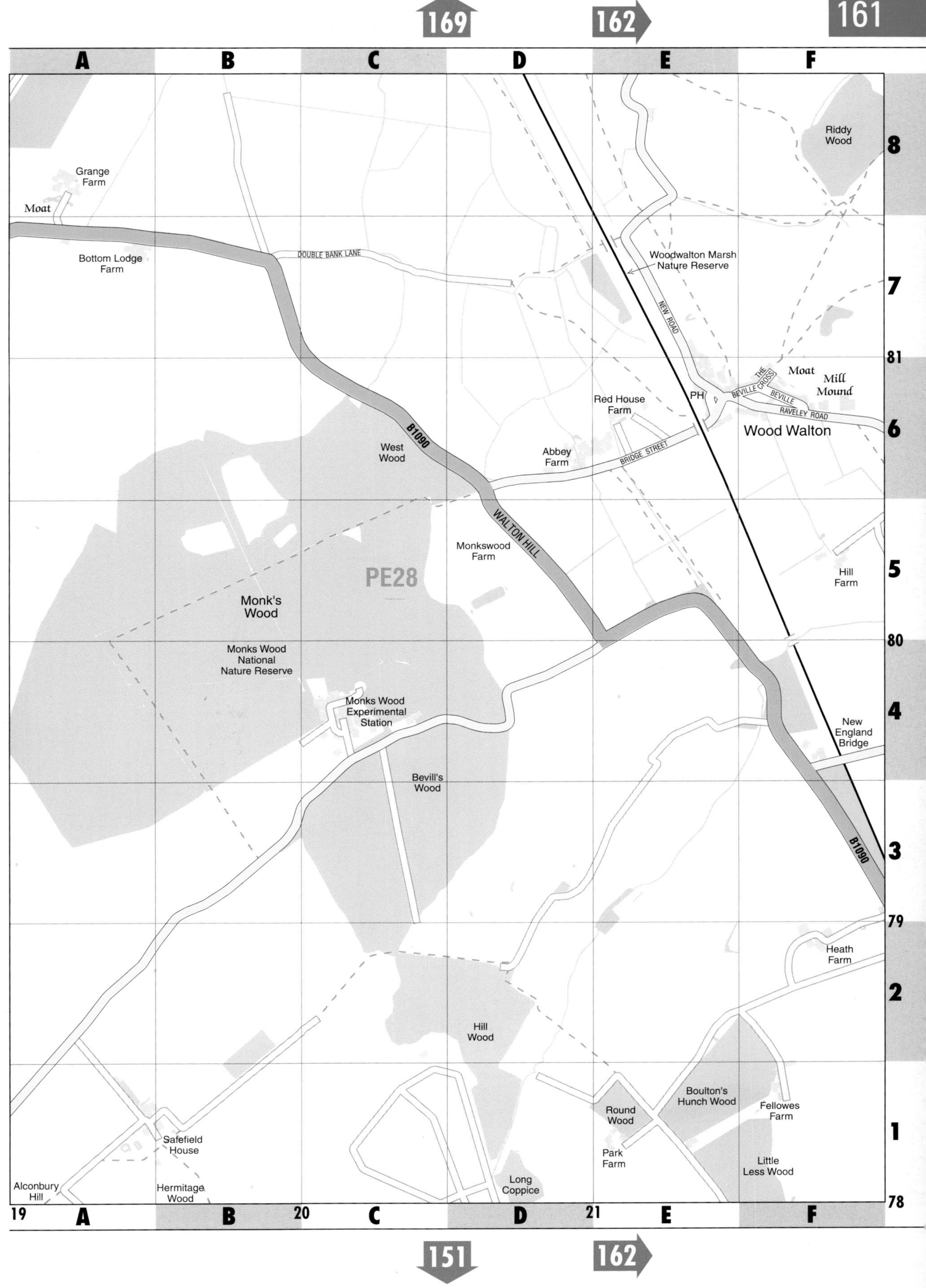

A B C D E F

Riddy Wood 8

Grange Farm

Moat

Bottom Lodge Farm

DOUBLE BANK LANE 7

Woodwalton Marsh Nature Reserve

NEW ROAD

81

Moat Mill Mound

THE CROSS BEVILLE CROSS BEVILLE

PH RAVELEY ROAD

B1090 6

Wood Walton

West Wood

Red House Farm

Abbey Farm BRIDGE STREET

WALTON HILL

Monkswood Farm Hill Farm 5

PE28

Monk's Wood

80

Monks Wood National Nature Reserve

Monks Wood Experimental Station New England Bridge 4

Bevill's Wood

B1090 3

79

Heath Farm

2

Hill Wood

Boulton's Hunch Wood

Round Wood Fellowes Farm

Park Farm Little Less Wood 1

Safefield House

Alconbury Hill Hermitage Wood Long Coppice 78

161
170

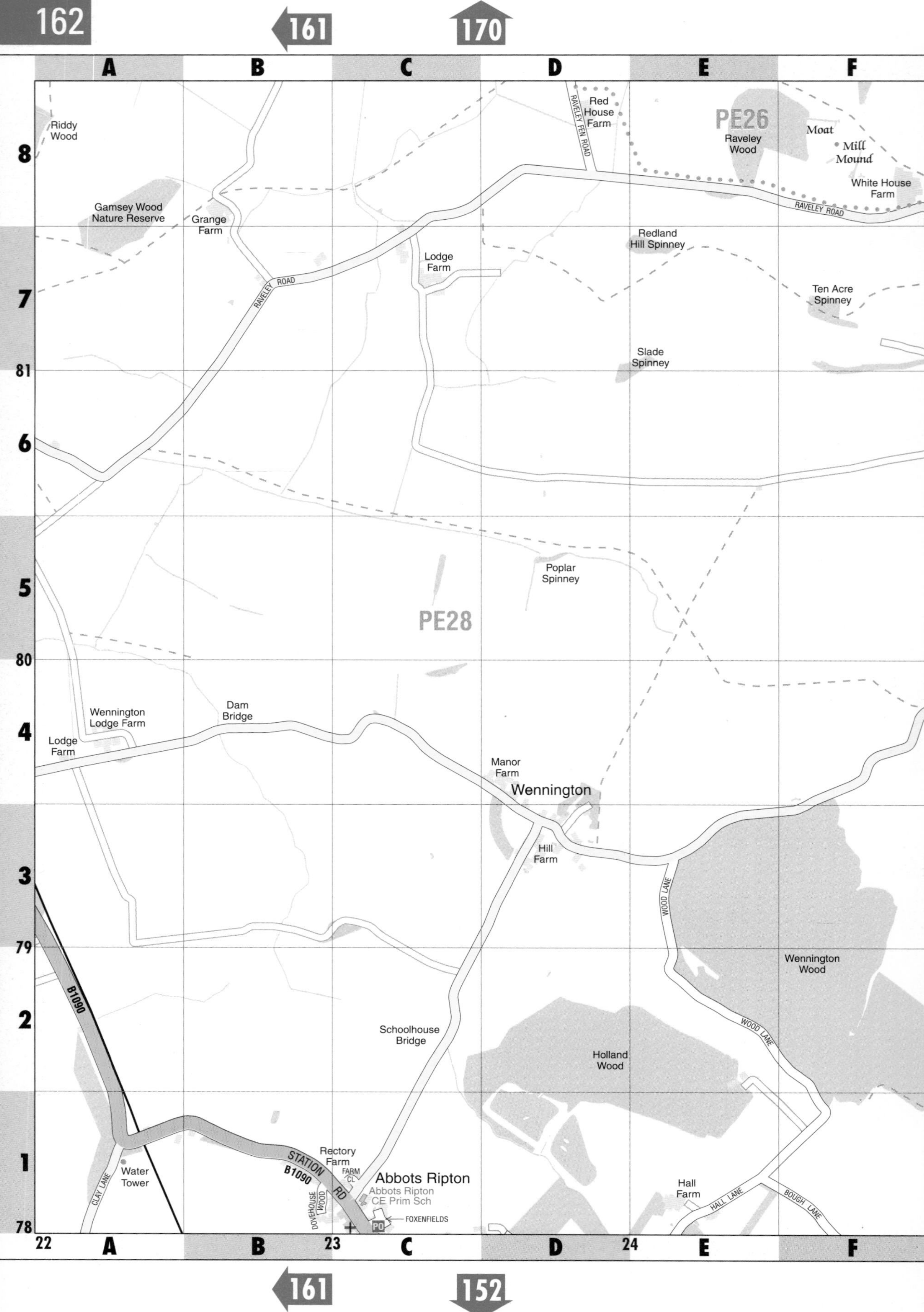
A
B
C
D
E
F
8
7
81
6
5
80
4
3
79
2
1
78
22
23
24
Riddy Wood
Red House Farm
RAVELEY FEN ROAD
PE26
Raveley Wood
Moat
Mill Mound
White House Farm
RAVELEY ROAD
Gamsey Wood Nature Reserve
Grange Farm
Redland Hill Spinney
Lodge Farm
RAVELEY ROAD
Ten Acre Spinney
Slade Spinney
Poplar Spinney
PE28
Wennington Lodge Farm
Dam Bridge
Lodge Farm
Manor Farm
Wennington
Hill Farm
WOOD LANE
Wennington Wood
B1090
Schoolhouse Bridge
WOOD LANE
Holland Wood
Rectory Farm
FARM CL
Abbots Ripton
Abbots Ripton CE Prim Sch
STATION RD
B1090
DOVEHOUSE WOOD
FOXENFIELDS
PO
Water Tower
CLAY LANE
Hall Farm
HALL LANE
BOUGH LANE

161
152

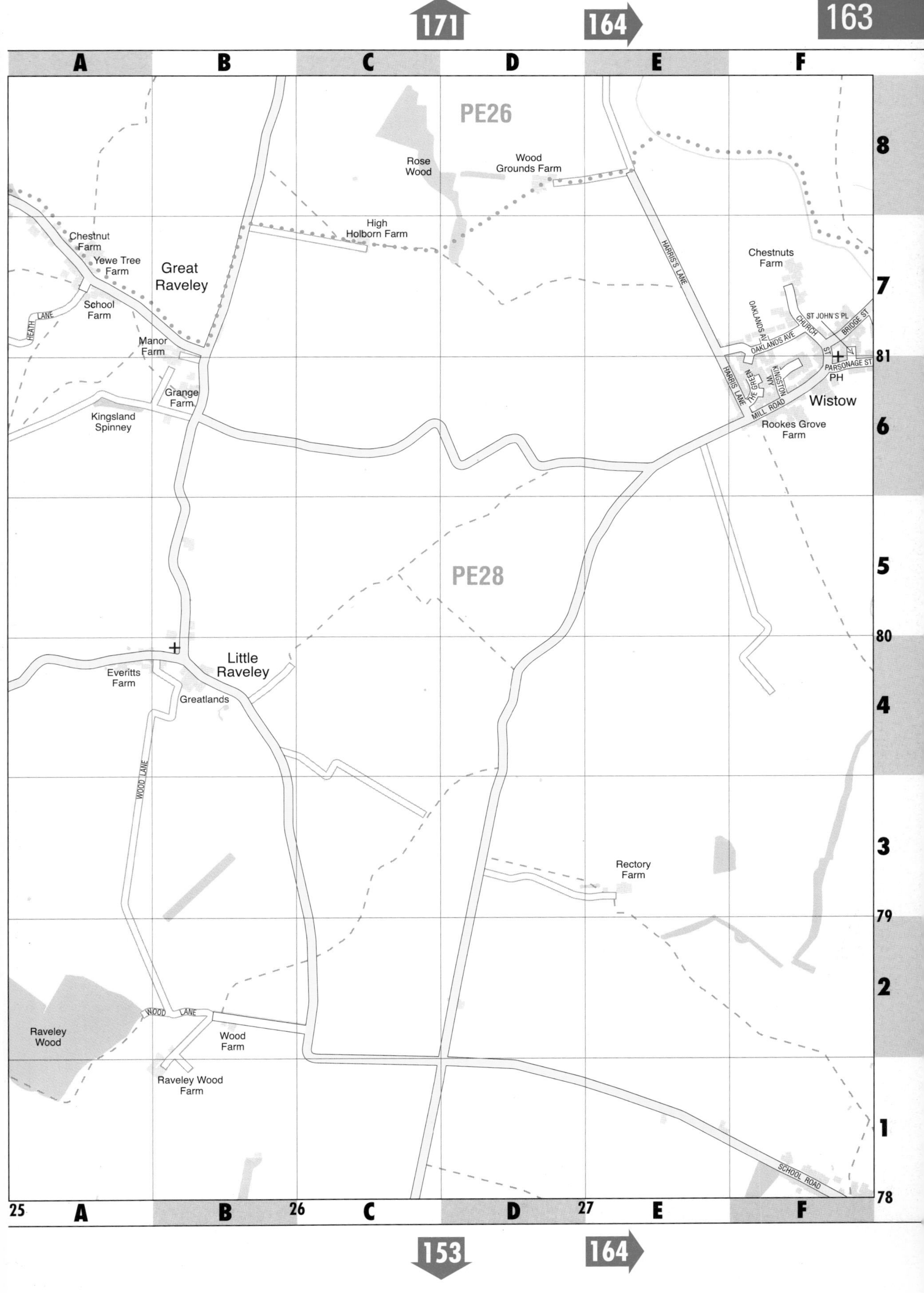

A **B** **C** **D** **E** **F**

8

PE26

Rose
Wood

Wood
Grounds Farm

High
Holborn Farm

Chestnut
Farm

Yewe Tree
Farm

HARRIS'S LANE

Chestnuts
Farm

7

Great
Raveley

School
Farm

HEATH LANE

OAKLANDS AVE

ST JOHN'S PL

CHURCH ST

BRIDGE ST

81

Manor
Farm

GREEN WAY

KINGSTON WAY

PARSONAGE ST

PH

Grange
Farm

HARRIS'S LANE

MILL ROAD

Wistow

Kingsland
Spinney

Rookes Grove
Farm

6

PE28

5

80

Little
Raveley

Everitts
Farm

Greatlands

4

WOOD LANE

Rectory
Farm

3

79

2

Raveley
Wood

WOOD LANE

Wood
Farm

Raveley Wood
Farm

1

SCHOOL ROAD

78

163
172

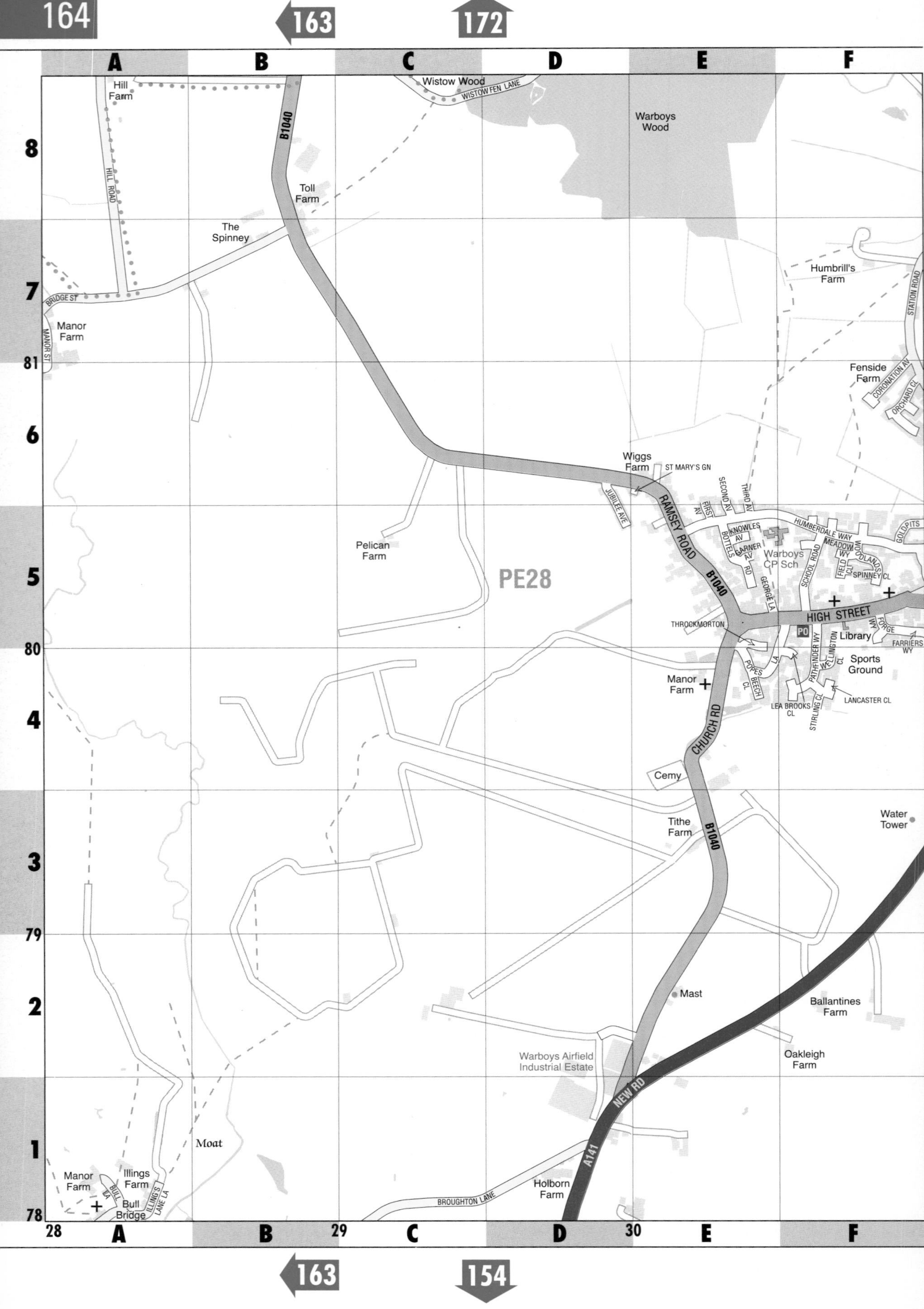
A
B
C
D
E
F
8
7
81
6
5
80
4
3
79
2
1
78
28
29
30
Hill Farm
Wistow Wood
WISTOW FEN LANE
Warboys Wood
B1040
HILL ROAD
Toll Farm
The Spinney
BRIDGE ST
Manor Farm
MANOR ST
Humbrill's Farm
STATION ROAD
Fenside Farm
CORONATION AV
ORCHARD CL
Wiggs Farm
ST MARY'S GN
JUBILEE AVE
RAMSEY ROAD
FIRST AV
SECOND AV
THIRD AV
KNOWLES AV
BOTTELS
GARNER AV
RD
GEORGE LA
Warboys CP Sch
HUMBERDALE WAY
MEADOW WY
SCHOOL ROAD
FIELD CL
WOODLANDS
SPINNEY CL
GOLDPITS
Pelican Farm
PE28
HIGH STREET
THROCKMORTON
PO
PATHFINDER WY
WELLINGTON CL
Library
FORGE WY
FARRIERS WY
Sports Ground
POPES LA
BEECH CL
Manor Farm
LEA BROOKS CL
STIRLING CL
LANCASTER CL
CHURCH RD
Cemy
Tithe Farm
Water Tower
Mast
Ballantines Farm
Oakleigh Farm
Warboys Airfield Industrial Estate
NEW RD
A141
Moat
Manor Farm
Illings Farm
BULL LA
Bull Bridge
ILLINGS LANE LA
BROUGHTON LANE
Holborn Farm

163
154

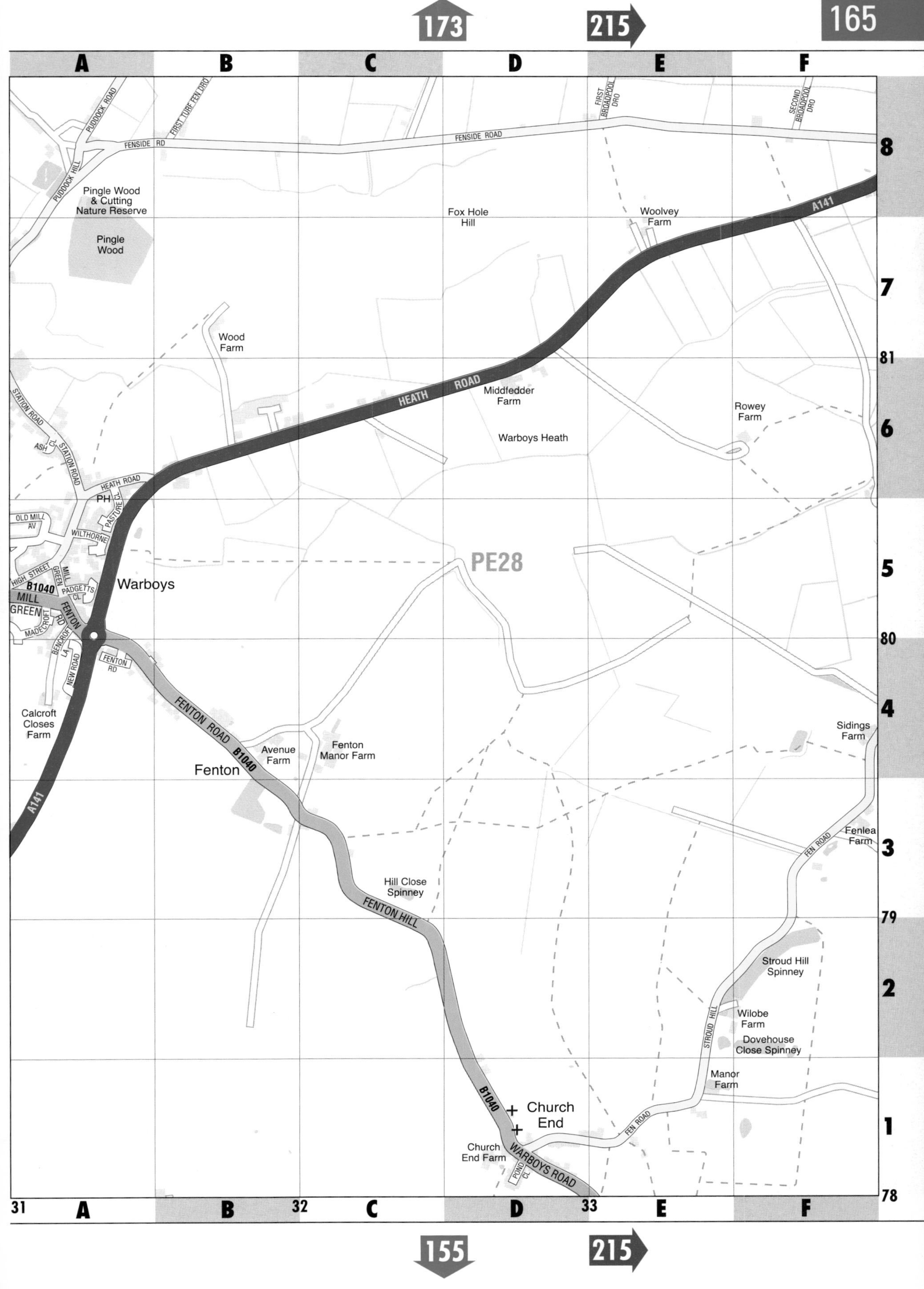
173
215
A
B
C
D
E
F
8
7
81
6
5
80
4
3
79
2
1
78
31
32
33
PUDDOCK ROAD
FIRST TURF FEN DRO
FIRST BROADPOOL DRO
SECOND BROADPOOL DRO
PUDDOCK HILL
FENSIDE RD
FENSIDE ROAD
Pingle Wood & Cutting Nature Reserve
Pingle Wood
Fox Hole Hill
Woolvey Farm
A141
Wood Farm
HEATH ROAD
Middfedder Farm
Rowey Farm
Warboys Heath
STATION ROAD
ASH CL
HEATH ROAD
PH
PASTURE CL
OLD MILL AV
WILTHORNE
HIGH STREET
MILL GREEN
B1040
PADGETTS CL
Warboys
MILL GREEN
FENTON RD
MADECROFT
BENCROFT LA
NEW ROAD
FENTON RD
PE28
Calcroft Closes Farm
FENTON ROAD
B1040
Avenue Farm
Fenton Manor Farm
Fenton
Sidings Farm
Fenlea Farm
FEN ROAD
Hill Close Spinney
FENTON HILL
Stroud Hill Spinney
Wilobe Farm
STROUD HILL
Dovehouse Close Spinney
Manor Farm
B1040
Church End
FEN ROAD
Church End Farm
POND CL
WARBOYS ROAD
155
215

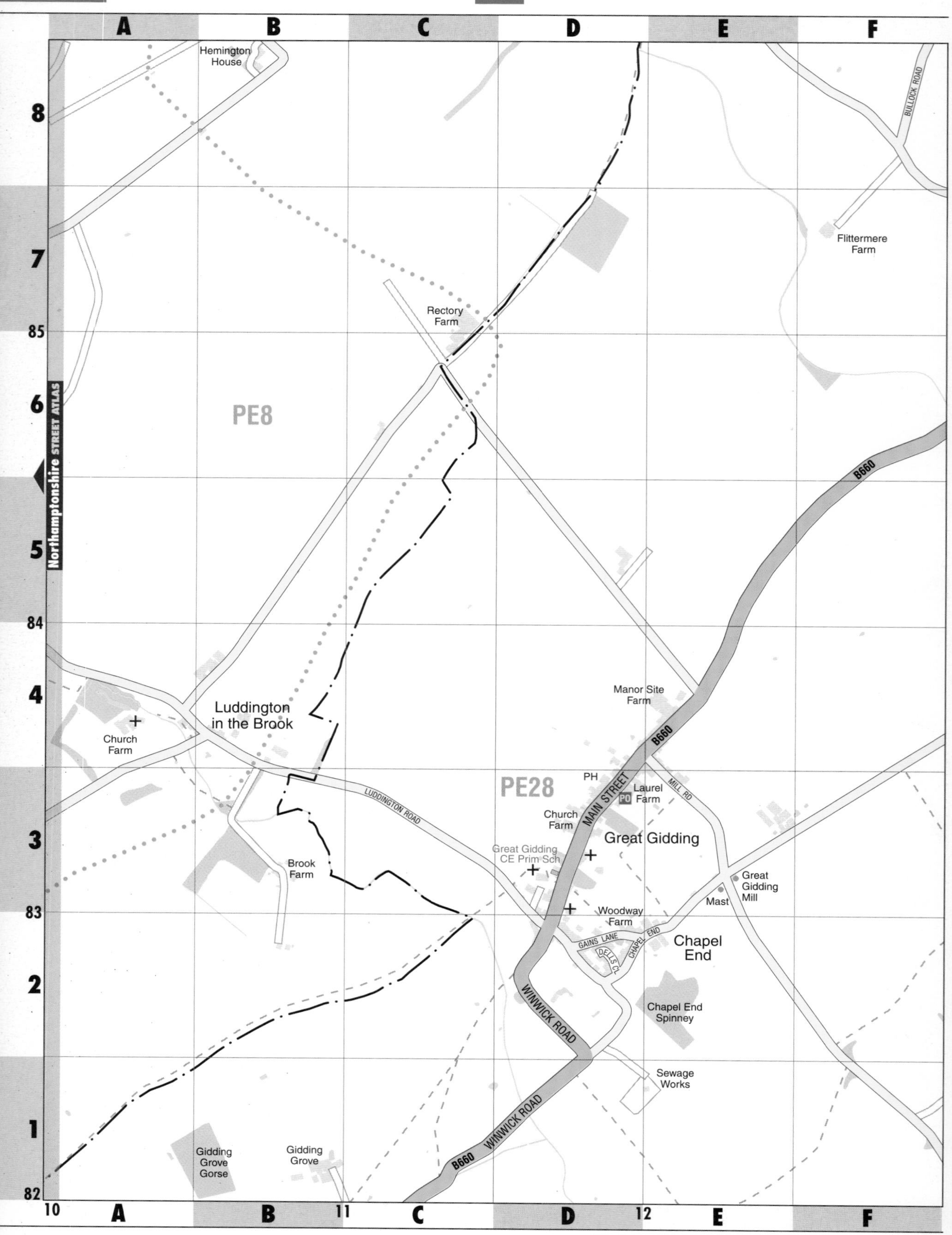

Northamptonshire STREET ATLAS

8

7

85

6

PE8

5

84

4

Church Farm

Luddington in the Brook

3

83

2

1

82

10   A   B   11   C   D   12   E   F

Hemington House

Flittermere Farm

BULLOCK ROAD

Rectory Farm

B660

Manor Site Farm

B660

PE28

Main Street

PH

PO

Laurel Farm

Mill Rd

Church Farm

Great Gidding

Great Gidding CE Prim Sch

Great Gidding Mill

Mast

Woodway Farm

Gains Lane

Delts Cl

Chapel End

Chapel End

Chapel End Spinney

Winwick Road

Sewage Works

B660

Winwick Road

Gidding Grove Gorse

Gidding Grove

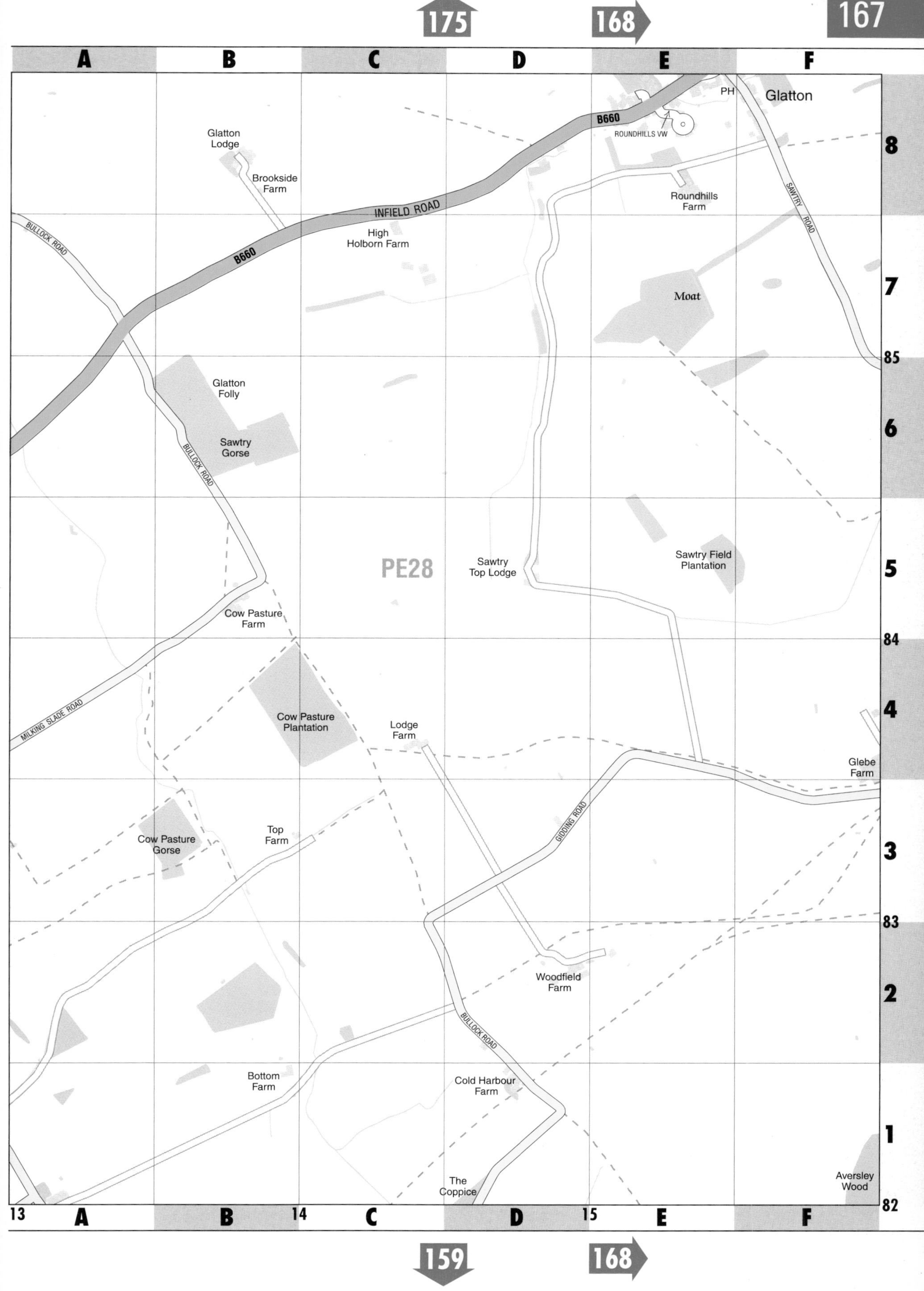

A B C D E F

8
7
85
6
5
84
4
3
83
2
1
82

Glatton
PH
B660
ROUNDHILLS VW
Glatton Lodge
Brookside Farm
INFIELD ROAD
B660
High Holborn Farm
Roundhills Farm
SAWTRY ROAD
BULLOCK ROAD
Moat
Glatton Folly
Sawtry Gorse
BULLOCK ROAD
PE28
Sawtry Top Lodge
Sawtry Field Plantation
Cow Pasture Farm
MILKING SLADE ROAD
Cow Pasture Plantation
Lodge Farm
Glebe Farm
Cow Pasture Gorse
Top Farm
GIDDING ROAD
Woodfield Farm
Bottom Farm
BULLOCK ROAD
Cold Harbour Farm
The Coppice
Aversley Wood

13 A B 14 C D 15 E F

167
176

A B C D E F

8

Yew Tree Farm
CONINGTON LANE
Conington
COTTON CL
BRUCES CL
CHURCH ROAD
CHURCH LA

Palmer's Grove

PE7

Spot's Grove

7

B1043
A1(M)

High Fen

85

Middlemarsh Farm
SAWTRY RD

Duckpit Fen

6

GLATTON ROAD

15

Bruce's Castle Farm
Castle Grove Moat

COOKS LANE
CREASE ROAD

Little Common Farm

5

Brookside Industrial Estate
BROOKSIDE
SALTERS WY
WESTERMAN CL
WARREN CT
PARK RD
TORT HL
RECTORY CL
B1043

Little Common

84

WHITEHOUSE RD
SHANLEY ROAD
FARFIELD RD
ROWELL VIEW
PIPPINS CL
DEERPARK
CHESTNUT CL
CHURCH STREET
HIGH ST
ANNESLEY CL
CHURCH CW
TINKERS LANE

Manor Farm
+

1 BLOOMFIELD WY
2 THE GRANARY
3 ALL SAINTS WY
4 ST DAVID'S WY
5 HUNTINGS DR

4

GLEBE RD
MILL VW
HATFIELD RD
ABBEY CL
BELGRAVE SQ
PH
THE MALTINGS
FEN LANE
NEWTON RD
MANOR CL
CHAPEL END
ST ANDREWS WAY
A1(M)
OLD NORTH ROAD

Glebe Farm
GIDDING ROAD
PAPYRUS WY
WOODFIELD DR
WESTFIELD RD
+
Liby
Sawtry Com Coll
FEN LANE
MOYNE CL
CAVENDISH CL
PETLEYS
Black Horse Farm

Sawtry Leisure Centre
HILLFIELD RD
MIDDLEFIELD ROAD
COLLEGE CY
GREEN END ROAD
LOUTHE WY
MOYNE RD
ERMINE WY
STRAIGHT DROVE

Great Common

3

ASHDALE CL 1
OAKLEY DR 2
HUNTERS WY 3
HAWTHORN WY 4
WINDSOR RD 5
DEVONSHIRE CL 6
WINDSOR RD
THE BRIARS
Sawtry Jun & Inf Schs
CROMWELL WY
RANGWORTH RD
BEAUMARIS RD
STANCH HL RD
FEN LANE

Sawtry
LAUREL CL
MAPLE CL
CRABAPPLE WY
ROCHAMPTON RD
BLINDS
BEDFORD CL
DURHAM CL
PH
SAXON CL

83

ELM BRYMBLE
MONKS
CAMBRIDGE
ALDWIN
HOLBEIN RD
SOOTHEY WY
PO
CHESHAM CL
CHESHAM RD
BUCKINGHAM WY
BLY
Stanch-hill Bridge

PE28

P
CAMBS
AVERSLEY GRANGE
BILL HALL WAY

Common Barn Farm
Sawtry Roughs

2

Wood End Farm
High Holborn Hill
Green End

Manor House Farm

15

1

ST JUDITH'S LANE
C2
1 EWINGSWOOD
2 WHEATSHEAVES
3 STANEGATE
4 STUMPCROSS
5 COTTON CL

Aversley Wood

B1043
A1(M)

82

16 A B 17 C D 18 E F

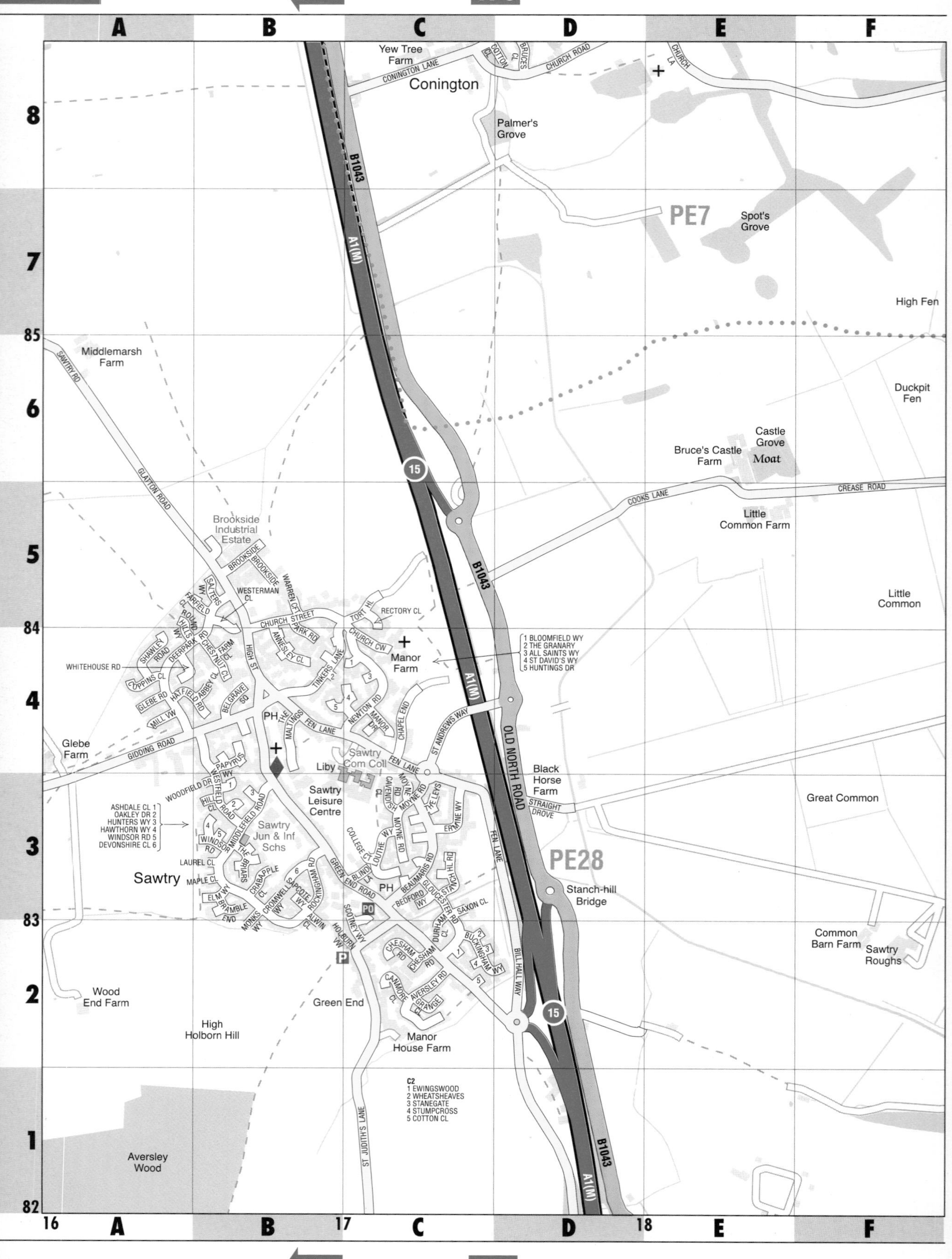

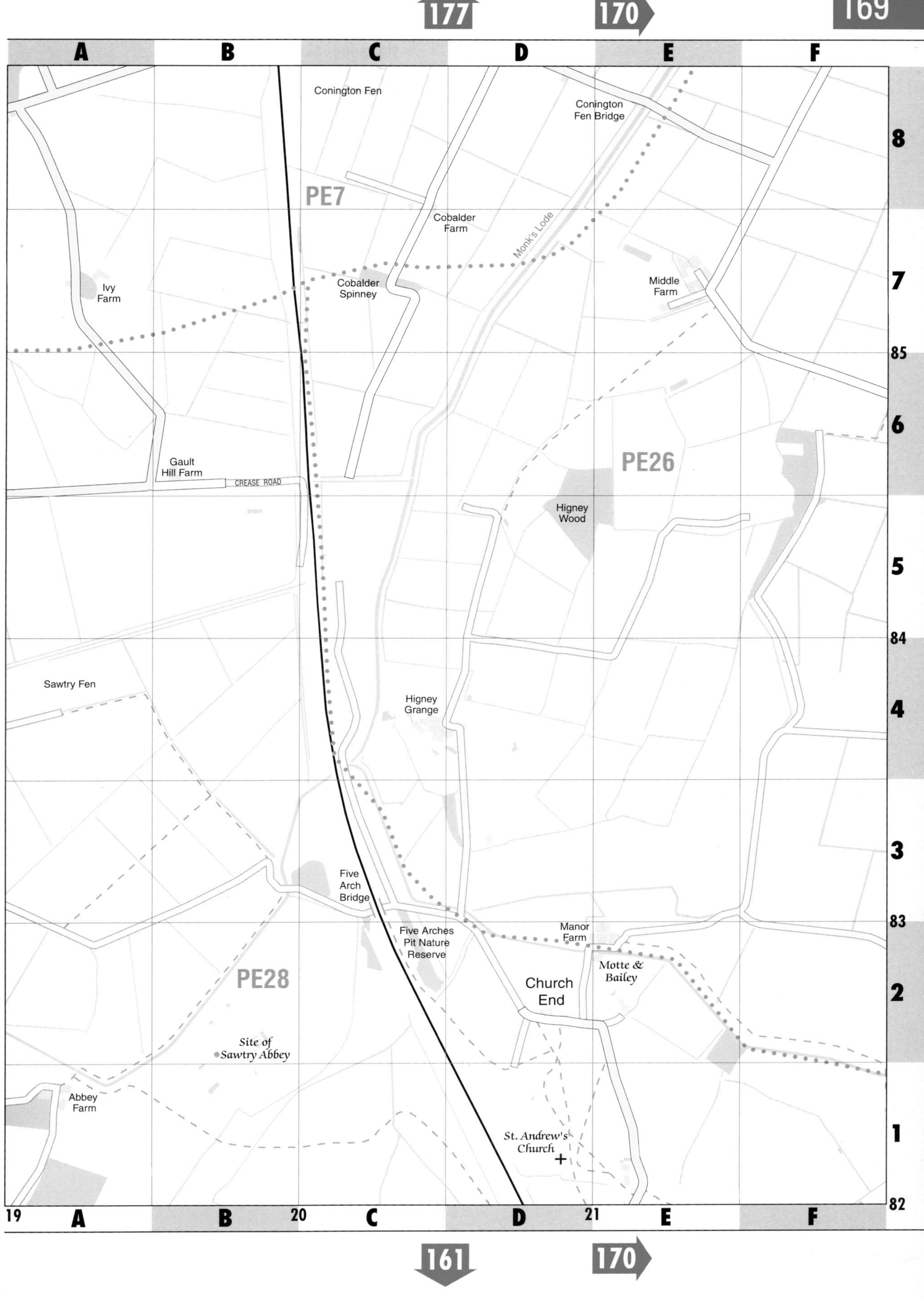

177
170

A   B   C   D   E   F

8

Conington Fen

Conington
Fen Bridge

PE7

Cobalder
Farm

Monk's Lode

7

Ivy
Farm

Cobalder
Spinney

Middle
Farm

85

6

Gault
Hill Farm

CREASE ROAD

PE26

Higney
Wood

5

84

Sawtry Fen

Higney
Grange

4

3

83

Five
Arch
Bridge

Five Arches
Pit Nature
Reserve

Manor
Farm

PE28

Motte &
Bailey

Church
End

2

Site of
Sawtry Abbey

Abbey
Farm

St. Andrew's
Church

1

82

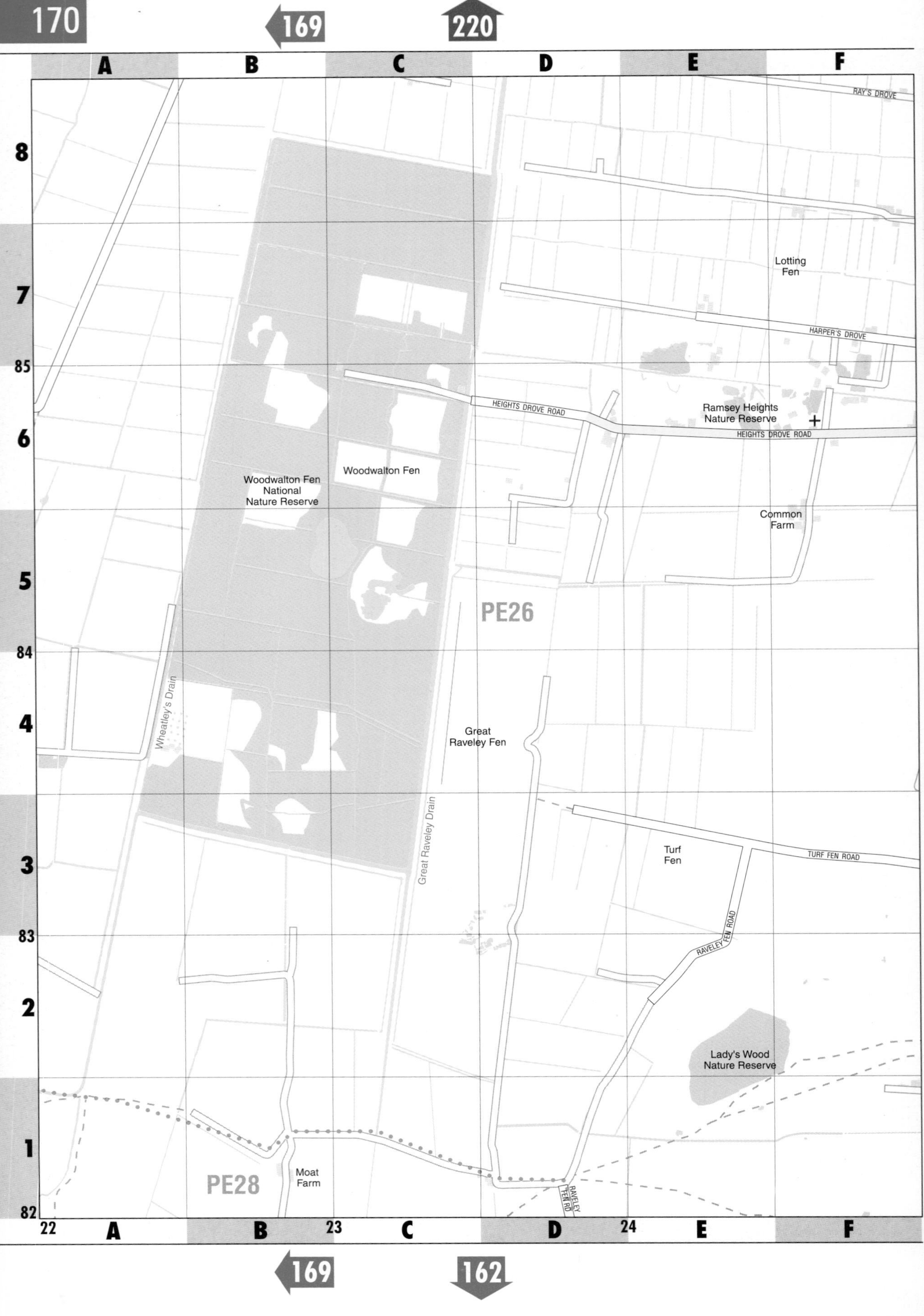

169
220

A · B · C · D · E · F

8

7

85

6

5

84

4

83

2

1

82

RAY'S DROVE

Lotting
Fen

HARPER'S DROVE

Heights Drove Road

Ramsey Heights
Nature Reserve

HEIGHTS DROVE ROAD

Woodwalton Fen
National
Nature Reserve

Woodwalton Fen

Common
Farm

PE26

Wheatley's Drain

Great
Raveley Fen

Great Raveley Drain

Turf
Fen

TURF FEN ROAD

RAVELEY FEN ROAD

Lady's Wood
Nature Reserve

PE28

Moat
Farm

RAVELEY
FEN RD

22 · A · B · 23 · C · D · 24 · E · F

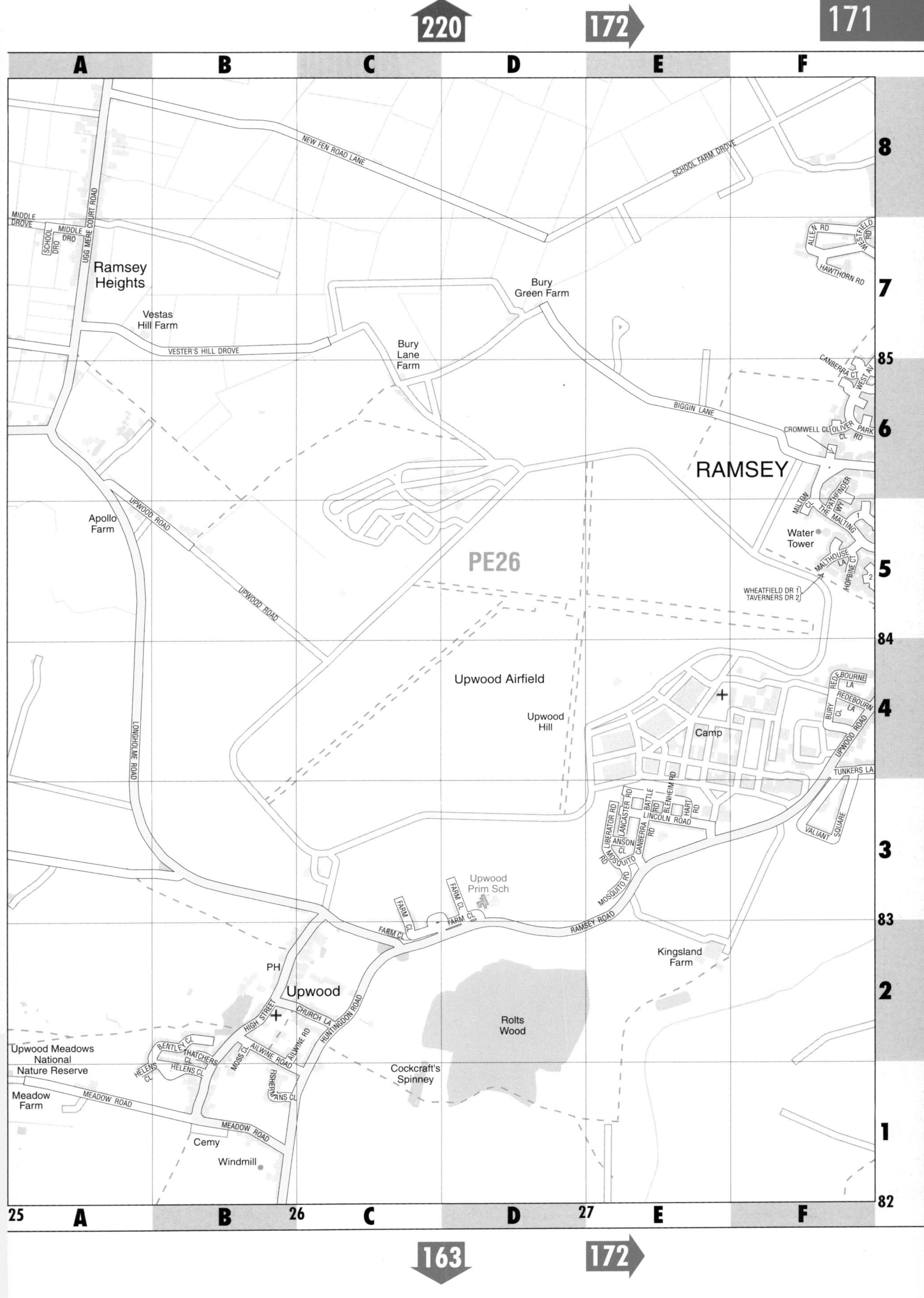
220
172
A
B
C
D
E
F
8
7
85
6
5
84
4
3
83
2
1
82
25
26
27
NEW FEN ROAD LANE
SCHOOL FARM DROVE
MIDDLE DROVE
SCHOOL DRO
MIDDLE DRO
UGG MERE COURT ROAD
Ramsey Heights
Vestas Hill Farm
VESTER'S HILL DROVE
Bury Green Farm
Bury Lane Farm
BIGGIN LANE
RAMSEY
ALLEN RD
WESTFIELD RD
HAWTHORN RD
CANBERRA CT
WEST AV
CROMWELL CL
OLIVER CL
PARK RD
MILTON CL
PATHFINDER WY
THE MALTINGS
Water Tower
MALTHOUSE LA
HOPBINE CT
WHEATFIELD DR 1
TAVERNERS DR 2
Apollo Farm
UPWOOD ROAD
PE26
Upwood Airfield
Upwood Hill
Camp
REDEBOURNE LA
BURY CL
UPWOOD ROAD
TUNKERS LA
VALIANT SQUARE
LONGHOLME ROAD
LIBERATOR RD
LANCASTER RD
BATTLE RD
BLENHEIM RD
HART RD
LINCOLN ROAD
ANSON CL
CANBERRA RD
MOSQUITO RD
Upwood Prim Sch
FARM CL
RAMSEY ROAD
Kingsland Farm
PH
Upwood
HIGH STREET
CHURCH LA
HUNTINGDON ROAD
AILWINE RD
AILWINE ROAD
MOSS CL
FISHERMANS CL
BENTLEY CL
THATCHERS CL
HELENS CL
Rolts Wood
Cockcraft's Spinney
Upwood Meadows National Nature Reserve
Meadow Farm
MEADOW ROAD
Cemy
Windmill
163
172

A B C D E F

8

B1040
ST MARY'S ROAD

STOCKING FEN ROAD

WOOD LANE

B1096

Park
Farm

PH
STATION GD

LIME RD   STAR LA
PRINCE'S ST
STAR LANE
FIELD ROAD
PRINCE'S STREET
FLETCHERS
FLOWERS CL
GREAT
WHYTE
MILL FIELDS
MILL
BECKET'S CL
Cemetery

ABBEY
FIELDS

7

WESTFIELD
SLADE CL
STATION
AM OBO
VINERY CT
ORCH
GREAT WHYTE
SCHOOL RD
WHYTEFIELD ROAD
WILLOW WK
NEW RD
MILL ST
SILVER ST
TOWER CL
NEW RD
WHELLANS YARD
NEWTOWN ROAD
SPINES CL
DRIVERS LA
ABBEY CL
OATES WY
LAWRENCE RD
Ramsey
Rural
Museum

P
P
P
LITTLE WHYTE
Ramsey
Abbey Sch

Ramsey Jun Sch
BLENHEIM ROAD
THE AVENUE
WEST AV
Liby
NEW RY
HIGH ST
B1096
Ramsey
Abbey Gatehouse

85

CHARLES AV
WEST
QUEEN MARY
SERJEANTS CL
THE AVENUE
CRICKETFIELD LA
HIGH STREET
B1040
LION
BROWN WY
PH
Ramsey
Leisure
Centre

6

FELLOWES DR
PARK RD
Football
Club
Spinning
Infant Sch
FAIRFIELD
WYATT CL
BRYANT CL
MUGGLESTONS LA
RAMSEY
Ailwyn
Sch
ABBEY RD

BIGGIN LANE
BURY ROAD
HOLLOW LANE

Hollow
Head Farm

5

CH'HOUSE WY
MALTING
W DRAYHORSE RD
BRANDS CL
FOUNDRY WK
LION WK
WARD CL
GRENFELL
CLOSE
UPWOOD RD
GRE
ELMWOOD C
Bury Fen
PE26
LONG DROVE

84

TAVERNERS DR
HIGH ST
BARN CL
OWL'S END
GARDEN CL
BROOM'S WY
UPWOOD ROAD
B1040
Bury
THE GLEBE
MEADOW LANE

4

SUNFIELD CL
GROVE
TUNKERS LA
POUND RD
HIGH WK
BURYFIELD
BURYFIELD
3
4
5
Bury CE
Prim Sch
HILL EST
Bury
Lug Fen

1 BADER CL
2 ROWELL WK
3 OLD STABLE WK
4 RINGWOOD CL
5 WOODFIELD
Manor
House
Hall
Farm
JACK'S CORNER DROVE

3

Jack's
Corner
Spinney
Milestone
Farm
STRAIGHT DROVE

83

2

Manor
Farm
PE28

Dorringtons
Farm

1

SHILLOW HILL
The
Spinney
Wistow Wood
Nature Reserve
CROSS DROVE
WISTOW FEN LANE

82

Hill
Farm
HILL RD
B1040
WISTOW FEN LA
Warboys
Wood

28 A 29 B C 30 D E F

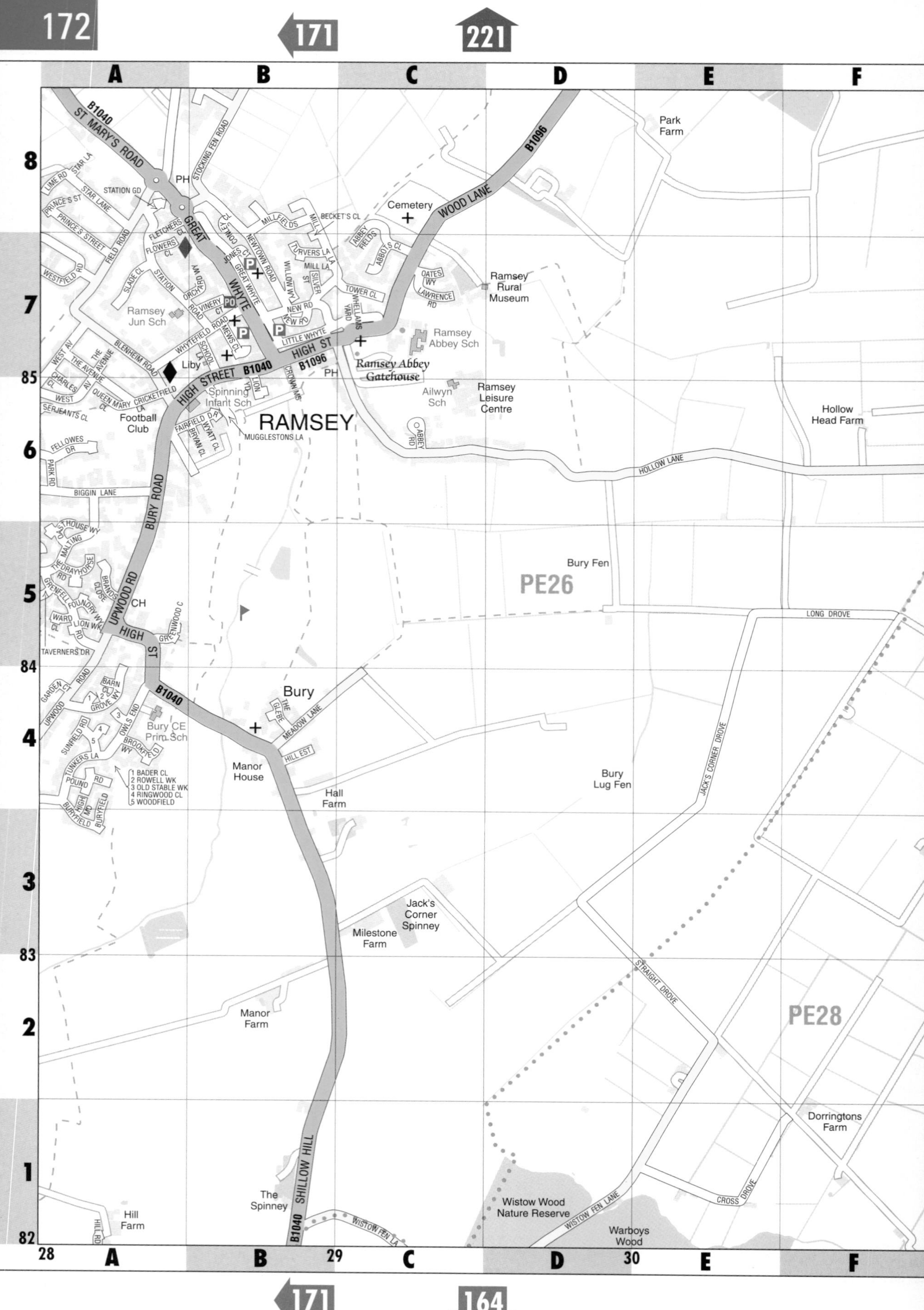

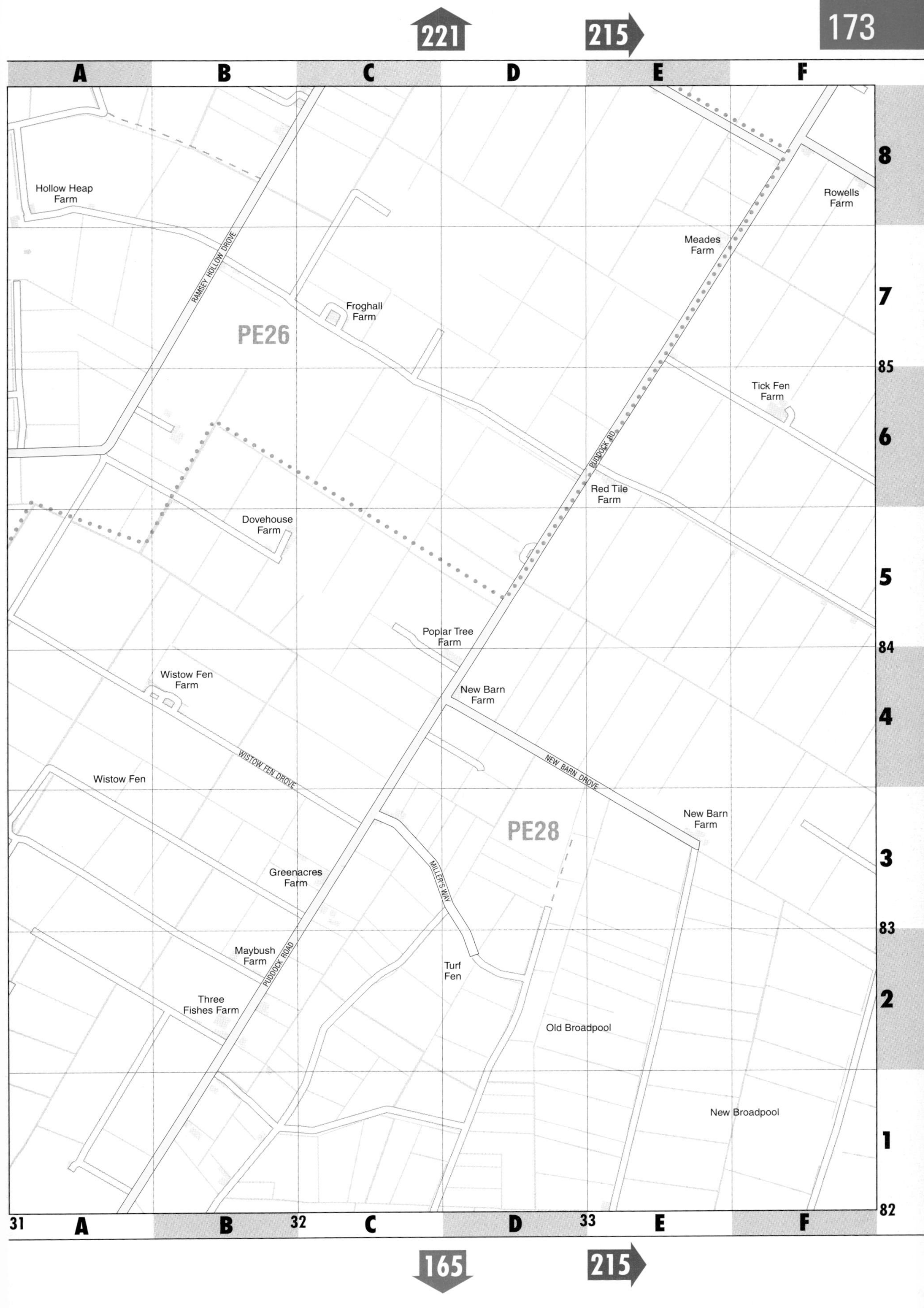

A   B   C   D   E   F

8

Hollow Heap
Farm

Rowells
Farm

Meades
Farm

7

Froghall
Farm

PE26

85

Tick Fen
Farm

6

RAMSEY HOLLOW DROVE

BUDDOCK RD.

Red Tile
Farm

Dovehouse
Farm

5

Poplar Tree
Farm

84

Wistow Fen
Farm

New Barn
Farm

4

WISTOW FEN DROVE

NEW BARN DROVE

Wistow Fen

New Barn
Farm

PE28

3

Greenacres
Farm

MILLER'S WAY

PUDDOCK ROAD

83

Maybush
Farm

Turf
Fen

2

Three
Fishes Farm

Old Broadpool

New Broadpool

1

82

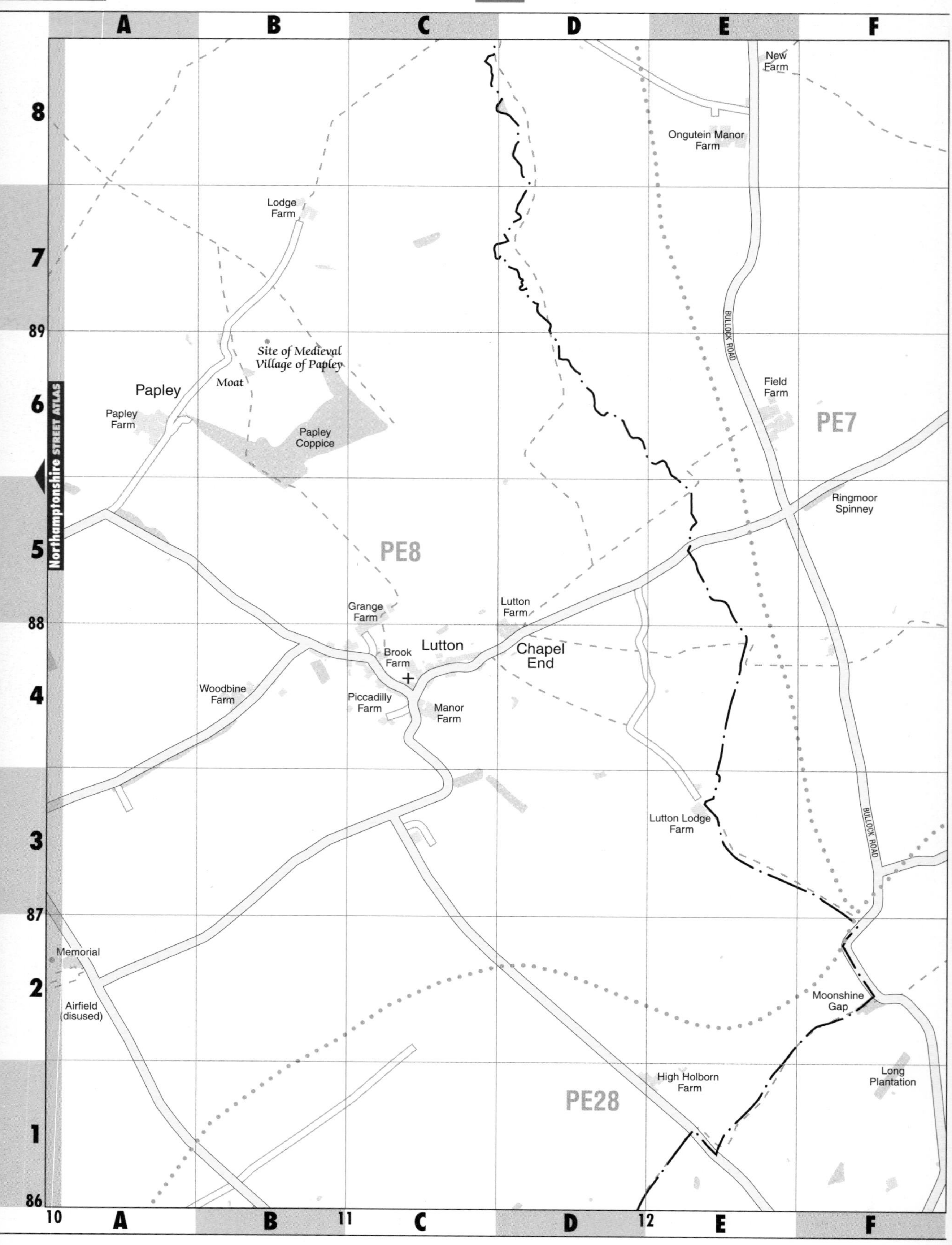

A　　B　　C　　D　　E　　F

8

7

89

6

Papley

PE7

5

PE8

88

4

3

87

2

PE28

1

86

10　A　　B　11　C　　D　12　E　　F

Northamptonshire STREET ATLAS

New Farm

Ongutein Manor Farm

Lodge Farm

Site of Medieval Village of Papley

Moat

Papley Farm

Papley Coppice

Field Farm

Ringmoor Spinney

BULLOCK ROAD

Grange Farm

Lutton Farm

Brook Farm

Lutton

Chapel End

Woodbine Farm

Piccadilly Farm

Manor Farm

Lutton Lodge Farm

Memorial

Airfield (disused)

Moonshine Gap

BULLOCK ROAD

High Holborn Farm

Long Plantation

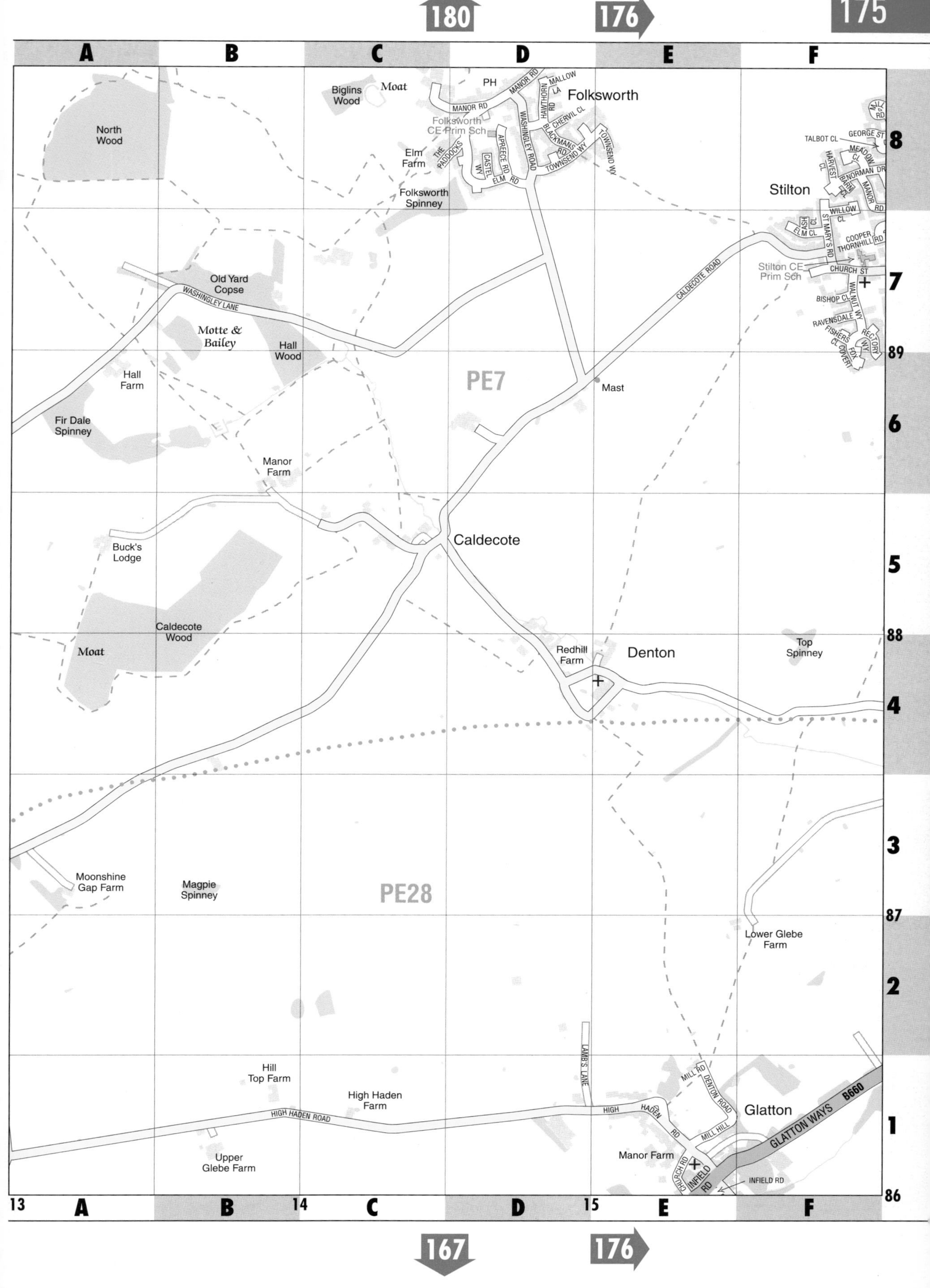

A B C D E F

North Wood

Biglins Wood
Moat
PH
MANOR RD
HIGHLOW
MALLOW
Folksworth
Folksworth CE Prim Sch
MANOR RD
CHERVIL CL
WASHINGLEY ROAD
BLACKMANS RD
TOWNSEND WY
Elm Farm
THE PADDOCKS
APRECE RD
CASTLE WY
ELM RD
TOWNSEND WY

Stilton
TALBOT CL
GEORGE ST
MEADOW CL
HARVEST CL
NORMAN DR
MANOR RD
WILLOW CL
ELM CL
ASH CL
ST MARY'S RD
COOPER
THORNHILL RD
Stilton CE Prim Sch
CHURCH ST
BISHOP CL
WALNUT WY
RAVENSDALE
FISHERS CL
FOX COVERT
RECTORY WY

Folksworth Spinney

8

Old Yard Copse
WASHINGLEY LANE
Motte & Bailey
Hall Wood

7

89

Hall Farm

PE7

Mast

6

Fir Dale Spinney

Manor Farm

Buck's Lodge

Caldecote

5

Caldecote Wood

88

Moat

Redhill Farm
Denton
Top Spinney

4

PE28

3

Moonshine Gap Farm
Magpie Spinney

Lower Glebe Farm

87

2

Hill Top Farm
High Haden Farm
LAMB'S LANE
MILL RD
DENTON ROAD
Glatton
GLATTON WAYS
B660
HIGH HADEN ROAD
HIGH HADEN RD
MILL HILL

1

Upper Glebe Farm
Manor Farm
CHURCH RD
INFIELD RD
INFIELD RD

86

13 A B 14 C D 15 E F

175
181

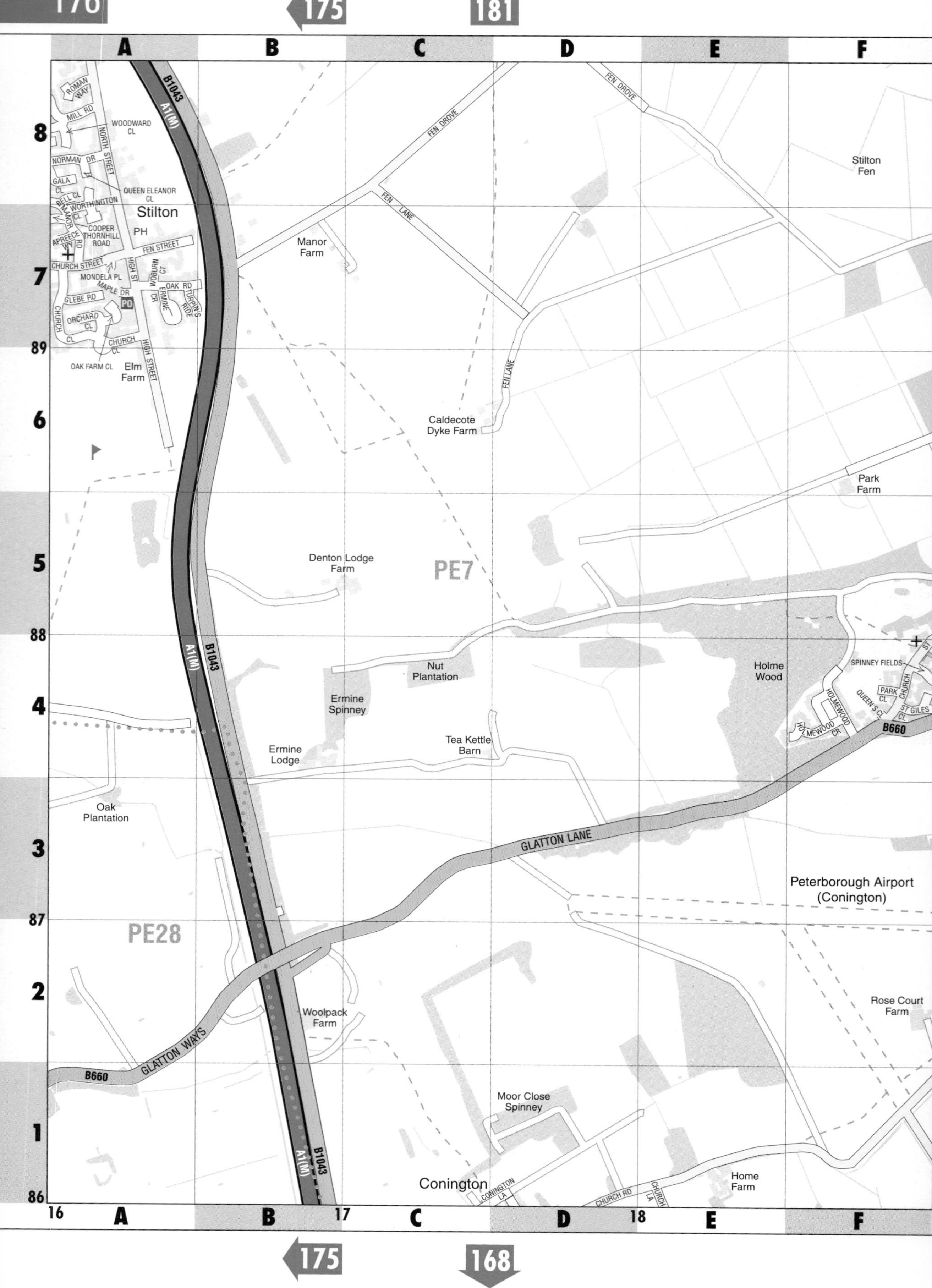
A
B
C
D
E
F
8
7
89
6
5
88
4
3
87
2
1
86
16
17
18
ROMAN WAY
MILL RD
WOODWARD CL
NORTH STREET
NORMAN DR
GALA CL
QUEEN ELEANOR CL
BELL CL
WORTHINGTON CL
MANOR RD
Stilton
COOPER THORNHILL ROAD
PH
APREECE WY
FEN STREET
CHURCH STREET
HIGH ST
MONDELA PL
MAPLE DR
OAK RD
ERMINE CR
TURPIN'S RIDE
GLEBE RD
PO
ORCHARD CL
CHURCH CL
CHURCH CL
HIGH STREET
OAK FARM CL
Elm Farm
B1043
A1(M)
FEN DROVE
FEN DROVE
FEN LANE
FEN LANE
Manor Farm
Stilton Fen
Caldecote Dyke Farm
Park Farm
Denton Lodge Farm
PE7
Nut Plantation
Ermine Spinney
Holme Wood
SPINNEY FIELDS
PARK CL
CHURCH
QUEEN'S CL
HOLMEWOOD
HOLMEWOOD CR
ST GILES CL
B660
Ermine Lodge
Tea Kettle Barn
Oak Plantation
GLATTON LANE
Peterborough Airport (Conington)
PE28
Woolpack Farm
Rose Court Farm
GLATTON WAYS
B660
Moor Close Spinney
Conington
CONINGTON LA
CHURCH RD
CHURCH LA
Home Farm

175
168

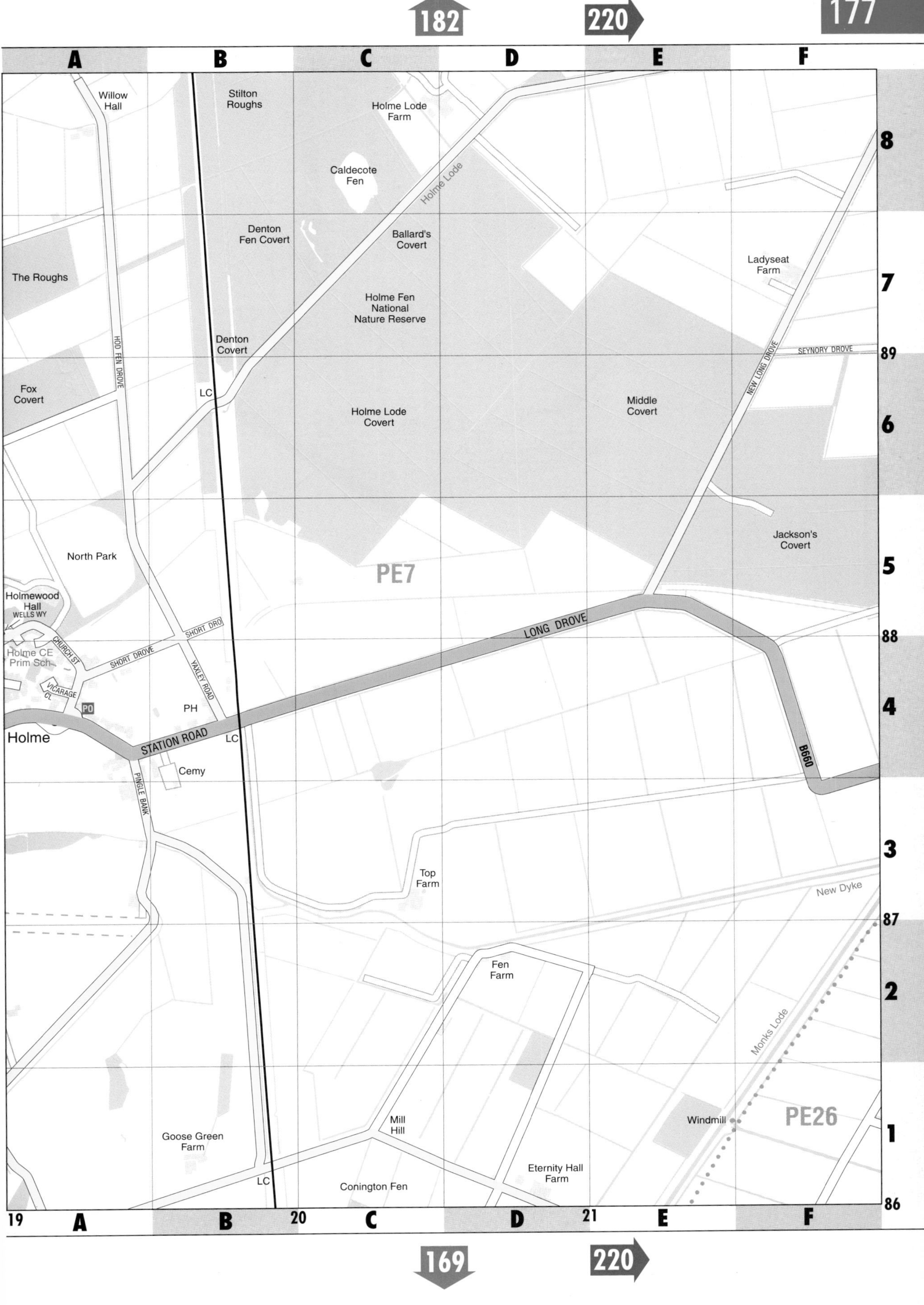

A **B** **C** **D** **E** **F**

8

Willow
Hall

Stilton
Roughs

Holme Lode
Farm

Caldecote
Fen

Holme Lode

Denton
Fen Covert

Ballard's
Covert

Ladyseat
Farm

The Roughs

7

Holme Fen
National
Nature Reserve

Denton
Covert

NEW LONG DROVE

SEYNORY DROVE

89

Fox
Covert

LC

Holme Lode
Covert

Middle
Covert

6

Jackson's
Covert

North Park

PE7

5

Holmewood
Hall
WELLS WY

SHORT DRO

LONG DROVE

88

Holme CE
Prim Sch

CHURCH ST

SHORT DRIVE

VALLEY ROAD

4

VICARAGE
CL

PO

PH

Holme

STATION ROAD

LC

B660

PINGLE BANK

Cemy

New Dyke

3

87

Top
Farm

Fen
Farm

2

Monks Lode

Goose Green
Farm

Mill
Hill

Windmill

PE26

1

LC

Eternity Hall
Farm

86

Conington Fen

183

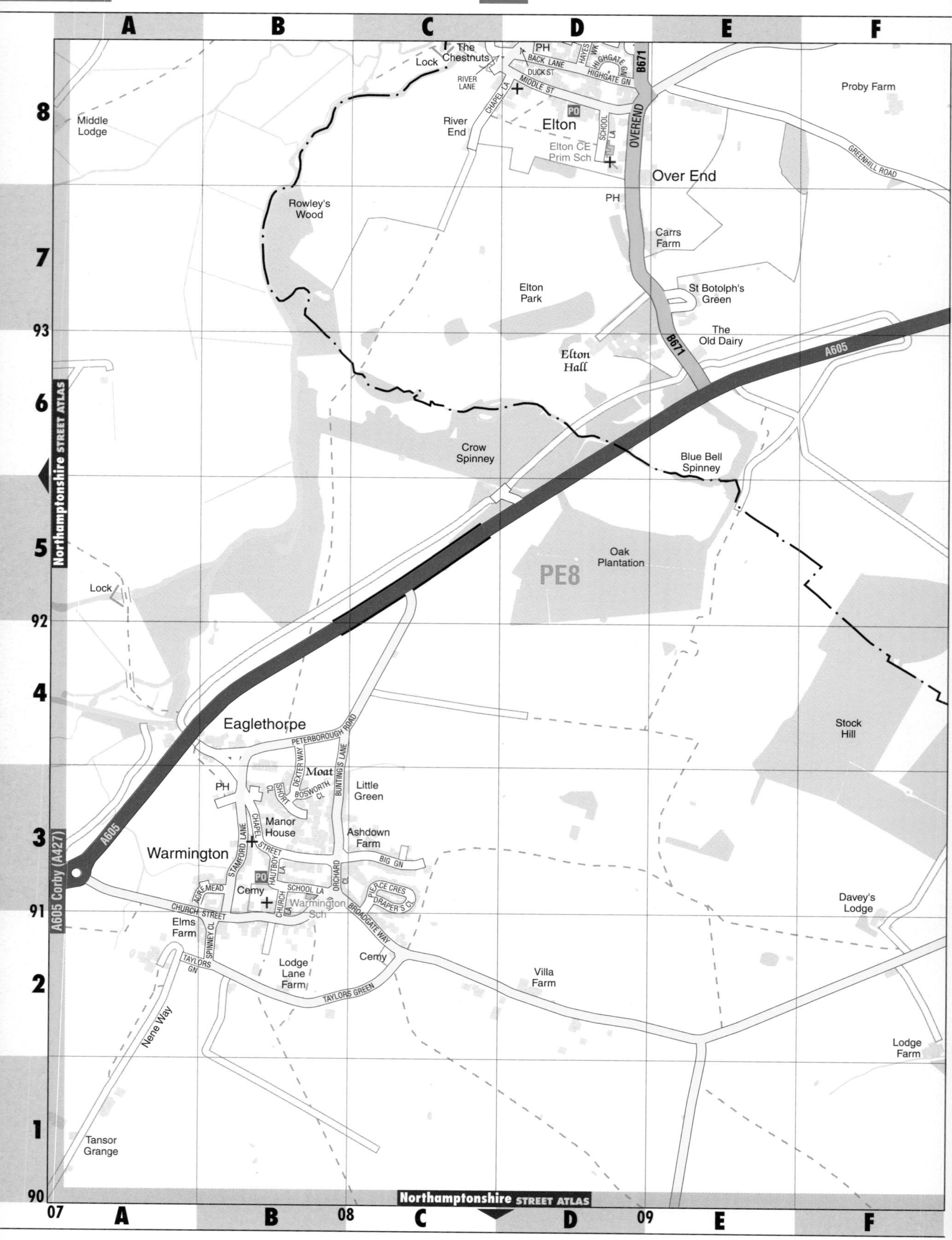

A
B
C
D
E
F
The Chestnuts
Lock
PH
BACK LANE
HAYES WK
HIGHGATE GN
DUCK ST
HIGHGATE GN
B671
RIVER LANE
MIDDLE ST
Proby Farm
8
Middle Lodge
CHAPEL LA
River End
PO
Elton
SCHOOL LA
OVEREND
Elton CE Prim Sch
GREENHILL ROAD
Over End
PH
Rowley's Wood
Carrs Farm
7
Elton Park
St Botolph's Green
93
The Old Dairy
B671
Elton Hall
A605
6
Northamptonshire STREET ATLAS
Crow Spinney
Blue Bell Spinney
5
Oak Plantation
PE8
Lock
92
4
Eaglethorpe
PETERBOROUGH ROAD
DEXTER WAY
Moat
BUNTINGS LANE
Little Green
PH
SHORT CL
BOSWORTH CL
Manor House
CHAPEL STREET
Ashdown Farm
STAMFORD LANE
Stock Hill
3
A605
Warmington
HAUTBOY LA
BIG GN
PO
ORCHARD CL
ACRE MEAD
Cemy
SCHOOL LA
PIERCE CRES
DRAPER'S CL
A605 Corby (A427)
CHURCH LA
Warmington Sch
Davey's Lodge
91
CHURCH STREET
BROADGATE WAY
Elms Farm
SPINNEY CL
Cemy
TAYLORS GN
Lodge Lane Farm
Villa Farm
2
TAYLORS GREEN
Nene Way
Lodge Farm
1
Tansor Grange
90
07
A
B
08
C
D
09
E
F

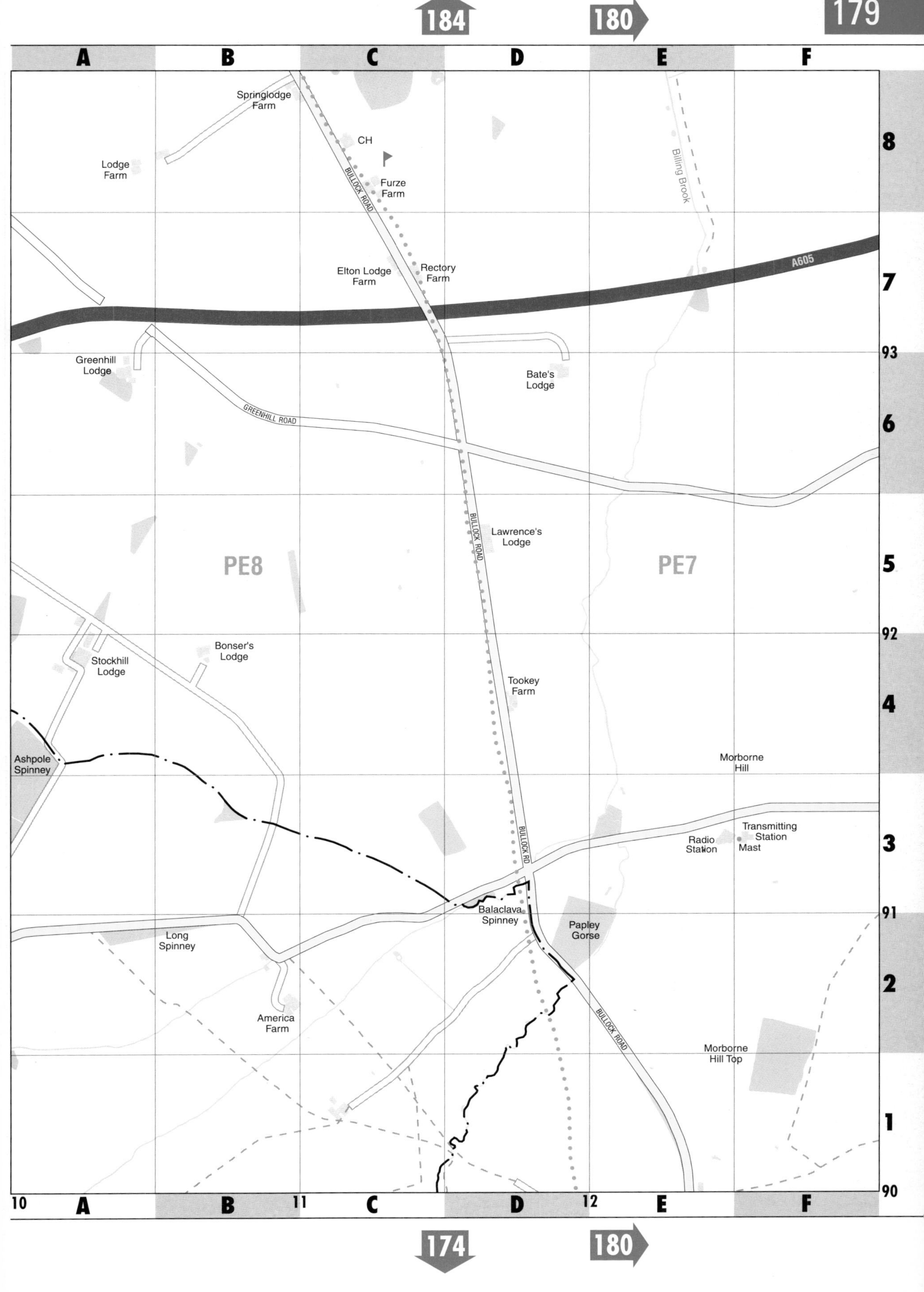

Springlodge Farm

CH

Lodge Farm

BULLOCK ROAD

Furze Farm

Elton Lodge Farm

Rectory Farm

A605

Billing Brook

Greenhill Lodge

GREENHILL ROAD

Bate's Lodge

PE8

Lawrence's Lodge

PE7

Bonser's Lodge

BULLOCK ROAD

Stockhill Lodge

Tookey Farm

Morborne Hill

Ashpole Spinney

Radio Station

Transmitting Station Mast

Long Spinney

BULLOCK RD

Balaclava Spinney

Papley Gorse

America Farm

BULLOCK ROAD

Morborne Hill Top

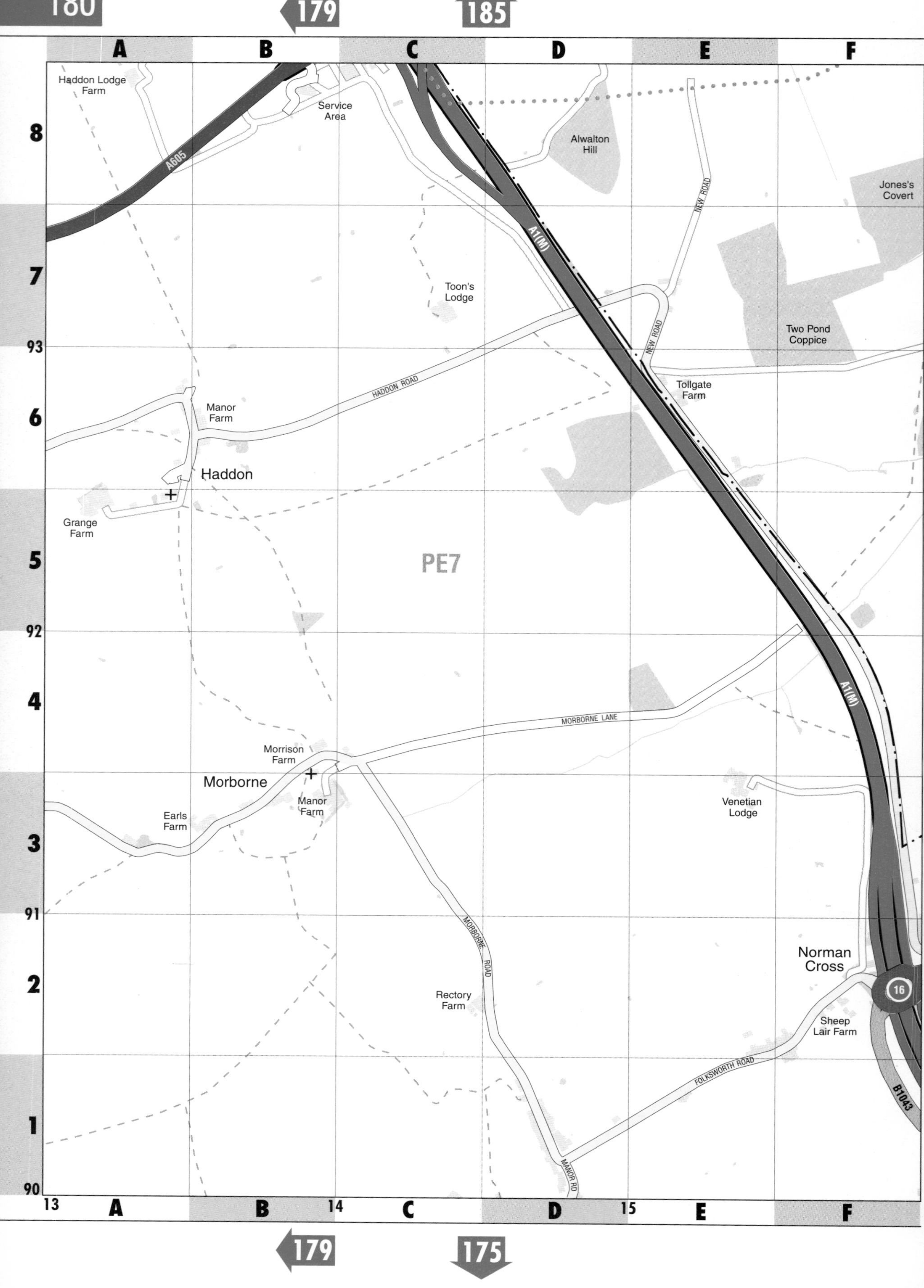

179
185

A   B   C   D   E   F

8

7

93

6

5

92

4

91

2

1

90

13   A   B   14   C   D   15   E   F

Haddon Lodge
Farm

Service
Area

Alwalton
Hill

Jones's
Covert

A605

A1(M)

NEW ROAD

Two Pond
Coppice

Toon's
Lodge

HADDON ROAD

Tollgate
Farm

Manor
Farm

Haddon

Grange
Farm

PE7

MORBORNE LANE

A1(M)

Morrison
Farm

Morborne

Manor
Farm

Earls
Farm

Venetian
Lodge

MORBORNE ROAD

Norman
Cross

16

Rectory
Farm

Sheep
Lair Farm

FOLKSWORTH ROAD

MANOR RD

B1043

179
175

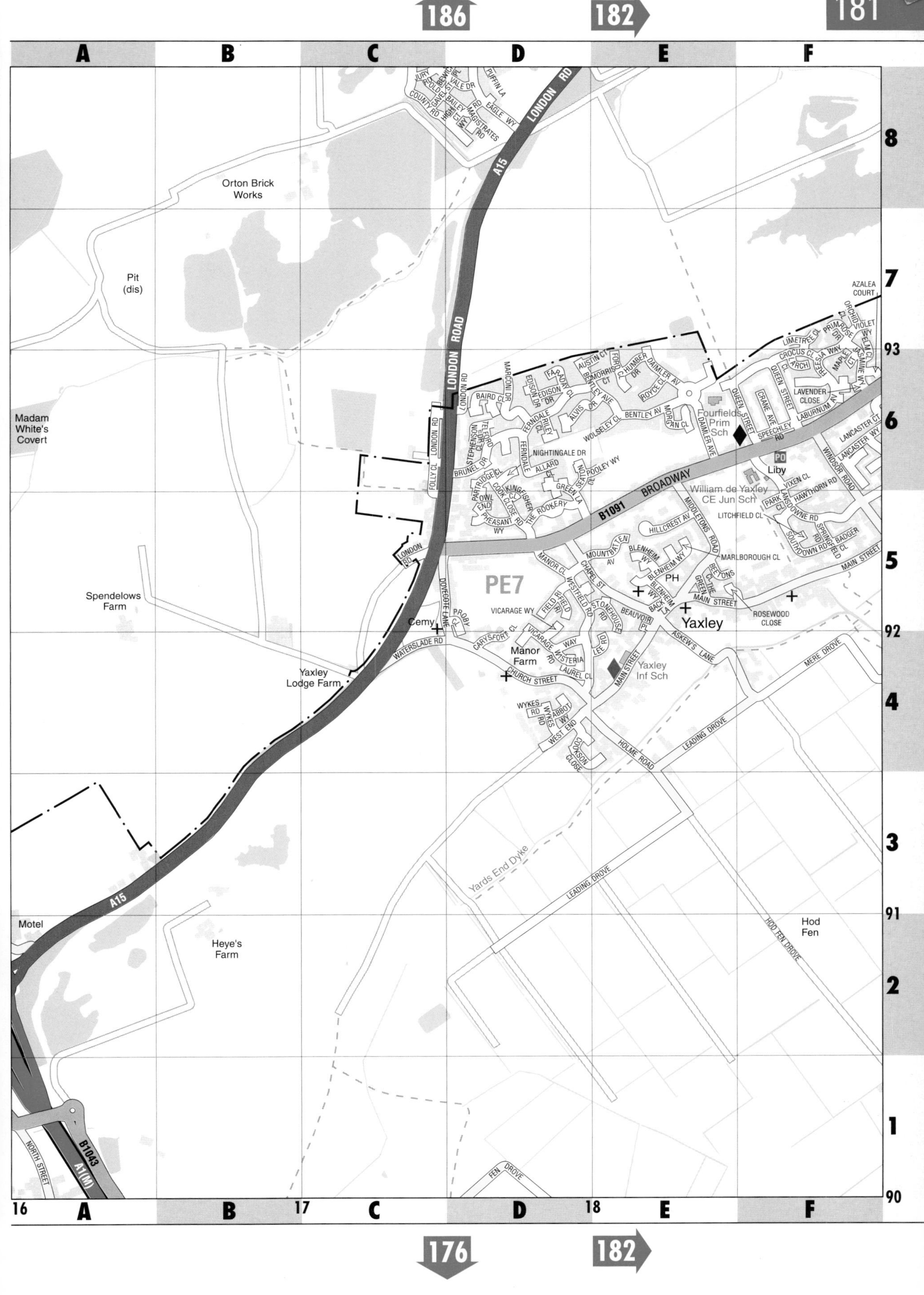
186
182
A
B
C
D
E
F
8
7
6
5
4
3
2
1
93
92
91
90
16
17
18
Orton Brick Works
Pit (dis)
Madam White's Covert
Spendelows Farm
Yaxley Lodge Farm
Motel
Heye's Farm
LONDON ROAD
A15
PE7
Yaxley
Cemy
Manor Farm
PH
Liby
PO
Fourfields Prim Sch
William de Yaxley CE Jun Sch
Yaxley Inf Sch
B1091 BROADWAY
HOLME ROAD
LEADING DROVE
MERE DROVE
HOD FEN DROVE
FEN DROVE
Yards End Dyke
Hod Fen
B1043
A1(M)
NORTH STREET
ROSEWOOD CLOSE
LAVENDER CLOSE
AZALEA COURT
MAIN STREET
CHURCH STREET
WATERSLADE RD
ASKEW'S LANE
176
182

181
187
220

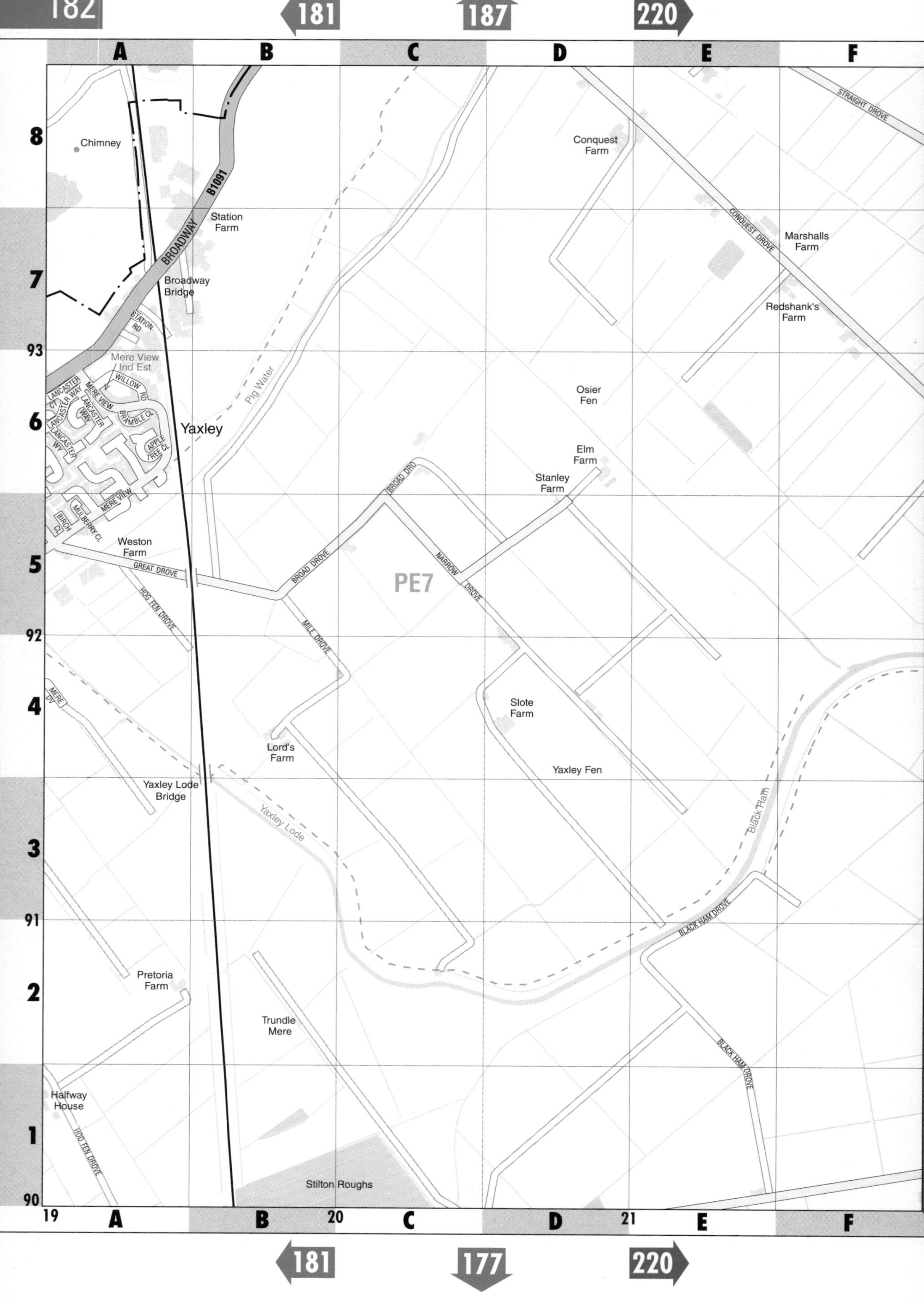
Chimney
B1091
BROADWAY
Station Farm
Broadway Bridge
STATION RD
Mere View Ind Est
WILLOW RD
LANCASTER CT
LANCASTER WAY
MERE VIEW
LANCASTER WAY
BRAMBLE CL
APPLE TREE CL
LANCASTER WY
Yaxley
Pig Water
MERE VIEW
MULBERRY CL
BIRCH CL
Weston Farm
GREAT DROVE
HOG FEN DROVE
BROAD DROVE
BROAD DRO
NARROW DROVE
MILE DROVE
PE7
Conquest Farm
STRAIGHT DROVE
CONQUEST DROVE
Marshalls Farm
Redshank's Farm
Osier Fen
Elm Farm
Stanley Farm
Slote Farm
Yaxley Fen
Lord's Farm
MERE DV
Yaxley Lode Bridge
Yaxley Lode
Black Ham
BLACK HAM DROVE
Pretoria Farm
Trundle Mere
BLACK HAM DROVE
Halfway House
HOG FEN DROVE
Stilton Roughs

181
177
220

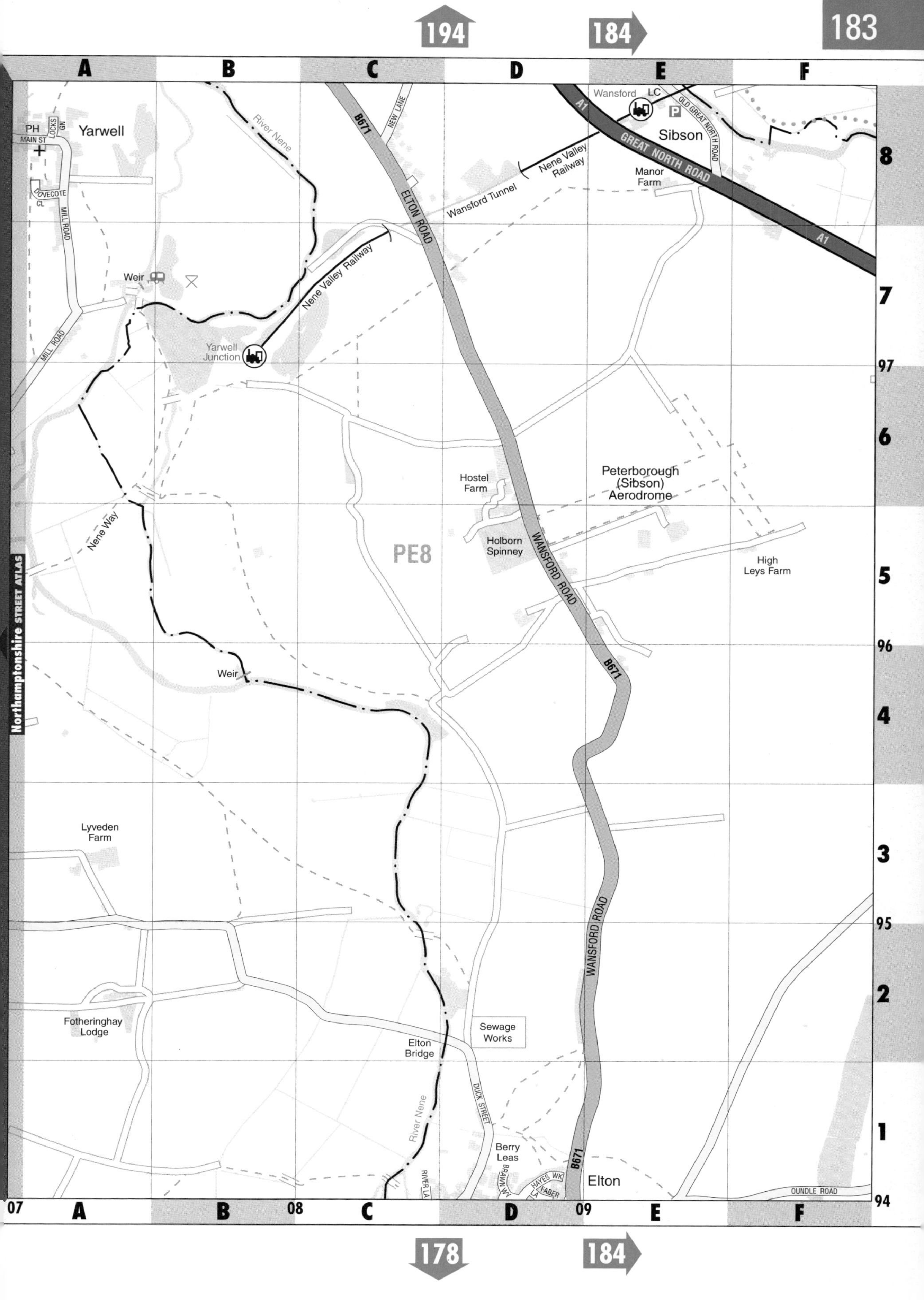

A   B   C   D   E   F

8

Yarwell
PH
MAIN ST
LOCKS GN
River Nene
B671
NEW LANE
ELTON ROAD
Wansford   LC
P
OLD GREAT NORTH ROAD
Sibson
GREAT NORTH ROAD
Manor
Farm
A1

DOVECOTE
CL
MILL ROAD

Nene Valley
Railway

Wansford Tunnel

7

Weir

Nene Valley Railway

MILL ROAD

97

Yarwell
Junction

6

Nene Way

Hostel
Farm

Peterborough
(Sibson)
Aerodrome

PE8

Holborn
Spinney

WANSFORD ROAD

High
Leys Farm

5

96

Weir

B671

4

Northamptonshire STREET ATLAS

Lyveden
Farm

3

95

Fotheringhay
Lodge

2

Elton
Bridge

Sewage
Works

WANSFORD ROAD

River Nene

DUCK STREET

1

Berry
Leas

River Nene

HAYES WK
BRAMW...
FABER

B671

Elton

OUNDLE ROAD

94

183
195

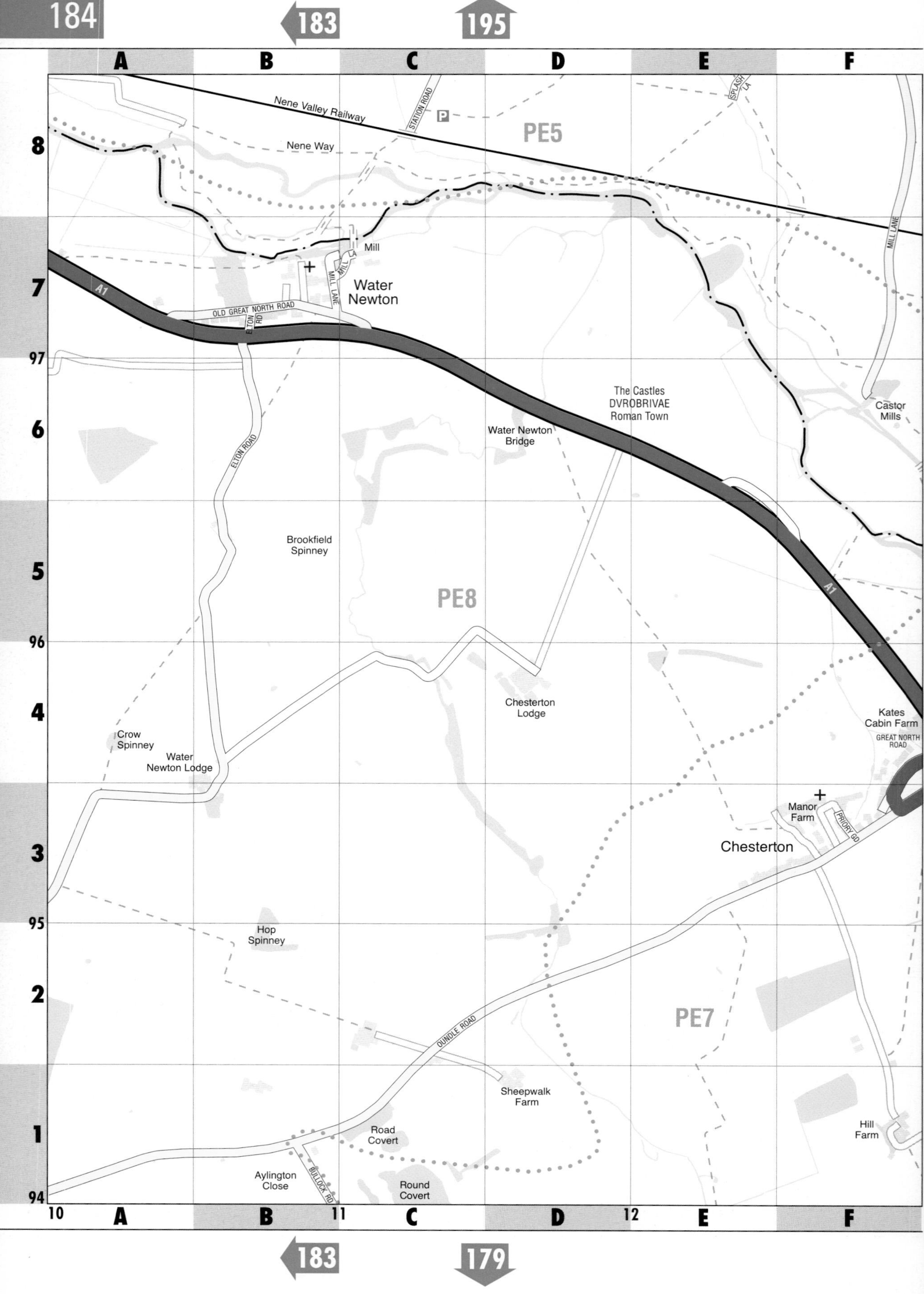
A
B
C
D
E
F
8
7
97
6
5
96
4
3
95
2
1
94
10
11
12
Nene Valley Railway
STATION ROAD
SPLASH LA
PE5
Nene Way
Mill
MILL LA
MILL LANE
Water Newton
A1
OLD GREAT NORTH ROAD
ELTON RD
ELTON ROAD
MILL LANE
The Castles
DVROBRIVAE
Roman Town
Castor Mills
Water Newton Bridge
Brookfield Spinney
PE8
Chesterton Lodge
Kates Cabin Farm
GREAT NORTH ROAD
Crow Spinney
Water Newton Lodge
Manor Farm
PRIORY GD
Chesterton
Hop Spinney
PE7
OUNDLE ROAD
Sheepwalk Farm
Road Covert
Hill Farm
Aylington Close
BULLOCK RD
Round Covert

183
179

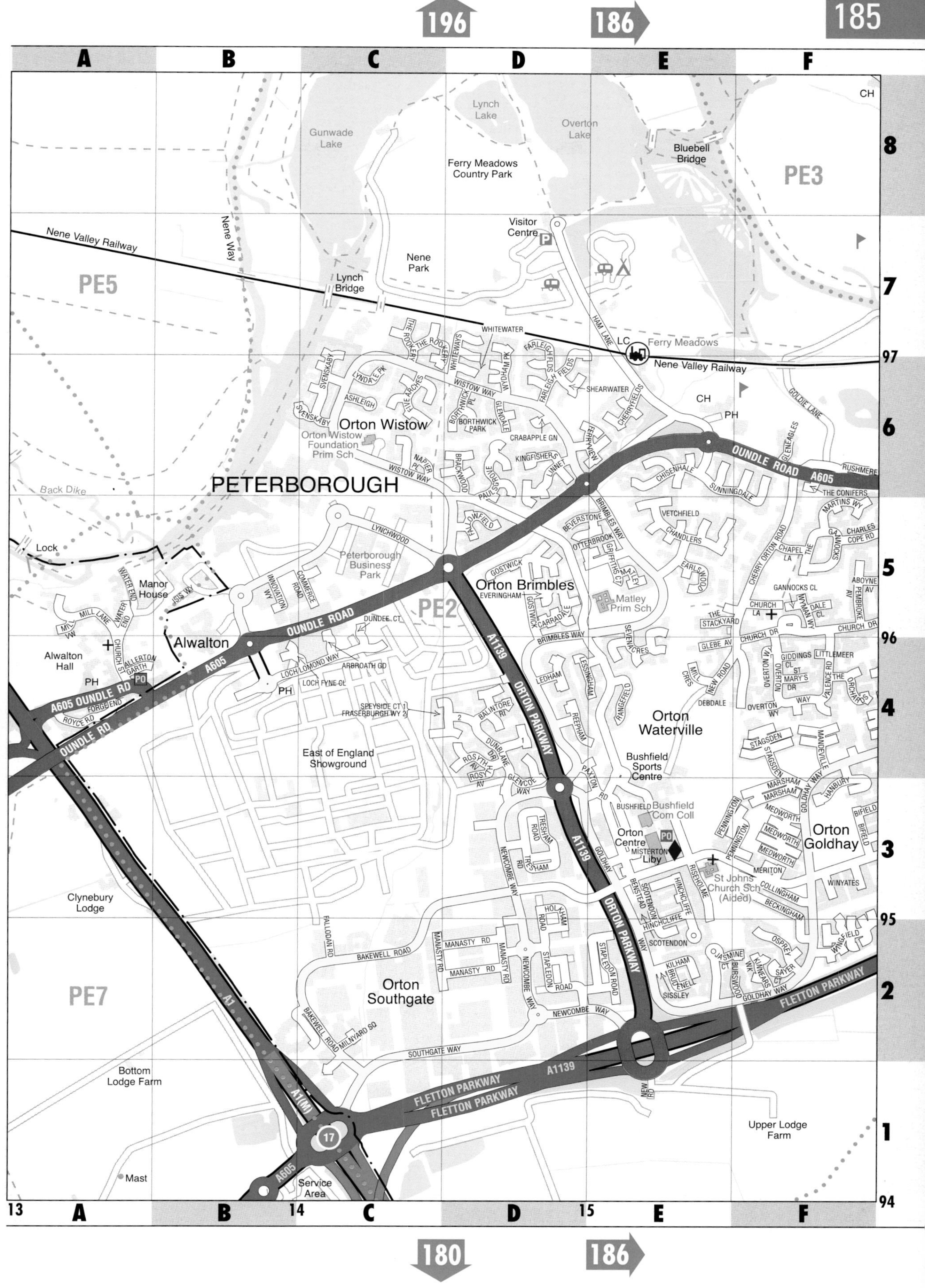

A   B   C   D   E   F

CH

Lynch
Lake

Gunwade
Lake

Overton
Lake

Bluebell
Bridge

8

Ferry Meadows
Country Park

PE3

Nene Valley Railway

Visitor
Centre
P

Nene Way

PE5

Nene
Park

7

Lynch
Bridge

🚉 🏕

WHITEWATER

LC

Ferry Meadows

97

Nene Valley Railway

THE ROOKERY
THE ROOK

WHITEWAYS

FARLEIGH FIELDS

SHEARWATER

CH

PH

GOLDIE LANE

6

SVENSKABY

LYNDA CR
ASHLEIGH

FIVE ARCHES

BORTHWICK PL

MK WHOLM

FARLEIGH FIELDS

GLENDALE

CHERRYFIELDS

BIRCH VIEW

OUNDLE ROAD   A605

RUSHMERE

MARTINS WY

GLENEAGLES

THE CONIFERS

Orton Wistow

BORTHWICK
PARK

CRABAPPLE GN

GA
GANNOCKS

CHARLES
COPE RD

Orton Wistow
Foundation
Prim Sch

NAPIER
CL

KINGFISHER PL

CHISENHALE

SUNNINGDALE

VETCHFIELD

THE
STACKYARD

GANNOCKS CL

ABOYNE
AV

PEMBROKE
AV

PETERBOROUGH

BRACKNWOOD

WISTOW WAY

PAIGNELS
JESSOP

LINNET

CHANDLERS

EARLSMOOR

CHURCH
LA

WYMAN
CL

DALE
CL

CHURCH DR

LOWFIELD

BEVERSTONE

BRIMBLES WAY

GRIFFITHS CL

MATLEY CL

SEVENACRES

GLEBE AV

GIDDINGS
CL   LITTLEMEER

CHURCH DR

OVERTON WY

Lock

LYNCHWOOD

Peterborough
Business
Park

GOSTWICK

Orton Brimbles

EVERINGHAM

GOSTWICK

OTTERBROOK

CARRADALE

Matley
Prim Sch

MILES
CRES

NEW ROAD

ST MARY'S
DR

DEBDALE

VALENCE
WAY

THE
ORCHARD

5

Manor
House

INNOVATION
WY

COMMERCE
ROAD

PE2

CARRADALE

BRIMBLES WAY

LEDHAM

LESSINGHAM

REEPHAM

PANGEFIELD

OVERTON
WY

96

Alwalton Hall

CHURCH
GARTH

Alwalton

OUNDLE ROAD

A605

Dundee CT

LOCH LOMOND WAY

ARBROATH GD

BALINTORE
RD

PAXTON
RD

Orton
Waterville

STAGSDEN

STAGSDEN

MARSHAM

MANVILLE WAY

HAMBURY

4

PH

MILL LANE

WATER END

ROYCE RD
FORGE END
A605 OUNDLE RD

PH

PO

LOCH FYNE DL

SPEYSIDE CT
FRASERBURGH WY 2

ROSYTH
DRIV
ROSYTH AV

DUNBAR
LANE

GLENCOE
WAY

Bushfield
Sports
Centre

MARSHAM

MEDWORTH

BIFIELD

OUNDLE RD

East of England
Showground

2

BUSHFIELD
COM COLL

Bushfield
Com Coll

PENNINGTON

PENNINGTON

MEDWORTH

MEDWORTH

Orton
Goldhay

BIFIELD

3

Clynebury
Lodge

TRESHAM
ROAD

NEWCOMBE WAY

TRESHAM

Orton
Centre
Liby

MISTERTON RD

PO

RISEHOLME

ST JOHNS
CHURCH SCH
(Aided)

MERITON

COLLINGHAM

BECKINGHAM

WINYATES

95

HINCHCLIFFE

A1139

ORTON PARKWAY

HOLLYHAM
ROAD

BENSTEAD

SCOTENDON
WAY

HINCHCLIFFE

SCOTENDON

WINGFIELD

OSPREY

PE7

BAKEWELL
ROAD

MILNYARD SQ

FALLODAN RD

BAKEWELL ROAD

MANASTY RD

MANASTY RD

MANASTY RD

STAPLE DON ROAD

STAPLE DON ROAD

KILHAM
BRUNELL
SISSLEY

JASMINE
WK

BURSWOOD

KINNEARS
SATER

GOLDHAY WAY

FLETTON PARKWAY

2

Orton
Southgate

NEWCOMBE
WAY

NEWCOMBE WAY

NEW
RD

Bottom
Lodge Farm

A1

A1(M)

SOUTHGATE WAY

A1139

FLETTON PARKWAY

Upper Lodge
Farm

1

17

FLETTON PARKWAY

FLETTON PARKWAY

Mast

A605

Service
Area

94

13   A   14   B   C   15   D   E   F

185
197

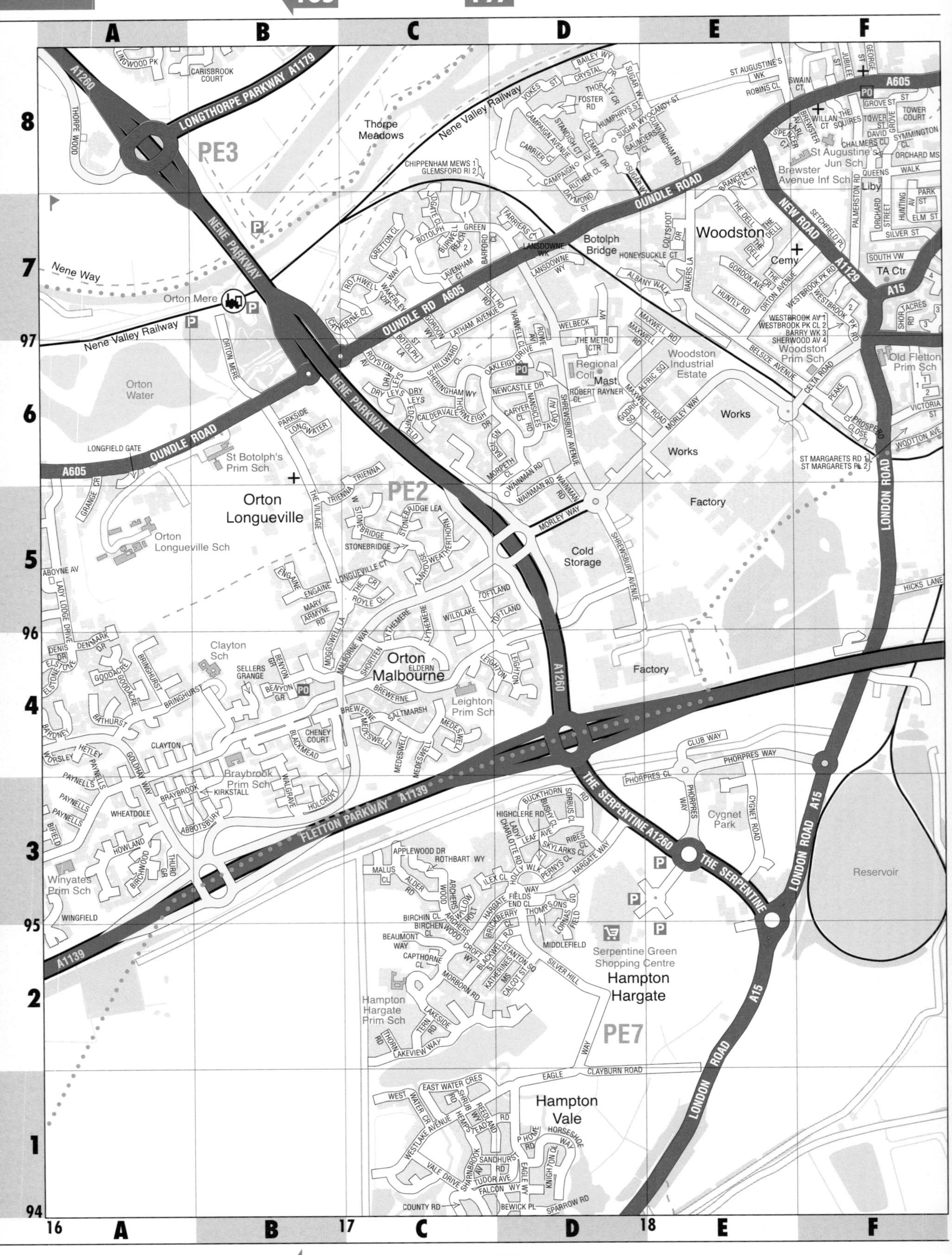
A
B
C
D
E
F
8
7
97
6
5
96
4
3
95
2
1
94
16
17
18
PE3
PE2
PE7
Thorpe Meadows
Nene Valley Railway
Nene Way
Orton Mere
Orton Water
LONGTHORPE PARKWAY A1179
A1260
NENE PARKWAY
OUNDLE ROAD
OUNDLE RD A605
A605
Botolph Bridge
Woodston
Cemy
TA Ctr
A15
A1129
NEW ROAD
LONDON ROAD
St Augustine's Jun Sch
Brewster Avenue Inf Sch
Liby
Old Fletton Prim Sch
Woodston Prim Sch
Woodston Industrial Estate
Regional Coll
Mast
THE METRO CTR
Works
Factory
Cold Storage
St Botolph's Prim Sch
Orton Longueville
Orton Longueville Sch
Clayton Sch
Orton Malbourne
Leighton Prim Sch
Braybrook Prim Sch
Winyates Prim Sch
FLETTON PARKWAY A1139
A1139
THE SERPENTINE A1260
THE SERPENTINE
Cygnet Park
Reservoir
Serpentine Green Shopping Centre
Hampton Hargate
Hampton Hargate Prim Sch
Hampton Vale
MORLEY WAY
SHREWSBURY AVENUE
LONGFIELD GATE
THE VILLAGE
CLUB WAY
PHORPRES WAY
HICKS LANE
WOOTTON AVE
CLAYBURN ROAD

A B C D E F
16 17 18

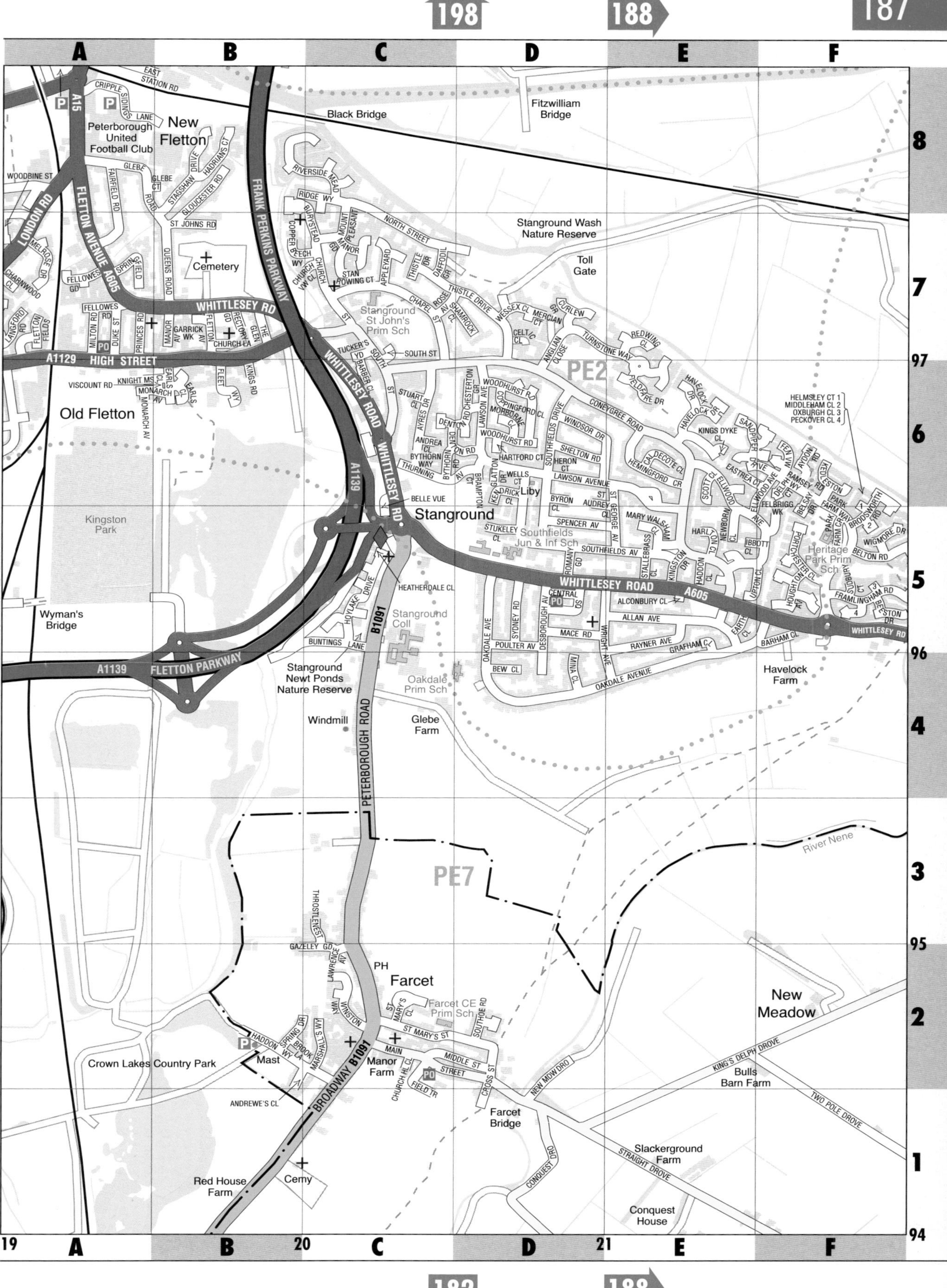

198
188

A   B   C   D   E   F

8

7

97

6

5

96

4

3

95

2

1

94

East Station Rd
P
A15
P
CRIPPLE SIDINGS LANE
Peterborough United Football Club
New Fletton
Black Bridge
Fitzwilliam Bridge

WOODBINE ST
GLEBE
HADRIANS DRIVE
RIVERSIDE MEAD
FRANK PERKINS PARKWAY

FAIRFIELD RD
STASHAW DRIVE
GLEBE CT
SLOUGESTER RD
RIDGE WY
COPPER BEECH
NORTH STREET
Stanground Wash Nature Reserve

FLETTON AVENUE A605
QUEENS ROAD
St JOHNS RD
MOUNT PLEASANT
APPLEYARD
Toll Gate

LONDON RD
Cemetery
ST OWING CT
THISTLE DR
DAPPOOL
MERCIAN
CELT CL
PE2

MELROSE RD
SPRINGFIELD
CHURCH
CHURCH VW CL
STAN
Stanground St John's Prim Sch
THISTLE DRIVE
WESSEX CL
ANGLIAN CLOSE
CURLEW
REDWING
HELMSLEY CT 1
MIDDLEHAM CL 2
OXBURGH CL 3
PECKOVER CL 4

CHARNWOOD
FELLOWES GD
WHITTLESEY RD
CHAPEL ROAD
SHAMROCK AV
TURNSTONE WAY
CLOXTRE DR

LANGFORD
FELLOWES RD
RECTORY RD
SOUTH ST
WOODHURST RD
CONEYGREE ROAD
HAVELOCK CL

FLETTON FIELDS
MILTON RD
PRINCES RD
THE GLEN
STUART AV
PINGFORD CL
WINDSOR DR
HAVELOCK DR
KINGS DYKE

A1129 HIGH STREET
PO
DUKE ST
GARRICK WK
AYRES DR
DENTON RD
MORBOROUGH
SHELTON RD
HEMINGFORD CR
SANDOPER

VISCOUNT RD
KNIGHT MS
MONARCH
CHURCH RD
ANDREA CE
BYTHORN WAY
WELLS
DRICK CL
HARTFORD CT
HERON CL
DECOTE CL
EASTREA DR

EARLS
MONARCH AV
KINGS RD
FLEET WY
THURNING
BYRON CL
Liby
SPENCER AV
LAWSON AVENUE
SCOTT CL
ELLWOOD
RAMSEY CL

Old Fletton
EARLS WY
BELLE VUE
Stanground
STUKELEY CL
Southfields Jun & Inf Sch
MARY WALSHAM
HARL
NEWBORN
IBBOTT CL
FELBRIGG WK
WIGMORE DR

Kingston Park
A1139
WHITTLESEY ROAD
HEATHERDALE CL
SOUTHFIELDS AV
CENTRAL PO
STALLEBRASS
HADDON
Heritage Park Prim Sch
BELTON RD

Wyman's Bridge
HOYLAKE DRIVE
B1091
Stanground Coll
SYDNEY RD
WRIGHT AVE
ALLAN AVE
ALCONBURY CL
FRAMLINGHAM RD
RESTON DR

A1139 FLETTON PARKWAY
BUNTINGS LANE
OAKDALE AVE
DESBOROUGH
MACE RD
RAYNER AVE
GRAFHAM CL
BARHAM CL
WHITTLESEY RD

Stanground Newt Ponds Nature Reserve
Oakdale Prim Sch
POULTER AV
BEW CL
OAKDALE AVENUE
Havelock Farm

Windmill
Glebe Farm
PETERBOROUGH ROAD

River Nene

PE7

THROSTLE NEST
GAZELEY GD
PH
Farcet
Farcet CE Prim Sch
New Meadow

LAWRENCE AV
St MARY'S CL
SOUTHGE RD
KING'S DELPH DROVE
Bulls Barn Farm

Crown Lakes Country Park
P
HADDON RD
SPRING BROOK
WINSTON
MAIN
St MARY'S ST
MIDDLE STREET
NEW MOW DRO
TWO POLE DROVE

Mast
BROADWAY B1091
MARSHALL
Manor Farm
CHURCH CL
FIELD TR
CROSS ST
Slackerground Farm
STRAIGHT DROVE

ANDREWE'S CL
PO
Farcet Bridge
CONQUEST RD

Red House Farm
Cerny
Conquest House

19   A   B   20   C   D   21   E   F

182
188

187
199

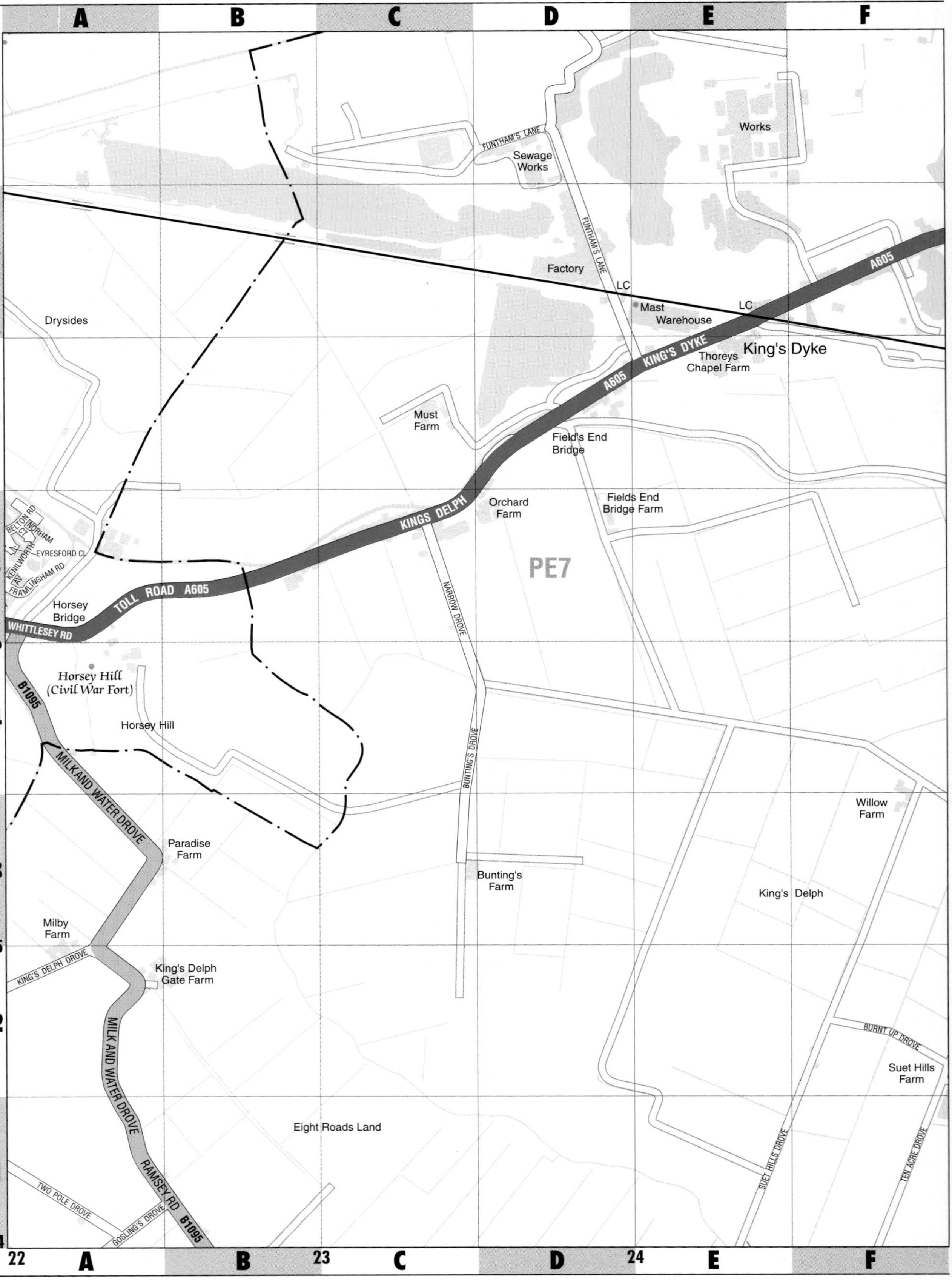

A | **B** | **C** | **D** | **E** | **F**

8

FUNTHAM'S LANE

Sewage
Works

Works

7

Factory

LC

A605

KING'S DYKE

Mast
Warehouse

LC

King's Dyke

97

Drysides

Thoreys
Chapel Farm

A605

6

Must
Farm

Field's End
Bridge

KINGS DELPH

Orchard
Farm

Fields End
Bridge Farm

PE7

5

BELTON RD
NORHAM
KENILWORTH
EYRESFORD CL
FRAMLINGHAM RD

TOLL ROAD A605

Horsey
Bridge

NARROW DROVE

WHITTLESEY RD

96

B1095

Horsey Hill
(Civil War Fort)

4

MILK AND WATER DROVE

Horsey Hill

Willow
Farm

BUNTING'S DROVE

Paradise
Farm

3

Bunting's
Farm

King's Delph

Milby
Farm

95

KING'S DELPH DROVE

King's Delph
Gate Farm

2

MILK AND WATER DROVE

BURNT UP DROVE

SUET HILLS DRIVE

Suet Hills
Farm

Eight Roads Land

TEN ACRE DROVE

1

TWO POLE DROVE

RAMSEY RD B1095

GOSLING'S DROVE

94

22 | **A** | **B** | 23 | **C** | | **D** | 24 | **E** | | **F**

187
220

200
190

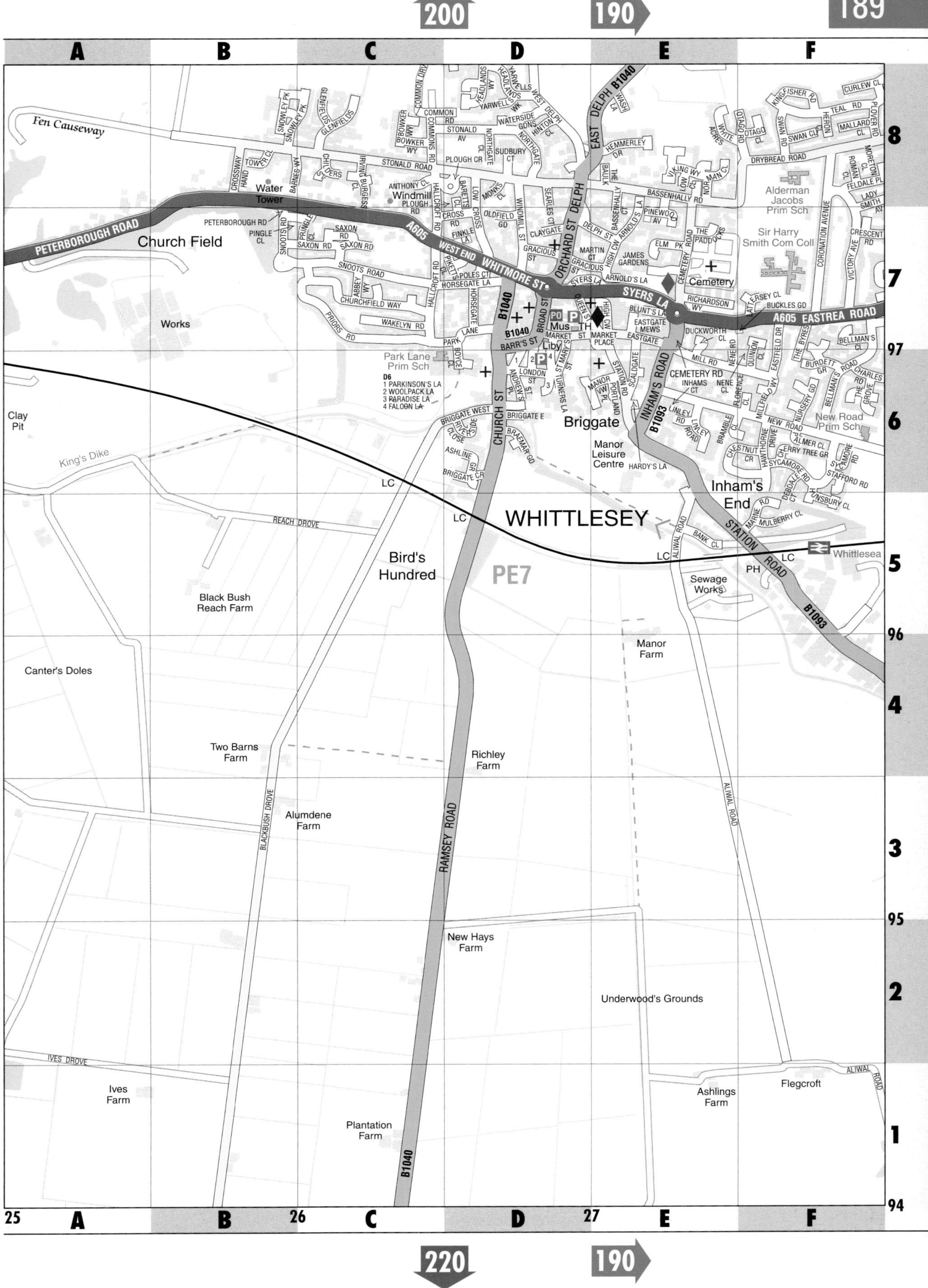
A
B
C
D
E
F
8
7
97
6
5
96
4
3
95
2
1
94
25
26
27
Fen Causeway
PETERBOROUGH ROAD
Church Field
Water Tower
Windmill
Works
Park Lane Prim Sch
D6
1 PARKINSON'S LA
2 WOOLPACK LA
3 PARADISE LA
4 FALCON LA
Clay Pit
King's Dike
LC
REACH DROVE
Bird's Hundred
PE7
WHITTLESEY
Briggate
Manor Leisure Centre
HARDY'S LA
Inham's End
Black Bush Reach Farm
Canter's Doles
Two Barns Farm
Richley Farm
Alumdene Farm
Manor Farm
Sewage Works
PH
Whittlesea
BLACKBUSH DROVE
RAMSEY ROAD
CHURCH ST
B1040
B1093
A605
WEST END
WHITMORE ST
SYERS LA
A605 EASTREA ROAD
EAST DELPH
ORCHARD ST
DELPH
INHAM'S ROAD
STATION ROAD
ALIWAL ROAD
Mus
TH
Liby
PO
MARKET PLACE
MARKET ST
BARR'S ST
BROAD ST
BRIGGATE WEST
BRIGGATE E
Cemetery
Alderman Jacobs Prim Sch
Sir Harry Smith Com Coll
New Road Prim Sch
STONALD ROAD
DRYBREAD ROAD
CORONATION AVENUE
BASSENHALLY RD
NEW ROAD
CEMETERY RD
New Hays Farm
Underwood's Grounds
IVES DROVE
Ives Farm
Plantation Farm
Ashlings Farm
Flegcroft

220
190

189
201

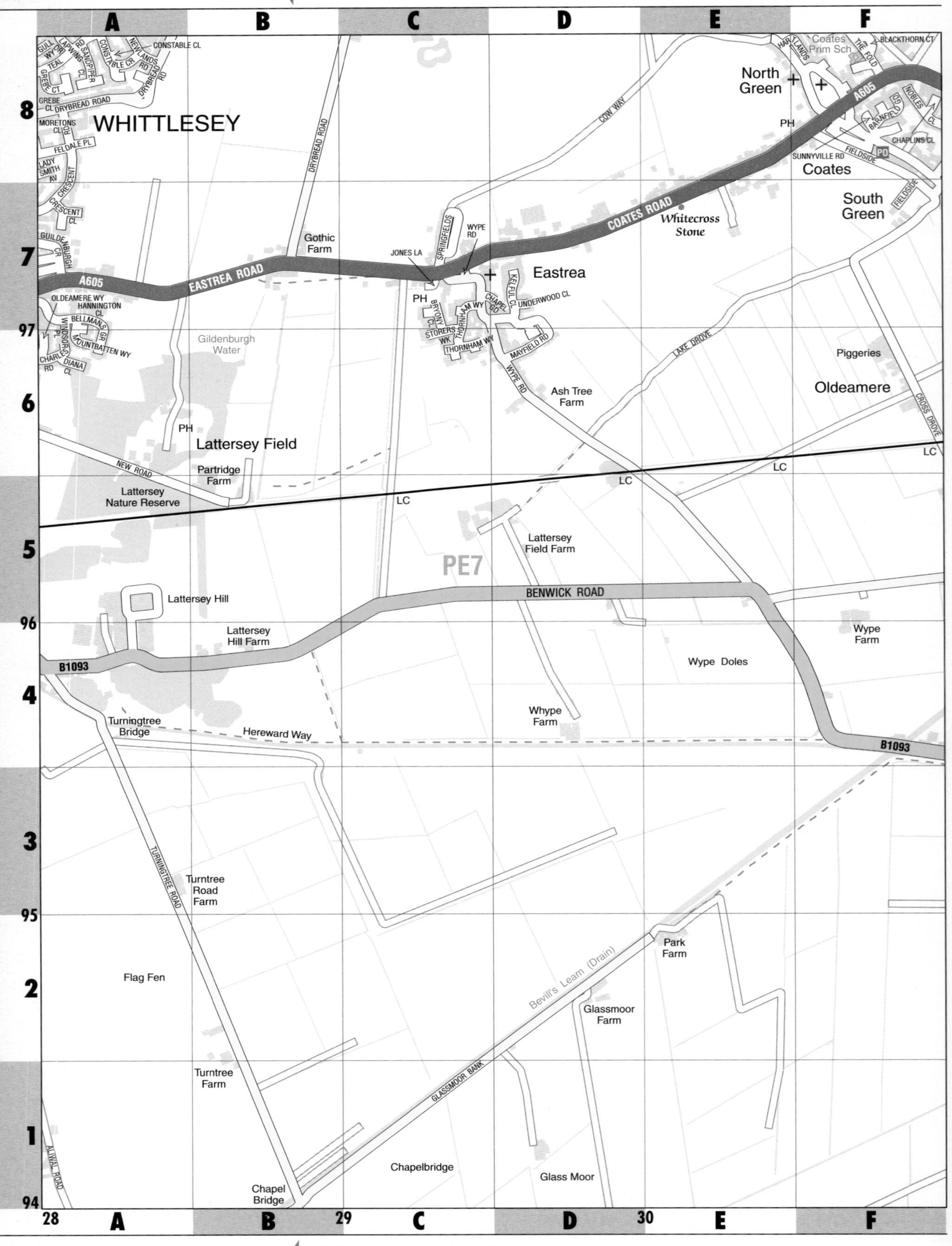
WHITTLESEY
Eastrea
North Green
Coates
South Green
Oldeamere
Coates Prim Sch
A605
EASTREA ROAD
COATES ROAD
DRYBREAD ROAD
Gothic Farm
Whitecross Stone
Piggeries
Ash Tree Farm
Gildenburgh Water
Lattersey Field
Partridge Farm
Lattersey Nature Reserve
NEW ROAD
Lattersey Field Farm
PE7
BENWICK ROAD
Lattersey Hill
Lattersey Hill Farm
B1093
Wype Farm
Wype Doles
Whype Farm
Turningtree Bridge
Hereward Way
TURNINGTREE ROAD
Turntree Road Farm
Flag Fen
Park Farm
Bevill's Leam (Drain)
Glassmoor Farm
Turntree Farm
GLASSMOOR BANK
Chapelbridge
Glass Moor
Chapel Bridge
ALIWAL ROAD
LAKE DROVE
COW WAY
CROSS DROVE
WYPE RD
LC

189
221

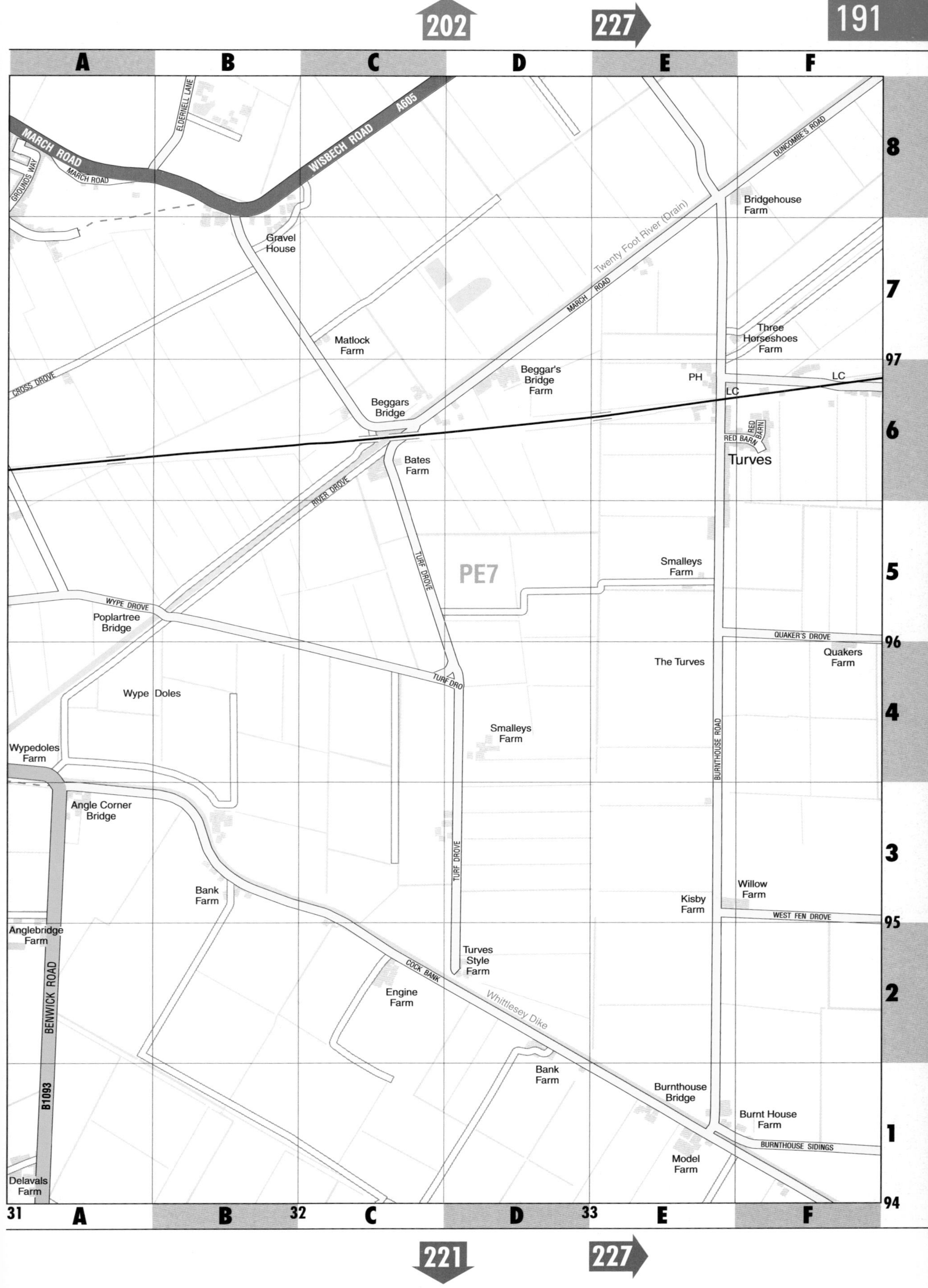

A **B** **C** **D** **E** **F**

GROUNDS WAY

MARCH ROAD

MARCH ROAD

ELDERNELL LANE

WISBECH ROAD A605

DUNCOMBE'S ROAD

8

Gravel House

Bridgehouse Farm

Twenty Foot River (Drain)

7

Matlock Farm

MARCH ROAD

Three Horseshoes Farm

CROSS DROVE

Beggar's Bridge Farm

PH

LC

LC

97

Beggars Bridge

LC

6

Bates Farm

RED BARN

RED BARN

Turves

RIVER DROVE

PE7

TURF DROVE

Smalleys Farm

5

WYPE DROVE

Poplartree Bridge

QUAKER'S DROVE

96

TURF DRO

The Turves

Quakers Farm

Wype Doles

Smalleys Farm

BURNTHOUSE ROAD

4

Wypedoles Farm

Angle Corner Bridge

TURF DROVE

3

Bank Farm

Willow Farm

Kisby Farm

WEST FEN DROVE

95

Anglebridge Farm

BENWICK ROAD

COCK BANK

Whittlesey Dike

Turves Style Farm

2

Engine Farm

B1093

Bank Farm

Burnthouse Bridge

Burnt House Farm

BURNTHOUSE SIDINGS

1

Model Farm

Delavals Farm

94

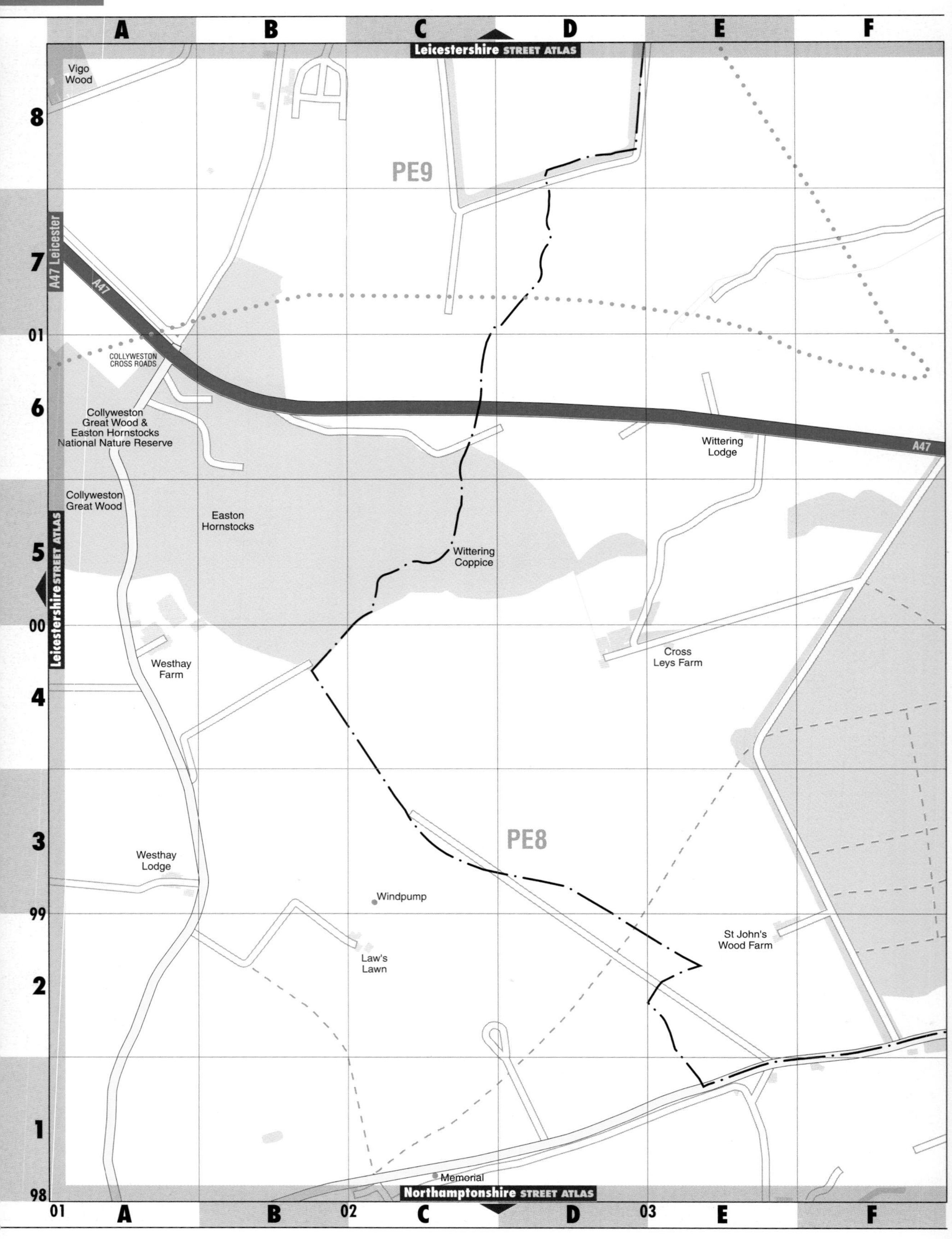

A B C D E F

Vigo
Wood

8

PE9

A47 Leicester

A47

7

01

COLLYWESTON
CROSS ROADS

6

Collyweston
Great Wood &
Easton Hornstocks
National Nature Reserve

Wittering
Lodge

A47

Collyweston
Great Wood

Leicestershire STREET ATLAS

Easton
Hornstocks

Wittering
Coppice

5

00

Cross
Leys Farm

Westhay
Farm

4

Westhay
Lodge

PE8

3

Windpump

99

St John's
Wood Farm

Law's
Lawn

2

1

Memorial

98

01 A B 02 C D 03 E F

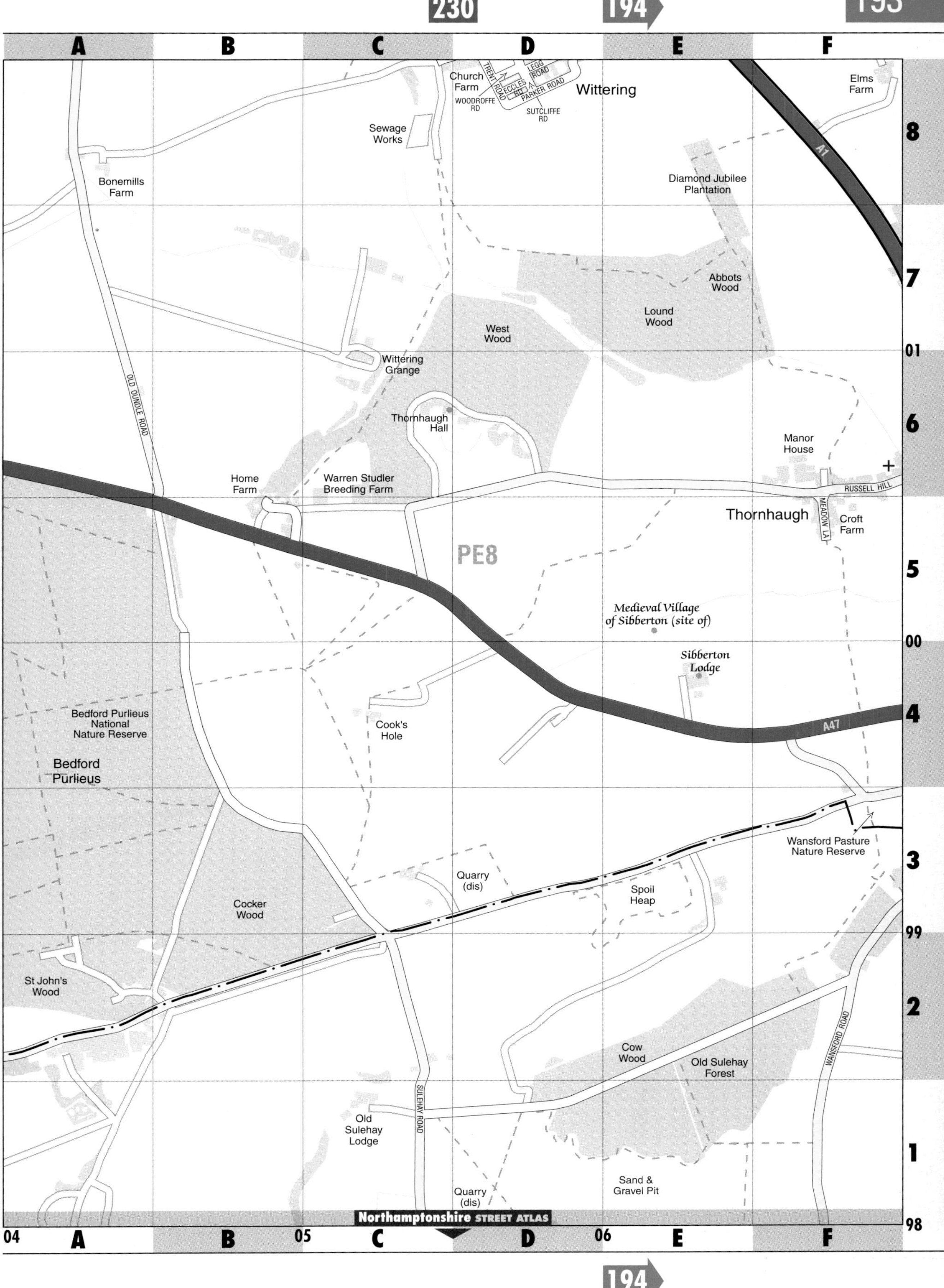

A   B   C   D   E   F

8

Wittering

Church Farm
TRENT ROAD
LEGG ROAD
ECCLES RD
PARKER ROAD
WOODROFFE RD
SUTCLIFFE RD

Elms Farm

A1

Sewage Works

Bonemills Farm

Diamond Jubilee Plantation

7

Abbots Wood

Lound Wood

01

West Wood

Wittering Grange

6

Manor House

Thornhaugh Hall

+

OLD DUMBLE ROAD

Home Farm

Warren Studler Breeding Farm

RUSSELL HILL

MEADOW LA

Thornhaugh

Croft Farm

PE8

5

Medieval Village of Sibberton (site of)

00

Sibberton Lodge

Bedford Purlieus National Nature Reserve

Cook's Hole

4

A47

Bedford Purlieus

Wansford Pasture Nature Reserve

3

Quarry (dis)

Spoil Heap

Cocker Wood

99

St John's Wood

WANSFORD ROAD

2

Cow Wood

Old Sulehay Forest

SULEHAY ROAD

Old Sulehay Lodge

1

Sand & Gravel Pit

Quarry (dis)

98

04   A   B   05   C   D   06   E   F

193
230

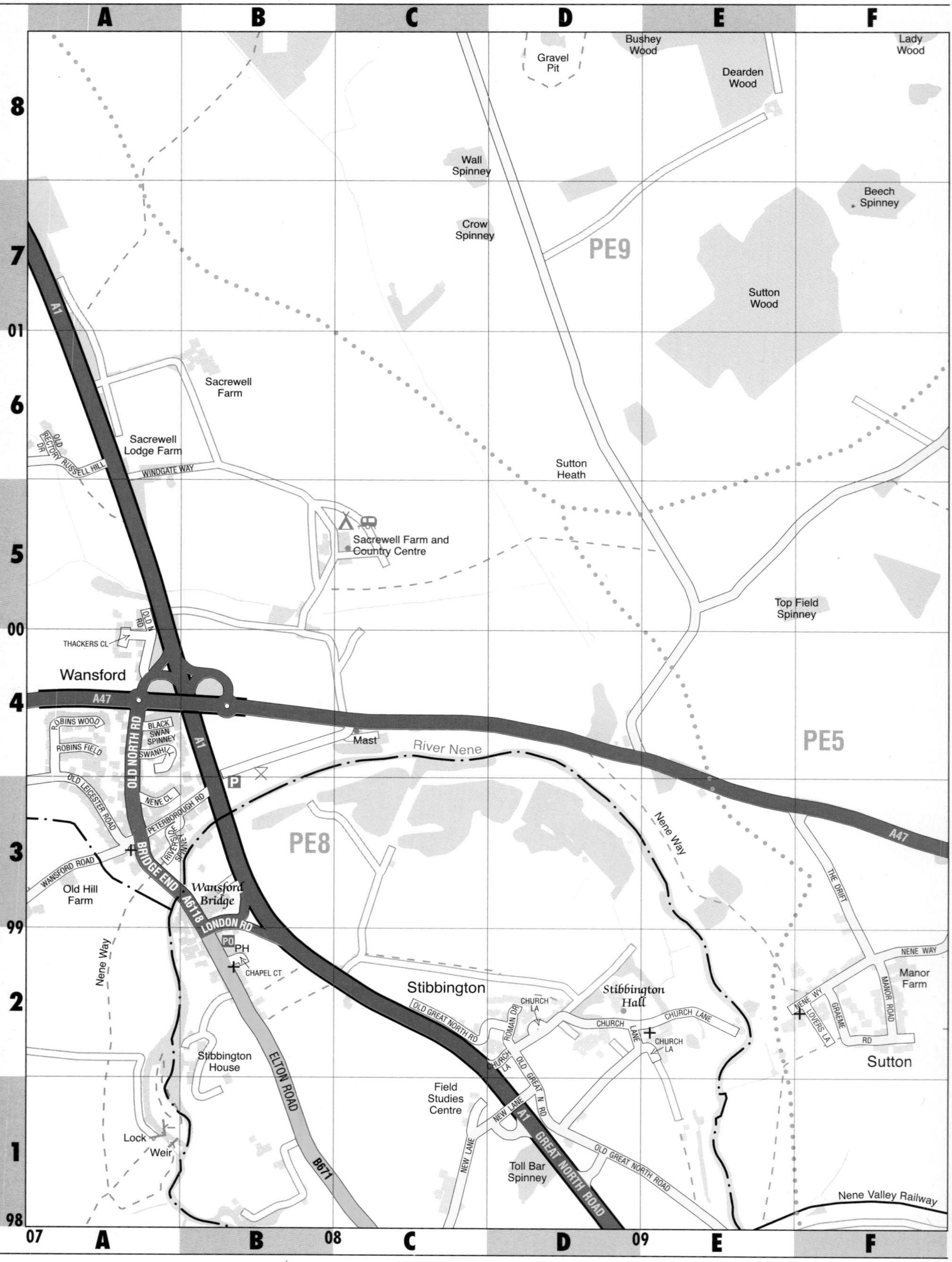
A
B
C
D
E
F
8
7
01
6
5
00
4
3
99
2
1
98
07
08
09
Gravel Pit
Bushey Wood
Dearden Wood
Lady Wood
Wall Spinney
Beech Spinney
Crow Spinney
PE9
Sutton Wood
A1
Sacrewell Farm
Sacrewell Lodge Farm
OLD RECTORY DR
RUSSELL HILL
WINDGATE WAY
Sutton Heath
Sacrewell Farm and Country Centre
Top Field Spinney
OLD N RD
THACKERS CL
Wansford
A47
ROBINS WOOD
BLACK SWAN SPINNEY
SWANHILL
ROBINS FIELD
OLD NORTH RD
Mast
River Nene
PE5
OLD LEICESTER ROAD
P
NENE CL
PETERBOROUGH RD
Nene Way
PE8
RIVERSIDE SPINNEY
WANSFORD ROAD
BRIDGE END
A6118
Wansford Bridge
Old Hill Farm
THE DRIFT
LONDON RD
PO
PH
CHAPEL CT
NENE WAY
Manor Farm
Stibbington
Stibbington Hall
CHURCH LA
OLD GREAT NORTH RD
ROMAN DR
CHURCH LANE
CHURCH
NENE WY
LOVERS LA
GRAEME
MANOR ROAD
RD
Sutton
Stibbington House
ELTON ROAD
Field Studies Centre
OLD GREAT N RD
NEW LANE
GREAT NORTH ROAD
OLD GREAT NORTH ROAD
Lock
Weir
B671
Toll Bar Spinney
Nene Valley Railway

193
183

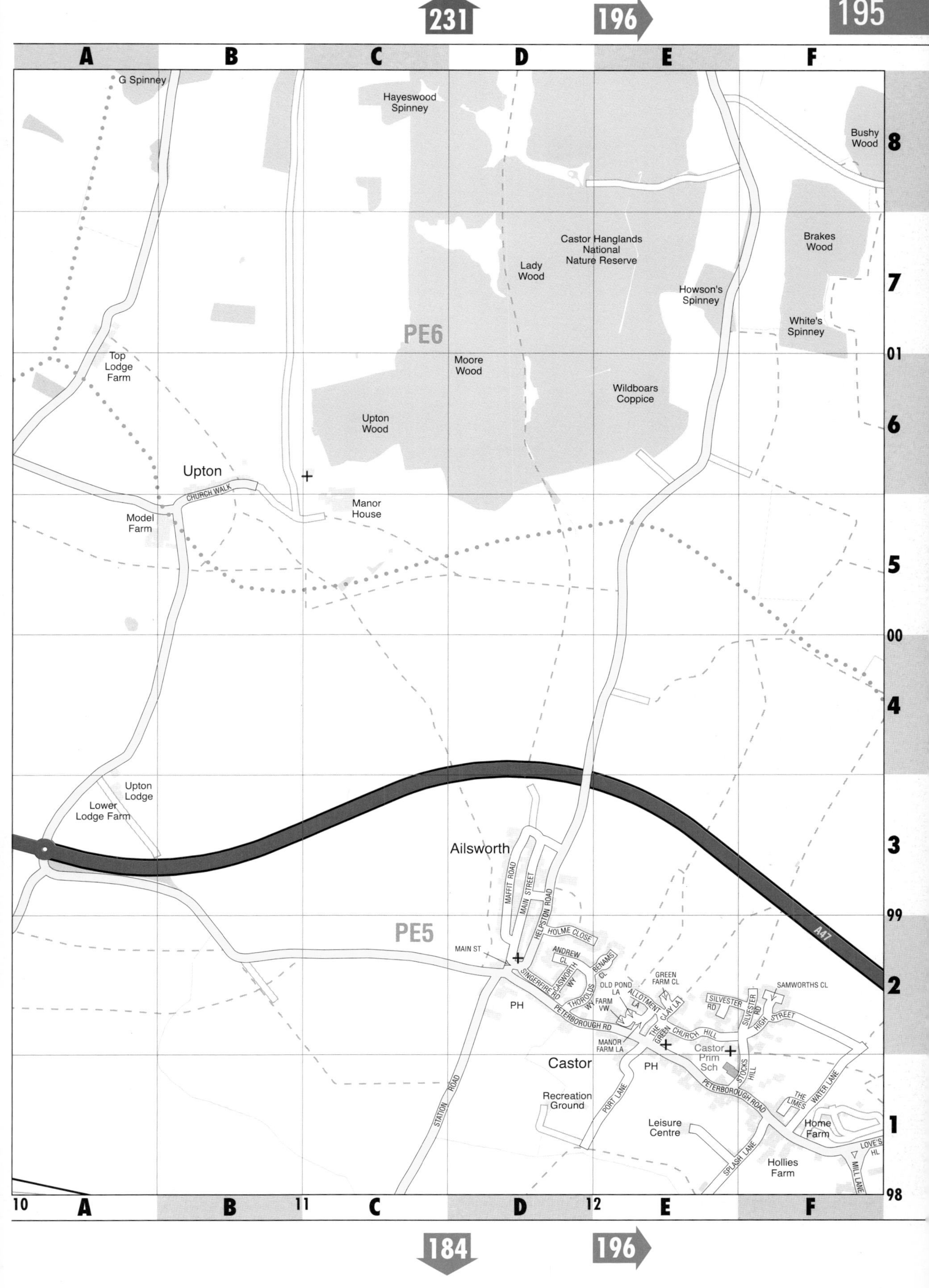

A   B   C   D   E   F

G Spinney

Hayeswood
Spinney

Bushy
Wood   8

Castor Hanglands
National
Nature Reserve

Brakes
Wood

Lady
Wood

Howson's
Spinney   7

White's
Spinney

PE6

Top
Lodge
Farm

Moore
Wood   01

Wildboars
Coppice   6

Upton
Wood

Upton

CHURCH WALK

Model
Farm

Manor
House

5

00

4

Upton
Lodge

Lower
Lodge Farm   3

Ailsworth

A47   99

PE5

MAFFIT ROAD
MAIN STREET
HELPSTON ROAD

HOLME CLOSE   2

MAIN ST

ANDREW
CL

BENHAMS
CL

GREEN
FARM CL

SAMWORTHS CL

SINGERFIRE RD
THOROLDS
CASWORTH WY

OLD POND
LA
WY
FARM VW

ALLOTMENT
LA

THE GREEN
CHURCH HILL

SILVESTER
RD

SILVESTER
RD

HIGH STREET

PH

PETERBOROUGH RD

MANOR
FARM LA

Castor
Prim
Sch

Castor

PH

STOCKS HILL   1

Recreation
Ground

PORT LANE

PETERBOROUGH ROAD

THE
LIMES

WATER LANE

STATION ROAD

Leisure
Centre

Home
Farm

LOVE'S HL

SPLASH LANE

Hollies
Farm

MILL LANE

98

195
203

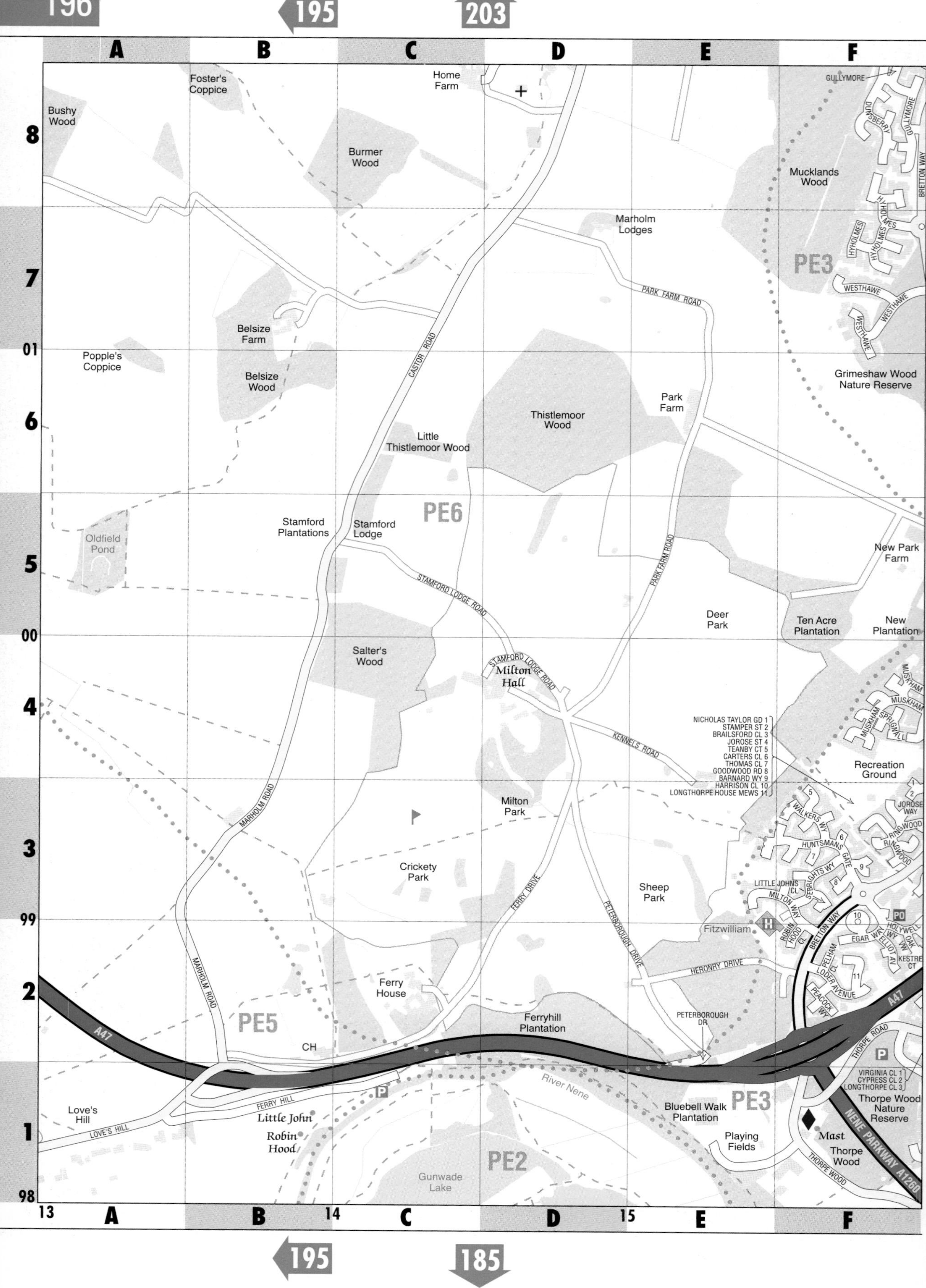
A
B
C
D
E
F
Foster's Coppice
Home Farm
Bushy Wood
Burmer Wood
Mucklands Wood
Marholm Lodges
GULLYMORE
DUNSBERRY
GULLYMORE
BRETTON WAY
HYHOLMES
HYHOLMES
HY HOLMES
PE3
WESTHAWE
WESTHAWE
WESTHAWE
PARK FARM ROAD
Belsize Farm
Popple's Coppice
Belsize Wood
CASTOR ROAD
Grimeshaw Wood Nature Reserve
Park Farm
Thistlemoor Wood
Little Thistlemoor Wood
PE6
Stamford Plantations
Stamford Lodge
Oldfield Pond
New Park Farm
PARK FARM ROAD
STAMFORD LODGE ROAD
Deer Park
Ten Acre Plantation
New Plantation
Salter's Wood
STAMFORD LODGE ROAD
Milton Hall
MUSKHAM
MUSKHAM
MUSKHAM
SPRIGWELL
KENNELS ROAD
NICHOLAS TAYLOR GD 1
STAMPER ST 2
BRAILSFORD CL 3
JOROSE ST 4
TEANBY CT 5
CARTERS CL 6
THOMAS CL 7
GOODWOOD RD 8
BARNARD WY 9
HARRISON CL 10
LONGTHORPE HOUSE MEWS 11
Recreation Ground
JOROSE WAY
RINGWOOD
RINGWOOD
Milton Park
MARHOLM ROAD
WALKERS WY
HUNTSMANS GATE
Crickety Park
Sheep Park
LITTLE JOHNS CL
SEBRIGHTS WY
MILTON WAY
FERRY DRIVE
PETERBOROUGH DRIVE
Fitzwilliam
ROBIN HOOD CL
BRETTON WAY
PO
HOLYWELL WY
EGAR WAY
ELLIOT AV
OAK WY
KESTREL CT
PELHAM CL
LODER AVENUE
PEACOCK WY
HERONRY DRIVE
MARHOLM ROAD
Ferry House
Ferryhill Plantation
PETERBOROUGH DR
A47
A47
PE5
CH
THORPE ROAD
P
VIRGINIA CL 1
CYPRESS CL 2
LONGTHORPE CL 3
River Nene
P
FERRY HILL
Love's Hill
LOVE'S HILL
Little John
Robin Hood
Bluebell Walk Plantation
PE3
Thorpe Wood Nature Reserve
NENE PARKWAY A1260
Mast
Playing Fields
Thorpe Wood
THORPE WOOD
PE2
Gunwade Lake
8
7
01
6
5
00
4
3
99
2
1
98
13
14
15
A
B
C
D
E
F

195
185

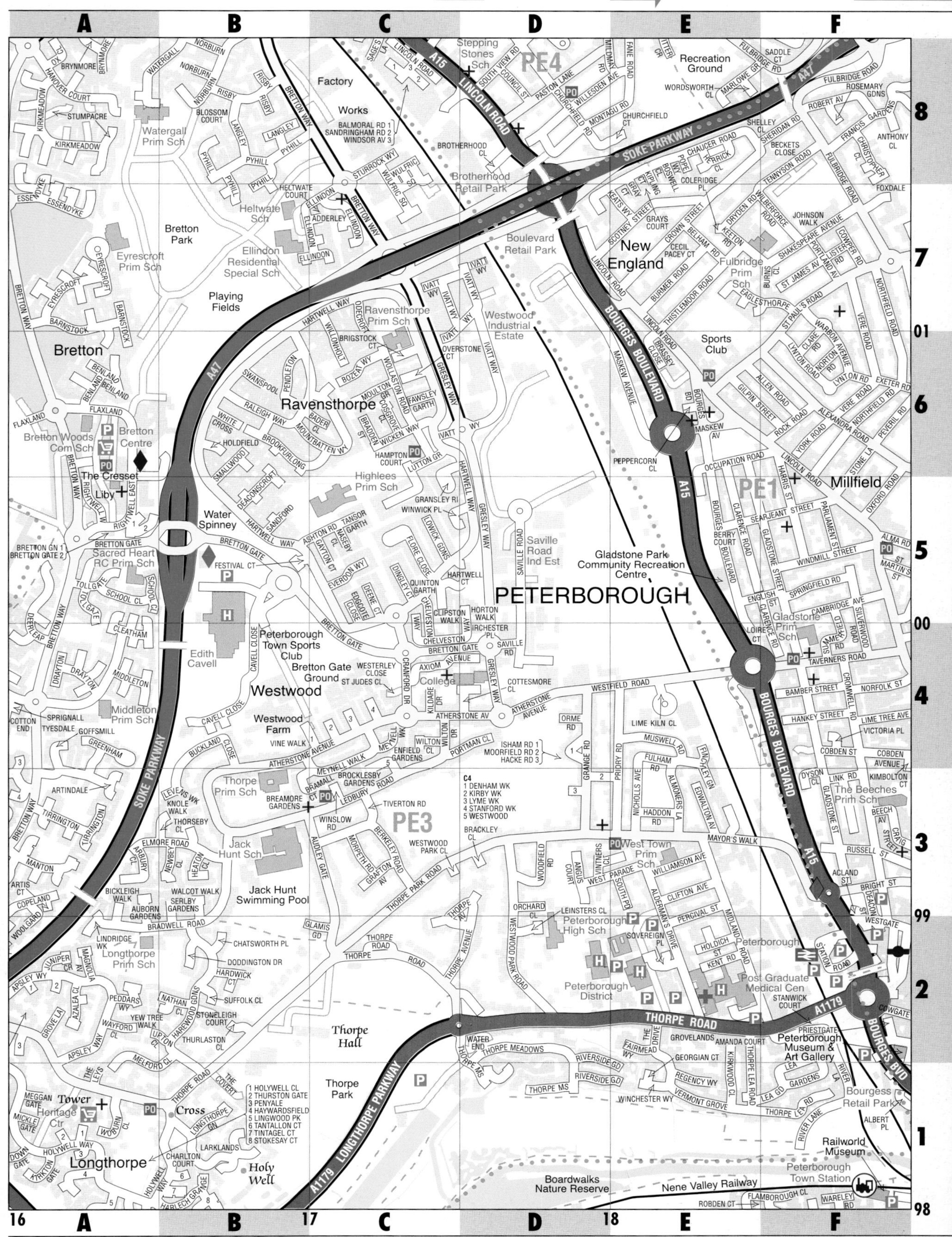
A
B
C
D
E
F
8
7
01
6
5
00
4
3
99
2
1
98
16
17
18
PE4
PE1
PE3
PETERBOROUGH
Bretton
Bretton Park
Ravensthorpe
Westwood
New England
Millfield
Longthorpe
Factory
Works
Recreation Ground
Stepping Stones Sch
Watergall Prim Sch
Heltwate Sch
Ellindon Residential Special Sch
Eyrescroft Prim Sch
Playing Fields
Ravensthorpe Prim Sch
Brotherhood Retail Park
Boulevard Retail Park
Westwood Industrial Estate
Fulbridge Prim Sch
Sports Club
Bretton Woods Com Sch
Bretton Centre
The Cresset
Liby
Water Spinney
Sacred Heart RC Prim Sch
Highlees Prim Sch
Saville Road Ind Est
Gladstone Park Community Recreation Centre
Gladstone Prim Sch
Edith Cavell
Peterborough Town Sports Club
Bretton Gate Ground
College
Westwood Farm
Middleton Prim Sch
Thorpe Prim Sch
Jack Hunt Sch
Jack Hunt Swimming Pool
The Beeches Prim Sch
West Town Prim Sch
Peterborough High Sch
Peterborough District
Post Graduate Medical Cen
Peterborough
Longthorpe Prim Sch
Thorpe Hall
Thorpe Park
Tower
Heritage Ctr
Cross
Holy Well
Peterborough Museum & Art Gallery
Bourgess Retail Park
Railworld Museum
Peterborough Town Station
Boardwalks Nature Reserve
Nene Valley Railway
SOKE PARKWAY
LINCOLN ROAD
BOURGES BOULEVARD
THORPE ROAD
LONGTHORPE PARKWAY
A15
A47
A1179
BALMORAL RD 1
SANDRINGHAM RD 2
WINDSOR AV 3
ISHAM RD 1
MOORFIELD RD 2
HACKE RD 3
C4
1 DENHAM WK
2 KIRBY WK
3 LYME WK
4 STANFORD WK
5 WESTWOOD
1 HOLYWELL CL
2 THURSTON GATE
3 PENYALE
4 HAYWARDSFIELD
5 LINGWOOD PK
6 TANTALLON CT
7 TINTAGEL CT
8 STOKESAY CT
BRETTON GN 1
BRETTON GATE 2

198

A3
1 BURGHLEY RD
2 BURGHLEY SQ
3 ST MARK'S CT

197

205

PETERBOROUGH

PE1

Dogsthorpe

Newark

Eastfield

Fengate

D7
1 SOMERBY GARTH
2 HUNGARTON CT
3 ALLEXTON GD
4 ROTHERBY GR
5 WHETSTONE CT

D3
1 WETHERBY WY
2 RASEN CT
3 HEXHAM CT
4 NORTH BANK RD
5 VICARAGE FARM RD

A1
1 WENTWORTH ST
2 BRIDGE ST
3 RIVERGATE
4 EMBANKMENT RD

A2
1 KING ST
2 QUEEN ST
3 TRINITY ST
4 PRIESTGATE
5 CATTLE MARKET WAY

B2
1 FENGATE CL
2 HEREWARD CL

B3
1 CRAWTHORNE ST
2 JORDAN MS

Power Station

Refuse Tip

Rugby Club

Sports Ground

Central Park

Peterborough Cathedral

Peterborough Regional Coll

Key Theatre

Council Offices

Lido Swimming Pool

Queensgate Centre

Broadway Theatre

A15 A1139 EYE ROAD PASTON PARKWAY FRANK PERKINS PARKWAY POTTERS WAY BOULEVARD LONDON RD

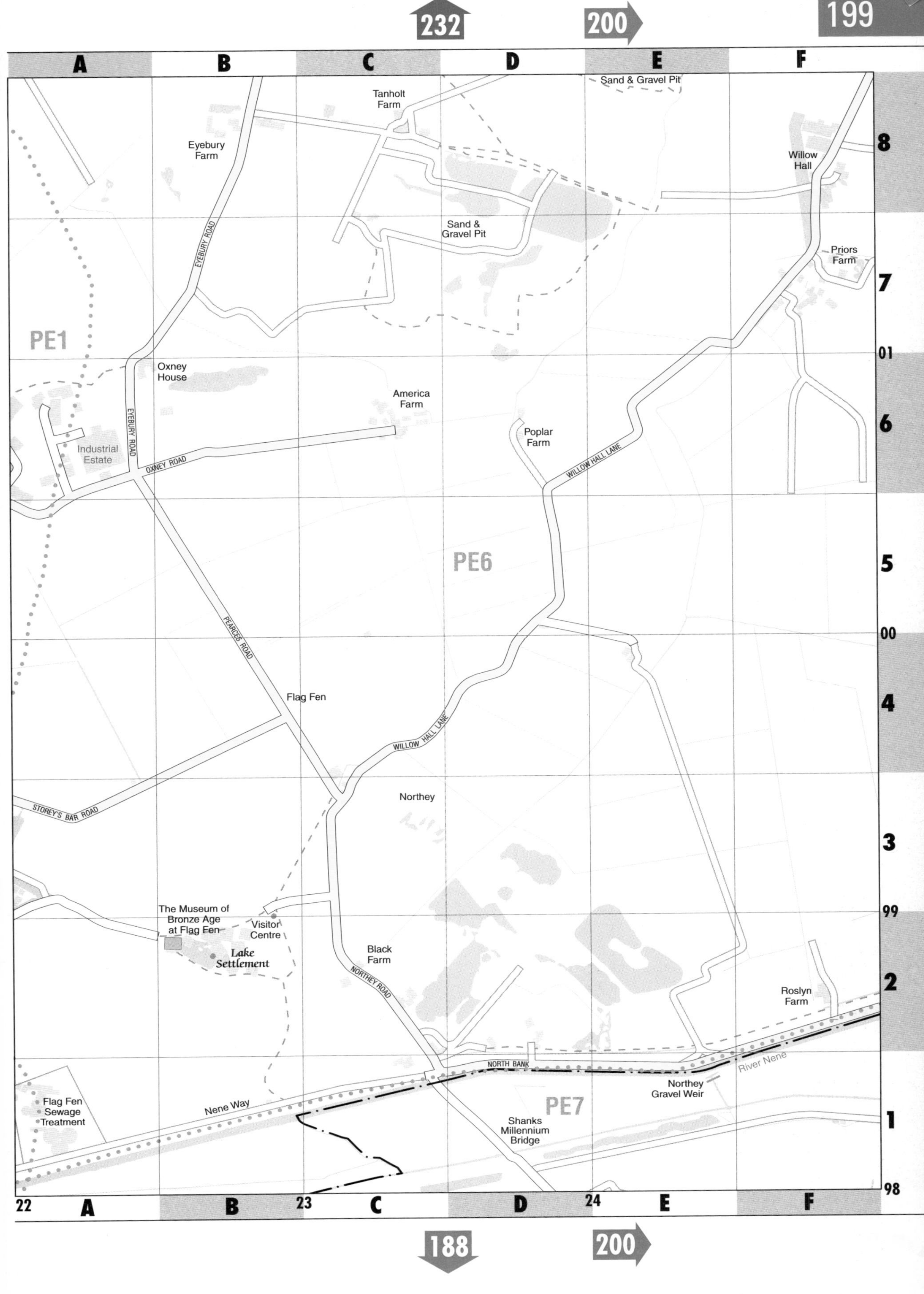
232
200
A
B
C
D
E
F
8
7
01
6
5
00
4
3
99
2
1
98
22
23
24
Sand & Gravel Pit
Tanholt Farm
Eyebury Farm
Willow Hall
Sand & Gravel Pit
Priors Farm
EYEBURY ROAD
PE1
Oxney House
America Farm
Industrial Estate
EYEBURY ROAD
OXNEY ROAD
Poplar Farm
WILLOW HALL LANE
PE6
PEARCES ROAD
Flag Fen
WILLOW HALL LANE
STOREY'S BAR ROAD
Northey
The Museum of Bronze Age at Flag Fen
Visitor Centre
Lake Settlement
Black Farm
NORTHEY ROAD
Roslyn Farm
NORTH BANK
River Nene
Northey Gravel Weir
Flag Fen Sewage Treatment
Nene Way
PE7
Shanks Millennium Bridge
188
200

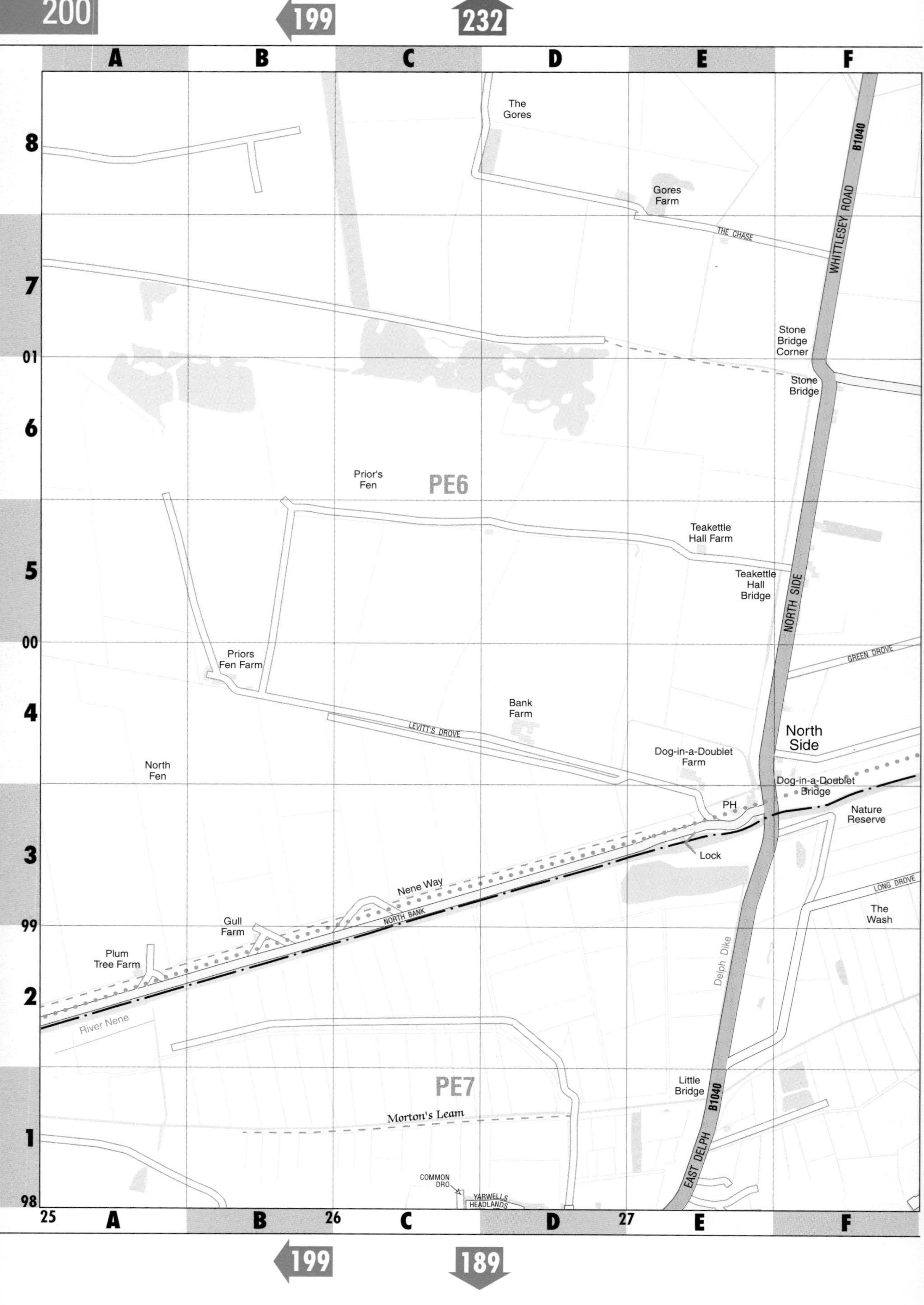

A B C D E F

8

7

01

6

The Gores

Gores Farm

THE CHASE

WHITTLESEY ROAD

B1040

Stone Bridge Corner

Stone Bridge

Prior's Fen

PE6

5

00

Teakettle Hall Farm

Teakettle Hall Bridge

NORTH SIDE

Priors Fen Farm

GREEN DROVE

4

North Fen

LEVITT'S DROVE

Bank Farm

Dog-in-a-Doublet Farm

North Side

Dog-in-a-Doublet Bridge

3

PH

Lock

Nene Way

NORTH BANK

Nature Reserve

LONG DROVE

The Wash

99

Gull Farm

Plum Tree Farm

River Nene

Delph Dike

2

Little Bridge

B1040

1

PE7

Morton's Leam

EAST DELPH

98

COMMON DRO

YARWELL'S HEADLANDS

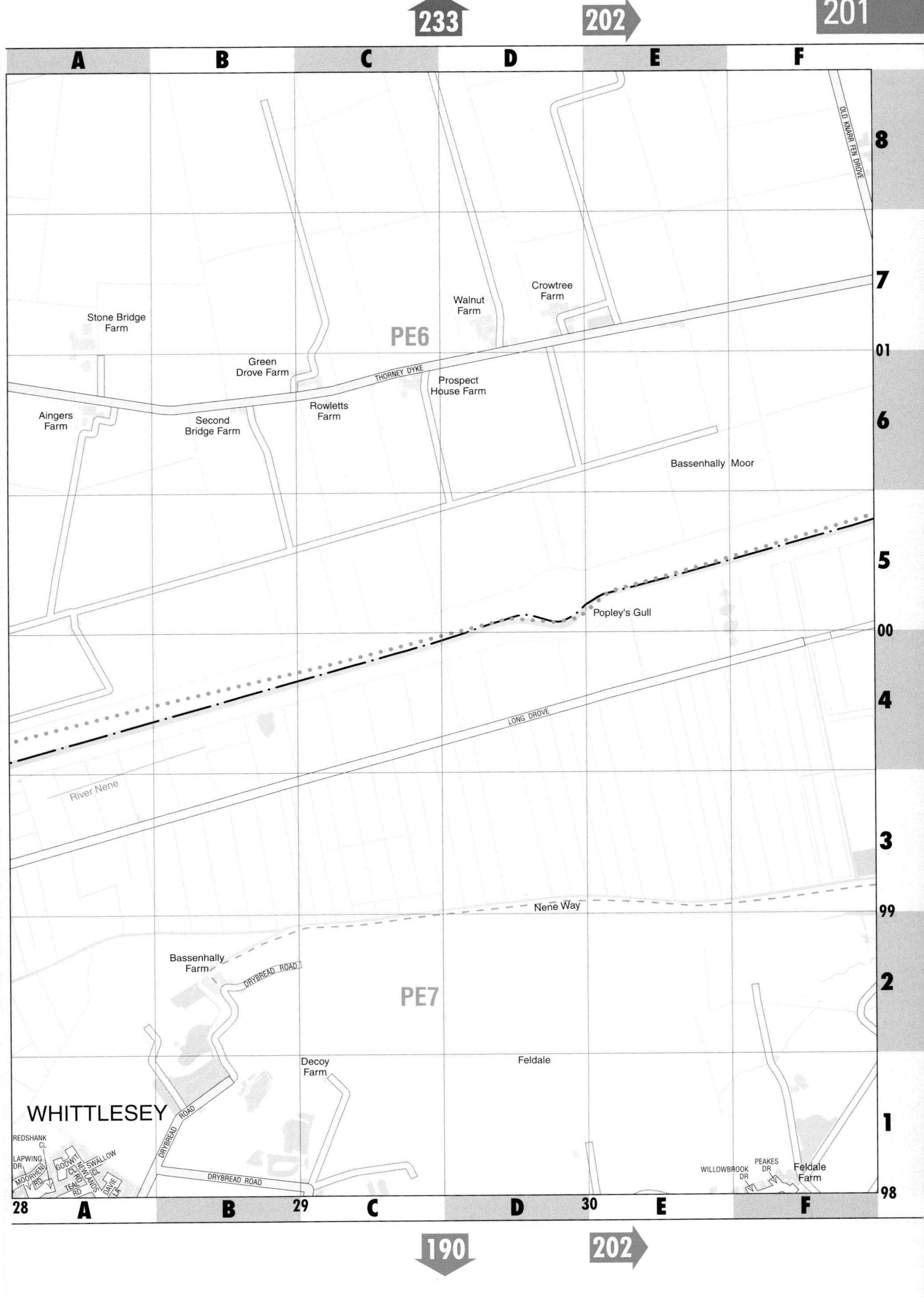

A   B   C   D   E   F

PE6

Stone Bridge
Farm

Walnut
Farm

Crowtree
Farm

Green
Drove Farm

THORNEY DYKE

Prospect
House Farm

Aingers
Farm

Rowletts
Farm

Second
Bridge Farm

Bassenhally Moor

OLD KNARR FEN DROVE

Popley's Gull

LONG DROVE

River Nene

Nene Way

Bassenhally
Farm

DRYBREAD ROAD

PE7

Decoy
Farm

Feldale

WHITTLESEY

REDSHANK
CL

LAPWING
DR

MOORHEN
VIEW

GODWIT
CL
TEAL CL
CURLEW CL
FENLANDS
RD

SWALLOW
CL

DALE
LA

DRYBREAD
ROAD

DRYBREAD ROAD

WILLOWBROOK
DR

PEAKES
DR

Feldale
Farm

A B C D E F

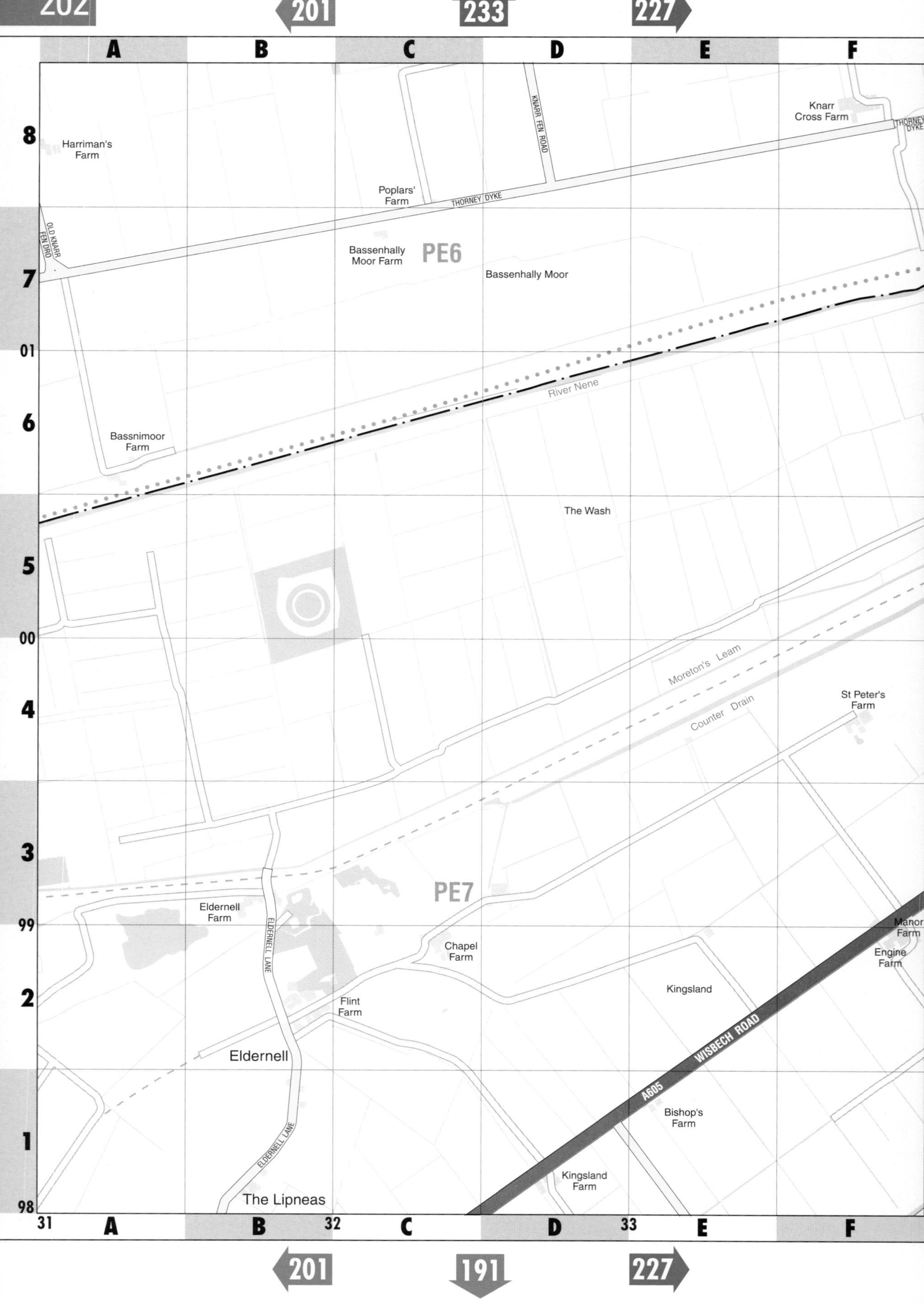

8 — Harriman's Farm

Knarr Cross Farm

THORNEY DYKE

Poplars' Farm

7 — OLD KNARR FEN DRO

Bassenhally Moor Farm

PE6

Bassenhally Moor

01

River Nene

6 — Bassnimoor Farm

The Wash

5 —

00

Moreton's Leam

4 — Counter Drain

St Peter's Farm

3 —

PE7

99 — Eldernell Farm

Chapel Farm

Manor Farm

Engine Farm

ELDERNELL LANE

2 — Flint Farm

Kingsland

WISBECH ROAD

Eldernell

A605

1 — Bishop's Farm

Kingsland Farm

ELDERNELL LANE

98 — The Lipneas

31 A B 32 C D 33 E F

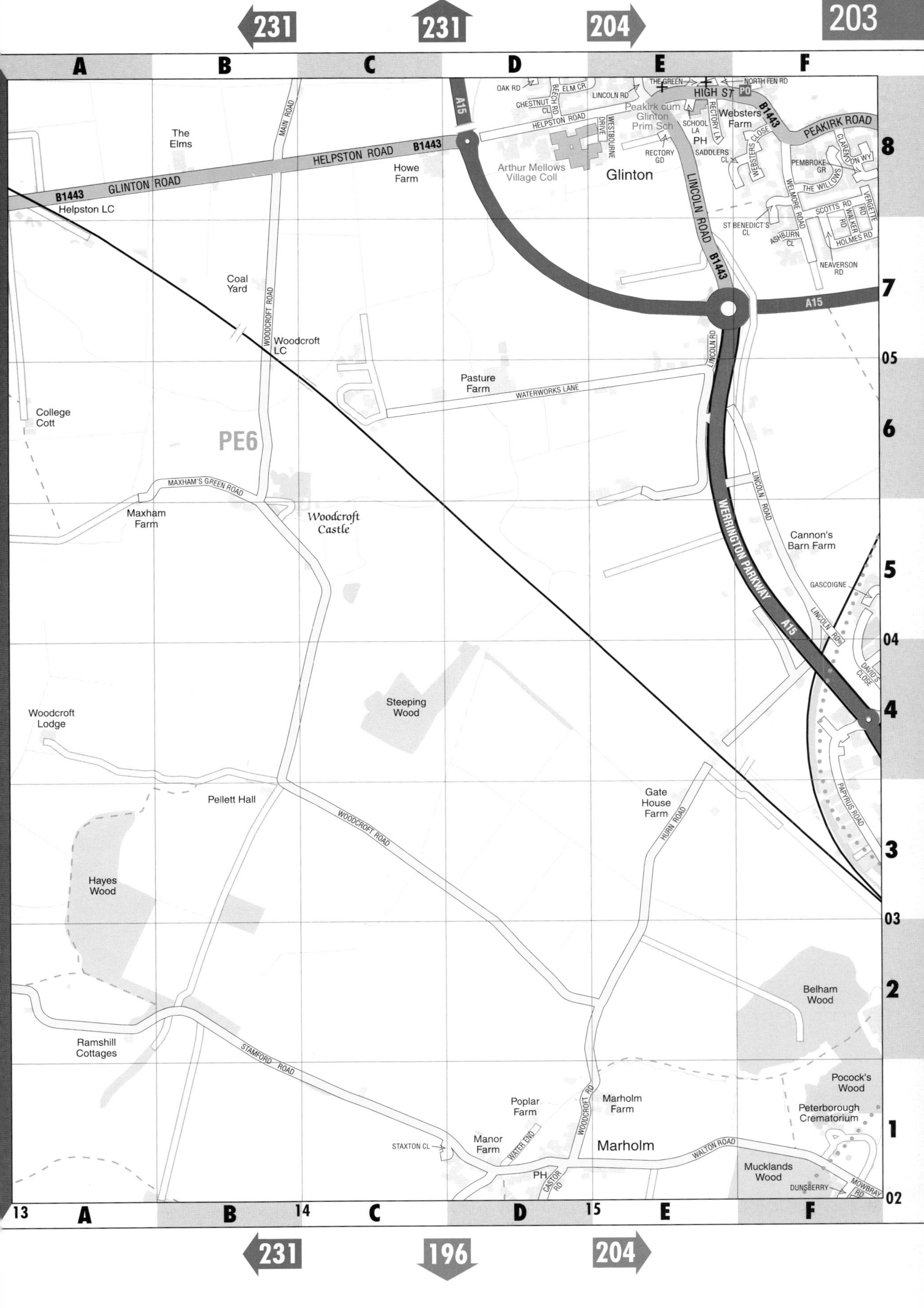

A B C D E F

231 231 204

8

OAK RD
THE GREEN
NORTH FEN RD
HIGH ST
PO
Helpston Road
CHESTNUT CLI
ELM CR
LINCOLN RD
Peakirk cum
Glinton Prim Sch
Websters Farm
B1443
PEAKIRK ROAD
BEECH RD
WESTBOURNE DRIVE
SCHOOL LA
PH
RECTORY LA
SADDLERS CL
WEBSTERS CLOSE
CLARENSON WY
PEMBROKE GR
THE WILLOWS
WELMORE ROAD
VERGETTE
The Elms
HELPSTON ROAD
B1443
Howe Farm
Arthur Mellows Village Coll
Glinton
RECTORY GD
ST BENEDICT'S CL
ASHBURN CL
SCOTTS RD
WALKER RD
HOLMES RD
NEAVERSON RD

GLINTON ROAD
B1443
Helpston LC
LINCOLN ROAD
B1443
A15
7

Coal Yard
Woodcroft LC
WOODCROFT ROAD
MAIN ROAD
A15
A15
05

College Cott
PE6
Pasture Farm
WATERWORKS LANE
LINCOLN RD
6

Maxham Farm
MAXHAM'S GREEN ROAD
Woodcroft Castle
LINCOLN ROAD
WERRINGTON PARKWAY
A15
Cannon's Barn Farm
GASCOIGNE
04
5

Woodcroft Lodge
Steeping Wood
DAVID'S CLOSE
4

Pellett Hall
WOODCROFT ROAD
Gate House Farm
HURN ROAD
PAPYRUS ROAD
03
3

Hayes Wood
Belham Wood
2

Ramshill Cottages
STAMFORD ROAD
Poplar Farm
WOODCROFT RD
Marholm Farm
WATER END
WALTON ROAD
Pocock's Wood
Peterborough Crematorium
1

STAXTON CL
Manor Farm
PH
CASTOR RD
Marholm
Mucklands Wood
DUNSBERRY
MOWBRAY RD
02

13 A 14 B C 15 D E F

203 206

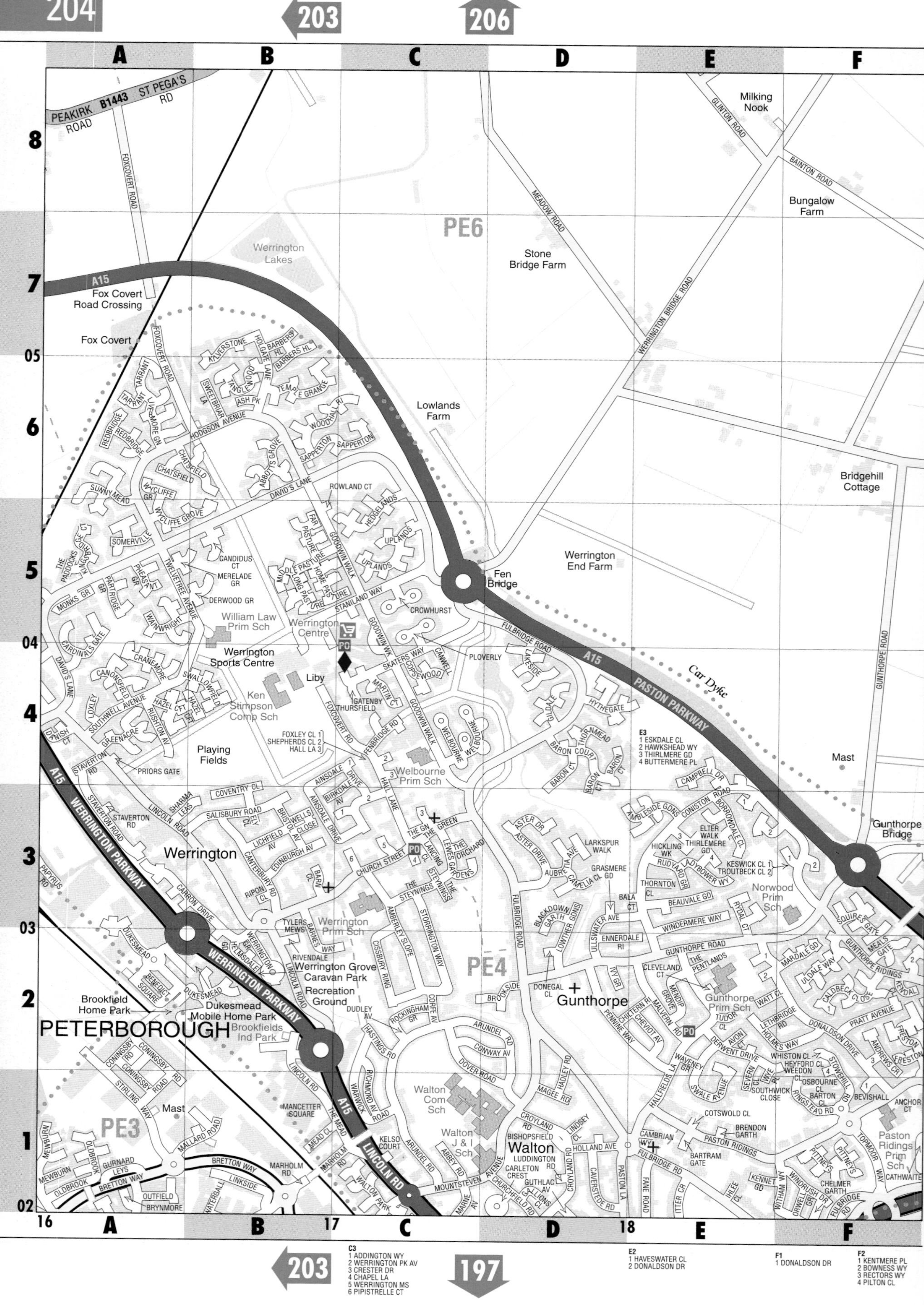
A B C D E F
8 7 05 6 5 04 4 3 03 2 1 02
16 17 18
PEAKIRK ROAD
B1443 ST PEGA'S RD
FOXCOVERT ROAD
Milking Nook
GLINTON ROAD
BAINTON ROAD
Bungalow Farm
MEADOW ROAD
PE6
Werrington Lakes
Stone Bridge Farm
WERRINGTON BRIDGE ROAD
A15
Fox Covert Road Crossing
Fox Covert
Lowlands Farm
Bridgehill Cottage
Werrington End Farm
Fen Bridge
HODGSON AVENUE
DAVID'S LANE
ABBOTS GROVE
SAPPERTON
TEMPLE GRANGE
KILVERSTONE
HOLGATE LANE
BARBERS HL
SWEETBRIAR LA
CHATSFIELD
WYCLIFFE GROVE
SOMERVILLE
TWELVETREE AVENUE
CANDIDUS CT
MERELADE GR
DERWOOD GR
MONKS GR
PARTRIDGE GR
PHEASANT GR
WAINWRIGHT
GOODWIN WALK
UPLANDS
HEDGELANDS
ROWLAND CT
STANILAND WAY
CROWHURST
PLOVERLY
FULBRIDGE ROAD
LAKESIDE
SKATERS WAY
COPSEWOOD
CAMWELL
William Law Prim Sch
Werrington Centre
Werrington Sports Centre
Liby
Ken Stimpson Comp Sch
CARDINALS GATE
CRANEMORE
CANONSFIELD
SOUTHWELL AVENUE
SWALLOWFIELD
HAZEL CFT
RUSHTON AV
LOXLEY
GREENACRE
STAVERTON RD
PRIORS GATE
Playing Fields
FOXCOVERT RD
FENBRIDGE RD
GATENBY
THURSFIELD
MARTIN CT
FOXLEY CL 1
SHEPHERDS CL 2
HALL LA 3
Welbourne Prim Sch
WELBOURNE
Car Dyke
PASTON PARKWAY
HYTHEGATE
GILDALE
THORNAMEAD
BARON COURT
BARON CT
E3
1 ESKDALE CL
2 HAWKSHEAD WY
3 THIRLMERE GD
4 BUTTERMERE PL
Mast
GUNTHORPE ROAD
Gunthorpe Bridge
CAMPBELL DR
CONISTON ROAD
BORROWDALE CL
AMBLESIDE GDNS
ELTER WALK
THIRLMERE GD
HICKLING WK
LADYBOWER WY
KESWICK CL 1
TROUTBECK CL 2
ASTER DR
ASTER DRIVE
AUBRETIA AVE
LARKSPUR WALK
GRASMERE GD
CAMELLIA CL
THORNTON CL
BEAUVALE GD
BALA CT
RYDAL CT
Norwood Prim Sch
WINDERMERE WAY
ULLSWATER AVE
ENNERDALE RI
BLACKDOWN GARTH
LOWTHER GDNS
SQUIRES GATE
MEADS GATE
GUNTHORPE RIDINGS
COVENTRY CL
SALISBURY ROAD
LINCOLN ROAD
SHARMA LEYS
STAVERTON ROAD
LICHFIELD AV
BRISTOL AV
WELLS CLOSE
EDINBURGH AV
CANTERBURY RD
RIPON CL
AINSDALE DRIVE
BIRKDALE AV
HALL LANE
THE GREEN
THE GN
LANCING CL
LEWES GARDENS
THE ORCHARD
CHURCH STREET
BARN CL
THE STEYNINGS
STEYNINGS
Werrington
WERRINGTON PARKWAY
PAPYRUS RD
CARRON DRIVE
DUKESMEAD
BENEDICT SQUARE
HELMSDALE GR
WERRINGTON GR
TYLERS MEWS
BARNES WAY
RIVENDALE
Werrington Prim Sch
Werrington Grove Caravan Park
Recreation Ground
AMBERLEY SLOPE
STORRINGTON WAY
CISSBURY RING
PE4
FULBRIDGE ROAD
BROOKSIDE
DONEGAL CL
Gunthorpe
IVY GR
CLEVELAND CT
THE PENTLANDS
MENDIP GROVE
Gunthorpe Prim Sch
WATT CL
MARDALE GD
ULDALE WAY
CALDBECK CLOSE
KENDAL
PRATT AVENUE
DONALDSON DRIVE
PRESTON
ANDREWS CR
Brookfield Home Park
Dukesmead Mobile Home Park
PETERBOROUGH
Brookfields Ind Park
DUDLEY AV
ROCKINGHAM GR
CORFE AV
ARUNDEL RD
CONWAY AV
DOVER ROAD
HASTINGS RD
RICHMOND AV
WARWICK ROAD
Walton Com Sch
HADLEY RD
MAGEE RD
CHILTERN RI
PENNINE WAY
CHEVIOT AV
MALVERN RD
TUDOR CL
AVON CT
DERWENT DRIVE
WAVENEY GR
SWALE AVENUE
SEVERN CL
WYE PL
LETHBRIDGE RD
HOLMES WAY
WHISTON CL
HEYFORD CL
WEEDON CL
STOWEHILL RD
OSBOURNE CL
BARTON CL
SOUTHWICK CLOSE
RINGSTEAD RD
BEVISHALL
ANCHOR CT
HALLFIELDS LA
COTSWOLD CL
BRENDON GARTH
PASTON RIDINGS
BARTRAM GATE
CAMBRIAN WY
FULBRIDGE RD
Paston Ridings Prim Sch
TOPMOOR WAY
CATHWAITE
PITTNEYS
CHELMER GARTH
FULBRIDGE
WINDRUSH DR
ORWELL GR
WITHAM WY
KENNET GD
IHLEE CL
ITTER CR
FANE ROAD
PASTON LA
CAVERSTEDE RD
HOLLAND AVE
LINDSEY CL
CROYLAND RD
CROYLAND AV
GUTHLAC AV
GALLIONS CL
CHURCHFIELD RD
BISHOPSFIELD
Walton
LUDDINGTON RD
CARLETON CREST
MOUNTSTEVEN AVENUE
MARNE AV
Walton J & I Sch
ABBEY RD
KELSO COURT
ARUNDEL RD
LINCOLN RD
MANCETTER SQUARE
THE MEAD
MEAD CL
MARHOLM RD
WALTON PARK
CONINGSBY RD
CONINGSBY ROAD
STIRLING WAY
Mast
MALLARD ROAD
PE3
NEWBURN
OLDBROOK
MEWBURN
GURNARD LEYS
BRETTON WAY
LINKSIDE
WATERGALL
OUTFIELD
BRYNMORE
C3
1 ADDINGTON WY
2 WERRINGTON PK AV
3 CRESTER DR
4 CHAPEL LA
5 WERRINGTON MS
6 PIPISTRELLE CT
E2
1 HAVESWATER CL
2 DONALDSON DR
F1
1 DONALDSON DR
F2
1 KENTMERE PL
2 BOWNESS WY
3 RECTORS WY
4 PILTON CL

203 197

207
232

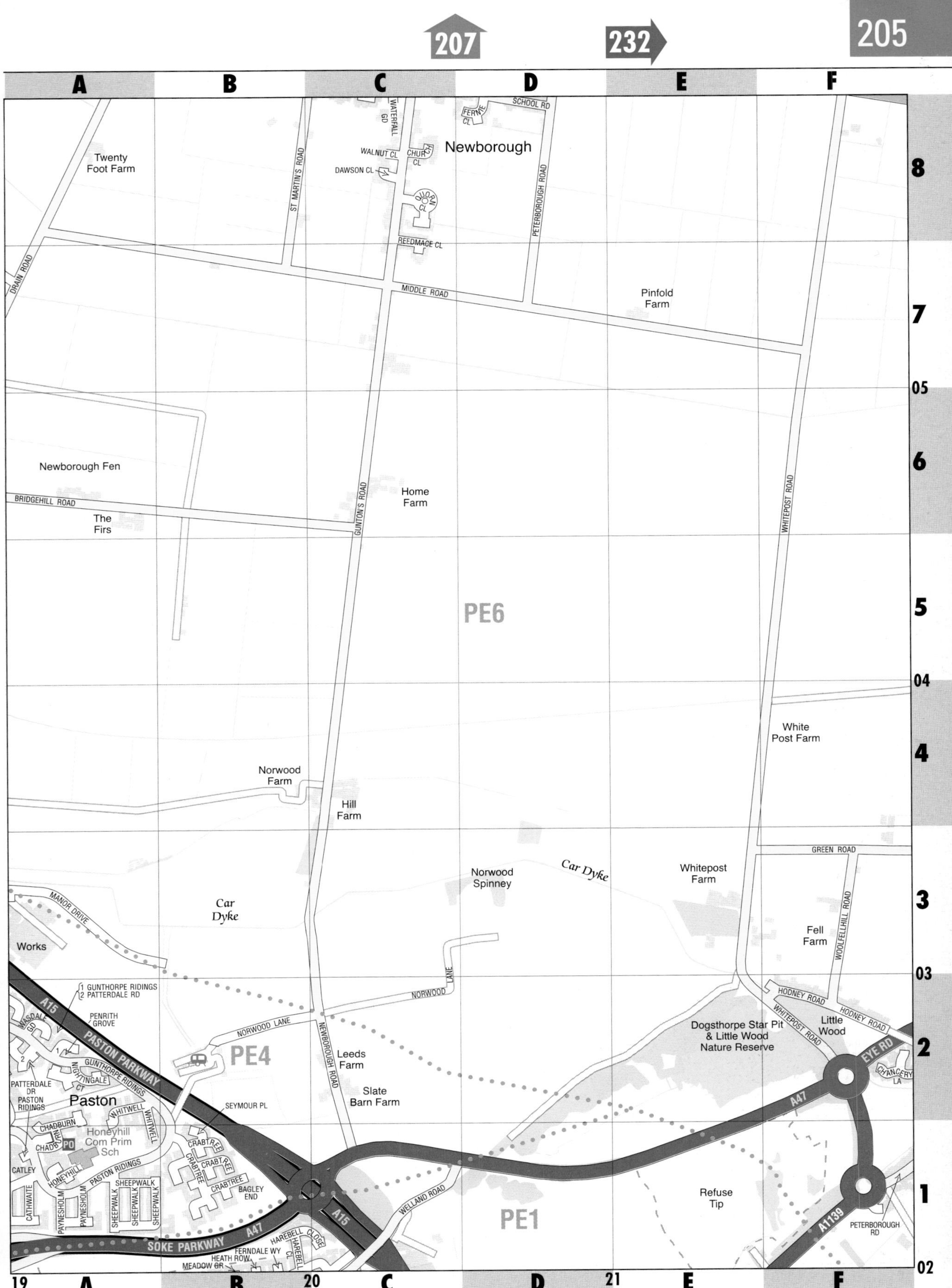
A
B
C
D
E
F
8
7
6
5
4
3
2
1
05
04
03
02
19
20
21
Newborough
Twenty Foot Farm
SCHOOL RD
FERNIE CL
WATERFALL GD
WALNUT CL
CHURCH CL
DAWSON CL
QUORN CL
REEDMACE CL
ST MARTIN'S ROAD
PETERBOROUGH ROAD
DRAIN ROAD
MIDDLE ROAD
Pinfold Farm
Newborough Fen
BRIDGEHILL ROAD
The Firs
GUNTON'S ROAD
Home Farm
WHITEPOST ROAD
PE6
White Post Farm
Norwood Farm
Hill Farm
GREEN ROAD
Norwood Spinney
Car Dyke
Whitepost Farm
MANOR DRIVE
Car Dyke
WOOLFELLHILL ROAD
Fell Farm
Works
1 GUNTHORPE RIDINGS
2 PATTERDALE RD
NORWOOD LANE
HODNEY ROAD
HODNEY ROAD
WHITEPOST ROAD
Little Wood
Dogsthorpe Star Pit & Little Wood Nature Reserve
EYE RD
CHANCERY LA
A15
PASTON PARKWAY
PENRITH GROVE
WASDALE GD
NORWOOD LANE
NEWBOROUGH ROAD
PE4
Leeds Farm
GUNTHORPE RIDINGS
NIGHTINGALE CT
PATTERDALE DR
PASTON RIDINGS
Paston
WHITWELL
SEYMOUR PL
Slate Barn Farm
A47
CHADBURN
CHADBURN
PO
Honeyhill Com Prim Sch
CRABTREE
CRABTREE
CRABTREE
CRABTREE
CATLEY
HONEYHILL
PASTON RIDINGS
SHEEPWALK
SHEEPWALK
SHEEPWALK
SHEEPWALK
BAGLEY END
WELLAND ROAD
Refuse Tip
CATHWAITE
PAYNESHOLM
PAYNESHOLM
A15
PE1
A1139
PETERBOROUGH RD
HAREBELL CLOSE
HAREBELL CL
SOKE PARKWAY
A47
FERNDALE WY
HEATH ROW
MEADOW GR

198
232

231

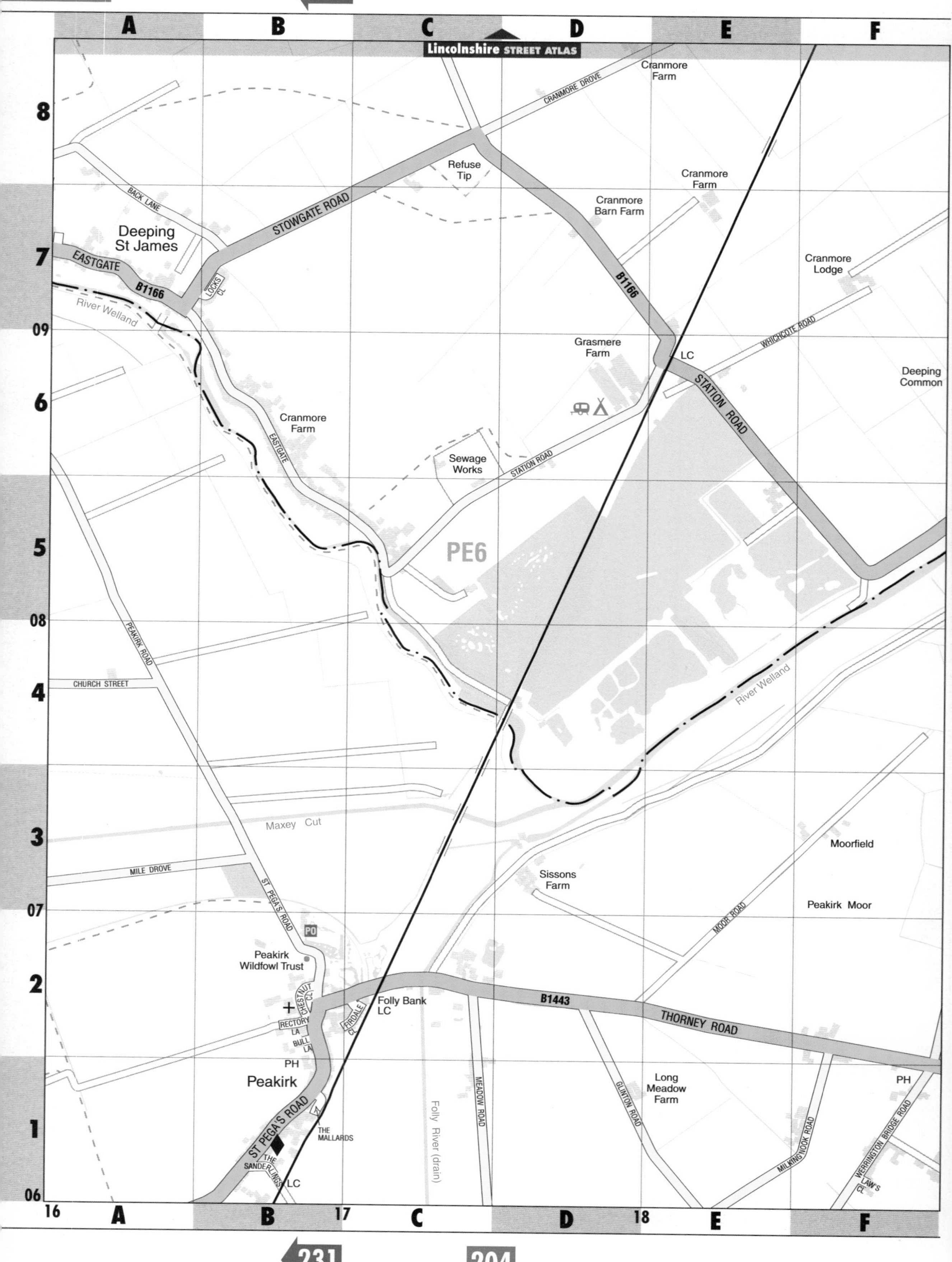

Lincolnshire STREET ATLAS

A   B   C   D   E   F

8

Cranmore Drive

Cranmore
Farm

Refuse
Tip

Cranmore
Farm

STOWGATE ROAD

Cranmore
Barn Farm

Deeping
St James

7

EASTGATE

B1166

B1166

LOCKS CL

BACK LANE

Cranmore
Lodge

River Welland

WHICHCOTE ROAD

09

Grasmere
Farm

LC

6

Deeping
Common

EASTGATE

Cranmore
Farm

STATION ROAD

Sewage
Works

STATION ROAD

5

PE6

08

PEAKIRK ROAD

4

CHURCH STREET

River Welland

3

Maxey   Cut

Moorfield

MILE DROVE

Sissons
Farm

Peakirk Moor

07

ST PEGA'S ROAD

PO

MOOR ROAD

2

Peakirk
Wildfowl Trust

CHESTNUT CL

Folly Bank
LC

B1443

THORNEY ROAD

RECTORY
LA

BIRDALE

PH

BULL LA

Long
Meadow
Farm

PH

GUNTON ROAD

Peakirk

MEADOW ROAD

Folly River (drain)

MILKINGNOOK ROAD

WERRINGTON BRIDGE ROAD

1

ST PEGA'S ROAD

THE
SANDERLINGS

THE
MALLARDS

LAW'S
CT

06

LC

16   A   B   17   C   D   18   E   F

231

204

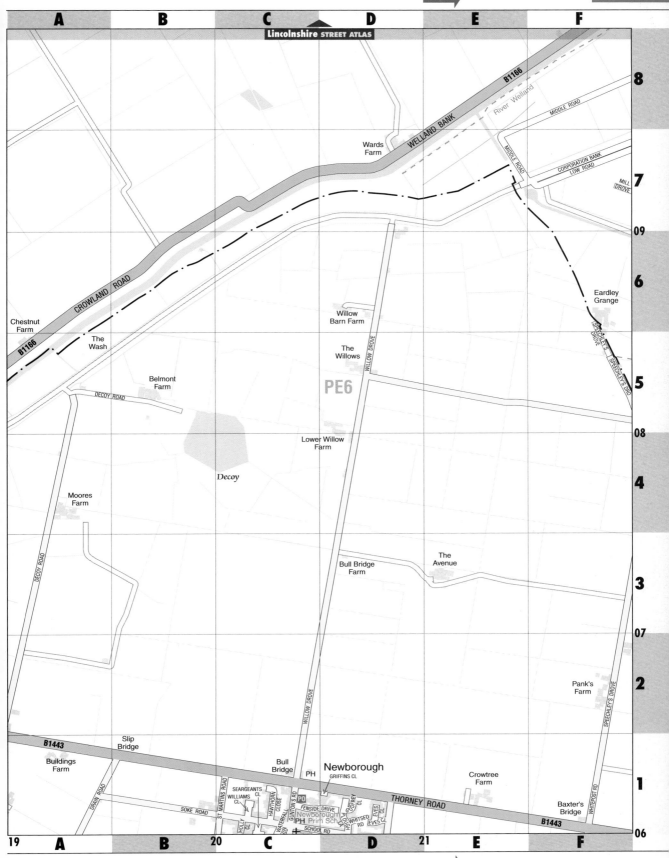

Lincolnshire STREET ATLAS

A   B   C   D   E   F

8
B1166
River Welland
MIDDLE ROAD
WELLAND BANK
Wards Farm
MIDDLE ROAD
CORPORATION BANK
LOW ROAD
7
MILL DROVE
09
6
Eardley Grange
SPEECHLEY'S DRIVE
Chestnut Farm
B1166
CROWLAND ROAD
The Wash
Willow Barn Farm
WILLOW DRIVE
The Willows
SPEECHLEY'S DRO
5
PE6
Belmont Farm
DECOY ROAD
08
Lower Willow Farm
Decoy
4
Moores Farm
DECOY ROAD
The Avenue
Bull Bridge Farm
3
07
Pank's Farm
SPEECHLEY'S DRIVE
2
WILLOW DRIVE
B1443
Slip Bridge
Buildings Farm
Bull Bridge
PH
Newborough
GRIFFINS CL
Crowtree Farm
1
DRAIN ROAD
SOKE ROAD
ST MARTINS ROAD
SEARGEANTS CL
WILLIAMS CL
HOLLY CL
HAWTHORN CLOSE
WATERFALL CLO
GUNTON'S RD
PO
FENSIDE DRIVE
Newborough PH Prim Sch
SCHOOL RD
GODFREY CL
HOW
WHITSED RD
EYES CL
EYES CL
THORNEY ROAD
Baxter's Bridge
WHITEPOST RD
B1443
06

19   A   B   20   C   D   21   E   F

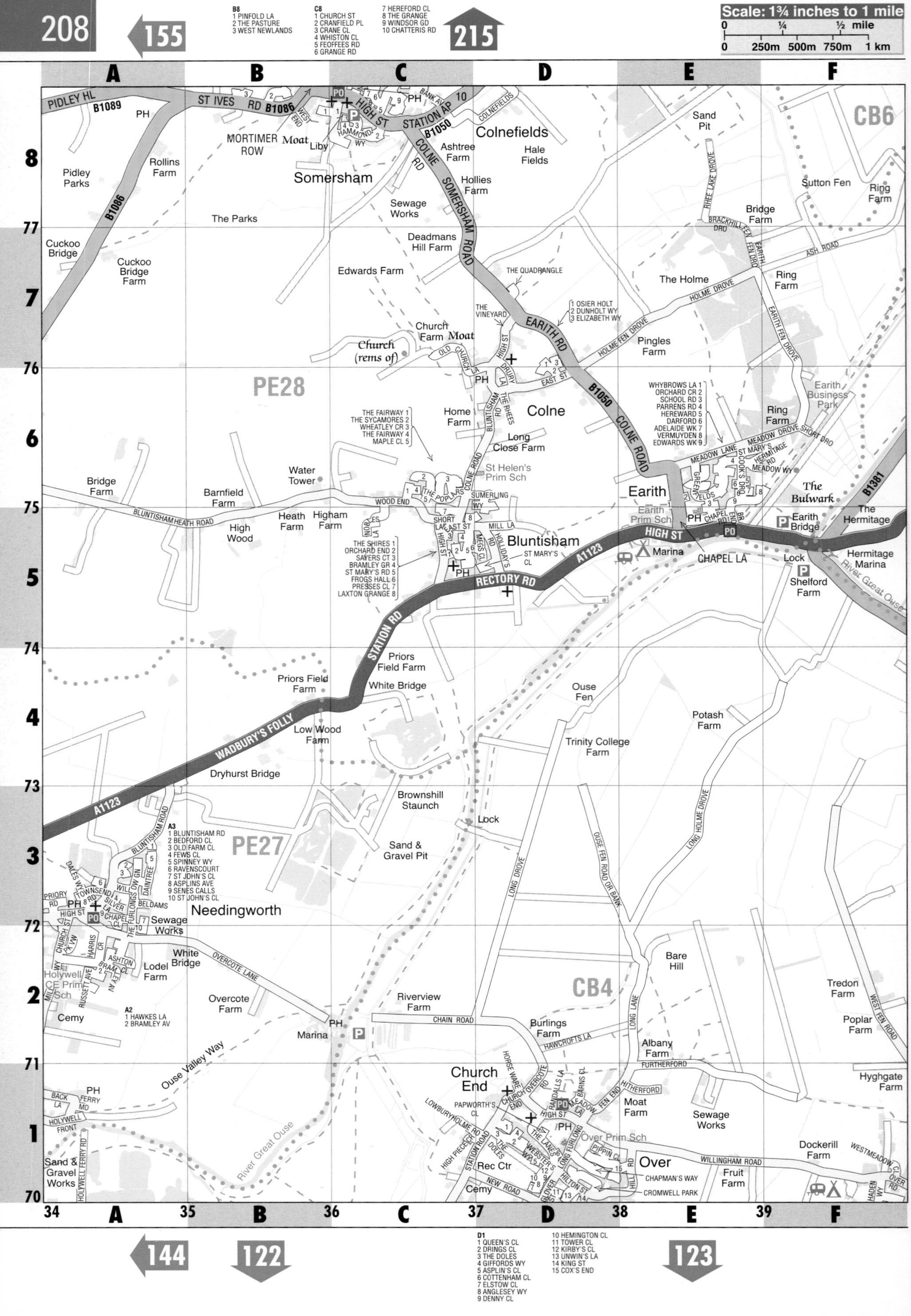

208
155
215
144
122
123
B8
1 PINFOLD LA
2 THE PASTURE
3 WEST NEWLANDS
C8
1 CHURCH ST
2 CRANFIELD PL
3 CRANE CL
4 WHISTON CL
5 FEOFFEES RD
6 GRANGE RD
7 HEREFORD CL
8 THE GRANGE
9 WINDSOR GD
10 CHATTERIS RD
Scale: 1¾ inches to 1 mile
0 ¼ ½ mile
0 250m 500m 750m 1 km
A B C D E F
8 77 7 76 6 75 5 74 4 73 3 72 2 71 1 70
34 35 36 37 38 39
PIDLEY HL
B1089
ST IVES RD B1086
PH
MORTIMER ROW
Moat
Liby
Somersham
HIGH ST
STATION AP
B1050
COLNEFIELDS
Colnefields
Ashtree Farm
Hale Fields
Sand Pit
CB6
Pidley Parks
Rollins Farm
B1086
COLNE RD
SOMERSHAM ROAD
Hollies Farm
Sewage Works
Sutton Fen
Ring Farm
RHEE LAKE DROVE
Bridge Farm
BRACKHILL FEN DRO
EARITH FEN DRO
ASH ROAD
The Parks
Cuckoo Bridge
Cuckoo Bridge Farm
Deadmans Hill Farm
Edwards Farm
THE QUADRANGLE
The Holme
Ring Farm
HOLME DROVE
THE VINEYARD
1 OSIER HOLT
2 DUNHOLT WY
3 ELIZABETH WY
EARITH RD
HOLME FEN DROVE
Pingles Farm
EARITH FEN DROVE
Church Farm
Moat
Church (rems of)
OLD CHURCH LA
HIGH ST
DRURY LA
EAST ST
B1050
PE28
WHYBROWS LA 1
ORCHARD CR 2
SCHOOL RD 3
PARRENS RD 4
HEREWARD 5
DARFORD 6
ADELAIDE WK 7
VERMUYDEN 8
EDWARDS WK 9
Earith Business Park
THE FAIRWAY 1
THE SYCAMORES 2
WHEATLEY CR 3
THE FAIRWAY 4
MAPLE CL 5
Home Farm
BLUNTISHAM RD
THE RHEES
Colne
Long Close Farm
COLNE ROAD
Ring Farm
MEADOW DROVE
SHORT DRO
MEADOW LANE
ST MARY'S
HERMITAGE RD
MEADOW WY
COOK'S DRO
Water Tower
St Helen's Prim Sch
THE POPLARS
Bridge Farm
Barnfield Farm
WOOD END
SUMERLING WY
Earith
GREEN FIELDS
The Bulwark
B1381
BLUNTISHAM HEATH ROAD
Heath Farm
Higham Farm
High Wood
SHORT LA
EAST ST
MILL LA
Earith Prim Sch
PH
CHAPEL RD
BR END
HIGH ST
PO
Earith Bridge
The Hermitage
THE SHIRES 1
ORCHARD END 2
SAYERS CT 3
BRAMLEY GR 4
ST MARY'S RD 5
FROGS HALL 6
PRESSES CL 7
LAXTON GRANGE 8
Bluntisham
ST MARY'S CL
HOLLIDAY'S RD
A1123
Marina
CHAPEL LA
Lock
Hermitage Marina
River Great Ouse
Shelford Farm
RECTORY RD
STATION RD
Priors Field Farm
Priors Field Farm
White Bridge
Ouse Fen
Potash Farm
WADBURY'S FOLLY
Low Wood Farm
Trinity College Farm
Dryhurst Bridge
A1123
Brownshill Staunch
Lock
BLUNTISHAM ROAD
A3
1 BLUNTISHAM RD
2 BEDFORD CL
3 OLD FARM CL
4 FEWS CL
5 SPINNEY WY
6 RAVENSCOURT
7 ST JOHN'S CL
8 ASPLINS AVE
9 SENES CALLS
10 ST JOHN'S CL
PE27
Sand & Gravel Pit
OUSE FEN ROAD OR BANK
LONG HOLME DROVE
LONG DROVE
DALES WY
TOWNSEND RD
PRIORY RD
PH
HIGH ST
PO
SILVER
CHAPEL
BELDAMS
THE FURLONGS
DAINTREE
Needingworth
Sewage Works
CHURCH ST
HARRIS CR
ASHTON
BRAMLEY AV
Holywell CE Prim Sch
MILL WY
RUSSETT AVE
Lodel Farm
White Bridge
OVERCOTE LANE
Bare Hill
CB4
Tredon Farm
Overcote Farm
Riverview Farm
Cemy
A2
1 HAWKES LA
2 BRAMLEY AV
PH
Marina
CHAIN ROAD
Burlings Farm
HAWCROFTS LA
LONG LANE
Albany Farm
Poplar Farm
WEST FEN ROAD
Ouse Valley Way
FURTHERFORD
Hyghgate Farm
PH
BACK LA
FERRY MD
HOLYWELL FRONT
Church End
HORSE WARE
OVERCOTE RD
RANDALLS LA
BARNS CL
HITHERFORD
FEN END
MEADOW LA
Moat Farm
Sewage Works
PAPWORTH'S CL
LOWBURY HOLME RD
CHURCH END
PO
HIGH ST
PH
Over Prim Sch
Dockerill Farm
WESTMEADOW CL
Sand & Gravel Works
HOLYWELL FERRY RD
River Great Ouse
HIGH PIECE RD
STATION ROAD
THE DOLES
WEBSTER'S WY
LONG FURLONG
PIPPIN CL
HILL RD
Over
WILLINGHAM ROAD
Fruit Farm
OVER RD
HADEN WY
Rec Ctr
CHAPMAN'S WAY
CROMWELL PARK
NEW ROAD
GLOVER ST
HILTON ST
Cemy
D1
1 QUEEN'S CL
2 DRINGS CL
3 THE DOLES
4 GIFFORDS WY
5 ASPLIN'S CL
6 COTTENHAM CL
7 ELSTOW CL
8 ANGLESEY WY
9 DENNY CL
10 HEMINGTON CL
11 TOWER CL
12 KIRBY'S CL
13 UNWIN'S LA
14 KING ST
15 COX'S END

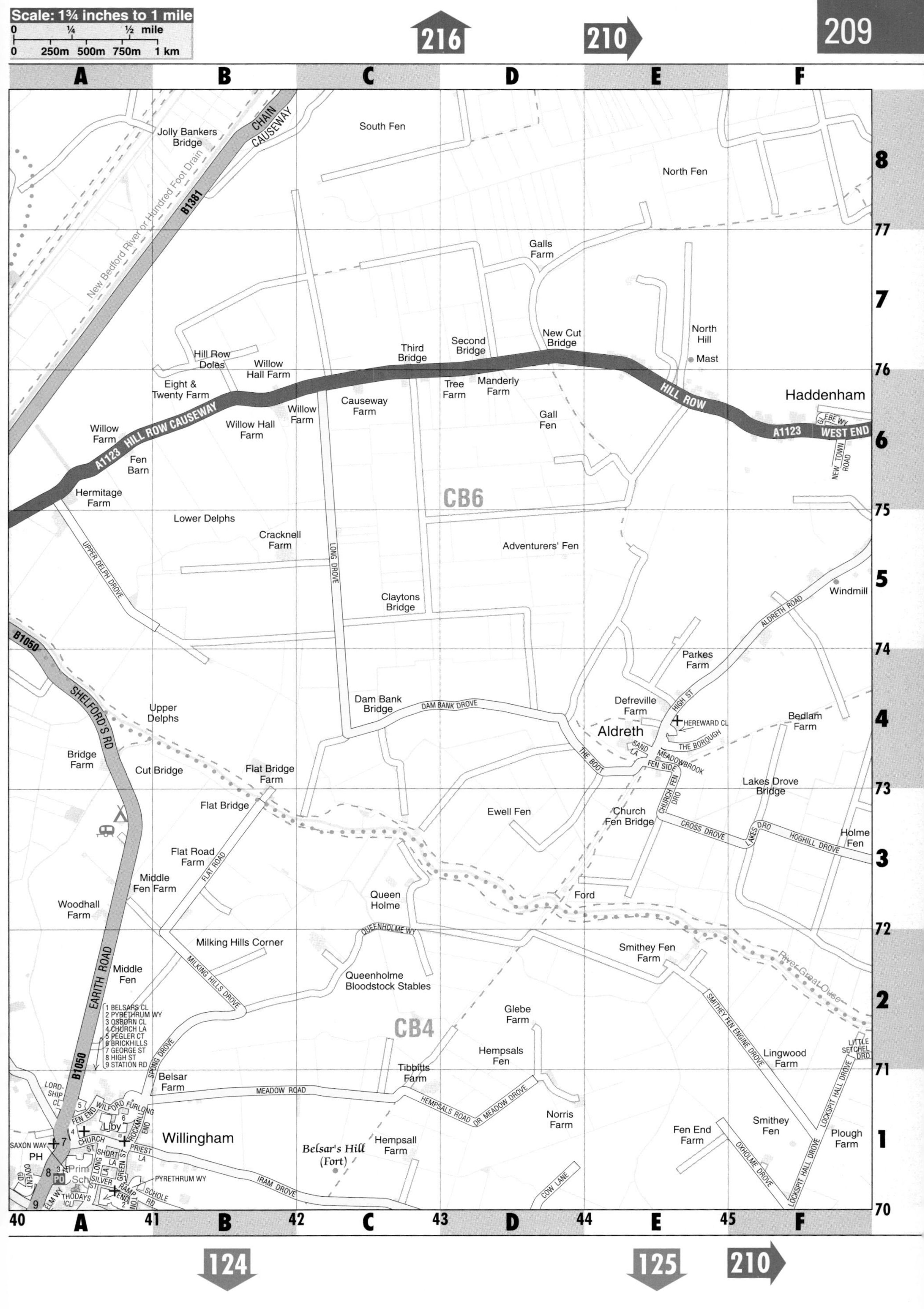
Scale: 1¾ inches to 1 mile
216
210
South Fen
North Fen
Jolly Bankers Bridge
CHAIN CAUSEWAY
B1381
New Bedford River or Hundred Foot Drain
Galls Farm
North Hill
Mast
New Cut Bridge
Second Bridge
Third Bridge
Hill Row Doles
Willow Hall Farm
Eight & Twenty Farm
Tree Farm
Manderly Farm
HILL ROW
Haddenham
Causeway Farm
Willow Farm
Willow Hall Farm
Gall Fen
A1123 WEST END
NEW TOWN ROAD
Willow Farm
A1123 HILL ROW CAUSEWAY
Fen Barn
Hermitage Farm
CB6
Lower Delphs
Cracknell Farm
Adventurers' Fen
UPPER DELPH DROVE
LONG DROVE
Claytons Bridge
Windmill
ALDRETH ROAD
B1050
Parkes Farm
SHELFORD'S RD
Upper Delphs
Dam Bank Bridge
DAM BANK DROVE
Defreville Farm
HIGH ST
HEREWARD CL
Aldreth
THE BOROUGH
Bedlam Farm
Bridge Farm
Cut Bridge
Flat Bridge Farm
THE BOOT
SAND LA
MEADOWBROOK
FEN SIDE
Lakes Drove Bridge
Flat Bridge
Ewell Fen
Church Fen Bridge
CHURCH FEN DRO
CROSS DROVE
LAKES DRO
HOGHILL DROVE
Holme Fen
Flat Road Farm
FLAT ROAD
Middle Fen Farm
Queen Holme
Ford
Woodhall Farm
Milking Hills Corner
QUEENHOLME WY
Smithey Fen Farm
River Great Ouse
EARITH ROAD
Middle Fen
MILKING HILLS DROVE
Queenholme Bloodstock Stables
1 BELSARS CL
2 PYRETHRUM WY
3 OSBORN CL
4 CHURCH LA
5 PEGLER CT
6 BRICKHILLS
7 GEORGE ST
8 HIGH ST
9 STATION RD
CB4
Glebe Farm
SMITHEY FEN ENGINE DROVE
LITTLE SETCHEL DRO
Hempsals Fen
Lingwood Farm
SPONG DROVE
Tibbitts Farm
Belsar Farm
MEADOW ROAD
LORDSHIP CL
WILFORD FURLONG
FEN END
HEMPSALS ROAD OR MEADOW DROVE
Norris Farm
Smithey Fen
LOCKSPIT HALL DROVE
Liby
Fen End Farm
Plough Farm
Willingham
CHURCH ST
PRIEST LA
SAXON WAY
PH
SHORT LA
Belsar's Hill (Fort)
Hempsall Farm
Prim Sch
PO
SILVER ST
GREEN ST
PYRETHRUM WY
IRAM DROVE
COW LANE
OXHOLME DROVE
COVENT GD
ELM WY
THODAYS CL
RAMPTON END
SCHOLE RD
A B C D E F
40 41 42 43 44 45
70 71 72 73 74 75 76 77
1 2 3 4 5 6 7 8
124
125
210

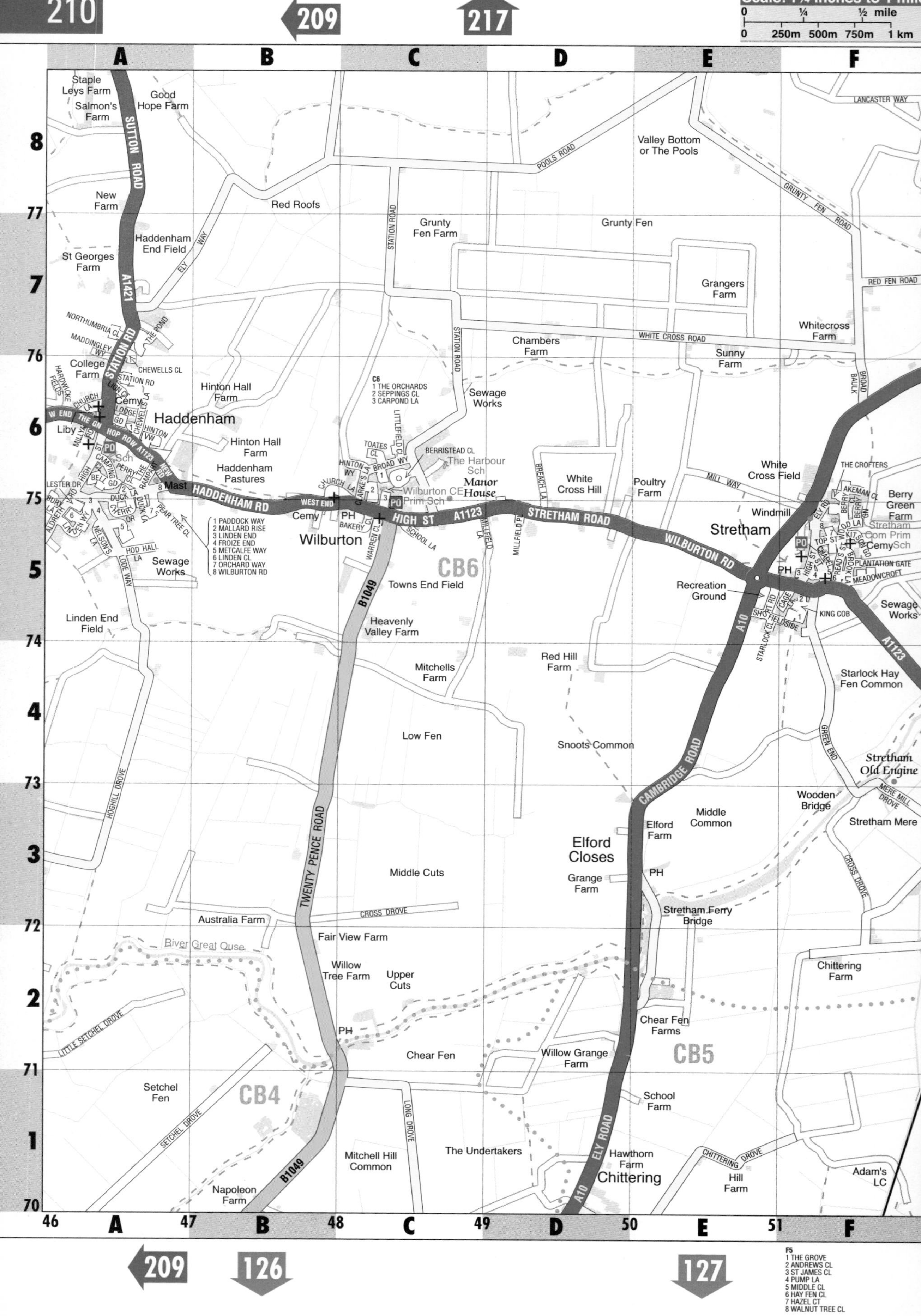

218
212

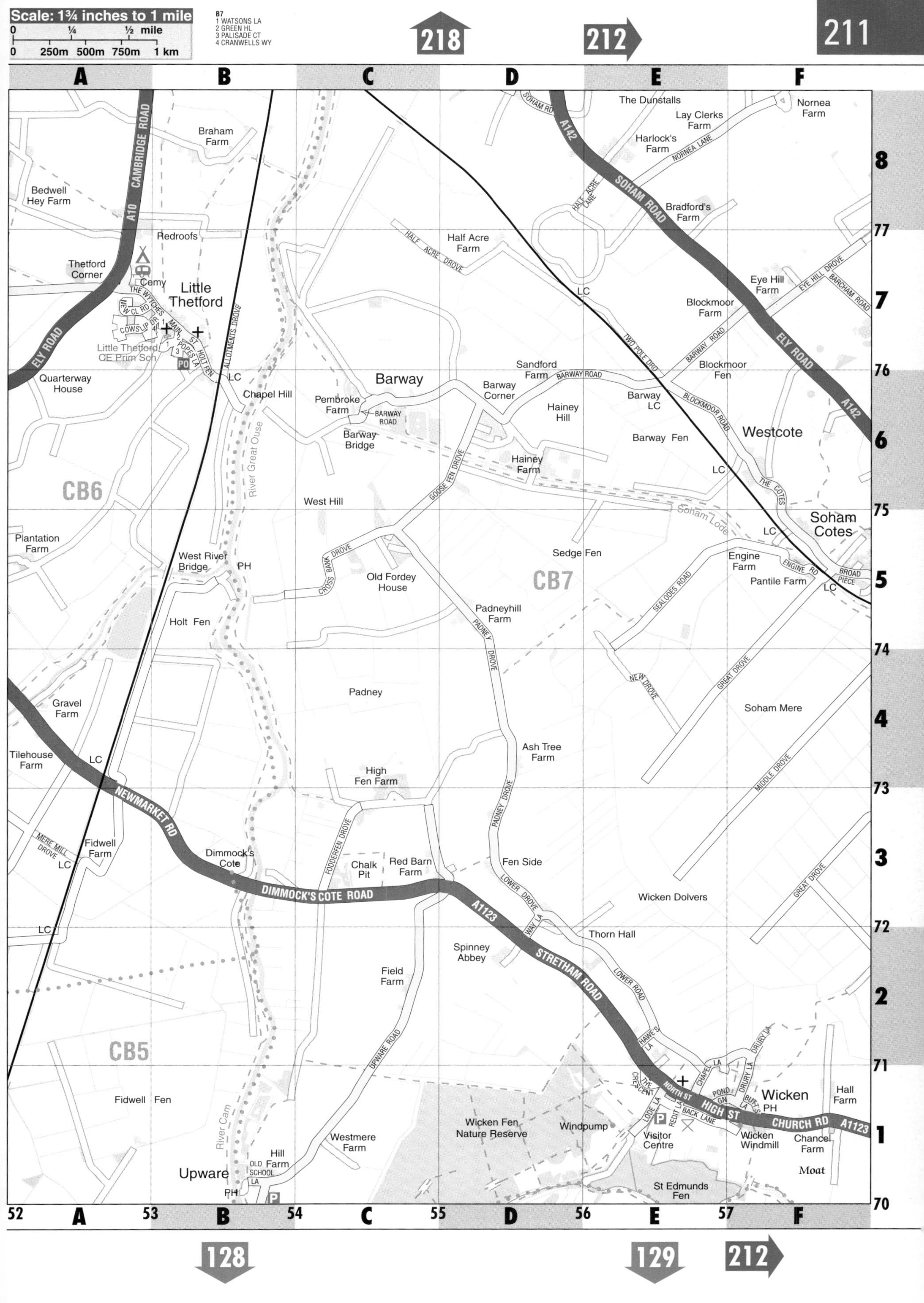
Scale: 1¾ inches to 1 mile
0 ¼ ½ mile
0 250m 500m 750m 1 km
B7
1 WATSONS LA
2 GREEN HL
3 PALISADE CT
4 CRANWELLS WY
A
B
C
D
E
F
8
77
7
76
6
75
5
74
4
73
3
72
2
71
1
70
52
53
54
55
56
57
A10 CAMBRIDGE ROAD
Braham Farm
Bedwell Hey Farm
Redroofs
Thetford Corner
Cemy
Little Thetford
THE WYTCHES
NEW CL RD
COWSLIP DR
MAIN ST
POPES LA
HOLT FEN
Little Thetford CE Prim Sch
PO
ELY ROAD
Quarterway House
ALLOTMENTS DROVE
LC
Chapel Hill
River Great Ouse
CB6
Plantation Farm
West River Bridge
PH
Holt Fen
Gravel Farm
Tilehouse Farm
NEWMARKET RD
MERE MILL DROVE
Fidwell Farm
Dimmock's Cote
DIMMOCK'S COTE ROAD
CB5
Fidwell Fen
River Cam
Upware
OLD SCHOOL LA
Hill Farm
UPWARE ROAD
Westmere Farm
Field Farm
Spinney Abbey
FODDERFEN DROVE
Chalk Pit
Red Barn Farm
High Fen Farm
Padney
Old Fordey House
CROSS BANK DROVE
West Hill
GOOSE FEN DROVE
Barway Bridge
Pembroke Farm
BARWAY ROAD
Barway
Half Acre Farm
HALF ACRE DROVE
Barway Corner
Sandford Farm
Hainey Hill
Hainey Farm
Padneyhill Farm
PADNEY DROVE
Ash Tree Farm
Fen Side
LOWER DROVE
WAY LA
A1123
STRETHAM ROAD
Thorn Hall
LOWER ROAD
HAWE'S LA
THE CRESCENT
LODE LA
REDIT LA
NORTH ST
HIGH ST
BACK LANE
CHAPEL LA
POND GN
DRURY LA
BUTTS LA
CHURCH RD
Wicken
PH
Wicken Windmill
Hall Farm
Chancel Farm
Moat
Wicken Fen Nature Reserve
Windpump
Visitor Centre
St Edmunds Fen
Wicken Dolvers
GREAT DROVE
MIDDLE DROVE
Soham Mere
NEW DROVE
SEALODES ROAD
Sedge Fen
CB7
Soham Lode
Engine Farm
ENGINE RD
Pantile Farm
BROAD PIECE
Soham Cotes
THE COTES
Westcote
Barway Fen
Barway LC
BLOCKMOOR ROAD
Blockmoor Fen
BARWAY ROAD
TWO POLE DRO
Blockmoor Farm
Eye Hill Farm
EYE HILL DROVE
BARCHAM ROAD
ELY ROAD
A142
SOHAM ROAD
HALF ACRE LANE
Bradford's Farm
Harlock's Farm
NORNEA LANE
Lay Clerks Farm
The Dunstalls
Nornea Farm
SOHAM RD

128
129
212

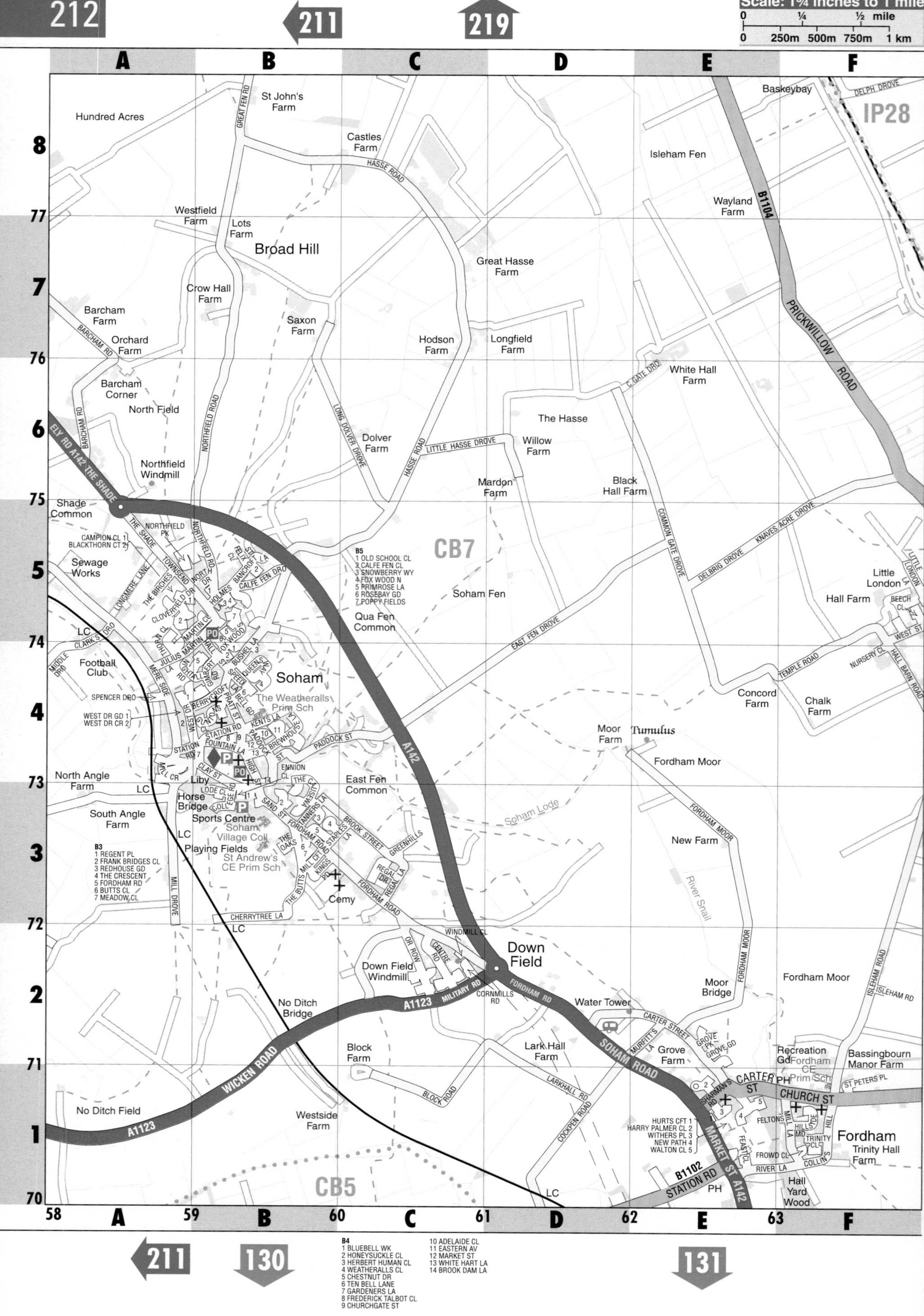
211
219
Scale: 1¾ inches to 1 mile
0 ¼ ½ mile
0 250m 500m 750m 1 km
A B C D E F
8
77
7
76
6
75
5
74
4
73
3
72
2
71
1
70
58 59 60 61 62 63
Hundred Acres
St John's Farm
GREAT FEN RD
Castles Farm
HASSE ROAD
Baskeybay
DELPH DROVE
IP28
Isleham Fen
Wayland Farm
B1104
Westfield Farm
Lots Farm
Broad Hill
Great Hasse Farm
Crow Hall Farm
Barcham Farm
BARCHAM RD
Orchard Farm
Saxon Farm
Hodson Farm
Longfield Farm
PRICKWILLOW ROAD
White Hall Farm
C GATE DRO
Barcham Corner
North Field
NORTHFIELD ROAD
LONG DOLVER DROVE
The Hasse
Dolver Farm
HASSE ROAD
LITTLE HASSE DROVE
Willow Farm
ELY RD A142 THE SHADE
Northfield Windmill
Mardon Farm
Black Hall Farm
Shade Common
THE SHADE
NORTHFIELD PK
CAMPION CL 1
BLACKTHORN CT 2
COMMON GATE DROVE
KNAVES ACRE DROVE
DELBRIG DROVE
CB7
Sewage Works
B5
1 OLD SCHOOL CL
2 CALFE FEN CL
3 SNOWBERRY WY
4 FOX WOOD N
5 PRIMROSE LA
6 ROSEBAY GD
7 POPPY FIELDS
Soham Fen
Little London
LITTLE LONDON LA
Hall Farm
BEECH CL
WEST ST
Qua Fen Common
EAST FEN DROVE
LC
CLARK'S DRO
Football Club
MIDDLE DRO
Soham
The Weatheralls Prim Sch
NURSERY CL
TEMPLE ROAD
HALL BARN ROAD
SPENCER DRO
Concord Farm
Chalk Farm
WEST DR GD 1
WEST DR CR 2
Moor Farm
Tumulus
PADDOCK ST
Fordham Moor
North Angle Farm
Liby
Horse Bridge
East Fen Common
A142
South Angle Farm
Sports Centre
Soham Village Coll
Soham Lode
FORDHAM MOOR
New Farm
B3
1 REGENT PL
2 FRANK BRIDGES CL
3 REDHOUSE GD
4 THE CRESCENT
5 FORDHAM RD
6 BUTTS CL
7 MEADOW CL
Playing Fields
St Andrew's CE Prim Sch
BROOK STREET
GREENHILLS
River Snail
MILL DROVE
Cemy
FORDHAM ROAD
CHERRYTREE LA
WINDMILL CL
Down Field
Down Field Windmill
FORDHAM MOOR
Moor Bridge
Fordham Moor
ISLEHAM ROAD
ISLEHAM RD
No Ditch Bridge
A1123
MILITARY RD
CORNMILLS RD
FORDHAM RD
Water Tower
CARTER STREET
Block Farm
Lark Hall Farm
Grove Farm
GROVE PK
GROVE GD
Recreation Gd
Fordham CE Prim Sch
Bassingbourn Manor Farm
WICKEN ROAD
SOHAM ROAD
LARKHALL RD
BLOCK ROAD
CARTER ST
CHURCH ST
ST PETERS PL
No Ditch Field
A1123
Westside Farm
COCKPEN ROAD
HURTS CFT 1
HARRY PALMER CL 2
WITHERS PL 3
NEW PATH 4
WALTON CL 5
MARKET ST A142
FELTONS
Fordham
Trinity Hall Farm
FROWD CL
RIVER LA
COLLINS
CB5
B1102
STATION RD
PH
Hall Yard Wood
LC
211
130
131
B4
1 BLUEBELL WK
2 HONEYSUCKLE CL
3 HERBERT HUMAN CL
4 WEATHERALLS CL
5 CHESTNUT DR
6 TEN BELL LANE
7 GARDENERS LA
8 FREDERICK TALBOT CL
9 CHURCHGATE ST
10 ADELAIDE CL
11 EASTERN AV
12 MARKET ST
13 WHITE HART LA
14 BROOK DAM LA

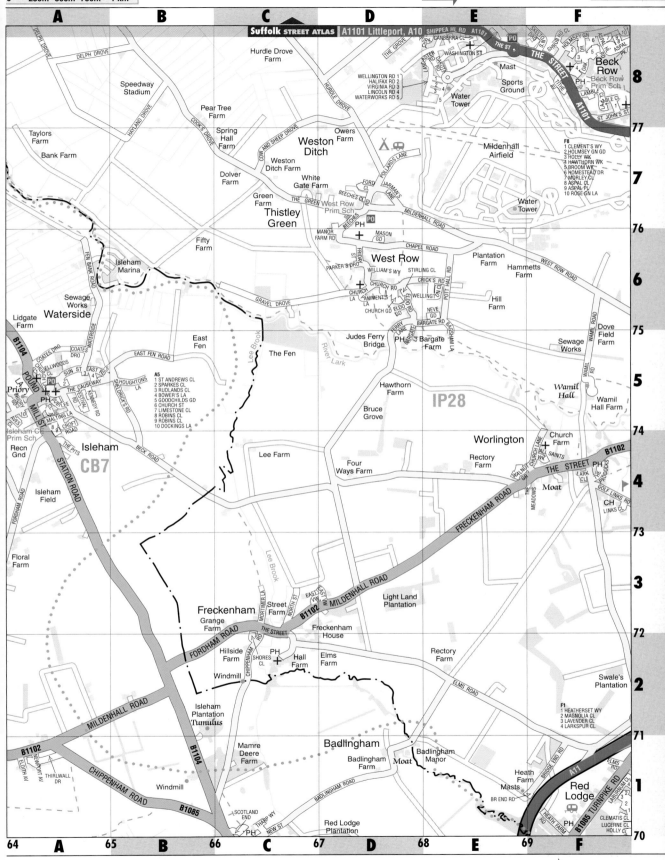

Scale: 1¾ inches to 1 mile

0   ¼   ½   mile
0 250m 500m 750m 1 km

A   B   C   D   E   F

8
77
7
76
6
75
5
74
4
73
3
72
2
71
1
70

Beck Row
Beck Row Prim Sch

F8
1 CLEMENT'S WY
2 HOLMSEY GN GD
3 HOLLY WK
4 HAWTHORN WK
5 BROOM WK
6 HOMESTEAD DR
7 MORLEY CL
8 ASPAL CL
9 ASPAL PL
10 ROSE GN LA

WELLINGTON RD 1
HALIFAX RD 2
VIRGINIA RD 3
LINCOLN RD 4
WATERWORKS RD 5

Washington St
Mast
Sports Ground
Water Tower

Speedway Stadium
Taylors Farm
Bank Farm
Pear Tree Farm
Spring Hall Farm
Dolver Farm

Hurdle Drove Farm
Owers Farm
Weston Ditch
Weston Ditch Farm
White Gate Farm
Green Farm

Mildenhall Airfield
Water Tower

Thistley Green
West Row Prim Sch
PO
PH

Fifty Farm
Isleham Marina

Sewage Works
Waterside
Lidgate Farm

East Fen
East Fen Road
The Fen

A5
1 ST ANDREWS CL
2 SPARKES CL
3 RUDLANDS CL
4 BOWER'S LA
5 GOODCHILDS GD
6 CHURCH ST
7 LIMESTONE CL
8 ROBINS CL
9 ROBINS CL
10 DOCKINGS LA

Manor Farm Rd
West Row
Plantation Farm
Hammetts Farm

Parker's Dro
Church La
Church Gd

Hill Farm

Judes Ferry Bridge
PH
Bargate Farm

Hawthorn Farm
Bruce Grove

IP28

Sewage Works

Dove Field Farm

Wamil Hall
Wamil Hall Farm

Priory
PH
Isleham CE Prim Sch
Recn Gnd
Isleham
CB7

Lee Farm

Four Ways Farm

Rectory Farm
Worlington
Church Farm
All Saints
B1102
PH
Moat
CH
GOLF LINKS RD
LINKS CL

Isleham Field

FREKENHAM ROAD
THE STREET

Floral Farm

Lee Brook

Light Land Plantation

Freckenham
Grange Farm
Street Farm
Freckenham House
B1102 Mildenhall Road

Rectory Farm

Swale's Plantation

Hillside Farm
PH
Windmill
Hall Farm
Elms Farm
Elms Road

F1
1 HEATHERSET WY
2 MAGNOLIA CL
3 LAVENDER CL
4 LARKSPUR CL

Isleham Plantation
Tumulus

Mamre Deere Farm
Badlingham
Badlingham Farm
Moat
Badlingham Manor

Heath Farm Masts

Red Lodge

B1104
B1102
NEWPORT AV
ELDITH AV
THIRLWALL DR
Windmill
CHIPPENHAM ROAD
B1085
SCOTLAND END
THARP WY
NEW ST
PH
Badlingham Road
Red Lodge Plantation
BR END RD
PH
A11
B1085 TURNPIKE RD
CLEMATIS CL
LUCERNE CL
HOLLY CL

MILDENHALL ROAD
FORDHAM ROAD
STATION ROAD
FORDHAM ROAD

64   65   66   67   68   69

A   B   C   D   E   F

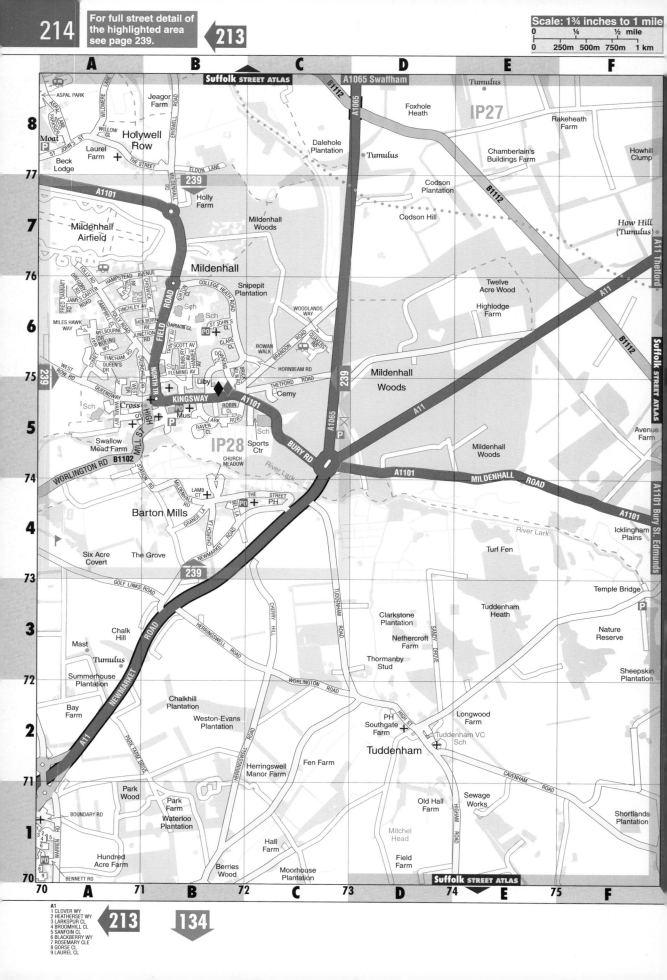

214

For full street detail of
the highlighted area
see page 239.

213

Scale: 1¾ inches to 1 mile
0   ¼   ½ mile
0   250m 500m 750m 1 km

A B C D E F

8

← ASPAL PARK
ASPAL LANE
PARSING LANE
WILDMERE LANE
ERISWELL ROAD
WILLOW CL

Jeagor
Farm

Suffolk STREET ATLAS

A1065 Swaffham

B1112

A1065

IP27

Foxhole
Heath

Tumulus

Rakeheath
Farm

Moat
P
Holywell
Row

77

Beck
Lodge
Laurel
Farm
ST JOHN'S ST
THE STREET
ELDON LANE
239
THURLOW RD

Dalehole
Plantation

Tumulus

Chamberlain's
Buildings Farm

Howhill
Clump

A1101

Holly
Farm

Codson
Plantation

B1112

7

Mildenhall
Airfield

Mildenhall
Woods

Codson Hill

How Hill
(*Tumulus*)

76

FOLLY RD
GREGORY RD
FRED DANNATT
JAMES CARTER
CAMPBELL ROAD
FINCHLEY AV
Ind
Est
Sch
CHISWICK RD
HAMPSTEAD AVENUE
NUNS CL
GIFFORD RD
COLLEGE HEATH ROAD
FIELD ROAD
NORTH TR

Mildenhall

Snipepit
Plantation

WOODLANDS
WAY

A11 Thetford

B1112

Suffolk STREET ATLAS

Twelve
Acre Wood

Highlodge
Farm

6

MILES HAWK
WAY
MELBOURNE
DR
BOEING
WY
COMET CL
FINCHAM RD
QUEEN'S
DR
HOLBORN CL
PO
DARWIN CL
TRINITY AV
SCOTT AV
JUNCTION
RD
BLUBELL
HAMMER
FLEMING AV
ST JOHN'S
CL
CLARE
CL
DOWNING
CL
BRICK
KILN RD
BRANDON ROAD
CLIMERS
CL
Sch
ROWAN
WALK
HORNBEAM RD
THETFORD   ROAD

Mildenhall
Woods

Avenue
Farm

75

239
WEST
ROW RD
QUEENSWAY
HIGH ST
WEST
ST
CROSS
Sch
PO
Mus
P
KINGSWAY
ROBIN
CL
LARK
ROAD
RAVEN
CL
Libry
A1101
Cemy
239
A1065
A11

Mildenhall
Woods

5

Swallow
Mead Farm
IP28
Sports
Ctr
Sch
CHURCH
MEADOW
BURY RD
P

Mildenhall
Woods

Avenue
Farm

74

WORLINGTON RD
B1102
STATION RD
MILDENHALL
RD
LAMB
CT
BELL LA
PO
THE
STREET
PH
River Lark
A1101   MILDENHALL   ROAD
A1101 Bury St. Edmunds

4

Six Acre
Covert
The Grove
Barton Mills
GRANGE LA
CHURCH LA
NEWMARKET
ROAD
TUDDENHAM
ROAD
SANDY
DROVE

River Lark

Turf Fen

Icklingham
Plains

73

GOLF LINKS ROAD
239
CHERRY
HILL

Clarkstone
Plantation

Tuddenham
Heath

Temple Bridge
P

3

Mast
Chalk
Hill
Tumulus
ROAD
HERRINGSWELL   ROAD

Nethercroft
Farm
Thormanby
Stud

Nature
Reserve

72

Summerhouse
Plantation
Chalkhill
Plantation
NEWMARKET
WORLINGTON   ROAD

Sheepskin
Plantation

2

Bay
Farm
A11
PARK FARM DRIVE
Weston-Evans
Plantation
HERRINGSWELL   ROAD
Fen Farm
PH
Southgate
Farm
HIGH ST
Tuddenham VC
Sch
Longwood
Farm

Tuddenham

71

BOUNDARY RD
WARREN RD
Park
Wood
Park
Farm
Herringswell
Manor Farm
Old Hall
Farm
Sewage
Works
HIGHAM
ROAD
CAVENHAM   ROAD
Shortlands
Plantation

1

1
2
3 4
5
6
7
8
9
PO
BENNETT RD
Waterloo
Plantation
Hall
Farm
Mitchel
Head
Field
Farm

70

Hundred
Acre Farm
Berries
Wood
Moorhouse
Plantation

Suffolk STREET ATLAS

A 70 71 B 72 C 73 D 74 E 75 F

A1
1 CLOVER WY
2 HEATHERSET WY
3 LARKSPUR CL
4 BROOMHILL CL
5 SANFOIN CL
6 BLACKBERRY WY
7 ROSEMARY CLE
8 GORSE CL
9 LAUREL CL

213

134

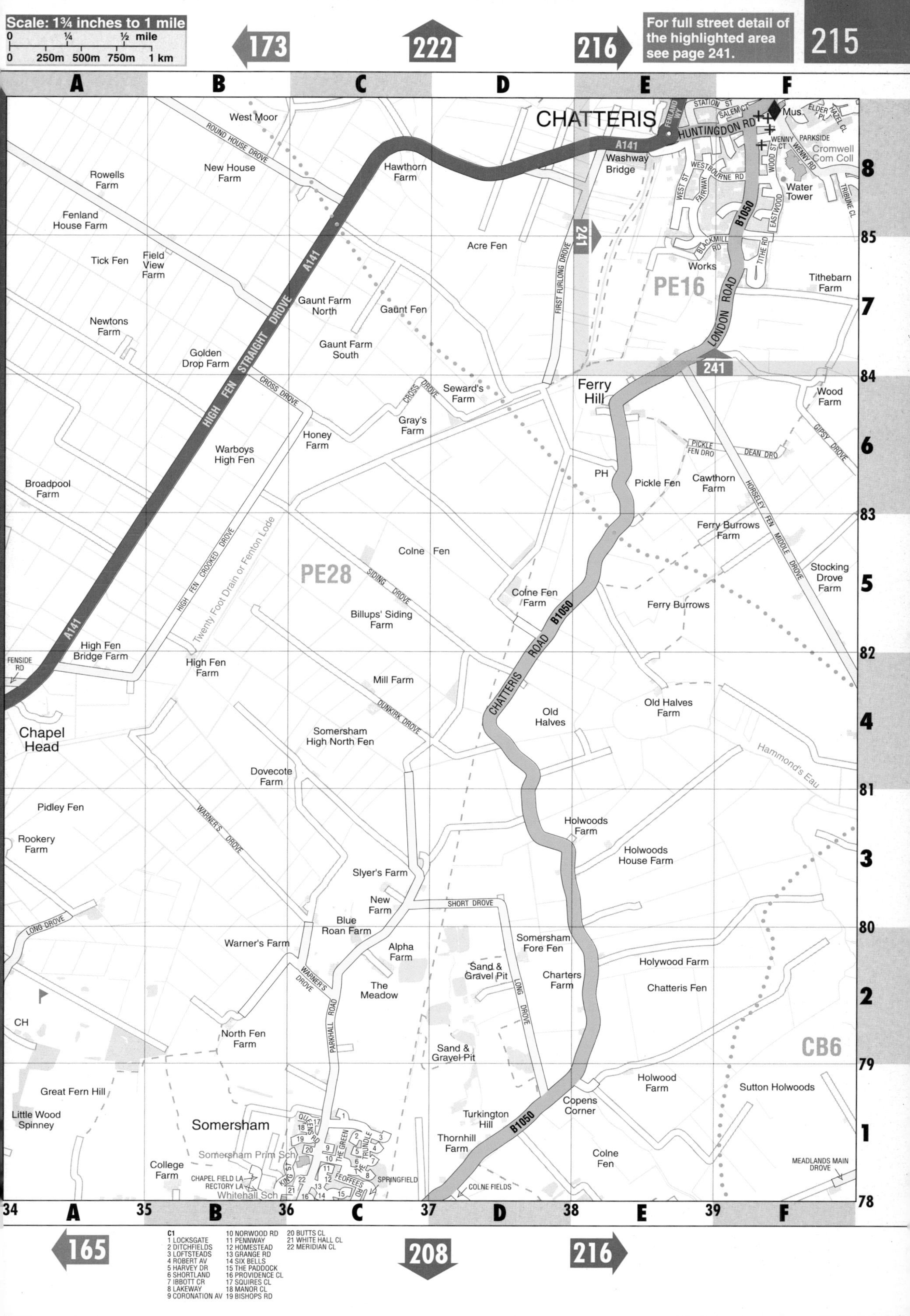

Scale: 1¾ inches to 1 mile

0   ¼   ½   mile
0   250m 500m 750m   1 km

173

222

216

For full street detail of
the highlighted area
see page 241.

215

A   B   C   D   E   F

West Moor

ROUND HOUSE DROVE

CHATTERIS

Rowells
Farm

New House
Farm

Hawthorn
Farm

Washway
Bridge

HUNTINGDON RD

STATION ST
SALEM CT

Mus.
ELDER HAZEL PL

WENNY PARKSIDE

Cromwell
Com Coll

8

Fenland
House Farm

WEST ST

PARKWAY

WESTBOURNE RD

WOOD ST

WENNY RD

Water
Tower

TRIBUNE CL

85

Tick Fen

Field
View
Farm

Acre Fen

FIRST FURLONG DROVE

241

BLACKMILL RD

B1050

PE16

Works

LONDON ROAD

TITHE RD

Titheborn
Farm

7

Newtons
Farm

HIGH FEN STRAIGHT DROVE

A141

Gaunt Farm
North

Gaunt Fen

241

84

Golden
Drop Farm

Gaunt Farm
South

CROSS DROVE

Seward's
Farm

Ferry
Hill

Wood
Farm

GYPSY DROVE

6

Broadpool
Farm

HIGH FEN CROOKED DROVE

Honey
Farm

CROSS DROVE

Gray's
Farm

PH

Pickle Fen

PICKLE
FEN DRO

DEAN DRO

Cawthorn
Farm

HORSELEY FEN MIDDLE DROVE

83

A141

Twenty Foot Drain or Fenton Lode

PE28

Warboys
High Fen

Colne Fen

SIDING DROVE

Ferry Burrows
Farm

Stocking
Drove
Farm

5

High Fen
Bridge Farm

Billups' Siding
Farm

Colne Fen
Farm

B1050

Ferry Burrows

82

FENSIDE
RD

High Fen
Farm

Mill Farm

DUNKIRK DROVE

CHATTERIS ROAD

Old Halves
Farm

Hammond's Eau

4

Chapel
Head

Somersham
High North Fen

Old
Halves

81

Pidley Fen

Dovecote
Farm

WARNER'S DROVE

Holwoods
Farm

Holwoods
House Farm

3

Rookery
Farm

Slyer's Farm

New
Farm

SHORT DROVE

LONG DROVE

80

LONG DROVE

Warner's Farm

Blue
Roan Farm

Alpha
Farm

Somersham
Fore Fen

Holywood Farm

Chatteris Fen

2

CH

The
Meadow

PARKHALL ROAD

Sand &
Gravel Pit

Charters
Farm

CB6

North Fen
Farm

Sand &
Gravel Pit

79

Great Fern Hill

Holwood
Farm

Sutton Holwoods

MEADLANDS MAIN
DROVE

Little Wood
Spinney

WARNER'S DROVE

Somersham

QUEENS
RD

KINGS ST

THE GREEN

TC TRUNDLE

SPRINGFIELD

Turkington
Hill

Thornhill
Farm

B1050

Copens
Corner

Colne
Fen

1

College
Farm

Somersham Prim Sch

CHAPEL FIELD LA
RECTORY LA

Whitehall Sch

FEOFFEES

COLNE FIELDS

78

34   A   35   B   36   C   37   D   38   E   39   F   78

C1
1 LOCKSGATE
2 DITCHFIELDS
3 LOFTSTEADS
4 ROBERT AV
5 HARVEY DR
6 SHORTLAND
7 IBBOTT CR
8 LAKEWAY
9 CORONATION AV
10 NORWOOD RD
11 PENNWAY
12 HOMESTEAD
13 GRANGE RD
14 SIX BELLS
15 THE PADDOCK
16 PROVIDENCE CL
17 SQUIRES CL
18 MANOR CL
19 BISHOPS RD
20 BUTTS CL
21 WHITE HALL CL
22 MERIDIAN CL

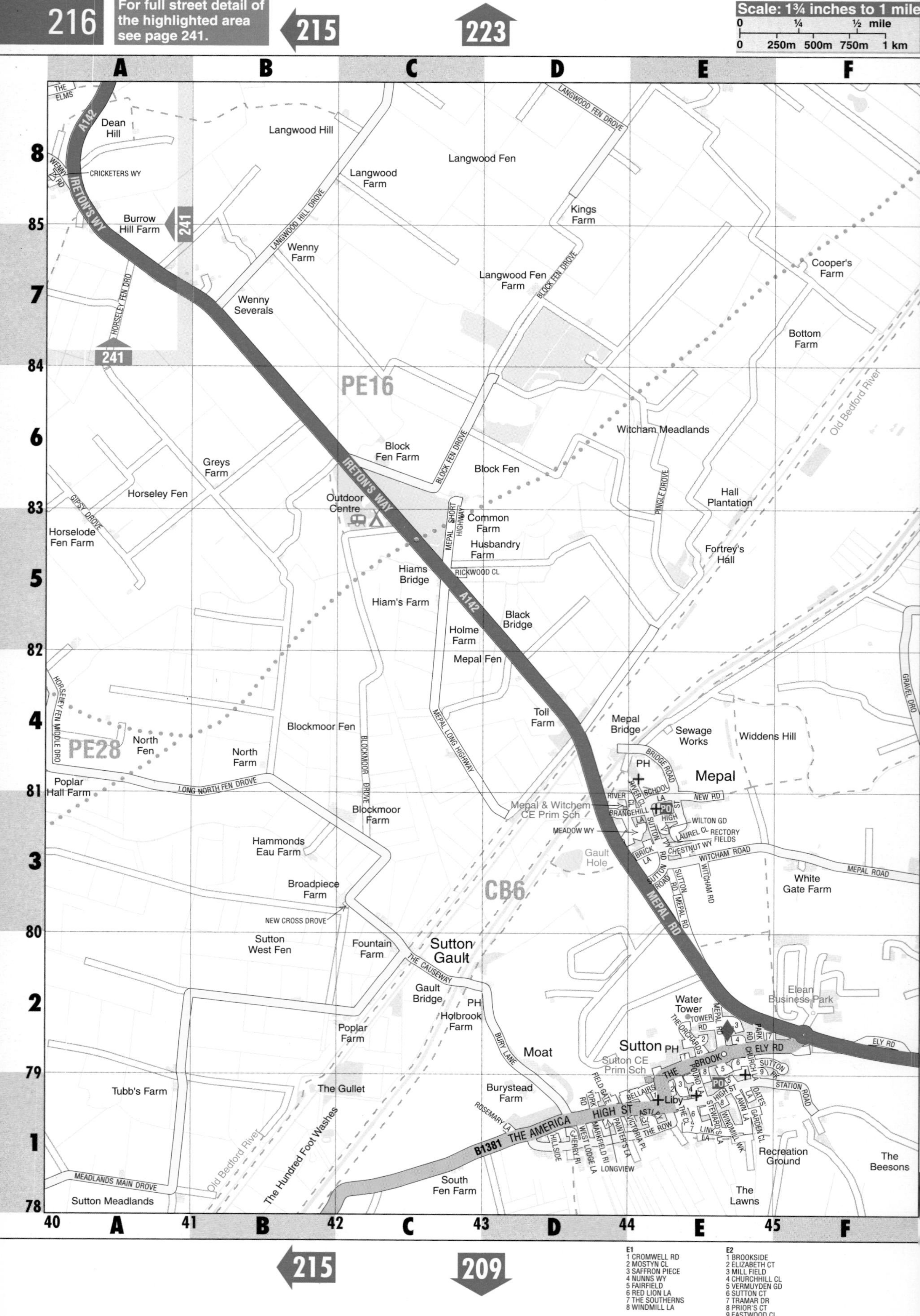
216
For full street detail of the highlighted area see page 241.
215
223
Scale: 1¾ inches to 1 mile
0 ¼ ½ mile
0 250m 500m 750m 1 km
A B C D E F
THE ELMS
Dean Hill
A142
WENNY RD
CRICKETERS WY
IRETON'S WY
Langwood Hill
Langwood Farm
Langwood Fen
LANGWOOD FEN DROVE
Kings Farm
Burrow Hill Farm
241
LANGWOOD HILL DROVE
Wenny Farm
Langwood Fen Farm
BLOCK FEN DROVE
Cooper's Farm
HORSELEY FEN DRO
Wenny Severals
Bottom Farm
PE16
Old Bedford River
Witcham Meadlands
Block Fen Farm
Greys Farm
Block Fen
Horseley Fen
IRETON'S WAY
Outdoor Centre
MEPAL SHORT HIGHWAY
Common Farm
PINGLE DROVE
Hall Plantation
GIPSY DROVE
Horselode Fen Farm
Husbandry Farm
Fortrey's Hall
Hiams Bridge
RICKWOOD CL
Hiam's Farm
A142
Black Bridge
Holme Farm
Mepal Fen
GRAVEL DRO
HORSELEY FEN MIDDLE DRO
Toll Farm
Mepal Bridge
Sewage Works
Widdens Hill
Blockmoor Fen
MEPAL LONG HIGHWAY
BLOCKMOOR DROVE
PE28
North Fen
North Farm
BRIDGE ROAD
PH
Mepal
Poplar Hall Farm
LONG NORTH FEN DROVE
RIVER CL
SCHOOL LA
NEW RD
RIVER
Mepal & Witchem CE Prim Sch
BRANGEHILL LA
PO
HIGH ST
WILTON GD
Blockmoor Farm
MEADOW WY
SUTTON RD
LAUREL CL
RECTORY FIELDS
CHESTNUT WY
Hammonds Eau Farm
BRICK LA
WITCHAM ROAD
Gault Hole
MEPAL ROAD
White Gate Farm
SUTTON ROAD
SUTTON RD
MEPAL RD
WITCHAM RD
Broadpiece Farm
CB6
MEPAL RD
NEW CROSS DROVE
Sutton West Fen
Fountain Farm
Sutton Gault
THE CAUSEWAY
Elean Business Park
Gault Bridge
PH
Water Tower
TOWER RD
Holbrook Farm
Poplar Farm
THE ORCHARDS
PARK RD
ELY RD
BURY LANE
Moat
Sutton
PH
THE BROOK
CHURCH LA
Sutton CE Prim Sch
SUTTON PK
FIELD GATE
BELLAIRS
Tubb's Farm
The Gullet
Burystead Farm
YORK RD
GROUND LA
PO
STATION ROAD
Liby
HIGH ST
OATES LA
ROSEMARY LA
THE AMERICA
HIGH ST
ASTLEY
STEWARD'S LA
LAWN LA
GARDEN CL
The Hundred Foot Washes
B1381
PAINTER'S LA
THE ROW
THE CL
LINK LA
WINDMILL WK
Old Bedford River
HILLSIDE
CHERRY RI
MARKFIELD RI
WEST LODGE LA
VICTORIA PL
Recreation Ground
The Beesons
MEADLANDS MAIN DROVE
LONGVIEW
South Fen Farm
The Lawns
Sutton Meadlands
8
85
7
84
6
83
5
82
4
81
3
80
2
79
1
78
40 41 42 43 44 45
215
209
E1
1 CROMWELL RD
2 MOSTYN CL
3 SAFFRON PIECE
4 NUNNS WY
5 FAIRFIELD
6 RED LION LA
7 THE SOUTHERNS
8 WINDMILL LA
E2
1 BROOKSIDE
2 ELIZABETH CT
3 MILL FIELD
4 CHURCHHILL CL
5 VERMUYDEN GD
6 SUTTON CT
7 TRAMAR DR
8 PRIOR'S CT
9 EASTWOOD CL

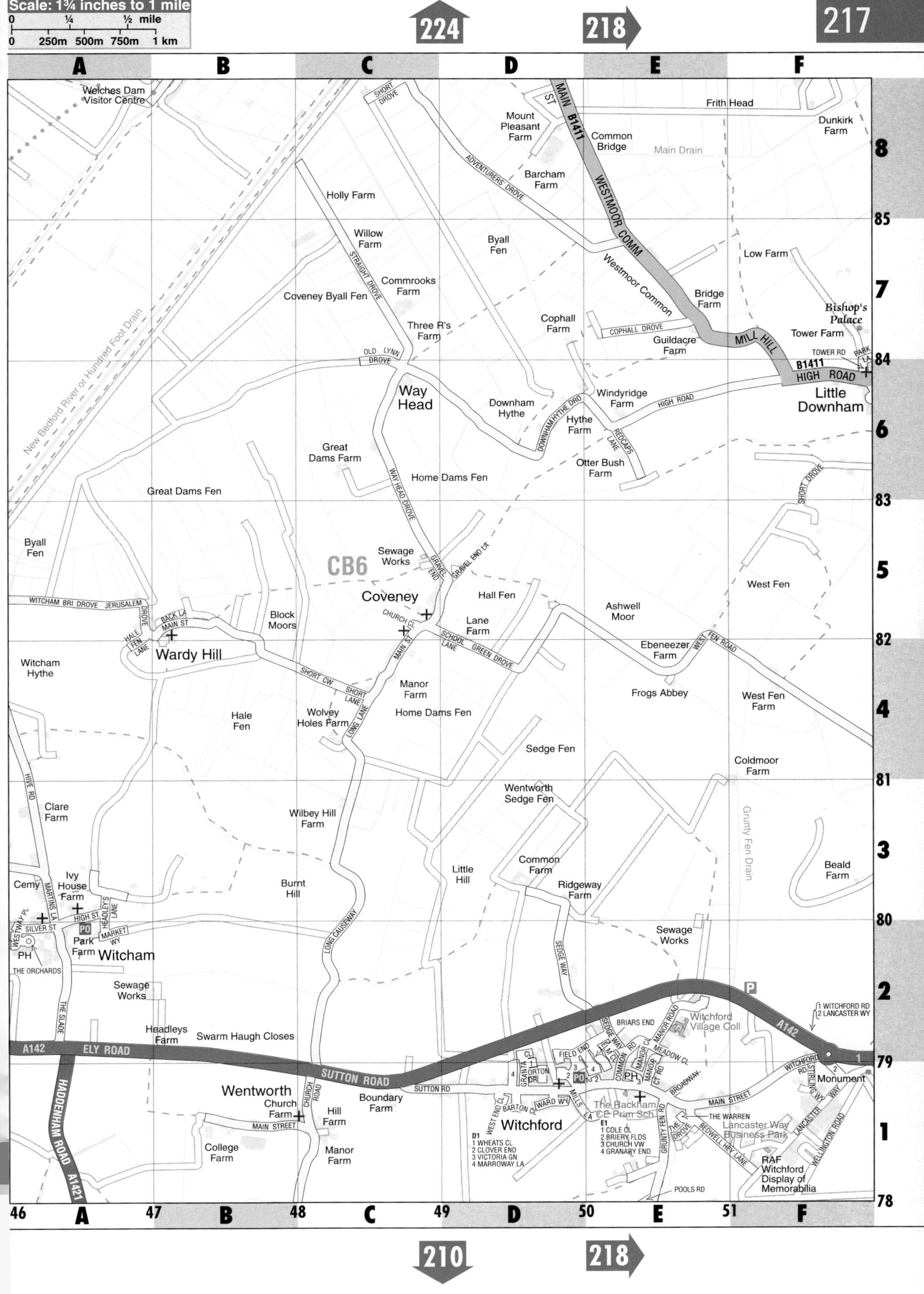

Scale: 1¾ inches to 1 mile

0   ¼   ½   mile
0   250m   500m   750m   1 km

A   B   C   D   E   F

224
218

Welches Dam Visitor Centre

Frith Head

Dunkirk Farm

8

Main Drain

Mount Pleasant Farm

ST

B1411

Common Bridge

Barcham Farm

Holly Farm

85

WESTMOOR COMM

Willow Farm

Byall Fen

Low Farm

7

Commrooks Farm

Coveney Byall Fen

STRAIGHT DROVE

Westmoor Common

Bridge Farm

Bishop's Palace

Tower Farm

Three R's Farm

Cophall Farm

COPHALL DROVE

Guildacre Farm

MILL HILL

TOWER RD

PARK LA

84

OLD LYNN DROVE

Way Head

Downham Hythe

Windyridge Farm

B1411

HIGH ROAD

Little Downham

DOWNHAMHYTHE DRO

Hythe Farm

HIGH ROAD

6

Great Dams Farm

REDCARS LANE

Otter Bush Farm

WAY HEAD DROVE

Home Dams Fen

83

Great Dams Fen

SHORT DROVE

Byall Fen

Sewage Works

West Fen

5

CB6

GRANGE END

Coveney

Hall Fen

Ashwell Moor

WITCHAM BRI DROVE   JERUSALEM

CHURCH CL

GRAVEL END LA

Lane Farm

WEST FEN ROAD

BACK LA

MAIN ST

SCHOOL LANE

GREEN DROVE

Ebeneezer Farm

82

HALE FEN LANE

Wardy Hill

MAIN ST

Frogs Abbey

Witcham Hythe

SHORT CW

Manor Farm

Home Dams Fen

West Fen Farm

4

SHORT LANE

Hale Fen

Wolvey Holes Farm

LONG LANE

Sedge Fen

Coldmoor Farm

81

Clare Farm

Wilbey Hill Farm

HIVE RD

Wentworth Sedge Fen

Grunty Fen Drain

Beald Farm

3

Ivy House Farm

Burnt Hill

Little Hill

Common Farm

Ridgeway Farm

Cemy

MARTINS LA

HIGH ST

HEADLEY LANE

LONG CAUSEWAY

Sewage Works

80

WESTWA PL

SILVER ST

PO

MARKET WY

SEDGE WAY

P

A142

1 WITCHFORD RD
2 LANCASTER WY

PH

Park Farm

Witcham

THE ORCHARDS

THE SLADE

Sewage Works

Headleys Farm

Swarm Haugh Closes

BRIARS END

Witchford Village Coll

2

SEDGE WAY NTH

MANOR ROAD

MEADOW CL

Monument

A142

ELY ROAD

SUTTON ROAD

CL

FIELD END

MANOR CL

Witchford

RD

BROADWAY

WITCHFORD RD

WELLINGTON WAY

79

HADDENHAM ROAD

A1421

Wentworth

Church Farm

CHURCH ROAD

Hill Farm

Boundary Farm

SUTTON RD

GRANTA

MORTON CL

BARTON CL

WARD

MILLS

WEST END CL

PO

PH

The Rackham CE Prim Sch

Lancaster Way Business Park

THE WARREN

MAIN STREET

LANCASTER ROAD

BIDWELL NEY LANE

1

MAIN STREET

Witchford

D1
1 WHEATS CL
2 CLOVER END
3 VICTORIA GN
4 MARROWAY LA

E1
1 COLE CL
2 BRIERY FLDS
3 CHURCH VW
4 GRANARY END

GRUNTY FEN RD

RAF Witchford Display of Memorabilia

College Farm

MAIN STREET

Manor Farm

POOLS RD

78

46   A   47   B   48   C   49   D   50   E   51   F

210
218

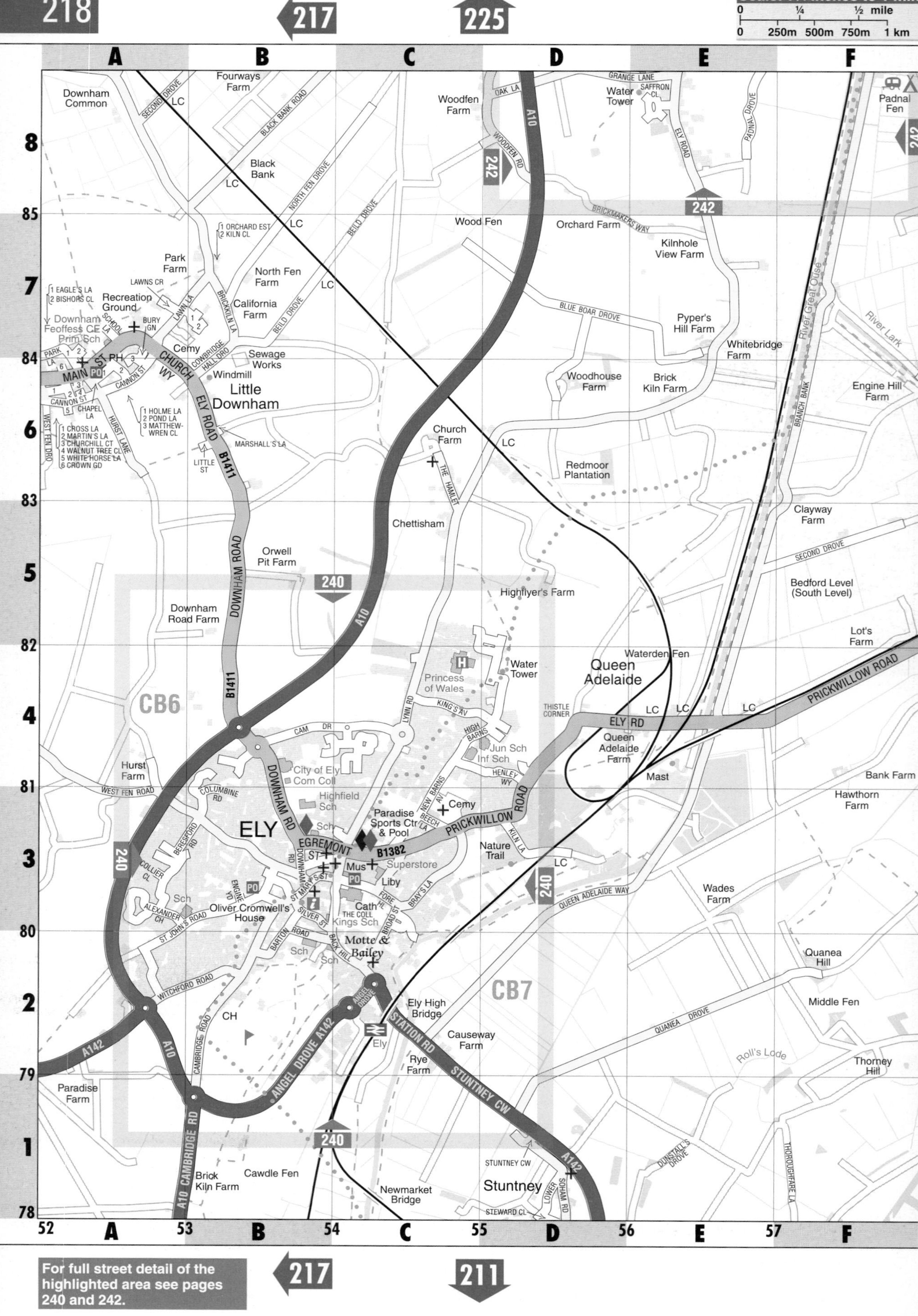

Scale: 1¾ inches to 1 mile
0   ¼   ½ mile
0   250m 500m 750m 1 km

A   B   C   D   E   F

Downham Common
Fourways Farm
Second Drove
LC
Black Bank Road
Black Bank
North Fen Drove
Beld Drove
LC
Woodfen Farm
Oak La
A10
Woodfen Rd
242
Water Tower
Grange Lane
Saffron Cl
Padnal Drive
Ely Road
Padnal Fen
242

8

LC
1 ORCHARD EST
2 KILN CL
LC
Wood Fen
Brickmakers Way
242
Orchard Farm
Kilnhole View Farm
River Lark

85

Park Farm
Lawns Cr
North Fen Farm
Beld Drove
LC
Blue Boar Drove
Pyper's Hill Farm
Whitebridge Farm
River Great Ouse

7

1 EAGLE'S LA
2 BISHORS CL
Recreation Ground
Downham Feoffess CE Prim Sch
School Dro
Lawn La
Bury Gn
Brackln La
California Farm
Cambridge Hall Dro
Sewage Works
Woodhouse Farm
Brick Kiln Farm
Branch Bank
Engine Hill Farm

84

Park La
Main St
PH
Church Wy
Windmill
Little Downham
Church Farm
The Hamlet
LC
Redmoor Plantation
Cannon St
Chapel La
1 CROSS LA
2 MARTIN'S LA
3 CHURCHILL CT
4 WALNUT TREE CL
5 WHITE HORSE LA
6 CROWN GD
Ely Road
1 HOLME LA
2 POND LA
3 MATTHEW-WREN CL
Marshall's La
B1411
Little St

6

West Fen Dro
Chettisham
Clayway Farm
Second Drove

83

Downham Road
Orwell Pit Farm
240
Highflyer's Farm
Bedford Level (South Level)
Lot's Farm

5

Downham Road Farm
A10
Water Tower
Queen Adelaide
Waterden Fen
Prickwillow Road

82

CB6
B1411
Princess of Wales
H
King's Av
Lynn Rd
Thistle Corner
Ely Rd
LC LC LC
Queen Adelaide Farm
Bank Farm
Hawthorn Farm

4

Hurst Farm
West Fen Road
Cam Dr
City of Ely Com Coll
Columbine Rd
Highfield Sch
Sch
High Barns
Jun Sch Inf Sch
Henley Wy
New Barns
Prickwillow Road
Mast

81

ELY
Downham Rd
Beech Av
Cemy
Kiln La
Beccford Rd
Collier Cl
Sch
Egremont St
Mus PO
Paradise Sports Ctr & Pool
Superstore
Liby
Nature Trail
Queen Adelaide Way
A10
LC
Wades Farm

3

Alexander Ch
Engine Yd
PO
Oliver Cromwell's House
St John's Road
St Mary's St
Cath
THE COLL
Kings Sch
Fore
Broad St
Box's La
Barton Road
Back Hill
Motte & Bailey
Sch
240

2

Witchford Road
CH
Angel Drove A142
Angel Bridge
Ely High Bridge
Station Rd
Ely
Causeway Farm
CB7
Quanea Drove
Quanea Hill
Middle Fen

A142
A10
Cambridge Road
Rye Farm
Stuntney Cw
Roll's Lode
Thorney Hill

79

Paradise Farm
240
Cawdle Fen
Newmarket Bridge
Stuntney
A142
Soham Rd
Lower Rd
Dunstall's Drive
Thoroughfare La

1

A10 Cambridge Rd
Brick Kiln Farm
Stuntney CW
Steward Cl

78

52 A 53 B 54 C 55 D 56 E 57 F

For full street detail of the highlighted area see pages 240 and 242.

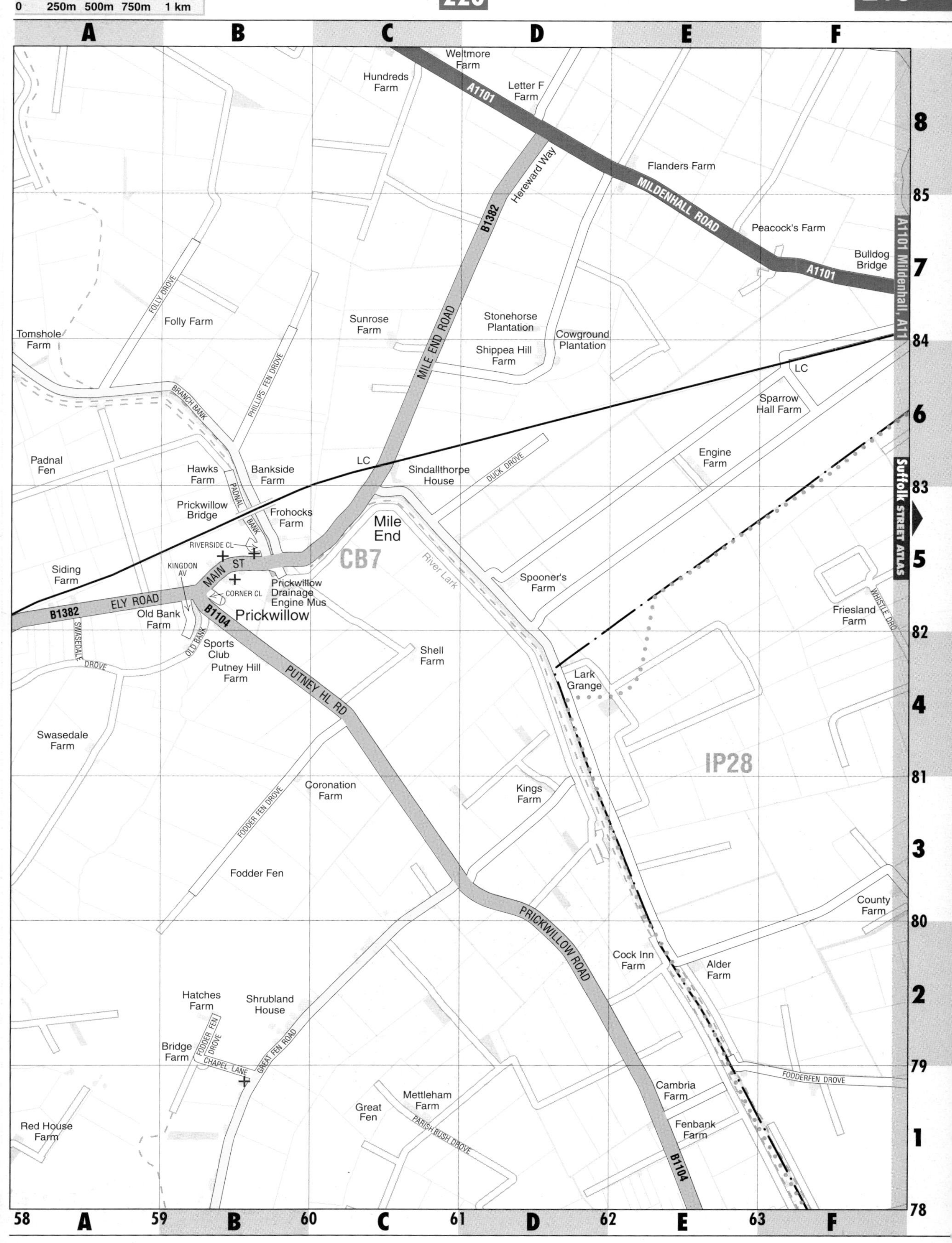

A   B   C   D   E   F

8
85
7
84
6
83
5
82
4
81
3
80
2
79
1
78

Weltmore Farm
A1101
Letter F Farm
Hundreds Farm
Hereward Way
MILDENHALL ROAD
Flanders Farm
Peacock's Farm
B1382
Bulldog Bridge
A1101
A1101 Mildenhall, A11

Suffolk STREET ATLAS

Tomshole Farm
Folly Farm
FOLLY DROVE
PHILLIPS FEN DROVE
Sunrose Farm
MILE END ROAD
Stonehorse Plantation
Shippea Hill Farm
Cowground Plantation
LC
Sparrow Hall Farm

Padnal Fen
BRANCH BANK
Hawks Farm
Bankside Farm
PADNAL BANK
LC
Sindallthorpe House
DUCK DROVE
Engine Farm

Prickwillow Bridge
Frohocks Farm
Mile End
River Lark
Spooner's Farm
WHISTLE DROVE
Friesland Farm

Siding Farm
RIVERSIDE CL
MAIN ST
KINGDON AV
CORNER CL
CB7
Prickwillow Drainage Engine Mus

Lark Grange

SWASEDALE DROVE
B1382
ELY ROAD
Old Bank Farm
OLD BANK
B1104
Prickwillow
Sports Club
Putney Hill Farm
Shell Farm

Swasedale Farm
FODDER FEN DROVE
PUTNEY HL RD
Coronation Farm
Kings Farm
IP28
County Farm

Fodder Fen
PRICKWILLOW ROAD
Cock Inn Farm
Alder Farm

Hatches Farm
Shrubland House
FODDER FEN DROVE
GREAT FEN ROAD
FODDERFEN DROVE

Bridge Farm
CHAPEL LANE
Mettleham Farm
Great Fen
PARISH BUSH DROVE
Cambria Farm
Fenbank Farm

Red House Farm
B1104

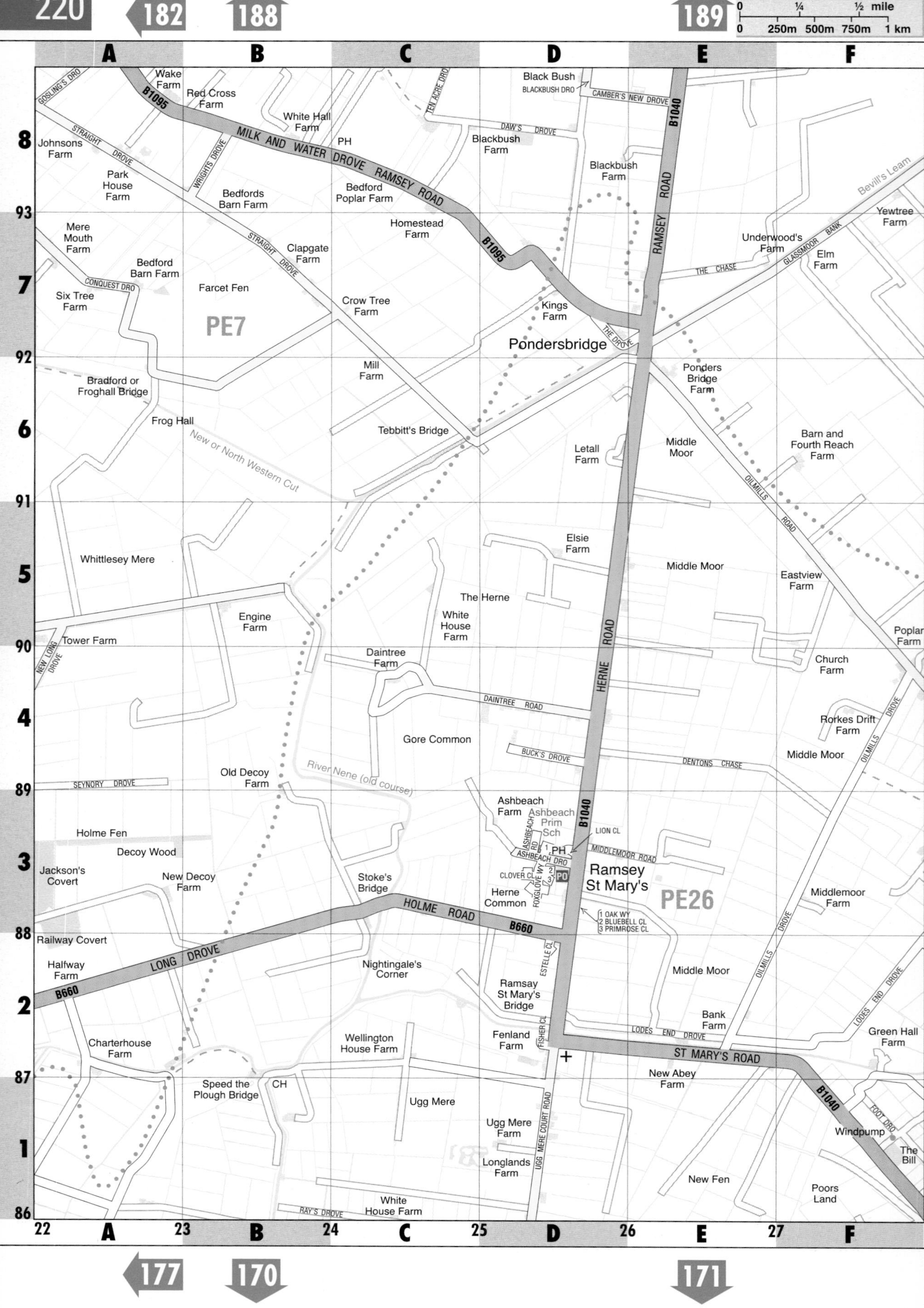

Wake Farm
Red Cross Farm
White Hall Farm
PH
Black Bush
BLACKBUSH DRO
Blackbush Farm
CAMBER'S NEW DROVE
Johnsons Farm
Park House Farm
Bedfords Barn Farm
Bedford Poplar Farm
Homestead Farm
Blackbush Farm
Underwood's Farm
Yewtree Farm
THE CHASE
Elm Farm
GLASSMOOR BANK
Bevill's Leam
Mere Mouth Farm
Bedford Barn Farm
Clapgate Farm
Crow Tree Farm
CONQUEST DRO
STRAIGHT DRIVE
Six Tree Farm
PE7
Farcet Fen
Kings Farm
Pondersbridge
THE DRO
Ponders Bridge Farm
Mill Farm
Bradford or Froghall Bridge
Letall Farm
Middle Moor
Barn and Fourth Reach Farm
Frog Hall
Tebbitt's Bridge
New or North Western Cut
OILMILLS ROAD
Whittlesey Mere
Elsie Farm
Middle Moor
Eastview Farm
Engine Farm
The Herne
White House Farm
Tower Farm
NEW LONG DROVE
Daintree Farm
DAINTREE ROAD
Poplar Farm
Church Farm
Gore Common
BUCK'S DROVE
DENTONS CHASE
Rorkes Drift Farm
Middle Moor
SEYNORY DROVE
Old Decoy Farm
River Nene (old course)
Ashbeach Farm
Ashbeach Prim Sch
LION CL
MIDDLEMOOR ROAD
Holme Fen
Decoy Wood
PH
Ramsey St Mary's
PE26
Middlemoor Farm
Jackson's Covert
New Decoy Farm
Stoke's Bridge
HERNE ROAD
CLOVER CL WY
PD
ASHBEACH DRO
FOXGLOVE WY
Herne Common
1 OAK WY
2 BLUEBELL CL
3 PRIMROSE CL
Railway Covert
HOLME ROAD
B660
Nightingale's Corner
Ramsay St Mary's Bridge
Middle Moor
Halfway Farm
LONG DROVE
Bank Farm
Green Hall Farm
B660
Fenland Farm
LODES END DROVE
LODES END DROVE
Charterhouse Farm
Wellington House Farm
Speed the Plough Bridge
CH
Ugg Mere
FISHER CL
ESTELLE CL
New Abey Farm
ST MARY'S ROAD
B1040
Windpump
FOOT DRO
The Bill
Ugg Mere Farm
UGG MERE COURT ROAD
Longlands Farm
New Fen
Poors Land
RAY'S DROVE
White House Farm

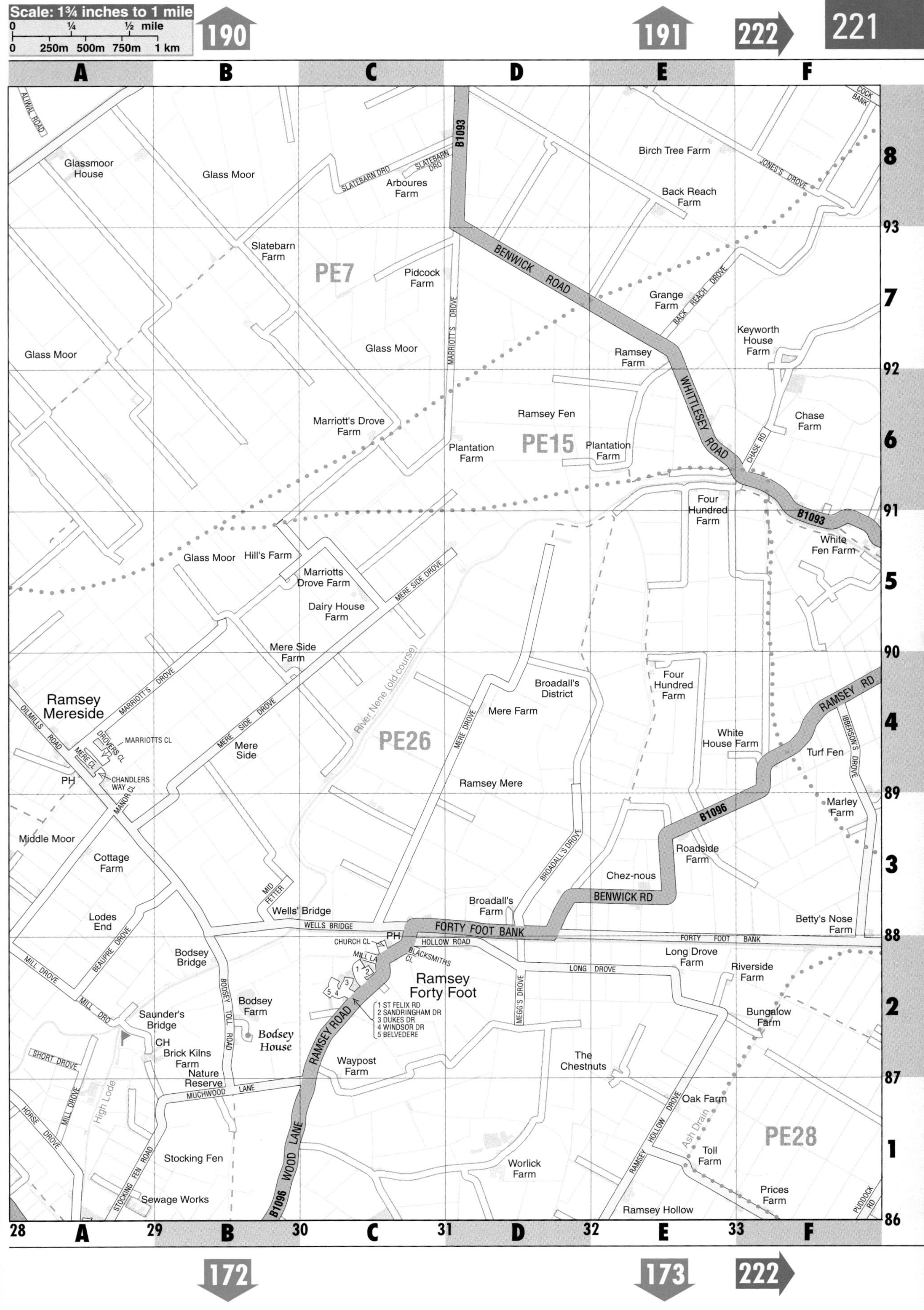
Scale: 1¾ inches to 1 mile
0 ¼ ½ mile
0 250m 500m 750m 1 km
190
191
222
A B C D E F
8 93 7 92 6 91 5 90 4 89 3 88 2 87 1 86
28 29 30 31 32 33
Glassmoor House
Glass Moor
Slatebarn Farm
PE7
Arboures Farm
Pidcock Farm
Glass Moor
Glass Moor
Marriott's Drove Farm
Glass Moor
Hill's Farm
Marriotts Drove Farm
Dairy House Farm
Mere Side Farm
Ramsey Mereside
Mere Side
PE26
River Nene (old course)
Mere Farm
Ramsey Mere
Broadall's District
Plantation Farm
PE15
Ramsey Fen
Plantation Farm
Ramsey Farm
Birch Tree Farm
Back Reach Farm
Grange Farm
Keyworth House Farm
Chase Farm
Four Hundred Farm
White Fen Farm
Four Hundred Farm
White House Farm
Turf Fen
Marley Farm
Roadside Farm
Chez-nous
Broadall's Farm
Betty's Nose Farm
Middle Moor
Cottage Farm
Lodes End
Bodsey Bridge
Bodsey Farm
Bodsey House
Saunder's Bridge
Brick Kilns Farm
Nature Reserve
Stocking Fen
Sewage Works
High Lode
Waypost Farm
Ramsey Forty Foot
Wells' Bridge
Long Drove Farm
Riverside Farm
Bungalow Farm
The Chestnuts
Oak Farm
Ash Drain
Toll Farm
PE28
Worlick Farm
Prices Farm
Ramsey Hollow
B1093
BENWICK ROAD
WHITTLESEY ROAD
B1096
RAMSEY RD
BENWICK RD
FORTY FOOT BANK
WELLS BRIDGE
HOLLOW ROAD
LONG DROVE
MEGG'S DROVE
RAMSEY ROAD
WOOD LANE
MUCHWOOD LANE
BODSEY TOLL ROAD
STOCKING FEN ROAD
MILL DROVE
MILL DRO
BEAUPRE DROVE
SHORT DROVE
HORSE DROVE
OILMILLS ROAD
MARRIOTT'S DROVE
MERE SIDE DROVE
MERE DROVE
BROADALL'S DROVE
MID FETTER
MARRIOTT'S DROVE
SLATEBARN DRO
ALWAL ROAD
JONES'S DROVE
COCK BANK
BACK REACH DROVE
CHASE RD
IBBERSON'S DROVE
RAMSEY HOLLOW DROVE
PUDDOCK RD
DROVERS CL
MARRIOTTS CL
MERE CL
CHANDLERS WAY
MANOR CL
CHURCH CL
MILL LA
BLACKSMITHS CL
PH
CH
1 ST FELIX RD
2 SANDRINGHAM DR
3 DUKES DR
4 WINDSOR DR
5 BELVEDERE
172
173
222

222

221

227

Scale: 1¾ inches to 1 mile
0   ¼   ½ mile
0   250m 500m 750m 1 km

A   B   C   D   E   F

8

Ransonmoor Grange

Flood's Ferry Farm

KNIGHT'S END ROAD

Flood's Ferry

Ranson Moor

LAND DROVE

PARSON'S

93

Mast

Perkins Farm

Flood's Drain

Ransonmoor Farm

White Fen Farm

FLOOD'S FERRY ROAD

7

PE15

Ranson Moor

RANSONMOOR DROVE

92

White Fen

Capolder Farm

Crawdam Farm

Bridgstock Farm

PARSON'S LAND DROVE

Ranson Moor

Copalder Farm

HOSPITAL ROAD

HOSPITAL ROAD

6

Bedford Level (Middle Level)

Ranson Moor

Thacker's Farm

Ransonmoor Farm

South View Farm

Askham House

Doddington

Mast

Copalder Corner

Thickens Farm

Parson's Land Farm

H

Windmill

91

River Nene (old course)

B1093

Benwick Road

B1093

DODDINGTON RD

OAKTREE CL

PO

B1093

WHITTLESEY RD

New World Poultry Farm

Post Mill Farm

PH

5

HIGH ST

THE ORCHARD

Boardenhouse Farm

Dyke Moor

NEWGATE ST

LITHOLT RD

CHAPEL GD

COOK'S CH

Benwick

Dykemoor Dro N

PRIMROSE HILL

TURF FEN LANE

CHURCH LA

PO

PH

Benwick Prim Sch

Lilly Holt

Dykemoor Farm

How Moor

90

RAMSEY RD

Copalder

DYKEMOOR DRO

DYKEMOOR   DROVE

Howmoor Farm

Turf Fen

B1096

Dyke Moor

Barway Farm

4

Households Farm

Curf Farm

89

Beezlings Farm

BEEZLING FEN DROVE

CURF FEN DROVE

A142

Benwick Mere

Barrots Farm

Swingbrow

Leonard Childs Bridge

Curf Fen

DODDINGTON ROAD

3

Stanley Hall Farm

Granary Farm

Beezling Fen

Carter's Bridge Farm

Aspen Farm

Curf

PE26

Bank Farm

FORTY   FOOT   BANK

BADNEY DROVE

Dock Bridge

Willow Farm

Betty Nose Farm

BADNEY DROVE

Westmoor Farm

88

Puddock Bridge

Beazling Farm

A141

241

DOCK RD

Lambe's Plantation

PE16

WESTMOOR DROVE

Westmoor Farm North

DODDINGTON ROAD

Sewage Works

2

PUDDOCK ROAD

Dawson's Farm

Morley's Farm

Purrant's Farm

ALBERT WAY

SHORT NIGHTLAYER'S DRO

87

CHATTERIS

241

Slade Field

Womb Farm

BRIDGE ST

HIGH ST

PE28

Westmoor Farm South

West Moor

FENLAND WAY

LODE WAY

Cemy

NEW ROAD

1

PUDDOCK RD

Round House Farm

West Moor

Honeysome Farm

Isle Coll

GULL WY

Cemy

HIGH ST

ROUND HOUSE DROVE

HONEYSOME ROAD

Sch

OLDFORGE GD

Liby

Sch

86

34   A   35   B   36   C   37   D   38   E   39   F

A5
1 NENESIDE
2 RIVER CL
3 CRICKETERS WY
4 SKIEFS ROW
5 WHITE HART DR
6 GREEN LA

F5
1 CORNFIELDS
2 MILLER CL
3 ANCASTER WY
4 HUNTS CL
5 RONALDSWAY
6 FEN VIEW

For full street detail of the highlighted area see page 241.

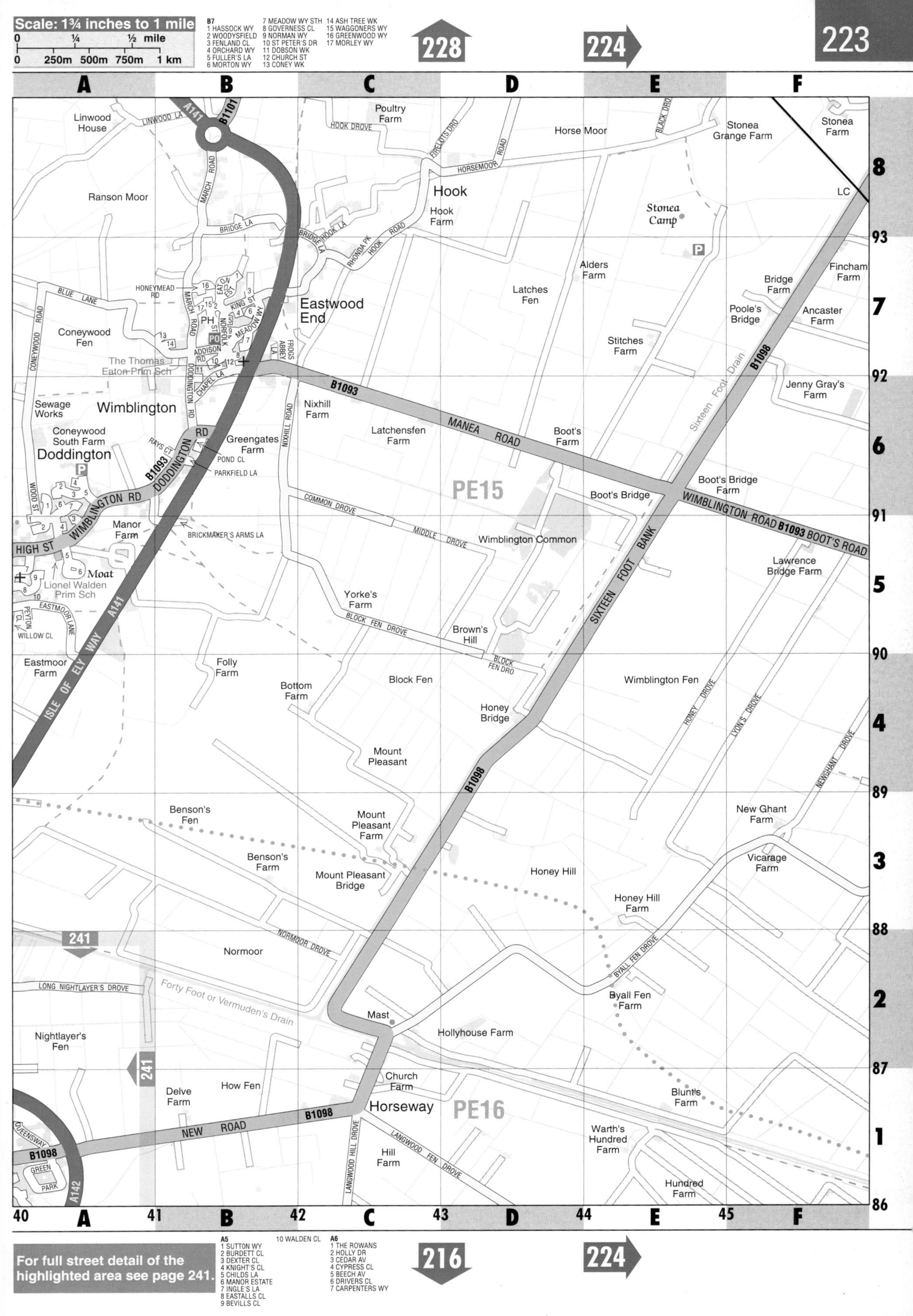
Scale: 1¾ inches to 1 mile
0 ¼ ½ mile
0 250m 500m 750m 1 km
B7
1 HASSOCK WY
2 WOODYSFIELD
3 FENLAND CL
4 ORCHARD WY
5 FULLER'S LA
6 MORTON WY
7 MEADOW WY STH
8 GOVERNESS CL
9 NORMAN WY
10 ST PETER'S DR
11 DOBSON WK
12 CHURCH ST
13 CONEY WK
14 ASH TREE WK
15 WAGGONERS WY
16 GREENWOOD WY
17 MORLEY WY
228
224
223
A B C D E F
Linwood House
LINWOOD LA
A141
B1101
Poultry Farm
HOOK DROVE
FIELDS DRO
HORSEMOOR ROAD
Horse Moor
BLACK DRO
Stonea Grange Farm
Stonea Farm
8
LC
MARCH ROAD
Ranson Moor
Hook
Hook Farm
Stonea Camp
BRIDGE LA
HOOK LA
RHONDA PK
HOOK ROAD
93
Alders Farm
Latches Fen
Bridge Farm
Fincham Farm
HONEYMEAD RD
BLUE LANE
KING ST
MEADOW WY
Eastwood End
Poole's Bridge
Ancaster Farm
7
CONEYWOOD ROAD
Coneywood Fen
PH
PO
NORFOLK ST
ADDISON RD
FROGS ABBEY LA
Stitches Farm
The Thomas Eaton Prim Sch
CHAPEL LA
DODDINGTON RD
B1093
Sixteen Foot Drain
B1098
92
Jenny Gray's Farm
Sewage Works
Wimblington
Nixhill Farm
Latchensfen Farm
MANEA ROAD
Boot's Farm
Coneywood South Farm
Doddington
RAYS CT
Greengates Farm
POND CL
PARKFIELD LA
NIXHILL ROAD
6
PE15
Boot's Bridge Farm
Boot's Bridge
WOOD ST
WIMBLINGTON RD
COMMON DROVE
MIDDLE DROVE
WIMBLINGTON ROAD B1093 BOOT'S ROAD
91
Manor Farm
BRICKMAKER'S ARMS LA
Wimblington Common
HIGH ST
Moat
Lionel Walden Prim Sch
SIXTEEN FOOT BANK
Lawrence Bridge Farm
5
EASTMOOR LANE
PEYTON CL
WILLOW CL
ISLE OF ELY WAY
Yorke's Farm
BLOCK FEN DROVE
Brown's Hill
BLOCK FEN DRO
90
Eastmoor Farm
Folly Farm
Bottom Farm
Block Fen
Wimblington Fen
HONEY DROVE
LYON'S DROVE
Honey Bridge
4
Mount Pleasant
NEWGHANT DROVE
89
Benson's Fen
Mount Pleasant Farm
New Ghant Farm
Benson's Farm
Mount Pleasant Bridge
Honey Hill
Vicarage Farm
3
Honey Hill Farm
241
NORMOOR DROVE
Normoor
BYALL FEN DROVE
88
LONG NIGHTLAYER'S DROVE
Forty Foot or Vermuden's Drain
Byall Fen Farm
2
Mast
Nightlayer's Fen
Hollyhouse Farm
241
Church Farm
87
Delve Farm
How Fen
Horseway
PE16
Blunt's Farm
QUEENSWAY
B1098
NEW ROAD
GREEN PARK
A142
LANGWOOD HILL DROVE
LANGWOOD FEN DROVE
Hill Farm
Warth's Hundred Farm
1
Hundred Farm
86
40 A 41 B 42 C 43 D 44 E 45 F
For full street detail of the highlighted area see page 241.
A5
1 SUTTON WY
2 BURDETT CL
3 DEXTER CL
4 KNIGHT'S CL
5 CHILDS LA
6 MANOR ESTATE
7 INGLE'S LA
8 EASTALLS CL
9 BEVILLS CL
10 WALDEN CL
A6
1 THE ROWANS
2 HOLLY DR
3 CEDAR AV
4 CYPRESS CL
5 BEECH AV
6 DRIVERS CL
7 CARPENTERS WY
216
224

223
229

Scale: 1¾ inches to 1 mile

0   ¼   ½   mile
0   250m 500m 750m 1 km

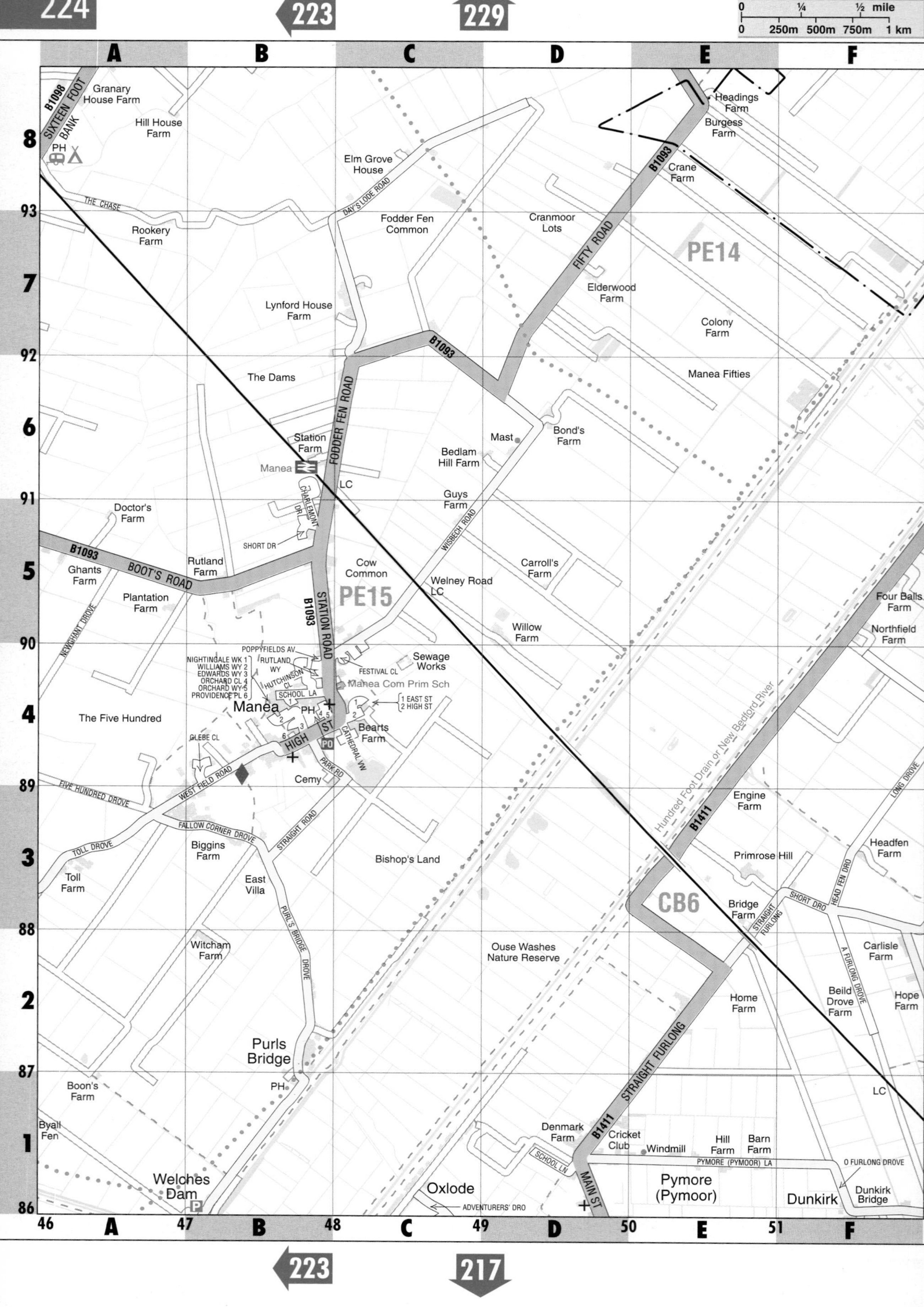

B1098 SIXTEEN FOOT BANK
Granary House Farm
PH
Hill House Farm
THE CHASE
Rookery Farm
Elm Grove House
DAY'S LODE ROAD
Fodder Fen Common
Lynford House Farm
The Dams
FODDER FEN ROAD
Station Farm
Manea
LC
CHARLEMONT DR
SHORT DR
Doctor's Farm
B1093 BOOT'S ROAD
Ghants Farm
Plantation Farm
Rutland Farm
STATION ROAD
B1093
PE15
Cow Common
Welney Road LC
NEWGRANT DROVE
The Five Hundred
POPPYFIELDS AV
NIGHTINGALE WK 1
WILLIAMS WY 2
EDWARDS WY 3
ORCHARD CL 4
ORCHARD WY 5
PROVIDENCE PL 6
RUTLAND WY
HUTCHINSON CL
SCHOOL LA
FESTIVAL CL
Manea Com Prim Sch
Manea
PH
1 EAST ST
2 HIGH ST
HIGH ST
GLEBE CL
Bearts Farm
CATHEDRAL VW
PARK RD
PO
Cemy
WEST FIELD ROAD
FIVE HUNDRED DROVE
FALLOW CORNER DROVE
STRAIGHT ROAD
Biggins Farm
East Villa
Bishop's Land
TOLL DROVE
Toll Farm
Witcham Farm
PURL'S BRIDGE DROVE
Purls Bridge
PH
Boon's Farm
Byall Fen
Welches Dam
P
Oxlode
ADVENTURERS' DRO

PE14
Headings Farm
Burgess Farm
B1093
Crane Farm
Cranmoor Lots
FIFTY ROAD
Elderwood Farm
Colony Farm
Manea Fifties
Mast
Bond's Farm
Bedlam Hill Farm
Guys Farm
WISBECH ROAD
Carroll's Farm
Willow Farm
Sewage Works
Four Balls Farm
Northfield Farm
Engine Farm
Hundred Foot Drain or New Bedford River
B1411
Primrose Hill
CB6
Bridge Farm
STRAIGHT FURLONG
SHORT DRO
HEAD FEN DRO
Headfen Farm
A FURLONG DROVE
Carlisle Farm
Beild Drove Farm
Hope Farm
LONG DROVE
Home Farm
Ouse Washes Nature Reserve
Denmark Farm
B1411
SCHOOL LN
Cricket Club
Windmill
MAIN ST
Hill Farm
Barn Farm
PYMORE (PYMOOR) LA
O FURLONG DROVE
Pymore (Pymoor)
Dunkirk
Dunkirk Bridge
LC

223
217

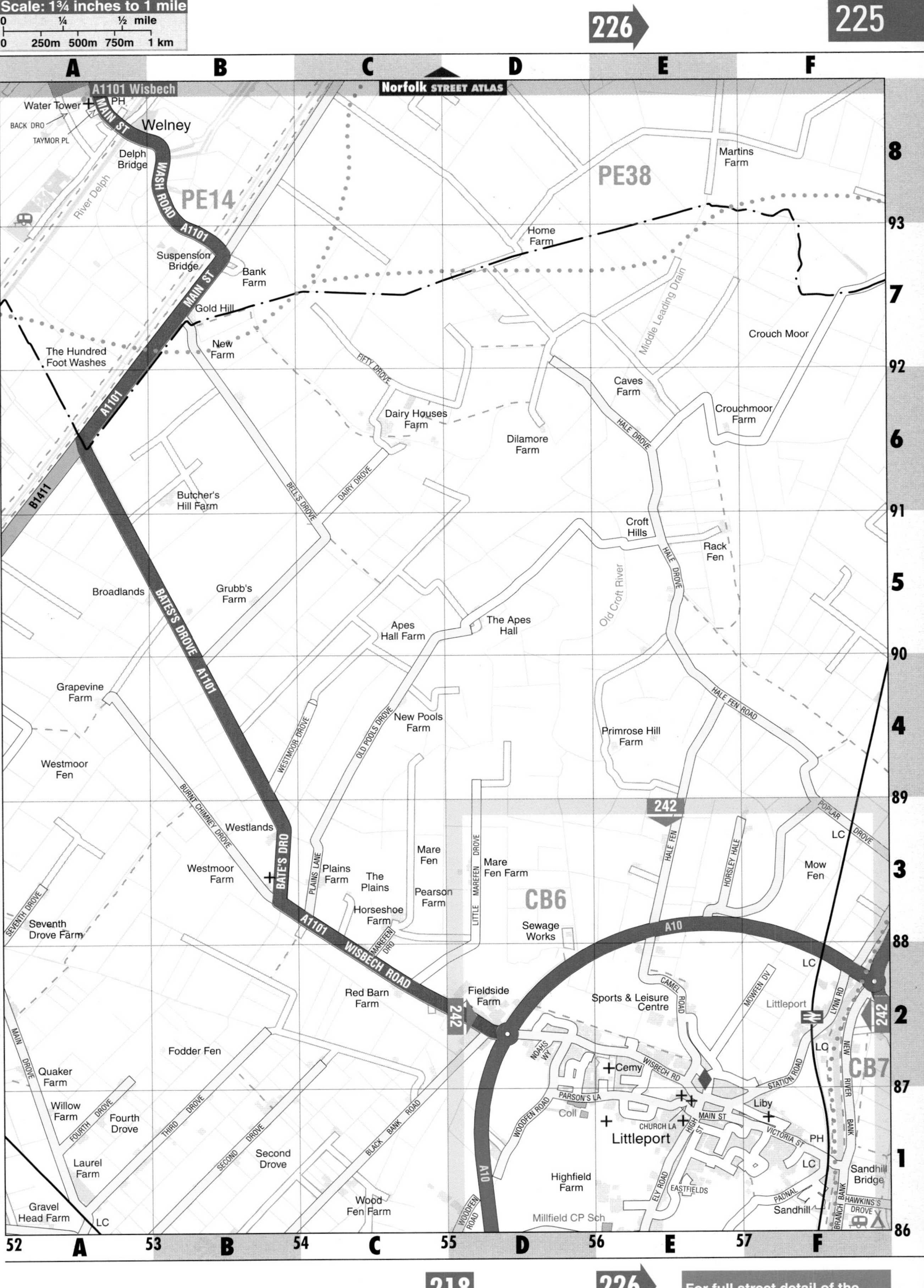

Norfolk STREET ATLAS

A1101 Wisbech
Water Tower
PH
BACK DRO
TAYMOR PL
MAIN ST
Welney
Delph Bridge
River Delph
PE14
WASH ROAD
A1101
Suspension Bridge
MAIN ST
Bank Farm
Gold Hill
New Farm
The Hundred Foot Washes
B1411
A1101
FIFTY DROVE
Dairy Houses Farm
Dilamore Farm
PE38
Home Farm
Martins Farm
Crouch Moor
Caves Farm
Crouchmoor Farm
Middle Leading Drain
HALE DROVE
Croft Hills
Rack Fen
Butcher's Hill Farm
BELL'S DROVE
DAIRY DROVE
Old Croft River
HALE DROVE
Broadlands
Grubb's Farm
BATE'S'S DROVE A1101
Apes Hall Farm
The Apes Hall
Grapevine Farm
WESTMOOR DROVE
OLD POOLS DROVE
New Pools Farm
Primrose Hill Farm
HALE FEN ROAD
POPLAR DROVE
LC
Westmoor Fen
BURNT CHIMNEY DROVE
242
HALE FEN
HORSLEY HALE
Mow Fen
Westlands
BATE'S DRO
A1101
PLAINS LANE
Westmoor Farm
Plains Farm
The Plains
MARE FEN DRO
Mare Fen
LITTLE MAREFEN DROVE
Mare Fen Farm
CB6
A10
SEVENTH DROVE
Seventh Drove Farm
Horseshoe Farm
Pearson Farm
Sewage Works
WISBECH ROAD
MAREFEN DRO
Red Barn Farm
242
Fieldside Farm
Sports & Leisure Centre
CAMEL ROAD
MOWFEN DV
Littleport
LC
242
CB7
A10
NOAH'S WY
Cemy
Wisbech Rd
Liby
STATION ROAD
LQ
MAIN DROVE
Quaker Farm
Fodder Fen
WOODFEN ROAD
PARSON'S LA
Coll
MAIN ST
PH
RIVER BANK
NEW RD
OLD NR1
LC
Willow Farm
FOURTH DROVE
Fourth Drove
THIRD DROVE
SECOND DROVE
BLACK BANK ROAD
CHURCH LA
Littleport
VICTORIA ST
Sandhill Bridge
Laurel Farm
Second Drove
Highfield Farm
ELY ROAD
EASTFIELDS
PADNAL
Sandhill
HAWKINS'S DROVE
Gravel Head Farm
LC
Wood Fen Farm
WOODFEN ROAD
Millfield CP Sch
BRANCH BANK

218

226

For full street detail of the highlighted area see page 242.

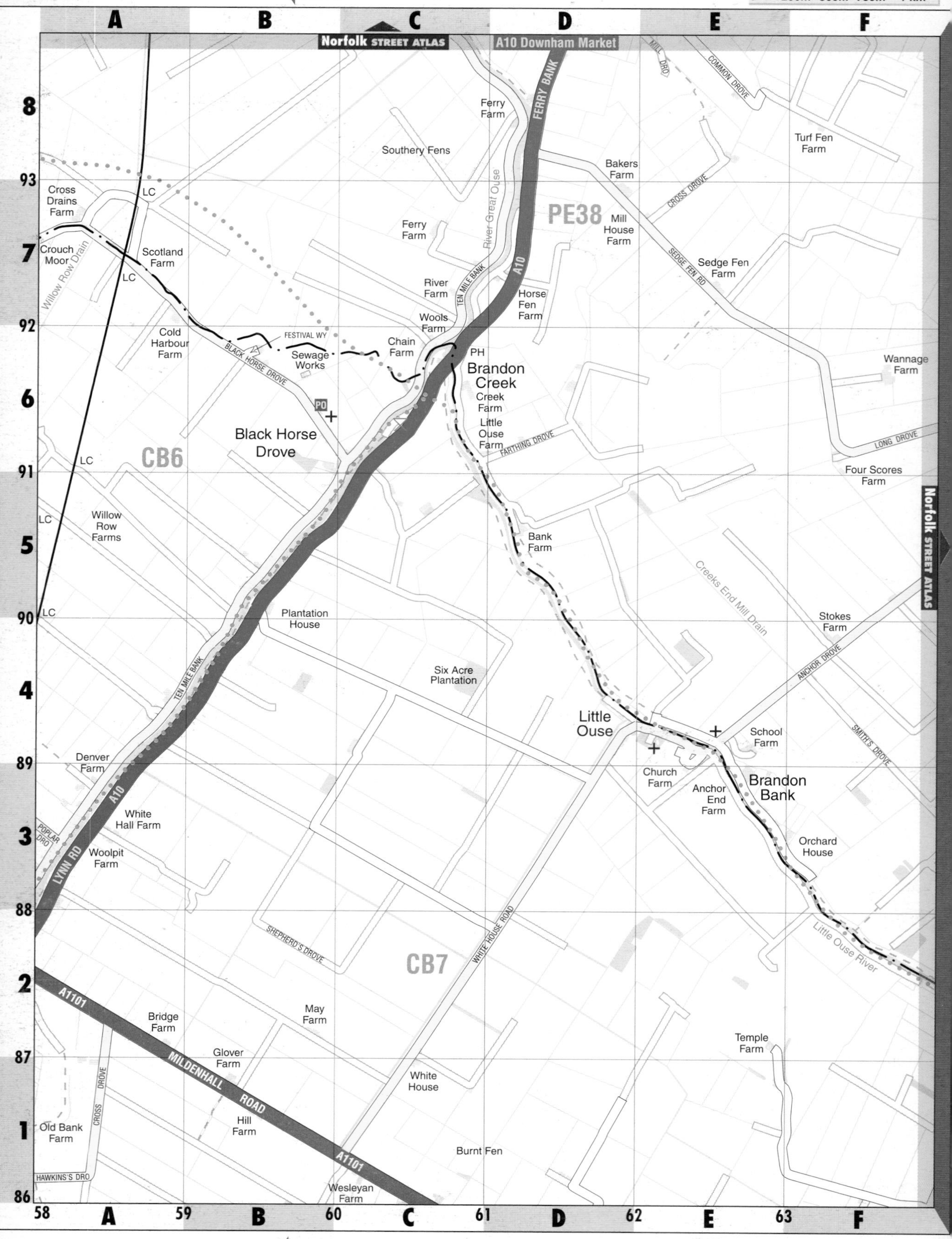

Norfolk STREET ATLAS

A10 Downham Market

PE38

CB6

Black Horse Drove

Brandon Creek

Little Ouse

Brandon Bank

CB7

Ferry Farm

Southery Fens

Bakers Farm

Turf Fen Farm

Cross Drains Farm

Scotland Farm

Crouch Moor

Ferry Farm

Mill House Farm

Sedge Fen Farm

Wannage Farm

Cold Harbour Farm

FESTIVAL WY

Sewage Works

Chain Farm

River Farm

Wools Farm

Horse Fen Farm

Creek Farm

Little Ouse Farm

FARTHING DROVE

Four Scores Farm

LONG DROVE

Willow Row Farms

Plantation House

Bank Farm

Creeks End Mill Drain

Stokes Farm

Six Acre Plantation

ANCHOR DROVE

SMITH'S DROVE

School Farm

Denver Farm

White Hall Farm

Church Farm

Anchor End Farm

Orchard House

Woolpit Farm

SHEPHERD'S DROVE

WHITE HOUSE ROAD

Little Ouse River

A1101

Bridge Farm

May Farm

Temple Farm

Glover Farm

White House

Old Bank Farm

Hill Farm

MILDENHALL ROAD

A1101

Burnt Fen

HAWKINS'S DRO

Wesleyan Farm

PO

PH

LC

Norfolk STREET ATLAS

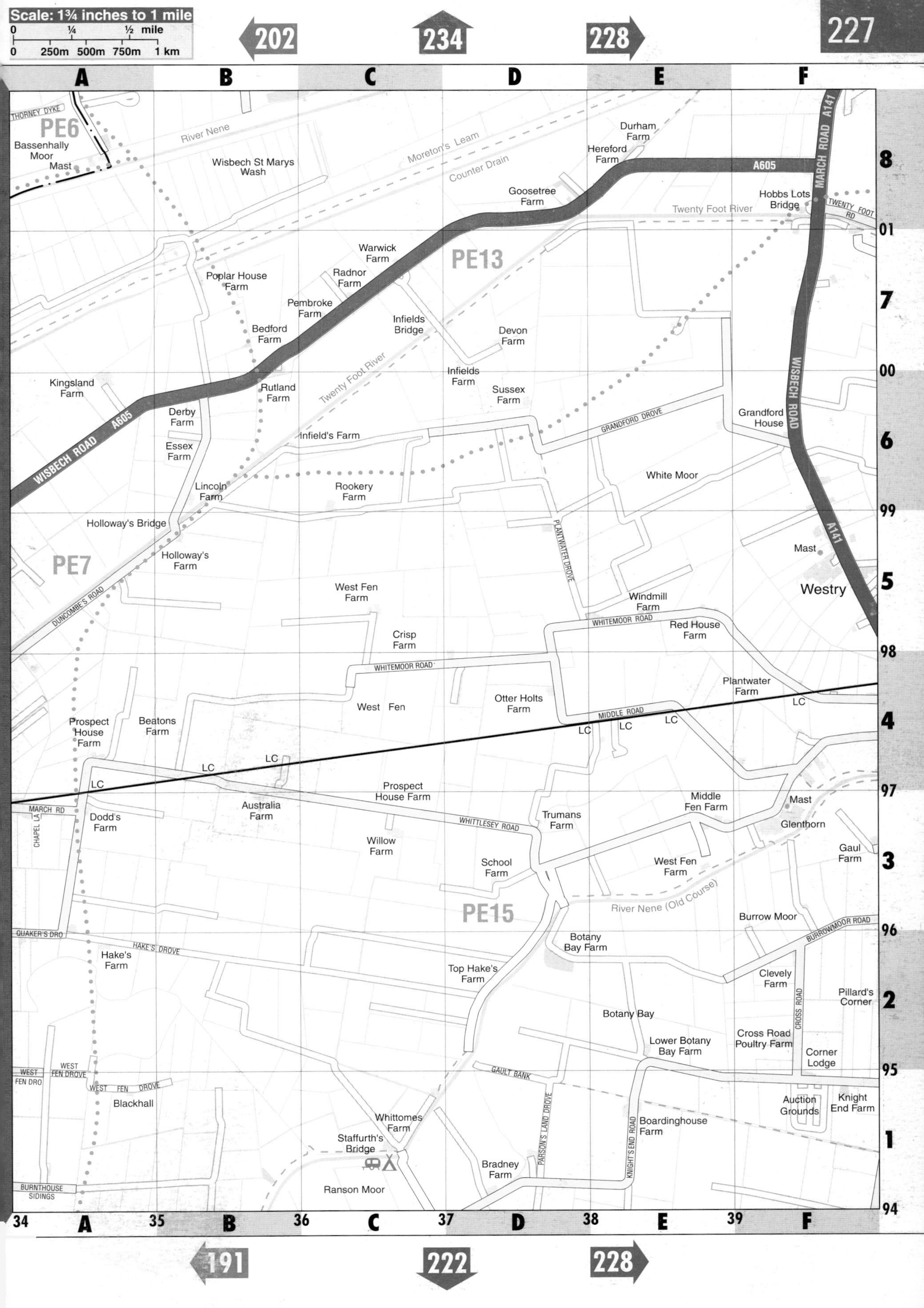

A   **B**   **C**   **D**   **E**   **F**

THORNEY DYKE

PE6

Bassenhally
Moor
Mast

River Nene

Wisbech St Marys
Wash

Moreton's Leam

Counter Drain

Durham
Farm

Hereford
Farm

A605

Goosetree
Farm

Twenty Foot River

Hobbs Lots
Bridge

TWENTY FOOT RD

MARCH ROAD A141

8

01

Warwick
Farm

Poplar House
Farm

Radnor
Farm

Pembroke
Farm

Bedford
Farm

PE13

Infields
Bridge

Devon
Farm

7

Kingsland
Farm

Derby
Farm

Rutland
Farm

Twenty Foot River

Infields
Farm

Sussex
Farm

Grandford Drove

Grandford
House

WISBECH ROAD

00

6

WISBECH ROAD A605

Essex
Farm

Infield's Farm

White Moor

A141

99

Lincoln
Farm

Rookery
Farm

Mast

Holloway's Bridge

PLANTWATER DROVE

Westry

5

PE7

Holloway's
Farm

West Fen
Farm

Windmill
Farm

WHITEMOOR ROAD

Red House
Farm

98

DUNCOMBE'S ROAD

Crisp
Farm

Otter Holts
Farm

Plantwater
Farm

LC

4

Prospect
House
Farm

Beatons
Farm

West Fen

WHITEMOOR ROAD

MIDDLE ROAD

LC   LC   LC

LC

LC

LC   LC

Prospect
House Farm

97

MARCH RD

Dodd's
Farm

Australia
Farm

WHITTLESEY ROAD

Trumans
Farm

Middle
Fen Farm

Mast

Glenthorn

Gaul
Farm

3

CHAPEL LA

Willow
Farm

School
Farm

West Fen
Farm

PE15

River Nene (Old Course)

Burrow Moor

BURROWMOOR ROAD

96

QUAKER'S DRO

HAKE'S DROVE

Hake's
Farm

Top Hake's
Farm

Botany
Bay Farm

Clevely
Farm

CROSS ROAD

Pillard's
Corner

2

WEST
FEN DRO

WEST
FEN DROVE

WEST FEN DROVE

Blackhall

Botany Bay

Lower Botany
Bay Farm

Cross Road
Poultry Farm

Corner
Lodge

95

Whittomes
Farm

GAULT BANK

PARSON'S LAND DROVE

Boardinghouse
Farm

KNIGHT'S END ROAD

Auction
Grounds

Knight
End Farm

1

Staffurth's
Bridge

Bradney
Farm

BURNTHOUSE
SIDINGS

Ranson Moor

94

34   **A**   **35**   **B**   **36**   **C**   **37**   **D**   **38**   **E**   **39**   **F**

Scale: 1¾ inches to 1 mile
0   ¼   ½ mile
0   250m 500m 750m 1 km

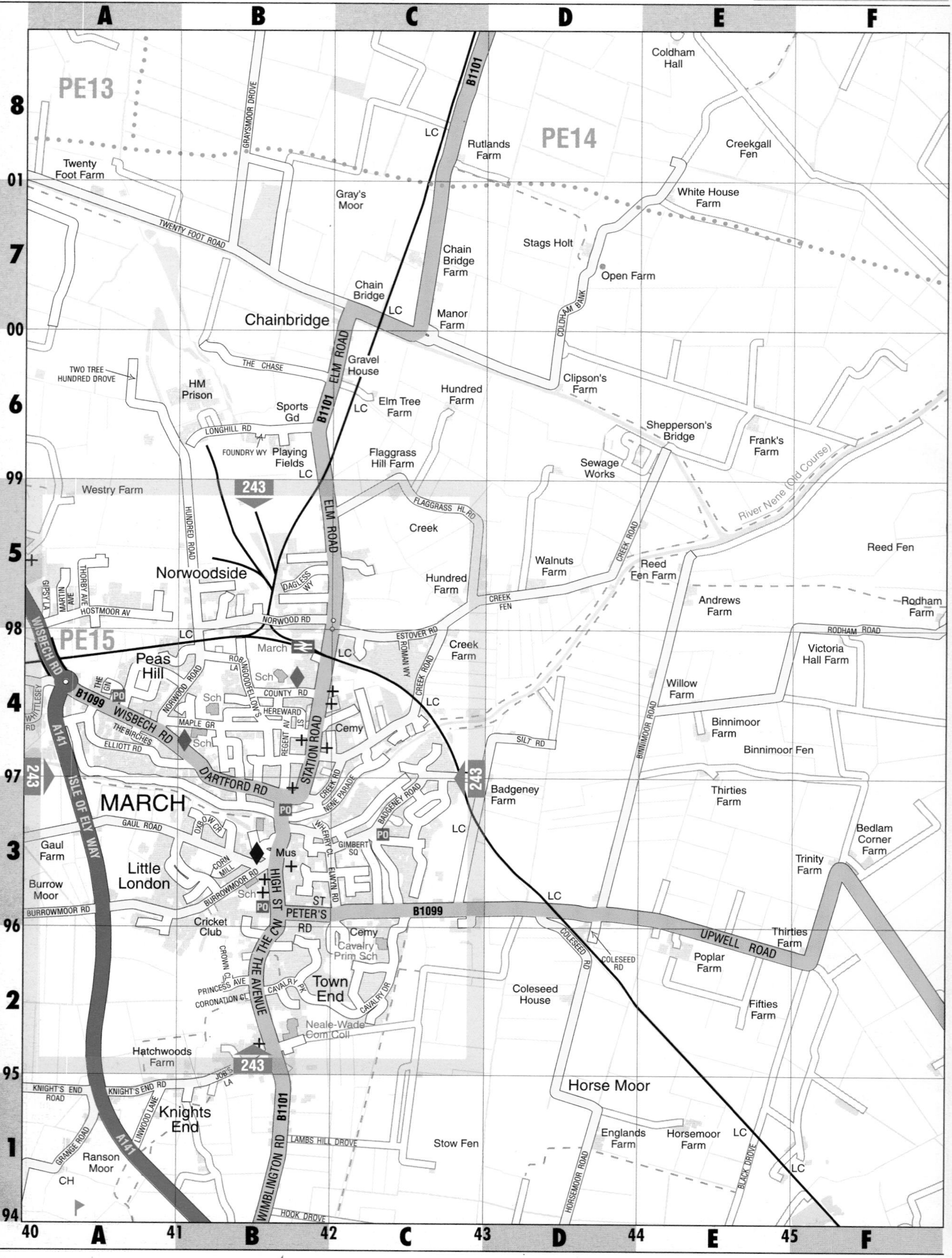

A   B   C   D   E   F

8

PE13

Coldham Hall

PE14

01

Twenty Foot Farm

Gray's Moor

Creekgall Fen

White House Farm

GRAYSMOOR DRIVE

7

TWENTY FOOT ROAD

Rutlands Farm

Stags Holt

Open Farm

B1101

Chain Bridge Farm

00

Chainbridge

Chain Bridge

Manor Farm

Clipson's Farm

COLDHAM BNK

THE CHASE

ELM ROAD

LC

Gravel House

6

Two Tree Hundred Drove

HM Prison

Sports Gd

Elm Tree Farm

Hundred Farm

Shepperson's Bridge

Frank's Farm

LONGHILL RD

B1101

LC

Sewage Works

FOUNDRY WY

Playing Fields

99

243

Westry Farm

LC

Flaggrass Hill Farm

FLAGGRASS HL RD

River Nene (Old Course)

HUNDRED ROAD

ELM ROAD

Creek

CREEK ROAD

Reed Fen

5

Norwoodside

DAGLESS WY

Hundred Farm

Walnuts Farm

Reed Fen Farm

Andrews Farm

Rodham Farm

GIPSY LA

THORBY AVE

MALLARD LANE

HOSTMOOR AV

NORWOOD RD

CREEK FEN

RODHAM ROAD

98

WISBECH RD

PE15

LC

March

ESTOVER RD

ROMAN WY

Creek Farm

Victoria Hall Farm

Peas Hill

ROBINGOODFELLOW'S LA

Sch

COUNTY RD

LC

CREEK ROAD

LC

Willow Farm

BINNIMOOR RD

4

B1099

WISBECH RD

Sch

HEREWARD

Cemy

SILT RD

Binnimoor Farm

A141

ABBOTTS WAY

THE BIRCHES

NORWOOD ROAD

MAPLE GR

REGENT ST

STATION ROAD

NENE PARADE

Binnimoor Fen

97

ELLIOTT RD

DARTFORD RD

243

CREEK RD

Badgeney Farm

Thirties Farm

243

ISLE OF ELY WAY

MARCH

DIXON CT

Mus

WHERRY CT

BADGENEY ROAD

GIMBERT SQ

LC

Bedlam Corner Farm

3

Gaul Farm

GAUL ROAD

Little London

CORN MILL

ELWYN RD

PO

LC

Trinity Farm

Burrow Moor

BURROWMOOR RD

Sch

HIGH ST

PETER'S RD

B1099

UPWELL ROAD

Thirties Farm

96

BURROWMOOR RD

Cricket Club

THE CW ST

Cemy

Cavalry Prim Sch

COLESEED RD

COLESEED RD

Poplar Farm

CROWN RD

THE AVENUE

CAVALRY DR

Town End

Coleseed House

Fifties Farm

2

PRINCESS AVE

CORONATION AVE

CAVALRY RD

Neale-Wade Com Coll

95

Hatchwoods Farm

JOB'S LA

243

Horse Moor

KNIGHT'S END ROAD

KNIGHT'S END RD

WIMBLINGTON RD

B1101

LAMBS HILL DROVE

Stow Fen

Englands Farm

Horsemoor Farm

LC

BLACK DROVE

1

Knights End

GRANGE ROAD

LINWOOD LANE

A141

HORSEMOOR ROAD

LC

CH

Ranson Moor

HOOK DROVE

94

40   A   41   B   42   C   43   D   44   E   45   F

For full street detail of the highlighted area see page 243.

Scale: 1¾ inches to 1 mile

236

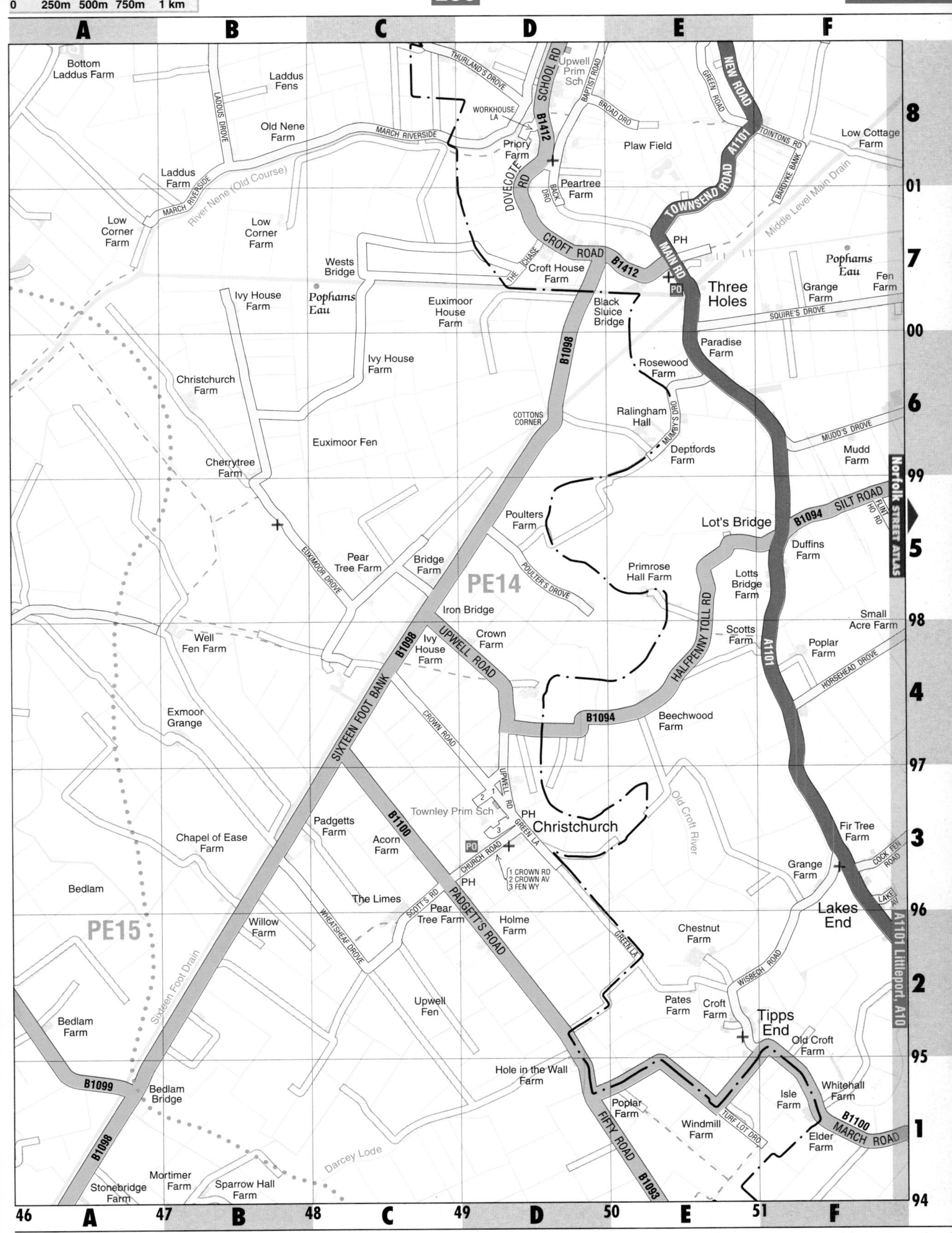

Bottom Laddus Farm
Laddus Fens
Old Nene Farm
Laddus Farm
Low Corner Farm
Low Corner Farm
Wests Bridge
Pophams Eau
Ivy House Farm
Euximoor House Farm
Ivy House Farm
Christchurch Farm
Euximoor Fen
Cherrytree Farm
Pear Tree Farm
Bridge Farm
PE14
Iron Bridge
Well Fen Farm
Ivy House Farm
Crown Farm
Exmoor Grange
Chapel of Ease Farm
Padgetts Farm
Acorn Farm
Bedlam
PE15
Willow Farm
The Limes
Pear Tree Farm
Holme Farm
Upwell Fen
Bedlam Farm
Bedlam Bridge
Hole in the Wall Farm
Mortimer Farm
Stonebridge Farm
Sparrow Hall Farm
Darcey Lode
Sixteen Foot Drain
Upwell Prim Sch
Priory Farm
Plaw Field
Peartree Farm
Croft House Farm
Black Sluice Bridge
Three Holes
Paradise Farm
Rosewood Farm
Ralingham Hall
Deptfords Farm
Poulters Farm
Primrose Hall Farm
Lot's Bridge
Lotts Bridge Farm
Scotts Farm
Beechwood Farm
Townley Prim Sch
Christchurch
Old Croft River
Chestnut Farm
Pates Farm
Croft Farm
Tipps End
Old Croft Farm
Poplar Farm
Windmill Farm
Isle Farm
Whitehall Farm
Elder Farm
Low Cottage Farm
Pophams Eau
Fen Farm
Grange Farm
Middle Level Main Drain
Mudd Farm
Duffins Farm
Small Acre Farm
Poplar Farm
Fir Tree Farm
Grange Farm
Lakes End
River Nene (Old Course)
COTTONS CORNER
1 CROWN RD
2 CROWN AV
3 FEN WY
Norfolk STREET ATLAS
A1101 Littleport, A10

224

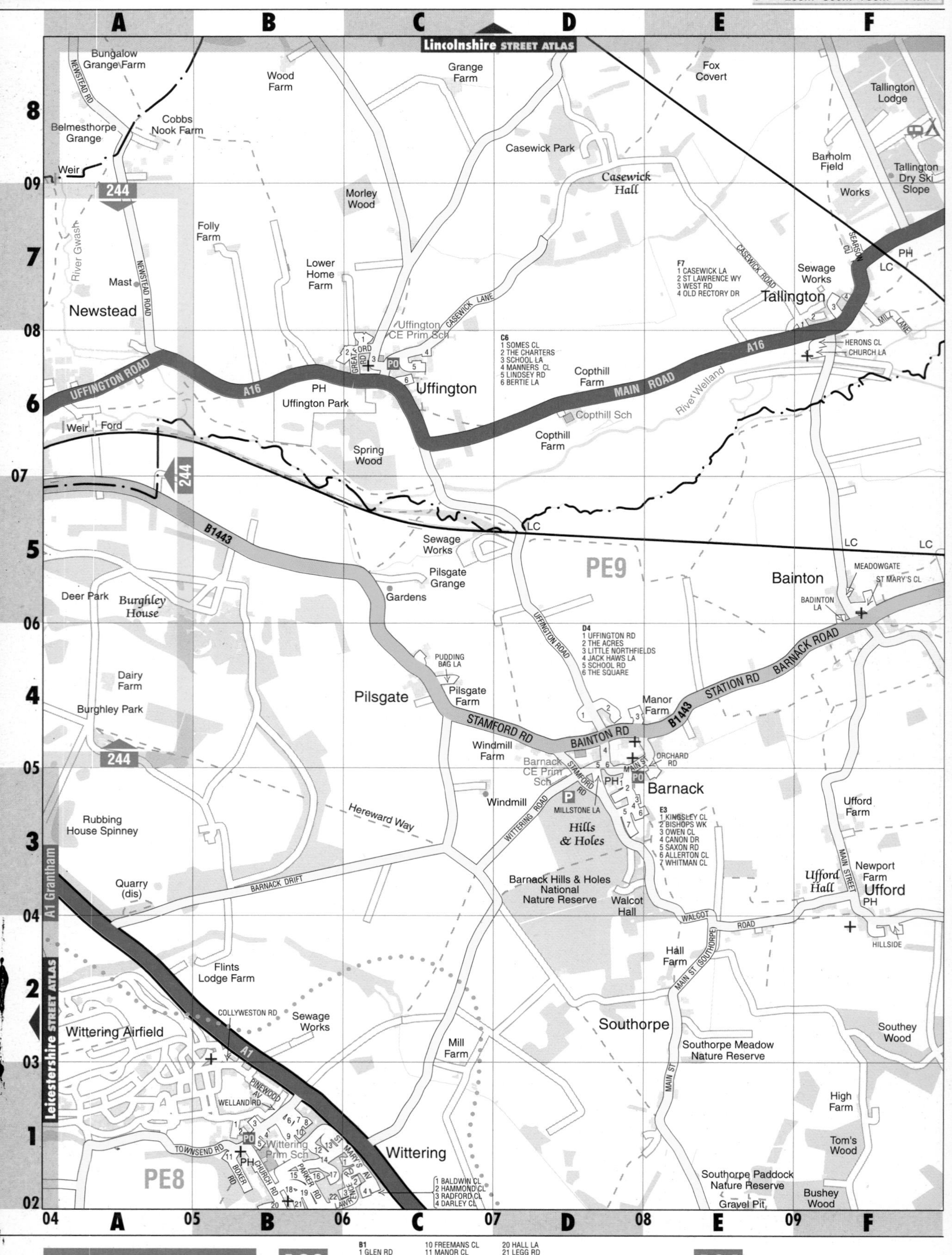

Scale: 1¾ inches to 1 mile

0   ¼   ½ mile
0   250m   500m   750m   1 km

Lincolnshire STREET ATLAS

8

09

7

08

6

07

5

06

4

05

3

04

2

03

1

02

A   B   C   D   E   F

Labels on map (selected):

Bungalow Grange Farm

Wood Farm

Grange Farm

Fox Covert

Tallington Lodge

Belmesthorpe Grange

Cobbs Nook Farm

Casewick Park

Barholm Field

Tallington Dry Ski Slope

Weir

244

Morley Wood

Casewick Hall

Works

Folly Farm

River Gwash

Lower Home Farm

Mast

Newstead

Casewick Lane

F7
1 CASEWICK LA
2 ST LAWRENCE WY
3 WEST RD
4 OLD RECTORY DR

Sewage Works

Tallington

CASEWICK ROAD

PH

LC

Uffington CE Prim Sch

UFFINGTON ROAD

GREAT FORD RD

PD

A16

C6
1 SOMES CL
2 THE CHARTERS
3 SCHOOL LA
4 MANNERS CL
5 LINDSEY RD
6 BERTIE LA

HERONS CL
CHURCH LA

MILL LANE

PH

Uffington Park

Uffington

Copthill Farm

MAIN ROAD

A16

Weir   Ford

244

Spring Wood

Copthill Sch

Copthill Farm

River Welland

LC

B1443

Sewage Works

LC

LC

LC

Pilsgate Grange

PE9

Bainton

MEADOWGATE
ST MARY'S CL

Deer Park

Burghley House

Gardens

BADINTON LA

D4
1 UFFINGTON RD
2 THE ACRES
3 LITTLE NORTHFIELDS
4 JACK HAWS LA
5 SCHOOL RD
6 THE SQUARE

UFFINGTON ROAD

BARNACK ROAD

STATION RD

PUDDING BAG LA

Dairy Farm

Pilsgate Farm

Pilsgate

Manor Farm

B1443

Burghley Park

244

STAMFORD RD

BAINTON RD

Windmill Farm

Barnack CE Prim Sch

ORCHARD RD

Ufford Farm

Hereward Way

Windmill

P

MILLSTONE LA

PH

PD

Barnack

E3
1 KINGSLEY CL
2 BISHOPS WK
3 OWEN CL
4 CANON DR
5 SAXON RD
6 ALLERTON CL
7 WHITMAN CL

Rubbing House Spinney

WITTERING ROAD

Hills & Holes

Ufford Hall

Newport Farm

Ufford

MAIN STREET

PH

Quarry (dis)

BARNACK DRIFT

Barnack Hills & Holes National Nature Reserve

Walcot Hall

HILLSIDE

A1 Grantham

Leitestershire STREET ATLAS

Flints Lodge Farm

COLLYWESTON RD

Sewage Works

Hall Farm

WALCOT ROAD

Southey Wood

Wittering Airfield

A1

Southorpe

MAIN ST (SOUTHORPE)

Mill Farm

Southorpe Meadow Nature Reserve

High Farm

PINEWOOD AV

WELLAND RD

Tom's Wood

PD

PH

Wittering Prim Sch

Wittering

ST MARY'S DR

PARKER RD

BOXER RD

CHURCH RD

Southorpe Paddock Nature Reserve
Gravel Pit

Bushey Wood

PE8

B1
1 BALDWIN CL
2 HAMMOND CL
3 RADFORD CL
4 DARLEY CL

04   A   05   B   06   C   07   D   08   E   09   F

For full street detail of the highlighted area see page 244.

193

194

B1
1 GLEN RD
2 NENE CL
3 CHATER RD
4 HARVEY CL
5 THE LIMES
6 BROWNES RD
7 EXETER RD
8 THE HOLT
9 BURGHLEY AV
10 FREEMANS CL
11 MANOR CL
12 ST MICHAEL'S RD
13 ST JOHN'S RD
14 ST GEORGE'S RD
15 BROADHURST RD
16 NEWMAN CL
17 MALTBY CL
18 CARNEGIE RD
19 EMBRY RD
20 HALL LA
21 LEGG RD
22 JEFFERSON CL

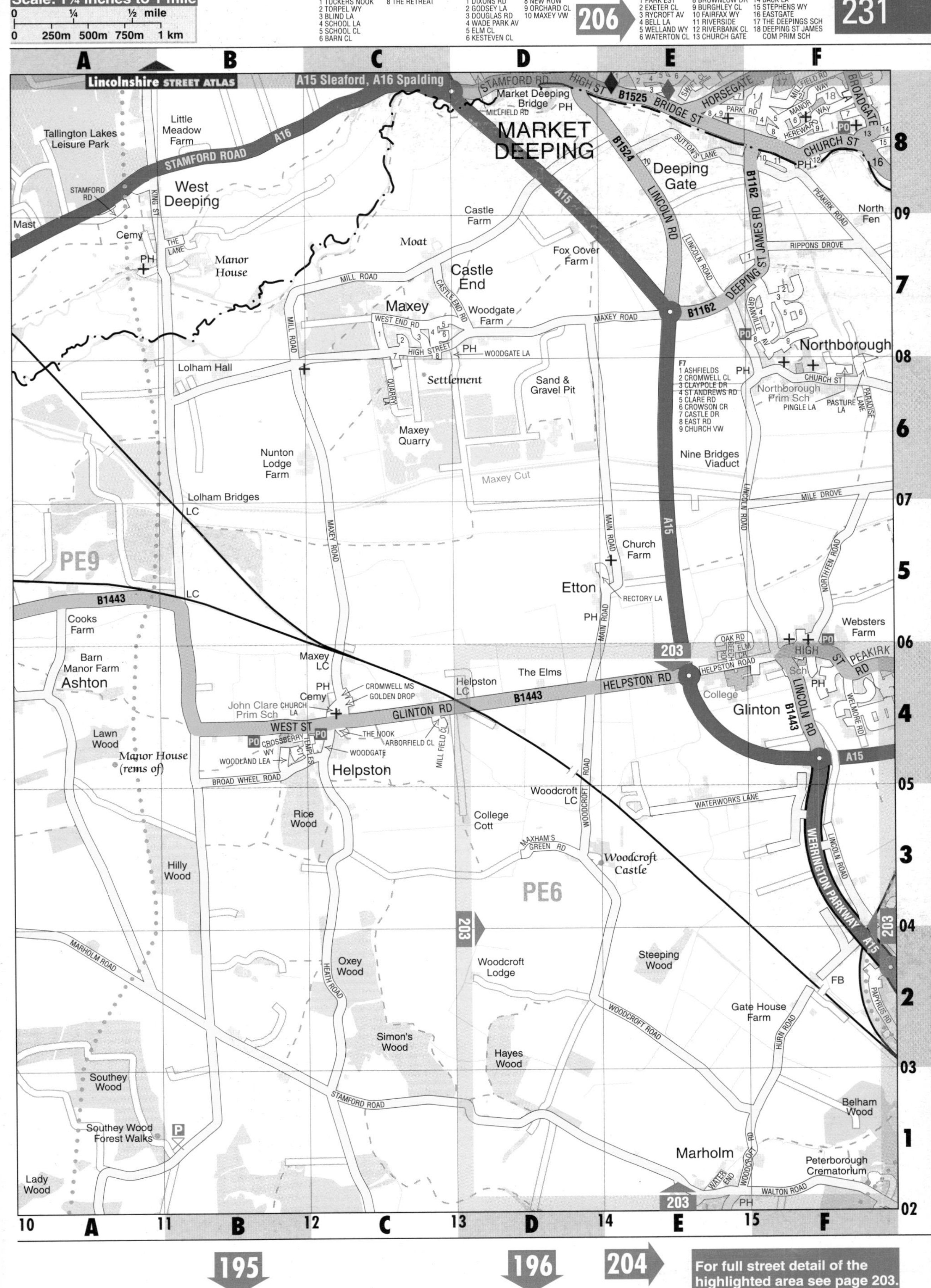

207

B8
1 ABBOTS DR
2 GLEBE GD
3 CORONATION AV
4 CHAPEL ST
5 STRICKLANDS DR
6 ALDERLANDS CL

7 PENWALD CL
8 TATWIN DR
9 BECCELM DR

Scale: 1¾ inches to 1 mile

0   ¼   ½   mile
0   250m 500m 750m 1 km

A1073 Spalding (A16) **Lincolnshire** STREET ATLAS

Middle Rd
Crowland High Wash
Corporation Bank
Low Rd
Low Rd
Crowland
Broadway
Thorney Rd
A1073
B1040
Barbers Drove

C8
1 SNOWDON CL
2 CRAWFORD GD
3 KENNULPHS CL

Green Drove
Sheppard's Drove
Old South Eau
Empsons Farm

Plank Drove
Crease Drove
Peterborough Road
Harvester Way
Alderlands
Harrington Dr
Carrington's Drove
Greenbank Farm
Green Drove
South Eau Farm
Falls Bridge
Empsons Farm
Fall's Drove
Blue Bell Farm

Mill Drove
Ashley's Barn
Vine House Farm
Blue Bell Bridge

Kennulph's Farm
Poplar Farm
Eardley Grange Farm
Wright's Drove
Peterborough Road
Toll House Farm
Nene Terrace
St Vincent's Cross Farm
French Drove
Old Hall Farm
Bell Drove

Speechley's Dro
Old Farm
Hundreds Farm
Hundreds Road
St Vincent's Cross
Bennett's Pieces

Pepper Lake Farm
Horseshoe Bridge
Singlesole Farm
Hangman's Corner

Moor's Farm
Gray's Farm
Cross
B1040
Singlecote Farm
Crowland Road

A1073
Olympia Farm
Hill Farm
PE6
Lodge Farm

Steam House Farm
Little Tower's Fen
Buke Horn Farm
B1443

Flood Farm
B1443 Thorney Road
Powder Blue Farm
Cat's Water Plantation
Bukehorn Road
Buke Horn Plantation

Hill Farm
Fletchers Farm
Mason's Bridge
Thorney Road
B1443
Rose Farm

Hurn Farm
Crowland Rd
Bedford Level (North Level)
The Reaches
Cat's Water

ASH CL 1
LAUREL DR 2
BERBERIS CL 3
ORCHARD CT 4

Turves Farm
Elm Tree Farm
Oakhurst Farm
Cat's Water Plantation
Middle West Farm
Great Towers Fen
Windmill

Northolm Farm
Nipcut Road
Catwater Farm
Hightrees Farm
A47
Abbey House

Turves Road
Northolme Coppice
The Causeway

Northam Cl
Eye Green
Causeway Toll Farm
Pode Hole Farm
Guys Fen

Newstead Cl
A1073
PH
Pershore Rd
Eye Green Nature Reserve
Pasture House Farm
Toneham Farm

Green Rd
Eye Green Ind Est
Guilsborough Rd
Thorney Road
Hayne's Farm
Willow Hall Lane
Toneham Lane

Crowland Rd
Cerny Liby
Thorney Road
Chicell's Hurst
Thorney River

A47 Eye Road
PH
PO
Fountains Pl
Eye Prim Sch
Bar Pastures
Bar Pasture Farm
Barlees Fen
Hill Farm
Whittlesey Rd

Peterborough Rd
Leeston Ct
Lindisfarne Rd
Eyebury Rd
Eye
Sand & Gravel Pit

205   199   200

A1
1 BEAULIEU CT
2 HODNEY RD
3 TINTERN RI
4 MOORE'S LA
5 ST BENET'S GD
6 CHANCERY LA
7 BEECH LA
8 IXWORTH CL
9 DELAPRE CT

10 WALSINGHAM WY
11 GLASTONBURY CL
12 CARTMEL WY
13 DEERHURST WY
14 BOXGROVE CL
15 NEW RD
16 WESTMINSTER GD
17 MONKS DR
18 ST BEE'S DR
19 ST OLAVE'S DR

20 ST ALBAN'S DR

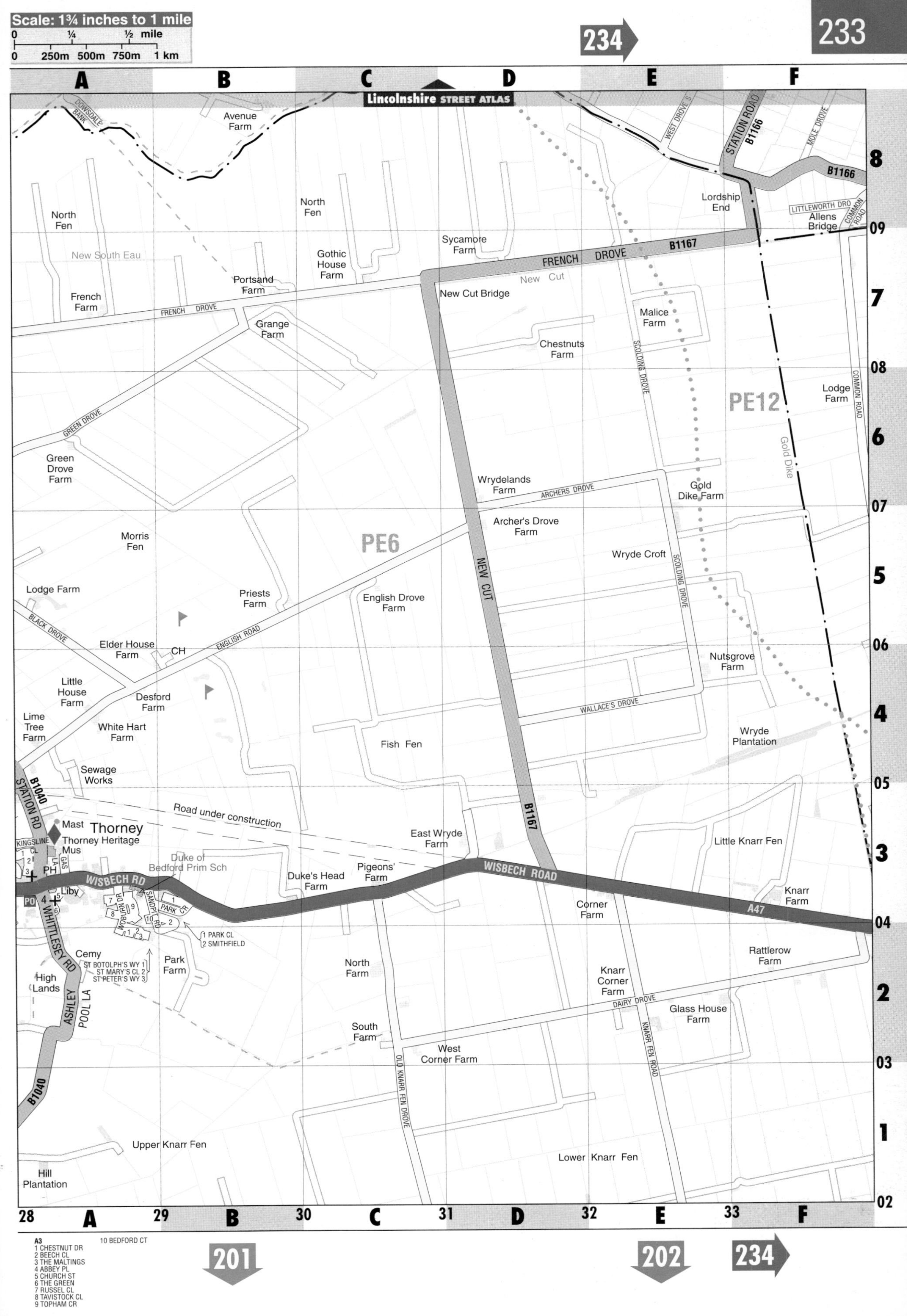

Scale: 1¾ inches to 1 mile

0   ¼   ½   mile
0   250m 500m 750m 1 km

Lincolnshire STREET ATLAS

A B C D E F

DOWSDALE BANK
Avenue Farm
North Fen
North Fen
WEST DROVE
STATION ROAD
MOLE DROVE
B1166
B1166
8
Lordship End
Sycamore Farm
FRENCH DROVE B1167
LITTLEWORTH DRO
Allens Bridge
COMMON ROAD
09
New South Eau
Gothic House Farm
New Cut
7
Portsand Farm
Malice Farm
French Farm
FRENCH DROVE
New Cut Bridge
08
Grange Farm
Chestnuts Farm
PE12
Lodge Farm
GREEN DROVE
SCOLDING DROVE
COMMON ROAD
6
Green Drove Farm
Wrydelands Farm
ARCHERS DROVE
Gold Dike Farm
Gold Dike
07
Morris Fen
Archer's Drove Farm
Wryde Croft
5
Lodge Farm
PE6
NEW CUT
SCOLDING DROVE
BLACK DROVE
Priests Farm
English Drove Farm
06
Elder House Farm
CH
ENGLISH ROAD
Nutsgrove Farm
Little House Farm
Desford Farm
WALLACE'S DROVE
4
Lime Tree Farm
White Hart Farm
Fish Fen
Wryde Plantation
Sewage Works
05
B1040
Road under construction
STATION RD
B1167
Mast
Thorney
Thorney Heritage Mus
East Wryde Farm
Little Knarr Fen
3
KINGSLINE
GAS
PH
Duke of Bedford Prim Sch
Pigeons' Farm
WISBECH ROAD
Liby
Duke's Head Farm
Corner Farm
Knarr Farm
WISBECH RD
A47
PO
1 PARK CL
2 SMITHFIELD
Rattlerow Farm
04
WHITTLESEY RD
Cemy
ST BOTOLPH'S WY 1
ST MARY'S CL 2
ST PETER'S WY 3
Park Farm
North Farm
Knarr Corner Farm
2
High Lands
ASHLEY
POOL LA
DAIRY DROVE
Glass House Farm
KNARR FEN ROAD
South Farm
OLD KNARR FEN DROVE
West Corner Farm
03
B1040
Upper Knarr Fen
1
Lower Knarr Fen
Hill Plantation
02

28 A 29 B 30 C 31 D 32 E 33 F

A3
1 CHESTNUT DR
2 BEECH CL
3 THE MALTINGS
4 ABBEY PL
5 CHURCH ST
6 THE GREEN
7 RUSSEL CL
8 TAVISTOCK CL
9 TOPHAM CR
10 BEDFORD CT

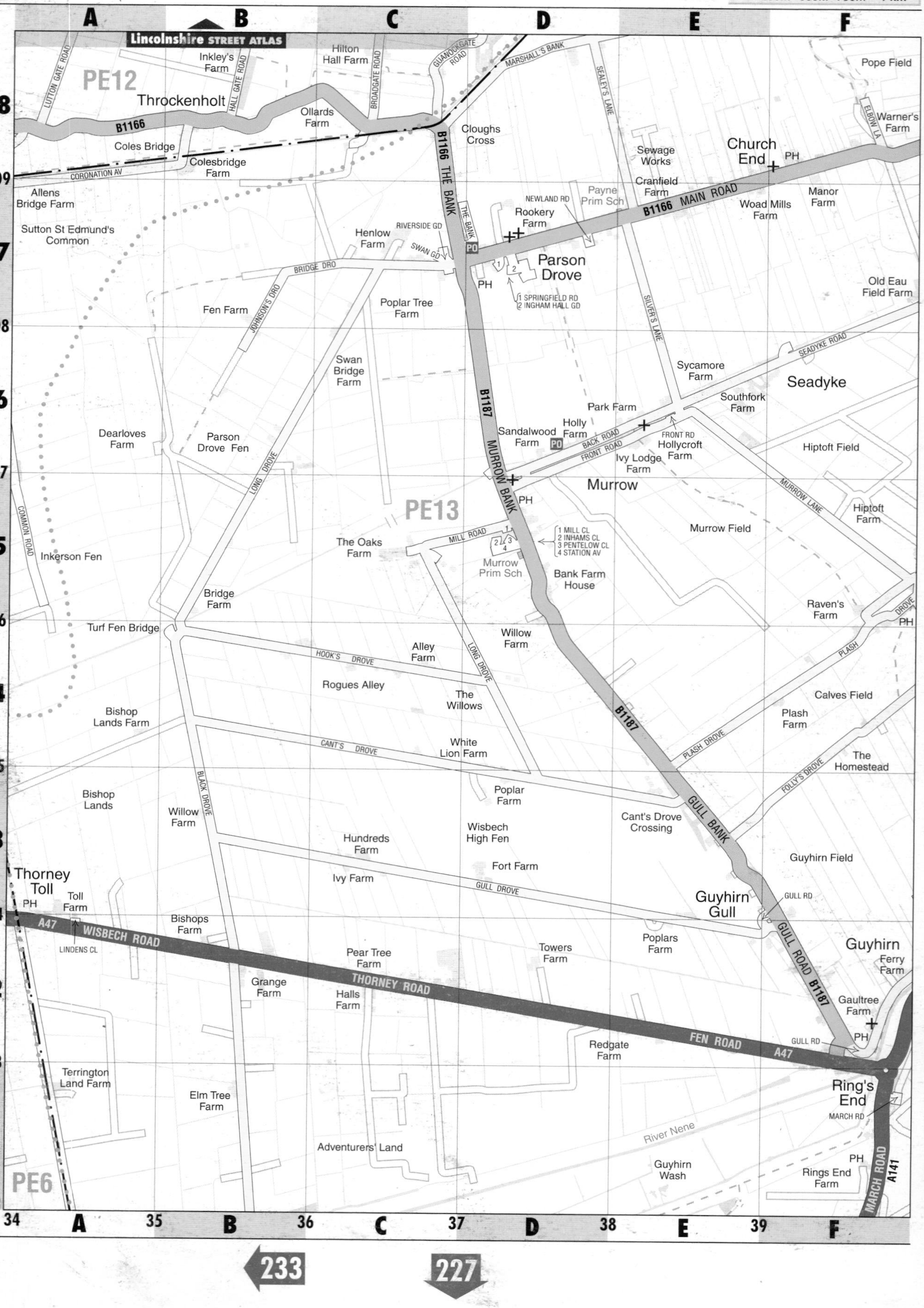

A | B | C | D | E | F

Lincolnshire STREET ATLAS

8

PE12

LUTTON GATE ROAD
Throckenholt
Inkley's Farm
HALL GATE ROAD
Hilton Hall Farm
BROADGATE ROAD
GUANOCKGATE ROAD
MARSHALL'S BANK
SEALEY'S LANE
Pope Field
ELROW TA
Warner's Farm

B1166
Coles Bridge
Ollards Farm
B1166 THE BANK
Cloughs Cross
Sewage Works
Cranfield Farm
Church End PH
B1166 MAIN ROAD
Woad Mills Farm
Manor Farm

09

Colesbridge Farm
CORONATION AV

Allens Bridge Farm

NEWLAND RD
Payne Prim Sch
Rookery Farm

Old Eau Field Farm

7

Sutton St Edmund's Common

Henlow Farm
RIVERSIDE GD
SWAN GD
PO
Parson Drove
PH
1 SPRINGFIELD RD
2 INGHAM HALL GD

SILVER'S LANE

BRIDGE DRO
JOHNSON'S DRO
Fen Farm
Poplar Tree Farm

08

Sycamore Farm
SEADYKE ROAD
Seadyke

6

Swan Bridge Farm

B1187 MURROW BANK
Sandalwood Farm
Holly Farm PO
Park Farm
BACK ROAD
FRONT RD
FRONT RD
Southfork Farm
Hollycroft Farm
Ivy Lodge Farm

Hiptoft Field

Dearloves Farm
LONG DROVE
Parson Drove Fen

07

PH
Murrow
MURROW LANE
Hiptoft Farm

PE13

COMMON ROAD

5

Inkerson Fen
The Oaks Farm
MILL ROAD
1 2 3 4
1 MILL CL
2 INHAMS CL
3 PENTELOW CL
4 STATION AV
Murrow Field

Bank Farm House

DROVE
PH

Bridge Farm
Murrow Prim Sch

Raven's Farm

06

Turf Fen Bridge
HOOK'S DROVE
Alley Farm
LONG DROVE
Willow Farm

PLASH

4

Rogues Alley
The Willows

B1187
Calves Field
PLASH DROVE
Plash Farm

Bishop Lands Farm
CANT'S DROVE
White Lion Farm

05

BLACK DROVE
Poplar Farm
PLASH DROVE
The Homestead

3

Bishop Lands
Willow Farm
Hundreds Farm
Wisbech High Fen
Cant's Drove Crossing
FOLLY'S DROVE

GULL BANK
Guyhirn Field

Ivy Farm
Fort Farm
GULL RD

04

Thorney Toll
PH
Toll Farm
GULL DROVE
Guyhirn Gull
Guyhirn

A47 WISBECH ROAD
Bishops Farm
GULL ROAD B1187
Ferry Farm

2

LINDENS CL
Grange Farm
Pear Tree Farm
Halls Farm
THORNEY ROAD
Towers Farm
Poplars Farm
Gaultree Farm
PH
GULL RD

FEN ROAD A47

03

Terrington Land Farm
Redgate Farm
Ring's End
MARCH RD

1

Elm Tree Farm
River Nene

PH
MARCH ROAD
A141
Rings End Farm

PE6
Adventurers' Land
Guyhirn Wash

02

34 | A | 35 | B | 36 | C | 37 | D | 38 | E | 39 | F

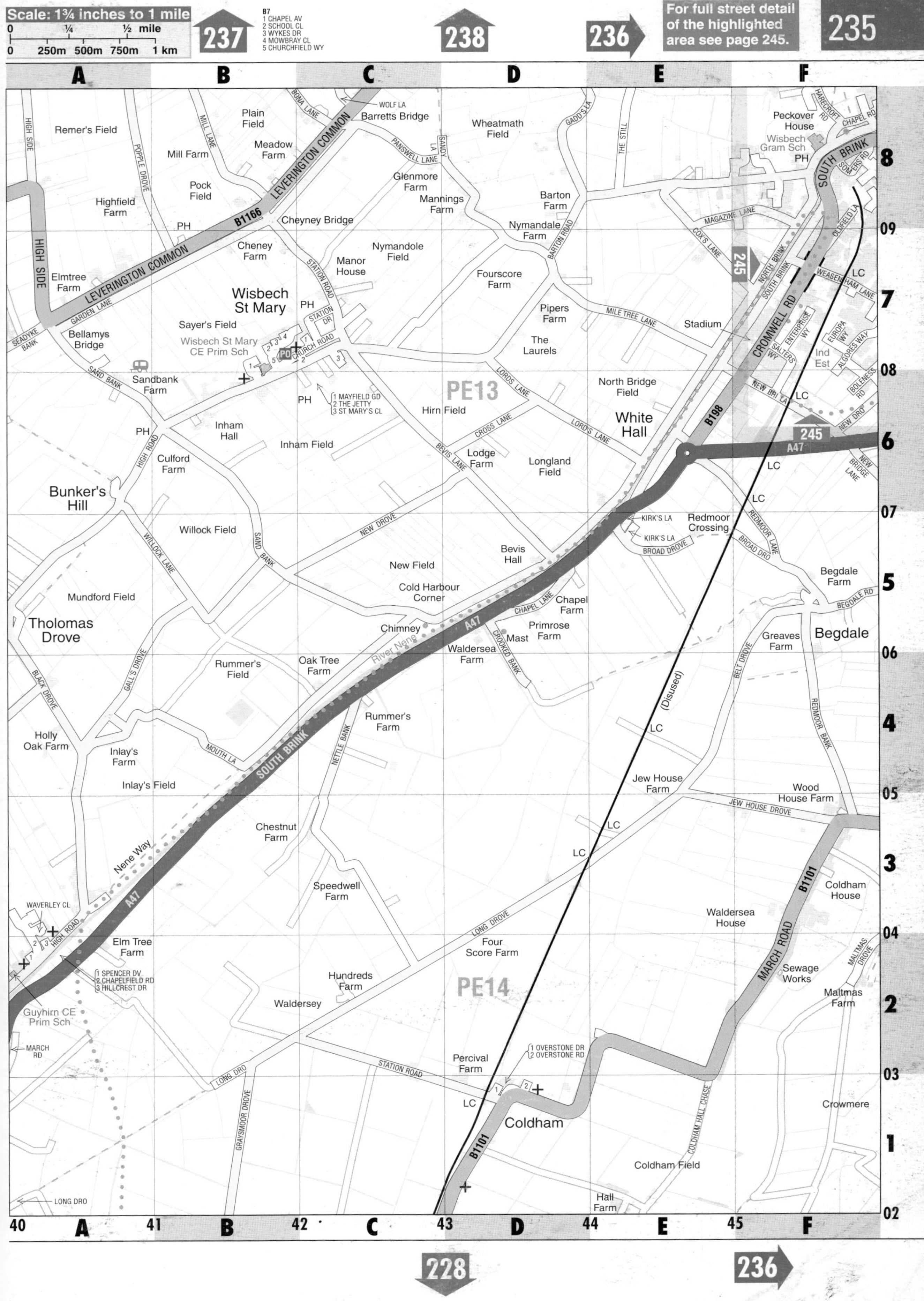

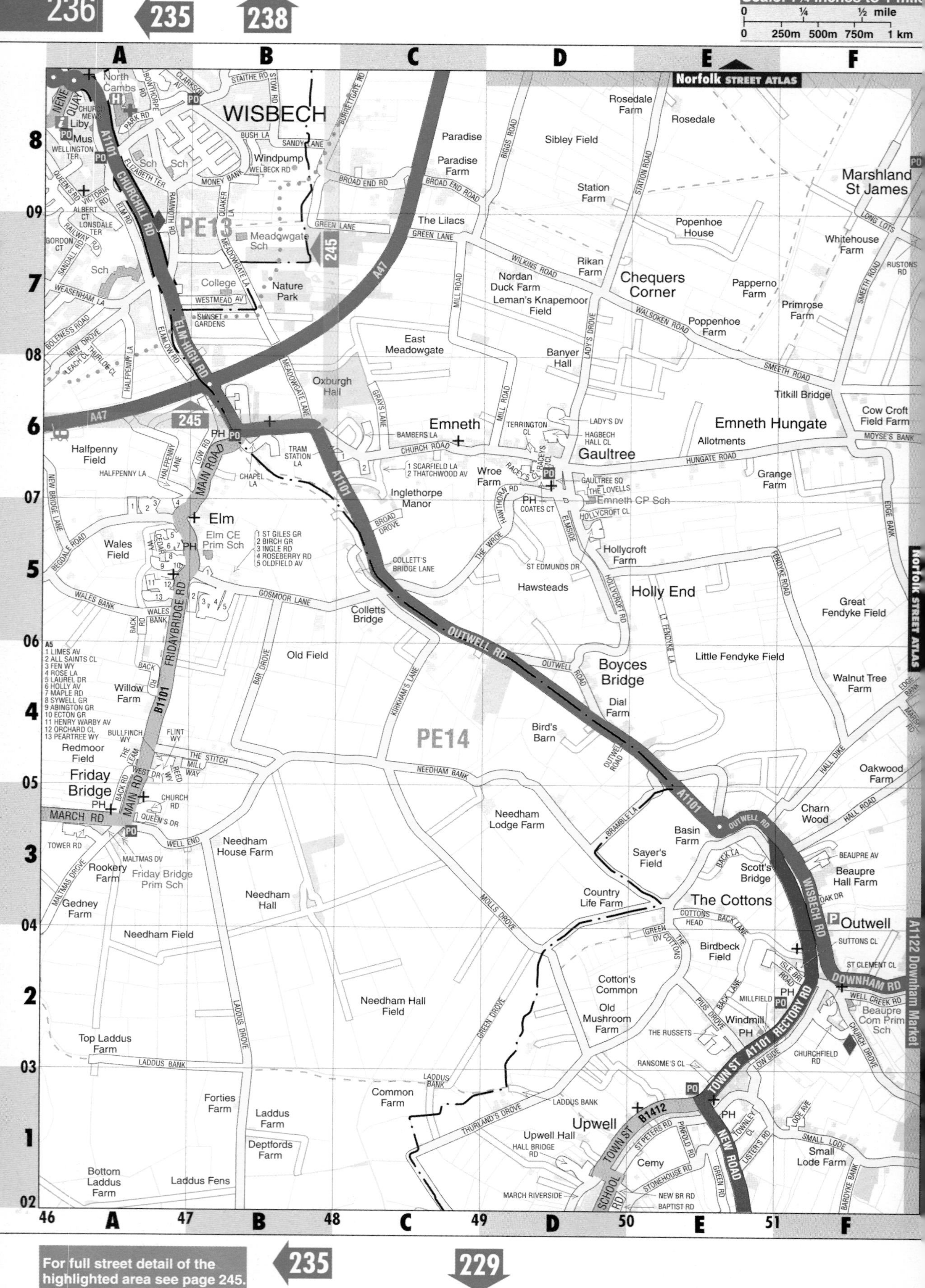

Scale: 1¾ inches to 1 mile

0   ¼   ½ mile

0   250m 500m 750m 1 km

A   B   C   D   E   F

Norfolk STREET ATLAS

North
Cambs
Liby
Mus
CHURCH
CHURCH
MEWS
Staithe Rd
CLARKSON
AV
PO
BUSH LA
SANDY LANE
WISBECH
Windpump
WELBECK RD
BROAD END RD
Paradise
Paradise
Farm
Biggs Road
Sibley Field
Rosedale
Farm
Rosedale
Marshland
St James

8

Wellington
Ter
MONEY BANK
QUAKER
The Lilacs
Station
Farm
Popenhoe
House
Whitehouse
Farm
Rustons
Rd

09
Albert
Ct
Lonsdale
Ter
Balwary
Rd
Gordon
Ct
Sandall Rd
Meadowgate
La
PE13
Meadowgate
Sch
245
BROAD END ROAD
Green Lane
GREEN LANE
Wilkins Road
Rikan
Farm
Chequers
Corner
Papperno
Farm
Primrose
Farm

7
Weasenham La
Sch
College
WESTMEAD AV
A47
Nordan
Duck Farm
Leman's Knapemoor
Field
Poppenhoe
Farm

Nature
Park
SUNSET
GARDENS
Sch
Oxburgh
Hall
East
Meadowgate
Banyer
Hall
Walsoken Road

08
New Drove
HALFPENNY
LANE
ELM LOW RD
ELM HIGH RD
245
Bambers La
Emneth
CHURCH ROAD
Terrington
Cl
Lady's Dv
Smeeth Road
Titkill Bridge
Cow Croft
Field Farm

6
A47
Halfpenny
Field
HALFPENNY LA
PH
PO
TRAM
STATION LA
CHAPEL
LA
A1101
1 SCARFIELD LA
2 THATCHWOOD AV
Wroe
Farm
HAGBECH
HALL CL
Gaultree
Gaultree Sq
THE LOVELLS
Allotments
Emneth Hungate
Moyse's Bank
Grange
Farm

07
LOW RD
MAIN ROAD
Elm
Inglethorpe
Manor
BROAD DROVE
RACEY'S CL
COATES CT
PH
Emneth CP Sch
HOLLYCROFT CL
Hungate Road
Edge Bank

Elm CE
Prim Sch
1 ST GILES GR
2 BIRCH GR
3 INGLE RD
4 ROSEBERRY RD
5 OLDFIELD AV
THE WROE
Hollycroft
Farm
ELMSIDE
HOLLYCROFT RD

5
Wales
Field
FRIDAYBRIDGE RD
PH
GOSMOOR LANE
Colletts
Bridge
Collett's
Bridge Lane
St Edmunds Dr
Hawsteads
Holly End
LT FENDYKE LA
FENDYKE ROAD
Great
Fendyke Field

REGDALE ROAD
WALES BANK
BACK
WALES
BANK
Old Field
OUTWELL RD
OUTWELL RD
Little Fendyke Field
Walnut Tree
Farm

06
AS
1 LIMES AV
2 ALL SAINTS CL
3 FEN WY
4 ROSE LA
5 LAUREL DR
6 HOLLY AV
7 MAPLE RD
8 SYWELL GR
9 ABINGTON GR
10 ECTON GR
11 HENRY WARBY AV
12 ORCHARD CL
13 PEARTREE WY
Willow
Farm
BAR DROVE
KIRKHAM'S LANE
Boyces
Bridge
Dial
Farm

4
B1101
BULLFINCH WY
FLINT
WY
THE STITCH
MILL
WAY
PE14
OUTWELL
ROAD
Bird's
Barn
Hall Dike
Oakwood
Farm

Redmoor
Field
THE TEAM
WEST DR
REED
NEEDHAM BANK
A1101
Charn
Wood
Hall Road

05
Friday
Bridge
PH
MARCH RD
MAIN RD
CHURCH
RD
QUEEN'S DR
Needham
Lodge Farm
Basin
Farm
BACK LA
Scott's
Bridge
Beaupre Av
Beaupre
Hall Farm

3
TOWER RD
Rookery
Farm
PO
WELL END
MALTMAS DV
Friday Bridge
Prim Sch
Needham
House Farm
BRAMBLE LA
Sayer's
Field
OUTWELL RD
WISBECH RD
The Cottons
OAK DR
Outwell
A1122 Downham Market

04
MALTMAS DROVE
Gedney
Farm
Needham Field
Needham
Hall
MOLLS DROVE
LADDUS DROVE
Country
Life Farm
GREEN DROVE
COTTONS
HEAD
BACK LANE
Birdbeck
Field
SUTTONS CL
ST CLEMENT CL

2
Top Laddus
Farm
Needham Hall
Field
Cotton's
Common
Old
Mushroom
Farm
THE RUSSETS
Windmill
PH
A1101
RECTORY RD
MILLFIELD
WELL CREEK RD
Beaupre
Com Prim
Sch

03
LADDUS BANK
Forties
Farm
Laddus
Farm
LADDUS BANK
Ransome's Cl
TOWN ST
CHURCHFIELD
RD
CHURCH DROVE

1
Bottom
Laddus
Farm
Deptfords
Farm
THURLAND'S DROVE
Common Farm
Upwell Hall
HALL BRIDGE
RD
Upwell
TOWN ST
B1412
ST PETERS RD
LISTERS RD
PH
NEW ROAD
SMALL
LODE CL
Small
Lode Farm

02
Laddus Fens
Cemy
SCHOOL
RD
PINFOLD RD
STONEHOUSE RD
GREEN RD
BARDYKE BANK

MARCH RIVERSIDE
NEW BR RD
BAPTIST RD

46   A   47   B   48   C   49   D   50   E   51   F

For full street detail of the
highlighted area see page 245.
235
229

Scale: 1¾ inches to 1 mile
0 ¼ ½ mile
0 250m 500m 750m 1 km

238

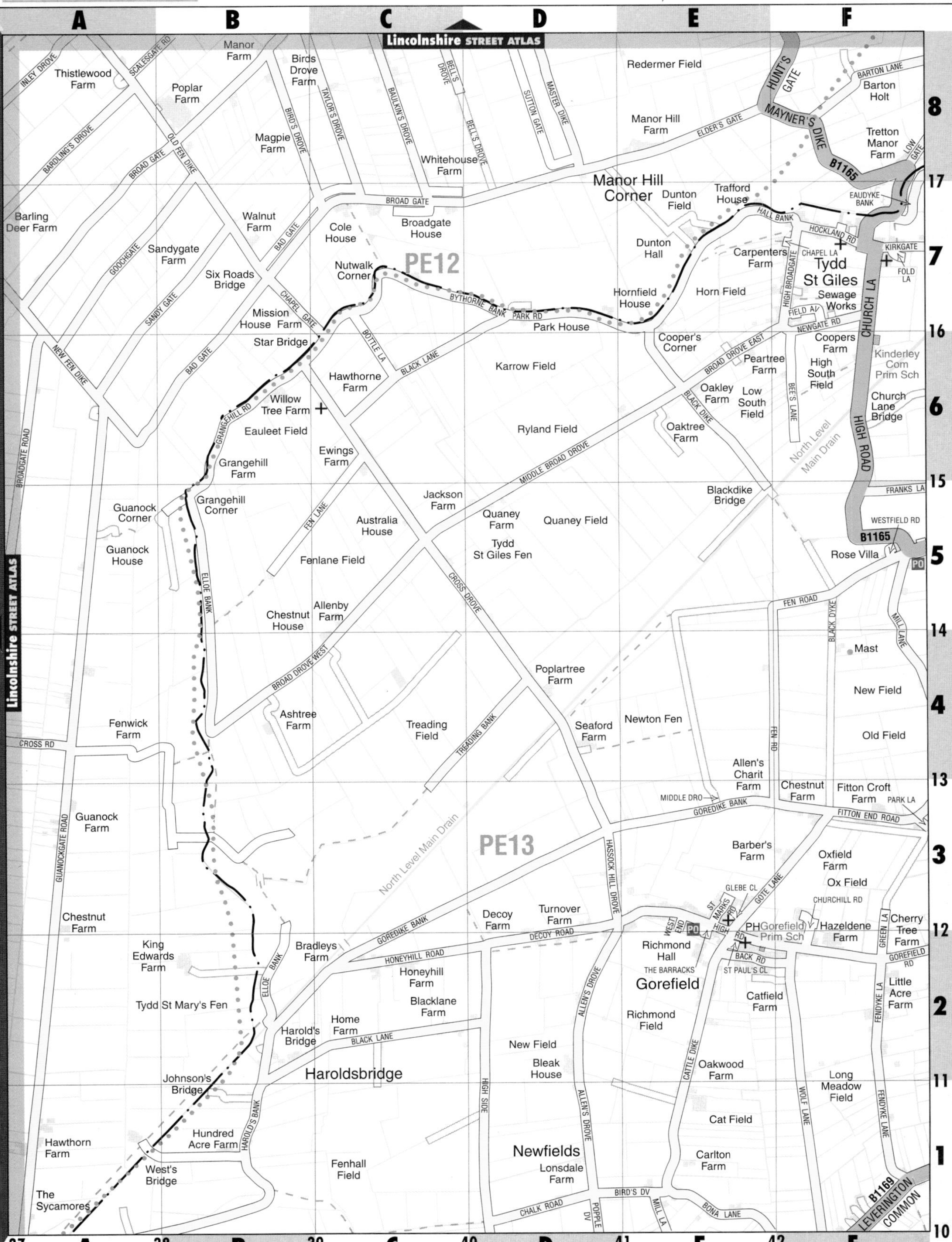

Lincolnshire STREET ATLAS
A
B
C
D
E
F
8
17
7
16
6
15
5
14
4
13
3
12
2
11
1
10
37
38
39
40
41
42
Thistlewood Farm
Manor Farm
Birds Drove Farm
Redermer Field
Poplar Farm
Barton Holt
Manor Hill Farm
Tretton Manor Farm
Magpie Farm
Whitehouse Farm
Manor Hill Corner
Trafford House
Dunton Field
Barling Deer Farm
Walnut Farm
Broadgate House
Cole House
Sandygate Farm
Six Roads Bridge
Nutwalk Corner
PE12
Dunton Hall
Carpenters Farm
Tydd St Giles
Sewage Works
Horn Field
Hornfield House
Mission House
Farm
Star Bridge
Park House
Cooper's Corner
Coopers Farm
Kinderley Com Prim Sch
Hawthorne Farm
Karrow Field
Peartree Farm
High South Field
Willow Tree Farm
Oakley Farm
Low South Field
Church Lane Bridge
Eauleet Field
Ryland Field
Oaktree Farm
Ewings Farm
Grangehill Farm
North Level Main Drain
Blackdike Bridge
Grangehill Corner
Jackson Farm
Guanock Corner
Quaney Farm
Quaney Field
Australia House
Tydd St Giles Fen
Guanock House
Rose Villa
Fenlane Field
Allenby Farm
Chestnut House
Mast
Poplartree Farm
New Field
Ashtree Farm
Fenwick Farm
Treading Field
Seaford Farm
Newton Fen
Old Field
Allen's Charit Farm
Chestnut Farm
Fitton Croft Farm
Guanock Farm
PE13
Barber's Farm
Oxfield Farm
Ox Field
Chestnut Farm
Turnover Farm
Decoy Farm
Cherry Tree Farm
Hazeldene Farm
Gorefield Prim Sch
King Edwards Farm
Bradleys Farm
Richmond Hall
Honeyhill Farm
THE BARRACKS
Gorefield
Tydd St Mary's Fen
Blacklane Farm
Catfield Farm
Little Acre Farm
Richmond Field
Home Farm
Harold's Bridge
New Field
Bleak House
Oakwood Farm
Haroldsbridge
Johnson's Bridge
Long Meadow Field
Cat Field
Hawthorn Farm
Hundred Acre Farm
Newfields
Fenhall Field
Carlton Farm
West's Bridge
Lonsdale Farm
The Sycamores
INLEY DROVE
SCALESGATE RD
BARDLING'S DROVE
BROAD GATE
OLD FEN DIKE
BIRD'S DROVE
TAYLOR'S DROVE
BAULKIN'S DROVE
BELL'S DROVE
SUTTON GATE
MASTER DIKE
ELDER'S GATE
HUNT'S GATE
MAYNER'S DIKE
B1165
BARTON LANE
LOW GATE
EAUDYKE BANK
HALL BANK
HOCKLAND RD
KIRKGATE
FOLD LA
CHAPEL LA
HIGH BROADGATE
CHURCH LA
FIELD AV
NEWGATE RD
BROAD GATE
BAD GATE
GOOCHGATE
SANDY GATE
CHAPEL GATE
BYTHORNE BANK
PARK RD
BOTTLE LA
BLACK LANE
NEW FEN DIKE
BAD GATE
GRANGEHILL RD
BROAD DROVE EAST
BLACK DIKE
BEE'S LANE
HIGH ROAD
BROADGATE ROAD
MIDDLE BROAD DROVE
FRANKS LA
WESTFIELD RD
B1165
PO
FEN LANE
ELLOE BANK
CROSS DROVE
FEN ROAD
BLACK DYKE
MILL LANE
BROAD DROVE WEST
CROSS RD
TREADING BANK
FEN RD
MIDDLE DRO
GOREDIKE BANK
PARK LA
FITTON END ROAD
GUANOCKGATE ROAD
HASSOCK HILL DROVE
GLEBE CL
GOTE LANE
ST MARKS RD
WEST END
HIGH RD
PH
CHURCHILL RD
GOREDIKE BANK
DECOY ROAD
HONEYHILL ROAD
BACK RD
ST PAUL'S CL
GREEN LA
GOREFIELD RD
ELLOE BANK
ALLEN'S DROVE
FENDYKE LANE
BLACK LANE
CATTLE DIKE
HIGH SIDE
HAROLD'S BANK
WOLF LANE
ALLEN'S DROVE
FENDYKE LANE
BIRD'S DV
MILL LA
CHALK ROAD
POPPLE DV
BONA LANE
B1169
LEVERINGTON COMMON

234
235
238

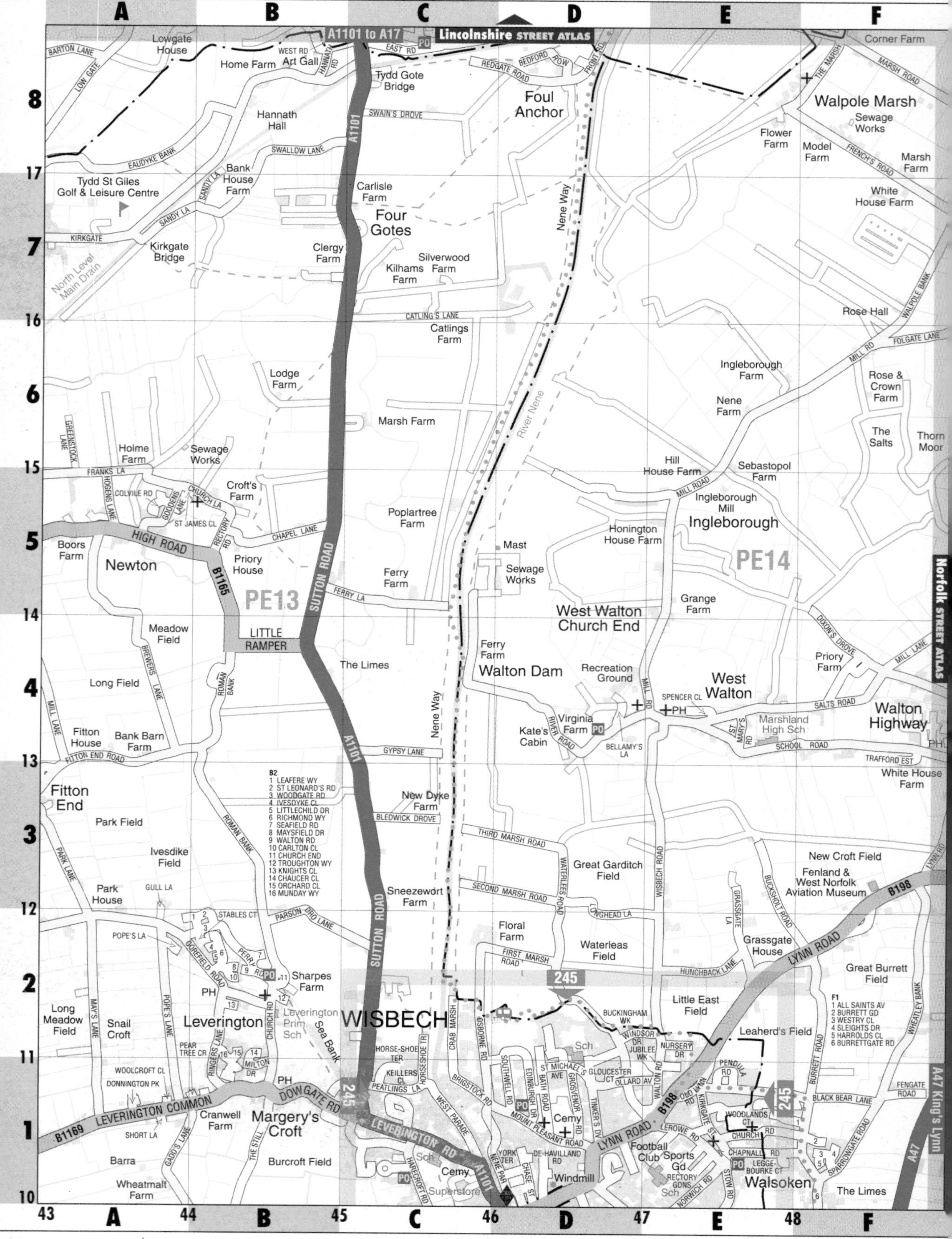

Scale: 1¾ inches to 1 mile

0   ¼   ½ mile

0   250m 500m 750m 1 km

Lincolnshire STREET ATLAS

A   B   C   D   E   F

Barton Lane

Lowgate House

LOW GATE

EAUDYKE BANK

Tydd St Giles Golf & Leisure Centre

North Level Main Drain

KIRKGATE

Kirkgate Bridge

SANDY LA

Home Farm

WEST RD

HANNATH RD

Art Gall

Hannath Hall

SWALLOW LANE

Bank House Farm

GROVERS LANE

CHURCH LA

RECTORY RD

St James Cl

St James Cl

HIGH ROAD

Boors Farm

Newton

PE13

B1165

Priory House

A1101 to A17

Tydd Gote Bridge

SWAIN'S DROVE

Carlisle Farm

Four Gotes

Clergy Farm

Silverwood Farm

Kilhams Farm

CATLING'S LANE

Catlings Farm

Lodge Farm

Marsh Farm

Holme Farm

Sewage Works

Croft's Farm

CHAPEL LANE

Poplartree Farm

Ferry Farm

A1101

SUTTON ROAD

FERRY LA

LITTLE RAMPER

The Limes

ROMAN BANK

Meadow Field

Long Field

Fitton House

Bank Barn Farm

FITTON END ROAD

MILL LANE

BREWERS LANE

Fitton End

Park Field

Ivesdike Field

Park House

PARK LANE

GULL LA

ROMAN BANK

STABLES CT

PARSON'S LANE

POPE'S LA

MAY'S LANE

POPE'S LA

Snail Croft

Long Meadow Field

FOREFIELD ROAD

PH

PERRY RD

CHURCH RD

Sharpes Farm

Leverington

PEAR TREE CR

RINGERS LA

MILTON DR

PH

Leverington Prim Sch

Sea Bank

WISBECH

GYPSY LANE

New Dyke Farm

BLEDWICK DROVE

Sneezewort Farm

B2
1 LEAFERE WY
2 ST LEONARD'S RD
3 WOODGATE RD
4 IVESDYKE CL
5 LITTLECHILD DR
6 RICHMOND WY
7 SEAFIELD RD
8 MAYSFIELD DR
9 WALTON RD
10 CARLTON CL
11 CHURCH END
12 TROUGHTON WY
13 KNIGHTS CL
14 CHAUCER CL
15 ORCHARD CL
16 MUNDAY WY

THIRD MARSH ROAD

SECOND MARSH ROAD

WATERLESS ROAD

Great Garditch Field

Floral Farm

Waterleas Field

FIRST MARSH ROAD

LONGHEAD LA

WISBECH ROAD

245

BUCKINGHAM WK

Little East Field

WINDSOR DR

JUBILEE WK

NURSERY DR

WOOLCROFT CL

DONNINGTON PK

SHORT LA

B1169

LEVERINGTON COMMON

CRANWELL FARM

Margery's Croft

THE STILL

GAOD'S LANE

Barra

Wheatmalt Farm

Burcroft Field

DOWGATE RD

A1101

245

LEVERINGTON RD

HORSE-SHOE TER

HORSESHOE TER

KEILLERS CL

PEATLINGS LA

WEST PARADE

PO

Sch

BRIGSTOCK RD

HARECROFT RD

THE STILL

Cemy Superstore

SOUTHWELL RD

OSBORNE RD

CRAB MARSH

YORK TER

CHASE ST

NENE PAR

ASHLINE

ST MICHAEL'S AVE

EDINBURGH DR

MOUNT PLEASANT

BATH RD

GROSVENOR RD

GLOUCESTER CT

OLLARD AV

DE-HAVILLAND RD

Windmill

Foul Anchor

REDGATE ROAD

BEDFORD ROW

FRONT RD

Nene Way

River Nene

West Walton Church End

Ferry Farm

Walton Dam

Mast

Sewage Works

Virginia Farm

Kate's Cabin

BELLAMY'S LA

Recreation Ground

SPENCER CL

PH

PH

Honington House Farm

Hill House Farm

Grange Farm

MILL RD

DIXON'S DROVE

SALTS ROAD

ST MARY'S RD

Marshland High Sch

SCHOOL ROAD

West Walton

TRAFFORD EST

White House Farm

Great Gardiech Field

GRASSGATE LA

Grassgate House

HUNCHBACK LANE

Fenland & West Norfolk Aviation Museum

BLACKSHORT ROAD

LYNN ROAD

B198

Great Burrett Field

F1
1 ALL SAINTS AV
2 BURRETT GD
3 WESTRY CL
4 SLEIGHTS DR
5 HARROLDS CL
6 BURRETTGATE RD

Leaherd's Field

PENDULA RD

PRIORY RD

245

BLACK BEAR LANE

OLD INN RD

HARKGATE RD

Woodlands Ct

CHAPNALL RD

PO

LEGGE-BOURKE CT

Walsoken

The Limes

Football Club Sports Gd

RECTORY GDNS

NORWICH RD

STOW RD

LEROWE RD

CHURCH RD

SPARROWGATE RD

FENGATE ROAD

WHEATLEY BANK

BURRETT ROAD

A47 King's Lynn

A47

Corner Farm

THE MARSH

MARSH ROAD

Walpole Marsh

Sewage Works

Flower Farm

Model Farm

FRENCH'S ROAD

Marsh Farm

White House Farm

WALPOLE BANK

Rose Hall

MILL RD

FOLGATE LANE

Ingleborough Farm

Nene Farm

Rose & Crown Farm

The Salts

Thorn Moor

Sebastopol Farm

Ingleborough Mill

Ingleborough

PE14

Priory Farm

MILL LANE

Walton Highway

PH

Norfolk STREET ATLAS

8

17

7

16

6

15

5

14

4

13

3

12

2

11

1

10

43   A   44   B   45   C   46   D   47   E   48   F

For full street detail of the highlighted area see page 245.

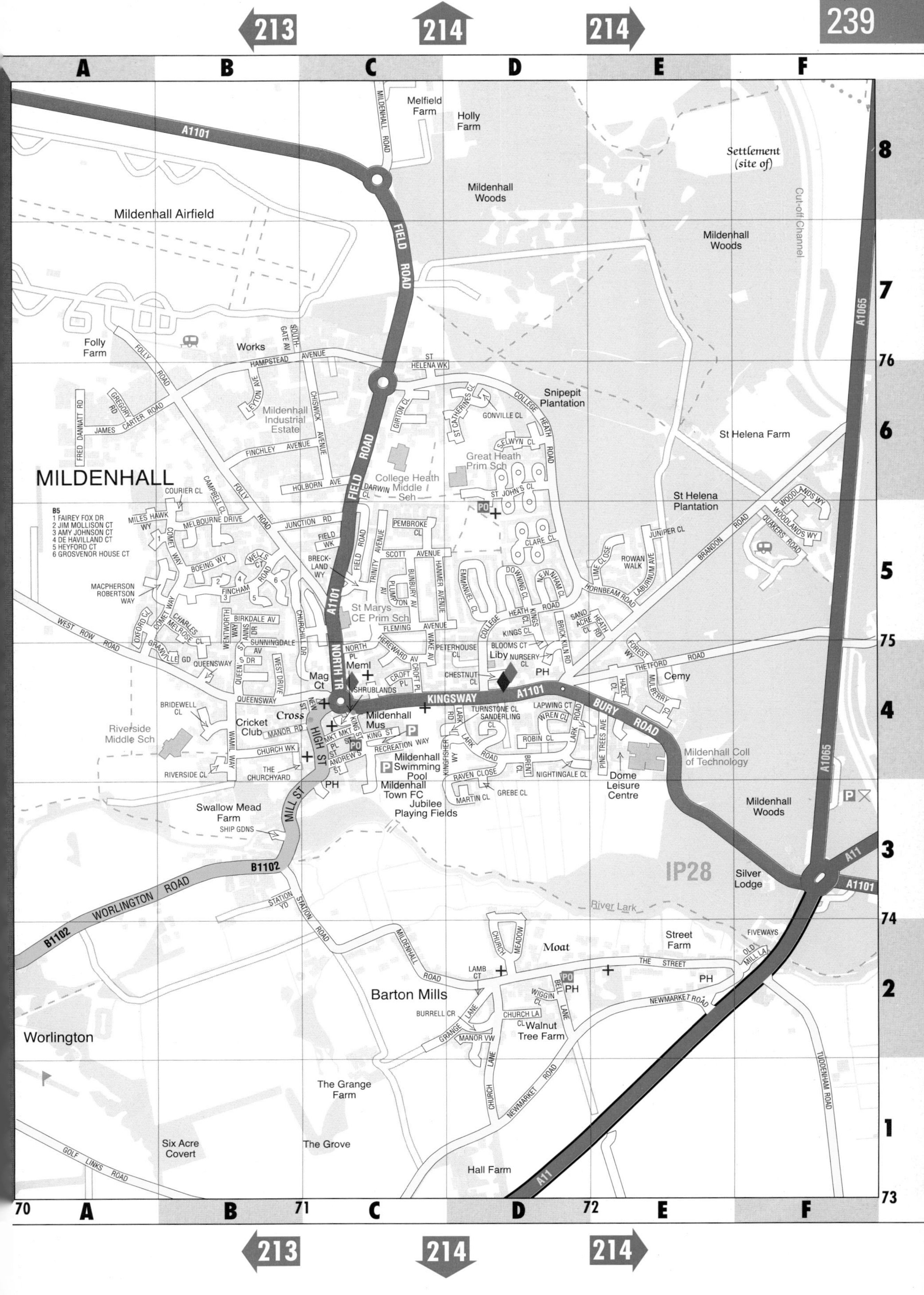
213
214
214
A
B
C
D
E
F
A1101
Melfield Farm
Holly Farm
MILDENHALL ROAD
Settlement (site of)
Mildenhall Woods
Mildenhall Airfield
FIELD ROAD
Cut-off Channel
Mildenhall Woods
A1065
Folly Farm
Works
SOUTHGATE AV
HAMPSTEAD AVENUE
ST HELENA WK
FOLLY ROAD
GREGORY RD
JAMES CARTER ROAD
LEYTON AVE
Mildenhall Industrial Estate
CHISWICK AVENUE
GIRTON CL
ST CATHERINES CL
COLLEGE HEATH ROAD
GONVILLE CL
Snipepit Plantation
St Helena Farm
FRED DANNATT RD
FINCHLEY AVENUE
SELWYN CL
Great Heath Prim Sch
MILDENHALL
COURIER CL
CAMPBELL CL
HOLBORN AVE
College Heath Middle Sch
DARWIN CL
ST JOHN'S CL
St Helena Plantation
B5
1 FAIREY FOX DR
2 JIM MOLLISON CT
3 AMY JOHNSON CT
4 DE HAVILLAND CT
5 HEYFORD CT
6 GROSVENOR HOUSE CT
MILES HAWK WY
MELBOURNE DRIVE
JUNCTION RD
FIELD WK
PEMBROKE CL
CLARE CL
JUNIPER CL
BRANDON ROAD
WOODLANDS WY
QUAKERS' ROAD
COMET WAY
BOEING WY
WELLS CT
BRECKLAND WY
SCOTT AVENUE
TRINITY AVENUE
HANMER AVENUE
ROWAN WALK
LIME CLOSE
LABURNUM AVE
MACPHERSON ROBERTSON WAY
FINCHAM ROAD
PLUMPTON AV
BUNBURY AV
EMMANUEL CL
DOWNING CL
NEWNHAM CL
HORNBEAM ROAD
WEST ROW ROAD
OXFORD CL
CHARLES MELROSE CL
BIRKDALE AV
WENTWORTH WAY
ST ANNS DR
CHURCHILL DR
St Marys CE Prim Sch
FLEMING AVENUE
COLLEGE HEATH ROAD
KINGS CL
SANDACRE CL
HEATH RD
BRICK KILN RD
SUNNINGDALE AV
GRANVILLE GD
QUEENSWAY
QUEEN'S DR
WEST DRIVE
NORTH TR
NORTH PL
HEREWARD AV
WAKE AV
PETERHOUSE CL
BLOOMS CT
Liby
NURSERY CL
PH
FOREST WY
THETFORD ROAD
Cemy
Mag Ct
Meml
CROFT PL
CROFT PL
CHESTNUT CL
SHRUBLANDS
QUEENSWAY
KINGSWAY
A1101
HAZEL CL
MULBERRY CL
BRIDEWELL CL
NEW ST
Cross
Mildenhall Mus
TURNSTONE CL
SANDERLING CL
LAPWING CT
WREN CL
BURY ROAD
Riverside Middle Sch
Cricket Club
MANOR RD
HIGH ST
MKT ST
KING ST
P
WAMIL WAY
CHURCH WK
PL ST
ST ANDREW'S ST
PO
RECREATION WAY
KINGFISHER RD
LARK RD
ROBIN CL
LARK RD
PINE TREES AVE
Mildenhall Coll of Technology
Mildenhall Swimming Pool
RIVERSIDE CL
THE CHURCHYARD
PH
Mildenhall Town FC
RAVEN CLOSE
BRENT CL
NIGHTINGALE CL
Dome Leisure Centre
A1065
Jubilee Playing Fields
MARTIN CL
GREBE CL
Mildenhall Woods
Swallow Mead Farm
MILL ST
SHIP GDNS
B1102
IP28
Silver Lodge
A11
A1101
WORLINGTON ROAD
STATION YD
STATION ROAD
River Lark
B1102
MILDENHALL ROAD
CHURCH MEADOW
Moat
Street Farm
FIVEWAYS
OLD MILL LA
LAMB CT
THE STREET
PO
PH
PH
Barton Mills
BELL LANE
WIGGIN CL
NEWMARKET ROAD
BURRELL CR
GRANGE LANE
CHURCH LA
CL
Walnut Tree Farm
MANOR VW
Worlington
CHURCH LANE
NEWMARKET ROAD
TUDDENHAM ROAD
The Grange Farm
Six Acre Covert
The Grove
GOLF LINKS ROAD
Hall Farm
A11
8
7
76
6
5
75
4
3
74
2
1
73
70
71
72
A
B
C
D
E
F
213
214
214

218 218 218

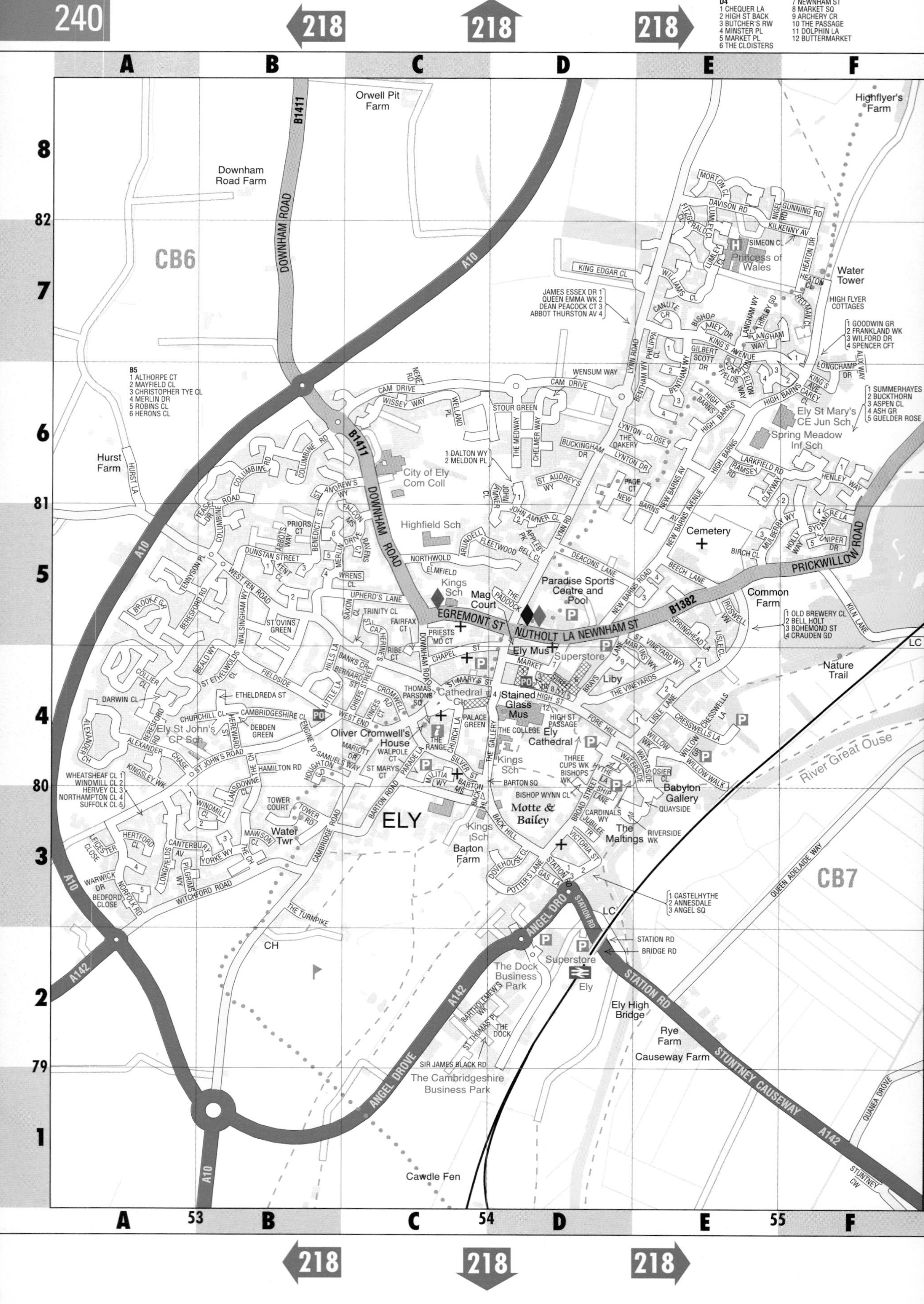
D4
1 CHEQUER LA
2 HIGH ST BACK
3 BUTCHER'S RW
4 MINSTER PL
5 MARKET PL
6 THE CLOISTERS
7 NEWNHAM ST
8 MARKET SQ
9 ARCHERY CR
10 THE PASSAGE
11 DOLPHIN LA
12 BUTTERMARKET
A
B
C
D
E
F
8
82
7
6
81
5
4
80
3
2
79
1
53
54
55
Orwell Pit Farm
Highflyer's Farm
Downham Road Farm
CB6
B1411
DOWNHAM ROAD
A10
Water Tower
HIGH FLYER COTTAGES
JAMES ESSEX DR 1
QUEEN EMMA WK 2
DEAN PEACOCK CT 3
ABBOT THURSTON AV 4
1 GOODWIN GR
2 FRANKLAND WK
3 WILFORD DR
4 SPENCER CFT
B5
1 ALTHORPE CT
2 MAYFIELD CL
3 CHRISTOPHER TYE CL
4 MERLIN DR
5 ROBINS CL
6 HERONS CL
1 SUMMERHAYES
2 BUCKTHORN
3 ASPEN CL
4 ASH GR
5 GUELDER ROSE
Princess of Wales
KING EDGAR CL
MORTON CL
DAVISON RD
GUNNING RD
KILKENNY AV
SIMEON CL
HEATON DR
WILLIAMS CL
CANUTE CR
BISHOP LANEY DR
LANGHAM WY
KING'S AVENUE
GILBERT SCOTT DR
LONGCHAMP DR
ALIX WAY
HIGH BARNS
Ely St Mary's CE Jun Sch
Spring Meadow Inf Sch
Hurst Farm
HURST LA
City of Ely Com Coll
1 DALTON WY
2 MELDON PL
CAM DRIVE
WISSEY WAY
WENSUM WAY
STOUR GREEN
THE MEDWAY
CHELMER WAY
WELLAND PL
LYNN ROAD
BUCKINGHAM DR
LYNTON CLOSE
LYNTON DR
ST AUDREY'S WY
LARKFIELD RD
RAMSEY RD
HENLEY WAY
Highfield Sch
Cemetery
PRICKWILLOW ROAD
JOHN AMNER CL
NORTHWOLD
ELMFIELD
FLEETWOOD
DEACONS LANE
NEW BARNS AVENUE
BEECH LANE
SYCAMORE LA
JUNIPER DR
BIRCH CL
COLUMBINE RD
DUNSTAN STREET
WEST FEN ROAD
TENNYSON PL
PRIORS CT
Paradise Sports Centre and Pool
Kings Sch
Mag Court
Common Farm
B1382
EGREMONT ST
NUTHOLT LA
NEWNHAM ST
1 OLD BREWERY CL
2 BELL HOLT
3 BOHEMOND ST
4 CRAUDEN GD
LC
Ely Mus
Superstore
Liby
Nature Trail
ST OVINS GREEN
FIELDSIDE
ETHELDREDA ST
DARWIN CL
CHURCHILL CL
CAMBRIDGESHIRE CL
DEBDEN GREEN
Ely St John's CP Sch
ST JOHN'S ROAD
HAMILTON RD
WEST END
Thomas Parsons Sq
Cathedral Ct
Stained Glass Mus
Oliver Cromwell's House
Ely Cathedral
Kings Sch
River Great Ouse
WHEATSHEAF CL 1
WINDMILL CL 2
HERVEY CL 3
NORTHAMPTON CL 4
SUFFOLK CL 5
BARTON SQ
BISHOP WYNN CL
Babylon Gallery
QUAYSIDE
TOWER COURT
ELY
Motte & Bailey
Water Twr
The Maltings
RIVERSIDE WK
Barton Farm
WITCHFORD ROAD
CAMBRIDGE ROAD
BARTON ROAD
1 CASTELHYTHE
2 ANNESDALE
3 ANGEL SQ
CB7
QUEEN ADELAIDE WAY
THE TURNPIKE
CH
LC
STATION RD
BRIDGE RD
A142
ANGEL DROVE
The Dock Business Park
Superstore
Ely
Ely High Bridge
Rye Farm
Causeway Farm
STATION RD
STUNTNEY CAUSEWAY
SIR JAMES BLACK RD
The Cambridgeshire Business Park
QUANEA DROVE
STUNTNEY CW
Cawdle Fen
A10

218 218 218

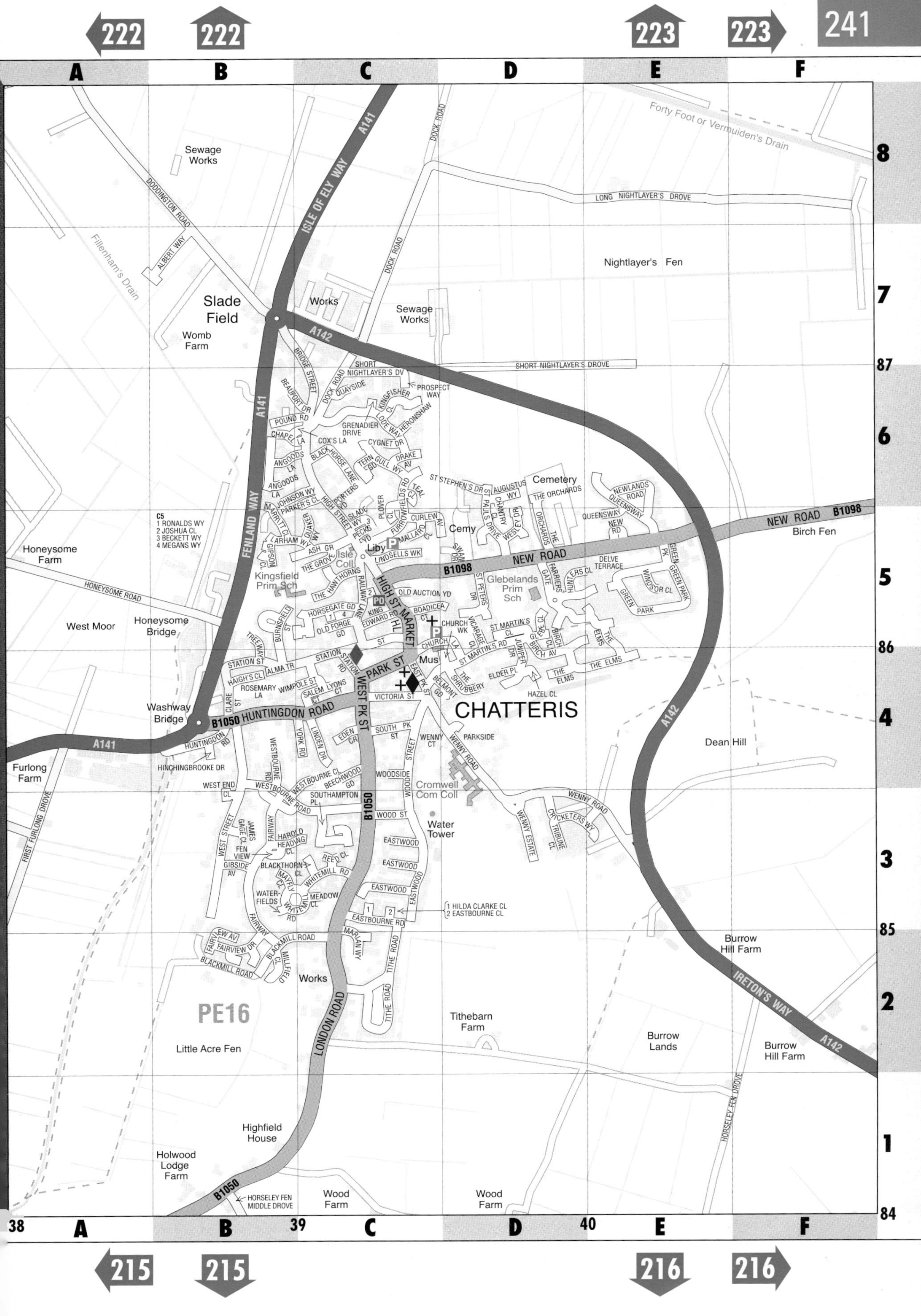
222
222
223
223
A
B
C
D
E
F
8
7
87
6
5
86
4
3
85
2
1
84
38
39
40
215
215
216
216
CHATTERIS
Slade Field
Womb Farm
Sewage Works
Works
Nightlayer's Fen
Forty Foot or Vermuiden's Drain
LONG NIGHTLAYER'S DROVE
SHORT NIGHTLAYER'S DROVE
ISLE OF ELY WAY
A141
A142
DODDINGTON ROAD
ALBERT WAY
Fillenham's Drain
DOCK ROAD
FENLAND WAY
Honeysome Farm
HONEYSOME ROAD
Honeysome Bridge
West Moor
Washway Bridge
B1050 HUNTINGDON ROAD
Furlong Farm
FIRST FURLONG DROVE
HINCHINGBROOKE DR
Kingsfield Prim Sch
Isle Coll
Liby
Cemy
Cemetery
Glebelands Prim Sch
NEW ROAD
B1098
Birch Fen
HIGH ST
MARKET HL
PARK ST
WEST PK ST
Mus
Cromwell Com Coll
Water Tower
Dean Hill
Burrow Hill Farm
IRETON'S WAY
Burrow Lands
Tithebarn Farm
PE16
Little Acre Fen
LONDON ROAD
Works
Highfield House
Holwood Lodge Farm
Wood Farm
Wood Farm
HORSELEY FEN MIDDLE DROVE
HORSELEY FEN DROVE
C5
1 RONALDS WY
2 JOSHUA CL
3 BECKETT WY
4 MEGANS WY
1 HILDA CLARKE CL
2 EASTBOURNE CL
WENNY ROAD
WENNY ESTATE
CRICKETERS WY
TRIBUNE CL
PARKSIDE
HAZEL CL
THE ELMS
ST MARTIN'S RD
STATION ST
ALMA TR
HAIGH'S CL
ROSEMARY LA
WIMPOLE ST
VICTORIA ST
SOUTH PK ST
WESTBOURNE RD
WEST STREET
BLACKMILL ROAD
FAIRVIEW DR
MILLFIELD CL
TITHE ROAD
EASTWOOD
WOOD ST
WOODSIDE
BEECHWOOD GD
SOUTHAMPTON PL

225 225 226

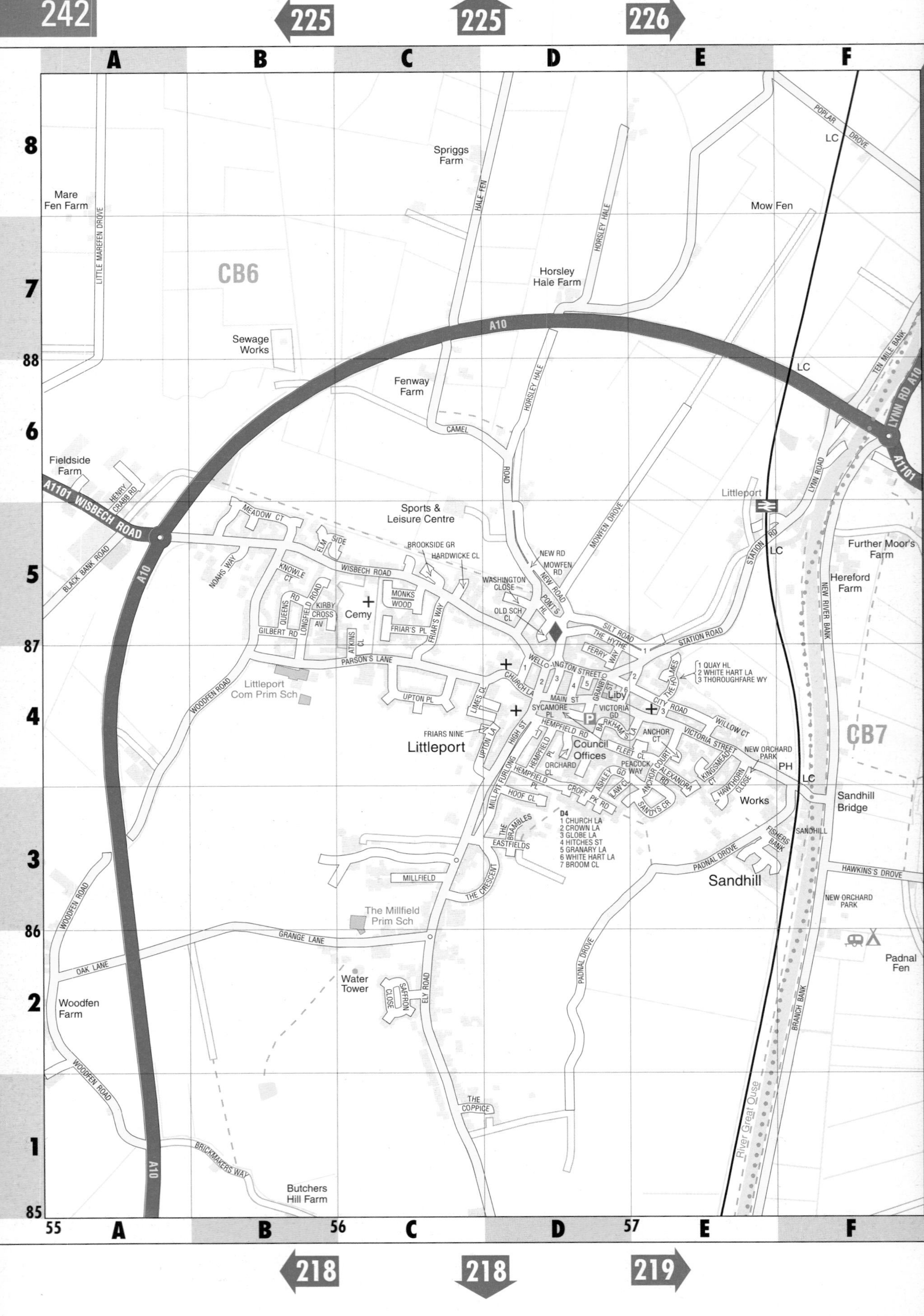
A
B
C
D
E
F
8
7
88
6
5
87
4
3
86
2
1
85
55
56
57
Spriggs Farm
Mare Fen Farm
LITTLE MAREFEN DROVE
HALE FEN
HORSLEY HALE
Horsley Hale Farm
Mow Fen
POPLAR DROVE
LC
CB6
Sewage Works
A10
Fenway Farm
CAMEL
HORSLEY HALE
TEN MILE BANK
LYNN RD A10
A1101
Fieldside Farm
HENRY CRABB RD
A1101 WISBECH ROAD
BLACK BANK ROAD
MEADOW CT
Sports & Leisure Centre
MOWFEN DROVE
Littleport
LYNN ROAD
STATION RD
Further Moor's Farm
Hereford Farm
NEW RIVER BANK
NOAHS WAY
KNOWLE CT
ELM SIDE
WISBECH ROAD
BROOKSIDE GR
HARDWICKE CL
NEW RD
MOWFEN RD
NEW ROAD
WASHINGTON CLOSE
PONTS HL
OLD SCH CL
MONKS WOOD
FRIAR'S PL
FRIAR'S WAY
QUEENS RD
LONGFIELD ROAD
KIRBY CROSS AV
GILBERT RD
Cemy
ATKINS CL
PARSON'S LANE
SILT ROAD
THE HYTHE
FERRY WAY
STATION ROAD
WELLINGTON STREET
CHURCH LA
GRANBY ST
THE HOLMES
1 QUAY HL
2 WHITE HART LA
3 THOROUGHFARE WY
Littleport Com Prim Sch
WOODFEN ROAD
UPTON PL
LIMES CL
MAIN ST
Liby
CITY ROAD
SYCAMORE PL
VICTORIA GD
BARKHAMS LA
WILLOW CT
FRIARS NINE
Littleport
UPTON LA
HIGH ST
HEMPFIELD RD
HEMPFIELD PL
Council Offices
ANCHOR CT
VICTORIA STREET
NEW ORCHARD PARK
CB7
FLEET CL
ORCHARD CL
PEACOCK WAY
ANCHOR COURT
KINGSMEAD CT
PH
LC
HEMPFIELD PL
ASHLEY GD
LAW CL
ALEXANDRA RD
HAWTHORN CLOSE
MILLPIT FURLONG
HOOF CL
CROFT PK RD
SANDYS CR
Works
Sandhill Bridge
D4
1 CHURCH LA
2 CROWN LA
3 GLOBE LA
4 HITCHES ST
5 GRANARY LA
6 WHITE HART LA
7 BROOM CL
THE BRAMBLES
EASTFIELDS
FISHERS BANK
SANDHILL
PADNAL DROVE
HAWKINS'S DROVE
Sandhill
MILLFIELD
THE CRESCENT
NEW ORCHARD PARK
The Millfield Prim Sch
GRANGE LANE
OAK LANE
WOODFEN ROAD
PADNAL DROVE
Padnal Fen
Water Tower
SAFFRON CLOSE
ELY ROAD
BRANCH BANK
Woodfen Farm
WOODFEN ROAD
THE COPPICE
River Great Ouse
BRICKMAKERS WAY
A10
Butchers Hill Farm

218 218 219

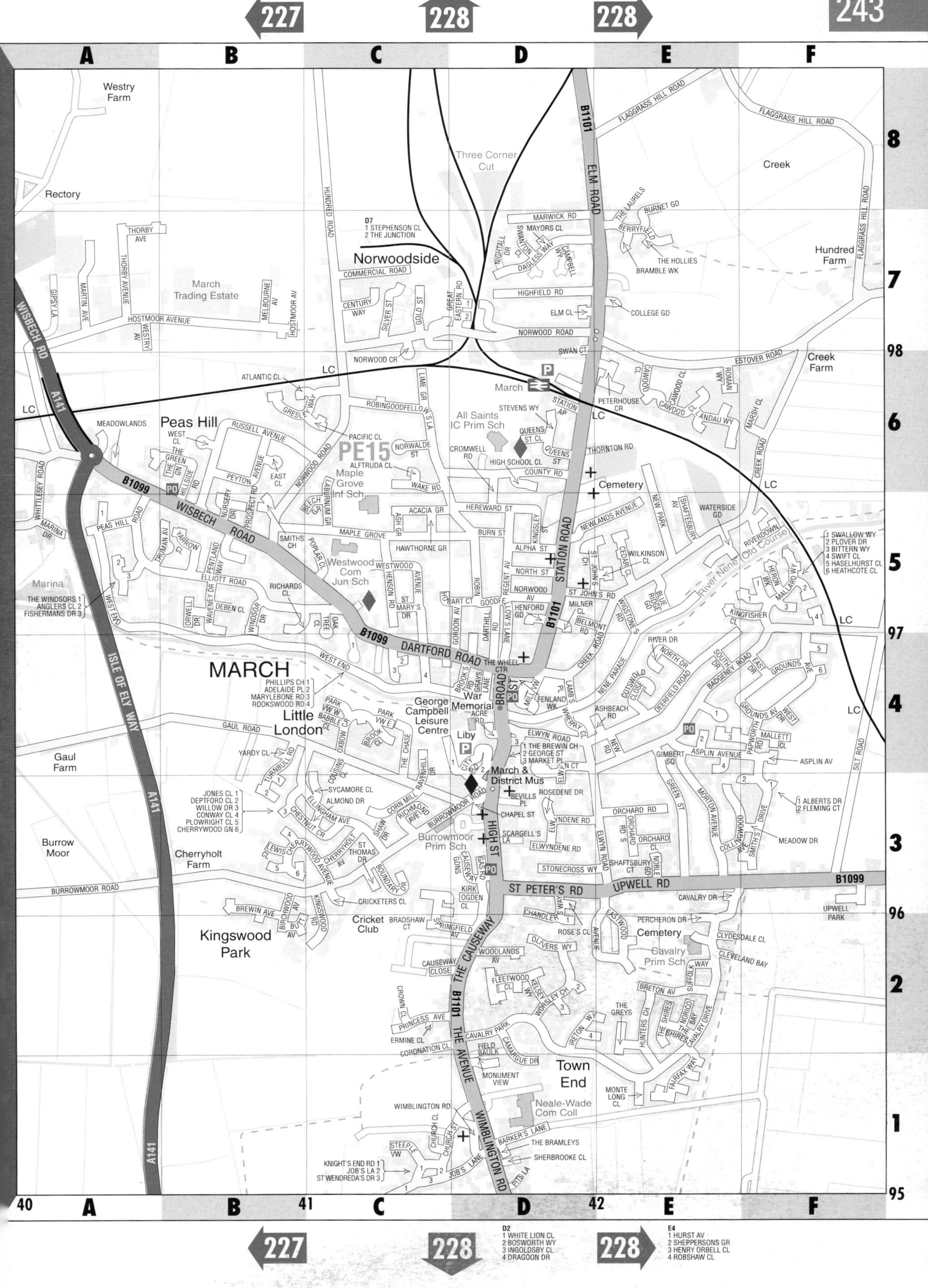
227
228
228
A
B
C
D
E
F
8
7
98
6
5
97
4
3
96
2
1
95
40
41
42
Westry Farm
Rectory
Three Corner Cut
Creek
Hundred Farm
Creek Farm
FLAGGRASS HILL ROAD
B1101
ELM ROAD
HUNDRED ROAD
D7
1 STEPHENSON CL
2 THE JUNCTION
Norwoodside
THORBY AVE
THORBY AVENUE
March Trading Estate
WISBECH RD
GIPSY LA
MARTIN AVE
MELBOURNE AV
HOSTMOOR AV
HOSTMOOR AVENUE
WESTRY AV
COMMERCIAL ROAD
CENTURY WAY
SILVER ST
GOLD ST
GREAT EASTERN RD
NORWOOD CR
NORWOOD ROAD
MARWICK RD
MAYORS CL
NIGHTALL DR
SWANTON CL
DAGLESS WAY
CAMPBELL WK
THE LAURELS
BURNET GD
BERRYFIELD
THE HOLLIES
BRAMBLE WK
HIGHFIELD RD
ELM CL
COLLEGE GD
SWAN CT
ESTOVER ROAD
CAWOOD CL
ROMAN WY
LC
ATLANTIC CL
LIME GR
W'S LA
March
STATION AP
STEVENS WY
All Saints IC Prim Sch
PETERHOUSE CR
LANDAU WY
MARSH CL
CREEK ROAD
A141
MEADOWLANDS
Peas Hill
RUSSELL AVENUE
GRESLEY WAY
ROBINGOODFELLOW'S LA
PACIFIC CL
PE15
NORWALDE ST
QUEENS ST CL
QUEENS ST
THORNTON RD
WEST CL
THE GREEN
THE GN
HILLSIDE RD
PEYTON AVENUE
EAST CL
NORWOOD ROAD
ALFTRUDA CL
Maple Grove Inf Sch
CROMWELL RD
HIGH SCHOOL CL
COUNTY RD
Cemetery
B1099
PO
NURSERY RD
PROSPECT RD
WAKE RD
BEECH GR
LABURNUM GR
ACACIA GR
HEREWARD ST
WHITTLESEY ROAD
MARINA DR
PEAS HILL ROAD
WISBECH ROAD
ASH GR
NEW PARK
SHAFTESBURY AV
WATERSIDE GD
NEWLANDS AVENUE
KINGSLEY ST
STATION ROAD
SMITHS CH
POPLAR CL
MAPLE GROVE
HAWTHORNE GR
BURN ST
RIVERDOWN
River Nene Old Course
1 SWALLOW WY
2 PLOVER DR
3 BITTERN WY
4 SWIFT CL
5 HASELHURST CL
6 HEATHCOTE CL
TRUMAN AV
YARROW CL
PENTLAND WAY
Westwood Com Jun Sch
WESTWOOD
ALPHA ST
NORTH ST
ST JOHN'S CH
CEDAR CL
WILKINSON CL
HERON WK
MALLARD WY
Marina
THE WINDSORS 1
ANGLERS CL 2
FISHERMANS DR 3
WEST END
ELLIOTT ROAD
RICHARDS CL
HENSON RD
AVENUE
ST MARY'S DR
ROBIN
GORDON AV
DARTHILL RD
REGENT AV
NORWOOD AV
ST JOHN'S RD
MILNER CL
BLUE RIDGE GD
WIGSTONES
KINGFISHER CL
ORWELL DR
WAVENEY DR
DEBEN CL
WINDSOR DR
OAK TREE CL
BART CT
GOODFE
HENFORD GD
BELMONT RD
B1101
B1099
DARTFORD ROAD
THE WHEEL CTR
RIVER DR
NORTH DR
SOUTH DR
BADGENEY ROAD
EAST DR
GROUNDS AVE
MARCH
PHILLIPS CH 1
ADELAIDE PL 2
MARYLEBONE RD 3
ROOKSWOOD RD 4
BROOK'S RD
GRAYS LANE
BROAD ST
MILL VW
FENLAND WK
LAMB'S PL
CREEK ROAD
NENE PARADE
COTSWOLD CLOSE
DEERFIELD ROAD
WEST END
PARK VW W
BABBLE CR
George Campbell Leisure Centre
War Memorial
ACRE RD
Little London
ASHBEACH RD
WHERRY CL
GROUNDS AV
WEST
GAUL ROAD
OXBOW CR
PARK VW E
BROOK CL
THE CHASE
Liby
ELWYN ROAD
1 THE BREWIN CH
2 GEORGE ST
3 MARKET PL
NEW RD
PAPWORTH RD
MALLETT CL
Gaul Farm
YARDY CL
TURNBULL RD
COUSINS CL
RAVENHILL DR
CITY RD
March & District Mus
ELWYN CT
GIMBERT SQ
ASPLIN AVENUE
ASPLIN AV
SYCAMORE CL
ALMOND DR
CORN MILL
BEVILLS PL
ROSEDENE DR
GREEN ST
MORTON AVENUE
1 ALBERTS DR
2 FLEMING CT
JONES CL 1
DEPTFORD CL 2
WILLOW DR 3
CONWAY CL 4
PLOWRIGHT CL 5
CHERRYWOOD GN 6
ELLINGHAM AVE
CHESTNUT CR
RICHMOND AVE
BURROWMOOR ROAD
CHAPEL ST
ELWYNDENE RD
ORCHARD RD
ORCHARD RD S
ORCHARD CL
COLLINGWOOD AVE
SMITH'S DRIVE
MEADOW DR
Burrow Moor
Cherryholt Farm
LEWIS CL
CHERRYWOOD AVENUE
CHERRYHOLT AV
ST THOMAS RD
SHAW DR
Burrowmoor Prim Sch
SCARGELL'S LA
HIGH ST
ELWYNDENE RD
ELWYN ROAD
SHAFTSBURY CT
NOBLE CL
SILT ROAD
GAS RD
CAUSEWAY GDNS
STONECROSS WY
BOUNDARY DR
BURROWMOOR ROAD
ST PETER'S RD
UPWELL RD
B1099
CAVALRY DR
KINGSWOOD RD
BIRCHWOOD AV
BUTT AV
BREWIN AVE
CRICKETERS CL
KIRK
OGDEN CL
UPWELL PARK
Cricket Club
BRADSHAW CT
SPRINGFIELD AV
THE CAUSEWAY
CHANDLER
PERCHERON DR
Kingswood Park
ROSE'S CL
EASTWOOD AVENUE
Cemetery
CLYDESDALE CL
Cavalry Prim Sch
CLEVELAND BAY
OLIVERS WY
WOODLANDS AV
CAUSEWAY CLOSE
SUFFOLK WAY
FLEETWOOD CL
KELSEY WY
WORSLEY CH
BRETON AV
B1101
THE AVENUE
CROWN CL
PRINCESS AVE
THE GREYS
HUNTERS CH
THE SHIRES
NORICO
THE BAY
CAVALRY DRIVE
ERMINE CL
CAVALRY PARK
IRETON WY
CORONATION CL
FIELD BAULK
CAMARGUE DR
Town End
FAIRFAX WAY
MONUMENT VIEW
MONTE LONG CL
WIMBLINGTON RD
Neale-Wade Com Coll
CHURCH CL
CHURCH ST
WIMBLINGTON RD
BARKER'S LANE
THE BRAMLEYS
SHERBROOKE CL
STEEPLE VW
KNIGHT'S END RD 1
JOB'S LA 2
ST WENDREDA'S DR 3
JOB'S LANE
PITS LA
A141
ISLE OF ELY WAY
A141
D2
1 WHITE LION CL
2 BOSWORTH WY
3 INGOLDSBY CL
4 DRAGOON DR
E4
1 HURST AV
2 SHEPPERSONS GR
3 HENRY ORBELL CL
4 ROBSHAW CL
227
228
228

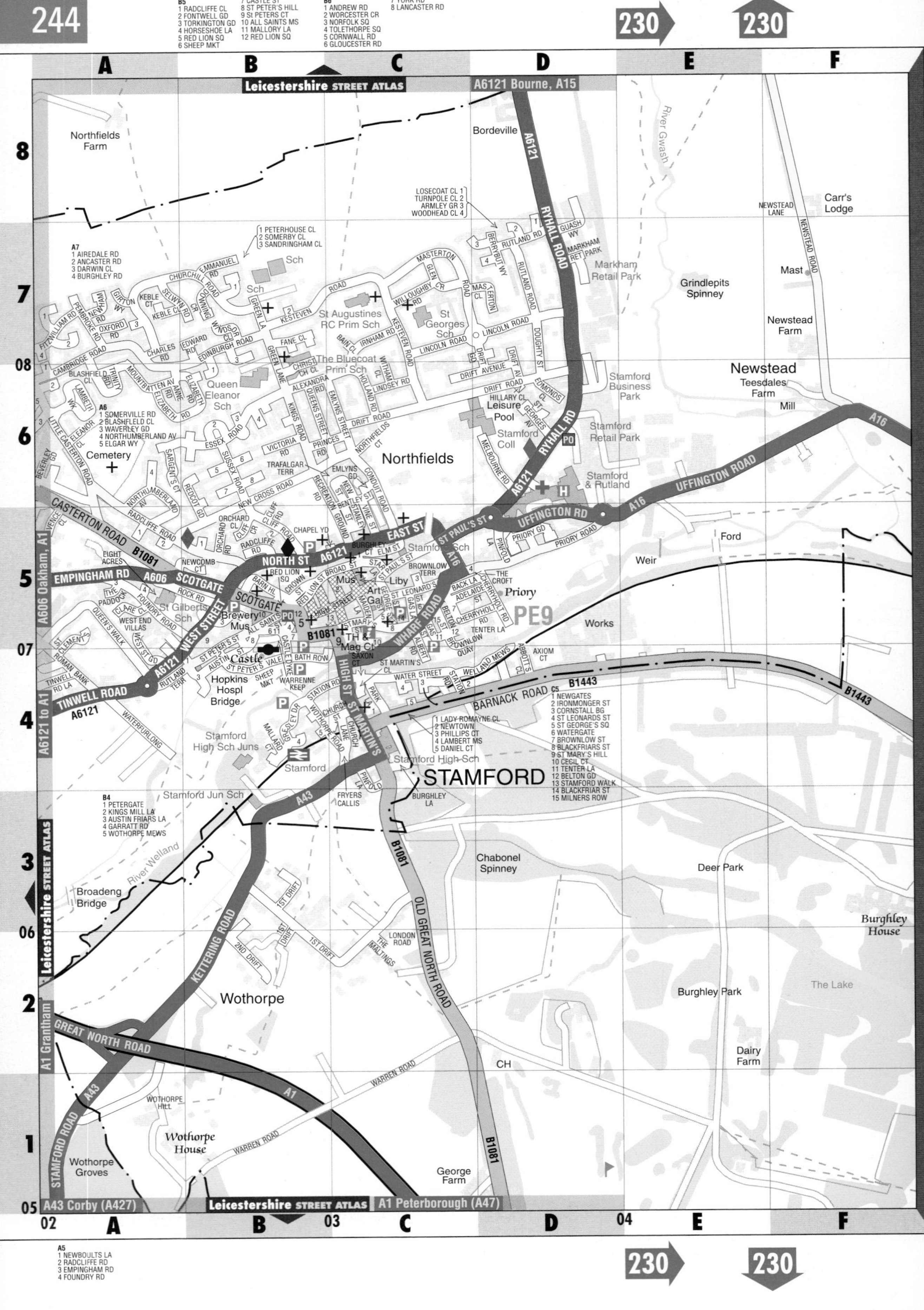
B5
1 RADCLIFFE CL
2 FONTWELL GD
3 TORKINGTON GD
4 HORSESHOE LA
5 RED LION SQ
6 SHEEP MKT
7 CASTLE ST
8 ST PETER'S HILL
9 St PETERS CT
10 ALL SAINTS MS
11 MALLORY LA
12 RED LION SQ
B6
1 ANDREW RD
2 WORCESTER CR
3 NORFOLK SQ
4 TOLETHORPE SQ
5 CORNWALL RD
6 GLOUCESTER RD
7 YORK RD
8 LANCASTER RD
230
230
A
B
C
D
E
F
Leicestershire STREET ATLAS
A6121 Bourne, A15
8
7
08
6
5
07
4
3
06
2
1
05
Northfields Farm
Bordeville
River Gwash
A6121
RYHALL ROAD
LOSECOAT CL 1
TURNPOLE CL 2
ARMLEY GR 3
WOODHEAD CL 4
NEWSTEAD LANE
Carr's Lodge
NEWSTEAD ROAD
Mast
Grindlepits Spinney
Newstead Farm
Newstead
Teesdales Farm
Mill
A16
1 PETERHOUSE CL
2 SOMERBY CL
3 SANDRINGHAM CL
A7
1 AIREDALE RD
2 ANCASTER RD
3 DARWIN CL
4 BURGHLEY RD
Sch
MASTERTON
GLEN CR
RUTLAND RD
GUASH WY
MARKHAM RET PARK
Markham Retail Park
CHURCHILL RD
EMMANUEL RD
KESTEVEN RD
St Augustines RC Prim Sch
WILLOUGHBY RD
St Georges Sch
LINCOLN ROAD
DOUGHTY ST
GIRTON WY
KEBLE CT
KEBLE CL
SELWYN RD
FITZWILLIAM RD
PEMBROKE RD
NEWNHAM RD
OXFORD RD
CAMBRIDGE ROAD
CHARLES RD
EDWARD RD
EDINBURGH ROAD
GREEN LANE
FANE CL
IRNHAM RD
BAIN CL
KESTEVEN ROAD
CHRIST CH CL
The Bluecoat Prim Sch
DRIFT AVENUE
DRIFT ROAD
EDMONDS CL
Stamford Business Park
BLASHFIELD CL
TRINITY RD
MOUNTBATTEN AV
Queen Eleanor Sch
ALEXANDRA RD
QUEENS STREET
EMLYNS STREET
HOLLAND RD
LINDSEY RD
HILLARY CL
Leisure Pool
Stamford Coll
ST GEORGES AV
Stamford Retail Park
PO
LAMBETH WK
A6
1 SOMERVILLE RD
2 BLASHFIELD CL
3 WAVERLEY GD
4 NORTHUMBERLAND AV
5 ELGAR WY
ELEANOR CL
LITTLE CASTERTON ROAD
Cemetery
ESSEX ROAD
SUSSEX ROAD
VICTORIA RD
PRINCES RD
NORTHFIELDS CT
Northfields
MELBOURNE RD
Stamford & Rutland
H
UFFINGTON ROAD
UFFINGTON RD
BEVERLEY GD
SARGENT'S CT
TRAFALGAR TERR
EMLYNS GD
CONDUIT ROAD
REDCOT RD
NEW CROSS ROAD
RECREATION GROUND RD
NEW BENTLEY ST
STANLEY ST
VINE ST
NORTHUMBERLAND AV
CASTERTON ROAD
RADCLIFFE ROAD
ORCHARD CL
CLIFF RD
CLIFF CL
CHAPEL YD
EAST ST
ST PAUL'S ST
PRIORY GD
PRIORY ROAD
PINFOLD LA
Ford
Weir
A606 Oakham, A1
EIGHT ACRES
B1081
NEWCOMB CT
ORCHARD RD
RADCLIFFE RD
NORTH ST
A6121
BURGHLEY CT
ELM ST
Stamford Sch
EMPINGHAM RD
A606
SCOTGATE
BARN HILL
RED LION SQ
CROWN ST
BROAD ST
Mus
STAR LA
ST PAUL'S ST
BROWNLOW TERR
Liby
THE CROFT
Priory
THE PADDOCK
ROCK RD
SCOTGATE
FOUNDRY ROAD
CLARE CL
St Gilberts Sch
WEST STREET
Brewery Mus
RED LION ST
HIGH STREET
Art Gal
ST GEORGE ST
ST LEONARD'S ST
GAS LA
WHARF ROAD
BACK LA
ADELAIDE ST
CHERRYHOLT RD
CHERRYHOLT RD
BELTON ST
PE9
Works
WEST END VILLAS
QUEEN'S WALK
WEST ST GD
ALL SAINTS PL
B1081
ST MARY'S ST
TH & Mag Ct
TENTER LA
BROWNLOW QUAY
ST CLEMENT'S
07
ROMAN BANK
A6121
ST PETER'S ST
AUSTIN ST
Castle
ST PETER'S VALE
CASTLE DYKE
BATH ROW
SAXON CT
ST MARTIN'S CL
WELLAND MEWS
ABBOTTS CL
AXIOM CT
TINWELL RD LA
TINWELL ROAD
RUTLAND TERR
Hopkins Hospl Bridge
SHEEP MKT
WARRENNE KEEP
HIGH ST ST MARTIN'S
WATER STREET
STATION RD
B1443
BARNACK ROAD
A6121 to A1
A6121
WATERFURLONG
STATION RD
WOTHORPE RD
CHURCH LA
PARK LA
C5
1 NEWGATES
2 IRONMONGER ST
3 CORNSTALL BG
4 ST LEONARDS ST
5 ST GEORGE'S SQ
6 WATERGATE
7 BROWNLOW ST
8 BLACKFRIARS ST
9 ST MARY'S HILL
10 CECIL CT
11 TENTER LA
12 BELTON GD
13 STAMFORD WALK
14 BLACKFRIAR ST
15 MILNERS ROW
1 LADY ROMAYNE CL
2 NEWTOWN
3 PHILLIPS CT
4 LAMBERT MS
5 DANIEL CT
Stamford High Sch Juns
MALLARD CT
Stamford
Stamford High Sch
STAMFORD
PINFOLD LA
B4
1 PETERGATE
2 KINGS MILL LA
3 AUSTIN FRIARS LA
4 GARRATT RD
5 WOTHORPE MEWS
Stamford Jun Sch
A43
FRYERS CALLIS
BURGHLEY LA
B1081
Chabonel Spinney
Deer Park
River Welland
Broadeng Bridge
1ST DRIFT
KETTERING ROAD
1ST DRIFT
2ND DRIFT
LONDON ROAD
THE MALTINGS
OLD GREAT NORTH ROAD
Burghley House
Wothorpe
Burghley Park
The Lake
A1 Grantham
GREAT NORTH ROAD
Dairy Farm
CH
WARREN ROAD
A43
A1
WOTHORPE HILL
STAMFORD ROAD
Wothorpe House
WARREN ROAD
B1081
Wothorpe Groves
George Farm
A43 Corby (A427)
Leicestershire STREET ATLAS
A1 Peterborough (A47)
02
03
04
A5
1 NEWBOULTS LA
2 RADCLIFFE RD
3 EMPINGHAM RD
4 FOUNDRY RD
230
230

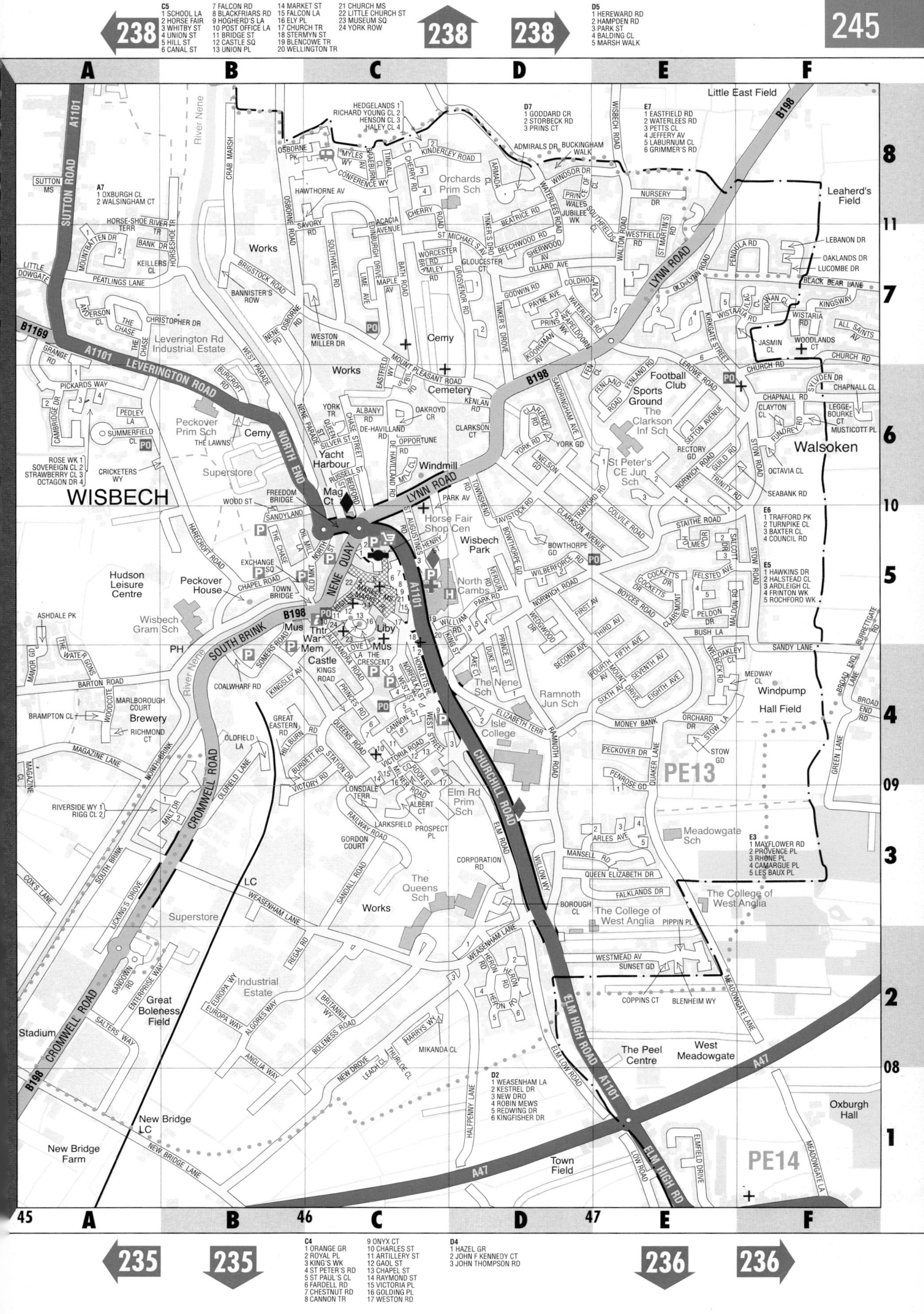
245
238
C5
1 SCHOOL LA
2 HORSE FAIR
3 WHITBY ST
4 UNION ST
5 HILL ST
6 CANAL ST
7 FALCON RD
8 BLACKFRIARS RD
9 HOGHERD'S LA
10 POST OFFICE LA
11 BRIDGE ST
12 CASTLE SQ
13 UNION PL
14 MARKET ST
15 FALCON LA
16 ELY PL
17 CHURCH TR
18 STERMYN ST
19 BLENCOWE TR
20 WELLINGTON TR
21 CHURCH MS
22 LITTLE CHURCH ST
23 MUSEUM SQ
24 YORK ROW
238
238
D5
1 HEREWARD RD
2 HAMPDEN RD
3 PARK ST
4 BALDING CL
5 MARSH WALK
A B C D E F
Little East Field
D7
1 GODDARD CR
2 STORBECK RD
3 PRINS CT
E7
1 EASTFIELD RD
2 WATERLEES RD
3 PETTS CL
4 JEFFERY AV
5 LABURNUM CL
6 GRIMMER'S RD
HEDGELANDS 1
RICHARD YOUNG CL 2
HENSON CL 3
HALEY CL 4
A7
1 OXBURGH CL
2 WALSINGHAM CT
Orchards Prim Sch
Leaherd's Field
Works
Cemy
Cemetery
Leverington Rd Industrial Estate
Peckover Prim Sch
Yacht Harbour
Windmill
WISBECH
Walsoken
Football Club
Sports Ground
The Clarkson Inf Sch
St Peter's CE Jun Sch
Horse Fair Shop Cen
Wisbech Park
North Cambs
Superstore
Hudson Leisure Centre
Peckover House
Wisbech Gram Sch
Mag Ct
Mus
Thtr
War Mem
Castle
Liby
Mus
The Nene Sch
Ramnoth Jun Sch
Isle College
Brewery
Windpump
Hall Field
E6
1 TRAFFORD PK
2 TURNPIKE CL
3 BAXTER CL
4 COUNCIL RD
E5
1 HAWKINS DR
2 HALSTEAD CL
3 ARDLEIGH CL
4 FRINTON WK
5 ROCHFORD WK
PE13
Elm Rd Prim Sch
Meadowgate Sch
E3
1 MAYFLOWER RD
2 PROVENCE PL
3 RHONE PL
4 CAMARGUE PL
5 LES BAUX PL
The Queens Sch
Works
Superstore
The College of West Anglia
The College of West Anglia
Industrial Estate
Great Boleness Field
Stadium
The Peel Centre
West Meadowgate
D2
1 WEASENHAM LA
2 KESTREL DR
3 NEW DRO
4 ROBIN MEWS
5 REDWING DR
6 KINGFISHER DR
New Bridge LC
New Bridge Farm
Town Field
Oxburgh Hall
PE14
A1101
B198
B1169
A47
8 11 7 6 10 5 4 09 3 2 08 1
45 46 47
C4
1 ORANGE GR
2 ROYAL PL
3 KING'S WK
4 ST PETER'S RD
5 ST PAUL'S CL
6 FARDELL RD
7 CHESTNUT RD
8 CANNON TR
9 ONYX CT
10 CHARLES ST
11 ARTILLERY ST
12 GAOL ST
13 CHAPEL ST
14 RAYMOND ST
15 VICTORIA PL
16 GOLDING PL
17 WESTON RD
D4
1 HAZEL GR
2 JOHN F KENNEDY CT
3 JOHN THOMPSON RD
235
235
236
236

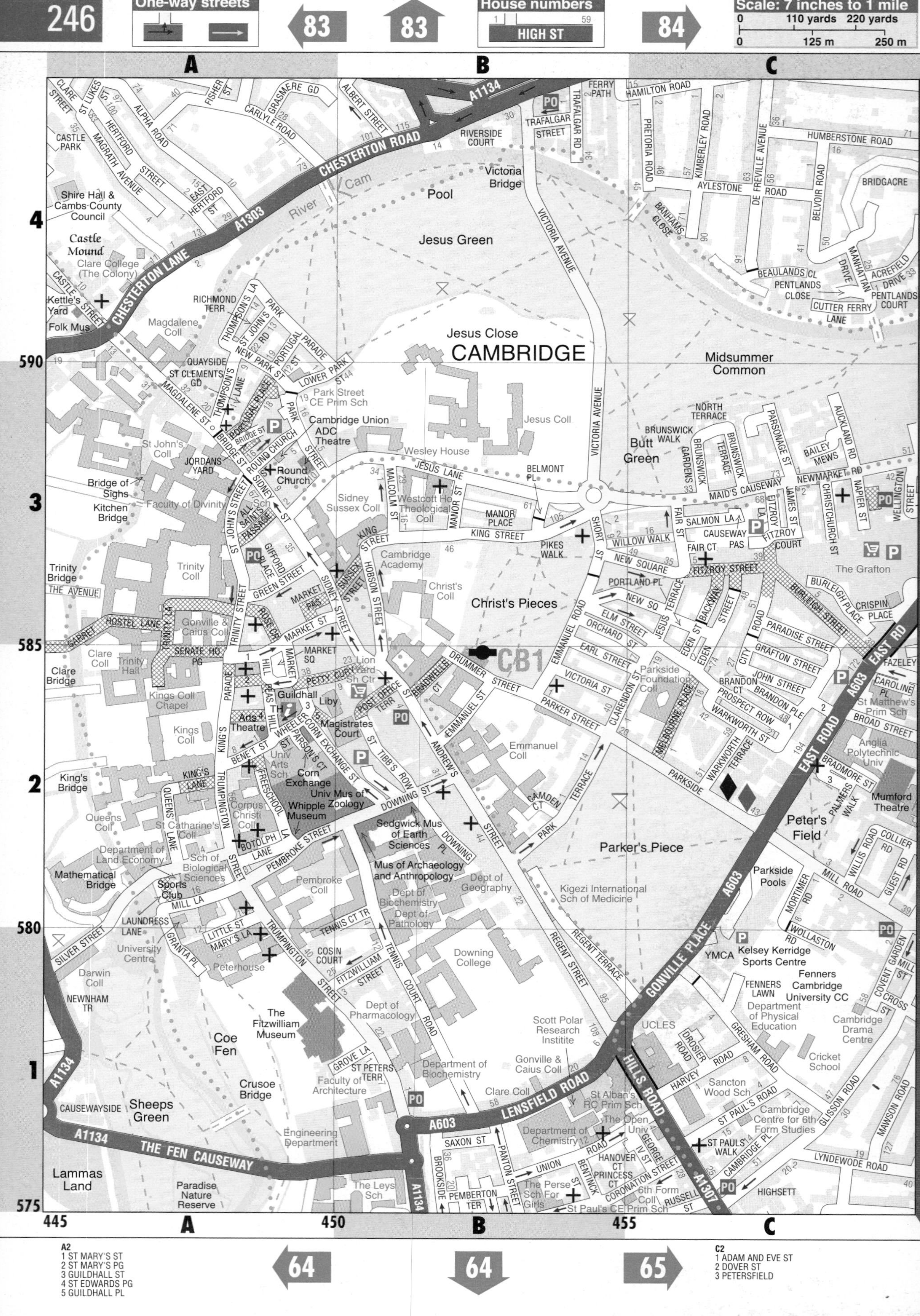
246
One-way streets
83
83
House numbers
1
59
HIGH ST
84
Scale: 7 inches to 1 mile
0
110 yards
220 yards
0
125 m
250 m
A
B
C
CAMBRIDGE
CB1
Jesus Green
Jesus Close
Midsummer Common
Butt Green
Christ's Pieces
Parker's Piece
Peter's Field
Coe Fen
Sheeps Green
Lammas Land
Paradise Nature Reserve
Pool
River Cam
Victoria Bridge
Castle Mound
Shire Hall & Cambs County Council
Clare College (The Colony)
Kettle's Yard
Folk Mus
Magdalene Coll
St John's Coll
Bridge of Sighs
Kitchen Bridge
Faculty of Divinity
Round Church
Cambridge Union
ADC Theatre
Park Street CE Prim Sch
Wesley House
Jesus Coll
Sidney Sussex Coll
Westcott Ho Theological Coll
Cambridge Academy
Christ's Coll
Trinity Bridge
Trinity Coll
Gonville & Caius Coll
Clare Coll
Trinity Hall
Clare Bridge
Kings Coll Chapel
Kings Coll
King's Bridge
Queens Coll
Guildhall
TH
Liby
Arts Theatre
Lion Yard Sh Ctr
Magistrates Court
Univ Arts Sch
Corn Exchange
Univ Mus of Zoology
Whipple Museum
Corpus Christi Coll
St Catharine's Coll
Department of Land Economy
Sch of Biological Sciences
Mathematical Bridge
Sports Club
Sedgwick Mus of Earth Sciences
Mus of Archaeology and Anthropology
Pembroke Coll
Dept of Biochemistry
Dept of Pathology
Dept of Geography
Emmanuel Coll
Parkside Foundation Coll
Anglia Polytechnic Univ
Mumford Theatre
St Matthew's Prim Sch
The Grafton
Parkside Pools
Kigezi International Sch of Medicine
YMCA
Kelsey Kerridge Sports Centre
Fenners Cambridge University CC
Department of Physical Education
Cambridge Drama Centre
Cricket School
University Centre
Darwin Coll
Peterhouse
Downing College
Dept of Pharmacology
The Fitzwilliam Museum
Crusoe Bridge
Faculty of Architecture
Department of Biochemistry
Engineering Department
Scott Polar Research Institite
Gonville & Caius Coll
UCLES
Sancton Wood Sch
Cambridge Centre for 6th Form Studies
St Alban's RC Prim Sch
The Open Univ
Department of Chemistry
The Perse Sch For Girls
6th Form Coll
St Paul's CE Prim Sch
The Leys Sch
CHESTERTON ROAD
CHESTERTON LANE
A1303
A1134
THE FEN CAUSEWAY
A603
LENSFIELD ROAD
GONVILLE PLACE
EAST ROAD
HILLS ROAD
A1307
VICTORIA AVENUE
MAID'S CAUSEWAY
NEWMARKET RD
EMMANUEL ROAD
PARKSIDE
PARK TERRACE
REGENT STREET
TRUMPINGTON STREET
KING'S PARADE
TRINITY STREET
ST JOHN'S STREET
BRIDGE ST
SIDNEY STREET
HOBSON STREET
KING STREET
JESUS LANE
DOWNING ST
PEMBROKE STREET
TENNIS COURT ROAD
MILL ROAD
LYNDEWODE ROAD
HIGHSETT
445
450
455
575
580
585
590
1
2
3
4
A
B
C
64
64
65
A2
1 ST MARY'S ST
2 ST MARY'S PG
3 GUILDHALL ST
4 ST EDWARDS PG
5 GUILDHALL PL
C2
1 ADAM AND EVE ST
2 DOVER ST
3 PETERSFIELD

Index

Church Rd **6** Beckenham BR2..........**53** C6

Place name	Location number	Locality, town or village	Postcode district	Page and grid square
May be abbreviated on the map	Present when a number indicates the place's position in a crowded area of mapping	Shown when more than one place has the same name	District for the indexed place	Page number and grid reference for the standard mapping

Public and commercial buildings are highlighted in magenta **Places of interest** are highlighted in blue with a star ★

Abbreviations used in the index

Acad	**Academy**	Comm	**Common**	Gd	**Ground**	L	**Leisure**	Prom	**Prom**
App	**Approach**	Cott	**Cottage**	Gdn	**Garden**	La	**Lane**	Rd	**Road**
Arc	**Arcade**	Cres	**Crescent**	Gn	**Green**	Liby	**Library**	Recn	**Recreation**
Ave	**Avenue**	Cswy	**Causeway**	Gr	**Grove**	Mdw	**Meadow**	Ret	**Retail**
Bglw	**Bungalow**	Ct	**Court**	H	**Hall**	Meml	**Memorial**	Sh	**Shopping**
Bldg	**Building**	Ctr	**Centre**	Ho	**House**	Mkt	**Market**	Sq	**Square**
Bsns, Bus	**Business**	Ctry	**Country**	Hospl	**Hospital**	Mus	**Museum**	St	**Street**
Bvd	**Boulevard**	Cty	**County**	HQ	**Headquarters**	Orch	**Orchard**	Sta	**Station**
Cath	**Cathedral**	Dr	**Drive**	Hts	**Heights**	Pal	**Palace**	Terr	**Terrace**
Cir	**Circus**	Dro	**Drove**	Ind	**Industrial**	Par	**Parade**	TH	**Town Hall**
Cl	**Close**	Ed	**Education**	Inst	**Institute**	Pas	**Passage**	Univ	**University**
Cnr	**Corner**	Emb	**Embankment**	Int	**International**	Pk	**Park**	Wk, Wlk	**Walk**
Coll	**College**	Est	**Estate**	Intc	**Interchange**	Pl	**Place**	Wr	**Water**
Com	**Community**	Ex	**Exhibition**	Junc	**Junction**	Prec	**Precinct**	Yd	**Yard**

Index of localities, towns and villages

A

Abbotsley 57 C5
Abbots Ripton 162 C1
Abington Piggots 11 E5
Ailsworth 195 D3
Alconbury 150 E4
Alconbury Weston 150 D6
Aldreth 209 E4
Alwalton 185 B4
Arbury 83 D6
Arrington 44 C1
Ashdon 21 B1
Ashley 91 F7
Ashton 231 A4
Ashwell 2 E4
Ashwell End 2 A5

B

Babraham 50 E1
Badlingham 213 D1
Bainton 230 F5
Balsham 53 A2
Barham 149 B3
Bar Hill 102 C3
Barley 6 F2
Barnack 230 E3
Barrington 29 E8
Bartlow 21 A7
Barton 63 B3
Barton Mills 239 C2
Barway 211 C6
Bassingbourn 12 F4
Beck Row 213 F8
Begdale 235 F5
Benwick 222 A5
Bird's Hundred 189 C5
Blackhall 227 A1
Black Horse Drove 226 B6
Bluntisham 208 D5
Bordeville 244 D8
Bottisham 86 F6
Bourn 60 C6
Boxworth 101 B5
Boxworth End 123 E3
Boyces Bridge 236 D4
Brampton 140 C2
Brampton Lodge 140 A1
Brampton Park 140 D1
Brandon Bank 226 E3
Brandon Creek 226 D6
Bretton 197 A6
Briggate 189 E6
Brington 147 D4
Brinkley 70 E2
Broad Green Newmarket 91 D4
Broad Green Royston 8 C3
Brook End 136 B6
Broughton 153 F8
Buckden 118 B3
Buckworth 149 E6
Bunker's Hill 235 A6
Burrough End 70 E4
Burrough Green 70 F3
Burton End 37 C8
Burwell 130 C2
Bury 172 B4
Bythorn 146 D4

C

Caldecote Highfields 61 B7
Caldecote Highfields 80 B1
Caldecote Stilton 175 D5
Caldecote St Neots 76 B1
Calford Green 24 F7
Cambourne 79 D4
Cambridge 246 A2
Camps End 22 A1
Cardinal's Green 37 B1
Carlton 55 A7
Carlton Green 55 A4
Carlton Hill 55 A8
Castle Camps 22 F4
Castle End 231 D7
Castor 195 D1
Catworth 136 D7
Caxton 78 F1
Chainbridge 228 B7
Chapel End 174 D4
Chatteris 241 D4
Cherry Hinton 65 F5
Chesterford Park 19 D1
Chesterton Cambridge 84 A6
Chesterton Peterborough 184 E3
Cheveley 91 C6
Childerley 80 C8
Childerley Gate 80 D4
Chippenham 133 D8
Chittering 127 B8
Chrishall 8 D4
Christchurch 229 D3
Church End Catworth 136 E7
Church End Eltisley 77 D4
Church End Great Stukeley 151 F2
Church End Over 208 C1
Church End Pidley 165 D1
Church End Swavesey 122 E7
Church End Woodwalton 169 D2
Church Field 189 B7
Clayhithe 106 D5
Claypit Hill 61 D2
Clopton 156 E5
Coates 190 F8
Cockayne Hatley 25 C8
Coldham 235 D1
Coldham Hall 228 E8
Coldham's Common 84 D2
Coleseed House 228 D2
Colne 208 D6
Colnefields 208 D8
Comberton 62 C5
Commercial End 108 C3
Conington Fenstanton 121 C1
Conington Sawtry 168 C8
Corner Lodge 227 F2
Coton 82 B2
Cottenham 126 C3
Coveney 217 C5
Covington 135 D2
Cowlinge 73 D1
Crawley End 8 D5
Cropley Grove 92 D3
Crow End 60 D7
Crowland 232 B8
Croxton 76 F4
Croydon 27 A7

D

Dalham 92 E8
Deeping Gate 231 E8
Deeping St James 206 A7
Denny End 105 F8
Denton 175 E4
Diddington 96 A8
Dillington 94 C7
Ditton Green 90 E1
Doddington 223 A6
Dogsthorpe 198 C7
Down Field 212 D2
Downham Hythe 217 D6
Dry Drayton 102 C1
Duck End 97 F5
Duckpuddle Bush 4 F2
Dullingham 70 D8
Dullingham Ley 71 A5
Duloe 74 A6
Dunkirk 224 F1
Duxford 17 D8
Dyer's Green 13 C8

E

Eaglethorpe 178 A4
Earith 208 E6
Eastfield 198 D4
Eastgate 198 B2
East Hatley 43 B1
Easton 138 C4
East Perry 116 E3
Eastrea 190 D7
Eaton Ford 74 C5
Eaton Socon 74 B3
Eldernell 202 B2
Ellington 139 A4
Ellington Thorpe 139 A2
Elm 236 B5
Elmdon 9 A4
Elsworth 100 C4
Eltisley 77 E4
Elton 178 D8
Ely 240 C3
Emmaus 127 E2
Emneth 236 C6
Emneth Hungate 236 E6
Etton 231 D5
Everton 40 C3
Exmoor Grange 229 B4

Exning 110 A8
Eye 232 B1
Eye Green 232 B2
Eynesbury 74 F3

F

Farcet 187 C2
Fen Ditton 84 F5
Fen Drayton 122 F6
Fen End 57 D6
Fengate 198 D2
Fenstanton 122 C5
Fenton 165 B4
Fitton End 238 A3
Flint Cross 15 B2
Folksworth 175 D8
Fordham 212 F1
Fowlmere 15 D8
Foxton 30 C5
Freckenham 213 C3
Friday Bridge 236 A4
Fulbourn 66 F4

G

Gamlingay 41 D5
Gamlingay Cinques 41 B6
Gamlingay Great Heath 40 E3
Garden Cottage 93 D5
Gatley End 3 C7
Gaultree 236 D6
Gimbers End 115 B2
Girton 82 F8
Glatton 175 F1
Glenthorn 227 F3
Glinton 203 E8
Godmanchester 141 E2
Gorefield 237 E2
Grafham 116 A7
Grandford House 227 F6
Grantchester 64 A4
Graveley 97 F4
Gravel House 228 C6
Great Abington 34 C6
Great Bradley 55 F7
Great Cambourne 79 B2
Great Chesterford 18 D2
Great Chishill 7 F2
Great Eversden 45 E8
Great Gidding 166 E3
Great Gransden 58 D5
Great Paxton 96 E4
Great Raveley 163 B7
Great Shelford 48 F5
Great Staughton 93 F6
Great Stukeley 152 A2
Great Wilbraham 68 A7
Great Wratting 39 D5
Green End Comberton 62 B6
Green End Great Stukeley 152 A1
Green End Little Staughton .93 A3
Guilden Morden 10 E4
Gunthorpe 204 D2
Guyhirn 234 F2

H

Haddenham 210 B6
Haddon 180 B6
Hadstock 20 C6
Hail Weston 95 B1
Hamerton 159 B4
Hampton Hargate 186 D2
Hanchet End 38 C1
Hanchett Village 23 B8
Hardwick Buckden 117 A5
Hardwick Cambridge 81 B3
Hare Park 88 A3
Harlton 46 D5
Haroldsbridge 237 C2
Harston 48 A3
Hartford 142 A6
Haslingfield 47 B6
Hatley End 25 B5
Hatley St George 43 A3
Hauxton 48 B4
Haverhill 24 C8
Hawthorn Lodge 93 D5
Hazel Stub 23 C7
Helpston 231 C4
Hemingford Abbots 142 E3
Hemingford Grey 143 E1
Herringswell 113 E8
Heydon 8 A5
High Cross 82 E2
Highfields 80 D2
High Harthay 139 E3
Hildersham 34 F5
Hilton 121 B1
Hinxton 18 A7
Histon 104 C4

Holly End 236 E5
Holme 177 A4
Holywell 144 F2
Holywell Row 214 A8
Hook 223 D8
Horningsea 106 A1
Horseheath 37 A3
Horse Moor 228 D1
Houghton 143 A5
Huntingdon 141 F4

I

Ickleton 18 A4
Impington 104 C2
Ingleborough 238 E5
Inham's End 189 F6
Islands Common 74 E7
Isleham 213 A5

K

Kennett 134 F5
Kennett End 113 A2
Kentford 113 B2
Keyston 146 B3
Kimbolton 113 F6
King's Dyke 188 E6
Kings Hedges 83 E7
Kings Ripton 153 C5
Kingston 61 A3
Kingswood Park 243 B2
Kirtling 72 D6
Kirtling Green 72 C4
Kirtling Towers 72 D7
Knapwell 100 E2
Kneesworth 13 A6
Knights End 228 A1

L

Laddus Fens 236 B1
Lakes End 229 F3
Landbeach 105 D7
Landwade 132 C4
Lark Hall Corner 69 A1
Lattersea Field 190 B6
Leighton Bromswold 148 D3
Leverington 238 B2
Lidgate 73 E8
Linton 35 E3
Litlington 12 B2
Little Abington 34 B7
Littlebury Green 9 F2
Little Catworth 137 A6
Little Chishill 1 C7
Little Ditton 90 F2
Little Downham 218 B6
Little End 74 C1
Little Eversden 46 A7
Little Gidding 158 F8
Little Gransden 58 D3
Little Green 178 C3
Little Heath 41 C4
Little Linton 35 B3
Little London 243 C4
Little Ouse 226 D4
Little Paxton 96 B2
Littleport 242 C4
Little Raveley 163 B4
Little Shelford 48 E3
Little Staughton 93 B2
Little Stukeley 151 C4
Little Thetford 211 B7
Little Wilbraham 86 E1
Little Wratting 39 D3
Lode 107 C2
Lolworth 101 F5
Long Meadow 107 F2
Longstanton 124 E2
Longstowe 59 F3
Longthorpe 197 A1
Lower Cambourne 78 F4
Luddington in the Brook
.....166 B4
Lutton 174 C4

M

Madingley 81 E5
Manea 224 B4
March 243 B4
Margery's Croft 238 B1
Marholm 203 E1
Market Deeping 231 D8
Marshland St James 236 F8
Maxey 231 C7
Melbourn 14 C5
Meldreth 29 A2
Mepal 216 E4

Mildenhall 239 A6
Mile End 219 C5
Mill End 72 E5
Millfield 197 F5
Mill Green 22 D7
Milton 105 E2
Molesworth 147 A5
Morborne 180 B3
Morden Green 11 C1
Moulton 112 E6
Murrow 234 D5

N

Needingworth 208 B3
Nene Terrace 232 D6
Newark 198 E6
Newborough 207 E7
New England 197 E7
Newfields 237 D1
New Fletton 187 B8
Newmarket 111 B5
New Meadow 187 F2
Newnham 64 C8
Newnham Croft 64 D7
Newstead 244 E6
Newton Harston 31 C8
Newton Wisbech 238 A5
Newtown Cambridge 64 E7
Newtown Huntingdon 141 E5
Newtown Kimbolton 114 A5
New Wimpole 28 B8
Norman Cross 180 F2
Northborough 231 F7
Northfields 244 C6
North Green 190 A6
North Side 200 F4
Norwoodside 243 C7
Nosterfield End 22 F5

O

Oakington 103 B5
Odsey 3 C1
Offord Cluny 118 F3
Offord D'Arcy 118 F1
Old Fletton 187 A6
Old Hurst 154 C7
Old Weston 148 A8
Old Wimpole 44 F3
Orton Brimbles 185 D5
Orton Goldhay 185 D4
Orton Longueville 186 B5
Orton Malbourne 186 A5
Orton Southgate 185 C2
Orton Waterville 185 E4
Orton Wistow 185 C6
Orwell 45 E1
Outwell 236 F3
Over 208 E1
Over End 178 F2
Owl End 152 A3
Oxlode 224 C1

P

Pale Green 23 D1
Pampisford 33 B5
Papworth Everard 99 B3
Papworth St Agnes 98 D5
Papworth Village
Settlement 99 A2
Parson Drove 234 D7
Paston 205 A1
Peakirk 206 B1
Peas Hill 243 B6
Peterborough 197 D5
Pidley 155 E8
Pilsgate 230 C4
Place House 93 E6
Pondersbridge 220 D7
Prickwillow 219 B5
Pymore (Pymoor) 224 E1

Q

Queen Adelaide 218 D4

R

Ralingham Hall 229 E6
Rampton 125 F4
Ramsey 172 B6
Ramsey Forty Foot 221 C2
Ramsey Heights 171 A7
Ramsey Mereside 221 A4
Ramsey St Mary's 220 D3

Ravensthorpe 197 C6
Reach 130 C1
Red Lodge 213 F1
Ring's End 234 F1
Romsey Town 65 B8
Royston 5 B6

S

St Ives 143 E7
St Neots 74 E4
Sandhill 242 E3
Sapley 141 F8
Sawston 33 A7
Sawtry 168 A3
Saxon Street 91 B3
Seadyke 234 F6
Sewell's Barn 138 A2
Shepreth 29 E4
Shingay 26 F2
Shudy Camps 22 B5
Sibson 183 E8
Six Mile Bottom 68 F7
Slade Field 241 B7
Snailwell 133 B4
Soham 212 B4
Soham Cotes 211 F5
Somersham 215 B1
Somersham Park 208 C8
South Green 190 F7
Southoe 95 E5
Southorpe 230 D2
Spaldwick 137 F6
Stags Holt 228 D7
Stamford 244 D4
Stanground 187 C5
Stapleford 49 D4
Staughton Green 94 B4
Staughton Highway 94 A5
Steeple Gidding 159 B7
Steeple Morden 11 B2
Stetchworth 90 A2
Stetchworth Ley 71 B7
Steventon End 21 C2
Stibbington 194 C2
Stilton 176 A7
Stirloe 118 B2
Stonely 115 B3
Stourbridge Common 84 B4
Stow Cum Quy 86 A6
Stow Longa 137 C2
Streetly End 37 A5
Strethall 9 F4
Stretham 210 C5
Studlands Park 110 F8
Stukeley 141 B6
Stuntney 218 D1
Sturmer 24 F4
Sutton Ailsworth 194 F2
Sutton Ely 216 E2
Sutton Gault 216 C2
Swaffham Bulbeck 108 B1
Swaffham Prior 108 E1
Swavesey 123 E6
Swingbrow 222 D3

T

Tadlow 26 A3
Tallington 230 E7
Temple End 55 D2
Tetworth 40 F7
Teversham 85 C1
The Cottons 236 E3
The Green 121 D1
The Limes 229 C3
The Lipneas 202 B1
The Meadow 215 C2
The Severals 111 B5
Thistley Green 213 C2
Tholomas Drove 235 A5
Thorney 233 A3
Thorney Toll 234 A3
Thornhaugh 193 F5
Three Holes 229 E7
Thriplow 31 C2
Throckenholt 234 B8
Tilbrook 114 B7
Tipps End 229 F2
Toft 61 E4
Top End 93 B1
Toseland 97 D2
Town End 243 D2
Trumpington 64 E2
Tuddenham 214 D2
Turves 191 F6
Tydd St Giles 237 F7

U

Uffington 230 C6
Ufford 230 F3

Upend 92 A1
Upend Green 91 F2
Upton Ailsworth 195 B6
Upton Alconbury 160 C2
Upware 211 B1
Upwell 236 D1
Upwood 171 C2

W

Walpole Marsh 238 F8
Walsoken 245 F6
Walton 204 D1
Walton Dam 238 D4
Walton Highway 238 F4
Wansford 194 A4
Warboys 165 A5
Wardy Hill 217 B4
Waresley 57 E2
Warmington 178 A3
Waterbeach 106 C7
Water End 25 B3
Water Newton 184 C7
Waterside 213 A6
Way Head 217 C6
Wayside 138 C5
Weald 76 B4
Welches Dam 224 A1
Welney 225 B8
Wendy 27 C4
Wennington 162 A4
Wentworth 217 B1
Werrington 204 B3
Westcote 211 F6
West Deeping 231 B8
West End 155 A5
Westley Bottom 69 C2
Westley Waterless 70 C5
Weston Colville 54 B7
Weston Ditch 213 C2
Weston Green 54 D5
West Perry 116 C2
West Row 213 D6
Westry 227 F5
West Walton 238 E4
West Walton Church End
.....238 D5
Westwick 103 E7
West Wickham 37 B7
Westwood 197 B4
West Wratting 53 E5
Whaddon 28 C1
White Hall 235 E6
Whittlesey 189 D5
Whittlesford 32 B5
Wicken 211 F1
Wiggens Green 23 E2
Wilburton 210 B5
Willingham 209 B1
Willingham Green 54 D8
Wimblington 223 A6
Wintringham 75 F4
Winwick 158 B6
Wisbech 245 A6
Wisbech St Mary 235 C6
Wistow 163 F6
Witcham 217 A2
Witchford 217 D1
Withersfield 38 C4
Wittering 230 C1
Woodditton 90 E3
Woodhurst 155 B4
Woodland Green 24 E7
Woodston 186 E7
Wood Walton 161 F6
Woolley 149 E1
Worlington 213 E4
Wothorpe 244 B2
Wrestlingworth 25 C4
Wyton 142 F5

Y

Yarwell 183 A8
Yaxley 181 F4
Yelling 98 C1

A

A Furlong Dro CB6	224	F2
Abbey Cl Burwell CB5	130	B1
Sawtry PE28	168	B4
Abbey Fields PE26	172	C7
Abbey La Lode CB5	107	C2
Swaffham Bulbeck CB5	108	B3
Abbey Mdws Prim Sch		
CB5	84	D2
Abbey Pl 4 Thorney PE6	233	A3
Waterbeach CB5	127	B1
Abbey Rd		
Cambridge CB5	84	A3
Peterborough PE4	204	C1
Ramsey PE26	172	C6
Abbey St Cambridge CB1	84	A2
Ickleton CB10	17	F3
Abbey Way PE7	189	C7
Abbey Wlk CB1	84	A2
Abbot Thurston Ave		
CB6	240	E6
Abbot Way PE7	181	D4
Abbot's Cl PE28	155	A5
Abbots Cl		
Cambridge CB4	83	E7
Hemingford Abbots		
PE28	142	F3
Ramsey PE26	172	C7
Abbots Cres PE27	144	A6
Abbots Dr 1 PE6	232	B8
Abbots Ripton CE Prim Sch		
PE28	162	C1
Abbots Way Ely CB6	240	B5
Horningsea CB5	106	A1
Abbotsbury PE2	186	A3
Abbotsley Rd PE19	57	E8
Abbotsmede Prim Sch		
PE1	198	C4
Abbott Cl PE28	140	C3
Abbott's Cl PE9	244	D4
Abbott's Gr Cotts CB9	24	F3
Abbotts Cl SG8	12	C4
Abbotts Ct 2 CB9	24	E5
Abbotts Rd PE4	204	B6
Abbotts Rd CB9	39	A1
Abercorn Ct CB9	23	F6
Abercorn Pl 6 CB4	83	E8
Abington Gr 6 PE14	236	A5
Abington Pl CB4	39	A1
Abington Rd SG8	11	F2
Aboyne Ave PE2	185	F5
Abrahams Cl CB4	105	D6
Abram's La SG8	8	C4
Acacia Ave		
Peterborough PE1	198	B8
St Ives PE27	143	E6
Wisbech PE13	245	C8
Acacia Gr March PE15	243	C5
St Neots PE19	75	A6
Acer Rd PE1	198	B6
Acheson Rd PE28	117	E8
Ackerman Gdns 4 PE19	74	C2
Ackerman St PE19	74	C2
Ackroyd Rd 2 SG8	5	E8
Acland St PE1	197	F3
Acorn Ave CB3	102	C4
Acorn La CB3	79	C4
Acre Rd Carlton CB8	55	B8
March PE15	243	D4
Acre The PE28	150	F4
Acrefield Dr CB4	246	C4
Acremead PE8	178	A3
Acres The 2 PE9	230	D4
Acton Way CB4	83	D5
Adam and Eve St 1		
CB1	246	C1
Adam's La PE19	96	E4
Adams Ct CB5	106	C7
Adams Rd		
Cambridge CB3	83	B2
Swaffham Prior CB5	108	D5
Adastral Cl CB8	110	E4
Addenbrookes Hospl		
CB2	65	A3
Adderley PE3	197	C7
Addington Way 1 PE4	204	C3
Addison Rd PE15	223	B7
Adelaide Cl 10 CB7	212	B4
Adelaide Pl PE15	243	C4
Adelaide St PE9	244	C5
Adelaide Wlk PE28	208	E6
Admirals Dr PE13	245	D8
Admirals Way PE19	74	A2
Adventurers' Dro CB6	224	C1
Ailwine Rd PE26	171	B2
Ailwyn Sch PE26	172	C6
Aingers Rd CB4	104	B4
Ainsdale CB1	65	F5
Ainsdale Dr PE4	204	B4
Ainsworth Ct 4 CB1	84	A1
Ainsworth Pl CB1	84	B1
Ainsworth St CB1	84	A1
Aintree Rd SG8	5	F6
Airedale Cl PE1	198	A6
Airedale Rd 1 PE9	244	A7
Airport Way CB1	85	B2
Akeman Cl CB6	210	F6
Akeman St		
Cambridge CB4	83	C5
Landbeach CB4	105	C6
Akerly Dr CB3	79	A4
Alamein Ct PE19	74	C5
Albany Rd PE13	245	C6
Albany Wlk PE2	186	D7
Albemarle Rd PE27	143	F2
Albemarle Way CB4	83	E7

Albert Ct PE13	245	C3
Albert Pl PE3	197	F1
Albert Rd Stamford PE9	244	C5
Stow cum Quy CB5	86	A5
Albert St CB4	246	B4
Alberta Cres PE29	141	E5
Albert's Dr PE15	243	F3
Albion Row 6 CB3	83	C3
Albion Yd 5 CB3	83	C3
Alconbury CE Prim Sch		
PE28	150	F5
Alconbury Cl PE2	187	E5
Alde Rd CB9	39	A1
Aldeburgh Cl 21 CB9	23	E7
Alder Cl 1 PE19	74	B5
Alder Dr Bourn CB3	79	C3
Huntingdon PE29	141	D5
Alder Rd PE7	186	C5
Alderlands Rd CB6	232	B8
Alderlands Cl 6 PE6	232	B8
Alderman Jacobs Prim Sch		
PE7	189	F8
Alderman's Dr PE3	197	E3
Aldham Ct 12 CB9	23	E7
Aldreth Rd CB6	209	F5
Aldsworth Cl PE1	198	D6
Alec Rolph Cl CB1	66	D5
Alex Wood Rd CB4	83	E6
Alexander Chase CB6	240	A4
Alexander Rd SG19	25	D3
Alexandra Rd		
Littleport CB6	242	E4
Peterborough PE1	197	F6
Stamford PE9	244	B6
Wisbech PE13	245	C5
Alfric Sq PE2	186	B6
Alftruda Cl PE15	243	C6
Algar Dr CB8	70	F8
Algores Way PE13	245	B2
Alington Rd PE19	74	E1
Aliwal Rd PE7	189	F1
Alix Way CB7	240	F7
All Saints Ave PE13	245	F7
All Saints CE Prim Sch		
CB8	111	B3
All Saints Cl		
St Ives PE27	144	A6
2 Wisbech PE14	236	A5
All Saints IC Prim Sch		
PE15	243	D6
All Saints Jun Sch		
PE1	198	A6
All Saints Mews 10 PE9	244	B5
All Saints Pas		
Cambridge CB2	246	A3
6 Huntingdon PE28	141	D4
All Saints Rd		
Fulbourn CB1	66	F5
Newmarket CB8	111	A3
All Saints' Rd PE1	198	A5
All Saints' St PE9	244	B5
All Saints Way PE28	168	C4
All Saints Wlk IP28	213	F4
All Souls La CB3	83	B4
Allan Ave PE7	187	E5
Allard Cl PE7	181	D6
Allen Ct CB2	64	D2
Allen Farm Cl PE29	141	E1
Allen Rd		
Peterborough PE1	197	E6
Ramsey PE26	171	F7
Allen's Dro PE13	237	D1
Allen's Orch PE28	140	E1
Allens Cl CB3	63	B4
Allerton Cl 6 PE9	230	D3
Allerton Garth PE7	185	A4
Allexton Gdns 3 PE1	198	D7
Allington Wlk CB9	23	E8
Allotment La PE5	195	E2
Allotments Dro PE6	211	B7
Alma Rd PE1	197	F5
Alma Terr PE16	241	B4
Almond Cl PE29	142	A1
Almond Dr PE15	243	C6
Almond Gr CB3	102	C4
Almond Rd		
Peterborough PE1	198	B7
St Neots PE19	74	F6
Almoners' Ave CB1	65	C3
Almoners La CB1	197	E3
Alms Cl PE29	141	C7
Alms Hill CB3	60	D7
Alms La SG7	2	D4
Alnwick Ct 1 PE19	74	F2
Alpha La PE28	151	E3
Alpha Rd CB4	246	A4
Alpha St PE15	243	D5
Alpha Terr CB2	64	D3
Alstead Rd CB4	104	B5
Alsyke Cl PE28	116	A7
Althorpe Ct 1 CB6	240	D5
Alvis Dr PE7	181	D6
Alwin Cl PE28	168	B3
Alwyn Cl PE27	144	B6
Alwyne Rd CB1	65	C2
Amanda Cl PE3	197	E2
Amberley Slope PE4	204	B4
Ambleside Gdns CB4	204	D3
Ambrose Way CB4	104	C4
Ambury Hill PE29	141	E5
Ambury Rd PE29	141	D5
Ambury Rd S PE29	141	D5
Amcotts CB3	60	B8
America The CB6	216	D1
American Air Mus★ CB2 16	F8
American La PE29	141	E5

Amwell Rd CB4	83	F8
Amy Johnson Ct 3		
IP28	239	B5
Ancaster Rd 2 PE9	244	A7
Ancaster Way		
Cambridge CB1	65	C7
3 Doddington/Wimblington		
PE15	222	F5
Anchor Ct		
Littleport CB6	242	E3
Peterborough PE4	205	F1
Anchor Dro PE38	226	F4
Anchor La CB5	130	B4
Anderson Cl PE13	245	A7
Anderson Cres PE29	142	A2
Anderson Rd		
Boxworth CB4	101	D8
Swavesey CB4	122	D1
Andrea Cl PE2	187	C6
Andrew Cl PE5	195	D2
Andrew Rd		
Newmarket CB8	110	E5
St Neots PE19	74	F2
1 Stamford PE9	244	B6
Andrewe's Cl PE7	187	B1
Andrews Cl 2 CB5	210	F5
Andrews Cres PE4	204	F2
Angel Dro CB7	240	D2
Angel Sq CB7	240	D3
Angell's Mdw SG7	2	D4
Angle End CB1	67	F8
Angle La SG8	29	E5
Anglers Cl PE15	243	A5
Anglers Way CB4	84	C5
Angles Theatre The★		
PE13	245	C5
Anglesey Abbey (& remains		
of Priory)★ CB5	107	B1
Anglesey Way 8 CB4	208	D1
Anglia Polytechnic Univ		
CB1	246	C2
Anglia Way PE13	245	B2
Anglian Bsns Pk SG8	5	B7
Anglian Cl PE2	187	D6
Angoods La PE16	241	B6
Angus Cl 2 CB1	65	A8
Angus St PE3	197	D3
Ann Suckling Rd CB9	39	A2
Anne Rd PE9	244	A6
Anne's Cl CB8	110	B8
Annesdale CB7	240	D3
Annesley CB1	65	C5
Annesley Cl PE28	168	B4
Annington Cres SG8	13	A8
Ann's Rd CB5	84	E4
Ansley Way PE27	143	E5
Anson Cl PE26	171	E3
Anson Dr PE27	143	F6
Anson Pl PE19	74	A2
Anstey Way CB2	64	D2
Antelope Way CB1	66	A7
Anthony Cl		
Peterborough PE1	197	F8
Whittlesey PE7	189	C8
Antonia Cl PE28	24	E7
Anvil Ave SG8	12	A2
Anvil Cl CB2	49	C4
Apeldoorn Wlk PE13	245	D7
Apley Way CB3	79	A4
Apollo Way CB4	83	E8
Apple Acre Rd CB9	38	C1
Apple Cl PE15	96	F8
Apple Gr PE19	74	C4
Apple Orch The PE28	143	D2
Apple Tree Cl PE7	182	A6
Appleby Pk CB2	240	D5
Appletree Cl CB4	125	D1
Appletree Gr CB5	130	B4
Appletrees CB3	102	C3
Applewood Cl CB1	65	F5
Applewood Dr PE7	186	C3
Appleyard PE2	187	C7
Approach Cotts CB9	38	D2
Apreece Rd PE7	175	D8
Apreece Way PE7	176	A7
Apsley Way PE3	197	A2
Apthorpe St CB1	66	F6
Apthorpe Way CB4	84	A7
Aragon Cl		
Buckden PE19	117	B4
Cambridge CB4	83	E7
Aragon Pl PE28	113	F5
Aragon Rd CB9	23	D6
Arber Cl CB5	86	E6
Arborfield Cl PE6	231	C4
Arbour La CB3	79	A4
Arbroath Gdns PE2	185	C4
Arbury Banks★ SG7	2	C5
Arbury Ct PE3	197	A3
Arbury Ct CB4	83	E6
Arbury Prim Sch CB4	83	E5
Arbury Rd CB4	83	E6
Arcadia Gdns CB4	103	C5
Archers Dro PE6	233	D6
Archers Wood Rd PE7	186	C3
Archers Wood Nature		
Reserve★ PE28	160	C7
Archery Cres 9 CB7	240	D4
Archway Ct CB3	64	B7
Arden Rd CB4	83	F7
Ardleigh Cl 3 PE15	245	E6
Ardross Cl CB8	68	F6
Argyle St CB1	65	B8
Argyll Ct CB9	23	F6
Arles Ave PE13	245	D5
Armada Cl PE13	245	D8
Armingford Cres SG8	14	E7

Armitage Way CB4	83	F8
Armley Gr PE9	244	D7
Armshold La CB3	61	D2
Armstrong Cl		
Newmarket CB8	111	B3
Perry PE28	115	D3
Armstrong Ct 1 PE29	141	F8
Arnhem Cl PE13	74	C5
Arnold's La PE7	189	E7
Arran Cl CB1	65	F6
Arran Way PE27	144	A8
Arrendene Rd CB9	38	F1
Arthur Mellows Village Coll		
PE6	203	D8
Arthur St CB4	83	C4
Arthur's Mdw Nature		
Reserve★ PE28	120	C7
Artillery St 11 PE13	245	C4
Artindale PE3	197	A3
Artis Ct PE3	197	A3
Arundel Cl CB4	83	C5
Arundel Cres PE19	74	E2
Arundel Rd		
Huntingdon PE29	142	A6
Peterborough PE4	204	C1
Arundel Wlk 1 CB9	23	E8
Arundell CB6	240	C5
Ascham La CB2	32	B4
Ascham Rd CB4	83	E4
Ascot Dr PE1	198	B6
Ascot Rd SG8	5	F6
Ash Cl Huntingdon PE29	141	E7
Peterborough PE1	198	C7
Stilton PE7	175	F7
Thorney PE6	232	F3
Warboys PE28	165	A6
Ash Ct Brampton PE28	140	C3
Peterborough PE1	198	C7
Ash Gn CB10	18	D1
Ash Gr Burwell CB5	130	B2
Chatteris PE16	241	C5
Ely CB7	240	F5
Haverhill CB9	38	E1
March PE15	243	C5
Melbourn SG8	14	C5
Ash Pk PE4	204	B6
Ash Rd Earith PE28	208	F7
Peterborough PE1	198	C7
Ash Tree Cl 14 PE15	223	B7
Ashbeach Dro PE26	220	D3
Ashbeach Prim Sch		
PE26	220	D3
Ashbeach Rd		
March PE15	243	D4
Ramsey PE26	220	D3
Ashburn Cl PE6	203	F7
Ashbury Cl CB1	65	B6
Ashcroft PE19	98	B2
Ashcroft CB4	83	E7
Ashcroft Gdns PE1	198	C5
Ashdale Cl PE28	168	B3
Ashdale Pk PE15	245	A5
Ashdon Pl CB10	21	C2
Ashdon CP Sch CB10	21	B5
Ashen Gn CB2	49	A5
Ashfield PE28	113	F5
Ashfield Rd CB4	84	B5
Ashfields 1 PE6	231	F7
Ashlea Cl CB9	24	B6
Ashlea Rd CB9	24	A6
Ashleigh PE2	185	C6
Ashley Ct 9 CB1	84	A1
Ashley Gdns CB6	242	D3
Ashley Hill Sch CB8	91	F8
Ashley Pool La PE6	233	A2
Ashley Rd		
Cheveley CB8	112	A1
Newmarket CB8	111	E2
Ashley Way CB2	32	E8
Ashline Gr PE7	189	D6
Ashmead Dr CB3	81	A3
Ashton Cl PE27	208	A2
Ashton Gdns PE29	141	D5
Ashton Rd PE3	197	B5
Ashvale CB4	83	D7
Ashwell & Morden Sta		
SG7	3	D2
Ashwell Bury SG7	2	C5
Ashwell Prim Schol SG7	2	D4
Ashwell Rd		
Guilden Morden SG8	10	F2
Newnham SG7	2	A1
Ashwell St Ashwell SG7	2	D4
Bassingbourn cum Kneesworth		
SG8	13	A3
Ashwell Village Mus★		
SG7	2	D4
Askers Field CB3	78	E2
Askew's La PE7	181	E4
Aspal Cl 8 IP28	213	E8
Aspal Hall Rd IP28	213	F8
Aspal La IP28	214	A8
Aspal Pk		
Beck Row, Holywell		
Row & Kenny Hill IP28	214	A8
Mildenhall IP28	213	E8
Aspal Pl 9 IP28	213	E8
Aspen Cl Ely CB7	240	D5
Haverhill CB9	38	E1
Aspen Gn PE29	141	E5
Asplin Ave PE15	243	E4
Asplin's Cl 5 CB4	208	D1
Asplin's La PE19	117	F3
Asplins Ave 8 PE27	208	A3
Aster Dr PE4	204	D5
Astilbe La PE29	141	D5
Astley Cl CB6	216	E1

Astore Pk PE1	198	E3
Atherstone Ave PE3	197	B4
Atherton Cl CB4	83	E5
Athlone 7 CB1	84	A1
Athlone CB3	99	A3
Atkins Cl Cambridge CB4	84	A7
Littleport CB6	242	C5
Atkinson St PE1	198	C2
Atlantic Cl PE15	243	B6
Atterton Rd CB9	38	D1
Auberry Way CB3	78	F3
Auborn Gdns PE3	197	A3
Aubretia Ave PE4	204	D3
Auckland Rd CB5	246	C3
Audley Cl SG19	58	E4
Audley Gate PE3	197	C3
Audley Way CB1	37	A3
Augers Rd 4 CB1	65	F6
Augusta Cl PE1	198	E6
Augustus Cl		
4 Cambridge CB4	83	E8
Haverhill CB9	24	D1
Augustus Way PE16	241	D6
Aureole Wlk CB8	110	E8
Austin Ct PE7	181	D6
Austin Friars La 3 PE9	244	B4
Austin St PE9	244	B4
Australia Ct CB3	83	B4
Avenells Way 2 SG19	41	D5
Avenue Rd		
Huntingdon PE29	141	D5
St Neots PE19	74	F6
Avenue The		
Borough Fen PE6	207	E3
Burwell CB5	130	C3
Cambridge CB3	246	A3
Girton CB3	103	B1
Godmanchester PE29	141	E3
Leighton PE28	148	C3
Madingley CB3	81	F7
March PE15	243	D2
Newmarket CB8	111	A3
Ramsey PE26	172	A7
Aversley Rd PE28	168	C2
Aversley Wood Nature		
Reserve★ PE28	159	F8
Aves Cl CB7	213	A5
Avon Ct		
Eaton Socon PE19	74	C3
Peterborough PE4	204	E2
Avro Ct PE29	141	B8
Axiom Ave PE3	197	C4
Axiom Ct PE29	244	D4
Axis Way 6 PE19	74	B5
Aydon Rd PE7	187	F6
Aylesborough Cl 4 CB4	83	D7
Aylesford Way CB4	49	B4
Aylestone Rd CB4	246	C4
Aylington Cl PE8	184	B1
Ayre Ct 5 PE19	75	A5
Ayres Dr PE2	187	C6
Azalea Cl PE3	197	A2
Azalea court PE7	181	F6

B

Babble Cl PE15	243	C4
Babraham CE Prim Sch		
CB2	50	D1
Babraham Institute		
CB2	50	D2
Babraham Rd		
Babraham CB2	50	B1
Cambridge CB2	65	C2
Fulbourn CB1	50	E8
Great Shelford CB2	49	E8
Sawston CB2	32	F8
Stapleford CB2	50	B6
Babylon Gall★ CB7	240	E3
Back Dro Upwell PE14	229	D8
Welney PE14	225	A8
Back Hill Ely CB7	240	D3
Hadstock CB1	20	B6
Back La Bourn CB3	79	B4
Burrough Green CB8	70	F4
Cambourne CB3	79	C4
Coveney CB6	217	B5
14 Deeping St James PE6	231	F8
Elton PE8	178	D8
Ely CB7	240	D4
Eye PE6	232	A1
Haslingfield CB3	47	B4
Holywell-cum-Needingworth		
PE27	144	F2
Ickleton CB10	18	A3
Market Deeping PE6	206	A7
Melbourn SG8	14	C4
Outwell PE14	236	E3
Stamford PE9	244	C5
Wicken CB7	211	E1
Yaxley PE7	181	E5
Back Rd Elm PE14	236	A5
Gorefield PE13	237	E2
Linton CB1	35	C3
Murrow PE13	234	D6
Wisbech PE14	236	A1
Back Reach Dro PE15	221	E7
Back St Bourn CB3	2	D3
Bacon's Yd SG7	2	D4
Bacton Rd CB3	47	B5
Badcock Rd CB3	47	B5
Bader Cl		
Peterborough PE3	197	B6
Ramsey PE26	172	A4

Badgeney Rd PE15 243 E4
Badger Cl PE7 181 F5
Badinton La PE9 230 F5
Badlingham Rd CB7 213 C1
Badminton Cl CB4 83 C6
Badney Dro PE16 222 D3
Bagley End PE4 205 B1
Bagot Pl 5 CB4 83 F8
Bagsham La IP28 213 E6
Bahram Cl CB8 110 E4
Bailey Cl CB9 24 D7
Bailey Mews CB5 246 C3
Bailey Way PE2 186 D8
Bain Cl PE9 244 C7
Baines Coney CB9 38 D1
Bainton Rd
Barnack PE9 230 D4
Newborough PE6 204 F8
Baird Cl PE7 181 D6
Bakehouse Hill CB8 70 E8
Baker Dr CB5 130 C3
Bakers Cl CB3 62 D6
Bakers Field CB3 102 C1
Bakers La Barley SG8 6 F3
Linton CB1 35 D2
Peterborough PE2 186 E7
Bakers Link PE19 74 E2
Bakers Row CB8 111 A4
Bakers Way PE28 115 E2
Bakery Cl Fen Ditton CB5 84 E5
Wilburton CB6 210 C5
Bakewell Rd PE2 185 C2
Bala Ct PE4 204 E3
Balaton Pl CB8 111 A6
Balding Cl 4 PE13 245 D5
Baldock Rd SG8 4 C4
Baldock St SG8 5 D6
Baldock Way CB1 65 B5
Baldwin Cl PE8 230 C1
Baldwins Cl CB3 60 C5
Baldwin's Cnr SG7 2 E5
Baldwins Manor SG19 58 D4
Balingdon La CB1 35 D3
Balintore Rise PE2 185 D4
Balland Field CB4 124 A8
Ballard Cl CB4 105 D3
Balmoral Dr 5 CB9 23 E8
Balmoral Rd PE4 197 C8
Balmoral Way PE19 74 E2
Balsham Rd
Fulbourn CB1 67 B2
Linton CB1 35 D3
Bamber St PE1 197 F4
Bambers La PE14 236 C6
Bancroft Cl CB1 65 B6
Bancroft La CB7 212 B5
Bandon Rd CB3 82 F6
Banff Cl 2 CB4 83 E7
Banhams Cl CB4 246 C4
Bank Ave PE28 208 C8
Bank Cl PE7 189 E5
Bank Dr PE13 245 A7
Bank The PE13 234 C7
Bankes Mead CB2 32 D1
Banks Cnr CB6 240 C4
Banks Ct PE19 74 E2
Bank's End PE28 142 D6
Bannister Gdns SG8 5 E8
Bannister's Row PE13 245 B7
Bannold Ct CB5 106 B8
Bannold Dro CB5 106 C8
Bannold Rd CB5 106 D8
Banworth La CB4 105 D6
Baptist Rd PE14 229 D8
Bar Cl CB2 49 C5
Bar Dro PE14 236 B4
Bar Hill Prim Sch CB4 102 B4
Bar La Hatley SG19 42 E2
Stapleford CB2 49 C4
Tadlow SG19 25 E8
Barbara Stradbroke Ave
CB8 89 B7
Barber Cl PE2 187 C7
Barbers Dro PE6 232 C8
Barbers Hill PE4 204 B7
Barcham Rd CB7 211 F7
Bardling's Dro PE12 237 A8
Bardney PE2 186 A4
Bardyke Bank PE14 229 F7
Baretts Cl PE7 189 D8
Barford Cl PE2 186 C7
Barford Rd PE19 74 E2
Bargate La IP28 213 D5
Bargate Rd IP28 213 D6
Barham Cl PE2 187 F5
Barham Ct SG8 14 D6
Barham Rd PE28 149 D6
Barker Cl
Hail Weston PE19 95 A1
Waterbeach CB5 106 B8
Barker's La PE15 243 D1
Barkham's La CB6 242 D4
Barkston Dr PE1 198 B6
Barkway Rd SG8 5 E5
Barkway St SG8 5 D5
Barkways CB5 130 C1
Barleuy Ct 6 PE19 74 D5
Barley Rd
Eaton Socon PE19 74 C3
Great & Little Chishill SG8 7 A7
Barley VP Sch SG8 7 A2
Barley Way CB1 35 D2
Barlings Ct CB8 111 A4
Barn Cl
Huntingdon PE29 142 A7
Barn Cl *continued*
6 Maxey PE6 231 C7
Peterborough PE4 204 B3
Ramsey PE26 172 A4
Stilton PE7 175 F8
Barn Hill PE9 244 B5
Barnabas Ct CB4 105 D1
Barnabas Oley CE Prim Sch
SG19 58 E4
Barnack CE Prim Sch
PE9 230 D4
Barnack Drift PE9 230 B3
Barnack Hills & Holes
National Nature Reserve★
PE9 230 D3
Barnack Rd
Bainton PE9 230 E4
St Martin's Without PE9 244 C4
Barnard Cl 1 PE19 74 F1
Barnard Way
1 Cambridge CB4 83 D5
Peterborough PE3 196 F3
Barnes Cl
Cambridge CB5 84 D2
St Neots PE19 74 E6
Barnes Way
Peterborough PE4 204 B3
Whittlesey PE7 189 B8
Barnfield Gdns PE7 190 F8
Barnfield La PE28 98 D7
Barns Cl CB4 208 D1
Barns The PE19 117 B4
Barnstock PE3 197 A7
Barnwell Dr CB1 84 E2
Barnwell Rd CB1 84 D1
Baron Ct
Eaton Socon PE19 74 B4
Peterborough PE4 204 D4
Baron's Way CB3 99 B3
Barons La CB2 30 C5
Baros Cl CB1 22 A7
Barra PE13 238 A1
Barracks The PE13 237 E2
Barringer Way PE19 74 F7
Barrington CE Prim Sch
CB2 46 F1
Barrington Nature Reserve★
CB2 29 F8
Barrington Rd
Orwell SG8 45 F1
Shepreth SG8 29 D6
Barron's Gn SG8 29 F4
Barrons Way 1 CB3 62 C5
Barrow Cl CB2 64 E5
Barrow La CB3 79 A4
Barrow Rd CB2 64 E5
Barrowcrofts CB4 104 B5
Barrowfield PE1 198 E7
Barr's St PE7 189 D7
Barry Lynham Dr CB8 111 C2
Barry Wlk PE2 186 F7
Barsey Cl CB9 38 C1
Barston Dro CB5 108 C7
Bartholemew's Wlk
CB7 240 C2
Bartholomew Cl CB10 18 E2
Bartlow Hills (Tumuli)★
CB1 21 B6
Bartlow Pl CB9 39 B1
Bartlow Rd
Castle Camps CB1 22 D4
Hadstock CB1 20 D7
Linton CB1 35 E2
Barton CE Prim Sch
CB3 63 B4
Barton Cl Cambridge CB3 64 B8
Peterborough PE4 204 F1
Witchford CB6 217 D1
Barton Holt PE13 237 F8
Barton La PE13 237 E8
Barton Mews CB7 240 C4
Barton Rd
Cambridge CB3 64 B8
Comberton CB3 62 D5
Ely CB7 240 C3
Haslingfield CB3 47 A7
Wisbech PE13 245 A4
Barton Sq CB7 240 D4
Bartons Cl CB1 53 B2
Bartons Pl CB8 110 E5
Bartram Gate PE4 204 E1
Barway Cnr CB7 211 D6
Barway Rd CB7 211 E7
Bascraft Way PE29 142 A1
Basil Gn PE2 186 D6
Bassenhally Ct PE7 189 E7
Bassenhally Rd PE7 189 E8
Bassenthwaite PE29 141 B6
Basset Cl 3 CB4 83 F8
Bassett Cl CB4 83 F8
Bassingboum Barracks
SG8 12 F8
Bassingbourn Prim Sch
SG8 12 D4
Bassingbourn Rd SG8 12 B3
Bassingbourn Village Coll
SG8 12 E4
Bateman Mews CB2 64 E7
Bateman St CB2 64 E7
Bate's Dro CB6 225 B3
Bateson Rd CB4 83 D4
Bates's Dro CB6 225 B5
Bath Cres PE28 143 B8
Bath Rd PE13 245 C7
Bath Row PE9 244 B4
Bathurst PE2 186 A4
Battle Gate CB3 80 A8
Battle Gate Rd CB3 80 A8
Battle Rd PE26 171 E3
Baulk La SG19 43 A3
Baulk The Thriplow SG8 31 B2
Whittlesey PE7 189 E8
Baulkin's Dro PE12 237 C8
Baulks The CB2 32 E7
Bawtree Cres CB1 35 E3
Baxter Cl 3 PE13 245 E6
Baxter Dr 4 PE19 74 E2
Baycliffe Cl 1 CB1 65 D5
Bayfield Dr CB5 130 C2
Bayford Pl 1 CB4 83 F8
Bayliss PE29 118 F7
Beach Rd CB4 125 F3
Beachampstead Rd 1
PE19 93 F6
Beacon Cl PE29 141 A6
Beaconsfield Ct 4 CB9 23 F7
Beaconsfield Terr CB4 83 D4
Beald Way CB6 240 B4
Beale Ct 2 PE29 141 F8
Beales Way CB4 84 A7
Bean Cl 2 PE19 75 A6
Bear La SG7 2 D4
Beatrice Rd PE13 245 D7
Beatty Rd PE19 74 B2
Beauchamp Cl PE19 74 B3
Beaufort Ct 3 CB9 23 F7
Beaufort Dr
Chatteris PE16 241 B6
Hardwick PE19 117 A5
Beaulands Cl CB4 246 C4
Beaulieu Ct 1 PE6 232 A1
Beaumaris Rd PE28 168 C3
Beaumont Cl PE29 141 F8
Beaumont Cres CB1 65 D3
Beaumont Ct CB9 24 B6
Beaumont Rd CB1 65 D3
Beaumont Vale CB9 24 B6
Beaumont Way PE7 186 C2
Beaupre Ave PE14 236 F3
Beaupre Com Prim Sch
PE14 236 F2
Beaupre Dro PE26 221 A2
Beauvale Gdns PE4 204 E3
Beauvoir Pl PE7 181 E5
Beaver Cl 8 PE19 74 B5
Bec Rd PE19 74 E5
Beccelm Dr 9 PE6 232 B8
Beche Rd CB5 84 A2
Beche Way CB4 105 C7
Beck Rd CB7 213 B4
Beck Row Prim Sch
IP28 213 F8
Becket's Cl PE26 172 B8
Beckets Cl PE1 197 F8
Beckett Way 3 PE16 241 C5
Beckingham PE2 185 F3
Bede Pl PE1 198 A6
Bedford Ave PE28 143 B8
Bedford Cl Ely CB6 240 A3
2 Needingworth PE27 208 A3
St Ives PE27 143 F7
Bedford Ct
5 Haverhill CB9 23 F7
10 Thorney PE6 233 A3
Bedford Purlieus National
Nature Reserve★
PE8 193 A4
Bedford Row PE13 238 D8
Bedford St
Peterborough PE1 198 B4
St Neots PE19 74 E6
Wisbech PE13 245 C6
Bedford Way PE28 168 C3
Bedwell Hey La CB6 217 E1
Beech Ave
7 Doddington/Wimblington
PE15 223 A6
Little Stukeley PE28 152 A2
Peterborough PE1 197 F3
Beech Cl
Great Shelford CB2 48 E3
Huntingdon PE29 141 E7
Isleham CB7 212 F5
2 Thorney PE6 233 A3
Warboys PE28 164 E4
Beech Croft CB8 70 D2
Beech Dr PE27 143 F5
Beech End PE28 150 F4
Beech Gr Haverhill CB9 23 E8
March PE15 243 C5
St Neots PE19 74 F6
Beech La Ely CB7 240 E5
7 Eye PE6 232 A1
Pampisford CB2 33 B5
Beech Rd PE6 203 D8
Beech Way CB1 35 C2
Beeches Cl IP28 213 D7
Beeches Prim Sch The
PE1 197 F3
Beeches Rd IP28 213 D7
Beeches The CB4 83 F5
Beechside SG19 41 C6
Beechwood Ave
Bottisham CB5 86 F6
Melbourn SG8 14 C5
Beechwood Cl
Exning CB8 110 C8
Peterborough PE1 198 C7
Beechwood Gdns
PE16 241 C4
Beechwood Nature Reserve★
CB1 65 F2
Beechwood Rd PE13 245 D7
Beehive Ctr Ret Pk CB1 84 B2
Bee's La PE13 237 F6
Beeson Cl PE19 95 F2
Beeston Dr PE7 187 F5
Beeton Cl SG8 14 C6
Beetons Cl PE7 181 E5
Beevor Ct PE19 152 E1
Beezling Cl 9 PE19 74 C6
Beezling Fen Dro
PE26 222 D3
Begdale Rd PE14 235 F5
Begwary Cl 7 PE19 74 B5
Beild Dro CB6 218 B7
Belbin Way CB2 32 D8
Beldam Ave SG8 5 E5
Beldam's Cl CB3 61 D4
Beldams PE27 208 A3
Belgic Sq PE2 198 E3
Belgrave Rd CB1 65 C8
Belgrave Sq PE28 168 B4
Belham Rd PE1 197 E7
Bell Cl Ely CB6 240 D5
Meldreth SG8 14 A8
Stilton PE7 176 A7
Bell Dro PE6 232 F6
Bell Foundry Cl 1 SG19 41 D5
Bell Gdns
Haddenham CB6 210 A6
Soham CB7 212 B4
Bell Hill CB4 104 B4
Bell Holt CB7 240 E4
Bell La Alconbury PE28 150 F4
Barton Mills IP28 239 D2
Fenstanton PE28 121 B5
4 Market Deeping PE6 231 F8
Nuthampstead SG8 1 A2
Southoe & Midloe PE19 95 E6
Bell Rd CB5 86 E5
Bellairs CB6 216 E1
Bellamy Cl PE19 74 E2
Bellamy's La PE14 238 D4
Bell's Dro
Littleport CB6 225 B6
Sutton St James PE12 237 C8
Bell's Pl PE1 198 A2
Belle Isle PE28 140 B3
Belle Isle Cres PE28 140 B3
Belle Vue PE2 187 C6
Bellman's Cl PE7 189 F7
Bellman's Rd PE7 189 F6
Bellmans Gr PE7 190 A7
Bells Mdw SG8 11 A5
Belmont Ct 8 CB9 23 F7
Belmont Gdns PE16 241 C4
Belmont Pl CB5 246 B3
Belmont Rd PE15 243 D5
Belmore Cl 1 CB4 83 C5
Belsar's Hill (Fort)★
CB4 209 C1
Belsars Cl CB4 209 A1
Belsay Ct CB9 23 D8
Belsay Dr PE2 187 F5
Belsize Ave PE2 186 E6
Belt Dro PE14 235 F4
Belt The CB8 73 D8
Belton Rd PE7 187 F5
Belton St PE9 244 C5
Belton's Hill PE28 137 F7
Belvedere PE26 221 C2
Belvoir Ct 4 CB9 23 E8
Belvoir Rd CB4 246 C4
Belvoir Terr CB2 64 E7
Belvoir Way PE1 198 C8
Benams Cl PE5 195 E2
Bencroft La PE28 165 A4
Bendyshe Way
Barrington CB2 30 A8
Harston CB2 47 A1
Benedict Sq PE4 204 A2
Benedict St CB6 240 B5
Benefield Rd CB8 112 F6
Benet Cl CB4 105 C1
Bene't St CB2 246 A2
Benians Ct CB3 83 B3
Benland PE3 197 A6
Bennett Rd IP28 214 A1
Benny's Way CB3 82 B2
Benson Pl 5 CB4 83 C4
Benson St 4 CB4 83 C4
Benstead PE2 185 E3
Bensteads End CB1 68 A8
Bentham Way CB6 240 E6
Bentinck St CB2 246 B1
Bentley Ave PE7 181 E6
Bentley Cl PE26 171 B2
Bentley Rd CB2 64 E5
Bentley St PE9 244 C5
Benwick Prim Sch
PE15 222 A5
Benwick Rd
Doddington PE15 222 D5
Ramsey PE26 221 E3
Whittlesey PE7 221 D7
Benyon Gr PE2 186 B4
Berberis Cl PE6 232 F3
Beresford Rd CB6 240 A5
Bergamont Cl 5 PE29 118 F8
Bergamot Rd CB9 23 C8
Bergholt Cl 4 CB5 84 E4
Berkeley Rd PE3 197 C3
Berkley Ct 1 PE19 74 E4
Berkley St PE19 74 E4
Bermuda Rd CB4 83 C4
Bermuda Terr CB4 83 C4
Bernard Cl PE29 141 D6
Bernard Rd PE28 140 D3
Bernard St CB6 240 B4
Berristead Cl CB6 210 C6
Berry Cl CB6 210 F5
Berry Ct PE1 197 E5
Berry Gn CB6 210 F5
Berry Gn Pk NN14 156 E5
Berry La PE29 118 C8
Berry Leas PE8 183 D1
Berrybut Way PE9 244 D7
Berrycroft Soham CB7 212 B4
Willingham CB4 124 A8
Berryfield PE15 243 E7
Bertie La 6 PE9 230 C6
Betjamin Rd SG8 5 D8
Betjeman Rd SG8 13 D1
Betony Vale SG8 5 E5
Betony Wlk CB9 23 D8
Bettles Cl PE1 198 A6
Betts Cl PE29 141 F1
Between Cl Dro CB4 125 D2
Bevan Cl PE29 141 E6
Beverley Cl SG8 5 B8
Beverley Gdns PE9 244 A6
Beverley Way 4 CB2 64 D3
Beverstone PE2 185 D5
Beville PE28 161 F6
Bevills Cl 16 PE15 223 A5
Bevills Pl PE15 243 D3
Bevington Way PE19 74 E2
Bevis La PE13 235 C6
Bevishall PE4 204 F1
Bew Cl PE2 187 D4
Bewick Pl PE7 181 D8
Bewicks Mead CB5 130 C2
Bickerley Ct CB3 79 A3
Bickleigh Wlk PE3 197 A3
Bicton Ind Est PE28 114 B7
Bifield PE2 185 F3
Big Gn PE8 178 C3
Biggen The CB2 17 E8
Biggin Abbey★ CB5 84 F8
Biggin La Fen Ditton CB5 84 F8
Ramsey PE26 171 E6
Biggs Rd PE14 236 D8
Bigram's La PE19 114 C7
Bilberry Cl 1 PE19 74 C5
Bilberry End CB1 20 C7
Bill Hall Way PE28 168 D2
Bill Rickaby Dr CB8 111 A5
Binnimoor Rd PE15 228 E4
Biotechnology Ctr CB3 82 D7
Birch Ave PE16 241 D5
Birch Cl Cambridge CB4 83 F5
Chatteris PE16 241 D5
Ely CB7 240 E5
Yaxley PE7 182 A5
Birch Dr PE28 151 E3
Birch Gr PE14 236 B5
Birch Trees Rd CB2 49 A6
Birchen Cl PE7 186 C3
Birches The CB7 212 A5
Birchin Cl PE7 186 C3
Birchtree Ave PE1 198 A7
Birchwood PE2 186 A3
Birchwood Ave PE15 243 B2
Bird Farm Rd CB1 66 E5
Bird La PE19 95 A1
Bird's Dro
Gorefield PE13 237 D1
Sutton St James PE12 237 B8
Birds Cl CB10 18 A3
Birdwood Rd CB1 65 D6
Birkdale Ave
Mildenhall IP28 239 B5
Peterborough PE4 204 B3
Birt La PE27 144 A3
Biscay Cl CB9 24 C7
Bishop Cl PE7 175 F7
Bishop Creighton Prim Sch
PE1 198 B2
Bishop Laney Dr CB6 240 E7
Bishop Way CB4 104 C3
Bishop Wynn Cl CB7 240 D3
Bishop's Ct CB2 64 C1
Bishop's Rd
Cambridge CB2 64 D1
Peterborough PE1 198 A1
Bishops Cl Haverhill CB9 23 E8
Little Downham CB6 218 A7
Peterborough PE1 198 D5
Bishops Ct 8 CB9 23 E8
Bishops Rd
St Neots PE19 74 F2
19 Somersham PE28 215 C1
Bishops Way
Buckden PE19 117 B4
Great Paxton PE19 96 E4
Bishops Wlk
2 Barnack PE9 230 D3
Ely CB7 240 D4
Bishopsfield PE4 204 D1
Bittern Cl PE27 143 F7
Bittern Way PE15 243 F5
Black Bank CB6 218 B8
Black Bank Rd CB6 218 B8
Black Bear La
Leverington PE13 245 F7
Newmarket CB8 110 F3
Walsoken PE14 238 F1
Black Dike PE13 237 E6
Black Dro March PE15 223 E8
Thorney PE6 233 A5
Wisbech St Mary PE13 234 B3
Black Dyke PE13 237 F4
Black Ham Dro PE7 182 E2
Black Hill Rd PE27 143 E6
Black Horse Dro CB6 226 B6
Black Horse La
Chatteris PE16 241 C6
Swavesey CB4 122 E6
Black La Gorefield PE13 237 C2
Tydd St Giles PE13 237 C6

Black Swan Spinney
PE8 194 A4
Blackberry Droveway
CB5 108 C8
Blackberry Way 6 IP28 214 A1
Blackbird Way PE28 150 E4
Blackbush Dro PE7 220 D8
Blackdown Garth PE4 204 D3
Blacked-Out Britain War Mus★ PE29 141 D4
Blackfriar St 14 PE9 244 C5
Blackfriars Rd 8 PE13 245 C5
Blackfriars St 8 PE9 244 C5
Blackhall Rd CB4 83 C7
Blackmans Rd PE7 175 D8
Blackmead PE2 186 B4
Blackmill Rd PE16 241 B2
Blackmore Cl 4 CB9 38 F1
Blacksmith Cl SG19 40 C3
Blacksmiths Cl
Abbotsley PE19 57 B5
Ramsey Forty Foot PE26 221 C2
Blacksmiths La
Abbotsley PE19 57 B5
Ellington PE28 139 A4
Shudy Camps CB1 22 C5
Blackstone Rd PE29 141 C7
Blackthorn Cl
Cambridge CB4 83 F6
Chatteris PE16 241 C3
Blackthorn Ct
Coates/Eastrea PE7 190 F8
Soham CB7 212 A5
Blackwell Rd PE7 186 C2
Blackwood Rd PE19 74 B3
Bladon Way CB9 39 B1
Blair Par CB9 23 E8
Blair Way PE19 74 E2
Blake Cl SG8 13 D1
Blakeland Hill CB2 17 D8
Blakes Way PE19 74 B2
Blandford Gdns PE1 198 E7
Blandford Wlk 1 CB4 83 C6
Blanford Wlk CB4 83 C7
Blashfeld Cl 2 PE9 244 A6
Blaxhall Ct 13 CB9 23 E7
Blea Wr PE29 141 B6
Bledwick Dro PE13 238 C3
Blench La CB1 34 F6
Blencowe Terr 19 PE13 245 C5
Blenheim Cl
2 Cambridge CB1 65 E5
3 Eaton Socon PE19 74 C4
Haverhill CB9 39 B1
Shepreth SG8 29 E4
Blenheim Dr PE27 143 F7
Blenheim Gr PE19 96 F8
Blenheim Rd
Ramsey PE26 172 A7
Upwood PE26 171 E3
Blenheim Way
Emneth PE14 245 E2
1 Hardwick CB3 81 A4
Yaxley PE7 181 E5
Blethan Dr PE29 141 A6
Blinco Gr CB1 65 B5
Blind La 3 Maxey PE6 231 C7
Sawtry PE28 168 C3
Bliss Way CB1 66 A6
Block Fen Dro
Chatteris PE16 216 C6
Wimblington PE15 223 C5
Block Rd CB7 212 C1
Blockmoor Dro CB6 216 C4
Blockmoor Rd CB7 211 E6
Blois Rd CB9 24 F1
Bloomfield Cl PE19 95 E1
Bloomfield Way PE28 168 C4
Blooms Ct IP28 239 D4
Bloomsfield CB5 130 C1
Blossom Ct PE3 197 B8
Blossom St 3 CB1 84 A1
Blue Boar Dro CB6 218 D7
Blue La PE15 223 A7
Blue Ridge Gdns PE15 243 E5
Bluebell Ave PE1 198 A8
Bluebell Cl PE26 220 D3
Bluebell Wlk 1 CB7 212 B4
Bluecoat Prim Sch The
PE9 244 B6
Bluegate PE29 118 F7
Bluntisham Heath Rd
PE28 155 F3
Bluntisham Rd
Bluntisham/Colne PE28 208 D6
1 Needingworth PE27 208 A3
Blunt's La PE7 189 E7
Blythe Gn PE28 115 D2
Blythe Way
Caldecote CB3 80 C1
Gamlingay SG19 41 D5
Blyton Rd CB3 99 A3
Boadicea Ct PE16 241 C5
Boardman Cl PE19 95 F2
Boardwalks Nature Reserve★
PE3 197 D1
Bodiam Way PE19 74 F2
Bodian Wlk 3 CB9 23 E8
Bodsey Toll Rd PE26 221 B2
Boeing Way IP28 239 B5
Bogmoor Rd SG8 7 C1
Bogs Gap La SG8 11 B3
Bohemond St CB7 240 E5
Boleness Rd PE13 245 C2
Boleyn Way CB9 23 D7
Boleyn Wlk CB8 111 C3
Bolton Cl CB5 130 A2
Bona La PE13 235 B8
Boongate PE1 198 C3
Boot La CB2 29 E8
Boot The CB6 209 D4
Booth Way PE19 95 F1
Boot's Rd PE15 223 F6
Boretree Way PE29 141 A7
Borough Cl PE13 245 D3
Borough The CB6 209 E4
Borrowdale CB4 83 C6
Borrowdale Cl PE4 204 E3
Borthwick Pk PE2 185 D6
Borthwick Pl PE2 185 D6
Bossert's Way CB3 80 C2
Boswell Cl PE1 197 E8
Bosworth Cl PE8 178 B3
Bosworth Rd CB1 65 D5
Bosworth Way 2 PE15 243 D2
Botolph Gn PE2 186 C7
Botolph La CB2 246 A2
Bottels Rd PE28 164 E5
Bottisham Com Prim Sch
CB5 86 F5
Bottisham Pk★ CB5 86 F7
Bottisham Swimming Pool
CB5 86 E6
Bottisham Village Coll
CB5 86 E6
Bottle La PE13 237 C7
Bough La PE28 162 F1
Boulevard Ret Pk PE1 197 D7
Boundary Dr PE15 243 C3
Boundary Rd
Haverhill CB9 24 D5
Red Lodge IP28 214 A1
Boundary Rd Ind Est
CB9 24 C5
Bourdillon Ct 1 PE28 121 B6
Bourges Bvd PE1 197 D7
Bourgess Ret Pk PE3 197 F1
Bourn Bridge Rd CB1 34 A8
Bourn CE Prim Sch
CB3 60 C6
Bourn Rd CB3 59 F8
Bourn Windmill★ CB3 79 A1
Bourne Rd
Cambridge CB4 84 C5
Haverhill CB9 24 B8
Bourns The CB1 67 A4
Bower Cl PE1 198 C5
Bower's La 4 CB7 213 A5
Bowers Croft CB1 65 C3
Bowker Way PE7 189 C8
Bowlings Ct PE27 144 A3
Bowness Way 2 PE4 204 F2
Bowsers CB10 20 D3
Bowsers La CB10 20 B2
Bowthorpe Gdns
PE13 245 D5
Boxer Rd PE8 230 B1
Boxford Ct 20 CB9 23 E7
Boxgrove Cl 14 PE6 232 A1
Boxworth End CB4 122 E3
Boxworth Rd CB3 100 C4
Boyce Cl PE7 189 D7
Boyces Rd PE13 245 E5
Boyton Cl CB9 39 A2
Bozeat Way PE3 197 C6
Brackenbury Cl CB4 104 C3
Brackenwood PE2 185 D6
Brackhill Fen Dro
PE28 208 E8
Brackley Cl
3 Cambridge CB4 83 D6
Peterborough PE3 197 D3
Brackwood PE2 185 D6
Brackyn Rd CB1 65 B7
Bradden St PE3 197 C6
Bradegate Dr PE1 198 E7
Bradford's Cl CB5 86 E6
Bradley Rd CB8 72 F1
Bradmore St CB1 246 C2
Bradrushe Fields CB3 82 F3
Bradshaw Cl PE29 141 E6
Bradshaw Ct PE15 243 C2
Bradwell Rd PE3 197 A2
Bradwells Ct CB1 246 B2
Braeburn Ave PE13 245 C8
Braemar Gdns PE7 189 D6
Braggs La
Hemingford Grey PE28 143 C1
Wrestlingworth SG19 25 B4
Brailsford Cl PE3 197 A4
Bramall Ct PE3 197 C3
Bramble Cl
Haverhill CB9 38 D1
Whittlesey PE7 189 E6
Yaxley PE7 182 A6
Bramble Ct 2 PE28 140 C3
Bramble End
Alconbury PE28 150 F5
Sawtry PE28 168 B3
Bramble La PE14 236 D3
Bramble Wlk PE15 243 E7
Brambles The
Balsham CB1 53 C1
Bar Hill CB3 102 D3
Cambridge CB2 64 D2
Girton CB3 83 A6
Hemingford Grey PE27 143 F1
Littleport CB6 242 D3
3 Royston SG8 5 E5
Bramley Ave
Melbourn SG8 14 D6
Needingworth PE27 208 A2
Bramley Cl
Cottenham CB4 125 D3
Offord Cluny PE19 118 A1
Bramley Ct CB4 84 B6
Bramley Dr PE19 118 A1
Bramley Gr PE28 208 C5
Bramley Rd
Haverhill CB9 23 C7
St Ives PE27 144 B5
Wisbech PE13 245 C7
Bramley Way CB3 81 A4
Bramleys The
March PE15 243 D1
Shepreth SG8 29 E4
Brampton Cl PE13 245 A4
Brampton Ct PE2 187 D6
Brampton Gdns PE19 75 A4
Brampton Inf Sch
PE28 140 C2
Brampton Jun Sch
PE28 140 C2
Brampton Rd
Buckden PE19 117 C6
Cambridge CB1 84 B1
Grafham PE28 116 B7
Huntingdon PE29 141 B3
Royston SG8 5 F6
Brampton Wood Nature Reserve★ PE19 139 D1
Brancepeth Pl PE2 186 E7
Branch Bank Ely CB7 218 F6
Littleport CB7 242 F2
Branch Rd CB3 62 C7
Brandon Ct CB1 246 C2
Brandon Pl CB1 246 C2
Brandon Rd IP28 239 E5
Brands Cl PE26 172 A5
Brangehill La CB6 216 D3
Brassey Cl PE1 197 E6
Bravo La PE28 151 E3
Brawn Way PE8 183 D1
Bray 6 CB1 84 A1
Braybrook PE2 186 A3
Braybrook Prim Sch
PE2 186 B4
Brays La CB7 240 D4
Brazilian Terr CB8 110 F3
Breach La CB6 210 D6
Breach Rd PE28 116 A7
Bream Cl PE28 149 D6
Breamore Gdns PE3 197 B3
Breckenwood Rd CB1 66 E6
Breckland Way IP28 239 C5
Brecon Way PE29 141 A4
Brenda Gautrey Way
CB4 125 E3
Brendon Garth PE4 204 E1
Brent Cl IP28 239 D4
Brentwood Cl 6 CB5 84 E4
Brentwood Ct CB5 84 E4
Breton Ave PE15 243 E2
Bretton Ctr PE3 197 A6
Bretton Gate PE3 197 A5
Bretton Gn PE3 197 A5
Bretton Way
Bretton PE3 197 A7
Peterborough PE3 196 F2
Bretton Woods Com Sch
PE3 197 A6
Brewerne PE2 186 C4
Brewers Cl CB4 123 F3
Brewers La PE13 238 A4
Brewery La SG8 29 B2
Brewery Rd CB2 33 A5
Brewhouse La CB7 212 B4
Brewin Ave PE15 243 B3
Brewin Chase The
PE15 243 D4
Brewster Ave PE2 186 F8
Brewster Ave Inf Sch
PE2 186 E8
Briar Way PE1 198 C5
Briars End CB6 217 E2
Briars The PE28 168 B3
Briary La SG8 5 C5
Brick Kiln Rd IP28 239 D5
Brick Kilns PE29 118 F8
Brick La CB6 216 E3
Brick Row SG8 8 D3
Brickberry Cl PE7 186 C2
Brickfields Ave CB8 110 D7
Brickhills CB4 209 A1
Brickkiln La CB6 218 B7
Brickmaker's Arms La
PE15 223 B5
Brickmakers Way CB6 242 B1
Bridewell Cl IP28 239 B4
Bridewell Rd CB1 66 A5
Bridgacre CB1 246 C4
Bridge Cl CB2 48 F6
Bridge Dro PE13 234 B7
Bridge End Earith PE28 208 E5
Wansford PE8 194 A3
Bridge End Rd IP28 213 E1
Bridge La
Great Shelford CB2 48 E4
Wimblington PE15 223 B8
Bridge of Sighs★ CB3 246 A3
Bridge Pl PE29 141 E3
Bridge Rd
Broughton PE28 153 F8
Ely CB7 240 E2
Histon CB4 104 C2
Impington CB4 83 C8
Mepal CB6 216 E4
Bridge St
Cambridge CB2 246 A3
Chatteris PE16 241 B7
Market Deeping PE6 231 E8
Moulton CB8 112 F5
2 Peterborough PE1 198 A1
St Ives PE27 144 A3
Bridge St *continued*
Whaddon SG8 13 B8
11 Wisbech PE13 245 C5
Wistow PE28 163 F7
Wood Walton PE28 161 E6
Bridgefoot
Great & Little Chishill SG8 15 B2
St Ives PE27 144 A3
Bridgehill Rd PE6 205 A6
Bridle End PE19 98 B2
Bridle Way CB3 63 F4
Brierley Wlk CB4 83 C7
Briery Fields 2 CB6 217 E1
Briggate Cres PE7 189 C6
Briggate E PE7 189 D6
Briggate W PE7 189 C6
Bright St PE1 197 F3
Brigland Cl PE29 141 B6
Brigstock Ct PE3 197 C6
Brigstock Rd PE13 245 B7
Brimbles Way PE2 185 E5
Brimley Rd CB4 83 D6
Bringhurst PE2 186 A4
Brington CE Prim Sch
PE28 147 C4
Brington Rd PE28 147 F7
Brinkley Rd Brinkley CB8 69 A6
Carlton CB8 54 F8
Westley Waterless CB8 70 D3
Weston Colville CB1 54 C8
Brinkman Rd CB1 35 D3
Bristol Ave PE4 204 B3
Britannia Way PE13 245 C2
Britannic Way CB1 65 F7
British Antarctic Survey
CB3 82 E3
British Horse Racing Sch
CB8 111 B8
Britten Pl CB1 65 D7
Broad Baulk CB6 210 F6
Broad Cl PE1 198 D5
Broad Dro
Emneth PE14 236 C5
Upwell PE14 229 D8
Wisbech PE14 235 F5
Yaxley PE7 182 B5
Broad Dro E PE13 237 E6
Broad Dro W PE13 237 B4
Broad End CB3 100 A4
Broad End La PE13 245 F4
Broad End Rd PE14 245 F4
Broad Gate PE12 237 A8
Broad Hill CB7 212 B7
Broad La
Cottenham CB4 125 E5
Haslingfield CB3 47 A5
Broad Leas PE27 144 A4
Broad Piece CB7 211 F5
Broad St Bourn CB3 79 B4
Cambridge CB1 246 C2
Ely CB7 240 D3
Haverhill CB9 23 F8
March PE15 243 D4
Stamford PE9 244 B5
Whittlesey PE7 189 D7
Broad Way CB6 210 C6
Broad Wheel Rd PE6 231 B4
Broad Wlk The PE19 74 E3
Broadall's Dro PE26 221 D3
Broadcroft Cres CB9 23 E8
Broadgate La PE6 231 F8
Broadgate Rd PE12 234 C8
Broadgate Way PE8 178 B3
Broadhurst Rd 15 PE8 230 B1
Broadlands CB6 225 A5
Broadlands The PE1 198 E5
Broadmeadow CB2 49 F1
Broads Rd CB5 130 C6
Broadway Bourn CB3 60 D8
Cambourne CB3 79 E3
Crowland PE6 232 B8
Farcet PE7 187 C1
Grantchester CB3 64 A4
Witchford CB6 217 E1
Yaxley PE7 181 E5
Broadway Gdns PE1 198 B5
Broadway The
Oakington/Longstanton
CB4 103 B5
Romsey Town CB1 65 B8
St Ives PE27 144 A3
Broadway Theatre★
PE1 198 F3
Broadweir PE28 138 C4
Brockholt Rd CB3 78 E2
Brocklesby Gdns PE3 197 C3
Brockley Rd CB3 100 B4
Brocks Bsns Ctr CB9 23 F5
Brockwood Cl 2 SG19 41 D6
Brodsworth Rd PE7 187 F5
Bromholme La PE28 141 A3
Brook Cl
Alconbury PE28 150 F4
Histon CB4 104 B4
March PE15 243 C4
Brook Dam La 14 CB7 212 B4
Brook End SG8 11 C3
Brook La Coton CB3 82 C2
Farcet PE7 187 B2
Stretham CB6 210 F5
Brook Rd
Bassingbourn cum Kneesworth
SG8 12 D4
Eaton Socon PE19 74 C4
Kimbolton PE28 114 B7
Newton CB2 31 B6
Brook Service Rd CB9 24 A8
Brook St Elsworth CB3 100 B3
Brook St *continued*
Peterborough PE1 198 A2
St Neots PE19 74 E5
Soham CB7 212 C3
Brook The CB6 216 E1
Brook's Rd PE15 243 D4
Brookdale CB3 102 C3
Brooke Gr CB6 240 A5
Brooke Rd SG8 5 D8
Brookfield Cl CB2 32 F5
Brookfield Dr CB4 123 F3
Brookfield Home Pk
PE4 204 B2
Brookfield Rd
Coton CB3 82 B2
Papworth Everard CB3 99 A4
Sawston CB2 32 F5
Brookfield Way
Cambourne CB3 79 A3
Ramsey PE26 172 A4
Brookfields CB1 65 D7
Brookfields Cl CB8 111 B5
Brookfields Hospl CB1 65 C8
Brookfields Ind Pk
PE4 204 B2
Brookfurlong PE3 197 B6
Brookhampton St CB10 18 A5
Brooklands PE28 150 F2
Brooklands Ave CB2 64 E6
Brooks Rd CB1 65 D8
Brookside
Alconbury PE28 150 F4
Cambridge CB2 246 B1
Dalham CB8 92 E8
Exning CB8 110 C8
Great Paxton PE19 96 D4
Huntingdon PE29 141 D5
Moulton CB8 112 F5
Oakington/Longstanton
CB4 123 F2
Orwell SG8 45 D1
Peterborough PE4 204 D2
St Ives PE28 143 B5
Sawtry PE28 168 B5
1 Sutton CB6 216 E2
Toft CB3 61 D4
Brookside Gr CB6 242 C5
Brookside Ind Est
PE28 168 B5
Brookside La 1 CB2 64 E7
Broom Cl
7 Littleport CB7 242 D4
Peterborough PE1 198 A8
Broom Way PE27 144 B5
Broom Wlk 5 IP28 213 F8
Broomhill Cl 4 IP28 214 A1
Brotherhood Cl PE4 197 D8
Brotherhood Ret Pk
PE4 197 D8
Brothers Pl CB1 65 D6
Broughton House Gall★
CB1 246 B3
Broughton La PE28 154 B8
Brownes Rd 6 PE8 230 B1
Browning Dr PE19 74 C6
Brownlow Dr 8 PE6 231 F8
Brownlow Quay PE9 244 C5
Brownlow Rd
Cambridge CB4 83 C6
Peterborough PE1 198 A6
Brownlow St 7 PE9 244 C5
Brownlow Terr PE9 244 C5
Brown's Sq 6 PE19 74 F5
Brownshill Staunch
PE27 208 C3
Broxbourne Cl CB1 66 A7
Bruces Cl PE7 168 D8
Brudenell PE2 185 E2
Brunel Dr PE7 181 D6
Brunswick Ct CB1 66 E5
Brunswick Gdns CB5 246 C3
Brunswick Terr CB5 246 C3
Brunswick Wlk CB1 246 C3
Bryan Cl PE26 172 B6
Brybank Rd CB9 38 C1
Brynmore PE3 204 A1
Bryony Cl
Coates/Eastrea PE7 190 C7
Haverhill CB9 38 E1
Buchan St CB4 83 E7
Buckden CE Prim Sch
PE19 117 B4
Buckden Marina PE19 117 E3
Buckden Rd
Brampton PE28 117 D7
Grafham PE28 116 A6
Bucking Way Rd CB3 101 D8
Buckingham Dr CB6 240 D6
Buckingham Rd
Cambridge CB3 83 C3
Haverhill CB9 23 E7
Buckingham Way
PE28 168 C2
Buckingham Wlk
PE13 245 D8
Buckingway Bsns Pk
CB4 101 E8
Buckland Cl PE3 197 B4
Buckle St PE1 198 C3
Buckles Gdns PE7 189 F7
Buckley Rd PE19 74 E4
Buck's Dro PE26 220 D4
Buck's La CB3 45 F7
Buckshot Rd PE14 238 E3
Buckthorn CB7 240 F6

Buckthorn Rd PE7 186 D3
Buckworth Rd PE28 150 C5
Budge Cl PE28 140 E2
Budleigh Cl CB1 65 D7
Buff La SG19 43 A1
Buffalo Way CB1 66 A7
Building End SG8 1 F8
Building End Rd SG8 1 F7
Bukehorn Rd PE6 232 D4
Bulbeck Mill CB2 29 F7
Bull La Broughton PE28 164 A1
Langley CB11 1 F2
Peakirk PE6 206 B2
West Wratting CB1 53 F6
Bullard Laboratories CB3 83 A4
Bullen Cl CB1 65 D5
Bullfinch Way
Cottenham CB4 125 D5
Friday Bridge PE14 236 A4
Bullock Rd Elton PE8 184 B1
Folksworth & Washingley PE7 174 E7
Great Gidding PE28 167 B6
Little Gidding PE28 167 D2
Bullrush La CB3 79 C3
Bulstrode Gdns CB3 83 A2
Bulteel Cl CB4 105 C3
Bumpstead Rd CB9 24 B5
Bunbury Ave IP28 239 C5
Bunting's Dro PE7 188 C4
Bunting's La PE8 178 B3
Buntings Cres CB5 130 B3
Buntings La PE7 187 B5
Buntings Path CB5 130 B3
Bunyan Cl 4 SG19 41 D5
Burberry Rd PE19 117 B3
Burcroft Rd PE13 245 B6
Burdett Cl 3 PE15 223 A5
Burdett Gr PE7 189 F6
Burdett Rd PE13 245 B4
Bure Cl PE27 144 B6
Bures Ct 14 CB9 23 E7
Burford Way PE1 198 D6
Burgess Rd CB5 106 B7
Burgess's Dro CB5 106 C7
Burghley Ave 9 PE8 230 B1
Burghley Cl 9 PE6 231 F8
Burghley Ct PE9 244 C5
Burghley House★ PE9 244 F3
Burghley La PE9 244 C3
Burghley Rd
1 Peterborough PE1 198 A3
4 Stamford PE9 244 A7
Burghley Rise CB5 130 C2
Burghley Sq 2 PE1 198 A3
Burgoynes Farm Cl CB4 104 D3
Burgoyne's Rd CB4 104 D3
Buristead Rd CB2 48 F5
Burkett Way CB4 104 B5
Burleigh Pl CB1 246 C3
Burleigh Rd PE27 143 F8
Burleigh St CB1 246 C3
Burleigh Terr PE27 144 A3
Burling Ct CB1 65 C6
Burling Wlk CB4 105 D3
Burlington Way PE28 143 C1
Burma Rd CB2 32 A1
Burmer Rd PE1 197 E7
Burmoor Cl PE29 141 B6
Burn St PE15 243 D5
Burnaby Cl PE28 140 C3
Burnet Gdns PE15 243 E7
Burnett Way PE29 141 F8
Burnham Cl CB1 66 A6
Burns Cl PE1 197 F7
Burns Ct 3 PE19 74 D5
Burns Rd SG8 5 C8
Burns Way PE27 143 F6
Burnsfield St PE16 241 B5
Burnside CB1 65 D7
Burnt Chy Dro CB6 225 B4
Burnt Cl
Grantchester CB3 64 A4
St Neots PE19 74 E3
Burnt House Cl CB9 38 C1
Burnt Up Dro PE7 188 F2
Burnthouse Rd PE7 191 E4
Burnthouse Sidings PE7 191 F1
Burntwood End CB10 19 E2
Burrel Rd PE27 144 B6
Burrell Cres IP28 239 C2
Burrell Way CB1 53 B2
Burrett Gdns 2 PE14 238 F1
Burrett Rd PE14 238 F1
Burrettgate Rd
6 Leverington PE14 238 F1
Walsoken PE13 245 F5
Burrough Field CB4 104 C1
Burrough Gn Endowed CE Prim Sch CB8 70 F4
Burrowmoor Prim Sch PE15 243 C3
Burrowmoor Rd PE15 243 C3
Burrows Dr PE29 141 C3
Burstellars PE27 144 A6
Burswood PE2 185 F2
Burton Cl CB9 23 E7
Burton Ct PE1 198 C3
Burton End
Haverhill CB9 23 E7
West Wickham CB1 37 C8
Burton End CP Sch CB9 23 D7
Burton Hill CB9 38 D5
Burton St PE1 198 C3
Burton Way PE28 137 F6
Burwell Castle (site of)★ CB5 130 B1
Burwell Mus★ CB5 130 C1
Burwell Rd
Eaton Socon PE19 74 C6
Exning CB8 110 A8
Reach CB5 129 E1
Swaffham Prior CB5 108 E5
Burwell Reach PE2 186 C7
Burwell Village Coll CB5 130 B3
Bury CE Prim Sch PE26 172 A4
Bury Cl Ramsey PE26 171 F4
St Ives PE27 143 F5
Bury Gn CB6 218 A7
Bury La Chrishall SG8 8 D1
Haddenham CB6 210 A5
Lidgate CB8 73 F8
Meldreth SG8 14 A5
Moulton CB8 112 F6
Sutton CB6 216 D2
Bury Plantation SG8 5 F6
Bury Rd
Great Shelford CB2 49 C4
Kentford CB8 134 B2
Mildenhall IP28 239 E4
Newmarket CB8 111 C5
Ramsey PE26 172 A5
Snailwell CB8 111 E8
Bury The CB5 86 C5
Bury Way PE27 143 F5
Buryfield PE26 172 A4
Burystead PE2 187 B8
Bush Cl CB3 62 D5
Bush La PE13 245 E5
Bushel La CB7 212 B4
Bushey Cl PE29 141 E5
Bushfield PE2 185 E3
Bushfield Com Coll PE2 185 E3
Bushfield Sports Ctr PE2 185 E4
Bushmead Gdns PE19 74 B3
Bushmead Jun Sch PE19 74 A3
Bushmead Prim Sch PE19 74 A3
Bushmead Rd PE19 74 A3
Bushy Cl PE7 186 D3
Bustard Hill PE28 113 D8
Bustler's Rise CB2 17 D8
Butcher Cl CB4 105 C3
Butcher's Hill CB10 18 A4
Butcher's La SG19 25 B4
Butcher's Row 3 CB7 240 D4
Bute Ct CB9 23 F6
Butler Way
Cambridge CB4 83 D6
Haslingfield CB3 47 A5
Butlers Way CB2 32 F7
Butley Ct 2 CB9 23 E6
Butt Ave PE15 243 B2
Butt La
Great Wilbraham CB1 68 A7
Milton CB4 105 B3
Butt's La CB7 211 F1
Buttermarket CB6 240 D4
Buttermel Cl 1 PE29 118 F8
Buttermere PE29 141 B6
Buttermere Pl 4 PE4 204 E3
Button End CB2 47 D4
Butts Cl 6 Soham CB7 212 B3
20 Somersham PE28 215 C1
Butts The Fowlmere SG8 15 D8
Soham CB7 212 B3
Buttsgrove Way PE29 141 F7
Buxtons La SG8 10 F3
Buzzard Cl PE28 142 B8
Byall Fen Dro PE15 223 E2
Bydand La PE19 95 F2
Byfield Rd CB3 99 B3
Byng Cl PE19 74 B2
Byres The PE7 189 F7
Byron Cl
Huntingdon PE29 141 F6
Peterborough PE2 187 D6
Byron Pl 10 PE19 74 C6
Byron Rd 4 SG8 5 E8
Byron Sq CB2 64 D2
Bythorn Rd PE2 187 C6
Bythorn Way PE2 187 C6
Bythorne Bank PE13 237 C7

C

Cabbage Moor CB2 48 E8
Cadenham Rd CB5 108 E3
Cadwin Field CB4 83 F7
Caernarvon Rd PE19 74 F2
Caernarvon Wlk CB9 23 E8
Cage Hill CB5 108 D5
Cage La
Great Staughton PE19 94 B6
Stretham CB6 210 F5
Cairns CB8 131 A3
Caithness Ct CB4 83 E8
Calcot St PE7 186 D2
Caldbeck Cl PE4 204 F2
Caldecote Cl PE2 187 E6
Caldecote Prim Sch CB3 80 C2
Caldecote Rd
St Neots PE19 74 E3
Stilton PE7 175 E7
Caldervale PE2 186 C6
Caledon Way 3 CB4 83 E8
Calfe Fen Cl 2 CB7 212 B5
Calfe Fen Dro CB7 212 B5
Calford Dr CB9 23 C8
California Rd
Huntingdon PE29 141 E6
St Ives PE27 143 E6
Callander Cl CB4 83 D7
Calvin Cl CB4 125 F3
Cam Cl PE27 144 A7
Cam Cswy CB4 84 B6
Cam Dr CB6 240 C6
Camargue Dr PE15 243 D2
Camargue Pl 4 PE13 245 E3
Cambanks CB4 84 A4
Camber's New Dro PE7 220 D8
Cambourne Bsns Pk CB3 79 B5
Cambourne Rd CB3 79 B5
Cambrian Way PE4 204 E1
Cambridge & Cty Folk Mus★ CB3 246 A4
Cambridge Acad CB1 246 B3
Cambridge Airport CB1 84 F2
Cambridge Ave PE1 197 F5
Cambridge Bsns Pk CB4 84 C7
Cambridge Cl
Haverhill CB9 38 E1
St Ives PE27 143 F8
Cambridge Cres SG8 13 A8
Cambridge Ct 10 PE19 74 F5
Cambridge Ctr for Sixth Form Studies CB1 246 C1
Cambridge Dr
St Ives PE27 143 F8
Wisbech PE13 245 A6
Cambridge Drama Ctr CB1 246 C1
Cambridge Gdns PE19 74 F5
Cambridge Pl CB1 246 C1
Cambridge Rd
Babraham CB2 50 D4
Balsham CB1 52 F2
Barley SG8 7 A3
Barton CB3 62 E1
Ely CB7 240 B3
Eynesbury Hardwicke PE19 76 B4
Fenstanton PE28 121 A6
Foxton CB2 30 C7
Fulbourn CB1 66 A5
Girton CB3 82 E8
Godmanchester PE29 141 F2
Great Shelford CB2 48 F7
Hardwick CB3 81 B3
Hauxton CB2 48 A5
Histon CB4 83 C8
Madingley CB3 81 F5
Melbourn SG8 14 E7
Milton CB4 105 C1
Newton CB2 31 B8
Oakington/Longstanton CB4 103 C4
Orwell SG8 45 C1
St Neots Rural PE19 75 C5
Sawston CB2 32 E8
Stamford PE9 244 A6
Stretham CB6 210 E3
Thetford CB6 211 A8
Thriplow SG8 30 F3
Waterbeach CB5 105 F7
Wimpole SG8 27 F6
Cambridge Regional Coll CB4 83 F8
Cambridge Ret Pk CB5 84 B3
Cambridge Science Pk CB4 84 B8
Cambridge Sq PE28 143 B7
Cambridge St
Godmanchester PE29 141 F2
St Neots PE19 75 A5
Cambridge Sta CB1 65 A7
Cambridge Summer Sch of Tech CB3 64 B7
Cambridge Univ Botanic Gdn★ CB2 64 F7
Cambridge Univ Ctr CB2 246 A1
Cambridge Univ Press CB2 64 F5
Cambridge Way CB9 38 E1
Cambridgeshire Cl CB6 240 B4
Camden Ct CB1 246 B2
Camel Rd CB6 242 C6
Camelia Cl PE4 204 D3
Cameron Rd CB4 83 E7
Campaign Ave PE2 186 D8
Campbell Cl IP28 239 B6
Campbell Dr PE4 204 E4
Campbell La CB2 64 C2
Campbell St 1 CB1 65 B8
Campbell Way PE15 243 D7
Camping Cl CB6 210 A6
Campion Cl CB7 212 A5
Campion Rd PE1 198 B8
Campion Way SG8 5 E5
Campkin Ct CB4 83 F7
Campkin Rd CB4 83 F7
Camps Cl CB5 106 B7
Camps Rd Bartlow CB1 21 B7
Haverhill CB9 23 F7
Camps Rd *continued*
Helions Bumpstead CB9 23 B1
Camside CB4 84 A4
Canal St 6 PE13 245 C5
Canberra Cl
Bassingbourn SG8 13 B5
Mildenhall IP28 213 E8
Canberra Ct PE26 171 F7
Canberra Dr PE27 143 F7
Canberra Rd PE26 171 E3
Candidus Ct PE4 204 B5
Candy St PE2 186 E8
Cangle Junc CB9 24 A8
Canmore Cl PE28 168 C2
Canners Cl CB3 61 E5
Cannon St
Little Downham CB6 218 A6
Wisbech PE13 245 C4
Cannon Terr 8 PE13 245 C4
Cannon's Cl SG8 10 F5
Canon Cl CB9 39 A1
Canon Dr 4 PE9 230 D3
Canonsfield PE4 204 A4
Cantelupe Rd CB3 47 C7
Canterbury Ave CB6 240 A3
Canterbury Cl CB4 83 C4
Canterbury Rd PE4 204 B3
Canterbury St CB4 83 C4
Cant's Dro PE13 234 C4
Canute Cres CB6 240 E7
Canwell PE4 204 C4
Capper Rd CB5 127 C1
Capstan Cl CB4 84 A3
Capthorne Cl PE7 186 C2
Capuchin Ct CB1 66 A7
Capulet Cl PE19 74 C3
Capulet Ct PE29 141 F7
Car Dyke Rd
Landbeach CB5 105 F6
Waterbeach CB5 106 A6
Caravere Cl 2 CB4 83 F8
Caraway Rd CB1 66 E5
Cardiff Pl SG8 13 A8
Cardigan St CB8 111 A3
Cardinal Distribution Pk PE29 142 B1
Cardinal Way
Godmanchester PE29 142 B1
5 Haverhill CB9 38 F1
Cardinals Gate PE4 204 A5
Cardinals Way CB7 240 D4
Carey Cl CB7 240 F6
Caribou Way CB1 66 A7
Carisbrook Ct PE3 186 B8
Carisbrooke Rd CB4 83 C5
Carisbrooke Way 8 PE19 74 F2
Carleton Crest PE4 204 D1
Carlisle Terr PE27 144 B3
Carlow 9 CB1 84 A2
Carlton Cl Haverhill CB9 38 F2
10 Leverington PE13 238 B2
Carlton Gn Rd CB8 55 A6
Carlton Rd CB8 70 E1
Carlton Rise SG8 14 D5
Carlton Way CB4 83 D5
Carlyle Rd CB4 246 A4
Carmel St CB10 18 D2
Carmen St CB10 18 D3
Carnation Way IP28 133 F8
Carnegie Rd 18 PE8 230 B1
Caroline Pl CB1 246 C2
Carpenters Way 9 PE15 223 A6
Carpond La 3 CB6 210 C6
Carr Rd PE1 198 D3
Carradale PE2 185 D5
Carrick Cl CB1 65 E5
Carrier Cl PE2 186 D8
Carrington Pl PE28 140 C3
Carrington's Dro PE6 232 B8
Carron Dr PE4 204 A3
Carrops The CB8 134 A6
Carr's Lodge PE9 244 F8
Carsey Hill CB1 22 B6
Carson Wlk CB8 110 F6
Carter Cl
Brampton PE28 140 C3
Duxford CB2 17 E8
Carter Rd CB5 130 C3
Carter St CB7 212 E1
Carter's Way CB4 122 E5
Carters Cl PE3 196 F3
Carters Croft CB10 21 B1
Cartmel Way 12 PE6 232 A1
Cartwright Rd 5 SG8 5 D5
Caryer Cl PE2 186 D6
Carysfort Cl PE7 181 D4
Casburn's La CB5 130 A3
Casewick La 1 PE9 230 F7
Casewick Rd PE9 230 E7
Castel Way PE7 175 D8
Castelhythe CB7 240 D3
Casterton Rd PE9 244 A6
Castle Ave CB9 23 E7
Castle Camps CB1 22 D1
Castle Camps CE Prim Sch CB1 22 E3
Castle Dr 7 PE6 231 F7
Castle Dyke PE9 244 B5
Castle End Rd PE6 231 C7
Castle Gdns PE28 113 F4
Castle Hill PE29 141 D3
Castle Hill Cl PE19 74 C2
Castle Hill Ct PE29 141 E4
Castle Hill Gall★ CB4 83 C4
Castle Hill Mid Sch CB9 23 D7
Castle La CB9 23 E8
Castle Manor Com Upper Sch CB9 23 E8
Castle Moat Rd PE29 141 D4
Castle Pk CB1 246 A4
Castle Row 8 CB3 83 C3
Castle Sq 12 PE13 245 C5
Castle St
Cambridge CB3 246 A4
7 Stamford PE9 244 B5
Castle Wlk CB9 23 E8
Castor Hanglands National Nature Reserve★ PE6 195 E7
Castor Mills PE8 184 F6
Castor Prim Sch PE5 195 E2
Castor Rd Castor PE6 196 C6
Marholm PE6 203 D1
Casworth Way PE5 195 D2
Cat Field PE13 237 E1
Catharine St CB1 65 B8
Cathedral Sq PE3 198 A2
Cathedral View PE15 224 C4
Catherine Cl PE2 186 B7
Cathwaite PE4 204 F1
Catkin Cl CB9 38 E1
Catley PE4 205 A1
Catley Pk CB1 19 D6
Catling's La PE13 238 C7
Cattell's La CB5 106 B8
Cattle Dike PE13 237 E2
Cattle Mkt Rd PE1 198 A2
Cattle Mkt Way 6 PE4 198 A2
Causeway
Godmanchester PE29 141 E1
Great Staughton PE19 93 F6
Pampisford CB2 33 C5
Causeway Cl
Great Staughton PE19 93 F6
March PE15 243 C2
Causeway Gdns PE15 243 D3
Causeway Pas CB1 246 C3
Causeway Rd PE28 154 A8
Causeway Sch The PE1 198 C3
Causeway The
Bassingbourn SG8 13 A5
Burwell CB5 130 B2
Elsworth CB3 100 B4
Haverhill CB9 23 E8
Isleham CB7 213 A5
March PE15 243 D2
Soham CB7 212 B4
Sutton CB6 216 C2
Thorney PE6 233 E2
West Wratting CB1 53 E5
Causewayside CB1 246 A1
Cavalry Dr PE15 243 E2
Cavalry Pk PE15 243 D2
Cavalry Prim Sch PE15 243 E2
Cavell Cl PE3 197 B4
Cavendish Ave CB1 65 B5
Cavendish Cl PE28 168 C3
Cavendish Ct 5 CB9 23 E6
Cavendish Rd CB1 84 B1
Cavendish St PE1 198 B4
Cavendish Way CB3 80 C1
Cavenham Rd IP28 214 E2
Caverstede Rd PE4 204 D1
Cavesson Ct CB4 83 C6
Caville White CB9 23 C8
Cawdor Pl 6 PE19 74 F2
Cawood Cl PE15 243 E6
Caxton End Bourn CB3 60 B7
Eltisley PE19 77 F3
Caxton La CB2 30 B5
Caxton Rd Bourn CB3 60 C7
Great Gransden SG19 58 E5
St Ives PE27 144 B6
Cecil Ct 10 PE9 244 C5
Cecil Lodge Cl CB8 110 F3
Cecil Pacey Ct PE1 197 E7
Cecil Rd PE1 198 A6
Cedar Ave 5 PE15 223 A6
Cedar Cl Grafham PE28 115 F7
March PE15 243 E5
Melbourn SG8 14 C5
Cedar Cres SG8 5 B6
Cedar Ct CB7 242 D4
Cedar Dr PE28 151 E3
Cedar Gr PE1 198 B8
Cedar Rd PE27 143 F6
Cedar Wlk CB5 86 F6
Celta Rd PE2 186 F6
Celtic Cl PE2 187 D7
Cemetery Hill CB8 110 D7
Cemetery Rd
St Neots PE19 74 F5
Whittlesey PE7 189 E6
Cenacle The 1 CB3 64 C7
Centenary Way PE28 140 C2
Central Ave
Brampton PE28 140 D1
Peterborough PE1 198 C7
Central Sq PE2 187 D5
Centre Dr CB8 111 D2
Centre for Mathematical Sciences CB3 83 B2
Centre Rd CB7 212 C2
Centurion Way PE29 142 B1
Century Way PE15 243 C7
Cerris Rd PE1 198 B7
Chadburn PE4 205 A1
Chadley La PE29 141 F2
Chaffinch Way CB3 79 C4
Chain Cl PE1 198 B6
Chain Cswy CB6 209 B8

Chain Rd CB4 208 C2
Chainbridge La PE28 135 F8
Chalfont Cl 2 CB1 65 F6
Chalk Gr CB1 65 D4
Chalk Rd PE13 237 D1
Chalkhill Barrow SG8 14 C4
Chalklands CB1 35 C3
Chalkstone Mid Sch
CB9 24 A8
Chalkstone Way CB9 39 A1
Chalky La SG8 8 D2
Chalky Rd CB1 34 C3
Challis Cl CB2 29 F8
Challis Gn CB2 29 F8
Chalmers Rd CB1 65 C6
Chamberlain Way PE19 74 F7
Chamois Cl CB2 32 F6
Champions Cl SG8 15 E8
Champneys Wlk CB3 64 C8
Chancellor Cl PE29 141 C7
Chancellors Wlk 2 CB4 83 C6
Chancery La 6 PE6 232 A1
Chandler's Way PE15 243 D2
Chandlers PE2 185 E5
Chandlers Ct CB5 130 B3
Chandlers Way PE26 221 A4
Chantry Cl
Cambridge CB4 83 F4
Chatteris PE16 241 D6
Peterborough PE1 198 A5
Swavesey CB4 122 E6
Chantry The CB1 67 A5
Chapel Ave 1 PE13 235 B7
Chapel Cl Hilton PE28 120 B1
Litlington SG8 12 A2
Needingworth PE27 208 A3
Waterbeach CB5 106 B7
Wrestlingworth SG19 25 B4
Chapel Ct PE8 194 B2
Chapel End
Great Gidding PE28 166 D2
Sawtry PE28 168 C4
Chapel Field SG19 41 D4
Chapel Field La PE28 215 B1
Chapel Gate PE12 237 B7
Chapel Gdns
Benwick PE15 222 A5
Coates/Eastrea PE7 190 C7
Chapel Hill CB2 47 A3
Chapel La
Chatteris PE16 241 B6
Downham CB6 218 A6
Easton PE28 138 B4
Elm PE14 236 B6
Elton PE8 178 C8
Fowlmere SG8 15 E8
Harston CB2 47 F3
Kirtling CB8 72 C5
Melbourn SG8 14 C6
Newton PE13 238 B5
Alwalton PE2 185 F5
4 Peterborough PE4 204 C3
Reach CB5 129 D1
Houghton PE28 143 A5
St Ives PE27 144 A3
Soham CB7 219 B2
Tydd St Giles PE13 237 F7
Whittlesey PE7 227 A3
Wicken CB7 211 E1
Willingham CB4 208 E5
Wimblington PE15 223 B6
Wisbech PE14 235 D5
Chapel Rd
Beck Row, Holywell
Row & Kenny Hill IP28 213 D6
Earith PE28 208 E5
Great Eversden CB3 45 F8
Weston Colville CB1 54 B5
Wisbech PE13 245 B5
Chapel Row CB8 91 F8
Chapel St
Alconbury PE28 150 F4
Cambridge CB4 84 A4
4 Crowland PE6 232 B8
Duxford CB2 32 D1
Ely CB6 240 C4
Exning CB8 110 B8
March PE15 243 D3
Stanground PE2 187 C7
Peterborough PE1 198 B2
Stretham CB6 210 F5
Warmington PE8 178 B3
Waterbeach CB5 106 B7
13 Wisbech PE13 245 C4
Yaxley PE7 181 D5
Chapel Yd
Kimbolton MK44 113 E1
Stamford PE9 244 C5
Chapelfield Rd PE13 235 A2
Chapelfield Way CB2 32 F8
Chaplains Cl 6 CB9 38 F1
Chaplin's Ct CB1 66 F5
Chaplins Cl PE7 190 F8
Chapman Ct CB4 83 E7
Chapman Way PE19 74 E1
Chapman's Cl SG8 14 C6
Chapman's Way CB4 208 E1
Chapmans Cl CB4 105 C7
Chapmans Dr 5 CB3 79 C3
Chapnall Cl PE13 245 F6
Chapnall Rd PE13 245 F6
Chapple Dr CB9 38 F1
Charcoal La PE28 140 C3
Charding Cres SG8 5 C7
Charlemont Dr PE15 224 B5
Charles Cl
Newmarket CB8 110 E3
Ramsey PE26 172 A7
Charles Cope Rd PE2 185 F5
Charles Dr PE29 142 A6
Charles Melrose Cl
IP28 239 B5
Charles Rd
Stamford PE9 244 A7
Whittlesey PE7 189 F6
Charles St
Cambridge CB1 65 B7
Peterborough PE1 198 B3
Charles' St PE19 74 F5
Charles St 10 PE13 245 C4
Charlton Ct PE3 197 B1
Charnocks Cl 3 SG19 41 D5
Charnwood Cl PE2 187 A7
Charrington Cl CB9 24 C6
Charters The 2 PE9 230 C6
Chartfield Rd CB1 65 F6
Chase Cl CB9 39 A1
Chase Rd PE15 221 F6
Chase St PE13 245 C6
Chase The Ely CB6 240 B4
March PE15 243 C4
Thorney PE6 200 E7
Upwell PE14 229 D7
Whittlesey PE7 220 E7
Wimblington PE15 224 A8
Wisbech PE13 245 A7
Chaston Rd CB2 49 A5
Chater Rd 3 PE8 230 B1
Chatsfield PE4 204 A6
Chatsworth Ave CB4 83 C5
Chatsworth Pl PE3 197 B2
Chatteris Mus★ PE16 241 C4
Chatteris Rd
Chatteris PE28 215 D4
10 Somersham PE28 208 C8
Chaucer Cl
Cambridge CB2 64 E6
14 Wisbech PE13 238 B2
Chaucer Pl PE19 74 D6
Chaucer Rd
Cambridge CB2 64 D7
Peterborough PE1 197 E8
Royston SG8 5 C8
Chaucer Way PE27 143 F6
Chauntry Rd CB9 23 F7
Chawston Cl 9 PE19 74 C5
Chedburgh Pl CB9 39 B1
Cheddars La CB5 84 B3
Chedworth St CB3 64 C7
Cheere Way CB3 99 B3
Chelmer Cl PE27 144 B7
Chelmer Garth PE4 204 F1
Chelmer Rd CB9 24 B8
Chelmer Way CB6 240 D6
Cheltenham Cl PE1 198 B6
Chelveston Way PE3 197 C5
Chelwood Rd CB1 65 F6
Cheney Ct PE2 186 C4
Cheney Way CB4 84 C5
Chequer La 1 CB7 240 D4
Chequer St PE28 121 B6
Chequers Cl
Alconbury Weston PE28 150 C6
Cambridge CB1 65 F5
Fenstanton PE28 121 B6
Chequers Cnr PE14 236 E7
Chequers Croft PE28 120 B2
Chequers Ct 1 PE29 141 D4
Chequers La CB3 99 B3
Chequers Rd CB4 104 C2
Chequers Way PE29 141 D4
Cherry Bounds Rd CB3 82 E8
Cherry Cl Cambridge CB1 65 E5
Linton CB1 35 B3
Milton CB4 105 D3
Cherry Ct CB3 79 A4
Cherry Dr SG8 5 E7
Cherry Hill IP28 214 C3
Cherry Hinton CE Inf Sch
CB1 65 F6
Cherry Hinton Cl Limekiln
Close Nature Reserve★
CB1 65 F4
Cherry Hinton Com Jun Sch
CB1 66 A6
Cherry Hinton Rd
Cambridge CB1 65 B6
Great Shelford CB2 65 D1
Teversham CB1 66 A8
Cherry Hinton W Pit Nature
Reserve★ CB1 65 E4
Cherry Holt La PE9 244 D5
Cherry Orch
Fulbourn CB1 66 D5
Haddenham CB6 210 A5
Oakington/Longstanton
CB4 103 C5
Cherry Orton Rd PE2 185 F5
Cherry Rd PE13 245 C8
Cherry Rise CB6 216 D1
Cherry Tree CB7 128 C5
Cherry Tree Ave CB2 49 C4
Cherry Tree Cl
Huntingdon PE29 141 C6
Litlington SG8 12 A1
Cherry Tree Gr PE7 189 F6
Cherry Tree Way
PE28 121 B6
Cherry Trees CB2 48 E7
Cherryfields PE2 185 E6
Cherryholt Ave PE15 243 C3
Cherryholt Rd PE9 244 D5
Cherrytree Gr PE1 198 C6
Cherrytree La CB7 212 B3
Cherrywood Ave PE15 243 B3
Cherrywood Gn PE15 243 B3
Chervil Cl PE7 175 D8
Chervil Way 1 CB3 79 C3
Cherwell Ct CB3 64 C7
Chesham Rd PE28 168 C2
Chesnut Gr CB4 83 F4
Chester Ct 3 CB9 23 E6
Chester Rd
Peterborough PE1 198 C3
Wyton Airfield PE28 143 B7
Chester Way PE29 142 B1
Chesterfield Rd CB4 84 A6
Chesterfield Way 3
PE19 74 E2
Chesterton Com Coll
CB4 83 E4
Chesterton Gr PE2 187 D6
Chesterton Hall Cres
CB4 83 F4
Chesterton Hospl CB4 83 F4
Chesterton La CB4 246 A4
Chesterton Rd CB4 246 A4
Chestnut Ave PE1 198 C6
Chestnut Cl
Brampton PE28 140 D2
Glinton PE6 203 D8
Grafham PE28 116 A7
Haslingfield CB3 47 B4
Haverhill CB9 23 F8
Huntingdon PE29 141 E7
Mildenhall IP28 239 D4
Peakirk PE6 206 B2
Sawston CB2 32 E7
Sawtry PE28 168 B4
Chestnut Cres
March PE15 243 B3
Whittlesey PE7 189 E6
Chestnut Dr
5 Soham CB7 212 B4
1 Thorney PE6 233 A3
Chestnut Gr
Cambridge CB4 83 F4
Little Stukeley PE28 152 A2
St Neots PE19 74 F4
Chestnut La SG8 13 B6
Chestnut Rd
St Ives PE27 143 F6
7 Wisbech PE13 245 C4
Chestnut Rise
Bar Hill CB3 102 D3
Burwell CB5 130 B4
Chestnut Way CB6 216 E3
Chestnut Wlk 6 SG8 5 E5
Chestnuts The
Elton PE8 178 C8
Harston CB2 48 A4
Chettisham CB6 218 C5
Cheveley CE Prim Sch
CB8 91 C7
Cheveley Rd
Newmarket CB8 111 C3
Woodditton CB8 91 C3
Cheviot Ave PE4 204 E2
Chewells Cl CB6 210 A6
Chewells La CB6 210 A6
Cheyney Cl SG8 11 B1
Cheyney St SG8 11 B1
Chichester Way PE28 115 D2
Chiefs St CB6 240 C4
Chigwell Ct 7 CB5 84 E4
Chilcourt SG8 5 C6
Childerley Hall★ CB3 80 D8
Childers St PE7 189 C8
Childs La 12 PE15 223 A5
Child's Pond Rd PE19 75 A6
Chilford Hall Vineyard★
CB1 35 D6
Chiltern Rise PE4 204 D2
Chimswell Way CB9 23 C8
Chippenham Fen National
Nature Reserve★
CB7 132 B7
Chippenham Mews
PE2 186 C7
Chippenham Rd
Chippenham CB8 133 C2
Fordham CB7 213 A1
Moulton CB8 133 D1
Chisenhale PE2 185 E6
Chishill Rd Barley SG8 7 A2
Great & Little Chishill SG8 7 F3
Heydon SG8 8 A4
Chishill Windmill★ SG8 7 C2
Chiswick Ave IP28 239 C6
Chiswick End SG8 14 A7
Chittering Dro CB5 127 C8
Chivers Rd CB9 23 D7
Chivers Way CB4 104 B2
Chrishall Rd SG8 15 F6
Christ Church Cl PE9 244 B6
Christchurch St CB1 246 C3
Christie Dr PE29 141 A5
Christopher Cl PE1 197 F8
Christopher Dr PE13 245 A7
Christopher Tye Cl 3
CB6 240 B5
Christ's Coll CB1 246 B3
Church Cl
Bassingbourn SG8 12 E5
Cottenham CB4 125 F6
Coveney CB6 217 C5
Dullingham CB8 70 E8
Exning CB8 110 C8
Great & Little Abington
CB1 34 C7
Great Wilbraham CB1 67 F7
Newborough PE6 205 C8
Ramsey PE26 221 C2
Stilton PE7 176 A7
Church Cl *continued*
The Stukeleys PE28 151 F2
Whittlesford CB2 32 C5
Church Cswy PE28 168 C4
Church Dr PE2 185 F5
Church Dro PE14 236 F2
Church End
Arrington SG8 44 D1
Barley SG8 7 A1
Cambridge CB1 65 F8
Coton CB3 82 B2
Everton SG19 40 C3
Gamlingay SG19 41 E5
Hilton PE28 99 B8
Horningsea CB5 106 A2
11 Leverington PE13 238 B2
Over CB4 208 D1
Parson Drove PE13 234 E8
Rampton CB4 124 F4
Weston Colville CB1 54 A7
Whaddon SG8 28 B2
Church Farm La SG8 11 B1
Church Fen Dro CB6 209 E3
Church Gate 13 PE6 231 F8
Church Gdns IP28 213 D6
Church Gn CB10 18 B7
Church Hill Castor PE5 195 E2
Grafham PE28 115 F6
Church Hill Cl PE7 187 C1
Church La
Abington Pigotts SG8 11 F6
Arrington SG8 44 D1
Ashwell SG7 2 D4
Balsham CB1 53 B2
Barton CB3 63 B4
Barton Mills IP28 239 D1
Beck Row, Holywell
Row & Kenny Hill IP28 213 D6
Brington & Molesworth
PE28 147 C4
Burwell CB5 130 B1
Cambridge CB2 64 C2
Castle Camps CB1 22 E3
Chatteris PE16 241 C4
Cheveley CB8 91 C6
Comberton CB3 62 C3
Conington PE7 168 E8
Cottenham CB4 125 F6
Covington PE28 135 C2
Croydon SG8 27 A8
Doddington/Wimblington
PE15 222 F5
Ellington PE28 138 F4
Elsworth CB3 100 B4
Ely CB7 240 C4
Exning CB8 110 C8
Fenstanton PE28 121 B6
Fulbourn CB1 67 A5
Gamlingay SG19 41 D5
Girton CB3 82 E8
Graveley PE19 97 F5
Great & Little Abington
CB1 34 B7
Great Paxton PE19 96 D5
Guilden Morden SG8 10 F5
Haddenham CB6 210 A6
Helpston PE6 231 B4
Hemingford Abbots
PE28 143 A3
Hemingford Grey PE28 143 C2
Hilton PE28 120 B1
Huntingdon PE29 142 A5
Isleham CB7 213 A5
Kennett CB8 133 F5
Kingston CB3 61 B3
Leighton PE28 148 D3
Linton CB1 35 C2
Little Eversden CB3 46 A7
Little Staughton MK44 93 B2
1 Littleport CB6 242 D4
Madingley CB3 81 E4
Milton CB4 105 D2
Newmarket CB8 111 A3
Newton PE13 238 A5
Pampisford CB2 33 B5
Papworth Everard CB3 99 A2
Alwalton PE2 185 F5
Peterborough PE2 187 B7
Ramsey PE26 171 B2
Royston SG8 5 D6
Sawston CB2 32 F7
Sibson cum Stibbington
PE8 194 E2
Snailwell CB8 132 A3
Spaldwick PE28 137 F6
Stamford PE9 244 C4
Stetchworth CB8 90 A2
Stow Longa PE28 137 B3
Sutton CB6 216 E2
Tallington PE9 230 F6
Tilbrook PE28 113 B7
Tydd St Giles PE13 237 F6
Warmington PE8 178 B2
Westley Waterless CB8 70 B5
Whittlesford CB2 32 C5
Wilburton CB6 210 B6
Willingham CB4 209 A1
Worlington IP28 213 F4
Wrestlingworth SG19 25 B3
Church La Cl IP28 239 D2
Church Leys PE28 121 C6
Church Mdw IP28 239 D2
Church Mdws PE19 74 F5
Church Mews 21 PE13 245 C5
Church Path CB1 20 B6
Church Pl PE29 141 E2
Church Rate Wlk CB3 64 C8
Church Rd
Brampton PE28 140 E2
Buckworth PE28 149 D6
Carlton CB8 55 A6
Catworth PE28 136 D7
Chrishall SG8 8 D3
Christchurch PE14 229 D3
Conington PE7 168 D8
Easton PE28 138 B4
Everton SG19 40 C3
Glatton PE28 175 E1
Grafham PE28 115 E7
Great Wilbraham CB1 67 F8
Hauxton CB2 48 A5
Leverington PE13 245 F7
Little Stukeley PE28 151 F2
Little Wilbraham CB1 86 F2
Moulton CB8 112 F5
Shepreth SG8 29 E4
Shudy Camps CB1 22 C5
Stow cum Quy CB5 85 F4
Teversham CB1 85 B2
Thistley Green IP28 213 D6
Toft CB3 61 E4
Warboys PE28 164 E4
Wentworth CB6 217 C1
Wicken CB7 211 F1
Friday Bridge PE14 236 A3
Wisbech PE13 238 B1
Wisbech St Mary PE13 235 B7
Wittering PE8 230 B1
Church St Ashley CB8 91 F8
Bourn CB3 60 C5
Buckden PE19 117 A4
Cambridge CB4 84 A4
12 Doddington/Wimblington
PE15 223 B7
Exning CB8 110 C8
Fen Ditton CB5 84 E6
Fen Drayton CB4 121 F5
Fenstanton PE28 121 B6
Fordham CB7 212 F1
Gamlingay SG19 41 D5
Great Chesterford CB10 18 D2
Great Eversden CB3 45 E7
Great Gransden SG19 58 E4
Great Shelford CB2 48 E4
Stapleford CB2 49 C4
Great Wilbraham CB1 67 F8
Guilden Morden SG8 10 F4
Harston CB2 47 D2
Haslingfield CB3 47 A5
Hemingford Grey PE28 143 C2
Histon CB4 104 B5
Holme PE7 176 F4
Ickleton CB10 18 A4
6 Isleham CB7 213 A5
Litlington SG8 12 A2
Little Gransden SG19 58 E3
March PE15 243 C1
Market Deeping PE6 231 F8
Needingworth PE27 208 A2
Northborough PE6 231 F6
Old Hurst PE28 154 D7
Alwalton PE7 185 A4
Stanground PE2 187 C7
Peterborough PE1 198 A2
Werrington PE4 204 C3
St Ives PE27 143 F4
St Neots PE19 74 F5
Sawtry PE28 168 B4
1 Somersham PE28 208 C8
Stamford PE9 244 B4
Steeple Morden SG8 11 B1
Stilton PE7 175 F7
5 Thorney PE6 233 A3
Thriplow SG8 31 C1
Warmington PE8 178 A3
Whaddon SG8 28 B2
Whittlesey PE7 189 D6
Willingham CB4 209 A1
Wistow PE28 163 F7
Withersfield CB9 38 C4
Woodhurst PE28 155 B5
Yaxley PE7 181 D4
Church Terr 17 PE13 245 C5
Church View
Keyston PE28 146 A3
9 Northborough PE6 231 F7
Oakington/Longstanton
CB4 103 C6
4 St Neots PE19 74 F5
3 Witchford CB6 217 E1
Church View Cl PE2 187 B7
Church Way
Alconbury PE28 150 E5
Downham CB6 218 A7
Haslingfield CB3 47 A5
Little Stukeley PE28 151 D4
Church Wlk
Chatteris PE16 241 D5
Little Gransden SG19 58 E3
Mildenhall IP28 239 B4
Peterborough PE1 198 A3
6 St Neots PE19 74 E5
Stow Longa PE28 137 B3
Sturmer CB9 24 E5
Upton PE6 195 B5
Churchfield SG8 7 A1
Churchfield Ave CB2 32 F8
Churchfield Ct
Girton CB3 103 E2
Peterborough PE4 197 E8
Churchfield Rd
Peterborough PE4 197 D8

Churchfield Rd *continued*
Upwell PE14 .... 236 F2
Churchfield Way
Whittlesey PE7 .... 189 C7
[5] Wisbech St Mary PE13 . 235 B7
Churchgate St [9] CB7 .. 212 B4
Churchill Cl [4] CB6 ... 216 E2
Churchill Ave
Haverhill CB9 .... 39 B1
Houghton & Wyton PE28 .. 143 B7
Newmarket CB8 .... 110 D5
Churchill Cl CB6 ...... 240 A4
Churchill Coll CB3 ...... 83 B3
Churchill Ct
Little Downham CB6 ...... 218 A6
Newmarket CB8 .... 110 F3
Churchill Dr IP28 ..... 239 B5
Churchill Rd
Gorefield PE13 .... 237 F3
Stamford PE9 .... 244 B7
Wisbech PE13 .... 245 D4
Churchyard The IP28 .. 239 B4
Cinques Rd SG19 ...... 41 C6
Cinques The SG19 ...... 41 B6
Cissbury Ring PE4 .... 204 C2
City of Ely Com Coll
CB6 .... 240 C6
City Rd Cambridge CB1 .. 246 C2
Littleport CB6 .... 242 E4
March PE15 .... 243 D4
Peterborough PE1 .... 198 A2
Civic Ind Est CB9 ...... 23 F5
Clack La PE28 .... 135 D8
Clare Cl
Mildenhall IP28 .... 239 D5
Stamford PE9 .... 244 A5
Waterbeach CB5 .... 106 A8
Clare Coll (The Colony)
CB4 .... 246 A4
Clare Coll CB2 .... 246 A2
Clare Coll Pavilion CB2 . 64 F5
Clare Ct PE27 .... 144 A4
Clare Dr CB3 .... 80 C2
Clare Pl CB8 .... 111 B2
Clare Rd Cambridge CB3 .. 64 C8
Huntingdon PE29 .... 142 A7
[5] Northborough PE6 .... 231 F7
Peterborough PE1 .... 197 F6
Clare St Cambridge CB4 . 246 A4
Chatteris PE16 .... 241 B4
Claremont [1] CB1 ...... 64 F7
Claremont Rd PE13 .... 245 E5
Clarence Rd
Peterborough PE1 .... 197 E5
Wisbech PE13 .... 245 D6
Clarendale Est CB8 .... 55 F6
Clarendon Rd
Cambridge CB2 .... 64 F6
Haverhill CB9 .... 23 F7
Clarendon St CB1 .... 246 B2
Clarendon Way PE6 ... 203 F8
Clark Rd SG8 .... 5 D7
Clark's Dro CB7 ...... 212 A4
Clarke's La CB6 ...... 210 C5
Clarkes Way SG8 ...... 12 F5
Clarkson Ave PE13 .... 245 D5
Clarkson Cl CB3 ...... 83 B2
Clarkson Ct PE13 ...... 245 D6
Clarkson Inf Sch The
PE13 .... 245 E6
Clarkson Rd CB3 ...... 83 B2
Claudian Cl CB9 ...... 24 D7
Clay Cl La CB4 ...... 104 D3
Clay La
Abbots Ripton PE28 ..... 162 A1
Castor PE5 .... 195 E2
Little Stukeley PE28 .... 151 F7
Clay St Histon CB4 .... 104 B5
Soham CB7 .... 212 B4
Clayburn Rd PE7 ..... 186 C1
Claybush Rd SG7 ...... 2 D3
Claydon Cl CB1 ...... 22 E4
Claygate PE7 .... 189 D7
Claygate Rd CB1 ...... 65 F6
Clayhithe Rd CB5 .... 106 C5
Clayhive Dr [6] CB9 .... 23 F7
Claypole Dr [3] PE6 .... 231 F7
Clayton PE2 .... 186 A4
Clayton Cl PE13 ...... 245 F6
Clayton Sch PE2 ...... 186 B4
Claytons Way PE29 .... 141 F5
Clayway CB7 .... 240 E6
Clear Cres SG8 ...... 14 D5
Cleatham PE3 .... 197 A4
Clematis Cl IP28 ...... 213 F1
Clement Dr PE2 ...... 186 D8
Clement's La CB9 ...... 23 F7
Clement's Way [1] IP28 . 213 F8
Clements Cl CB9 ...... 23 F7
Clements CP Sch CB9 ... 23 F7
Clements Dr CB9 ...... 23 F7
Clerk Maxwell Rd CB3 .. 83 A2
Cleve Pl PE6 .... 232 A1
Cleveland Bay PE15 ... 243 E2
Cleveland Ct PE4 ...... 204 E2
Cleves Rd CB9 .... 23 D6
Cley Ct CB9 .... 38 C1
Clifden Cl SG8 .... 44 D1
Cliff Cres PE9 .... 244 B5
Cliff Rd PE9 .... 244 B5
Clifton Ave PE3 ...... 197 E3
Clifton Ct CB1 .... 65 A6
Clifton Rd
Cambridge CB1 .... 65 A6
Huntingdon PE29 ...... 141 D7
Clipston Wlk PE3 ...... 197 C5
Clive Hall Dr CB4 ...... 124 A1
Cliveden Cl CB4 .... 83 C5
Cloisters The [6] CB7 ... 240 D4
Close The Babraham CB2 . 50 E2
Godmanchester PE29 .... 142 A1
Kennett CB8 .... 133 F5
Papworth Everard CB3 .... 99 B3
Royston SG8 .... 5 F7
St Neots PE19 .... 74 E6
Sutton CB6 .... 216 E1
Close Victoria SG19 .... 25 B4
Cloughs Cross PE13 ... 234 D8
Clover Cl PE26 .... 220 D3
Clover Ct Cambridge CB1 . 66 A5
Linton CB1 .... 35 D2
Clover End [2] CB6 ..... 217 D1
Clover Field CB9 ...... 23 D8
Clover Rd PE19 .... 74 C3
Clover Way [1] IP28 .... 214 A1
Cloverfield Dr CB7 ... 212 A5
Club Way PE7 .... 186 E4
Clydesdale Cl PE15 .... 243 E2
Clydesdale Rd [6] SG8 ..... 5 E6
Coach Dr CB3 .... 46 D5
Coach House La CB2 .... 31 B7
Coach La CB8 .... 91 D5
Coalwharf Rd PE13 .... 245 B4
Coates Ct PE14 .... 236 D6
Coates Dro CB7 ...... 213 A5
Coates Prim Sch PE7 .. 190 F8
Coates Rd PE7 .... 190 D7
Cob Pl PE29 .... 118 F7
Cobbet Pl PE1 .... 198 B3
Cobble Yd CB1 .... 246 C3
Cobden Ave PE1 ...... 197 F4
Cobden St PE1 .... 197 F4
Cobholm Pl [4] CB4 ...... 83 F8
Cobwebs PE28 .... 142 D8
Cock Bank PE7 .... 191 C2
Cock Fen Rd PE14 ..... 229 F3
Cockbrook La
Brington & Molesworth
PE28 .... 147 C8
Old Weston PE28 ...... 157 C2
Cockburn St CB1 ...... 65 B8
Cockcroft Pl CB3 ...... 83 B2
Cockerell Rd CB4 ...... 83 D5
Cockerton Rd CB3 ...... 103 E1
Cocketts Dr PE13 ...... 245 E5
Cockfen La CB4 ...... 105 C7
Cockhall Cl SG8 .... 12 A1
Cockhall La SG8 .... 12 A1
Cockle Cl CB2 .... 31 C7
Cockpen Rd CB7 ...... 131 A8
Codling Wlk CB3 ...... 78 F4
Codrington Ct [2] PE19 ... 74 B3
Cody Rd CB5 .... 127 B1
Coggeshall Cl [5] CB5 .... 84 E4
Cohort Way PE29 ...... 142 B1
Colbron Cl SG7 .... 2 C4
Colbrook CB1 .... 66 D6
Cold Arbour SG19 ...... 56 A1
Cold Harbour SG7 ...... 2 E7
Cold Harbour Cnr
PE13 .... 235 C5
Coldham Bank PE15 ... 228 D6
Coldham Hall Chase
PE14 .... 235 E1
Coldham's Gr CB1 ...... 84 C1
Coldham's La CB1 ...... 84 C2
Coldham's Rd CB1 ...... 84 B2
Coldhams Cres PE29 .. 141 F6
Coldhams N PE29 ...... 141 F6
Coldhams S PE29 ...... 141 F5
Coldhorn Cres PE13 .... 245 D7
Cole Cl [1] CB6 .... 217 D1
Coleridge Com Coll
CB1 .... 65 C7
Coleridge Ct [1] PE19 .... 74 C6
Coleridge Pl PE1 ...... 197 E8
Coleridge Rd CB1 ...... 65 B6
Coles La Brinkley CB8 .... 70 D2
Linton CB1 .... 35 C2
Oakington/Longstanton
CB4 .... 103 C6
Coles Rd CB4 .... 105 D2
Coleseed Rd PE15 ..... 228 D2
Colesfield CB4 .... 123 E2
Coll of Animal Welfare The
PE29 .... 119 C5
Coll of W Anglia CB4 .. 105 D3
College Cl CB5 .... 86 E6
College Cres CB3 ...... 47 B5
College Ct PE28 ...... 168 C3
College Fields CB4 ..... 83 F6
College Gdns PE15 .... 243 E7
College Heath Mid Sch
IP28 .... 239 C6
College Heath Rd
IP28 .... 239 D6
College Pk PE1 .... 198 C5
College Rd Histon CB4 .. 104 B1
Soham CB7 .... 212 B3
College The CB7 ...... 240 D4
Collett's Bridge La
PE14 .... 236 C5
Collier Rd CB1 .... 246 C2
Collier Way CB2 .... 49 C4
Colliers La CB5 .... 86 A6
Collingham PE2 .... 185 F3
Collings Pl CB8 .... 110 E5
Collingwood Ave
PE15 .... 243 E3
Collingwood Ct SG8 ...... 5 E7
Collingwood Rd PE19 .... 74 B2
Collin's Hill CB7 ...... 212 F1
Collyweston Great Wood & Easton Hornstocks National Nature Reserve★
PE8 .... 192 A6
Collyweston Rd PE9 ... 230 B2
Colmworth Bsns Pk
PE19 .... 74 C1
Colmworth Gdns [5] PE19 74 C2
Colne Fields
Colne PE28 .... 215 D1
Somersham PE28 ...... 208 D8
Colne Rd
Bluntisham PE28 ...... 208 C6
Colne PE28 .... 208 C8
Earith PE28 .... 208 D6
Colne Valley Rd CB9 .... 24 A7
Colour Ct PE29 .... 141 D7
Colts Croft SG8 .... 7 E2
Coltsfoot Cl CB1 ...... 66 A5
Coltsfoot Dr
Peterborough PE2 ...... 186 E7
Royston SG8 .... 5 E6
Columbine Rd CB6 .... 240 B6
Colvile Rd
Newton PE13 .... 238 A5
Wisbech PE13 .... 245 E5
Colville Prim Sch CB1 .. 65 F5
Colville Rd CB1 .... 65 F6
Colwyn Cl CB4 .... 83 D5
Comberton Rd
Barton CB3 .... 62 F5
Little Eversden CB3 ...... 46 C8
Toft CB3 .... 61 E5
Comberton Village Coll
CB3 .... 62 A4
Comet Rd PE29 .... 143 A8
Comet Way
Mildenhall IP28 .... 239 B5
St Ives PE27 .... 144 A7
Comfrey Ct CB1 .... 66 A5
Commerce Rd PE2 .... 185 C5
Commercial Rd PE15 .. 243 C7
Common Acre La CB6 .225 D6
Common Dro
Southery PE38 .... 226 E8
Whittlesey PE7 .... 189 C8
Wimblington PE15 ...... 223 C6
Common Gate Dro
CB7 .... 212 E5
Common La Ashwell SG7 .. 2 B6
Chrishall SG8 .... 1 F7
Hemingford Abbots
PE28 .... 142 F3
Sawston CB2 .... 32 D7
Common Rd
Parson Drove PE12 ...... 233 F7
West Wratting CB1 ...... 54 E2
Weston Colville CB1 ...... 54 E4
Whittlesey PE7 .... 189 C8
Witchford CB6 .... 217 E1
Common The CB1 ...... 53 F4
Commons Rd PE7 ...... 189 C8
Compton Fields CB7 .. 240 E7
Computer Laboratory
CB3 .... 83 A3
Conder Cl CB4 .... 105 C3
Conduit Head Rd CB3 ... 82 F3
Conduit Rd PE9 .... 244 C6
Coneygear Ct PE29 .... 141 E7
Coneygear Rd PE29 .... 141 E8
Coneygree Rd PE2 .... 187 D6
Coneywood Rd PE15 .... 223 A7
Conference Way PE13 .245 C8
Conifers The PE2 ...... 185 F6
Coningsby Rd PE3 ...... 204 A2
Conington La PE7 ...... 168 C8
Conington Rd CB3 ...... 121 B3
Coniston Cl PE29 ...... 141 B6
Coniston Rd
Cambridge CB1 .... 65 B6
Peterborough PE4 ...... 204 E3
Conley Cl PE26 .... 172 B7
Connaught Rd CB9 ...... 23 E7
Connor's Cl SG8 .... 10 F4
Conquest Dro PE7 ..... 187 D1
Constable Ave [4] PE19 .. 74 D5
Constable Cl PE7 ...... 190 A8
Constable Cres PE7 ... 190 A8
Constable Rd
[1] Haverhill CB9 .... 38 D1
St Ives PE27 .... 144 A7
Constables Leys PE28 .. 113 F5
Consul Ct [8] CB4 .... 83 E7
Control Twr Mus★ SG8 .. 12 F8
Convent Dr CB5 .... 105 F8
Conway Ave PE4 ...... 204 C2
Conway Cl
[3] Cambridge CB1 ...... 65 F6
Haverhill CB9 .... 23 D8
March PE15 .... 243 B3
Conway Pl [4] PE19 ...... 74 F2
Cook Cl CB4 .... 84 B6
Cook Cl Rd PE7 ...... 181 D6
Cook's Dro
Beck Row, Holywell
Row & Kenny Hill IP28 .. 213 B8
Earith PE28 .... 208 E6
Cook's Gn PE15 ...... 222 F5
Cook's Hole PE8 ...... 193 C4
Cooks La PE28 .... 168 D5
Cookson Cl PE7 ...... 181 D4
Coolidge Gdns CB4 .... 125 F4
Coombe Rd SG8 .... 4 A1
Coombelands SG8 ...... 13 E1
Coombelands Rd [3] SG8 .. 5 E8
Cooper Thornhill Rd [1]
PE7 .... 175 F7
Cooper's Cl CB8 .... 90 A1
Cootes La CB4 .... 121 E5
Cootes Mdw PE27 ...... 144 B3
Copalder Cnr PE15 .... 222 B6
Copel Cl CB3 .... 80 B1
Copeland PE3 .... 197 A3
Copellis Cl CB9 .... 39 A2
Copes Cl PE19 .... 117 B4
Cophall Dro CB6 ...... 217 E7
Coploe Rd CB10 .... 17 F3
Copper Beech Way
PE2 .... 187 B7
Copperbeech Cl PE27 .144 A5
Copperfields SG8 ...... 5 B6
Coppice Ave CB2 ...... 49 B6
Coppice Dr CB3 .... 79 A4
Coppice The
Histon CB4 .... 104 C1
Littleport CB6 .... 242 C1
Coppingford Cl PE2 ... 187 D6
Coppins Cl PE28 ...... 168 A4
Coppins Ct PE14 ...... 245 E2
Copsewood PE4 .... 204 C4
Copy Hill CB9 .... 23 E3
Coral Pk Trading Est
CB1 .... 84 B2
Corbett St CB4 .... 125 E4
Cordell Cl PE27 .... 143 E6
Cordon St PE13 .... 245 C4
Coree Cl CB2 .... 65 A5
Corfe Ave PE4 .... 204 C2
Corfe Pl [3] PE19 .... 74 F2
Cormas Cl [5] SG8 .... 5 E8
Corn Exchange St
CB2 .... 246 A2
Corn Mill PE15 .... 243 C3
Corner Cl CB7 .... 219 B5
Cornfields [1] PE15 .... 222 F5
Cornish Cl CB1 .... 37 A3
Cornmills Rd CB7 ...... 212 D2
Cornstall Bldgs [3] PE9 .244 C5
Cornwall Ct PE19 .... 74 B4
Cornwall Rd
[6] Stamford PE9 .... 244 B6
Wyton Airfield PE28 .... 143 A8
Cornwallis Dr PE19 ...... 74 A3
Cornwallis Rd CB9 ...... 23 F6
Corona Rd CB4 .... 83 E4
Coronation Ave
[3] Crowland PE6 .... 232 B8
Huntingdon PE29 ...... 141 E5
Parson Drove PE12 ...... 234 A7
Royston SG8 .... 5 C5
[9] Somersham PE28 .... 215 C1
Warboys PE28 .... 164 F6
Whittlesey PE7 .... 189 F7
Coronation Cl
March PE15 .... 243 C2
Waterbeach CB5 .... 106 A7
Coronation Mews [2] CB2 64 E7
Coronation Pl CB2 ...... 64 E7
Coronation St CB2 .... 246 B1
Corporation Bank PE6 .207 F7
Corporation Rd PE13 .. 245 D3
Corpus Christi Coll
CB2 .... 246 A2
Corpus Christi La
PE29 .... 141 E1
Corrie Rd CB1 .... 65 B7
Corsican Pine Cl CB8 .. 110 F5
Corunna Cl [7] PE19 ...... 74 C5
Corvus Cl SG8 .... 5 E8
Cosgrove Cl PE3 ...... 197 C6
Cosin Ct CB1 .... 246 A1
Cotes The CB7 .... 211 F6
Coton CE Prim Sch
CB3 .... 82 B2
Coton Rd CB3 .... 63 E5
Cotswold Cl
March PE15 .... 243 E4
Peterborough PE4 ...... 204 E1
Cottenham Cl [6] CB4 .. 208 D1
Cottenham Prim Sch
CB4 .... 125 D4
Cottenham Rd
Histon CB4 .... 104 B5
Landbeach CB4 .... 126 B1
Cottenham Village Coll
CB4 .... 125 E3
Cottesmore Cl PE3 .... 197 D4
Cotton Cl
Conington PE7 .... 168 C8
[5] Sawtry PE28 .... 168 C2
Cotton Ct [1] PE29 ...... 141 F7
Cotton End PE3 .... 197 A4
Cotton End Rd CB8 .... 110 C8
Cotton La PE19 .... 97 C7
Cotton's Field CB3 .... 102 B1
Cottons Cnr PE14 ...... 229 D6
Cottons Head PE14 .... 236 E3
Cottons The PE14 ...... 236 E2
Cottrell's La CB3 ...... 100 B4
Coulson Cl CB4 .... 105 C2
Coulson Way PE28 .... 150 F4
Council Rd [4] PE13 .... 245 E6
Council St PE4 .... 197 D8
Countess Cl PE19 ...... 74 B3
County Rd
Hampton Vale PE7 ...... 181 C8
March PE15 .... 243 D6
Coupals Cl CB9 .... 24 C6
Coupals CP Sch CB9 ... 24 D7
Coupals Rd CB9 .... 24 E6
Courier Cl IP28 .... 239 B6
Courtland Ave CB1 ...... 65 C5
Courtney Way CB4 ...... 83 E4
Courtyard Way CB4 .... 125 E5
Courtyards CB2 .... 48 F3
Cousins Cl PE15 .... 243 C4
Covehite Ct [6] CB9 ...... 23 E6
Covent Gdn CB1 .... 246 C1
Covent Gdns CB4 ...... 209 A1
Coventry Cl PE4 .... 204 B3
Covert Cl CB9 .... 39 A1
Covert The
[1] Comberton CB3 ...... 62 D6
Peterborough PE3 ...... 197 B1
Cow and Hare Pas
PE27 .... 144 A3
Cow and Sheep Dro
IP28 .... 213 C7
Cow Brook La CB3 ...... 99 A3
Cow Fen Rd CB4 ...... 122 E6
Cow La Fulbourn CB1 .... 66 E5
Godmanchester PE29 .... 142 C2
Great Chesterford CB10 .. 19 A4
Rampton CB4 .... 124 F6
Cow Way PE7 .... 190 D8
Cowbridge Hall Dro
CB6 .... 218 B6
Cowdell End CB3 ...... 100 B4
Cowgate PE1 .... 197 F2
Cowley Cl PE28 .... 115 D3
Cowley Pk CB4 .... 84 B7
Cowley Rd CB4 .... 84 C7
Cowlinge Cnr CB8 ...... 73 D8
Cowper Rd
Cambridge CB1 .... 65 B6
Huntingdon PE29 ...... 141 D5
Peterborough PE1 ...... 197 F7
Cowpers Ct [4] PE19 ...... 74 D6
Cowslip Cl SG8 .... 5 F5
Cowslip Dr CB6 .... 211 A7
Cox's Cl CB2 .... 49 C4
Cox's Dro CB1 .... 66 F6
Cox's End [15] CB4 ...... 208 D1
Cox's La Chatteris PE16 . 241 C6
Wisbech PE13 .... 245 A3
Coxons Cl PE29 .... 141 E5
Coxs Cl CB1 .... 23 C7
Crab Apple Way SG19 ... 41 C5
Crab Marsh PE13 ...... 245 B8
Crabapple Cl PE28 .... 168 B3
Crabapple Gdns PE2 .. 185 D6
Crabtree PE4 .... 205 B1
Crabtree Croft CB1 ...... 35 B3
Craft Way SG8 .... 11 B2
Crafts Way CB3 .... 102 C3
Craig St PE1 .... 197 F3
Craister Ct CB4 .... 83 E7
Cramswell Cl CB1 ...... 23 E6
Crandal Way CB2 ...... 49 A4
Crane Ave PE7 .... 181 F6
Crane Cl [3] PE28 ...... 208 C8
Crane St PE28 .... 140 C3
Cranemore PE4 .... 204 A4
Crane's La CB3 .... 61 A2
Cranfield Pl [2] PE28 ... 208 C8
Cranfield Way
Brampton PE28 .... 140 D2
Buckden PE19 .... 117 A3
Cranford Dr PE3 ...... 197 C4
Cranleigh Cl CB2 ...... 64 D1
Cranmer Rd CB3 .... 83 B1
Cranmore Dro PE6 .... 206 D8
Cranny The PE19 ...... 117 F2
Cranwells Way [4] CB6 .. 211 B7
Crathern Way CB4 ...... 83 F7
Cratherne Way CB4 ..... 83 F7
Crauden Gdns CB7 .... 240 E5
Craven Cl CB2 .... 64 D2
Craven Way CB8 ...... 110 E6
Crawford Gdns [2] PE6 .. 232 C8
Crawley End SG8 .... 8 D4
Crawthorne Rd PE1 .... 198 A3
Crawthorne St [1] PE1 .. 198 B3
Crease Dro PE6 .... 232 B8
Crease Rd
Conington PE28 .... 168 F5
Sawtry PE28 .... 169 B6
Crecy Ct PE19 .... 74 C5
Creek Fen PE15 .... 228 D5
Creek Rd PE15 .... 243 D4
Crescent Cl PE7 .... 190 A7
Crescent Rd
Histon CB4 .... 104 C1
Whittlesey PE7 .... 189 F7
Crescent The
Cambridge CB3 .... 83 B3
Dullingham CB8 .... 89 C1
Eaton Socon PE19 ...... 74 C3
Eye PE6 .... 232 A1
Impington CB4 .... 104 C1
Littleport CB6 .... 242 C3
Peterborough PE2 ...... 186 E7
St Ives PE27 .... 144 A5
St Neots PE19 .... 74 F6
[4] Soham CB7 .... 212 B3
Wicken CB7 .... 211 E1
Wisbech PE13 .... 245 C4
Cressbrook Dr CB3 ...... 79 C3
Cressener Terr [3] PE19 .. 74 F5
Cresset The PE3 .... 197 A6
Cresswells La CB7 .... 240 E4
Crester Dr [3] PE4 ...... 204 C3
Criccieth Way PE19 ...... 74 F1
Cricket Field Rd CB8 .. 111 B2
Cricket Sch CB1 .... 246 C1
Cricketers Cl PE15 .... 243 C3
Cricketers Way
[3] Benwick PE15 ...... 222 A5
Chatteris PE16 .... 241 D3
Wisbech PE13 .... 245 A6
Cricketfield La PE26 .... 172 A6
Crick's Rd IP28 .... 213 D6
Cripple Sidings La
PE2 .... 187 A8

Crishall CE Prim Sch
SG8 ....8 C3
Crispin Cl Haverhill CB9 ..23 D7
1 Impington CB4 ....83 D7
Crispin Pl CB1 ....246 C3
Crockfords Rd CB8 ....111 A2
Crocus Cl PE7 ....181 F6
Crocus Gr PE1 ....198 A8
Croft Cl Brampton PE28 .140 D2
Histon CB4 ....104 B5
Croft Gdns CB3 ....64 C7
Croft La Haverhill CB9 ..24 B6
Oakington/Longstanton
CB4 ....103 B6
Croft Pk Rd 242 D3
Croft Pl IP28 ....239 C4
Croft Rd Isleham CB7 ..213 A5
Newmarket CB8 ....110 E5
Outwell PE14 ....229 D7
Croft The Fulbourn CB1 ..66 E5
Stamford PE9 ....244 D5
Croft Way PE7 ....186 C2
Crofters The PE6 ......210 F6
Croftfield Rd PE29 ....141 F1
Croftgate CB3 ....64 A7
Crofts The PE19 ....95 F1
Crome Ditch Cl CB3 .....64 A4
Cromwell Cl
2 Northborough PE6 ....231 F7
Ramsey PE26 ....171 F6
Cromwell Com Coll
PE16 ....241 C4
Cromwell Ct **4** PE19 ..74 F3
Cromwell Gdns **4** PE19 .75 A5
Cromwell House★
PE29 ....141 D5
Cromwell Mews PE6 ....231 C4
Cromwell Mus★ PE29 .141 D4
Cromwell Pk CB4 ......208 E1
Cromwell Pk Prim Sch
PE29 ....141 A5
Cromwell Pl PE27 .....144 B3
Cromwell Rd
Cambridge CB1 ....84 B1
Ely CB6 ....240 C4
March PE15 ....243 D6
Peterborough PE1 .....197 F4
St Neots PE19 ....74 F3
1 Sutton CB6 ....216 E1
Wisbech PE13 ....245 B3
Cromwell Sq PE29 .....141 D5
Cromwell Terr PE27 ...144 B3
Cromwell Way PE28 ...168 B3
Cromwell Wlk PE29 ....141 D5
Crooked Bank PE14 ...235 D5
Croots Cl PE28 ....140 B2
Cropston Rd PE1 ......198 E7
Crosfield Ct CB4 ....83 E7
Cross Bank Dro CB7 ...211 C5
Cross Cl CB9 ....39 A1
Cross Dro
Haddenham CB6 ......209 E3
Littleport CB7 ....226 A1
Southery PE38 ....226 F2
Stretham CB6 ....210 F3
Tydd St Giles PE13 ....237 C5
Warboys PE28 ....215 C6
Waterbeach CB5 ......127 D4
Whittlesey PE7 ....190 F6
Wilburton CB6 ....210 C3
Wistow PE28 ....172 E1
Cross Farm Cl PE28 ..120 C2
Cross Gn CB8 ....70 F8
Cross Hall Rd PE19 ....74 D6
Cross Keys Ct CB4 ....125 D3
Cross La
Little Downham CB6 ...218 A6
Melbourn SG8 ....14 C6
Wisbech PE13 ....235 D6
Cross La Cl SG8 ....45 E1
Cross Rd March PE15 .227 F2
Sutton St Edmund PE12 .237 A4
Whittlesey PE7 ....189 C7
Cross St
Cambridge CB1 ......246 C1
Covington PE28 ....135 D2
Farcet PE7 ....187 D1
Huntingdon PE29 .....141 E5
Peterborough PE1 ....198 A2
Cross The PE28 ....161 F6
Crossberry Way PE6 ..231 B4
Crosshall Inf Sch PE19 ..74 C6
Crosshall Jun Sch
PE19 ....74 C6
Crosshall Marina★
PE19 ....74 E7
Crosshall Rd PE19 .....74 D6
Crossroad Cotts CB10 .17 C2
Crossway Hand PE7 ..189 B8
Crossways Barley SG8 ..6 F1
Linton CB1 ....35 D2
Crossways Gdns CB2 ..64 C2
Crow Dean CB3 ....79 A3
Crow Hill La CB3 ....79 B3
Crow Spinney La
PE28 ....115 C4
Crow Tree St SG19 ....58 D4
Crowhill **6** PE29 ....118 F8
Crowhurst PE4 ....204 C5
Crowland Rd
Deeping St James PE6 .207 A6
Eye PE6 ....232 A3
Haverhill CB9 ....23 F8
Newborough PE6 .....232 A2
Thorney PE6 ....232 E5
Crowland Way CB4 .....83 F7
Crowlands CB4 ....125 D4
Crown Ave PE14 ......229 D3

Crown Cl
Hail Weston PE19 ......95 A1
March PE15 ....243 C2
St Ives PE27 ....144 A4
Crown Gdns
Alconbury PE28 ......150 E4
Little Downham CB6 ..218 A6
Crown La **2** CB6 ....242 D4
Crown Lakes Ctry Pk★
PE7 ....187 B2
Crown Mews PE26 ....172 B7
Crown Pl PE27 ....144 A3
Crown Rd PE14 ......229 D3
Crown St
Peterborough PE1 ....197 E7
St Ives PE27 ....144 A3
Stamford PE9 ....244 B5
Crown Wlk
Newmarket CB8 ......111 A4
St Ives PE27 ....144 A3
Crowson Cres **6** PE6 .231 F7
Crowthorne Cl CB1 ....65 F6
Croxton Gdns PE28 ...136 D6
Croydon Hill SG8 ......26 E8
Croydon Rd
Arrington SG8 ....44 C1
Croydon SG8 ....27 B8
Croyland Rd PE4 .....204 D1
Crummock Wr PE29 ..141 C5
Crunch Croft CB9 ......24 E5
Crystal Dr PE2 ....186 D8
Cuckoo La
Lolworth CB3 ....101 F5
Rampton CB4 ....124 E3
Culloden Cl PE19 ......74 C5
Cumberland Way **3**
PE19 ....74 F1
Cundell Dr CB4 ......125 E4
Cunningham Cl CB4 ....83 E6
Cunningham Rd PE2 ..186 E4
Cunningham Way PE19 .74 A2
Curf PE16 ....222 F3
Curf Fen Dro PE16 ...222 F2
Curlew Ave PE16 .....241 C5
Curlew Cl PE7 ....189 F8
Curlew Cres **6** SG8 ...5 E8
Curlew Gr PE2 ....187 D7
Curlew Pl **2** PE7 ....75 B6
Cutter Ferry Cl CB4 ....84 A3
Cutter Ferry La CB4 ..246 C4
Cygnet Dr PE16 ......241 C6
Cygnet Pk PE7 ....186 E3
Cygnet Rd PE7 ....186 E3
Cypress Cl
6 Doddington PE15 ..223 A6
Peterborough PE3 ....197 A2
Cyprus Rd CB1 ....65 C7

D

Da Vinci Cl PE27 .....144 A4
Dacre Gn SG8 ....5 F6
Daffodil Gr PE4 ......187 C7
Dagless Way PE15 ....243 D7
Daimler Ave PE7 .....181 E6
Daintree PE27 ....208 A3
Daintree Rd PE26 ....220 D4
Daintree Way PE15 ..143 D1
Daintrees Rd CB4 ....121 F6
Dairy Dro
Littleport CB6 ....225 C6
Thorney PE6 ....233 E2
Daisy Cl CB4 ....83 D7
Dakota Rd PE28 ......213 E8
Dalby Ct PE1 ....198 C5
Dale Cl PE7 ....185 F5
Dale The CB4 ....123 F4
Dale Way CB2 ....32 F8
Dalegarth CB4 ....83 F4
Dales Way PE27 .....208 A3
Dalham Pl CB9 ....24 B8
Dalham Rd Ashley CB8 .92 B7
Moulton CB8 ....112 F4
Dalton Sq CB4 ....84 B5
Dalton Way CB6 .....240 D6
Dam Bank Dro CB6 ..209 C4
Dane Dr CB3 ....83 A1
Dane Hill CB3 ....133 E5
Dane Hill Rd CB8 ....133 D5
Danes Cl PE1 ....198 C4
Danesbury Ct CB1 .....84 C1
Daniel Ct PE9 ....244 C4
Danish Ct PE4 ....204 A4
Daphmoir Cl CB2 ......29 F8
Darford PE28 ....208 E6
Darley Cl PE8 ....230 C1
Darrington Cl **1** PE19 .74 B3
Dart Cl PE27 ....144 B6
Darthill Rd PE15 ....243 D5
Dartmoor Dr PE29 ...141 A4
Darwin Cl Ely CB6 ...240 A4
Mildenhall IP28 .....239 C6
3 Stamford PE9 ....244 B4
Darwin Coll★ CB3 ...246 A1
Darwin Dr CB4 ....83 D5
Darwin Pl CB8 ....111 B1
Darwood Ct PE27 ....144 B3
Daules Rd PE28 ......140 E1
Davey Cl CB4 ....104 C3
Davey Cres CB2 ....49 C4
David Bull Way CB1 ..105 D3
David Chalmers Cl
PE2 ....186 F8
David St **5** CB1 .....65 A8
David's Cl PE4 ....203 F4
David's La PE4 ......204 B6

Davie La PE7 ....201 A1
Davis Cl PE19 ....96 A2
Davison Rd CB6 .....240 E8
Davy Rd CB1 ....65 B7
Daw's Dro PE7 ......220 D8
Daws Cl **5** CB1 .....65 F6
Dawson Cl PE6 ......205 C8
Daymond St PE2 ....186 D7
Day's Cl SG8 ....5 C5
Day's Lode Rd PE15 ..224 C7
De Bec Cl PE1 ......198 C3
De Freville Ave CB4 ...246 C4
De Freville Rd CB2 ....49 A6
De Havilland Ct **4** IP28 239 B5
De Havilland Rd PE13 .245 C6
De La Haye Cl CB3 ....99 B3
De La Warre Way CB3 ..79 B4
De Vere Cl PE28 .....143 B1
Deacon St PE1 ......197 F3
Deacons La CB7 ....240 D5
Deacons Rd PE1 ....198 B5
Deaconscroft PE3 ...197 B5
Deal Cl PE29 ....141 E8
Deal Gr CB2 ....32 F8
Dean Dr CB1 ....65 B4
Dean Dro PE16 ......215 F6
Dean Peacock Ct CB6 .240 E6
Dean Rd CB1 ....21 B8
Deans Cl CB9 ....39 A1
Debdale Pl PE2 ......185 E4
Debdale Ct PE7 ......189 F5
Debden Gn CB6 .....240 B4
Deben Ave PE27 ....144 A7
Deben Cl PE15 ......243 B5
Deben Rd CB9 ....24 B8
Decoy Rd
Borough Fen PE6 ....207 A3
Gorefield PE13 ......237 D2
Deene Ct PE3 ....197 C5
Deeping St James Com Prim
Sch **18** PE6 ....231 F8
Deeping St James Rd
PE6 ....231 E7
Deepings Sch The **17**
PE6 ....231 F8
Deerfield Rd PE15 ...243 E4
Deerhurst Way **13** PE6 .232 A1
Deerleap PE3 ....197 A5
Deerpark Rd PE28 ...168 A4
Degas Dr PE27 ......144 A7
De-Havilland Rd PE13 .245 C6
Deighton Cl PE27 ...144 B5
Delamere Cl
Little Wilbraham CB8 ..68 F6
Peterborough PE1 ...198 C5
Delapre Ct **9** PE6 ..232 A1
Delbrig Dro CB7 .....212 E5
Dell The
Peterborough PE2 ...186 E7
Royston SG8 ....5 C5
Dells Cl PE28 ....166 D2
Delph Ct PE7 ....189 D7
Delph Dro IP28 .....212 F8
Delph St PE7 ....189 D7
Delta La PE27 ......151 E3
Delve Terr PE16 ....241 D5
Dendys PE21 ....143 D1
Dengaine Cl CB3 ......99 B2
Denham Rd CB8 ......92 E8
Denham Wlk **1** PE3 .197 C4
Denis Dr PE2 ....186 A4
Denmark Dr PE2 ....186 A4
Denmark Rd CB4 ...125 E3
Dennis Gn SG19 .....41 C4
Dennis Rd CB5 ....84 F4
Dennis Wilson Ct CB2 .64 D4
Denny Abbey★ CB5 .127 A6
Denny Cl **9** CB4 ...208 D1
Denny End Rd CB5 ..105 F8
Denson Cl CB5 ......106 A8
Denton Rd
Glatton PE28 ....175 E1
Peterborough PE2 ...187 C6
Dentons Chase PE26 .220 E4
Depot Rd CB8 ....110 E6
Deptford Cl PE15 ...243 B3
Derby Dr PE1 ....198 C6
Derby Rd CB1 ....65 B6
Derby St CB3 ....64 C7
Derby Way CB3 .....110 D5
Derwent Cl
Cambridge CB1 ......65 D5
Huntingdon PE29 ...141 B5
St Neots PE19 ....144 B6
Derwent Dr PE4 ....204 E2
Derwood Gr PE4 ....204 B5
Desborough Ave PE2 .187 D5
Desborough Rd PE29 .142 A6
Desmond Ave CB1 ....65 F6
Devana Cl PE28 .....119 F8
Devills Pl PE16 .....243 D4
Devil's Dyke Nature
Reserve★ CB5 ......109 B5
Devoke Cl PE29 ....141 B6
Devon Cl PE27 .....144 A8
Devon Rd PE28 ....154 A1
Devonshire Ct PE28 .168 B3
Devonshire Mews CB3 .80 C1
Devonshire Rd CB1 ...65 A8
Dewpond Cl **4** PE19 .75 A4
Dexter Cl **10** PE15 ..223 A5
Dexter Way PE8 ....178 B3
Dial Cl PE19 ....95 F2
Diamond Cl CB2 ......64 E5
Diana Cl PE7 ....190 A4
Dickasons SG8 ....14 D7
Dickens St PE1 .....198 B3

Dickerson Cl **1** SG19 ..41 D6
Digby Ct **3** PE19 ....74 F3
Dimmock's Cote CB6 .211 B3
Dimmock's Cote Rd
CB7 ....211 B3
Dingley Ct PE3 .....197 C5
Dip The CB8 ....111 C2
Ditchburn Pl CB1 ....84 A1
Ditchfield CB5 ......108 D8
Ditchfields **2** PE28 .215 C1
Ditton Cl CB8 ....111 A1
Ditton Fields CB5 ....84 C3
Ditton Gn CB8 ....90 D1
Ditton La CB5 ....84 E4
Ditton Lodge Fst Sch
CB8 ....111 B2
Ditton Wlk CB5 ....84 C4
Dixies SG7 ....2 D3
Dixon's Dro PE14 ...238 F5
Dixons Rd **1** PE6 ..231 E8
Dobson Wlk **11** PE15 .223 B7
Dock Bsns Pk The
CB7 ....240 D2
Dock La CB5 ....106 A2
Dock Rd PE16 ......241 C6
Dock The CB7 ......240 D2
Dockings La **10** CB7 .213 A5
Doctor's Cl CB4 ....104 D3
Docwra Rd CB3 ......99 A3
Docwra's Cl SG8 .....29 D5
Doddington Dr PE3 ..197 B2
Doddington Hospl
PE15 ....222 F6
Doddington Rd
Benwick PE15 ......222 A5
Chatteris PE16 .....241 A8
Doddington/Wimblington
PE15 ....223 B6
Dodds Mead CB8 .....47 A5
Dodford La CB3 ....103 E2
Dog Kennel La SG8 ...5 D6
Dogget La CB1 ......66 F4
Doggett Rd CB1 ......65 E6
Dogsthorpe Gr PE1 ..198 A5
Dogsthorpe Jun & Inf Sch
PE1 ....198 B2
Dogsthorpe Rd PE1 ..198 A5
**Dogsthorpe Star Pit & Little
Wood Nature Reserve**★
PE6 ....205 E2
Dole The CB4 ......104 C3
Doles The **3** CB4 ..208 D1
Dolls Cl CB1 ....53 C1
Dolphin Cl
Cambridge CB1 ......66 A7
Linton CB1 ....35 C1
Dolphin La **11** Ely CB7 .240 D4
Dolphin Way CB2 .....49 B4
Dolphins Way SG19 ..41 D6
Dome Leisure Ctr
IP28 ....239 E4
Donaldson Dr **2** PE4 .204 E2
Donegal **7** CB1 ......84 A2
Donegal Cl PE4 ....204 D2
Donne Cl SG8 ....5 C8
Donnington Pk PE13 .238 A1
Dorchester Cres **3** PE1 198 D7
Dorchester Way PE3 .143 B7
Doris St CB8 ....110 F3
Dorling Way CB4 ...140 B3
Dorral Dean CB3 .....80 B1
Dorvis La CB10 ....21 B7
Double Bank La PE28 .161 B7
Doug Smith Cl CB8 ..110 F6
Doughty St PE9 ....244 D7
Douglas House Hospl
CB2 ....64 E5
Douglas Rd **3** PE6 ..231 E8
Douglas Way CB3 .....79 B3
Dove Cl PE28 ....121 C5
Dove Cote Cl CB4 ..121 F5
Dove House Rd CB9 ..24 B4
Dovecote Cl
Peterborough PE1 ...198 A7
Yarwell PE8 ....183 A8
Dovecote La PE7 ...181 C5
Dovecote Rd
Great Paxton PE19 ...96 D3
Upwell PE14 ....229 D7
Dovehouse Cl Ely CB7 .240 D3
Fowlmere SG8 ....15 E8
Godmanchester PE29 .142 A1
St Neots PE19 ....74 F6
Dovehouse Wood
PE28 ....162 B1
Dover Cl PE29 .....141 E8
Dover Rd PE4 ......204 C2
Dover St **2** CB1 ....246 C2
Dovey Cl PE27 .....144 B6
Dowding Way CB4 ....83 D6
Dowgate Rd PE13 ..238 B1
Down Gate PE3 ....197 A1
Downe Cl CB3 ....99 A2
**Downham Feoffees CE Prim
Sch** PE28 ....218 A4
Downham Hythe Dro
CB6 ....217 D6
Downham Rd Ely CB6 .240 D4
Outwell PE14 ....236 F2
Downham's La CB4 ...84 A6
Downing Cl
Bottisham CB5 ....86 E6
Mildenhall IP28 .....239 D5
Newmarket CB8 ....111 A2
Downing Coll CB2 ..246 B1
Downing Cres PE9 ..244 B7
Downing Ct CB5 ....108 A1

Downing Pl CB2 ....246 B2
Downing St CB2 ....246 B2
Downlands SG8 ....5 C6
Downs Cres CB9 ......23 F8
Downs Pl CB9 ....23 F8
Downton Dr CB9 .....23 E8
Dowsdale Bank PE6 .233 A8
Dragoon Dr **4** PE15 .243 D2
Drain Rd PE6 ....205 A7
Drake Ave PE16 ....241 C6
Drake Cl PE29 .....141 F6
Drake Rd PE19 ......74 B2
Drake Way CB4 ....104 C5
Draper's Cl PE8 ....178 C3
Drapers La CB9 ......23 B2
Drapery Row **1** CB8 .111 A3
Drayhorse Rd PE26 .172 A5
Drayton PE3 ....197 A4
Drayton Cl CB1 ......66 A5
Drayton Rd CB1 ......66 A5
Drewels La PE19 .....56 D4
Drift Ave PE9 ......244 D7
Drift Gdns PE9 ....244 D7
Drift Rd PE9 ....244 C4
Drift The Elsworth CB3 .100 A4
Exning CB8 ....110 A8
Oakington/Longstanton
CB4 ....103 B5
Sutton PE5 ....194 F3
Drings Cl **2** CB4 ...208 D1
Drinkwater Cl CB8 ..110 E4
Drive The Perry PE28 .115 D1
Peterborough PE3 ...197 C2
St Ives PE27 ....143 F4
Drivers Ave PE29 ..141 E5
Drivers Cl **8** PE15 .223 A6
Drosier Rd CB2 ....246 C1
Drove Rd SG19 ......41 A6
Drove The Farcet PE26 .220 D7
Witchford CB6 .....217 E1
Drovers Cl PE26 ...221 A4
Drummer St CB1 ...246 B2
Drury La
Bluntisham/Colne PE28 .208 D7
Melbourn SG8 ......14 C6
Wicken CB7 ....211 F2
Dry Drayton CE Prim Sch
CB3 ....102 C1
Dry Drayton Rd
Madingley CB3 ....81 D7
Oakington & Westwick
CB4 ....103 A4
Dry Leys PE2 ....186 C6
Drybread Rd PE7 ...189 F8
Dryden Cl PE27 ....143 E6
Dryden Ct **7** PE19 ...75 A5
Dryden Rd PE1 .....197 E7
Dubbs Knoll Rd SG8 ..10 F5
Duberly Cl PE28 ...115 E2
Duchess Cl PE19 .....74 A3
Duchess Dr
Newmarket CB8 ....111 D2
Woodditton CB8 .....90 B8
Duck Dro CB7 ......219 D5
Duck End Girton CB3 ..82 D8
Godmanchester PE29 .141 F1
Duck La
Haddenham CB6 ...210 A4
St Neots PE19 ....74 F4
Duck St PE8 ....178 D8
Ducks La CB8 ......110 C2
Duckworth Cl PE7 ..189 E7
Duddery Hill CB9 ....23 F6
Duddery Rd CB9 ......24 A7
Dudley Ave PE4 ....204 C2
Dudley Rd CB5 ....84 E4
Duke of Bedford Prim Sch
PE6 ....233 B3
Duke St
Peterborough PE2 ...187 A7
Wisbech PE13 .....245 D4
Dukes Dr PE26 .....221 C2
Dukes Mdw CB2 .....49 C5
Dukes Rd PE19 ......74 B4
Dukesmead PE4 ....204 A2
Dukesmead Mobile Home Pk
PE4 ....204 B2
Dullingham Rd
Newmarket CB8 ....110 F1
Stetchworth CB8 .....89 D3
Woodditton CB8 .....89 F7
Dullingham Sta CB8 ..89 B2
Duloe Rd PE19 ....74 B5
Dunblane Dr PE2 ...185 D4
Duncan Way PE29 ..141 F4
Duncock La CB3 ....110 E8
Duncombe's Rd PE7 .191 F8
Dundee Cl CB4 ......84 A5
Dundee Ct PE2 .....185 C5
Dungate La CB1 ......52 B7
Dunholt Way PE28 ..208 D6
Dunkirk Dro PE28 ..215 C4
Dunmowe Way CB1 ..66 E5
Dunsberry
Marholm PE3 ......203 F1
Peterborough PE3 ...196 F8
Dunsbridge Turnpike
SG8 ....29 F2
Dunsey Wood Cl CB9 ..38 E1
Dunsmore Cl CB5 ....84 E4
Dunstal Field CB4 ..125 D2
Dunstall's Dro CB7 .218 E1
Dunstan St CB4 ....246 B5
Dunster Dr CB9 ......23 E8
Durham Cl PE28 ...168 C2

Durham Rd PE1 ....198 C3
Durham Way
Newmarket CB8 ....110 E5
Wyton Airfield PE28 ....143 B8
Durnford Way CB4 ....83 E5
Duxford Airfield CB2 ....17 A8
Duxford Camp CB2 ....31 F1
Duxford CE Com Prim Sch CB2 ....32 D1
Duxford Rd
Hinxton CB10 ....18 A7
Ickleton CB10 ....17 F5
Whittlesford CB2 ....32 D4
Dwyer-joyce Cl CB4 ....104 B4
Dykemoor Dro PE15 ....222 C4
Dykemoor Dro N PE15 ....222 E5
Dyson Cl
Peterborough PE1 ....197 F3
The Stukeleys PE29 ....141 A5
Dyson's Dro CB5 ....130 B5

E

Eachard Rd CB3 ....83 B5
Eagle Ct PE19 ....75 B7
Eagle La CB8 ....89 D1
Eagle Way PE29 ....142 A8
Eagle's La CB6 ....218 A7
Eaglesthorpe PE1 ....197 E7
Eames Gdns PE1 ....198 E6
Eardley Grange PE6 ....207 F6
Earith Bsns Pk PE28 ....208 F6
Earith Fen Dro PE28 ....208 F7
Earith Prim Sch PE28 ....208 E5
Earith Rd
Bluntisham/Colne PE28 ....208 D7
Willingham CB4 ....209 A2
Earl Cl 1 PE19 ....74 B4
Earl Spencer Ct PE2 ....186 E8
Earl St CB1 ....246 B2
Earls Cl PE2 ....187 B6
Earls Hill Gdns SG8 ....5 C6
Earlswood PE2 ....185 E5
Earning St PE29 ....141 F1
Earth Cl PE2 ....187 E5
East Chadley La PE29 ....141 F2
East Cl PE15 ....243 B6
East Delph PE7 ....189 E8
East Dr Caldecote CB3 ....80 C1
March PE15 ....243 F4
East Fen Comm CB7 ....212 C4
East Fen Dro CB7 ....212 D4
East Fen Rd CB7 ....213 B5
East Hatley SG19 ....43 A1
East Hertford St CB4 ....246 A4
East La SG19 ....41 C6
East Meadowgate PE14 ....236 C7
East of England Showground★ PE2 ....185 C4
East Perry PE28 ....115 E2
East Pk St PE16 ....241 C4
East Rd Cambridge CB1 ....246 C2
Isleham CB7 ....213 A5
8 Northborough PE6 ....231 F7
Tydd St Mary PE13 ....238 C8
East St
Bluntisham/Colne PE28 ....208 C5
Great Gransden SG19 ....58 E4
Huntingdon PE29 ....141 F5
1 Kimbolton PE28 ....113 F4
Manea PE15 ....224 C4
St Ives PE27 ....144 A3
St Neots PE19 ....74 F5
Stamford PE9 ....244 C5
East Sta Rd PE2 ....187 A8
East View IP28 ....213 C3
East Villa PE15 ....224 B3
East Way CB2 ....50 A1
East Wr Cres PE7 ....186 C1
Eastalls Cl 15 PE15 ....223 A5
Eastbourne Cl 2 PE16 ....241 C3
Eastbourne Rd PE16 ....241 C3
Eastern Ave
Haverhill CB9 ....23 E8
Peterborough PE1 ....198 C8
11 Soham CB7 ....212 B4
Eastern Cl PE1 ....198 D7
Eastern Ind Est PE1 ....198 E3
Eastfield CB4 ....84 A5
Eastfield Dr PE7 ....189 F6
Eastfield Gr PE1 ....198 B4
Eastfield Inf Sch PE27 ....144 A4
Eastfield Rd
Peterborough PE1 ....198 C4
Royston SG8 ....5 E6
1 Wisbech PE13 ....245 E7
Eastfield Way PE13 ....245 C6
Eastfields CB6 ....242 C3
Eastgate
Great Chesterford CB10 ....18 D2
15 Market Deeping PE6 ....231 F8
Peterborough PE1 ....198 B2
Whittlesey PE7 ....189 E7
Eastgate Mews PE7 ....189 E7
Eastholm Cl PE1 ....198 C3
Eastholm Cty Sch PE1 ....198 C4
Eastleigh Rd PE1 ....198 C3
Eastmoor La PE15 ....223 A5
Easton Rd PE19 ....114 C3
Eastrea Ct PE2 ....187 E6
Eastrea Rd PE7 ....189 F7
Eastwood PE16 ....241 C3
Eastwood Ave PE15 ....243 E3
Eastwood Cl CB6 ....216 E2
Eastwood End PE15 ....223 C7
Eaton Cl Cambridge CB4 ....84 A6
Huntingdon PE29 ....142 A7
Eaton Est PE15 ....223 B7
Eaudyke Bank PE13 ....237 F7
Eayre Ct PE19 ....75 A5
Eccles Rd PE8 ....193 D8
Echo Hill SG8 ....5 C5
Echo La PE28 ....151 E3
Ecton Gr 7 PE14 ....236 A5
Eden Cres PE16 ....241 C4
Eden Rd CB9 ....24 A7
Eden St CB1 ....246 C3
Eden St Backway CB1 ....246 C2
Edendale Cl CB1 ....65 C5
Edenfield PE2 ....186 C6
Edgcote Cl PE3 ....197 C5
Edge Bank PE14 ....236 F6
Edgeborough Cl CB8 ....134 A1
Edgecombe CB4 ....83 F7
Edgerley Drain Rd PE1 ....198 F5
Edinburgh Ave
Peterborough PE4 ....204 B3
Sawston CB2 ....32 F8
Edinburgh Dr
Eaton Socon PE19 ....74 B4
St Ives PE27 ....143 F7
Wisbech PE13 ....245 C8
Edinburgh Rd
Cambridge CB4 ....84 A5
Newmarket CB8 ....110 E4
Stamford PE9 ....244 B7
Edis Way CB2 ....30 C5
Edison Dr PE7 ....181 D6
Edison Rd PE27 ....144 C6
Edith Cavell Hospl PE3 ....197 B4
Edmonds Cl PE9 ....244 D6
Edmund Cl Haverhill CB9 ....23 F7
Milton CB4 ....105 C2
Edwalton Ave PE3 ....197 E3
Edward Rd
St Neots PE19 ....74 F2
Stamford PE9 ....244 B7
Edward St CB1 ....84 A1
Edwards Way PE15 ....224 B4
Edwards Wlk PE28 ....208 E6
Edwinstowe Cl CB2 ....64 E6
Egar Way PE3 ....196 F2
Egerton Cl CB5 ....84 D4
Egerton Rd CB5 ....84 E4
Egremont Rd CB3 ....81 A3
Egremont St CB6 ....240 C5
Eight Acres PE9 ....244 A5
Eighth Ave PE13 ....245 E4
Ekin Rd CB5 ....84 D4
Ekin Wlk CB5 ....84 D3
Eland Way CB1 ....66 A7
Elbourn Way SG8 ....12 F5
Elbow La PE13 ....234 F8
Elder Cl Cambridge CB4 ....83 F6
Sawston CB2 ....32 D8
Elder Pl PE16 ....241 D4
Eldern PE2 ....186 C4
Eldernell La PE7 ....191 B8
Elder's Gate PE12 ....237 E8
Eldith Ave CB7 ....213 A1
Eldo Gdns IP28 ....213 D6
Eldo Rd IP28 ....213 D6
Eldon La IP28 ....214 B8
Elean Bsns Pk CB6 ....216 F2
Eleanor Cl PE9 ....244 A6
Elecks La SG8 ....11 D8
Elfleda Rd CB5 ....84 C3
Elford Closes CB6 ....210 E3
Elgar Way 5 PE9 ....244 A6
Elin Way SG8 ....14 B8
Eliot Rd SG8 ....5 D8
Elizabeth Ave CB8 ....110 E5
Elizabeth Ct
5 Eaton Socon PE19 ....74 C4
Hemingford Grey PE27 ....143 F1
Peterborough PE1 ....198 A5
2 Sutton CB6 ....216 E2
Elizabeth Dr PE29 ....142 B6
Elizabeth Par CB8 ....110 E5
Elizabeth Rd PE9 ....244 A6
Elizabeth Terr PE13 ....245 D4
Elizabeth Way
Bluntisham/Colne PE28 ....208 D7
Burrough Green CB8 ....70 F4
Cambridge CB4 ....83 F4
Gamlingay SG19 ....41 C6
Elizabethan Way PE28 ....140 B2
Ellesmere Rd CB4 ....83 D6
Ellindon PE3 ....197 B7
Ellindon Residential Specl Sch PE3 ....197 B7
Ellingham Ave PE15 ....243 C3
Ellington Rd PE28 ....149 E1
Elliot Ave PE3 ....196 F2
Elliott Cl CB8 ....111 A6
Elliott Rd PE15 ....243 B5
Ellis Cl CB4 ....125 D3
Ellison Cl CB4 ....83 D7
Ellison La CB3 ....81 A4
Elloe Bank
Newton PE13 ....237 B2
Tydd St Giles PE13 ....237 B5
Ellwood Ave PE2 ....187 E5
Ellwoods Cl CB7 ....213 A5
Elm CE Prim Sch PE14 ....236 B5
Elm Cl Dullingham CB8 ....70 D8
Haverhill CB9 ....23 F8
Huntingdon PE29 ....141 E7
Elm Cl *continued*
March PE15 ....243 D7
5 Market Deeping PE6 ....231 E8
Stilton PE7 ....175 F7
Witchford CB6 ....217 E2
Yaxley PE7 ....181 F7
Elm Cres PE6 ....203 D8
Elm Croft PE19 ....95 F3
Elm Ct Elmdon CB11 ....9 B4
5 Sturmer CB9 ....24 E5
Elm Dr
Little Stukeley PE28 ....151 E3
Offord Cluny PE19 ....118 A2
St Ives PE27 ....143 F6
Elm End PE28 ....150 F4
Elm High Rd PE14 ....245 E1
Elm Low Rd PE14 ....245 D2
Elm Pk PE7 ....189 E7
Elm Rd Folksworth PE7 ....175 D8
Little Stukeley PE28 ....152 A2
March PE15 ....243 D8
Wisbech PE13 ....245 D3
Elm Rd Prim Sch PE13 ....245 D4
Elm Side CB6 ....242 B5
Elm St Cambridge CB1 ....246 B3
Peterborough PE2 ....186 F7
Stamford PE9 ....244 C5
Elm Tree Cl CB3 ....79 C3
Elm Tree Dr SG8 ....12 F4
Elm Way Melbourn SG8 ....14 C5
Papworth Everard CB3 ....99 A3
Sawtry PE28 ....168 B3
Willingham CB4 ....209 A1
Elm Wlk SG8 ....5 F7
Elmdon Lee CB11 ....9 E1
Elmdon Pl CB9 ....24 B8
Elmfield CB6 ....240 C5
Elmfield Dr PE14 ....245 E1
Elmfield Rd
Cambridge CB4 ....84 A5
Peterborough PE1 ....198 A7
Elmhurst Cl CB9 ....24 B7
Elmondbury CB11 ....9 A4
Elmore Rd PE3 ....197 A3
Elm's Ave CB2 ....49 A5
Elms Cl CB2 ....32 D1
Elms Rd
Freckenham IP28 ....213 E2
Red Lodge IP28 ....213 F1
Elms The
Chatteris PE16 ....241 E4
Great Chesterford CB10 ....18 E3
Haslingfield CB3 ....47 C5
Milton CB4 ....105 C2
Elmside PE14 ....236 D5
Elsie's Way PE29 ....141 F6
Elstone PE2 ....186 A4
Elstow Cl 7 CB4 ....208 D1
Elsworth CE Prim Sch CB3 ....100 A4
Elsworth Cl PE27 ....144 C5
Elsworth Pl CB1 ....65 A6
Elsworth Rd
Boxworth CB3 ....101 A5
Conington CB3 ....100 C8
Elter Wlk PE4 ....204 E3
Elter Wr PE29 ....141 B5
Eltisley Ave CB3 ....64 C7
Eltisley Rd SG19 ....58 E6
Elton CE Prim Sch PE8 ....178 D8
Elton Hall★ PE8 ....178 D6
Elton Rd
Sibson cum Stibbington PE8 ....183 C8
Water Newton PE8 ....184 B7
Elvedon Way CB8 ....110 E5
Elwyn Ct PE15 ....243 D3
Elwyn Rd PE15 ....243 D4
Elwyndene Rd PE15 ....243 D3
Ely Cath CB7 ....240 D4
Ely Cl PE4 ....204 B3
Ely Mus★ CB7 ....240 D4
Ely Pl 16 PE13 ....245 C5
Ely Rd Downham CB6 ....218 B6
Ely CB7 ....218 D4
Landbeach CB5 ....105 F8
Littleport CB6 ....242 C2
Milton CB4 ....105 E3
Soham CB7 ....211 F7
Stretham CB6 ....210 F5
Sutton CB6 ....216 F2
Waterbeach CB5 ....126 E3
Wentworth CB6 ....217 A2
Ely St John's CP Sch CB6 ....240 A4
Ely St Mary's CE Jun Sch CB7 ....240 F6
Ely Way CB6 ....210 A7
Embankment Rd 4 PE1 ....198 A1
Embry Rd 19 PE8 ....230 B1
Emery Cl PE28 ....140 C3
Emery Pl PE19 ....74 F7
Emery Rd CB1 ....84 A1
Emery St CB1 ....84 A1
Emlyns Gdns PE9 ....244 C6
Emlyns St PE9 ....244 C6
Emmanuel Cl IP28 ....239 D5
Emmanuel Coll CB1 ....246 B2
Emmanuel Rd
Cambridge CB1 ....246 B2
Stamford PE9 ....244 B7
Emmanuel St CB1 ....246 B2
Emneth CP Sch PE14 ....236 D6
Emperor Ct 8 CB4 ....83 E8
Empingham Rd PE9 ....244 A5
Empire Theatre★ PE13 ....245 C5
Empress Swimming Pool PE16 ....241 C4
Empson Rd PE1 ....198 F5
Emson's Cl CB1 ....35 D2
Enderbys Wharf PE27 ....144 A3
Enfield 8 CB1 ....84 A2
Enfield Gdns PE3 ....197 C4
Engaine PE2 ....186 B5
Engine Rd CB7 ....211 F5
Engine Yd CB6 ....240 B4
Engleric SG8 ....8 D4
English Rd PE6 ....233 B4
English St PE1 ....197 E5
Ennerdale Cl PE29 ....141 B6
Ennerdale Rise PE4 ....204 D2
Ennion Cl CB7 ....212 B3
Ennisdale Cl 9 CB4 ....83 E7
Enniskillen Rd CB4 ....84 B5
Enterprise Way PE13 ....245 A2
Erasmus Cl CB4 ....83 D5
Erica Rd PE27 ....144 A6
Eriswell Rd
Beck Row, Holywell Row & Kenny Hill IP28 ....214 B8
Haverhill CB9 ....24 B8
Ermine Bsns Ctr PE29 ....141 B8
Ermine Bsns Pk PE29 ....141 B8
Ermine Cl March PE15 ....243 C2
Royston SG8 ....5 D8
Ermine Cres PE7 ....176 A7
Ermine Ct PE29 ....141 C5
Ermine St Caxton CB3 ....78 E2
Huntingdon PE29 ....141 C5
Little Stukeley PE28 ....151 F2
The Stukeleys PE28 ....141 A8
Ermine St N CB3 ....99 A4
Ermine St S CB3 ....78 C8
Ermine Way
Arrington SG8 ....44 C4
Sawtry PE28 ....168 C3
Erratts Hill CB8 ....73 D1
Eskdale Cl 1 PE4 ....204 E3
Essendyke PE3 ....197 A7
Essex Cl CB4 ....83 E5
Essex Hill CB11 ....9 B2
Essex Rd
Huntingdon PE29 ....141 E8
5 Stamford PE9 ....244 B6
Estelle Cl PE26 ....220 D2
Estover Rd PE15 ....243 E6
Etheldreda St CB6 ....240 B4
Eurocentre Sch CB2 ....64 F7
Europa Way PE13 ....245 B2
Euston St PE29 ....141 E4
Euximoor Dro PE14 ....229 B5
Evans Cl
Brampton PE28 ....140 D3
Royston SG8 ....5 D7
Evans Way CB2 ....32 E8
Evelyn Hospl The CB2 ....64 E6
Ever Gn CB8 ....55 F6
Everdon Way PE3 ....197 C5
Evergreen La CB8 ....55 F7
Evergreens CB4 ....84 B5
Everingham PE2 ....185 D5
Eversden Church Sch CB3 ....46 A7
Eversden Cl CB3 ....61 D5
Eversden Rd CB3 ....46 C5
Eversley Cl CB4 ....125 D4
Everton Hill SG19 ....40 B3
Everton Lower Sch SG19 ....40 D3
Everton Rd
Gamlingay Great Heath SG19 ....40 E3
Sandy SG19 ....40 B1
Eves Cl PE6 ....207 D1
Ewingswood 1 PE28 ....168 C2
Exchange Sq PE13 ....245 B5
Exchange St PE1 ....198 A2
Exeter Cl Cambridge CB2 ....64 D1
2 Market Deeping PE6 ....231 F8
Exeter Ct 10 CB9 ....23 E6
Exeter Rd
Newmarket CB8 ....111 A4
Peterborough PE1 ....197 F6
7 Wittering PE8 ....230 B1
Exmoor Cl PE29 ....141 A4
Exning CP Sch CB8 ....110 B8
Exning Rd CB8 ....110 D6
Eye Gn Ind Est PE6 ....232 A2
Eye Gn Nature Reserve★ PE6 ....232 B2
Eye Hill Dro CB7 ....211 F7
Eye Prim Sch PE6 ....232 B1
Eye Rd PE1 ....198 E7
Eyebury Rd PE6 ....199 A6
Eyeworth Rd SG19 ....25 B2
Eynesbury CE Prim Sch PE19 ....74 E4
Eynesbury Gn PE19 ....74 F4
Eynesford Cl PE7 ....188 A5
Eyrescroft PE3 ....197 A7
Eyrescroft Prim Sch PE3 ....197 A7
Eyresford Cl PE7 ....188 A5

F

Faber La PE8 ....183 D1
Fair Ct CB1 ....246 C3
Fair Gn The CB5 ....129 D1
Fair St CB1 ....246 C3
Fairacre CB10 ....18 C3
Fairbairn Rd CB4 ....84 C5
Fairchild Way PE1 ....198 A7
Fairey Ave PE29 ....141 F1
Fairey Fox Dr 1 IP28 ....239 B5
Fairfax Ct Ely CB6 ....240 C4
St Neots PE19 ....74 F3
Fairfax Rd CB1 ....84 B1
Fairfax Way
March PE15 ....243 E1
10 Market Deeping PE6 ....231 F8
Fairfield Gamlingay SG19 ....41 C5
5 Sutton CB6 ....216 E1
Fairfield Dr PE26 ....172 A6
Fairfield Rd PE2 ....187 A8
Fairfield Way CB1 ....35 D3
Fairfields St Ives PE27 ....144 B4
Sawston CB2 ....50 A1
Fairfields Cres PE27 ....144 B4
Fairhaven Cl CB5 ....107 C2
Fairhaven Way CB8 ....110 E5
Fairlawns CB8 ....110 F2
Fairlawns Rd CB8 ....110 F2
Fairmead Way PE3 ....197 E2
Fairstead House Sch CB8 ....111 B4
Fairview Ave PE16 ....241 B2
Fairview Dr PE16 ....241 B2
Fairview Gr CB5 ....108 E5
Fairway Chatteris PE16 ....241 B3
Girton CB3 ....103 E2
Fairway The
Bar Hill CB3 ....102 D3
Bluntisham/Colne PE28 ....208 C6
Falcon Cl Haverhill CB9 ....24 C8
5 St Neots PE19 ....75 B7
Falcon Dr PE29 ....142 B7
Falcon La
4 Whittlesey PE7 ....189 D6
15 Wisbech PE13 ....245 C5
Falcon Mews CB6 ....240 B5
Falcon Rd 7 PE13 ....245 C5
Falcon Way
Buckden PE19 ....117 B3
Peterborough PE7 ....186 C1
Falconer Rd CB9 ....24 C5
Falklands Dr PE13 ....245 E3
Falklands Rd CB9 ....39 A1
Falkner Rd CB2 ....33 A8
Fallodan Rd PE2 ....185 C3
Fallow Cnr Dro PE15 ....224 A3
Fallow Dr PE19 ....74 B5
Fallowfield
Cambridge CB4 ....84 B5
Peterborough PE2 ....185 D5
Fallowfield Ct 8 CB9 ....23 E7
Fall's Dro PE6 ....232 F7
Falmouth Ave CB8 ....110 F3
Falmouth Gdns CB8 ....111 A6
Falmouth St CB8 ....110 F3
Falstaff Rd PE19 ....74 C3
Fane Cl PE9 ....244 B7
Fane Rd PE4 ....197 E8
Fanshawe Rd CB1 ....65 A6
Far Pasture PE4 ....204 B5
Faraday Cl PE7 ....181 D6
Farcet CE Prim Sch PE7 ....187 C2
Farcet Cl 5 PE19 ....74 C6
Fardell Rd 6 PE13 ....245 C4
Fardell's La CB3 ....100 A4
Farendon Rd PE28 ....140 E1
Farfield Cl PE28 ....168 A5
Farleigh Fields PE2 ....185 D7
Farm Cl
Abbots Ripton PE28 ....162 C1
Ramsey PE26 ....171 C3
Sawtry PE28 ....168 B4
Farm La
Papworth Everard CB3 ....99 C2
Thriplow SG8 ....31 B1
Farm Rise CB2 ....32 C5
Farm View PE5 ....195 E2
Farmer's End CB3 ....61 E5
Farmer's Row CB1 ....66 E4
Farmland Mus★ CB5 ....127 A5
Farmstead Cl CB4 ....104 B5
Farrier Ct SG8 ....5 C7
Farriers Ct PE2 ....186 D7
Farriers Gate PE16 ....241 D5
Farriers Way PE28 ....164 F5
Farringdon Cl PE1 ....198 D6
Farringford Cl 4 CB4 ....83 C6
Farthing Dro PE38 ....226 D6
Farthing La PE27 ....144 B4
Fassage Cl CB5 ....107 C2
Fastnet Cl CB9 ....24 D8
Faulkner Cl CB4 ....105 C2
Fawcett Prim Sch CB2 ....64 D3
Fawsley Garth PE3 ....197 C6
Fayway NN14 ....156 F2
Fazeley CB1 ....246 C2
Feast Cl CB7 ....212 E1
Feilden Way CB8 ....110 E5
Felbrigg Wlk PE2 ....187 F6
Feldale Pl PE7 ....189 F8
Fellowes Dr PE26 ....172 A6
Fellowes Gdns PE2 ....187 A7
Fellowes Rd PE2 ....187 A7
Felsham Chase CB5 ....130 C2
Felsted Ave PE13 ....245 E5
Felton St CB1 ....65 A8
Felton Way CB7 ....240 E6
Feltons CB7 ....212 E1
Feltwell Pl 1 CB9 ....24 B8
Fen Bank Rd CB7 ....213 A6
Fen Cl PE13 ....245 E6
Fen Cswy★ PE7 ....189 A8
Fen Cswy The CB3 ....246 A1

Fen Ditton CP Sch CB5 .84 F5
Fen Drayton Nature Reserve★ CB4 .121 F7
Fen Drayton Prim Sch CB4 .121 F6
Fen Drayton Rd CB4 .122 C5
Fen Dro PE7 .176 C8
Fen End Over CB4 .208 D1
Willingham CB4 .209 A1
Fen La Sawtry PE28 .168 C3
Stilton PE7 .176 C8
Swaffham Bulbeck CB5 .108 A4
Tydd St Giles PE13 .237 B5
Fen Rd
Bassingbourn cum Kneesworth SG8 .12 B7
Little Wilbraham CB1 .86 D2
Lode CB5 .107 B4
Milton CB4 .84 D6
Newton PE13 .237 E4
Pidley cum Fenton PE28 .165 E1
Shingay cum Wendy SG8 .26 F1
Wisbech St Mary PE13 .234 E2
Fen Side
Haddenham CB6 .209 E4
Wicken CB7 .211 D3
Fen St PE7 .176 A7
Fen The PE28 .121 B6
Fen View
Chatteris PE16 .241 B3
Christchurch PE14 .229 D3
6 Doddington/Wimblington PE15 .222 F5
Peterborough PE2 .187 F6
Fen Way 3 PE14 .236 A5
Fenbridge Rd PE4 .204 C4
Fendon Cl CB1 .65 B3
Fendon Rd CB1 .65 B3
Fendyke La PE13 .237 F1
Fendyke Rd PE14 .236 E5
Fengate PE1 .198 D1
Fengate Cl 1 PE1 .198 B2
Fengate Mobile Home Pk PE1 .198 D1
Fengate Rd PE14 .238 F1
Fengate Trad Est PE1 .198 D2
Fenhall Field PE13 .237 C1
Fenland & W Norfolk Aviation Mus★ PE14 .238 F3
Fenland Cl 3 PE15 .223 B7
Fenland Rd PE13 .245 E6
Fenland Way PE16 .241 B5
Fenland Wlk PE15 .243 D4
Fenleigh Cl CB5 .106 B8
Fennec Cl CB1 .66 B6
Fennels Cl CB9 .24 A7
Fenners Lawn CB1 .246 C1
Fenny La SG8 .29 A1
Fenside Dr PE6 .207 C1
Fenside Rd PE28 .165 D8
Fenstanton & Hilton Prim Sch PE28 .121 C6
Fenton Hill PE28 .165 C3
Fenton Rd Haverhill CB9 .24 B8
Warboys PE28 .165 A4
Feoffees Rd 5 PE28 .208 C8
Fern Gr CB9 .23 E8
Ferndale Teversham CB1 .66 C8
Yaxley PE7 .181 D6
Ferndale Cl CB8 .111 B5
Ferndale Rise CB5 .84 C4
Ferndale Way PE1 .205 B1
Ferndown Dr PE29 .118 F8
Fernie Cl PE6 .205 D8
Fernlea Cl CB1 .65 F7
Ferrars Ave PE19 .74 E4
Ferrars Ct 4 PE29 .141 D4
Ferrars Rd PE29 .141 D5
Ferrars Way CB4 .83 D6
Ferriman Rd PE28 .137 F6
Ferry Bank PE38 .226 D8
Ferry Cutter La CB4 .246 C4
Ferry Dr PE6 .196 D3
Ferry Hill Castor PE5 .196 B1
Chatteris PE16 .215 E6
Ferry La
Beck Row, Holywell Row & Kenny Hill IP28 .213 D5
Cambridge CB4 .84 B4
Newton PE13 .238 B5
Ferry Mdw PE27 .208 A1
Ferry Mdws Ctry Pk★ PE2 .185 D8
Ferry Path CB1 .246 B4
Ferry Way CB6 .242 D4
Ferryview PE2 .185 E6
Festival Cl PE15 .224 C4
Festival Ct PE3 .197 B5
Festival Rd CB7 .213 A5
Festival Way CB6 .226 B6
Fews Cl 4 PE27 .208 A3
Field Ave PE13 .237 F7
Field Baulk PE15 .243 D2
Field Bell PE28 .140 F3
Field Cl Abbotsley PE19 .57 A6
Alconbury PE28 .150 F5
Buckden PE19 .117 B4
Grafham PE28 .116 A7
Linton CB1 .35 B2
Little Paxton PE19 .95 F2
Warboys PE28 .164 F5
Field Cottage Rd PE19 .74 C3
Field Cres SG8 .5 F7
Field End Balsham CB1 .53 B2
Witchford CB6 .217 D2
Field Farm Cotts CB10 .18 F7
Field Gate CB6 .216 D2
Field La CB5 .84 E6
Field Rd Kingston CB3 .61 B3
Mildenhall IP28 .239 C5
Ramsey PE26 .172 A7
Field Rise PE7 .181 D5
Field Row CB3 .61 B3
Field Terr PE7 .187 C2
Field Terr Rd CB8 .110 F5
Field View Bar Hill CB3 .102 B2
Harston CB2 .48 A4
Field Way CB1 .65 C3
Field Wlk
Mildenhall IP28 .239 C5
Peterborough PE1 .198 B2
Fielden Way CB8 .110 E5
Fieldfare Dr PE2 .187 E6
Fieldfare Way 10 SG8 .5 E8
Fielding Ct 2 PE19 .74 C6
Fielding Pl PE19 .97 F4
Fields End Cl PE7 .186 D3
Fieldside Ely CB6 .240 B4
Stretham CB6 .210 E5
Whittlesey PE7 .190 F8
Fifth Ave PE13 .245 E4
Fifty Dro CB6 .225 C7
Fifty Rd
Christchurch PE14 .229 D1
Manea PE14 .224 D7
Figtree Wlk PE1 .198 B8
Fillance The SG8 .12 D5
Finch Rd CB4 .83 D5
Fincham Rd IP28 .239 B5
Fincham's Cl CB1 .35 D2
Finchfield PE1 .198 F7
Finchley Ave IP28 .239 B6
Finchley Gn PE3 .197 E4
Finch's Cl CB2 .49 C5
Finch's Field CB3 .46 A7
Finch's Rd CB3 .46 A7
Finkle La PE7 .189 D7
Firdale Cl PE6 .206 C2
Firelots Dro PE15 .223 C8
Firs The CB2 .32 D2
First Ave Warboys PE28 .164 E6
Wisbech PE13 .245 D5
First Broadpool Dro PE28 .165 E8
First Drift PE9 .244 B2
First Dro Burwell CB5 .130 C7
Peterborough PE1 .198 D7
First Furlong Dro PE16 .241 A3
First Marsh Rd PE14 .238 D2
First Turf Fen Dro PE28 .165 B8
Fish Hill SG8 .5 D6
Fisher Cl Duxford CB2 .17 E8
Haverhill CB9 .24 D7
Ramsey St Mary's PE26 .220 D2
Fisher St CB4 .246 A4
Fisher's La
Cambridge CB1 .65 F6
Orwell SG8 .45 D2
Fishermans Cl PE26 .171 B1
Fishermans Dr PE15 .243 A5
Fishers Bank CB6 .242 E3
Fishers Cl PE7 .175 F7
Fishers Way PE29 .118 F8
Fishers Yd 4 PE19 .74 E5
Fison Rd CB5 .84 E4
Fitton End Rd PE13 .237 F3
Fitzgerald Cl CB6 .240 E8
Fitzroy Ct CB1 .246 C3
Fitzroy La CB5 .246 C3
Fitzroy St
Cambridge CB1 .246 C3
Newmarket CB8 .111 A3
Fitzwilliam Coll CB3 .83 B4
Fitzwilliam Hospl PE6 .196 E2
Fitzwilliam Mus The★ CB2 .246 A1
Fitzwilliam Rd
Cambridge CB2 .64 F6
Stamford PE9 .244 A7
Fitzwilliam St
Cambridge CB2 .246 B1
Peterborough PE1 .198 A3
Five Arches PE2 .185 C6
Five Arches Pit Nature Reserve★ PE28 .169 C2
Five Hundred Dro PE15 .224 A4
Fiveways IP28 .239 F2
Flackdale Rd PE28 .120 B1
Flag Bsns Exchange PE1 .198 E3
Flag Fen Rd PE1 .198 C4
Flaggrass Hill Rd PE15 .243 E8
Flambards Cl SG8 .14 B8
Flamborough Cl PE2 .197 E1
Flamsteed Dr PE29 .140 F5
Flamsteed Rd CB1 .65 A6
Flat Rd CB4 .209 B3
Flat The CB8 .111 F7
Flatford Rd CB9 .23 C8
Flavian Cl CB9 .24 D7
Flawn Way PE19 .74 D2
Flaxfields CB1 .35 C3
Flaxland PE3 .197 A6
Fleam Dyke Cotts CB1 .67 C2
Flecks La
Shingay cum Wendy SG8 .26 D1
Steeple Morden SG8 .11 D8
Fleet Cl CB6 .242 D4
Fleet The SG8 .5 C6
Fleet Way PE2 .187 B6
Fleetwood CB6 .240 C5
Fleetwood Cl PE15 .243 D2
Flegcroft PE7 .189 F1
Fleming Ave IP28 .239 C5
Fleming Ct PE15 .243 F3
Fletcher Ave CB5 .127 C1
Fletcher's Terr 3 CB1 .65 A8
Fletchers Cl PE26 .172 A7
Fletton Ave PE2 .187 A8
Fletton Fields PE2 .187 A7
Fletton Parkway PE2 .185 F2
Flint Ct PE28 .140 C2
Flint House Rd PE14 .229 F5
Flint La CB5 .126 E3
Flint Way Elm PE14 .236 A4
St Neots PE19 .74 E2
Flood's Ferry PE15 .222 A8
Flood's Ferry Rd PE15 .222 B7
Flore Cl PE3 .197 C5
Florence Cl PE7 .189 F6
Florida Ave PE29 .141 F8
Flower St 2 CB1 .84 A1
Flowers Cl PE26 .172 A7
Flowmere Rd SG8 .8 A5
Fodder Fen Dro CB7 .219 B3
Fodder Fen Rd PE15 .224 C6
Fodderfen Dro
Beck Row, Holywell Row & Kenny Hill IP28 .219 F1
Wicken CB7 .211 C3
Fold La PE13 .237 F7
Fold The PE7 .190 F8
Folgate La PE14 .238 F6
Folk Mus★ CB1 .246 A4
Folksworth CE Prim Sch PE7 .175 D8
Folksworth Rd PE7 .180 E1
Folly Cl PE7 .181 C5
Folly Dro CB7 .219 A7
Folly Rd IP28 .239 B6
Folly's Dro PE13 .234 F3
Fontwell Ave CB4 .83 C5
Fontwell Gdns 2 PE9 .244 B5
Foot Dro PE26 .220 F1
Footpath The CB3 .82 C2
Ford Cl
Beck Row, Holywell Row & Kenny Hill IP28 .213 D7
Eaton Socon PE19 .74 D5
Yaxley PE7 .181 C6
Ford End
Alconbury PE28 .150 F4
Hail Weston PE19 .95 B1
Fordham Abbey★ CB7 .131 E8
Fordham CE Prim Sch CB7 .212 F1
Fordham Cl SG7 .2 D5
Fordham Moor CB7 .212 E3
Fordham Rd
Exning CB8 .131 E3
Freckenham IP28 .213 B2
Isleham CB7 .213 A4
Newmarket CB8 .110 F8
5 Royston SG8 .5 E5
Snailwell CB8 .132 A5
5 Soham CB7 .212 B3
Fordham Way SG8 .14 D5
Fordwich Cl 1 CB4 .83 D6
Fore Hill CB7 .240 D4
Foreman's Rd SG8 .31 B2
Forest End CB8 .134 A6
Forest Glade CB9 .38 F2
Forest Rd CB1 .65 E5
Forest Way IP28 .239 E4
Forge Cl PE19 .74 B2
Forge End
Great Shelford CB2 .49 C4
Peterborough PE7 .185 A4
Forge Way PE28 .164 F5
Forster Rd PE28 .140 E1
Forsythia Rd PE27 .144 A6
Fortescue Rd CB4 .83 E6
Forties Cl CB9 .24 D8
Fortune Way SG8 .12 E5
Forty Acre Rd PE1 .198 D2
Forty Foot Bank
Doddington PE26 .222 C3
Ramsey PE26 .221 E2
Ramsey Forty Foot PE26 .221 C3
Forum Ct 7 CB4 .83 E7
Foster Ct PE29 .141 F7
Foster Rd
Cambridge CB2 .64 D2
Peterborough PE2 .186 D8
Foster Way CB3 .79 B3
Foul Anchor PE13 .238 D8
Foundry Cl CB4 .125 D3
Foundry Rd PE9 .244 A5
Foundry Way
Eaton Socon PE19 .74 B1
March PE15 .228 B6
Ramsey PE26 .172 A5
Foundry Wlk PE27 .144 A3
Fountain La
Haslingfield CB3 .47 B5
Soham CB7 .212 B4
Fountains Pl PE6 .232 B1
Four Acres
Fenstanton PE28 .121 C6
Great Chesterford CB10 .18 D3
Four Gotes PE13 .238 C7
Four Went Ways CB1 .51 A1
Fourfields Prim Sch PE7 .181 E6
Fourth Ave PE13 .245 E4
Fourth Dro
Downham CB6 .225 A1
Peterborough PE1 .198 F3
Fowlmere Nature Reserve★ SG8 .15 B8
Fowlmere Prim Sch SG8 .15 D8
Fowlmere Rd
Foxton SG8 .30 D3
Heydon SG8 .7 F8
Newton CB2 .31 B6
Shepreth SG8 .29 F4
Thriplow SG8 .31 A2
Fox Cl PE19 .75 A5
Fox Cnr SG8 .10 F5
Fox Covert PE7 .175 F7
Fox Gn CB8 .55 F7
Fox Gr PE29 .141 F2
Fox Hill SG8 .11 A5
Fox Hill Rd SG8 .10 F5
Fox Hollow CB3 .102 C4
Fox Rd Balsham CB1 .52 F3
Bourn CB3 .60 D5
Catworth PE28 .136 D8
Fox St SG19 .58 E5
Fox Wood N 4 CB7 .212 B5
Fox Wood S CB7 .212 B4
Foxburrow Cl CB9 .38 F1
Foxcovert Rd
Peakirk PE6 .204 A8
Werrington PE4 .204 B4
Peterborough PE4 .204 A7
Foxdale PE1 .197 F7
Foxenfields PE28 .162 C1
Foxglove Bank SG8 .5 F5
Foxglove Cl 3 PE19 .74 C5
Foxglove Way PE26 .220 D3
Foxley Cl PE4 .204 C4
Fox's Cl CB4 .105 D2
Fox's Way CB3 .62 D6
Foxton Prim Sch CB2 .30 C5
Foxton Rd
Barrington CB2 .29 F8
Foxton CB2 .30 A7
Foxton Sta CB2 .30 C6
Foxtrot La PE28 .151 F3
Framlingham Rd PE7 .187 F5
Francis Cl CB9 .23 F8
Francis Darwin Ct CB4 .83 C5
Francis Gdns PE1 .197 F8
Francis Pas 3 CB2 .64 E7
Frank Bridges Cl 2 CB7 .212 B3
Frank Perkins Parkway PE2 .187 B8
Frank Perkins Way PE1 .198 D4
Frankland Wlk CB7 .240 F6
Franklin Cres PE1 .198 E6
Franklin Gdns CB4 .125 D4
Frank's La CB4 .84 B5
Franks La PE13 .237 F5
Fraser Dr PE27 .144 A7
Fraser Rd CB4 .84 A6
Fraserburgh Way 2 PE2 .185 C4
Freckenham Rd IP28 .213 E3
Fred Archer Way CB8 .111 A3
Fred Dannatt Rd IP28 .239 A6
Frederick Talbot Cl 8 CB7 .212 B4
Free Church Pas PE27 .144 A3
Free Sch La CB2 .246 A2
Freedom Bridge PE13 .245 B6
Freeman Cl 10 PE8 .230 B1
Freemantle Ct 5 PE19 .74 B3
Freesia Way PE7 .181 F6
Freewood La CB11 .9 B3
French Dro PE6 .232 E7
French's Rd
Cambridge CB4 .83 D4
Walpole PE14 .238 F8
Freshfields CB8 .110 F4
Freston PE4 .204 F2
Friar Cl CB9 .38 F1
Friar's Cl CB1 .65 F5
Friar's Pl CB6 .242 C5
Friar's Way CB6 .242 C5
Friars Nine CB6 .242 C4
Friday Bridge Prim Sch PE14 .236 A3
Friday St IP28 .213 D6
Fridaybridge Rd PE14 .236 A4
Friends Cl PE19 .98 C2
Frinton Way 4 PE13 .245 E5
Fritton Ct 7 CB9 .23 E6
Frobisher Cl PE29 .141 F6
Frog End
Great Wilbraham CB1 .67 F7
Haslingfield CB3 .47 A6
Little Wilbraham CB1 .86 C2
Shepreth SG8 .29 F2
Frogge St CB10 .18 B3
Frogmore CB8 .110 B7
Frogs Abbey CB6 .217 E4
Frogs Abbey La PE15 .223 B7
Frogs Hall PE28 .208 C5
Froize End CB6 .210 A5
Froment Way CB4 .105 C3
Fromont Cl CB1 .66 E4
Front Rd Murrow PE13 .234 D6
Tydd St Giles PE13 .238 D8
Frowd Cl CB7 .212 E1
Frumetty La PE28 .150 F4
Fryers Callis PE9 .244 C3
Fryth Cl CB9 .39 A1
Fulbourn Hospl
Cambridge CB2 .65 B3
Fulbourn CB1 .66 C5
Fulbourn Nature Reserve★ CB1 .67 B4
Fulbourn Old Drift CB1 .66 A6
Fulbourn Prim Sch CB1 .66 F5
Fulbourn Rd
Cambridge CB1 .65 F5
Fulbourn CB1 .66 D7
Fulbridge Prim Sch PE1 .197 F7
Fulbridge Rd PE1 .197 F8
Fulbrooke Rd CB3 .64 A7
Fulham Rd PE3 .197 E4
Fullards Cl PE29 .155 B4
Fuller Cl PE28 .137 F6
Fuller's La 5 PE15 .223 B7
Fundrey Rd PE13 .245 F6
Funtham's La PE7 .188 D7
Furlong Way CB3 .80 B1
Furlongs The PE27 .208 A2
Furrells The CB1 .35 C3
Furrowfields Rd PE16 .241 C5
Furrows The PE27 .144 A4
Furtherford CB4 .208 E1
Furze Gr SG8 .5 E5
Furze Ride PE1 .198 B8
Fydell Ct PE19 .75 B7

G

Gables Cl SG8 .29 A1
Gables The PE28 .121 A5
Gadd's La PE13 .235 D8
Gage Cl SG8 .5 D8
Gains La PE28 .166 D2
Gainsborough Ave 6 PE19 .74 C5
Gainsborough Cl CB4 .84 B6
Gainsborough Dr PE27 .144 A7
Gainsborough Rd CB9 .38 D1
Gala Cl PE7 .176 A8
Galfrid Rd CB5 .84 D2
Gallery The CB7 .240 D4
Gallions Cl PE4 .204 D1
Gallows Hill (Tumulus)★ SG7 .3 E1
Gall's Dro PE13 .235 A4
Gamlingay Cinques Nature Rerserve★ SG19 .41 A7
Gamlingay Fst Sch SG19 .41 D5
Gamlingay Mdws Nature Reserve★ SG19 .41 A4
Gamlingay Rd
Gamlingay SG19 .41 D8
Potton SG19 .41 C1
Waresley SG19 .57 E1
Gamlingay Village Coll SG19 .41 E5
Gamlingay Wood Nature Reserve★ SG19 .41 E8
Gamsey Wood Nature Reserve★ PE28 .162 A8
Gannet Cl CB9 .24 C8
Gannocks Cl PE2 .185 F5
Gannocks The PE2 .185 F5
Ganwick Cl CB9 .38 F2
Gaol St 12 PE13 .245 C4
Garden Cl Royston SG8 .5 E7
St Ives PE27 .144 A6
Sutton CB6 .216 E1
Garden Ct Burwell CB5 .130 C4
Ramsey PE26 .172 A4
Garden End SG8 .14 D5
Garden End Rd PE1 .198 B6
Garden Fields CB2 .48 E3
Garden La Royston SG8 .5 D5
Wisbech St Mary PE13 .235 A7
Garden Rd PE1 .198 A6
Garden Wlk
Cambridge CB4 .83 D4
Histon CB4 .104 C5
Royston SG8 .5 E7
Gardeners La 7 CB7 .212 B4
Gardens The PE15 .243 A6
Gardiners La SG7 .2 D4
Garlic Row CB5 .84 B3
Garner Ave PE28 .164 E5
Garner Cl CB4 .105 C3
Garner Ct PE29 .141 F7
Garratt Rd 4 PE9 .244 B4
Garret Hostel La CB2 .246 A2
Garrick Wlk PE2 .187 B7
Garry Dr CB4 .84 A7
Garton St PE1 .198 A5
Gas La Ely CB7 .240 D3
Stamford PE9 .244 C5
Thorney PE6 .233 A3
Gas Rd PE15 .243 D3
Gas St PE9 .244 C5
Gascoigne PE6 .203 F5
Gatenby PE4 .204 C4
Gateways CB8 .90 F6
Gaul Rd PE15 .243 B4
Gault Bank PE15 .227 D1
Gaultree Sq PE14 .236 D6
Gavel St PE7 .181 C8
Gayton Cl 3 CB2 .64 D3
Gayton Ct PE3 .197 C5
Gazeley Gdns PE7 .187 B2
Gazeley Rd Ashley CB8 .92 A8
Cambridge CB2 .64 D4
Kentford CB8 .134 C1
Moulton CB8 .112 F6
Gazelle Cl 4 PE19 .74 B5
Gazelle Way CB1 .66 B7

Geneva St PE1 ...198 A3
Geoffrey Bishop Ave CB1 ...67 A4
George Campbell Leisure Ctr PE15 ...243 C4
George Gibson Cl CB8 ...110 C8
George IV St CB2 ...246 C4
George La
  Buckden PE19 ...117 A4
  Royston SG8 ...5 D5
  Warboys PE28 ...164 E5
George Lambton Ave CB8 ...110 F6
George Nuttall Cl CB4 ...84 A6
George Pateman Ct 2 CB1 ...64 F7
George Pl 7 PE19 ...74 F2
George St
  Cambridge CB4 ...83 F4
  Huntingdon PE29 ...141 D4
  March PE15 ...243 D4
  Peterborough PE2 ...186 F4
  Stilton PE7 ...175 F8
  Willingham CB4 ...209 A1
Georgian Ct PE3 ...197 E2
Gerard Cl CB8 ...84 C2
Gerard Rd CB5 ...84 D3
Gery Ct PE19 ...74 C5
Giant's Hill★ CB4 ...125 A5
Gibralter La CB2 ...122 E5
Gibside Ave PE16 ...241 B3
Gibson Cl CB5 ...106 A7
Gidding Gr PE28 ...166 B1
Gidding Rd PE28 ...167 D3
Giddings Cl PE2 ...185 F4
Gifford Pl CB2 ...246 A3
Gifford's Cl CB8 ...82 E8
Giffords Way 4 CB4 ...208 C4
Gilbert Cl CB4 ...83 C5
Gilbert Rd
  Cambridge CB4 ...83 D5
  Littleport CB6 ...242 B5
Gilbert Scott Dr CB6 ...240 E7
Gildale PE4 ...204 D4
Gildenburgh Ave PE1 ...198 D5
Gill's Hill CB3 ...60 D5
Gilmerton Ct CB2 ...64 D4
Gilmorton Dr PE1 ...198 D7
Gilpin St PE1 ...197 E6
Gilvan Cl PE19 ...95 E1
Gimber Ct 5 PE29 ...141 F7
Gimbert Rd CB7 ...212 B5
Gimbert Sq PE15 ...243 E4
Gipping Cl 4 CB9 ...23 E6
Gipsey Cnr PE19 ...56 C5
Gipson Cl PE16 ...241 B5
Gipsy Dro PE16 ...215 F6
Gipsy La PE15 ...243 A7
Girton Cl
  Mildenhall IP28 ...239 C1
  Woodditton CB8 ...111 B1
Girton Coll CB3 ...83 B2
Girton Cres PE29 ...142 A7
Girton Glebe Prim Sch CB3 ...103 E1
Girton Rd Girton CB3 ...82 F7
  Haverhill CB9 ...24 B1
Girton Way PE9 ...244 A7
Gisborne Rd CB1 ...65 C6
Gladeside CB3 ...102 C4
Gladstone Pk Com Recn Ctr PE1 ...197 F5
Gladstone Prim Sch PE1 ...197 F5
Gladstone St PE1 ...197 F3
Gladstone Way CB1 ...65 F5
Glamis Cl CB9 ...23 D8
Glamis Gdns PE1 ...197 B2
Glassmoor Bank PE7 ...220 F7
Glastonbury Cl 11 PE6 ...232 A1
Glatton Dr PE2 ...187 D6
Glatton La PE7 ...176 D3
Glatton Rd PE28 ...168 A6
Glatton Ways PE28 ...175 F1
Glebe Ave PE15 ...185 E4
Glebe Cl
  Chatteris PE16 ...241 D5
  Gorefield PE13 ...237 E3
  Great Paxton PE19 ...96 E4
  Toft CB3 ...61 E5
  Wimblington PE15 ...224 B4
Glebe Cres CB2 ...33 B4
Glebe Ct PE2 ...187 A8
Glebe Gdns 2 PE6 ...232 B8
Glebe La Buckden PE19 ...117 A3
  Cambourne CB3 ...79 C4
Glebe Rd Barrington CB2 ...29 F8
  Brampton PE28 ...140 E2
  Cambridge CB1 ...65 B4
  Hemingford Grey PE28 ...143 D1
  Huntingdon PE29 ...141 D7
  Perry PE28 ...115 D3
  Peterborough PE2 ...187 A8
  Sawtry PE28 ...168 A4
  Stilton PE7 ...176 A7
  Waterbeach CB5 ...106 A7
Glebe The Haverhill CB9 ...39 A1
  Ramsey PE26 ...172 B4
Glebe Way
  Haddenham CB6 ...209 F6
  Histon CB4 ...104 C4

Glebelands Prim Sch PE16 ...241 D5
Glemsford Pl 2 CB9 ...24 B8
Glemsford Rise PE2 ...186 C7
Glen Cres PE9 ...244 C2
Glen Rd 1 PE8 ...230 B1
Glen The PE7 ...187 B7
Glenacre Cl 3 CB1 ...65 E5
Glencoe Way PE2 ...185 D3
Glendale PE2 ...185 D6
Gleneagles PE2 ...185 E5
Glenfields PE2 ...189 C8
Glenmere Cl CB1 ...65 D5
Glenton St PE1 ...198 C2
Glenville Cl CB1 ...85 B1
Glinton Rd
  Helpston PE6 ...203 A8
  Newborough PE6 ...204 E8
Glisson Rd CB1 ...246 C1
Global Ctr Ind Est PE1 ...198 E4
Globe La
  Alconbury PE28 ...150 E3
  Littleport 3 CB6 ...242 D4
Gloucester Ct PE13 ...245 D4
Gloucester Rd
  Brampton PE28 ...140 D1
  Haverhill CB9 ...23 F7
  Peterborough PE2 ...187 B7
  Sawtry PE28 ...168 C3
  Stamford 7 PE9 ...244 B6
  Wyton Airfield PE28 ...143 B8
Glover Cl CB2 ...32 F6
Glover St CB4 ...208 D1
Goddard Cres 1 PE13 ...245 D7
Godeby Cl 4 PE29 ...141 F8
Godesdone Rd CB5 ...84 A3
Godfrey Cl PE6 ...207 D1
Goding Way CB4 ...105 E2
Godmanchester Com Swimming Pool PE29 ...141 E2
Godmanchester Prim Sch PE29 ...141 F2
Godric Sq PE2 ...186 D6
Godsey La 2 PE6 ...231 E8
Godwin Cl CB1 ...65 C4
Godwin Rd PE13 ...245 D7
Godwin Way CB1 ...65 C4
Godwit PE7 ...201 A1
Goffers Knoll (Tumulus)★ SG8 ...14 E1
Goffsmill PE3 ...197 A4
Gog Magog Way CB2 ...49 C5
Gold St PE15 ...243 C7
Goldcrest Cl 3 CB3 ...79 C3
Golden Drop PE6 ...231 C4
Golden Miller Cl CB8 ...110 D7
Golden Road 8 PE29 ...118 F8
Goldhay Way PE2 ...185 F2
Goldie La PE2 ...185 F6
Golding Pl 15 PE13 ...245 C4
Golding Rd CB1 ...65 B6
Goldings Cl CB9 ...39 A2
Goldpits PE28 ...164 F5
Golf La PE28 ...151 F3
Golf Links Rd
  Barton Mills IP28 ...214 A3
  Worlington IP28 ...239 A1
Gonville & Caius Coll CB2 ...246 B1
Gonville Cl IP28 ...239 D6
Gonville Pl CB1 ...246 C1
Goochgate PE12 ...237 D3
Goodacre PE2 ...186 A4
Goodchilds Gdns 5 CB7 ...213 A5
Goode Cl CB4 ...125 D4
Goodens La PE13 ...238 A5
Goodliffe Ave CB1 ...53 C2
Goodwin Gr CB7 ...240 F7
Goodwin Wlk PE4 ...204 C4
Goodwood Rd
  Peterborough PE3 ...196 F3
  Royston SG8 ...5 F6
Goose Cross CB3 ...80 B1
Goose Fen Dro CB7 ...211 C6
Gordon Ave
  March PE15 ...243 D4
  Peterborough PE2 ...186 E7
Gordon Cl PE19 ...95 F1
Gordon Ct PE13 ...245 C3
Gordon Fendick Sch PE13 ...245 D8
Gordon Rd PE19 ...95 F1
Gordon Richards Cl CB8 ...110 F6
Gordon Way PE2 ...186 C7
Gore Tree Rd PE28 ...120 C7
Goredike Bank PE13 ...237 E3
Gorefield Prim Sch PE13 ...237 E2
Gorefield Rd PE13 ...237 F2
Gorse Cl 8 IP28 ...214 A1
Gorse Gn PE1 ...198 B8
Gorse Way PE27 ...144 B5
Goshawk Cl PE29 ...142 A8
Gosling Way CB2 ...33 A8
Gosling's Dro PE2 ...220 A8
Gosmoor La PE14 ...236 B5
Gosslan Cl PE27 ...144 A6
Gostwick PE2 ...185 D5
Gote La PE13 ...237 E3
Gough Way CB3 ...64 A8
Governess Ct 8 PE15 ...223 B7
Gower Rd SG8 ...5 C7
Gowers The CB3 ...103 E1
Grace Sch of Medicine CB1 ...65 A8

Gracious St PE7 ...189 D7
Graeme Rd PE5 ...194 F2
Grafham Cl PE2 ...187 E4
Grafham Rd PE28 ...138 F4
Grafham Wr Ex Ctr★ PE28 ...116 B5
Grafham Wr Nature Reserve★ PE28 ...115 C3
Grafton Ave PE3 ...197 C3
Grafton Cl PE27 ...143 F8
Grafton Ctr CB1 ...246 C3
Grafton St CB1 ...246 C2
Grain Cl CB2 ...49 A5
Grainger Ave PE29 ...118 F8
Grammar Sch Wlk PE29 ...141 D4
Granary Cl PE29 ...141 E1
Granary End 4 CB6 ...217 E1
Granary La 5 CB6 ...242 D4
Granary Rd CB8 ...111 B2
Granary The
  Old Hurst PE28 ...154 D7
  Sawtry PE28 ...168 B4
Granary Way CB3 ...79 B3
Granby St
  Littleport CB6 ...242 D4
  Newmarket CB8 ...111 B3
  Peterborough PE2 ...198 B2
Grandford Dro PE15 ...227 E6
Grandridge Cl CB1 ...66 F4
Grange Ave PE2 ...198 A6
Grange Bottom SG8 ...5 B7
Grange Cl PE28 ...168 C2
Grange Cres PE2 ...186 A5
Grange Cl CB3 ...64 B8
Grange Dr CB3 ...82 E7
Grange Farm Cl PE19 ...57 B5
Grange Farm The IP28 ...239 C1
Grange La
  Barton Mills IP28 ...239 C2
  Littleport CB6 ...242 E4
Grange Rd
  Cambridge CB3 ...64 B8
  Duxford CB2 ...17 A6
  Ickleton CB10 ...9 A8
  March PE15 ...228 A1
  Peterborough PE2 ...197 D4
  6 Somersham PE28 ...208 C8
  Wisbech PE13 ...245 A7
Grange The
  Meldreth SG8 ...14 B8
  8 Somersham PE28 ...208 C8
Grangehill Rd PE13 ...237 B6
Granham's Rd
  Cambridge CB1 ...65 C1
  Great Shelford CB2 ...49 A7
Granhams Cl CB2 ...49 A6
Gransden Rd
  Abbotsley PE19 ...57 E6
  Caxton CB3 ...59 D8
Gransley Rise PE3 ...197 C5
Granta Cl
  Great Chesterford CB10 ...18 D1
  St Ives PE27 ...144 B7
  Witchford CB6 ...217 D1
Granta Cotts CB10 ...18 C2
Granta Leys CB1 ...35 B3
Granta Pk CB1 ...34 A6
Granta Pl CB2 ...246 A1
Granta Rd CB2 ...32 E5
Granta Terr CB2 ...49 B4
Granta Vale CB1 ...35 D2
Grantchester Mdws CB3 ...64 C7
Grantchester Rd
  Barton CB3 ...63 D7
  Cambridge CB2 ...64 B2
  Coton CB3 ...82 C1
  Grantchester CB3 ...64 B6
Grantchester Rise CB5 ...130 B5
Grantchester St 3 CB3 ...64 C7
Grantham Cl SG8 ...5 B8
Granville Ave PE6 ...231 F7
Granville Gdns IP28 ...239 A4
Granville Pl 1 PE1 ...198 A4
Grasmere PE29 ...141 B6
Grasmere Gdns
  Cambridge CB1 ...246 A4
  Peterborough PE4 ...204 D3
Grass Plant Cotts CB8 ...131 B4
Grass Yd 3 PE28 ...113 F4
Grassgate La PE14 ...238 E3
Gravel Bridge Rd CB4 ...123 C6
Gravel Dro
  Beck Row, Holywell Row & Kenny Hill IP28 ...213 C6
  Witcham CB6 ...216 F4
Gravel End CB6 ...217 C5
Gravel End La CB6 ...217 D5
Gravel Pit Hill SG8 ...16 C8
Gravel Wlk PE1 ...198 A2
Graveley Rd PE19 ...97 A8
Graveley Way PE28 ...98 E8
Gray Ct PE1 ...197 E8
Gray Rd CB1 ...65 D6
Gray's Rd SG19 ...41 D6
Grayling Cl CB4 ...84 A4
Grays Cl SG8 ...5 C8
Grays Gn MK44 ...93 B2
Grays La Emneth PE14 ...236 C6
  March PE15 ...243 D4
Graysmoor Dro PE14 ...228 B8
Great & Little Shelford CE Prim Sch CB2 ...48 F4
Great Abington Prim Sch CB1 ...34 C5

Great Chesterfield CE Prim Sch CB10 ...18 D2
Great Chesterford Sta CB10 ...18 C1
Great Cl CB3 ...63 B4
Great Dro Soham CB7 ...211 F3
  Swaffham Prior CB7 ...128 C6
  Yaxley PE7 ...182 A5
Great Eastern Rd
  March PE15 ...243 D7
  Wisbech PE13 ...245 B4
Great Eastern St CB1 ...65 B8
Great Farthing Cl PE27 ...144 B4
Great Fen Rd CB7 ...212 B8
Great Gidding CE Prim Sch PE28 ...166 D3
Great Heath Prim Sch IP28 ...239 D6
Great How PE27 ...143 F7
Great La CB5 ...129 C1
Great N Fen Dro CB4 ...125 C6
Great N Rd
  Alconbury PE28 ...150 A4
  Buckden PE19 ...117 A5
  Eaton Socon PE19 ...74 B2
  Peterborough PE2 ...185 A4
  St Neots PE19 ...74 C7
  Sibson cum Stibbington PE8 ...183 E8
  Southoe & Midloe PE19 ...95 F4
  Wothorpe PE9 ...244 C2
Great Northern St PE29 ...141 D5
Great Parlow Cl PE19 ...97 E7
Great Paxton CE Prim Sch PE19 ...96 E5
Great Staughton Prim Sch PE19 ...93 F6
Great Whyte PE26 ...172 A4
Great Wilbraham CE Prim Sch CB1 ...67 F8
Great Wilbraham Rd CB1 ...86 F1
Greater Foxes CB1 ...66 F5
Greatford Rd PE9 ...230 C6
Greatlands PE28 ...163 B4
Grebe Cl
  Mildenhall IP28 ...239 D3
  Whittlesey PE7 ...190 A8
Grebe Ct PE7 ...190 A8
Grebe Way 3 PE19 ...75 B7
Green Acres SG19 ...41 C5
Green Bank Rd CB5 ...108 B2
Green Butts CB2 ...32 D5
Green Cl PE19 ...94 A6
Green Drift SG8 ...5 B6
Green Dro
  Coveney CB6 ...217 D4
  Crowland PE6 ...232 D8
  Elm PE14 ...236 D2
  Northside PE6 ...200 F4
  Thorney PE6 ...233 B4
Green End
  Comberton CB3 ...62 C6
  Fen Ditton CB5 ...84 E6
  Gamlingay SG19 ...41 C5
  Landbeach CB4 ...105 D8
  Little Staughton MK44 ...93 A3
  Little Stukeley PE28 ...152 A1
  Sawtry PE28 ...168 B3
  Stretham CB6 ...210 F4
Green End Rd
  Cambridge CB4 ...84 B6
  St Neots PE19 ...75 A5
  Sawtry PE28 ...168 B3
Green Farm Cl PE5 ...195 E2
Green Head Rd CB5 ...108 B4
Green Hedges Sch The CB2 ...49 C4
Green Hill 2 CB6 ...211 B7
Green How PE27 ...143 E6
Green La Ashwell SG7 ...2 A1
  6 Benwick PE15 ...222 A5
  Brampton PE28 ...140 D2
  Christchurch PE14 ...229 D3
  Ellington PE28 ...138 F4
  Everton SG19 ...40 C3
  Great Staughton PE19 ...93 F6
  Hail Weston PE19 ...95 A1
  Leverington PE13 ...237 C2
  Linton CB1 ...35 C2
  Peterborough PE1 ...198 A4
  St Ives PE27 ...143 A5
  Stamford PE9 ...244 B7
  Upton & Coppingford PE28 ...160 C2
  Walsoken PE14 ...245 F4
  Yaxley PE7 ...181 D6
Green Leys PE27 ...143 F5
Green Man La PE27 ...47 E3
Green Pk Brinkley CB8 ...70 D2
  Cambridge CB4 ...84 B6
  Chatteris PE16 ...241 E5
Green Rd
  Newborough PE6 ...205 F3
  Newmarket CB8 ...111 B2
  Upwell PE14 ...229 E8
Green Rd The CB2 ...33 A8
Green Side CB5 ...106 B7
Green St
  Cambridge CB2 ...246 A3
  Duxford CB2 ...32 D1
  March PE15 ...243 E3
  Royston SG8 ...5 D8
  Willingham CB4 ...209 A1
Green The Ashley CB8 ...91 F8

Green The continued
  Beck Row, Holywell Row & Kenny Hill IP28 ...213 C7
  Brampton PE28 ...140 D2
  Cambridge CB4 ...84 B5
  Castor PE5 ...195 E2
  Foxton CB2 ...30 B5
  Glinton PE6 ...203 E8
  Great Staughton PE19 ...93 F7
  Haddenham CB6 ...210 A6
  Kingston CB3 ...61 B3
  Kirtling CB8 ...72 C5
  Lolworth CB3 ...101 F5
  Peterborough PE4 ...204 C3
  Royston SG8 ...5 D6
  Snailwell CB8 ...132 A3
  Somersham PE28 ...215 C1
  Steeple Morden SG8 ...11 C1
  6 Thorney PE6 ...233 A3
  Yaxley PE7 ...181 E5
Green Tiles Cl PE29 ...152 E1
Greenacres Duxford CB2 ...32 D1
  Peterborough PE4 ...204 A4
Greenbanks SG8 ...14 C5
Greendale PE29 ...141 A6
Greenfield SG8 ...5 B7
Greenfield Cl CB2 ...49 D4
Greenfields
  Earith PE28 ...208 E6
  Eltisley PE19 ...77 E4
  Hemingford Grey PE27 ...143 F1
  Newmarket CB8 ...111 C3
  1 St Neots PE19 ...75 A6
Greenfields Way CB9 ...23 F6
Greenford Cl SG8 ...28 D8
Greengage Cl SG8 ...14 C4
Greengage Rise SG8 ...14 C5
Greengarth PE27 ...144 A5
Greengate Ct PE1 ...198 C4
Greenham PE3 ...197 A4
Greenhaze La CB3 ...79 B3
Greenhill Rd PE8 ...178 F8
Greenhills CB7 ...212 C3
Greenlands CB2 ...65 B3
Greenleas CB4 ...104 B5
Greenlow SG8 ...14 A4
Green's Rd CB4 ...83 E4
Greenside Cl CB4 ...122 E6
Greenstock La PE13 ...238 A6
Greenway PE19 ...117 B4
Greenwood Cl
  1 Haverhill CB9 ...23 E7
  Ramsey PE26 ...172 A5
Greenwood Way 16 PE15 ...223 B7
Gregory Rd IP28 ...239 A6
Grenadier Dr PE16 ...241 C6
Grenadier Rd PE19 ...74 B2
Greneway Sch The SG8 ...5 E7
Grenfell Rd PE26 ...172 A5
Grenville Way PE19 ...74 B2
Gresham Rd CB1 ...246 C1
Gresley Dr PE9 ...244 B4
Gresley Way
  March PE15 ...243 B6
  Peterborough PE3 ...197 C6
Gretton Cl PE2 ...186 C7
Greville Rd CB1 ...65 B7
Greville Starkey Ave CB8 ...110 F5
Greys SG8 ...5 A4
Greys The PE15 ...243 E2
Greystoke Ct 1 CB1 ...65 E5
Greystoke Rd CB1 ...65 E5
Grieve Ct CB4 ...84 C5
Griffins Cl PE6 ...207 D1
Griffiths Ct PE2 ...185 E5
Grimeshaw Wood Nature Reserve★ PE3 ...196 F6
Grimmer's Rd 6 PE13 ...245 E7
Grimshaw Rd PE1 ...198 B6
Grip The CB1 ...35 B1
Groat La SG19 ...41 D8
Grosvenor Gdns PE19 ...74 E6
Grosvenor House Ct 6 IP28 ...239 B5
Grosvenor Rd PE13 ...245 D7
Grosvenor Yd CB8 ...111 A3
Grounds Ave PE15 ...243 F4
Grounds Way PE7 ...191 A8
Grove Cl CB3 ...80 B1
Grove Ct
  Little Paxton PE19 ...95 F2
  St Ives PE27 ...144 A4
Grove End PE28 ...120 C1
Grove Gdns CB7 ...212 C2
Grove La
  Brampton PE28 ...140 D3
  Cambridge CB1 ...246 B1
  Peterborough PE3 ...197 A2
Grove Pk CB2 ...212 C2
Grove Prim Sch The CB4 ...83 F6
Grove Rd
  Little Paxton PE19 ...95 F2
  Sawston CB2 ...33 A8
Grove St PE2 ...186 F4
Grove The
  Cambridge CB4 ...84 B6
  Chatteris PE16 ...241 C5
  Huntingdon PE29 ...142 B6
  Linton CB1 ...35 B3
  Mildenhall IP28 ...213 D8
  Orwell SG8 ...28 D8
  St Neots PE19 ...74 E6
  1 Stretham CB6 ...210 F4
  Whittlesey PE7 ...189 F6

Grove The *continued*
Wistow PE28 .... 163 F6
Grove Way PE26 ...... 172 A4
Grovelands PE3 ...... 197 E2
Grovemere Ct PE28 .... 114 B7
Grunty Fen Rd CB6 .... 210 F8
Guanockgate Rd PE12 . 234 C8
Guash Way PE9 ...... 244 D7
Guelder Rose CB7 ..... 240 F5
Guest Rd CB1 .... 246 C2
Guild Rd PE13 .... 245 E6
Guilden Morden CE Prim Sch
SG8 .... 10 F5
Guildenburgh Cres
PE7 .... 190 A7
Guildhall Pl 5 CB1 .... 246 A2
Guildhall St 3 CB1 .... 246 A2
Guilsborough Rd PE6 .. 232 B2
Guineas Cl CB8 .... 110 E6
Guise La SG8 .... 12 D6
Gull Bank PE13 .... 234 E3
Gull Dro PE13 .... 234 D3
Gull La PE13 .... 238 A3
Gull Rd PE13 .... 234 F3
Gull Way
Chatteris PE16 .... 241 C6
Whittlesey PE7 .... 190 A8
Gullymore PE3 .... 196 F8
Gunhild Cl CB1 .... 65 D5
Gunhild Ct CB1 .... 65 C5
Gunhild Way CB1 .... 65 C5
Gunnell Cl CB4 .... 105 D2
Gunning Rd CB6 ...... 240 E8
Gunning Way CB4 ...... 83 C6
Gunnings Way PE28 ... 143 C1
Gunthorpe Prim Sch
PE4 .... 204 E2
Gunthorpe Rd
Newborough PE6 .... 204 F4
Peterborough PE4 ...... 204 E2
Gunthorpe Ridings
PE4 .... 205 A2
Gunton's Rd PE6 ...... 205 C6
Guntons Cl CB7 .... 212 B4
Gurlings Cl CB9 .... 39 A2
Gurnard Leys PE3 ..... 204 A1
Gurney Way CB4 .... 83 E4
Guthlac Ave PE4 ...... 204 D1
Guyatt Ct CB5 .... 130 B2
Guyhirn CE Prim Sch
PE13 .... 235 A2
Guyhirn Gull PE13 ..... 234 E3
Gwydir St CB1 .... 65 A8
Gypsy Cnr PE28 ...... 150 B6
Gypsy La PE13 .... 238 C4

H

Hacke Rd PE3 .... 197 D3
Haddenham End Field
CB6 .... 210 A7
Haddenham Rd CB6 ... 217 A1
Haddon Cl PE2 .... 187 E5
Haddon Rd
Haddon PE7 .... 180 C6
Peterborough PE3 ...... 197 E3
Haddon Way PE7 ...... 187 B2
Haddow's Cl CB4 ..... 123 F2
Haden Way Over CB4 .. 208 F1
Willingham CB4 .... 123 F8
Hadleigh Ct CB5 .... 84 E4
Hadley Rd PE4 .... 204 D1
Hadrian Cl CB9 .... 24 D7
Hadrians Ct PE2 ...... 187 B8
Hadstock Rd CB1 ...... 35 B1
Hagbech Hall Cl PE14 . 236 D6
Hagger's Cl SG8 .... 14 D6
Haggis Gap CB1 .... 66 F5
Haig Ct CB4 .... 84 A4
Haigh's Cl PE16 ...... 241 B4
Hake's Dro PE15 ...... 227 A2
Halcyon Ct PE29 ...... 141 C6
Hale Ave CB4 .... 83 D4
Hale Cl SG8 .... 14 D6
Hale Dro CB6 .... 225 E6
Hale Fen CB6 .... 242 C8
Hale Fen La CB6 ..... 217 A4
Hale Fen Rd CB6 ..... 225 E4
Haley Cl
Hemingford Grey PE28 ... 143 B1
Wisbech PE13 .... 245 C8
Half Acre Dro CB7 .... 211 C7
Half Acre La CB7 ..... 211 D8
Halfpenny La PE14 .... 245 D1
Halfpenny Toll Rd
PE14 .... 229 E4
Halifax Rd
Cambridge CB4 .... 83 B4
Mildenhall IP28 .... 213 E8
Halifax Way CB8 ...... 110 E5
Hall Bank PE13 .... 237 E7
Hall Barn Rd CB7 ..... 212 F4
Hall Bridge Rd PE14 .. 236 D1
Hall Cl Bourn CB3 ...... 60 C5
Foxton CB2 .... 30 B6
Huntingdon PE29 .... 142 A6
Little Paxton PE19 .... 95 F2
Hall Cres CB2 .... 33 A7
Hall Dike PE14 .... 236 F4
Hall Dr Hardwick CB3 .... 80 F3
Highfields CB3 .... 80 C2
Hall End CB4 .... 105 D2
Hall Farm La SG19 ..... 58 D4
Hall Farm Rd 2 CB4 .... 83 D5
Hall Gate Rd PE12 .... 234 B8
Hall Gn La PE28 ...... 121 B6
Hall La
Abbots Ripton PE28 ..... 152 D8
Brinkley CB8 .... 70 E2
Burwell CB5 .... 130 B1
Great & Little Chishill SG8 ... 7 F2
Peterborough PE4 ...... 204 C4
Tilbrook PE28 .... 113 C8
20 Wittering PE8 .... 230 B1
Hall Rd Outwell PE14 ... 236 F3
St Neots PE19 .... 74 E3
Hall St CB7 .... 212 B5
Hallards The 6 PE19 .... 74 C6
Hallaton Rd PE1 ...... 198 D8
Hallcroft Rd PE7 ..... 189 C8
Hallfields La PE4 ..... 204 E1
Hallwyck Gdns CB8 ... 110 F2
Halstead Cl 2 PE13 ... 245 E5
Ham La PE2 .... 185 E7
Hamden Way CB3 ...... 99 B3
Hamerton Rd
Alconbury Weston PE28 .. 150 C7
Buckworth PE28 .... 149 D6
Winwick PE28 .... 158 C5
Hamerton Zoo Pk★
PE28 .... 159 B5
Hamilton Ct CB8 ...... 110 E2
Hamilton Rd
Cambridge CB4 .... 246 B4
Ely CB6 .... 240 B4
Newmarket CB8 .... 110 E3
Hamiltons The CB8 .... 110 E2
Hamlet Cl PE29 .... 141 F6
Hamlet Rd CB9 .... 24 B7
Hamlet The CB6 ...... 218 C6
Hammond Cl
Newmarket CB8 .... 110 E6
Pampisford CB2 .... 33 B5
Wittering PE8 .... 230 C1
Hammond Way PE28 .. 208 C8
Hampden Rd 2 PE13 .. 245 D5
Hampden Rise SG8 ...... 5 D4
Hampden Way PE19 .... 75 A3
Hampshire Rd PE28 ... 143 B8
Hampstead Ave IP28 .. 239 B6
Hampton Cl PE28 ..... 121 C6
Hampton Ct PE3 ...... 197 C6
Hampton Hargate Prim Sch
PE7 .... 186 C2
Hanaper Dr SG8 .... 6 F1
Hanbury PE2 .... 185 F3
Hanchet End CB9 ...... 38 B1
Hankey St PE1 .... 197 F4
Hanmer Ave IP28 ..... 239 C5
Hannath Rd PE13 ..... 238 B8
Hannington Cl PE7 ... 190 A7
Hanover Cl
Bar Hill CB3 .... 102 B3
Eaton Socon PE19 .... 74 D5
Hanover Ct
Brampton PE28 .... 140 D3
Cambridge CB1 .... 246 B1
Peterborough PE3 ...... 197 A8
Hansell Rd PE28 ..... 140 B3
Hanson Ct CB4 .... 83 E7
Harbins La PE19 .... 57 C6
Harbour Ave CB3 ...... 62 D6
Harbour Sch The CB6 . 210 C6
Harcombe Rd CB1 ..... 65 E6
Harcourt PE29 .... 142 A2
Harding Cl 1 CB5 .... 106 A7
Harding Way
Cambridge CB4 .... 83 C5
Histon CB4 .... 104 B4
St Ives PE27 .... 144 B5
Hardman Rd CB2 ...... 30 C5
Hardwick Com Prim Sch
CB3 .... 81 A3
Hardwick Ct PE3 ..... 197 B2
Hardwick La PE19 .... 117 A5
Hardwick Rd
Haverhill CB9 .... 24 B8
St Neots PE19 .... 74 E3
Toft CB3 .... 61 E6
Hardwick St CB3 ...... 64 C7
Hardwicke Cl CB6 .... 242 C5
Hardwicke Fields CB6 . 210 A6
Hardwicke La PE19 .... 57 B6
Hardwicke Rd SG19 .... 58 F6
Hardy Cl PE29 .... 141 F6
Hardy Dr SG8 .... 5 D8
Hardy Pl 1 PE19 ...... 74 D6
Hardy's La PE7 .... 189 E6
Harebell Cl
Cambridge CB1 .... 66 A5
Huntingdon PE29 .... 141 D6
Peterborough PE1 ...... 205 B1
Harecroft Rd PE13 .... 245 B5
Harefield Rise CB1 .... 35 E2
Harewood Gdns PE3 .. 197 B2
Hargate Way PE7 ..... 186 D3
Hargood Ct 4 PE19 .... 74 B3
Hargreaves Rd 6 SG8 ... 5 D5
Harland Rd PE19 ...... 74 E6
Harlech Ct 5 PE19 .... 74 F2
Harlech Grange PE3 .. 197 B1
Harlestones Rd CB4 .. 125 D4
Harley Ind Pk PE19 .... 96 D2
Harlton Cl PE2 ...... 187 E5
Harlton Rd
Great Eversden CB3 ...... 45 F7
Haslingfield CB3 .... 46 F5
Harold Heading Cl
PE16 .... 241 B3
Harold's Bank PE13 ... 237 B1
Harper's Dro PE26 .... 170 F7
Harradine Cl PE29 .... 155 B5
Harrier Cl PE29 ...... 142 A8
Harrington Dr PE6 ... 232 C8
Harris Cres PE27 ..... 208 A2
Harris La PE28 .... 163 E6
Harris Rd CB4 .... 83 D6
Harris St PE1 .... 197 F6
Harrison Cl PE3 ...... 196 F3
Harrison Way PE27 ... 144 B3
Harrison's Dro
Burwell CB5 .... 129 A8
Swaffham Prior CB7 ..... 128 D7
Harris's La PE28 ..... 163 E7
Harrolds Cl 5 PE14 ... 238 F1
Harrow Rd CB9 .... 23 E7
Harry Palmer Cl CB7 .. 212 E1
Harry Scott Ct CB4 .... 83 E7
Harrys Way PE13 ..... 245 C2
Harston & Newton CP Sch
CB2 .... 47 F2
Harston Mill CB2 ...... 47 D2
Harston Rd
Haslingfield CB3 .... 47 C4
Newton CB2 .... 31 B8
Hart Cl CB9 .... 38 F1
Hart Rd PE26 .... 171 E3
Hartfield Rd CB8 ...... 70 E4
Hartford Com Jun & Inf Sch
PE29 .... 141 F5
Hartford Ct PE2 ...... 187 D6
Hartford Rd PE29 ..... 141 E4
Hartington Gr CB1 ..... 65 A5
Hartlands PE7 .... 190 E8
Hartley Cl CB5 .... 106 B8
Hartwell Ct PE3 ...... 197 C5
Hartwell Way PE3 .... 197 B5
Harvest Cl PE7 ...... 175 F8
Harvest Ct PE27 ..... 144 A4
Harvest Way CB1 ...... 84 A2
Harvester Way
Crowland PE6 .... 232 B8
Peterborough PE1 ...... 198 C1
Harvey Cl 4 PE8 ..... 230 B1
Harvey Dr 5 PE28 .... 215 C1
Harvey Goodwin Ave
CB4 .... 83 D4
Harvey Goodwin Gdns
CB4 .... 83 D4
Harvey Rd CB1 .... 246 C1
Harvey St 3 PE19 ...... 74 E4
Haselhurst Cl PE15 ... 243 F4
Haslingfield Prim Sch
CB3 .... 47 A5
Haslingfield Rd
Barrington CB2 .... 29 F8
Barton CB3 .... 63 B2
Harlton CB3 .... 46 E6
Hasse Rd CB7 .... 212 C8
Hassock Hill Dro
PE13 .... 237 D3
Hassock Way 1 PE15 . 223 B7
Hastings Rd PE4 ..... 204 C2
Hatchet La PE19 ..... 114 B2
Hatfield Rd PE28 ..... 168 A4
Hathaway Cl PE19 ..... 74 C3
Hatherdene Cl CB1 .... 65 E8
Hatley Cl PE19 .... 75 A7
Hatley Dr CB5 .... 130 B3
Hatley Pk★ SG19 .... 42 F2
Hatley Rd
Gamlingay SG19 .... 41 F4
Wrestlingworth &
Cockayne Hatley SG19 ... 25 B7
Hatton Pk Prim Sch
CB4 .... 123 F2
Hatton's Pk CB4 ..... 123 F2
Hatton's Rd CB4 ..... 102 D6
Hautboy La PE8 ..... 178 B3
Hauxton CP Sch CB2 ... 48 C4
Hauxton Rd
Cambridge CB2 .... 48 C8
Great Shelford CB2 ...... 48 D4
Havelock Cl SG19 ...... 41 C5
Havelock Dr PE2 ..... 187 E6
Haven The CB1 .... 66 F5
Haverhill Arts Ctr★
CB9 .... 24 A7
Haverhill Bsns Pk CB9 .. 24 A5
Haverhill Leisure Ctr
CB9 .... 24 B7
Haverhill Rd
Castle Camps CB1 .... 22 E4
Horseheath CB1 .... 37 A3
Little Wratting CB9 .... 39 F3
Stapleford CB2 .... 49 E5
Steeple Bumpstead CB9 ... 24 B1
Haveswater Cl 1 PE4 . 204 E2
Haviland Way CB4 ..... 83 F6
Hawcrofts La CB4 .... 208 D2
Hawe's La CB7 .... 211 E2
Haweswater PE29 ..... 141 C5
Hawk Dr PE29 .... 142 B7
Hawkes End PE28 .... 140 E2
Hawkes La PE27 ..... 208 A2
Hawkesden Rd PE19 ... 75 B6
Hawkesford Way PE19 .. 74 F7
Hawkins Cl PE28 ..... 115 D3
Hawkins Dr 1 PE13 ... 245 E5
Hawkins Rd CB4 ...... 83 F7
Hawkins's Dro CB7 ... 242 F3
Hawkshead Way 2 PE4 204 E3
Hawthorn Ave
Hauxton CB2 .... 48 B4
Sawston CB2 .... 32 F6
Hawthorn Cl
Little Paxton PE19 .... 95 F2
Littleport CB6 .... 242 E3
Newborough PE6 .... 207 C1
Royston SG8 .... 5 F7
Hawthorn Dr PE29 .... 141 D5
Hawthorn End 1 PE28 . 150 F5
Hawthorn Rd
Emneth PE14 .... 236 D5
Folksworth PE7 .... 175 D8
Haverhill CB9 .... 38 D1
Peterborough PE1 ...... 198 C6
Ramsey PE26 .... 171 F7
St Neots PE19 .... 74 E6
Yaxley PE7 .... 181 F5
Hawthorn Way
Burwell CB5 .... 130 C3
Cambridge CB4 .... 83 F4
Royston SG8 .... 5 F7
St Ives PE27 .... 144 A5
Sawtry PE28 .... 168 B3
Hawthorn Wlk 4 IP28 . 213 F8
Hawthorne Ave PE13 .. 245 C8
Hawthorne Dr PE7 ... 189 F6
Hawthorne Gr PE15 ... 243 C5
Hawthorne Rd CB2 ..... 49 B4
Hawthorns The PE16 . 241 C5
Hay Cl CB1 .... 53 B1
Hay Fen Cl 6 CB6 .... 210 F5
Hay St SG8 .... 11 B2
Haycocks Rd CB9 ...... 23 C8
Haycraft Cl PE28 ..... 116 A7
Haycroft The PE19 ... 117 F2
Haydock Rd SG8 .... 5 F6
Hayes Wlk PE8 ...... 178 D8
Hayfield Ave CB2 ...... 32 F7
Hayland Dro IP28 .... 213 B7
Hayley Wood Nature
Reserve★ CB3 .... 43 C6
Hayling Ave PE19 ...... 96 A2
Hayling Cl 4 PE29 .... 118 F7
Hayman's Way CB3 .... 99 A2
Haymarket Rd 7 CB3 ... 83 C3
Hayster Dr CB1 .... 65 E6
Hayter Cl CB1 .... 53 F4
Haywardsfield PE3 .... 197 A1
Haywoods La SG8 .... 5 E7
Hayzen Cl CB2 .... 29 F8
Hazel Cl Chatteris PE16 . 241 D4
Haverhill CB9 .... 23 E7
Mildenhall IP28 .... 239 E4
Hazel Croft PE4 ..... 204 A4
Hazel Ct 7 CB6 ...... 210 F5
Hazel Gdns 1 PE13 ... 245 D4
Hazel La CB3 .... 79 C5
Hazel Way PE27 ...... 144 B4
Hazelwood Cl CB4 ..... 83 D6
Hazelwood Wlk PE29 .. 141 F7
Head Fen Dro CB6 .... 224 F3
Headford Cl CB5 ...... 84 D4
Headington Cl CB1 .... 65 F5
Headington Dr CB1 .... 65 F5
Headlake Dro CB5 .... 128 E1
Headland Ave CB9 ..... 23 E7
Headlands
Fenstanton PE28 .... 121 C5
Huntingdon PE29 .... 141 C3
Headlands Way PE7 .. 189 D8
Headley Gdns CB2 ..... 49 B4
Headley's La CB6 .... 217 A2
Heasman Cl CB8 ..... 110 F5
Heath Ave SG8 .... 5 C6
Heath Farm Rd IP28 .. 213 F1
Heath House CB4 ..... 84 A5
Heath La PE28 .... 163 A7
Heath Rd Bottisham CB1 .. 87 B4
Burwell CB5 .... 109 D5
Exning CB8 .... 110 B6
Gamlingay SG19 .... 41 A4
Helpston PE6 .... 231 C2
Mildenhall IP28 .... 239 E5
Newmarket CB8 .... 111 C3
Swaffham Bulbeck CB5 ... 108 B2
Swaffham Prior CB5 ..... 109 A3
Warboys PE28 .... 165 C6
Heath Row PE1 ...... 205 B1
Heathbell Rd CB8 .... 111 C3
Heathcote Cl PE15 ... 243 F4
Heather Ave PE1 ..... 198 A8
Heatherdale Cl PE7 .. 187 C5
Heatherset Way 1 IP28 213 F1
Hathersett Cl CB8 ... 110 E7
Heathfield Royston SG8 ... 5 B6
Thriplow CB2 .... 31 E1
Heaton Cl Ely CB6 .... 240 F7
Peterborough PE3 ...... 197 B3
Heaton Dr CB6 ...... 240 F7
Hectare The CB2 ...... 48 F7
Heddon Way PE27 .... 144 B6
Hedgelands
Peterborough PE4 ...... 204 C5
Wisbech PE13 .... 245 C8
Hedgerley Cl CB3 ..... 83 A2
Heffer Cl CB2 .... 49 C4
Heights Dro Rd PE26 . 170 D6
Helen Cl 3 CB5 .... 84 E4
Helens Cl PE26 ...... 171 B1
Helions Bumpstead Rd
CB9 .... 23 F5
Helions Pk Ave CB9 .... 24 A7
Helions Pk Gdns CB9 ... 24 A7
Helions Pk Gr CB9 ..... 24 A7
Helions Service Rd
CB9 .... 24 A7
Helions Wlk CB9 ...... 24 A7
Helmsdale Gdns PE4 .. 204 B2
Helmsley Ct PE7 ..... 187 F5
Helpston Rd
Castor PE5 .... 195 D2
Etton PE6 .... 203 C8
Heltwate Ct PE3 ..... 197 C7
Heltwate Sch PE3 .... 197 B7
Hemingford Cres PE2 . 187 E6
Hemingford Grey Prim Sch
PE28 .... 143 D2
Hemingford Rd
Cambridge CB1 .... 65 B8
Hemingford Grey PE27 ... 143 F2
Hemington Cl 10 CB4 .. 208 D1
Hemlocks The CB3 ..... 47 B5
Hemmerley Dr PE7 ... 189 E8
Hempfield Pl CB6 .... 242 D4
Hempfield Rd CB6 .... 242 D4
Hempsals 12 PE19 ...... 74 C6
Hempsals Rd or Mdw Dro
CB4 .... 209 C1
Hempstead Rd
2 Haverhill CB9 .... 38 C1
Peterborough PE7 ...... 186 C1
Hen Brook PE19 ...... 74 F4
Henderson Cl CB9 ..... 38 C1
Henford Gdns PE15 .. 243 D5
Henley Rd CB1 .... 84 B2
Henley Way CB7 ..... 240 F6
Henry Cl CB9 .... 23 D6
Henry Crabb Rd CB6 .. 242 A6
Henry Morris Rd
Histon CB4 .... 104 C3
Sawston CB2 .... 33 A8
Henry Orbell Cl 3 PE15 243 E4
Henry St
Peterborough PE1 ...... 198 A4
Wisbech PE13 .... 245 C5
Henry Warby Ave 3
PE14 .... 236 A5
Henshaw PE1 .... 198 E6
Henson Cl PE13 ...... 245 C8
Henson Rd PE15 ..... 243 C5
Herbert Human Cl 3
CB7 .... 212 B4
Herbert St CB4 .... 83 E4
Herbert Twinn Ct CB5 .. 84 D4
Hercules Cl 5 CB4 ..... 83 E8
Hereford Cl 7 PE28 ... 208 C8
Hereward PE28 ...... 208 E6
Hereward Ave IP28 ... 239 C5
Hereward Cl
Haddenham CB6 .... 209 E4
Histon CB4 .... 104 C3
2 Peterborough PE1 .... 198 B2
Hereward Com Coll
PE1 .... 198 D5
Hereward Rd
Peterborough PE1 ...... 198 B2
1 Wisbech PE13 .... 245 D5
Hereward St Ely CB6 .. 240 B4
March PE15 .... 243 D5
Hereward Way PE6 ... 231 F8
Herewood Cross Sh Ctr
PE1 .... 198 A2
Heritage Pk Prim Sch
PE7 .... 187 F5
Hermitage Rd PE28 ... 208 E6
Herne Rd PE26 ...... 220 D4
Heron Cl PE7 .... 189 F8
Heron Ct
Peterborough PE2 ...... 187 D6
1 St Neots PE19 .... 75 B6
Heron Pk PE1 .... 198 F6
Heron Rd PE13 ...... 245 D2
Heron Way PE27 ..... 143 F7
Heron Wlk PE15 ..... 243 F5
Heronry Dr PE6 ..... 196 E2
Heron's Cl CB1 .... 65 D4
Herons Cl 6 Ely CB6 .. 240 B5
Tallington PE9 .... 230 F6
Heronshaw PE16 ..... 241 C6
Herrick Cl PE1 ...... 197 E8
Herring's Cl CB5 ...... 85 F5
Herringswell Rd
Herringswell IP28 .... 214 B2
Kentford CB8 .... 134 B4
Herschel Rd CB3 ...... 83 B1
Hertford Cl CB6 ..... 240 A3
Hertford La SG8 .... 8 E5
Hertford St CB4 ..... 246 A4
Hervey Cl CB6 ...... 240 B3
Hethersett Cl CB8 ... 110 E8
Hetley PE2 .... 186 A4
Hexham Ct 3 PE1 ... 198 D3
Heydon La Elmdon CB11 ... 8 F4
Heydon SG8 .... 8 B5
Heydon Rd SG8 .... 7 E2
Heyford Cl PE4 ..... 204 F2
Heyford Ct 5 IP28 .. 239 B5
Hickling Wlk PE4 .... 204 E3
Hicks La Girton CB3 ..... 82 E8
Peterborough PE7 ...... 186 F5
Hicks Way 4 CB9 ..... 24 E5
Hide Cl CB2 .... 32 F6
High Barns CB7 ..... 240 E6
High Broadgate PE13 .. 237 F7
High Cl SG8 .... 8 A5
High Cswy PE7 ...... 189 E7
High Ct Way PE7 .... 181 D8
High Ditch Rd CB5 .... 85 A4
High Fen Crooked Dro
PE28 .... 215 B5
High Fen Straight Dro
PE28 .... 215 B6
High Flyer Cotts CB7 . 240 F7
High Gn Abbotsley PE19 .. 57 B6
Great Shelford CB2 ...... 49 A6
High Haden Rd PE28 . 175 B1
High Leys PE27 ..... 143 F5
High Mdw Harston CB2 .. 47 F3
Ramsey PE26 .... 172 A3
High Piece Cres CB4 .. 208 C1
High Pk Cnr CB7 .... 132 D5
High Rd Downham CB6 .. 217 F6

High Rd *continued*
Gorefield PE13 237 E3
Newton PE13 238 A5
Tydd St Giles PE13 237 F6
Wisbech St Mary PE13 235 A6
High Sch Cl PE15 243 D6
High Side PE13 235 A8
High St Abbotsley PE19 57 B6
Abington Pigotts SG8 11 F5
Alconbury PE28 150 F4
Alconbury Weston PE28 150 D6
Ashley CB8 91 F8
Ashwell SG7 2 D4
Babraham CB2 33 D8
Balsham CB1 53 A2
Barley SG8 6 F2
Barrington CB2 29 E8
Barton CB3 63 B4
Bassingbourn SG8 12 F4
Benwick PE15 222 A5
Bluntisham/Colne PE28 208 C5
Bottisham CB5 86 F5
Bourn CB3 60 C6
Boxworth CB3 101 B5
Brampton PE28 140 E2
Brinkley CB8 70 D2
Buckden PE19 117 A4
Burwell CB5 109 B8
Cambourne CB3 79 B3
Castle Camps CB1 22 E3
Castor PE5 195 F2
Catworth PE28 136 D7
Chatteris PE16 241 C5
Cherry Hinton CB1 66 A7
Cheveley CB8 91 C7
Chippenham CB7 132 E8
Chrishall SG8 8 D3
Conington CB3 121 C1
Coton CB3 82 B2
Cottenham CB4 125 E4
Croxton PE19 76 F4
Croydon SG8 27 A7
Doddington/Wimblington PE15 223 A5
Dry Drayton CB3 102 B1
Earith PE28 208 E5
Ellington PE28 139 A4
Ely CB7 240 D4
Eye PE6 232 A1
Eyeworth SG19 10 A8
Fen Ditton CB5 84 E5
Fen Drayton CB4 121 F5
Fenstanton PE28 121 A6
Fowlmere SG8 15 E8
Foxton CB2 30 B5
Fulbourn CB1 66 F5
Girton CB3 103 E1
Glinton PE6 203 E8
Grantchester CB3 64 A4
Graveley PE19 97 F5
Great & Little Abington CB1 34 C6
Great Chesterford CB10 18 E2
Great Eversden CB3 45 E8
Great Paxton PE19 96 D4
Great Shelford CB2 48 E3
Great Wilbraham CB1 67 F7
Guilden Morden SG8 10 F4
Haddenham CB6 209 E4
Hail Weston PE19 74 B8
Harlton CB3 46 D5
Harston CB2 47 F3
Haslingfield CB3 47 B5
Hauxton CB2 48 C5
Haverhill CB9 24 A7
Hemingford Abbots PE28 143 A3
Hemingford Grey PE28 143 C2
Hildersham CB1 34 E5
Hilton PE28 120 B1
Hinxton CB10 18 B7
Histon CB4 104 B4
Holywell-cum-Needingworth PE27 144 F5
Horningsea CB5 106 A1
Huntingdon PE29 141 D4
Kimbolton PE28 113 F4
Knapwell CB3 100 E3
Landbeach CB4 105 D6
Linton CB1 35 C2
Little Paxton PE19 95 F2
Little Staughton MK44 93 B1
Little Wilbraham CB1 86 E1
Littleport CB6 242 D4
Lode CB5 107 C2
Longstanton CB4 123 F3
Longstowe CB3 59 F2
Madingley CB3 81 F5
Manea PE15 224 C4
March PE15 243 D3
Market Deeping PE6 231 D8
Maxey PE6 231 C7
Melbourn SG8 14 C5
Meldreth SG8 14 B8
Mepal CB6 216 E3
Mildenhall IP28 239 C4
Milton CB4 105 D2
Needingworth PE27 208 A3
Newmarket CB8 110 F3
Oakington CB4 103 C6
Offord Cluny PE19 96 F8
Orwell SG8 45 E1
Over CB4 208 D1
Pampisford CB2 33 B5
Peterborough PE2 187 A6
High St *continued*
Pidley cum Fenton PE28 155 E8
Rampton CB4 124 E5
Ramsey PE26 172 A6
Royston SG8 5 D6
St Neots PE19 74 E5
Sawston CB2 32 F6
Sawtry PE28 168 B4
Shepreth SG8 29 E4
Soham CB7 212 B4
Somersham PE28 208 C8
Spaldwick PE28 137 F6
Stamford PE9 244 B5
Stetchworth CB8 90 A2
Stilton PE7 176 A7
Stourbridge Common CB4 84 A4
Stretham CB6 210 F5
Sutton CB6 216 D1
Swaffham Bulbeck CB5 108 B1
Swaffham Prior CB5 108 D5
Swavesey CB4 122 E6
Tadlow SG8 26 A3
Teversham CB1 66 C8
Tilbrook PE28 113 B6
Toft CB3 61 D4
Tuddenham IP28 214 D2
Upwood PE26 171 B2
Warboys PE28 164 F5
Waterbeach CB5 106 B8
West Wickham CB1 37 A7
West Wratting CB1 53 F5
Whittlesford CB2 32 C5
Wicken CB7 211 E1
Wilburton CB6 210 C5
Willingham CB4 209 A1
Wisbech PE13 245 C5
Witcham CB6 217 A3
Wrestlingworth SG19 25 B4
Yelling PE19 98 C1
High St Back 2 CB7 240 D4
High St Pas CB7 240 D4
High St St Martin's PE9 244 C4
Higham Rd IP28 214 E1
Highbury St PE1 198 A5
Highclere Cl CB8 110 D8
Highclere Rd PE7 186 D3
Highdene Rd CB1 66 A6
Highfield Ave
Alconbury Weston PE28 150 D6
Cambridge CB4 83 E5
Highfield Cl CB2 17 D8
Highfield Cotts SG8 4 B7
Highfield Gate CB1 66 F6
Highfield Rd
Histon CB4 104 C1
March PE15 243 D7
Highfield Sch CB6 240 C5
Highfields Rd CB3 80 C2
Highgate Gn PE8 178 D8
Highlands SG8 5 E6
Highlands The CB8 110 D8
Highlees Prim Sch PE3 197 C6
Highsett CB1 246 C1
Hightown Dro CB5 129 C4
Highway The PE19 94 A6
Highworth Ave CB4 83 F5
Hilda Clarke Cl 1 PE16 241 C3
Hilda St CB4 83 D4
Hildersham Mill CB1 34 F5
Hildersham Rd CB1 34 D7
Hill Cl
Brington & Molesworth PE28 147 C5
Little Stukeley PE28 151 F1
Newmarket CB8 110 E3
Peterborough PE1 198 D5
Sawtry PE28 168 B3
Hill Cres CB9 39 A1
Hill Est Ramsey PE26 172 B4
St Ives PE28 143 B5
Hill Farm Rd CB2 32 B3
Hill Farms CB1 66 C2
Hill La CB9 24 F3
Hill Rd Over CB4 208 E1
Wistow PE26 164 A8
Hill Rise St Ives PE27 143 E7
St Neots PE19 75 A5
Hill Row CB6 209 E6
Hill Row Cswy CB6 209 A6
Hill St 5 PE13 245 C5
Hill View
Dry Drayton CB3 102 D1
Lidgate CB8 73 F8
Hillary Cl PE9 244 D6
Hillburn Rd PE13 245 B4
Hillcrest CB3 102 C3
Hillcrest Ave PE7 181 E5
Hillcrest Dr PE13 235 A2
Hillfield Alconbury PE28 150 F5
Foxton CB2 30 C5
Hillfield Rd CB3 62 D6
Hills Ave CB1 65 B5
Hills La CB6 240 B4
Hills Rd CB2 246 C1
Hills Rd Sixth Form Coll CB1 65 A6
Hillside Orwell SG8 45 E2
Royston SG8 5 D5
Sawston CB2 32 F8
Sutton CB6 216 D1
Hillside Cl
Ellington PE28 138 F4
Ufford PE9 230 F2
Hillside Cotts PE28 146 A4
Hillside La SG8 44 C4
Hillside Mdw CB7 212 F1
Hillside Rd PE15 243 B5
Hillstead CB2 49 D7
Hillward Cl PE2 186 C6
Hillway CB1 35 C2
Hilsdens Dr PE29 142 A1
Hilton Rd PE28 120 E3
Hilton St CB4 208 D1
Hinchcliffe PE2 185 E2
Hinchinbrooke Rd PE28 117 D8
Hinchingbrooke Ctry Pk★ PE29 140 F4
Hinchingbrooke Dr PE16 241 B4
Hinchingbrooke Hospl PE29 141 B5
Hinchingbrooke House★ PE29 141 B3
Hinchingbrooke Sch PE29 141 A4
Hines Cl CB3 63 A4
Hines La CB3 62 C5
Hinkins Cl SG8 14 D6
Hinton Ave CB1 65 C5
Hinton Cl PE7 189 D8
Hinton Rd CB1 66 D5
Hinton View CB6 210 A6
Hinton Way
Great Shelford CB2 49 C6
Wilburton CB6 210 C6
Hinxton Rd CB2 17 E8
Hinxworth Rd SG7 2 B4
Histon & Impington Inf Sch CB4 104 B3
Histon & Impington Jun Sch CB4 104 C4
Histon Rd
Cambridge CB4 83 C4
Cottenham CB4 104 C8
Histon Sch CB4 104 B4
Hitches St 4 CB6 242 D4
Hitherford CB4 208 E1
Hive Rd CB6 217 A4
Hives The PE19 74 D4
Hoadly Rd CB3 83 B5
Hobart Ct PE15 243 C5
Hobart Rd CB1 65 C7
Hobbledodds Cl CB4 122 E6
Hobby Cl PE29 142 B6
Hobson St CB1 246 B3
Hockland Rd PE13 237 F7
Hockley Cl CB1 22 B5
Hod Fen Dro
Denton & Caldecote PE7 177 A7
Yaxley PE7 181 F2
Hod Hall La CB6 210 A5
Hodgson Ave PE4 204 B6
Hodley Pl CB3 99 B1
Hodney Rd 2 PE6 232 A1
Hodson's Dr PE29 141 E5
Hodwell SG7 2 D4
Hog Fen Dro PE7 182 A5
Hogarth Cl PE27 144 A7
Hogarth Pl 2 PE19 74 D5
Hogens La PE13 238 A5
Hogherd's La 9 PE13 245 C5
Hoghill Dro CB6 209 F3
Hog's La SG8 8 D3
Holbein Rd PE27 144 A7
Holben Cl CB3 63 B3
Holborn Ave IP28 239 B6
Holbrook Rd
Cambridge CB1 65 B4
Haverhill CB9 23 E6
Holburn View PE28 168 B2
Holcroft PE2 186 B3
Holden End CB10 21 B2
Holdfield PE3 197 B6
Holdich St PE3 197 E2
Holdsworth Valley CP Sch CB8 110 F3
Holgate La PE4 204 B7
Holkham Mead CB5 130 C2
Holkham Rd PE2 185 D3
Holland Ave PE4 204 D1
Holland Pk CB8 91 C7
Holland Rd PE9 244 C6
Hollands Bsns Ctr CB9 24 B6
Hollands Rd CB9 24 A6
Hollands Road Ind Est CB9 24 A6
Hollesley Ave CB9 23 C8
Holliday's Rd PE28 208 D5
Hollies Cl SG8 5 E6
Hollies The PE15 243 E7
Hollmans Cl CB1 66 F4
Hollow Hill CB9 38 B4
Hollow La PE26 172 E6
Hollow Rd Chrishall SG8 8 D1
Elmdon CB11 9 C4
Ramsey Forty Foot PE26 221 C2
Hollow The PE29 142 B6
Holly Ave PE14 236 A5
Holly Cl
Newborough PE6 207 C1
Red Lodge IP28 213 F1
Holly Dr 4 PE15 223 A6
Holly Way 7 PE6 231 E8
Holly Wlk Ely CB7 240 F5
3 Mildenhall IP28 213 F8
Peterborough PE7 186 D3
Hollybush Way CB1 35 D3
Hollycroft Cl PE14 236 D5
Hollycroft Rd PE14 236 D5
Hollymount 6 CB1 84 A2
Hollytrees CB3 102 C3
Holme CE Prim Sch PE7 177 A4
Holme Cl Castor PE5 195 D2
Oakington/Longstanton CB4 103 C5
Holme Dro PE28 208 E7
Holme Fen Dro PE28 208 D7
Holme Fen National Nature Reserve★ PE7 177 C7
Holme La CB6 218 A6
Holme Rd
Ramsey PE26 220 C3
Yaxley PE7 181 E4
Holme Way CB2 32 F8
Holmehill PE29 118 F8
Holmes Dr PE13 245 E5
Holmes La CB7 212 B5
Holmes Rd PE6 203 F7
Holmes The CB6 242 E4
Holmes Way PE4 204 E2
Holmewood PE7 176 F4
Holmewood Cres PE7 176 F4
Holmsey Gn IP28 213 F8
Holmsey Gn Gdns 2 IP28 213 F8
Holt Cl 8 PE8 230 B1
Holt Fen CB6 211 B7
Holyrood Cl CB4 83 C6
Holywell CE Prim Sch PE27 208 A2
Holywell Cl PE3 197 A1
Holywell Ferry Rd CB4 121 F6
Holywell Front PE27 144 F2
Holywell Way PE3 196 F2
Home Cl Grafham PE28 116 A6
Histon CB4 104 B4
Home End CB1 67 A4
Home Farm Cl
Abbotsley PE19 57 B6
Hilton PE28 120 B1
Rampton CB4 124 F4
Home Farm Rd PE28 143 B5
Home Pasture PE4 204 B5
Homefield Cl CB4 104 C3
Homefield Rd CB9 23 F5
Homefield Rd Units CB9 23 F5
Homerton Coll CB2 65 A5
Homerton St CB2 65 A6
Homestall Cres CB9 38 B4
Homestead 12 PE28 215 C1
Homestead Dr 6 IP28 213 F8
Homing The CB5 84 E3
Honey Dro PE15 223 E4
Honey Hill
9 Cambridge CB3 83 C3
Fen Drayton CB4 122 A4
Fenstanton PE28 121 B6
Gamlingay SG19 41 D4
West Wratting CB1 53 E5
Honey Hill Mews CB3 83 C3
Honeydon Ave PE19 74 B5
Honeyhill PE4 205 A1
Honeyhill Com Prim Sch PE4 205 A1
Honeyhill Rd PE13 237 C2
Honeymead Rd PE15 223 B7
Honeysome Rd PE16 241 A5
Honeysuckle Cl
Haverhill CB9 38 E1
Red Lodge IP28 134 A8
2 Soham CB7 212 B4
Honeysuckle Ct PE2 186 D7
Honeyway SG8 5 E6
Hoo Cl PE19 117 B4
Hoof Cl CB6 242 D3
Hook Dro PE15 228 B1
Hook La PE15 223 C7
Hook Rd PE15 223 C7
Hook's Dro PE13 234 C4
Hook's Mill SG8 10 E7
Hooper St CB1 84 A1
Hop Row CB6 210 A6
Hopbine Ct PE26 171 F5
Hope St CB1 65 B8
Hopkins Cl CB4 84 A6
Hopton Rise CB9 38 B1
Horn La Kirtling CB8 72 B5
Linton CB1 35 B2
Hornbeam Rd IP28 239 D5
Horningsea Rd
Fen Ditton CB5 84 F6
Horningsea CB5 85 A8
Horse and Gate St CB4 121 F5
Horse Comm Cl PE29 141 E5
Horse Comm La PE29 141 E5
Horse Dro PE26 221 A1
Horse Fair Sh Ctr PE13 245 C5
Horse Ware CB4 208 D2
Horsegate
Market Deeping PE6 231 E8
Whittlesey PE7 189 D7
Horsegate Gdns PE16 241 C5
Horsegate La PE7 189 C7
Horsehead Dro PE14 229 F4
Horseheath Gn CB1 37 C1
Horseheath Pk CB1 37 D3
Horseheath Rd
Linton CB1 35 D2
Withersfield CB9 38 A4
Horseley Fen Dro PE16 241 E1
Horseley Fen Mid Dro PE16 241 B1
Horsemoor Rd PE15 223 D8
Horseshoe Cl
Balsham CB1 53 C2
Horseshoe Cl *continued*
Elmdon CB11 9 B4
Horseshoe La
4 Haverhill CB9 23 E7
4 Stamford PE9 244 B5
Horseshoe Terr PE13 245 B7
Horse-shoe Terr PE13 245 A7
Horseshoe Way PE7 186 D1
Horseshoes La CB1 54 D5
Horseshoes Way PE28 140 D2
Horseway PE16 223 C1
Horsey Hill (Civil War Fort)★ PE7 188 A4
Horsham Cl 3 CB9 38 C1
Horsley Hale CB6 242 D6
Horton Wlk PE3 197 D5
Hospital Rd PE15 222 E6
Hostmoor Ave PE15 243 A7
Hotel La PE28 151 F3
Houghton Ave PE2 187 F5
Houghton Gdns CB6 240 B4
Houghton Grange PE28 143 C5
Houghton Hill Rd PE28 143 B5
Houghton Mdws Nature Reserve★ PE28 143 C4
Houghton Mill★ PE28 143 A4
Houghton Prim Sch PE28 143 A5
Houghton Rd PE27 143 E5
Houghtons La CB7 213 B5
Houldsworth Terr CB8 110 F3
Housman Ave SG8 5 C8
How Hill (Tumulus)★ IP27 214 F7
Howard Cl CB5 84 D4
Howard Ct CB5 84 E4
Howard De Walden Way CB8 111 A4
Howard Rd
Cambridge CB5 84 E4
Eaton Socon PE19 74 C1
Meldreth SG8 14 A8
Howard Rd Ind Est PE19 74 C1
Howard's La CB1 37 A2
Howe Rd CB9 38 F1
Howes Pl CB3 83 A5
Howgate Rd CB4 83 D7
Howitt's Gdns PE19 75 A2
Howitt's La 5 PE19 74 F3
Howitts La PE19 74 F4
Howland PE2 186 A3
Howlett Way CB5 86 E6
Howletts Hill PE13 245 C4
Hoylake Dr PE7 187 C5
Huddleston Way CB2 33 A7
Hudpool PE29 118 F7
Hudson Cl 1 CB9 24 C6
Hudson Leisure Ctr PE13 245 A5
Hulatt Rd CB1 65 C4
Humber Dr PE7 181 E6
Humber Rd PE29 141 F7
Humberdale Way PE28 164 F5
Humberley Cl 1 PE19 74 F3
Humberstone Rd CB4 246 C4
Humphreys Rd CB4 83 E6
Humphries Way CB4 105 D3
Humphrys St PE2 186 D8
Hunchback La PE14 238 E2
Hundon Pl CB9 24 B8
Hundred Rd PE15 243 C8
Hundreds Rd PE6 232 C6
Hungarton Ct 2 PE1 198 D7
Hungate Rd PE14 236 E6
Hunsbury Cl PE7 189 F6
Hunters Chase PE15 243 E2
Hunters Cl PE16 241 D5
Hunters Way
Kimbolton PE28 113 F5
Royston SG8 5 E6
Sawtry PE28 168 B3
Hunting Ave PE2 186 F7
Hunting Gr CB3 101 B5
Huntingdon Boat Club PE29 141 F4
Huntingdon Jun & Inf Sch PE29 141 E6
Huntingdon Leisure Ctr PE29 141 D6
Huntingdon Racecorse PE28 140 C5
Huntingdon Rd
Boxworth CB3 101 E7
Brampton PE28 141 A2
Cambridge CB3 83 A5
Chatteris PE16 241 B4
Fen Drayton CB4 121 D4
Houghton & Wyton PE28 142 F5
Lolworth CB3 102 B5
Ramsey PE26 171 C2
St Neots PE19 75 A8
Sawston CB2 33 A8
Huntingdon St PE19 74 F6
Huntingdon Sta PE29 141 C4
Huntingdonshire Coll
Huntingdon PE29 141 E6
St Neots PE19 74 F6
Huntings Dr PE28 168 B4
Huntley Cl CB5 84 E4
Huntly Gr PE1 198 B4
Huntly Rd PE2 186 E7
Hunts Cl 4 PE15 222 F5
Hunts End PE19 117 B4

Hunt's Gate PE12 .....237 F8
Hunts La CB10 .....18 B7
Hunts Rd CB2 .....17 D8
Huntsmans Gate PE3 ..196 F3
Huntsmill CB1 .....66 E4
Hurdle Dro IP28 .....213 D8
Hurdleditch Rd SG8 ....28 D8
Hurdles Way CB2 .....31 E1
Hurn Rd PE6 .....203 E3
Hurrell Rd CB4 .....83 C6
Hurrell's Row CB2 .....42 E2
Hurricane Cl PE29 .....141 B8
Hurrys Cl CB2 .....32 E7
Hurst Ave 1 PE15 .....243 E4
Hurst La CB6 .....240 A6
Hurst Pk Ave CB4 .....83 E5
Hurstingstone PE27 ...144 A5
Hurts Croft CB7 .....212 E1
Hut Field La CB3 .....99 A3
Hutchinson Cl PE15 ...224 A4
Huttles Gn SG8 .....29 E4
Hyholmes PE3 .....196 F7
Hyll Cl CB10 .....18 D3
Hyperion Way CB8 ....110 D8
Hythe Cl CB5 .....130 A3
Hythe La Burwell CB5 ...130 A3
Ely CB7 .....240 D4
Hythe The CB6 .....242 D5
Hythegate PE4 .....204 D4

I

Ibberson's Dro PE15 ...221 F4
Ibbott Cl PE2 .....187 E5
Ibbott Cres 7 PE28 ....215 C1
Iceni Way CB8 .....110 B8
Icewell Hill CB8 .....111 A4
Ickleton Grange CB10 ..17 A1
Ickleton Pl CB9 .....24 B8
Ickleton Rd Duxford CB2 .17 E7
Elmdon CB11 .....9 A4
Great Chesterford CB10 ...18 C2
Hinxton CB10 .....18 B6
Icknield Cl Cheveley CB8 .91 C5
Ickleton CB10 .....18 A3
Icknield Prim Sch The
CB2 .....33 A8
Icknield Wlk SG8 .....5 F6
Icknield Wlk Fst Sch
SG8 .....5 F7
Ida Darwin Hospl CB1 ..66 D5
Ihlee Cl PE4 .....204 E1
Ilex Cl PE7 .....186 C3
Ilex Rd PE27 .....144 B6
Illing's La La PE28 .....164 A1
Illingworth Way CB2 ....30 C5
Illston Pl PE1 .....198 D7
Impala Dr CB1 .....66 A7
Imperial War Mus*
CB2 .....31 F1
Impett's La CB1 .....67 A4
Impington La CB4 .....104 C3
Impington Village Coll
CB4 .....104 D3
India La PE28 .....151 F2
Infield Rd PE28 .....167 C7
Ingham Hall Gdns
PE13 .....234 D7
Ingham Rd CB9 .....24 A8
Ingle Rd PE14 .....236 B5
Ingleborough PE1 .....198 A5
Ingleborough Mill
PE14 .....238 E5
Ingle's La 14 PE15 .....223 A5
Ingoldsby Cl 3 PE15 ...243 D2
Ingram St PE29 .....141 E4
Inham's Rd PE7 .....189 E6
Inhams Cl PE13 .....234 D5
Inhams Ct PE7 .....189 E6
Inhams Way PE28 .....116 A7
Inkerman Rise PE19 ....74 C5
Inley Dro PE12 .....237 A8
Innovation Way PE2 ...185 B5
Institute of Astronomy
CB3 .....83 A3
Institute of Public Health
CB2 .....65 B2
Interchange Ind Est The
PE29 .....141 C8
International Extension Coll
CB1 .....65 A8
Inverness Cl CB4 .....84 A5
Iram Dro CB4 .....209 B1
Irchester Pl PE3 .....197 D4
Ireton Cl PE19 .....74 F3
Ireton Way PE15 .....243 D2
Ireton's Way
Chatteris PE16 .....241 F2
Mepal PE16 .....216 C6
Irnham Rd PE9 .....244 C7
Ironmonger St 2 PE9 ..244 C5
Irving Burgess Cl PE7 .189 C8
Isaacson Rd CB5 .....109 C8
Isham Rd PE3 .....197 D4
Isherwood Cl SG8 .....5 C8
Isinglass Cl CB8 .....111 E2
Isis Way PE2 .....185 B5
Isle Bridge Rd PE14 ...236 F2
Isle Coll Chatteris PE16 .241 C5
Wisbech PE13 .....245 D4
Isle of Ely Way
Chatteris PE16 .....241 C7
March PE15 .....243 A4
Isleham CE Prim Sch
CB7 .....213 A5
Isleham Marina IP28 ..213 B6
Isleham Rd CB7 .....212 F2
Isons Cl SG8 .....15 E8
Itter Cres PE4 .....197 E8
Ivan Clark's Cnr CB1 ....34 C7
Ivatt St CB4 .....125 E5
Ivatt Way PE3 .....197 C7
Ivel Cl PE19 .....74 C4
Ivelbury Cl PE19 .....117 A3
Iver Cl CB1 .....65 F7
Ives Dro PE7 .....189 A2
Ivesdyke Cl 4 PE13 ....238 B2
Ivett's Cl CB3 .....45 E7
Ivy Field CB3 .....63 B4
Ivy Gr PE4 .....204 D2
Ivy Way PE28 .....138 A6
Ivydene CB5 .....128 A2
Ixworth Cl 8 PE6 .....232 A1
Ixworth Rd 3 CB9 .....23 E6
Izaak Walton Way CB4 ..84 C5
Izzard Rise PE19 .....96 E4

J

Jack Haws La 4 PE9 ...230 D4
Jack Hunt Sch PE3 ....197 B3
Jack Hunt Swimming Pool
PE3 .....197 B3
Jack Jarvis Cl 5 CB8 ..111 A3
Jack Warren Gn CB5 ....84 F3
Jack's Cnr Dro PE26 ...172 E3
Jackson Cl CB2 .....48 C5
Jackson's La CB10 .....18 D3
Jackson's Sq CB10 .....18 D3
Jackson's Way SG8 .....15 E8
James Carter Rd IP28 .239 A6
James Ct PE19 .....74 F2
James Essex Dr CB6 ...240 E7
James Gage Cl PE16 ..241 B3
James Gdns PE7 .....189 E7
James Nurse Cl CB1 ....66 A6
James St CB5 .....246 C3
Janus Cl CB9 .....24 D6
Jarman Way SG8 .....5 B7
Jarman's La IP28 .....213 D7
Jarvis Way CB8 .....110 E5
Jasmin Cl PE13 .....245 F7
Jasmine Ct
Cambridge CB1 .....65 C5
Peterborough PE2 .....185 E2
Jasmine Way PE7 .....181 F6
Jay Cl CB9 .....24 C7
Jaywick Rd CB9 .....24 A8
Jeavons La 6 CB3 .....79 C3
Jedburgh Cl 3 CB4 .....83 E7
Jefferson Cl 22 PE8 ....230 B1
Jeffery Ave 4 PE13 ....245 E7
Jeffrey Cl SG8 .....5 C8
Jellicoe Pl PE19 .....74 A2
Jenkins Cl PE19 .....74 B2
Jennings Ave PE19 .....74 E2
Jenyns Cl CB5 .....86 E7
Jepps La SG8 .....5 D6
Jermyn Cl CB4 .....83 D6
Jerusalem Dro CB6 ...217 A5
Jesus Coll CB5 .....246 B3
Jesus La CB1 .....246 B3
Jesus Terr CB1 .....246 C3
Jetty The PE13 .....235 C7
Jew House Dro PE14 ...235 E3
Jim Mollison Ct 2 IP28 239 B5
Jj Thompson Ave CB3 ...82 F2
Job's La PE15 .....243 C1
John Amner Cl CB6 ...240 D6
John Breay Cl SG8 .....29 D4
John Clare Prim Sch
PE6 .....231 B4
John Clarke Ct CB4 ....84 A6
John Conder Ct CB1 ....65 C7
John F Kennedy Ct 2
PE13 .....245 D4
John Falkner Com Inf Sch
CB2 .....32 E7
John Impey Way SG8 ...14 D6
John Mansfield Sch
PE1 .....198 B8
John Paxton Jun Sch
CB2 .....32 F8
John Sale Cl SG7 .....2 C4
John St Cambridge CB1 .246 C2
Royston SG8 .....5 D6
John Thompson Rd 3
PE13 .....245 D4
John's Cl SG8 .....15 E8
Johnson Way PE16 .....241 C6
Johnson Wlk PE1 .....197 F7
Johnson's Dro PE13 ...234 B7
Joiner's Ct CB1 .....35 B2
Joiner's Rd CB1 .....35 B2
Jolley Way CB4 .....83 F6
Jones Cl PE15 .....243 B3
Jones Ct PE26 .....172 B7
Jones Dr CB3 .....99 A3
Jones La PE7 .....190 C7
Jones's Dro PE7 .....221 F8
Jopling Way CB2 .....48 C4
Jordan Mews 2 PE1 ....198 B3
Jordans Yd CB1 .....246 A3
Jorose St PE3 .....197 A3
Jorose Way PE3 .....197 F3
Joscelynes CB2 .....49 C4
Joshua Cl 2 PE16 .....241 C5
Josiah Ct CB5 .....106 C8
Joyce's Cl CB2 .....32 F6
Jubilee Ave PE28 .....164 D6
Jubilee Cl Isleham CB7 .213 A5
Little Paxton PE19 .....95 F2
Waterbeach CB5 .....106 A8
Jubilee Ct CB8 .....90 A1
Jubilee End SG8 .....11 B2
Jubilee St PE2 .....186 F8
Jubilee Terr CB7 .....240 D3
Jubilee Way SG8 .....11 B2
Jubilee Wlk
Haverhill CB9 .....24 A7
Wisbech PE13 .....245 D8
Judson Ct 3 PE29 .....141 F8
Julian Cl CB9 .....24 D7
Julius Martin La CB7 ..212 A4
Junc The 2 PE15 .....243 D7
Junction Rd IP28 .....239 B5
Juniper Cl IP28 .....239 E5
Juniper Cres PE3 .....197 A2
Juniper Dr
Chatteris PE16 .....241 D5
Ely CB7 .....240 F5
Jupiter Cl 2 CB9 .....24 C6
Jury Rd PE7 .....181 C8
Justinian Cl CB9 .....24 D6
Jutland Rise PE19 .....74 C5

K

Kaldor Ct CB4 .....83 E7
Kathleen Elliot Way
CB1 .....65 F7
Kay Hitch Way CB4 ....104 B2
Keates Rd CB1 .....66 A5
Keats Cl SG8 .....5 C8
Keats Ct PE19 .....74 C6
Keats Way PE1 .....197 D7
Keble Cl PE9 .....244 A7
Keble Ct PE9 .....244 A7
Kedleston Rd PE7 .....187 F6
Keep The CB9 .....23 E7
Keeton Rd PE1 .....197 E7
Kefford Cl SG8 .....12 F5
Keillers Cl PE13 .....245 A7
Kelful Cl PE7 .....190 D7
Kelsey Cres CB1 .....66 A7
Kelsey Kerridge Sports Ctr
CB1 .....246 C1
Kelsey Way PE15 .....243 D2
Kelso Ct PE4 .....204 C1
Kelvin Cl CB1 .....65 D5
Kemmann La CB3 .....79 B3
Ken Stimpson Comp Sch
PE4 .....204 B4
Kendal Cl PE4 .....204 F2
Kendal Way CB4 .....84 A6
Kendrick Cl PE2 .....187 D6
Kenilworth Ave PE7 ....188 A5
Kenilworth Cl 3 PE19 ...74 C3
Kenlan Rd PE13 .....245 D6
Kennedy Croft CB4 .....126 A7
Kennedy Rd CB7 .....213 A5
Kennels Rd PE6 .....196 D4
Kennet Gdns PE4 .....204 E1
Kennetside CB8 .....73 D1
Kennett Com Prim Sch
CB8 .....133 F5
Kennett Rd or Moulton Road
CB8 .....112 F7
Kennett Sta CB8 .....133 F3
Kennulphs Cl 3 PE6 ....232 C8
Kent Cl Ely CB6 .....240 B5
St Ives PE27 .....143 F7
Kent Rd
Huntingdon PE29 .....141 E8
Peterborough PE3 .....197 E2
Kent Way CB4 .....83 F7
Kentings CB3 .....62 B5
Kentmere Pl 1 PE4 ....204 F2
Kents La CB7 .....212 B4
Kentwell Pl CB5 .....130 C2
Kenwood Gdns CB1 .....35 E2
Kerridge Cl CB1 .....84 A1
Kespar CB8 .....73 D6
Kesters Cl CB3 .....81 B2
Kesteven Cl 6 PE6 .....231 E8
Kesteven Rd PE9 .....244 B7
Kesteven Wlk PE1 .....198 B2
Kestrel Cl
Cottenham CB4 .....125 E5
Huntingdon PE29 .....142 A7
Kestrel Ct PE3 .....197 F2
Kestrel Dr 2 PE14 .....245 D2
Kestrel Pl 4 PE19 .....75 B7
Kestrel Rd CB9 .....24 C7
Kestrel Way 7 SG8 .....5 E8
Keswick Cl PE4 .....204 F3
Kettering Rd PE9 .....244 B2
Kettlefields CB8 .....89 F1
Kettlefields Prim Sch
CB8 .....89 F1
Kettles Cl CB4 .....103 C5
Kettle's Yd* CB1 .....246 A4
Key Theatre* PE1 .....198 A1
Keynes Rd CB5 .....84 D4
Keyston Rd PE28 .....135 D2
Kidmans Cl Hilton PE28 .120 B1
Newton CB2 .....31 B7
Kigezi Int Sch of Medicine
CB1 .....246 B2
Kildare Dr PE3 .....197 C4
Kilham PE2 .....185 E2
Kilkenny Ave CB6 .....240 E7
Killem's Gn CB11 .....1 E4
Kilmaine Cl CB4 .....83 F8
Kiln Cl
2 Little Downham CB6 ...218 B7
St Ives PE27 .....143 E6
Kiln House Yd SG8 .....5 C6
Kiln La CB7 .....240 F5
Kilverstone PE4 .....204 B6
Kim Rd PE28 .....114 A7
Kimberley Rd CB4 .....246 C4
Kimbolton Ct PE1 .....197 F3
Kimbolton Prep Sch
PE28 .....113 E5
Kimbolton Rd
Hail Weston PE19 .....74 A8
Pertenhall MK44 .....113 D1
Kimbolton Sch PE28 ...113 F4
Kinderley Com Prim Sch
PE13 .....237 F6
Kinderley Rd PE13 ....245 C8
King Cob CB6 .....210 F5
King Edgar Cl CB6 ....240 D7
King Edward Rd PE16 .241 C5
King Edward VII Rd
CB8 .....110 E5
King George Ave CB8 ..110 B8
King Hedges Prim Sch
CB4 .....83 F7
King James Way SG8 ....5 D6
King St Cambridge CB1 ..246 B3
Doddington/Wimblington
PE15 .....223 B7
Mildenhall IP28 .....239 C4
14 Over CB4 .....208 D1
1 Peterborough PE1 ....198 A2
Rampton CB4 .....124 E4
Somersham PE28 .....215 B1
West Deeping PE6 .....231 A8
Wisbech PE13 .....245 C5
King's Ave CB7 .....240 E7
King's Delph Dro PE7 ..187 E2
King's Dyke PE7 .....188 E6
King's Gate CB3 .....78 E1
King's Gdns
Huntingdon PE29 .....141 D5
Peterborough PE1 .....198 A5
King's Hedges Rd CB4 ..83 D7
King's La
Cambridge CB1 .....246 A2
Elmdon CB11 .....9 A3
St Neots PE19 .....75 A5
King's Par CB2 .....246 A2
King's Rd CB3 .....64 B7
King's Wk 3 PE13 .....245 C4
Kingdon Ave CB7 .....219 B5
Kingfisher Cl Bourn CB3 .60 C6
Chatteris PE16 .....241 C6
Haverhill CB9 .....24 C8
Little Paxton PE19 .....96 A2
March PE15 .....243 E5
Sawston CB2 .....32 E6
Yaxley PE7 .....181 D5
Kingfisher Dr
Burwell CB5 .....130 B4
6 Wisbech PE14 .....245 D2
Kingfisher Gn PE27 ....143 F7
Kingfisher Rd PE7 .....189 F8
Kingfisher Way
Cottenham CB4 .....125 D5
Mildenhall IP28 .....239 D4
The Stukeleys PE29 .....141 A6
Kingfishers PE2 .....185 D6
Kings Cl
Huntingdon PE29 .....142 A7
Mildenhall IP28 .....239 D5
Kings Coll CB2 .....246 A2
Kings Coll Sch CB3 .....83 C1
Kings Ct CB8 .....110 B8
Kings Delph PE7 .....188 C5
Kings Dr CB8 .....111 B1
Kings Dyke Cl PE2 ....187 E6
Kings Gr CB3 .....63 B4
Kings Hedges PE27 ....144 A6
Kings Mead CB8 .....91 C7
Kings Mill La
Great Shelford CB2 .....48 F4
2 Stamford PE9 .....244 B4
Kings Par CB7 .....212 B3
Kings Rd
Eaton Socon PE19 .....74 B3
Hardwick CB3 .....81 A2
Peterborough PE2 .....187 B6
St Ives PE27 .....144 A4
St Neots PE19 .....74 F6
Stamford PE9 .....244 B6
Wisbech PE13 .....245 C4
Kings Ride SG8 .....4 C3
Kings Ripton Rd PE29 .152 D1
Kings Sch PE1 .....198 A4
Kings Sch The CB6 ....240 C5
Kingsbridge Ct PE4 ....204 A5
Kingsbrook PE27 .....144 A5
Kingsfield Prim Sch
PE16 .....241 B5
Kingsland Way SG7 .....2 D4
Kingsley Ave PE13 .....245 B4
Kingsley Cl 1 PE9 .....230 D3
Kingsley Rd PE1 .....198 C4
Kingsley St PE15 .....243 D5
Kingsley Wlk CB6 .....240 A4
Kingsline Cl PE6 .....233 A3
Kingsmead Ct CB6 ....242 E4
Kingston Cl PE29 .....141 E8
Kingston Dr PE2 .....187 E5
Kingston Pas 2 CB8 ...111 A3
Kingston Rd CB3 .....61 D1
Kingston St CB1 .....65 A8
Kingston Vale SG8 .....5 E5
Kingston Way PE28 ....163 F6
Kingsway Arbury CB4 ....83 D6
Duxford Airfield CB2 .....31 F1
Leverington PE13 .....245 F7
Mildenhall IP28 .....239 C4
Newmarket CB8 .....110 F4
Royston SG8 .....5 D8
Kingswood Rd PE15 ....243 C3
Kinnaird Way CB1 .....65 C4
Kinnears Wlk PE2 .....185 F2
Kinross Rd CB4 .....84 A5
Kintbury CB2 .....17 D8
Kipling Ct PE1 .....197 E8
Kipling Pl 1 PE19 .....74 D5
Kipling Rd 1 SG8 .....5 E8
Kirby Cl CB4 .....83 F5
Kirby Cross Ave CB6 ..242 B5
Kirby Rd CB5 .....127 C1
Kirby Terr CB5 .....127 B1
Kirby Wlk PE3 .....197 C5
Kirby's Cl 12 CB4 .....208 D1
Kirk Ogden Cl PE15 ...243 D3
Kirkgate PE13 .....237 F7
Kirkgate St PE13 .....245 E7
Kirkham's La PE14 .....236 C4
Kirkmeadow PE3 .....197 A8
Kirk's La PE14 .....235 E5
Kirkstall PE2 .....186 B3
Kirkton Gate PE3 .....197 A1
Kirkwood Cl PE3 .....197 E2
Kirkwood Rd CB4 .....83 F7
Kirtling Pl 5 CB9 .....24 B8
Kirtling Rd Kirtling CB8 ..72 D7
Woodditton CB8 .....90 E1
Kisby Ave PE29 .....142 A1
Kite Cl PE29 .....142 A7
Kitson Gdns CB6 .....210 F5
Knapp Rise CB3 .....47 A5
Knapp The CB3 .....47 A5
Knaresborough Ct 10
PE19 .....74 F1
Knarr Fen Rd PE6 .....202 D8
Knaves Acre Dro CB7 ..212 E5
Kneesworth House (Hospital)
SG8 .....13 C5
Kneesworth Rd SG8 ....13 F8
Kneesworth St SG8 .....5 C7
Knight Mews PE2 .....187 A6
Knight's Cl 11 PE15 ....223 A5
Knight's End Rd PE15 ..243 C1
Knighton Cl PE7 .....186 D1
Knights Cl
Eaton Socon PE19 .....74 B4
13 Leverington PE13 ....238 B2
Knights Ct CB9 .....23 E7
Knights Way CB4 .....105 D3
Knipe Cl PE29 .....141 B7
Knole Wlk PE3 .....197 B3
Knowle Ct CB6 .....242 B5
Knowles Ave PE28 .....164 E5
Knowles Cl PE28 .....140 E2
Knox End CB10 .....21 A2
Knutsford Rd SG8 .....12 E4
Kooreman Ave PE13 ...245 D7
Kyle Cres PE28 .....140 D2
Kym Rd PE19 .....74 C4

L

Laburnhum Gr PE1 ....198 B8
Laburnum Ave
Mildenhall IP28 .....239 E5
Yaxley PE7 .....181 F6
Laburnum Cl
Cambridge CB4 .....83 F4
Red Lodge IP28 .....213 F1
5 Wisbech PE13 .....245 E7
Laburnum Gr PE15 ....243 C6
Laburnum La CB5 .....130 A3
Laburnum Way PE27 ..144 A5
Lacey's La CB8 .....110 B7
Lacey's Way CB2 .....32 D1
Lacks Cl CB4 .....125 D3
Laddus Bank PE14 .....236 C1
Laddus Dro PE14 .....229 B8
Lady Adrian Sch The
CB4 .....83 E5
Lady Charlotte Rd
PE7 .....186 D3
Lady Jermy Way CB1 ...85 B1
Lady Lodge Dr PE2 ...186 A5
Lady Margaret Rd 1
CB3 .....83 C3
Lady Romayne Cl PE9 .244 C4
Lady Smith Ave PE7 ...189 F8
Lady Way PE19 .....74 B4
Ladybower Way PE4 ...204 E3
Ladygate 1 CB9 .....23 E6
Lady's Dro PE14 .....236 D6
Lady's Wood Nature
Reserve* PE26 .....170 E2
Ladywalk CB4 .....123 F3
Lake Ave PE14 .....229 F3
Lake Ct PE13 .....245 D4
Lake Dro PE7 .....190 E6
Lake Way PE29 .....141 C5
Lakefield Ave PE19 .....96 A2
Lakes Dro CB6 .....209 F3
Lakeside
Hamrton Hargate PE7 ....186 C2
Peterborough PE4 .....204 D4
Lakeside Cl
Little Paxton PE19 .....96 A2
Perry PE28 .....115 D3
Lakeside Leisure Ctr
PE2 .....186 A5
Lakeview Way PE7 ....186 C2
Lakeway 8 PE28 .....215 C1
Lamb Fair Ct CB1 .....35 D2
Lambert Mews PE9 ....244 C4
Lambeth Wlk PE9 .....244 A6
Lamble Cl IP28 .....213 F8
Lambourn Cl 1 CB2 ....64 D3

Lambourne Rd CB3 ....81 A3
Lambs' Cross CB4 ....103 F8
Lambs Hill Dro PE15 ..228 B1
Lamb's La
 Cottenham CB4 ....125 D3
 Glatton PE28 ....175 D2
Lamb's Pl PE15 ....243 D4
Lammas Field 4 CB3 ...64 C7
Lammas Gdns PE29 ....141 C5
Lammas Rd PE1 ....198 A7
Lammas Way
 St Ives PE27 ....143 F4
 St Neots PE19 ....74 E6
Lamport Dr PE29 ......141 F8
Lancaster Cl
 Old Hurst PE28 ....154 D6
 Warboys PE28 ....164 F4
Lancaster Ct PE7 ......181 F6
Lancaster Dr PE27 ....144 A6
Lancaster Rd
 Mildenhall IP28 ....213 E8
 Ramsey PE26 ....171 E3
 10 Stamford PE9 ....244 B6
Lancaster Way Ely CB6 .217 F1
 Godmanchester PE29 ...141 F2
 Huntingdon PE29 ......141 B8
 Yaxley PE7 ....181 F6
Lancaster Way Bsns Pk
 CB6 ....217 F1
Lancelot Way PE28 ....121 C5
Lancing Cl PE4 ....204 C3
Landau Way PE15 .....243 E6
Landbeach Rd CB4 ....105 D3
Landcliffe Cl PE27 .....144 B5
Lander Cl CB4 ....105 C4
Landseer Ct CB9 ....23 F6
Landwade Rd
 Exning CB8 ....131 B4
 Fordham CB8 ....131 D5
Lane End PE19 ....38 B1
Lane The Easton PE28 ..138 B4
 Hauxton CB2 ....48 B4
 Old Hurst PE28 ....154 E6
 Stow Longa PE28 ......137 B2
 West Deeping PE6 .....231 B7
Lanes The
 Great Wilbraham CB1 ...67 F8
 Over CB4 ....208 D1
 St Ives PE28 ....143 A5
Langdale Cl CB1 ....66 A7
Langdyke PE1 ....198 F6
Langford Rd PE2 ......187 A7
Langham Rd CB1 ....65 C6
Langham Way Ely CB7 .240 E7
 Haverhill CB9 ....38 B1
Langley PE3 ....197 B8
Langley Cl PE27 ....144 A4
Langley Ct PE27 ....144 A4
Langley Lawn CB11 ....1 D2
Langley Way PE28 .....143 B1
Langton Rd PE1 ....198 D7
Langwood Cl 7 PE19 ..74 C6
Langwood Fen Dro
 PE16 ....216 D8
Langwood Hill Dro
 PE16 ....216 B7
Lankester Rd CB8 ......5 C5
Lansbury Cl 4 PE19 ...74 E4
Lansdowne Cl CB6 ....240 B3
Lansdowne Rd
 Cambridge CB3 ....82 F3
 Yaxley PE7 ....181 F6
Lansdowne Way PE2 ..186 D7
Lansdowne Wlk PE2 ..186 D7
Lantree Cres CB2 ......64 D1
Lanwades Pk CB8 .....133 F1
Lapwing Ct IP28 ......239 D4
Lapwing Dr PE7 ....190 A8
Lapwings Cl CB1 ......85 B1
Larch Cl PE7 ....181 F6
Larch Gr PE1 ....198 C6
Larham Way PE16 ....241 B5
Lark Cl IP28 ....213 E4
Lark Cres PE29 ......142 A6
Lark End PE19 ....117 B3
Lark Grange CB7 ....219 D4
Lark Hill CB8 ....112 E5
Lark Rd IP28 ....239 D4
Lark Rise PE9 ....80 F3
Lark Way PE28 ......150 E4
Larkfield Rd CB7 ....240 E6
Larkhall Rd CB7 .....212 D1
Larkin Cl Cambridge CB4 .84 A6
 Royston SG8 ....13 D1
Larkin Pl SG8 ....13 D1
Larkins Rd SG8 ....26 F6
Larklands PE3 ....197 B1
Larks Cl CB9 ....24 C7
Larkspur Cl 4 IP28 ...213 F1
Larkspur Wlk PE4 ....204 D3
Larmor Dr CB3 ....83 B3
Latham Ave PE2 ......186 C6
Latham Cl CB2 ....64 D6
Latham Rd
 Cambridge CB2 ....64 D6
 Huntingdon PE29 .....141 C8
Latimer Cl CB5 ....84 E3
Latin Cl PE19 ....118 A2
Lattersey Cl PE7 ......189 F7
Lattersey Nature Reserve*
 PE7 ....190 B6
Laundress La CB3 ....246 A2
Laundry La CB1 ....65 D5
Laureate CP Sch CB8 .110 E6
Laureate Gdns CB8 ...110 E6
Laureate Paddocks
 CB8 ....110 E6
Laureate Sch Rd CB8 .110 E6
Laurel Cl Haverhill CB9 .38 D2
 Mepal CB6 ....216 E3
 9 Red Lodge IP28 ....214 A1
 Sawtry PE28 ....168 A3
 Yaxley PE7 ....181 B4
Laurel Dr Elm PE14 ...236 A5
 Thorney PE6 ....232 F3
Laurels Cl PE19 ....74 F4
Laurels The PE15 .....243 E7
Lauriston Pl 1 CB4 ...83 E8
Lavender
 3 Red Lodge IP28 ....213 F1
 Yaxley PE7 ....181 F6
Lavender Cres PE1 ...198 B8
Lavender Ct 4 PE29 ..141 F7
Lavender Field CB9 ...23 D8
Lavender Rd CB4 ......84 A7
Lavender Way PE27 ..144 A6
Lavenham Ct PE2 ....186 C7
Lavington Grange PE1 .198 E6
Law Cl CB6 ....242 D3
Law's Cl PE6 ....206 F1
Law's Lawn PE8 ......192 C2
Lawn Ave PE1 ....198 A7
Lawn La
 Little Downham CB6 ..218 A7
 Sutton CB6 ....216 E1
Lawn The CB2 ....32 C5
Lawns Cres CB2 ......218 A7
Lawns Ct SG8 ....5 D6
Lawns The
 Cambridge CB3 ....83 A2
 Everton SG19 ....40 C3
 Melbourn SG8 ....14 C5
 Wisbech PE13 ....245 B6
Lawrance Lea CB2 ....47 F2
Lawrence Ave PE7 ...187 C2
Lawrence Cl CB3 .....82 D8
Lawrence Rd
 Eaton Socon PE19 ...74 C5
 Ramsey PE26 ....172 C7
 Wittering PE8 ....230 B1
Lawrence Way CB4 ..83 F7
Laws Cres PE28 ......140 C4
Lawson Ave PE2 .....187 D6
Laxton Ave CB3 ......81 A3
Laxton Cl PE19 ......74 C4
Laxton Grange PE28 .208 C5
Laxton Way CB4 .....84 C5
Layer Rd CB9 ....23 E7
Layston Pk SG8 ......5 D5
Layton Cres PE28 ...140 D2
Lea Brooks Cl PE28 ..164 F4
Lea Gdns PE3 ....197 F1
Lea Rd PE28 ....143 C1
Leach Cl PE13 ....245 C2
Leaden Hill SG8 ......28 D8
Leaden's La PE19 ....117 C3
Leader's Way CB8 ...110 E4
Leading Dro PE13 ...181 E4
Leaf Ave PE7 ....186 D3
Leafere Way 1 PE13 .238 B2
Leam The PE14 .....236 A4
Leather La CB9 ......23 E7
Lebanon Dr PE13 ...245 F7
Ledbury Rd PE3 .....197 C3
Ledger Ct PE27 .....144 A6
Ledham PE2 ....185 D4
Ledo Rd CB2 ....31 F2
Lee Cl Sutton CB4 ...125 D3
 Hanchet End CB9 ....38 D2
Lee Rd PE7 ....181 E4
Leechcroft PE28 .....121 C6
Lees La PE19 ....95 E5
Lees Way CB3 ....103 E1
Leete Pl SG8 ....5 C7
Leete Rd CB1 ....65 F5
Leete's La CB3 ....46 A8
Leeway Ave CB2 ....49 B5
Legg Rd 21 PE8 .....230 B1
Legge-bourke Ct
 PE13 ....245 F6
Legion Ct CB4 ....83 E7
Legion Way PE29 ...142 B1
Leicester Cl CB6 ....240 A3
Leighton PE2 ....186 C4
Leighton Prim Sch
 PE2 ....186 C4
Leinsters Cl PE3 ....197 D3
Leiston Ct PE6 ......232 A1
Leiston Rd CB1 ......23 E7
Lemur Dr CB1 ....66 B7
Lensfield Rd CB2 ...246 B1
Lenton Cl PE28 .....140 D2
Lents Way CB4 ......84 C5
Leofric Sq PE1 ......198 E3
Leonard Cl 2 CB5 ...84 E4
Leopold Wlk PE4 ...204 D3
Lerowe Rd PE13 ....245 E7
Les Baux Pl 5 PE13 .245 E7
Leslie Gn Rd PE28 ..143 B5
Lessingham PE2 ....185 D4
Lester Dr CB6 ....210 A6
Lester Piggott Way
 CB8 ....110 F6
Lethbridge Rd PE4 .204 E2
Lettice Martin Croft
 CB2 ....32 C5
Levellers La PE19 ..74 F3
Levens Wlk PE3 ....197 B3
Leverington Comm
 PE13 ....235 B8
Leverington Prim Sch
 PE13 ....238 B2

Leverington Rd PE13 ..245 A6
Leverington Rd Ind Est
 PE13 ....245 B7
Levers Wr PE29 ......141 C5
Levitt's Dro PE6 .....200 C4
Lewes Gdns PE4 ....204 C3
Lewis Cl
 Great & Little Abington
  CB1 ....34 C5
 March PE15 ....243 B3
Lewis Cres CB1 ......34 C5
Lexington Cl 3 CB4 ..83 C5
Ley Rd CB8 ....90 A1
Leyburn Cl CB1 .....66 A7
Leys Ave CB4 ....83 F5
 St Neots PE19 ......74 E6
Leys Rectory PE19 ..117 F2
Leys Sch The CB2 ..246 B1
Leys Sports Ctr The
 CB2 ....64 E7
Leys The
 Alconbury PE28 .....150 F4
 Little Gransden SG19 .58 E3
 Peterborough PE3 ..197 A1
 Sawtry PE28 ....168 C3
Leys Wlk CB2 ....48 C4
Leyton Ave IP28 ....239 B6
Liberator Rd PE26 ..171 E3
Lichfield Ave CB4 ...204 B3
Lichfield Rd CB1 ....65 B6
Licking's Dro PE13 .245 A2
Lidgate Cl PE2 ......186 C7
Lidgate Rd CB8 .....92 E7
Lilac Cl Haslingfield CB3 .47 B5
 Wisbech PE13 .....245 F7
Lilac Ct CB1 ....65 C5
Lilac End CB3 ......47 B4
Lilac Rd PE1 ....198 C7
Lilac Way PE27 ....144 B6
Lilley Cl CB4 ....84 B5
Lilyholt Rd PE15 ...222 A5
Lime Ave PE13 ....245 C7
Lime Cl Burwell CB5 .130 C1
 Mildenhall IP28 ...239 E5
Lime Gr March PE15 .243 C6
 Royston SG8 ....5 E8
 St Neots PE19 .....74 F6
Lime Kiln Cl PE7 ..197 E4
Lime Rd PE26 .....172 A8
Lime Tree Ave PE1 .197 F4
Limekiln Cl SG8 ...5 E5
Limekiln Rd CB1 ..65 E3
Limes Ave 1 PE14 .236 A5
Limes Cl
 Bassingbourn SG8 .12 E5
 Littleport CB6 .....242 C4
Limes Ct PE27 ....143 F1
Limes Pk Rd PE27 .143 F1
Limes Rd CB3 .....81 A3
Limes The
 Bassingbourn SG8 .12 E5
 Castor PE5 ....195 F1
 Harston CB2 ......47 F2
 Sawston CB2 .....32 F8
 5 Wittering PE8 ..230 B1
Limestone Cl 7 CB7 .213 A5
Limetree Cl
 3 Cambridge CB1 ..65 D5
 Yaxley PE7 ....181 F7
Limlow SG8 ....4 B8
Linclare Pl 7 PE19 ..74 C4
Lincoln Ave CB4 ...143 F7
Lincoln Cl PE19 ...117 A5
Lincoln Rd
 Deeping Gate PE6 .231 E4
 Mildenhall IP28 ..213 E8
 Peterborough PE4 .197 C8
 Ramsey PE26 .....171 E3
 Stamford PE9 ....244 D7
 Wyton Airfield PE28 .143 A8
Linden Cl
 Cambridge CB4 ...83 C4
 Haddenham CB6 ..210 A5
Linden Dr PE16 ...241 C4
Linden End CB6 ..210 A5
Linden Gr PE29 ..141 F2
Linden Way CB6 .210 A5
Lindens Cl PE13 .234 A2
Lindeth Cl PE29 .141 A7
Lindisfarne Cl 9 PE19 .74 F1
Lindisfarne Rd PE6 .232 A1
Lindridge Wlk PE3 .197 A2
Lindsay Cl SG8 ...13 C1
Lindsells Wlk PE16 .241 C5
Lindsey Cl PE4 ...204 D1
Lindsey Rd
 Stamford PE9 ...244 C6
 5 Uffington PE9 .230 C6
Ling Garth PE1 ..198 B8
Lingfield Way CB8 .5 E6
Lingholme Cl 2 CB4 .83 C5
Lingmoor PE29 ...141 A6
Lingrey Ct CB2 ...64 D2
Lingwood Pk PE3 .197 A1
Link Dr PE28 .....140 C3
Link La CB6 ......216 E1
Link Rd
 Peterborough PE1 .197 F3
 Sawston CB2 .....32 F8
Links Cl IP28 .....213 E4
Links The CB8 ...89 D8
Links Way PE27 .143 F4
Linkside PE3 .....204 B1
Linley Rd St Neots PE19 .74 E3
 Whittlesey PE7 ..189 E6
Linlithgow Cl CB3 .99 A3
Linnet PE2 ....185 D6

Linton CE Inf Sch CB1 ..35 C2
Linton Cl CB8 ....110 F5
Linton Hts Jun Sch
 CB1 ....35 D2
Linton Liby CB1 .....35 C2
Linton Pl CB9 ....24 B8
Linton Rd Balsham CB1 .52 F2
 Great Abington CB1 ..34 D6
 Hadstock CB1 ....20 B8
 Horseheath CB1 ....36 F3
Linton Village Coll
 CB1 ....35 B2
Linton Zoological Gdns★
 CB1 ....35 B1
Linwood La PE15 ...223 A8
Lion Cl CB8 ....220 D3
Lion Ct CB6 ....210 A6
Lion Wlk PE26 .....172 A5
Lion Yd PE26 ......172 B6
Lion Yd Sh Ctr CB1 .246 B2
Lionel Walden Prim Sch
 PE15 ....223 A5
Lions Cross PE29 ..119 A8
Lisburn Rd CB8 ...111 B3
Lisle Cl CB7 ....240 E5
Lisle La CB7 ......240 E4
Lisle Wlk CB1 .....66 A6
Lister Rd PE1 .....197 F7
Lister's Rd PE14 ..236 E1
Litchfield Cl PE7 .181 F5
Litlington Rd SG8 .11 E1
Little Back La The
 CB5 ....129 C1
Little Bowsers CB10 .20 D3
Little Casterton Rd
 PE9 ....244 A6
Little Chilfords CB1 .35 B4
Little Chishill Rd SG8 .1 C6
Little Church St 22
 PE13 ....245 C5
Little Cl PE6 ......232 A1
Little Dowgate PE13 .245 A7
Little End Rd PE19 .74 B1
Little End Rd Ind Est
 PE19 ....74 B2
Little Farthing Cl
 PE27 ....144 B4
Little Fen Dro
 Burwell CB5 ......129 E6
 Swaffham Prior CB5 .129 A1
Little Fendyke La
 PE14 ....236 E5
Little Gn Cheveley CB8 .91 C5
 Guilden Morden SG8 .11 A7
Little Gransden La
 SG19 ....58 D4
Little Hasse Dro CB7 .212 A6
Little Heath SG19 ..41 C4
Little How PE27 ....143 E6
Little Johns Cl PE3 .196 F3
Little La Ely CB6 ...240 B4
 Great Gransden SG19 .58 E4
 Melbourn SG8 .....14 C6
Little London PE26 .212 F5
Little London Dro CB7 .212 F5
Little London La CB7 .212 F5
Little Marefen Dro
 CB6 ....242 A7
Little Mdw PE28 ..102 B2
Little Moor PE28 ..121 C5
Little Northfields 8
 PE9 ....230 D4
Little Paddocks PE13 .238 C1
Little Paxton La PE19 .95 F2
Little Paxton Prim Sch
 PE19 ....95 F1
Little Ramper PE13 .238 C1
Little Setchel Dro CB4 .209 F2
Little St CB6 ......218 B6
Little St Mary's La
 CB2 ....246 A1
Little Thetford CE Prim Sch
 CB6 ....211 B7
Little Whyte PE26 .172 B6
Little Wilbraham Rd
 CB1 ....86 D4
Littlechild Dr 5 PE28 .238 B2
Littlecotes Cl PE28 .137 F7
Littlefield Cl
 Godmanchester PE29 .118 F8
 Wilburton CB6 .....210 C6
Littlemeer PE2 .....185 F4
Littleport Com Prim Sch
 CB6 ....242 B4
Littleport Sta CB6 .242 E6
Littleworth Dr PE13 .233 F8
Littleworth End PE19 .118 A1
Livermore Cl PE4 ..204 A6
Loch Fyne Cl PE2 ..185 C4
Lock Lomond Way
 PE2 ....185 C4
Locks Cl PE6 .....206 B7
Locks Gn PE8 ....183 A8
Locksgate 1 PE28 .215 C1
Lockspit Hall Dro
 Cottenham CB4 ..125 F8
 Ottenham CB4 ...209 F1
Lode Ave Outwell PE14 .236 F1
 Waterbeach CB5 .106 B7
Lode Cl CB7 ......212 B3
Lode La PE7 .....211 E1
Lode Rd Bottisham CB5 .86 D7
 Lode CB5 ....107 D1
Lode Way
 Chatteris PE16 ..241 C6
 Haddenham CB6 .210 A5
Loder Ave PE3 ...196 F2
Lodes End Dro PE26 .220 F2
Lodge Cl PE29 ...141 C4

Lodge Gdns CB6 ....210 A6
Lodge Rd SG8 ......31 A1
Loftsteads 3 PE28 ..215 C1
Logan's Way CB4 ...84 A3
Loire Ct PE1 ......197 E4
Lomax Dr PE28 ...140 C3
Lombardy Dr PE1 ..198 B8
London La PE19 ...96 E4
London Rd Barley SG8 .6 F1
 Chatteris PE16 .....241 C2
 Fenstanton PE28 ..120 E7
 Fowlmere SG8 ....15 D5
 Godmanchester PE29 .141 F1
 Great Chesterford CB10 .18 C2
 Great Shelford CB2 .49 B4
 Harston CB2 .....48 B3
 Hemingford Grey PE27 .143 F1
 Kimbolton PE28 ..114 A4
 Peterborough PE7 .186 F3
 Royston SG8 .....5 D4
 Sawston CB2 ....32 F5
 Stamford PE9 ....244 C2
 Wansford PE8 ...194 B2
 Yaxley PE7 .....181 C5
London St
 Godmanchester PE29 .141 F1
 Whittlesey PE7 ..189 D6
Lone Tree Ave CB4 .83 C8
Lone Tree Gr CB4 .83 C8
Long Cswy
 Peterborough PE1 .198 A2
 Witcham CB6 ....217 C2
Long Dolver Dro CB7 .212 B6
Long Dro Bury PE26 .172 F5
 Cottenham CB4 ..125 F3
 Downham CB6 ...224 F3
 Elm PE14 ....235 B1
 Feltwell PE38 ...226 F6
 Haddenham CB6 .209 C5
 Holme PE7 ......177 D5
 Over CB4 ....208 D3
 Parson Drove PE13 .234 B5
 Ramsey PE26 ...221 D2
 Somersham PE28 .215 D2
 Waterbeach CB5 .106 D8
 Whittlesey PE7 .200 F3
Long Furlong CB4 .208 D1
Long Holme Dro CB4 .208 E3
Long La Coveney CB6 .217 C3
 Fowlmere SG8 ..15 D8
 Gamlingay SG19 .41 F3
 Hemingford Grey PE28 .120 C8
 Linton CB1 ....35 C1
 Over CB4 ......208 E2
 Spaldwick PE28 .137 F5
 Willingham CB4 .124 A8
Long Lots PE14 ..236 F8
Long Mdw Field PE13 .237 F2
Long Mdws Rd PE5 .107 F2
Long N Fen Dro CB6 .216 A4
Long Nightlayer's Dro
 PE16 ....241 E8
Long Pasture PE4 .204 B5
Long Rd Cambridge CB2 .64 F4
 Comberton CB3 ..81 D2
Long Rd Sixth Form Coll
 CB2 ....64 F3
Long Reach Rd CB4 .84 C6
Longchamp Dr CB7 .240 F6
Longfellow Ave 5 PE19 .74 D5
Longfield Gate PE2 .186 A6
Longfield Rd CB6 ..242 B5
Longfields CB6 ...240 A3
Longhead La PE14 .238 D3
Longhill Rd PE15 ..228 B8
Longholme Rd PE26 .171 A4
Longmere La CB7 .212 A5
Longsands Com Coll
 PE19 ....75 A6
Longsands Par 3 PE19 .75 A5
Longsands Rd PE19 .75 A5
Longstaff Way PE29 .142 A6
Longstanton Rd
 Oakington/Longstanton
  CB4 ....103 B3
 Over CB4 ......123 B7
Longthorpe Cl PE3 .197 A2
Longthorpe Gn PE3 .197 B1
Longthorpe House Mews
 PE3 ....196 F2
Longthorpe Parkway
 PE3 ....186 A8
Longthorpe Prim Sch
 PE3 ....197 A2
Longueville Ct PE2 .186 B5
Longview CB6 ...216 D1
Longwater PE2 ..186 B6
Longwood CB3 ..81 B8
Longworth Ave CB4 .84 A3
Lonsdale CB1 ....35 E2
Lonsdale Terr PE13 .245 C3
Loop Rd PE28 ...146 A4
Lophams Cl CB9 .38 C2
Lord's Croft La CB9 .24 A7
Lord's Gd Dro CB5 .128 D2
Lords La PE13 ...235 D7
Lord's La PE13 ..235 D6
Lordship Cl Orwell SG8 .45 E1
 Willingham CB4 .209 A1
Lordship Dr SG8 .14 C7
Lordship End PE12 .233 E8
Loris Ct CB1 ....66 A7
Lorna Ct PE27 ..143 F6
Lornas Field PE7 .186 D2
Losecoat Cl PE9 .244 D7
Lotfield St SG8 .45 E1
Lottings Way PE19 .74 C6

Loughborough Univ of
  Peterborough PE1 ...198 A3
Loughrigg Cl PE29 ....141 B7
Loughton Ct CB5 .....84 E4
Louthe Way PE28 .....168 C3
Love La Ashwell SG7 .....2 A5
  Houghton & Wyton PE28 ...143 A5
  Wisbech PE13 ....245 C4
Lovell Rd CB4 ....84 A7
Lovells The PE14 .....236 D6
Lovers La PE5 ....194 F2
Love's Cl CB4 ....104 C2
Love's Hill PE5 ......195 F1
Low Cl PE7 ....189 E8
Low Cross PE7 ....189 D8
Low Fen Dro Way CB5 ..85 B4
Low Gate PE13 ....237 F8
Low Harthay PE28 ....139 D3
Low Pk Cnr CB7 ......133 A6
Low Rd Burwell CB5 ...130 B2
  Crowland PE6 ....207 F7
  Fenstanton PE28 .....121 A7
  Hemingford Grey PE28 ..144 A1
  Little Stukeley PE28 ...151 D3
  The Stukeleys PE28 ...140 C7
  Wisbech PE14 ....245 E1
Low Side PE14 ....236 E2
Lowbury Cres CB4 ....103 B6
Lowburyholme Rd
CB4 ....208 C1
Lower Downs Slade
CB9 ....24 A8
Lower Dro CB7 ....211 D3
Lower End CB5 ....108 E5
Lower Gn CB11 ....1 F1
Lower Gower Rd SG8 ...5 D8
Lower King St SG8 .....5 D6
Lower Pk St CB5 .....246 A3
Lower Rd Croydon SG8 ..26 D5
  Ely CB7 ....218 D1
  Wicken CB7 ....211 E2
Lower St SG8 ....31 B1
Lower Wood Nature
Reserve★ CB8 ....54 C6
Lower Yd CB8 ....132 A2
Lowerfield SG8 ....6 D5
Loweswater PE29 .....141 C5
Lowfields CB3 ....46 B8
Lowick Gdns PE3 ....197 C6
Lowndes Dro PE27 ...144 F7
Lowry Cl Haverhill CB9 ..38 D1
  St Ives PE27 ....144 A7
Lowry Rd PE19 ....74 C6
Lowther Gdns PE4 ...204 D2
Lowther St CB8 ......110 F3
Loxley PE4 ....204 A4
Loxley Gn PE28 ......142 F5
Luard Cl CB2 ....65 A4
Luard Rd CB2 ....65 A5
Lucas Ct PE29 ....141 F7
Lucas La SG7 ....2 E4
Lucerne Cl
  Cambridge CB1 ....66 A6
  Red Lodge IP28 ......213 F1
Lucketts Cl CB4 .....104 B5
Luck's La PE19 ....117 A4
Lucombe Dr PE13 ....245 F7
Lucy Cavendish Coll
CB3 ....83 C3
Luddington Cl PE19 ..96 E4
Luddington Rd
  Great Gidding PE28 ...166 C3
  Peterborough PE4 ....204 D1
Ludlow La CB1 ....67 A5
Lug Fen Droveway
CB5 ....107 A5
Luke St PE19 ....74 E4
Lulworth Dr CB9 .....23 E8
Lumen Rd SG8 ....5 D7
Lumley Cl CB6 ....240 E8
Lundy Cl CB9 ....24 D7
Lutton Gate Rd PE12 .234 A8
Lutton Gr PE3 ....197 C6
Lye Cl PE19 ....94 A6
Lyles Rd CB4 ....125 D4
Lymage Rd PE28 .....115 D3
Lyme Wlk PE3 ....197 C6
Lynch La SG8 ....15 E8
Lynchwood PE2 ......185 C5
Lyndale Pk PE2 ......185 C6
Lyndewode Rd CB1 ..246 C1
Lyndhurst Cl CB4 ....105 C2
Lynfield La CB4 ......84 A4
Lynn Rd Ely CB6 .....240 D6
  Littleport CB6 ....242 F6
  Wisbech PE13 ....245 C6
Lynton Cl CB6 ....240 D6
Lynton Dr CB6 ....240 D6
Lynton Rd PE1 ....197 F6
Lynton Way CB2 ......33 A8
Lynx The CB1 ....66 A7
Lyons Ct PE16 ....241 C4
Lyon's Dro PE15 .....223 F4
Lysander Cl PE27 ....143 F7
Lythemere PE2 ......186 C4
Lyvelly Gdns PE1 ....198 E6

M

Macaulay Ave CB2 ....49 B6
MacBeth Cl PE29 ....141 F6
Mace Rd PE2 ....187 D5
MacFarlane Cl CB4 ..104 C2
MacKenzie Rd CB1 ...84 A1
MacKerel Hall CB8 ...5 B6
MacPherson Robertson Way
IP28 ....239 A5

Maddingley Way CB6 .210 A7
Madecroft PE28 ......165 A5
Madeley Ct PE28 ....143 C2
Madingley Hall★ CB3 ..81 E5
Madingley Rd
  Cambridge CB3 ....83 B3
  Dry Drayton CB3 .....102 B1
Madingley Sch CB3 ...81 F5
Madingley Wood CB3 ..82 A4
Madras Rd PE1 ....65 C7
Maffit Rd PE5 ....195 D3
Magazine Cl PE13 ...245 A4
Magazine La PE13 ...245 A4
Magdalene Cl CB4 ...123 F2
Magdalene St CB2 ...246 A3
Magee Rd PE4 ....204 D1
Magistrates Ct PE7 ..181 D8
Magna Cl CB1 ....34 C6
Magnolia Ave PE3 ...197 A2
Magnolia Cl
  Cambridge CB1 ....65 B5
  Red Lodge IP28 ......213 F1
Magrath Ave CB4 ....246 A4
Maiden La PE9 ....244 C5
Maid's Cswy CB5 ....246 C3
Mailes Cl CB3 ....63 B4
Main Dro CB6 ....225 A2
Main Rd Etton PE6 ...203 B8
  Little Gransden SG19 ..58 D3
  Parson Drove PE13 ...234 E7
  Uffington PE9 ....230 D6
  Upwell PE14 ....229 F7
  Wisbech PE14 ....236 A3
Main St Ailsworth PE5 .195 D2
  Barnack PE9 ....230 D3
  Bythorn & Keyston PE28 .146 D4
  Caldecote CB3 ....61 B6
  Castor PE5 ....195 D3
  Coveney CB6 ....217 B5
  Downham PE7 ....217 D8
  Ely CB7 ....219 B5
  Farcet PE7 ....187 C2
  Great Gidding PE28 ...166 D3
  Hardwick CB3 ....81 A1
  Hatley SG19 ....43 A3
  Huntingdon PE29 .....142 A6
  Little Downham CB6 ..218 A6
  Littleport CB6 ....242 D4
  Old Weston PE28 .....147 F7
  Shudy Camps CB1 .....21 F6
  Southorpe PE9 ....230 E1
  Stow cum Quy CB5 ....85 F5
  Thetford CB6 ....211 B7
  Ufford PE9 ....230 F3
  Welney PE14 ....225 A8
  Wentworth CB6 ......217 B1
  Witchford CB6 ....217 E1
  Yarwell PE8 ....183 A8
  Yaxley PE7 ....181 E5
Maio Rd CB4 ....83 F5
Maitland Ave CB4 ....84 B6
Malborne Way PE2 ...186 B4
Malcolm St CB1 .....246 B3
Malcolm Way CB8 ...111 B5
Malden Cl CB5 ....84 D3
Malden Way PE19 ....74 D2
Maldon Rd PE13 ....245 E6
Malecoff PE29 ....118 F7
Males Cl CB4 ....125 E5
Malin Cl CB9 ....24 D7
Mallard Cl
  Chatteris PE16 ......241 C5
  Whittlesey PE7 ......189 F8
Mallard La PE9 ......244 B4
Mallard La PE19 .....75 A4
Mallard Rd
  Peterborough PE3 ...204 A1
  Royston SG8 ....5 C6
Mallard Rise CB6 ....210 A6
Mallard Way PE15 ...243 F5
Mallards The
  Peakirk PE6 ....206 B1
  St Ives PE27 ....143 F7
Mallett Cl PE15 .....243 F4
Malletts Rd CB1 .....66 A5
Mallory La PE9 ......244 B5
Mallory Rd PE1 .....198 C2
Mallow La PE7 ......175 D8
Mallow Wlk
  Haverhill CB9 ....23 C8
  Royston SG8 ....5 E5
Mallows Cl CB3 .....62 D6
Malory Pl CB3 ....99 A3
Malt Dr PE13 ....245 B3
Malta Rd CB1 ....65 B7
Maltby Cl PE8 ......230 B1
Malthouse Cl PE29 ..141 D4
Malthouse La PE26 ..171 F5
Malthouse Way CB2 ..29 F8
Malting End CB8 .....72 D4
Malting La
  Cambridge CB3 ....64 C3
  Ellington PE28 ....139 A4
  Foxton CB22 ....30 C5
  Isleham CB7 ....213 A5
  Litlington SG8 ....12 A2
Malting The PE26 ...171 F5
Maltings Cl
  Moulton CB8 ....112 E5
  Royston SG8 ....5 C7
Maltings La CB8 ......7 E2
Maltings Pl SG19 ....41 D5
Maltings The
  Alconbury PE28 ......150 E5
  Cambourne CB23 .....80 B2
  Eaton Socon PE19 ....74 C5
  Gamlingay SG19 .....41 D6

Maltings The continued
  St Martin's Without PE9 .244 C2
  Sawtry PE28 ....168 B4
  Thorney PE6 ....233 A3
Maltmas Dro PE14 ..235 F2
Malton La SG8 ....29 B4
Malton Rd SG8 ......45 F1
Maltsters Way CB4 ...84 A4
Malus Cl PE7 ....186 C3
Malvern Cl CB8 .....111 B2
Malvern Rd
  Cambridge CB1 ....65 E6
  Peterborough PE4 ....204 E2
Manasty Rd PE2 .....185 D2
Mancetter Sq PE4 ...204 B1
Manchester Rd PE28 .117 D8
Manchester Way
PE27 ....144 A8
Mandene Gdns SG19 ..58 E4
Mander Way CB1 .....65 C5
Manderston Rd CB8 .110 E4
Mandeville
  Burwell CB5 ....109 B8
  Peterborough PE2 ...185 F4
Mandeville Rd PE28 .140 C3
Mandrill Cl CB1 ......66 A7
Manea Com Prim Sch
PE15 ....224 C4
Manea Rd PE15 .....223 D6
Manea Sta PE15 ....224 B6
Maners Way CB1 .....65 C4
Mangers La CB2 .....32 D1
Manhattan Dr CB4 ..246 C4
Manners Ct PE9 .....230 C6
Manor Ave PE2 ......187 B7
Manor Cl
  Brampton PE28 ......140 E2
  Buckden PE19 ....117 A3
  Graveley PE19 ....98 A5
  Great Staughton PE19 ..93 F6
  Harston CB2 ....47 F3
  Little Paxton PE19 ....95 F7
  Little Wilbraham CB1 ..86 D1
  Ramsey Forty Foot PE26 .221 A3
  St Ives PE28 ....142 F5
  Somersham PE28 ....215 C1
  Witchford CB6 ....217 E1
  Wittering PE8 ....230 B1
  Yaxley PE7 ....181 D5
Manor Com Coll CB4 ..83 F6
Manor Cres CB3 ....81 A1
Manor Ct CB3 ....64 B8
Manor Ct Rd CB6 ...217 E1
Manor Dr
  Fenstanton PE28 .....121 B6
  Peterborough PE6 ...205 A3
  Sawtry PE28 ....168 C4
Manor Est PE15 .....223 A5
Manor Farm Cl
  Haverhill CB9 ....24 B7
  Oakington & Westwick
  CB4 ....103 C6
Manor Farm Ct PE28 .115 D2
Manor Farm La PE5 ..195 E2
Manor Farm Rd
  Beck Row, Holywell
  Row & Kenny Hill IP28 .213 D7
  Girton CB3 ....103 E2
  St Neots PE19 ....75 A5
  Waresley SG19 ......57 E2
Manor Gdns
  Buckden PE19 ....117 A4
  Peterborough PE2 ...187 C7
  Wisbech PE13 ....245 A4
Manor Gr PE19 ......75 A5
Manor House Cl PE19 .74 C2
Manor House St PE1 .198 A3
Manor La
  Alconbury PE28 ......150 F5
  Boxworth CB3 ....101 C6
  Great Chesterford CB10 ..18 C2
  Great Gransden SG19 ..58 D4
Manor Leisure Ctr
PE7 ....189 E6
Manor Pk CB4 ......104 A4
Manor Pl CB4 ....246 B3
Manor Rd
  Folksworth PE7 ......180 D1
  Gamlingay SG19 ......41 D6
  Haverhill CB9 ....24 B7
  Hemingford Grey PE28 .143 B1
  Little Shelford CB2 ...48 E4
  Meldreth SG8 ....29 A1
  Mildenhall IP28 ......239 B4
  Sutton PE5 ....194 F2
  Witchford CB6 ....217 E2
Manor St
  Cambridge CB1 ......246 B3
  Wistow PE28 ....164 A7
Manor View
  Barton Mills IP28 ....239 D2
  Whittlesey PE7 ......189 D6
Manor Way
  Hail Weston PE19 .....95 A1
  Market Deeping PE6 ..231 F8
Manor Wlk CB1 .....67 A5
Manse Dr CB4 ......125 C3
Mansel Ct CB4 ....83 E6
Mansel Way CB4 ....83 E6
Mansell Rd PE13 ....245 D3
Mansfield Cl CB4 ...105 C4
Mansfield Ct PE1 ...198 C5
Manton PE3 ....197 A3
Maple Ave Sawston CB2 .32 F5
  Wisbech PE13 ....245 C4
Maple Cl
  Bluntisham/Colne PE28 .208 C6
  Bottisham CB5 ....86 F5

Maple Cl continued
  Bourn CB3 ....79 C3
  Cambridge CB4 ......83 F5
  Linton CB1 ....35 B3
  Sawtry PE28 ....168 A3
Maple Ct
  Gamlingay SG19 ......41 C5
  Yaxley PE7 ....181 E6
Maple Dr
  Huntingdon PE29 .....141 E8
  Little Stukeley PE28 ..151 E8
  Stilton PE7 ....176 A7
Maple End PE28 .....150 F4
Maple Gr March PE15 .243 C5
  Peterborough PE1 ...198 C7
Maple Gr Inf Sch
PE15 ....243 C5
Maple Rd PE14 ......236 A5
Maple Way
  Melbourn SG8 ....14 C5
  Royston SG8 ....5 E8
Maple Wlk PE7 .....186 C2
Maples The
  Fulbourn CB1 ....66 C5
  Peterborough PE2 ...198 F5
March & District Mus★
PE15 ....243 D4
March La CB1 ....65 F8
March Rd
  Coates/Eastrea PE7 ..191 A8
  Elm PE13 ....227 F8
  Coldham PE14 ......235 F2
  Guyhirn PE13 ....235 A2
  Welney PE14 ....229 F1
  Whittlesey PE7 ......191 B9
  Wimblington PE15 ...223 B7
March Riverside PE14 .229 C8
March Sta PE15 .....243 D6
March Trad Est PE15 .243 B7
Marchioness Way
  ....74 B4
March's Cl CB1 ......66 E5
Marconi Dr PE7 .....181 D6
Marcus Cl 24 D7
Mardale Gdns PE4 ..204 F2
Mare Fen Nature Reserve★
CB4 ....122 F8
Marefen Dro CB6 ...225 C3
Marfleet Cl CB2 ......48 F7
Margett St CB4 .....125 E4
Margetts PE28 ......143 D1
Marholm Rd
  Castor PE6 ....196 B3
  Peterborough PE3 ...204 B1
  Ufford PE9 ....231 A2
Marian Way PE16 ...241 C2
Marigold Dr IP28 ...133 F8
Marina Dr PE15 ....243 A5
Mariner's Way CB4 ..84 A3
Marion Cl CB3 ....83 B4
Maris Gn CB2 ....49 A6
Maris La CB2 ....64 C2
Markby Cl CB2 ....17 D8
Market Hill
  Cambridge CB2 ......246 A2
  Chatteris PE16 ......241 C5
  Haverhill CB9 ....24 A8
  Huntingdon PE29 ....141 D4
  Royston SG8 ....5 D6
  St Ives PE27 ....144 A3
Market La Linton CB1 ..35 B2
  St Ives PE27 ....144 A3
Market Mews PE13 ..245 C5
Market Pas CB1 .....246 A3
Market Pl Ely CB7 ....240 D4
  Little London PE15 ..243 D4
  Mildenhall IP28 ......239 C4
  St Neots PE19 ....74 E5
  Whittlesey PE7 ......189 E7
  Wisbech PE13 ....245 C5
Market Rd PE27 ....144 B3
Market Sq
  Cambridge CB2 ......246 A2
  Ely CB7 ....240 D4
  St Neots PE19 ....74 E5
Market St
  Cambridge CB2 ......246 A3
  Ely CB7 ....240 D4
  Fordham CB7 ....212 E1
  Mildenhall IP28 ......239 C4
  Newmarket CB8 .....111 A3
  Old Chapel CB7 ......212 B4
  Swavesey CB4 ....122 E6
  Whittlesey PE7 ......189 D7
  Wisbech PE13 ....245 C5
Market Way CB6 ....217 A2
Markfield Rise CB6 ..216 D1
Markham Cl CB4 .....84 A7
Markham Ret Pk PE9 .244 D7
Markhams Cl CB9 ...38 E1
Mark's Way CB3 ....103 E1
Marlborough Cl
  St Ives PE27 ....143 F7
  Yaxley PE7 ....181 D5
Marlborough Ct
  Haverhill CB9 ....23 E7
  Newnham CB3 ....64 B8
  Wisbech PE13 ....245 A4
Marley Rd PE27 ....143 F5
Marlowe Ct PE19 ...74 D6
Marlowe Gr PE4 ....197 E8
Marlowe Rd CB3 ....64 C7
Marmora Rd CB1 ....65 B7
Marne Ave PE4 .....204 C1
Marne Rd PE7 ......189 F5
Marquis Cl PE9 .....74 B4
Marriott Cl PE1 ....198 C5
Marriott Dr CB6 ...240 C4

Marriott's Dro PE26 .221 A4
Marriotts Cl PE26 ...221 A4
Marritt Cl PE16 .....241 B6
Marroway La CB6 ...217 D1
Marsh Cl PE15 ......243 F6
Marsh La PE28 ......143 D1
Marsh Rd Outwell PE14 .236 F4
  Walpole PE14 ....238 F8
Marsh The PE14 ....238 F8
Marsh Wlk PE13 ....245 D5
Marshall Rd CB1 ....65 A5
Marshall's Bank PE13 .234 D8
Marshall's Cl CB1 ...85 A1
Marshall's La CB6 ..218 A6
Marshall's Way PE7 .187 C2
Marsham PE2 ......185 F3
Marshfields Sch PE1 .198 D7
Marshland High Sch
PE14 ....238 E4
Marston Rd PE19 ...75 A3
Martin Ave PE15 ....243 A7
Martin Cl
  Godmanchester PE29 .119 A8
  Mildenhall IP28 ......239 D3
  Soham CB7 ....212 A5
Martin Ct
  Peterborough PE4 ...204 C4
  Whittlesey PE7 ......189 E7
Martin Rd CB5 ......130 B3
Martin's La CB6 .....218 A6
Martindale Way CB2 ..32 E8
Martingale Cl CB4 ..83 C6
Martingale Rd SG8 ...5 E6
Martins La Linton CB1 ..35 E2
  Witcham CB6 ....217 A3
Martins Mews CB9 ..38 C1
Martins Way PE2 ...185 F5
Martinsbridge PE1 .198 F7
Marwick Rd PE15 ..243 D7
Mary Armyne Rd PE2 .186 B5
Mary Walsham Cl PE2 .187 E5
Maryland Ave
  Huntingdon PE29 ....141 F8
  Swaffham Bulbeck CB5 .108 B2
Marylebone Rd CB5 .243 C4
Masefield Ave PE19 ..74 C6
Masefield Way SG8 ..13 C1
Maskew Ave PE1 ....197 E6
Mason Gdns IP28 ...213 D6
Mason Rd CB5 ......130 B5
Master Dike PE12 ..237 D8
Masterton Cl PE9 ..244 A4
Masterton Rd PE9 ..244 C7
Matley PE2 ....185 E5
Matley Prim Sch PE2 .185 E5
Matt Dawson Cl CB8 .110 F6
Matthew Parker Cl
  CB4 ....105 D7
Matthew Wren Cl CB6 .218 A6
Matthews La CB8 ...55 F6
Maule Cl
  Huntingdon PE29 ....141 E6
  St Neots PE19 ....74 E1
Maurice Cl PE28 ...113 F5
Mawson Cl CB6 ....240 B3
Mawson Rd CB1 ...246 C1
Maxey Cl Helpston PE6 .231 C5
  Northborough PE6 ...231 E8
Maxey View PE6 ...231 E8
Maxham's Gn Rd PE6 .203 B6
Maxwell Rd PE2 ....186 D6
May St SG8 ....7 E2
Mayfair Gdns PE13 .235 C7
Mayfield PE19 ......117 A3
Mayfield Cl CB6 ....240 B5
Mayfield Cres PE2 ..141 F6
Mayfield Prim Sch CB4 .83 C5
Mayfield Rd
  Coates/Eastrea PE7 ..190 D7
  Girton CB3 ....82 F8
  Huntingdon PE29 ....141 F6
  Peterborough PE1 ...198 A6
Mayflower Rd PE13 .245 E3
Mayfly Cl PE16 .....241 B6
Maynards CB2 ......32 C5
Mayner's Dike PE12 .237 D6
Mayor's Wlk PE3 ...197 E3
Mayors Cl PE15 ....243 D7
Maypole Croft CB1 .37 C8
Maypole La CB8 ....90 E3
May's Ave CB1 ......53 A2
May's La PE13 ......84 C5
Mays Way CB4 ......83 C5
Maysfield Dr PE13 ..238 B2
Maytrees PE27 .....143 F4
Maze Rd PE28 .....120 C1
McCalmont Way CB8 .111 E2
Mead Cl PE3 ....204 B1
Mead The PE4 .....204 B1
Mead View CB4 ....103 B5
Meadenvale PE1 ...198 F5
Meadlands Main Dro
CB6 ....215 F1
Meadow Bsns Ctr The
PE27 ....144 B2
Meadow Cl
  Chatteris PE16 ......241 C3
  Little Paxton PE19 ....95 F2
  St Ives PE27 ....144 B3
  Soham CB7 ....212 D5
  Stilton PE7 ....175 F8
  Witchford CB6 ......217 C2
Meadow Ct CB6 ....242 B5
Meadow Dr PE15 ...243 A5
Meadow Drift CB3 ..100 B5

Meadow Dro PE28 .....208 E6
Meadow Farm Cl CB4 .103 D6
Meadow Gr PE1 ....205 B1
Meadow How PE27 ....143 F6
Meadow La
Earith PE28 ....208 E6
Hemingford Abbots
PE28 ....142 F3
Hemingford Grey PE28 ...143 D3
Houghton & Wyton PE28 ..143 B4
Linton CB1 ....35 B2
Newmarket CB8 ....111 D1
Offord Darcy PE19 ......117 F2
Over CB4 ....208 D1
Ramsey PE26 ....172 B4
St Ives PE27 ....144 C3
Thornhaugh PE8 ....193 F5
Meadow Prim Sch The
CB1 ....53 B2
Meadow Rd
Great Chesterford CB10 ...18 D3
Great Gransden SG19 .....58 B5
Newborough PE6 ....204 D8
Peakirk PE6 ....206 C1
Ramsey PE26 ....171 B1
Willingham CB4 ....209 B1
Meadow Rise CB3 ......60 C6
Meadow View PE19 .....77 E4
Meadow Way
Doddington/Wimblington
PE15 ....223 B7
Earith PE28 ....208 E6
Godmanchester PE29 ....142 A2
Great Paxton PE19 ....96 E4
Harston CB2 ....48 A3
Mepal CB6 ....216 E3
Warboys PE28 ....164 F5
Meadow Way S 7 PE15 223 B7
Meadow Wlk CB1 ......34 C6
Meadowbrook CB6 ....209 E4
Meadowcroft CB6 .....210 F5
Meadowcroft Way SG8 ..28 E8
Meadowfield Rd CB2 ...32 E6
Meadowgate PE9 ......230 F5
Meadowgate La PE14 ..245 E2
Meadowgate Sch
PE13 ....245 E3
Meadowground PE28 ...116 A7
Meadowlands
Burwell CB5 ....130 B1
March PE15 ....243 A6
Meadowlands Rd CB5 ..84 E3
Meadows Cl 5 PE19 ....74 F5
Meadows The
Haslingfield CB3 ....47 B5
Worlington IP28 ....213 F4
Meadowsweet PE19 ....74 B6
Meadowsweet Cl
2 Cambourne CB3 ....79 A4
Haverhill CB9 ....38 E1
Meals Gate PE4 ....204 F2
Medallion Ct 1 PE19 ....74 F5
Medbourne Gdns PE1 .198 C8
Medcalfe Way SG8 .....14 D6
Medeswell PE2 ....186 C4
Medieval Village of Clopton
(site of)★ SG8 ....26 E6
Medieval Village of Croydon
(site of)★ SG8 ....27 B8
Medieval Village of Great
Childerley (site of)★
CB3 ....80 D8
Medieval Village of
Landbeach (site of)★
CB4 ....105 C7
Medieval Village of Papley
(site of)★ PE8 ....174 B7
Medieval Village of Sawtry
(site of)★ PE28 ....169 B2
Medieval Village of Sibberton
(site of)★ PE8 ....193 E5
Medieval Village of
Wintringham★ PE19 ...75 F4
Medland Gr 6 PE19 .....75 A5
Medway Cl PE13 ......245 E4
Medway Rd PE29 ......141 E7
Medway The CB6 ......240 D6
Medworth PE2 ....185 F3
Meeting La
Litlington SG8 ....12 A2
Melbourn SG8 ....14 C6
Meeting Wlk CB9 ......24 B8
Megans Way 4 PE16 ...241 C5
Meggan Gate PE3 .....197 A1
Megg's Dro PE26 ......221 D2
Megs Cl PE28 ....208 D5
Melbourn Bury SG8 ....14 B5
Melbourn Prim Sch
SG8 ....14 C6
Melbourn Rd SG8 ....5 D7
Melbourn Science Pk
SG8 ....14 D7
Melbourn St SG8 ....5 D6
Melbourn Village Coll
SG8 ....14 C7
Melbourne Ave PE15 ..243 B7
Melbourne Dr IP28 ....239 B5
Melbourne Pl CB1 ....246 C2
Melbourne Rd PE9 ....244 D6
Meldon Pl CB6 ....240 D5
Meldreth Manor Sch & Orch
House SG8 ....29 A1
Meldreth Rd
Shepreth SG8 ....29 D4
Whaddon SG8 ....28 C1
Meldreth Sta SG8 ......14 B7
Meldrith Prim Sch SG8 ..14 B8
Melford Cl Burwell CB5 .130 C2
Peterborough PE3 ......197 A2
Mellis Cl CB9 ....38 B1
Mellows Cl PE1 ....198 C3
Melrose Dr PE2 ....187 A7
Melrose Gdns CB8 ....110 E4
Melton Cl 1 CB8 ......111 B2
Melvin Way CB4 ......104 A4
Memorial Ct CB3 ....83 C1
Mendip Gr PE4 ....204 E2
Mepal & Witchem CE Prim
Sch CB6 ....216 D3
Mepal Long Highway
CB6 ....216 C4
Mepal Outdoor Ctr
PE16 ....216 C6
Mepal Rd CB6 ....216 E2
Mepal Short Highway
CB6 ....216 C5
Mercers Row CB5 ......84 B4
Mercian Ct PE2 ....187 D7
Mere Cl PE26 ....221 A4
Mere Dro Ramsey PE26 .221 D4
Yaxley PE7 ....181 F4
Mere Mill Dro CB6 ....210 F4
Mere Side CB7 ....212 A4
Mere Side Dro PE26 ...221 B4
Mere View PE7 ....182 A5
Mere View Ind Est
PE7 ....182 A6
Mere Way
Cambridge CB4 ....83 E6
Hemingford Grey PE28 ...120 B5
Houghton & Wyton PE28 ..143 A6
Merelade Gr PE4 ......204 B5
Meridian Cl 22 PE28 ....215 C1
Meridian Prim Sch CB3 .62 C5
Meridian Sch SG8 ....5 E7
Meriton PE2 ....185 F3
Merle Way CB3 ....79 A4
Merlin Cl
Huntingdon PE29 ....142 B7
St Neots PE19 ....75 B7
Merlin Dr 4 CB6 ......240 B5
Merritt St PE29 ....141 C5
Merton Grange SG19 ....41 F5
Merton Rd CB4 ....104 B3
Merton St CB3 ....64 C7
Mertoun Paddocks
CB8 ....90 A8
Metcalfe Rd CB4 ....83 D5
Metcalfe Way CB6 ....210 A5
Metro Ctr The PE2 ....186 D6
Mewburn PE3 ....204 A1
Mews Cl PE26 ....172 B7
Meynell Gdns CB8 ....111 A5
Meynell Wlk PE3 ......197 B3
Michael's Cl CB3 ......103 E1
Mickle Gate PE3 ......197 A1
Mickle Hill PE28 ......135 D7
Mid Career Coll CB1 ....67 B4
Mid Fetter PE26 ....221 B3
Middle Broad Dro
PE13 ....237 D5
Middle Cl 5 CB6 ......210 F5
Middle Drift SG8 ....5 C6
Middle Dro
Newton PE13 ....237 E3
Ramsey PE26 ....171 A7
Soham CB7 ....211 F3
Wimblington PE15 ......223 C5
Middle Pasture PE4 ...204 B5
Middle Rd
Crowland PE6 ....207 E7
March PE15 ....227 E4
Newborough PE6 ....205 C7
Middle St Elton PE8 ...178 D8
Farcet PE7 ....187 C2
Great Gransden SG19 .....58 E4
Litlington SG8 ....12 A2
Thriplow SG8 ....31 B1
Middle Watch CB4 ....122 E5
Middle Way CB2 ....50 A1
Middlefield PE7 ....186 D3
Middlefield Com Prim Sch
PE19 ....74 F2
Middlefield Rd PE28 ...168 B3
Middleham Cl PE7 ....187 F5
Middlemiss View
PE29 ....118 F8
Middlemoor Rd
Ramsey PE26 ....220 D3
Whittlesford CB2 ....32 A5
Middleton PE3 ....197 A4
Middleton Prim Sch
PE3 ....197 A4
Middleton Way CB4 ...121 E4
Middletons Rd PE7 ....181 E5
Midfield CB4 ....103 D4
Midgate PE1 ....198 A2
Midhurst Cl CB4 ....84 A5
Midland Rd PE3 ....197 E3
Midloe Grange PE19 ....95 A6
Mikanda Cl PE14 .....245 C2
Milburn Dro CB8 ......112 E5
Mildenhall Airfield
IP28 ....239 B8
Mildenhall Coll of Tecnology
IP28 ....239 E4
Mildenhall Ind Est
IP28 ....239 B6
Mildenhall Mus★
IP28 ....239 C4
Mildenhall Pl CB9 ......24 B8
Mildenhall Rd
Barton Mills IP28 ....239 C2
Mildenhall Rd *continued*
Beck Row, Holywell
Row & Kenny Hill IP28 ..239 C8
Ely CB7 ....219 E8
Fordham IP28 ....213 A2
Freckenham IP28 ....213 D3
Icklingham IP28 ....214 E4
Littleport CB7 ....242 F6
Mildenhall Swimming Pool
IP28 ....239 C4
Mildmay Rd PE4 ......197 D8
Mile Dro Glinton PE6 ...231 F5
Yaxley PE7 ....182 B5
Mile End Rd CB7 ......219 C6
Mile Rd CB2 ....50 C4
Mile Tree La PE13 .....235 E7
Miles Hawk Way IP28 .239 A5
Milford St CB1 ....84 A1
Military Rd CB7 ....212 C2
Militia Way CB7 ....240 C4
Milk and Wr Dro PE7 ..188 A4
Milk and Wr Dro Ramsey Rd
PE7 ....188 A2
Milking Hills Dro CB4 .209 B2
Milking Nook Rd PE6 ..206 E1
Milking Slade Rd
PE28 ....167 A4
Mill Cl Burwell CB5 ....130 B1
Exning CB8 ....110 B8
Hemingford Grey PE28 ...143 D2
Huntingdon PE29 ....142 A6
Murrow PE13 ....234 D5
The Stukeleys PE28 .....151 D3
Wisbech PE13 ....245 C6
Mill Cnr CB7 ....212 A4
Mill Comm PE29 ......141 C3
Mill Cres PE2 ....185 E4
Mill Croft CB7 ....212 B3
Mill Cswy SG8 ....8 C5
Mill Ct CB2 ....49 A5
Mill Dro Crowland PE6 ..207 F7
Lode CB5 ....128 A1
Ramsey PE26 ....221 A2
Soham CB7 ....212 A3
Southery PE38 ....226 E8
Mill End SG19 ....25 A4
Mill End Cl CB1 ....65 F5
Mill End Rd CB1 ....65 E6
Mill Field 3 CB6 ......216 E2
Mill Field Cl PE6 .....231 C4
Mill Gn PE28 ....165 A5
Mill Hill Conington PE7 ..177 C1
Downham CB6 ....217 F7
Glatton PE28 ....175 E1
Haverhill CB9 ....23 F7
Newmarket CB8 ....111 A4
Royston SG8 ....5 E4
Swaffham Prior CB5 ....108 E5
Weston Colville CB1 .....54 C6
Mill Hill End PE28 ....120 B1
Mill Hill Rd 7 PE19 ....74 D5
Mill Hole CB2 ....33 E8
Mill La Arrington SG8 ...44 C3
Barrington CB2 ....29 E8
Bassingbourn SG8 ....12 D5
Bluntisham/Colne PE28 ..208 D5
Burwell CB5 ....130 B1
Cambridge CB2 ....246 A2
Castor PE5 ....184 F7
Duxford CB2 ....32 E1
Exning CB8 ....110 B8
Fordham CB7 ....212 F1
Gorefield PE13 ....235 B8
Hauxton CB2 ....48 A6
Hemingford Grey PE28 ...143 D3
Hinxton CB10 ....18 A7
Histon CB4 ....104 D6
Ickleton CB10 ....18 B4
Impington CB4 ....104 D5
Linton CB1 ....35 C2
Little Paxton PE19 ....95 E1
Newton PE13 ....237 F5
Peterborough PE7 ....185 A5
Potton SG19 ....40 D1
Ramsey PE26 ....172 B8
St Neots PE19 ....74 F8
Sawston CB2 ....32 E7
Shingay cum Wendy SG8 ..27 B4
Stetchworth CB8 ....89 F1
Swaffham Bulbeck CB5 ..108 B3
Tallington PE9 ....230 F7
Toft CB3 ....61 D5
Water Newton PE8 ......184 C7
West Walton PE14 ......238 F4
Whittlesford CB2 ....32 D5
Mill Pit Furlong CB6 ..242 D3
Mill Rd Alconbury PE28 ..150 E4
Ashley CB8 ....91 F8
Buckden PE19 ....117 C3
Cambridge CB1 ....246 C2
Emneth PE14 ....236 D6
Fen Drayton CB4 ....121 D5
Glatton PE28 ....175 E1
Great Gidding PE28 .....166 E3
Great Wilbraham CB1 ....67 F7
Harston CB2 ....47 D2
Haverhill CB9 ....24 A7
Histon CB4 ....104 B1
Huntingdon PE29 ....142 A6
Kirtling CB8 ....72 E5
Little Gransden SG19 ....58 E4
Little Stukeley PE28 .....151 D4
Little Wilbraham CB1 ....86 D1
Lode CB5 ....107 C2
Maxey PE6 ....231 C7
Nassington PE8 ....183 A7
Oakington/Longstanton
CB4 ....103 D6
Mill Rd *continued*
Royston SG8 ....5 D7
Stilton PE7 ....175 F8
Walpole PE14 ....238 F6
Waterbeach CB5 ....106 A7
West Walton PE14 ......238 D4
West Wickham CB1 ....36 E8
West Wratting CB1 ....53 F2
Whittlesey PE7 ....189 E6
Wisbech St Mary PE13 ...234 C5
Wistow PE28 ....163 F6
Mill Reef Cl CB8 .....110 D7
Mill St Ashwell SG7 ......2 D4
Cambridge CB1 ....246 C1
Gamlingay SG19 ....41 D5
Isleham CB7 ....213 A5
Mildenhall IP28 ....239 B3
St Ives PE28 ....143 A5
Mill View March PE15 ..243 D4
Peterborough PE7 ....185 A5
Sawtry PE28 ....168 A4
Mill View Ct PE19 ......74 C2
Mill Way
Grantchester CB3 ....64 A3
Holywell-cum-Needingworth
PE27 ....144 F3
Stretham CB6 ....210 E6
Swavesey CB4 ....122 C6
Wisbech PE14 ....236 A4
Mill Yd PE29 ....141 E2
Millards La CB5 ......107 D2
Millbank CB8 ....110 F4
Miller Cl
2 Doddington/Wimblington
PE15 ....222 F5
Godmanchester PE29 ....118 F8
Offord Cluny PE19 ......118 A2
Miller Way
Brampton PE28 ....140 C3
Cambourne CB3 ....79 B3
Miller's Rd CB3 ....61 D5
Miller's Way PE28 .....173 C3
Millers Cl CB1 ....35 D3
Millfield Littleport CB6 ..242 C3
Upwell PE14 ....236 E2
Willingham CB4 ....124 A8
Millfield Cl PE16 .....241 B2
Millfield La CB6 ......210 C5
Millfield Pl CB6 ......210 D5
Millfield Prim Sch The
CB6 ....242 C3
Millfield Rd
Market Deeping PE6 .....231 F8
Maxey PE6 ....231 D8
Millfield Way PE7 .....189 F6
Millfields Ramsey PE26 .172 B8
Stetchworth CB8 ....89 F1
Millfields Way CB9 .....24 B8
Millington Rd CB3 .....64 C7
Mills La
Longstanton CB4 ....124 A1
Witchford CB6 ....217 D1
Millstone La PE9 .....230 D3
Millyard CB6 ....210 A6
Milner Cl March PE15 ..243 D5
Sawston CB2 ....32 E7
Milner Rd
Comberton CB3 ....62 D6
Wisbech PE13 ....245 C4
Milners Row 15 PE9 ....244 C5
Milnyard Sq PE2 ......185 C2
Milton Ave PE19 ....74 C6
Milton CE Prim Sch
CB4 ....105 C2
Milton Cl
Huntingdon PE29 ....141 E6
Ramsey PE26 ....171 F5
Royston SG8 ....13 C1
St Ives PE27 ....143 F6
Milton Ctry Pk★ CB4 ..105 D1
Milton Dr PE13 ....238 B1
Milton Rd
Cambridge CB4 ....246 B4
Impington CB4 ....104 F4
Peterborough PE2 ....187 A7
Milton Rd Prim Sch
CB4 ....83 E4
Milton Way PE3 ......196 E3
Mina Cl PE2 ....187 D4
Minden Ct 8 PE19 .....74 C5
Minerva Cl CB9 ....24 D6
Minerva Way CB4 ......83 E8
Mingle La CB2 ....49 B5
Minster Pl 4 CB7 .....240 D4
Minster Precincts
PE1 ....198 B2
Minster Rd
Haverhill CB9 ....39 A1
Royston SG8 ....5 C8
Mint La PE19 ....96 E4
Minter Cl CB5 ....86 A5
Minton Ent Pk CB8 ...110 F7
Missleton Ct CB1 ......65 C5
Misterton PE2 ....185 E3
Misty Mdws CB5 ....84 D4
Mitchell Cl PE1 ......198 C2
Mitchells CB10 ....20 B1
Mitchells Cotts CB10 ...20 B1
Moat La
Abbots Ripton PE28 .....152 C8
Melbourn SG8 ....14 D7
Perry PE28 ....115 D1
Moat Way CB4 ....122 E6
Moat Wlk CB9 ....23 E8
Moats' Way PE28 .....119 E7
Mobb's Hole SG7 ......10 C4
Moggswell La PE2 ....186 B4
Mole Dro PE12 ....233 F8
Molewood Cl CB4 ......83 C6
Molls Dro PE14 ....236 C3
Monarch Ave PE2 .....187 A6
Monarch Rd PE19 ......74 B4
Moncrieff Cl 1 CB4 ....83 E7
Mondela Pl PE7 ....176 A7
Monet Cl PE27 ....144 A7
Money Bank PE13 .....245 E4
Money Hill (Tumulus)★
CB3 ....47 B3
Moneypiece Cl 1 CB9 ...38 F1
Monk Dr CB3 ....79 C4
Monkfield La CB3 ......79 C3
Monkfield Pk Prim Sch
CB3 ....79 B4
Monks Cl PE7 ....189 D8
Monks Dr 17 PE6 .....232 A1
Monks Gr PE4 ....204 A5
Monks Hardwick PE19 ..75 E8
Monks Mdw PE6 ......232 B8
Monks Way PE28 .....168 B2
Monks Wood National Nature
Reserve★ PE28 ....161 B4
Monkswell CB2 ....64 D3
Monkswood CB6 ......242 C5
Montagu Ct 2 PE19 ....74 E4
Montagu Gdns PE28 ...113 E5
Montagu Rd
Huntingdon PE29 ....141 E4
Little Stukeley PE28 .....151 F2
Peterborough PE4 ....197 D8
Montagu Sq PE19 ......74 E4
Montagu St PE19 ......74 E4
Montague Rd PE28 ....117 D8
Monte Long Cl PE15 ..243 E1
Montford Cl CB5 .....130 C4
Montfort Ct 9 CB9 .....23 F7
Montfort Way CB4 .....83 E6
Montgomery Rd CB4 ...83 E6
Montreal Rd CB1 ......65 C7
Montrose Cl CB4 ......83 E7
Monument St PE1 .....198 A3
Monument View PE15 .243 D1
Moon Hall La CB9 .....24 A6
Moonhall Bsns Pk CB9 ..24 A5
Moor End SG8 ....29 D3
Moor Pasture Way CB9 .39 B4
Moor Rd
Great Staughton MK44 ....93 B1
Newborough PE6 ....206 E2
Moor The SG8 ....14 C7
Moore Cl CB4 ....84 A6
Moore's La 4 PE6 ....232 A1
Moores Wlk PE19 ......74 F5
Moorfield PE6 ....206 F3
Moorfield Rd
Duxford CB2 ....32 E3
Peterborough PE3 ....197 D3
Moorfield Way PE28 ...151 F2
Moorhen Rd PE7 ......201 A1
Moorhouse Dr PE29 ...141 E7
Moory Croft Cl PE19 ...94 A6
Moot Way PE28 ....155 A5
Morborne Cl PE2 .....187 D6
Morborne La PE7 .....180 D4
Morborne Rd PE7 .....180 C2
Morden Rd CB3 ....99 B3
More's Mdw CB2 ....48 F6
Moreton Cl PE7 ......189 F8
Moretons Cl PE7 .....190 A8
Morgan Cl PE7 ....181 E6
Morgans CB4 ....125 D4
Morland Way PE27 ....144 A7
Morley Cl 7 IP28 .....213 F8
Morley Meml Prim Sch
CB1 ....65 B5
Morley Way
17 Eastwood End PE15 ...223 B7
Peterborough PE2 ....186 D5
Morpeth Cl PE2 ......186 C6
Morpeth Rd PE3 ......197 C3
Morrice Gn SG8 ....1 A3
Morris Cl PE19 ....117 A3
Morris Ct PE7 ....181 E6
Morris St PE1 ....198 B3
Mortimer La IP28 .....213 C3
Mortimer Rd
Cambridge CB1 ....246 C2
Royston SG8 ....5 E6
Mortimers La CB2 ......30 C5
Mortlock Ave CB4 .....84 B6
Mortlock Cl SG8 ....14 C6
Mortlock Gdns CB1 ....34 C5
Mortlock St SG8 ....14 C6
Morton Ave PE15 .....243 E3
Morton Cl CB6 ....240 E8
Morton St SG8 ....5 D7
Morton Way 6 PE15 ...223 B7
Morton's Leam★ PE7 ..200 C1
Mosquito Rd PE26 ....171 E3
Moss Bank CB4 ....84 C5
Moss Cl PE26 ....171 B1
Moss Dr CB3 ....47 C5
Mostyn Cl 2 CB6 .....216 E1
Motocross Circuit CB3 ..78 F8
Moules La CB1 ....20 C6
Moulton Ave CB8 .....134 A2
Moulton CE VC Fst Sch
CB8 ....112 E6
Moulton Gr PE3 ......197 C6
Moulton Paddocks
CB8 ....111 F6
Moulton Rd
Ashley CB8 ....112 D1
Cheveley CB8 ....91 D8
Newmarket CB8 ....111 D4
Moulton Road or Kennett Rd
CB8 ....112 F7

Mount Dr PE13 ....245 E4
Mount Pleasant
3 Cambridge CB3 ....83 C3
Great Paxton PE19 ....96 E4
Peterborough PE2 ....187 C7
Spaldwick PE28 ....137 E6
Mount Pleasant Rd
PE13 ....245 C7
Mount Pleasant Wlk 2
CB3 ....83 C3
Mount Rd CB9 ....24 A7
Mount The Barley SG8 ....6 E1
Toft CB3 ....61 D5
Mountbatten Ave
Stamford PE9 ....244 A6
Yaxley PE7 ....181 D5
Mountbatten Ct 6 PE19 .74 C4
Mountbatten Dr PE13 .245 A7
Mountbatten Way
Peterborough PE3 ....197 B6
Whittlesey PE7 ....190 A6
Mounteagle 2 SG8 ....5 D5
Mountford Cl CB2 ....48 C4
Mountfort Cl 3 PE19 ....74 F3
Mountsteven Ave PE4 .204 C1
Mouth La PE13 ....235 B4
Mowbray Cl 4 PE13 ...235 B7
Mowbray Rd
Bretton PE3 ....203 F1
Cambridge CB1 ....65 C4
Mowfen Rd CB6 ....242 D5
Mowlam Cl CB4 ....104 C2
Moyne Cl CB4 ....83 D7
Moyne Rd PE28 ....168 C3
Moyse's Bank PE14 ....236 F6
Muchwood La PE26 ...221 B1
Mudd's Dro PE14 ....229 F6
Mugglestons La PE26 ..172 B6
Mulberry Cl
Bottisham CB5 ....86 F6
Cambridge CB4 ....83 F5
Mildenhall IP28 ....239 E4
Whittlesey PE7 ....189 F5
Yaxley PE7 ....182 A5
Mulberry Way CB7 ....240 E5
Mullard Radio Astronomy
Obsy★ CB3 ....46 E7
Mullein Cl 4 PE19 ....74 C5
Mumby's Dro PE14 ....229 E6
Mumford Theatre★
CB1 ....246 C2
Muncey Wlk CB4 ....104 C5
Munday Way 16 PE13 ...238 B2
Munnings Cl CB9 ....38 D1
Muntjac Cl 5 PE19 ....74 B5
Murfitt Way SG19 ....41 D6
Murfitt's La CB7 ....212 E2
Muriel Cl CB3 ....99 B2
Murrell Cl PE19 ....74 F7
Murrell Ct PE19 ....74 F7
Murrow Bank PE13 ....234 D6
Murrow La PE13 ....234 F5
Murrow Prim Sch
PE13 ....234 D5
Murton Cl CB5 ....130 A3
Museum of Archaeology &
Anthropology★ CB2 ..246 B2
Museum of Bronze Age at
Flag Fen The★ PE6 ...199 B2
Museum of Classical
Archaeology★ CB3 ....64 C8
Museum of Technology★
CB5 ....84 B3
Museum Sq 23 PE13 ...245 C5
Musgrave Way
Fen Ditton CB5 ....84 F6
7 St Neots PE19 ....74 F5
Musker Pl CB3 ....99 B1
Muskham PE3 ....196 F4
Musticott Pl PE13 ....245 F6
Mustill's La CB4 ....123 B8
Muswell Rd PE3 ....197 E4
Mutlow Hill (Tumulus)★
CB1 ....67 F1
Myles Way PE13 ....245 C8
Myrtle Ave PE1 ....198 C7
Myrtle Ct PE1 ....198 C7
Myrtle Gn PE27 ....144 A5
Myrtle Gr PE1 ....198 C7
Myrtle House Cvn Pk
PE1 ....198 E5
Myrtle Way PE27 ....144 A5

N

Nansicles Rd PE2 ....186 D6
Napier Pl PE2 ....185 C6
Napier St CB1 ....246 C3
Narrow Dro
Whittlesey PE7 ....188 C5
Yaxley PE7 ....182 C5
Narrow La CB4 ....104 B4
Naseby Cl PE3 ....197 C5
Naseby Gdns PE19 .....75 A4
Nash Rd 7 SG8 ....5 D5
Nat Flatman St CB8 ...111 B3
Natal Rd CB1 ....65 C7
Nathan Cl PE3 ....197 B2
National Extension Coll
CB2 ....64 F7
National Horse Racing Mus★
CB8 ....111 A3
Navigation Wharf 6
PE19 ....74 E5
Nayland Rd CB9 ....23 E6
Neale Cl CB1 ....65 F7
Neale-wade Com Coll
PE15 ....243 D1
Neaverson Rd PE6 ....203 F7
Nedderworth Rd PE27 .144 B3
Needham Bank PE14 ..236 C4
Needingworth Rd
PE27 ....144 B4
Nelson Gdns PE13 ....245 D6
Nelson Rd
Eaton Socon PE19 ....74 B3
Huntingdon PE29 ....142 A6
Nelson's La CB6 ....210 A5
Nene Cl Wansford PE8 ..194 A3
Whittlesey PE7 ....189 F6
2 Wittering PE8 ....230 B1
Nene Par March PE15 ..243 E4
Wisbech PE13 ....245 B7
Nene Parkway PE3 ....196 F1
Nene Pk★ PE2 ....185 C7
Nene Quay PE13 ....245 C5
Nene Rd
Eaton Socon PE19 ....74 C4
Ely CB6 ....240 C6
Huntingdon PE29 ....141 E8
Kimbolton PE28 ....114 A7
Whittlesey PE7 ....189 E6
Nene Sch The PE13 ...245 D4
Nene St PE1 ....198 B2
Nene Way St Ives PE27 .144 A7
Sutton PE5 ....194 F2
Warmington PE8 ....178 A2
Neneside 1 PE15 ....222 A5
Neptune Cl CB4 ....83 E7
Ness Rd CB5 ....130 C3
Nether Gr CB4 ....123 F2
Netherhall Sch The
CB1 ....65 E4
Netherhall Way CB1 ....65 D4
Nettle Bank PE14 .....235 C4
Neve Gdns IP28 ....213 E6
Neville Rd CB1 ....65 C6
New Barn Dro PE28 ...173 D4
New Barns Ave CB7 ....240 D6
New Barns Rd CB7 ....240 D5
New Bridge La
Elm PE14 ....235 F6
Wisbech PE14 ....245 A1
New Bridge Rd PE14 ..236 E1
New Broadpool PE28 ..173 F1
New Cangle CP Sch
CB9 ....38 F1
New Cheveley Rd CB8 .111 C2
New Cl SG8 ....12 B2
New Cl Rd CB6 ....211 A7
New Cross Dro CB6 ...216 B3
New Cross Rd PE9 ....244 B5
New Cut
Newmarket CB8 ....111 A3
Thorney PE6 ....233 D5
New Dro Soham CB7 ....211 E4
3 Wisbech PE13 ....245 D2
Wisbech St Mary PE13 ...235 C5
New England PE28 ....120 B2
New Farm Cl SG8 ....15 E8
New Farm Cotts CB1 ...20 E7
New Fen Dike PE12 ....237 A6
New Fen Rd La PE26 ..171 C8
New Field
Gorefield PE13 ....237 D2
Newton PE13 ....237 F4
New Hall CB3 ....83 C3
New Hall La CB3 ....79 C4
New La PE8 ....183 C8
New Long Dro PE7 ....177 F6
New Mdw Dro PE7 ....187 D1
New Orch Pk CB6 ....242 E4
New Path CB7 ....212 E1
New Pk PE15 ....243 E5
New Pk St CB5 ....246 A4
New Rd Barton CB3 ....63 B4
Burwell CB5 ....130 B3
Chatteris PE16 ....241 E5
Cottenham CB4 ....125 E4
Exning CB8 ....110 B8
15 Eye PE6 ....232 A1
Great & Little Chishill SG8 ..15 B1
Guilden Morden SG8 ....11 A5
Haddenham CB6 ....210 A6
Harston CB2 ....47 F3
Haslingfield CB3 ....47 B5
Hemingford Abbots
PE28 ....143 A1
Hinxton CB10 ....18 B6
Histon CB4 ....104 C3
Littleport CB6 ....242 D5
March PE15 ....243 E4
Melbourn SG8 ....14 E4
Mepal CB6 ....216 E3
Offord Cluny PE19 ....118 A2
Outwell PE14 ....236 E1
Over CB4 ....208 D1
Peterborough PE2 ....185 E4
Ramsey PE26 ....172 B7
St Ives PE27 ....144 B3
Sawston CB2 ....32 E8
Shudy Camps CB1 ....22 C7
Upwell PE14 ....229 E8
Warboys PE28 ....165 A4
Whittlesey PE7 ....189 F6
Wood Walton PE28 ....161 E7
Woodston PE2 ....186 F7
New Rd Prim Sch PE7 .189 F6
New River Bank CB7 ...242 F5
New River Gn CB8 ....110 B8
New Row 8 PE6 ....231 E8
New Sch Rd CB4 ....104 B3
New Sq CB1 ....246 B3
New St Cambridge CB1 ...84 A2
New St *continued*
Chippenham CB7 ....132 E8
Doddington/Wimblington
PE15 ....222 F5
Godmanchester PE29 ....141 F1
Mildenhall IP28 ....239 C4
St Neots PE19 ....74 E5
Stamford PE9 ....244 C6
New Town Rd CB6 .....209 F6
Newark Ave PE1 ....198 C6
Newark Cl SG8 ....5 C8
Newark Hill Prim Sch
PE1 ....198 D6
Newark Rd PE1 ....198 F4
Newbey Cl PE3 ....197 B3
Newbolt SG8 ....5 D8
Newborn Cl PE2 ....187 E5
Newborough Prim Sch
PE6 ....207 C1
Newborough Rd PE4 ..205 C2
Newboults La PE9 .....244 A5
Newcastle Dr PE2 .....186 D6
Newcomb Ct PE9 ....244 B5
Newcombe Way PE2 ..185 D2
Newell Cl SG8 ....44 D1
Newell Wlk CB1 ....65 F7
Newgate Rd PE13 .....237 F6
Newgate St PE15 .....222 F5
Newgates 1 PE9 ....244 C5
Newghant Dro PE15 ...223 F4
Newham Rd PE9 ....244 A7
Newington CB4 ....124 B8
Newlands Ave PE15 ...243 D5
Newlands Bldgs SG19 ..42 D4
Newlands Rd
Chatteris PE16 ....241 E6
Parson Drove PE13 .....234 D7
Whittlesey PE7 ....190 A8
Newman Ave SG8 ....5 F6
Newman Cl 16 PE8 ....230 B1
Newmarket Cl PE1 ....198 B6
Newmarket Hospl
CB8 ....111 A5
Newmarket Leisure Ctr
CB8 ....110 F4
Newmarket Rd
Ashley CB8 ....91 E8
Barton Mills IP28 ....239 D1
Burwell CB5 ....130 C1
Cambridge CB5 ....246 C3
Cheveley CB8 ....91 C8
Cowlinge CB8 ....73 D3
Fen Ditton CB1 ....85 D3
Fordham CB7 ....131 D7
Great Chesterford CB10 ...18 C3
Lidgate CB8 ....73 C6
Moulton CB8 ....112 E5
Royston SG8 ....5 F6
Snailwell CB8 ....132 B2
Stow cum Quy CB5 ....85 F4
Stretham CB6 ....211 A3
Newmarket Sports Ctr
CB8 ....110 F4
Newmarket Sta CB8 ...111 A2
Newmarket Swimming Pool
CB8 ....110 F3
Newmarket Upper Sch
CB8 ....110 F4
Newnham Cl
Huntingdon PE29 ....142 A7
Mildenhall IP28 ....239 D5
Newnham Coll CB3 .....64 C8
Newnham Croft Prim Sch
CB3 ....64 C7
Newnham Croft St 2
CB3 ....64 C7
Newnham Dro CB5 ....129 C5
Newnham La CB5 .....130 B3
Newnham Rd CB3 .....64 C7
Newnham St 7 CB7 ...240 D4
Newnham Terr
Cambridge CB1 ....246 A1
Newnham CB3 ....64 C8
Newnham Way SG7 ......2 B2
Newnham Wlk CB3 ....64 C8
Newport Ave CB7 .....213 A1
Newstead Cl PE6 .....232 A2
Newstead La PE9 .....244 F8
Newstead Rd PE9 .....230 A8
Newton Fen PE13 .....237 E4
Newton Pl 9 CB9 ....24 B8
Newton Prim Sch The
PE19 ....77 E3
Newton Rd
Cambridge CB2 ....64 E5
Great Shelford CB2 ....48 D3
Harston CB2 ....47 F1
Newton CB2 ....31 A8
Sawtry PE28 ....168 C4
Newton Way PE1 .....198 D2
Newtons Ct PE29 .....141 E4
Newtown
Hail Weston PE19 ....74 B8
Kimbolton PE28 ....113 F5
Stamford PE9 ....244 C4
Newtown La PE28 .....113 F5
Newtown Rd PE26 ....172 B7
Next Odsey SG7 ....3 C3
Nicholas Taylor Gdns
PE3 ....196 F3
Nicholls Ave PE3 .....197 E3
Nicholson Way CB4 .....83 E6
Nigel Rd CB6 ....240 E8
Nightall Dr PE15 .....243 D7
Nightall Rd CB7 .....212 A4
Nightingale Ave
Bassingbourn SG8 ....13 A5
Cambridge CB1 ....65 C3
Nightingale Cl IP28 ...239 D4
Nightingale Ct PE4 ...205 A2
Nightingale Dr PE7 ...181 D6
Nightingale Way
Royston SG8 ....5 E8
1 St Neots PE19 ....75 B7
Nightingale Wlk PE15 .224 B4
Nimbus Way CB8 .....110 E8
Nine Chimneys La CB1 ..53 B2
Nipcut Rd PE6 ....232 C2
Nixhill Rd PE15 ....223 B6
Noahs Way CB6 ....242 B5
Noble Gdns PE15 .....243 E3
Nobles Cl PE7 ....190 F8
Nobles La PE28 ....208 C5
Noel Murless Dr CB8 ..110 F5
Nook The PE6 ....231 C4
Norburn PE3 ....197 B8
Norfolk Ave CB8 .....110 E5
Norfolk Rd Ely CB6 ....240 A3
Huntingdon PE29 ....141 E8
St Ives PE27 ....144 A8
Wyton Airfield PE28 .....143 B8
Norfolk Sq 3 PE9 .....244 B6
Norfolk St
Cambridge CB1 ....84 A1
Doddington/Wimblington
PE15 ....223 B7
Peterborough PE1 ....197 F4
Wisbech PE13 ....245 C4
Norfolk Terr CB1 ....84 A1
Norgett's La SG8 ....14 D6
Norham Ct PE7 ....188 A5
Norico Bay PE15 .....243 E2
Norman Cl PE7 ....189 E8
Norman Dr PE7 ....175 F8
Norman Pk CB3 ....102 C4
Norman Rd PE1 ....198 C4
Norman Way
9 Doddington/Wimblington
PE15 ....223 B7
Over CB4 ....123 B7
Norman's La 8 SG8 ......5 D5
Normanton Rd PE1 ...198 D7
Normanton Way CB4 ..104 B5
Normoor Dro PE16 ....223 B2
Nornea La CB7 ....211 F8
Norris Mus★ PE27 ....144 A3
Norris Rd PE27 ....144 A4
North Ave CB9 ....23 E8
North Bank PE6 ....199 D1
North Bank Rd 4 PE1 .198 D3
North Brink PE13 .....245 A4
North Brook End SG8 ...11 B6
North Cambridgeshire Hospl
PE13 ....245 D5
North Cl SG8 ....5 C8
North Cotts CB2 ....64 D4
North Dr March PE15 ...243 E4
Newmarket CB8 ....110 F5
Soham CB7 ....212 B5
North End
Bassingbourn cum Kneesworth
SG8 ....12 D6
Exning CB8 ....130 F3
Meldreth SG8 ....29 B2
Wisbech PE13 ....245 B6
North End Rd CB10 .....18 A8
North Fen Dro CB6 ....218 B8
North Fen Rd PE6 ....231 F5
North La SG19 ....41 B7
North Lodge Dr CB3 ....99 B2
North Pl IP28 ....239 C4
North Rd
Alconbury Weston PE28 ..150 D5
Brampton PE28 ....140 D1
Great Abington CB1 ....33 F5
St Ives PE27 ....144 A4
Whittlesford CB2 ....32 B6
North Side PE6 ....200 F5
North St Burwell CB5 ...130 B4
Cambridge CB4 ....83 C4
Folksworth & Washingley
PE7 ....181 A1
Freckenham IP28 ....213 C3
Huntingdon PE29 ....141 E5
March PE15 ....243 D5
Peterborough PE1 ....198 A2
Stamford PE9 ....244 B5
Stilton PE7 ....176 A8
Wicken CB7 ....211 E1
Wisbech PE13 ....245 C5
North Terr
Cambridge CB1 ....246 C3
Mildenhall IP28 ....239 C4
Peterborough PE1 ....198 E7
Sawston CB2 ....32 F5
Northam Cl PE6 ....232 A2
Northampton Cl CB6 ..240 A3
Northampton St CB3 ...83 C2
Northborough Prim Sch
PE6 ....231 F6
Northey Rd PE6 ....199 C2
Northfield Fulbourn CB1 ..67 A5
Girton CB3 ....103 E2
Northfield Cl SG19 ....41 C6
Northfield Pk CB7 .....212 A5
Northfield Rd
Ashwell SG7 ....2 C7
Peterborough PE1 ....197 F7
Soham CB7 ....212 A5
Wyboston PE19 ....74 A1
Northfields Ave CB4 ....83 E7
Northfields Ct PE9 ....244 C6
Northfields Rd CB5 ...107 D2
Northgate PE7 ....189 D8
Northgate Cl PE7 .....189 D8
Northminster PE1 .....198 A3
Northumberland Ave 4
PE9 ....244 A6
Northumberland Cl 2
CB4 ....83 D6
Northumbria Cl CB6 ...210 A7
Northwold CB6 ....240 C5
Norton Cl
Cambridge CB5 ....84 D3
Papworth Everard CB3 ....99 A2
Norton Rd Haverhill CB9 .23 E6
Peterborough PE1 ....197 F6
Norwalde St PE15 .....243 C6
Norwich Rd PE13 .....245 D5
Norwich St CB2 ....64 E7
Norwood Ave PE15 ...243 D5
Norwood Cres PE15 ...243 C6
Norwood La PE4 ....205 B2
Norwood Prim Sch
PE4 ....204 F3
Norwood Rd
March PE15 ....243 D7
10 Somersham PE28 ....215 C1
Notley Dr CB9 ....38 C1
Nottingham Way PE1 ..198 C6
Nuffield Cl CB4 ....84 B7
Nuffield Rd
Cambridge CB4 ....84 B6
St Ives PE27 ....144 C6
Nunns Way 4 CB6 .....216 E1
Nun's Orch CB4 ....104 B4
Nuns Way CB4 ....83 F7
Nursery Cl Isleham CB7 .212 F4
Mildenhall IP28 ....239 D4
Peterborough PE1 ....198 A4
Nursery Dr March PE15 .243 B5
Wisbech PE13 ....245 E8
Nursery Gdns
Little Paxton PE19 ....96 A2
St Ives PE27 ....144 B5
Whittlesey PE7 ....189 F6
Nursery La PE1 ....198 D2
Nursery Rd
Huntingdon PE29 ....141 E4
St Neots PE19 ....74 F4
Nursery Way 2 CB3 .....62 C5
Nursery Wlk
Brampton PE28 ....140 C3
Cambridge CB4 ....83 C5
Nutholt La CB6 ....240 D5
Nutters Cl CB3 ....64 A4
Nuttings Rd CB1 ....84 D1

O

O Furlong Dro CB6 ....224 F1
Oak Cl PE19 ....75 A5
Oak Dr Brampton PE28 ..140 C4
Little Stukeley PE28 .....151 F3
Mildenhall IP28 ....213 F8
Outwell PE14 ....236 F3
Oak End PE28 ....150 F4
Oak Farm Cl PE7 .....176 A7
Oak La Cheveley CB8 .....91 C4
Littleport CB6 ....242 A2
Oak Rd Glinton PE6 .....231 E5
Stilton PE7 ....176 A7
Oak Tree Ave CB4 ....83 F5
Oak Tree Cl
March PE15 ....243 C5
St Ives PE27 ....143 F5
Oak Tree Way CB4 .....104 B3
Oak View PE3 ....196 F2
Oak Way PE26 ....220 D3
Oakdale Ave PE2 .....187 D4
Oakdale Prim Sch
PE7 ....187 C4
Oakery The CB7 ....240 D6
Oakington Barracks
CB4 ....124 B1
Oakington CE Prim Sch
CB4 ....103 C5
Oakington Rd
Cottenham CB4 ....125 B1
Dry Drayton CB3 ....102 D2
Girton CB3 ....103 E3
Oakington & Westwick
CB4 ....103 E7
Oaklands
Fenstanton PE28 ....121 B5
Peterborough PE1 ....198 B4
Oaklands Ave PE28 ....163 F7
Oaklands Dr PE13 .....245 F7
Oakleaf Rd PE1 ....198 C6
Oakleigh Cres PE29 .....141 F1
Oakleigh Dr PE2 ....186 C6
Oakley Cl PE13 ....245 E4
Oakley Dr PE28 ....168 B3
Oakrits SG8 ....14 B8
Oakroyd Cres PE13 ....245 C6
Oaks Bsns Pk The
CB8 ....110 E7
Oaks Dr CB8 ....110 F7
Oaks The Milton CB4 ....105 C2
Soham CB7 ....212 B3
Oaktree Cl PE15 ....222 F5
Oaktree Rd CB4 ....121 D6
Oasthouse Way PE26 ..172 A5
Oates' La CB6 ....216 E1
Oates Way PE26 ....172 C7
Oatlands Ave CB3 .....102 B4
Occupation Rd
Cambridge CB1 ....84 A2
Peterborough PE1 ....197 E6
Ockendon Cl PE19 ....74 B3

Octagon Dr PE13 245 A6
Octavia Cl PE13 245 F6
Octavia Hill Birthplace Mus The★ PE13 245 B5
Odecroft PE3 197 C7
Offa Lea CB2 31 B7
Offord Prim Sch PE19 118 A2
Offord Rd PE19 97 F6
Ogden Cl SG8 14 D6
Oil Mill La PE13 245 B5
Oilmills Dro PE26 220 F4
Oilmills Rd PE26 220 E6
Old Auction Yd PE16 241 C5
Old Bailey Rd PE7 181 C8
Old Bank CB7 219 B4
Old Brewery Cl CB7 240 E4
Old Broadpool PE28 173 D2
Old Church La PE28 208 C7
Old Clements La 7 CB9 23 F7
Old Ct Hall PE29 141 E1
Old Farm Cl
Histon CB4 104 B5
3 Needingworth PE27 208 A3
Old Fen Dike PE12 237 B8
Old Field PE13 237 F4
Old Fletton Prim Sch PE2 186 F6
Old Ford La PE19 114 B2
Old Forge Way CB2 32 E8
Old Glebe PE28 150 E5
Old Great N Rd
St Martin's Without PE9 244 C3
Sibson cum Stibbington PE8 194 C2
Old Haverhill Rd CB9 39 E4
Old Houghton Rd PE29 142 B6
Old House Rd CB1 53 C2
Old Knarr Fen Dro PE6 233 C2
Old Leicester Rd PE8 194 A3
Old Lynn Dro CB6 217 C7
Old Lynn Rd PE13 245 E7
Old Mill Ave PE28 165 A5
Old Mill Cl CB2 29 D7
Old Mill La IP28 239 F2
Old Mkt PE13 245 C5
Old N Rd
Bassingbourn cum Kneesworth SG8 13 B4
Longstowe CB3 60 A3
Royston SG8 5 C7
Sawtry PE28 168 D4
Wansford PE8 194 A3
Old Orch The PE15 222 A5
Old Oundle Rd PE8 193 A6
Old Pinewood Way CB3 99 B4
Old Pond La PE5 195 E2
Old Pools Dro CB6 225 C4
Old Pound Cl PE28 143 D2
Old Ramsey Rd
St Ives PE28 143 E8
Woodhurst PE28 154 E2
Old Rectory Dr
Dry Drayton CB3 102 B1
4 Tallington PE9 230 F7
Thornhaugh PE8 194 A6
Old Rly Ind Est PE27 144 D4
Old Rope Wlk CB9 23 E7
Old Rorge Gdns PE16 241 C5
Old Sch Cl Burwell CB5 130 C3
Littleport CB6 242 D5
1 Soham CB7 212 B5
Old Sch Gdns 3 PE19 74 C2
Old Sch La Brinkley CB8 70 E1
Milton CB4 105 D2
Wicken CB7 211 B1
Old Sta Rd CB8 111 B4
Old Stable Wlk PE26 172 A4
Old W Est PE15 222 A5
Old Weston Rd PE28 158 A5
Oldbrook PE3 204 A1
Oldeamere Way PE7 190 A7
Oldfield Ave PE14 236 B5
Oldfield Gdns PE7 189 D7
Oldfield La PE13 245 B4
Oldforge Gdns PE16 241 C5
Oldhurst Rd PE28 155 E8
Olive Rd PE1 198 C7
Oliver Cl PE26 171 F6
Oliver Cromwell's House★ CB7 240 C4
Oliver Rd PE27 144 B3
Olivers Way PE15 243 D2
Olivia Rd PE28 140 C3
Ollard Ave PE13 245 D7
Ongar Ct CB5 84 F4
Onyx Ct 9 PE13 245 C4
Open Univ The CB2 246 C1
Opportune Rd PE13 245 C6
Orange Gr 1 PE13 245 C4
Orchard Ave CB4 83 E5
Orchard Cl Balsham CB1 52 F3
Bassingbourn SG8 13 A5
Cottenham CB4 125 C3
Eaton Socon PE19 74 C4
Elsworth CB3 100 B4
Girton CB3 103 E1
Hail Weston PE19 95 A1
Haverhill CB9 23 F7
Lidgate CB8 73 E8
Little Wilbraham CB1 86 E2
Littleport CB6 242 D4
Manea PE15 224 B4
March PE15 243 E3
Orchard Cl *continued*
9 Market Deeping PE6 231 E8
Peterborough PE3 197 D3
Stamford PE9 244 B5
Stilton PE7 176 A7
Warboys PE28 164 F6
Warmington PE8 178 B3
9 Wisbech PE14 236 A5
15 Wisbech PE13 238 B2
Orchard Cres PE28 208 E6
Orchard Ct PE6 232 F3
Orchard Dr Girton CB3 82 E7
Waterbeach CB5 127 B1
Wisbech PE13 245 E4
Orchard End
Bluntisham/Colne PE28 208 C5
Rampton CB4 124 E4
Orchard Est
Cambridge CB1 65 F7
1 Little Downham CB6 218 B7
Orchard Gate SG8 14 C6
Orchard Gdns PE28 121 B5
Orchard La
Brampton PE28 140 E3
Huntingdon PE29 141 E4
Orchard Mews PE2 186 F8
Orchard Pightle CB1 20 B6
Orchard Rd
Barnack PE9 230 E4
Eaton Socon PE19 74 C4
Great Shelford CB2 49 B6
Haslingfield CB3 47 B5
Histon CB4 104 C5
March PE15 243 E3
Melbourn SG8 14 C5
Royston SG8 5 B7
Sawston CB2 32 F7
Stamford PE9 244 B5
Orchard Rd S PE15 243 E3
Orchard Row CB7 212 C2
Orchard St
Cambridge CB1 246 B3
Peterborough PE2 186 F7
Stow cum Quy CB5 85 F5
Whittlesey PE7 189 D7
Orchard Terr
St Ives PE27 144 A4
Whittlesford CB2 32 C4
Orchard The Ashley CB8 91 F7
Fen Drayton CB4 121 F5
Little Paxton PE19 95 F2
Peterborough PE4 204 C3
Orchard View CB5 127 B1
Orchard Way
Burwell CB5 130 B3
Cambourne CB3 79 A3
4 Doddington/Wimblington PE15 223 B7
Godmanchester PE29 141 F2
Haddenham CB6 210 A5
Manea PE15 224 B4
Melbourn SG8 14 D6
Oakington/Longstanton CB4 103 C5
Offord Cluny PE19 97 A8
Ramsey PE26 172 A7
Royston SG8 5 C8
Orchards Prim Sch PE13 245 D8
Orchards The
Cambridge CB1 65 F5
Chatteris PE16 241 D5
Great Shelford CB2 49 B6
Peterborough PE2 185 F4
Sutton CB6 216 E2
1 Wilburton CB6 210 C6
Witcham CB6 217 A2
Orchid Cl
13 Eaton Socon PE19 74 C6
Yaxley PE7 181 F7
Orchid Fare CB3 80 C2
Orford Rd CB9 23 F6
Orkney Cl CB9 24 D7
Orme Rd PE3 197 D4
Orthwaite PE29 141 B6
Orton Ave PE2 186 E7
Orton Dr CB6 217 D1
Orton Longueville Sch PE2 186 A5
Orton Mere PE2 186 B7
Orton Parkway PE2 185 D4
Orton Wistow Foundation Prim Sch PE2 185 C6
Orwell Cl PE27 144 A6
Orwell Dr PE15 243 B5
Orwell Furlong CB4 84 C7
Orwell Gr PE4 204 F1
Orwell Rd CB2 29 C8
Osborn Cl CB4 209 A1
Osborne Pk PE13 245 C8
Osborne Rd PE13 245 B7
Osbourne Cl PE4 204 F1
Osier Cl CB7 240 E4
Osier Ct 4 PE19 74 C6
Osier Holt PE28 208 D6
Osier Way CB3 79 C5
Osiers The PE19 117 A3
Oslar's Way CB1 66 E5
Osprey PE2 185 F2
Osprey Cl PE29 142 A7
Osprey Rd CB9 24 C7
Osric Ct PE1 198 C5
Otago Cl PE7 189 F8
Otago Rd PE7 189 E8
Othello Cl PE29 142 A7
Otter Cl CB3 102 B4
Otter Way 9 PE19 74 B5
Otterbrook PE2 185 D5
Oundle Rd Elton PE8 183 F1
Peterborough PE2 185 E6
Ouse Fen Rd Or Bank CB4 208 D3
Ouse Rd
Eaton Socon PE19 74 C4
Kimbolton PE28 114 B7
St Ives PE27 144 A7
Ouse Valley Way PE19 117 E4
Ouse Washes Nature Reserve★ CB6 224 D2
Ouse Wlk PE29 141 E4
Outfield PE3 204 A1
Outwell Rd
Boyces Bridge PE14 236 D4
Elm PE14 236 C5
Outwell PE14 236 E3
Over Hall La CB10 21 D2
Over Prim Sch CB4 208 D1
Over Rd Swavesey CB4 122 F8
Willingham CB4 208 F1
Overchurch Cl CB9 23 F7
Overcote La PE27 208 B2
Overcote Rd CB4 208 D1
Overend PE8 178 D8
Overhall Gr Nature Reserve★ CB3 100 F3
Overhills Prim Sch PE28 113 F5
Overstone Ct PE3 197 C6
Overstone Dr 1 PE14 235 D1
Overstone Rd 2 PE14 235 D1
Overton Way PE2 185 F4
Overwater Cl PE29 141 A6
Ovington Pl 3 CB9 24 B8
Owall Wlk 8 SG8 5 E8
Owen Cl 3 PE9 230 D3
Owen Dr SG8 13 D1
Owl End
The Stukeleys PE28 151 F2
Yaxley PE7 181 D5
Owl Way PE29 142 B7
Owls End PE26 172 A4
Owlstone Rd CB3 64 C7
Ox Cl PE3 197 A8
Ox Field PE13 237 F3
Oxbow Cres PE15 243 C4
Oxburgh Cl
Peterborough PE7 187 F5
Wisbech PE13 245 A7
Oxford Cl
Bassingbourn SG8 12 F7
Mildenhall IP28 239 A5
Wyton PE29 143 B8
Oxford Rd
Cambridge CB4 83 B4
Peterborough PE1 197 F5
St Ives PE27 144 A4
Stamford PE9 244 A7
Oxford St CB8 110 B8
Oxholme Dro CB4 209 F1
Oxney Rd PE1 198 D5
Oyster Row CB5 84 B3

P

Pacific Cl PE15 243 C6
Paddock Cl CB4 104 C4
Paddock Row CB3 100 B4
Paddock St CB7 212 B4
Paddock The
Eaton Socon PE19 74 D4
Ely CB6 240 D5
Harston CB2 47 F2
Huntingdon PE29 141 E5
15 Somersham PE28 215 C1
Stamford PE9 244 A5
Paddock Way
Haddenham CB6 210 A6
Sawston CB2 32 F7
Paddocks Chase PE19 118 A3
Paddocks CP Sch CB8 110 E4
Paddocks Dr CB8 111 A1
Paddocks The
Alconbury PE28 150 F5
Burwell CB5 130 B1
Cambridge CB1 84 C1
Folksworth PE7 175 D8
Hilton PE28 120 B2
Little Wilbraham CB8 68 F6
Peterborough PE4 204 A5
Whittlesey PE7 189 E7
Woodhurst PE29 155 B4
Worlington IP28 213 F4
Padgett's Rd PE14 229 C3
Padgetts Cl PE28 165 A5
Padholme Rd PE1 198 C3
Padholme Rd E PE1 198 E3
Padlock Rd CB1 53 F4
Padnal Bank CB7 219 B6
Padnal Dro CB6 242 E3
Padney Dro CB7 211 D5
Page Ct CB7 240 D6
Pages Way 3 PE28 140 C3
Paget Cl CB2 64 E3
Paget Pl CB8 111 A6
Paget Rd CB2 64 D2
Painter's La CB6 216 D1
Pakenham Cl CB4 84 A5
Pakenham Pl CB9 24 B7
Palace Gdns SG8 5 C6
Palace Gn CB7 240 C4
Palace La CB7 132 D8
Palace St CB8 111 A3
Palisade Ct 3 CB6 211 B7
Palm Ct PE1 198 B8
Palmer Cl PE7 189 F6
Palmers Cl CB1 35 B3
Palmers La
Alconbury PE28 150 F4
Chrishall SG8 8 C4
Palmers Rd PE1 198 F5
Palmers Way SG8 14 D6
Palmers Wlk CB1 246 C2
Palmerston Rd PE2 186 F7
Pamment's La IP28 213 D6
Pampisford Rd CB1 34 C5
Pamplin Ct 1 CB1 65 F6
Panswell La PE13 235 C8
Panther Way CB1 66 A7
Pantile La CB5 130 A3
Pantiles CB1 20 B7
Panton St CB2 246 B1
Papley Gr Farm Cotts PE19 77 E7
Papley Hollow PE19 77 F8
Papworth Hospl CB3 99 C2
Papworth Rd
Graveley PE19 98 A5
March PE15 243 F4
Papworth's Cl CB4 208 D1
Papyrus Rd PE4 203 F3
Papyrus Way PE28 168 B4
Parade La CB7 240 C4
Paradise Ctr & Pool CB7 240 D5
Paradise La
Northborough PE6 231 F6
3 Whittlesey PE7 189 D6
Paradise Nature Reserve★ CB1 246 A1
Paradise St CB1 246 C3
Paragon Rd PE27 144 A5
Parcell Wlk PE29 118 F8
Parish Bush Dro CB7 219 C1
Park Ave Histon CB4 104 A4
Little Paxton PE19 95 F1
Newmarket CB8 111 B3
St Ives PE27 144 B4
Wisbech PE13 245 C6
Park Cl
Bassingbourn SG8 12 E5
Holme PE7 176 F4
Little Paxton PE19 95 E1
Moulton CB8 112 F5
Thorney PE6 233 B3
Yaxley PE7 181 F5
Park Cotts CB8 111 B3
Park Cres
Little Paxton PE19 95 F2
Peterborough PE1 198 B5
Thorney PE6 233 B3
Waterbeach CB5 106 C8
Park Dr Histon CB4 104 C3
Little Paxton PE19 95 F1
Park End CB5 87 B8
Park Est 1 PE6 231 F8
Park Farm Cotts CB10 18 F6
Park Farm Cres PE7 187 F5
Park Farm Dr IP28 214 A2
Park Farm La SG8 1 A2
Park Farm Rd PE6 196 E5
Park Farm Way PE7 187 F6
Park Hill CB1 37 C2
Park Home Rd PE7 186 D1
Park La Brampton PE28 117 D8
Castle Camps CB1 22 F3
Dry Drayton CB3 81 C8
Fen Drayton CB4 121 F6
Godmanchester PE29 141 F2
Histon CB4 103 F4
Kimbolton PE19 113 F2
Langley CB11 1 F2
Leverington PE13 238 A3
Little Downham CB6 217 F6
Longstowe CB3 59 F3
Madingley CB3 81 F6
Newmarket CB8 111 B3
Newton PE13 237 F3
Peterborough PE1 198 C4
Stamford PE9 244 C4
Whittlesey PE7 189 C7
Park La Prim Sch PE7 189 C6
Park Par CB5 246 A4
Park Rd Brampton PE28 140 C2
Buckden PE19 117 B4
Burwell CB5 130 B2
Cheveley CB8 91 C6
Great Chesterford CB10 18 E5
Haverhill CB9 23 D8
Manea PE15 224 B4
Market Deeping PE6 231 E8
Peterborough PE1 198 A3
Ramsey PE26 171 F6
St Ives PE27 144 B4
St Neots PE19 74 F6
Sawston CB2 32 F5
Sawtry PE28 168 B5
Sutton CB6 216 E2
Tydd St Giles PE13 237 D7
Wisbech PE13 245 D5
Park Side
Little Paxton PE19 95 E1
St Ives PE27 144 B4
Park St Cambridge CB5 246 A3
Chatteris PE16 241 C4
Dry Drayton CB3 102 C1
Peterborough PE2 186 F7
2 Wisbech PE13 245 D5
Park St CE Prim Sch CB5 246 A3
Park Terr
Cambridge CB1 246 B2
Peterborough PE1 198 A6
Park View
Bassingbourn SG8 12 E5
Little Stukeley PE28 151 F1
Needingworth PE27 208 A2
Park View E PE15 243 C4
Park View W PE15 243 C4
Park Way
Little Paxton PE19 95 F1
Offord Cluny PE19 118 A2
St Neots PE19 74 F7
Parker Cl PE19 74 E2
Parker Rd PE8 230 B1
Parker St CB1 246 B2
Parker's Cl PE16 241 B5
Parker's Dro IP28 213 D6
Parker's Terr 2 CB1 84 A2
Parkers Wlk CB8 110 E8
Parkfield La PE15 223 B6
Parkgate PE29 141 C6
Parkhall Rd PE28 215 C2
Parkinson's La 1 PE7 189 D6
Parklands SG8 5 E6
Parkside
Cambridge CB1 246 C2
Chatteris PE16 241 D4
Chippenham CB7 132 E8
Haverhill CB9 23 F6
Mildenhall IP28 214 A8
Peterborough PE2 186 B6
Parkside Foundation Coll CB1 246 C2
Parkside Pools CB1 246 C2
Parkway St Ives PE27 144 B4
Shudy Camps CB1 22 C6
The Stukeleys PE29 141 A5
Parkway Mid Sch CB9 23 D8
Parliament St PE1 197 F5
Parlour Cl CB4 104 B5
Parnwell Prim Sch PE1 198 E7
Parnwell Way PE1 198 F6
Parr Cl CB4 104 C3
Parr Rd CB9 23 D6
Parrens Rd PE28 208 E6
Parson Dro La PE13 238 B2
Parsonage Barns CB5 86 F5
Parsonage Cl
Burwell CB5 130 B2
Duxford CB2 17 E8
Parsonage Farm La CB8 90 F2
Parsonage Gdns 2 CB9 23 E7
Parsonage La CB5 130 B2
Parsonage St
Cambridge CB5 246 C3
Wistow PE28 163 F6
Parsonage Way CB1 35 D2
Parson's Ct CB2 246 A2
Parson's Dr PE28 139 A4
Parson's La CB6 242 C4
Parson's Land Dro PE15 222 D6
Parsons Gn PE27 144 C4
Parthia Cl SG8 5 E6
Partridge Cl PE7 181 D5
Partridge Dr CB3 102 B3
Partridge Gr PE4 204 A5
Partridge Hill SG7 2 C3
Paske Ave CB9 23 F7
Passage The 10 CB7 240 D4
Paston La PE4 197 D8
Paston Parkway PE4 204 E4
Paston Ridings PE4 204 E1
Paston Ridings Prim Sch PE4 204 F1
Pasture Cl PE28 165 A5
Pasture La PE6 231 F6
Pasture The 2 PE28 208 B8
Pastures The CB3 81 A1
Pates Cl CB3 47 A6
Pathfinder Way
Ramsey PE26 171 F5
Warboys PE28 164 F4
Wyton PE28 143 A8
Patterdale Dr PE4 205 A2
Patterdale Rd PE4 205 A2
Paulsgrove PE2 185 D5
Pavement The PE27 144 A3
Pavilion Ct Haverhill CB9 24 B7
7 Kings Hedges CB4 83 E8
Paxton Cl CB4 125 E3
Paxton Hill PE19 96 D2
Paxton Pitts Nature Reserve★ PE19 96 A3
Paxton Rd
Offord Darcy PE19 96 F7
Peterborough PE2 185 D4
Payne Ave PE13 245 D7
Payne Prim Sch PE13 234 D7
Paynells PE2 186 A3
Paynes Mdw CB1 35 C3
Paynesholm PE4 205 A1
Payton Way CB5 106 B7
Peacock Dr CB5 86 F7
Peacock Way
Littleport CB6 242 E4
Peterborough PE3 196 F2
Peacocks CB2 49 A4
Peake Cl PE2 186 F6
Peakes Dr PE7 201 F1
Peakirk cum Glinton Prim Sch PE6 203 E8
Peakirk Rd
Deeping Gate PE6 231 F8
Glinton PE6 203 F8
Northborough PE6 206 A4
Peakirk Wildfowl Trust★ PE6 206 B2

Peaks Ct PE29 ....141 A5
Pear Tree PE13 ....234 C2
Pear Tree Cl
  Fenstanton PE28 ....121 A5
  Haddenham CB6 ....210 A5
Pear Tree Cres PE13 ....238 A2
Pearce Cl CB3 ....64 B8
Pearces Rd PE6 ....199 B5
Pearl Leisure Ctr PE5 .195 E1
Pearmain Ct CB4 ....84 C5
Pearmains Cl SG8 ....45 E1
Pearson Cl Milton CB4 .105 D1
  St Neots PE19 ....74 E2
Peartree Way 10 PE14 .236 A5
Peas Hill CB2 ....246 A2
Peas Hill Rd PE15 ....243 A5
Pease Way CB4 ....103 F4
Peate Cl PE29 ....141 F1
Peatlings La PE13 ....245 A7
Peckover Cl PE7 ....187 F5
Peckover Ct PE13 ....245 E4
Peckover House★
  PE13 ....245 B5
Peckover Prim Sch
  PE13 ....245 B6
Pecks Cl PE28 ....120 C1
Pecks Yd PE16 ....241 C5
Peddars Way PE3 ....197 A2
Pedley La PE13 ....245 A6
Peer Rd PE19 ....74 B4
Pegler Cl CB4 ....209 A1
Peldon Dr PE13 ....245 E5
Pelham Cl
  Cottenham CB4 ....125 D3
  Peterborough PE3 ....196 F2
Pelham Ct CB4 ....83 C6
Pelham Way CB4 ....125 D3
Pelican Prep Sch CB1 .65 B4
Pemberton Terr CB2 .246 B1
Pembroke Ave
  Peterborough PE2 ....185 F5
  9 St Neots PE19 ....74 E2
  Waterbeach CB5 ....105 F8
Pembroke Cl
  Huntingdon PE29 ....141 F7
  Mildenhall IP28 ....239 C5
  2 Newmarket CB8 ....111 B2
Pembroke Coll CB2 .246 A2
Pembroke Gr PE6 ....203 F8
Pembroke La CB1 ....35 E2
Pembroke Rd PE9 ....244 A7
Pembroke St CB2 ....246 A2
Pembroke Way CB1 ....85 B1
Pen Cl CB1 ....66 A6
Pen Hills Nature Reserve★
  SG8 ....4 E3
Penarth Pl CB3 ....64 A8
Pendleton PE3 ....197 B6
Pendragon Com Prim Sch
  CB3 ....99 A3
Pendragon Hill CB3 ....99 A4
Pendula Rd PE13 ....245 E7
Pennine Way PE4 ....204 D2
Pennington PE2 ....185 E3
Pennington Rd PE29 ....142 A7
Pennway 11 PE28 ....215 C1
Penrith Gr PE4 ....205 D4
Penrose Gdns PE13 ....245 E4
Penrwyn 5 PE19 ....74 F1
Pentelowes The PE28 .135 D2
Pentland Way PE15 ....243 B5
Pentlands Cl CB4 ....246 C4
Pentlands Cl CB1 ....246 C4
Pentlands The PE4 ....204 D4
Pentlow Hawke Cl CB9 .24 B7
Penwald Cl 7 PE6 ....232 B8
Penyale PE3 ....197 A1
Pepper Cl SG8 ....12 F4
Peppercorn Cl PE1 ....197 E6
Peppercorns La 2 PE19 .74 C2
Pepperslade CB2 ....31 F1
Peppin Brown Gall The★
  CB2 ....32 C5
Pepys House★ PE28 .140 F2
Pepys Rd
  Brampton PE28 ....140 F2
  St Neots PE19 ....75 A4
Pepys Terr CB4 ....104 C1
Pepys Way CB3 ....82 E8
Percheron Cl CB4 ....104 D3
Percheron Dr PE15 ....243 C4
Percival St PE1 ....197 E2
Peregrine Cl PE29 ....142 A7
Perkins La 7 PE6 ....231 C7
Perne Ave CB1 ....65 C6
Perne Rd CB1 ....65 C6
Pernys Cl PE7 ....186 D3
Perowne St CB1 ....84 A1
Perry Cl CB6 ....210 A6
Perry Ct CB3 ....83 C4
Perry Dr SG8 ....5 C7
Perry Rd Buckden PE19 .116 F3
  Leverington PE13 ....238 B2
Perse Boys Sch The
  CB2 ....65 A4
Perse Girls 6th Form Coll
  CB1 ....246 C1
Perse Prep Sch CB2 .64 E4
Perse Sch For Girls The
  CB2 ....246 B1
Perse Way CB4 ....83 D5
Pershore Rd CB3 ....81 A3
Pershore Way PE6 ....232 B2
Persimmon Wlk CB8 .110 E8
Peter Goodin Cl CB4 .105 C2
Peterborough Airport
  (Conington) PE7 .....176 F3

Peterborough Bsns Pk
  PE2 ....185 C5
Peterborough Cath (St
  Peter's)★ PE1 ....198 A2
Peterborough Coll of Adult
  Ed PE1 ....198 B3
Peterborough District
  PE3 ....197 E2
Peterborough Dr
  Bretton PE6 ....196 E2
  Castor PE6 ....196 D3
Peterborough High Sch
  PE3 ....197 D2
Peterborough Mus & Art
  Gall★ PE3 ....197 D2
Peterborough Rd
  Castor PE5 ....195 E1
  Crowland PE6 ....232 B8
  Eye PE6 ....205 F1
  Newborough PE6 ....205 D8
  Peterborough PE7 ....187 C3
  Wansford PE8 ....194 A3
  Warmington PE8 ....178 B4
  Whittlesey PE7 ....189 B7
Peterborough Regional Coll
  Peterborough PE1 ....198 B5
  Woodston PE2 ....186 D6
Peterborough Sta PE1 .197 F2
Peterhouse CB2 ....246 A1
Petergate 1 PE9 ....244 B4
Peterhouse Cl
  Mildenhall IP28 ....239 D4
  Stamford PE9 ....244 B7
Peterhouse Cres PE13 243 E6
Peterhouse Dr CB8 ....111 A2
Peterhouse Tech Pk
  CB1 ....66 A4
Petersfield 3 CB1 .246 C2
Petersfield CE Sch SG8 .28 D8
Petersfield Rd CB2 ....17 D8
Petersfield St CB5 ....86 E5
Petingo Cl CB8 ....110 D7
Pettis Rd PE27 ....143 E6
Pettis Wlk PE27 ....143 F7
Pettits Cl CB1 ....66 F4
Pettitt's Cl CB3 ....102 C2
Pettitt's La CB3 ....102 C1
Petts Cl 3 PE13 ....245 E7
Petts La CB10 ....19 E1
Petty Cury CB2 ....246 A2
Petworth St CB1 ....84 A2
Peverel Cl CB5 ....84 D3
Peverel Rd CB5 ....84 D3
Peveril Rd PE1 ....197 F6
Peyton Ave PE15 ....243 B6
Peyton Cl PE15 ....223 A5
Pheasant Gr PE4 ....204 A5
Pheasant Rise CB3 ....102 A3
Pheasant Way PE7 ....181 D5
Philip Gdns PE19 ....74 F2
Philippa Cl CB6 ....240 F2
Philipps Cl CB8 ....110 D4
Phillips Ave SG8 ....5 D4
Phillips Chase PE15 ..243 C4
Phillips Ct PE7 ....244 C4
Phillips' Fen Dro CB7 .219 B6
Phoenix Rd CB9 ....24 A5
Phoenix Sq PE19 ....74 E6
Phorpres Cl PE7 ....186 D3
Phorpres Way PE7 ....186 E4
Pickards Way CB4 ....245 A6
Pickle Fen Dro PE16 .215 E6
Picknage Rd SG8 ....7 A2
Pidley Hill PE28 ....208 A8
Pidley Sheep La PE28 .155 F7
Pieces La CB5 ....106 B8
Pieces Terr CB5 ....106 B7
Pierce Cres PE8 ....178 C3
Pierce La CB1 ....66 F5
Pig La PE27 ....144 B5
Pigeons Cl SG8 ....31 C2
Pightle Cl Harston CB2 .47 D2
  Royston SG8 ....5 C7
Pightle The
  Bottisham CB5 ....86 E6
  Grafham PE28 ....116 A4
  Haverhill CB9 ....24 A8
Pikes Wlk CB1 ....246 B3
Piketts Cl PE7 ....189 D7
Pilgrims Cl CB10 ....18 D4
Pilgrims Way CB6 ....240 A3
Pilton Cl 4 PE4 ....204 F2
Pinder Cl PE29 ....118 F7
Pine Gr CB4 ....122 E3
Pine Tree Cl PE1 ....198 B4
Pine Trees Ave IP28 .239 E4
Pine View CB4 ....126 A4
Pines Ind Est The CB8 .131 F4
Pinewood Ave
  Whittlesey PE7 ....189 E7
  Wittering PE8 ....230 B1
Pinfold Cl
  Godmanchester PE29 ..141 F1
  1 Somersham PE28 ..208 B8
  Stamford PE9 ....244 D5
Pinfold La PE14 ....236 D1
Pingle Bank PE7 ....177 A4
Pingle Cl PE13 ....189 D7
Pingle Dro PE16 ....216 E6
Pingle La PE6 ....231 F6
Pingle Wood & Cutting
  Nature Reserve★
  PE28 ....165 A8
Pinhoe Dr SG8 ....23 C8
Pinkeneys SG8 ....8 D5
Pinza Cl CB8 ....110 E8
Pipe La PE1 ....198 B2

Piperell Way CB9 ....24 A5
Pipers Cl CB9 ....24 C7
Pipers La PE29 ....141 F1
Pipistrelle Cl PE19 ....96 A2
Pipistrelle Ct 6 PE4 .204 C3
Pippin Cl
  Offord Darcy PE19 ....117 F1
  Over CB4 ....208 D1
Pippin Dr CB4 ....84 C6
Pippin Gr SG8 ....5 C7
Pippin Pk CB8 ....73 E8
Pippin Pl PE13 ....245 E2
Pippin Wlk CB3 ....81 A3
Pitfield Cl PE28 ....121 C5
Pits La PE15 ....243 D1
Pits The CB7 ....213 A4
Pitsdean Rd PE19 ....57 A4
Pittneys PE4 ....204 F1
Pius Dro PE14 ....236 E2
Place Farm Com Prim Sch
  CB9 ....23 F8
Plains La CB6 ....225 C3
Plaistow Way SG8 ....7 E2
Plane Tree Cl SG19 ....41 C6
Plank Dro PE6 ....232 B8
Plantation Gate CB6 .210 F5
Plantation Rd CB2 ....33 A7
Plantwater Dro PE15 .227 D5
Plash Dro PE13 ....234 F4
Playles Yd SG8 ....12 C5
Plough Cl SG8 ....3 B8
Plough Cres PE7 ....189 C8
Plough La PE6 ....207 D1
Plough Rd PE7 ....189 D8
Plover Cl PE16 ....241 C5
Plover Dr PE15 ....243 F5
Plover Rd PE7 ....189 F8
Ploverly PE4 ....204 C4
Plowright Cl PE15 ....243 B3
Plum Tree Cl 3 CB4 ....83 D7
Plumian Way CB1 ....53 C2
Plumpton Ave IP28 .239 C5
Polecat La PE28 ....150 E5
Poles Ct PE7 ....189 D7
Pollards La IP28 ....213 D7
Pond Cl
  Eastwood End PE15 ..223 B6
  Pidley cum Fenton PE28 .165 D1
  The Stukeleys PE29 ...140 F5
Pond Gn CB7 ....211 E1
Pond La CB6 ....218 A6
Pond The CB6 ....210 A7
Pont's Hill CB6 ....242 D5
Pooley Way PE7 ....181 D6
Pools Rd CB6 ....210 D8
Poor's Land SG8 ....6 D4
Poorsfield Rd 2 CB5 .106 A7
Pope Rd PE19 ....74 E4
Pope Way PE1 ....197 E8
Popes Ct 3 CB9 ....24 E5
Pope's La PE13 ....238 A2
Popes La Thetford CB6 .211 B7
  Warboys PE28 ....164 E4
Popham Cl PE19 ....74 A3
Pophams Eau★ PE14 .229 C7
Poplar Ave PE1 ....198 C8
Poplar Cl
  Great Gransden SG19 ...58 D4
  Great Shelford CB2 ....49 A5
  Haverhill CB9 ....38 D1
  Huntingdon PE29 ....141 E7
  March PE15 ....243 C5
  Royston SG8 ....5 E7
Poplar Dr SG8 ....5 E7
Poplar Farm Cl SG8 ....12 D4
Poplar Rd CB4 ....104 B3
Poplar Way CB2 ....49 C4
Poplars Cl CB5 ....130 B2
Poplars The PE28 ....208 C6
Popple Dro PE15 ....235 A8
Poppy Fields 7 CB7 .212 B5
Poppyfields Ave PE15 .224 B4
Porch Cl PE29 ....141 F1
Porson Ct CB2 ....64 E4
Porson Rd CB2 ....64 D5
Port La PE5 ....195 E1
Portchester Cl PE2 ....187 F5
Porters Yd PE16 ....241 C6
Portland Ave PE1 ....197 F7
Portland Gn CB8 ....110 E3
Portland Pl
  Cambridge CB1 ....246 C3
  Whittlesey PE7 ....189 E6
Portland Rd CB8 ....110 E3
Portman Cl PE3 ....197 C4
Portobello La CB7 ....32 E7
Portugal Pl CB2 ....246 A3
Portugal St CB2 ....246 A3
Portway SG8 ....14 E7
Portway Rd CB3 ....81 A1
Post Office La 10 PE13 .245 C5
Post Office Terr CB1 ..246 B2
Post St PE29 ....141 E2
Pott Hall Rd IP28 ....213 E6
Potter's La CB7 ....240 D3
Potters Way PE1 ....198 B1
Potton End PE19 ....77 E3
Potton Rd Everton SG19 .40 C3
  Fenstanton PE28 ....120 C3
  Gamlingay SG19 ....41 D3
  Gamlingay Great Heath
   SG19 ....40 F3
  Guilden Morden SG8 ....10 F6
  Hilton PE28 ....99 B8
  St Neots PE19 ....74 F2
  Wrestlingworth SG8 ....25 A1

Potton Wood★ SG19 ....25 A8
Poulter Ave PE2 ....187 D5
Poulter's Dro PE14 ....229 D5
Pound Cl Bottisham CB5 ..86 E7
  Burwell CB5 ....130 B2
  Hail Weston PE19 ....95 B1
  Spaldwick PE28 ....137 F6
Pound Gn SG8 ....10 F5
Pound Hill CB3 ....83 C3
Pound La Isleham CB7 .213 A5
  Kimbolton PE28 ....113 F4
  Sutton CB6 ....216 E2
Pound Rd
  Chatteris PE16 ....241 B6
  Hemingford Grey PE28 .143 D1
  Ramsey PE26 ....172 A4
Pound The PE27 ....144 A5
Pound Way CB5 ....108 B2
Powell Cl CB3 ....61 D5
Powis Pl 2 PE19 ....74 F1
Pratt Ave PE4 ....204 F2
Pratt St CB7 ....212 B4
Prentice Cl CB4 ....123 F2
Presses Cl PE28 ....208 C5
Preston Cl CB3 ....61 D5
Pretoria Rd CB4 ....246 C4
Priam's Way CB2 ....49 B4
Prickwillow Drainage Engine
  Mus★ CB7 ....219 B5
Prickwillow Rd Ely CB7 .240 F5
  Isleham CB7 ....212 F7
  Soham CB7 ....219 D3
Priest La CB4 ....209 A1
Priestgate 4 PE1 ....198 A2
Priests Mdw Ct CB6 .240 C5
Primary Ct CB4 ....84 B5
Prime Cl SG8 ....14 C6
Primes Cl CB2 ....29 D7
Primrose Cl
  Cambridge CB1 ....66 A5
  Peterborough PE1 ....198 A8
  Ramsey St Mary's PE26 .220 D3
Primrose Dr PE7 ....181 F7
Primrose Farm Rd CB1 .86 E2
Primrose Hill
  Doddington PE15 ....222 E5
  Haverhill CB9 ....23 F7
  Little Gransden SG19 ....58 E3
Primrose La
  Huntingdon PE29 ....141 E5
  5 Soham CB7 ....212 B5
  Waterbeach CB5 ....106 A8
Primrose St CB4 ....83 D4
Primrose View SG8 ....5 F5
Prince Andrew's Cl 1
  SG8 ....5 D5
Prince Cl PE19 ....74 E6
Prince of Wales Cl
  PE13 ....245 D6
Prince S Rd PE13 ....245 D5
Prince St PE13 ....245 D5
Prince William Ct 6 CB4 83 C4
Prince William Way
  CB2 ....32 F6
Prince's St
  Huntingdon PE29 ....141 D4
  Peterborough PE1 ....198 A1
  Ramsey PE26 ....172 A4
Princes Cl CB1 ....53 C1
Princes Dr PE19 ....74 A6
Princes Gate PE1 ....198 B4
Princes Gdns PE1 ....198 A4
Princes Mews SG8 ....5 C6
Princes Rd
  Peterborough PE2 ....187 A4
  Stamford PE9 ....244 B6
Princess Ave PE15 ....243 C2
Princess Ct CB1 ....246 B1
Princess Dr CB2 ....49 F1
Princess of Wales Hospl
  CB6 ....240 E7
Princess Way
  Haverhill CB9 ....23 E8
  Newmarket CB8 ....110 E4
Pringle Cl PE7 ....189 C7
Pringle Ct PE28 ....151 D4
Pringle Way PE28 ....151 D4
Prins Ave PE13 ....245 D7
Prins Ct 3 PE13 ....245 D7
Prior's Cl CB4 ....104 B4
Prior's Ct 8 CB6 ....216 E2
Priors Ct CB6 ....240 D5
Priors Gate PE4 ....204 A4
Priors Rd
  Hemingford Grey PE28 .143 C1
  Whittlesey PE7 ....189 C7
Priory Ave Haverhill CB9 .23 F7
  Swavesey CB4 ....122 C5
Priory Cl Burwell CB5 .130 B2
  Ickleton CB10 ....18 A3
  7 Market Deeping PE6 .231 F8
  Royston SG8 ....5 E6
Priory Dro CB5 ....129 D7
Priory Gdns
  Peterborough PE7 ....184 D5
  Stamford PE9 ....244 D5
  Waterside CB7 ....213 A6
Priory Gr PE29 ....141 E5
Priory Hill PE19 ....75 B7
Priory Hill Rd PE19 ....75 A7
Priory Jun Sch PE19 ....75 A6
Priory La
  Huntingdon PE29 ....141 E5
  Royston SG8 ....5 D5
  St Neots PE19 ....74 E6
Priory Mews
  St Ives PE27 ....144 A3
  St Neots PE19 ....74 E6

Priory Pk Inf Sch PE19 .74 F6
Priory Rd
  Cambridge CB5 ....84 A3
  Holywell-cum-Needingworth
   PE27 ....208 A3
  Horningsea CB5 ....106 A1
  Huntingdon PE29 ....141 E5
  Needingworth PE27 ....144 F5
  Peterborough PE3 ....197 B3
  St Ives PE27 ....144 A2
  St Neots PE19 ....74 E6
  Stamford PE9 ....244 D5
Priory St 3 CB4 ....83 C4
Priory The PE19 ....74 E5
Priory Wlk CB3 ....79 C3
Proby Cl PE7 ....181 D5
Prospect Pl PE13 ....245 C4
Prospect Rd PE15 ....243 B5
Prospect Row
  Cambridge CB1 ....246 C2
  9 St Neots PE19 ....74 E6
Prospect Way PE16 ....241 C6
Prospero Cl PE2 ....186 F6
Prospero Way PE29 ....141 F7
Provence Pl 2 PE13 .245 E3
Provence Rd PE29 ....141 A6
Providence Cl 16 PE28 .215 C1
Providence Pl PE15 .224 B4
Providence Way CB5 .127 A1
Pryor Cl CB4 ....105 D2
Pudding Bag La PE9 .230 C4
Pudding La SG8 ....7 A1
Puddock Hill PE28 ....165 A8
Puddock Rd
  Ramsey PE28 ....221 F1
  Warboys PE28 ....165 A8
Pudgell The SG8 ....7 E2
Puffin La PE7 ....181 D8
Pump La 2 Hardwick CB3 .81 A3
  4 Stretham CB6 ....210 F5
Purbeck Rd CB2 ....65 A5
Purl's Bridge Dro
  PE15 ....224 B3
Purley Rd 1 CB3 ....79 A4
Purls Bridge PE15 ....224 B2
Putney Hill Rd CB7 .219 B4
Pye Terr CB4 ....84 A4
Pyecroft PE1 ....198 B6
Pyhill PE3 ....197 B8
Pymore (Pymoor) La
  CB6 ....224 E1
Pyrecroft CB3 ....79 A3
Pyrethrum Way CB4 .209 A1

Q

Quadrangle The PE28 .208 D7
Quadrant The
  Royston SG8 ....5 C8
  St Ives PE27 ....144 B3
Quail Wlk 8 SG8 ....5 E8
Quainton Cl CB5 ....84 D3
Quaker Cl PE28 ....153 C6
Quaker La PE13 ....245 E3
Quaker Way PE16 ....241 C5
Quaker's Dro PE7 ....191 F5
Quaker's La CB9 ....24 A7
Quakers' Rd IP28 ....239 F5
Quanea Dro CB7 ....240 F1
Quarry La
  Haslingfield CB3 ....47 B4
  Maxey PE6 ....231 C6
  Swaffham Bulbeck CB5 .108 B1
Quay Ct CB7 ....144 A3
Quay Hill CB6 ....242 E4
Quay The PE27 ....144 A3
Quayside
  Cambridge CB1 ....246 A3
  Chatteris PE16 ....241 C6
  Ely CB7 ....240 E6
Queen Adelaide Way
  CB7 ....240 E3
Queen Edith Com Prim Sch
  CB1 ....65 C4
Queen Edith's Way CB1 .65 D4
Queen Eleanor Cl PE7 .176 A8
Queen Eleanor Sch
  PE9 ....244 B6
Queen Elizabeth Dr
  PE13 ....245 D3
Queen Emma Wlk
  CB6 ....240 E6
Queen Mary Cl PE26 .172 A6
Queen St Cowlinge CB8 .73 C1
  Haverhill CB9 ....24 A8
  Newmarket CB8 ....111 B3
  2 Peterborough PE1 .198 A2
  Whittlesey PE7 ....189 D7
  Wisbech PE13 ....245 C6
  Yaxley PE7 ....181 F6
Queen's Cl Holme PE7 .176 F4
  1 Over CB4 ....208 D1
Queen's Dr
  Mildenhall IP28 ....239 B4
  Wisbech PE14 ....245 A3
Queen's Dr Inf Sch
  PE1 ....198 A5
Queen's Dr W PE1 ....198 A5
Queen's Gdns PE1 ....198 A5
Queen's Marlborough Coll
  The CB2 ....64 E7
Queen's Mdw CB1 ....65 F7
Queen's Rd CB3 ....64 C8
Queen's Wlk PE9 ....244 A5

Queenholme Way
CB4 . . . .**209** C2
Queens Cl Balsham CB1 . .**52** F2
Harston CB2 . . . .**48** A3
St Ives PE27 . . . .**144** A5
Queens Coll CB3 . . . . . .**246** A2
Queens Ct
Eaton Socon PE19 . . . .**74** B3
7 Haverhill CB9 . . . .**23** E8
Queens Dr PE29 . . . . . .**141** F5
Queens Gdns PE19 . . . . .**74** B4
Queens' La CB2 . . . .**246** A2
Queens Rd
Littleport CB6 . . . .**242** B5
Peterborough PE2 . . . . . .**187** B7
Royston SG8 . . . .**5** D7
Somersham PE28 . . . . . .**215** C1
Wisbech PE13 . . . .**245** C4
Queens Sch The PE13 . . .**245** D3
Queens Sq CB9 . . . .**24** A8
Queens St March PE15 . . .**243** D3
Stamford PE9 . . . .**244** B6
Withersfield CB9 . . . .**38** C4
Queens St Cl PE15 . . . . .**243** D6
Queens View CB8 . . . . .**110** A8
Queens Way CB4 . . . . . .**103** C6
Queens Wlk PE2 . . . . . .**186** F8
Queensberry Rd CB8 . . .**111** A3
Queensgate Ctr PE1 . . . .**198** A2
Queensway
Cambridge CB2 . . . .**64** E6
Chatteris PE16 . . . .**241** D5
Exning CB8 . . . .**110** B8
Haverhill CB9 . . . .**23** E8
Mildenhall IP28 . . . .**239** A4
Royston SG8 . . . .**5** D7
St Neots PE19 . . . .**74** F7
Sawston CB2 . . . .**32** F8
Soham CB7 . . . .**212** B4
Quendon Pl CB9 . . . .**24** B8
Quickset Rd CB11 . . . .**9** B5
Quidditch La CB3 . . . . . .**79** A4
Quince Rd CB3 . . . .**81** A3
Quinion Cl PE7 . . . .**189** F6
Quinton Garth PE3 . . . .**197** C5
Quorn Cl PE6 . . . .**205** C4
Quy Rd CB5 . . . .**86** B8

R

Racey's Cl PE14 . . . .**236** D6
Raceys Cl PE14 . . . .**236** D6
Rachel Cl **1** CB5 . . . .**84** E4
Rackham CE Prim Sch The
CB6 . . . .**217** E1
Rackham Cl CB4 . . . .**83** C4
Radcliffe Cl **1** PE9 . . . . .**244** B5
Radcliffe Rd PE9 . . . . . .**244** A5
Radegund Rd CB1 . . . . . .**65** B7
Radegunds CB2 . . . .**32** C5
Radford Cl PE8 . . . .**230** C1
Radwinter Rd CB10 . . . . .**21** B1
RAF Molesworth PE28 .**147** C8
RAF Witchford Display of
Memorabilia ★ CB6 . . . .**217** F1
RAF Wyton PE28 . . . . . .**143** A8
Ragdale Cl PE1 . . . .**198** E7
Railway Cl CB5 . . . .**109** B8
Railway La PE16 . . . . . .**241** C5
Railway Rd PE13 . . . . . .**245** C3
Railway St CB1 . . . .**65** F7
Railworld Mus ★ PE2 .**197** F1
Raine Ave CB9 . . . .**23** D8
Raleigh Cl PE19 . . . .**74** A2
Raleigh Way PE19 . . . . .**197** B6
Ramnoth Jun Sch
PE13 . . . .**245** D4
Ramnoth Rd PE13 . . . . .**245** D4
Rampart The CB6 . . . . .**210** A6
Ramper Rd CB4 . . . .**123** A3
Rampley La PE19 . . . .**95** F2
Rampleys The PE28 . . . .**143** D2
Ramply Cl PE19 . . . .**95** F1
Rampton Drift CB4 . . . .**124** B2
Rampton End CB4 . . . . .**209** A1
Rampton Rd
Cottenham CB4 . . . .**125** B4
Longstanton CB4 . . . . . .**124** A2
Oakington/Longstanton
CB4 . . . .**123** F1
Willingham CB4 . . . .**124** B7
Ramsden Sq CB4 . . . .**84** A7
Ramsey Abbey Gatehouse ★
PE26 . . . .**172** C7
Ramsey Abbey Sch
PE26 . . . .**172** C7
Ramsey Hollow Dro
PE26 . . . .**173** B7
Ramsey Hts Nature Reserve ★
PE26 . . . .**170** E6
Ramsey Jun Sch PE26 .**172** A7
Ramsey Leisure Ctr
PE26 . . . .**172** C7
Ramsey Rd
Benwick PE15 . . . .**221** F4
Ely CB7 . . . .**240** E6
Kings Ripton PE28 . . . . .**153** C5
Old Hurst PE28 . . . .**154** D6
Ramsey PE26 . . . .**221** C2
St Ives PE27 . . . .**143** F7
Upwood & The Raveleys
PE26 . . . .**171** D2
Warboys PE28 . . . .**164** E6
Whittlesey PE7 . . . .**220** E7

Ramsey Rural Mus ★
PE26 . . . .**172** D7
Ramsey Way PE2 . . . . . .**187** F6
Ramshill Cotts PE6 . . . .**203** A2
Randalls La CB4 . . . .**208** D1
Range The CB7 . . . .**240** C4
Rangefield PE2 . . . .**185** E4
Ransome's Cl PE14 . . . .**236** E2
Ransonmoor Dro
PE15 . . . .**222** D7
Ransonmoor Grange
PE15 . . . .**222** F8
Raptor Foundation The ★
PE28 . . . .**155** A4
Rasen Ct **2** PE1 . . . . . .**198** D3
Ratcliffe Ct PE1 . . . . . .**198** D7
Ratfords Yd CB1 . . . .**68** A8
Rathmore Cl CB1 . . . .**65** A5
Rathmore Rd CB1 . . . . . .**65** A6
Raveley Fen Rd PE28 . . .**162** D8
Raveley Rd PE28 . . . . . .**161** F6
Raven Cl
Mildenhall IP28 . . . .**239** D4
St Neots PE19 . . . .**75** B7
Ravenhill Dr PE15 . . . . .**243** C3
Ravens Ct CB6 . . . .**240** C5
Ravenscourt **6** PE27 . . .**208** A3
Ravensdale PE7 . . . .**175** F7
Ravensthorpe Prim Sch
PE3 . . . .**197** C7
Ravensworth Gdns CB1 . .**65** A7
Rawlin Cl CB5 . . . .**84** D3
Rawlin Cl CB5 . . . .**84** D3
Rawlyn Rd CB5 . . . .**84** D3
Ray's Dro PE26 . . . .**220** B1
Rayes La CB8 . . . .**111** A4
Rayleigh Cl CB2 . . . .**64** E5
Raymond St **14** PE13 . . .**245** C4
Rayner Ave PE2 . . . .**187** E5
Rayner's Cl SG8 . . . .**30** D1
Rays Ct PE15 . . . .**223** B6
Rayson Way CB5 . . . .**84** D3
Reach Dro PE7 . . . .**189** B5
Reach Rd Burwell CB5 . .**109** B8
Reach CB5 . . . .**129** F1
Reaches The PE6 . . . . . .**232** C3
Read's St CB6 . . . .**210** F5
Ream Cl PE19 . . . .**74** E2
Recreation Cl CB4 . . . . .**105** D1
Recreation Gd Rd PE9 .**244** B6
Recreation Rd CB9 . . . . . .**23** F7
Recreation Way IP28 . . .**239** C4
Rectors Way **3** PE4 . . . .**204** F2
Rectory Cl
Brampton PE28 . . . .**140** E2
Great Paxton PE19 . . . . . .**96** E4
Oakington/Longstanton
CB4 . . . .**123** F1
Sawtry PE28 . . . .**168** C5
Rectory Farm Rd CB1 . . .**86** F7
Rectory Fields CB6 . . . .**216** E3
Rectory Gdns
Glinton PE6 . . . .**203** E8
Godmanchester PE29 . . .**141** F2
Peterborough PE2 . . . . . .**187** B7
Wisbech PE13 . . . .**245** E6
Rectory La Ashdon CB10 . .**21** A1
Etton PE6 . . . .**231** E5
Fowlmere SG8 . . . .**15** E8
Glinton PE6 . . . .**203** E8
Kingston CB3 . . . .**61** B3
Peakirk PE6 . . . .**206** B2
St Ives PE28 . . . .**142** F5
Somersham PE28 . . . . . .**215** B1
Southoe & Midloe PE19 . . .**95** D6
Rectory Rd
Bluntisham/Colne PE28 . .**208** D5
Duxford CB2 . . . .**17** E8
Newton CB22 . . . .**238** B5
Outwell PE14 . . . .**236** F2
Rectory Way PE7 . . . . . .**175** F7
Red Barn PE7 . . . .**191** E6
Red Cross La CB2 . . . . . .**65** B3
Red Dock La CB8 . . . .**73** F1
Red Fen Rd CB6 . . . .**210** F7
Red Hill Cl CB2 . . . .**48** E8
Red Hill La CB2 . . . .**48** E8
Red Lion Cl PE28 . . . . . .**150** F4
Red Lion La **6** CB6 . . . .**216** E1
Red Lion Sq **5** PE9 . . . .**244** B5
Red Lion St **12** PE9 . . . .**244** B5
Red Roofs CB6 . . . .**210** B8
Redbridge PE4 . . . .**204** A6
Redcaps La CB2 . . . .**217** E6
Redcot Gdns **8** PE9 . . . .**244** B6
Redcott Gdns PE9 . . . . .**244** B5
Redebourne La PE26 . . .**171** F4
Redfern Cl CB4 . . . .**83** E6
Redgate Ct PE1 . . . .**198** E2
Redgate Rd Girton CB3 . .**82** E8
Tydd St Giles PE13 . . . . .**238** C4
Redhouse Gdns **3** CB7 .**212** B3
Redit La CB7 . . . .**211** E1
Redlands SG8 . . . .**8** E8
Redlands Rd CB3 . . . . . .**101** C5
Redman Cl PE7 . . . .**240** F7
Redmile Wlk PE1 . . . . . .**198** D8
Redmoor Bank PE14 . . .**235** F4
Redmoor Cl PE27 . . . . . .**144** B7
Redmoor La PE14 . . . . . .**235** F5
Redroofs CB6 . . . .**211** B7
Redshank Cl
Haverhill CB9 . . . .**24** C7
Whittlesey PE7 . . . .**201** A1
Redwell St PE27 . . . . . .**143** E5
Redwing Cl PE2 . . . .**187** E5
Redwing Dr Royston SG8 . . .**5** E8
5 Wisbech PE14 . . . . . .**245** D2

Redwing Pl **2** PE19 . . . .**75** B7
Redwing Rise SG8 . . . . . .**5** E8
Redwongs Way PE29 . . .**141** D7
Reed Cl Cambridge CB2 . .**64** E1
Chatteris PE16 . . . .**241** C3
Reed Way PE14 . . . .**236** A4
Reedland Way PE7 . . . . .**186** C1
Reedmace Cl PE6 . . . . . .**205** C8
Reeds La CB9 . . . .**24** A8
Reepham PE2 . . . .**185** D4
Rees Thomas Sch CB4 . .**83** F6
Reeve Hill SG8 . . . .**8** A6
Reeves Pightle SG8 . . . . . .**7** F3
Reeves Way PE1 . . . .**198** D5
Regal Dr CB7 . . . .**212** C3
Regal La CB7 . . . .**212** C3
Regal Rd PE13 . . . .**245** B2
Regatta Ct CB5 . . . .**84** B4
Regency Sq CB1 . . . .**65** A7
Regency Way PE3 . . . . . .**197** C1
Regent Ave PE15 . . . . . .**243** D5
Regent Cl PE19 . . . .**74** B4
Regent Pl **1** CB7 . . . . . .**212** B3
Regent St CB2 . . . .**246** B1
Regent Terr CB2 . . . . . .**246** B1
Regents Ct CB8 . . . .**110** F3
Regional Swimming Pool
PE1 . . . .**198** B1
Reilly Way CB1 . . . .**65** F8
Rembrandt Way PE27 . .**144** A7
Renoir Cl PE27 . . . .**144** A7
Resbury Cl PE27 . . . .**50** A1
Retreat The **8** PE6 . . . .**231** F8
Reubens Rd CB4 . . . . . .**105** C7
Reynold's Cl CB9 . . . .**38** D1
Reynolds Cl PE27 . . . . . .**144** A7
Reynolds Ct **6** PE19 . . . .**74** D6
Reynolds Dr PE19 . . . . . .**95** F1
Reynolds' Dro CB4 . . . . .**124** D3
Rhee Lake Dro PE28 . . .**208** E8
Rhees The PE28 . . . .**208** D6
Rhonda Pk PE15 . . . . . .**223** C7
Rhone Pl **3** PE13 . . . . . .**245** E3
Rhugarve Gdns CB1 . . . . .**35** D2
Rhymers Gate PE28 . . . .**142** F5
Ribble Cl PE27 . . . .**144** B6
Ribe Ct CB6 . . . .**240** C4
Ribes Cl PE7 . . . .**186** D3
Ribston Way CB4 . . . .**84** C6
Richard Young Cl
PE13 . . . .**245** C8
Richards Cl PE15 . . . . . .**243** B5
Richardson Way PE7 . . .**189** E7
Richmond Ave
March PE15 . . . .**243** C3
Peterborough PE4 . . . . . .**204** C2
Richmond Cl
Huntingdon PE29 . . . . . .**141** E8
7 St Neots PE19 . . . . . .**74** F1
Richmond Ct PE13 . . . . .**245** A4
Richmond Field PE13 . . .**237** E2
Richmond Rd CB4 . . . . . .**83** B4
Richmond Terr CB1 . . . .**246** A4
Richmond Way **6** PE13 .**238** B2
Rickard Cl CB1 . . . .**65** E6
Rickwood Cl CB6 . . . . . .**216** C5
Rickyard The SG7 . . . .**2** D3
Riddiford Cres PE28 . . . .**140** C2
Riddy Cl CB2 . . . .**48** B5
Riddy La CB3 . . . .**60** C5
Rideaway PE28 . . . .**119** F8
Ridge Way PE2 . . . .**187** B8
Ridgefield Prim Sch
CB1 . . . .**65** C7
Ridgeway
Papworth Everard CB3 . . .**99** A4
Perry PE28 . . . .**115** D2
St Neots PE19 . . . .**74** F2
Ridgeway The CB1 . . . . . .**35** E2
Ridley Hall Rd CB3 . . . . . .**64** C8
Rigg Cl PE13 . . . .**245** B3
Rightwell PE3 . . . .**197** A6
Rightwell E PE3 . . . .**197** A5
Rightwell W PE3 . . . . . .**197** A5
Riley Cl PE7 . . . .**181** D6
Ringers La PE13 . . . .**238** B2
Ringstead Rd PE4 . . . . .**204** F1
Ringwood PE3 . . . .**196** F3
Ringwood Cl PE26 . . . . .**172** A4
Ripon Cl PE4 . . . .**204** B3
Rippons Dro PE26 . . . . .**231** F7
Risby PE3 . . . .**197** B8
Riseholme PE2 . . . .**185** E3
Rivar Pl CB1 . . . .**84** A1
Rivendale PE4 . . . .**204** B2
River Bank CB7 . . . .**128** C6
River Cl **2** Benwick PE15 .**222** A5
Little Paxton PE19 . . . . . .**95** F1
Mepal CB6 . . . .**216** E4
River Dr PE15 . . . .**243** E4
River Dro PE7 . . . .**191** C5
River End PE7 . . . .**178** C8
River La Brampton PE28 .**140** E1
Cambridge CB5 . . . .**84** A3
Elton PE8 . . . .**178** C8
Fordham CB7 . . . .**212** E1
Great Paxton PE19 . . . . . .**96** D3
Haslingfield CB3 . . . .**47** C5
Peterborough PE3 . . . . . .**197** F2
River Mdw PE28 . . . . . .**142** F3
River Terr
3 St Neots PE19 . . . . . .**74** E5
Wisbech PE14 . . . .**245** A8
Riverbank Cl **12** PE6 . . .**231** F8

Riverdown PE15 . . . . . .**243** F5
Rivergate **3** PE1 . . . . . .**198** A1
Rivergate Sh Ctr PE1 . . .**198** A1
Rivermill Gall ★ PE19 . .**74** C2
Riverside Cambridge CB5 .**84** B3
11 Market Deeping PE6 .**231** F8
Riverside Cl Ely CB7 . . . .**219** B5
Mildenhall IP28 . . . .**239** B4
Whittlesey PE7 . . . .**189** D6
Riverside Ct CB5 . . . . . .**246** B4
Riverside Gdns
Parson Drove PE13 . . . . .**234** C7
Peterborough PE3 . . . . . .**197** D5
Riverside Mead PE2 . . . .**187** B8
Riverside Mid Sch
IP28 . . . .**239** A4
Riverside Rd PE29 . . . . .**141** E4
Riverside Spinney
PE8 . . . .**194** A3
Riverside Way PE13 . . . .**245** B3
Riverside Wlk CB7 . . . . .**240** E3
Riversmead PE19 . . . . . .**74** E6
Rivey Cl CB1 . . . .**35** D3
Rivey Way CB1 . . . .**35** D2
Roan Wlk **8** SG8 . . . .**5** E6
Robbs Wlk PE27 . . . . . .**144** A3
Robden Ct PE2 . . . .**197** E1
Robert Arkenstall Prim Sch
The CB6 . . . .**210** A4
Robert Ave
Peterborough PE1 . . . . . .**197** F8
4 Somersham PE28 . . .**215** C1
Robert Jennings Cl
CB4 . . . .**84** A6
Robert May Cl CB1 . . . . .**65** D7
Robert Rayner Cl PE2 . .**186** D6
Roberts Cl PE19 . . . .**74** B2
Robertson Way PE29 . . .**152** L1
Robin Cl Bar Hill CB3 . . .**100** F5
Haverhill CB9 . . . .**24** C7
Mildenhall IP28 . . . .**239** D4
Robin Goodfellow's La
PE15 . . . .**243** D5
Robin Hood Cl PE7 . . . .**196** F2
Robin Mews **4** PE14 . . .**245** D2
Robingoodfellow's La
PE15 . . . .**243** C6
Robins Cl **5** Ely CB6 . . . .**240** B5
8 Isleham CB7 . . . .**213** A5
Peterborough PE2 . . . . . .**186** E8
Robins Field PE8 . . . . . .**194** A4
Robins' La CB3 . . . .**101** F5
Robins Wood PE4 . . . . . .**194** A4
Robinson Coll CB3 . . . . . .**83** B1
Robinson Way CB2 . . . . . .**65** A3
Robshaw Cl **4** PE15 . . . .**243** E4
Rocester Way SG8 . . . .**5** D8
Rochford Wlk **5** PE13 . .**245** C5
Rochfort Ave CB8 . . . . .**110** E5
Rock Rd Cambridge CB1 . .**65** A6
Peterborough PE1 . . . . . .**197** F6
Royston SG8 . . . .**5** C8
Stamford PE9 . . . .**244** B5
Rockall Cl CB9 . . . .**24** D7
Rockingham Gr PE4 . . . .**204** C2
Rockingham Rd PE28 . . .**168** B3
Rockingham Yd CB8 . . . .**90** D8
Rockmill End CB4 . . . . .**209** A1
Rodham Rd PE15 . . . . . .**228** F5
Rodings The CB5 . . . .**84** E4
Rodney Rd PE29 . . . . . .**142** A6
Roe Gn PE19 . . . .**74** B5
Roedeer Cl CB1 . . . .**66** A7
Roe's Cl CB2 . . . .**32** F8
Roger's Cl CB3 . . . .**100** B4
Rogers End CB10 . . . . . .**21** B1
Rogers Rd CB5 . . . .**108** E6
Rogues La CB3 . . . .**99** D5
Roland Cl CB4 . . . .**83** E5
Rolleston Garth PE1 . . . .**198** C8
Rollys La SG7 . . . .**2** D4
Roman Bank
Newton PE13 . . . .**238** B4
Stamford PE9 . . . .**244** C4
Roman Cl Burwell CB5 . .**130** A2
Whittlesey PE7 . . . .**189** F8
Roman Courts CB4 . . . . . .**83** E8
Roman Dr PE8 . . . .**194** D2
Roman Drift CB3 . . . .**80** C1
Roman Hill CB3 . . . .**63** C4
Roman Way
Haverhill CB9 . . . .**24** D7
March PE15 . . . .**243** C6
Perry PE28 . . . .**115** D2
Stilton PE7 . . . .**176** A8
Roman Way Fst Sch SG8 . .**5** D8
Romany Gdns PE27 . . . .**187** D5
Romney Cl PE27 . . . .**144** A7
Romney Ct **2** PE19 . . . . .**74** C5
Romsey Jun Sch CB1 . . . .**65** B8
Romsey Mews CB1 . . . . . .**65** B7
Romsey Rd CB1 . . . .**65** C8
Romsey Terr PE16 . . . . .**241** C5
Ronalds Way PE16 . . . . .**241** C5
Ronaldsway **5** PE15 . . .**222** F5
Rook Gr CB4 . . . .**209** A1
Rookery Cl
Great Chesterford CB10 . .**144** C4
St Ives PE27 . . . .**144** C4
Waterbeach CB5 . . . . . .**106** A8
Rookery Pl PE28 . . . . . .**121** C5
Rookery Sh Ctr The
CB8 . . . .**111** A4
Rookery The
Balsham CB1 . . . .**53** A2
Little Paxton PE19 . . . . . .**95** F2
8 Newmarket CB8 . . . .**111** A3
Peterborough PE2 . . . . . .**185** C7

Rookery The continued
Yaxley PE7 . . . .**181** D5
Rookery Way PE28 . . . . .**121** B5
Rooks St CB4 . . . .**125** C4
Rookswood Rd PE15 . . . .**243** C4
Rookwood Way CB9 . . . . .**24** A6
Roscrea Terr PE29 . . . . .**141** D4
Rose and Crown Rd
CB4 . . . .**122** C3
Rose Ave PE2 . . . .**187** C7
Rose Cres CB2 . . . .**246** A3
Rose Croft PE28 . . . . . .**115** C2
Rose Ct **8** PE19 . . . .**74** C4
Rose Gn La **10** IP28 . . . .**213** F8
Rose Hill CB9 . . . .**38** D5
Rose La **4** Elm PE14 . . . .**236** A5
Great Chesterford CB10 . .**14** C6
Melbourn SG8 . . . .**14** C6
Rose Wlk Royston SG8 . . . .**5** C7
Wisbech PE13 . . . .**245** A6
Rosebay Gdns **6** CB7 . . .**212** B5
Roseberry Rd PE14 . . . .**236** B5
Rosebery Way CB8 . . . . .**110** C5
Rosedale PE14 . . . .**236** E8
Rosedene Dr PE15 . . . . .**243** D3
Rosefinch Cl CB9 . . . .**24** C7
Roseford Rd CB4 . . . .**83** D6
Roselea CB4 . . . .**104** C3
Rosemary Cl **7** IP28 . . . .**214** A1
Rosemary Gdns PE1 . . . .**197** B5
Rosemary Greene Cl
CB3 . . . .**78** E2
Rosemary La
Cambridge CB1 . . . .**65** E7
Chatteris PE16 . . . .**241** B4
Sutton CB6 . . . .**216** C1
Rosemary Rd CB5 . . . . .**106** B7
Rose's Cl PE15 . . . .**243** D2
Rosewood Cl PE7 . . . . . .**181** E5
Rosie Hospl CB2 . . . .**65** A3
Ross Cl CB9 . . . .**24** D6
Ross Piers Sports Ctr The
CB7 . . . .**212** B3
Ross St CB1 . . . .**65** B8
Roswell View CB7 . . . . .**240** E5
Rosyth Ave PE2 . . . .**185** D3
Rotherby Gr **4** PE1 . . . .**198** D7
Rotherwick Way CB1 . . . .**65** C3
Rothleigh Rd **2** CB1 . . . .**65** D5
Rothwell Way PE27 . . . .**144** A4
Round Church St CB2 . . .**246** A3
Round Hills Way PE28 . .**168** A5
Round House Dro
PE28 . . . .**222** A1
Roundhills View PE28 . .**167** A8
Roundhouse Cl PE1 . . . .**198** D3
Roundhouse Dr PE28 . . .**115** D3
Rous Rd CB8 . . . .**111** B3
Row The CB6 . . . .**216** E1
Rowan Ave
Peterborough PE1 . . . . . .**198** C6
Sawston CB2 . . . .**32** F6
Rowan Cl Bottisham CB5 . .**86** F6
Hanchet End CB9 . . . . . .**38** E1
Huntingdon PE29 . . . . . .**141** C5
Wisbech PE13 . . . .**245** F7
Rowan Wlk IP28 . . . . . .**239** E5
Rowans The
2 Doddington/Wimblington
PE15 . . . .**223** A6
Milton CB4 . . . .**105** C1
Rowe Ave PE2 . . . .**186** D7
Rowell Cl CB9 . . . .**39** A2
Rowell Wlk PE26 . . . . . .**172** A4
Rowells The CB4 . . . . . .**125** C3
Rowland Ct PE4 . . . .**204** B6
Rowlands Cl CB2 . . . .**30** C5
Rowles Way CB4 . . . . . .**101** D8
Rowley Ct
Newmarket CB8 . . . .**110** E3
1 Sturmer CB9 . . . .**24** E5
Rowley Dr CB8 . . . .**110** F4
Rowley Gdns CB5 . . . .**86** E6
Rowley Rd PE19 . . . .**75** B7
Rowlinson Way CB4 . . . . .**84** B3
Rows The CB8 . . . .**110** F3
Roxburgh Rd CB4 . . . . . .**83** E7
Royal Anglian Regiment Mus
The ★ CB2 . . . .**16** F8
Royal Cl **2** PE19 . . . .**74** B4
Royal Oak La CB2 . . . . .**143** A2
Royal Pal Cl CB8 . . . . . .**110** D7
Royal Pl **2** PE13 . . . . . .**245** C4
Royce Cl PE7 . . . .**181** E6
Royce Ct PE27 . . . .**144** B7
Royce Rd Alwalton PE7 . .**185** A4
Eastfield PE1 . . . .**198** D3
Royle Cl PE2 . . . .**186** C5
Royse Gr SG8 . . . .**5** C8
Roysia Mid Sch SG8 . . . . .**5** D8
Royston Ave
Peterborough PE2 . . . . . .**186** C6
Spaldwick PE28 . . . .**137** F6
Royston Hospl SG8 . . . . . .**5** D4
Royston La
Comberton CB3 . . . .**62** C3
Elmdon CB11 . . . .**9** C6
Royston Mus ★ SG8 . . . . .**5** C6
Royston Outdoor Pool
SG8 . . . .**5** C8
Royston Rd Barley SG8 . . . .**6** F3
Caxton CB3 . . . .**59** F7
Duxford CB2 . . . .**32** D3
Foxton CB2 . . . .**30** A5
Harston CB2 . . . .**47** D1
Litlington SG8 . . . .**12** B1
Royston Sta SG8 . . . .**5** C6
Rubens Way PE27 . . . . .**144** A7

Ruddles La PE28 ......142 E6
Rudlands Cl **3** CB7 .....213 A5
Rudyard Gr PE4 .....204 E3
Ruffles Rd CB9 ....24 C7
Rupert Brooke Mus★
............................64 A3
Rush Gr CB1 ....66 A6
Rushbrook Cl CB3 .....59 F3
Rushington Cl PE27 ...144 B5
Rushmere PE2 ....185 F6
Rushton Ave PE4 .....204 A4
Ruskin Cl **2** CB9 ......38 D1
Russell Ave PE15 .....243 B6
Russell Cl
  Steeple Morden SG8 ....11 B2
  7 Thorney PE6 ....233 A3
Russell Ct
  Cambridge CB2 ......64 E7
  St Neots PE19 ....74 F6
Russell Hill PE8 ......193 F6
Russell St
  Cambridge CB2 .....246 C1
  Peterborough PE1 ....197 F3
  St Neots PE19 ....74 E6
  Wisbech PE13 ....245 C6
Russet Cl PE27 ......144 B5
Russet Ct CB4 ....84 C6
Russet Way SG8 ......14 D6
Russet Wlk **3** CB3 ....81 A3
Russets The PE14 ....236 E2
Russett Ave PE27 ....208 A2
Rustat Ave CB1 ....65 A7
Rustat Rd CB1 ....65 A6
Rustons Rd PE14 .....236 F7
Rustons The CB2 ......32 D1
Rusts La PE28 ......150 F4
Rutherford Rd CB2 ....64 E4
Rutland Cl
  Cambridge CB4 ......83 D6
  St Ives PE27 ....143 F7
Rutland Ct **5** CB8 .....23 E7
Rutland Gn PE28 .....120 B1
Rutland Rd PE9 ......244 D7
Rutland Terr PE9 .....244 A4
Rutland Way PE15 ....224 B4
Rutner Cl PE2 ....186 D8
Rycroft Ave
  3 Deeping St James PE6 .231 F8
  St Neots PE19 ....74 E6
Rydal Cl PE29 ....141 B6
Rydal Ct PE4 ....204 E3
Rye Cl **4** PE19 ......74 F1
Rye Ct **10** CB9 ....23 E7
Ryecroft La SG8 ......15 E8
Ryhall Rd PE9 ......244 D6

S

Sable Cl CB1 ....66 A7
Sackville Cl CB4 ......83 E7
Sackville St CB8 .....111 B4
Sackville Way CB3 .....79 C4
Sacred Heart RC Prim Sch
  PE3 ....197 A5
Sacrewell Farm & Ctry Ctr★
  PE8 ....194 C5
Saddle Ct PE4 ....197 E8
Saddlers Cl PE6 .....203 E8
Saddlers Pl SG8 ....5 C7
Sadlers Cl Coton CB3 ...82 B2
  Hardwick CB3 ....81 A1
Sadlers Way PE28 ....143 D1
Saffron Cl CB6 ......242 C2
Saffron Piece **3** CB6 ..216 E1
Saffron Rd Histon CB4 ..104 B3
  Sawston CB2 ....33 A8
Saffron St SG8 ....5 F5
Sage's La PE4 ....197 C8
Saggers Cl SG8 ......12 D1
Sainfoin Cl CB2 ......33 A8
Sainsfoins CB2 ....48 F1
St Alban's Dr **20** PE6 ...232 A1
St Alban's RC Prim Sch
  CB2 ....246 B1
St Albans CB8 ....111 A6
St Albans Rd CB4 .....83 D6
St Andrew CB8 ......111 A4
St Andrew's CE Com Jun Sch
  CB4 ....84 C6
St Andrew's CE Prim Sch
  CB7 ....212 B3
St Andrew's Cl CB2 ....49 C4
St Andrew's Hill CB5 ..106 B7
St Andrew's Pk CB4 ...104 B5
St Andrew's Pl PE7 ...189 D6
St Andrew's Rd CB4 ....84 A3
St Andrew's St
  Cambridge CB2 .....246 B2
  Mildenhall IP28 .....239 C4
St Andrew's Way CB6 ..240 B6
St Andrews Cl **1** CB8 ..213 A5
St Andrews Hill CB5 ..106 B7
St Andrews La **2** PE6 ..113 F4
St Andrews Rd **4** PE6 ..231 F7
St Andrews Way
  Histon CB4 ....104 E4
  Sawtry PE28 ....168 C4
St Ann's La PE29 ....141 F1
St Annes CE Prim Sch
  PE29 ....118 F8
St Anns Dr IP28 .....239 B4
St Anselm Pl **1** PE19 ...74 E5
St Anthony **2** CB8 ....111 A4
St Anthonys Wlk CB2 ...64 E7
St Arleys La PE27 ....144 A5
St Audrey Cl
  Peterborough PE2 ...187 D6

St Audrey Cl continued
  St Ives PE27 ....144 B5
St Audrey's Cl CB4 ...104 A4
St Audrey's Way CB6 ..240 D6
St Augustine's Jun Sch
  PE2 ....186 F8
St Augustine's Wlk
  PE2 ....186 E8
St Augustines Inf Sch
  PE13 ....245 D8
St Augustines RC Prim Sch
  PE9 ....244 C7
St Augustines Rd
  PE13 ....245 C5
St Barnabas Ct **3** PE29 .141 F7
St Barnabas Rd CB1 ...65 A8
St Bartholomew's Ct
  CB5 ....84 B3
St Bede's Cres CB1 ....65 E6
St Bede's Gdns CB1 ...65 E6
St Bede's Inter Church Comp
  Sch CB1 ....65 D6
St Bee's Dr **18** PE6 ...232 A1
St Benedict's Ct PE6 ..203 F7
St Benedicts Ct **5** PE29 .141 D4
St Benet's Gdns **5** PE6 .232 A1
St Botolph La PE2 ....186 C6
St Botolph's Gn PE8 ..178 E7
St Botolph's Prim Sch
  PE2 ....186 B6
St Botolph's Way
  Haverhill CB9 ....23 F8
  Thorney PE6 ....233 A2
St Botolphs Pl CB9 ....23 E7
St Catharine's Coll
  CB2 ....246 A2
St Catharines Hall CB3 .82 C2
St Catharines Sq CB4 ..83 C7
St Catherine's CB6 ...240 C5
St Catherine's Cl IP28 .239 D6
St Catherines Prep Sch
  CB2 ....64 E7
St Catherines Rd
  CB2 ....246 A2
St Christophers Ave **2**
  CB4 ....83 C4
St Clement Cl PE14 ...236 F2
St Clement's CB4 ....244 A5
St Clements Gdns
  CB1 ....246 A3
St Clements Pas PE29 .141 E4
St Colettes Prep Sch
  CB1 ....64 F7
St David CB8 ....111 A4
St David's Sq PE11 ...198 D1
St David's Way PE28 ..168 C4
St Denys **3** CB8 ....111 A4
St Edmunds Coll CB3 ...83 C3
St Edmunds Dr PE14 ..236 F2
St Edwards Pas **4** CB1 .246 A2
St Ethelwolds Cl CB6 ..240 B4
St Fabians Cl CB8 ....110 F5
St Faiths Sch CB2 .....64 E6
St Felix CE VC Mid Sch
  CB8 ....110 F6
St Felix Cl CB7 ......212 B5
St Felix RC Prim Sch
  CB8 ....23 D7
St Felix Rd PE26 ....221 C2
St George **1** CB8 ....111 A4
St George Ave PE2 ...187 E6
St George's Rd
  St Ives PE27 ....144 A4
  14 Wittering PE8 ....230 B1
St George's Sq **5** PE9 ..244 C5
St Georges Ave PE9 ..244 C5
St Georges Piece PE28 ..140 E1
St Georges Ct **3** PE29 .141 D4
St Georges Sch
  Peterborough PE1 ....198 A7
  Stamford PE9 ......244 C7
St Georges Way CB4 ..104 E4
St Germain St PE29 ..141 D4
St Germain Wlk **8**
  PE29 ....141 D4
St Gilberts Sch PE9 ..244 B5
St Giles Cl PE7 ......176 F4
St Giles Gr PE14 ....236 B5
St Helena Farm IP28 ..239 F6
St Helena Wlk IP28 ..239 C7
St Helen's Prim Sch
  PE28 ....208 D4
St Hugh's Rd PE19 ...117 A4
St Ives Rd Elsitsley PE19 ..77 E6
  Hemingford Grey PE28 .143 D2
  Old Hurst PE28 .....154 D6
  Papworth Everard CB3 ..98 F2
  St Ives PE28 ....143 A5
  Somersham PE28 ....208 B8
St Ivo Leisure Ctr
  PE27 ....143 F4
St Ivo Sch PE27 .....143 F5
St James CB8 ....111 A4
St James Ave PE1 ...197 F7
St James Cl
  Newton PE13 ....238 A5
  3 Stretham CB6 ....210 F5
St James Ct **5** CB9 ...23 E8
St James Rd PE19 ....95 F3
St John Fisher RC Sch
  PE29 ....198 C4
St John's CE Prim Sch
  PE29 ....141 E7
St John's Chase PE15 .243 D5
St John's Cl
  Mildenhall IP28 .....239 D6
  7 Needingworth PE27 .208 A3
  Waterbeach CB5 ....106 B7
St John's Coll CB2 ..246 A3

St John's La CB5 ....106 A2
St John's Pl
  Cambridge CB4 ....83 C3
  Wistow PE28 ....163 F7
St John's Rd
  Cambridge CB5 .....246 A4
  Coton CB3 ....82 B2
  Ely CB6 ....240 A4
  March PE15 ....243 D5
  18 Wittering PE8 ....230 B1
St John's St
  Beck Row, Holywell
  Row & Kenny Hill IP28 .214 A8
  Cambridge CB2 .....246 A3
  Duxford CB2 ....32 D1
  Mildenhall IP28 .....213 F8
  Peterborough PE1 ...198 B2
St Johns Ave CB8 ....111 A1
St Johns Church Sch (Aided)
  PE2 ....185 F3
St Johns Cl PE28 ....155 B5
St Johns Coll Sch CB3 ..83 C2
St John's Innovation Ctr
  CB4 ....84 C8
St Johns La CB3 ......99 B2
St Johns Mews PE19 ...96 E4
St Johns Rd PE2 ....187 B7
St Johns St PE29 ....141 D5
St Johns Way CB3 ....79 A4
St Judes Cl PE3 .....197 C4
St Judith's La PE28 ..160 B6
St Katherines Mews
  PE7 ....186 C3
St Kilda Ave CB4 .....84 A7
St Laurence Rd CB4 ...30 C5
St Laurence's RC Prim Sch
  CB4 ....83 D7
St Lawrence Way **2**
  PE9 ....230 F7
St Leonard's Rd **2** PE13 .238 B2
St Leonard's St **4** PE9 .244 C5
St Louis RC VA Prim Sch
  CB8 ....111 A4
St Luke's CE Prim Sch
  CB4 ....83 C4
St Lukes Cl PE29 ....141 D5
St Lukes Mews CB4 ...83 D4
St Lukes St CB4 ....246 A4
St Margaret's Rd CB4 ..82 F6
St Margaret's Sq CB1 ..65 B5
St Margarets Pl PE2 ..186 F6
St Margarets Rd PE2 ..186 F6
St Margarets Way
  PE29 ....141 C6
St Mark's Ct **3** PE1 ..198 A3
St Marks Ct CB3 ......64 C8
St Marks Rd PE13 ....237 E3
St Marks St PE1 .....198 A3
St Martin's Cl
  Chatteris PE16 ......241 D5
  Exning CB8 ....110 C7
  Stamford PE9 ......244 C4
St Martin's Rd
  Chatteris PE16 ......241 D4
  Newborough PE6 ....205 B8
  Wisbech PE13 ......245 E7
St Martin's St PE1 ...197 F5
St Martins Wlk CB7 ..240 D5
St Mary's Earith PE28 .208 E6
  Gamlingay SG8 ....41 E5
St Mary's Ave PE8 ...230 B1
St Mary's CE Prim Sch
  PE19 ....75 A5
St Mary's Cl
  Bainton PE9 ....230 F5
  Bluntisham PE28 ....208 D5
  Farcet PE7 ....187 C2
  Peterborough PE1 ...198 B4
  Thorney PE6 ....233 A2
  Wisbech St Mary PE13 .235 C7
St Mary's Dr
  March PE15 ....243 C5
  Peterborough PE2 ...185 F4
St Mary's Gn PE28 ...164 E6
St Mary's Hill **9** PE9 ..244 C5
St Mary's Pas **2** CB1 .246 A2
St Mary's RC JMI Sch
  SG8 ....5 D7
St Mary's Rd
  Bluntisham/Colne PE28 .208 C5
  Ramsey PE26 ......220 E2
  Sawston CB2 ....33 A7
  Stilton PE7 ....175 F8
  West Walton PE14 ...238 E4
St Mary's St
  1 Cambridge CB1 ....246 A2
  Ely CB7 ....240 C4
  Farcet PE7 ....187 C2
  St Neots PE19 ....74 E4
  Stamford PE9 ......244 C5
  Whittlesey PE7 .....189 D6
St Mary's Wlk
  Everton SG19 ....40 C3
  Fowlmere SG8 ....15 E8
St Marys CE Prim Sch
  IP28 ....239 C5
St Marys Ct Ely CB7 ..240 C4
  Peterborough PE1 ...198 B2
St Marys Pas **3** PE19 ..141 A4
St Marys Pk SG8 ......5 D6
St Marys Sch CB7 ....240 C4
St Marys Sq **7** CB8 ...111 A3
St Marys St **9** PE29 ..141 D4
St Matthew's Ct **5** CB1 .84 A2
St Matthews Gdns CB1 ..84 A2
St Matthew's Prim Sch
  CB1 ....246 C2
St Matthew's St CB1 ...84 A2

St Michael's Ave PE13 .245 C7
St Michael's Gate PE1 ..198 F7
St Michael's Rd **12** PE8 .230 B1
St Michaels CB4 .....103 A8
St Michaels La
  Longstanton CB4 ....124 A1
  Oakington/Longstanton
  CB4 ....103 A8
St Neots Com Coll
  PE19 ....74 E3
St Neots Comm Nature
  Reserve★ PE19 ......74 E7
St Neots Leisure Ctr
  PE19 ....74 E2
St Neots Mus★ PE19 ...74 E5
St Neots Rd
  Abbotsley PE19 ......57 A7
  Comberton PE23 .....81 D3
  Coton CB3 ....82 B3
  Eaton Socon PE19 ...74 C4
  Eltisley PE19 ....77 D4
  Hardwick CB3 ....80 E4
  Knapwell CB3 ....79 D5
  Madingley CB3 ......81 F3
St Neots Sta PE19 ....75 B6
St Olave's Dr **19** PE6 ..232 A1
St Ovins Gn CB6 .....240 B5
St Patrick **4** CB8 ....111 A4
St Paul's CE Prim Sch
  CB2 ....246 B1
St Paul's Cl
  Gorefield PE13 ......237 E2
  5 Wisbech PE13 ....245 C4
St Paul's Rd
  Cambridge CB1 .....246 C1
  Peterborough PE1 ...197 F7
St Paul's St **5** PE9 ...244 C5
St Pauls Dr PE16 ....241 D6
St Pauls Wlk CB1 ....246 C1
St Pega's Rd PE6 ....204 A8
St Peter's CE Jun Sch
  PE13 ....245 E6
St Peter's Dr **10** PE15 ..223 B7
St Peter's Hill **8** PE9 ..244 B5
St Peter's Rd Coton CB3 .82 B2
  Huntingdon PE29 ....141 D7
  March PE15 ....243 D3
  4 Wisbech PE13 ....245 C4
St Peter's Sch PE29 ..141 D6
St Peter's St
  Cambridge CB3 ......83 C3
  Caxton CB3 ....59 E8
  Duxford CB2 ....17 D8
  Stamford PE9 ......244 B4
St Peter's Vale PE9 ..244 B4
St Peter's Way
  Ellington PE28 ......139 A4
  Thorney PE6 ....233 A2
St Peters Ave CB8 ...112 F4
St Peters Cl PE28 ...112 F5
St Peters Ct **9** PE9 ..244 B5
St Peters Dr PE16 ...241 D5
St Peters Pl CB7 ....212 F1
St Peters Rd
  Outwell PE14 ....236 E1
  Peterborough PE1 ...198 A2
St Peters Terr CB1 ..246 B1
St Philip's CE Prim Sch
  CB1 ....84 C1
St Philip's Rd CB1 ....65 B8
St Philips Rd
  Cambridge CB1 ......65 C8
  Newmarket CB8 .....110 E4
St Regis CB4 ....83 F4
St Stephen's Dr PE16 .241 C6
St Stephen's Pl **1** CB4 .83 C4
St Thomas PE19 ......77 E4
St Thomas Cl CB3 .....62 D6
St Thomas Dr PE15 ..243 C3
St Thomas Moore RC Prim
  Sch PE1 ....198 D4
St Thomas' Pl CB1 ...240 C2
St Thomas's Sq CB1 ...65 D6
St Tibb's Row CB2 ...246 B2
St Vigor's Rd CB1 .....66 F4
St Vincent's Cl CB3 ...82 E3
St Wendreda's Dr
  PE15 ....243 C1
St Wendred's Way
  CB8 ....110 B7
Salcott Dr PE13 .....245 E6
Salem Ct PE16 ......241 C4
Salisbury Ct PE7 ....143 F8
Salisbury Ct **1** CB9 ...23 F7
Salisbury Rd PE4 ....204 B3
Salisbury Villas CB1 ...64 F7
Sallowbush Rd PE29 ..141 D6
Sallows PE28 ....121 C6
Sallows Rd PE1 .....198 B6
Salmon La CB1 .....246 C3
Salon Way PE29 .....141 B7
Saltergate PE1 ......198 E7
Salters Way
  Sawtry PE28 ....168 B5
  Wisbech PE13 ......245 B5
Saltersgate PE1 .....198 F7
Saltmarsh PE2 ......186 C4
Salts Rd PE14 ......238 F4
Sambar Ct **3** PE19 ...74 B5
Sames Ct CB4 ......125 E5
Samian Cl CB2 ....80 C2
Samuel Pepys Sch
  PE19 ....75 A4
Samuel Ward Upper Sch
  CB9 ....39 B1
Samuels Way CB6 ...240 C4
Samworths Cl PE5 ...195 F2

Sancton Wood Sch
  CB1 ....246 C1
Sand Acre Cl IP28 ...239 D5
Sand Bank PE13 .....235 A7
Sand Dro CB5 ....127 C8
Sand La CB6 ....209 E4
Sand Rd SG19 ....58 F5
Sand St CB7 ....212 B3
Sandall Rd PE13 ....245 C3
Sanderling Cl IP28 ..239 D4
Sanderlings The PE6 ..206 B1
Sanders Cl PE28 ....151 D3
Sandfields Rd PE19 ...74 F4
Sandford PE3 ....197 B5
Sandhill CB6 ....242 F3
Sandhurst Rd PE7 ...186 C1
Sandown Rd PE13 ...245 A2
Sandpiper Cl
  Haverhill CB9 ....24 B7
  Whittlesey PE7 .....190 A8
Sandpiper Dr PE2 ...187 E6
Sandpit Rd PE6 .....233 A3
Sandringham Ave
  PE13 ....245 D6
Sandringham Cl PE9 ..244 B7
Sandringham Dr PE26 .221 C2
Sandringham Rd PE4 ..197 C8
Sandwich Cl
  Huntingdon PE29 ....141 E7
  St Ives PE27 ....143 F8
Sandwich Rd
  Brampton PE28 .....140 D1
  St Neots PE19 ....75 A5
Sandwick Cl **2** CB4 ...83 E8
Sandy Dro IP28 ......214 D3
Sandy Gate PE12 ....237 A7
Sandy La Cambridge CB4 .83 F4
  Kimbolton PE28 .....113 C6
  Tydd St Giles PE13 ..238 B7
  Wisbech PE13 ......245 F4
Sandy Rd Everton SG19 ..40 B2
  Lode CB5 ....107 C6
Sandyland PE13 .....245 B5
Sandys Cres CB6 ....242 E3
Sanfoin Cl **5** IP28 ..214 A1
Sapcote Way PE28 ..168 B3
Sapley Pk PE29 .....141 F8
Sapley Rd PE29 .....152 F1
Sapley Spinneys Nature
  Reserve★ PE28 ....152 E1
Sapley Sq PE29 .....141 E7
Sapperton PE4 ......204 B6
Sargent's Ct PE9 ....244 A6
Sascombe Vineyard★
  CB8 ....72 F3
Saunders Cl
  Huntingdon PE29 ....141 D6
  Peterborough PE2 ...186 E8
Saunders Ct CB3 .....79 B3
Savile Way SG8 ......15 E8
Savile's Cl PE19 .....74 D7
Saville Rd PE3 ......197 D5
Saville Rd Ind Est PE3 .197 D5
Savory Rd PE13 .....245 B6
Sawpit La PE28 .....159 A4
Sawston Rd CB2 ......33 D8
Sawston Village Coll
  CB2 ....32 E8
Sawtry Com Coll PE28 .168 C4
Sawtry Jun & Inf Sch
  PE28 ....168 B3
Sawtry Leisure Ctr
  PE28 ....168 B3
Sawtry Rd
  Conington PE28 .....167 F8
  Sawtry PE28 ....168 A4
Sawtry Roughs PE28 ..168 F2
Sawtry Way PE28 ....153 E2
Sawtry Way Cotts
  PE28 ....143 C6
Saxby Gdns PE1 ....198 C8
Saxham Ct CB9 ......38 B1
Saxon Cl Ely CB6 ....240 C5
  Exning CB8 ....110 D8
  Godmanchester PE29 .141 F1
  Sawtry PE28 ....168 C3
Saxon Dr CB5 ....130 B1
Saxon Pl PE19 ....74 F4
Saxon Rd
  5 Barnack PE9 ....230 D3
  Cambridge CB5 ......84 A3
  Peterborough PE1 ...198 C4
  Whittlesey PE7 .....189 C7
Saxon St CB2 ....246 B1
Saxon St Rd CB8 .....91 D4
Saxon Way Bar Hill CB3 .102 B2
  Melbourn SG8 ....14 C4
  3 Waterbeach CB5 ..106 A7
Sayer Ct PE2 ....185 F2
Sayer St PE29 ......141 C5
Sayers Ct PE28 .....208 C5
Scaldgate PE7 ......189 E6
Scalesgate Rd PE12 ..237 A8
Scalford Dr PE2 .....198 C8
Scaltback Cl CB8 ....110 E6
Scaltback Mid Sch
  CB8 ....110 E5
Scarfield La PE14 ...236 C6
Scargell's La PE15 ..243 D3
Scarlett's La CB1 .....53 D4
Scarsdale Cl CB4 .....84 B6
Sch of Clinical Medicine
  CB2 ....65 B3
Schlumberger Laboratories
  CB3 ....82 E3

Scholars Ave PE29 141 C4
Schole Rd CB4 209 A1
School Cl Cheveley CB8 91 C6
Gamlingay SG19 41 D5
5 Maxey PE6 231 C7
Peterborough PE3 197 A5
2 Wisbech St Mary PE13 235 B7
School Dro PE26 171 A7
School Farm Dro
PE26 171 E8
School Hill CB4 104 B4
School La
Alconbury PE28 150 F5
Barley SG8 7 A1
Barton CB3 63 B4
Bourn CB3 79 B3
Boxworth CB3 101 B5
Buckden PE19 117 B4
Burwell CB5 130 B1
Bythorn & Keyston PE28 146 D4
Conington CB3 121 C1
Coveney CB6 217 D5
Downham CB6 218 A7
Pymore CB6 224 D1
Eaton Socon PE19 74 C2
Elton PE8 178 D8
Fenstanton PE28 121 B6
Fulbourn CB1 66 F4
Glinton PE6 203 E8
Haslingfield CB3 47 B5
Haverhill CB9 23 D8
Histon CB4 104 C3
Kings Ripton PE28 153 C6
Little Paxton PE19 96 A2
Longstanton CB4 123 F1
Longstowe CB3 60 A3
Manea PE15 224 B4
4 Maxey PE6 231 C7
Mepal CB6 216 E3
Ramsey PE26 172 B7
St Neots PE19 74 E4
Swavesey CB4 122 E6
Thriplow SG8 31 B2
Toft CB3 61 D4
3 Uffington PE9 230 C6
Warmington PE8 178 B3
Waterbeach CB5 127 B8
Wilburton CB6 210 C5
1 Wisbech PE13 245 C5
School Rd
5 Barnack PE9 230 D4
Broughton PE28 153 F8
Earith PE28 208 E6
Great Wratting CB9 39 E5
Moulton CB8 112 F6
Newborough PE6 205 D8
Outwell PE14 229 D8
Warboys PE28 164 F5
West Walton PE14 238 E4
Woodditton CB8 91 A3
School St CB10 18 D2
School Wlk CB3 99 A2
Scolding Dro PE6 233 E5
Scorney PE28 121 C6
Scotendon PE2 185 E3
Scotenoon PE2 185 E3
Scotgate PE9 244 A5
Scotland Cl CB4 84 B5
Scotland End CB7 213 C1
Scotland Rd
Cambridge CB4 84 A5
Dry Drayton CB3 81 A6
Scotney St PE1 197 E7
Scotney Way PE28 168 C3
Scotred Cl CB5 109 B8
Scotsdowne Rd CB2 64 D3
Scott Ave IP28 239 C5
Scott Cl
Peterborough PE2 187 E6
Royston SG8 13 D1
Scott Polar Research Institite
CB2 246 B1
Scott's Rd PE14 229 C2
Scotts Cl PE28 120 B1
Scotts Cres PE28 120 B1
Scotts Gdns CB2 32 C5
Scotts Rd PE6 203 F8
Scotts Yd CB3 47 B5
Scrolans PE27 143 E6
Seabank Rd PE13 245 F6
Seadyke Bank PE13 235 A7
Seadyke Rd PE13 234 F6
Seafield Rd 7 PE13 238 B2
Sealey's La PE13 234 D8
Sealodes Rd CB7 211 E5
Seargeants Cl PE6 207 C1
Searjeant St PE1 197 E5
Searle St CB4 83 D4
Searles Ct PE7 189 D8
Searles Mdw CB3 102 B1
Sears Cl PE29 118 F8
Searson Cl PE9 230 F7
Seathwaite PE29 141 B6
Seaton Cl PE7 181 D6
Sebrights Way PE3 196 F3
Second Ave
Warboys PE28 164 E6
Wisbech PE13 245 D4
Second Broadpool Dro
PE28 165 F8
Second Drift PE9 244 B2
Second Dro
Downham CB6 218 A8
Littleport CB6 225 B1
Ely CB7 218 F5
Second Dro *continued*
Peterborough PE1 198 D1
St Ives PE27 144 C2
Second Dro Ind Est
PE1 198 D1
Second Marsh Rd
PE14 238 C3
Sedge Fen Rd PE38 226 E7
Sedge Way CB6 217 D2
Sedgwick Mus of Earth
Sciences★ CB2 246 B2
Sedgwick St CB1 65 B8
Sedley Inf Sch CB1 65 C7
Sedley Taylor Rd CB2 64 F4
Sefton Ave PE13 245 E6
Sefton Cl CB2 64 D3
Sefton Way CB8 110 D5
Selby Ct 2 PE29 141 F7
Sellers Grange PE2 186 B4
Selsingen Way CB2 32 F7
Selwyn Cl
Great Shelford CB2 49 A5
Mildenhall IP28 239 D6
Newmarket CB8 111 A1
Selwyn Coll CB3 64 B8
Selwyn Gdns CB3 64 B8
Selwyn Rd
Cambridge CB3 64 B7
Stamford PE9 244 A7
Senate House Pas
CB2 246 A2
Senes Calls 9 PE27 208 A3
Seppings Cl 2 CB6 210 C6
Serby Ave SG8 5 C8
Serjeants Cl PE26 172 A6
Serlby Gdns PE3 197 B3
Serpentine Gn Sh Ctr
PE7 186 D3
Setchel 11 PE19 74 C6
Setchel Dro CB4 125 F7
Setchell Cl PE19 97 F5
Setchfield Pl PE2 186 F7
Seven Rides SG8 5 D3
Sevenacres PE2 185 E5
Seventh Ave PE13 245 E4
Seventh Dro CB6 225 A3
Severn Cl PE4 204 E1
Severn Pl CB1 84 A2
Seymore Dr CB9 23 D7
Seymour Cl CB8 111 C3
Seymour Cl CB1 65 C8
Seymour Pl PE4 205 B2
Seymour St CB1 65 C8
Seynory Dro PE7 177 F7
Shade The CB7 212 A5
Shadowbush Cl 2 CB9 38 F1
Shady Wlk 2 PE19 74 F5
Shaftenhoe End Rd SG8 7 A1
Shaftesbury Ave
March PE15 243 E5
St Neots PE19 74 F5
Shaftesbury Ct 17 CB1 23 E7
Shaftesbury Rd CB2 64 F6
Shaftesbury Way SG8 5 E5
Shaftsbury Ct PE15 243 E3
Shakespeare SG8 5 D8
Shakespeare Ave PE1 197 F7
Shakespeare Rd
Eaton Socon PE19 74 C3
St Ives PE27 143 F6
Shamrock Cl PE2 187 C7
Shannon Cl CB9 24 D7
Shardlow Cl 1 CB9 38 C1
Sharma Leas PE4 204 A3
Sharman's Rd CB7 212 E1
Sharnbrook Ave PE7 186 C1
Sharps La PE28 150 F3
Shaw Dr PE15 243 C3
Shawley Rd PE28 168 A4
Shearling Dr CB3 79 A4
Shearwater PE2 185 D6
Sheep Mkt
St Ives PE27 144 B3
6 Stamford PE9 244 B5
Sheep St PE28 148 D3
Sheepfold PE27 144 C5
Sheepfold La CB3 79 B5
Sheepwalk PE4 205 A1
Sheldrick's Rd CB7 213 B5
Shelford Mill CB2 48 F4
Shelford Pk Ave CB2 49 A5
Shelford Rd
Cambridge CB2 48 E8
Fulbourn CB1 66 C3
Harston CB2 48 C3
Whittlesford CB2 32 A6
Shelford Sta CB2 49 B5
Shelford's Rd CB4 209 A4
Shelley Cl
Huntingdon PE29 141 F6
Peterborough PE1 197 E8
Royston SG8 13 D1
Shelley Pl 5 PE19 74 D6
Shelly Gdn CB3 83 C3
Shelly Row 4 CB3 83 C3
Shelton Rd PE2 187 D6
Shepherd Cl SG8 5 E5
Shepherd Dr PE19 74 E2
Shepherd's Cl
Cambridge CB1 66 A6
Fen Ditton CB5 84 F5
Shepherd's Dro CB7 226 B2
Shepherds Cl PE4 204 C4
Shepherds Ct 9 CB9 23 E7
Sheppard Way CB1 85 B1
Sheppard's Dro PE6 232 D8
Sheppersons Gr 2
PE15 243 E4
Shepreth L-Moor Nature
Reserve★ SG8 29 D3
Shepreth Rd
Barrington CB2 29 D7
Foxton CB2 30 A4
Shepreth SG8 30 B3
Shepreth Sta SG8 29 E5
Shepreth Wildlife Pk★
SG8 29 E5
Sheralds Croft La SG8 31 A2
Sherborne Rd PE1 198 D6
Sherbourne Cl CB4 84 B6
Sherbrooke Cl PE15 243 D1
Sheridan Rd PE1 197 F8
Sheriffs Ct CB8 70 F3
Sheringham Way PE2 186 C6
Sherlock Cl CB3 83 B4
Sherlock Ct CB3 83 B4
Sherlock Rd CB3 83 B5
Sherwood Ave
Peterborough PE2 186 F7
Wisbech PE13 245 D7
Shetland Rd CB9 24 D8
Shillow Hill PE26 172 B1
Shingay La CB2 32 F7
Ship Gdns IP28 239 B3
Ship La CB7 240 D3
Shippea Hill Rd IP28 213 E8
Shirdley Rd PE19 74 F4
Shire Ct 7 CB9 23 E7
Shire Gr PE1 198 C5
Shires The
Bluntisham/Colne PE28 208 C5
March PE15 243 E2
Royston SG8 5 E6
Shirley Cl CB4 105 E2
Shirley Gr CB4 84 B5
Shirley Inf Sch CB4 84 B5
Shirley Rd CB4 104 B3
Shooter's Hollow
PE19 116 D3
Shores Cl IP28 213 C3
Short Cl PE8 178 B3
Short Cswy CB6 217 C4
Short Dr PE15 224 B5
Short Dro
Cottenham CB4 125 F2
Little Downham CB6 217 F5
Pymore CB6 217 C8
Downham CB6 224 F3
Earith PE28 208 F6
Holme PE7 177 A4
Ramsey PE26 221 A2
Somersham PE28 215 D3
Short La
Bluntisham/Colne PE28 208 C5
Coveney CB6 217 C4
Willingham CB4 209 A1
Wisbech PE13 238 A1
Short Nightlayer's Dro
PE16 241 C6
Short Rd Exning CB8 131 F2
Snailwell CB8 132 A3
Stretham CB6 210 E5
Short St Bourn CB3 60 C5
Cambridge CB1 246 B3
Shortacres Rd PE2 186 F7
Shortfen PE2 186 C4
Shortland 6 PE28 215 C1
Shortsands Yd 3 PE19 75 A5
Shrewsbury Ave PE2 186 D5
Shropshire Pl PE1 198 B2
Shrub House Cl IP28 213 F8
Shrub Rd PE7 186 C1
Shrubberies The CB8 111 D1
Shrubbery Gr SG8 5 D4
Shrubbery The PE16 241 D4
Shrublands IP28 239 C4
Shudy Camps Pk CB1 22 C6
Sibson Aerodrome
PE8 183 E6
Sidgwick Ave CB3 64 C8
Siding Dro PE28 215 C5
Sidney Farm Rd CB1 65 E6
Sidney Gdns CB3 47 B6
Sidney St CB2 246 A3
Sidney Sussex Coll
CB1 246 B3
Siggin's La CB1 20 D6
Silhalls Cl CB8 91 F7
Silt Rd Littleport CB6 242 D5
March PE15 243 F4
Upwell PE14 229 F5
Silver Birch Ave PE27 143 F6
Silver Birch Cl PE29 141 E7
Silver Hill PE7 186 D3
Silver La PE27 208 A3
Silver Lodge IP28 239 F3
Silver St Ashwell SG7 2 D4
Buckden PE19 117 B4
Burwell CB5 130 B4
Cambridge CB3 246 A1
Ely CB7 240 C4
Godmanchester PE29 118 E8
Guilden Morden SG8 10 F4
Litlington SG8 12 A2
March PE15 243 C7
Peterborough PE2 186 F7
Ramsey PE26 172 B7
St Neots PE19 74 E4
Willingham CB4 209 A1
Wisbech PE13 245 C6
Witcham CB6 217 A2
Withersfield CB9 38 A4
Silverdale Ave CB3 82 B2
Silverdale Cl CB3 82 A2
Silverley Way CB8 91 F7
Silver's La PE13 234 E7
Silverweed PE19 74 C5
Silverwood Cl CB1 84 B2
Silverwood Rd PE1 197 F5
Silvester Rd PE5 195 E2
Simeon Cl CB6 240 F7
Simmer Piece PE28 121 C5
Simpkin Cl PE19 74 B2
Singerfire Rd PE5 195 D2
Sir Harry Smith Com Coll
PE7 189 F7
Sir James Black Rd
CB7 240 C2
Siskin Cl SG8 5 E8
Sissley PE2 185 E2
Six Bells 14 PE28 215 C1
Six Mile Bottom Rd
CB1 69 A1
Sixteen Foot Bank
Christchurch PE14 229 C4
Wimblington PE15 223 E5
Sixth Ave PE13 245 E4
Skaters Way PE4 204 C4
Skeets Ct PE29 141 F7
Skeggles Cl PE29 141 B5
Skeifs Row 4 PE15 222 A5
Skelton Pl PE27 144 B5
Skelton's Dro IP28 213 F8
Skipper's La
West Wickham CB1 37 F8
West Wratting CB1 54 E1
Withersfield CB9 38 A5
Skiver Cl CB2 32 F6
Skylark Pl 9 SG8 5 E8
Skylarks Cl PE7 186 D3
Slade Cl PE26 172 A7
Slade The
Witcham CB6 217 A2
Wrestlingworth &
Cockayne Hatley SG19 25 B3
Slade Way PE16 241 C5
Slatebarn Dro PE7 221 C8
Sleaford St CB1 84 A1
Sleford Cl CB1 53 B2
Sleights Dr 4 PE14 238 F1
Slid La CB2 29 F8
Slipe Cotts PE28 146 A6
Small Lode PE14 236 F1
Smallwood PE3 197 B5
Smeefield PE28 99 B8
Smeeth Rd
Emneth PE14 236 E6
Marshland St James
PE14 236 F7
Smith Dr PE19 117 B3
Smith St CB3 100 A4
Smith's Dr PE15 243 F3
Smith's Dro PE38 226 F4
Smith's End La SG8 6 F1
Smithey Fen Engine Dro
CB4 209 E2
Smithfield PE6 233 B3
Smiths Chase PE15 243 B5
Smiths Yd PE19 94 A6
Snail Croft PE13 238 A2
Snailwell Rd
Fordham CB8 131 F5
Newmarket CB8 111 B6
Snailwell Short Rd
CB8 131 E1
Snoots Rd PE7 189 B7
Snowberry Way 3 CB7 212 B5
Snowden Cl 1 PE6 232 C8
Snowdon Ct 9 CB9 23 E6
Snowdonia Way PE29 141 A4
Snowley Pk PE7 189 B8
Snowy Way PE29 142 B6
Soham Mere CB7 211 F4
Soham Rd Ely CB7 211 D8
Fordham CB7 212 D2
Soham Village Coll
CB7 212 B3
Soke Parkway PE3 197 A3
Soke Rd PE6 207 B1
Sokemans Way PE28 117 D8
Somerby Cl PE9 244 B7
Somerby Garth 1 PE1 198 D7
Somers Rd PE13 245 B4
Somerset Cl CB4 83 D7
Somerset Ct 16 CB9 23 E7
Somerset Rd
Histon CB4 104 A3
Wyton Airfield PE28 143 B8
Somersham Prim Sch
PE28 215 C1
Somersham Rd
Bluntisham PE28 155 E2
Colne PE28 208 C8
Holywell-cum-Needingworth
PE27 144 C7
Somervell Ct 5 CB4 83 E7
Somerville PE4 204 A5
Somerville Rd 1 PE9 244 A6
Somes Cl 1 PE9 230 C6
Sorbus Cl PE7 186 D3
Sorrel Cl SG8 5 F5
Sorrel Wlk CB9 38 D1
Sorrell Cl SG8 5 F5
South Brink Elm PE14 235 B4
Wisbech PE13 245 A3
South Cl SG8 5 B7
South Dr March PE15 243 E4
Newmarket CB8 110 F4
South End SG8 12 E3
South Gn Rd CB3 64 C7
South La 3 CB3 62 C5
South Par PE3 197 E3
South Pk Dr CB3 99 B1
South Pk St PE16 241 C4
South Rd
Brampton PE28 117 D8
Great Abington CB1 33 F4
Histon CB4 104 B1
South St Comberton CB3 62 C4
Great Chesterford CB10 18 D2
Huntingdon PE29 141 F5
Litlington SG8 12 A2
Peterborough PE1 198 B2
5 St Neots PE19 74 E5
Woodhurst PE28 155 A4
South Terr CB2 32 F5
South View PE2 186 F7
South View Rd PE4 197 D8
Southacre Cl CB2 64 E6
Southacre Dr CB2 64 E6
Southampton Pl PE16 241 C3
Southbrook Field CB3 99 A2
Southbrooke Cl 2 CB2 64 D3
Southcourts CB2 48 F3
Southdown Rd PE7 181 F5
Southerns The 7 CB6 216 E1
Southey Wood★ PE9 231 A1
Southfield CB10 18 A3
Southfields Ave PE2 187 D5
Southfields Cl
Newmarket CB8 110 E4
Wisbech PE13 245 E7
Southfields Dr PE2 187 D6
Southfields Jun & Inf school
PE2 187 D5
Southgate Ave IP28 239 B7
Southgate Way PE2 185 C2
Southlands Ave PE1 198 A6
Southoe Rd PE7 187 D2
Southorpe Mdw Nature
Reserve★ PE9 230 E2
Southorpe Paddock Nature
Reserve★ PE9 230 E1
Southside Ct CB4 84 A5
Southwell Ave PE4 204 A4
Southwell Rd PE13 245 C8
Southwick Cl PE4 204 E1
Sovereign Cl PE13 245 A6
Sovereign Pl PE3 197 E2
Sovereign Way CB4 125 E3
Spalding Way CB1 65 D4
Spaldings La CB4 105 D7
Spaldwick Prim Sch
PE28 137 F5
Spaldwick Rd PE28 137 C3
Sparkes Cl 2 CB7 213 A5
Sparrow Cl PE29 141 E5
Sparrow Dr PE28 150 E4
Sparrow Rd PE7 186 D1
Sparrow Way PE28 120 B1
Sparrowgate Rd PE14 238 F1
Sparrowhawk Way
PE29 142 B7
Sparrows Cl PE28 117 D8
Speechley Rd PE7 181 F6
Speechley's Dro PE6 207 F2
Speed La CB7 212 B4
Speedwell Cl CB1 66 A6
Spencer Ave PE2 187 D5
Spencer Cl
3 Eaton Socon PE19 74 D6
West Walton PE14 238 E4
Spencer Croft CB7 240 E6
Spencer Dr
Melbourn SG8 14 D6
St Ives PE27 144 A7
Spencer Dro
Guyhirn PE13 235 A2
Soham CB7 212 A4
Spencer Rd CB10 18 D3
Spens Ave CB3 64 B8
Spenser Cl SG8 13 D1
Speyside Ct 1 PE2 185 D4
Spiggots Cl CB4 123 E2
Spindle Rd CB9 38 D1
Spinney Abbey CB7 211 D2
Spinney Cl
Brampton PE28 140 D3
Warboys PE28 164 F5
Warmington PE8 178 B2
Spinney Dr CB2 49 A4
Spinney Field PE28 138 F3
Spinney Fields PE7 176 F4
Spinney La PE28 150 F5
Spinney Prim Sch The
CB1 65 E6
Spinney The
Bar Hill CB3 102 B3
Cottenham CB4 125 E5
Huntingdon PE29 142 B6
Spinney Way
5 Needingworth PE27 208 A3
St Ives PE27 144 A6
Spinning Inf Sch PE26 172 B6
Spires End PE28 150 D6
Spitfire Cl PE29 141 B8
Spittals Way
Huntingdon PE29 141 C7
The Stukeleys PE29 152 C1
Splash La Castor PE5 184 E8
St Ives PE28 142 F6
Split Dro CB5 129 A4
Spong Dro CB4 209 B1
Spooners Cl CB8 70 F8
Sprignall PE3 196 F4
Spring Cl Burwell CB5 130 B1
Histon CB4 104 C4
Huntingdon PE29 141 E6
Spring Comm Sch
PE29 141 F6
Spring Dr PE7 187 B2
Spring Hill MK44 93 A3

Spring La
Bassingbourn SG8 ..12 F3
Bottisham CB5 ..86 F6
Spring Mdw Inf Sch
CB7 ..240 E6
Spring Pl PE19 ..95 A1
Springbrook PE19 ..74 F4
Springfield
Huntingdon PE29 ..141 E5
Peterborough PE2 ..187 A7
Somersham PE28 ..215 C1
Springfield Ave PE15 ..243 C2
Springfield Cl
Buckden PE19 ..117 A3
2 St Neots PE19 ..75 A5
Springfield Rd
Alconbury Weston PE28 ..150 D5
Cambridge CB4 ..83 E4
1 Parson Drove PE13 ..234 D7
Peterborough PE1 ..197 F5
Sawston CB2 ..32 F5
Yaxley PE7 ..181 F5
Springfield Terr 1 CB4 ..83 E4
Springfields PE7 ..190 C7
Springhead SG7 ..2 D4
Springhead La CB7 ..240 E5
Springhill Rd CB4 ..121 E6
Spruce Dr PE28 ..151 F2
Spurgeons Ave CB5 ..106 B8
Spurgeon's Cl CB1 ..85 B1
Spurling Cl CB8 ..91 C5
Square The
6 Barnack PE9 ..230 D4
Stow cum Quy CB5 ..86 A6
Squire's Dr PE14 ..229 F7
Squire's Field The CB1 ..67 F7
Squires Cl 17 PE28 ..215 C1
Squires Ct
5 Eaton Socon PE19 ..74 B4
Haverhill CB9 ..23 E7
Squires Gate PE4 ..204 F3
Squires The PE2 ..186 F8
St Johns Bsns Pk
PE29 ..141 C8
Stable Yd CB3 ..79 B3
Stables Ct PE13 ..238 B2
Stackyard The
Ickleton CB10 ..18 A3
Peterborough PE2 ..185 E5
Stafford Rd PE7 ..189 F6
Staffordshire Gdns 8
CB1 ..84 A1
Staffordshire St CB1 ..84 A2
Stagsden PE2 ..185 F4
Stagshaw Dr PE2 ..187 B8
Stained Glass Mus★
CB7 ..240 D4
Staithe Rd PE13 ..245 E5
Stake Piece Rd SG8 ..5 C5
Stakings The CB2 ..32 D7
Stallebrass Cl PE2 ..187 E5
Stamford & Rutland Hospl
PE9 ..244 D6
Stamford Arts Ctr
PE9 ..244 C5
Stamford Ave SG8 ..5 D7
Stamford Cl SG8 ..5 D7
Stamford Coll PE9 ..244 D6
Stamford Endowed Sch
PE9 ..244 C5
Stamford High Sch
PE9 ..244 C4
Stamford High Sch Juns
PE9 ..244 B4
Stamford Jun Sch
PE9 ..244 B3
Stamford La PE8 ..178 B3
Stamford Leisure Ctr
PE9 ..244 D6
Stamford Lodge Rd
PE6 ..196 D4
Stamford Mus★ PE9 ..244 C5
Stamford Rd
Barnack PE9 ..230 C4
Easton on the Hill PE9 ..244 A1
Helpston PE6 ..231 C1
Marholm PE6 ..203 B2
Market Deeping PE6 ..231 D8
Tallington PE9 ..231 A8
Stamford Ret Pk PE9 ..244 D6
Stamford Sch PE9 ..244 C5
Stamford St 3 CB8 ..111 B2
Stamford Sta PE9 ..244 B4
Stamford Theatre★
PE9 ..244 C5
Stamford Wlk 13 PE9 ..244 C5
Stamford Yd SG8 ..5 C6
Stamfords Artists Gall
PE9 ..244 C5
Stamper St PE3 ..196 F3
Stan Rowing Ct PE2 ..187 C7
Stanbury Cl CB5 ..84 E6
Stanch Hill Rd PE28 ..168 C3
Standish Ct PE2 ..186 D8
Stanegate 3 PE28 ..168 C2
Stanesfield Rd CB5 ..84 D3
Stanford Bus Pk PE9 ..244 D7
Stanford Wlk PE3 ..197 C7
Stanground Coll PE7 ..187 C5
Stanground Newt Ponds
Nature Reserve★
PE7 ..187 C4
Stanground St John's Prim
Sch PE1 ..187 C7
Stanground Wash Nature
Reserve★ PE2 ..187 D7
Staniland Way PE4 ..204 B5
Stanley Ct CB5 ..84 B3
Stanley Rd
Cambridge CB5 ..84 B3
Great Chesterford CB10 ..18 E3
Newmarket CB8 ..111 C3
Peterborough PE1 ..198 A3
Stanley St PE9 ..244 C5
Stanpoint Way PE27 ..144 A5
Stansfield Gdns CB1 ..66 F5
Stansgate Ave CB2 ..65 B3
Stanton Mere Way
CB4 ..124 A6
Stanton Sq PE7 ..186 D2
Stanwick Ct PE3 ..197 F2
Stapledon Rd PE2 ..185 D2
Stapleford Com Prim Sch
CB2 ..49 C4
Staples La CB7 ..212 B3
Star And Garter La CB8 .91 C7
Star Cl PE1 ..198 C3
Star La Ramsey PE26 ..172 A8
Stamford PE9 ..244 C5
Star Mews PE1 ..198 C2
Star Rd PE1 ..198 C2
Stargoose Cl CB3 ..80 B1
Starling Cl
Alconbury PE28 ..150 E4
Milton CB4 ..105 D3
Starlock Cl CB6 ..210 E4
Stathern Rd PE1 ..198 D7
Station App
March PE15 ..243 D6
Newmarket CB8 ..111 A2
Somersham PE28 ..208 C8
Station Ave PE13 ..234 D5
Station Dr
Wisbech PE13 ..245 C4
Wisbech St Mary PE13 ..235 C7
Station Gate CB5 ..109 B8
Station Gdns PE26 ..172 A8
Station La PE19 ..117 F3
Station Rd
Abbots Ripton PE28 ..162 B1
Ailsworth PE5 ..184 C8
Ashwell SG7 ..2 E4
Barnack PE9 ..230 E4
Bluntisham PE28 ..208 C4
Cambridge CB1 ..64 F7
Catworth PE28 ..136 D5
Chatteris PE16 ..241 C4
Deeping St James PE6 ..206 E6
Dullingham CB8 ..89 C2
Elm PE14 ..235 C2
Ely CB7 ..240 D3
Fordham CB7 ..131 A8
Foxton CB2 ..30 B6
Fulbourn CB1 ..67 A5
Gamlingay SG19 ..41 E5
Gedney Hill PE12 ..233 F8
Great Shelford CB2 ..49 A5
Haddenham CB6 ..210 A6
Harston CB2 ..47 F2
Haverhill CB9 ..24 A8
Histon CB4 ..104 C3
Holme PE7 ..177 A4
Isleham CB7 ..213 A4
Kennett CB8 ..133 F5
Linton CB1 ..35 B2
Littleport CB6 ..242 E4
Lode CB5 ..107 C2
Longstanton CB4 ..123 F4
Manea PE15 ..224 B5
March PE15 ..243 D5
Meldreth SG8 ..14 B6
Mildenhall IP28 ..239 B3
Oakington & Westwick
CB4 ..103 D7
Over CB4 ..122 F8
Pampisford CB2 ..33 F6
Peterborough PE3 ..197 F2
Ramsey PE26 ..172 A7
St Ives PE27 ..144 B3
St Neots PE19 ..75 B5
Shepreth SG8 ..29 E5
Soham CB7 ..212 B4
Stamford PE9 ..244 B4
Steeple Morden SG8 ..3 B7
Stow cum Quy CB5 ..106 E1
Sutton CB6 ..216 F1
Swaffham Bulbeck CB5 ..108 A2
Swaffham Prior CB5 ..108 C5
Swavesey CB4 ..122 E7
Thorney PE6 ..233 A4
Tilbrook PE28 ..113 B7
Walsoken PE14 ..236 E8
Warboys PE28 ..164 F7
Waterbeach CB5 ..106 B7
Whittlesey PE7 ..189 E5
Wilburton CB6 ..210 C7
Willingham CB4 ..124 A7
Wisbech St Mary PE13 ..235 C7
Yaxley PE7 ..182 A7
Station Rd E CB2 ..32 E3
Station Rd W CB2 ..32 E3
Station St PE16 ..241 B4
Station Yd IP28 ..239 B3
Staughton Pl 2 PE19 ..74 C4
Staunch Hill PE28 ..148 C3
Staverton Rd PE4 ..204 A3
Staxton Cl PE6 ..203 C1
Steam Brewery Mus★
PE9 ..244 B5
Stearne's Yd CB3 ..47 B5
Steeple Morden CE Prim Sch
SG8 ..11 B2
Steeple View PE15 ..243 C1
Stephen Cl CB9 ..23 F8
Stephens Way 15 PE6 ..231 F8
Stephenson Cl
1 March PE15 ..243 D7
Royston SG8 ..5 B7
Yaxley PE7 ..181 D6
Stephenson Ct PE1 ..198 B2
Stephenson Rd PE27 ..144 B6
Stepping Stones PE28 .143 D1
Stepping Stones Sch
PE4 ..197 D8
Stermyn St 18 PE13 ..245 C5
Sterndale Cl CB3 ..82 E8
Sterne Cl CB1 ..65 B6
Sternes Way CB2 ..49 C4
Stetchworth Rd
Dullingham CB8 ..70 F8
Stetchworth CB8 ..71 C8
Stevens Cl CB4 ..125 D4
Stevens Way PE15 ..243 D6
Stevenson Ct
Cambridge CB5 ..84 A3
Eaton Socon PE19 ..74 D6
Steward Cl CB7 ..211 D8
Steward's La CB6 ..216 E1
Stewart Cl PE28 ..140 C2
Steynings The PE4 ..204 C3
Stickle Cl PE29 ..141 B7
Stile Plantation SG8 ..5 E6
Stiles The PE29 ..141 F1
Still The PE13 ..238 B1
Stilton CE Prim Sch
PE7 ..175 F7
Stirling Cl
Beck Row, Holywell
Row & Kenny Hill IP28 ..213 D6
Cambridge CB4 ..84 A5
Warboys PE28 ..164 F4
Stirling Dr CB9 ..23 E8
Stirling Gdns CB8 ..110 E4
Stirling Rd PE27 ..144 A7
Stirling Way
Papworth Village CB3 ..99 C1
Peterborough PE3 ..204 A1
Witchford CB6 ..217 F1
Stirtloe La PE19 ..117 A2
Stitch The PE14 ..236 B4
Stocker Way 2 PE19 ..74 E2
Stocking Fen Rd PE26 .221 A1
Stocking La
Nuthampstead SG8 ..1 A2
Spaldwick PE28 ..114 E8
Stockley Cl CB9 ..24 C7
Stocks Cl CB5 ..86 E5
Stocks Hill PE5 ..195 F1
Stocks La
Gamlingay SG19 ..41 D4
Orwell SG8 ..45 E1
Stockwell St CB1 ..65 B8
Stokes Cl CB4 ..123 F1
Stokesay Ct PE3 ..197 B1
Stonald Ave PE7 ..189 D8
Stonald Rd PE7 ..189 C8
Stone Field CB3 ..102 A3
Stone La Meldreth SG8 ..29 C3
Peterborough PE1 ..197 F5
Stone St CB1 ..84 B1
Stone Terr CB1 ..84 B1
Stonea Camp★ PE15 ..223 E8
Stonebridge PE2 ..186 C5
Stonebridge La CB1 ..67 A4
Stonebridge Lea PE2 ..186 C5
Stonecross Way PE15 .243 D3
Stonehill PE29 ..141 C7
Stonehill Rd CB2 ..48 E7
Stonehouse Rd
Upwell PE14 ..236 E1
Yaxley PE7 ..181 E5
Stoneleigh Ct PE3 ..197 B2
Stonely Rd PE28 ..138 B3
Stoney Cl PE29 ..141 F8
Storbeck Rd 2 PE13 ..245 D7
Storers Wlk PE7 ..190 C6
Stores Hill CB8 ..92 E8
Storey's Bar Rd PE6 ..199 A3
Storey's Way CB3 ..83 B3
Storrington Way PE4 .204 C3
Stott Gdns CB4 ..84 A6
Stour Cl PE27 ..144 A6
Stour Gn CB6 ..240 D6
Stour Valley Rd CB9 ..24 B7
Stourbridge Gr CB1 ..84 C1
Stow Gdns PE13 ..245 E4
Stow La PE13 ..245 E4
Stow Rd
Kimbolton PE28 ..113 F5
Spaldwick PE28 ..137 F6
Stow cum Quy CB5 ..85 F5
Wisbech PE13 ..245 F5
Stowehill Rd PE4 ..204 F2
Stowgate Rd PE6 ..206 B7
Straight Dro
Bury PE26 ..172 D3
Coveney CB6 ..217 C7
Farcet PE7 ..187 E1
Sawtry PE28 ..168 D3
Wistow PE28 ..172 E2
Straight Furlong CB6 ..224 E2
Straight Rd PE15 ..224 B3
Strangeways Rd CB1 ..65 D4
Strasbourg Sq 6 CB9 ..24 B8
Stratfield Cl CB4 ..83 B5
Stratford Pl PE19 ..74 C3
Strathcarron Ct CB4 ..83 E7
Strawberry Cl PE13 ..245 A6
Strawberry Fields CB9 ..23 D7
Street The
Barton Mills IP28 ..239 E2
Beck Row, Holywell
Row & Kenny Hill IP28 ..214 A8
Street The *continued*
Dalham CB8 ..92 E8
Freckenham IP28 ..213 C3
Great Bradley CB8 ..55 F7
Great Wratting CB9 ..39 E6
Kirtling CB8 ..72 D6
Lidgate CB8 ..73 D8
Mildenhall IP28 ..213 E8
Moulton CB8 ..112 F5
Snailwell CB8 ..132 A4
Westley Waterless CB8 ..70 C5
Woodditton CB8 ..91 B2
Worlington IP28 ..213 F4
Streetly End CB1 ..37 B5
Streetways CB8 ..68 E7
Stretham Com Prim Sch
CB6 ..210 F5
Stretham Old Engine★
CB6 ..210 F4
Stretham Rd
Wicken CB7 ..211 D2
Wilburton CB6 ..210 D5
Stretten Ave CB4 ..83 D4
Stretton Ave CB8 ..111 B2
Stricklands Dr 5 PE6 ..232 B8
Strollers Way CB8 ..90 A2
Stroud Hill PE28 ..165 E2
Strympole Way CB3 ..80 B1
Stuart Cl
Godmanchester PE29 ..142 A1
Peterborough PE2 ..187 C6
Stuart Ct PE1 ..198 B4
Stuart Dr SG8 ..5 D8
Stubbs Cl 3 Haverhill CB9 38 D1
St Ives PE27 ..144 A7
Studlands Pk Ave
CB8 ..110 D6
Studlands Rise SG8 ..5 E6
Studlands Rise Fst Sch
SG8 ..5 E5
Stukeley Cl
Cambridge CB3 ..64 A8
Peterborough PE2 ..187 D5
Stukeley Mdws Ind Es
PE29 ..141 C8
Stukeley Mdws Prim Sch
PE29 ..141 C6
Stukeley Pk PE28 ..152 A2
Stukeley Rd PE29 ..141 C6
Stulp Field Rd CB3 ..64 A4
Stump Cross CB10 ..18 D5
Stumpacre PE3 ..197 A8
Stumpcross 4 PE28 ..168 C2
Stuntney Cswy CB7 ..240 E2
Sturmer Cl 6 CB4 ..83 C7
Sturmer Rd CB9 ..24 B7
Sturmer Road Ind Est
CB9 ..24 C6
Sturrock Way PE3 ..197 C8
Sturton St CB1 ..84 A1
Sudbury Ct
Peterborough PE7 ..187 F5
Whittlesey PE7 ..189 D8
Sudeley Gr CB3 ..81 A3
Suet Hills Dro PE7 ..188 E1
Suez Rd CB1 ..65 C7
Suffolk Cl Ely CB6 ..240 A3
Huntingdon PE29 ..141 F6
Peterborough PE3 ..197 B2
St Ives PE27 ..144 A8
Suffolk Rd 5 SG8 ..5 E6
Suffolk Way
March PE15 ..243 E2
Newmarket CB8 ..110 E5
Sugar Way PE2 ..186 D8
Sulehay Rd PE8 ..193 C1
Sumerling Way PE28 ..208 C6
Summerfield CB3 ..64 C8
Summerfield Cl PE13 ..245 A6
Summerfield Rd PE1 ..197 F4
Summerhayes CB7 ..240 F6
Sun Hill SG8 ..5 C5
Sun La 6 CB8 ..111 A3
Sun St 1 Cambridge CB1 ..84 A2
Isleham CB7 ..213 A5
Sunderland Ave CB2 ..33 A8
Sundew Cl PE19 ..74 B6
Sunfield Rd PE26 ..172 A4
Sunflower St CB4 ..83 D7
Sunmead Wlk CB1 ..66 A6
Sunningdale PE2 ..185 E6
Sunningdale Ave IP28 .239 B4
Sunnybank 1 PE19 ..75 A5
Sunnymead PE4 ..204 A6
Sunnyside CB5 ..84 E2
Sunnyville Rd PE7 ..190 F8
Sunset Gdns PE13 ..245 E2
Sunset Sq 2 CB4 ..83 D7
Surrey Rd PE29 ..141 E8
Sussex Rd
Stamford PE9 ..244 B6
Wyton Airfield PE28 ..143 B8
Sussex St CB2 ..246 B3
Sutcliffe Rd PE8 ..193 D8
Sutton CE Prim Sch
CB6 ..216 E1
Sutton Cl CB4 ..105 D3
Sutton Ct 6 CB6 ..216 E2
Sutton Gate PE12 ..237 D8
Sutton Mdws PE13 ..245 A8
Sutton Pk CB6 ..216 E2
Sutton Rd
Eyeworth SG19 ..10 A8
Haddenham CB6 ..210 A8
Mepal CB6 ..216 E3
Newton PE13 ..238 B6
Wentworth CB6 ..217 C1
Wisbech PE13 ..245 A7
Sutton Rd *continued*
Witchford CB6 ..217 C1
Sutton Way 1 PE15 ..223 A5
Sutton's La PE6 ..231 E8
Suttons Cl PE14 ..236 F2
Svenskaby PE2 ..185 C6
Swaffham Bulbeck CE Prim
Sch CB5 ..108 B1
Swaffham Heath Rd
CB5 ..108 C1
Swaffham Prior CE Com Prim
Sch CB5 ..108 D5
Swaffham Rd
Bottisham CB5 ..107 E1
Burwell CB5 ..109 A7
Reach CB5 ..108 E8
Swain Ct PE2 ..186 F8
Swain's Dro PE13 ..238 C8
Swale Ave PE4 ..204 E1
Swallow Cl PE7 ..201 A1
Swallow Ct 3 PE19 ..75 B6
Swallow La PE13 ..238 B8
Swallow Way PE15 ..243 F5
Swallowfield PE4 ..204 A4
Swan Cl St Ives PE27 ..143 F7
Whittlesey PE7 ..189 F8
Swan Ct PE15 ..243 D6
Swan Dr PE16 ..241 D5
Swan End PE19 ..117 B4
Swan Gdns
Fenstanton PE28 ..121 B5
Parson Drove PE13 ..234 C7
Peterborough PE1 ..198 E6
Swan Gr CB8 ..110 B8
Swan La Exning CB8 ..110 B8
Guilden Morden SG8 ..10 F4
Haverhill CB9 ..24 A8
Swan Rd
Fenstanton PE28 ..121 B5
Whittlesey PE7 ..189 F8
Swan St SG7 ..2 D4
Swanhill PE8 ..194 A4
Swann Rd CB5 ..84 C4
Swann's Cl SG8 ..26 A3
Swann's Rd CB5 ..84 B4
Swann's Terr 4 CB1 ..65 A8
Swansley La CB3 ..79 A4
Swanspool PE3 ..197 B6
Swanton Cl PE15 ..243 D7
Swasedale Dro CB7 ..219 A5
Swavesey Prim Sch
CB4 ..122 E6
Swavesey Rd CB4 ..122 A4
Swavesey Village Coll
CB4 ..122 E5
Swayne's La CB3 ..62 C5
Sweetbriar La PE4 ..204 B6
Sweeting Ave PE19 ..95 F1
Sweetings Rd PE29 ..118 F8
Swift Cl March PE15 ..243 F5
Market Deeping PE6 ..231 E8
Royston SG8 ..13 D1
St Neots PE19 ..75 B6
Swifts Cnr CB1 ..66 F5
Swinburne Cl SG8 ..13 D1
Swinnell Cl SG8 ..13 A5
Sybil Rd PE13 ..245 C6
Sycamore Ave PE1 ..198 C6
Sycamore Cl
4 Cambridge CB1 ..65 D5
March PE15 ..243 C3
Sycamore Dr PE29 ..141 E8
Sycamore La CB7 ..240 F5
Sycamore Pl CB6 ..242 D4
Sycamore Rd PE7 ..189 F6
Sycamores The
Bluntisham/Colne PE28 ..208 C6
Little Paxton PE19 ..95 F2
Milton CB4 ..105 C2
Sydney Rd PE2 ..187 D5
Syers La PE7 ..189 D7
Sylton Cl PE29 ..141 F1
Sylvden Dr PE13 ..245 F6
Sylvester Rd CB3 ..83 B1
Symmington Cl PE2 ..186 F8
Symonds Cl CB4 ..104 B4
Symonds La CB1 ..35 B3
Sywell Gr 5 PE14 ..236 A5

T

Tabrum Cl CB3 ..63 F4
Tadlow Rd SG19 ..25 C3
Taggart Tile Mus★
PE19 ..93 E6
Tait Cl PE1 ..198 C5
Talbot Ave PE2 ..186 D6
Talbot Cl PE7 ..175 F8
Tall Trees 3 SG8 ..5 E6
Tallington Dry Ski Slope
PE9 ..230 F8
Tallington Lakes Leisure Pk★
PE9 ..231 A8
Tall's La PE28 ..121 B6
Tamar Cl PE27 ..144 B6
Tamarin Gdns CB1 ..66 A6
Tan House La CB5 ..109 B8
Tan Yd PE19 ..74 E5
Tanglewood
Alconbury Weston PE28 ..150 E6
Peterborough PE4 ..204 B6
Tanhouse PE2 ..186 C5
Tanners La CB7 ..212 B3

Tannersfield Way CB8 .110 F4
Tannery Cl SG8 ....5 C6
Tannery Drift SG8 ....5 C7
Tannery Drift Sch SG8 ...5 C6
Tannery Rd CB2 ....32 F6
Tansor Garth PE3 ....197 C5
Tansor Grange PE8 ...178 A1
Tansur Ct PE19 ....74 F8
Tansy Cl 2 PE19 ....74 B5
Tantallon Ct PE3 ....197 B1
Tanyard The SG8 ....12 E4
Tarrant PE4 ....204 A6
Tasman Rd CB9 ....24 C7
Tates Field CB3 ....59 E8
Tatwin Dr 8 PE6 ....232 B8
Taunton Cl CB1 ....65 D7
Taverners Dr PE26 ....171 F5
Taverners Rd PE1 ....197 F4
Tavistock Cl 8 PE6 ....233 A3
Tavistock Rd
Cambridge CB4 ....83 C6
Wisbech PE13 ....245 D5
Tawny Cres PE29 ....142 B7
Tay Cl PE27 ....144 B7
Taylor's Dro PE12 ....237 C8
Taylor's La CB4 ....122 D6
Taylors Field CB8 ....70 F8
Taylors Gn PE8 ....178 A2
Taylors La PE19 ....116 F5
Taymor Pl PE14 ....225 A8
Tea Kettle La CB8 ....89 F1
Teal Cl Chatteris PE16 ..241 C6
St Ives PE27 ....143 F7
Teal Rd PE7 ....189 F8
Teanby Ct PE3 ....196 F3
Teasdale Cl SG8 ....13 D1
Teasel Cl
15 Eaton Socon PE19 ....74 C6
2 Royston SG8 ....5 E5
Teasel Dr CB6 ....240 B5
Teasel Way CB1 ....66 A5
Tebbutts Rd PE19 ....74 E5
Tedder Way CB4 ....83 C6
Telegraph St CB4 ....125 E4
Telford Dr PE7 ....181 D6
Templars Ct CB9 ....23 E7
Temple Cl Duxford CB2 ..32 D1
Huntingdon PE29 ....141 E4
Temple Ct 4 CB4 ....83 E7
Temple End
Great Wilbraham CB1 ....68 A8
Little Thurlow CB9 ....55 F2
Temple Grange PE4 ....204 B6
Temple Rd CB7 ....212 F4
Templemore Cl CB1 ....65 B4
Temples Ct PE6 ....231 B4
Tempsford Rd SG19 ....40 A4
Ten Acre Dro PE7 ....220 C8
Ten Bell La 6 CB7 ....212 B4
Ten Mile Bank CB6 ....242 F6
Tenby Cl CB1 ....66 A6
Tenby Way 6 PE19 ....74 F1
Tenison Ave CB1 ....64 F7
Tenison Manor CB4 ....125 D4
Tenison Rd CB1 ....65 A8
Tennis Ct Ave PE29 ....141 E5
Tennis Ct Rd CB2 ....246 B1
Tennis Ct Terr CB2 ....246 A1
Tennyson Ave PE27 ....143 F6
Tennyson Cl
Huntingdon PE29 ....141 F6
Royston SG8 ....13 D1
Tennyson Pl
Eaton Socon PE19 ....74 D6
Ely CB6 ....240 A5
Tennyson Rd PE1 ....197 F7
Tenter La PE9 ....244 C5
Tenterleas PE27 ....144 B3
Tern Cl CB9 ....24 C7
Tern Gdns PE16 ....241 C6
Tern Rd PE7 ....186 C2
Tern Way 4 PE19 ....75 B6
Terr The CB8 ....111 A3
Terrington Cl PE14 ....236 D6
Tetworth Hill SG19 ....41 A7
Teversham CE Prim Sch CB1 ....85 B2
Teversham Drift CB1 ....66 A7
Teversham Rd CB1 ....66 E6
Teversham Way CB2 ....50 A1
Teynham Cl CB1 ....65 D7
Thackeray Cl SG8 ....13 D1
Thackers Cl PE8 ....194 A4
Thackray Cl PE29 ....141 E7
Thames Rd PE29 ....141 F8
Tharp Way CB7 ....213 C1
Thatcher Stanfords Cl SG8 ....14 C7
Thatchers Cl PE26 ....171 B2
Thatchers Wood CB4 ....123 F1
Thatchwood Ave PE14 .236 C6
Thetford Cnr CB6 ....211 A7
Thetford Rd IP28 ....239 E4
Thetford Terr CB5 ....84 E2
Thicket Rd PE28 ....143 B4
Thickwillow 2 PE29 ....118 F8
Third Ave
Warboys PE28 ....164 E6
Wisbech PE13 ....245 E5
Third Dro
Downham CB6 ....225 B1
Peterborough PE1 ....198 E2
Third Marsh Rd PE14 ..238 C3
Thirlby Gdns CB7 ....240 E7
Thirleby Cl CB4 ....83 D5
Thirlemere Gdns PE4 ..204 E3
Thirlmere PE29 ....141 B6
Thirlmere Gdns 3 PE4 .204 E3
Thirlwall Dr CB7 ....213 A1
Thistle Cnr CB7 ....218 D4
Thistle Dr PE2 ....187 C7
Thistle Gn CB4 ....122 E6
Thistlemoor Rd PE1 ...197 E7
Thoday St CB1 ....65 B8
Thodays Cl CB4 ....209 A1
Thomas Christian Way CB5 ....86 E7
Thomas Cl PE3 ....196 F3
Thomas Eaton Prim Sch The PE15 ....223 B7
Thomas King Dr PE29 .141 C6
Thomas Parsons Sq CB7 ....240 C4
Thomas Rd CB1 ....66 D5
Thomas Way SG8 ....13 D1
Thomas Wlk CB11 ....9 F1
Thompsons Gd PE7 ...186 D3
Thompson's La CB2 ...246 A3
Thompsons Mdw SG8 ..11 A4
Thongsley PE29 ....141 F7
Thongsley Fields Prim Sch PE29 ....141 F7
Thorby Ave PE15 ....243 A7
Thorley Cres PE2 ....186 D8
Thorleye Rd CB5 ....84 C2
Thorn Cl CB7 ....212 A4
Thorn Rd PE7 ....186 C2
Thorndown Cl PE27 ...143 E6
Thorndown Com Inf Sch PE27 ....143 E6
Thorndown Com Jun Sch PE27 ....143 E6
Thorney Dyke PE6 ....201 C6
Thorney Heritage Mus* PE6 ....233 A3
Thorney Rd Eye PE6 ...232 B1
Newborough PE6 ....206 E2
Wisbech St Mary PE13 ...234 C2
Thornham Way PE7 ....190 C6
Thornhill Pl CB4 ....123 F2
Thornleigh Dr PE2 ....186 C6
Thornmead PE4 ....204 D4
Thornton Cl Girton CB3 ..82 F6
Peterborough PE4 ....204 E3
Thornton Rd Girton CB3 ..82 F7
March PE15 ....243 D6
Thornton Way CB3 ....83 A6
Thorolds Way PE5 ....195 D2
Thoroughfare La CB7 ..218 F1
Thoroughfare Way CB6 ....242 E4
Thorpe Ave PE3 ....197 C2
Thorpe Lea Rd PE3 ....197 F1
Thorpe Mdws PE3 ....197 D1
Thorpe Pk Rd PE3 ....197 C3
Thorpe Prim Sch PE3 ..197 B3
Thorpe Rd PE3 ....197 B1
Thorpe The PE28 ....143 B1
Thorpe Way CB5 ....84 F4
Thorpe Wood PE3 ....196 F1
Thorpe Wood Nature Reserve* PE3 ....196 F1
Thorseby Cl PE3 ....197 B3
Thrapston Rd
Brampton PE28 ....140 B4
Catworth PE28 ....147 C2
Kimbolton PE28 ....113 F5
Spaldwick PE28 ....137 F6
Three Cups Wlk CB7 ..240 D4
Three Hills CB1 ....21 A7
Three Shires Way PE28 ....135 E4
Thrifts Wlk CB4 ....84 A4
Thriplow CE Prim Sch SG8 ....31 B2
Thriplow Rd SG8 ....30 F1
Throckmorton PE28 ...164 E5
Throckmorton Rd PE28 ....117 D8
Throstlenest PE7 ....187 C3
Thruffle Way CB3 ....102 C3
Thulborn Cl CB1 ....85 B1
Thurland's Dro PE14 ...229 C8
Thurlaston Cl PE3 ....197 B2
Thurley Cl PE19 ....95 E5
Thurloe Cl PE13 ....245 C2
Thurlow Rd CB9 ....39 C6
Thurnall Ave SG8 ....5 D5
Thurning Ave PE2 ....187 C6
Thurning Rd PE28 ....157 F7
Thuro Gr PE2 ....186 A3
Thursfield PE4 ....204 C4
Thurston Gate PE3 ....197 A1
Tiberius Cl CB9 ....24 D7
Tilbrook Mill MK44 ....113 A7
Tilbrook Rd PE28 ....113 D6
Tillbrooks Hill CB8 ....73 C1
Tillyard Way CB1 ....65 D4
Tilton Ct PE1 ....198 C8
Tindall Cl PE13 ....245 C8
Tinker's Dro PE13 ....245 D8
Tinker's La CB3 ....61 C2
Tinkers La PE28 ....168 B4
Tintagel Ct
Peterborough PE3 ....197 B1
2 St Neots PE19 ....74 F2
Tintern Rise 3 PE6 ....232 A1
Tinwell Rd PE9 ....244 A4
Tinwell Rd La PE9 ....244 A4
Tipplers' Rd CB4 ....122 E2
Tiptree Cl CB5 ....84 F4
Tirrington PE3 ....197 A3
Tithe Ave IP28 ....213 F8
Tithe Cl PE28 ....120 B2
Tithe Rd PE16 ....241 C2
Tithe Way CB3 ....79 C3
Tiverton Rd PE3 ....197 C3
Tiverton Way CB1 ....65 C7
Toates Cl CB6 ....210 C6
Toft La CB1 ....67 F7
Toftland PE2 ....186 D5
Tointons Rd PE14 ....229 F8
Tolethorpe Sq 4 PE9 ....244 B6
Toll Bar La PE28 ....146 B5
Toll Dro PE15 ....224 A3
Toll House Rd PE2 ....186 C7
Toll Rd PE7 ....188 A5
Tollfield PE28 ....113 F4
Tollgate PE3 ....197 A5
Tom Jennings Cl CB8 ..110 F5
Tomlinson Ct PE29 ...141 F8
Toneham La PE6 ....232 F1
Top La PE19 ....57 B5
Top St CB6 ....210 F5
Topcliffe Way CB1 ....65 C3
Topham Cres 9 PE6 ....233 A3
Topham Ct PE19 ....74 F7
Topham Way CB4 ....83 D6
Topmoor Way PE4 ....204 F1
Torkington Gdns 3 PE9 ....244 B5
Torpel Way 2 PE6 ....231 C7
Tort Hill PE28 ....168 C5
Toseland Rd PE19 ....97 E4
Tothill Rd CB5 ....108 D4
Touthill Cl PE1 ....198 A2
Tower Cl
Bassingbourn SG8 ....12 F5
Cottenham CB4 ....125 D3
Huntingdon PE29 ....141 D8
11 Over CB4 ....208 D1
Ramsey PE26 ....172 C7
Whittlesey PE7 ....189 B8
Tower Ct Ely CB6 ....240 B3
Haverhill CB9 ....23 E7
Peterborough PE2 ....186 F8
Tower Rd
Downham CB6 ....217 F7
Elm PE14 ....236 A3
Ely CB7 ....240 B3
Sawston CB2 ....33 A8
Sutton CB6 ....216 E2
Tower Sq PE29 ....152 D1
Tower St PE2 ....186 F8
Tower View CB1 ....35 D3
Towgood Way PE19 ....96 D4
Towler St PE1 ....198 A3
Town Bridge PE13 ....245 B5
Town Cl CB2 ....32 E7
Town End Cl CB9 ....38 F1
Town Farm Cl SG8 ....10 F4
Town Gn Rd SG8 ....28 D8
Town La CB2 ....33 B5
Town Orch PE19 ....95 E5
Town St Newton CB2 ....31 B7
Outwell PE14 ....236 E1
Town The PE19 ....93 E6
Towne Rd SG8 ....5 D5
Townley Cl PE14 ....236 E1
Townley Prim Sch PE14 ....229 D3
Townsend CB7 ....212 A5
Townsend Cl CB4 ....105 D3
Townsend Rd
Needingworth PE27 ....208 A3
Upwell PE14 ....229 E7
Wittering PE8 ....230 A1
Townsend Way PE7 ....175 D8
Townshend Rd PE13 ...245 D6
Toyse Cl CB5 ....130 C4
Toyse La CB5 ....130 B4
Trafalgar Rd
Cambridge CB4 ....246 B4
Eaton Socon PE19 ....74 C5
Trafalgar St CB4 ....246 B4
Trafalgar Terr PE9 ....244 B6
Trafalgar Way CB3 ....102 B5
Trafford Est PE14 ....238 F4
Trafford Pk 1 PE13 ....245 E6
Trafford Rd PE13 ....245 D5
Tram Sta La PE14 ....236 B6
Tramar Dr 7 CB6 ....216 E2
Trap Rd SG8 ....11 A4
Treading Bank PE13 ....237 C4
Treading Field PE13 ....237 C4
Tredegar Cl CB4 ....83 E6
Tredgold La CB1 ....246 C3
Treeway PE16 ....241 B5
Trefoil Ct 2 CB9 ....23 F7
Trent Cl PE27 ....144 A7
Trent Rd PE8 ....193 D8
Tresham Rd PE2 ....185 D3
Trevone Pl CB1 ....65 D7
Tribune Cl PE16 ....241 D3
Tribune Ct CB4 ....83 E7
Trienna PE2 ....186 B5
Trigg Way SG8 ....14 D6
Trinity Ave IP28 ....239 C5
Trinity Cl Balsham CB1 ....53 B2
Bottisham CB5 ....86 F6
Ely CB6 ....240 C5
Fordham CB7 ....212 F1
Great Paxton PE19 ....96 E4
Haslingfield CB3 ....47 B5
Trinity Coll CB2 ....246 A3
Trinity Dr CB8 ....111 B2
Trinity La CB2 ....246 A2
Trinity Link CB9 ....39 A1
Trinity Pl PE29 ....141 E4
Trinity Rd
Stamford PE9 ....244 A6
Trinity Rd *continued*
Wisbech PE13 ....245 E6
Trinity St
Cambridge CB2 ....246 A2
3 Peterborough PE1 ....198 A2
Triplow Mdws Nature Reserve* SG8 ....31 B2
Troughton Way 12 PE13 .238 B2
Troutbeck Cl PE4 ....204 F3
Truman Ave PE15 ....243 A5
Trumpington Gall* CB4 ....83 E4
Trumpington High St CB2 ....64 D3
Trumpington Rd CB2 ...64 E5
Trumpington St CB2 ..246 A2
Trundle Mere PE7 ....182 B2
Trundle The PE28 ....215 C1
Trundley Cl CB9 ....38 F1
Tucker's Yd PE2 ....187 C7
Tuckers Nook 1 PE6 ...231 C7
Tuddenham Rd IP28 ...239 F2
Tuddenham VC Sch IP28 ....214 E2
Tudor Ave PE7 ....186 C1
Tudor Cl PE4 ....204 E2
Tudor Ct
Bassingbourn cum Kneesworth SG8 ....13 B4
Kimbolton PE28 ....113 F5
Tudor Rd PE29 ....141 F2
Tulyar Wlk CB8 ....110 E8
Tunbridge Cl
Bottisham CB5 ....86 E6
Burwell CB5 ....130 B2
Tunbridge La CB5 ....86 E6
Tunkers La PE26 ....171 F4
Tunwells Cl CB2 ....49 A5
Tunwells La CB2 ....49 A5
Turberville Ct PE28 ....143 C1
Turf Dro PE7 ....191 C5
Turf Fen La PE15 ....222 F5
Turf Fen Rd PE26 ....170 F3
Turf Lot Dro PE14 ....229 E1
Turf Maze* PE28 ....120 C1
Turnbull Rd PE15 ....243 B3
Turner Cl CB9 ....38 D1
Turner Rd
Eaton Socon PE19 ....74 C5
St Ives PE27 ....144 A7
Turners La PE7 ....189 D6
Turningtree Rd PE7 ...190 A3
Turnpike Cl 2 PE13 ....245 E6
Turnpike Hill CB9 ....38 C4
Turnpike La IP28 ....133 E8
Turnpike Rd IP28 ....133 E8
Turnpike The CB7 ....240 B3
Turnpole Cl PE9 ....244 D7
Turnstone Cl IP28 ....239 D4
Turnstone Way PE2 ...187 D7
Turpin's Ride
4 Royston SG8 ....5 D5
Stilton PE7 ....176 A7
Turpyn Ct CB4 ....83 E6
Turvers La PE26 ....172 B7
Turves Rd PE6 ....232 A2
Tuyar Wlk CB8 ....110 E8
Tweed Cl CB8 ....112 F6
Tweedale CB1 ....65 F5
Twelvetree Ave PE4 ...204 A5
Twenty Foot Rd PE15 ..227 F8
Twenty Pence Rd
Cottenham CB4 ....125 F6
Wilburton CB6 ....210 B3
Two Pole Dro
Farcet PE7 ....187 F1
Soham CB7 ....211 E7
Two Tree Hundred Dro PE15 ....228 A6
Twyford Gdns PE1 ....198 D7
Tydd St Giles Golf & Leisure Ctr PE13 ....238 A7
Tyesdale PE3 ....197 A4
Tylers Mews PE4 ....204 B3
Tyrrell Pk PE1 ....198 D2
Tythe Piece PE28 ....121 C5

U

UCLES CB1 ....246 C1
Uffen Way CB2 ....32 E8
Uffington Rd
1 Barnack PE9 ....230 D4
Stamford PE9 ....244 D5
Uffington Sch PE9 ....230 C6
Ufford Pl 7 CB9 ....24 B8
Ugg Mere Ct Rd PE26 .220 D1
Uldale Way PE4 ....204 F2
Ullswater PE29 ....141 C5
Ullswater Ave PE4 ....204 D2
Underwood Cl PE7 ....190 D7
Union La CB4 ....83 F5
Union Pl 13 PE13 ....245 C5
Union Rd CB2 ....246 B1
Union St 4 PE13 ....245 C5
Univ Arts Sch CB2 ....246 A2
Univ Museum of Zoology* CB2 ....246 B2
Univ of Cambridge
Cambridge CB1 ....84 A2
Madingley CB3 ....81 E6
University Concert Hall CB3 ....83 C2
University Music Sch CB3 ....83 C1
Unwin's La 13 CB4 ....208 D1
Uphall Rd CB1 ....84 D1
Upherd's La CB6 ....240 C5
Uplands PE4 ....204 C5
Upper Delph Dro CB6 .209 A5
Upper Gatley End SG8 ..3 D6
Upper Gwydir St 1 CB1 .84 A1
Upper King St SG8 ....5 D6
Upton Cl
Stanground PE2 ....187 E5
Longthorpe PE3 ....197 A2
Upton Gdn PE28 ....160 C1
Upton La CB6 ....242 D4
Upton Pl CB6 ....242 C4
Upware Rd
Swaffham Prior CB7 ....128 D8
Wicken CB7 ....211 C1
Upwell Pk PE15 ....243 F3
Upwell Prim Sch PE14 ....229 D8
Upwell Rd
Christchurch PE14 ....229 C4
March PE15 ....243 E3
Upwood Airfield
Polebrook PE8 ....174 A2
Ramsey PE26 ....171 D4
Upwood Mdws National Nature Reserve* PE26 ....171 A2
Upwood Prim Sch PE26 ....171 D3
Upwood Rd PE26 ....171 B5

V

Valarian Cl 14 PE19 ....74 C6
Vale Dr PE7 ....186 C1
Valence Rd PE2 ....185 F4
Valerian Ct CB1 ....66 A5
Valiant Rd PE27 ....143 F7
Valiant Sq PE26 ....171 F3
Valley Rise SG8 ....5 E6
Valley The CB3 ....62 D6
Valley Way CB8 ....110 E4
Valparaiso Univ CB3 ...83 C3
Van Diemans Way PE28 ....116 A7
Van Dyke Pl PE27 ....144 A7
Van Gogh Pl PE27 ....144 A7
Vange Pl CB9 ....24 B8
Vanners Rd CB9 ....24 A7
Varrier Jones Dr CB3 ..99 A3
Varrier Jones Pl CB3 ..99 A3
Veasey Rd PE29 ....142 A7
Velos Wlk CB5 ....84 E4
Vence Cl PE9 ....244 A5
Ventress Cl CB1 ....65 D5
Ventress Farm Ct CB1 ..65 E5
Verdun Rd PE13 ....245 D5
Vere Rd PE1 ....197 F7
Vergette Rd PE6 ....203 F8
Vergette St PE1 ....198 B4
Vermont Gr PE3 ....197 E1
Vermuyden PE28 ....208 E6
Vermuyden Gdns 5 CB6 ....216 E2
Vermuyden Way CB4 ..121 F5
Verulam Way CB4 ....83 D6
Vester's Hill Dro PE26 .171 B7
Vetch Wlk CB9 ....38 D1
Vetchfield PE2 ....185 E5
Vicarage Ave CB2 ....32 F7
Vicarage Cl
Chatteris PE16 ....241 D5
Dullingham CB8 ....89 C1
Holme PE7 ....177 A4
Melbourn SG8 ....14 C6
Oakington/Longstanton CB4 ....103 D6
Swaffham Bulbeck CB5 ..108 A1
Waterbeach CB5 ....106 A7
Vicarage Dr CB3 ....64 A3
Vicarage Farm Rd 5 PE1 ....198 D3
Vicarage Farm Yd PE19 .57 B6
Vicarage La
Swaffham Prior CB5 ....108 D4
Whittlesford CB2 ....32 B5
Woodditton CB8 ....90 D3
Vicarage Rd
Newmarket CB8 ....111 B3
Waresley SG19 ....58 A2
Vicarage Terr CB1 ....84 A1
Vicarage Way PE7 ....181 D5
Vicarage Wlk PE19 ....93 F6
Viceroy Cl PE19 ....74 A3
Victor Cl PE27 ....144 A7
Victoria Ave CB5 ....246 B3
Victoria Cres
Royston SG8 ....5 D7
St Ives PE28 ....143 A5
Victoria Gdns CB6 ....242 D4
Victoria Gn 3 CB6 ....217 D1
Victoria Pk CB4 ....83 D4
Victoria Pl
Peterborough PE1 ....197 F4
Sutton CB6 ....216 D1
16 Wisbech PE13 ....245 C4
Victoria Rd
Cambridge CB4 ....83 D4
Haverhill CB9 ....23 D7
Stamford PE9 ....244 B6
Wisbech PE13 ....245 C4
Victoria Sq PE29 ....141 E4
Victoria St
Cambridge CB1 ....246 B2
Chatteris PE16 ....241 C4
Ely CB7 ....240 D3
Littleport CB6 ....242 E4

Victoria St *continued*
Old Fetton PE2 .186 F6
Peterborough PE1 .198 A5
Victoria View CB4 .125 F7
Victoria Way CB8 .110 E7
Victory Ave PE7 .189 F7
Victory Rd PE13 .245 B3
Victory Way CB4 .125 D4
Victory Wlk 7 SG8 .5 E5
Viersen Platz PE1 .198 A1
Viking Cl CB1 .53 E5
Viking Way
Bar Hill CB3 .102 B4
Whittlesey PE7 .189 E8
Villa Ct CB4 .83 E8
Villa Pl CB4 .104 C2
Villa Rd CB4 .104 C2
Village The PE2 .186 B5
Vincent Cl CB8 .110 E7
Vinces Ct CB6 .240 C4
Vine Cl
Great Shelford CB2 .49 C4
Hemingford Grey PE27 .143 E2
Vine St PE9 .244 C5
Vine Wlk PE3 .197 B4
Vinegar Hill PE28 .150 E7
Vinery Ct PE26 .172 B7
Vinery Pk CB1 .84 C1
Vinery Rd CB1 .65 C8
Vinery Way CB1 .84 C1
Viney Cl PE1 .198 D5
Vineyard Rd PE1 .198 B2
Vineyard The PE28 .208 D7
Vineyard Way
Buckden PE19 .117 B3
Ely CB7 .240 E5
Vineyard Wlk CB5 .86 F6
Vineyards The CB7 .240 D4
Vintner Cl CB3 .99 A3
Vintners Cl PE3 .197 D3
Violet Cl CB1 .66 A5
Violet Way PE7 .181 F7
Virginia Cl PE3 .197 A2
Virginia Rd IP28 .213 E8
Virginia Way PE27 .143 E6
Viscount Ct PE19 .74 B3
Viscount Rd PE2 .187 A6
Vixen Cl PE7 .181 F6
Vokes St PE2 .186 D8
Vulcan Way PE19 .74 B1

W

Wadbury's Folly PE27 .208 B4
Waddelow Rd CB5 .106 A8
Wade Pk Ave 4 PE6 .231 E8
Wadloes Rd CB5 .84 D4
Waggoners Way 15
PE15 .223 B7
Wagstaff Cl CB4 .83 F7
Wainman Rd PE2 .186 D5
Wainwright PE4 .204 A5
Waits The PE27 .144 A3
Wake Ave IP28 .239 C5
Wake Rd March PE15 .243 C6
Peterborough PE1 .198 B2
Wakefield Cl CB10 .18 D3
Wakelin Ave CB2 .49 F1
Wakelyn Rd PE7 .189 C7
Wakerley Dr PE2 .186 C7
Walcot Rd PE9 .230 E2
Walcot Wlk PE3 .197 B3
Walden Cl 17 PE15 .223 A5
Walden Gr PE29 .141 D4
Walden Rd
Great Chesterford CB10 .18 E3
Hadstock CB1 .20 B6
Huntingdon PE29 .141 D4
Walden Way CB2 .48 F6
Wales Bank PE14 .236 A5
Walgrave PE2 .186 B4
Walker Ct CB4 .83 E6
Walker Rd PE6 .203 F7
Walkers Way PE3 .196 F3
Walkling Way CB4 .105 D1
Walks E The 7 PE29 .141 D4
Walks N The PE29 .141 D4
Wallace Ct PE29 .142 A8
Wallace's Dro PE6 .233 D4
Waller's Cl SG8 .7 F2
Wallman's La CB4 .122 E6
Walnut Cl
Newborough PE6 .205 C8
Royston SG8 .5 D6
Walnut Gr IP28 .213 E4
Walnut Tree Ave CB5 .84 A3
Walnut Tree Cl
Bassingbourn SG8 .12 E5
Little Downham CB6 .218 A6
8 Stretham CB6 .210 F5
Walnut Tree Cres
PE28 .121 B5
Walnut Tree Dr PE29 .141 C6
Walnut Tree Gr PE28 .140 D3
Walnut Tree Way CB4 .83 C7
Walnut Way PE7 .175 F7
Walpole Bank PE14 .238 F7
Walpole Ct CB7 .240 C4
Walpole Rd CB1 .65 D6
Walsingham Ct PE13 .245 A7
Walsingham Way
Ely CB6 .240 B5
10 Eye PE6 .232 A1
Walsoken Rd PE14 .236 E7
Waltham Cl PE1 .198 D8
Walton Cl CB7 .212 E1
Walton Com Sch PE4 .204 C1
Walton Hill PE28 .161 D5
Walton J & I Sch PE4 .204 C1
Walton Pk PE4 .204 C1
Walton Rd
9 Leverington PE13 .238 B2
Marholm PE6 .203 E1
Wisbech PE13 .245 E7
Waltons CB10 .21 C3
Wamil Rd IP28 .213 F5
Wamil Way IP28 .239 B4
Wandlebury Ctry Pk★
CB2 .50 B8
Wansford Pasture Nature
Reserve★ PE8 .193 F3
Wansford Rd
Elton PE8 .183 D5
Wansford PE8 .194 A3
Yarwell PE8 .193 F2
Wantage Gdns PE19 .96 A2
Warbon Ave PE1 .197 F7
Warboys Airfield Ind Est
PE28 .164 D2
Warboys Cl CB3 .61 D5
Warboys CP Sch PE28 .164 E5
Warboys Rd PE28 .155 E8
Ward Cl
Peterborough PE1 .198 B3
Ramsey PE26 .172 A5
St Ives PE28 .143 A5
Ward Rd CB1 .65 D6
Ward Way CB6 .217 D1
Warden Hill SG19 .40 C3
Ware La PE28 .142 F5
Ware Rd PE19 .74 E6
Wareley Rd PE2 .197 F1
Waresley & Gransden Woods
Nature Reserve★
SG19 .58 C2
Waresley Rd
Gamlingay SG19 .41 D6
Great Gransden SG19 .58 B3
Warkworth St CB1 .246 C2
Warkworth Terr CB1 .246 C2
Warmington Sch PE8 .178 B3
Warner's Dro
Pidley cum Fenton PE28 .215 B3
Somersham PE28 .215 C2
Warners Gr PE27 .144 A4
Warren Cl St Ives PE28 .142 F6
Wilburton CB6 .210 C5
Warren Croft PE28 .168 B5
Warren Ct 6 CB9 .23 E7
Warren La
Bythorn & Keyston PE28 .146 D4
Titchmarsh PE28 .156 F1
Warren Pl CB8 .111 F5
Warren Rd
Cambridge CB4 .84 A6
Herringswell CB8 .134 A7
Red Lodge IP28 .214 A1
St Ives PE27 .144 B4
Wothorpe PE9 .244 B1
Warren The
3 Royston SG8 .5 D5
Witchford CB6 .217 E1
Warren Twrs CB8 .111 E4
Warrene Keep PE9 .244 B4
Warrington St CB8 .111 A2
Warwick Ct
Eaton Socon PE19 .74 C3
2 Haverhill CB9 .23 E8
Warwick Dr CB6 .240 A3
Warwick Rd
Cambridge CB4 .83 C5
Peterborough PE4 .204 C1
Wasdale Gdns PE4 .205 A2
Wash La PE7 .189 E8
Wash Rd PE14 .225 B8
Washbank Rd PE19 .74 E4
Washingley La PE7 .175 B7
Washingley Rd
Folksworth PE7 .175 D8
The Stukeleys PE29 .141 C8
Washington Cl CB6 .242 D5
Washington St IP28 .213 E8
Washpit La CB3 .46 D7
Washpit Rd CB3 .82 C8
Wastwater PE29 .141 B6
Water End
Alwalton PE7 .185 A5
Marholm PE6 .203 D1
Peterborough PE3 .197 D2
Wrestlingworth SG19 .25 B3
Water La Bourn CB3 .60 D6
Cambridge CB4 .84 B5
Castor PE5 .195 F1
Cottenham CB4 .126 A7
Great Bradley CB8 .55 F8
Histon CB4 .104 C3
Melbourn SG8 .14 C5
Oakington/Longstanton
CB4 .103 C5
Sturmer CB9 .24 F5
Water St Cambridge CB4 .84 B4
Stamford PE9 .244 C4
Waterbeach CP Sch
CB5 .106 B8
Waterbeach Rd CB4 .105 E7
Waterbeach Sta CB5 .106 C6
Watercourse The CB8 .111 A4
Waterfall Gdns PE6 .207 C1
Waterfields PE16 .241 B3
Waterfurlong PE9 .244 A4
Watergall PE3 .197 B8
Watergall Prim Sch
PE3 .197 A8
Watergate 6 PE9 .244 C5
Waterlees Rd 2 PE13 .245 E7
Waterloo Cl
Brampton PE28 .140 D3
Newmarket CB8 .110 D8
Waterloo Dr 2 PE19 .74 F3
Waterloo Rd PE1 .198 A5
Watermead CB3 .102 C3
Watermead Cres CB3 .79 A3
Waterside Ely CB7 .240 E4
Isleham CB7 .213 A5
Waterside Gdns
March PE15 .243 E5
Whittlesey PE7 .189 D8
Waterslade Rd PE7 .181 C4
Watersmead PE19 .117 E3
Waterton Cl 6 PE6 .231 F8
Waterwick Hill CB11 .1 F1
Waterworks La PE6 .203 D6
Waterworks Rd IP28 .213 E8
Watsons La 1 CB6 .211 B7
Watt Cl PE4 .204 E2
Wattle Cl CB3 .79 A4
Wavell Way CB4 .83 E6
Waveney Dr PE15 .243 B5
Waveney Gr PE4 .204 E2
Waveney Rd PE27 .144 A7
Waveney Terr CB9 .24 B7
Waverley Cl PE13 .235 A3
Waverley Gdns 3 PE9 .244 A6
Way Head Dro CB6 .217 C6
Way La
Waterbeach CB5 .106 B8
Wicken CB7 .211 D2
Way The Fowlmere SG8 .15 E8
Fowlmere SG8 .30 E1
Wayford Cl PE3 .197 A2
Weasenham La 1 PE13 245 D2
Weatheralls Cl 4 CB7 .212 B4
Weatheralls Prim Sch The
CB7 .212 B4
Weatherthorn PE2 .186 C5
Weavers Field CB3 .82 E7
Webbs Mdw SG19 .58 D4
Webb's Rd CB1 .36 F5
Webster's Way CB4 .208 D1
Websters Cl PE6 .203 F8
Weddell Rd CB9 .24 C6
Wedgewood Dr CB1 .65 F6
Wedgwood Dr PE13 .245 D5
Weedon Cl PE4 .204 F2
Weir Cl Buckden PE19 .117 A3
Hemingford Grey PE28 .143 D1
Weir Rd PE28 .143 D1
Weirs Dro CB5 .129 F1
Welbeck Rd PE13 .245 E4
Welbeck Way PE2 .186 D7
Welbourne PE4 .204 C4
Welbourne Prim Sch
PE4 .204 C4
Welby Cl PE28 .115 D3
Welches Dam Visitor Ctr★
CB6 .217 A8
Well Bottom CB8 .112 B8
Well Creek Rd PE14 .236 F2
Well End PE14 .236 A3
Welland Bank PE6 .207 D7
Welland Cl
Peterborough PE1 .198 A7
St Ives PE27 .144 A7
Welland Ct 9 PE19 .74 C4
Welland Mews PE9 .244 C4
Welland Pl CB6 .240 D6
Welland Prim Sch
PE1 .198 C8
Welland Rd
Peterborough PE1 .198 B8
Wittering PE8 .230 B1
Welland Way 5 PE6 .231 F8
Wellbrook Way CB3 .82 F7
Wellcome Trust Genome
Campus CB10 .18 B6
Wellingly Ct CB3 .79 A3
Wellington Ave PE27 .143 F7
Wellington Cl
Old Hurst PE28 .154 E7
Thistley Green IP28 .213 D6
Warboys PE28 .164 F4
Waterbeach CB5 .106 B7
Wellington Ct 3 CB1 .84 A2
Wellington Pl SG8 .13 B5
Wellington Rd Ely CB6 .217 F1
Mildenhall IP28 .213 E8
Wellington St
4 Cambridge CB1 .84 A2
Littleport CB6 .242 D4
4 Newmarket CB8 .111 A3
Peterborough PE1 .198 B2
St Ives PE27 .144 A3
Wellington Terr
15 Haverhill CB9 .23 E7
20 Wisbech PE13 .245 C5
Wells Bridge PE26 .221 C3
Wells Cl Haslingfield CB3 .47 A5
Peterborough PE4 .204 B3
Wells Ct
Mildenhall IP28 .239 B5
Peterborough PE2 .187 D6
Wells Way PE7 .177 A5
Wellsfield PE29 .141 E6
Wellum Cl 18 CB9 .23 E7
Welmore Rd PE6 .203 F8
Welstead Rd CB1 .66 A6
Wenny Ct PE16 .241 C4
Wenny Est PE16 .241 D3
Wenny Rd PE16 .241 E3
Wenny Severals PE16 .216 B7
Wensum Cl PE27 .144 B6
Wentworth Dr IP28 .239 B4
Wentworth Rd CB4 .83 C4
Wentworth St 1 PE1 .198 A1
Wentworth Terr 6 CB9 .23 E8
Wenvoe Cl CB1 .65 F6
Werrington Bridge Rd
PE6 .204 E7
Werrington Gr PE4 .204 B2
Werrington Gr Cvn Pk
PE4 .204 B2
Werrington Mews 5
PE4 .204 C3
Werrington Parkway
PE6 .203 E5
Werrington Pk Ave 2
PE4 .204 C3
Werrington Prim Sch
PE4 .204 C3
Werrington Sports Ctr
PE4 .204 B4
Wertheim Way PE29 .141 B6
Wesley Dr PE16 .241 D5
Wesley House CB5 .246 B3
Wesleyan Rd PE1 .198 A7
Wessex Cl PE2 .187 D7
West Ave PE26 .171 F6
West Brook PE28 .120 B2
West Brook Cl PE28 .120 B2
West Cl
Alconbury Weston PE28 .150 D6
March PE15 .243 B6
Waresley SG19 .57 F2
West Delph PE7 .189 D8
West Dr
Friday Bridge PE14 .236 A4
Highfields CB3 .80 C2
March PE15 .243 F4
Mildenhall IP28 .239 B4
Soham CB7 .212 B4
West Dr Cres CB7 .212 A4
West Dr Gdns CB7 .212 A4
West Dro S PE12 .233 E8
West End Ashwell SG7 .2 C3
Brampton PE28 .140 C3
Ely CB6 .240 C4
Gorefield PE13 .237 E3
Haddenham CB6 .209 F6
March PE15 .243 B4
Somersham PE28 .208 B8
Whittlesey PE7 .189 C7
Whittlesford CB2 .32 B4
Wilburton CB6 .210 B5
Woodditton CB8 .71 D8
Yaxley PE7 .181 D4
West End Cl PE16 .241 B4
West End La CB9 .38 E8
West End Rd
Fenstanton PE28 .121 A5
Maxey PE6 .231 C7
West End Villas PE9 .244 A5
West Fen Dro
Downham CB6 .218 A6
March PE7 .227 A1
Whittlesey PE7 .191 F3
West Fen Rd
Coveney CB6 .217 E4
Ely CB6 .240 B5
Willingham CB4 .208 F2
Witchford CB6 .218 A3
West Field CB1 .34 B7
West Field Rd PE15 .224 A3
West Gn CB2 .29 D7
West Hill Rd CB2 .30 B4
West Leys PE27 .143 F4
West Lodge La CB6 .216 D1
West Meadowgate
PE14 .245 E2
West Moor Ave CB2 .32 E8
West Newlands 3 PE28 208 B8
West Par
Peterborough PE3 .197 D3
Wisbech PE13 .245 B7
West Perry PE28 .115 D2
West Pk St PE16 .241 C4
West Rd Cambridge CB3 .83 C1
Gamlingay SG19 .41 C4
Histon CB4 .104 B3
3 Tallington PE9 .230 F7
Tydd St Giles PE13 .238 B8
West Row Prim Sch
IP28 .213 D7
West Row Rd
Beck Row, Holywell
Row & Kenny Hill IP28 .213 F6
Mildenhall IP28 .239 A5
West St Chatteris PE16 .241 B3
Godmanchester PE29 .141 E1
Great Gransden SG19 .58 D4
Helpston PE6 .231 B4
Huntingdon PE29 .141 E5
Isleham CB7 .212 F5
Over CB4 .123 A8
St Ives PE27 .144 A4
St Neots PE19 .74 E5
Stamford PE9 .244 B4
Toft CB3 .62 B5
Wisbech PE13 .245 C4
West St Gdns PE9 .244 A5
West Stonebridge
PE2 .186 C5
West Town Prim Sch
PE3 .197 E3
West View
Cambridge CB3 .64 C7
Little Stukeley PE28 .151 F1
West Way Meldreth SG8 .28 F1
Sawston CB2 .50 A1
West Wickham Rd
Balsham CB1 .53 C1
Horseheath CB1 .37 A3
West Wlk CB5 .86 F6
West Wr Cres PE7 .186 C1
West Wratting Rd CB1 .53 B2
Westberry Ct CB3 .64 B8
Westbourne Cl PE16 .241 B3
Westbourne Ct CB9 .24 A8
Westbourne Dr PE6 .203 E8
Westbourne Rd PE16 .241 B4
Westbrook Ave PE2 .186 F7
Westbrook Cl
1 Brampton PE28 .140 C3
Steeple Morden SG8 .3 B8
Westbrook Pk Cl PE2 .186 F7
Westbrook Pk Rd PE2 .186 F7
Westbury Rd PE27 .143 F4
Westcombe Sq PE1 .198 D4
Westcott House Theological
Coll CB1 .246 B3
Westcroft 4 CB3 .62 B4
Westering The CB5 .84 E2
Westerley Cl PE3 .197 C4
Westerman Cl PE28 .168 B5
Western Ave
Haverhill CB9 .38 E1
Peterborough PE1 .198 B7
Westfield CB4 .124 A6
Westfield Com Prim Sch
CB9 .24 B7
Westfield Jun Sch
PE27 .144 A4
Westfield La CB4 .83 C4
Westfield Rd
Fowlmere SG8 .15 D8
Great Shelford CB2 .48 E7
Newton PE13 .237 F5
Peterborough PE3 .197 E4
Ramsey PE26 .171 F7
Sawtry PE28 .168 B4
Wisbech PE13 .245 E7
Yaxley PE7 .181 D5
Westfields CB3 .99 A2
Westgate Cambridge CB1 .65 E5
Peterborough PE1 .197 F2
Westhawe PE3 .196 F7
Westhorpe CB5 .130 B4
Westlake Ave PE7 .186 C1
Westlands
Comberton CB3 .62 B4
Littleport CB6 .225 B3
Westley Bottom Rd
CB8 .69 B8
Westmead Ave PE13 .245 E2
Westmeadow Cl CB4 .208 F1
Westminster & Cheshunt
Colleges CB3 .83 C3
Westminster Gdns 16
PE6 .232 A1
Westminster Pl PE1 .198 F5
Westmoor Comm CB6 .217 E8
Westmoor Dro
Chatteris PE16 .222 D2
Littleport CB6 .225 B4
Westmoreland Gdns
PE1 .198 B2
Weston Ave SG8 .5 C7
Weston Cl PE19 .95 A1
Weston Colville Rd
CB8 .70 D1
Weston Ct PE19 .74 C4
Weston Gr CB1 .66 E5
Weston Miller Dr
PE13 .245 C7
Weston Rd PE13 .245 C3
Weston Way CB8 .110 F6
Westry Ave PE15 .243 A7
Westry Cl 3 PE14 .238 F1
Westway Pl CB6 .217 A2
Westwick Hall★ CB4 .103 E7
Westwood PE3 .197 C8
Westwood Ave PE15 .243 C5
Westwood Com Jun Sch
PE15 .243 C5
Westwood Ind Est
PE3 .197 D7
Westwood Pk Cl PE3 .197 C3
Westwood Pk Rd PE3 .197 D2
Westwood Rd PE27 .144 A4
Wetenhall Rd CB1 .65 B8
Wetherby Way 1 PE1 .198 D3
Weymouth Way PE1 .198 D6
Whaddon Gap SG8 .28 A1
Whaddon Rd SG8 .28 E2
Whaddons The PE29 .141 F6
Whalley St PE1 .198 B3
Wharf Rd PE9 .244 C4
Wheat Croft CB1 .35 D3
Wheatdole PE2 .186 A3
Wheatfield Cres 2 SG8 .5 E6
Wheatfield Dr PE26 .171 F5
Wheatfield Jun & Inf Sch
PE27 .144 A6
Wheatfields PE27 .144 A6
Wheatley Bank PE14 .238 F2
Wheatley Cres PE28 .208 C6
Wheats Cl 1 CB6 .217 D1
Wheatsheaf Cl CB6 .240 A3
Wheatsheaf Dro PE14 .229 C3
Wheatsheaf Rd
Alconbury Weston PE28 .150 D6
Eaton Socon PE19 .74 C3
Woodhurst PE28 .155 D4
Wheatsheaf Way CB1 .35 D3
Wheatsheaves 2 PE28 .168 C2
Wheel Ctr The PE15 .243 D4
Wheel Yd PE1 .198 A2

Wheeler St CB2 246 A2
Wheeler's Cl CB3 46 A7
Wheeler's Way CB3 46 A7
Wheelers CB2 49 B6
Wheelwright Way CB5 86 A5
Whellams Yd PE26 172 C7
Wherry Cl PE15 243 D4
Whetstone Ct 5 PE1 198 D7
Whichcote Rd PE6 206 E6
Whines La CB4 123 B8
Whinfell Cl PE29 141 A7
Whipple Mus of the History of Science★ CB1 246 A2
Whippletree Rd CB2 32 A5
Whistler Rd 5 PE19 74 C5
Whistlers The PE27 144 A7
Whiston Cl
Peterborough PE4 204 F2
4 Somersham PE28 208 C8
Whitacre PE1 198 E6
Whitby St 3 PE13 245 C5
White Acres PE7 189 E8
White Cross PE3 197 B6
White Cross Hill CB6 210 D6
White Cross Rd CB6 210 E7
White Droveway CB5 108 A3
White Fen Droveway CB5 107 B5
White Field Way CB2 32 D8
White Hall Cl 21 PE28 215 C1
White Hart Ct PE27 144 A3
White Hart Dr 5 PE15 222 A5
White Hart La
Godmanchester PE29 142 A1
6 Littleport CB6 242 D4
St Ives PE27 144 A3
13 Soham CB7 212 B4
White Horse La CB6 218 A6
White House Rd CB7 226 C2
White Lion Cl 1 PE15 243 D2
White Rose Wlk 5 CB4 83 D7
Whitecroft Rd SG8 14 A8
Whitecross PE27 144 A4
Whitefriars CB4 84 B5
Whitegate Cl Girton CB3 82 E8
Swavesey CB4 122 D6
Whitegates CB8 111 C3
Whitehall Gdns CB2 31 E1
Whitehall Sch PE28 215 B1
Whitehall Way PE28 115 D2
Whitehall Wlk PE19 74 F4
Whitehill Cl CB1 84 D2
Whitehill Rd CB5 84 C2
Whitehouse La CB3 83 A5
Whitehouse Rd PE28 168 A4
Whitemill Rd PE16 241 C3
Whitemoor Rd PE15 227 C4
Whitepost Rd
Borough Fen PE6 207 F1
Newborough PE6 205 F6
Whitewater PE2 185 D6
Whiteway Dro CB5 107 F8
Whiteways PE2 185 D6
Whitfield Cl CB4 83 E7
Whitgift Rd CB1 85 B1
Whitlocks CB2 64 D2
Whitman Cl 7 PE9 230 D3
Whitmore St PE7 189 D7
Whitmore Way CB5 106 B6
Whitsed Rd PE6 207 D1
Whitsed St PE1 198 B3
Whittets Cl SG19 58 D4
Whittington PE1 198 E7
Whittlesea Sta PE7 189 F5
Whittlesey Mus★ PE7 189 D7
Whittlesey Rd
Benwick PE15 221 E6
March PE15 243 A5
Peterborough PE2 187 B7
Thorney PE6 200 F7
Whittlesford Rd
Little Shelford CB2 48 F2
Newton CB2 31 D7
Whittlesford Sta CB2 32 E3
Whitton Cl CB4 122 E5
Whitwell PE4 205 A2
Whitwell Way CB3 82 A2
Whybrows La PE28 208 E6
Whydale Rd 4 SG8 5 E5
Whytefield Rd PE26 172 A7
Whytford Cl CB4 84 A3
Wicken Fen National Nature Reserve★ CB7 211 D1
Wicken Rd CB7 212 B1
Wicken Way PE3 197 C6
Widgham Gn CB8 71 D3
Wiggin Cl IP28 239 D2
Wigmore Cl PE29 141 E1
Wigmore Dr PE7 187 F5
Wigstone's Rd PE15 243 E5
Wilberforce Rd
Cambridge CB3 83 B2
Peterborough PE1 197 E7
Wisbech PE13 245 D5
Wilbraham Rd
Bottisham CB1 86 F3
Fulbourn CB1 67 C7
Wilbraham Temple CB1 68 A8
Wilburton CE Prim Sch CB6 210 C6
Wilburton Rd CB6 210 A6
Wild Acres CB5 130 B1
Wild Goose Leys PE28 152 D5
Wildber Cl PE19 74 F4
Wilderness The PE27 144 B3
Wilderspin Cl CB3 82 F6
Wilding Wlk CB4 84 A5
Wildlake PE2 186 C5
Wildmere La IP28 214 A8
Wiles Cl Cambridge CB4 84 A7
Waterbeach CB5 106 A8
Wilff Cl PE29 152 E1
Wilford Dr CB7 240 E6
Wilford Furlong CB4 209 A1
Wilkin St 1 CB1 65 A8
Wilkins Rd PE14 236 D7
Wilkinson Cl
Eaton Socon PE19 74 B3
March PE15 243 E5
Willan Ct PE2 186 F8
Willesden Ave PE4 197 D8
William Blake Ct CB9 38 E1
William de Yaxley CE Jun Sch
Yaxley PE7 181 F6
Yaxley PE7 181 E6
William Dr 8 PE19 74 F1
William Law Prim Sch PE4 204 B5
William Rd PE13 245 C5
William Smith Cl CB1 65 A7
William Westley CE Prim Sch CB2 32 D5
William's Way IP28 213 D6
Williams Cl
Brampton PE28 140 C3
Ely CB6 240 E7
Newborough PE6 207 C1
Williams Way PE15 224 B4
Williamson Ave PE3 197 E3
Willie Snaith Rd CB8 110 F6
Willingham Gn Rd CB8 54 D8
Willingham Prim Sch CB4 209 A1
Willingham Rd CB4 208 E1
Willis Rd CB1 246 C2
Willmott Rd SG8 12 F5
Willock La PE13 235 A5
Willonholt PE3 197 C7
Willoughby Ct PE1 198 E8
Willoughby Rd PE9 244 C7
Willow Ave PE1 198 B7
Willow Cl
Beck Row, Holywell Row & Kenny Hill IP28 214 A8
Brampton PE28 140 C2
Doddington PE15 222 A5
Haverhill CB9 38 D1
Little Paxton PE19 95 F1
St Neots PE19 74 F3
Stilton PE7 175 F7
Willow Cres
Milton CB4 105 D2
Newmarket CB8 111 B2
Willow Ct CB6 242 E4
Willow Dr PE15 243 B3
Willow Dro PE6 207 D4
Willow End PE28 150 F4
Willow Farm Cl PE28 150 D7
Willow Gn PE27 208 A3
Willow Gr Ely CB7 240 E4
Lode CB5 107 C2
Willow Hall La PE6 199 D6
Willow Holt PE7 186 C3
Willow La CB3 79 C3
Willow Rd PE7 182 A6
Willow Row Farms CB6 226 A5
Willow Way
Bottisham CB5 86 F6
Hauxton CB2 48 B4
Ramsey PE26 172 B7
St Ives PE27 144 C4
Wisbech PE13 245 D3
Willow Wlk
Cambridge CB1 246 B3
Ely CB7 240 E4
Willowbrook Dr PE7 201 F1
Willows The
Glinton PE6 203 F8
Great Chesterford CB10 18 D3
Willowside Way SG8 5 C8
Wilson Cl CB4 84 A7
Wilson Way
Brampton PE28 117 E8
Milton CB4 105 D2
Wilson's Rd CB4 103 A8
Wilsons La SG7 2 C4
Wilthorne PE28 165 A5
Wilton Cl PE3 197 C4
Wilton Dr PE3 197 C4
Wilton Gdns CB6 216 E3
Wiltshire Rd PE28 154 B1
Wimbish Rd CB3 99 A2
Wimblington Rd
Doddington/Wimblington PE15 223 A5
March PE15 243 C1
Wimblington PE15 223 E6
Wimborne Dr PE1 198 E7
Wimbridge Cl SG8 27 F6
Wimpole Ave★ SG8 27 F5
Wimpole Hall★ SG8 44 F3
Wimpole Home Farm★ SG8 44 F3
Wimpole Pk★ SG8 44 E3
Wimpole Rd Barton CB3 63 A2
Great Eversden CB3 45 E7
Wimpole St PE16 241 B4
Winchester Way PE3 197 E1
Winchfield SG19 58 E5
Winchmore Dr CB2 64 C3
Winderemere Cl CB1 66 A7
Windermere PE29 141 B6
Windermere Way PE4 204 E3
Winders La CB4 104 B5
Windgate Way PE8 194 A6
Windlesham Cl CB4 83 E6
Windmill Cl
Ellington PE28 138 F4
Ely CB6 240 B3
Sawston CB2 32 F8
Soham CB7 212 C2
Windmill Hill CB8 110 C8
Windmill La
Fulbourn CB1 66 E4
Histon CB4 104 B4
8 Sutton CB6 216 E1
Windmill Sch The CB1 66 D5
Windmill St
Peterborough PE1 197 F5
Whittlesey PE7 189 D8
Windmill Wlk CB6 216 E1
Windover Rd PE29 141 D7
Windrush Dr PE4 204 F1
Windsor Ave PE4 197 C8
Windsor Cl
Chatteris PE16 241 E5
St Ives PE27 143 F8
10 St Neots PE19 74 F2
Stamford PE9 244 B7
Windsor Dr
March PE15 243 B5
Peterborough PE2 187 D6
Ramsey PE26 221 C2
Wisbech PE13 245 D8
Windsor Gdns 9 PE28 208 C8
Windsor Pl PE7 190 A7
Windsor Rd
Cambridge CB4 83 C5
Godmanchester PE29 142 A1
Newmarket CB8 110 E4
Royston SG8 5 F6
Sawtry PE28 168 B3
Yaxley PE7 181 F6
Windsor Terr CB9 23 D8
Windsors The PE15 243 A5
Winfold Rd CB5 106 A8
Wingate Cl CB2 64 D3
Wingate Way CB2 64 D3
Wingfield PE2 185 F3
Winhills Prim Sch PE19 75 A4
Winship Rd CB4 105 C1
Winslow Rd PE3 197 C3
Winston Way PE7 187 C2
Wintringham Rd 8 PE19 74 F5
Winwick Pl PE3 197 C5
Winwick Rd PE28 158 B8
Winyates PE2 185 F3
Winyates Prim Sch PE2 186 A3
Wisbech Castle★ PE13 245 C4
Wisbech Gram Sch PE13 245 B5
Wisbech Rd
Littleport CB6 242 A6
Manea PE15 224 C5
March PE15 243 A7
Outwell PE14 236 F3
Thorney PE6 233 A3
Walsoken PE13 245 E8
Welney PE14 229 E2
Whittlesey PE7 191 C8
Wisbech St Mary PE13 234 A2
Wisbech St Mary CE Prim Sch PE13 235 B7
Wisbech Yacht Harbour★ PE13 245 C6
Wissey Way CB6 240 C6
Wistaria Rd PE13 245 F7
Wisteria Rd PE7 181 D4
Wistow Ct 3 PE19 74 C6
Wistow Fen Dro PE28 173 B4
Wistow Fen La PE28 164 C8
Wistow Way PE2 185 D6
Wistow Wood Nature Reserve★ PE28 172 D1
Witcham Bridge Dro CB6 217 A5
Witcham Rd CB6 216 E3
Witchford Rd Ely CB6 240 A3
Witchford CB6 217 F1
Witchford Village Coll CB6 217 E2
Witham Cl PE9 244 C6
Witham Way PE4 204 F1
Withers Pl CB7 212 E1
Withersfield Rd
Haverhill CB9 38 E1
Withersfield CB9 38 F7
Wittering Airfield PE8 230 A2
Wittering Prim Sch PE8 230 B1
Wittering Rd PE9 230 D3
Woburn Cl
Cambridge CB4 83 E7
Peterborough PE3 197 A1
Woburn Ct PE7 176 A7
Woburn Dr PE6 233 A2
Woburn Pl CB2 31 F1
Wolf La Gorefield PE13 237 F1
Wisbech PE13 235 C8
Wolfson Coll CB3 64 B8
Wollaston Rd
Cambridge CB1 246 C1
Peterborough PE3 197 C6
Wolseley Cl PE7 181 E6
Wolsey Gdns PE19 117 A5
Wolsey Way CB1 65 F7
Wood End
Bluntisham/Colne PE28 208 C6
Pertenhall MK44 113 D1
Wood La
Abbots Ripton PE28 162 E2
Broughton PE28 163 A2
Papworth Everard CB3 99 A4
Ramsey PE26 172 C8
Stretham CB6 210 F5
Wood St Chatteris PE16 241 C4
Doddington/Wimblington PE15 223 A6
Huntingdon PE29 141 E4
Wisbech PE13 245 B6
Wood View PE28 140 B4
Woodbine St PE2 187 A8
Woodbrook Cl CB3 99 B2
Woodbyth Rd PE1 198 A6
Woodcock Cl
Haverhill CB9 24 C7
Histon CB4 104 D3
Woodcock Rd 10 SG8 5 E8
Woodcote Cl PE1 198 A7
Woodcote Pk PE13 245 A4
Woodcroft Castle★ PE6 203 C5
Woodcroft Rd
Etton PE6 203 B7
Glinton PE6 203 C3
Marholm PE6 203 D1
Woodditton Rd
Kirtling CB8 72 B5
Newmarket CB8 111 A1
Woodditton CB8 90 B8
Woodfen Rd CB6 242 A2
Woodfield Ave PE26 172 A4
Woodfield Dr PE28 168 A3
Woodfield La CB3 79 A3
Woodfield Rd PE3 197 D3
Woodforde Cl SG7 2 E4
Woodgate PE6 231 C4
Woodgate La PE6 231 D7
Woodgate Rd 3 PE13 238 B2
Woodhall La CB1 53 A1
Woodhall Rise PE4 204 B6
Woodhead Cl PE9 244 D7
Woodhead Dr CB4 83 F6
Woodhead Pl CB3 99 B3
Woodhouse Way CB4 84 A7
Woodhurst Rd PE2 187 D6
Woodland Lea PE6 231 B4
Woodland Rd CB2 32 F8
Woodland Wlk 2 CB3 79 C3
Woodlands 1 Royston SG8 5 E6
St Neots PE19 75 A7
Warboys PE28 164 F5
Woodlands Ave PE15 243 D2
Woodlands Cl
Girton CB3 103 D1
Great Shelford CB2 49 A4
Woodlands Ct PE13 245 F7
Woodlands Dr SG8 14 B8
Woodlands Pk CB3 103 D1
Woodlands Rd CB2 49 A4
Woodlands The
Linton CB1 35 B4
Peterborough PE1 198 D5
Woodlands Way IP28 239 F5
Woodlark Dr CB4 125 D4
Woodlark Rd CB3 83 B5
Woodmans Way CB4 105 D2
Woodroffe Rd PE8 193 D8
Woods Cl CB9 24 E5
Woodside
Chatteris PE16 241 C4
Oakington/Longstanton CB4 123 F1
Woodside Way PE27 144 B5
Woodston Ind Est PE2 186 E6
Woodston Prim Sch PE2 186 F7
Woodwalton Fen National Nature Reserve★ PE26 170 B6
Woodwalton Marsh Nature Reserve★ PE28 161 E7
Woodward Cl PE7 176 A8
Woodysfield 2 PE15 223 B7
Woolcroft Cl PE13 238 A1
Woolfellhill Rd PE6 205 F3
Woolgard PE3 197 A3
Woollards La CB2 49 A4
Woolley Cl PE28 140 D3
Woolley Hill PE28 138 D6
Woolley Rd PE28 149 B3
Woolpack La
St Ives PE27 144 A3
2 Whittlesey PE7 189 D6
Woolpack Way SG8 29 B1
Woolthwaite La CB3 79 A4
Wooton Field SG19 41 D4
Woottens Cl CB3 62 C5
Wootton Ave PE2 186 F6
Wootton Way CB3 64 A8
Worboys Ct SG8 10 F5
Worcester Ave CB3 81 A4
Worcester Cres 2 PE9 244 B6
Worcester Rd PE13 245 C7
Worcester Way SG8 14 E6
Wordsworth Ave PE19 74 D6
Wordsworth Cl
Peterborough PE4 197 E8
Royston SG8 13 D1
Wordsworth Gr CB3 64 C8
Workhouse La PE14 229 D8
Worlington Rd
Barton Mills IP28 214 C3
Worlington Rd
Worlington IP28 239 A3
Worsley PE2 186 A4
Worsley Chase PE15 243 D2
Wortham Pl 2 CB9 24 A8
Wortham Rd SG8 5 E4
Worthington Cl PE7 176 A7
Worts' Cswy CB1 65 C2
Wothorpe Hill PE9 244 A1
Wothorpe Mews 5 PE9 244 B4
Wothorpe Rd PE9 244 B4
Wr Gdns The PE13 245 A5
Wragg Dr CB8 111 A6
Wratting Rd
Great Thurlow CB9 39 B8
Haverhill CB9 24 A8
Wren Cl IP28 239 D4
Wren Pk CB2 32 B4
Wrens Cl CB6 240 B5
Wrestlingworth Lower Sch SG19 25 B3
Wrexham Terr SG8 5 D7
Wright Ave PE2 187 D5
Wright's Cl CB5 84 E6
Wright's Dro PE6 232 B7
Wrights Dro PE7 220 B8
Wrights Gr CB1 66 F4
Wroe The PE14 236 C5
Wulfric Sq PE3 197 C8
Wulfstan Ct CB1 65 C4
Wulfstan Way CB1 65 C4
Wyatt Cl PE26 172 B6
Wyboston Ct 1 PE19 74 C4
Wycliffe Gr PE4 204 A5
Wycliffe Rd CB1 65 C8
Wydham Pk PE2 185 D6
Wye Pl PE4 204 E1
Wykes Dr 3 PE13 235 B7
Wykes Rd PE7 181 D4
Wyman Way PE2 185 F5
Wynborne Cl CB4 83 E5
Wyndham Way CB8 111 A6
Wynford Way CB4 83 F7
Wype Dro PE7 191 A5
Wype Rd PE7 190 C7
Wysing Arts Ctr★ CB3 60 C3
Wytches The CB6 211 A7
Wyton Airfield PE28 153 F2
Wyton Prim Sch PE28 143 B8

Y

Yardy Cl PE15 243 B4
Yarmouth Pl 1 CB9 24 A8
Yarrow Cl PE15 243 B5
Yarrow Rd CB1 66 A5
Yarwell Cl PE2 186 D7
Yarwells Headlands PE7 189 D8
Yarwells Wlk PE7 189 D8
Yaxley Inf Sch PE7 181 E4
Yaxley Rd PE7 177 B4
Yeats Cl SG8 13 D1
Yeldham Pl CB9 24 A8
Yeomans Cl PE28 136 D7
Yerril Gdn 3 CB9 23 E7
Yew Tree Wlk PE4 197 A2
York Cl
Godmanchester PE29 141 F1
Mildenhall IP28 213 D8
York Gdns PE13 245 D6
York Rd Chatteris PE16 241 C4
Haverhill CB9 23 E7
Peterborough PE1 197 F6
9 Stamford PE9 244 B6
Sutton CB6 216 D1
Wisbech PE13 245 D6
Wyton Airfield PE28 143 A8
York Row 24 PE13 245 C5
York Sq PE28 143 B8
York St CB1 84 A1
York Terr
Cambridge CB1 84 A1
Wisbech PE13 245 C6
York Way Royston SG8 5 B8
St Ives PE27 144 A8
Yorke Way CB6 240 B3
Young St CB1 84 A2
Youngman Ave CB4 104 C5
Youngman Cl CB4 104 C5

Z

Zetland Wlk CB1 65 D7

Name and Address	Telephone	Page	Grid reference

NG	NH	NJ	NK	

Using the Ordnance Survey National Grid

NG	NH	NJ	NK
NM	NN	NO	NP
NR	NS	NT	NU
NX	NY	NZ	
SC	SD	SE	TA
SH	SJ	SK	TF	TG
SM	SN	SO	SP	TL	TM
SR	SS	ST	SU	TQ	TR
SW	SX	SY	SZ	TV

Any feature in this atlas can be given a unique reference to help you find the same feature on other Ordnance Survey maps of the area, or to help someone else locate you if they do not have a Street Atlas.

The grid squares in this atlas match the Ordnance Survey National Grid and are at 500 metre intervals. The small figures at the bottom and sides of every other grid line are the National Grid kilometre values (**00** to **99** km) and are repeated across the country every 100 km (see left).

To give a unique National Grid reference you need to locate where in the country you are. The country is divided into 100 km squares with each square given a unique two-letter reference. Use the administrative map to determine in which 100 km square a particular page of this atlas falls.

The bold letters and numbers between each grid line (**A** to **F**, **1** to **8**) are for use within a specific Street Atlas only, and when used with the page number, are a convenient way of referencing these grid squares.

Example   The railway bridge over DARLEY GREEN RD in grid square B1

Step 1: Identify the two-letter reference, in this example the page is in **SP**

Step 2: Identify the 1 km square in which the railway bridge falls. Use the figures in the southwest corner of this square: Eastings **17**, Northings **74**. This gives a unique reference: **SP 17 74**, accurate to 1 km.

Step 3: To give a more precise reference accurate to 100 m you need to estimate how many tenths along and how many tenths up this 1 km square the feature is (to help with this the 1 km square is divided into four 500 m squares). This makes the bridge about **8** tenths along and about **1** tenth up from the southwest corner.

This gives a unique reference: **SP 178 741**, accurate to 100 m.

Eastings (read from left to right along the bottom) come before Northings (read from bottom to top). If you have trouble remembering say to yourself "Along the hall, THEN up the stairs"!

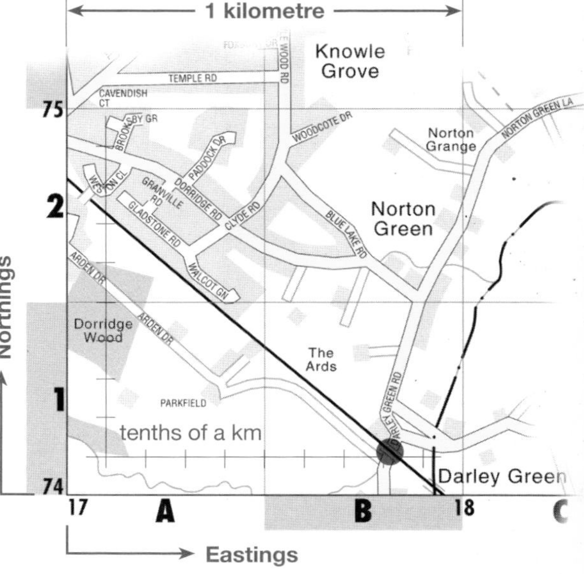

PHILIP'S MAPS

the Gold Standard for serious driving

◆ Philip's street atlases cover every county in England and Wales, plus much of Scotland.

◆ All our atlases use the same style of mapping, with the same colours and symbols, so you can move with confidence from one atlas to the next

◆ Widely used by the emergency services, transport companies and local authorities.

◆ Created from the most up-to-date and detailed information available from Ordnance Survey

◆ Based on the National Grid

BEST BUY • BEST BUY
Auto EXPRESS
BEST BUY • BEST BUY

PHILIP'S STREET ATLAS London
The definitive Lon...
from Britain's national m...
PHILIP'S

PHILIP'S STREET ATLAS Devon
Unique comprehensive coverage
BEST BUY Auto Express
Includes Lyme Regis, Seaton and Wellington, plus Exeter and Plymouth city centres at extra-large scale
with time-saving through-routes

PHILIP'S STREET ATLAS Norfolk
Unique comprehensive coverage
BEST BUY Auto Express
Includes Norwich city centre at extra-large scale, plus town maps of Bury St Edmunds and Lowestoft
with time-saving through-routes

PHILIP'S STREET ATLAS Cumbria
Unique comprehensive coverage
BEST BUY Auto Express
Every named street, road and lane
Plus town maps of Dumfries and Morecambe, with Carlisle city centre at extra-large scale

PHILIP'S BRITAIN'S MOST DETAILED ROAD ATLAS
NAVIGATOR Britain
Ultra-large scale mapping 1½ miles to 1 inch
Scottish Highlands and islands at 2½ miles to 1 inch
50 fully indexed town plans
'Extremely clear maps with the most detail by far'
Auto Express
Recommended by the Institute of Advanced Motorists

For national mapping, choose **Philip's Navigator Britain** – the most detailed road atlas available of England, Wales and Scotland. Hailed by Auto Express as 'the ultimate road atlas', this is the only one-volume atlas to show every road and lane in Britain.

Currently available street atlases

England

Bedfordshire	Suffolk
Berkshire	Surrey
Birmingham and West Midlands	East Sussex
Bristol and Bath	West Sussex
Buckinghamshire	Tyne and Wear Northumberland
Cambridgeshire	Warwickshire
Cheshire	Birmingham and West Midlands
Cornwall	Wiltshire and Swindon
Cumbria	Worcestershire
Derbyshire	East Yorkshire Northern Lincolnshire
Devon	North Yorkshire
Dorset	South Yorkshire
County Durham and Teesside	West Yorkshire
Essex	**Wales**
North Essex	Anglesey, Conwy and Gwynedd
South Essex	Cardiff, Swansea and The Valleys
Gloucestershire	Carmarthenshire, Pembrokeshire and Swansea
North Hampshire	Ceredigion and South Gwynedd
South Hampshire	Denbighshire, Flintshire, Wrexham
Herefordshire Monmouthshire	Herefordshire Monmouthshire
Hertfordshire	Powys
Isle of Wight	**Scotland**
East Kent	Aberdeenshire
West Kent	Ayrshire
Lancashire	Edinburgh and East Central Scotland
Leicestershire and Rutland	Fife and Tayside
Lincolnshire	Glasgow and West Central Scotland
London	Inverness and Moray
Greater Manchester	
Merseyside	
Norfolk	
Northamptonshire	
Nottinghamshire	
Oxfordshire	
Shropshire	
Somerset	
Staffordshire	

All England and Wales coverage

How to order

Philip's maps and atlases are available from bookshops, motorway services and petrol stations. You can order direct from the publisher by phoning **01903 828503** or online at **www.philips-maps.co.uk**
For bulk orders only, phone 020 7644 6940